The Negro Leagues Book, Volume 2:
The Players, 1862 - 1960

BOOKS by LARRY LESTER

* * *

THE NEGRO LEAGUES BOOK
With Dick Clark

BLACK BASEBALL'S NATIONAL SHOWCASE
The East-West All-Star Game, 1933-1953
Reprinted in 2020, Expanded Edition 1933-1962

BLACK BASEBALL IN KANSAS CITY
With Sammy J. Miller

BLACK BASEBALL IN DETROIT
With Sammy J. Miller and Dick Clark

BLACK BASEBALL IN CHICAGO
With Sammy J. Miller and Dick Clark

BLACK BASEBALL IN PITTSBURGH
With Sammy J. Miller

BASEBALL'S FIRST COLORED WORLD SERIES
1924 Meeting of the Hilldale Giants and the Kansas City Monarchs

RUBE FOSTER IN HIS TIME
On the Field and in the Papers with Black Baseball's Greatest Visionary

BLACK BASEBALL IN NEW YORK CITY
An Illustrated History, 1885 - 1959

The Negro Leagues Book, Volume 2:
The Players, 1862 – 1960
Edition 1.2

By Larry Lester & Wayne Stivers
With a foreword by Gary Ashwill

www.Seamheads.com

Published by NoirTech Research, Inc.
Copyright 2020 by NoirTech Research, Inc.
All Rights Reserved

For information about permissions to reproduce selections from this book, contact:
NoirTech Research, Inc.
P.O. Box 380146
Kansas City, MO 64138
NTResearch@comcast.net

ISBN: 978-1-7344944-2-6
ISBN: 978-1-7344944-0-2 eBook

1. African American Athletes, 2. Baseball, 3. Race Relations, 4. Sports, 5. Negro Leagues, 6. All-Star games, 7. World Series games, 8. Military, 9. Collegiate, 10. History, 11. Black Baseball, 12. Colored Baseball, 13. Uniform numbers, 14. Cemeteries, 15. Sports History, 16. Sports Literature

Printed in the United States of America

Book Cover Design by: Artrocity
https://artrocity.wixsite.com/

E-book formatting by Sebastian Banker

Table of Contents

Foreword i
Introduction ii
Dedicated to Dick Clark, R.I.P. iii
IN THE BEGINNING 1
ALL-TIME NEGRO BASEBALL REGISTER 23
APPENDIX A: WOMEN IN BLACK BASEBALL 224
    Owners: 224
    Officers: 227
    Players: 228
APPENDIX B: 230
    MAJOR LEAGUE AND NEGRO LEAGUE CONNECTIONS 230
    Debut Dates of Black Players onto Major League Teams 232
    Negro League Players Who Went Directly into the Major Leagues 239
    BROWN BARRIER BREAKERS 242
        Tan players who played in both the Major & Negro Leagues before 1947 242
    Special Negro Leagues Draft by MLB 244
        American League Teams: 244
        National League Teams: 245
APPENDIX C: 246
    All-Star Register for the annual East-West Classic, 1933-1960 246
    East-West All-Stars by Team, 1933 to 1960 257
    Major League Baseball players who played in the East-West All-Star Classic 266
    Future NBBHOF Inductees who played in the East-West All-Star Classic 268
    Latin American players in the East-West All-Star Classic 272
    1949 to 1999, 50 Years of Major League All-Star History 273
APPENDIX D: 276
    All-Time World Series Rosters by players 276
    MLB players who played in the Negro League World Series 282
    All-Time Negro League World Series Rosters - by Teams 283
APPENDIX E: 286
    International Baseball Hall of Fames 287

- Negro Leaguers in the National Basketball Hall of Fame ... 291
- National Baseball Hall of Famers who played in both the Negro Leagues and the Major Leagues ... 291
- List of National Baseball Hall of Famers by cities ... 294
- List of Cooperstown Hall of Famers by Teams ... 305
- Teams with the Most Negro League Hall of Famers in the National Baseball Hall of Fame in Cooperstown, New York. ... 310
- Shrine of the Eternals with Negro League Connections ... 310

APPENDIX F: Family Connections & Crossover Skills ... 311
- Negro Leaguers and executives who participated in other professional sports. ... 311
- List of Relatives in the Black Leagues ... 321
- Negro Leaguers with relatives in the Major Leagues, NBA, and NFL, along with entertainment and political connections ... 328

APPENDIX G: Uniform Numbers ... 330
- Retired Major League Uniform Numbers of former Negro League players. ... 331
- Uniform numbers of players compiled from photographs and printed rosters, home and road numbers ... 332

APPENDIX H: Military Service of African American Players ... 380
- Civil War, 1861 to 1865 ... 381
- Spanish American War, April to August 1898 ... 381
- World War I, 1914 to 1918 ... 381
- Defense Workers during World War II ... 384
- World War II, 1939 to 1945 ... 384
- Korean War, 1950 to 1953 ... 389

APPENDIX I: Collegians ... 390

APPENDIX J: Tributes to Negro Leaguers & Teams ... 400
- Streets and Highways named after Black Ballplayers ... 400
- Ball Parks, Historic Markers, Statues and Other Landmarks named in honor of Negro League players and Teams ... 403
- Honors, awards and postage stamps of Negro Leaguers ... 419
- Black Stars on the Silver Screen ... 425

APPENDIX K: Cemeteries ... 434

APPENDIX L: BOOKS, THESES, DISSERTATIONS, and NEWSPAPERS RESEARCHED ... 465
- Books Authored by Former Negro League Players: ... 465
- Selected Bibliography of Theses & Dissertations ... 467

- Other Related Theses & Dissertations ... 471
- Major & Minor Newspapers Researched ... 474
- Contributing Libraries located in non-major Negro League cities: ... 479
- Contributing Researchers: ... 480

Authors: ... 481

Foreword
By Gary Ashwill

You hold in your hands the results of a decades-long collaborative project to make sense of one of the murkiest and most misunderstood chapters in American history—the era of racially segregated baseball. On the White side of the color line, the major and minor leagues saw their games avidly reported in the local and national press, and carefully recorded for posterity. But for African American teams and leagues, and their many hundreds of professional players, there was nothing comparable. Despite the efforts of a relatively small number of sportswriters at Black newspapers, the records of the Negro Leagues that have come down to us are sparse and often confusing, with many gaps and contradictions.

Nevertheless the situation is not hopeless. Even if statistics were not reliably compiled and made available to the public, between the Black weeklies and mainstream daily papers, thousands of box scores and game stories were printed. Living veterans of the leagues have donated their time and memories to the cause, helping historians reconstruct the rosters of teams from 30, 40, 50 or more years before. Archives, government records, maps, and other caches of information still exist that contain important traces of the Black men and women who played baseball for a living even as they were barred from the White-dominated majors and minors.

In 1907 the famed player and manager Sol White published his *Official Base Ball Guide*, the first book about the African American experience in baseball. It would take 62 years for the second book to arrive. When Robert L. Peterson released *Only the Ball Was White* in 1969, it spurred the modern reconstruction of segregation-era Black baseball history. Particularly important was Peterson's Appendix C, an "All-Time Register of Players and Officials 1884-1950," which represented the first attempt at a systematic listing of players and their teams and served as a starting point and guide for the many historians who would follow up Peterson's efforts.

The heart of the present book is a continuation of Peterson's register, corrected, extended, and massively expanded by decades of new research, spearheaded by Larry Lester, Wayne Stivers, and the now departed Dick Clark. As the guiding lights behind SABR's Negro Leagues Committee as well as the Negro League Researchers and Authors Group, this trio has put Negro Leagues research on a solidly empirical basis. They have also served as mentors and examples to generations of fledgling researchers (including me). The 2006 induction of 17 Negro league figures into the National Baseball Hall of Fame stands as a tribute to their work and influence.

The new register's listing of 6,000 players and officials extends alphabetically from Aaron to Zuber, and chronologically from Robert Henson, pitcher and manager for the eponymous Henson Base Ball Club of Jamaica, Long Island, in 1859, to Odell Daniels, a pitcher/outfielder for the 1964 Satchel Paige All-Stars. Like any comparably sprawling, encyclopedic undertaking, it is not perfect, it is not absolutely complete, and it will likely never be finished. *The Negro Leagues Book, Volume 2: Black Baseball Players, 1862-1960* is the best sort of reference work, an authoritative guide that also serves as a spur to future research.

Gary Ashwill is the lead researcher for the Seamheads.com Negro Leagues Database (http://www.seamheads.com/NegroLgs/index.php) and writes the blog Agate Type: Reconstructing Negro League & Latin American Baseball History (http://agatetype.typepad.com).

Introduction
by Larry Lester

As an advocate and activist for recognition of these "invisible men" into baseball's finest memorial, the National Baseball Hall of Fame and Museum in Cooperstown, New York, the acceptance of these forgotten athletes has been a sensitive subject for baseball fans everywhere. Until recently, the oral history of these outstanding athletes had long been the only source for verification of their accomplishments. At times, searching for statistical and biographical validation of their contributions has been an exercise in frustration.

Frustration if you ever tried to solve a Rubik Cube. In the mid-1970s, the multi-colored layer of small cubes, arranged in a systematic pattern of colors, amazing many Americans. The challenge was to twist and rotate these colors, creating a seemingly impossible disarray of orderliness, and later to be rearranged until its original color sequence was retained. The solution to this puzzle has befuddled the inquisitive minds of many and likewise the solutions to discovering the best-practices for accurately researching the Negro Baseball Leagues has puzzled many sports historians.

Many cynics have claimed that these records do not exist and therefore a players' credibility can never be validated. These same critics contend African Americans were apathetic about their heritage and did not record players' achievements and contributions to baseball. Such historical assassination of these men and women has inspired us to prove these naysayers wrong with facts and figures.

At times this exercise by Dick Clark, Wayne Stivers and I felt like the mortal Sisyphus, of Greek mythology, who was subjected to the dreadful punishment and hopeless labor of eternally rolling a rock to the top of a mountain, only to have the stone fall back to ground zero from its own weight. While baseball research can be therapeutic and intoxicating, all at the same time, this body of research has become an art form for many historians.

Despite our gallant and dedicated efforts, this project will never be fully completed. We welcome your feedback and edits to any section of *The Negro Leagues Book, Volume 2: The Players, 1862-1960*.

Dedicated to Dick Clark, R.I.P.

By Larry Lester

There were two real McCoys from Ypsilanti, Michigan: inventor Elijah McCoy and historian Richard Clifford Clark. Dick Clark was the most genuine person known to mankind. Liked by all, respected by many. Diogenes stopped looking for an honest man when he met Sir Richard. He was charming, brilliant, and bitter — sometimes all at the same time. Clark's opinions were honest and sometimes unfiltered. You have to respect a man for that! As many of us who knew him, we are better men and women, fathers, mothers, husbands and wives for knowing him.

Clark was a dog's best friend. And he was this canine's best friend. Richard "Dick" Clark, 68 years old, my mentor, my buddy, my homey, my roomy, uncle to my daughters, even ate my wife's cooking, and an inspirational leader to many, passed away Monday morning, December 8, 2014.

Like our mutual friend Jerry Malloy, he was someone who didn't compromise on being the person only he could be. Dick Clark was someone who didn't hold back on sharing his gifts to research, fact check or befriend a ball player or historian in need. He was a Negro League savant. No one, absolutely no one, knew more about Negro League history than Dick Clark. We had to ban him from Trivia Contests because he knew the answers before the questions were asked. He had a mathematical mind palace, and probably could have moon walked with Einstein or Tesla. Dick's brilliancy often shined thru his unique sense of humor.

More than 30 years ago, I joined the Society for American Baseball Research (SABR) with Dick Clark serving as chairman of the Negro Leagues Committee. Before technology took over, he welcomed me to the organization by mail, and each week we faithfully wrote, and also ran up some significant long distance telephone bills. Back in the day, you had to have a lot of postage stamps to keep up with his correspondences. Two years later, 1987, we met in person for the first time in Washington, D.C., at the 17th SABR National Convention, and became best-buds immediately.

The avid diet-Pepsi drinker was my co-editor (or co-pilot) for *The Negro Leagues Book*, called by some the bible of Black Baseball. He also contributed to more than 100 books on Negro Leagues history. Some of his last words from his hospice bed in Detroit, Michigan were, *"I'm Sorry Larry, but I'm Going Home!"* Dick, Wayne Stivers and myself wanted to complete the ultimate Negro League Encyclopedia, before either of us were called home. To fill that directive is volume two of *The Negro Leagues Book*.

Our constant companion, Rick Meister (now deceased), who had been on bedside watch since day one, was part of the quartet that often broke bread together. We had sleepovers at each of our homes. The Four Tops worked on several committees, conferences, letter-writing campaigns, and through collaborative efforts with like-minded individuals, we re-opened the doors of Cooperstown in 1987, to get 25 more Black ball veterans in the National Baseball Hall of Fame and Museum, beginning with Ray Dandridge.

Still, all good things must come to an end. We all have a reservation in the upper room, without the privilege of cancellation. Despite our best game, Father Time is still undefeated.

Well the dogs are now whistling a new tune, barking at the new moon. I will miss my dear friend and will carry his thoughts with me each and every day, until my call to home comes. Clark was as fine a gentleman as one could meet.

From his hospice bed Dick whispered, *"Please keep the legacy alive!* And this volume of work is in that direction

.

IN THE BEGINNING

The Gentlemen's Agreement and the Color Line:

Snapshots of the early days of Black Baseball and its significance in American history

It's time to recognize the legacy of Black Baseball as durable Americana. Former Major League Baseball Commissioner and President of Yale University, A. Bart Giamatti wrote in "A Life of A. Bartlett Giamatti: By Him and About Him:"

"When baseball desegregated itself in 1947 on the field, the first American institution to do so voluntarily, baseball changed America. Baseball changed how Blacks and Whites felt about themselves and about each other. For the first time, a Black American was on America's most privileged version of a level field. He was there as an equal because of his skill, as those Whites who preceded him had been and those Blacks and Whites who succeeded him would be. Merit will win, it was promised by baseball which touches upon race relations, immigration and assimilation, ethnicity, language, math, statistics, labor and management, money and all these things, as well as being a social barometer of where America has been."

One such barometer was the "Gentlemen's Agreement." It became the clay tablets that commanded baseball owners and forced Black players to play in a world where only the ball was white. Black players were slaves to a segregated sport and were unfree in a free country.

The Negro Baseball Leagues were a product of segregated America, created to give opportunity where opportunity did not exist. The Leagues were a peephole into this country's bigotry-bigotry aimed at individuals a shade darker than the hide of a dirty baseball. In the process, it forced the best non-White athletes to play shadow ball in an oasis between the white foul lines.

Their competitive play was colorblind, but the country's mindset was not. For years, they listened to airbrushed excuses from the powers that be; "You are not ready for the Show," "Our fans are not ready for Colored ballplayers," or the dubious compliment, "If you were only White!" But prejudice could not whitewash their talents. The talents of these soulful men exhibited an explosion of raw skills, intoxicating excitement, and a curious appeal to many fans.

Quarantined from baseball's mainstream, the world of Black Baseball became a fortress of stability, offering the preservation of ancestry, a towering strength of credibility, instilled with the highest class of play, athleticism, leadership, professionalism, and innovative play, coupled with an unselfish pride in sports achievement. As the Negro Leagues reached its zenith of credibility and prosperity, Black and White audiences saw sepia stars as a welcome diversion to the Great Recession and later war times, as they flocked to games to watch this up-tempo style of play on the diamonds.

To follow are snapshots of how Black Baseball evolved from before the Civil War up through 1900.

October 24, 1855 - *Newark Daily Mercury*

BASE BALL — A match game of Base Ball was played between the St. John's and Union Cubs (Colored) yesterday afternoon. Two innings were played when it commenced to rain. The St. John's Club made ten runs and the Union Club only two. The game is to be played again on Friday at 2 o'clock, on the grounds of the St. John's Club [in East Orange, NJ], foot of Chestnut Street.

December 10, 1859 – *New York Anglo-African*

The first recorded game with a box score between two Black teams occurred on this date.

"Mr. Editor: A match was played between the Henson Base Ball Club of Jamaica, and the Unknown, of Weeksville, at Jamaica, L.I., on Tuesday, November 15th, which resulted in another victory for the Henson."

The Henson Base Ball Club defeated the Unknown(s), 54 to 43.

October 17, 1862 - *Brooklyn Daily Eagle*

Base Ball
A New Sensation in Base Ball Circles - Sambo as a Ball Player, and Dinah as an Emulator
Unknown Club of Weeksville vs. Monitor of Brooklyn

Negro Leagues Book #2: The Players

The return match between the Atlantic and Harlem Clubs did not take place as appointed yesterday afternoon, but was postponed on account of the unfit condition of the grounds for playing. Among the large crowd that visited the grounds was our reporter, who, on learning that the match would not be played, went on a perambulating tour through the precincts of Bedford, waiting for something to "turn up."

He had not proceeded far when he discovered a crowd assembled on the grounds in the vicinity of the Yucatan Skating Pond, and on repairing of the locality found a match in progress between the Unknown and Monitor Clubs - both of African descent. Quite a large assemblage encircled the contestants, where everyone was as black as the ace of spades.

Among the assemblage we noticed a number of old and well known players, who seemed to enjoy the game more heartily than if they had been the players themselves. The dusky contestants enjoyed the game hugely and to use a common phrase, they "did the thing genteelly."

Dinah, all eyes, was there to applaud to have a very jolly time, and the little piccaninnies laughed with the rest. It would have done Beecher, Greeley, or any other of the luminaries of the radical wing of the Republican Party good to have been present. The playing was quite spirited, and the faces decreed a victory for the Unknowns. The occasion was the first of a series.

This is the first match to our knowledge that has been played in this city between players of African descent.

The First Gentlemen's Agreement or the Color Line

This unofficial but very real agreement is understood to be an oral agreement or rule that racially excluded African Americans from playing in the Major Leagues. This restriction was based on hues of skin pigmentation. Below are perhaps the first official written declarations of banning Black players from the national pastime, along with some early day accounts of Colored or Black Baseball.

October 3, 1867 - *Ball Players Chronicle*

Championship of the Colored Clubs - Arrangements have been made to play a series of games of base ball for the championship between the Excelsiors of Philadelphia and the Unique and Monitor clubs of Brooklyn - Colored clubs. The games will be played today and to-morrow, on the Satellite Grounds, Brooklyn. We have no doubt they will excite considerable attention and draw quite a large crowd, from the novelty of Colored clubs contending for the championship. We understand that Mr. J. J. Grum, of the Eckford Club, has kindly consented to stand as umpire.

> **Editor's note:** In seven innings, the Excelsiors defeated the Uniques by a score of 42-37. A few days later, the Monitors defeated the Excelsiors 32-18.

October 19, 1867 *New York Clipper*

EXCELSIOR VS. UNIQUE. One of the first box scores found between Black teams.

"The Excelsior Club, of Philadelphia, and the Unique Club, of Brooklyn, composed of American citizens of African scent [sic.] played a game at the Satellite Grounds, Williamsburg, on Thursday, Oct. 3rd. The affair was decidedly unique, and afforded considerable merriment to several hundred of the white trash' of this city and Brooklyn. The game was a Comedy of Errors' from beginning to end, and the decisions of the umpire—a gentlemanly looking light-colored party from the Bachelor Club of Albany—excelled anything ever witnessed on the ball field. Disputes between the players occurred every few minutes and the game finally ended in a row. At 5 1/2 o'clock, while the Brooklyn club was at the bat, with every prospect of winning the game, the Excelsiors, profiting by the examples set by their White brothers, declared that it was too dark' to continue the game, and the umpire called it and awarded the ball to the Philadelphians. Confusion worse confounded reigned supreme for full an hour at one time for a riot, but the police, who were present in large force, kept matters pretty quiet, and the crowd finally dispersed.

October 16, 1867 - The Pythians, a prominent Black club from Philadelphia, file a petition to join the Pennsylvania Base Ball Association, at a meeting held at the Court House, in Harrisburg, PA.

December 9, 1867 - At their 12th annual convention in Philadelphia, the Nominating Committee of the National Association of Base Ball Players (NABBP) reports:

"It is not presumed by your Committee that any club who have applied are composed of persons of color, or any portion of them; and the recommendation of your Committee in this report are based upon this view, and they unanimously report against the admission of any club which may be composed of one or more colored persons... If colored clubs were admitted, there would be in all probability some division of feeling — whereas by excluding them, no injury could result to anybody."

December 18, 1867 - After reviewing an application for league entry by the Philadelphia Pythians, the National Association of Base Ball Players bans Black players "on political grounds."

Editor's Note: A four page hand-written letter to the Pythian team was transcribed verbatim by eminent historian Jerry Malloy below. Malloy was considered by many researchers to be the most knowledgeable authority on nineteenth-century Black Baseball.

Philadelphia, Dec. 18th, 1867

To the President & Members of the Pythian B.B.C.

Gentlemen:

The delegate appointed by this Club to represent them in the Pa. State Convention of Base Ball Players, which met at Harrisburg on the 16th of October last, respectfully.

Reports that in the night of the 15th of Oct. he proceeded to Harrisburg and put up at the [illegible] House where he met Messrs. Hayhurst and Ellis of the Athletic B.B.C. and other delegates to the Convention. The next morning he proceeded to the Court House where the Convention assembled and was introduced by Mr. Hayhurst to President Rose, Sec. Domer and others. On the Convention being called to order, and the roll called, Messrs. Evans Rogers, Saml. Hayhurst and Wm. Cramer were appointed a Com. on Credentials. Whilst this Com. were making up their report the delegates clustered together in small groups to discuss what action ought to be taken on the admittance of the Pythians delegate, and your delegate himself was waited on by Sec. Domer who stated that he & Mr. Hayhurst had both been discussing the matter of our admittance, and canvassing the other delegates, and tho' they and the President were in favor of our acceptance, still the majority of the delegates were opposed to it and they would advise me to withdraw my application, as they thought it were better for us to withdraw than to have it on record that we were black balled. This your delegate declined to do, and waited for the Com. to report, which they shortly did and reported favorably in all the credentials presented to them save that of the Pythian which they purposely left out of their general report. On their report being read a resolution was hastily passed and Mr. Ellis quickly springing to his feet moved that the Com. be discharged. Your delegate was about to say that as they had not finished their business they ought not to be discharged, when Mr. Rodgers arose & said that there was one other credential in their hands which they were bound to report, from the Pythian B.B.C. a colored organization from Philadelphia, and they had presented it alone that the Convention might take such action on it as they should deem fit. It having been read by the Secretary, Mr. Ellis moved that it be laid on the table, which motion was seconded by at least two thirds of the Convention, and but for the timely interference of Messrs. Rogers (of the Batchelor Club of this city) and Hayhurst, Mr. Ellis' motion would have passed. These gentlemen [illegible] that as there were but a few delegates present (some 20 in all) that the matter be deferred till evening, when in all probability there would be a larger no. present, and they thought it unfair that this few present should take the responsibility of rejecting a delegate (for so the most of them seem disposed) when perhaps a greater proportion of those present in the evening would be in favor [of their] acceptance. To this Mr. Ellis and Mr. Rogers, of the Chester Club, the mover and seconder of the motion to table agreed together with the rest of the delegates. The Convention then proceeded to [crossed out: "an election of officers"] the adoption of a Constitution and

---

[Inserted: 36 lines clipped from a column of an unidentified newspaper, probably *The Ball Players' Chronicle*, October 24, 1867 (Vol. I: No. 21), p. 1. The "Chronicle" stated that their account was "taken from the Philadelphia Sunday Mercury. The clipping covered the end of the convention, including an announcement of members of Committee on Constitution and By-Laws, the results of the election of new officers, the recitation of a poem composed by a delegate, and adjournment. None of this material addresses the issue of African American membership. Not included was the Chronicle's report that "The [Credentials] Committee reported that an application had been received from the Pythian Base Ball Club of Philadelphia (Colored), the consideration of which was laid over until evening," or that "Before its adjournment, the delegate from the Pythian Club withdrew his application."]

After the adjournment in the morning the members of the Convention clustered around your delegate and whilst all expressed sympathy for our club, a few only[,] such as Messrs. Hayhurst, Domer, Rose, Stimel of the Chestnut St. Theater, and Rogers of the Batchelor expressed a willingness to move for our admission, while numbers of others openly said that they would in justice to the opinion of the clubs they represented be compelled, though against their personal feelings, to vote against our admission.

Messrs. Hayhurst & Domer again requested the withdrawal of our credentials, and were seconded in this request by most of the members. As your delegate did not feel at liberty to do this whilst there was any hope whatever of admission, he telegraphed home for instructions, and received word to fight if there was a chance. When evening came the delegates were in number about the same as the morning and as there seemed no chance for anything but being black balled, your delegate withdrew his application, and rec'd from Mr. Domer, the Sec.[,] a pass home over the Phila. Central R.R.

Before closing this already too lengthy report your delegate feels bound to state that all [underlined] the delegates seemed disposed to show their sympathy and respect for our club by [crossed out: their] showing him every possible courtecy [sic] & kindness. While at dinner Messrs. Hayhurst, Rogers and others invited him to attend the base ball match that was to be played that afternoon in company with them, which was accepted. And on the ["road"?, illegible] & at the match, your delegate cannot speak too highly of the kind attentions which these gentlemen showed him and their expressions of friendship for our club.

End of transcription.

December 19, 1867

The *Milwaukee Daily Sentinel* also reported, "First, rules of order are discussed; then additional clubs are admitted into the Association, and thirdly, and selfishly and cowardly, it is resolved that 'No club composed of persons of color, or having in its membership persons of color, shall be admitted into the National Association.' Great applause by the delegates and hisses in the galleries, whereupon the President, with more feeling than dignity, declared, as one having such authority, that if these demonstrations were repeated, he would 'order the galleries to be cleared immediately'." Sentinel information is courtesy of Skip McAfee.

1869 *New York Clipper*

"The prejudices of race are rapidly disappearing. A week or two ago we chronicled a game between the Pythian (Colored) and Olympics (White) clubs of Philadelphia. This affair was a great success, financially and otherwise."

August 24, 1870 - *The Sporting World*

"Base Ball from a Colored Point of View.

"Match Game Between American Clubs of African Descent.

"THE GAME FROM A COLORED STANDPOINT.

"Chicago has enjoyed a wide range of experience in base ball, having witnessed its representation in nearly every possible shape, but not until yesterday had an opportunity been afforded for seeing how the American citizens of African descent does it. Indeed, there were those so prejudiced as to maintain the base ball and the suffrage qualification were widely different, inasmuch as, while one was the creature of legislative enactment, the other was utter impossibility on anatomical grounds; in short, that tender shins and red-hot grounders were incompatible. This fallacy, like many other with reference to the same subject, was thoroughly exploded at Ogden Park yesterday afternoon. Our colored brethren can play base ball, an do it well into the bargain. For sometime past there has existed in Chicago an organization known as the Blue Stockings, which is made up exclusively of dusky athletes who are employed as waiters in the various hotels and restaurants. Under serious difficulties the necessary practice was obtained, owing to an idiosyncrasy of the rowdy element in monopolizing the lake front as a White man's park,' to the exclusion of colored ball-tossers.

At last, however, the Blue Stocking nine had mastered the preliminaries, and on the first of the present month they accepted the challenge of the Rockford Club, of Rockford, which is also made up of amendments, to play a match game. Be it known that the latter are the protégés of the Forest City boys, who have made it a special point to put them through the details, and have looked upon them as appendages, in some sort, to the crack amateur club. In the first game the Blue Stockings were beaten, and the contest yesterday was the second of the series. There were about four hundred spectators in attendance, being largely of the African persuasion, with about an equal apportionment of the sexes, while a small element of the pure and unadulterated (so-called) Caucasians were on hand for the sake of curiosity. With an astounding disregard of the distinguished precedents afforded by the White Stockings, Amateurs, etc., the rival nines were on hand soon after 2 o'clock, and they actually paid so little regard to base ball usages as to begin the game at the precise time advertised, viz., 2 1/2 o'clock. Such conduct could only be properly punished by expulsion from the State and National Associations, to which, unfortunately, neither the Blue Stockings nor the Rockfords belong. They should be admitted at once in order that such reflections upon the practices of their betters (?) might be rigorously dealt with.

The Blue Stockings wore a very tasty uniform, consisting of cap of broad blue and white stripes, blue shirt with a neat monogram on the breast, white flannel pants, blue stockings and regulation shoes. The rig of the Rockfords was made up of blue cap, and white shirt, and blue pants of full length. With the selection of Mr. R.C. Rickhoff, late of the Potter Palmers, as umpire, everything was in readiness, and the Blue Stockings, having won the toss, took the field. In each of the first and second innings the Rockfords were whitewashed in one-two-three order, by very fine fielding on the part of their opponents, who when they came to the bat, had no difficulty in hitting for five tallies in the first and three in the second inning, thus gaining a strong lead, which rapidly increased as the game proceeded, the final result showing 48 for the Blue Stockings and 14 for the Rockfords.

The game was an unusually interesting one throughout, besides being extremely creditable for the Chicago lads, whose general play in the field and at the bat were fully equal to that of any amateur club in the city. As a catcher, George Brown has no superiors here, and few equals, while as a Captain he displayed an energy and judgment, and enforced a discipline, of which a certain high-priced team we know of stands sadly in need. His foul tips, flies and bounds, would have excited Craver's envy, and his throwing to second was such that the plan of stealing from first was altogether abandoned by the other side. The other members of the nine played uniformly well, as will be seen by the fact that four blanks were visited upon the Rockfords, who are good batters. The latter also displayed some fine individual points, but in general they were outplayed in every respect, and they can go back to Rockford well supplied with reasons why they failed to deserve the $100 which the Forest City Club promised them, in the event of their beating the Blue Stockings.

To sum up the game in general, it need only be said that, saving the single item of color, it was like other well-played games. One peculiarity, however, was noticeable, whether accidental or usual we don't know. It consisted in an irresistible propensity for tumbling head over heels when in the act of running bases or going for fly catches. Somersaults, which would have permanently doubled up and disabled a White Stocking, were counted as nothing by they of the colored hose, and resulted in much amusement among the spectators; nothing more.

September 4, 1870 - *Chicago Tribune*
"Base Ball. The Amateur Tournament"
"A meeting of the Captains and members of the nines contemplating participation in the forthcoming tournament for the amateur championship of Chicago, was held last evening, at the office of A. Goodrich, No. 128 Dearborn street. The meeting was not formally organized, the proceedings taking the form of free discussion of the various questions connected with the tournament. Among other things, it was decided to reject the application of the Blue Stockings (Colored) for a place in the list of competing clubs. After other matters had been canvassed, the meeting adjourned until Tuesday evening next, when the Captains of the various nines are requested to assemble at Foley's billiard hall, thence to depart to a suitable place of meeting. It is now ascertained that the Amateurs, Aetnas, Athletics, Transits, and Actives will participate in the tournament, which will begin at Ogden Park on Thursday afternoon next."

September 17, 1870 - *Chicago Tribune*
"An evening paper pronounces the tournament a fizzle, because the colored club, known as the Blue Stockings, was not permitted to enter, and compete for the amateur championship and silver ball. Some weeks ago, this nine, composed of young colored men, met and badly worsted a similar organization from Rockford. They played a much better game than anyone would have supposed a party of hotel and restaurant waiters capable of doing, and they were encouraged to make application for admission to the tournament lists, which they did, but without any idea that the proposition would be seriously entertained. It was acted upon by the five clubs interested, and rejected, mainly because the Blue Stockings were not deemed of sufficient strength to be entitled to consideration. Probably their social standing had somewhat to do with the matter. Very naturally it would as the young men belonging to our leading amateur clubs are all respectable and of good standing, some of them being connected with the best families of Chicago. They were all thoroughly in earnest regarding the title of supremacy with the ball and bat and were not disposed to burlesque the tournament by the admission of a

colored club of inferior capacity, even though the gate receipts should suffer thereby. They were not playing for gate receipts, but for the championship and the silver ball, and, having the unquestioned right and power, they decided to rule out the Blue Stockings, and nothing more would have been heard of it but for the ill-natured and purely gratuitous comments of the evening contemporary, which seems to have resurrected this affair as a pretext for throwing cold water upon the laudable efforts of our amateur players to improve their play by engaging in a series of contests for the championship of the city, and its attendant honors and advantages. The tournament is by no means a fizzle. It is true that the attendance has not been commensurate with the merits of the clubs interested, but the games are spirited and attractive, and the affair will be continued to a successful and satisfactory termination."

September 20, 1870 - *Chicago Tribune*
"The Blue Stockings (Colored) beat a picked nine (White), 17 to 9."

September 21, 1870 - *Chicago Tribune*
"The Blue Stockings (Colored) were beaten by a White picked nine, 24 to 8."

September 29, 1870 - *Chicago Tribune*
Aetnas defeated Amateurs, 24-21, at Ogden Park to win tournament.

October 1, 1870 - *Chicago Tribune*
"Miscellaneous Games"
"The last game of the series for the colored championship of the State was played at Rockford on Thursday last, between the Blue Stockings, of Chicago, and the Rockfords, of Rockford, both colored. The Blue Stockings were victorious by a score of 30 to 18."

October 2, 1870 - *Chicago Tribune*
"The Hunters (Colored) beat the Monitors (White), 35 to 20."

October 9, 1870 - *Chicago Tribune*
"The Hunters (Colored) defeated the Union Turners, by a score of 22 to 0."

May 31, 1871 - *Chicago Tribune*
"GAMES IN CHICAGO. The Blue Stockings (Colored) were defeated yesterday by the Uniques (Colored) by a score of 39 to 5. The game was for the colored championship."

June 13, 1871- *Chicago Tribune*
"The Red Stockings (Colored) captured the Red Hands by 33 to 14."

September 17, 1871 - *Chicago Tribune*
"Colored Men's Match Game.
"Philadelphia, Sept. 16. —The colored men's base ball match to-day was largely attended. The score is: Uniques, Chicago, 19; Pythians, Philadelphia, 7. This is the first defeat for the Pythians in five years."

September 19, 1871 - *Chicago Tribune*
"The Uniques."
"This club, composed of young men of African descent, having inflicted the first defeat of their experience upon the Pythians, of Philadelphia, the colored champions of the East, now lay claim to the title of the colored champions of America. The Unique is composed of George Brown, Captain and catcher; Wm. Johnson, pitcher; T. Hambleton, short stop; Henry Hampton, second base; John Sanders, first base; Robert Johnson, third base; John Shaw, centre field; John Simms, right field; J. Tyler, left field. The Uniques play the Oclias, of Troy, N.Y., tomorrow, and in Pittsburgh on Saturday next."

June 26, 1870 - *Chicago Times*
The Shamrocks and Blue Stockings have met at last. The game was very close, the former winning, by the score of 15 to 14."

August 24, 1870 - *Chicago Times*

"A COLORED GAME"

"A game of ball was played on yesterday, at Ogden park, between two clubs composed entirely of negroes. One hailed from Rockford, and wore pink socks; the other is a home organization, and reveled in socks of blue. They were named respectively after the color of their hosiery. Both clubs played a very strong game, but the Chicago nine proved very easy victors. A very select crowd of 500 witnessed the highly-colored affair. The game was satisfactory to all parties. An admirer of the national was heard to say, at its conclusion, that the Chicago boys were liable to make it warm for any club in the country."

August 24, 1870 - *Chicago Times*

"The Amateurs of this city are about completing arrangements for a grand tournament for the [illegible] amateur championship of Chicago and a prize of $100, the latter being offered by the Amateur Club, to be given to the champion club. A moderate entrance fee, say $10, will be charged, in order that the tournament may not be flooded with clubs of no reasonable pretensions. Other prizes will be for the best players in several particulars. It is intended that the tournament that shall being in the 4th of September. The Blue Stockings (Colored) will probably be among the contestants. Why not?"

September 4, 1870 - *Chicago Times*

"The Amateur Tournament.

"An interesting meeting was held at Goodrich's law office on last evening, to take the preliminary steps for the forthcoming amateur tournament. There were only three clubs represented, although the attendance of members of each club was quite large. The fact that it was expected that colored clubs would be allowed to participate in the matches was probably the reason that more of the city organizations had no delegates present. But it was virtually decided on last evening that it would injure the prospects of the tournament to admitted colored nines, and so it is probable that those who have signified their intention of entering will be allowed to withdraw, to prevent any ill-feeling on account of race."

September 7, 1870 - *Chicago Times*

"BASE-BALL. THE AMATEUR TOURNAMENT.

"Announcements of the proposed tournament of the amateur base- ball clubs of the city have been published in The Times. The matter has now taken definite shape, and the following valuable prizes have been offered by various parties:

"One hundred dollars and an elegant silver ball, the latter manufactured and presented by Conger & Webb, jewelers, No. 125 South Clark street. A full description of the ball was given in this journal on yesterday. It is a beauty in every respect and is now on exhibition at Conger & Webb's establishment.

"Messrs. Goodrich & Kirby, No. 122 Dearborn street, offer a fine set of studs, mounted with jewels and oriental garnets, to the most popular base-ball reporter in the city. The individual who attends to that department of the Times knows very well that he is the person indicated, and that the prize is rightfully his, but, in justice to the unpopular reporters of other Chicago journals, he insists that they shall be allowed some slight chance to compete for Messrs. Goodrich & Kirby's beautiful prize.

"An elegant seal ring, valued at $20, will be awarded to the player making the most runs during the tournament. This prize is given by the Amateur club.

"A pair of buckskin shoes with patent spikes will be given to the swiftest runner by J.W.D. Kelley & Bros., No. 164 Lake street.

"J.A. Pierce & Co., of No. 61 Clark street, offer a pair of Indian clubs to the best thrower.

"Suitable prizes will be awarded to the players making the most fly catches, home runs, muffs, etc."

September 20, 1870 - *Chicago Times*

A DENIAL. The captain of the Blue Stockings—the colored nine that was not permitted to play in the amateur tournament—says that he did make a formal application on behalf of his club to be permitted to take part in the games, and that The Post knows nothing of the facts when it says he did not do so."

Negro Leagues Book #2: The Players

September 21, 1870 - *Chicago Times*
"THE BLUE STOCKINGS. This club, composed of colored players, are ready to meet any amateur nine in this city at a fair trial of base ball skill. Though excluded from the one-horse tournament, the Blue Stockings are still of the opinion that they can make a good game against any club in Chicago, except the professionals."

September 23, 1870 - *Chicago Times*
"THE BLUE STOCKINGS are evidently in earnest as regards their protest in the matter of not being permitted to join in the abortive amateur tournament, as will be seen from the subjoined card published in the latest issue of the New York Clipper:

"Chicago, Sept. 10, 1870.—Mr. Frank Queen, Editor, New York Clipper: We, the Blue Stockings (Colored), of Chicago, made application to play in the amateur tournament now in progress in this city, at Ogden park, but were not admitted, for what reason I cannot tell, unless it is because they are afraid of us beating them. If they are afraid to play us, why, then, do they put their names out as the champion amateur clubs of the city? Yours truly, W.P. Johnson, Secretary of the Blue Stocking B.B.C., 228 and 230 South Clark street."

September 25, 1870 - *Chicago Times*
"The Red Stockings defeated the Blue Stockings, 22 to 5."

September 28, 1870 - *Chicago Times*
"WHITE VS. BLACK. The Independents (White) and the Blue Stockings (Colored) played a game on yesterday, at Ogden park. The former were victorious, in a score of 17 to 15."

October 2, 1870 - *Chicago Times*
THE COLORED CHAMPIONSHIP. The third and decisive game for the colored championship of the state took place at Rockford on Friday last, between the Blue Stockings, of Chicago, and the Rockfords. The nine from the Garden city were again victorious, as the appended score by innings will show:

```
Blue Stockings      221 514 591—30.
Rockfords           533 040 300—18.
```

October 6, 1870 - *Chicago Times*
"The Blue Stockings, Colored, and the Independents play their return game at Ogden park this afternoon. A prize of $100 has been raised for the winners, and a lively game is anticipated."

October 7, 1870 - *Chicago* Times
"The Blue Stockings, Colored, and the Independents, contested an exciting game at Ogden park on yesterday afternoon, for a prize of $100. The stalwart youths of the blue hose and dusky faces were defeated, by a score of 25-24."

October 8, 1870 - *Chicago* Times
"THE BLUE STOCKINGS claim that in their late game with the Independents, the game was called at the end of the eighth inning, and in proof of their claim they state that they have been given the $100 purse, and they also forward the following score of the game by innings:"

```
Blue Stockings      010 423 58—23
Independents        423 047 02—22
```

May 31, 1871 - *Chicago Times*
"THE COLORED CHAMPIONSHIP. In the first game of a series between the Blue Stockings and the Uniques, for the Colored championship on the grounds of the Prairie club, corner State and Twenty-third streets, the Unique were the winners by a score of 39 to 5.

The Uniques are open to play any amateur club in the city. Clubs desiring to make matches may address all communications to W.D. Berry, corresponding secretary, No. 77 Clark street." [Historian Bob Pruter notes that William Johnson, Unique's pitcher, was also a member of the Blue Stockings in 1870]

September 26, 1871 - *Chicago Times*
"The Hunters beat the You Beta on yesterday, 33 to 23."

October 4, 1871 - *Chicago Times*
"The Hunters beat the Marines on yesterday by a score of 27 to 11."

October 12, 1875 - *Chicago Times*
"Senegambians at the Noble Sport in This City...

"A COLORED GAME. There is war in Africa. Yesterday, the colored Blue Stockings, of St. Louis, played the colored Uniques, of Chicago, a match game of base-ball on the grounds of the white, White Stockings, and walloped them to the tune of 12 to 8. The Uniques invaded The Times local rooms, last night, four strong or stronger, and claimed that their manager, Hall, had offered their pitcher $10 to throw' the game; that he being a little-hatched man, had owned up and said he refused the proffered bribe, but that Dyson, the catcher, had yielded to the charms of $25 and sold them out. They discovered the alleged treachery at the end of the seventh inning, and changed catchers, but too late to win the game. As another game is played on the same grounds by the same clubs Wednesday, the Uniques wished to start in with clean hands."

October 24, 1875 - *Chicago Times*
"A NEW COLORED CLUB. The Lake City Base-ball association, a colored organization, with a capital of $750, is now in the field. It proposes to get together the best nine that the colored population of the country can afford, and has elected the following officers: President, Harry P. Hall; vice president, H. Bearford; manager, William Berry."

August 22, 1881 - *The Louisville Commercial*
Cleveland Whites vs. Eclipse

The Utter Respectability of the Eclipse Nine Will Not Permit a Mulatto Catcher

How the Whites were Beaten

The Cleveland Whites were defeated yesterday by the Eclipse through errors and passed balls of the former's catcher. Walker, the regular catcher of the Whites, is a mulatto. He is as respectable looking as any ball player who has played here this season. When the club arrived they were informed that he could not play in the games here. Yesterday West, the first baseman, began as catcher, but one inning was sufficient to demonstrate that he could not catch. He gave out after he had allowed two runs to be scored on passed balls. The crowd raised a yell for "Walker" and after much persuasion, he came out.

He took a little preliminary practice before beginning to play and such throwing to bases as this has not been seen here since the days of the League clubs. When it was seen that Walker was going to play, a member of the Eclipse players left the grounds and refused to play if the "objectionable negro" was allowed to stay. After much talk it was agreed that he should not play and he started for his coat and collar, of which he had divested himself upon entering the field.

He had about reached them when Charles Fuller rushed up and endeavored to eject him summarily from the park. Some gentleman standing near interfered and prevented this, so took a seat among the crowd, and watched the game throughout.

Louisville is the first city whose base ball club has refused to allow him to play. He is well educated and probably more intelligent than sixteen out of the eighteen players. His parents are highly respectable and wealthy citizens of Cleveland. All the League [Western] clubs have played against him. It is hoped that he will be allowed to play in today's game. Another thing ardently to be desired is that the Eclipse club should have a watchman to guard Mr. Fuller who offered such an indignity to Mr. Walker yesterday.

Arandel, the pitcher for the Whites, is a host in himself. Only five hits were made off them, and with a catcher two, would have been all. The other three were made about abundant opportunity had been offered to put the side out. The six runs made by the Eclipse were all made by errors of the Cleveland's catcher.

Browning did the best playing for the Eclipse. A one-handed running pick-up of a seeming good base hit captured the crown.

Stockwell, the left fielder of the Whites, carried off the honors of the day, making several fine catches.

The final score was Eclipse - 6; Whites - 3.

Negro Leagues Book #2: The Players

July 5, 1883 - *Savanna (GA) Morning News*
"The Broadways and Athletics, two colored base ball clubs, crossed bats yesterday to the tune of 23 to 11 in favor of the Broadways."

September 10, 1883 - *Savanna (GA) Morning News*
"Considerable interest is taken in the contest at Base Ball Park to-day between the Athletic (Colored) Base Ball Club, of Jacksonville, and the Atlantics (Colored) of this city. The game will be called at 3:30 o'clock."

September 11, 1883 - *Savanna (GA) Morning News*
"The Colored Base Ballist - Florida Defeated by One Score.

The game between the Athletic Base Ball Club, colored, of Jacksonville, and the Atlantics of this city, for the championship of Georgia and Florida, at Base Ball Park yesterday afternoon was witnessed by about 500 people. The game was called at 3:30 o'clock and was concluded at 6:10, and was well played throughout, the total score being 17 to 16 in favor of the Atlantics.

This gives the championship to Georgia, since it was won by Florida in 1881.

The visiting club was entertained last night and will be given a picnic at Cedar Hammock today, returning home tomorrow morning."

September 13, 1883 - *Savanna (GA) Morning News*
"The Colored Base Ballist.

The game at Base Ball Park yesterday between the Athletic Base Ball Club, colored, of Jacksonville, and the Atlantics of this city, was witnessed by a fair crowd. The game was called at 3:30 o'clock, and was well played by the visitors throughout, and resulted in an even score on the close of the seventh inning, when the game was concluded. The score by innings is as follows:

```
                1 2 3 4 5 6 7
Athletics       0 3 3 4 1 1 0 - 12
Atlantics       0 0 0 5 4 1 3 - 12 (13)
```

The visiting club left for home last night, well pleased with their entertainment."

October 6, 1885 – *New York Times*
The Cuban Giants Beaten

There was a farcical game of ball at the Polo Grounds yesterday that served to amuse some 600 spectators. A nine of the ebon sons of Africa, running in all coffee shades from black Mocha to café au lait, who call themselves Cuban Giants, gave a minstrel performance on the diamond and the Mets enjoyed it and took their cue from the colored champions. The pitcher of the Giants was 6 feet 4 inches in height, and he twirled the ball like a Long Branch tray. The Mets made 9 runs in the first inning, and for the rest of the game the excitement was kept up by the gibes of the grandstand and the repartee of the players.

April 1, 1886 – *St. Louis Post-Dispatch*
"Gossip of the Game" - A call has been issued for the captains of all colored base ball clubs of Georgia, Florida, South Carolina, Alabama, and Tennessee that have a fair record and desire to enter the **Southern League of Colored Base Ballists**, Lock Box 298, Jacksonville, Florida.

Editor's note: the first game was played on June 7 between the Georgia Champions' Baseball Club of Atlanta, GA and the Eclipse Baseball Club of Memphis, TN. The Champions won 11 to 10. The league comprised of roughly 19 teams. The league officials were president, John W. Jones, manager Thomas T. Harden, treasurer L.H. Jones and secretary M.J. Christopher.

June 29, 1886 - *Trenton True American*
In Sol White's December 27, 1930 article in the *New York Age* newspaper, he cites perhaps the first attempt by a Major League team to sign an African American ballplayer since brothers Fleetwood and Welday Walker signed with the Toledo Blue Stockings of the American Association in 1884. The Philadelphia Athletics, who would finish in sixth place in 1886, made an offer, but Thomas declined. Arthur Thomas played from 1883 to 1991 as a catcher and first baseman for several top flight Black teams.

In The Beginning

KING SOLOMON "SOL" WHITE – The godfather of early day Black baseball was a native of Bellaire, Ohio. This prince of Bellaire played for several New York teams, the Gorhams in 1889, Cuban Giants (1889-94), Cuban X-Giants (1896-99, 1901), Columbia Giants (1900), Brooklyn Royal Giants (1910), and the Lincoln Giants (1911).

White wrote, "He was 6 feet 4 inches in height; his arms almost reached his knees; he was sorta sway-backed and gangled-legged; he had a moaning voice and actually would cry when his team lost a game. His facial expressions were paradoxical; when he laughed you would have to look twice to see whether he was crying. An extremely hard worker, he ruled the roost including the captain. Thomas was a great receiver behind the bat. With his long arms he would reach out and grab wild pitches and when the ball left his hand for second base it looked like a long snake. We don't know how Arthur would take with the players of today, but there is one thing I do know, that is, a player with the earnestness of Arthur Thomas would make a hit with the fans."

The National Colored Base Ball League or the League of Colored Base Ball Clubs - 1887

December 15, 1886 – *Sporting Life*

The Colored League

All the Preliminaries Arranged for a Colored Base Ball Association

The National League of Colored Base Ball Players held their first convention at Eureka Hall on Arthur Street, Pittsburg[h], Dec. 9. The representatives present selected Nelson M. Williams of Washington, as temporary chairman, and J. Will Gatewood as secretary. The following teams were represented: Philadelphia [Pythians] by Gilbert A. Ball and R.G. Still; Baltimore by J.J. Callis; Washington [Capitol Citys] by Nelson M. Williams; Cincinnati [Browns] by J.W. Fowler; Louisville [Falls City] by L. Condon; Pittsburg[h] [Keystones] by Walter S. Brown.

The following permanent officers were as follows: President Walter S. Brown of Pittsburg[h], vice president J.J. Callis of Baltimore [Lord Baltimores]; secretary of N.M. Williams of Washington; treasurer Gilbert A. Ball of Philadelphia; assistant secretary, M.A. Spriggs of Pittsburg[h]; board of directors, Horace McGee, J.J. Callis, L. Condon and R.G. Still; schedule committee, W.S. Brown, M.A. Spriggs, Horace McGee, L. Condon and R.G. Still; committee on constitution, J.J. Callis, J.W. Fowler, N.M. Williams and R.G. Still.

Upon taking his office President Brown welcomed the delegates in a neat address of welcome. The Spalding ball was adopted. On the question of the adoption of the National rules for 1887, as passed by the League and the Association committees, there was a lively debate, but the motion adopting them was carried. The convention adjourned to meet in March, at the call of President Brown. Boston and Cleveland both sent letters guaranteeing their acceptance of place in the league, and the teams were accordingly enrolled. The meeting was enthusiastic.

January 2, 1887 - *Democrat and Chronicle Rochester (NY)*

—A colored baseball league has been organized. It looks like a dark season for the national game—as reported in the Hartford Post.

January 26, 1887 - *Sporting Life*

Larkin's Colored Protégé

Walter Brown [of the Pittsburg Keystones], of the Colored League [president of the National Colored Base Ball League], will sign a pitcher next week named Malson [Malone, William H.]. He is a boilermaker of Reading [PA] and comes highly recommended. Larkin, of the Athletics, says that Malson [Malone] is a greater twirler, and that if his was of another color he would be in big demand from more than one first-class club. Five of the Colored League teams have agreed to the National Agreement, viz: Boston, Baltimore, Pittsburg, Cincinnati and Louisville. Washington and Philadelphia will likely follow suit, and New York, which asks admission, will probably do likewise. Some idea of the salaries of the League can be gathered from the statement that Malson [Malone] is to get $75 a month.

Negro Leagues Book #2: The Players

April 11, 1887 – *New York Times*

Sunday Ball Playing

It Attracts Great Throngs to Many Diamonds.

Between 2,000 and 3,000 people went out to the Long Island Grounds yesterday to see a game between the Newark nine and the Cuban Giants. The game had hardly got under way when the Queens County Sheriff and two Deputies made their appearance and ordered a cessation of hostilities. The crown, however, had come out to see ball played, so with a howl or rage they stood up as one man and then began to clamber over the seats toward the Sheriff. Cries of "slug him" and "lynch him" were heard from all sides, proceeding from those on the outskirts of the crowd. The Sheriff again ordered the game to be stopped and then went away. The players resumed their positions, the crowd fell back, and the interrupted work was taken up." The Cuban Giants lost to the Newark club, 4-1 in six innings.

After 17 league games played, the final league standings below:

```
Teams                        W      L      Pct%
Philadelphia Pythians        4      3      .571
Pittsburg Keystones          3      3      .500
Louisville Falls City        2      2      .500
Baltimore Lord Baltimores    4      5      .444
New York Gorhams             3      4      .429
Boston Resolutes             1      0     1.000
Cincinnati Browns            Did Not Play
Washington Capitol Citys     Did Not Play
```

April 13, 1887 - *Sporting Life*

Do They Need Protection?

The progress of the Colored League will be watched with considerable interest. There have been prominent colored base ball clubs throughout the country for many years past, but this is their initiative year in launching forth on a league scale by forming a league . . . representing . . . leading cities in the country. The League will attempt to secure the protection of the National Agreement. This can only be done with the consent of all National Agreement clubs in whose territories the colored clubs are located.

This consent should be obtainable, as these clubs can in no sense be considered rivals to the White clubs nor are likely to hurt the latter in the least financially. Still the league can get along without protection. The value of the latter to the White clubs lies in that it guarantees a club undisturbed possession of its players.

There is not likely to be much of a scramble for colored players. Only two such players are now employed on professional White clubs, and the number is not likely to be ever materially increased owing to the high standard of play required and to the popular prejudice against any considerable mixture of races.

> **Editor's note:** The National Colored Base Ball League was organized as an eight team league under the direction of Walter Brown of Pittsburg(h) with protection applied for, and granted, under the terms of the National Agreement. Although eight teams were originally included, only six of the teams were able to play. The Boston Resolutes and the New York Gorhams were added before the start of the 1887 season. While the Washington Capitol Citys and the Cincinnati Browns never opened their seasons.
>
> The first game was played on May 6 at Pittsburgh. The New York Gorhams won over the Pittsburgh Keystones, 11-8. The final game was also played in Pittsburgh, on May 19th, with the Keystone club victorious over the Lord Baltimores, 6-2. Overall, attendance over the two weeks, was poor with frequent rainouts.

September 12, 1887 - *New York Times*

"A Color Line in Baseball".

"The St. Louis Browns Refuse to Play with the Cuban Giants.

The Philadelphia Times will say tomorrow that for the first time in the history of baseball the color line has been drawn, and that the "world champions," the St. Louis Browns, are the men who have established the precedent that White players must not play with colored men. There have been little dissensions before, but only about a player here and there. The Browns were in open revolt last night. Some time ago President [Christian Wilhelm] Von Der Ahe arranged for his club to play an exhibition game at West Farms, near New York, with the Cuban Giants, the noted colored club. He was promised a big guarantee and it was expected that fully 15,000 persons would be present. The game was to have been played today, and President Von Der Ahe yesterday purchased railroad tickets for all his players and made all the arrangements for the trip. While he was at supper at the Continental Hotel last night thinking over the misfortune that had befallen Capt. [Charles] Comiskey, he was approached by "Tip" O'Neill, the heavy slugging left fielder, who laid a letter on the table and then hastily slipped out of the room.

The letter read as follows:

Philadelphia, Penn, Sept. 10.

To Chris Von Der Ahe, Esq.:

Dear Sir:

We, the undersigned members of the St. Louis Baseball Club, do not agree to play against negroes (sic) tomorrow. We will cheerfully play against White people at any time, and think, by refusing to play, we are only doing what is right, taking everything into consideration and the shape the team is in at present.

[signed] W.A. Latham, John Hoyle, J.E. O'Neill, R. L. Caruthers, W.E. Gleason, W.H. Robinson, Charles King, Curt Welch.

President Von Der Ahe did not wait to finish his meal. He left the table hastily and went down stairs into the corridor, where he found the players talking in a group. The sudden appearance of their manager among them surprised the players and they acted like a ship's crew about to mutiny. When Von Der Ahe asked the meaning of the letter he had just received nobody answered him. "Yank" Robinson hung his head and sneaked to the rear of the crowd. "Silver" King opened his mouth, but his tongue refused to move, and even Artie Latham, whose jaws are always going, couldn't get out a word. Receiving no reply, President Von Der Ahe said quietly: 'As it seems to be a matter of principle with you, you need not play tomorrow.'

President Von Der Ahe said to a Times reporter tonight: 'I am sorry to have disappointed the people of West Farms today, as I always fulfill my engagements. I was surprised at the action of my men, especially as they knew a week ago that the game was arranged, and yet they waited until the very last minute before they informed me of their opposition.

The St. Louis players were not disposed to talk of their action. Latham, Boyle and O'Neill were the leaders, it is said, and they had considerable trouble in securing the signatures of some of the men. Capt. Comiskey didn't know anything about the matter, and Knouff refused to sign the letter.

They had played with the Cuban Giants once before last season, and they seemed to enjoy it better than a contest with White players. Curtis Welch, the center fielder, played with the Toledo Club when [Moses Fleetwood] Walker, the colored player, was a member of the team. 'I think some of the boys wanted a day to themselves,' said Capt. Comiskey. 'They have played against colored clubs before without a murmur, and I think they are sorry for their hasty action already.'

The Cuban Giants were originally organized at Trenton about two years ago as an independent club. This season they have been in various places in close proximity of New York City. They are good players and the team has made money. They have played games with the Chicago, Indianapolis, Detroit, Louisville, Athletic, and other prominent clubs, and this is the first time that any club has refused to play with them on account of their color.

The International League recently adopted a resolution prohibiting the employment of colored players by its clubs. This was caused by opposition from the players, who objected to playing with second baseman [Charlie] Grant of the Buffalo club, and colored pitcher [George] Stovey, of the Newark club.

Negro Leagues Book #2: The Players

Editor's note: Chris von der Ahe was a German entrepreneur from Hille, Prussia. Earlier in 1885, Christian Friedrich Wilhelm von der Ahe erected a life-size statue of himself outside of St. Louis' Sportsman's Park. The former store and saloon owner purchased the team in 1882, also operated a farm club called the St. Louis Whites of the Western Association, in 1888.

October 15, 1887 - *New York Age*

The Cuban Giants, the great colored base ball nine, whose appearance [in Boston] created such interest and enthusiasm, and whose magnificent playing called forth vociferous plaudits, has an interesting and creditable history which shall be known of all colored and White lovers of the national sport.

July 28, 1888 - *New York Age*

Esteem and Respect for the Race

One fact cannot be doubted, and that is their extremely large following, by no means [all] colored, who flock in hundreds to see them [Cuban Giants]. For the last two seasons the residents of the old Dutch town owe much to the Cuban Giants for the amount of life they have given the place and the interest stimulated in this national sport. If any one doubts the popularity of this colored team, let him stand at 14th Street Ferry upon a Saturday afternoon and hear the comments and see the immense crowds flocking to their games . . . This is another way of cultivating esteem and respect for the race, and it is a good way, judging from appearances.

August 22, 1888 – *Chicago Daily Tribune*

The Pinchback Base-Ball Brigade

Chicago's Colored Champions Defeat Them in a Wildly Exciting Game.

The Pinchback Base-ball Club came all the way from New Orleans [more than a 1,000 mile trip] to play the Chicago Unions yesterday at the South Side Park. Both organizations enjoy an unrivaled reputation in the world of colored sport, and the Pinchbacks are so highly esteemed in Louisiana that five car-loads of gentlemen of their race came with them from the South. The betting on the contest was unprecedentedly heavy, a colored saloonkeeper, whose probity is held to be beyond question, having in his pockets 121 dollars, and 45 cents in cash, a ring with a stone popularly believed to be an amethyst, two pencil-cases, a watch-chain, and a promissory note, being the stakes in various wagers made upon the result, together with a bundle of gold-topped umbrellas, and canes with silver heads and elaborate monograms.

The New Orleans contingent sat to the right of the stand, the Chicago men to the left. There was not as much cordiality between them as hospitality demanded. A notice-board separated them. It read: "Please do not throw cushions."

The Southerners, being men of means, had all provided themselves with cushions. The Chicago men, being comparatively indigent, had to sit on the hard boards. The umpire, a tall, swarthy fellow, was unfortunately a gentleman of mild disposition. He stood in awe of the grandstand. A ragged enthusiast on whose coat there were big brown stains which looked like a map of the world, threatened to convert him into mincemeat.

"You won't use any profane language on these grounds," cried Mr. Jones, Captain of the Unions.

"Go along," retorted the man with a geographical coat, "You can't hit the ball with a shovel."

On this a partisan of the home team raised a cushion, which he purloined in the excitement from a Southerner, and brought it down with a resounding thwack on the head of the enthusiast, who was heard to exclaim as he sunk to rise no more, "Can't hit the ball with a shove."

Order being thus restored the game proceeded evenly until Mr. Turner of the Pinchbacks was struck out. "Get a new umpire," cried the excursionists from New Orleans. "The umpire's all right," returned the Chicago men.

Would you any gentleman in the audience like to act as umpire!" cried the Captain of the Pinchbacks.

"I would," screamed everybody in the crown, rising to his feet.

Two umpires were selected in place of the weakling whose infirmity of purpose had precipitated the crisis. And now the game became exciting. Before the sixth inning one run had been scored by both sides. Mr. Campbell of the home team prepared to resist the onslaught of Mr. Hopkins, the Pinchback pitcher. The corner of a scarlet handkerchief projected from his pocket.

"There's Thurman at the bat," cried a colored wit. "See his old bandana."

Encouraged by this ally, Mr. Campbell made a two-base hit. In an instant the grandstand went mad. One gentleman stood upon his head, his legs, being supported by two friends, who held him in this uncomfortable position until somebody bowled him over with a cushion. Another gentleman transformed himself into a windmill and swung his arms at an incredible speed. A third turned a succession of somersaults, landing at length in the midst of the New Orleans contingent, which, chafing at the prospect of defeat, lifting him bodily and dropped him over the stand.

Mr. Campbell's prowess speedily bore fruit. With the aid of Messrs. Jones and Smith he put three more runs to the credit of the Unions. The Southerners never recovered from the disaster. One of their supporters, whose face was so freckled that it looked like a fly-paper in a confectioner's window, announcing despairingly that all was over but the shouting. The saloonkeeper began his distribution of silver-headed canes and gold-topped umbrellas. Messrs. Williams, Ross, and Ferranda went out one after the other in the ninth inning, and the game was over. Score: Chicago Unions, 4: New Orleans Pinchbacks, 1.

Then the cushions flew.

The women pressed around the Unions, even going to the length of embracing them. Cigars were pressed upon the winners by their happy supporters.

"It's the poorest game we've played for months," said one of them. And it was.

September 5, 1888 - *New York Sun*

The Cuban Giants, who by the way, are neither giants nor Cubans, but thick-set and brawny colored men, make about as stunning an exhibition of ball playing as any team in the country.

November 5, 1888 – *New York Times*

The Whites Won the Game

New-Orleans, Nov. 4. – A few years ago a White baseball club could not be paid to play against a colored club, but to-day large crowds of both complexions sat in inclement weather and watched a fine fight between the Pinchbacks, the colored champions who recently made a tour of the North, and the Ben Theards, the champion White amateur nine. Both sides put up a magnificent fielding game, and ran bases with daring, but the Whites did the most hitting, and took the best advantage of errors, and won by a score of 4 to 1. The match was made for $100 a side and all the receipts, but only an exhibition game was played. The Pinchbacks have a young pitcher, [George] Hopkins, who could be made good enough for any nine in the country, but he is sick now, and the match will come off when he recovers. When he pitches the Whites will put in Mike Shea, who has pitched for Cincinnati [Red Stockings].

January 17, 1889 - *St. Augustine Weekly News*

The colored employees of the Hotel Ponce de Leon [built in 1888 by millionaire developer and Standard Oil co-founder Henry M. Flagler] will play a game today at the fort grounds with a picked nine from the Alcazar [the second luxury hotel constructed in 1888 by Flagler]. As both teams possess some of the best colored baseball talent in the United States, being largely composed of the famous Cuban Giants, the game is likely to be an interesting one.

February 23, 1889 - *New York Age*

The progressive Association of the United States of America
PREJUDICE ON THE DIAMOND
EVENTS OF THE SEASON AT ST. AUGUSTINE
Inaugurating a Course of Annual Sermons on Race Progress.
The Detroit Base Ball Club to Play the Cuban Giants at Richmond.
Special Correspondence of *THE AGE*.

St. Augustine, Fla., Feb. 11. —On last Monday evening a surprise party was given to Rev. Howard and wife at their residence. The company included a number of visiting ladies from Jacksonville, several young men from the North and the elite of St. Augustine's Society, numbering in all about eighteen couples. An enjoyable time was had. The Knights of Pythians had a public installation of officers on Tuesday, which was well attended. A social. gathering followed by a promenade concert finished the evening's entertainment. The visitors were well cared for and departed highly pleased with the attention paid them by the knights and the Ladies Auxiliary Corps of the Commander.

Negro Leagues Book #2: The Players

At the solicitation of Mr. F.P. Thompson, a meeting was called on Saturday, 9th inst., to inaugurate a course of annual sermons to the hotel men that come to St. Augustine each winter, and the citizens in general, upon our progress the past twenty-five years. The meeting was called to order by Mr. D.P. Slater and Messrs. Wm. De Cato and S.K. Govern elected secretaries. After it was decided to go into permanent organization, Mr. F.P. Thompson was elected president; W. De Cato, treasurer and S.K. Govern secretary. The name was then adopted, viz: The Progressive Association of the United States of America. The second Sunday in March at the Genevor's Opera House, 8 P.M., was fixed as the time and place of the first sermon. The secretary was instructed to solicit the services of an eminent and eloquent divine for the occasion. The following committees were then appointed. Arrangements—F.P. Thompson, chairman, C.H. Booker, A.G. Randolph, Wm. De Cato, S.K. Govern, Robert McKenny, H. Thomas, W.R. Dorsey, D.P. Slater, R.M. Hicks, B.F. Holmes, H.C. Jones, H.W. Scott, James Wharton, E.M. Gatewood, Hotel Ponce de Leon; George A. Smith, G.W. McKenzie, A.H Freeman J.L. Smith, Alcazar Hotel; C.C. Randolph, W. Palmer, J. Howard, J. Grimke, Cordova Hotel; H. Stewart, S.F. William, Hotel San Marco; Rev. D.S. Scott, R.Y. Meeks, Louis Whaley, H M. Emily, Baptist and Methodist Churches; F.E. Witzell, D.M. Papy, Wm. Greene,

-2-

Mr. Wm. Cook of Trenton, N.J., brother of the late Walter L. Cook, proprietor of the Cuban Giants, took lunch at the Ponce de Leon last Friday. The Standards defeated the Cuban Giants on Friday by a score of 7 to 4. Thomas pitched and Malone caught for the Standard, Boyd and Catto being the battery for the Giants. Clarence Williams, the king of base ball coaches, is quite sick and will not be able to play for at least a couple of weeks. Frye's shoulder is well and he is putting up a great game at shortstop for the Standard. The report going the rounds of the papers that the Detroit's have cancelled their games with the Cuban Giants at Richmond April 9 and 10 is incorrect. The Philadelphia Record stated that a number of Citizens of Richmond requested Mr. R.H. Leadley to cancel the games, as they do not want colored and White clubs to play there against each other. But Mr. Leadley has ignored the request and assured me he has no intention of cancelling the games and sees no reason why he should. If there were a few more R.H. Leadleys in the profession, color prejudice would soon be a thing of the past in the South.

Mr. F.P. Thompson devoted forty-five minutes on last Monday lecturing to his crew on the unpardonable sin of race prejudice in the South, [while] in the dining room of the Ponce de Leon. His eloquence brought forth many rounds of applause. At the close he invited the men to name any day on which they would speak on the subject and he would arrange for the occasion from time to time as they desired. Your correspondent, together 'With Messrs. D.P. Slater and Charles Hinds, spoke on Thursday, taking for their theme the method by which color prejudice may be overcome. The marked attention and the many compliments expressed by the entire crew was a token of appreciation for the efforts of the speakers. The fact that several others have announced their desire to speak on the same subject is proof that their feelings have been awakened by the facts expressed.

signed S. K. Govern

Editor's note: Stanislaus Kostka (Cos) Govern was a native of St. Croix in the Virgin Islands and came to the United States at age 13, serving as a cabin boy aboard the training ship the *Monongahela*. The entrepreneurial Govern later worked in the hotel industry and was an editor for the *Philadelphia Tribune*. In Sol White's *History of Colored Base Ball, with Other Documents on the Early Black Game 1886-1936*, he called Govern a "smart fellow and shrewd baseball man." While Michael E. Lomax, author of *Black Baseball Entrepreneurs, 1860-1901: Operating by Any Means Necessary* claimed, "Cos was without question one of the two most successful early Black Baseball entrepreneurs. He not only established the business model for the Negro Leagues but also just might deserve credit as the father of Latin American winter ball."

June 16, 1889 - *Trenton Times*
All the Games Lost
Because the Giants Did Not Use the Official League Ball

The Middle States League held a special meeting at the Girard House in Philadelphia, last night. The delegates present were Charles E. Mason, of the Philadelphia Giants; Edward Cuthbert, Reading club; Terrance Connell and H.H. Hennsell, Lancaster club; J.C. Devine, York club; S. K. Govern, Cuban Giants and James Harrington, Harrisburg. The disputed game between the Reading club and Cuban Giants came up first.

This game was to have been played last Monday. The Readings were here and their manager on the ground, but a few minutes before 4 o'clock, which was the time of game, he ordered his men by telephone to pack up and go home. The Giants were delayed in reaching Trenton on account of missing a train and arrived here in time to be driven hastily to the grounds and be on the diamond a few minutes before 4. They went through the formality required by the rules and then claimed the game by a score of 9 to 0.

The dispute was finally settled by the Giants agreeing to pay the Reading club the amount guaranteed to them. This game will be played over in the near future.

The most interesting feature of the meeting was a long discussion over the charges that were made before the Board of Directors against the Giants.

The main charge was the playing of championship games without using the regulation ball adopted by the league. The Giants have maintained that there was no regulation ball, but the league directors claim that the Mason ball is the official ball and must be used in all games. Manager Govern explained that it was not the desire of the club to violate any laws, but that it was rather because of not fully understanding them.

Another charge made was that the Giants have been playing championship games with men who have not signed regular contracts.

There were several other minor charges which were discussed and satisfactorily explained away, and in the future the Trenton [Cuban] Giants will play according to law. The two remarkable games just played with the Philadelphia Giants do not count, owing to the fact that the Cubans did not use the Mason ball, and these will have to be played over again.

There is a disposition among some of the members to increase the circuit to eight clubs, and applications were presented from the Norristown, Pa., and Norwalk, Conn., clubs. Both were rejected, however, by a close vote, the League voting to continue with six clubs through the coming season.

July 23, 1889 - *Brooklyn Eagle*
Female Ball Players

How They Knocked Luke Kenny All Over the Diamond

Two colored women, named Mary E. Thompson and Mary Jackson, who live in the classic precincts of Crow Hill, are members of a lady's baseball club. Yesterday afternoon, while at practice. Luke Kenney, of 191 Buffalo Avenue, happened to pass. The two women picked Luke up for a ball and knocked him all over the field with base ball bats. Kenney objected to this sort of treatment and procured the arrest of the two Marys. This morning they were arraigned before Justice Kenna and held for trial on a charge of assault.

November 4, 1889 - *Brooklyn Eagle*
A Colored Base Ball Club

Pittsburgh, PA., November 4. Capitalist of Latrobe, Pa., have taken steps to put the Keystone Ball Club, of this city, composed of colored players, on an equal playing and financial footing with the celebrated Cuban Giants and Gorhams, the crack colored ball clubs of New York City. Arrangements have been made to have the Keystones compete with the clubs mentioned for the colored championship of the world, and play in every prominent city of the United States.

May 13, 1892 - *Cleveland Gazette*
Trenton, New Jersey, native Patrick Powers moved his Trenton team to Jersey City in 1885, and found himself in need of pitching. Powers returned to his hometown to raid the Trenton Cuban Giants of their star colored pitcher, George Stovey. An advocate for baseball to be played on Sunday, Powers often challenged social norms. He later wrote in the *Gazette*:

"By luck I happened to think of a colored pitcher named Stovey in Trenton, a fellow with a very light skin, who was playing on the Trenton team. It was my game to get him to Jersey City the next day in time for the game.

I telegraphed a friend to meet me in Trenton at midnight, and went to Stovey's house, roused him up, and got his consent to sign with Jersey City.

Meanwhile some Trenton people got into the scheme and notified the police to prevent Stovey from leaving town. I became desperate. I worked a member of 'Trenton's finish' all right, and finally hired a carriage, and amid a shower of missiles, drove Stovey to a station nearby, where we boarded a train for Jersey City.

Negro Leagues Book #2: The Players

I gave Stovey $20 to keep up his courage and dressed him in a new suit of clothes as soon as the stores opened in the morning. I then put him to bed and waited for the game.

When I marched my men onto the field the public was surprised and they [Newark's players] gave me a laugh. Stovey was put in to pitch for the home team, and dropped the Newarks out in one, two, three order.

The game ended with the score 1 to 0 in Jersey City's favor, and Stovey owned the town."

> **Editor's note:** Powers went on to state that the New York Giants [whom he later managed in 1892] wanted to sign Stovey for the last four games of the season. "Stovey had his grip packed and awaited the word," recalled Powers. Nevertheless that call never came.

March 15, 1896 - *New York Sun*

Cuban Giants will be known as the X Cuban Giants (sic). The following well known ball players have signed: Clarence Williams, O. [Oscar, OJax] Jackson, A. [Andrew, AJax] Jackson, B. [Bill, William] Jackson, [William] Selden, [John] Nelson, Sol White, and [Windsor] Terrell. Clubs wishing games can address manager E.B. Lamar, Jr., northeastern corner 134th Street and St. Ann's Avenue—Yours Truly E.B. Lamar, Jr.

June 1, 1896 - *New York Times*

Mr. Jackson Bet His Life
Tried to Drown Himself When the Cuban Giants Lost a Game
Hackensack, NJ, May 31 - The Cuban Giant baseball team came here yesterday and played a game with the Oritani Club. Samuel Jackson, a colored resident, had been waiting for the coming of the Giants for a week, and expected great things of them.

He said if they did not beat the local team he would drown himself in the Hackensack. Someone said he would not do it, and Sam made a bet of a dollar that he would. The Giants came and lost, and at the close of the game Jackson went to the river and jumped in.

Thus far he had carried out the terms of his bet, and when an attempt was made to rescue him, he tried to fulfill the terms to the letter. He was rescued with difficulty and sent to the hospital, where he is recovering.

July 10, 1899 - *Trenton Daily True American*

On July 9, William Seldon of the Cuban Giants against the Bordentowns, a team in the Middle States league, pitched a no-hitter. Seldon struck out three batters and walked two, en route to a 2-0 win. A full account of the game was reported in the *True American*. This is the first recorded no-hitter by a Black pitcher in baseball history.

March 24, 1901 - *Chicago Defender*

Manager John J. McGraw of the Baltimore club has signed a Cherokee Indian for his club this year, and is sanguine of the success of his find. His name is Tokohoma, is 22 years old, weighs about 175 pounds and is about 5 feet 8 inches in height.

"Tokie" as he is known, has been in Hot Springs some time for a visit, and saw McGraw and Clark Griffith [player-manager] of the Chicago [White Sox] club out on the big lawn of the Eastman Hotel playing ball a few mornings ago and "butted" in. At first Muggsey [McGraw] thought he was a Negro and was about to tell him to move on when he noticed his straight, black hair. He walked over and took a look at him, then asked him if he wasn't an Indian. Tokie said he wasn't anything else and he would show them guys how to play ball if he only had a chance, so Mac told him to come on. He encouraged the boy all he could and told him to come around next day.

Next morning, long before McGraw and Griffith had appeared, the Indian was on hand with a sweater and infielder's glove. He was tried on all kinds of hard ones, and the more McGraw saw him play the better he like him. The Indian stopped everything that his way, covering a large amount of ground and handling himself like a natural born ball player. Griffith got in front of him to see how he would handle the fast ones that he let go through him, and Tokie took to his kind of work like a duck to water.

McGraw then asked him where he had learned to play and he said, "I never learned; I already know how. I used to play second base on our team out in the Indian Nation, and I was supposed to be the best player on the team.

McGraw then tried him on batting. Griffith pitching him some wide ones and the Indiana showed that he was a good sticker. He was then signed for this year.

Tokohoma bats right handed, is fleet of foot and throws with quickness and ease, snapping the ball away with a graceful motion. He will be tried at second base, but will likely be moved to right field."

August 23, 1901 - *Philadelphia Inquirer*
"X-Giants Win Under Glare of Electric Lights."

"Under the glistening glare of seventeen electric arc lights the Cuban X-Giants defeated Frankford last night at Wistar Park by a score of 10 to 6. There were over 1800 people within the grounds when the game started and the powerful rays of the lights gave the spectators a fairly distinguishable view of the plays and players. The lights were arranged within a foot of the right and left field foul lines, extending past first and third bases about fifteen feet, whence they were run in a semi-circle around the infield, giving the outfielder a few yards in which to move around."

More interestingly, the press claimed, "The ball used was about twice the size of the regulation sphere, being soft and elastic, and when swatted by the batsmen it gave forth a sound very similar to that of an overripe cantaloupe hurtled by a mischievous boy at an old man's high hat."

Editor's note: This is almost three decades before the Negro and Major Leagues played under the artificial sun.

February 8, 1902 – *New York Sun*
The Cuban X-Giants Baseball Club as it stands to-day is the strongest combination of colored ball players ever gotten together in this country. The lineup is as follows: Pitchers, Dan McCullen [McClellan], James Robinson, Ed Wilson, and Harry Buckner; catchers, Robert Jordan and William Smith; first base, Ray Wilson; second base, Charles Grant; third base, William [Bill] Monroe; short stop, Grant [Home Run] Johnson; left field, [Big Bill] Smith or [Robert] Jordan; centre [sic] field, William Jackson; right field, a pitcher. In the list are three new players, Johnson, Grant and Buckner. Charles Grant is not only a good hitter but a fine fielder. He played part of last season with the Baltimore American League Club. Buckner has the reputation of being the best colored pitcher in the West to-day. All clubs desiring games with the Giants this season should address E.B. Lamar, Jr., 766 East 175th Street, New York city.

CHARLIE GRANT - A 1933 article in the *Chicago Defender* called Charlie Grant, ". . . a great ball player. Many figured him the peer of Babe Ruth, Ty Cobb and Hans Wagner." The paper added that "The old-time managers pointed out that his speed, great fielding and batting made him too valuable a man to be left out of the game on days he was not pitching and therefore, like Babe Ruth, he was converted into an infielder, where his bat could be expected to function properly and daily."

Editor's note: Grant never played for the Baltimore American League club. In 1901, Grant was working as a bellhop at the Eastman Hotel in Hot Springs, Arkansas, where many players enjoyed naturally heated springs and bathhouses. Oriole manager John J. McGraw saw Grant compete against fellow co-workers and thought his talent level was of major league quality. McGraw attempted to pass the straight-haired, high cheek-boned, cafe au lait-complexioned Charlie Grant, as a full-blooded Cherokee. The newly christened Charlie "Tokohama" was later exposed by Chicago White Sox president, Charlie Comiskey. Comiskey recognized Grant as the former Black second baseman of the Columbia Giants of Chicago and snitched to league officials, causing Grant to be expelled from the team, before the league started. Similar attempts by other liberal White managers met with similar fates.

July 18, 1903 - *The Gazette York (PA)* and *York (PA) Daily*
July 17 - Danny McClellan, with the Cuban X-Giants, pitched the first recorded perfect game by a Black pitcher, against the Penn Park Athletic Club of York, Pennsylvania, champions of the Tri-State League. McClellan struck out five batters in a 5-0 win.

April 19, 1905 - *The Washington Post*

Negro Leagues Book #2: The Players

Opening of Metropolitan League

The Metropolitan baseball league, composed of six of the best colored teams in the District, namely; Athletics, Colored Americans, Giants, Lafayettes, Treasury Department and Eastern Empires, will open its season Monday and will also pay on Tuesday and Wednesday in American League Park.

Monday's game will be between the Eastern Empires and the crack Treasury team; Tuesday, April 25, the Lafayettes will lock horns with the Athletics, while on Wednesday, the Colored Americans will tackle the Giants.

The season closes August 26, and 108 championship games will be played. In addition to several individual prizes, the firm of Spalding & Bro., has offered a $50 prize to the team winning the pennant. The schedule for the season will be announced later.

April 26, 1905 - *The Washington Post*

Metropolitan League Opening

More than 600 people attended the opening game of the Metropolitan League at American League Park, Seventh and Florida Avenue, Monday. The opposing clubs were the Treasury Department and the Eastern Empires. The score:

```
                                        R   H   E
Treasury         0  0  4  0  3  4  0  0  x  -  11  12  1
Eastern          0  0  3  0  3  0  0  0  0  -   6   8  4
```

Batteries - Treasury Department, Proctor and Webster; Eastern Empires, Young, Thomas and Hamilton. Struck out - by Proctor, 11; by Young, 7; by Thomas 4. Bases on balls—off Proctor 3; off Thomas 3. Umpire - Mr. Shaughnessy.

July 15, 1905 - *The Washington Post*

Tied Joe Gans' Team

Atlantics and Middle Section Giants at American Park

The game between the Middle Section Giants of Baltimore and the Atlantics, the strong team of the Metropolitan League, of this city, attracted over 1,700 people to the American League Park yesterday.

Joe Gans, the lightweight champion, is captain of the Giants and played first base. He showed that he can play ball as well as fight. Both teams showed up strong in the field, and while the base-hit column is small there was a number of long hits which were cleverly caught by the outfielders.

The feature of the game were the battery work of both teams and a one-hand catch of Cardoza [second baseman] of the Atlantics.

```
The score                                R  H  E
Atlantics              2  0  0  0  0  1  1  0  0  -  4  6  3
Middle Section Giants  0  2  0  0  2  0  0  0  0  -  4  5  3
```

International League of Independent Professional Base Ball Clubs - 1906

April 14, 1906 - *Sporting Life*

A New Local League

In addition to the American and National league games to be seen this season, there will also be twenty contests between the fastest independent clubs in the United States and Cuba, to be played on the grounds of the American and National league clubs. The newly launched league will be known as the International League of Independent Professional Base Ball Clubs, and William Freihofer, of this city, is president and will present a handsome silver cup to the club winning the championship. John A. O'Rourke, also of Philadelphia, is the secretary and treasurer of the new organization. The board of directors is Manuel Caps, of Brooklyn, N.Y.; A. Pastor of Havana, Cuba; Roderick McMahon, of New York City; E.B. Lamar, Dumont, N.J., and John A. O'Rourke, Philadelphia.

The membership of the new league includes the Cuban Stars, the champions of Santiago de Cuba [later changed named to Cuban Stars of Havana and owned by Manuel Camps, with booking done by E.B. Lamar]; Havana, champions of Cuba [later became the Havana Stars and owned by Alfredo Pastor, with booking by E.B. Lamar]; Philadelphia Professionals [owned by bakery chain owner William Freihofer], the crack independent club of this city; the Philadelphia Quaker Giants [owned by Jess and Ed McMahon], recently incorporated in New York, and which is claimed to be the fastest aggregation of negro ball players in the world. Last, but not least, the Cuban X-Giants [also owned/managed by E.B. Lamar], the genuine negro champions of the United States and Cuba.

The first championship games will be played on Decoration Day, on the Athletic grounds, when the Philadelphia Professionals will meet the Cuban Stars. Each club has agreed to post a bond of $500 as a guarantee it will finish the season.

Editor's note: The league consisted of two Black teams, two Cuban teams and one White club with plans to play an eight-game season, with each club playing the other teams twice. The Havana Stars were replaced in June by the Wilmington (DE) Giants, but another White team, the Riverton-Palmyra (NJ) Athletic Club eventually replaced the Giants, making two of the five teams comprised of all White players. The Riverton-Palmyra team failed to win any league games. The Philadelphia Giants won the Freihofer Trophy cup with an 8-1 won-lost record.

October 29, 1906 - *Philadelphia Evening Item*

National Association of Colored Base Ball Clubs of the United States and Cuba, 1907 - 1909

A meeting held Monday afternoon [October 22] at the Lion's Club, 87 Fleet Street, Brooklyn, resulted in the formation of the National Association of Colored Base Ball Clubs of the United States and Cuba. The association is composed of the:

Philadelphia Giants Base Ball Association, Inc.;
New York Cuban X-Giants
New York Cuban Giants
Brooklyn Royal Giants
Havana Cuban Stars

The organization was made a permanent one and H. Walter Schlichter, of the Philadelphia Giants, was elected president;
J. W. Connor, of the Royal Giants, vice president;
J. M. Bright of the Cuban Giants, treasurer;
Manuel Camps of the Cuban Stars, and
E. B. Lamar, Jr., of the Cuban X-Giants, with the president, Board of Trustees.
Nat C. Strong, of New York, was engaged as secretary.
Manager Grant [Home run] Johnson, of the Royal Giants, was present at the formation.

The association is modeled on the lines of the National and the American League White clubs, and the purposes of the organization is for the perpetuation of colored base ball by surrounding it with such safeguards as will warrant absolute public confidence in its integrity and methods and maintaining a high standard of skill and sportsmanship in its players.

The protection of the property rights of those engaged without sacrificing the spirit of competition in the conduct of the game.

The promotion of the welfare of colored ball players as a class by perfecting them in their profession and enabling them to secure adequate compensation for expertness.

The organization was made necessary by the financial results of the season of 1906, when every owner of a colored ball club in this vicinity lost money, due to the exorbitant salaries paid to the players and the keen competition among the various clubs.

The idea is to place colored base ball on a solid business basis and to protect both players and managers and prevent jumping from one club to another on the slightest pretext, as was done this last season. It is intended to protect the managers from unscrupulous and unreliable managers of independent clubs who engage the colored clubs and unceremoniously cancel the dates at the last moment if so inclined. It is intended to "cut out" all such clubs which treat any of the National agreement clubs in that manner.

The full text of the agreement as entered follows:

The National Agreement for the government of professional colored base ball, entered into this day, October 22nd, 1906, between the Philadelphia Giants Baseball and Athletic Association, Inc. of Philadelphia, PA, the Cuban X Giants Base Ball Club of New York, the Royal Giants Base Ball Club of Brooklyn, N.Y., the Cuban Giants Base Ball Club of New York and the Cuban Star Base Ball Club of Havana, Cuba.

This agreement made and entered into by and between the Philadelphia Giants Baseball and Athletic Association, Inc. of Philadelphia, PA, the Cuban X Giants Base Ball Club of New York, the Royal Giants Base Ball Club of Brooklyn, N.Y., the Cuban Giants Base Ball Club of New York and the Cuban Star Base Ball Club of Havana, Cuba, known as the National Association of Colored Base Ball Clubs of the United States and Cuba, shall be styled the National Agreement and shall have for its objects:

1. Perpetuation of colored base ball, in keeping with the national pastime of America by surrounding it with such safeguards as will warrant absolute public confidence in its integrity and methods, and by maintaining a high standard of skill and sportsmanship in its players.
2. Protection of the property rights of those engaged in colored base ball as a business without sacrificing the spirit of competition in the conduct of the clubs.
3. Promotion of the welfare of ball players as a class by developing and perfecting them in their profession and enabling them to secure adequate compensation for expertness.

Article 1.

Section 1: - This agreement shall be indissoluble except by the unanimous vote of the parties to it and if any of said parties withdraws from it or violates any of its fundamental principles the party so withdrawing or offending, shall be treated as the enemies of colored baseball.

Article 2.

Section 1: - Each party to this agreement retains the right to conduct its affairs and govern its players accordingly to its constitution and by-laws.

Section 2: - The annual meeting shall be held at a place designated by the President on the third Monday in October in each year.

Article 3.

Section 1: - Each member shall have one vote on all questions that may come before any meeting which may be held, and such meetings may be called at the request of one or more members of the parties to this agreement.

Section 2: - A secretary shall be elected yearly. The secretary's salary shall be . . . and his duties shall consist of keeping accurate minutes of the proceedings of this organization and giving every possible aid in securing engagements for the parties in this agreement.

Section 3: - Whenever two or more clubs cannot amicably arrange differences over a player the case shall be presented to the disinterested members of this agreement and the decision made by a majority vote, but should it be impossible to reach an agreement or the decision not satisfactory to those involved the question in dispute be submitted with all evidence in writing to the President of the National Commission, of White ball players whose decision shall be considered final and binding.

ALL-TIME NEGRO BASEBALL REGISTER
1862 - 1960

More than 7,000 entries covering 99 years of glory for more than 6,000 players, 375 executives, 200 umpires, 50 writers, plus bus drivers, scouts, batboys—who played, coached, scouted, managed, and owned pro and semipro Black teams.

The Negro Baseball League Register first appeared in Robert Peterson's landmark work *Only The Ball Was White* (Prentice-Hall 1970). Minor changes and updates were made in the reprint by McGraw-Hill in 1984 and Oxford Press's reissued release in 1992. The immense task undertaken by Peterson is difficult to comprehend considering his accomplishment was before the world wide web and online research tools. He emphasizes the dilemma of tracking players via microfilmed papers, pencils and notepads, with his spaghetti theory.

"Tracing the course of the organized Negro Leagues is rather like trying to follow a single black strand through a ton of spaghetti. The footing is infirm, and the strand has a tendency to break off in one's hand and slither back into the amorphous mass."

We are extremely grateful for Bob Peterson's pioneering efforts in this field.

Our goals were to add players and teams, fill in missing first names, and verify the years played. Because first names do not normally appear in box scores, we interviewed players and located scorecards to fill this void. We estimated that more than 3,500 additions and updates have been made to the original Peterson Register. This includes extending the register years through 1960, the last official year of play, from Peterson's original cut-off date of 1950.

We have attempted to provide the researcher and reader with the player's full legal name and nicknames. Some players have a name in brackets to indicate that they appear in stories or box scores under different names or variations of that name. In a few entries you will find, "See . . . " This is for players who were either misidentified in earlier Registers or played under an alias.

This project to include all former Negro League players is an on-going effort. We solicit your support for any additions, corrections or modifications.

Please send any changes to the editors:
SatchelPaige-Hof@comcast.net or Ntresearch@comcast.net

[KEY: legal name, nicknames, career years, primary positions, semipro & pro teams]

Negro Leagues Book #2: The Players

AARON, HENRY LOUIS (HANK, PORK CHOP)—1952—ss, 3b, Indianapolis Clowns

ABALLÍ, GABRIEL—1930—p, Cuban Stars (East)

ABBOTT, JAMES ISAAC (JIM)—1904-08, 1914—p, of, Famous Cuban Giants, Genuine Cuban Giants, Brooklyn Royal Giants, Lincoln (NY) Stars, New York Colored Giants

ABBOTT, LANGSTON—1939—p, Chicago Palmer House Stars

ABBOTT, ROBERT SENGSTACKE—1905-40—editor, *Chicago Defender, Abbott's Monthly*

ABERNATHY, ROBERT WILLIAM (JAMES)—1945-48—of, Boston Blues, Indianapolis Clowns, Kansas City Monarchs, New York Cubans

ABRAHAM, ____—1869—of, Rockford (IL) Rockfords

ABRAMS, GEORGE—1862—p, Brooklyn Monitors

ABRAMS, GEORGE M.—1911, 1913—manager, p, Indianapolis ABCs

ABRAMS, JAMES—1862—of, Brooklyn Monitors

ABREU [ABREAU], EUFEMIO—1918-25, 1930, 1932—c, 1b, 2b, ss, of, Cincinnati Cuban Stars, Indianapolis ABCs, Cuban Stars (East & West)

ABREU [ABREAU], JOSÉ (PEPE)—1930-35—p, Cuban Stars (East & West), Stars of Cuba

ACEA, ____—1910, 1915—of, Cuban Stars, Almendares Cubans

ACEDACO, ____—1924—p, Havana Cuban Stars

ACKERMAN, ____—1928—p. Gilkerson's Union Giants

ACKLYN, TED—1953—umpire, East/West game

ACOSTA y FERNÁNDEZ, JOSÉ (ACOSTICA)—1914-15—p, Long Branch (NJ) Cubans

ADAMS, ____—1871—c, Philadelphia Pythians

ADAMS, ____—1918-26—umpire, ECL

ADAMS, ____—1918—of, Havana Red Sox

ADAMS, ____—1928—p, Chicago Giants

ADAMS, ____—1942—c, Memphis Red Sox

ADAMS, BENJAMIN FRANKLIN (BEN)—1953, 1958-61—p, Memphis Red Sox, Kansas City Monarchs, Detroit Clowns, Detroit Stars

ADAMS, BILL (PACKINGHOUSE)—1938—3b, Kansas City Monarchs

ADAMS, CHARLES—1869-78—of, Chicago Blue Stockings

ADAMS, EMERY (ACE)—1932-46—p, of, Memphis Red Sox, Baltimore Elite Giants, New York Black Yankees, Philadelphia Stars

ADAMS, ERNEST—1947-48—of, Indianapolis Clowns, Baltimore Elite Giants

ADAMS, F.—1869-71—of, c, Chicago Blue Stockings

ADAMS, FRANK—1888—of, Chicago Gordons

ADAMS, JOSEPH—1886—of, Chicago Gordons

ADAMS, LEN—1927-28—3b, Birmingham Black Barons, Chattanooga Black Lookouts, Colored All-Stars

ADAMS, MALACHI—1887—umpire, NCBBL

ADAMS, OSCAR W.—1926-31—owner, Birmingham Black Barons

ADAMS, P.—1886—2b, Chicago Gordons

ADAMS, RAYFORD—1946—of, Fresno/San Diego Tigers

ADAMS, ROBERT L. (BOBBY, SKIN)—1957, 1960—3b, Indianapolis Clowns, Raleigh (NC) Tigers

ADAMS, WILLIE—1935—ss, New York Black Yankees

ADDISON, J.—1910-11—c, Philadelphia Giants

ADDISON, K.—1910-12—3b, 2b, of, Philadelphia Giants, Pittsburgh Giants

ADDISON, [REV.] T.H.—1920—manager, 2b, c, Atlanta Black Crackers

ADDISON, THOMAS (TOM)—1911-12—ss, Philadelphia Giants

ADJER, JR., DANIEL L.—1868—player, Philadelphia Pythians

ADJER, ROBERT M.—1868—player, Philadelphia Pythians

ADKINS, ____—1930—p, Colored House of David

ADKINS, CLARENCE—1931—c, 3b, Nashville Elite Giants

ADKINS, JOSHUA—1867-71—of, 3b, Philadelphia Excelsior, Philadelphia Pythians

ADKINS, STACY [see ATKINS, STACY]

AGNEW, CLYDE—1950—p, Baltimore Elite Giants

AGNEW, JOE LOUIS—1957-58—p, Detroit Stars, Detroit Clowns

AGROM, ____—1958—umpire, East/West game

AGUILLARD [AGUILAR, AQUILLARD], JR., RAY ANTHONY (PICKLE)—1956-57—c, Detroit Stars

AHRENS, ____—1930—of, p, Cuban Stars (East)

AKERS, CHARLEY—1921-32—ss, Hilldale Club, Cleveland Tate Stars, Gilkerson's Union Giants

ALBERTSON, JOHNNY—1936-39, 1942—ss, New York Black Yankees, Brooklyn Royal Giants

ALBERTUS, ____—1932—p, Cuban Stars (East)

ALBRECHT, R.—1928-29—p, Bacharach (AC) Giants

ALBRIGHT, THOMAS (PISTOL PETE)—1929, 1936—p, New York Cubans, Bacharach (AC) Giants

ALBRITTON, ALEXANDER C. (ALEX)—1920-25—p, Pittsburgh Stars of Buffalo, Baltimore Black Sox, Washington Potomacs, Hilldale Club, Bacharach (AC) Giants, Wilmington Potomacs

ALDERETTE, N.—1917-18—p, Cuban Stars (East)

ALEX, JOE—1928—p, Nashville Elite Giants

ALEXANDER, ____—1880—3b. Washington Manhattans

ALEXANDER, ____—1948—pr, Indianapolis Clowns

ALEXANDER, B. FREYL (B. F.)—1912-13—president, Homestead Grays

ALEXANDER, CALVIN—1922—p, New Orleans Crescent Stars

ALEXANDER, DEWEY—1942—batboy, Kansas City Monarchs

ALEXANDER, GEORGE A.—1946—p, Cincinnati Crescents

ALEXANDER, GROVER CLEVELAND (BUCK)—1923-26—p, Detroit Stars, Indianapolis ABCs, Cleveland Elites

ALEXANDER, HARVEY (CHUFFY)—1925-27, 1932-33—of, 1b, Birmingham Black Barons, Monroe (LA) Monarchs, Houston Black Buffaloes, New Orleans Black Pelicans

ALEXANDER, (HUB)—1910-14—c, p, French Lick (IN) Plutos, Chicago Union Giants, Chicago Giants

ALEXANDER, JESSE (ONE ARM)—1946—of, San Francisco Sea Lions

ALEXANDER, JOE—1950—c, Kansas City Monarchs

ALEXANDER, (KOKE)—1918-21—of, Dayton Marcos, Chicago Giants, Columbus Buckeyes

ALEXANDER, SPENCER—1940-49—of, Newark Eagles, Asheville Blues

ALEXANDER, THEODORE ROOSEVELT (TED, RED)—1938-49—p, Cleveland Bears, Cincinnati-Cleveland Buckeyes, Chicago American Giants, Kansas City Monarchs, Birmingham Black Barons, New York Black Yankees, Indianapolis ABCs, Detroit Black Sox, Homestead Grays

ALEXANDER, WILLIAM—1883—ss, Washington Manhattans

ALFONSO, ANGEL (COCO)—1924-30—ss, 3b, 2b, Cuban Stars (East & West)

ALLEN, ____—1867—c, 1b, Ithaca (NY) Actives

ALLEN, ____—1908—1b, Columbus Giants

ALLEN, ____—1910—p, Philadelphia Giants

ALLEN, ____—1919—of, Pittsburgh Stars of Buffalo

ALLEN, ____—1921—umpire, NNL

ALLEN, ____—1931, 1936-37—ss, St. Louis Stars, Memphis Red Sox, Chicago American Giants

ALLEN, ____—1946—p, Montgomery Dodgers

ALLEN, ALEX (POPEYE)—1940, 1943—of, Birmingham Black Barons, New York Black Yankees, Schenectady Mohawk Giants

ALLEN, JOE—1887—1b, Pittsburgh Keystones (NCBBL)

ALLEN, ANDREW—1910-25—manager, LeDroit (DC) Tigers

ALLEN, CLIFFORD (CROOKS, CLYDE)—1932-38—p, Hilldale Club, Homestead Grays, Memphis Red Sox, Philadelphia Stars, Bacharach (AC) Giants, Baltimore Black Sox

ALLEN, CLINEY—1932-33—p, Baltimore Black Sox, Bacharach (AC) Giants, Philadelphia Stars

ALLEN, DAVID (DAVE)—1887—c, Trenton (NJ) Cuban Giants (Middle States League), Pittsburgh Keystones

ALLEN, FRANK—1888—infield, Trenton (NJ) Cuban Giants

ALLEN, HERBERT TODD—1907-19, 1921, 1925-28—3b, manager, Jewell's ABCs, Pittsburgh Keystones, Bowser's ABCs, Indianapolis ABCs, Chicago American Giants, Lincoln (NY) Giants, Louisville White Sox, Royal Poinciana (FL)

ALLEN, HOMER (FOOTS)—1931-32—p, 1b, Monroe (LA) Monarchs, Knoxville Giants

ALLEN, HOSEA WALTER (BUSTER, LONG BOY)—1941-47—p, Jacksonville Red Caps, Cincinnati Ethiopian Clowns (NML), Cincinnati-Indianapolis Clowns, Indianapolis Clowns, Cleveland Buckeyes, Memphis Red Sox

ALLEN, J. MOORE—1932—p, of, John Donaldson All-Stars

ALLEN, JR., JOHN FRANCIS (HAP)—1921—3b, of, Pittsburgh Keystones

ALLEN, JOHNNY—1946—ss, Oakland Larks

ALLEN, JR., MAJOR ROBERT—1919-22—2b, Lincoln (NY) Giants, Baltimore Black Sox, Brooklyn Royal Giants

ALLEN, MOSES—1887—1b, Pittsburgh Keystones

ALLEN, NEWTON HENRY (NEWT, COLT, ASHES, LITTLE NAPOLEON)—1922-44, 1947—2b, ss, manager, All Nations, Kansas City Monarchs, St. Louis Stars, Homestead Grays, Indianapolis Clowns, Detroit Wolves, Philadelphia Royal Giants

ALLEN, SAMUEL LEWIS (SAM)—1957-60—of, Kansas City Monarchs, Raleigh (NC) Tigers, Memphis Red Sox

ALLEN, SR., TOUSSAINT L'OUVERTURE (TOM, T.A.)—1914-28—1b, Havana Red Sox, Hilldale Club, Wilmington Potomacs, Newark Stars, Schenectady Mohawk Giants, Philadelphia Tigers, Breakers Hotel (FL)

ALLEN, WILLIAM—1887—p, Cincinnati Browns (NCBBL)

ALLEN, WILMER—1953—umpire, NAL

ALLEN, ZACK—1932—p, Austin Black Senators

ALLISON, ____—1937—ss, New York Black Yankees

Negro Leagues Book #2: The Players

ALLISON, ____–1941–p, New York Cubans

ALLISON, ____–1943–3b, Cincinnati Clowns

ALLISON, AL–1946–umpire, NAL

ALLISON, AMOS (MOODY)–1915-17, 1920-25–1b, 2b, ss, 3b, Chicago Union Giants, Chicago American Giants, Nashville Elite Giants, Indianapolis ABCs

ALMAGRO, JORGE–1945–of, 1b, p, Pittsburgh Crawfords (USL)

ALMEIDA [D'ALMEIDA, ALMEYDA], RAFAEL (MIKE)–1904-07–3b, All Cubans, Cuban Stars

ALONSO, ROGELIO–1927-30–p, of, Cuban Stars (West)

ALONZO, JUAN–1948–of, New York Cubans

ALSOP, CLIFFORD–1920-22–p, Kansas City Monarchs

ALSTON, EDDIE–1958–2b, Detroit Clowns

ALSTON, THOMAS EDISON (TOM)–1948–1b, Greensboro (NC) Goshen Red Wings

ALTMAN, GEORGE LEE–1955–of, Kansas City Monarchs

ÁLVAREZ, RAÚL–1924-37–p, of, Cuban Stars (East & West), New York Cubans, Trujillo All-Stars (Ciudad Trujillo Dragons)

AMARO, DIONISIO (DAVE)–1953-55–p, Indianapolis Clowns

AMARO y OLIVIA, SANTOS (EL CANGURO [the KANGAROO], GANSO)–1946–utility, New York Cubans

AMES, ____–1919–2b, St. Louis Giants

AMOROS y ISASI, EDMUNDO (SANDY)–1950–1b, of, New York Cubans

AMOS, (COUNTRY)–1945–p, Boston Royal Giants

ANAS, A.–1935–p, New York Cubans

ANDERS, ____–1940–of, Newark Eagles

ANDERSON, ____–1896–of, Cuban Giants

ANDERSON, ____–1907–1b, Keystone (PA) Giants

ANDERSON, ____–1922–p, New Orleans Crescent Stars

ANDERSON, ____–1929–p, Wichita Falls Black Spudders

ANDERSON, ____–1931–of, Santop Broncos

ANDERSON, ANDREW W. (ANDY)–1948, 1951–of, Harlem Globetrotters, Chicago American Giants

ANDERSON, ARTHUR (BERT)–1889–p, Chicago Unions

ANDERSON, BILL–1946–umpire, WCBA

ANDERSON, C.W.–1859, 1862, 1867–2b, Unknown Base Ball Club (of Weeksville, NY), Brooklyn Unique, Brooklyn Monitors, Mutuals of Washington

ANDERSON, CHARLES–1945–of, Detroit Motor City Giants

ANDERSON, CHARLIE–1920–of, Pittsburgh Stars of Buffalo

ANDERSON, CURT (ANDY)–1951-52–p, Birmingham Black Barons, Chicago American Giants

ANDERSON, ELIJAH [ELIAS]–1887–umpire, NCBBL

ANDERSON, JAMES–1891–of, New York Colored Giants

ANDERSON, JAMES–1947–p, of, Birmingham Black Barons

ANDERSON, JOE–1954–p, Memphis Red Sox

ANDERSON, JOHN–1927–officer, Hilldale Club

ANDERSON, LEROY ANDERSON (BUDDY)–1929–of, Pullen's Royal Giants

ANDERSON, LEWIS–1930, 1933–c, Chicago American Giants, Baltimore Black Sox

ANDERSON, LOUIS (POP)–1938-39–p, Atlanta Black Crackers, Indianapolis ABCs

ANDERSON, OTHELLO D. [ORINTHAL or ORENTHAL]–1946–p, Los Angeles White Sox, Detroit Senators

ANDERSON, OTIS–1924–umpire, World Series

ANDERSON, RALPH–1927, 1932–of, Nashville Elite Giants, Indianapolis ABCs

ANDERSON, ROBERT JAMES (BOBBY)–1915-22–ss, 2b, Dayton Marcos, Chicago Union Giants, Pop Lloyd All-Stars, Chicago Giants, Philadelphia Giants, Gilkerson's Union Giants, Foster's Hartford Giants

ANDERSON, ROLAND (SCHOOL BOY)–1943-44–p, Homestead Grays

ANDERSON, ROY–1920–of, St. Louis Giants

ANDERSON, S.–1883–of, Washington Manhattans

ANDERSON, SAM–1908-12–p, 3b, Cuban Giants, Pittsburgh Giants, York (PA) Cuban Giants

ANDERSON, SHERRY–1958–infield, Detroit Clowns

ANDERSON, THEODORE M. (BUBBLES)–1922-25–2b, ss, 3b, Kansas City Monarchs, All Nations, Birmingham Black Barons, Washington Potomacs, Indianapolis ABCs

ANDERSON, TURNER–1883–of, Washington Manhattans

ANDERSON, W.–1908–p, Cuban Giants

ANDERSON, WILLIAM–1911–of, Brown's Tennessee Rats

ANDERSON, WILLIAM–1914-17–officer, Hilldale Club

ANDERSON, WILLIAM (BILL)–1925-31–of, Montgomery Grey Sox, Nashville Elite Giants, Birmingham Black Barons

ANDERSON, WILLIAM ALBERT (BILL, CHICK)–1938-47–p, New York Black Yankees, Brooklyn Royal Giants, New York Cubans, Newark Eagles

ANDREWS, ____–1928–of, Philadelphia Quaker City Giants

ANDREWS, ____–1932–of, 2b, Memphis Red Sox

ANDREWS, ____—1938—of, Birmingham Black Barons
ANDREWS, ____—1938—2b, Chicago American Giants
ANDREWS, ____—1939—p, Cleveland Bears
ANDREWS, BILL (CURLEY)—1943-45—3b, ss, 2b, 1b, Philadelphia Stars, New York Black Yankees, Pittsburgh Crawfords (USL)
ANDREWS, HERMAN (JABO)—1930-42—of, manager, Birmingham Black Barons, Memphis Red Sox, Indianapolis ABCs, Detroit Wolves, Homestead Grays, Columbus Blue Birds, Pittsburgh Crawfords, Washington Black Senators, Chicago American Giants, Jacksonville Red Caps, Cleveland Bears, New York Cubans
ANDREWS, JOHN (SUNNY)—1945—ss, Toledo Cubs/Rays
ANDREWS, (POP)—1905-19—p, of, 1b, 2b, Brooklyn Royal Giants, Pittsburgh Stars of Buffalo, Philadelphia Giants, Havana Red Sox, Pittsburgh Giants, Cuban Giants
ANGULO [ANYURA], GUILLERMO—1929-30—1b, Stars of Cuba
ANTHONY, ___—1945—of, Detroit Motor City Giants
ANTHONY, GEORGE—1858-60—3b, Henson Base Ball Club of Jamaica (NY)
ANTHONY, JAMES—1858-60—of, Henson Base Ball Club of Jamaica (NY)
ANTHONY, LAVANCE (PETE)—1950—c, Houston Eagles, New York Cubans
ANTHONY, THAD—1950—c, Baltimore Elite Giants
ANTONE, ____—1937—c, Washington Elite Giants
APPLEGATE, GIDEON SPENCE (RED)—1943, 1947, 1949—p, New York Cubans, New York Black Yankees, Asheville Blues, Newark Eagles
AQUILLARD, RAY [see AGUILAR, RAY]
ARAGÓN, ____—1930—of, Boston Black Sox
ARAGÓN y VALDÉS, SR., ÁNGEL (PETE)—1913—3b, Long Branch (NJ) Cubans
ARANGO [ORANGO], PEDRO LUIS—[a.k.a. Pedro Pablo]—1925-39—3b, 1b, New York Cubans, Cuban Stars (East & West), Stars of Cuba
ARANSON, ____—1917—ss, All Nations
ARBANS, ____—1931—of, Cuban Stars (East)
ARCHER, LUCIUS WILLIAM (LUKE)—1919-24—p, c, Lincoln (NY) Giants, Baltimore Black Sox, Philadelphia Giants, Havana Red Sox
ARENAS, SR., HIPOLITO KANTERRA (POPS) [a.k.a. TY TORRENTO]—1927-36—of, 3b, ss, 2b, 1b, Atlanta Black Crackers, Schenectady Mohawk Giants, Louisville Black Caps, Havana Cubans, Havana Black Cubans
ARENAS, [DR.] J.A. (CHICO)—1955-58—infielder, New York Black Yankees, Cuban Stars, Jacksonville Red Caps
ARENCIBIA, EDUARDO MARIO—1947-48—of, New York Cubans
ARGUELLES, MARTINANO, [see GARAY]
ARIOSA y FERNÁNDEZ, MARIO (HOMERO)—1947-49—of, New York Cubans
ARIOSA y FERNÁNDEZ, HOMERO—1947—of, New York Cubans
ARMAS [ALMAS], FELIPE—1925-26—p, Cuban Stars (West), Kansas City Monarchs
ARMENTEROS, JUAN—1915—of, Almendares Cubans
ARMENTEROS, JUAN FRANCIS (TEKY, ARMY)—1953-55—c, Kansas City Monarchs
ARMENTEROS, PABLO—1916—p, New York Cuban Stars
ARMOUR, ____—1946-47—p, Chattanooga Choo Choos
ARMOUR, ALFRED ALLEN (BUDDY)—1936-50—of, ss, St. Louis Stars, Indianapolis ABCs, North Classic Team, New Orleans-St. Louis Stars, Harrisburg-St. Louis Stars, Cleveland Buckeyes, Chicago American Giants, Homestead Grays, New York Black Yankees, New Orleans Creoles, Pittsburgh Crawfords (USL)
ARMOUR, JOHNNIE—1933—p, 3b, of, Detroit Stars
ARMSTEAD, CLIFFORD (SLIM)—1925—p, Bacharach (AC) Giants
ARMSTEAD JR., JAMES (JIMMIE)—1938-49—p, of, Birmingham Black Barons, Indianapolis ABCs, St. Louis Stars, Baltimore Elite Giants, Philadelphia Stars, New Orleans-St. Louis Stars, Nashville Cubs
ARMSTRONG, ____—1883, 1887—of, 3b, Louisville Falls City (NCBBL)
ARMSTRONG, ____—1869—of, Rockford (IL) Rockfords
ARMSTRONG, ____—1915—p, Baltimore Grays
ARMSTRONG, ____—1917—p, Penn Red Caps of NY, Chicago Union Giants
ARMSTRONG, BILL—1945—p, Indianapolis Clowns
ARMSTRONG, GEORGE—1946—owner, Brooklyn Brown Dodgers, Pittsburgh Stars
ARMSTRONG, GEORGE ISAAC (MULE, ARMY)—1909-13—1b, c, Chicago American Giants, Chicago Giants, Twin Cities Gophers, St. Paul Colored Gophers, French Lick (IN) Plutos
ARMSTRONG, JIM—1938—umpire, NAL
ARMSTRONG, MIKE—1946—umpire, NNL
ARMSTRONG, PETE—1946-owner, Brooklyn Brown Dodgers, Pittsburgh Stars

Negro Leagues Book #2: The Players

ARNETT, PUSEY DELL—1896, 1905—ss, of, Chicago Unions

ARNOLD, ____—1889—of, New Orleans Pinchbacks

ARNOLD, ____—1919—p, Dayton Marcos

ARNOLD, CHARLES EDWARD (CHUCK)—1953—54—p, Memphis Red Sox

ARNOLD, E.—1922—officer, Louisville Stars/White Sox

ARNOLD, J.A.—1922—president, Louisville Stars/White Sox

ARNOLD, JAMES—1886—p, Unions of New Orleans

ARNOLD, (LEFTY)—1946—p, Chattanooga Choo Choos, Birmingham Black Barons

ARNOLD, PAUL (SONNY, SAM)—1926-36—of, Brooklyn Royal Giants, Newark Dodgers, Bacharach (AC) Giants, Hilldale Club, Newark Browns, Lincoln (NY) Giants, Chicago American Giants, New York Cubans

ARNOLD, TOM—1920-21—p, Pensacola Giants, Calgary Black Sox

ARPEN, ____—1936—ph, Bacharach (AC) Giants

ART, ____—1928—c, Harrisburg Giants

ARTHUR, J.—1923—2b, Washington Potomacs

ARTHUR, ROBERT—1945-46—p, of, Pittsburgh Crawfords (USL), Philadelphia Hilldales (USL)

ARTON, ____—1928—p, Bacharach (AC) Giants

ARUMÍS [ARUMI], JOAQUÍN—1920—of, 2b, Kansas City Monarchs

ARTEZ [ARZEB], ____—1945—of, Philadelphia Stars

ASBURY, ORLANDO H.—1918, 1924—p, Lincoln (NY) Giants

ASCANIO, CARLOS (EARTHQUAKE)—1945-46—1b, New York Black Yankees

ASH, JAMES—1868—player, Philadelphia Pythians

ASH, RUDOLPH THEODEUS—1920, 1925-26—of, Chicago Giants, Pensacola Giants, Chicago American Giants, Newark Stars, Hilldale Club

ASHBY, EARL—1945-48—c, Cleveland Buckeyes, Birmingham Black Barons, Homestead Grays, Newark Eagles

ASHEY, CARL—1938—umpire, NAL

ASHFORD, LLOYD—1913—player, All Nations

ASHPORT, ____—1913—3b, Havana Red Sox

ASKEW, ____—1959—p, Memphis Red Sox

ASKAN, ____—1942—of, New Orleans Black Pelicans

ASKEW, JESSE—1936, 1939—ss, St. Louis Stars, St. Louis Giants

ATKINS, ABE—1923—ss, 3b, Toledo Tigers

ATKINS, JOHN—1948—3b, Kansas City Monarchs

ATKINS, JOSEPH OSCAR (JOE, LEROY)—1945-47—3b, of, Pittsburgh Crawfords (USL), Boston Blues, Cleveland Buckeyes

ATKINS, STACY—1950—p, Chicago American Giants

ATKINSON, WILBURN (PEPPER)—1946—of, Los Angeles White Sox

AUBREY, ____—1923— umpire, NNL

AUBURY, ____—1905—1b, Cuban X-Giants

AUGUSTINE, LEON—1923—umpire, NNL

AUGUSTUS, C.—1926-28—p, Memphis Red Sox, St. Louis Giants

AUSBROOK, DOUGLAS LEONARD—1946—c, Cleveland Clippers

AUSSA [see NEIL, RAY or WALKER, JESSE]

AUSTIN, DERO—1964—midget clown, Indianapolis Clowns

AUSTIN, FRANK SAMUEL SILVESTER (JUNIOR, BIN BIN, PEE WEE)—1944-48—ss, Philadelphia Stars, Biz Mackey All-Stars

AUSTIN, JAKE—1939—manager, New York Black Yankees

AUSTIN, JOHN—1887—player, Cincinnati Browns (NCBBL)

AUSTIN, RAYMOND (TANK)—1926, 1930-33—p, Chattanooga White Sox, Nashville Elite Giants, Birmingham Black Barons, Atlanta Black Crackers, Brooklyn Royal Giants, New York Black Yankees

AVENDORPH, JULIUS—1899—officer, Columbia Giants

AVERETT [AVERY], (SKIP)—1943, 1948—of, New York Black Yankees

AVERY, WILLIAM—1921—p, Calgary Black Sox

AWKARD, SR., RUSSELL ALFRED—1940-41—of, New York Cubans, Newark Eagles

AWKWARD, BOB—1925—p, Hilldale Club

AYBAR, [DR.] JOSÉ—1937—owner, Trujillo All-Stars (Ciudad Trujillo Dragons)

AYLOR, C. W.—1887—president, Philadelphia Pythians (NCBBL)

AYLOR, JAMES—1887—of, Philadelphia Pythians (NCBBL)

B

BABCOCK, ____—1872—1b, Amicable Club of New York
BACTORY, ____—1909—player, Harrisburg Giants
BADEAU, ____—1920—p, New Orleans Crescent Stars
BAETZEL [BARTZEL], ____—1925-26—umpire, ECL
BAEZ, ANDRÉS JULIO (GRILLO B)—1940—of, p, New York Cubans
BAEZA, JOSÉ M.—1902—of, All Cubans
BACON, EDWARD THOMAS (ED)—1925—batboy, Hilldale Club
BADEAU, ____—1920—p, New Orleans Crescent Stars
BAGBY, ____—1921—ph, Cleveland Tate Stars, Dayton Marcos
BAGLEY, ____—1937—c, Cincinnati Tigers
BAGLEY, ____—1951—of, Brooklyn Royal Giants
BAILEY, ____—1921—of, All Nations
BAILEY, ALONZA—1934-35—p, Newark Dodgers
BAILEY, GEORGE D.—1914-29—of, 3b, Baltimore Giants, Lincoln (NY) Stars, Penn Red Caps of NY
BAILEY, H.J.—1926—officer, Montgomery Grey Sox
BAILEY, JOHN—1929—p, Baltimore Black Sox
BAILEY, JOHN THOMAS—1910—c, Chicago Giants
BAILEY, JOSEPH—1875—3b, St. Louis Blue Stockings
BAILEY, OTHA WILLIAM (BILL, LITTLE CATCH)—1950-59—c, Cleveland Buckeyes, Houston Eagles, New Orleans Eagles, Birmingham Black Barons
BAILEY, PERCY (BILL, LEFTY)—1927-34—p, Baltimore Black Sox, Nashville Elite Giants, Detroit Stars, Cole's Chicago American Giants, New York Black Yankees, Newark Dodgers
BAILEY, ROBERT (BOB)—1932—of, Hilldale Club
BAILEY, RUSSELL—1926—c, Nashville Giants
BAIRD, THOMAS YOUNGER—1938-54—officer, owner, Kansas City Monarchs; booking agent for NAL exhibition games
BAKER, ____—1891—of, Cuban Giants
BAKER, ____—1917—2b, Los Angeles White Sox
BAKER, ____—1921—of, Chicago Union Giants
BAKER, ____—1927—of, Wilmington Potomacs
BAKER, ART—1958—utility, Detroit Clowns
BAKER, EDGAR (LEFTY)—1944-46—p, Harlem Globetrotters, Memphis Red Sox, Cleveland Clippers, Brooklyn Brown Dodgers, Chicago Brown Bombers (USL)
BAKER, EUGENE WALTER (GENE)—1948-50—ss, Kansas City Monarchs; scout, Pittsburgh Pirates, 1965-1988
BAKER, FRANK—1956—c, Kansas City Monarchs
BAKER, HENRY—1925-26, 1932—1b, of, Indianapolis ABCs, Dayton Marcos
BAKER, HOWARD (HOME RUN)—1910—utility, Leland Giants, Chicago Union Giants
BAKER, HUDSON ANDREW (BAKE)—1945-48—of, Brooklyn Brown Dodgers, Philadelphia Stars, Indianapolis Clowns
BAKER, JACOB T.—1859—ss, Unknown Base Ball Club (of Weeksville, NY)
BAKER, LAMAR—1950—p, New York Black Yankees
BAKER, NORMAN (BUD)—1937—p, Newark Eagles, New York Black Yankees
BAKER, RUFUS (SCOOP, REACH)—1943-50—2b, 3b, ss, of, New York Black Yankees, Newark Eagles
BAKER, SAMMY—1950—p, Chicago American Giants
BAKER, TOM—1940—p, Baltimore Elite Giants
BAKER, WELTON B.—1931, 1935-38—vice-president, NSL; business manager, Atlanta Black Crackers; officer, Norfolk Giants
BALDWIN, ____—1933—umpire, NNL
BALDWIN, ____—1947—ph, New York Black Yankees
BALDWIN, ROBERT LEE—1947, 1957—c, manager, 1b, 2b, Detroit Wolves, Detroit Stars, Birmingham Black Barons
BALDWIN, ROBERT WEST (TINY)—1923-35—2b, manager, Indianapolis ABCs, Cleveland Elites, Detroit Stars, Cleveland Tate Stars
BALES, ____—1911—of, Leland Giants
BALL, GILBERT A.—1887— officer, National League of Colored Base Ball Clubs; president, utility, Philadelphia Pythians (NCBBL)
BALL, WALTER THOMAS—1902-24—p, of, Cuban X-Giants, Augusta (GA), Leland Giants, Chicago Giants, Chicago American Giants, St. Louis Giants, Schenectady Mohawk Giants, Brooklyn Royal Giants, Chicago Union Giants, Milwaukee Giants, Lincoln (NY) Stars, Lincoln (NY) Giants, Minneapolis Keystones, Philadelphia Quaker City Giants, St. Paul Colored Gophers
BALLARD, ____—1910—p, Chicago Giants
BALLARD, HERSCHEL—1937—officer, Indianapolis Athletics
BALLARD, JACOB—1868—player, Philadelphia Pythians
BALLESTER y SAN MARTÍN, MIGUEL (PEDRO), [a.k.a. PABLO BALLESTER]—1948—ss, New York Cubans
BALLESTEROS, GERARDO P.—1915-16—p, of, Long Branch (NJ) Cubans

BALLEW, (BLUE)—1930—p, Louisville White Sox
BALLEY, ____—1937—p, Cincinnati Tigers
BAMES, ____—1937—c, Birmingham Black Barons
BANAHAM, ____—1942—umpire, East/West game
BANFIELD, ____—1870—ss, Boston Resolutes
BANG, ____—1914—of, Chicago Union Giants
BANKHEAD, DANIEL ROBERT (DAN)—1940-47—p, Birmingham Black Barons, Memphis Red Sox, Chicago American Giants, Cincinnati Crescents
BANKHEAD, FRED—1937-50—2b, 3b, Birmingham Black Barons, Memphis Red Sox, New York Black Yankees
BANKHEAD, JR., GARNETT—1948, 1950—p, Homestead Grays
BANKHEAD, JOSEPH CALVIN (JOE)—1948-50—p, Birmingham Black Barons, Harlem Globetrotters
BANKHEAD, SAMUEL HOWARD (SAM, JARRY)—1931-50—ss, of, 2b, manager, Birmingham Black Barons, Louisville Black Caps, Nashville Elite Giants, Kansas City Monarchs, Pittsburgh Crawfords, Trujillo All-Stars (Ciudad Trujillo Dragons), Toledo Crawfords, Homestead Grays, North Classic Team, South All-Stars, Denver Post Negro All-Stars
BANKS, ____—1869—of, Brooklyn Unique
BANKS, ____—1896—p, Cuban X-Giants
BANKS, ____—1907—2b, Harrisburg Giants
BANKS, ____—1908—c, Columbia Giants
BANKS, ____—1916—of, Bacharach (AC) Giants
BANKS, ____—1919—2b, Wilmington Giants
BANKS, ____—1924, 1930—2b, 3b, Hilldale Club, Harrisburg Giants
BANKS, ____—1929—of, Santop Broncos
BANKS, ____—1931—of, Philadelphia Quaker City Giants
BANKS, BENJAMIN LANDON (BEN)—1952—2b, Kansas City Monarchs
BANKS, (BUD)—1896—p, Cuban X-Giants
BANKS, ERNEST (ERNIE, ANDY, BINGO)—1950, 1953—ss, Kansas City Monarchs
BANKS, G.—1914-17—p, c, Lincoln (NY) Giants, Philadelphia Giants
BANKS, JAMES W.—1950-52, 1956-58—p, 1b, of, Baltimore Elite Giants, Memphis Red Sox
BANKS, SR., JOHN T. (JOHNNY)—1942, 1950—p, Philadelphia Daisies (NML), Philadelphia Stars
BANKS, NORMAN EARL (SKEETER)—1945-46—2b, 3b, Newark Eagles, Nashville Cubs
BANKS, RICHARD ALLEN—1944-47—c, Richmond (VA) Cardinals, Asheville Blues
BANKS, S.—1915-19—c, Philadelphia Giants, Lincoln (NY) Giants
BANKS, WILLIAM—1947—c, Newark Eagles
BANTON, ____—1914—p, Chicago American Giants, West Baden (IN) Sprudels
BAPTISTE, ____—1923-24—of, Bacharach (AC) Giants, Philadelphia Giants
BARANDA [BARADO], MANUEL—1914-18—3b, of, 2b, 1b, Long Branch (NJ) Cubans, Jersey City Cubans, Cuban Stars (East)
BARBEE, BOB—1942—1b, p, Philadelphia Stars
BARBEE, JOHN QUINCY ADAMS (BUD)—1949—of, Louisville Buckeyes, Kansas City Monarchs
BARBEE, WALTER BRATCHER (LAMB)—1937-51—p, 1b, manager, New York Black Yankees, Cincinnati Ethiopian Clowns (NML), Cincinnati-Indianapolis Clowns, Baltimore Elite Giants, Raleigh (NC) Tigers, Indianapolis Clowns, Brooklyn Royal Giants, Bacharach (AC) Giants
BARBER, [DR.] FLETCHER—1932—officer, Washington Pilots
BARBER, HERB—1938-39—p, Bacharach (AC) Giants
BARBER, JOHN—1946—of, Pittsburgh Crawfords
BARBER, RALPH—1932—officer, Washington Pilots
BARBER, SAMUEL (SAM)—1940-50—p, Birmingham Black Barons, Cleveland Clippers, Cleveland Buckeyes
BARBETTE, ____—1918—1b, Cuban Stars (East)
BARBÓN, ROBERTO (CHICO)—1950—infield, New York Cubans
BARBOUR [BARBER], ELMORE (BULL)—1920-25—2b, Hilldale Club, Kansas City Monarchs, Harrisburg Giants, Pittsburgh Keystones
BARBOUR [BARBER], JESSE BERNARD [PHANTOM, JESS]—1908-26—of, infield, Philadelphia Giants, Chicago American Giants, Bacharach (AC) Giants, Detroit Stars, Pittsburgh Keystones, Harrisburg Giants, St. Louis Giants, Indianapolis ABCs, Philadelphia Quaker City Giants, Chicago Giants, Hilldale Club, Louisville White Sox, Breakers Hotel (FL), Royal Poinciana (FL)
BARCELÓ [BORSEL(O)], JOAQUÍN—1921—p, All Cubans
BARENTTO, ____—1921—1b, Cuban Stars (East) [see BORROTO, MARIO]
BARKER, ____—1921—of, Montgomery Grey Sox
BARKER, ____—1923—of, Nashville Elite Giants
BARKER, JOE (JELLY ROLL)—1932—2b, 3b, of, John Donaldson All-Stars

BARKER, MARVIN (HACK, HANK)—1935-50—of, utility, manager, New York Black Yankees, Philadelphia Stars, Newark Dodgers, Bacharach (AC) Giants, Newark Eagles, North All-Stars

BARKIN, M. C.—1928—owner, Cleveland Tigers

BARKS, ALFRED (AL)—1957—1b, New York Black Yankees

BARLOW, ____—1940—p, New Orleans-St. Louis Stars

BARLOW, TOM G.—1867-70—of, 3b, Mutuals of Washington, Washington Alerts

BARNER, BOB—1940—p, Cincinnati Buckeyes

BARNER [BARNES], DON—1960—of, Detroit-New Orleans Stars

BARNES, ____—1895—c, Adrian (MI) Page Fence Giants, Philadelphia Giants

BARNES, ____—1920—of, Atlanta Black Crackers

BARNES, ____—1925—p, Kansas City Monarchs

BARNES, ____—1927—3b, Gilkerson's Union Giants

BARNES, ARTHUR—1932—officer, New York Black Yankees

BARNES, CLAUDE (RED)—1956—p, Birmingham Black Barons

BARNES, ED—1937-40—p, Kansas City Monarchs, Baltimore Elite Giants, Birmingham Black Barons

BARNES, EDWARD—1957—p, Birmingham Black Barons

BARNES, FRANK—1949-50—p, Kansas City Monarchs

BARNES, FRED—1924, 1926—p, Washington Potomacs, Washington Black Sox

BARNES, SR., HARRY (TACKHEAD, MOOCH)—1935-44, 1948-49—c, manager, Chattanooga Choo Choos, Birmingham Black Barons, Memphis Red Sox, Atlanta Black Crackers, Birmingham Black Barons

BARNES, HENRY—1956—c, Memphis Red Sox

BARNES, ISAAC (IKE)—1955-59—p, c, Memphis Red Sox

BARNES, JR., ISAAC V. (POISON IVY, I.V.)—1938-40—of, p, Kansas City Monarchs

BARNES, SR., JOE—1950-52—p, Memphis Red Sox, Kansas City Monarchs, Indianapolis Clowns

BARNES, JOHN C. (TUBBY, FAT, SOUPY)—1921-31—c, Cleveland Tate Stars, Cleveland Browns, Detroit Stars, St. Louis Stars, Cleveland Hornets, Cleveland Tigers, Memphis Red Sox, Toledo Tigers, Indianapolis ABCs, Cleveland Elites, Havana Red Sox

BARNES, JOHN C.—1952—p, Philadelphia Stars

BARNES MUTE—1938—p, Atlanta Black Crackers

BARNES, OSCAR—1932—officer, New York Black Yankees

BARNES, RAY—1951—p, Kansas City Monarchs

BARNES, RUBE—1906—ss, 3b, Wilmington Giants, Philadelphia Giants

BARNES, SANFORD L.—1932—p, Chicago American Giants

BARNES, TOBIAS (TED)—1937, 1940—3b, Chicago American Giants

BARNES, THOMAS B. (TOM)—1950-51, 1954-55—p, Memphis Red Sox

BARNES, VIRGIL—1917—p, All Nations

BARNES, WILLIAM (JIMMY, BILL)—1937-43, 1946-47—p, Baltimore Elite Giants, Memphis Red Sox, Indianapolis Clowns, New York Black Yankees

BARNES, WILLIAM H.—1887—officer, Baltimore Lord Baltimores (NCBBL)

BARNETT, ARCHIE BUTLER—1921, 1928—c, Pittsburgh Keystones, St. Louis Stars

BARNETT y LOBO, VICTOR—1944-45—of, Newark Eagles

BARNHILL, ____—1945-46—1b, Pittsburgh Crawfords (USL)

BARNHILL, DAVID (DAVE, IMPO)—1938-49—p, New Orleans-St. Louis Stars, New York Cubans, Jacksonville Red Caps, Ethiopian Clowns, North Classic Team, North Classic Stars, North All-Stars

BARNHILL, HERBERT EDWARD (BARNEY, HERB)—1936-46—c, Jacksonville Red Caps, Kansas City Monarchs, Chicago American Giants, Cleveland Bears

BARÓ, BERNARDO—1915-30—of, 1b, Almendares Cubans, Cuban Stars (East & West), New York Cuban Stars, Kansas City Monarchs, Cincinnati Cuban Stars

BARR, ____—1921-22—3b, ss, Kansas City Monarchs, Cuban Stars (West) [see BARÓ, BERNARDO, and CARR, GEORGE HENRY]

BARRANE, CLEVE—1947—p, Brooklyn Royal Giants

BARRETT, ____—1921-25—umpire, NNL

BARRETT, ____—1928—c, St. Louis Giants

BARRIOS, PEDRO—1947—2b, Havana Las Palomas

BARRONS, ____—1932—p, New Orleans Black Pelicans

BARROW, WESLEY (BIGGIE)—1945-47, 1957, 1960—c, of, manager, coach, New Orleans Black Pelicans, Nashville Cubs, Baltimore Elite Giants, New Orleans Bears, Detroit-New Orleans Stars, Harlem Globetrotters, Portland (OR) Rosebuds, Los Angeles White Sox

BARRY, ____—1940—p, Chicago Giants

BARRY, JACK—1915—p, Chicago Giants

BARTAMINO, ____—1904—manager, All Cubans

BARTE, ____–1934–of, Philadelphia Stars [see WHITE, CHANEY]
BARTEL, ____–1889–c, Philadelphia Giants
BARTENS, ____–1891–c, New York Gorhams
BARTHOLOMEW, ____–1910–ss, New Orleans Eagles
BARTLETT, RAYMOND HOWARD (HOMER, SAPHO)–1910-25–p, Jewell's ABCs, Indianapolis ABCs, Bowser's ABCs, Kansas City Monarchs, Lincoln (NY) Giants
BARTON, ____–1891–p, of, Ansonia Cuban Giants, New York Gorhams
BARTON, ____–1907–1b, Harrisburg Giants
BARTON, BERT–1919-33–owner, Detroit Stars
BARTON, EUGENE (GENE, CHEEKY, CHERRY)–1906-11–of, Minneapolis Keystones, Twin City Gophers, St. Paul Colored Gophers, Leland Giants
BARTON, GEORGE–1889–3b, of, Trenton (NJ) Cuban Giants (Middle States League)
BARTON, SHERMAN (BUCKY)–1896-1912–of, Chicago Unions, Columbia Giants, Philadelphia Quaker City Giants, Cuban X-Giants, St. Paul Colored Gophers, Chicago Giants, Chicago Union Giants, Leland Giants, Adrian (MI) Page Fence Giants, Algona (IA) Brownies
BASCOM, WORLEY–1868–player, Philadelphia Pythians
BASHUM, ____–1932–c, Indianapolis ABCs
BASKINS [HASKINS], WILLIAM H.–1889-92–2b, Chicago Unions
BASS, JESSE–1957-60–2b, Birmingham Black Barons, Detroit Stars
BASS, LEROY PERCY (RED, ROY)–1940–c, Homestead Grays
BASSETT, ____–1888–2b, Hoosier Black Stockings
BASSETT, LLOYD PEPPER (ROCKING CHAIR, TARZAN)–1934-54–c, New Orleans Crescent Stars, Philadelphia Stars, Chicago American Giants, Pittsburgh Crawfords, Cincinnati Ethiopian Clowns (NML), Cincinnati-Indianapolis Clowns, Birmingham Black Barons, Toledo Crawfords, Homestead Grays, Memphis Red Sox, Detroit Stars, Kansas City Royals (winter)
BATES, ____–1888–p, Bloomington (IL) Reds
BATES, ____–1909–p, Louisville Cubs
BATES, ____–1913–1b, Chicago Union Giants
BATISTA, ____–1924–p, Philadelphia Giants
BATL'D, ____–1904–ss, Cuban Giants
BATSON, CHARLES MAXWELL (CHARLIE)–1908-09–of, Genuine Cuban Giants, Philadelphia Giants
BATTIES, J.–1907–c, Trusty (PA) Giants
BATTIES, WILLIAM–1907–2b, Trusty (PA) Giants
BATTLE, FREDDIE–1960-63–manager, 1b, of, Indianapolis Clowns
BATTLE(S), RAYMOND (RAY)–1944-45–3b, Homestead Grays, Atlanta Black Crackers
BATTLE, RUFUS E.–1924–c, Harrisburg Giants, Birmingham Black Barons
BATTLES, WILLIAM JAMES (BILL)–1938-39, 1947-49–ss, p, Schenectady Mohawk Giants, Chicago American Giants
BATUM, G.W.–1885–2b, Brooklyn Remsens
BAUCHMAN [BOCKMAN], HARRY (PICK)–1911-23–2b, 3b, Minneapolis Keystones, All Nations, Chicago American Giants, Chicago Union Giants, Chicago Giants
BAUER, ____–1925–umpire, ECL
BAUGH, JOHN MAYNARD (JOHNNY, WIZARD)–1920-21–p, Lincoln (NY) Giants
BAUGH, MELVIN–1945–2b, Chicago Brown Bombers (USL)
BAUZA, MARCELINO–1929-30–ss, Cuban Stars (West), Havana Red Sox
BAXTER, ____–1922–umpire, NNL
BAXTER, ____–1907–2b, Harrisburg Giants
BAXTER, AL–1898-99–of, 2b, ss, Celoron (NY) Acme Colored Giants (Iron & Oil League), Cuban Giants
BAXTER, JAMES–1944–2b, Baltimore Elite Giants
BAXTER, ISABELLE–1933–utility, Cleveland Colored Giants
BAYLIS(S), HENRY JUNIOR (HANK)–1948-55–3b, c, Chicago American Giants, Baltimore Elite Giants, Birmingham Black Barons, Kansas City Monarchs
BAYLOCK, ____–1927–p, Harrisburg Giants
BAYLOR, JOE–1931–c, Philadelphia Quaker City Giants
BAYNARD, JAMES HOWARD (FRANK)–1913-28–of, c, Penn Red Caps of NY, Newark Stars, Hilldale Club, Bacharach (AC) Giants, Havana Red Sox, Lincoln (NY) Giants, Cuban X-Giants
BEA, DARIUS F. (BILL, BUZ, DOC)–1934, 1940-42–p, of, Baltimore Black Sox, New York Black Yankees, Philadelphia Stars, Otto Brigg's All-Stars, Philadelphia Daisies (NML)
BEACH, ROY–1958–p, Memphis Red Sox
BEADLE, ____–1888–3b, Bloomington (IL) Reds
BEAL, GIOVANNI (LEFTY)–1947–p, 1b, Newark Eagles
BEALE, HARRY–1926-30, 1934–p, officer, Pittsburgh Crawfords
BEAMONT, SKUDY–1925–of, Philadelphia Giants, Philadelphia Royal Giants

BEAR, J.—1948—c, Harlem Globetrotters
BEAR, W.—1948—of, Harlem Globetrotters
BEARCAR, ____—1906—2b, Philadelphia Giants [see BROKAW, FREDERICK RICKER]
BEATTY, BENJAMIN—1876—player, Chicago Uniques
BEAUFORD, H.—1874—vice-president, Chicago Uniques
BEAVER, TROY—1943, 1945—of, Brooklyn Royal Giants
BEAVERS, JIM (RED)—1932—utility, Atlanta Black Crackers
BEBLEY, ____—1925—p, Birmingham Black Barons
BEBOP, SPEC— [see BELL, RALPH]
BECAMPA, ____—1919—p, Philadelphia Giants
BECK, ____—1928—c, Chattanooga Black Lookouts
BECKER, ____—1932—pr, Indianapolis ABCs
BECKWITH, CHRISTOPHER JOHN (BECK)—1917-39, 1942, 1944—ss, 3b, c, of, manager, Chicago Giants, Chicago American Giants, Baltimore Black Sox, Homestead Grays, Harrisburg Giants, Lincoln (NY) Giants, Bacharach (AC) Giants, New York Black Yankees, Newark Dodgers, Brooklyn Royal Giants, Newark Browns, Darby Daisies, Jewell's ABCs, All Nations
BECKWITH, STANLEY—1916-17—c, ss, Montgomery Grey Sox, Chicago Giants, Jewell's ABCs
BEDFORD, WILLIAM—1908-09—2b, Birmingham Giants, Cuban Giants
BEDGATE, ____—1915—p, Lincoln (NY) Giants
BEHEL, ____—1888—1b, Rockford (IL) Rockfords
BEITIA, COSME—1926—of, Lincoln (NY) Giants
BEJERANO, AGUSTÍN (PIJINI)—1928-29—of, Cuban Stars (East), Lincoln (NY) Giants
BELFIELD, SKINNER—1947-48—c, Newark Eagles
BELGEN, ____—1915—c, St. Louis Giants
BELL, ____—1867-71—3b, of, Mutuals of Washington, Actives of Philadelphia
BELL, ____—1917-18—of, Baltimore Black Sox
BELL, ____—1929—infield, Evansville Giants
BELL, ____—1932—c, Bacharach (AC) Giants
BELL, ____—1943—of, Chicago American Giants
BELL, CHARLES—1887—c, Pittsburgh Keystones (NCBBL)
BELL, CHARLES (LEFTY)—1948—p, Homestead Grays
BELL, CLIFFORD W. (CLIFF, CHERRY, CEE BELL)—1921-32—p, Kansas City Monarchs, Memphis Red Sox, Cleveland Cubs, Nashville Elite Giants, Chicago American Giants
BELL, ELISHA B. (JAKE, PREACHER)—1941-42, 1946—2b, Philadelphia Daisies (NML), Philadelphia Stars, Otto Brigg's All-Stars
BELL, EUGENE—1911—1b, Brown's Tennessee Rats
BELL, EUGENE—1929—p, Colored House of David
BELL, G.—1900, 1908—p, of, Genuine Cuban Giants, Chicago Columbia Giants, Chicago Union Giants
BELL, FRANK—1887-92—of, c, Pittsburgh Keystones (NCBBL), Cuban Giants, New York Gorhams (Middle States League), Ansonia Cuban Giants (Connecticut St. League), Philadelphia Giants
BELL, ABE—1924, 1926—p, Washington Potomacs, Harrisburg Giants, Washington Black Sox
BELL, FRED (LEFTY)—1922-27, 1932—p, of, Toledo Tigers, St. Louis Giants, St. Louis Stars, Detroit Stars, Montgomery Grey Sox
BELL, HERMAN—1943-50—c, Birmingham Black Barons
BELL, JAMES (STEEL ARM)—1932-40—c, Montgomery Grey Sox, Indianapolis Crawfords, Jacksonville Red Caps
BELL, JAMES THOMAS (COOL PAPA)—1922-37, 1942-46, 1948—of, p, St. Louis Stars, Pittsburgh Crawfords, Detroit Wolves, Kansas City Monarchs, Chicago American Giants, Memphis Red Sox, Homestead Grays, Detroit Senators, North Classic Team, Denver Post Negro All-Stars, Trujillo All-Stars (Ciudad Trujillo Dragons), Kansas City Royals
BELL, JOE (LEFTY)—1932—p, Montgomery Grey Sox
BELL, JULIAN (JUTE)—1923-31—p, of, Birmingham Black Barons, Memphis Red Sox, Detroit Stars, Louisville White Sox, Chattanooga White Sox, Nashville Elite Giants
BELL, MADISON—1939—vice-president, New York Black Yankees
BELL, MILTON—1946—utility, Pittsburgh Stars
BELL, MITCHELL—1957—3b, Indianapolis Clowns
BELL, PIEDMONT—1922—manager, Louisville Stars/White Sox
BELL, RALPH (SPEC BEBOP)—1950-60—clown, Indianapolis Clowns
BELL, WILLIAM—1902-04—p, of, Philadelphia Giants; 1921—umpire, NNL
BELL, WILLIAM—1910—assistant secretary—St. Louis Giants
BELL, SR., WILLIAM (W BELL, CAMPANITA)—1923-48—p, manager, Kansas City Monarchs, Detroit Wolves, Homestead Grays, Pittsburgh Crawfords, Newark Dodgers, Newark Eagles, New York Harlem Stars
BELL, JR., WILLIAM REGINALD (LEFTY, BILL)—1949-54—p, Kansas City Monarchs, Birmingham Black Barons
BELLINGER, CHARLES (CHARLIE)—1905, 1909-10, 1918-20—owner, San Antonio Black Broncos
BELTRAN, Isidro—1954—of, Kansas City Monarchs

BELYER, ____—1915—of, St. Louis Giants
BEMA, ____—1929—of, Cuban Stars (West)
BEN, ____—1926—1b, of, New Orleans Algiers
BENAVIDES y BENAVIDES, PRUDENCIO—1904—of, All Cubans
BENITEZ, ____—1928—p, Harrisburg Giants, Philadelphia Tigers, Havana Red Sox
BENJAMIN, ____—1924—of, New Orleans-St. Louis Stars
BENJAMIN, EDWARD—1926—utility, New Orleans Black Pelicans
BENJAMIN, HENRY—1931-32—of, 2b, Memphis Red Sox
BENJAMIN, JERRY CHARLES—1931-48—of, manager, Knoxville Giants, Memphis Red Sox, Detroit Stars, Birmingham Black Barons, Homestead Grays, Toledo Crawfords (nee Christopher), New York Cubans, North Classic Team, South All-Stars, Norfolk Royals
BENNETT, ____—1916—2b, Chicago Union Giants
BENNETT, ____—1924-26—umpire ECL, NNL
BENNETT, ____—1942—of, Birmingham Black Barons, New Orleans Black Pelicans
BENNETT, ARTHUR—1955—of, Kansas City Monarchs
BENNETT, BRANSFORD (BRADFORD, BUCK)—1940-43, 1946—of, 1b, New Orleans-St. Louis Stars, New York Black Yankees, Boston Blues
BENNETT, CLYDE—1952—2b, Kansas City Monarchs
BENNETT, DON—1926, 1930-34—2b, Dayton Marcos, Cleveland Cubs, Memphis Red Sox, Birmingham Black Barons
BENNETT, FRANK—1918—manager, Bacharach (AC) Giants
BENNETT, JAMES THOMAS (JIM, FIREBALL)—1945-48, 1953—p, of, Cincinnati-Indianapolis Clowns, Indianapolis Clowns, Kansas City (KS) Giants, Havana Las Palomas
BENNETT, JEREMIAH H. (JERRY)—1951—p, Kansas City Monarchs
BENNETT, JOHN—1930-32—of, Birmingham Black Barons, Louisville Black Caps
BENNETT, LEROY—1946—p, Boston Blues
BENNETT, SAMUEL (SAM)—1909-27—of, c, San Antonio Black Broncos, St. Louis Giants, St. Louis Stars, Schenectady Mohawk Giants, Lincoln (NY) Giants, Louisville White Sox, Oklahoma City Giants, Chicago American Giants, Dayton Marcos
BENNETT, WILLIAM J. (WILLIE)—1952-55—ss, of, Kansas City Monarchs

BENNETTE, GEORGE CLIFFORD (JEW BABY)—1920-22—of, Columbus Buckeyes, Memphis Red Sox, Indianapolis ABCs, Detroit Stars, Chicago Giants, Chicago Union Giants, Pittsburgh Keystones, Kansas City Monarchs, Atlanta Black Crackers, Foster Memorial Giants
BENNING, ____—1937—2b, Indianapolis Athletics
BENNING, A.G.—1926—officer, Birmingham Black Barons
BENNINGTON, ____—1958—p, Birmingham Black Barons
BENSON, ____—1867—of, Ithaca (NY) Actives
BENSON, ____—1913—p, All Nations
BENSON, ____—1932—ss, Indianapolis ABCs
BENSON, ARGUSTA [AUGUSTA] (SPEEDY)—1937-40—p, Washington Elite Giants, Memphis Red Sox
BENSON, CLEO (BALDY)—1942, 1946—manager, c, Chicago American Giants, San Francisco Sea Lions
BENSON, EUGENE (GENE, SPIDER)—1933-48—of, Brooklyn Royal Giants, Bacharach (AC) Giants, Pittsburgh Crawfords, Philadelphia Stars, Newark Eagles, South All-Stars, Otto Brigg's All-Stars
BENSON, HERBERT C.—1951-52—1b, Indianapolis Clowns
BENSON, NORMAN (BUS)—1938—p, Philadelphia Stars
BENTION, [see BENSON, EUGENE]
BENTLY, ____—1923-29—umpire, ECL
BENTON, ____—1910—p, Louisville Cubs
BENTON, CHARLES—1946—p, Pittsburgh Stars
BENTON, JAMES ELBERT—1950—p, Memphis Red Sox
BENVENUTI, JULIUS—1938-39—vice-president, Chicago American Giants
BERDINE, LEO—1925-32—p, of, Birmingham Black Barons, Memphis Red Sox, Indianapolis ABCs, Houston Black Buffaloes, Knoxville Giants
BERENT, ____—1932—of, Washington Pilots
BERGEN, ____—1907—of, Brooklyn Royal Giants
BERGIN, JIMMY—1949, 1953—1b, Kansas City Monarchs, Kansas City (KS) Giants
BERKLEY, ____—1941—p, New Orleans-St. Louis Stars
BERKLEY, JOHN RANDOLPH—1919—c, Hilldale Club
BERN, ____—1942—p, Minneapolis-St. Paul Gophers
BERNAL, PLÁCIDO (PABLO, SLICK)—1941—p, New York Cuban Stars
BERNARD, PABLO (MANITO)—1949-50—2b, ss, Louisville Buckeyes, Cleveland Buckeyes
BERNARD, ROBERT H. (BOB)—1910-25—of, c, of, Brooklyn Royal Giants, Havana Red Sox, Pittsburgh Giants, Lincoln (NY) Stars, Cuban Giants, Philadelphia Giants, Lincoln (NY) Giants, Hilldale Club

BERNO, ____—1931—of, Indianapolis ABCs
BERRY, ____—1934—p, Baltimore Black Sox
BERRY, EDDIE—1930—ss, 2b, Memphis Red Sox, Detroit Stars
BERRY, HORACE—1887—ss, Wilmington Base Ball Club
BERRY, JAMES—1953, 1956—p, Memphis Red Sox, Birmingham Black Barons
BERRY, JOHN PAUL—1935-37, 1945—p, 1b, Kansas City Monarchs, St. Louis Stars
BERRY, LEON LYNN—1934—p, Newark Dodgers
BERRY, MICHAEL C. (MIKE, RED, CANNONBALL)—1943-50—p, Baltimore Elite Giants, Kansas City Monarchs, Harlem Globetrotters, Seattle Steelheads, Cleveland Buckeyes
BERRY, MORTON (BUCKY)—1938—p, of, Atlanta Black Crackers, Ethiopian Clowns
BERRY, WILLARD EDWARD (EDDIE)—1942-43, 1945—p, of, Richmond Hilldales (NML), Baltimore Elite Giants, Brooklyn Brown Dodgers
BERRY, WILLIAM D.—1871, 1874, 1876—of, business manager, Chicago Uniques
BERWER, ____—1947—ss, Chicago American Giants
BEST, ROSS—1904-07—p, 2b, Brooklyn Royal Giants, Cuban Giants, Famous Cuban Giants
BETTS, ____—1938—of, Kansas City Monarchs
BETTS, RUSSEL BOYD—1950-51—p, Kansas City Monarchs
BETUS, ____—1932—of, Colored House of David
BEVERLY, CHARLES GREEN (HOOKS, WOOGER)—1924-36—p, Cleveland Browns, Birmingham Black Barons, Kansas City Monarchs, Cleveland Stars, Pittsburgh Crawfords, New Orleans Crescent Stars, Newark Eagles, Nashville Elite Giants, Cole's Chicago American Giants, Houston Black Buffaloes, New Orleans Black Pelicans
BEVERLY, JESS—1936—p, Philadelphia Stars
BEVERLY, NUNNIE—1945—of, New Orleans Black Pelicans
BEVERLY, W.—1936—p, Houston Black Buffaloes
BEVERLY, WILLIAM WALDO (BILL, FIREBALL)—1950-55—p, Houston Eagles, New Orleans Eagles, Chicago American Giants, Birmingham Black Barons
BIBBS, JUNIUS LLOYD (ALEXANDER, RAINEY)—1933-44—2b, ss, 3b, Detroit Stars, Cincinnati Tigers, Chicago American Giants, Kansas City Monarchs, Indianapolis Crawfords, Cleveland Buckeyes
BIBLINS, ____—1934—p [see PIPKIN, ROBERT]

BIDWELL, CHARLES—1930-32—officer, Chicago American Giants
BIGBY, CHARLIE—1953—of, Indianapolis Clowns
BIGGS, VANE—1949—c, Kansas City Monarchs
BILAO, STEPHEN LIBORE—1917—owner, Houston Black Buffaloes
BILGAR [BIGBY], ____—1914—c, Chicago Giants
BILLINGS, ____—1948—c, Homestead Grays
BILLINGS, WILLIAM (KID)—1921-23, 1926—p, Nashville Elite Giants, Memphis Red Sox
BILLINGSLEY, JOHN ALBERT (LITTLE JOHN)—1949-51—c, Memphis Red Sox
BILLINGSLEY, LAURENCE—1958-59—p, Birmingham Black Barons
BILLINGSLEY, SAM—1950, 1958—p, Memphis Red Sox, Birmingham Black Barons
BINDER, JAMES (JIMMY)—1930-46—3b, manager, Memphis Red Sox, Brooklyn Eagles, Indianapolis ABCs, Detroit Stars, Homestead Grays, Washington Elite Giants, Pittsburgh Crawfords, Cleveland Clippers
BINGA, JESSE E.—1887—player, Washington Capital Citys
BINGA, WILLIAM HENRY—1895-1911—3b, c, Adrian (MI) Page Fence Giants, Columbia Giants, Philadelphia Giants, St. Paul Colored Gophers, Chicago Union Giants, Kansas City (KS) Giants, Adrian Reformers (Michigan St. League), Twin City Gophers, Leland Giants, Minneapolis Keystones, Philadelphia Quaker Giants
BINGHAM, WILLIAM HORACE. (W.H., BINGO)—1910-21—of, Chicago Union Giants, Chicago Giants, West Baden (IN) Sprudels; 1917—manager, Lost Island (IA) Giants
BIOT, JR., CHARLES AUGUSTUS (CHARLIE)—1939-43—of, Newark Eagles, New York Black Yankees, Baltimore Elite Giants, Philadelphia Stars
BIRAN, JACK—1916—2b, Chicago American Giants
BIRDINE, LEO (see LEO BERDINE)
BIRHGA, ____—1931—cf, Birmingham Black Barons
BISHOP, A.W.—1921—president, manager, Chattanooga Tigers
BISHOP, C.—1908—c, Indianapolis ABCs
BISHOP, LES—1946—umpire, WCBA
BISSANT, JEAN (CHAMP)—1926—p, New Orleans Algiers, New Orleans Black Pelicans
BISSANT, JOHN L.—1934-47—of, Cole's Chicago American Giants, Chicago American Giants, Birmingham Black Barons, Chicago Brown Bombers (USL), Cincinnati Tigers

BISSANT, ROBERT NORMAND (BOB)—1938, 1943, 1945, 1947, 2b, of, Miami Ethiopian Clowns, Baltimore Elite Giants, Portland (OR) Rosebuds, New Orleans Black Pelicans, Chicago American Giants
BIVENS, SAM—1934, 1943—p, New Orleans Caulfield Ads; officer, Atlanta Black Crackers
BIVINS, ____—1948—p, Memphis Red Sox
BIX, ____—1921—p, St. Louis Giants
BIZZLE, JAMES—1947-48—p, Birmingham Black Barons
BLACK, ____—1923—umpire, NNL
BLACK, ____—1923-24—of, Memphis Red Sox
BLACK, DANIEL NATHANIEL (DANMON)—1950-52—p, Nashville Cubs, Baltimore Elite Giants, Birmingham Black Barons
BLACK, GILBERT HERNÁNDEZ (GIL)—1955—p, of, Indianapolis Clowns
BLACK, HOWARD—1926-28—p, Cleveland Elites, Dayton Marcos, Brooklyn Cuban Giants
BLACK, JOSEPH (JOE, CHICO)—1943-50—p, Baltimore Elite Giants, New York Black Yankees; author
BLACK, ROY (TANK)—1946—p, Oakland Larks
BLACK, TROY—1916-17—p, Kansas City Tigers
BLACK, WILLIAM—1938—of, Atlanta Black Crackers
BLACKBURN, ____—1938—p, Kansas City Monarchs
BLACKBURN, HUGH R.—1919-20—p, 1b, Gilkerson's Union Giants, Kansas City Monarchs
BLACKMAN, ____—1867—of, Ithaca (NY) Actives
BLACKMAN, JESSE JAMES—1949—utility, Jacksonville Eagles
BLACKMAN, WARREN—1939—p, Memphis Red Sox
BLACKMON, CHARLES—1938—p, Birmingham Black Barons
BLACKMON [BLACKMAN], CLIFFORD (SPEED)—1937-41, 1945—p, Chicago American Giants, Memphis Red Sox, New York Cubans, Indianapolis ABCs, Homestead Grays, New Orleans-St. Louis Stars, Mobile Black Shippers
BLACKMON, HENRY (GALLOPING GHOST)—1920-24—3b, Indianapolis ABCs, Baltimore Black Sox
BLACKMORE, WILLIE—1951, 1954—c, Birmingham Black Barons, Memphis Red Sox
BLACKSTONE, WILLIAM—1887—player, Cincinnati Browns (NCBBL)
BLACKWELL, ____—1934—p, Philadelphia Stars
BLACKWELL, CHARLES H. (RUCKER)—1915-29—of, West Baden (IN) Sprudels, Bowser's ABCs, Jewell's ABCs, St. Louis Giants, St. Louis Stars, Birmingham Black Barons, Indianapolis ABCs, Detroit Stars, Nashville Elite Giants, Bacharach (AC) Giants
BLACKWELL, GOVERNAR—1934—officer, Chicago American Giants
BLAIR, SR., GARNETT E. (SCHOOLBOY)—1942-49—p, Homestead Grays
BLAIR, LONNIE J. (CHICO)—1949-50—p, 2b, Homestead Grays
BLAIR, JR., WILLIAM G. (BILL, RADIO)—1947-48—p, Detroit Senators, Indianapolis Clowns, Portland (OR) Rosebuds, Cincinnati Crescents, Washington Black Senators
BLAKE, FOSTER—1929—p, Colored House of David
BLAKE, FRANCIS (FRANK, BIG RED)—1932-35—p, Baltimore Black Sox, New York Black Yankees, New York Cubans
BLAKE, W.H.—1890—utility, Chicago Unions
BLAKE, WILLIAM—1952—p, Philadelphia Stars
BLAKELY, BERT—1934—c, of, Cincinnati Tigers
BLAKEMORE, WILLIAM (WILLIE)—1954—c, Memphis Red Sox, Kansas City Monarchs, Louisville Clippers
BLANCH, ____—1867—of, Utica (NY) Fearless
BLANCHARD, CHESTER AUGUSTUS—1926-33—ss, utility, Dayton Marcos, Cleveland Tigers
BLANCO, ____—1923—of, All Cubans
BLANCO, CARLOS—1938-41—1b, New York Cubans
BLANCO, HEBERTO M. (HARRY, HENNY)—1941-42—2b, New York Cubans
BLAND [BLANK], ____—1869—1b, Washington Alerts
BLAND, ALFRED PETER—1926—p, ss, Washington Black Sox, Philadelphia Royal Giants
BLAND, BILL (SPIKE)—1940-41—c, Birmingham Black Barons, Cincinnati Buckeyes
BLAND, JAMES (BEADY)—1960—2b, Indianapolis Clowns
BLANE, ____—1922—p, Bacharach (NY) Giants
BLANK, ____—1928—ph, Detroit Stars
BLANKENMEISTER, ____—1921—umpire, NNL
BLANKENSHIP, ____—1908—of, Chicago Union Giants, Cuban Giants
BLANTON, ____—1915—p, French Lick (IN) Plutos
BLATTNER, FRANK (BLUKOI)—1912-21—2b, All Nations, Kansas City Monarchs
BLAVIS, FOX—1936—3b, Homestead Grays
BLAYLOCK, FRED—1945—p, Homestead Grays
BLEACH, LARRY—1934-35, 1937—2b, Brooklyn Royal Giants, Detroit Stars
BLEDSLOE, ____—1937—of, St. Louis Stars

BLEVINS, NEWT (RED FOX)—1932, 1936, 1946—3b, Little Rock Grays, Oakland Larks, Homestead Grays
BLICK, AL—1946—of, Oakland Larks
BLOCKER, ____—1931—p, Detroit Stars
BLOUNT, JOHN T. (TENNY)—1919-33—owner, officer, Detroit Stars; vice-president, NNL
BLUE, FRANK—1898—1b, Celoron (NY) Acme Colored Giants (Iron & Oil League)
BLUEITT [BLUIETT, BLUITT], VIRGIL FINLEY—1915-20, 1937-49—2b, of, Chicago Union Giants; umpire, NAL, East/West game
BLUFORD, ____—1932—of, Harrisburg Giants
BLUFORD, JAMES—1931—of, Newark Browns
BLUKOI, FRANK [see BLATTNER, FRANK]
BOADA, LUCAS—1921-25—p, of, Cuban Stars (East & West), Cincinnati Cuban Stars
BOARD, GEORGE L.—1902-13—1b, manager, Indianapolis ABCs, St. Paul Colored Gophers
BOARDLEY, ____—1919-20—of, Baltimore Black Sox
BOATLEY, ____—1929—1b, Fort Worth Panthers
BOATNER, ____—1926—p, New Orleans Black Pelicans
BOBO, J. [see LEONARD, JAMES]
BOBO, R.—1924—of, Louisville Black Caps
BOBO, WILLIE ALPHONSO—1923-30—1b, All Nations, Kansas City Monarchs, St. Louis Stars, Nashville Elite Giants, Cleveland Tigers
BOERING, ____—1942—p, Twin Cities Gophers
BOGGS, JR., GEORGE—1921-34—p, of, Cleveland Tate Stars, Milwaukee Bears, Detroit Stars, Dayton Marcos, Cleveland Tigers
BOGGS, JIM—1928—p, Cleveland Tigers, Baltimore Black Sox
BOHANNON, ____—1926—p, Colored All-Stars
BOISDEN, JULIUS—1868—player, Philadelphia Pythians
BOLAN, ____—1902-03—ss, Cuban Giants, Genuine Cuban Giants
BOLDEN, EDWARD (ED, CHIEF)—1910-50—officer, owner, Hilldale Club, Darby Phantoms, Philadelphia Stars; officer, ECL, ANL, NNL
BOLDEN, JR., FRANK E.—1930-62—writer, *Pittsburgh Courier*
BOLDEN [SHORTER], HILDA MAE—1951-52—owner, Philadelphia Stars
BOLDEN, JAMES HOWARD (JIM, FIREBALL)—1946-47, 1952—p, Cleveland Buckeyes, Birmingham Black Barons
BOLDEN, L. W.—1885—player, Brooklyn Remsens

BOLDEN, OTTO H.—1909-10, 1920—c, p, San Antonio Broncos, Leland Giants, Chicago Giants, Oklahoma City Giants, Oklahoma City Monarchs
BOLDRIDGE, MANVILLE C. (BUZZ)—1920-32—3b, Colored House of David, John Donaldson All-Stars
BOLDS, CAESAR—umpire, ECL
BOLES, LEON—1911—c, 1b, Chicago American Giants
BOLIN, ____—1905—ss, Brooklyn Royal Giants
BOLIVAR, WILLIAM G.—1868—player, Philadelphia Pythians
BONAHAM, RAY—1942—umpire, NAL
BOND, ____—1940—p, Baltimore Elite Giants
BOND, MONTE ROY—1957, 1960-61—ss, of, Birmingham Black Barons, Detroit Stars, Kansas City Monarchs
BOND, THEODORE HERBERT (THEO, TIMOTHY, TED)—1935-40—ss, 3b, Pittsburgh Crawfords, Newark Dodgers, Chicago American Giants
BOND, WALTER FRANKLIN (WALT)—1956—of, Kansas City Monarchs
BONDS, ____—1927—c, Cleveland Hornets
BONDS, CURTIS—1958—ss, Indianapolis Clowns
BONETA, ____—1924—p, St. Louis Cubs
BONNER, DON—1959-60—of, Detroit Stars, Detroit-New Orleans Stars
BONNER, ROBERT L.—1921-26—1b, c, Cleveland Tate Stars, St. Louis Stars, Toledo Tigers, Cleveland Browns, Cleveland Elites
BOOKER, ____—1935—2b, Detroit Cubs
BOOKER, ____—1948—p, Chattanooga Choo Choos
BOOKER, BILLY—1898—2b, Celoron (NY) Acme Colored Giants (Iron & Oil League)
BOOKER, DAN—1908-10—p, Kansas City (MO) Royal Giants, New York Colored Giants
BOOKER, JAMES (PETE)—1903-19—c, 1b, Philadelphia Giants, Leland Giants, Lincoln (NY) Giants, Chicago American Giants, Chicago Giants, Schenectady Mohawk Giants, Brooklyn Royal Giants, Indianapolis ABCs
BOOKER, RICH—1952—of, Kansas City Monarchs
BOOKMAN, ____—1914—p, Chicago American Giants
BOONE, ____—1906, 1910—of, Illinois Giants, St. Louis Giants
BOONE, ALONZO DARN (BUSTER)—1929-50—p, manager, Cleveland Cubs, Birmingham Black Barons, Chicago American Giants, Cincinnati-Cleveland Buckeyes, Cleveland Buckeyes, Louisville Buckeyes, Memphis Red Sox, Cleveland Bears

37

Negro Leagues Book #2: The Players

BOONE, CHARLES (LEFTY, BOB, BULLET)—1940-46—p, New Orleans-St. Louis Stars, Harrisburg-St. Louis Stars, Cincinnati Buckeyes, Jacksonville Red Caps, Cleveland Buckeyes, New York Black Yankees, Memphis Red Sox, Philadelphia Stars, Pittsburgh Crawfords (USL), Boston Blues

BOONE, OSCAR—[a.k.a. Oscar Brown] 1939-42—c, Indianapolis ABCs, Chicago American Giants, Birmingham Black Barons, Baltimore Elite Giants

BOONE, ROBERT (SPIDER)—1909-12—of, p, San Antonio Broncos, Oklahoma City Monarchs, Oklahoma City Giants, Kansas City (KS) Giants; —1923-40—umpire, NNL

BOONE, STEVE (LEFTY)—1940—p, Memphis Red Sox

BOOTS, KID [see EDWARDS, CY]

BORDEN, A.—1912-14, 2b, of, Pittsburgh Giants, Philadelphia Giants, Cuban Giants

BORDEN, J. [see BIRDINE, EDGAR LEO]

BORGES, A.—1928—infield, Cuban Stars (West)

BORDES, ED—1940—utility, Cleveland Bears

BORGES, JOSÉ—1904-05, 1908—2b, All Cubans, Cuban Stars

BORROTO, MARIO—1920-21—c, of, 2b, Cuban Stars (East)

BOROWSKI, CHARLES—1950—umpire, NNL

BORTER, ____—1916—1b, Chicago Giants

BOSLEY, LOUIS—1945—2b, 3b, Detroit Motor City Giants

BOSTIC, JOSEPH WILLIAM (JOE)—1942-50—writer, People's Voice of Harlem, New York Amsterdam News, announcer, Madison Square Garden (1972-88)

BOSTIC, LEROY—1960—infield, Raleigh (NC) Tigers

BOSTICK, FRED—1923-24—of, Compton Hill Cubs, Milwaukee Bears, St. Louis Giants

BOSTOCK, SR., LYMAN WESLEY—1938-49—1b, Birmingham Black Barons, Chicago American Giants, Brooklyn Royal Giants, New York Cubans

BOSTON, ROBERT LEE (BOB)—1946, 1948—3b, Boston Blues, Homestead Grays

BOSWELL, WILLIAM LEE (DUCKY)—1926, 1939—c, Toledo Crawfords, Memphis Red Sox

BOUGILLE [BOUGUILLE], (RED)—1932, 1934—of, p, New Orleans Black Pelicans, New Orleans Caulfield Ads, New Orleans Crescent Stars

BOULDIN, ____—1869—of, Washington Alerts

BOUNDS, EARL (TUBBY)—1933—p, Philadelphia Stars

BOURNE, ____—1887—ss, Boston Resolutes

BOURNE, LIONEL (JACKIE)—1947—umpire, East/West game

BOURNE, ST. CLAIR C.—writer, filmmaker, New York Age, New York Amsterdam News

BOUZA, TOM—1942—p, Brooklyn Royal Giants

BOWDEN, CICERO—1918—c, Bacharach (AC) Giants

BOWDEN, TOM—1946—of, San Francisco Sea Lions, Los Angeles White Sox

BOWE, RANDOLPH (BOB, LEFTY)—1939-41—p, Kansas City Monarchs, Chicago American Giants, Ethiopian Clowns

BOWEN, ____—1950—p, Indianapolis Clowns

BOWEN, (CHUCK, CHICO)—1937-43—of, p, Indianapolis Athletics, Chicago Brown Bombers (NML)

BOWER, ____—1921—p, Lincoln (NY) Giants

BOWERS, ____—1887—of, Philadelphia Pythians (NCBBL), Lancaster (PA) Giants

BOWERS (BAUER, BEAUER), ____—1925—umpire, NNL

BOWERS, NORMAN (CHUCK)—1926-27—p, ss, Baltimore Black Sox

BOWERS, WILLIAM JULIUS (JULIE)—1947-50—c, New York Black Yankees, New York Black Travelers

BOWIE, ____—1869—of, Washington Alerts

BOWLDEN ____—1948—1b, New York Cubans

BOWLEG, ____—1930—1b, Havana Red Sox

BOWLES, ____—1911—1b, Leland Giants

BOWMAN, ____—1867-69—3b, Brooklyn Unique

BOWMAN, ____—1927—p, Baltimore Black Sox, Chieftain A.C.

BOWMAN, ____—1934—c, Pittsburgh Giants

BOWMAN, EMMETT (SCOTTY)—1903-16, 1934-35—3b, p, c, ss, of, Philadelphia Giants, Leland Giants, Brooklyn Royal Giants

BOWMAN, GEORGE—1908, 1910, 1916—ss, 2b, Cleveland Giants, St. Paul Colored Gophers, Chicago American Giants

BOWMAN, ROBERT—1946, 1949—p, manager, Asheville Blues

BOWMAN, WILLIAM (BILL)—1903-08—p, of, Cuban X-Giants, Philadelphia Giants

BOWSER, THOMAS A.—1912-17—owner, manager, Indianapolis ABCs, Bowser's ABCs

BOYCE, ____—1923—1b, Havana Red Sox

BOYD, ____—1929—3b, Cleveland Tigers

BOYD, BENJAMIN F. (BEN)—1883-92—2b, of, Washington Manhattans, Argyle Hotel, Cuban Giants, York (PA) Cuban Giants (Eastern Interstate League), New York Gorhams & Trenton (NJ) Cuban Giants (Middle States League), Ansonia Cuban Giants (Connecticut St. League), York (PA) Colored

Monarchs (Eastern Interstate League), Washington Douglass Club

BOYD, BILL—1921—c, Bacharach (AC) Giants

BOYD, CHARLES W.—1883—business manager, Douglass Club of Washington DC

BOYD, ALFRED (FRED)—1920-22—of, Chicago American Giants, Cleveland Tate Stars

BOYD, GEORGE—1930—of, Colored House of David

BOYD, HENDERSON EDWARD (EDDIE)—1920—of, Detroit Stars, Chicago American Giants

BOYD, JAMES (JIMMY)—1946—p, Newark Eagles

BOYD, J.B. CAINE—1920—officer, Nashville Elite Giants

BOYD, LEE—1945-46—3b, ss, Detroit Motor City Giants, Cleveland Clippers

BOYD, LINCOLN E.—1949-52, 1959—of, manager, Louisville Buckeyes, Indianapolis Clowns

BOYD, OLLIE—1908—ss, Columbus Giants

BOYD, OLLIE (TURK)—1933-34, 1938—p, of, Kansas City Monarchs, Colored House of David

BOYD, ROBERT RICHARD (BOB, ROPE)—1946-50—1b, Memphis Red Sox; scout, Baltimore Orioles

BOYD, WILLIE JAMES—1943, 1946—p, Homestead Grays, Newark Eagles

BOYER, HENRY—1868, 1902—c, Philadelphia Pythians, Philadelphia Giants

BOYLE, ____—1888—p, Hoosier Black Stockings

BOYLE, JOE—1912—2b, All Nations

BOYLE, PAT—1922-25—umpire, NNL

BRACEY, S.—1883—87—of, St. Louis Black Stockings

BRACHE, REYNALDO—1957—?, Detroit Stars

BRACKEN, HERBERT (DOC, HERB) [a.k.a. Alphonso Bragana in 1945-47]—1939-40, 1945-47—p, St. Louis Giants, New York Cubans, New Orleans-St. Louis Stars, Cleveland Buckeyes, Brooklyn Brown Dodgers, Great Lakes Bluejackets

BRACY, ____—1867—ss, Philadelphia Excelsior

BRACY, ____—1883—of, St. Louis Black Stockings

BRADDOCK, ____—1911—2b, Leland Giants

BRADFORD, CHARLES WILLIAM (CHARLIE, MULE)—1910-28—p, of, coach, Lincoln (NY) Giants, Philadelphia Giants, Philadelphia Colored Giants of New York

BRADFORD, WILLIAM (BILL, CARBONDALE FLASH)—1936-50—of, New Orleans Creoles, Indianapolis ABCs, St. Louis Stars, Memphis Red Sox, Birmingham Black Barons, Chicago American Giants, Harlem Globetrotters, Atlanta Black Crackers

BRADLEY, ____—1889—p, Philadelphia Giants

BRADLEY, BOBBY—1931—of, Newark Browns

BRADLEY, FRANK E.—1937-41—p, Montgomery Grey Sox, Kansas City Monarchs

BRADLEY, OWEN—1922—umpire, NNL

BRADLEY, PHILIP (PHIL)—1905-27—c, 1b, Brooklyn Royal Giants, Lincoln (NY) Giants, Paterson (NJ) Smart Set, Pittsburgh Colored Stars, Pittsburgh Stars of Buffalo, Schenectady Mohawk Giants, Famous Cuban Giants, Philadelphia Giants, Pop Watkins Stars, Cuban Giants, Pittsburgh Giants

BRADLEY, PROVINE [PROVINCE] (RED)—1937-41—p, Kansas City Monarchs

BRADLEY, (RED)—1927, 1932—p, Baltimore Black Sox, Atlanta Black Crackers

BRADLEY, RICHARD (DICK, PEE WEE)—1937, 1939, 1946—p, manager, Cincinnati Tigers, Memphis Red Sox, Fresno/San Diego Tigers

BRADSHAW, ____—1926—of, Dayton Marcos

BRADY, FARMER (LEFTY)—1919, 1921, 1924—p, Cleveland Giants, Cleveland Tate Stars, Cleveland Browns

BRADY, JOHN—1887—of, Pittsburgh Keystones (NCBBL)

BRADY, S.—1883-87—of, St. Louis Black Stockings

BRAGAÑA, RAMÓN (EL PROFESOR)—1928-37—p, utility, Cuban Stars (East), Stars of Cuba, New York Cubans, Philadelphia Stars

BRAGG, EUGENE—1925—c, Chicago American Giants

BRAGG, JESSE M.—1907-19—3b, ss, 2b, Genuine Cuban Giants, Cuban Giants, Brooklyn Royal Giants, Schenectady Mohawk Giants, Lincoln (NY) Giants, Philadelphia Giants, Penn Red Caps of NY, Lincoln (NY) Stars, Brooklyn Cuban Giants, New York Colored Giants, Grand Central Terminal Red Caps

BRAM, ____—1927, 1930—ss, Baltimore Black Sox, Hilldale Club

BRAMMELL, ____—1932—c, Indianapolis ABCs

BRANCH, ____—1915—of, West Baden (IN) Sprudels

BRANCH, CHARLES—1956—of, Indianapolis Clowns

BRANCH, OTIS—1946—utility, Memphis Red Sox, Asheville Blues

BRANDALL ELMER—1914—of, All Nations

BRANDON, MACK—1950-51—of, Chicago American Giants

BRANHAM, ____—1926—p, Chattanooga Black Lookouts

BRANHAM, ESKER—1956—2b, Memphis Red Sox

BRANHAM [BRANAHAN], FINIS [FINEST] ERNEST (SLIM, LEGS, IRONMAN)—1920-27, 1931—p, Dayton Marcos, Cleveland Tate Stars, Harrisburg Giants, Detroit Stars,

Cleveland Elites, St. Louis Stars, Indianapolis ABCs, Cleveland Hornets, New York Black Yankees
BRANHAM, GEORGE FRANCIS—1917—p, Jewell's ABCs
BRANHAM, LUTHER HUMPHREY—1949-50—infield, Birmingham Black Barons, Chicago American Giants, San Francisco Sea Lions
BRANNON, NATHAN—1945-46—1b, Atlanta Black Crackers, Asheville Blues
BRANTLEY, OLLIE O.—1950-53—p, Memphis Red Sox
BRANSON, ROBERT—1946—p, Atlanta Black Crackers
BRASTU [BREATU], ALBERT—1890—3b, Chicago Unions
BRATHWAITE, ARCHIBALD (ARCHIE, LAFFY)—1944-48—of, Newark Eagles, Philadelphia Stars
BRATHWAITE, HIRAM ALONZO (JACKIE)—often confused with minor leaguer Archie Brathwaite. Hiram Alonzo did not play in the Negro Leagues.
BRAUSEN, ____—1924—umpire, NNL
BRAY, JAMES HOWARD—1920-31—c, Chicago Union Giants, Chicago Giants, Chicago American Giants, Chicago Columbia Giants
BRAXTON, ____—1880—ss, Washington Douglass Club
BRAXTON, W.—1883—of, Washington Manhattans
BRAZELTON, CLARKSON (JOHN)—1915-17—c, Chicago American Giants, Chicago Giants
BRAZZLE, JABE—1922—of, All Nations
BREAUX, ____—1926—2b, 3b, New Orleans Algiers, New Orleans Black Pelicans
BREDA, WILLIAM BERNARD (BILL, CHIPPY)—1950-51, 1953-54—of, Kansas City Monarchs, Birmingham Black Barons
BREEDLOVE, LEROY D.—1950—p, Kansas City Monarchs
BREEDLOVE, MACEO (SUITCASE)—1931-32, 1938—of, Colored House of David
BREEN, W.—1928, 1935—1b, of, Philadelphia Tigers, Pittsburgh Crawfords
BREGAN, ____—1928—3b, Cuban Stars (East)
BREMBLE, ____—1931—2b, Birmingham Black Barons
BREMER [BREMMER], SR., EUGENE JOSEPH (GENE)—1932-49—p, New Orleans Crescent Stars, Cincinnati Tigers, Memphis Red Sox, Kansas City Monarchs, Cincinnati-Cleveland Buckeyes, Cleveland Buckeyes, Louisville Buckeyes, Chicago American Giants, Washington (Yakima) Browns
BRENNAN, ____—1905—p, Philadelphia Giants
BRENNER, ____—1917—p, Chicago American Giants
BRESCIA, MATTY (MARTY)—1954-publicity & public relations, Memphis Red Sox

BRETT, ____—1912—p, Louisville Cubs
BREWER, CHESTER ARTHUR (CHET)—1924-49—p, Gilkerson's Union Giants, Kansas City Monarchs, Washington Pilots, New York Cubans, Philadelphia Stars, Chicago American Giants, Cleveland Buckeyes, Louisville Buckeyes, Philadelphia Royal Giants, Denver Post Negro All-Stars, Chet Brewer's Kansas City Royals; 1957-74—scout, Pittsburgh Pirates
BREWER, JR., CHESTER ARTHUR (CHET)—1947—p, Kansas City Royals
BREWER, GUY R.—1933-48—officer, New York Black Yankees
BREWER, LUTHER—1918-21—1b, of, Chicago Giants
BREWER, McKINLEY—1919—p, Indianapolis ABCs
BREWER, SHERWOOD (SHERRY, WOODY)—1946-61—of, 1b, 2b, ss, 3b, manager, Seattle Steelheads, Cincinnati Crescents, Indianapolis Clowns, Kansas City Monarchs, Detroit Clowns, Harlem Globetrotters, New York Cubans
BREWSTER, ____—1936-37—p, Detroit Stars, St. Louis Stars
BREWSTER, JACK—1956—p, Birmingham Black Barons
BREWSTER, SAMUEL—1950—of, Cleveland Buckeyes
BREWTON, OLEY—1936—p, Birmingham Black Barons
BRICE, ____—1932—of, Nashville Elite Giants
BRICE, GEORGE EDWARD (THREE FINGER)—1914—p, Cuban Giants
BRICE, JOHN E.—1950-51, 1956—of, Baltimore Elite Giants, Detroit Stars, Asheville Blues
BRICKLEY, ____—1909—p, St. Louis Giants
BRIDDLE, J.—1871—of, Chicago Blue Stockings
BRIDGEFORT, ROBERT (SOO)—1922—president, Chattanooga Tigers;—1932—officer, Cleveland Cubs
BRIDGEFORTH, WILLIAM SOUSA (SOO)—1950-54—owner, officer, Birmingham Black Barons, Baltimore Elite Giants
BRIDGEWATER, HENRY—1882-90—manager, St. Louis Black Stockings
BRIDGES, JOHN—1954—p, Memphis Red Sox
BRIDGES, MARSHALL—1951-54—p, of, Memphis Red Sox
BRIDGES, WILLIAM—1960—of, Raleigh (NC) Tigers
BRIGGAN [BIRGHAM], ____—1929—p, Wichita Falls Black Spudders
BRIGGERY, (BO)—1932—ss, 1b, Atlanta Black Crackers
BRIGGS, OTTO (MIRROR)—1914-41—of, manager, West Baden (IN) Sprudels, Indianapolis ABCs, Dayton Marcos, Hilldale Club, Philadelphia Quaker City Giants, Bacharach

(Philly) Giants, Santop's Broncos, Louisville Giants, Detroit Giants, Otto Brigg's All-Stars
BRIGHAM, ____–1924–p, Harrisburg Giants
BRIGHT, JOE–1932–of, Nashville Elite Giants
BRIGHT, JOHN M.–1887-1913–manager, p, Cuban Giants, Buffalo Cuban Giants, Famous Cuban Giants, Trenton (NJ) Cuban Giants (Middle States League), York (PA) Colored Monarchs (Eastern Interstate League), Genuine Cuban Giants
BRIGHT, JOHNNY–1907-08–p, The Cuban Giants, Cleveland Starlight Champs, Royal Poinciana (FL)
BRIMMER, ____–1934–of, c, Chicago American Giants, New Orleans Crescent Stars
BRINDLEY, ____–1914–c, All Nations
BRINSON, ____–1938–of, Chicago American Giants
BRISON, (BIRMINGHAM) SAM–1950-65–clown, actor, 2b, Indianapolis Clowns
BRISCOE, ____–1927–p, Washington Black Sox
BRISCOE, ____–1936–p, St. Louis Stars
BRISCOE, JESSE–1907-14–of, Indianapolis ABCs, Louisville White Sox, New York Black Sox, Chicago American Giants, Minneapolis Keystones, West Baden (IN) Sprudels
BRISKER, WILLIAM LEE–1950–general manager, Cleveland Buckeyes
BRISTER, ____–1867–of, Philadelphia Excelsior
BRISTER, ____–1921–p, Atlanta Black Crackers
BRITT, CHARLES (CHARLIE) [see BRITTON, GEORGE W. below]
BRITTON, AL–1941-42–p, Chicago American Giants
BRITTON [BRITT], GEORGE W. (CHIPPY, CHARLIE)–1917-44–p, c, 2b, ss, 3b, of, Indianapolis ABCs, Dayton Marcos, Columbus Buckeyes, Baltimore Black Sox, Hilldale Club, Homestead Grays, Newark Dodgers, Columbus Buckeyes, Washington Black Senators, Jacksonville Red Caps, Brooklyn Royal Giants, Chicago American Giants, Detroit Wolves, Cincinnati-Cleveland Buckeyes, Harrisburg Giants, Cleveland Buckeyes, Baltimore Elite Giants
BRITTON, JR., JOHN A. (JACK)–1940-50–3b, New Orleans-St. Louis Stars, Cincinnati Ethiopian Clowns (NML), Birmingham Black Barons, Indianapolis Clowns, Detroit Black Sox, Minneapolis-St. Paul Colored Gophers
BROADEST, ____–1897–p, Adrian (MI) Page Fence Giants
BROADLEY, ____–1919–of, Baltimore Black Sox
BROADNAX, MACEO (BABY BOY)–1931-32–p, of, Kansas City Monarchs
BROADNAX, WILLIE (BROADWAY)–1928-29–p, of, Memphis Red Sox

BROCK, CLYDE (BOMBER)–1942–of, Chicago Brown Bombers (NML)
BRODIE, MILLEDGE T.–1917–p, Bacharach (AC) Giants
BROILES, [see BROYLES]
BROKAW (BROWCOW), FREDERICK RICKER (FRED)–1905-06–2b, Brooklyn Royal Giants
BRONSON, ____–1936–pr, Philadelphia Stars
BROOKS, ____–1887–2b, Louisville Falls City (NCBBL)
BROOKS, ____–1926–p, Memphis Red Sox
BROOKS, ____–1929–p, Tulsa Black Oilers
BROOKS, ALPHONSO–1942–2b, Philadelphia Daisies (NML)
BROOKS, AMEAL (MACON, EMIL, ALEX, ALVIN, ARDMILLA)–1928-49–c, of, 2b, Chicago American Giants, Cleveland Cubs, Cole's Chicago American Giants, Pittsburgh Crawfords, Chicago Giants, Foster Memorial Giants, Columbus Blue Birds, Cincinnati Ethiopian Clowns (NML), New York Black Yankees, New York Cubans, Homestead Grays, Newark Eagles, Philadelphia Stars, Memphis Red Sox, Harlem Globetrotters, Brooklyn Royal Giants, North Classic Team, St. Louis Giants
BROOKS, BEATTIE–1918-21–2b, 3b, Lincoln (NY) Giants, Brooklyn Royal Giants, Philadelphia Giants, Breakers Hotel (FL)
BROOKS, BILL–1939–c, New York Black Yankees
BROOKS, CHARLES (CHARLIE) [see BROOKS, SIDNEY WILLIAM]
BROOKS, CHESTER A. [see BROOKS, IRVIN WOODBERRY]
BROOKS, E.–1936–p, Kansas City Monarchs
BROOKS, EARLE (SUNNY)–1915–ph, Cuban Giants
BROOKS, EDWARD (EDDIE)–1949-55–2b, Houston Eagles, Memphis Red Sox, New Orleans Eagles, Birmingham Black Barons
BROOKS, GUSTAVUS B. (GUS)–1893-95–of, Adrian (MI) Page Fence Giants, Chicago Unions
BROOKS, HENRY–1880–ss, Washington Keystones
BROOKS, IRVIN WOODBERRY–1918-31–p, c, of, Breakers Hotel (FL), Brooklyn Royal Giants, Bacharach (AC) Giants, Royal Poinciana (FL) Lincoln (NY) Giants
BROOKS, JAMES–1887–c, Baltimore Lord Baltimores (NCBBL)
BROOKS, JAMES–1923–utility, Lincoln (NY) Giants
BROOKS, JAMES–1938–p, Atlanta Black Crackers
BROOKS, JAMES (JIM, BUD)–1939–c, Philadelphia Stars

BROOKS, JESSE L.–1934-37–3b, Cleveland Red Sox, Kansas City Monarchs
BROOKS, JOE–1945-48–p, New Orleans Black Pelicans, Cincinnati Crescents, Harlem Globetrotters
BROOKS, JOHN O.–1942, 1944–p, Memphis Red Sox, Chicago American Giants
BROOKS, MARCELL (MARDY)–1933-34–2b, Schenectady Mohawk Giants
BROOKS, MOXIE–1945–p, Toledo Cubs/Rays
BROOKS, P.–1880–p, Washington Keystones
BROOKS, SIDNEY WILLIAM [CHARLES]–1919-23–of, 2b, 1b, 3b, p, St. Louis Giants, St. Louis Stars
BROOKS, W.M.–1920–secretary, Negro Southern League; manager, Knoxville Giants
BROOKS, WALLACE–1948–p, Baltimore Elite Giants
BROOME, ALEXANDER (a.k.a. AL BROWNE)–1940-44–p, Cleveland Bears, Jacksonville Red Caps
BROOME, JOHN B. (J.B.)–1947–of, New York Black Yankees
BROWN, ____–1871–c, Chicago Uniques
BROWN, ____–1871–p, Philadelphia Pythians
BROWN, ____–1880–p, Washington Douglass Club
BROWN, ____–1880–of, Washington Manhattans
BROWN, ____–1884–ss, Newark Dusky Boys
BROWN, ____–1900–p, Philadelphia Giants
BROWN, ____–1906, 1909–of, Philadelphia Quaker City Giants
BROWN, ____–1908–of, Indianapolis ABCs, Pop Watkins Stars
BROWN, ____–1910–1b, Cuban Giants
BROWN, ____–1913–p, Washington Giants
BROWN, ____–1913–of, Havana Red Sox
BROWN, ____–1915–of, All Nations
BROWN, ____–1916–p, Baltimore Black Sox
BROWN, ____–1916–p, Cuban X-Giants
BROWN, ____–1917–3b, Chicago Union Giants
BROWN, ____–1920–2b, New Orleans Crescent Stars
BROWN, ____–1922–2b, Cuban X-Giants
BROWN, ____–1922–1b, Buffalo Stars
BROWN, ____–1923–of, Richmond Giants
BROWN, ____–1922-30–umpire, NNL
BROWN, ____–1927–p, Shreveport Black Sports
BROWN, ____–1927–3b, Chappie Johnson's All-Star
BROWN, ____–1928–of, Kansas City (KS) Giants
BROWN, ____–1929–1b, Long Branch Cubans
BROWN, ____–1929–p, Hilldale Club
BROWN, ____–1929–of, Dallas Black Giants
BROWN, ____–1929–p, Wichita Falls Black Spudders
BROWN, ____–1932–of, Homestead Grays
BROWN, ____–1934–c, New York Black Yankees
BROWN, ____–1939–p, St. Louis Stars
BROWN, ____–1946–3b, Montgomery Dodgers
BROWN, ____–1951–of, Brooklyn Royal Giants
BROWN, A.–1920-23–c, Birmingham Black Barons, Nashville Elite Giants
BROWN, ABRAM–1867–officer, Actives of Philadelphia
BROWN, AL–1909–treasurer, Louisville Cubs
BROWN, ALFRED (BOMBER)–1947–p, Nashville Cubs, Birmingham Black Barons
BROWN, ANDREW–1891-92–of, 3b, Cuban Giants
BROWN, ARNOLD–1920-22–ss, 2b, Hilldale Club, Bacharach (AC) Giants, Harrisburg Giants, Washington Braves
BROWN, B.–1914-18–of, p, New York Stars, Brooklyn All-Stars, Washington Red Caps, Lincoln (NY) Stars, Baltimore Black Sox, Philadelphia Giants
BROWN, B.–1927–of, Memphis Red Sox
BROWN, B. L. (BILL)–1945–p, of, Memphis Red Sox
BROWN, (BALDY)–1921–3b, Norfolk Giants
BROWN, BARNEY (BRINQUITOS)–1929-49–p, of, Havana Red Sox, Cuban Stars (West), Philadelphia Stars, New York Black Yankees
BROWN, BEN–1899-1903–p, of, Genuine Cuban Giants
BROWN, BENNY–1931-32–ss, Newark Browns, Bacharach (Philly) Giants
BROWN, BOBBY–1959–of, Birmingham Black Barons
BROWN, BOOKER–1929–1b, Louisville Black Caps
BROWN, C.–1916–p, Montgomery Grey Sox
BROWN, C.–1929–p, Dallas Black Giants
BROWN, CHARLES–1886-87–p, Cuban Giants, Pittsburgh Keystones (NCBBL)
BROWN, CHARLEY–1920–3b, Birmingham Black Barons
BROWN, CLARENCE–1941–p, Kansas City Monarchs
BROWN, SR., CLEOPHUS LAMARR (BUDDY BUDDY, MOUSE)–1954-55–1b, p, Louisville Clippers, Detroit Stars
BROWN, CLIFFORD (QUACK)–1951-54–ss, p, Philadelphia Stars, Indianapolis Clowns, Detroit Stars
BROWN, CURTIS–1947, 1950–1b, New York Black Yankees
BROWN, D.–1925–p, St. Louis Stars
BROWN, D.–1955–infield, New York Black Yankees

BROWN, DAVID—1918-21—of, 1b, Dayton Marcos, Columbus Buckeyes, Detroit Stars, Cleveland Tate Stars [see BROWN, GEORGE DAVID]
BROWN, DAVID (DAVE, LEFTY)—1918-25—p, Chicago American Giants, Lincoln (NY) Giants
BROWN, DAVID G. (DAVE)—1925-27—p, St. Louis Stars, Kansas City Monarchs
BROWN, E.—1914-19—p, 1b, 3b, Brooklyn All-Stars, Cuban Giants, Chicago Union Giants
BROWN, EARL—1923-26—p, of, Lincoln (NY) Giants, Baltimore Black Sox, Harrisburg Giants
BROWN, ED (EDDIE)—1946—of, Portland (OR) Rosebuds
BROWN, EDWARD—1923—c, Milwaukee Bears, Chicago American Giants, Memphis Red Sox
BROWN, EDWARD (ED)—1920-24—p, Detroit Stars, Indianapolis ABCs, Chicago Giants, Chicago American Giants
BROWN, ELIAS [see BRYANT, ELIAS]
BROWN, ELMER CLAY—1921—3b, Indianapolis ABCs
BROWN, ELMORE—1947, 1954—p, Birmingham Black Barons, Louisville Clippers
BROWN, F.—1918—2b, Chicago Union Giants
BROWN, FRED—1909-10—of, San Antonio Black Broncos, Oklahoma Monarchs
BROWN, FRED—1932—umpire, EWL
BROWN, G.—1888—infield, Providence Grays
BROWN, G. GEORGE—1869-71, 1874, 1879—c, manager, Chicago Blue Stockings, Chicago Uniques
BROWN, GEORGE—1867-68, 1871—p, Philadelphia Pythians, Actives of Philadelphia
BROWN, GEORGE W. [DAVID]—1910-21—of, 3b, manager, West Baden (IN) Sprudels, Jewell's ABCs, Indianapolis ABCs, St. Louis Giants, Dayton Marcos, Columbus Buckeyes, Cleveland Tate Stars, Detroit Stars
BROWN, GEORGE—1939-46—of, Cincinnati-Cleveland Buckeyes, Baltimore Elite Giants, Philadelphia Stars, Chicago American Giants, Baltimore Grays
BROWN, GEORGE—1927—p, Kansas City Monarchs
BROWN, GEORGE—1930—c, Colored House of David
BROWN, H.—1906, 1910, 1913-15—1b, of, Illinois Giants, Schenectady Mohawk Giants, Brooklyn Royal Giants
BROWN, H. (HOOKS)—1939—ss, Memphis Red Sox (see BROWN, T.J.)
BROWN, HARRY—1910-20—3b, p, St. Paul Colored Gophers, Chicago Giants, Cuban Giants, New York Stars, Chicago Union Giants, Brooklyn All-Stars, Twin City Gophers
BROWN, HENRY LEE—1956, 1959—p, Kansas City Monarchs
BROWN, HUGH M.—1867-71—1b, 2b, ss, Mutuals of Washington
BROWN, ISSAC (IKE)—1960-61—ss, Kansas City Monarchs
BROWN, J.—1917-20—c, Jewell ABCs, Knoxville Giants, Indianapolis ABCs
BROWN, J.—1920—ss, Baltimore Black Sox
BROWN, J.—1939, 1946-c, of, Homestead Grays, Fresno/San Diego Tigers
BROWN, J.—1946—of, Fresno/San Diego Tigers
BROWN, JACK—1946—c, San Francisco Sea Lions
BROWN, JAMES (BILL)—1945—of, Detroit Motor City Giants
BROWN, JAMES (BLACK RIDER)—1938, 1947—p, Atlanta Black Crackers, Cincinnati-Indianapolis Clowns
BROWN, JAMES R. (JIM)—1918-42—c, 1b, 2b, ss, 3b, of, manager, Chicago American Giants, Louisville Black Caps, Foster Memorial Giants, Chicago Giants, Minneapolis-St. Paul Colored Gophers, Chicago Columbia Giants, Cleveland Cubs, Montgomery Grey Sox, Louisville Black Caps
BROWN, JAMES PHILIP—1938-39, 1941-43—p, of, Newark Eagles
BROWN, JEROME—1949—infield, Houston Eagles
BROWN, JESSE (BLACK RIDER)—1890—2b, ss, Lincoln (NE) Giants
BROWN, JESSE J. (PROFESSOR, LEFTY)—1938-44—p, New York Black Yankees, Baltimore Elite Giants, Boston Royal Giants
BROWN, JIM [see BROWN, WILLARD]
BROWN, JIM (LEFTY, AL)—1946—p, San Francisco Sea Lions
BROWN, JOHN—1887—officer, Philadelphia Pythians (NCBBL)
BROWN, JOHN—1936—officer, St. Louis Stars
BROWN, JOHN W.—1942-49—p, Cleveland Buckeyes, Houston Eagles, Louisville Buckeyes
BROWN, JOHNNY (BUBBLES)—1938—p, Atlanta Black Crackers
BROWN, JOSEPH—1887—manager, Washington Capital Citys
BROWN, JOSEPH A.—1947—officer, Detroit Senators
BROWN, JULIUS—1946—p, Indianapolis Clowns
BROWN, K.—1867-71—c, Mutuals of Washington
BROWN, L.—1914—2b, Indianapolis ABCs
BROWN, L.—1939—p, Homestead Grays

BROWN, L.A.—1926-27—officer, St. Louis Stars
BROWN, LARRY (IRON MAN)—1919-49—c, manager, Birmingham Black Barons, Pittsburgh Keystones, Indianapolis ABCs, Memphis Red Sox, Detroit Stars, Chicago American Giants, Lincoln (NY) Giants, New York Black Yankees, Cole's Chicago American Giants, Philadelphia Stars, Knoxville Giants, New York Harlem Stars, Pittsburgh Stars
BROWN, LAWRENCE JAMES (LEFTY)—1931-46—p, Claybrook (AR) Tigers, Memphis Red Sox, Richmond Hilldales (NML), Philadelphia Stars, Newark Eagles, San Francisco Sea Lions
BROWN, (LEFTY)—1942—p, Twin Cities Gophers
BROWN, M. [see BROWN, W. (MIKE)]
BROWN, M.—1946—p, San Francisco Sea Lions
BROWN, MALCOLM ELMORE ARNOLD (SCRAPPY, BILL DICK)—1918-37—ss, p, Washington Red Caps, Lincoln (NY) Giants, Baltimore Black Sox, Brooklyn Royal Giants, Hilldale Club, Homestead Grays, Schenectady Mohawk Giants, Providence Giants, Harrisburg Giants, Philadelphia Tigers, Bacharach (AC) Giants, Royal Poinciana (FL)
BROWN, MAYWOOD P.—1917-25, 1931—p, Montgomery Grey Sox, Lincoln (NY) Giants, Indianapolis ABCs, Chicago American Giants
BROWN, MIKE—1912-16—of, Brooklyn Royal Giants, Philadelphia Giants, Lincoln (NY) Giants
BROWN, JR., MORRIS—1868—player, Philadelphia Pythians
BROWN, O.C. (PIGGY)—1927, 1929—2b, Shreveport Black Sports, Bacharach (AC) Giants
BROWN, OLIVER (OLLIE, BUTT)—1931-32—business manager, Newark Browns; writer, *New Jersey Herald News*
BROWN, OSCAR [see BOONE, OSCAR]
BROWN, OSSIE—1935-39—p, Cole's Chicago American Giants, Indianapolis Athletics, Indianapolis ABCs, St. Louis Stars
BROWN, PERRY—1910—owner, New York Black Sox
BROWN, PINEY—1925-27—owner, Kansas City Royal American Giants
BROWN, R.—1920—p, Bacharach (AC) Giants
BROWN, RALPH—1954—ss, 2b, Birmingham Black Barons
BROWN, RAY—1939-40—c, Brooklyn Royal Giants, Chicago American Giants (see ULYSSES BUSTER BROWN)
BROWN, RAYMOND L. (RAY)—1930-48, 1950—p, of, Dayton Marcos, Indianapolis ABCs, Detroit Wolves, Homestead Grays
BROWN, RICH—1952—infield, Chicago American Giants
BROWN, ROBERT—1945—c, Chicago Brown Bombers (USL)
BROWN, ROBERT B.—1887—of, Boston Resolutes (NCBBL)
BROWN, SR., ROGER (STUD)—1959-60—3b, of, Kansas City Monarchs, Detroit-New Orleans Stars
BROWN, RONNIE—1943—1b, Harrisburg-St. Louis Stars
BROWN, ROOSEVELT—1931—p, Indianapolis ABCs
BROWN, ROY—1931-32—p, of, Kansas City Monarchs, Cleveland Cubs
BROWN, S.—1884—2b, Chicago Gordons
BROWN, S.—1916—of, Montgomery Grey Sox
BROWN, S.—1929—p, Dallas Black Giants
BROWN, SAM—1932—c, Louisville Black Caps
BROWN, SAM—writer, *Memphis World*
BROWN, SAMUEL R.—1942—president, New Orleans Eagles
BROWN, SCRAPPY [see BROWN, MALCOLM ELMORE ARNOLD]
BROWN, T.C.—1927, 1929—p, Shreveport Black Sports, Dallas Black Giants
BROWN, TED (JED)—1942-43, 1949—ss, Richmond Hilldales, Baltimore Elite Giants, Chicago American Giants
BROWN, THEO—1911-12—3b, Chicago Union Giants
BROWN, THOMAS—1869-79—1b, 3b, Chicago Uniques, Chicago Blue Stockings
BROWN, JR., THOMAS JEFFERSON (T. J., TOM), a.k.a. Hooks Brown—1939-50—ss, manager, Memphis Red Caps, New York Black Yankees, Memphis Red Sox, Cleveland Buckeyes, Indianapolis Clowns, Harrisburg-St. Louis Stars, Louisville Buckeyes, Chicago American Giants
BROWN, TOM—1917-20—p, of, Brooklyn Royal Giants, Chicago American Giants, Lincoln (NY) Giants
BROWN, (TUTE)—1918—3b, Washington Red Caps
BROWN, ULYSSES D. (BUSTER, JOE)—1937-42, 1944—c, Newark Eagles, Jacksonville Red Caps, Cincinnati-Cleveland Buckeyes, Chicago American Giants, Brooklyn Royal Giants, Homestead Grays
BROWN, W.—1920—2b, Chicago Union Giants
BROWN, W.—1932—ph, Chicago American Giants
BROWN, W.—1945—1b, Brooklyn Brown Dodgers
BROWN, W. (MIKE)—1904-18—p, 1b, of, Brooklyn Royal Giants, Buffalo Cuban Giants, Schenectady Mohawk Giants, Cuban Giants, Lincoln (NY) Stars, Lincoln (NY) Giants, Bacharach (AC) Giants, Philadelphia Giants
BROWN, W.A.—1911—manager, Brown's Tennessee Rats

BROWN, W.G.—1862, 1867—c, officer, Brooklyn Monitors
BROWN, W.M.—1920—secretary, Nashville Elite Giants, Knoxville Giants
BROWN, WALTER S.—1887— president, National League of Colored Base Ball Clubs; manager, Pittsburgh Keystones (NCBBL); writer, *Cleveland Gazette*
BROWN, WILLARD JESSIE (HOME RUN, ESE HOMBRE, SONNY)—1934-52, 1958—of, ss, Monroe (LA) Monarchs, Kansas City Monarchs
BROWN, WILLIAM—1900, 1902, 1905-06, 1910—ss, Philadelphia Giants, Chicago Columbia Giants, Chicago Unions, Brooklyn Royal Giants, Illinois Giants, Chicago Union Giants
BROWN, WILLIAM—1904-06—secretary, Chicago Union Giants; assistant manager, Leland Giants
BROWN, WILLIAM H.—1884, 1887—ss, 1b, p, of, Chicago Gordons, Pittsburgh Keystones (NCBBL), Chicago Unknowns
BROWN, WILLIAM HARRIS (CAP, WILLIE)—1951-55—ss, Birmingham Black Barons, Indianapolis Clowns
BROWN, WILLIAM M. (WIL, W.M.)—1931-36—officer, owner, Montgomery Grey Sox
BROWNE, H. (HAP)—1924—p, Cleveland Browns
BROWNIE, AL [see BROOME, ALEXANDER]
BROWNING, JAMES ROYAL [SKINK]—1930—c, Brooklyn Royal Giants
BROYLES, [BROILES] —1925-27—p, St. Louis Stars
BROYLES, B. —1912—p, Indianapolis ABCs
BRUCE, CLARENCE—1946-50—2b, Homestead Grays, Brooklyn Brown Dodgers
BRUCE, JACK—1946—of, Cleveland Clippers
BRUCE, LLOYD—1940—p, Chicago American Giants
BRUTON, CHARLES JOHN (JACK, DIZZY)—1928-41—p, of, 1b, 2b, 3b, Cleveland Bears, New Orleans-St. Louis Stars, Birmingham Black Barons, New York Black Yankees
BRUTON, CHUCK (NIP)—1950—p, Cleveland Buckeyes
BRUTON [BURTON], WALTER (WALT)—1938-39—p, Philadelphia Stars
BRUTON, WILLIAM HARON (BILLY) [a.k.a. JAMES or BILL JOHNSON]—1948-49—of, Louisville Buckeyes, Philadelphia Stars
BRYAN, ____—1929—p, Santop Broncos
BRYANT, ____—1889—c, New Orleans Pinchbacks
BRYANT, ____—1929—ss, Fort Worth Panthers
BRYANT, JR., ALLEN (LEFTY)—1937-47, 1953—p, All Nations, Kansas City Monarchs, Memphis Red Sox, Kansas City (KS) Giants
BRYANT, CLAUDE—1934—of, Brooklyn Royal Giants
BRYANT, EDDIE—1925-29—2b, Penn Red Caps of NY, Harrisburg Giants, Chattanooga White Sox
BRYANT, ELIAS (COUNTRY BROWN)—1918-34—3b, 2b, of, Bacharach (AC) Giants, Bacharach (NY) Giants, Brooklyn Royal Giants, Washington Potomacs, Wilmington Potomacs, Lincoln (NY) Giants, Breakers Hotel (FL)
BRYANT, JOHNNIE—1950—of, p, Cleveland Buckeyes
BRYANT, R. B.—1937—ss, Memphis Red Sox
BRYON, EDWARD—1946—1b, 2b, Asheville Blues
BRYSON, CLAUDE—1910—3b, Kansas City Cyclones
BUBBLES, JOHNNY [see BROWN, JOHNNY]
BUCHANAN, CHESTER FLOYD (BUCK)—1931-44—p, Philadelphia Stars, Bacharach (Philly) Giants, Brooklyn Royal Giants, Philadelphia Daisies
BUCHANAN, FLOYD (BUCK)—1914-16—p, Hilldale Club
BUCHANAN, OSCAR—1926—officer, Birmingham Black Barons
BUCK, ____—1923—p, Birmingham Black Barons
BUCKLEY, ____—1888—3b, Hoosier Black Stockings
BUCKLEY, CODY—1909-10—1b, Kansas City (MO) Royal Giants
BUCKNER, ____—1914—ss, Chicago Giants
BUCKNER, HARRY EDWARD (HOSS, GREEN RIVER, GOAT HEAD, DOC, IRON MAN)—1896-1918—p, of, Chicago Unions, Chicago Union Giants, Columbia Giants, Philadelphia Giants, Cuban X-Giants, Brooklyn Royal Giants, Philadelphia Quaker City Giants, Lincoln (NY) Giants, Paterson (NJ) Smart Set, Chicago Giants, Schenectady Mohawk Giants, Louisville White Sox;—1920-38—trainer, Milwaukee Brewers (AA)
BUCKNER, JOSEPH JAMES (JOE)—1946—p, Chicago American Giants, Boston Blues
BUCKNER, WILLIAM A. (DOC)—1918-33—trainer, conditioner, Chicago White Sox (MLB)
BUDBILL, ____—1950—p, Houston Eagles
BUDDLES, ____—1925—infield, Chicago American Giants
BUFORD, JAMES (BLACK BOTTOM)—1925-34—3b, 2b, Nashville Elite Giants, Cleveland Cubs, Detroit Stars, Louisville Red Caps, Birmingham Black Barons, Memphis Red Sox
BUFORD, ORA—1913-14—p, Chicago Giants, Indianapolis ABCs
BULGER, ____—1914—c, Chicago Giants
BULLOCK, ____—1890—p, of, Lincoln (NE) Giants
BULLOCK, ROYSTER H.—1921—p, Pittsburgh Keystones, Cleveland Tate Stars

Negro Leagues Book #2: The Players

BUMPLE, ____—1931—2b, Birmingham Black Barons
BUMPUS, EARL—1944-48—p, of, 1b, Kansas City Monarchs, Birmingham Black Barons, Chicago American Giants
BUNCE, ____—1867—of, Brooklyn Unique
BUNCH, JR., SIDNEY THOMAS—1949-50, 1954-55—of, Baltimore Elite Giants, Birmingham Black Barons
BUNEL, ____—1919-20—c, Baltimore Black Sox
BUNES, ____—1891—of, p, New York Colored Giants
BUNN, WILLIE BILL—1943—p, Atlanta Black Crackers
BURAN, ____—1932—of, Washington Pilots
BURBAGE, KNOWLINGTON OTTOWAY (BUDDY)—1927-51—of, Schenectady Mohawk Giants, Hilldale Club, Pittsburgh Crawfords, Baltimore Black Sox, Bacharach (AC) Giants, Newark Dodgers, Homestead Grays, Washington Black Senators, Brooklyn Royal Giants, Philadelphia Stars, New York Black Yankees, Detroit Giants, Washington Pilots, Otto Brigg's All-Stars, Philadelphia Daisies (NML), Bacharach (Philly) Giants, Baltimore Elite Giants
BURCH, ALONZO—1915—p, Chicago Union Giants
BURCH, EDGAR DANIEL—1914-17—p, Indianapolis ABCs, Chicago Union Giants, Louisville White Sox, All Nations
BURCH, JOHN WALTER—1927, 1931-47—c, 2b, ss, 3b, manager, Schenectady Mohawk Giants, Bacharach (Philly) Giants, Baltimore Black Sox, Cleveland Bears, St. Louis Stars, New Orleans-St. Louis Stars, Cincinnati-Cleveland Buckeyes, Cleveland Buckeyes, Chicago American Giants, Newark Dodgers, Washington Pilots, Homestead Grays, Brooklyn Brown Dodgers, Detroit Senators
BURDINE, LEO (see LEO BERDINE)
BURGEE, LOUIS—1910, 1915-17—p, 2b, Hilldale Club
BURGEN, ____—1947—1b, Newark Eagles
BURGESS, ____—1922—3b, Cuban X-Giants
BURGESS, P.—1942—p, Chicago American Giants
BURGETT, P.—1920—of, St. Louis Giants
BURGIN [BERGIN, BERGEN], RALPH D.—1913-43—3b, of, Hilldale Club, New York Harlem Stars, New York Black Yankees, Philadelphia Stars, Brooklyn Royal Giants, Baltimore Black Sox, Pittsburgh Crawfords, Bacharach (Philly) Giants, Havana Red Sox
BURGIN, JOHN (JOHNNY)—1928—utility, Hilldale Club
BURGOS, JOSÉ [see BORGES, JOSÉ]
BURGOS, JOSÉ ANTONIO—1949-50—2b, Birmingham Black Barons
BURKE (BURCH, BURT), ____—1925-26—umpire, NSL
BURKE, ROY—1938—p, Atlanta Black Crackers
BURKE, BILLY—1942-44—3b, Boston Royal Giants
BURKE, CHARLES (BUSTER)—1936-37, 1945—ss, of, Chicago Giants, Indianapolis Athletics, Toledo Cubs/Rays
BURKE, ERNEST—1914—of, Indianapolis ABCs
BURKE, ERNEST ALEXANDER (LITTLE ABNER)—1946-48—p, Baltimore Elite Giants
BURKE, WALTER (PING)—1937—p, Atlanta Black Crackers
BURKOCH, ____—1917—1b, All Nations
BURLEY, ____—1867—3b, Mutuals of Washington
BURLEY, DANIEL GARDNER (DAN)—1928-57—writer, *New York Amsterdam News, Chicago Defender, Chicago Sunday Bee, New York Age, Ebony, Jet, The Owl, The Original Handbook of Harlem Jive;* sportscaster, WWRL Radio - New York
BURNETT, FRED (TEX)—1921-46—c, 1b, of, coach, manager, Pittsburgh Keystones, Indianapolis ABCs, Lincoln (NY) Giants, Harrisburg Giants, Brooklyn Royal Giants, New York Harlem Stars, New York Black Yankees, Baltimore Black Sox, Homestead Grays, Brooklyn Eagles, Newark Eagles, Bacharach (AC) Giants, Nashville Cubs, Newark Dodgers, Havana Red Sox, Pittsburgh Crawfords (USL), Schenectady Mohawk Giants
BURNETT, HINEY—1938—c, Indianapolis ABCs
BURNETT, MARSHAL B.—1928—officer, Memphis Red Sox
BURNHAM, WILLIE (BEE)—1929-34—p, Monroe (LA) Monarchs, Shreveport Black Sports
BURNS, GEORGE—1931—infield, Montgomery Grey Sox
BURNS, CLOYCE—1946—p, Boston Blues
BURNS, F.—1942—p, of, Twin Cities Gophers
BURNS, J.—1942—1b, of, Twin Cities Gophers
BURNS, PETER (PETE)—1890-1902—c, Adrian (MI) Page Fence Giants, Columbia Giants Chicago Unions, Adrian Reformers (Michigan St. League), Algona (IA) Brownies, Philadelphia Giants
BURNS, WILLIAM TATUM (WILLIE, LEFTY)—1935-46—p, Memphis Red Sox, Cincinnati-Indianapolis Clowns, Newark Dodgers, Philadelphia Stars, Baltimore Elite Giants, Chicago American Giants, New York Black Yankees, Newark Eagles, Philadelphia Daisies (NML)
BURR, RAYMOND J.— 1867-68—of, officer, Philadelphia Pythians
BURRELL, ____—1917-20—of, Baltimore Black Sox
BURRELL, EDWARD—1868—player, Philadelphia Pythians
BURRELL, GEORGE—1884-85—p, c, Baltimore Atlantics

BURRIS, JR., SAMUEL JAMES (SPEED)—1937-41—p, Memphis Red Sox, Birmingham Black Barons, New Orleans-St. Louis Stars
BURROUGHS, ____—1942—of, Chicago American Giants
BURROWS, ____—1926—p, Chattanooga White Sox
BURROWS, ____—1940—p, Indianapolis Crawfords
BURTON, ____—1867, 1887—of, Monrovia Club of Harrisburg, Pittsburgh Keystones (NCBBL)
BURTON, H.—1886-87—c, Pittsburgh Keystones (NCBBL)
BURTON, HARRY (LEFTY)—1927, 1929-30—p, Royal Poinciana (FL), Pittsburgh Crawfords
BURTON, W. (SHORTY, BILLY) 1917-18, 1926—c, of, Bacharach (AC) Giants, Newark Stars
BURTON, WALTER [see BRUTON, WALTER]
BURTON, WILLIAM—1923-24, 1931—umpire, ECL
BUSBY, ____—1899—c, Chicago Unions
BUSBY, JIMMY—1933—of, 3b, Detroit Stars
BUSBY, MAURICE (LEFTY)—1920-22—p, Bacharach (AC) Giants, All Cubans, Baltimore Black Sox
BUSCH [BUSH], RONALD (DO)—1959-60—infield, Raleigh (NC) Tigers
BUSH, ELIJAH (SCUTTER)—1946—p, Cleveland Buckeyes
BUSTAMENTE, LUIS (ANGUILLA, "the EEL")—1904-13—ss, New York Cuban Stars, All Cubans, Brooklyn Royal Giants, Havana Stars
BUSTER, HERBERT—1943—ss, Chicago American Giants
BUTCHER, SPENCER (BUTCH)—1929—of, Pullen's Royal Giants
BUTLER, ____—1907—of, Keystone (PA) Giants
BUTLER, ____—1917—of, Lincoln (NY) Giants
BUTLER, BENJAMIN M.—1886-89—manager, New York Gorhams
BUTLER, BOOKER (DOC)—1950—c, Memphis Red Sox
BUTLER, CHARLES H.—1887—1b, Pittsburgh Keystones (NCBBL)
BUTLER, E. J.—1923—officer, Washington Potomacs
BUTLER, ED—1937-38, 1943, 1945—3b, ss, Pittsburgh Crawfords, Newark Eagles, Homestead Grays, Brooklyn Brown Dodgers
BUTLER, FRANK—1894-95, 1897—of, p, Chicago Unions
BUTLER, H.—1923—of, All Nations
BUTLER, J.—1884—p, Philadelphia Mutual B.B.C.
BUTLER, LEE—1923—2b, of, All Nations
BUTLER, RANDOLPH (RAN, THE SENATOR)—1902-12—officer, owner, manager, Indianapolis ABCs
BUTLER, SAM—1911—1b, Brown's Tennessee Rats

BUTLER, SOLOMON W. (K.C., SOL)—1925—p, Kansas City Monarchs; —1927—sports editor, *Chicago Bee*, *Chicago Defender*
BUTTERFIELD, (SKINNER)—1948—c, Newark Eagles
BUTTS, HARRY T.—1949-51—p, Indianapolis Clowns
BUTTS, THOMAS [ROBERT] LEE (TOMMY, PEE WEE, PEA EYE, COOL BREEZE)—1938-54—ss, Atlanta Black Crackers, Indianapolis ABCs, Baltimore Elite Giants, Memphis Red Sox, Birmingham Black Barons, Philadelphia Stars, Homestead Grays, Jacksonville Red Caps
BYAS [BAYAS], RICHARD THOMAS (SUBBY)—1931-42—c, 1b, Kansas City Monarchs, Foster Memorial Giants, Chicago American Giants, Newark Dodgers, Memphis Red Sox, Chicago Giants
BYATT [see BIOT, JR., CHARLES]
BYERS, HENRY—1887—2b, Pittsburgh Keystones (NCBBL)
BYERS, J. W. (BILL)—1918-21—umpire, NNL
BYRD, JAMES F.—1927-30—officer, Hilldale Club
BYRD, OLLIE—1920-21, 1925, 1927—1b, Chicago Union Giants, Chicago Giants, Gilkerson's Union Giants
BYRD, PRENTICE (PRIME) C.—1933-34—officer, owner, Akron Grays, Cleveland Giants, Cleveland Red Sox
BYRD, WILLIAM (BILL)—1932-50—p, of, Columbus Turfs, Columbus Blue Birds, Columbus Elite Giants, Washington Elite Giants, Baltimore Elite Giants, Nashville Elite Giants, Cleveland Red Sox, Philadelphia Stars, South All-Stars

C

CABALLERO, LUIS PÉREZ [a.k.a. LUIS PÉREZ]—1948-50—3b, Indianapolis Clowns, New York Cubans
CABAÑAS, ARMANDO (CHINO)—1910, 1912—2b, Stars of Cuba, All Nations
CABELL, FRANK—1887—utility, St. Louis Black Stockings
CABINAS, ____—1913—of, All Nations
CABLE, ____—1930—of, Louisville White caps
CABNESS, WILLIAM—1934—p, Birmingham Black Barons
CABRERA, A.—1921—umpire, NNL
CABRERA, ALFREDO A. (PÁJARO)—1905—1b, ss, All Cubans
CABRERA, ARMANDO—1915—of, Almendares Cubans
CABRERA, E.—1948—of, Indianapolis Clowns
CABRERA, LORENZO (CHIQUITÍN)—1947-50—1b, New York Cubans
CABRERA, LUIS RAÚL—1948—p, Indianapolis Clowns
CABRERA y GÓMEZ, RAFAEL VILLA (RAFE)—1944, 1948—p, of, Indianapolis Clowns
CABRIALES, ROBUSTINO—1947—3b, Havana Las Palomas
CADE, JOSEPH NATHAN (JOE)—1927-29—p, Bacharach (AC) Giants, Philadelphia Royal Giants, Cleveland Royal Giants, Pullen's Royal Giants
CADREAU, WILLIAM (BILL, CHIEF CHOUNEAU)—1911, 1917—p, Chicago Union Giants; 1910—p, Chicago White Sox (AL)
CAFFEY, CHARLES C.—1923—owner, Houston Black Buffaloes
CAFFIE, JOSEPH CLIFFORD (JOE, RABBIT)—1950—of, Cleveland Buckeyes
CAIN, MARLON (SUGAR)—1932, 1937-61—p, manager, Nashville Elite Giants, Pittsburgh Crawfords, Brooklyn Royal Giants, Indianapolis Clowns, New York Black Yankees, Kansas City Monarchs, Birmingham Black Barons, Bacharach (Philly) Giants, Detroit Stars, Oakland Larks
CALARAI, ____—1933—p, Cuban Stars
CALDERÍN, EVELIO—1917-24—p, Havana Stars, Cuban Stars (West)
CALDERÓN, BENITO L. (TOTI)—1926-28—c, Cuban Stars (West), Cuban Havana Stars, Homestead Grays
CALDWELL, ____—1933—of, Birmingham Black Barons
CALDWELL, EUGENE—1886-87—3b, Chicago Gordons
CALDWELL, FRANK—1947—p, Cleveland Buckeyes
CALHOUN, JIM—1921-23—2b, Toledo Tigers, Illinois Giants
CALHOUN, PAUL—1942—p, Philadelphia Stars, New York Black Yankees
CALHOUN [CALHAN], ROLAND C.—1938—p, Washington Black Senators
CALHOUN, WALTER ALLEN (LEFTY, BEARCAT)—1931-46—p, Birmingham Black Barons, Montgomery Grey Sox, Washington Black Senators, Pittsburgh Crawfords, Indianapolis ABCs, St. Louis Stars, New Orleans-St. Louis Stars, New York Black Yankees, Harrisburg-St. Louis Stars, Cleveland Buckeyes, Philadelphia Stars, Memphis Red Sox, Indianapolis Athletics, Louisville Black Colonels, Boston Blues
CALHOUN, WESLEY—1950—infield, of, Cleveland Buckeyes
CALL, F.—1884-85—3b, Baltimore Atlantics
CALLAWAY [CALLOWAY], THOMAS (TOM)—1921, 1925—of, 1929—manager, Houston Black Buffaloes, Oklahoma City Indians
CALLIS, JESSE JOSEPH—1887— officer, National League of Colored Base Ball Clubs; manager, Baltimore Lord Baltimores
CALLOWAY, ANDREW—1932—umpire, EWL
CALLOWAY, JIMMY—1945—ss, Detroit Motor City Giants
CALLOWAY, WILLIAM—[see GALLOWAY, WILLIAM HOWARD]
CALVO y GONZÁLEZ, JACINTO (JACK) DEL—1913-16, 1923—of, Long Branch (NJ) Cubans, All Cubans
CALVERT, CHARLIE (SMOKY)—1931—p, Brooklyn Royal Giants
CALVO y GONZÁLEZ, TOMÁS DEL (TOMMY)—1913-16—of, c, Long Branch (NJ) Cubans, Jersey City Cubans
CAM, ____—1891—of, Ansonia Cuban Giants (Connecticut St. League)
CAMBRIA, JOE—1933—owner, officer, Baltimore Black Sox
CAMPANELLA, ROY (CAMPY)—1937-45—c, of, Baltimore Elite Giants, Washington Elite Giants, Bacharach (Philly) Giants, Philadelphia Stars; 1946—scout, Brooklyn Dodgers
CAMPBELL, ____—1921—of, Jewell ABCs
CAMPBELL, ____—1927—c, Baltimore Black Sox, Ebenezer Royals
CAMPBELL, ____—1923—of, All Nations
CAMPBELL, ____—1930—1b, Birmingham Black Barons
CAMPBELL, ____—1942—c, Philadelphia Daisies (NML)
CAMPBELL, A.—1890—of, Chicago Union Giants

CAMPBELL, ANDREW (ANDY)—1901-11—c, ss, Chicago Union Giants, Leland Giants, Twin City Gophers, Minneapolis Keystones, St. Paul Colored Gophers, Cuban Giants

CAMPBELL, CHARLEY—1946—of, Detroit Stars

CAMPBELL, DAVID (DAVE, GYPSY)—1935-42—2b, Schenectady Mohawk Giants, New York Black Yankees, Philadelphia Stars

CAMPBELL, EDDIE—1926—of, Colored All-Stars

CAMPBELL, EMMET GRANVILLE—1922—3b, of, Pittsburgh Keystones

CAMPBELL, GRANT—1884, 1887-93—infield, of, Chicago Unions, Chicago Gordons

CAMPBELL, HUNTER—1937-42—manager, officer, Ethiopian Clowns, Cincinnati Ethiopian Clowns (NML)

CAMPBELL, JEFF CHRISTOPHER (BO)—1937—p, Homestead Grays

CAMPBELL, JOE—1884-93—p, of, Chicago Gordons, Chicago Unions

CAMPBELL, JOE—1930—of, Nashville Elite Giants

CAMPBELL, ROBERT (BUDDY)—1929-32—c, Cole's Chicago American Giants, Bacharach (Philly) Giants, Pittsburgh Crawfords, Memphis Red Sox

CAMPBELL, WILLIAM HENRY (ZIP, BULLET, VIN)—1923-30—p, Washington Potomacs, Philadelphia Giants, Hilldale Club, Lincoln (NY) Giants, Richmond Giants (NAA), Brooklyn Royal Giants, Cleveland Tigers, Providence Giants

CAMPINI, JOSEPH L. (JOE)—1948—c, Baltimore Elite Giants

CAMPOS y TOLEDO, FRANCISCO (TATICA)—1915-22, 1930—3b, 1b, 2b, p, Cuban Stars (East & West)

CAMPOS y LÓPEZ, FRANCISCO JOSÉ (FRANK)—1946—of, New York Cubans

CAMPOS, JOSÉ—1911—1b, All Cubans

CAMPOS, ROBERTO (MANZANILLO)—1923—of, p, Cuban Stars (West)

CAMPS [CAMPOS], MANUEL—1906-09—manager, Cuban Stars

CANADA, ERNIE—1951—p, Philadelphia Stars

CANADA [CANADY], JAMES (CAT, JIM, FLASH, SHORTNECK)-1936-45, 1948-60—1b, manager, Birmingham Black Barons, Memphis Red Sox, Baltimore Elite Giants, Jacksonville Red Caps, Atlanta Black Crackers, Durham (NC) Eagles, Chattanooga Choo Choos

CANEGATA [CANAGATA], WILLIAM (BILLY) FITZPATRICK—1957-58—ss, Indianapolis Clowns

CANIZARES, AVELINO—1945—ss, Cleveland Buckeyes

CANNADY, JESSE CLIFTON (HOSS)—1942-45—3b, 2b, Chicago American Giants, Cincinnati-Indianapolis Clowns, Homestead Grays, New York Cubans, Cincinnati Ethiopian Clowns (NML)

CANNADY, WALTER I. (REV, SAM)—1921-41—2b, ss, of, 3b, 1b, p, manager, Columbus Buckeyes, Dayton Marcos, Cleveland Tate Stars, Homestead Grays, Harrisburg Giants, Hilldale Club, Lincoln (NY) Giants, Darby Daisies, Pittsburgh Crawfords, New York Black Yankees, Philadelphia Stars, Brooklyn Royal Giants

CANNON, JOHN—1867-71—3b, p, Philadelphia Pythians

CANNON, RICHARD K. (SPEED BALL)—1928-34—p, St. Louis Stars, Nashville Elite Giants, Birmingham Black Barons, Louisville Red Caps, Cleveland Cubs, Louisville Black Caps, Louisville White Sox

CANTILLON, ____—1888—2b, Rockford (IL) Rockfords

CANTON [CANTER], LEWIS—1883-87—ss, St. Louis Black Stockings

CANTON, DENIO (TOTO)—1941—p, New York Cubans

CANTRO, ____—1948—ph, New York Cubans

CANTWELL, ____—1930—p, Chicago Giants

CANTY, ____—1938—1b, Birmingham Black Barons

CAPENEMZI, ____—1924—of, Bacharach (AC) Giants

CAPERS, ____—1942—p, Boston Colored Giants

CAPERS, GEORGE EDWARD (HEADACHE BAND)—1911-14—2b, ss, 3b, Pittsburgh Giants, Philadelphia Giants, Baltimore Giants

CAPERS, (LEFTY)—1929-32—p, Louisville White Sox, Hilldale Club, Louisville Black Caps, Montgomery Grey Sox

CARABALLO, ESTERIO—1939—of, New York Cubans

CARD, AL [see CURD, WILLIAM]

CÁRDENAS, LUCIO FRANCISCO (PANCHITO)—1920-21, 1924-27—c, of, Knoxville Giants, Birmingham Black Barons, Cuban Stars (East & West), Montgomery Grey Sox

CÁRDENAS [CARDONIAS, CARDINAS], OSCAR—1956-57—p, Kansas City Monarchs

CARDLE, ____—1920—2b, Jacksonville Stars

CARDSWELL, LLOYD—1949—p, Harlem Globetrotters

CARDWELL, JACK—1948—infield, Baltimore Elite Giants

CAREY, ____—1896—c, Cuban Giants

CAREY, ARTHUR [see CARY, ARTHUR]

CARITHENS, WARREN—1957—of, Detroit Stars

CARLISLE, MATTHEW (LICK. MATT)—1931-48—2b, ss, Birmingham Black Barons, Montgomery Grey Sox, Memphis Red Sox, Homestead Grays, New Orleans Crescent Stars, Harlem Globetrotters, New York Cubans

CARLSON, ____–1916–c, Chicago American Giants
CARLING, CHARLES [see CATLING, CHARLES]
CARLYLE, SYLVESTER JUNIUS (PEE WEE)–1945, 1947–2b, Kansas City Monarchs, Detroit Senators, Satchel Paige All-Stars
CARMICHAEL, ALFONZA–1960–infield, Raleigh (NC) Tigers
CARMICHAEL, LUTHER–1948–secretary, NSL
CARMON, ____–1913–ss, All Nations
CARNEY, ____–1918–of, Bacharach (AC) Giants
CARNEY, CLEMENT (TED, GABBY)–1932–c, infield, Washington Pilots
CARO, MANUEL–1946–c, Los Ángeles White Sox
CARPENTER, ____–1920-21, 1923, 1925, 1927–of, Nashville White Sox, Memphis Red Sox, Nashville Elite Giants, Montgomery Grey Sox
CARPENTER, ____–1944–p, Philadelphia Stars
CARPENTER, ARTHUR (BUDDY)–1909-14–ss, Harrisburg Giants
CARPENTER, ANDREW (ANDY)–1954-56–p, Detroit Stars, Kansas City Monarchs
CARPENTER, CLAY–1920, 1925-26–p, 3b, of, Montgomery Grey Sox, Nashville White Sox, Baltimore Black Sox, Philadelphia Giants
CARR, ____–1932–of, Little Rock Grays
CARR, SR., AUSTIN GEORGE–1948–1b, Homestead Grays
CARR, CHARLEY–1924–p, Baltimore Black Sox
CARR, ED–1890–of, Lincoln (NE) Giants
CARR, GEORGE HENRY (TANK)–1912-34–1b, 3b, of, c, Los Angeles White Sox, Kansas City Monarchs, Hilldale Club, Bacharach (AC) Giants, Philadelphia Stars, Lincoln (NY) Giants, Washington Pilots, Baltimore Black Sox, Royal Poinciana (FL), Pullen's Royal Giants, Philadelphia Royal Giants
CARR, JOHN W. (JOHNNY)–1916-20–1b, of, Dayton Marcos
CARR, WAYNE–1920-28–p, St. Louis Giants, Indianapolis ABCs, Baltimore Black Sox, Washington Potomacs, Bacharach (AC) Giants, Wilmington Potomacs, Newark Stars, Brooklyn Royal Giants, Lincoln (NY) Giants, Los Angeles White Sox
CARRERAS, CLEMENTE (SUNGO)–1933, 1938-41–2b, 3b, New York Cubans
CARRILLO, BERNARDO –1899-1904, 1906-07–ss, 1b, p, All Cubans, Havana Stars, Cuban Stars

CARRINGTON, FRITZ–1921, 1925-26–of, Houston Black Buffaloes, Brooklyn Cuban Giants
CARROLL, ____–1880–of, Washington Douglass Club
CARROLL, ____–1880–c, Washington Eagles
CARROLL, ____–1880–c, Washington Uniques
CARROLL, ____–1920–of, Bacharach (AC) Giants
CARROLL, ____–1940–p, Homestead Grays
CARROLL, HAL–1887–player, Cincinnati Browns (NCBBL)
CARROLL, JR., REGINALD RANDOLPH (SONNY)–1950–p, Baltimore Elite Giants
CARROLL, VERNON–1913–1b, Louisville Cubs
CARRUTHERS, WARREN–1955-58–p, of, Detroit Stars, Detroit Clowns, Kansas City Monarchs
CARSON, ____–1910–3b, West Baden (IN) Sprudels
CARSON, ____–1912–ss, Brown's Tennessee Rats
CARSON, JOHN–[see CASON, JOHN]
CARSWELL, FRANK–1944-53–p, Cleveland Buckeyes, Indianapolis Clowns, Chicago American Giants, Harlem Globetrotters
CARTER, ____–1880–p, Washington Eagles
CARTER, ____–1899–of, Cuban Giants
CARTER, ____–1946–umpire, WCBA
CARTER, ____–1944–ss, New York Black Yankees, Charleston's Cuban Yanks
CARTER, ALFRED–1934-42–of, p, Philadelphia Stars, Pittsburgh Crawfords, New York Cubans, Nashville Elite Giants, Homestead Grays, Toledo Crawfords, Satchel Paige's All-Stars
CARTER, ART ISAAC (IKE)–1883-84–2b, St. Louis Black Stockings
CARTER, ARTHUR–writer, *Afro-American* newspapers
CARTER, ARTHUR H.–1947–p, Philadelphia Stars
CARTER, [DR.] AUDREY B.–1932-33–officer, Memphis Red Sox, 1933–vice-president, NSL
CARTER, BILL [see CARTER, JAMES]
CARTER, (BO)–1931–president, Chattanooga Black Lookouts
CARTER, BOBBY–1959–of, Raleigh (NC) Tigers
CARTER, CHARLES (CHUCK)–1943–p, Baltimore Elite Giants, Homestead Grays
CARTER, CHARLES (KID)–1897-13–p, of, Philadelphia Giants, Wilmington Giants, Brooklyn Royal Giants, Philadelphia Quaker City Giants, Genuine Cuban Giants, Cuban Giants, Celoron (NY) Acme Colored Giants (Iron & Oil League)

CARTER, CLIFFORD—1923-34—p, Baltimore Black Sox, Bacharach (AC) Giants, Harrisburg Giants, Philadelphia Tigers, Hilldale Club, Philadelphia Stars, Providence Giants

CARTER, CORNELL—1932, 1938—p, Baltimore Black Sox, Birmingham Black Barons

CARTER, CURTIS—1946-48—p, Montgomery Dodgers, Jacksonville Eagles, Memphis Red Sox

CARTER, ELMER (SNAKE EYES)—1930-32—ss, 1b, p, Birmingham Black Barons, Kansas City Monarchs

CARTER, ERNEST C. (SPOON, WHIP)—1932-49—p, manager, Pittsburgh Crawfords, Memphis Red Sox, Cleveland Red Sox, Toledo Crawfords, Indianapolis Crawfords, Newark Eagles, Philadelphia Stars, Homestead Grays, Birmingham Black Barons, Louisville Black Caps, Akron Tyrites, Cleveland Giants, Montgomery Dodgers, St. Louis Stars, Denver Post Negro All-Stars

CARTER, FLINT B.—1869—1b, Chicago Blue Stockings

CARTER, FLOYD—1932—of, Hilldale Club

CARTER, FRANK—1917—p, St. Louis Giants, Havana Red Sox

CARTER, SR., HERMAN LEROY (LEE)—1940—ss, Philadelphia Stars

CARTER, ISAAC (IKE)—1882—2b, Bridgewater's Black Stockings

CARTER, J.—1929—p, Hilldale Club

CARTER, JAMES (JIMMY)—1938-39, 1943—p, Philadelphia Stars, Baltimore Elite Giants

CARTER, JAMES AYAH (JIM)—1946, 1948-49—p, Newark Eagles, Houston Eagles, Pittsburgh Crawfords

CARTER, JOHNNY—1945, 1947—of, 1b, Chicago Brown Bombers (USL), Detroit Senators

CARTER, KENNETH—1950—c, Cleveland Buckeyes

CARTER, MARK—1935—officer, Chattanooga Black Lookouts

CARTER, MARK (HANK)—1954-55—p, Detroit Stars, Louisville Clippers

CARTER, MARLIN THEODORE (MEL, PEE WEE)—1932-53—3b, Cincinnati Tigers, Atlanta Black Crackers, Memphis Red Sox, Chicago American Giants, Monroe (LA) Monarchs, Austin Black Senators

CARTER, MARVIN—1958—3b, Memphis Red Sox

CARTER, MATHEW—1954—p, Kansas City Monarchs

CARTER, OGELL—1937—of, Pittsburgh Crawfords

CARTER, PAUL (NICK)—1924-36—p, Hilldale Club, Darby Daisies, Philadelphia Stars, New York Black Yankees, Pittsburgh Crawfords

CARTER, ROBERT—1947—p, Homestead Grays

CARTER, T.C.—1927—1b, Shreveport Black Sports

CARTER, W.H. —1905—umpire, Metropolitan Colored Baseball League

CARTER, WAYNE—1909-10, 1914-18—2b, ss, 3b, Louisville White Sox, Louisville Cubs, Chicago Giants, New York Black Sox

CARTER, WILLIAM—1932, 1934—2b, Little Rock Grays, Little Rock Travelers, Louisville Red Caps

CARTER, WILLIAM—1946—p, Pittsburgh Crawfords (USL)

CARTER, WILLIAM (BILL)—1936-37, 1943—3b, 1b, St. Louis Stars, Birmingham Black Barons, Harrisburg-St. Louis Stars,

CARTER, WILLIAM (BILL)—1938, 1943, 1946—c, 2b, 1b, 3b, ss, of, Chicago American Giants

CARTER, WILLIAM HENRY—1920—c, Detroit Stars

CARTLEDGE, MENSKE (ROBBIE, MENNY)—1948, 1951-55—p, Raleigh (NC) Tigers, Philadelphia Stars, Birmingham Black Barons

CARTMAN, EVA—1954—secretary, treasurer— Memphis Red Sox

CARTMILL, JR., ALFRED FRANKLIN (AL)—1948-51, 1955—2b, Kansas City Monarchs

CARTWRIGHT, ____—1872—2b, Amicable Club of New York

CARTWRIGHT, JR., CLAIBORN (CLAY)—1946, 1953-54—utility, Nashville Cubs, Memphis Red Sox, Louisville Clippers, Detroit Stars

CARVALLO [see CASTILLO, JULIÁN]

CARVILLE, ____—1923—1b, All Nations

CARY [CAREY, CARRY], ARTHUR (KID)—1916-22, 1927—p, 3b, 2b, St. Louis Giants, Dayton Marcos, Brooklyn Royal Giants, Buffalo Stars

CASANAS, ____—1921—of, Bacharach (AC) Giants

CASANOVA y ORTIZ, PAULINO (PAUL)—1960-61—c, Indianapolis Clowns

CASE, ____—1932—of, Cleveland Stars

CASE, COS—1958—utility, Detroit Clowns

CASEY, ____—1921—2b, Brooklyn Royal Giants

CASEY, A.—1909—c, St. Louis Giants

CASEY, FRANK—1915—p, West Baden (IN) Sprudels

CASEY, [CARSON, CARTER] JOSEPH SYLVESTER (JOE)—1920-23—p, St. Louis Giants, Cleveland Tate Stars. Birmingham Black Barons

CASEY, WILLIAM (MICKEY)—1930-43—c, manager, Baltimore Black Sox, Bacharach (Philly) Giants, Philadelphia

Stars, Washington Black Senators, New York Cubans, Baltimore Grays, New York Black Yankees, Hilldale Club, Pittsburgh Crawfords, Baltimore Elite Giants, Newark Eagles
CASH, WAYMAN TREADWELL L.—1940s—c, Philadelphia Meteors
CASH, WILLIAM WALKER (BILL, READY)—1941-50—c, Otto Brigg's All-Stars, Philadelphia Daisies (NML), Philadelphia Stars
CASHER, LESLIE—1940—of, Chicago American Giants
CASON, JOHN—1917-31—c, 2b, ss, 1b, Brooklyn Royal Giants, Norfolk Stars, Hilldale Club, Lincoln (NY) Giants, Bacharach (AC) Giants, Baltimore Black Sox, Birmingham Black Barons, Havana Red Sox
CASPER, ____—1946—p, Homestead Grays
CASS, ____—1929—p, Tulsa Black Oilers
CASSELBERRY [CASTLEBERRY, CASTLEBURY], JAYCEE (J. C.)—p, c, utility—1957-59—Indianapolis Clowns
CASSELL, NEELY (NEAL)—1944-45—of, Philadelphia Hilldales (USL), Philadelphia Stars, Harrisburg-St. Louis Stars
CASTAINER, ____—1913-14—1b, ss, All Nations
CASTAÑO, TONY—1937—of, Trujillo All-Stars (Ciudad Trujillo Dragons)
CASTEN, ____—1897—p, Cuban Giants [see CARTER, CHARLES (KID)]
CASTILLE, IRVIN [IRVAN] (CHUCK)—1951-53—ss, 3b, Birmingham Black Barons
CASTILLO, ____—1930—2b, Boston Black Sox
CASTILLO, JOSÉ (JOE) GUARINO—c—1957, Detroit Stars
CASTILLO, JULIÁN—1911—1b, All Cubans, Cuban Stars
CASTONE, GEORGE WILLIAM—1888-93—p, of, manager, Kansas City (MO) Maroons, Lincoln Browns/Kearney (Nebraska State League), Lincoln (NE) Giants, Aspen (Colorado St. League), Bright's Cuban Giants
CASTONE, WILLIAM [see CASTONE, GEORGE WILLIAM]
CASTRO, ANTONIO—1927-29—c, Havana Red Sox, Cuban Stars (East), Stars of Cuba
CAT EYE, ____—1920—3b, Chicago Black Sox
CATES, JOE (RABBIT)—1931-38—ss, 2b, 3b, Louisville White Sox, Louisville Red Caps, Louisville Black Colonels, Louisville Black Caps, Nashville Elite Giants
CATHEY, WILLIS (JIM, BILL, WILLIE)—1948-52—p, Indianapolis Clowns
CATLING, CHARLES—1887—umpire, NCBBL
CATO, HARRY—1887-96—2b, p, of, ss, Cuban X-Giants, Cuban Giants, New York Gorhams (Middle States League), Genuine Cuban Giants, Philadelphia Giants, Trenton (NJ) Cuban Giants (Middle States League), Lancaster (PA) Giants
CATTO [GATTO], OCTAVIUS VALENTINE—1867-69—2b, ss, Philadelphia Pythians
CAULFIELD, FRED—1920-35—p, manager, New Orleans Caulfield Ads, New Orleans Crescent Stars, New Orleans Black Pelicans
CAVENS, JEFFERSON—1867-68—1b, Philadelphia Pythians
CELADA, ARMANDO—1928-29—ss, 2b, 3b, Cuban Stars (West)
CENTRE, ____—1908—2b, Chicago Union Giants
CEPEDA, PEDRO ANÍBAL (PERUCHO, THE BULL)—1937, 1941— of, 1b, Trujillo All-Stars (Ciudad Trujillo Dragons), Listed on the 1941 New York Cubans roster, but never played in a league game.
CEPHUS [CEPHAS], GOLDSBIRGH ARTHUR MONROE (GOLDIE)—1925-38—ss, of, Philadelphia Giants, Bacharach (Philly) Giants, Birmingham Black Barons, Newark Dodgers, Brooklyn Royal Giants, Philadelphia Quaker City Giants
CEREBEBES, ____—1929—of, Boston Black Sox
CHACÓN y CORTINA, PELAYO—1910-31—ss, manager, Stars of Cuba, Cuban Stars (East & West), All Cubans, Breakers Hotel (FL)
CHACÓN, JR., PELAYO—1930—3b, Stars of Cuba
CHADWICK, DAVID—1959—p, Raleigh (NC) Tigers
CHALLOWER, MARK—1944-45—secretary, Professional Negro Umpire Association
CHALMERS, MARVIN T.—1959—ss, Detroit Stars
CHAMBERLAIN, ED—1888-92—1b, c, New York Gorhams (Middle States League), Cuban Giants
CHAMBERS, ARTHUR (RUBE)—1924-27—p, Lincoln (NY) Giants, Wilmington Potomacs, Washington Potomacs
CHAMBERS, HOMER—1920—p, New Orleans Crescent Stars
CHANDLER, ____—1916—p, Bowser's ABCs
CHANDLER, ____—1931—3b, Cleveland Cubs
CHANDLER, JOHN—1958-59—p, Indianapolis Clowns
CHANEY, JR., JOHN E. (DUTCH, LEFTY)—1947, 1952—p, New York Black Yankees, Philadelphia Stars
CHAPEL, ____—1939—of, Toledo Crawfords
CHAPLIN, ____—1946—ss, New York Black Yankees
CHAPMAN, ____—1871—of, Boston Resolutes
CHAPMAN, ____—1915—of, St. Louis Cubs
CHAPMAN, ____—1944—1b, Baltimore Elite Giants

CHAPMAN, ARTHUR SIMMONS (ART)—1958—ss, Memphis Red Sox
CHAPMAN, CHARLES—1955—p, Detroit Stars
CHAPMAN, EDWARD—1927-28, 1931—of, Detroit Stars, Chicago Columbia Giants
CHAPMAN, JOHN—1887—player, Cincinnati Browns (NCBBL)
CHAPMAN, JOSEPH W.—1887—player, Cincinnati Browns (NCBBL)
CHAPMAN, LEONARDO MEDINA [see MEDINA, LÁZARO]
CHAPMAN, JR., ROY LLOYD (RAY)—1949-50—p, New York Black Yankees
CHAPPELL, ____—1939—of, Montgomery Grey Sox
CHARLES, ____—1869—c, Philadelphia Excelsior
CHARLESTON, BENJAMIN FRANKLIN (BENNIE)—1930-31—of, Homestead Grays, Indianapolis ABCs
CHARLESTON, J. (RED)—1920-34, 1942—c, Nashville Elite Giants, Baltimore Black Sox, Birmingham Black Barons, Memphis Red Sox, Montgomery Grey Sox, Cincinnati Buckeyes, Albany (GA) Giants, Nashville White Sox
CHARLESTON, OSCAR McKINLEY (CHARLIE)—1915-54—of, 1b, manager, umpire, Bowser's ABCs, Indianapolis ABCs, Lincoln (NY) Stars, Chicago American Giants, St. Louis Giants, Harrisburg Giants, Hilldale Club, Homestead Grays, Pittsburgh Crawfords, Toledo Crawfords, Indianapolis Crawfords, Philadelphia Stars, Brooklyn Brown Dodgers, Philadelphia Hilldales (USL), Indianapolis Clowns, Schenectady Mohawk Giants, Royal Poinciana (FL)
CHARLESTON, PORTER R.—1927-35, 1939—p, Hilldale Club, Darby Daisies, Philadelphia Stars, Baltimore Black Sox
CHARNOOK, THOMAS—1868—player, Philadelphia Pythians
CHARTER, WILLIAM M. (BABY, BILL)—1933-36, 1941, 1943—of, 1b, Louisville Red Caps, Detroit Black Sox, Louisville Black Colonels, St. Louis Stars, Kansas City Monarchs
CHASE, ____—1920—ss, New Orleans Crescent Stars
CHASE, ____—1920-23—of, p, Detroit Stars, Chicago Giants, Toledo Tigers, Cleveland Tate Stars
CHATMAN, ____—1922—p, Cleveland Tate Stars
CHATMAN, ARTHUR—1944—3b, Chicago American Giants
CHATMAN, CHARLES HOWARD (SLEEPY)—1955-58—p, Detroit Stars, Detroit Clowns, Birmingham Black Barons
CHATMAN, EDGAR—1944-46—p, Memphis Red Sox
CHAUNCEY, ____—1869—of, Philadelphia Excelsior

CHAUVIN, S.—1883-87—3b, St. Louis Black Stockings
CHAVERS, ____—1917—of, Dayton Marcos
CHAVIS, ____—1917—p, Jewell's ABCs
CHAVOUS, JAMES H.—1895-96—p, of, Adrian (MI) Page Fence Giants
CHEATHAM, GEORGE—1930-34—p, Baltimore Black Sox, Pittsburgh Crawfords, Homestead Grays, Bacharach (Philly) Giants
CHEATHAM, WALTER EDWIN—1918, 1920—of, Pennsylvania Giants, Madison Stars, Pittsburgh Stars of Buffalo
CHEEKS, ROBERT (BOB)—1946—p, Newark Eagles
CHENAULT, JOHN—1907-09—c, Indianapolis ABCs
CHERRY, HUGH—1949—officer, owner, Houston Eagles
CHERRY, JOE BOBBY (JOHNEY)—1958-61—p, c, Indianapolis Clowns
CHERRY, WILLIE—1929—c, Memphis Red Sox
CHESNUT, ____—1928—of, Chattanooga Black Lookouts
CHESNUTT, ____—1926—p, Albany Giants
CHESTER, ____—1867—3b, Monrovia Club of Harrisburg
CHESTER, DAVID—1926-28—of, Harrisburg Giants, Chattanooga Black Lookouts
CHESTINE, CLYDE—1946—1b, Brooklyn Brown Dodgers, Pittsburgh Stars
CHESTNUT, ____—1929—of, Chattanooga Black Lookouts
CHESTNUT, HENRY (JOE)—1949-52—p, Indianapolis Clowns, Philadelphia Stars, Birmingham Black Barons, Raleigh Tigers
CHEVALIER, JOE [see WIGGINS, JOE]
CHEW, ____—1867—of, 2b, Mutuals of Washington, Washington Alerts
CHILDERS, WOLF—1935-36—c, Cincinnati Tigers
CHILDRESS, JOHNNY—1958—p, Detroit Clowns
CHILDS, ____—1922—p, Bacharach (AC) Giants
CHILDS, ANDY PETE—1936-45—2b, p, Indianapolis Athletics, Memphis Red Sox, St. Louis Stars, Indianapolis ABCs, Cincinnati Tigers
CHILDS, CARL—1946—c, Cleveland Clippers
CHILDS, CHARLES—1909—p, Kansas City (MO) Royal Giants
CHILDS, SON—1929, 1931—ss, Memphis Red Sox, Chicago American Giants, Chicago Giants
CHIRBAN, LOUIS J.—1950—p, Chicago American Giants
CHISHOLM, ____—1922—umpire, NNL
CHISHOLM, JOE—1945, 1948, 1953, 1957—p, 2b, Philadelphia Stars, Chattanooga Choo Choos, Memphis Red Sox, Detroit Stars

CHISM, ELIJAH (ELI, LITTLE CHIS)—1936-42, 1946-51—3b, of, St. Louis Stars, Birmingham Black Barons, Cleveland Buckeyes, St. Louis Giants, New Orleans Black Pelicans, St. Louis Giants
CHITARAS, ____—1880—1b, Washington Uniques
CHRETIAN, ERNEST JOSEPH (ROLLIN)—1949-50—of, infield, Kansas City Monarchs, Philadelphia Stars
CHRISAPE, M.—1884—utility, Chicago Unknowns
CHRISPO, JOHN—1878—utility, Chicago Uniques
CHRISTIAN, JOHN—1935—of, New York Black Yankees
CHRISTIANO, TONY—1931-38—groundskeeper, Bedford Land Company— Greenlee Field
CHRISTIANSON, CAP—1946—umpire, WCBA
CHRISTIE, ____—1896—of, Cuban Giants
CHRISTOPHER, M.J.—1886—secretary, Southern League of Colored Base Ballists
CHRISTOPHER, THADIST B. (TED)—1934-46—c, of, 1b, Newark Eagles, Pittsburgh Crawfords, New York Black Yankees, Cincinnati-Cleveland Buckeyes, Cincinnati Ethiopian Clowns (NML), Cleveland Buckeyes, Nashville Elite Giants, Washington Elite Giants, Baltimore Elite Giants, Jacksonville Red Caps, Toledo Crawfords, Havana Las Palomas, Homestead Grays, Atlanta Black Crackers
CHRISTY, LEVI—1895-1890—editor, *Indianapolis Colored World*
CHUNN, J. C.—1945—officer, NSL; officer, Atlanta Black Crackers
CHURCH, R.S.—1887—manager, Boston Resolutes (NCBBL)
CHURCHILL, ____—1870-71—2b, Boston Resolutes
CHURCHILL, ____—1921—c, Norfolk Giants
CISCO [SISCO], J.—1884-85—player, Philadelphia Mutual B.B.C., Philadelphia Manhatten Club
CISCO, —1941—2b, Otto Brigg's All-Stars
CITRIANO, R.—1934—officer, Baltimore Black Sox
CLARIZIO, JR., LOUIS (THE GREY CAT)—1950—of, Chicago American Giants
CLARK, ____—1887—c, Louisville Falls City (NCBBL)
CLARK, ____—1867, 1871—3b, Philadelphia Excelsior, Philadelphia Pythians
CLARK, ____—1908-09-11—2b, of, p, Brooklyn Colored Giants, Brooklyn Royal Giants, Philadelphia Giants
CLARK, ____—1928—of, Evansville (IL) Giants
CLARK, ____—1929—of, Harrisburg Giants
CLARK, ____—1930—3b, Santop Broncos
CLARK, ____—1931—p, Kansas City Monarchs
CLARK, ____—1937—of, Kansas City Monarchs
CLARK SR., ALBERT D. (A.D.)—1919-20—p, of, Dayton Marcos, Cleveland Tate Stars
CLARK, ALEX W.—1928, 1931-32—of, ss, 2b, St. Louis Giants, Louisville White Sox, Birmingham Black Barons, Cleveland Stars
CLARK, BILL—1926-30—umpire, ECL
CLARK, BENNY—1926—p, Dayton Marcos, Atlanta Black Crackers, Cuban Stars (West), Chattanooga White Sox
CLARK, CHARLES W. (SENSATION, CHARLIE)—1922-24, 1926-28—p, 2b, Pittsburgh Keystones, Indianapolis ABCs, Memphis Red Sox, Cleveland Browns, Chicago American Giants, Homestead Grays, Atlanta Black Crackers, Chattanooga Black Lookouts
CLARK, CLEVELAND CHIFLAN—1945-50—of, New York Cubans
CLARK, ELMER—1957—p, 1b, of, Kansas City Monarchs
CLARK, ESTABAN—1955—1b, Kansas City Monarchs
CLARK, F. R.—1933—officer, Newark Dodgers
CLARK, HARRY (LEFTY)—1915-25—p, Brooklyn Royal Giants, Hilldale Club, Bacharach (AC) Giants
CLARK, J. L.—1946—p, Homestead Grays
CLARK[E], JOHN L.—1932-46—business manager, Pittsburgh Crawfords; public relations man, Homestead Grays; secretary, NNL
CLARK, LONEY (LONNIE)—1917—ss, Texas All-Stars (WES)
CLARK, M.—1958—p, Memphis Red Sox
CLARK, MACEO RICHARD—1923-25—p, Washington Potomacs, Wilmington Potomacs, Indianapolis ABCs, Bacharach (AC) Giants, Homestead Grays
CLARK, MARCELL—1941—c, Birmingham Black Barons
CLARK, JR., MILTON J.—1937-38—secretary, Chicago American Giants
CLARK, MORTEN AVERY (SPECS, MORTY)—1910-23—ss, of, 2b, 3b, p Philadelphia Giants, Indianapolis ABCs, Lincoln (NY) Stars, Lincoln (NY) Giants, Bacharach (AC) Giants, Washington Potomacs, Baltimore Black Sox, West Baden (IN) Sprudels, Chicago Black Sox, Royal Poinciana (FL)
CLARK, OLLIE—1941—1b, Detroit Stars
CLARK, RAYMOND—1930—p, Colored House of David
CLARK, RICHARD CLIFFORD (DICK)—1946—c, Detroit Wolves
CLARK, ROBERT WILLIAM (DELL)—1921—ss, 2b, St. Louis Giants, Pittsburgh Keystones
CLARK, ROY—1934-35—p, Newark Dodgers

CLARK, THOMAS (TOM)—1920-21—of, Chicago Giants, Jewell ABCs

CLARK, WILLIAM—writer, *New York Age*

CLARK, WILLIAM (BIFF)—1926, 1928—of, Memphis Red Sox, Chattanooga White Sox

CLARKE, ____—1867-69—p, c, Philadelphia Excelsior, Philadelphia Pythians

CLARKE, CALVIN (ALLIE)—1937-38, 1941—2b, of, Washington Black Senators, Detroit Stars, Newark Eagles

CLARKE, DICK—1942—2b, of, Richmond Hilldales (NML)

CLARKE, JOHN—1859—vice-president, 1b, Unknown Base Ball Club (of Weeksville, NY)

CLARKE, ROBERT ALFRED (KIKE, EGGIE, CAYUKA)—1922-48—c, manager, Richmond Giants (NAA), Baltimore Black Sox, New York Black Yankees, Philadelphia Stars, Baltimore Elite Giants, Philadelphia Tigers

CLARKE, VIBERT ERNESTO (WEBBO)—1946-53—p, Cleveland Buckeyes, Louisville Buckeyes, Memphis Red Sox

CLARKSON, [see BRAZELTON, JOHN]

CLARKSON, JAMES BUSTER (BUS)—1937-50—ss, of, 2b, Pittsburgh Crawfords, Toledo Crawfords, Indianapolis Crawfords, Newark Eagles, Philadelphia Stars, Baltimore Elite Giants

CLARKSON, LEROY (CANNONBALL)—1914-16—2b, Hilldale Club, Philadelphia Giants

CLARKSON, W.—1907—ss, Trusty (PA) Giants

CLARR, A.—1935—2b, Detroit Cubs

CLAXTON, JAMES EDWARD (JIMMIE)—1916, 1932—p, New York Cuban Stars, Oakland Oaks (PCL), Cuban Stars (West), Washington Pilots

CLAY, ____—1945—c, Newark Eagles

CLAY, ____—1947—of, Homestead Grays

CLAY, ALTON BROYEL (A.B.)—1949-50—of, New York Black Yankees

CLAY, HARRISON—1911—of, Brown's Tennessee Rats

CLAY, JOHN—1925-26—of, Bacharach (AC) Giants, Atlanta Black Crackers

CLAY, JR., LAWRENCE—1950s—p, Kansas City Monarchs

CLAY, JR., WILBRON A. (BUDDY)—1921—2b, Pittsburgh Keystones

CLAY, WILLIAM HENRY (LEFTY)—1931-36—p, Chicago American Giants, Kansas City Monarchs, Chicago Giants

CLAYBROOK, JR., JOHN C.—1929-38 (NSL)—owner, Claybrook (AR) Tigers

CLAYTON, JACK (SMILEY)—1943-46—c, New York Black Yankees, Oakland Larks, Chicago Giants, Chicago Brown Bombers (USL), Great Lakes Bluejackets

CLAYTON, ZACHARY M. (ZACK)—1932-44—1b, Bacharach (Philly) Giants, Baltimore Black Sox, Cole's Chicago American Giants, Chicago American Giants, Chicago Brown Bombers (NML), Brooklyn Eagles, Brooklyn Royal Giants, New York Black Yankees

CLEAGE, RALPH (PETE)—1920-21, 1924, 1926, 1928, 1936—of, 1b, Knoxville Giants, Chattanooga Black Lookouts, Chattanooga White Sox, St. Louis Stars; umpire, NNL

CLEARY, B.—1871—2b, Chicago Blue Stockings

CLEARY, CLINT—1879—p, Chicago Uniques

CLEMENTE y WILLIAMS, MIGUEL—1917—3b, of, p, Havana Cubans

CLEMMONS, RALPH—1910—owner, Dixie Park Baseball Club (Mobile, AL)

CLEVELAND, HOWARD (DUKE)—1938-46—of, Jacksonville Red Caps, Cleveland Bears, Cincinnati-Cleveland Buckeyes, Cleveland Buckeyes, Indianapolis Clowns

CLIFFORD, LUTHER (SHANTY)—1948-53—c, Homestead Grays, Kansas City Monarchs, Indianapolis Clowns

CLIFTON, (BUD)—1939—p, Bacharach (Philly) Giants

CLIFTON, NAT (SWEETWATER), [nee CLIFTON NATHANIEL]—1949, 1958—1b, of, Chicago American Giants, Detroit Clowns

CLINT, ____—1927-28—of, Evansville Giants

CLINTON, WILLIAM MELVIN—1917—3b, Bacharach (AC) Giants

CLISEN, ____—1913—p, St. Louis Giants

CLOSE, HERMAN—1887—manager, Philadelphia Pythians (NCBBL)

CLOUD, ____—1929—3b, Schenectady Mohawk Giants

CLOUD (RED)—1916—of, All Nations

CLUBBY, ____—1916—p, French Lick (IN) Plutos

COACHMAN, JAMES—1945—c, Chicago American Giants

COADY, ____—1914—c, All Nations

COATES, ____—1867—of, Philadelphia Excelsior

COATES, ____—1923—2b, Richmond Giants

COATES, LEROY JOSEPH—1944—of, Homestead Grays, Great Lakes Bluejackets

COBB, AL W.—1914-20, 1928, 1932—c, St. Louis Giants, Lincoln (NY) Giants, Jewell's ABCs, Indianapolis ABCs, St. Louis Stars, West Baden (IN) Sprudels, Little Rock Grays

COBB, LORENZA SAMUEL NATHANIEL—1920-35—officer, St. Louis Giants, Birmingham Black Barons, Memphis

Red Sox, Cleveland Elites; owner Cleveland Hornets; secretary, NSL

COBB, WILLIE—1908—of, 2b, Cuban Giants, Pop Watkins Stars

COBBIN, WILLIE JAMES (JIM)—1955-57, 1960—2b, of, Indianapolis Clowns, New York Black Yankees

COCHRAN, PHILLIP [see COCKRELL, PHILIP]

COCKERELL, PHIL, [see COCKRELL, PHILIP]

COCKERSHAM [COCKERHAM], JIMMY—1937-39—c, Indianapolis ABCs, Indianapolis Athletics

COCKRAN, ____—1920—of, Pittsburgh Stars of Buffalo

COCKRELL, PHILIP (PHIL, FISH, GEORGIA ROSE) [nee PHILIP WILLIAMS]—1913-46—p, of, Havana Red Sox, Lincoln (NY) Giants, Hilldale Club, Darby Daisies, Philadelphia Stars, Breakers Hotel (FL); umpire, NNL

COE, HARRY—1946—of, Brooklyn Brown Dodgers

COFFEE, ____—1921—p, Kansas City Monarchs

COFFEY, ____—1926—umpire, ECL

COFFEY, HOWARD (HARRY)—1951-54—p, Philadelphia Stars, Indianapolis Clowns

COFFEY, MARSHALL—1889-90—2b, Chicago Unions

COFFIE, CLIFFORD [see CAFFIE, JOSEPH]

COGDELL, JOHNNY—1946-48—p, Cincinnati Crescents, Harlem Globetrotters

COGLEMAN, ____—1926—umpire, NNL

COHEN, JAMES CLARENCE (JIM, FIREBALL)—1948-52—p, Indianapolis Clowns

COHEN, S.M.—1910—owner, Cohen Baseball Club (New Orleans, LA)

COHEN, WALTER LEWIS—1889—manager, New Orleans Pinchbacks

COIMBRE y ATILES, FRANCISCO (PANCHO, FRANK, AL)-1940-41, 1943-44—of, New York Cubans, North Classic Team, North All-Stars

COLAS y CUESTA, CARLOS CELESTINO SUCE (CHARLIE)—1940-41, 1949-51—c, New York Cubans, Memphis Red Sox

COLAS y CUELLA, JOSÉ LUIS—1945, 1947-52—of, manager, Memphis Red Sox, Pittsburgh Crawfords (USL)

COLE, ____—1880—3b, Washington Uniques

COLE, ____—1920—of, Pittsburgh Stars of Buffalo

COLE, ____—1946—p, Montgomery Dodgers

COLE, ARCHIBALD—1931-32—of, c, Nashville Elite Giants, Bacharach (Philly) Giants

COLE, ARCHIE S.—1923-24—p, of, Kansas City Monarchs, Detroit Stars, All Nations

COLE, CECIL EDWARD—1946—p, Newark Eagles; scout—Baltimore Orioles, Pittsburgh Pirates

COLE, HORACE—1929—2b, Evansville Giants

COLE, ROBERT ALEXANDER—1932-35—officer, owner, Chicago American Giants; treasurer, NNL; vice-president, NSL

COLE, WHEELER C.—1928—officer, Memphis Red Sox

COLE, WILLIAM—1896-99—c, p, Cuban Giants

COLEMAN, ____—1887—ss, South Baltimore Mutuals

COLEMAN, ____—1915-23—ss, St. Louis Cubs, St. Louis Giants, St. Louis Black Sox

COLEMAN, ____—1916—p, French Lick (IN) Plutos

COLEMAN, ARDIS—1944—p, Atlanta Black Crackers

COLEMAN, ARTHUR ALONZO—1919-21—p, of, 1b, Jewell's ABCs, Dayton Marcos, Columbus Buckeyes

COLEMAN, BENNY—1950—p, Chicago American Giants

COLEMAN, BOB—1960-61—p, of, Kansas City Monarchs

COLEMAN, CARL—1951—1b, Chicago American Giants

COLEMAN, CHARLES—1935-39, 1941-43—3b, p, of, Schenectady Mohawk Giants

COLEMAN, CLARENCE (CHOO CHOO)—1955-57—c, Indianapolis Clowns

COLEMAN, CLARENCE (POPS, CAPTAIN COLA)—1907, 1911-18—c, of, Chicago Giants, Chicago Union Giants, Indianapolis ABCs, Cleveland Tate Stars, Lincoln (NY) Giants, All Nations, Bowser's ABCs, Louisville Giants

COLEMAN, SR., ELLIOT HOYTE (JUNIOR)—1954-55—p, Birmingham Black Barons

COLEMAN, GILBERT—1927-33—of, 2b, Lincoln (NY) Giants, Brooklyn Cuban Giants, Bacharach (Philly) Giants, Newark Dodgers, Newark Browns

COLEMAN, HENRY (HERB, STRINGBEAN)—1934-43—p, Philadelphia Stars, Schenectady Mohawk Giants

COLEMAN, JIMMY (SLIM)—1945—p, Detroit Motor City Giants

COLEMAN, JOE—1955—p, Birmingham Black Barons

COLEMAN, JOHN (LEFTY)—1950-54—p, Baltimore Elite Giants, Birmingham Black Barons

COLEMAN, JOHN—1885—of, Brooklyn Remsens

COLEMAN, MELVIN (SLICK, MACAN)—1937-46—ss, c, Birmingham Black Barons, Atlanta Black Crackers

COLEMAN, ROSCOE—writer, *Philadelphia Inquirer*

COLEMAN, TOM—1951—p, Baltimore Elite Giants

COLEMAN, WORLEY (WIMPY)—1931-32, 1938—of, Colored House of David

COLES, RALPH HERMAN (PUNJAB, ASKARI)–1939-46–of, p, Jacksonville Red Caps, Cleveland Bears, Cincinnati Ethiopian Clowns (NML), Indianapolis Clowns, Havana Cuban Giants
COLLAZZO, A.–1929–utility, Havana Red Sox
COLLENDER, ____–1904–of, Philadelphia Giants
COLLEY, ____–1928–of, Buck Ewing's All-Stars
COLLIER, BOB–1928–c, of, Bacharach (AC) Giants
COLLIERS, LEONARD–1950-51–p, Cleveland Buckeyes, Birmingham Black Barons
COLLINS, ____–1909–c, Louisville Cubs
COLLINS, ____–1914–p, Indianapolis ABCs
COLLINS, ____–1918–c, Penn Red Caps of NY, Lincoln (NY) Giants
COLLINS, ____–1929–p, Colored House of David
COLLINS, ____–1946–umpire, WCBA
COLLINS, A.–1920–2b, Atlanta Black Crackers
COLLINS II, ARTHUR L. (FLASH)–1923-34, 1944–p, of, Harrisburg Giants, Toledo Tigers, Boston Royal Giants
COLLINS, B. A. (ED)–1925-28, 1932–p, Brooklyn Royal Giants, Baltimore Black Sox, Lincoln (NY) Giants
COLLINS, DON–1929–3b, Shreveport Black Sports
COLLINS, EUGENE MARVIN (GENE, RIP)–1947-51–p, Kansas City Monarchs
COLLINS, ARTHUR–1924–p, Baltimore Black Sox
COLLINS, FRANK–1934–p, Birmingham Black Barons
COLLINS, FRED–1888-92–c, of, New York Gorhams (Middle States League), Philadelphia Giants, Celoron (NY) Acme Colored Giants (Iron & Oil League), York (PA) Colored Monarchs (Eastern Interstate League)
COLLINS, GEORGE–1911–of, Cuban Giants
COLLINS, GEORGE (BOWLEGS)–1920-34–of, 2b, p, ss, New Orleans Crescent Stars, Milwaukee Bears, Toledo Tigers, Indianapolis ABCs, Nashville Elite Giants, New Orleans Caulfield Ads, Kansas City Monarchs
COLLINS, HARRY–1910-18–1b, New York Black Sox, Pittsburgh Giants, Brooklyn Royal Giants, Pittsburgh Stars of Buffalo
COLLINS, J.E.–1905–financial secretary, Metropolitan Colored Baseball League
COLLINS, MELVIN (SLIM, SLICK)–1946–ss, Fresno/San Diego Tigers
COLLINS, NATHAN F. (NAT)–1889–c, of, ss, New York Gorhams (Middle States League)
COLLINS, (SONNY)–1934-36–p, Bacharach (Philly) Giants, New York Black Yankees
COLLINS, WALTER–1947-52–p, Chicago American Giants, Memphis Red Sox, Indianapolis Clowns
COLLINS, WILLIE–1933–of, Nashville Elite Giants
COLLINS, WILLIE P. (JAMES, RIP)–1950-52–p, Birmingham Black Barons, Indianapolis Clowns
COLLON, ____–1930–2b, Colored House of David
COLTHIRST, ALEXANDER C. (ALEX)–1948–p, Indianapolis Clowns
COLVIN, ____–1946–p, Nashville Cubs
COLZIE, SR., JAMES C. (JIM, FIREBALL)–1937-49–p, Atlanta Black Crackers, Cincinnati-Indianapolis Clowns, Indianapolis Clowns
COMBS, A. CLARK (JACK)–1922-26–p, Detroit Stars
COMBS, J.–1883–utility, St. Louis Black Stockings
COMO, ARTHUR–1920, 1927–ss, Shreveport Black Sports
COMPTON ____– 1928–of, Cleveland Tigers
CONCEPCIÓN, RAMÓN (MONCEVILLE, MONCHILE)–1927-34–of, 3b, Philadelphia Giants, Cuban Stars (East), Philadelphia Quaker City Giants, Newark Browns, Bacharach (Philly) Giants, Lincoln (NY) Giants, Cuban House of David, Stars of Cuba
CONCEPCIÓN, ROBERTO (COVAS)–1929-30–p, c, Stars of Cuba
CONDON, ____–1924–umpire, ECL
CONDON, LAFAYETTE–1887– officer, National League of Colored Base Ball Clubs; p, of, manager, Louisville Falls City (NCBBL)
CONNELL, CHIEF–1913–p, Indianapolis ABCs
CONNELL, HARRY [see CORNETT, HARRY]
CONNELLY, ____–1921, 1929–umpire, ECL
CONNER, WILLIE–1950–c, Chicago American Giants
CONNOR, JOHN WILSON–1904-22–owner, officer, Brooklyn Royal Giants, Bacharach (AC) Giants
CONNORS, DICK (DOCK)–1954–ss, Kansas City Monarchs
CONRAD, ____–1927-29–umpire, NNL
CONRAD, ____–1930–p, Newark Browns
CONTAX, CHRIS–1921–president, Knoxville Giants
CONWAY, ____–1931–p, Little Rock Black Travelers
COOK, ____–1867–p, Washington Alerts
COOK, ____–1915–c, Cuban Giants
COOK, ____–1926, 1928, 1939–3b, 2b, Memphis Red Sox, St. Louis Giants
COOK, ____–1930–1b, Havana Red Sox
COOK, ____–1942–of, Twin Cities Gophers
COOK, (BUD)–1891–of, Cuban Giants

COOK, CHARLES—1935—p, Pittsburgh Crawfords
COOK, CHARLES—1862—of, Brooklyn Monitors
COOK, HENRY—1944—p, Cincinnati-Indianapolis Clowns
COOK, HOWARD (JOHNNY)—1937—p, Indianapolis Athletics
COOK, W.—1862—of, Brooklyn Monitors
COOK, WALTER L.—1886-88—officer, owner, Cuban Giants
COOK, WILLIAM—1886-88—officer, Cuban Giants
COOKE, JAMES (JAY)—1929-33—p, Baltimore Black Sox, Bacharach (Philly) Giants, Penn Red Caps of NY
COOLEY, WALTER (WALT)—1926, 1931—1b, Montgomery Grey Sox, Birmingham Black Barons
COOPER, ____—1920—p, Pittsburgh Stars of Buffalo
COOPER, ____—1925—p, Chappie Johnson's All-Stars
COOPER, ALEX—1927-28—of, Philadelphia Tigers, Harrisburg Giants
COOPER, ALFRED MAYART (ARMY)—1923-32—p, Kansas City Monarchs, Cleveland Stars
COOPER, ANDREW LEWIS (ANDY, LEFTY)—1920-41—p, manager, Detroit Stars, Chicago American Giants, Kansas City Monarchs, Philadelphia Royal Giants
COOPER, ANTHONY (ANT)—1926-35, 1940-41—ss, 2b, of, manager, Chattanooga Black Lookouts, Chattanooga White Sox, Birmingham Black Barons, Cleveland Stars, Baltimore Black Sox, Cleveland Red Sox, Louisville White Sox, Pittsburgh Crawfords, Newark Dodgers, Homestead Grays, New York Black Yankees, Bacharach (Philly) Giants, Memphis Red Sox, Brooklyn Royal Giants
COOPER, C.—1884—player, Philadelphia Mutual B.B.C.
COOPER, DARLTIE D. (DALTON, DOLLY, DALTIE)—1921-40—p, Nashville Elite Giants, Indianapolis ABCs, Harrisburg Giants, Lincoln (NY) Giants, Hilldale Club, Bacharach (Philly) Giants, Homestead Grays, Baltimore Black Sox, Newark Eagles, Washington Potomacs
COOPER, DAVID—1921—p, Nashville Elite Giants
COOPER, E. (JUDGE)—1910-28, 1930, 1933—1b, of, Leland Giants, Lincoln (NY) Stars, Cleveland Tate Stars, St. Louis Giants, Schenectady Mohawk Giants, Louisville White Sox, Lincoln (NY) Giants, Leland Giants, Philadelphia Colored Giants of New York, Philadelphia Giants, Penn Red Caps of NY, Los Angeles White Sox, Indianapolis ABCs, Grand Central Terminal Red Caps, Chicago American Giants
COOPER, EDWARD ELDER—1883-88—publisher, *Indianapolis Colored World*; 1888-1892—publisher, *Indianapolis Freeman*

COOPER, GEORGE (STRINGBEAN)—1946—p, Boston Blues
COOPER, HENRY (CHIEF)—1925-28—umpire, NNL
COOPER, HOUSTON—1934—of, Birmingham Black Barons
COOPER, JAMES—1938-47—p, Atlanta Black Crackers, New York Black Yankees, Newark Eagles, Philadelphia Stars, Cleveland Buckeyes
COOPER, RAY—1928-29—p, Hilldale Club [see COOPER, DARLTIE]
COOPER, SAMUEL (SAM)—1918-19, 1923-29—p, Richmond Giants, Detroit Stars, Chicago American Giants, Schenectady Mohawk Giants, Harrisburg Giants, Baltimore Black Sox, Bacharach (AC) Giants, Homestead Grays, Cleveland Stars, Cleveland Royal Giants, Pullen's Royal Giants
COOPER, THOMAS ROGER (TOM)—1947-53—1b, c, of, Kansas City Monarchs, Indianapolis Clowns
COOPER, W.—1935—of, Bacharach (Philly) Giants
COOPER, WILBUR—editor—*Cleveland Whip*
COOPER, WILLIAM THOMAS (BILL, W.T.)—1937-48—c, utility, Atlanta Black Crackers, Philadelphia Stars, New York Black Yankees, Asheville Blues
COPELAND, LAURENCE—1935—p, Brooklyn Eagles
CORBETT, CHARLES (GEECH, GEECHIE)—1921-28—p, Pittsburgh Keystones, Indianapolis ABCs, Harrisburg Giants, Hilldale Club
CORBETT, M.N.—1905—vice-president, Metropolitan Colored Baseball League
CORBIN, RUBE—1913—3b, All Nations
CORCORAN, TOM—1942—p, Homestead Grays
CÓRDOVA, SEVERINO (PETE)—1915-23—3b, ss, Almendares Cubans, Kansas City Monarchs, Cleveland Tate Stars, Toledo Tigers, Havana Cubans
CORIVOLIT, ____—1929—of, Boston Black Sox
CORLEY, J. B.—1942—p, Baltimore Grays
CORNELIUS, ____—1943—2b, Birmingham Black Barons
CORNELIUS, WILLIE—1921, 1929—of, Evansville Giants
CORNELIUS, WILLIAM McKINLEY (SUG)—1929-46—p, Atlanta Grey Sox, Nashville Elite Giants, Memphis Red Sox, Chicago American Giants, Cole's Chicago American Giants, Birmingham Black Barons, Cleveland Elites, Cincinnati-Cleveland Buckeyes
CORNETT, HARRY—1913—c, Indianapolis ABCs
CORREA, MARCELINO FRANCISCO (CUCO)—1922-37—ss, Cuban Stars (East & West), New York Cubans,

Padron's Cuban Giants, Trujillo All-Stars (Ciudad Trujillo Dragons)

CORTÉS [CORTEZ], AURELIO–1928-31, 1935–c, Cuban Stars (East & West), Philadelphia Tigers

CORTEZ, ____–1937–p, New York Cubans

COS, CELEDONIO HERVE [CELEDONCO. COSTIENZA, CONATIENZO, CALDONIA]–1954, 1957-58–p, Indianapolis Clowns, Detroit Stars, Detroit Clowns

COSA (COSS), ____–1932–of, ss, Little Rock Grays, Memphis Red Sox

COSSAR, WILLIE–1954–p, Memphis Red Sox

COSTELLO, ____–1922-24–umpire, NNL

COSTELLO, [see CASTILLO, JULIÁN]

COSTELLO, JOE–1957–c, Detroit Stars

COTTMAN, DARBY–1887-93–3b, of, Chicago Unions, Chicago Resolutes

COTTON, [see WILLIAMS, ROBERT A.]

COTTON, ____–1946–ss, Los Angeles White Sox

COTTON, DAVID–1916–p, 1921–manager, Montgomery Grey Sox

COTTON, JAMES–1945-46–officer, Chattanooga Choo Choos

COTTON, JOE CURTIS–1958-59–c, Detroit Clowns, Birmingham Black Barons

COTTON, LOUIS–1939-41–p, New Orleans Black Pelicans

COTTON, WILLIE–1933–p, Brooklyn Royal Giants

COTTRELL, ____–1923–c, Hilldale Club

COUNTEE, OTHELLO–1916-17–ss, Kansas City Tigers

COUSINS, JR., CLAUDE–1955–p, Indianapolis Clowns

COUTEAU, ____–1913-14–p, All Nations

COUTO, RAMÓN–1935–c, New York Cubans

COVILA, ____–1932–ss, Cuban Stars (West)

COVINGTON, JIM–1955–1b, New York Black Yankees

COVINGTON, JOHN WESLEY (WES)–1947-50–p, of, Raleigh Tigers

COWAN, EDDIE–1919-20–ss, Cleveland Tate Stars, New Orleans Crescent Stars, Atlanta Black Crackers

COWAN, JOHNNIE–1933-50–3b, 2b, Birmingham Black Barons, Cleveland Buckeyes, Memphis Red Sox, Cincinnati Buckeyes, Cuban Stars (East), Chattanooga Choo Choos

COWAN, WILLIAM R.–1913–officer, Colored National Base Ball League of the United States

COWANS, RUSSELL (RUSS)–1942-46–writer, *Detroit Tribune*; secretary, Negro Major Baseball League of America; executive secretary, United States League.

COX, ____–1910–2b, Kansas City Cyclones

COX, ____–1926–3b, Washington Black Sox

COX, ____–1943–ph, New York Black Yankees

COX, A.–1921–of, Atlanta Black Crackers

COX, CLAUDE–1921–3b, Atlanta Black Crackers

COX, COMER LANE (HANNIBAL, RUSS)–1930-31–of, Nashville Elite Giants, Cleveland Cubs

COX, JAMES–1947–p–Newark Eagles

COX, M. D. ALPHONSE–1936-43–p, Memphis Red Sox, Jacksonville Red Caps, Cleveland Bears

COX, ROBERT (BOB)–1945–p, Philadelphia Stars

COX, ROOSEVELT (INDIAN JOE, BENNY)–1936-44–3b, Detroit Stars, Kansas City Monarchs, New York Cubans, Memphis Red Sox

COX, TOM (LEFTY, RUBE)–1928-32–p, Lincoln (NY) Giants, Cleveland Cubs, Cleveland Tigers

COZART, HAYWOOD (HARRY, BIG TRAIN, JEFF)–1939-51–p, manager, Newark Eagles, Raleigh (NC) Tigers, Asheville Blues

CRADDOCK, WILLIAM [WALTER]–1927-29–of, Baltimore Black Sox

CRAIG, ALFRED–1939–p, Bacharach (Philly) Giants

CRAIG, CHARLES–1926-29–p, Lincoln (NY) Giants, Brooklyn Cuban Giants, Harrisburg Giants, Homestead Grays, Schenectady Mohawk Giants

CRAIG, DICK–1940-41–1b, Indianapolis Crawfords, Otto Brigg's All-Stars

CRAIG, HOMER–1934-35–p, Newark Dodgers

CRAIG, JOHN L.–1928-46, 1953–umpire, EWL, NNL

CRAIG, JOSEPH P. (JOE)–1940, 1945-46–1b, of, Indianapolis Crawfords, Philadelphia Stars, Brooklyn Brown Dodgers

CRAIN, A. C.–1887–of, Baltimore Lord Baltimores (NCBBL)

CRAIN, JOHN–1922–c, Bacharach (NY) Giants

CRAMER [CRANSON], ____–1922–p, Bacharach (NY) Giants

CRANSON, ____–1922–p, Bacharach (AC) Giants

CRAWFORD, ____–1910–of, New Orleans Eagles

CRAWFORD, ____–1922–umpire, NNL

CRAWFORD, EDGAR A.–1929–officer, Tulsa Black Oilers

CRAWFORD, HUBERT–1930, 1932, 1936, 1938–ss, 2b, Newark Browns, Newark Eagles, Bacharach (Philly) Giants

CRAWFORD, JOHN–1943–umpire, NNL

CRAWFORD, PETE–1960-61–of, Kansas City Monarchs

CRAWFORD, SAMUEL (SAM)–1910-39–p, manager, coach, New York Black Sox, Chicago Giants, Chicago

Negro Leagues Book #2: The Players

American Giants, Chicago Union Giants, Detroit Stars, Kansas City Monarchs, Brooklyn Royal Giants, Birmingham Black Barons, Chicago Columbia Giants, Cole's Chicago American Giants, Indianapolis Athletics, St. Louis Stars, Cleveland Tate Stars, Cleveland Tigers, Dayton Giants, Cleveland Cubs, Havana Red Sox, All Nations

CRAWFORD, WILLIE WALKER—1934, 1953-54—of, manager, Birmingham Black Barons, Chicago American Giants

CRAWLEY, (SPEED)—1931—2b, Bacharach (Philly) Giants

CREACY, ALBERT DEWEY (A.D., DEWEY)—1924-40—3b, Kansas City Monarchs, St. Louis Stars, Detroit Wolves, Washington Pilots, Columbus Blue Birds, Cleveland Giants, Philadelphia Stars, Brooklyn Royal Giants

CREEK, WILLIE—1924, 1929-32, 1934—c, Washington Potomacs, Brooklyn Royal Giants, Bacharach (Philly) Giants

CRELIN, WILBUR C.—1926—officer, Newark Stars

CRENSHAW, RUBE—1914-15—p, St. Louis Giants

CRESPO y QUIÑÓNEZ, ALEJANDRO (ALEX, HOME RUN)—1940-46—of, New York Cubans

CRESPO y HERNÁNDEZ, ROGELIO (FILETE)—1918-33—2b, 3b, Cuban Stars (East), Cuban Havana Stars, Gilkerson's Union Giants

CREWS, NELSON CAESAR—1911-24—owner, editor, *Kansas City Sun*

CRIGLER, ____—1948—1b, Philadelphia Stars

CRIST, ____—1944—utility, Jacksonville Red Caps

CRISUP, GEORGE M.—1875, 1884-86, 1889-90—c, ss, manager, Chicago Uniques, Chicago Unknowns, Chicago Resolutes

CRITTENDEN, ____—1904—of, Chicago Unions

CROCKENDALE, ____—1871—ss, Boston Resolutes

CROCKETT, FRANK—1916-23—of, Bacharach (AC) Giants, Brooklyn Royal Giants, Norfolk Stars

CROMARTIE, LEROY OLIVER (RAY, CRO)—1945—ss, Cincinnati-Indianapolis Clowns

CROMWELL, CHARLES H. (SQUARE DEAL)—1920-26—umpire, NNL

CROMWELL, JOHN—1918-26—umpire, NNL

CROOK, ____—1950—umpire, East/West game

CROOKS, CLYDE—1931—p, Knoxville Giants

CROSBY, RALPH JOSEPH—1954—infield, Birmingham Black Barons

CROSBY, JR., WALTER CHARLES (W.C.)—1944—c, Cleveland Buckeyes

CROSS, ____—1932—of, Memphis Red Sox, Little Rock Black Travelers

CROSS, ____—1960—2b, Raleigh (NC) Tigers

CROSS, BENNIE (BUNNIE)—1887—of, 1b, Boston Resolutes (NCBBL)

CROSS, NORMAN—1932-37, 1945—p, Cole's Chicago American Giants, Chicago American Giants, Chicago Brown Bombers (USL), Harlem Globetrotters, Atlanta Black Crackers

CROSSON, FRANK WARREN—1954-55—p, 1b, Memphis Red Sox

CROSSON, GEORGE DENNIS (DEEDY)—1919-21—ss, c, Lincoln (NY) Giants, Penn Red Caps of NY

CROUCH, ____—1913, 1916—p, of, All Nations

CROUSE, ____—1930—p, Louisville White Caps

CROUSE, MARTIN—1945—p, New York Black Yankees

CROW, SAM—1912-14—3b, All Nations

CROWDER, WILLIAM CHESTER (SMILING WILL)—1920, 1923-24—p, Madison Stars, Lincoln (NY) Stars, Lincoln (NY) Giants), Schenectady Mohawk Giants, Philadelphia Royal Giants, Nashville White Sox

CROWE, GEORGE DANIEL (BIG GEORGE)—1947-49—1b, New York Cubans, New York Black Yankees, Philadelphia Stars

CROWLEY, ____—1911—p, New York Black Sox

CROXTON, COLUMBUS (LUM)—1908-10—p, of, Cuban Giants, York (PA) Cuban Giants, Indianapolis ABCs

CRUDUP, ZEKE (BOB)—1924-28—p, Philadelphia Giants, Philadelphia Quaker City Giants

CRUE, JR., MARTÍN J. (MATTIE, MARTY, BILL)—1942-51—p, New York Cubans, Homestead Grays, New Orleans Eagles, New York Black Yankees

CRUISE, ____—1932—c, Hilldale Club

CRUM, GEORGE—1942, 1947—utility, Detroit Black Sox, Detroit Wolves

CRUMBIE, RALPH A.—1945-46—c, Pittsburgh Crawfords (USL)

CRUMBLEY, WILLIAM ALEXANDER (ALEX)—1933-38—of, Schenectady Mohawk Giants, New York Black Yankees, Atlanta Black Crackers, Pittsburgh Crawfords, Washington Black Senators

CRUMP, JAMES—1920-39—2b, Hilldale Club, Philadelphia Giants, Breakers Hotel (FL), Norfolk Giants, Norfolk Stars; umpire, NNL

CRUMP, WILLIS (SHORTY)—1916-23—of, 2b, c, Bacharach (AC) Giants

CRUTCHFIELD, JOHN WILLIAM (JIMMIE, COLONEL)—1930-39, 1941-45—of, Birmingham Black Barons, Indianapolis ABCs, Pittsburgh Crawfords, Newark Eagles, Toledo Crawfords, Indianapolis Crawfords, Chicago American Giants, Cleveland Buckeyes

CRUZ, F.—1930—p, Cuban Stars (East)

CRUZ, NESTOR SABATER—1926—of, Lincoln (NY) Giants, Newark Stars

CRUZ, RICHARD—1948—infield, Baltimore Elite Giants

CRUZ, TOMÁS (TOMMY) DE LA—1934—p, Havana Cuban Stars

CUELLA, JOSÉ LUIS—[see COLAS, JOSÉ]

CUERIA y OBRIT, BASILIO—1921-22, 1928-29—p, of, All Cubans, Cuban Stars (East & West), Havana Red Sox

CULVER [CULCRA], CHARLES—1916-22—3b, ss, of, Pittsburgh Stars of Buffalo, Penn Red Caps of NY, Cuban Stars (West), Lincoln (NY) Stars, Lincoln (NY) Giants, Philadelphia Giants

CUMMINGS, ____—1868—of, Actives of Philadelphia

CUMMINGS, (CHICK)—1909—ss, Cuban Giants

CUMMINGS, (CHICK)—1922, 1926, 1932—c, manager, Louisville Black Caps, Nashville Elite Giants, Memphis Red Sox;—1925-28—umpire, NNL

CUMMINGS, HARRY SYTHE (HUGH)—1887—manager, p, Baltimore Lord Baltimores (NCBBL)

CUMMINGS, NAPOLEON (NAP, CHANCE)—1916-29—1b, Bacharach (AC) Giants, Hilldale Club, Norfolk Stars, Madison Stars, Pennsylvania Red Caps, Atlanta Black Crackers, Royal Poinciana (FL), Breakers Hotel (FL)

CUNNINGHAM, ____—1918—p, Indianapolis ABCs

CUNNINGHAM, ____—1926-27—2b, Penn Red Caps of NY

CUNNINGHAM, EARL—1954-55, 1959—2b, of, Detroit Stars, Kansas City Monarchs

CUNNINGHAM, HERMAN (ROUNDER)—1916-31—ss, Montgomery Grey Sox

CUNNINGHAM, HARRY (BABY, CHIC)—1930-37—p, Memphis Red Sox, Birmingham Black Barons

CUNNINGHAM, JAMES—1921—2b, Montgomery Grey Sox

CUNNINGHAM, JOHN (JOHNNIE)—1917-21—ss, St. Louis Giants, Dayton Marcos, Columbus Buckeyes

CUNNINGHAM, L. (LITTLE HACK)—1929, 1932-34—of, Chattanooga White Sox, Baltimore Black Sox, Washington Pilots, Cuban Stars (East), Bacharach (Philly) Giants

CUNNINGHAM, LAWRENCE H. (LARRY)—1950-51—of, Memphis Red Sox, Houston Eagles, New Orleans Eagles

CUNNINGHAM, MARION (DADDY)—1916-26—1b, manager, Memphis Red Sox, Montgomery Grey Sox

CUNNINGHAM, PAT—1932—p, Baltimore Black Sox, Birmingham Black Barons

CUNNINGHAM, PAUL—1932—1b, c, John Donaldson All-Stars

CUNNINGHAM, REED—1920—1b, Montgomery Grey Sox

CUNNINGHAM, ROBERT (SLIM)—1950—p, Cleveland Buckeyes

CUNNINGHAM, SHERMAN [a.k.a. Satchel Paige, Jr.]—1963-64—p, Satchel Paige All-Stars

CUPA, ____—1913—of, Philadelphia Giants

CURD [CARD], WILLIAM H.—1884, 1887—3b, ss, Chicago Unions, Pittsburgh Keystones (NCBBL), Chicago Gordons

CURLEY, EARL C. [see GURLEY, EARL C.]

CURREN, ____—1920—2b, Chicago Black Sox

CURRIE [CURRY], REUBEN (RUBE, KING KURRIE, SPROUT)—1916-32—p, Kansas City (MO) Tigers, Chicago Union Giants, Kansas City Monarchs, Hilldale Club, Chicago American Giants, Detroit Stars, Cleveland Red Sox, Baltimore Black Sox

CURRY, HOMER (BLUE GOOSE)—1928-57—of, p, manager, Memphis Red Sox, Washington Elite Giants, New York Black Yankees, Newark Eagles, Baltimore Elite Giants, Philadelphia Stars, Nashville Elite Giants, Cleveland Tigers, Indianapolis Athletics, Monroe (LA) Monarchs, Louisville Clippers, Birmingham Black Barons

CURRY, LACEY K.—1949—ss, Kansas City Monarchs

CURRY, OSCAR J.—1887—p, Cuban Giants

CURRY, WILLIAM JACKSON (WILLIE, BO JACK)—1954-55—c, Louisville Clippers, Birmingham Black Barons

CURTIS, ____—1923-25—p, Harrisburg Giants

CURTIS, ____—1931-32—3b, c, Detroit Giants, Louisville Black Caps

CURTIS, [see RICKS, CURTISS]

CURTIS, WILLIAM (BILLY BOWLEGS)—1921, 1925, 1930—1b, Houston Black Buffaloes, Havana Red Sox

CURTIS, HARRY—1898—owner, manager, Celoron (NY) Acme Colored Giants (Iron & Oil League)

CUSACK, ____—1933—umpire, East/West game

CYRUS, HERB [see SOUELL, HERBERT]

D

D'MEZA, ANGEL— 1905-06—p, All Cubans, Havana Stars
DABNEY, SR., JOHN MILTON—1885-96—of, p, Argyle Hotel, Cuban X-Giants, Cuban Giants
DAILEY, ____—1888—of, Hoosier Black Stockings
DAILEY, JAMES—1945, 1948—1b, p, Birmingham Black Barons, Baltimore Elite Giants
DALEY, ____—1918—ss, Pennsylvania Giants
DALEY, ____—1931—c, Philadelphia Quaker City Giants
DALLARD, MAURICE JULIUS (MORRIS, EGGIE)— 1920-33—1b, of, Wilmington Potomacs, Baltimore Black Sox, Bacharach (AC) Giants, Hilldale Club, Philadelphia Quaker City Giants, Darby Daisies, Philadelphia Stars, Washington Potomacs, Madison Stars, Pennsylvania Giants, Lincoln (NY) Giants, Philadelphia Giants
DALLAS, BILL—1925—umpire supervisor, ECL
DALLAS, PORTER (BIG BOY)—1929-34—3b, Birmingham Black Barons, Monroe (LA) Monarchs, New Orleans Caulfield Ads, New Orleans Crescent Stars
DALTON, R. D. (ROSSIE)—1940—p, Chicago American Giants, Birmingham Black Barons
DALY, ____—1941—2b, Newark Eagles
DAMEN, LUNIE—1939—p, Toledo Crawfords
DANAGE, LUNIE D.—1920, 1925, 1929—2b, St. Louis Giants, Houston Black Buffaloes
DANCER, CARL—1954—of, Detroit Stars
DANCEY, ____—1906—ss, Wilmington Giants
DANCEY, J.C.—1905—treasurer, Metropolitan Colored Baseball League
DANCEY [DANCY], NATHANIEL (NATE)—1959-60—2b, Kansas City Monarchs
DANDRIDGE, JOHN—1949—p, Houston Eagles
DANDRIDGE, MOSES L.—1922-26—officer, Memphis Red Sox
DANDRIDGE, RAYMOND EMMETT (RAY, HOOKS, SQUATTY, MAMERTO, TALUA)—1933-49—3b, 2b, ss, manager, Detroit Stars, Nashville Elite Giants, Newark Dodgers, Newark Eagles, North Classic Team, New York Cubans, Homestead Grays; scout, San Francisco Giants
DANDRIDGE, RICHARD ALBERT (PING)—1914-19—2b, 3b, Philadelphia Giants, Lincoln (NY) Giants, Havana Red Sox
DANDRIDGE, TROY RASMUSSEN (DAN)—1926-29—3b, ss, Chicago Giants, Dayton Marcos
DANDY, ____—1923—ss, Nashville Elite Giants

DANDY, GEORGE—1915-17—p, Louisville White Sox, West Baden (IN) Sprudels, Lincoln (NY) Giants
DANIELS, ____—1910—ph, New York Black Sox
DANIELS, ____—1934—2b, Pittsburgh Giants
DANIELS, ____—1945—of, Chicago Brown Bombers (USL), Memphis Red Sox
DANIELS, ADAM. D. (A.D.)—1933-35—p, Philadelphia Royal Giants, Newark Dodgers
DANIELS, ALONZO—1954—infield, Birmingham Black Barons
DANIELS, CLIFFORD—1956—p, Kansas City Monarchs
DANIELS, ED—1922-23—officer, Memphis Red Sox
DANIELS, EDGAR (EDDIE, BERT)—1945-47—p, New York Cubans, Pittsburgh Crawfords (USL), Brooklyn Brown Dodgers
DANIELS, FRED—1919-28—p, of, St. Louis Giants, Bacharach (AC) Giants, Hilldale Club, Birmingham Black Barons, Lincoln (NY) Giants, Nashville Elite Giants, Detroit Stars
DANIELS, HAMMOND—1924-27—officer, Bacharach (AC) Giants
DANIELS, JAMES ED—1946-47—c, Knoxville Giants, Asheville Blues
DANIELS, JAMES GEORGE (JIM, SCHOOLBOY)— 1943—p, Birmingham Black Barons
DANIELS, JOE (JUMPING)—1926-28—p, Atlanta Grey Sox, Atlanta Black Crackers
DANIELS, JOHN—1955—p, Detroit Stars
DANIELS, SR., LEON THOMAS (PEPPER)—1921-35—c, Detroit Stars, Harrisburg Giants, Cuban Stars (East), Brooklyn Eagles, Bacharach (AC) Giants, Chicago Columbia Giants
DANIELS, ODELL—1964—of, p, Satchel Paige All-Stars
DANIELS, RAYMOND—1927—officer, Bacharach (AC) Giants
DANIELS, ROGER—1956-57—utility, New York Black Yankees
DANIELS, ZACHARIAS (ZACK)—1869-74—ss, Chicago Blue Stockings, Chicago Uniques
DANS, ____—1912—of, All Nations
DARBY, EDDY—1904—of, Philadelphia Giants
DARCY, DICK [see DORSEY, LUCIOUS]
DARDEN, CLARENCE—1938—3b, Atlanta Black Crackers
DARDEN, FLOYD—1950—2b, of, Baltimore Elite Giants
DARLO, ____—1935—2b, Havana Cubans
DARNBROUGH, ____—1888—p, Bloomington (IL) Reds
DARNELL, HERMAN—1951—1b, Indianapolis Clowns
DARRY, ____—1946—p, Brooklyn Brown Dodgers

DASLER, ____–1926–3b, Cleveland Elites
DAVAGE, EDWARD (ED)–1884–2b, Chicago Unknowns
DAVENPORT, LLOYD BENJAMON (BEAR MAN, DUCKY, HARAPOS [RAGS])–1934-51–of, manager, Monroe (LA) Monarchs, Philadelphia Stars, Cincinnati Tigers, Memphis Red Sox, Birmingham Black Barons, Chicago American Giants, Cleveland Buckeyes, Pittsburgh Crawfords, Louisville Buckeyes, Jacksonville Red Caps, New Orleans Crescent Stars, Cincinnati-Cleveland Buckeyes, Kansas City Monarchs
DAVIDS, CHARLIE–1926–owner, Newark Stars
DAVIDSON, ____–1909–p, Louisville Cubs
DAVIDSON, ____–1916–1b, West Baden (IN) Sprudels
DAVIDSON, CHARLES (SPECKS, SLIM)–1939-40, 1946-49–p, New York Black Yankees, Brooklyn Royal Giants, Baltimore Elite Giants, Memphis Red Sox
DAVIDSON, S.–1934–3b, Cleveland Red Sox
DAVIES, ____–1891–of, Cuban Giants
DAVIES, ____–1907–p, Philadelphia Giants
DAVIN, ____–1929–of, Boston Black Sox
DAVIS, ____–1867–c, Camden Resolutes
DAVIS, ____–1867–2b, Brooklyn Unique
DAVIS, ____–1879–of, Chicago Uniques
DAVIS, ____–1912–2b, Brown's Tennessee Rats
DAVIS, ____–1914-16–of, Indianapolis ABCs, Dayton Marcos
DAVIS, ____–1917–ss, Lost Island (IA) Giants
DAVIS, ____–1920–2b, p, Indianapolis ABCs
DAVIS, ____–1922–of, Cuban X-Giants
DAVIS, ____–1925–p, Gilkerson's Union Giants
DAVIS, ____–1926-27–1b, Cleveland Elites, Cleveland Hornets
DAVIS, ____–1928–p, Birmingham Black Barons
DAVIS, ____–1928–2b, Philadelphia Quaker City Giants
DAVIS, ____–1929–2b, Houston Black Buffaloes
DAVIS, ____–1929–ph, Schenectady Mohawks Giants
DAVIS, ____–1930–c, Colored House of David
DAVIS, ____–1930–ss, Havana Red Sox
DAVIS, ____–1930, 1934–p, Kansas City Monarchs
DAVIS, ____–1934–of, p, Gilkerson's Union Giants
DAVIS, ____–1935-37–of, 3b, p, Chicago Giants, Chicago American Giants
DAVIS, ____–1940–p, Brooklyn Royal Giants, New York Black Yankees
DAVIS, A. C.–1928–ss, Cleveland Tigers
DAVIS, A. G.–1887–umpire, NCBBL
DAVIS, A. L.–1924-25–ss, of, Indianapolis ABCs
DAVIS, ALBERT (GUNBOAT)–1925-37–p, Padron's Cuban Giants, Detroit Stars
DAVIS, AMBROSE–1886-97–ss, of, c, manager, Boston Resolutes (NCBBL), New York Gorhams (NCBBL)
DAVIS, ARTHUR–1916-17–of, Kansas City Tigers
DAVIS, AUSTIN–1941-46–ss, 3b, 2b, 1b, of, Newark Eagles, Homestead Grays, New York Black Yankees, Brooklyn Brown Dodgers
DAVIS, (BIG BOY)–1932–p, of, Indianapolis ABCs, Cuban Stars (East)
DAVIS, CHARLES (CHARLIE, LEFTY)–1953-55–p, Memphis Red Sox
DAVIS, (COUNTRY)–1939–of, Homestead Grays
DAVIS, DWIGHT–1930-31–p, Detroit Stars, Pittsburgh Crawfords
DAVIS, EARL (HAWK, HY, BUS)–1927-39–2b, Indianapolis ABCs, Bacharach (AC) Giants, Newark Browns, Hilldale Club, Philadelphia Giants, Newark Dodgers
DAVIS, EDWARD A. (EDDIE, PEANUTS, NYASSES)–1939-50–p, Cincinnati Ethiopian Clowns (NML), Cincinnati-Indianapolis Clowns, Indianapolis Clowns, Asheville Blues
DAVIS, EMMITT–1941-42–p, Detroit Black Sox
DAVIS, F. (RED)–1934, 1938–of, ss, Kansas City Monarchs, Jacksonville Red Caps
DAVIS, FRANK–1896-1904–officer, Cuban X-Giants
DAVIS, FRANK (BUNCH)–1906-11–ss, St. Paul Colored Gophers, Twin Cities Gophers, Minneapolis Keystones, Chicago American Giants
DAVIS, FRANK–1932–p, Cleveland Stars
DAVIS, FRANK–1945–p, Philadelphia Stars
DAVIS, FRED–1934–2b, Cleveland Red Sox
DAVIS, FRITZ [see DAVIS, OTIS]
DAVIS, G.–1938–c, Birmingham Black Barons
DAVIS, SR., GEORGE CARTER (CHIN)–1960-61–of, Kansas City Monarchs
DAVIS, (GOLDIE, RED)–1917, 1919, 1921, 1924–of, p, 1b, Indianapolis ABCs, Dayton Marcos
DAVIS, HORACE–1938–2b, Birmingham Black Barons
DAVIS, JACK–1918, 1922-25–ss, 3b, c, Bacharach (AC) Giants, Philadelphia Giants
DAVIS, JAMES–1920-21–p, Chicago Giants, Lincoln (NY) Giants, Kansas City Monarchs, Dayton Marcos
DAVIS, JAMES–1939–2b, Bacharach (Philly) Giants

DAVIS, JAMES (JIMMIE, NECKBONES)—1944, 1947-48—p, 3b, of, Jacksonville Eagles, Nashville Cubs, Chattanooga Choo Choos

DAVIS, JEFF—1926—p, ss, of, Montgomery Grey Sox

DAVIS, JOE—1909—p, Brooklyn Royal Giants, St. Paul Colored Gophers

DAVIS, JOE—1926-28—p, Atlanta Grey Sox

DAVIS, JOHN BARTON (JOHNNY)—1902-15—p, Chicago Columbia Giants, Leland Giants, Chicago Union Giants, Cuban Stars, Algona (IA) Brownies, St. Paul Colored Gophers, Twin City Gophers, French Lick (IN) Plutos, Chicago Giants

DAVIS, JOHN H.—1868—player, Philadelphia Pythians

DAVIS, JOHN HOWARD (CHEROKEE)—1940-50—of, Schenectady Mohawk Giants, Newark Eagles, North Classic Team, Houston Eagles, North All-Stars

DAVIS, JOHN HENRY (QUACK, DEADEYE, SMACK)—1907-10, 1913-15—of, p, Indianapolis ABCs, Louisville White Sox

DAVIS, L.B.—1929—officer, Shreveport Black Sports

DAVIS, LEE—1913-14, 1916—c, Chicago Union Giants

DAVIS, LEE ARTHUR—1945—p, Kansas City Monarchs, Philadelphia Stars

DAVIS, LELAND—1938—p, Chicago American Giants

DAVIS, LONNIE—1952—1b, Chicago American Giants

DAVIS, LORENZO (PIPER)—1942-50, 1958-59—1b, 2b, ss, manager, Birmingham Black Barons, North Classic Team, Homestead Grays, Washington (Yakima) Browns

DAVIS, JR., LORENZO (RUBINOFF, RUBE)—1959—of, 3b, c, Birmingham Black Barons

DAVIS, MARTIN LUTHER—1945—p, Chicago American Giants

DAVIS, NATHANIEL (NAT)—1945-51, 1959—1b, Brooklyn Brown Dodgers, New York Black Yankees, Philadelphia Stars, Raleigh (NC) Tigers

DAVIS, ODIE—1960-61—infield, of, Kansas City Monarchs

DAVIS, OTIS (FRITZ)—1945-47—ss, Detroit Motor City Giants, Cleveland Clippers, Detroit Wolves

DAVIS, (BIG PREACHER)—1920-21—3b, Jacksonville Stars, Atlanta Black Crackers, Columbus Buckeyes

DAVIS, RICHARD (DICK)—1887—c, Boston Resolutes (NCBBL)

DAVIS, RILEY MARCILOUS (PEACHES)—1916-18—p, Baltimore Black Sox

DAVIS, ROBERT—1912-23—3b, of, p, All Nations

DAVIS, ROBERT (DAGO, BIG)—1907-09—p, Cuban Giants, Philadelphia Giants

DAVIS, ROBERT LOMAX (BUTCH)—1944-50—of, Baltimore Elite Giants, Atlanta Black Crackers

DAVIS, ROOSEVELT (ROSEY, DURO, MACAN)—1924-45—p, St. Louis Stars, Columbus Blue Birds, Pittsburgh Crawfords, New York Black Yankees, Philadelphia Stars, Memphis Red Sox, Brooklyn Royal Giants, Baltimore Elite Giants, Chicago Brown Bombers (NML), Chicago American Giants, Cincinnati Ethiopian Clowns (NML), Cincinnati-Indianapolis Clowns, Indianapolis ABCs, Newark Eagles, Jacksonville Red Caps, Newark Dodgers, Cuban Stars (West)

DAVIS, ROSS (SATCHEL, SCHOOLBOY)—1940-47—p, Baltimore Elite Giants, Cleveland Buckeyes, Boston Blues, Birmingham Black Barons, New York Black Yankees

DAVIS, S.—1935—of, Chicago Giants

DAVIS, JR., SAUL HENRY (RAREBACK, DIXIE)—1921-31—3b, 2b, ss, Birmingham Black Barons, Cleveland Tigers, Memphis Red Sox, Chicago American Giants, Detroit Stars, Columbus Buckeyes, Chicago Giants

DAVIS, SHERMAN—1925—3b, Detroit Stars

DAVIS, SPENCER (JIMMY, BABE)—1936-48—of, ss, 2b, manager, Schenectady Mohawk Giants, Atlanta Black Crackers, Indianapolis ABCs, New York Black Yankees, Winston-Salem Giants, Brooklyn Eagles

DAVIS, SWELLIE—1912—c, Kansas City (KS) Giants

DAVIS, W.—1935—1b, Chicago Giants

DAVIS, WALTER C. (STEEL ARM)—1920-37—of, 1b, manager, Indianapolis ABCs, Detroit Stars, Chicago American Giants, Chicago Columbia Giants, Chicago Giants, Nashville Elite Giants, Brooklyn Eagles, Dayton Marcos, Washington (Yakima) Browns

DAVIS, WILLIAM (BUD)—1883-87—p, 3b, Chicago Gordons, Unions of New Orleans, St. Louis Blue Stockings, Boston Resolutes (NCBBL)

DAVIS, WILLIAM—1931—p, Baltimore Black Sox

DAVIS, WILLIAM (BILL)—1931-32—2b, Chicago Giants, Birmingham Black Barons

DAVIS, WILLIAM J.—1896-1904—officer, Cuban X-Giants

DAVIS, WILLIAM L. (BILL, BABE)—1935-40—3b, of, Chicago American Giants, St. Louis Stars, Atlanta Black Crackers, Indianapolis ABCs

DAVIS, WILLIAM NELSON (BILL, HOSS)—1938, 1940, 1945-47—p, Washington Black Senators, Newark Eagles, Jacksonville Red Caps, Philadelphia Stars

DAVIS, WILLIE—1945, 1957—officer, owner, Mobile Black Shippers, Mobile Havana Cuban Giants

DAVIS, WILSON—1939—p, Cleveland Bears

DAWKINS, ____–1921–umpire, NNL
DAWSON, ____–1910–p, Kansas City (KS) Giants
DAWSON, B.–1907-09–p, of, New York Colored Giants, Brooklyn Royal Giants, Cuban Giants
DAWSON, HOWARD–1931–p, Knoxville Giants
DAWSON, JOHNNY–1938-42–c, Memphis Red Sox, Kansas City Monarchs, Chicago American Giants, Birmingham Black Barons
DAWSON, LEROY (ROSSIE)–1946–manager, ph, Philadelphia Stars
DAY, EDWARD E. (EDDIE)–1891, 1898, 1902-04–of, ss, Philadelphia Giants, Cuban Giants, Celoron (NY) Acme Colored Giants (Iron & Oil League)
DAY, GUY–1885–c, Argyle Hotel
DAY, HENRY–1875–ss, St. Louis Blue Stockings
DAY, JEWELL–1946–1b, San Francisco Sea Lions
DAY, LEON–1934-50–p, utility, Baltimore Black Sox, Brooklyn Eagles, Newark Eagles, Baltimore Elite Giants, North All-Stars
DAY, WILSON CONNIE–1917, 1920-32, 1934, 1939–1b, 2b, 3b, ss, manager, Jewell's ABCs, Indianapolis ABCs, Baltimore Black Sox, Harrisburg Giants, Bacharach (AC) Giants, Hilldale Club, St. Louis Giants, Cleveland Royal Giants, Pullen's Royal Giants
DEAL, DAVID (JO JO)–1948–of, Newark Eagles
DEAN, BILL JOHNNY–1940-42–c, of, Philadelphia Stars
DEAN, CHARLES (CHARLIE)–1943, 1945, 1947–p, New York Black Yankees, New Orleans Black Pelicans
DEAN, GEORGIE–1943-45–c, New York Black Yankees, Philadelphia Hilldales (USL)
DEAN, JAMES ARTHUR (JIMMY)–1948-50–p, Philadelphia Stars
DEAN, NELSON–1925-33–p, Kansas City Monarchs, Cleveland Hornets, Cleveland Tigers, Detroit Stars, Cleveland Stars, Memphis Red Sox, Birmingham Black Barons, Detroit Giants
DEAN, ROBERT (BOBBY)–1923-34–3b, 2b, Schenectady Mohawk Giants, Philadelphia Royal Giants, Lincoln (NY) Giants, Penn Red Caps of NY, Homestead Grays
DEAN, ROBERT (BOB)–1937-40–p, St. Louis Stars, New Orleans-St. Louis Stars, Indianapolis ABCs
DEANE, ALPHEUS–1947–p, New York Black Yankees
DEAS, JAMES ALVIN (YANK)–1916-28–c, Bacharach (AC) Giants, Pennsylvania Giants, Lincoln (NY) Giants, Hilldale Club, Richmond Giants (NAA), Santop Broncos, Royal Poinciana (FL), Philadelphia Colored Giants of New York

DEASY, ____–1926–umpire, ECL
DEBERRY, C. I. (CHARLIE)–1948–manager, Greensboro (NC) Goshen Red Wings; vice-president, Negro American Association
DEBRAN, ROY–1940–of, New York Black Yankees
DEAGAN, ____–1888–of, Bloomington (IL) Reds
DEBOW, ____–1924–umpire, NNL
DEBRAN [DEBRAM], ROY–1940–of, New York Black Yankees
DECK [DEAK], WILLIAM (BILL)–1939–p, Bacharach (Philly) Giants, Philadelphia Stars
DECKER, CHARLES (DUSTY)–1929-38–c, 2b, ss, 3b, of, manager, Evansville Giants, Indianapolis ABCs, Montgomery Grey Sox, Detroit Stars, Memphis Red Sox, Louisville Black Colonels, Providence Giants, Cincinnati Tigers
DECUIR, LIONEL J.–1939-40–c, Kansas City Monarchs
DEDEAUX, RUSSELL LEWIS (RUSS)–1941, 1946–p, Newark Eagles, New York Black Yankees, Los Angeles White Sox
DEDMAN, ROY–1949–c, Durham (NC) Eagles
DEDRICK, JOHN L.–1935–booking agent, Brooklyn Eagles
DEES, CHARLES HENRY (CHARLIE)–1954–1b, Louisville Clippers
DEFRID, ____–1931–c, Newark Browns
DEGE, ____–1929–p, Cuban Stars (East)
DEIMER, ____–1930–p, Louisville White Caps
DEJERNETT, ____–1939–p, Indianapolis ABCs
DeJUAN [DEJUAM], ARMANDO–1923–of, All Cubans
De La CRUZ y RIVERO, TOMÁS (TOMMY)–1934–p, Cuban Havana Stars
DELANEY, FRED DOUGLAS (POP)–1904-05, 1910-12–2b, ss, of Brooklyn Royal Giants, Pittsburgh Giants
DELGADO, CLEMENTE De La CRUZ–1931-33–of, Philadelphia Royal Giants
DELGADO, FELIX RAFAEL (FELLE)–1936-41–of, New York Cubans, Cuban Stars
DELMAN, ____–1934–ss, Homestead Grays
DeLUGO, ____–1935–p, New York Cubans
DEMENT, ____–1928–c, Nashville Elite Giants
DEMERY, ARTIS T. (ART, SMOKEY)–1941, 1946–of, p, Baltimore Elite Giants, San Francisco Sea Lions
DeMEZA [see D'MEZA, ANGEL]
DeMOSS, ELWOOD (BINGO)–1905-46–2b, manager, Topeka (KS) Giants, Kansas City (KS) Giants, Oklahoma City Monarchs, Indianapolis ABCs, Chicago American Giants,

Chicago Giants, Detroit Stars, Cleveland Giants, Bowser's ABCs, Akron Tyrites, Newark Dodgers, Royal Poinciana (FL), Chicago Brown Bombers (NML)

DEMPSEY, ____—1921—p, Lincoln (NY) Giants

DENIKE, ____—1867—1b, Utica (NY) Fearless

DENIS, ____—1923—2b, All Cubans

DENNARD, RICHARD (DICK, DOCK)—1937, 1945-46—of, Jacksonville Eagles, Toledo Cubs/Rays, Detroit Stars

DENNIS, ____— 1923—p, Bacharach (AC) Giants

DENNIS, J.—1930—2b, Columbus Keystones

DENNIS, WESLEY LEWIS (DOC)—1943-55—1b, Baltimore Elite Giants, Philadelphia Stars, Birmingham Black Barons

DENNY, ____—1888—of, 3b, Hoosier Black Stockings

DENNY, ____—1924—p, All Nations

DENODER, ____—1927-28—umpire, NNL

DENT, ____—1869—2b, Washington Alerts

DENT, CARL JONVON—1950-55—ss, Indianapolis Clowns, Philadelphia Stars

DENTON, ____—1918—of, Penn Red Caps

DERMUND, ____—1884—2b, Brooklyn Alpines

DeROSE [DeROSS] ____—1936-37—umpire, NAL

DERR, DOLL—1925—umpire, World Series

DERRICK, EDWARD LEE (LEFTY)—1945-51—p, Nashville Black Vols, Nashville Cubs, Baltimore Elite Giants

DERRICK, LEON (L. B., LEO)—1925-27—secretary, Detroit Stars

DESHIELD, ____—1948—p, Philadelphia Stars

DESPERT [DESPERATE], DANIEL JAMES (HARRY, DANNY, DENNY)—1914-17—of, Lincoln (NY) Giants, Brooklyn Royal Giants, Philadelphia Giants; —1922-23, 1926—umpire, NNL, ECL

DEVEAN, ____—1908—c, New York Colored Giants

DEVEREAUX, ____—1902-06—c, 1b, Philadelphia Giants, Philadelphia Quaker City Giants

DEVERS, ____—1950—p, Houston Eagles

DEVINNEY, CHARLES—1876, 1887—of, Chicago Uniques

DEVOE, JAMES R. (JIMMIE, JIMMY, JOSH)—1915-19—c, Chicago Giants, Pittsburgh Keystones; 1921-23—business manager, Cleveland Tate Stars; 1923-24, 1935-41—umpire, NNL

DEVON, ____—1933—of, Philadelphia Stars [see DIXON, HERBERT ALBERT]

DEVORE, [see DEVOE, JOSH]—1923-24—umpire, ECL

DEVOTEZ, ____—1923—p, Cuban Stars (West)

DEWBERRY [DUBERRY], WILLIAM JAMES—1903-04, 1908—c, p, 2b, Minneapolis Keystones, Chicago Union Giants, Leland Giants

DEWITT, FRED—1922-30—1b, ss, Houston Black Buffaloes, Kansas City Monarchs, Cleveland Tigers, Memphis Red Sox, Hilldale Club

DeWITT, SAMUEL R. (EDDIE, S.R.)—1917-26—3b, 2b, Dayton Giants, Dayton Marcos, Indianapolis ABCs, Columbus Buckeyes, Toledo Tigers

DIAGO, MIXIMO—1952—c, Kansas City Monarchs

DIAL, KERMIT NATHERN—1932-40—2b, ss, 3b, of, p, Columbus Blue Birds, Cole's Chicago American Giants, Detroit Stars, Cincinnati Buckeyes

DIALS, OLAND CECIL (LOU)—1925-36—1b, of, Detroit Stars, Chicago American Giants, Memphis Red Sox, Hilldale Club, Cleveland Giants, Homestead Grays, Akron Tyrites, Birmingham Black Barons, New York Black Yankees

DIAMOND, (LEFTY) [see PIPKIN, ROBERT]

DÍAZ y PEDROSO, FERNANDO (EL BICHO)—1943-50—2b, of, p, New York Cubans

DÍAZ, HELIODORO EDOLFO (YOYO)—1926-39—p, New York Cubans, Cuban Stars (West)

DÍAZ, MARIO—1947—2b, New York Cubans

DÍAZ, PABLO MESA—1930-35—c, 1b, Cuban Stars (West), New York Cubans

DIBUT y VILLAFAÑA, PEDRO—1923—p, Cuban Stars (West)

DICK, [see DECK, WILLIAM]

DICKERSON, ____—1891—of, Cuban Giants, New York Gorhams

DICKERSON, JR., JOHN WILLIS—1950-51—of, 2b, Chicago American Giants, Memphis Red Sox

DICKERSON, JOHN FOUNT (BABE)—1947, 1950—p, Asheville Blues, Houston Eagles

DICKERSON, LOU—1921—p, Hilldale Club

DICKEY, WALTER CLAUDE (STEEL ARM, JOHN)—1920-22—p, Montgomery Grey Sox, St. Louis Stars, St. Louis Giants, Birmingham Black Barons, Knoxville Giants

DICKEY, JR., WILLIAM ALBERT (BILL)—1951, 1953—p, Kansas City Monarchs

DICKINS, ____—1945—p, Cincinnati Ethiopian Clowns (NML)

DICKINSON [DICKERSON], SAMUEL—1909-1911, owner, West Baden (IN) Sprudels

DICKSON, ____—1891—c, New York Colored Giants

DIDDLEY, ____—1948—p, Birmingham Clowns

DIECKERT, ____–1943–3b, New York Cubans

DIGGS, LEON–1953-56, 1960–of, 3b, Indianapolis Clowns, New York Black Yankees, Kansas City Monarchs, Raleigh (NC) Tigers

DIHIGO y LLANOS, MARTÍN [MARTEEN] MAGDALENO (EL MAESTRO, EL INMORTAL)–1923-45–2b, p, of, ss, 3b, 1b, manager, Cuban Stars (East), New York Cubans, Homestead Grays, Hilldale Club, Darby Daisies, Baltimore Black Sox

DILLARD, ____–1937–infield, St. Louis Stars

DILLARD, JAMES–1928–2b, Louisville White Sox

DILLARD, LAMON JACK (a.k.a. ARNIE)–1927, 1930-33–p, Lincoln (NY) Giants, Bacharach (Philly) Giants, Penn Red Caps of NY, Chicago American Giants, Brooklyn Cuban Giants

DILLON, ____–1931–umpire, ECL

DILLON, JIM (BIG MITT)–1947-51–3b, Colored House of David, Kansas City Monarchs, Satchel Paige All-Stars, Kansas City (KS) Giants

DILWORTH, ARTHUR–1916-19–p, of, c, Bacharach (AC) Giants, Hilldale Club, Lincoln (NY) Giants

DIMES, EDWIN CHARLES–1926, 1933, 1937–of, Dayton Marcos, Akron Tyrites, New York Black Yankees

DIREAUX [DIREUX], JIMMY–1937-39–p, of, Washington Elite Giants, Baltimore Elite Giants

DISMUKES, WILLIAM (DIZZY)–1909-58–p, manager, coach, NNL secretary, club secretary, Philadelphia Giants, Brooklyn Royal Giants, Schenectady Mohawk Giants, Indianapolis ABCs, Chicago American Giants, Dayton Marcos, Lincoln (NY) Stars, Pittsburgh Keystones, Memphis Red Sox, St. Louis Stars, Cincinnati Dismukes, Detroit Wolves, Homestead Grays, Columbus Blue Birds, Birmingham Black Barons, Kansas City Monarchs, West Baden (IN) Sprudels, Lincoln (NY) Giants, St. Louis Giants, Detroit Motor City Giants, Minneapolis Keystones, Detroit Tigers (independent)

DIXIE, ____–1912–of, Lincoln (NY) Giants

DIXON, ____–1922–umpire, ECL

DIXON, ____–1931–p, Cuban Stars (West)

DIXON, ____–1940–p, Chicago Giants

DIXON, EDDIE LEE (ED, BULLET)–1938-39–p, Atlanta Black Crackers, Indianapolis ABCs, Baltimore Elite Giants

DIXON, FRANK–1950–3b, Birmingham Black Barons

DIXON, GEORGE (TUBBY)–1914, 1917-31, 1934–c, Havana Red Sox, Chicago American Giants, Indianapolis ABCs, Birmingham Black Barons, Cleveland Hornets, Cleveland Tigers, Cleveland Cubs, Cleveland Red Sox, Royal Poinciana (FL)

DIXON, GLENN–1937-38–of, p, St. Louis Stars, Memphis Red Sox

DIXON, HERBERT ALBERT (RAP)–1922-37–of, manager, Harrisburg Giants, Baltimore Black Sox, Chicago American Giants, Hilldale Club, Darby Daisies, Pittsburgh Crawfords, Philadelphia Stars, Brooklyn Eagles, Homestead Grays, New York Cubans, Washington Potomacs, Newark Eagles, Philadelphia Royal Giants

DIXON, JOHN–1929-30–officer, Louisville Black Caps

DIXON, JOHN–1950–p, Chicago American Giants, Birmingham Black Barons, Homestead Grays

DIXON, JOHN ROBERT (JOHNNY BOB)–1926-34–p, Cleveland Tigers, Detroit Stars, Cuban Stars (East & West), Cleveland Giants, Cleveland Red Sox, Indianapolis ABCs, Chicago American Giants, Havana Red Sox, Cuban House of David, St. Louis Giants, Chattanooga Black/White Lookouts

DIXON, L.–1916–p, Montgomery Grey Sox

DIXON, LEONA–1929–officer, Louisville Black Caps

DIXON, SR., PAUL PERRY (DICK)–1931-38–of, Bacharach (Philly) Giants, Baltimore Black Sox, Washington Pilots, Philadelphia Stars, Newark Browns

DIXON, RANDY–1934–officer, Philadelphia Stars; writer, *Philadelphia Tribune*

DIXON, STEVEN–1914-16–p, Chicago American Giants, Chicago Giants

DIXON, TED–1955–of, Detroit Stars

DIXON, JR., THOMAS (TOM)–1930-40–c, Baltimore Black Sox, Bacharach (Philly) Giants, Hilldale Club, Washington Pilots, Baltimore Elite Giants, Providence Giants

DIXON, W.–1920–2b, ss, of, Nashville White Sox, Atlanta Black Crackers

DOBBINS, ED–1952–2b, Chicago American Giants

DOBBINS, NATHAN (NAT)–1921–ss, Hilldale Club

DOBY, SR., LAWRENCE (LARRY) EUGENE [a.k.a. LARRY WALKER]–1942-47–2b, Newark Eagles, Great Lakes Bluejackets

DOCK, LACY LEE–1918-19–ss, Dayton Marcos

DOCTOR, EDWARD W.–1883–1b, Cleveland Blue Stockings

DOHRMAN, ____–1869–of, Philadelphia Excelsior

DOLAN, TOM–1882–officer, St. Louis Black Stockings

DOLEMAN, EDWARD–1928-29–of, Louisville White Sox

DOMINGUEZ, JUSTO–1921, 1925–p, New York Cuban Stars, Cuban Stars (West)

DONALD, ____–1920–ph, Knoxville Giants
DONALD, ED or TED–1947–utility, Detroit Wolves [see TEASLEY, RONALD]
DONALD, GEORGE–1908-10–ss, manager, Birmingham Giants, San Antonio Black Broncos, Oklahoma City Monarchs, Oklahoma City Giants
DONALD, SYLVESTER–1959-60–infield, Kansas City Monarchs
DONALDSON, JOHN WESLEY–1908-34–p, of, Glasgow (MO) Hannaca Blues, Higbee (MO) Tigers, Brown's Tennessee Rats, All Nations, Kansas City Colts, Royal Poinciana (FL), LeHigh (IA), Bertha (MN), Lismore (MN), Madison (MN), Minneola (MN), Radville (SASK), Plentywood (MT), Moose Jaw (SASK), Melrose (MN), Scobey (MT), Gilkerson's Union Giants, Colored House of David, Cuban House of David, St. Cloud (MN), Los Angeles White Sox, Chicago Giants, Indianapolis ABCs, Kansas City Monarchs, Detroit Stars, Brooklyn Royal Giants, John Donaldson All-Stars, Satchel Paige All-Stars; 1949-?, scout, Chicago White Sox
DONALDSON, WILLIAM WILSON (W.W., BILLY)–1923-37–umpire, NNL
DONEGAN, ALBERT–1887–officer, Chicago Unions
DONELLY, ____–1938–3b, Memphis Red Sox
DONNELL, HERMAN (LEE)–1952–of, Indianapolis Clowns
DONNELLY, ____–1914–ph, All Nations
DONOSO y GALATA, LINO–1947-49–p, New York Cubans
DOOLAN, MIKE–1924–umpire, World Series
DOOLEY, ____–1933–of, Kansas City Monarchs
DOOLEY, ____–1934–p, Homestead Grays
DOOLEY, ____–1951–p, Kansas City Monarchs
DORIS, ____–1883–p, St. Louis Black Stockings
DORSEN, ANDREW–1867–manager, Brooklyn Monitors
DORSEY, ____–1927–p, Baltimore Black Sox
DORSEY, F. T.–1884-87–of, 2b, Baltimore Lord Baltimore, Baltimore Atlantics
DORSEY, HANK–1941–of, Philadelphia Stars, Otto Brigg's All-Stars
DORSEY, LUCIOUS–1941-42–of, Philadelphia Stars, Philadelphia Daisies (NML)
DORSEY, ROY–1910–of, p, Kansas City Cyclones, Kansas City (KS) Giants
DORTON, ____–1883–3b, p, Cleveland Blue Stockings
DOSTER, LEROY [a.k.a. Satchel Paige, Jr.]–1964–1b, p, Satchel Paige All-Stars

DOTSON, A.–1932–p, Bacharach (Philly) Giants
DOTSON, J.J.–1920–secretary, Texas Negro League, Fort Worth Black Panthers
DOUGHERTY, ____–1909–1b, Kansas City (MO) Royal Giants
DOUGHERTY, ____–1940–p, Chicago Giants
DOUGHERTY, CHARLES (PAT, KING)–1909-15–p, Leland Giants, Chicago American Giants, Chicago Giants
DOUGHERTY, GEORGE–1885–of, Brooklyn Remsens
DOUGHERTY, LON–1935–p, Brooklyn Eagles
DOUGHERTY, ROMEO LIONEL–1922-1935–writer, *New York Amsterdam News*
DOUGLAS, DALE FRED–1945–p, Indianapolis Clowns
DOUGLAS, EDDIE–1922–of, St. Louis Stars
DOUGLAS, GEORGE–1904–p, Cuban Giants
DOUGLAS, GEORGE WILLIAM–1885, 1891-92–of, p, Brooklyn Remsens, Ansonia Cuban Giants (Connecticut St. League), Cuban Giants
DOUGLAS, JESSE WARREN–1937-51–2b, 3b, ss, of, Kansas City Monarchs, Birmingham Black Barons, Chicago American Giants, Memphis Red Sox, New York Black Yankees, New Orleans Eagles
DOUGLAS, JIM–1951–p, Chicago American Giants
DOUGLASS, ____–1889–ss, New Orleans Pinchbacks
DOUGLASS, BILL–1870-71–of, p, Mutuals of Washington
DOUGLASS, CHARLES REMOND–1866-71–3b, of, p, secretary, Rochester Unexpected, Washington Alerts, Mutuals of Washington
DOUGLASS, E.–1912–1b, Kansas City (KS) Giants
DOUGLASS, EDWARD (EDDIE)–1918-29–1b, manager, Brooklyn Royal Giants, Lincoln (NY) Giants, Breakers Hotel (FL)
DOUSE, JOSEPH SOLOMON (JOE, SOL)–1952-53–p, of, Kansas City Monarchs
DOVE, ARTHUR–1946-50, 1958-61–owner, Raleigh (NC) Tigers
DOWNER, FREDERICK DOUGLASS (FRED)–1920-24–of, Pittsburgh Keystones, Baltimore Black Sox, Pittsburgh Crawfords, Cleveland Tate Stars, Knoxville Giants, Atlanta Black Crackers
DOWNING, ____–1880–cf, Washington Douglass Club
DOWNING, D. W.–1883–business manager, Douglass Club of Pittsburg(h)
DOWNS, ELLSWORTH–1887–player, Cincinnati Browns (NCBBL)

DOWNS, McKINLEY (BUNNY)—1915-43, 1955—2b, manager, St. Louis Giants, Bacharach (AC) Giants, Hilldale Club, Brooklyn Royal Giants, Brooklyn Cuban Giants, Philadelphia Tigers, Cincinnati (Ethiopian) Clowns, Indianapolis ABCs, West Baden (IN) Sprudels, Louisville White Sox, Harrisburg Giants, Richmond Giants (NAA), Indianapolis Clowns, Wilmington Potomacs, Montgomery Grey Sox, Breakers Hotel (FL)

DOYLE, JOSEPH S.—1926-60—umpire, ECL

DRAKE, ANDREW—1930-32—c, p, Birmingham Black Barons, Chattanooga Black Lookouts, Cole's Chicago American Giants, Nashville Elite Giants, Louisville Black Caps

DRAKE, ANDY—1939—p, St. Louis Stars

DRAKE, EMERY—1926, 1938, 1942-43—c, p, Memphis Red Sox, Indianapolis ABCs, Chicago Brown Bombers (NML)

DRAKE, SAMUEL HARRISON (SAMMY)—1953—3b, Kansas City Monarchs, Memphis Red Sox

DRAKE, [DR.] W. H.—1899—promoter, Adrian (MI) Page Fence Giants

DRAKE, WILLIAM P. (PLUNK, BILL)—1914-30—p, manager, All Nations, Brown's Tennessee Rats, St. Louis Giants, St. Louis Stars, Kansas City Monarchs, Indianapolis ABCs, Detroit Stars, Memphis Red Sox, Tulsa Black Oilers

DRAPER, ____—1918—of, Pennsylvania Giants

DREKE y VERDES, REYNALDO—1945-57—of, Cincinnati-Indianapolis Clowns, Indianapolis Clowns

DREKE [DRAKE], VALENTÍN—1919-28—of, Cuban Stars (East & West), Cincinnati Cuban Stars

DREW, ____—1899—3b, Cuban Giants

DREW, ____—1921, 1926—p, Jewell ABCs, Montgomery Grey Sox

DREW, JOHN M. (JOHNNY)—1931-32—officer, Darby Daisies, Hilldale Club

DREW, JR., LEVI (CHAMPIE)—1956—1b, of, New York Black Yankees

DREW, P. (LEFTY)—1939—of, p, Indianapolis ABCs

DRISCOLL, CLYDE—1958—p, Detroit Clowns

DRUMMER, ____—1911—of, Louisville Cubs

DRUMMER, ____—1948—p, Newark Eagles

DRUMMOND, JAMES J.—1959, 1961—manager, p, Raleigh (NC) Tigers

DRYDEN, ____—1916—of, Penn Red Caps of NY

DUANY y YEDRA, CLARO—1944-47—of, New York Cubans

DUBERRY, ____—1944—p, Birmingham Black Barons

DUBETS [DUBBETTS, DUBETTS], AL—1950—p, Chicago American Giants

DUBISSON, DANIEL J.—1932—officer; Little Rock Grays

DuBOSE, SR., [DeBOSE, DeBOIS], CLIFFORD JOE (POP)—1958—utility, Memphis Red Sox

DUCEY, EDWARD (EDDIE, GOLDIE)—1924-26, 1933—of, St. Louis Giants, Dayton Marcos, Bacharach (AC) Giants

DUCKETT, MAHLON NEWTON (JOHN, MAL, DUCK)—1940-50—3b, 2b, ss, Philadelphia Stars, Homestead Grays

DUCY, EDDIE—1946-47—2b, ss, Cincinnati Crescents, Homestead Grays, Portland (OR) Rosebuds

DUDLEY, JR., CHARLES ARTHUR (C.A., DOC)—1920-23—of, St. Louis Giants, St. Louis Stars

DUDLEY, EDWARD—1862—1b, Brooklyn Monitors

DUDLEY, EDWARD—1925-28, 1932—p, Lincoln (NY) Giants, Brooklyn Cuban Giants, Philadelphia Tigers, Washington Pilots, Newark Browns

DUDLEY, JAMES (BIG TRAIN)—1943-45—c, Baltimore Elite Giants, Nashville Black Vols

DUDLEY, JAMES H.—1882-83—manager, Richmond Swans

DUDLEY, WILLIAM (SMILING BILL)—1935, 1937—p, Detroit Cubs, Detroit Stars

DUEY, ____—1923—of, Havana Red Sox

DUFF, ERNEST—1925-32—of, Indianapolis ABCs, Cleveland Elites, Cleveland Hornets, Cleveland Tigers, Cuban Stars (West), Brooklyn Royal Giants, Chicago American Giants

DUFFEY, ____—1936—3b, Newark Eagles

DUFFY, ____—1910—2b, ss, French Lick (IN) Plutos

DUFFY, BILL—1946-47—c, Cincinnati Crescents, Kansas City Monarchs

DUGANS, ____—1918—of, Havana Red Sox

DUKE, JAMES M. (JIMMY)—1883—p, St. Louis Black Stockings

DUKES, ____—1912—1b, Brown's Tennessee Rats

DUKES, SR., TOMMIE (DIXIE)—1928-40, 1945—c, Chicago American Giants, Memphis Red Sox, Evansville Giants, Nashville Elite Giants, Columbus Elite Giants, Homestead Grays, Toledo Crawfords, Indianapolis Crawfords, Birmingham Black Barons, Cuban Stars (West)

DULA, LOUIS EDWARD—1933-39—p, of, Cincinnati Tigers, Homestead Grays

DUMAS, LAFAYETTE NAPOLEON (JIM)—1940-41—p, of, Memphis Red Sox

DUMOND, ____—1891—1b, New York Colored Giants

DUMPSON, SR., WILLIAM GARFIELD (BILL, SHOWBOAT)—1950-53—p, Indianapolis Clowns, Philadelphia Stars, New York Black Yankees
DUNBAR, ____—1888—of, Rockford (IL) Rockfords
DUNBAR, ART—1912-15—1b, of, All Nations
DUNBAR, ASHBY COLUMBUS—1907-20—of, Brooklyn Royal Giants, Lincoln (NY) Stars, Indianapolis ABCs, Penn Red Caps of NY, Lincoln (NY) Giants, Schenectady Mohawk Giants, Chicago American Giants, Louisville White Sox, Philadelphia Giants, Pittsburgh Giants, Chicago Black Sox, Paterson (NJ) Smart Set, Royal Poinciana (FL)
DUNBAR, JOHNNY (VET)—1930, 1934, 1937, 1941—c, Houston Black Buffaloes, New Orleans Crescent Stars, Memphis Red Sox, Indianapolis Athletics, Cincinnati Buckeyes
DUNCAN, ____—1926—umpire, ECL
DUNCAN, CHARLIE (SCOTTIE)—1938-40—p, Atlanta Black Crackers, Indianapolis ABCs, St. Louis Stars, Cincinnati Tigers, New Orleans-St. Louis Stars
DUNCAN, ED (DUKE)—1945, 1947—3b, Detroit Motor City Giants, Detroit Wolves
DUNCAN [DUNBAR], FRANK (PETE, REBEL)—1907-28—of, manager, Philadelphia Giants, Leland Giants, Chicago American Giants, Detroit Stars, Chicago Giants, Toledo Tigers, Cleveland Elites, Cleveland Hornets, Cleveland Tigers, Milwaukee Bears, Twin City Gophers, Royal Poinciana (FL)
DUNCAN, JR., FRANK LEE (DUNK, BAT BOY)—1920-48—c, of, manager, umpire, Chicago Giants, Kansas City Monarchs, New York Harlem Stars, Pittsburgh Crawfords, Homestead Grays, New York Cubans, Chicago American Giants, Philadelphia Royal Giants
DUNCAN, III, FRANK LEE—1941, 1945-49—p, Kansas City Monarchs, Baltimore Elite Giants, Chicago American Giants, Chicago Palmer House Stars
DUNCAN, JOE—1922, 1927—c, Bacharach (AC) Giants
DUNCAN, JR., JOSEPH T. (JOE)—1954—1b, p, Indianapolis Clowns
DUNCAN, MELVIN LUTHER (BUCK)—1949-51, 1955—p, of, Kansas City Monarchs, Detroit Stars
DUNCAN, WARREN—1922-27—of, Bacharach (AC) Giants, Bacharach (NY) Giants
DUNES, MEL [see DUNCAN, MELVIN]
DUNKIN, ESCOTTA (STRINGBEAN) [a.k.a. ISHOOKA DUNCAN]—1935-38—p, Pittsburgh Crawfords, Atlanta Black Crackers, Birmingham Black Barons
DUNLAP, HERMAN—1936-39—of, Chicago American Giants
DUNLAP, WALDO (CAVE CREEK)—1944, 1946, 1949-50—p, Atlanta Black Crackers, Asheville Blues
DUNMORE, AL—writer, *Pittsburgh Courier*
DUNN, ____—1888—c, Bloomington (IL) Reds
DUNN, ____—1917—p, Dayton Marcos
DUNN, ____—1954—ss, Detroit Stars, Louisville Clippers
DUNN, ALPHONSE (BLUE, ALLIE, AL)—1937-43, 1947-48—1b, Detroit Stars, New York Cubans, Birmingham Black Barons, Harlem Globetrotters, Cincinnati Crescents
DUNN, EUGENE—1945—2b, Asheville Blues
DUNN, JR., JOSEPH P. (JAKE)—1929-41—ss, of, 2b, manager, Pullen's Royal Giants, Detroit Stars, Washington Pilots, Nashville Elite Giants, Baltimore Black Sox, Philadelphia Stars, Baltimore Elite Giants
DUNN, WILLIE—1942—p, Jacksonville Red Caps
DUNSON, ____—1934—3b, Cincinnati Tigers
DUNVILLE, LARRY—umpire, NAL
DUPUIS (DUPREES), MURRAY (JOE)—1913—of, 2b, Indianapolis ABCs
DURAND, ____—1920—2b, ss, New Orleans Crescent Stars
DURANT, ____—1862—of, Unknown Base Ball Club (of Weeksville, NY)
DURANT, EDWARD (EAGLE) [see JURAN, ELI]
DURANTE, JIMMY—1960-61—infield, Raleigh (NC) Tigers
DURHAM, JOSEPH VAN (WINN, POP)—1951-52—of, Chicago American Giants
DURRUH, ____—1927—c, Baltimore Black Sox
DURVANT, ____—1923—p, Cuban Stars (West)
DUTTON, ____—1867—p, Camden Resolutes
DUVAL, CLARENCE—1888-89—mascot, Spalding Base Ball World Tour
DUVAL, PAUL—1939—3b, of, Philadelphia Stars
DWIGHT, SR., EDWARD JOSEPH (EDDIE, PEE WEE)—1924-37—of, Indianapolis ABCs, Kansas City Monarchs, Gilkerson's Union Giants
DYER, ARTHUR B.—1936—officer, St. Louis Stars
DYER, JOE—1946—utility, Pittsburgh Stars
DYKE, JR., WILLIAM ROBERT (LEFTY)—1942—p, Jacksonville Red Caps, Chicago American Giants, Newark Eagles
DYKES, A.—1927, 1929—2b, Evansville Giants, Birmingham Black Barons
DYKES, JONATHAN—1925-27, 1932—officer, Bacharach (AC) Giants, Washington Pilots
DYLL [DYALL], FRANK R.—1950—ss, Chicago American Giants
DYSON, BENJAMIN—1876, 1879—3b, 1b, Chicago Uniques

DYSON, MAJOR—1950—ss, New York Black Yankees

Courtesy of author, *Ebony*, December 1949

E

EACY, ____—1937—p, Pittsburgh Crawfords

EAGLE, ____—1931—of, Knoxville Giants

EAGLESTON, ____—1928—3b, Kansas City (KS) Giants

EARL, ____—1859—3b, Unknown Base Ball Club (of Weeksville, NY)

EARL, JOE—1964—p, Satchel Paige All-Stars

EARLE, CHARLES BABCOCK (FRANK, PELES)—1906-19—of, p, manager, Wilmington Giants, Cuban Giants, Philadelphia Giants, Brooklyn Royal Giants, Lincoln (NY) Giants, Bacharach (AC) Giants, Penn Red Caps of NY, Grand Central Terminal Red Caps

EARLE, JR., JAMES W.—1954—infield, Detroit Stars

EARLY, ____—1923—1b, Kansas City Monarchs [see ROGAN, BULLET]

EASLEY, HENRY (PETE)—1936—of, Memphis Red Sox

EASTE, ____—1923—p, Hilldale Club

EASTER, LUSCIOUS (LUKE)—1939, 1946-48—of, 1b, St. Louis Giants, Cincinnati Crescents, Homestead Grays

EASTERLING, HOWARD WILLIS (HO)—1936-49—3b, ss, 2b, Cincinnati Tigers, Chicago American Giants, Homestead Grays, New York Cubans, Indianapolis ABCs, South All-Stars, Washington (Yakima) Browns

EATMON [EATON, EATMAN], ELBERT BOE—1937-38—p, Birmingham Black Barons

ECHEVARRÍA, RAFAEL—1938—2b, New York Cubans

ECHOLS, ____—1924—umpire, NSL

ECHOLS [ECKLES], JOE—1939—of, Newark Eagles

ECHOLS, MELVIN JIM (SUNNY)—1943-46—p, of, manager, Atlanta Black Crackers

ECKELSON [EKELSON], JUAN (BICICLETA)—1925—p, Cuban Stars (West)

ECORA, ____—1926—p, Brooklyn Royal Giants

EDELIN, WILLIAM J.—1909—president, Washington Giants

EDGAR, J. NELSON—1858—secretary, Unknown Base Ball Club (of Weeksville, NY)

EDMOND, CARL—1934—p, Padron's Cuban Giants

EDSALL, GEORGE—1898—of, Celoron (NY) Acme Colored Giants (Iron & Oil League)

EDWARDS, CHANCELLOR D. (BIG JACK, PEP)—1928—c, Cleveland Tigers

EDWARDS, CY (a.k.a. KID BOOTS)—1908—of, Pop Watkins Stars, Brooklyn Royal Giants

EDWARDS, FRANK NUTINOUS (TEANNIE)—1936-37—c, St. Louis Stars, Cincinnati Tigers, Homestead Grays

EDWARDS, GEORGE (TACKY)—1945-47, 1950-51—ss, Boston Blues, Baltimore Elite Giants, Detroit Senators, Asheville Blues

EDWARDS, JACK—1925-27—p, Atlanta Black Crackers, Memphis Red Sox, St. Louis Stars

EDWARDS, JAMES (SMOKEY)—1913-22—p, of, c, Schenectady Mohawk Giants, Philadelphia Giants, Louisville White Sox, Lincoln (NY) Giants

EDWARDS, JESSE (JOHNNY)—1920-31—2b, of, Nashville Elite Giants, Birmingham Black Barons, Memphis Red Sox, Chattanooga Black Lookouts

EDWARDS, NATHANIEL (NATE, SNOOKUMS)—1918-19—of, p, Lincoln (NY) Stars, Bacharach (AC) Giants, Penn Red Caps of New York

EDWARDS, OSEE—1950—of, New York Black Yankees

EDWARDS, PHILIP NATHANIEL—1948—p, Birmingham Black Barons

EDWARDS, PRINCE—1922—umpire, Western League of Colored Baseball Clubs

EDWARDS, WILLIAM (WEEDY)—1944, 1947—p, Kansas City Monarchs, Newark Eagles

EGGLESTON, JR., MACAJAH MARCHAND (MACK, EGG, CAGER)—1917-34—c, of, 3b, 2b, ss, 1b, p, Dayton Giants, Dayton Marcos, Detroit Stars, Indianapolis ABCs, Washington Potomacs, Columbus Buckeyes, Wilmington Potomacs, Harrisburg Giants, Baltimore Black Sox, Bacharach (AC) Giants, Bacharach (Philly) Giants, New York Harlem Stars, Washington Pilots, Homestead Grays, Nashville Elite Giants, Lincoln (NY) Giants

EGGLESTON, WILLIAM—1885—ss, Argyle Hotel

EILER, ____—1921—umpire, NNL

EKELSON, [see ECKELSON, JUAN]

ELAM, ED—1932—p, Bacharach (Philly) Giants

ELAM, JR., JAMES THOMAS (JIM)—1943—p, Newark Eagles

ELBY, TRAVIS HENRY—1890—vice-president, Chicago Unions

ELDER, CHARLES—1913—ss, All Nations

ELDRIDGE, WILLIAM (BILLY) M.—1959-60—ss, Raleigh (NC) Tigers

ELLERBE, LACY (FOX)—1950—p, Baltimore Elite Giants

ELLERTON, ____—1922—p, Richmond Giants

ELLIOTT, EUGENE—1956—3b, Kansas City Monarchs

ELLIOTT, JOSEPH (JOE)—1954-59—p, Detroit Stars, Memphis Red Sox, Louisville Clippers, Birmingham Black Barons, New York Black Yankees
ELLIS, ____—1911—ss, West Baden (IN) Sprudels
ELLIS, ALBERT—1950—p, Cleveland Buckeyes
ELLIS, BILL (SPECS)—1940, 1942, 1944—p, of, Cleveland Browns, Birmingham Black Barons
ELLIS, GEORGE—1947—3b, Detroit Senators
ELLIS, JAMES MOONEY—1913, 1919, 1921-28—1b, 3b, of, Chicago Union Giants, Jewell's ABCs, Memphis Red Sox, Nashville Elite Giants, Cleveland Browns, Cleveland Tate Stars, St. Louis Giants
ELLIS, JOSH—1921—1b, Dayton Marcos
ELLIS, RAYMOND CHARLES [GLEN] (RUBE, RED, ROCKY)—1925-44—p, of, Hilldale Club, Philadelphia Stars, Homestead Grays, Jacksonville Red Caps, Baltimore Grays, Bacharach (Philly) Giants, Birmingham Black Barons
ELLISON, JEAN E. (EARLY BIRD)—1917-18, 1920—of, Foster's Hartford Giants, Chicago Union Giants
ELMORE, HENRY—1959-63—2b, 3b, Philadelphia Stars, Birmingham Black Barons
ELMORE, MONTE—1947—p, Jacksonville Eagles
ELSE, ____—1929—p, Oklahoma City Black Indians
ELSE, HARRY ELMO (SPEED)—1931-40—c, Monroe (LA) Monarchs, Kansas City Monarchs, Chicago American Giants, New Orleans Crescent Stars
ELSE, J.—1932—ss, New Orleans Black Pelicans
EMBRY [EMERY], WILLIAM ROSS (CAP)—1909-11—1b, of, Louisville Cubs, Chicago Union Giants, Minneapolis Keystones, 1923—umpire, NNL
ELY, ____—1932—p, Bacharach (Philly) Giants
EMERY, ____—1867—2b, Camden Resolutes
EMERY, ____—1933—c, John Donaldson All-Stars
EMMETT [EMMITT], (BUSTER)—1924—p, Indianapolis ABCs
EMMONS, ____—1917—of, Dayton Marcos
EMORY [EMERY], JOHN [JACK] F.—1906-22—p, of, Brooklyn Colored Giants, Philadelphia Giants, Paterson (NJ) Smart Set, Pittsburgh Colored Stars, Pittsburgh Stars of Buffalo, Brooklyn Royal Giants
EMORY [EMERY], SIMS V.—1887-89—c, 1b, New York Gorhams (Middle States League), Philadelphia Pythians (NCBBL), Boston Resolutes (NCBBL)
ENGLAND, CHARLES—1946—p, Newark Eagles
ENGLISH, ____—1890—2b, Lincoln (NE) Giants
ENGLISH, ____—1909—of, St. Louis Giants
ENGLISH, ____—1944—p, Birmingham Black Barons
ENGLISH, H. D.—1929-32—manager, officer, Houston Black Buffaloes, Fort Worth Black Cats, Monroe (LA) Monarchs
ENGLISH, JOE—1932—1b, New Orleans Black Pelicans
ENGLISH, LEWIS—1927-34—c, of, Evansville Giants, Louisville White Sox, Louisville Black Caps, Louisville Red Caps, Nashville Elite Giants, Detroit Stars, Memphis Red Sox
ENOCH, ____—1937—c, New York Black Yankees
ENSLEY, FRANK JAMES—1951-55—of, ss, Kansas City Monarchs, Indianapolis Clowns
ENTENZA [ESTENZA], LUIS A.—1927-28—p, of, 3b, c, Cuban Stars (West)
EPHRDIM, ____—1910—c, New Orleans Eagles
EPPS, HARVEY—1891—of, Cuban Giants
ERICKS, ____—1938—ph, Baltimore Elite Giants
ERMY, ____—1922—2b, Bacharach (AC) Giants
ERVIN, WILLIE LEE—1948—p, New York Black Yankees
ERYE, JOHN [see FRYE, JOHN H.]
ESCALANTE, FRANCISCO (NIMIN)—1931—1b, Cuban Stars (West), Cuban House of David
ESPINOZA [ESPENOSIA], TED—1946-47—2b, p, San Francisco Sea Lions, Indianapolis Clowns
ESTERBROOK, ____—1888—1b, Hoosier Black Stockings
ESTRADA, OSCAR—1924-25, 1931—p, of, Cuban Stars (East & West)
ETCHEGOYEN, CARLOS—1927-35—3b, Cuban Stars (East & West), Havana Red Sox, Cuban House of David
ETHERIDGE, (RED HORSE)—1911—p, Chicago American Giants
ETHRIDGE, JACK—1946—utility, Pittsburgh Stars
ETTINGER, ____—1889—of, Philadelphia Giants
ETZEL, ____—1915—ph, Hilldale Club
EUELL, ____—1927—ss, Washington Black Sox
EVANS, ____—1909—1b, St. Louis Giants
EVANS, ____—1920—of, Chicago Union Giants
EVANS, ____—1921—p, Illinois Giants
EVANS, ____—1939—ph, St. Louis Giants
EVANS, ____—1946—umpire, WCBA
EVANS, ALEX—1933-34—p, Louisville Red Caps
EVANS, BOOTS—1925-30—umpire, ECL
EVANS, CHARLES ALEXANDER (ALEC, SLOW-TIME)—1917-27—2b, p, of, Bacharach (AC) Giants, Penn Red Caps of NY, Baltimore Black Sox, Indianapolis ABCs, Houston Black Buffaloes, Philadelphia Royal Giants, Cleveland Royal Giants
EVANS, CLARENCE—1948-49—p, Homestead Grays

EVANS, CLAUDE—1937—of, Pittsburgh Crawfords
EVANS, JR., FELIX (CHIN, KALIHARI)—1934-49—p, of, Atlanta Black Crackers, Indianapolis ABCs, Memphis Red Sox, Birmingham Black Barons, Baltimore Elite Giants, Newark Eagles, St. Louis Stars, Chattanooga Choo Choos
EVANS, FRANK—1908, 1914-20—of, 3b, Kansas City (KS) Giants, All Nations, Kansas City Monarchs, New Orleans Bears
EVANS, FRANK BOWER—1950, 1956, 1959—of, Cleveland Buckeyes, Detroit Stars, Memphis Red Sox
EVANS, GEORGE—1887-91—2b, New York Gorhams (NCBBL), Ansonia Cuban Giants (Connecticut St. League)
EVANS, HERMAN—1938—of, Jacksonville Red Caps
EVANS, HEZIKIA (HANK)—1960—infield, Detroit-New Orleans Stars
EVANS, JAMES (STREAK)—1934—p, Homestead Grays
EVANS, JOHN J. – [see EVANS, GEORGE]
EVANS, JOHNNY J. (CHICO)—1954, 1957-58—2b, 3b, Indianapolis Clowns, Detroit Stars, Detroit Clowns, New Orleans Bears, Kansas City Monarchs
EVANS, LLOYD—1920—of, Kansas City Monarchs
EVANS, ROBERT J. (BOB)—1933-43—p, Baltimore Stars, Newark Dodgers, Newark Eagles, Jacksonville Red Caps, New York Black Yankees, Philadelphia Stars, Homestead Grays
EVANS, ROSS (RUSS)—1946—p, Atlanta Black Crackers
EVANS, TOM—1939—p, Philadelphia Stars
EVANS, ULYSSES (COWBOY)—1933-34, 1942-45—p, Louisville Red Caps, Cincinnati Ethiopian Clowns (NML), Chicago Brown Bombers (NML), Minneapolis-St. Paul Colored Gophers, Chicago American Giants, Detroit Motor City Giants (USL)
EVANS, W. P.—1916-25—2b, p, Baltimore Black Sox, Chicago American Giants, Lincoln (NY) Stars
EVANS, WALTER—1934—c, Monroe (LA) Monarchs
EVANS, WILLIAM—1903—c, of, Philadelphia Giants
EVANS, II, WILLIAM DEMONT (BILL, HAPPY, GREY GHOST)—1924-36—of, ss, 3b, p, Chicago American Giants, Brooklyn Royal Giants, Dayton Marcos, Cleveland Hornets, St. Louis Stars, Indianapolis ABCs, Homestead Grays, Washington Pilots, Detroit Wolves, Cincinnati Tigers, Memphis Red Sox
EVELYN, LIONEL RANDOLPH (LONNIE)—1948-50, 1955, 1959—ss, p, Brooklyn Royal Giants, New York Cubans, Indianapolis Clowns, New York Black Yankees, Kansas City Monarchs
EVERETT, BOB—1960—p, Raleigh (NC) Tigers
EVERETT, CURTIS—1950-52—c, of, Kansas City Monarchs
EVERETT, DEAN [see JAMES W. EVERETT below]
EVERETT, DWIGHT CLARENCE—1927-28—ss, Kansas City Monarchs, Detroit Stars
EVERETT, SR., JAMES WILLIAM (JIMMY, BLUE DEAN)—1929-43—p, Lincoln (NY) Giants, Penn Red Caps of NY, Cincinnati Ethiopian Clowns (NML), Newark Browns, Memphis Red Sox, Newark Eagles, New York Black Yankees, Jacksonville Red Caps
EVITT, ____—1928—1b, Gilkerson's Union Giants
EWELL, SR., WILMER LEWIS—1925-34—c, Indianapolis ABCs, Cincinnati Tigers, Cincinnati Giants, Louisville White Sox
EWING, COLUMBUS SPURLOCK—1931—of, Louisville White Sox
EWING, DORSEY—1916-17—of, Kansas City (MO) Tigers
EWING, ROWLAND (MONK)—1928-31, 1938, 1946—of, 1b, Louisville White Sox, San Francisco Sea Lions, Los Angeles White Sox, Colored House of David
EWING, SR., RUSSELL LEWIS—1929-30, 1935-39—c, business manager, officer, Cincinnati Tigers, Louisville White Sox, Louisville Black Caps, Nashville White Sox, Colored House of David, Nashville Cubs, Louisville Black Colonels
EWING, WILLIAM MONROE (BUCK, BILL)—1920-41—c, Chicago American Giants, Columbus Buckeyes, Indianapolis ABCs, Homestead Grays, Lincoln (NY) Giants, Cleveland Tate Stars, Schenectady Mohawk Giants
EYERS, HENRY [see BYERS, HENRY]

F

FABELO, JULIÁN—1916-23—3b, p, Cuban Stars (East & West), Havana Stars, New York Cuban Stars, All Cubans

FABORS, THOMAS—1942—p, Baltimore Elite Giants

FABRÉ y FONTRODONA, ISIDRO (PAPI)—1918-39—p, of, Cuban Stars (East & West), New York Cubans, All Cubans, New York Cuban Stars

FACE, ____—1924—3b, Harrisburg Giants

FAGAN, GARVIS DARIUS—1940, 1942-43—ss, 3b, 2b, of, Memphis Red Sox, Jacksonville Red Caps, Philadelphia Stars, Chicago Brown Bombers (NML), New York Black Yankees, Pittsburgh Crawfords

FAGEN [FAGAN, FAGIN], ROBERT W. (BOB)—1920-23, 1927-28—2b, manager, Kansas City Monarchs, St. Louis Stars, Philadelphia Royal Giants, Cleveland Royal Giants

FAGER, ____—1891—2b, Cuban Giants

FAIR, J.W.—1939—owner, Charlotte Ramblers (Black Hornets)

FAIRLEY, JOHNNY D. (CASINO)—1957-60—p, Raleigh (NC) Tigers, Detroit Stars, Birmingham Black Barons

FAIRMAN, ____—1867—p, Brooklyn Unique

FAISON, ____—1932—ss, Little Rock Grays

FALLINGS, JOHN—1947-48—p, New York Black Yankees

FARMER, ____—1867—of, Brooklyn Unique

FARMER, BOB—1934—p, Padron's Cuban Giants

FARMER, JR., GREENE (SCHOOLBOY)—1940-47—of, Cincinnati-Indianapolis Clowns, New York Cubans, New York Black Yankees, Jacksonville Red Caps, Cincinnati Crescents, Cincinnati-Cleveland Buckeyes

FARMER, WALTER MORAN—1913-33—stockholder, Colored National Base Ball League of the United States, and the Negro National League of Professional Baseball Clubs (NNL); officer, Chicago American Giants, Detroit Stars

FARRAR, ____—1956—p, Birmingham Black Barons

FARRELL, ____—1888—2b, Bloomington (IL) Reds

FARRELL, JOHN R.—1934—owner, Baltimore Black Sox, Washington Pilots

FARRELL, LUTHER ALANER (JACK, RED, FATS, LEFTY)—1919-34—p, of, Bacharach (AC) Giants, Lincoln (NY) Giants, New York Black Yankees, Chicago Giants, Chicago American Giants, Hilldale Club, St. Louis Giants, Gilkerson's Union Giants, Indianapolis ABCs, Cleveland Browns, Providence Giants

FARRELL, WILLIAM EDGAR—1899, 1902—1b, c, manager, Philadelphia Giants, Baltimore Blues

FARRINGTON, ____—1912—of, All Nations

FARRINGTON, FREDDIE (KING TUT II, JUNIOR)—1952—clown, Indianapolis Clowns

FATE, ____—1931—of, Knoxville Giants

FAULK, (STORMY)—1935-42—c, of, Boston Royal Giants

FAUNTROY, ____—1926—cf, Washington Black Sox

FAURIA, EDWIN—1930—assistant manager, New Orleans Black Pelicans

FAURIA, FRED—1922—officer, New Orleans Crescent Stars

FAVORS, THOMAS (MONK, TOM)—1947—of, Kansas City Monarchs, Jacksonville Eagles

FAZIO, ____—1941—p, Homestead Grays

FEARBRY, DON—1955—ss, Indianapolis Clowns, New York Black Yankees

FEARBRY, JR., MARVIN JAMES (BUTCH)—1955—2b, Indianapolis Clowns

FELDER, ____—1929—of, San Antonio Black Indians

FELDER, BENJAMIN FRANKLIN (BENNY)—1946-48, 1951—ss, 3b, Newark Eagles, Indianapolis Clowns, Philadelphia Stars, Brooklyn Brown Dodgers

FELDER, JAMES—1948—ss, Indianapolis Clowns

FELDER, KENDALL PERKINS (BUCK)—1944-47—ss, Memphis Red Sox, Chicago American Giants, Birmingham Black Barons, Chattanooga Choo Choos

FELIX, JAMES—1952—p, Chicago American Giants

FELKS, ____—1909—player, Harrisburg Giants

FELLOWS, ____—1937—p, c, Birmingham Black Barons

FELS, CARLTON—1924-26, 1928, 1930—of, Schenectady Mohawk Giants

FEMENELLA, JR., MICHAEL J.—1945-46—officer, Brooklyn Brown Dodgers

FENALI, ____—1912—c, All Nations

FENISON, TYLER—1957—p, Detroit Stars

FENNAR, ALBERTUS AVANT [a.k.a. DARIO] (AL, CLEFFIE)—1932-34, 1945—ss, Brooklyn Royal Giants, Cuban Stars (East), Bacharach (Philly) Giants

FENSON (FEARSON), ____—1907—p, Philadelphia Giants

FENTON, ____—1919-20—ss, Baltimore Black Sox

FERGUSON, ____—1880—of, Washington Eagles

FERGUSON, ____—1908—c, Cleveland Giants

FERGUSON, ____—1912—p, Baltimore Giants

FERGUSON, ____—1915—p, Cuban Giants

FERGUSON, ____—1916—p, Pittsburgh Giants

FERGUSON, ____—1930—umpire, ECL

FERGUSON, ____—1931—ss, Philadelphia Quaker City Giants

Negro Leagues Book #2: The Players

FERGUSON, WILLIAM—1890—2b, c, 1b, Chicago Unions
FERN, ____—1920—p, Kansas City Monarchs
FERNÁNDEZ, ____—1927—p, Brooklyn Cuban Giants
FERNÁNDEZ, BERNARDO (TOTO)—1938-39, 1941-49—p, Atlanta Black Crackers, Jacksonville Red Caps, Brooklyn Royal Giants, New York Black Yankees, Pittsburgh Crawfords (USL), Philadelphia Stars, Brooklyn Brown Dodgers
FERNÁNDEZ, EMANUEL—1941—of, p, New York Cubans
FERNÁNDEZ, CLARENCE—1945—2b, New Orleans Black Pelicans
FERNÁNDEZ, FLORENTINO (FLORITO)—1957—infield, Detroit Stars
FERNÁNDEZ, JR., JOSÉ M. (PEPE)—1948-50—c, New York Cubans
FERNÁNDEZ, SR., JOSÉ MARÍA (CUSO)—1916-50—c, manager, Gilkerson's Union Giants, Cuban Stars (East & West), New York Cubans, New York Cuban Stars, Cuban Havana Stars, All Cubans, Stars of Cuba
FERNÁNDEZ, OSCAR—1915—p, Havana Reds
FERNÁNDEZ, PABLO—1923—p, Cuban Stars (West)
FERNÁNDEZ, RENALDO—1950—of, New York Cubans
FERNÁNDEZ, RODOLFO (RUDY, VEN PORDIOS)—1932-46—p, New York Cubans, Cuban Stars (East & West), New York Black Yankees, Trujillo All-Stars (Ciudad Trujillo Dragons)
FERNÁNDEZ, T.—1941—p, New York Cubans
FERREND, ____—1889—of, New Orleans Pinchbacks
FERRERI, ____—1920—p, Bacharach (AC) Giants
FERRELL, JR., HOWARD LEROY (TOOTS)—1947-50—p, Baltimore Elite Giants, Newark Eagles
FERRELL, W. E.—1918—1b, Pennsylvania Giants
FERRELL, WILLIE TRUEHART (RED)—1937-43—p, Homestead Grays, Chicago American Giants, Cincinnati Ethiopian Clowns (NML), Birmingham Black Barons, Jacksonville Red Caps, Cleveland Bears
FERRER, CRESCENCIO—1915—c, Havana Reds
FERRER, EFIGENIO (COCO, AL)—1946-51—2b, ss, Indianapolis Clowns, Chicago American Giants, Havana Las Palomas
FERRER, PEDRO—1922-25, 1928-29—2b, ss, 3b, Cuban Stars (East), Havana Red Sox
FERRIS, ____—1907—p, Cuban Stars
FERRIS, JOSEPH1858-60—ss, Henson Base Ball Club of Jamaica (NY)
FERRO [FERRA], AMANCICO—1949—p, New York Cubans

FETHUM, ____—1925—of, Philadelphia Giants
FIALL, GEORGE GOODWIN—1918-30—ss, 3b, Lincoln (NY) Giants, Harrisburg Giants, Baltimore Black Sox, Birmingham Black Barons, Penn Red Caps of NY, Providence Giants, Brooklyn Royal Giants
FIALL, JR. THOMAS VIVIAN (TOM)—1917-25, 1931—of, York (PA) Cuban Giants, Brooklyn Royal Giants, Lincoln (NY) Giants, Hilldale Club, Penn Red Caps of NY, Grand Central Terminal Red Caps
FIBERIE, ____—1929—p, Havana Red Sox
FIELDS, ____—1887—1b, South Baltimore Mutuals
FIELDS, ____—1912-13—ss, Pittsburgh Giants
FIELDS, ____—1917—3b, Brown's Tennessee Rats
FIELDS, ____—1918—of, Bacharach (AC) Giants
FIELDS, ALEX—1946—2b, Boston Blues
FIELDS, ART—1917-24—umpire, NNL
FIELDS, BENNY—1930-38, 1941—2b, Memphis Red Sox, Cleveland Cubs, Birmingham Black Barons, Cleveland Stars, New York Black Yankees, Atlanta Black Crackers, Louisville Black Caps, Chattanooga White Sox
FIELDS, BOBBY—1948—of, Memphis Red Sox
FIELDS, C.—1934—3b, Pittsburgh Crawfords [see CRUTCHFIELD, JIMMIE]
FIELDS, CLIFFORD PETER—1950—of, Chicago American Giants
FIELDS, JAMES C.—1921—p, St. Louis Giants
FIELDS, LOUIS—1948—utility, Homestead Grays
FIELDS, RAYMOND E.—1946—officer, Nashville Cubs
FIELDS, ROMEY (BUDDY)—1918-26—p, Chicago American Giants, Cleveland Browns, St. Louis Giants, Dayton Marcos, Cleveland Elites, Nashville Elite Giants, Memphis Red Sox
FIELDS, TOM—1946—p, Homestead Grays
FIELDS, SR., WILMER LEON (RED, BILL, CHINKY)—1939-50—p, of, Homestead Grays; author
FIFER [PHIFFER], JOHN—1921—p, Indianapolis ABCs
FIGANZIE, ____—1859—2b, Unknown Base Ball Club (of Weeksville, NY)
FIGAROLA, RAFAEL [JOSÉ]—1904-15, 1918-21—c, 1b, Stars of Cuba, New York Cuban Stars, All Cubans, Cuban Havana Stars, Brooklyn Royal Giants, Cuban Stars (West)
FIGAROLO, ____—1915—p, All Nations
FIGUEROA, JOSÉ ANTONIO (TONO)—1940—p, New York Cubans
FIGUEROA, LUIS ENRIQUE (TITE, TITO)—1946—p, Baltimore Elite Giants

FILLEY, AARON—1875—1b, St. Louis Stockings

FILLMORE, JOE ALEXANDER (FIREBALL)—1941-52—p, Philadelphia Stars, Baltimore Grays

FINCH, ____—1933—of, Detroit Stars

FINCH, RAYFORD—1945, 1949-50—p, Cleveland Buckeyes, Louisville Buckeyes

FINCH [FITCH], ROBERT—1926—p, Lincoln (NY) Giants

FINDELL [PINDELL], THOMAS—1887—player, Washington Capital Citys

FINDLAY, JOHN—1945—p, Chicago Brown Bombers (USL)

FINE, CHARLIE [see HARMON, CHARLES (CHUCK) BYRON]

FINK, ____—1937-38—umpire, NNL

FINLEY, ____—1920—1b, Pensacola Giants

FINLEY [FINDLEY], ____—1938—of, Washington Black Senators

FINLEY, GWEN—1956—p, Birmingham Black Barons

FINLEY, JOHN THOMAS (TOM)—1922-33—3b, 2b, ss, Bacharach (AC) Giants, Lincoln (NY) Giants, Brooklyn Royal Giants, Penn Red Caps of NY, Darby Daisies, New York Harlem Stars, Baltimore Black Sox, Philadelphia Stars, Wilmington Potomacs, Washington Potomacs, Hilldale Club

FINNER [FINNAN], JOHNNIE CHARLEY (JOHN)—1918-27—p, St. Louis Giants, St. Louis Stars, Milwaukee Bears, Birmingham Black Barons, Atlanta Black Crackers, Memphis Red Sox, Albany (GA) Giants, Evansville Giants, Nashville Elite Giants

FINNEY, EDWARD LEWIS (MIKE, ED)—1948-50—3b, Baltimore Elite Giants

FINNICK, ____—1934—p, Memphis Red Sox

FISHBAUGH, JIM—1948-51—2b, Harlem Globetrotters, Asheville Blues, Chicago American Giants

FISHER, ____—1895—2b, Chicago Unions

FISHER, ____—1917—of, Bacharach (AC) Giants

FISHER, ____—1920—of, Atlanta Black Crackers

FISHER, ____—1937—ph, Kansas City Monarchs

FISHER, ____—1958—utility, Memphis Red Sox

FISHER, A.—1884—player, Philadelphia Mutual B.B.C.

FISHER, ELBERT (AL)—1908-10—p, of, Philadelphia Giants

FISHER, G.—1882—of, Philadelphia Orions

FISHER, GEORGE (TIPPER)—1920-23, 1926, 1930-34—of, Albany (GA) Giants, Atlanta Black Crackers, Richmond Giants (NAA), Harrisburg Giants, Columbus Turfs, Columbus Stars, Columbus Keystones

FISHER, HENRY N.—1875—p, Chicago Uniques; 1884—officer, Chicago Gordons

FISHER, J. F.—1884—p, Philadelphia Mutual B.B.C.

FISHER, JERRY—1908-11—p, of, Philadelphia Giants

FISHER, JIMMY—1932-33—p, Columbus Turfs, Columbus Blue Birds

FISHER, JONATHON—1955-56—p, Indianapolis Clowns, New York Black Yankees

FISHER, PETE—1867-71—of, p, Mutuals of Washington, Philadelphia Mutual B. B. C.

FISHER [FISHUE], PETE (THE WONDER)—1884-86—c, Philadelphia Mutual B. B. C., Philadelphia Manhatten Club, New York Gorhams

FISHER, W.—1884-85—player, Philadelphia Mutual B.B.C.

FISHER, WILLIAM—1884-87—president, Chicago Gordons

FISHER, YEOMAN—1891—of, Cuban Giants

FITZGERALD, ____—1912—p, All Nations

FITZGERALD, GERALD—1947-48—of, New York Black Yankees

FITZGERALD, JOHN (BUSTER)—1943, 1947-48—c, Newark Eagles

FITZGERALD, M.E.—1890—manager, Cuban Giants

FITZHUGH, ____—1929—p, Baltimore Black Sox

FLAMM, ____—1921—umpire, NNL

FLAMMER, ____—1921—of, Hilldale Club

FLANAGEN, ____—1917—p, All Nations

FLANLEY, GEORGE—1869—2b, Philadelphia Excelsior

FLEET, JOSEPH (JOE)—1930—p, Chicago American Giants, Memphis Red Sox

FLEIGER, ____—1924—umpire, ECL

FLEMING, ADOLPH (ART)—1933-37—p, of, Schenectady Mohawk Giants

FLEMING, BUDDY [see REEDY, JR., FLEMING]

FLEMING, SR., FRANK (BILL, BOONIE)—1946, 1951-53—p, 1b, of, Cleveland Buckeyes, Indianapolis Clowns, Asheville Black Tourists; 1961—manager, East West game

FLEMING, HENRY ALFORD—1911-19—owner, promoter, Jewell's ABCs, Indianapolis ABCs

FLETCHER, ____—1922—2b, Bacharach (AC) Giants

FLETCHER, AL—1955-56—c, of, New York Black Yankees, Indianapolis Clowns

FLIPPINS[G], ____—1931—ss, p, Chattanooga Black Lookouts

FLOOD, JESS—1919-20, 1927—c, Cleveland Tate Stars, Lincoln (NY) Giants, Cleveland Giants

FLOOD, TIM—1922—umpire, NNL

FLORES, ____—1936—2b, Cuban Stars (East)

FLORES, CONRADO—1954—p, Kansas City Monarchs

Negro Leagues Book #2: The Players

FLOURNEY, ____—1950—p, Cleveland Buckeyes
FLOURNOY, FRED EMMET—1928-33—c, Brooklyn Cuban Giants, Penn Red Caps of NY
FLOURNOY, WILLIS JEFFERSON (PUD, JESSE)—1919-34—p, Hilldale Club, Brooklyn Royal Giants, Baltimore Black Sox, Bacharach (Philly) Giants, Penn Red Caps of NY, Breakers Hotel (FL)
FLOWERS, JOHNNY (JAKE)—1941-43—3b, of, New York Black Yankees
FLOWERS, OLLIE—1946—of, 2b, Fresno/San Diego Tigers
FLOWERS, WILLIAM (BILL)—1946—3b, 2b, San Francisco Sea Lions, Los Angeles White Sox
FLOYD, ALBERT—1946—c, Fresno/San Diego Tigers
FLOYD, EARLE—1954-56, 1959—of, 1b, Detroit Stars, Kansas City Monarchs
FLOYD, FRANK JAMES (JEWBABY)—1920-55—trainer, Kansas City Monarchs
FLOYD, IRV—1954—p, of, Detroit Stars
FLOYD, JESSE—1913-16—of, Indianapolis ABCs, Bowser's ABCs
FLOYD, JESSE. J.—1932—officer, Little Rock Grays
FLOYD, LEO—1935-37—p, Brooklyn Eagles, Indianapolis Athletics
FLOYD, PORTER LEE [see HANNIBAL, JACK]
FOYE, ____—1871—p, Chelsea Auroras
FOLLIS, CHARLES W. (BLACK CYCLONE)—1908-09—of, c, Cleveland Giants, Cuban Giants, Cleveland Star Light Champions
FOOTE, JAKE—1929, 1944-45—c, Detroit Stars, Twin Cities Gophers (USL)
FOOTES, ROBERT—1895-1909—c, Chicago Unions, Philadelphia Giants, Brooklyn Royal Giants, Chicago Union Giants
FORBES, FRANK LINDSEY (STRANGLER, IRON MAN), [a.k.a. Frank Formita, Franklin Tidwillington Forbes]—1911-27—ss, 3b, of, 2b, p, Philadelphia Giants, Lincoln (NY) Stars, Harrisburg Giants, Lincoln (NY) Giants, Brooklyn Royal Giants, Bacharach (AC) Giants, Grand Central Terminal Red Caps, Royal Poinciana (FL), Breakers Hotel (FL), Penn Red Caps of NY, Chappie Johnson's All-Stars;—1929-43—umpire; owner, business manager, New York Cubans; NNL & ANL promoter;—1938-48—writer, *Chicago Defender*
FORBES, JOSEPH (JOE)—1917—p, Bacharach (AC) Giants
FORBES, JULIUS—1883-88—of, 3b, 1b, business manager, Orion Club of Philadelphia, Cuban Giants, Philadelphia Pythians (NCBBL), Lancaster (PA) Giants

FORBES, MINNIE L. WATKINS—1956—owner, Detroit Stars
FORCE, WILLIAM (BUDDIE)—1920-30, 1933—p, Detroit Stars, Baltimore Black Sox, Brooklyn Royal Giants, Baltimore Stars, Knoxville Giants
FORD, ____—1907—2b, Keystone (PA) Giants
FORD, ____—1908, 1919—1b, Cleveland Giants
FORD, ____—1914—p, Brooklyn Royal Giants
FORD, ____—1927—of, Chicago Giants
FORD, ____—1938—ss, Birmingham Black Barons
FORD, BILL—1931-33, 1941—officer, Cleveland Giants
FORD, C.—1918—p, Pennsylvania Giants
FORD, CARL (BUBBER)—1947—officer, Shreveport Tigers, Jacksonville Eagles
FORD, SR., ERVIN [ERWIN] LEE—1948-55—2b, of, Raleigh (NC) Tigers, Indianapolis Clowns, Greensboro Red Wings
FORD, FRANK—1915-18—c, Pennsylvania Giants, Hilldale Club
FORD, FRANK C. (CHINK)—1917-18—p, Pennsylvania Giants, Hilldale Club
FORD, GEORGE—1924, 1926-27—ss, Wilmington Black Sox, Washington Black Sox
FORD, HARRY—1938—3b, ss, Birmingham Black Barons
FORD, JAMES (JIMMY)—1931-46—3b, 2b, Memphis Red Sox, St. Louis Stars, New Orleans-St. Louis Stars, New York Black Yankees, Cincinnati Ethiopian Clowns (NML), Cincinnati-Cleveland Buckeyes, Philadelphia Stars, Baltimore Elite Giants, Harrisburg-St. Louis Stars, Washington Black Senators, Nashville Elite Giants, Cincinnati Crescents
FORD, JOHN DALLAS CECIL (CHINK)—1917—p, Hilldale Club
FORD, ROGERS—1940—p, Chicago American Giants
FORD, ROY—1921, 1925-26—ss, Pittsburgh Giants, Pittsburgh Keystones, Harrisburg Giants
FORD, WILLIAM H. (BILL)—1933—owner, Cleveland Giants
FORD, WILLIAM HENRY—1910—p, St. Paul Colored Gophers
FORD, WILLIAM HENRY—1915—ss, Chicago Giants, Leland Giants
FORD, WILLIAM JAMES (BILLY)—1954—c, Louisville Clippers
FOREMAN, (BUDDY)—1921—ss, Hilldale Club
FOREMAN, F. SYLVESTER (HOOKS)—1920-33—c, Kansas City Monarchs, Indianapolis ABCs, Washington Pilots,

Milwaukee Bears, Homestead Grays, Cleveland Browns, John Donaldson All-Stars

FOREMAN, JR., ZACHARIAH L. (ZACK)—1920-21—p, Kansas City Monarchs

FOREMAN, WILLIE—1951—player, Satchel Paige All-Stars

FORREST, CHARLES—1920—utility, St. Louis Giants

FORREST, JAMES DANIEL—1917-29—c, of, Lincoln (NY) Giants, Brooklyn Royal Giants, Philadelphia Colored Giants of New York

FORREST, PERCY—1938, 1943-46—p, of, Chicago American Giants, New York Black Yankees, Newark Eagles

FORGE, CLINTON—1959—c, Detroit Stars

FORGE, WILLIE JAMES—1954-55, 1959—c, Louisville Clippers, Kansas City Monarchs, Birmingham Black Barons

FORKINS, MARTY—1931—officer, New York Black Yankees

FORMENTAL [FORMENTHAL], PEDRO (PERICO, PERUCHO)—1947-50—of, Memphis Red Sox

FORNEY, CARL EDWARD (SATCH)—1957-61—p, of, manager, Indianapolis Clowns, Charlotte Ramblers (Black Hornets), Charlotte Pepsi Cola Giants

FORREST, ____—1917-29—of, c, Havana Red Sox, Lincoln (NY) Giants, Philadelphia Giants, Brooklyn Royal Giants, Philadelphia Colored Giants of New York

FORREST, JOE—1949—p, New York Black Yankees

FORREST, PERCY (PETE)—1938-49—p, Chicago American Giants, Newark Eagles, New York Black Yankees, Indianapolis Clowns, Baltimore Elite Giants

FORSYTHE, ____—1924—ph, Baltimore Black Sox

FORT, ____—1918—of, Chicago Union Giants

FORTSON, RALPH—1959-61—p, 1b, manager, Raleigh (NC) Tigers

FORTSON, T.J.—1928, 1930-32—officer, Atlanta Grey Sox, Atlanta Black Crackers

FORTUNE, T. (TIMOTHY) THOMAS—1891-1928—writer, New *York Age, New York Globe, New York Freeman, New York Amsterdam News, Norfolk Journal and Guide*

FOSTER, ____—1928—umpire, NNL

FOSTER, ____—1928—p, St. Louis Giants

FOSTER, ANDREW BISHOP (RUBE, CHIEF, JOCK)—1902-26—p, manager, owner, Chicago Union Giants, Cuban X-Giants, St. Paul Colored Gophers, Philadelphia Giants, Philadelphia Quaker City Giants, Leland Giants, Chicago American Giants, Louisville White Sox;—1920-26—founder, commissioner, president, and treasurer, The Negro National League of Professional Baseball Clubs (NNL); NNL

FOSTER, CHARLES B. (ALABAMA RED)—1909-10—1b, Kansas City, (KS), Giants, Oklahoma City Giants, San Antonio Broncos

FOSTER, EDWARD—1910—president, St. Louis Giants

FOSTER, FRANK—1947—p, Philadelphia Stars

FOSTER, GEORGE—1960—owner, Detroit-New Orleans Stars

FOSTER, JAMES (JIM)—1945-46—officer, Chicago Brown Bombers (USL)

FOSTER, JOHN—1888—utility, New York Gorhams

FOSTER, LELAND CHARLES (WOW)—1930-37—p, Houston Black Buffaloes, Monroe (LA) Monarchs, Tallulah (LA) Owls

FOSTER, LEONARD—1938—infield, Atlanta Black Crackers

FOSTER, PERCY—1938-39—p, Chicago American Giants

FOSTER, WILLIE HENDRICK (BILL)—1920-31—stockholder, The Negro National League of Professional Baseball Clubs (NNL); 1923-38—p, manager, Memphis Red Sox, Chicago American Giants, Homestead Grays, Kansas City Monarchs, Cole's Chicago American Giants, Birmingham Black Barons, Pittsburgh Crawfords, Washington (Yakima) Browns

FOULKE, ____—1912—of, Cuban Giants

FOUSE, ____—1911—p, Louisville Cubs

FOWLER, ELBERT—1959—ss, Memphis Red Sox

FOWLER, J.W. (BUD)—(nee John W. Jackson)—1878-1899—2b, p, of, 3b, c, ss, manager, Lynn (MA) Live Oaks (International Association), Stillwater, MN (Northwestern League); Omaha (NE) Omahogs, Keokuk (IA) Hawkeyes and Topeka (KS) Capitals (Western League); Binghamton, (NY) Crickets (International Association); Crawfordsville (IN) Hoosiers, Terre Haute (IN) Hoosiers, and Galesburg (Central Interstate league); Sterling, Galesburg, Burlington, and Davenport (Illinois-Iowa League); Evansville, New York Gorhams, All-American Black Tourists, Adrian (MI) Page Fence Giants; Lafayette, Indiana, Greenville (Michigan League); Adrian Reformers, Lansing Senators (Michigan St. League); Lincoln-Kearney (Nebraska St. League); Pueblo Pastimes (Colorado League); Portland (Eastern New England League); Worchester (New England Association); Santa Fe (New Mexico League), Montpelier (Vermont League), Jackson Base Ball Club of New York (NY), Chicago Unions, Black Wonders Base Ball Club (MO); officer, National League of Colored Base Ball Clubs

FOWLER, ROBERT (BOB)—1960-61—c, Raleigh (NC) Tigers, Birmingham Black Barons

FOWLKES, ERVIN—1946-48—ss, Chicago American Giants, Homestead Grays, Boston Blues, New York Black Yankees, Detroit Senators

FOWLKES, SAMUEL (BUDDY, JIMMY)—1946, 1948, 1950—p, Kansas City Monarchs, Cleveland Buckeyes, Boston Blues, Chicago American Giants

FOX, ____—1914—p, Brooklyn Royal Giants

FOX, ____—1923—of, Toledo Tigers

FOX, ____—1930—of, 2b, Nashville Elite Giants

FOX, ____—1936—3b, Homestead Grays

FOX, ____—1946—c, Newark Eagles

FOX, ORANGE W.—1887-88—of, Chicago Unions, Chicago Resolutes

FRANCIS, HORATIO—1867-68—2b, Philadelphia Excelsior, Philadelphia Pythians (NCBBL)

FRANCIS, JACOB—1885—umpire, Independent Colored teams

FRANCIS, OTIS WILBER (DEL, CAT, O.)—1908-20—2b, Indianapolis ABCs, Jewell's ABCs, Chicago Union Giants, Detroit Stars

FRANCIS, WILLIAM HENRY (BILLY, BRODIE)—1904-25—3b, Wilmington Giants, Cuban Giants, Philadelphia Giants, Lincoln (NY) Giants, Chicago American Giants, Hilldale Club, Bacharach (AC) Giants, Cleveland Browns, Chicago Giants, Schenectady Mohawk Giants, Royal Poinciana (FL), Breakers Hotel (FL)

FRANK, ____—1869—1b, Philadelphia Excelsior

FRANKLIN, ____—1908—ss, Brooklyn Colored Giants

FRANKLIN, ____—1926—1b, Albany Giants

FRANKLIN, [COL.] CHARLES B.—1936-38—officer, Louisville Black Lookouts

FRANKLIN, CHESTER ARTHUR—1919-55—owner, editor, *The Kansas City Call*

FRANKLIN, GEORGE—1890—p, Chicago Unions

FRANKLIN, LEON DELAND—1960-61—p, Kansas City Monarchs

FRANKLIN, PAUL—1929—2b, Fort Worth Panthers

FRANKLIN, WILLIAM B.—1887—manager, Louisville Falls City (NCBBL)

FRANKS, MICHAEL (MIKE) J.—1956-57—p, Indianapolis Clowns

FRASEL, JAMES—1942—of, Chicago Brown Bombers (NML)

FRAZIER, ____—1934—of, Pittsburgh Giants

FRAZIER, ALBERT EDWIN (COOL PAPA, POPS)—1932-44—2b, 3b, Jacksonville Red Caps, Cleveland Bears, Montgomery Grey Sox

FRAZIER, J. (FLASH)—1932—ss, Atlanta Black Crackers

FRAZIER, JOSHUA (POP)—1934-35—owner, Newark Dodgers

FRAZIER, ORAN FRANKLIN (DUCK)—1932—2b, Montgomery Grey Sox

FRAZIER, SR., SEVERN (SAM)—1932—utility, Montgomery Grey Sox

FREE, SR., KENNETH (KENNY) ALLEN—1959-60—3b, Raleigh (NC) Tigers, Cuban Giants

FREEHAN, JOHN B.—1924—umpire, World Series

FREEMAN, ____—1867—p, Utica (NY) Fearless

FREEMAN, ____—1929—c, Dallas Black Giants

FREEMAN, BILL (WILD BILL)—1925, 1929-1932—p, Indianapolis ABCs, John Donaldson All-Stars, Colored House of David

FREEMAN, BUCK—1925—umpire, World Series

FREEMAN, CHARLES (CHARLIE)—1913, 1916-17, 1927-32—3b, of, officer, Hilldale Club

FREEMAN, SR., ELZIE EUGENE (BUCK)—1940-43—p, Goldman Grays (Fort Smith, AR), Muskogee Hustlers, Tulsa Black Oilers

FREEMAN, GEORGE—1891-92—of, New York Gorhams

FREEMAN, LONNY [see GOODWIN, ALFRED ALONZO]

FREEMAN, W. J. (BUCK)—1908-11—p, Twin City Gophers, Minneapolis Keystones

FREEMAN, WILLIAM—1888-89—3b, Chicago Unions

FREEMONT, ____—1932—p, John Donaldson All Stars

FREIHOFER, WILLIAM—1906—president, International League of Independent Professional Base Ball Clubs

FRESNELL, ____—1939—of, Chicago American Giants

FREYER, JOHN—1870—Chicago Blue Stockings

FRIDAY, WILLIAM—1935—3b, Detroit Cubs

FRIELY, ____—1922—2b, Bacharach (AC) Giants

FRISBY, ____—1867—p, Camden Resolutes

FRISBY, ____—1883—p, Washington Manhattans

FRISBY, [DR.] NOBLE R.—1950—officer, Delta Giants (Greenville, MS); owner Frisby Stadium

FRITZ, ____—1904—of, Philadelphia Giants

FRITZ, ____—1928—p, Homestead Grays

FROEM, ____—1870—ss, Utica (NY) Fairless

FRYE, JOHN H. (JACK)—1883-96—1b, c, p, of, Cuban Giants, Reading, PA (Interstate League), Lewistown (Penn. St.

League), York (PA) Cuban Giants (Eastern Interstate League), Trenton (NJ) Cuban Giants (Middle States League), Ansonia Cuban Giants (Connecticut St. League), New York Gorhams (NCBBL), York (PA) Colored Monarchs (Eastern Interstate League)

FUATER, ____—1922—ph, Cuban Stars (West)

FULCHER, ROBERT—1940—p, Chicago American Giants, Birmingham Black Barons

FULLER, ____—1915—p, Brooklyn Royal Giants

FULLER, ALBIN—1946—p, Fresno/San Diego Tigers

FULLER, JAMES (JIMMY)—1912-22—c, York (PA) Cuban Giants, Bacharach (AC) Giants, Philadelphia Giants, Lincoln (NY) Stars, Havana Red Sox, Brooklyn Royal Giants, Hilldale Club, Grand Central Terminal Red Caps

FULLER, WILLIAM W. (CHICK)—1908-20—ss, 2b, Bacharach (AC) Giants, York (PA) Cuban Giants, Pennsylvania Giants, Cleveland Tate Stars, Hilldale Club, Brooklyn Colored Giants, New York Colored Giants, Penn Red Caps of NY, All Nations, Pittsburgh Stars of Buffalo, Cleveland Giants

FULLMAN, ____—1916—of, Baltimore Black Sox

FULTON, SAMUEL (SAM)—1955—p, Birmingham Black Barons

FUNES [FUMES], MAURICIO [MARINO]—1925-30—of, Cuban Stars (East & West), Stars of Cuba

FURNIER, ____—1910—1b, Indianapolis ABCs

FURR, ____—1921—ss, Lincoln (NY) Giants

FYFE, ____—1926—umpire, ECL

MR. ANDREW "RUBE" FOSTER, Manager.

G

GABBONS, ____—1946—pr, San Francisco Sea Lions
GABE, TED—1946—c, Oakland Larks, Portland (OR) Rosebuds
GABE, TILLMAN—1925—p, Lincoln (NY) Giants
GADSDEN, GUS—1932—of, 2b, Hilldale Club
GADSDEN, PAUL—1947—p, New York Black Yankees
GAICHEY, ____—1948—p, Memphis Red Sox
GAIDERIA, ____—1918—p, Cuban Stars
GAINES, ____—1927—of, Breakers Hotel (FL)
GAINES, ____—1929—of, Louisville White Sox
GAINES, JONAS GEORGE (LEFTY, a.k.a. RUFUS)—1937-51—p, Newark Eagles, Baltimore Elite Giants, Philadelphia Stars, Washington Elite Giants, Chicago American Giants, Houston Eagles
GAINES, LEON—1952—of, Philadelphia Stars
GAINES, WILLY (WILLIE)—1950-55—p, Philadelphia Stars, Indianapolis Clowns
GALATA, DOMINGO R.—1949-50—p, New York Cubans
GALATA y CAPOTE, RAÚL—1949-53—p, Indianapolis Clowns, New York Cubans
GALE, ____—1918—1b, Chicago Union Giants
GALES, WILLIAM—1887—3b, Wilmington Base Ball Club
GALETO, ____—1923-24—c, All Cubans, Cuban Stars (East)
GALEY, ____—1897—1b, of, Cuban Giants
GALLITON, THURMAN—1954—p, Detroit Stars
GALLOWAY, ____—1931—2b, Bacharach (Philly) Giants
GALLOWAY [GAUNT], VIC—1942—p, Minneapolis-St. Paul Colored Gophers
GALLOWAY, WILLIAM HIPPLE (BILL, HIPPO)—1899-06—of, 3b, 2b, Cuban X-Giants, Cuban Giants, Woodstock (Canadian League), Famous Cuban Giants, Genuine Cuban Giants
GALLOWAY, WILLIAM HOWARD—1958, 1960—p, Detroit Clowns, Detroit-New Orleans Stars
GÁLVEZ [GALBAE], FACUNDO (CUNDO, CUNEO)—1928-32—p, Cuban Stars (East & West), Cuban House of David
GALWAY, ____—1870—of, Utica (NY) Fairless
GAMBLE, JOHNNY—1939-42, 1945—p, Bacharach (Philly) Giants, Philadelphia Stars, Philadelphia Daisies (NML), Otto Brigg's All-Stars, Brooklyn Brown Dodgers
GAMBLE, L.H.—1942-43—owner, Chicago Brown Bombers (NML); officer Chicago Palmer House Stars
GAMBLE, WILLIAM—1921—p, Columbus Buckeyes
GAMBLEE, ELLSWORTH—1927—umpire, NNL
GÁMIZ, MÁRGARO (MAZIO, HARRY) [a.k.a. DOMINGO GÓMEZ]—1926-29, 1933-34—c, Harrisburg Giants, Philadelphia Tigers, Baltimore Black Sox, Cuban Stars (East), Havana Red Sox, Philadelphia Royal Giants
GAMP, ____—1917—of, Pittsburgh Stars of Buffalo
GANGGANG, ____—1916—p, of, Baltimore Black Sox
GANS, JOE [nee JOSEPH GANT]—1905—captain, 1b, Middle Section Giants of Baltimore
GANS, ROBERT EDWARD (JUDE, JUDY)—1908-38—of, manager, Brooklyn Royal Giants, Cuban Giants, Paterson (NJ) Smart Set, Lincoln (NY) Giants, Chicago American Giants, Chicago Giants, Lincoln (NY) Stars, Schenectady Mohawk Giants, Cleveland Tigers, Jewell's ABCs, Breakers Hotel (FL); umpire, EWL, NNL, ANL
GANT, HENRY—1887-91—3b, c, Pittsburgh Keystones (NCBBL), New York Gorhams, York Cuban Giants, Cuban Giants
GANTT, ____—1932—of, Chattanooga Black Lookouts
GANTZ, [see GÓMEZ, DOMINGO (HARRY)]
GARAY y ARGUELLES, MARTINIANO JOSÉ—1948-50—of, p, New York Cubans
GARCÍA, ANTONIO MARIA (EL INGLES)—1903-12—c, Genuine Cuban Giants, New York Cuban Stars, All Cubans, Cuban X-Giants
GARCÍA, ATARES (ANGEL)—1945-53—p, Indianapolis Clowns, Cincinnati-Indianapolis Clowns
GARCÍA, JOHN (JUAN)—1902-04—c, Cuban Giants, Genuine Cuban Giants
GARCÍA, JUAN (RENE)—1952—ss, Indianapolis Clowns
GARCÍA, MANUEL (COCAÍNA)—1926-36—p, of, New York Cubans, Cuban Stars (East & West), Stars of Cuba
GARCÍA, REGINO (MAMELO)—1905—c, 1b, All Cubans
GARCÍA, RAMONDO (CHANO)—1926-27—2b, Bacharach (AC) Giants, Lincoln (NY) Giants
GARCÍA, SERAFIN—1904-05—of, All Cubans
GARCÍA y RENDON, SILVIO—1937, 1940-47—ss, New York Cubans, Trujillo All-Stars (Ciudad Trujillo Dragons)
GARDEN, ____—1950—p, Chicago American Giants
GARDNER, ____—1914—of, Philadelphia Giants
GARDNER, ____—1920-23, 1926—of, Toledo Tigers, St. Louis Stars, Dayton Marcos, Baltimore Black Sox
GARDNER, ____—1928—p, Kansas City (KS) Giants
GARDNER, ____—1932—2b, Memphis Red Sox
GARDNER, A.—1883-87—utility, St. Louis Black Stockings

All-Time Register

GARDNER, FLOYD (JELLY)—1919-33—of, Detroit Stars, Chicago American Giants, Lincoln (NY) Giants, Homestead Grays, Royal Poinciana (FL), Dayton Marcos

GARDNER, GLOVER C. (GUS)—1920-23—c, of, Pensacola Giants, New Orleans Caulfield Ads

GARDNER, JAMES (CHAPPY)—1908-21—2b, 3b, ss, Brooklyn Royal Giants, Havana Red Sox, Cuban Giants, Brooklyn Colored Giants, Baltimore Black Sox

GARDNER, KENNETH FULLER (PING, STEEL ARM)—1918-32—p, umpire, Washington Red Caps, Brooklyn Royal Giants, Hilldale Club, Philadelphia Royal Stars, Philadelphia Royal Giants, Lincoln (NY) Giants, Harrisburg Giants, Bacharach (AC) Giants, Cleveland Tigers, Baltimore Black Sox, Newark Browns

GARDNER, SIMMIE—1945, 1948—p, Chicago Brown Bombers (USL), Chicago American Giants; —1951—umpire, East/West game

GAREY [GARVEY], ____—1925, 1929—c, p, Cuban Stars (West)

GARFIELD, ____—1930—of, Havana Red Sox

GARNER, ____—1886—3b, New York Gorhams

GARNER, HORACE T.—1946, 1948-49—of, p, Boston Blues, Indianapolis Clowns, Chicago American Giants

GARNER, RAYMOND—1914—of, Hilldale Club

GARO, ____—1937—c, New York Cubans

GARREN, ____—1905—c, All Cubans

GARRETT, ____—1921—of, Pittsburgh Stars of Buffalo

GARRETT, A. J. (JOHN)—1960—p, Raleigh (NC) Tigers

GARRETT, ALBERT [ALVIN] HAL—1886-87, 1899-1910—player, manager, officer, Cincinnati Browns (NCBBL), Columbia Giants, Leland Giants

GARRETT, FRANK—1883, 1887—ss, Louisville Falls City (NCBBL)

GARRETT, FRANK—1945-46—of, p, Brooklyn Brown Dodgers, Pittsburgh Crawfords (USL)

GARRETT, HENRY—1960—p, Raleigh (NC) Tigers

GARRETT, MARSHALL—1920—manager, Nashville White Sox; 1921—owner, Nashville Elite Giants

GARRETT JR., MITCHELL—1932—1b, p, Austin Black Senators

GARRETT, ROBERT (BOB)—1960—p, Raleigh (NC) Tigers

GARRETT, ROBERT WAYNE (FUZZY)—1951-52—umpire, NNL

GARRETT, SOLOMAN—1950—2b, New York Black Yankees

GARRETT, TOM—1926, 1930, 1936—1b, of, Bacharach (Philly) Giants, Harrisburg Giants, Birmingham Black Barons, New Orleans Black Pelicans, Houston Black Buffaloes

GARRETT, WILLIAM—1887—of, St. Louis Black Stockings

GARRETT, WILLIAM—1943—officer, New York Black Yankees

GARRIDO, ____—1918—of, Cuban Stars (East)

GARRIDO, SR., GIL L. GONZALO—1944-46—2b, 3b, ss, New York Cubans

GARRISON, ____—1872—c, Keystone Club of New Jersey

GARRISON, LEROY (DOC)—1934, 1942—1b, Bacharach (Philly) Giants, Brooklyn Royal Giants

GARRISON, RICHARD WILLIAM (BUSTER, DICK)—1907-11—p, Pittsburgh Giants, St. Paul Colored Gophers, Leland Giants, Twin City Gophers, Cleveland Giants, Pittsburgh Giants

GARRISON, ROSS (SNAPPER)—1889-1908—ss, 3b, York (PA) Cuban Giants (Eastern Interstate League), New York Gorhams (Middle States League), Cuban Giants, Cuban X-Giants

GARRY, ____—1919, 1922—of, Pittsburgh Stars of Buffalo

GARV, ____—1918—of, Cuban Stars (West)

GARVIN, LEEDELL—1940, 1942—p, of, 3b, Philadelphia Stars, Schenectady Mohawk Giants

GARY, ____—1918—of, Cuban Stars West

GARY, ____—1919—OF, Baltimore Black Sox

GARY, CHARLES—1948-50—3b, ss, Homestead Grays

GASKINS, AARON J.—1909—vice-president, treasurer, Washington Giants

GASTON, ALEX—1920—c, Bacharach (AC) Giants

GASTON, EDDIE—1945—p, Pittsburgh Crawfords (USL)

GASTON, HARRY—1921, 1926—ss, Hilldale Club, Harrisburg Giants

GASTON, HIRAM ALLAN (MIKE)—1952-53—p, Birmingham Black Barons

GASTON, ISAAC—1949—utility, Kansas City Monarchs

GASTON, ROBERT (JACK, RAB ROY)—1932-49—c, Homestead Grays, Brooklyn Brown Dodgers

GATEWOOD, C.D.—1938—p, Colored House of David

GATEWOOD, ERNEST WILLIS—1914-27—c, 1b, Lincoln (NY) Giants, Brooklyn Royal Giants, Bacharach (AC) Giants, Harrisburg Giants, Lincoln (NY) Stars, Schenectady Mohawk Giants, Philadelphia Giants

GATEWOOD, J. WILL—1887—secretary, National League of Colored Base Ball Clubs (NCBBL)

GATEWOOD, LOUIS [LEWIS]—1902-09—3b, Illinois Giants, Indianapolis ABCs
GATEWOOD, WILLIAM MILLER (BIG BILL)—1906-28—p, manager, Cuban X-Giants, Leland Giants, Chicago Giants, Chicago American Giants, St. Louis Giants, Detroit Stars, St. Louis Stars, Toledo Tigers, Albany (GA) Giants, Birmingham Black Barons, Memphis Red Sox, Milwaukee Bears, Lincoln (NY) Giants, St. Paul Colored Gophers, Indianapolis ABCs; umpire, ANL
GAUL, J.E.—1912—officer, All Nations
GAUTIER, JOHN—1955—p, Kansas City Monarchs
GAVIN, ____—1935—p, Brooklyn Eagles
GAVINS, ____—1911—p, Wilmington Giants
GAY, HERBERT—1929-30—p, Chicago American Giants, Birmingham Black Barons, Baltimore Black Sox
GAY, W.—1929—of, Chicago American Giants
GAY, WILLIAM HOWARD—1944-48—of, ss, 3b, Great Lakes Bluejackets, Seattle Steelheads, Harlem Globetrotters
GAYLE, JIM—1918—1b, Foster's Hartford Giants
GAYNOR, ____—1922—p, Philadelphia Giants
GAYNOR, MORGAN C.—1947—p, New York Black Yankees
GEARHART [GERHART], ____—1919-20—2b, of Brooklyn Royal Giants, Chicago American Giants
GEDDES, JOSEPH P.—1930—vice-president, New Orleans Black Pelicans
GEE, ____—1891—c, Cuban Giants
GEE, RICHARD RAYMOND (RICH)—1922-32—c, Lincoln (NY) Giants, New Orleans Crescent Stars, Schenectady Mohawk Giants, Harrisburg Giants
GEE, SAMUEL L. (SAMMY)—1948, 1955—ss, New York Cubans, Detroit Stars
GEE, JR., THOMAS HENRY (TOM)—1921, 1925-26—c, Ft. Worth Black Panthers, Lincoln (NY) Giants, Newark Stars
GEISEL, ____—1915—umpire, NNL
GEORGE, JOHN—1920-25—1b, ss, St. Louis Giants, New Orleans Crescent Stars, Chicago Giants, Harrisburg Giants, Chicago American Giants, Bacharach (AC) Giants, New Orleans Caulfield Ads
GERARD [GERALD, GERRARD], ALPHONSO (AL, HARLEM FLASH, PIGGY, CHICO)—1945-49—of, New York Black Yankees, Chicago American Giants, Indianapolis Clowns
GETSON, ____—1927—1b, St. Louis Giants
GETTLE, [see SETTLE]

GETTYS, SPENCER—1936—c, Bacharach (Philly) Giants; 1945—treasurer, NPUA
GHOLSTON, BERT E.—1923-43—umpire, NNL, EWL
GIAVANNI, BEALE [see GIOVANNI, BEALE]
GIBBONS, JAMES—1923—3b, Harrisburg Giants
GIBBONS, JOHN EDDIE (BAY)—1939-41, 1945, 1949—p, Toledo Crawfords, Harlem Globetrotters, Philadelphia Stars, Durham (NC) Eagles
GIBBONS, WALTER LEE (DIRK, BUBBLE GUM)—1948-49—p, Indianapolis Clowns; 1953-57—Winnipeg Giants, Brandon Grays, Minot Mallards (ManDak)
GIBBS, ____—1891—of, Philadelphia Orions
GIBBS, ____—1907—3b, Trusty (PA) Giants
GIBBS, S. R.—1910—owner, Fall City Stars (Louisville, KY)
GIBSON, ____—1918-19, 1923—p, Dayton Marcos, Illinois Giants
GIBSON, ____—1925—c, Chicago American Giants
GIBSON, ____—1927—of, Brooklyn Cuban Giants
GIBSON, B.—1927—p, Cleveland Hornets
GIBSON, JERRY WILLIAM—1934-43—of, p, Homestead Grays, Cincinnati Tigers, Cincinnati Ethiopian Clowns (NML), Cincinnati Buckeyes
GIBSON, JR., JOSHUA (JOSH)—1949-50—3b, 2b, Homestead Grays
GIBSON, SR., JOSHUA (JOSH, BOXER, TRUCUTU)—1928-46—c, of, Homestead Grays, Pittsburgh Crawfords, Trujillo All-Stars (Ciudad Trujillo Dragons), North Classic Team, South All-Stars
GIBSON, LANNIE—1933—of, Philadelphia Stars
GIBSON, PAUL—1934-35—p, Homestead Grays, Newark Dodgers
GIBSON, RALPH [RUFUS] [see GIPSON, RUFUS (GAP)
GIBSON [GIPSON], THEODORE (TED, RED SHIRT)—1940-42—p, c, Columbus Buckeyes, Chicago American Giants, Cincinnati Buckeyes, Birmingham Black Barons
GIBSON, WELDA HAROLD—1949-50—p, Houston Eagles
GIBSON, WILLIAM I.—writer, *Baltimore Afro-American*
GIDD'A, ____—1906—of, Cuban Stars
GID'WS, ____—1907—of, Harrisburg Giants
GIFFORD, ____—1891—of, Cuban Giants
GIGO, ____—1929—p, Chattanooga Black Lookouts
GILBERT, PAUL DEAN—1959-60—1b, Kansas City Monarchs
GILCREST [GILCHRIST], DENNIS—1930-35—c, 2b, ss, Indianapolis ABCs, Columbus Blue Birds, Cleveland Red Sox,

Brooklyn Eagles, Homestead Grays, Columbus Turfs, New York Black Yankees, Columbus Keystones

GILENDER, PLEASANT—1923—p, Bacharach (AC) Giants

GILES [GILERS], ____—1928—of, Birmingham Black Barons

GILES, CORNELIUS—1954—p, Indianapolis Clowns

GILES, SR., GEORGE FRANKLIN—1927-38—1b, Kansas City Monarchs, St. Louis Stars, Brooklyn Eagles, New York Black Yankees, Philadelphia Stars, Detroit Wolves, Homestead Grays, Pittsburgh Crawfords, Baltimore Black Sox

GILKERSON, ROBERT PAUL (GILKY)—1908-17—1b, 2b, owner, Cleveland Giants, Chicago Union Giants, Gilkerson's Union Giants, Twin City Gophers, Leland Giants, Lost Island (IA) Giants

GILL, WILLIAM—1931-37—1b, 3b, Detroit Stars, Louisville Red Caps, Indianapolis Athletics, Homestead Grays, Twin City Gophers, Colored House of David

GILLARD [GAILLARD, GILLEAD], ALBERT (HAMP)—1909-14, 1917—p, St. Louis Giants, Chicago American Giants, West Baden (IN) Sprudels, Birmingham Giants, Dayton Giants, Oklahoma City Giants, Kansas City (KS) Giants

GILLARD, LUTHER (PEN)—1934-42—of, 1b, Memphis Red Sox, Indianapolis Crawfords, Birmingham Black Barons, Monroe (LA) Monarchs

GILLESPIE, A.—1931—p, Cleveland Cubs

GILLESPIE, H.—1887—p, of, Louisville Falls City (NCBBL)

GILLESPIE, HENRY—1917-34—p, of, Pennsylvania Giants, Hilldale Club, Lincoln (NY) Giants, Bacharach (AC) Giants, Philadelphia Tigers, Philadelphia Quaker City Giants, New York Harlem Stars, Baltimore Black Sox, Harrisburg Giants, Madison Stars, Philadelphia Giants, Schenectady Mohawk Giants

GILLESPIE, MURRAY (LEFTY)—1930-32—p, Memphis Red Sox, Nashville Elite Giants, Monroe (LA) Monarchs

GILLHAM, ____—1917—c, Dayton Marcos

GILLIAM, ____—1906—c, Wilmington Giants

GILLIAM, SR., ELIJAH (SLIM)—1958-61—p, Raleigh (NC) Tigers, Birmingham Black Barons, New Orleans Stars

GILLIAM, JAMES WILLIAMS (JUNIOR, JIM)—1945-51—batboy, 2b, Nashville Black Vols, Baltimore Elite Giants

GILLIAM, JOHNNY—1960-61—of, Birmingham Black Barons, Indianapolis Clowns, Raleigh (NC) Tigers

GILLIAM, TED—1920-21, 1926—1b, p, Atlanta Black Crackers

GILLIAM, WILLIAM (WILLIE)—1929—c, Memphis Red Sox

GILLIAND, ____—1910—utility, Oklahoma City Giants

GILLIARD, ARTHUR LEE—1914—p, Louisville White Sox, Chicago American Giants, French Lick (IN) Plutos

GILLIS, SR., LOUIS CHARLES (SEA BOY)—1951—c, Birmingham Black Barons

GILMORE, (SPEED, SLATS)—1921, 1926-28—p, Pittsburgh Keystones, Lincoln (NY) Giants

GILMORE, JR., JAMES J. (SPEED)—1953-55—p, Kansas City Monarchs

GILMORE, QUINCY JORDAN [JARDIN]—1922-37—business manager, Kansas City Monarchs; secretary, treasurer, NNL; president, Texas-Oklahoma-Louisiana League

GILPIN, ____—1946—ph, Kansas City Monarchs

GILSON, ____—1922—of, Philadelphia Giants

GILYARD, C.—1929—ss, Tulsa Black Oilers

GILYARD, LUTHER—1937-39—1b, Chicago American Giants, St. Louis Stars

GIOVANNI [GIAVANNI], BEALE—1947-48—p. New York Black Yankees

GIPSON, ALVIN (BUBBER, SKEET)—1939-50—p, Chicago American Giants, Birmingham Black Barons, Houston Eagles, Detroit Senators, Cincinnati Crescents, New Orleans Crescent Stars, Cincinnati Buckeyes

GIPSON, RUFUS (GAP)—1951-61—2b, ss, manager, Birmingham Black Barons, Louisville Clippers, Memphis Red Sox, Detroit Stars, Raleigh (NC) Tigers

GISENTANER, WILLIAM (WILLIE, LEFTY)—1920-39—p, of, Atlanta Black Crackers, Columbus Buckeyes, Washington Potomacs, Kansas City Monarchs, Harrisburg Giants, Newark Stars, Lincoln (NY) Giants, Cuban Stars (East), Louisville White Sox, Pittsburgh Crawfords, Nashville Elite Giants, Louisville Red Caps, Homestead Grays, Louisville Black Caps, Chicago American Giants, Philadelphia Giants, Brooklyn Royal Giants, Havana Red Sox, Bacharach (AC) Giants, Jacksonville Stars, Montgomery Grey Sox

GIST, ROMMIE—1955—c, Indianapolis Clowns, New York Black Yankees

GIVENS, ____—1911—ss, Cuban Giants

GIVENS, ____—1927—ss, Cleveland Hornets

GIVENS, OSCAR C. (GIBBY)—1939, 1946-48—ss, Newark Eagles

GLADNEY, ____—1932—ss, Indianapolis ABCs

GLADSTONE, GRANVILLE A. (HAPPY)—1950—of, Indianapolis Clowns

GLASCOW, ANDREW—1867, 1871—1b, Philadelphia Excelsior, Philadelphia Pythians

GLASS, CARL LEE (BUTCH, LEFTY)—1921-37—p, of, manager, Memphis Red Sox, Cincinnati Tigers, St. Louis Stars, Birmingham Black Barons, Chicago American Giants, Kansas City Monarchs, Louisville White Sox, St. Louis Giants, Atlanta Black Crackers, Louisville Black Caps
GLASSCOCK, ____—1888—ss, Hoosier Black Stockings
GLEASON, BILL [see GREASON, [REV.] WILLIAM HENRY]
GLENN, ____—1917—of, Los Angeles White Sox
GLENN, HUBERT (COUNTRY)—1943-49—p, New York Black Yankees, Brooklyn Brown Dodgers, Indianapolis Clowns, Philadelphia Stars
GLENN, OSCAR (HAP)—1937-38—3b, Atlanta Black Crackers
GLENN, STANLEY RUDOLF (DOC)—1943-50—c, Philadelphia Stars, Brooklyn Brown Dodgers; author
GLOVER, THOMAS MOSS (LEFTY)—1934-45—p, Birmingham Black Barons, Cleveland Red Sox, New Orleans Black Pelicans, Washington Elite Giants, Memphis Red Sox, Baltimore Elite Giants, Columbus Elite Giants
GODFREY, SR., JAMES EDWARD CLEVELAND (CLEVE)—1951—p, Birmingham Black Barons
GODINEZ, MANUEL (MANOLO)—1946-49—p, Indianapolis Clowns, Cincinnati-Indianapolis Clowns
GOECKEL, EDWARD—1910-34—umpire, NNL
GOINES, OSCAR CHARLES—1915-17—c, of, Indianapolis ABCs, Bowser's ABCs, Jewell's ABCs, West Baden (IN) Sprudels
GOINES, WALTER—1932—p, Montgomery Grey Sox
GOLD, ____—1946—ph, Los Angeles White Sox
GOLDEN, CLYDE SHERMAN (BRUCE)—1946-52—p, Jacksonville Eagles, Newark Eagles, Homestead Grays, Houston Eagles, New Orleans Eagles, Chicago American Giants
GOLDEN, EUGENE (GOON)—1950-51—p, Cleveland Buckeyes
GOLDEN, FRANK—1888—umpire, Independent Colored teams
GOLDER, ____—1932—2b, Cuban Stars (West)
GOLDIE, [see DAVIS, GOLDIE, RED]
GOLDMAN, WILLIAM—1915—c, Hilldale Club
GOLDSMITH, ____—1928—1b, Kansas City (KS), Giants
GOLIAH [GOLIATH], FRED—1909-11, 1914, 1920—2b, of, Leland Giants, Chicago American Giants, Chicago Union Giants, Chicago Giants
GOMES, JOE—1925, 1932—p, of, Bacharach (AC) Giants

GÓMEZ, DAVID (MONOTEJAO)—1925-28, 1932—p, 3b, of, Cuban Stars (East & West), Philadelphia Tigers
GÓMEZ, DOMINGO (HARRY) [see GAMIZ, MARGARO]
GÓMEZ, RAFAEL EMILIO (JOE, JOSÉ, SIJO)—1925-33—p, Cuban Stars (East), Bacharach (Philly) Giants
GONZÁLEZ, ____—1918—3b, Dayton Marcos
GONZÁLEZ, ____—1945, 1947—p, Cincinnati-Indianapolis Clowns, New Orleans Creoles
GONZÁLEZ, A.—1912—p, Cuban Stars
GONZÁLEZ y LÓPEZ, EUSEBIO MIGUEL (MIKE, PAPO)—1931—1b, 2b, 3b, Philadelphia Royal Giants
GONZÁLEZ y CORDERO, MIGUEL ANGEL (MIKE, BAGUETTE, PANDE FLAUTA)—1911-14—c, 1b, Long Branch (NJ) Cubans
GONZÁLEZ y OJARUL, GERVASIO (STRIKE)—1910-18—1b, c, Cuban Stars (West), Long Branch (NJ) Cubans, Cuban Havana Stars, Breakers Hotel (FL)
GONZÁLEZ, PEDRO—1915-16—p, Havana Reds, Long Branch (NJ) Cubans
GONZÁLEZ, RENE—1950—of, New York Cubans
GONZÁLEZ, LUIS (CHICHO)—1908-12—p, of, Cuban Stars
GONZÁLEZ, RAMÓN (KAKÍN)—1916, 1919—3b, Long Branch (NJ) Cubans, New York Cuban Stars
GONZÁLEZ, RAÚL—1915—2b, Havana Reds
GOOD, ____—1884—p, Newark Dusky Boys
GOOD, ____—1890—of, York (PA) Cuban Giants (Eastern Interstate League)
GOOD, ____—1916—c, of, Lincoln (NY) Stars
GOOD, CLEVELAND—1937—p, Newark Eagles
GOODALL, ANDREW—1875—utility, St. Louis Blue Stockings
GOODALL, JAMES—1887—officer, Philadelphia Pythians (NCBBL)
GOODE, ____—1914—1b, Baltimore Giants
GOODE, MALVIN RUSSELL (MAL)—1948-1952—writer, *Pittsburgh Courier*
GOODELL, HERMAN—1911—2b, 3b, Brown's Tennessee Rats
GOODEN, ERNEST E. (PUD)—1921-24—2b, 3b, Pittsburgh Keystones, Toledo Tigers, Chicago American Giants, Cleveland Tate Stars, Detroit Stars
GOODGAME, JOHN W.—1912, 1917—p, Chicago Giants, Brooklyn Royal Giants
GOODMAN, JOE—1926-28—of, Harrisburg Giants

GOODMAN, W. —1923-38—umpire, NSL
GOODRICH, JOSEPH HENRY (JOE)—1923-26—2b, 3b, Washington Potomacs, Philadelphia Giants, Wilmington Potomacs, Harrisburg Giants
GOODSON, M. E.—1931-32—officer, New York Black Yankees
GOODWIN, ALFRED ALONZO (LONNIE, POP)—1920—officer, Lincoln (NY) Giants, California Winter League; Los Angeles White Sox, Philadelphia Royal Giants
GORDON, ____—1880—of, Washington Douglass Club
GORDON, ____—1920—p, Birmingham Black Barons
GORDON, ____—1923—of, p, Baltimore Black Sox
GORDON, ____—1925—of, Gilkerson's Union Giants
GORDON, ANDREW NATHANIEL (WILLIE, A.N.)—1921—2b, Calgary Black Sox
GORDON, (BUS)—1920—2b, Kansas City Monarchs
GORDON, CHARLES WILLIAM (CHARLIE, FLASH)—1939-42, 1946—of, p, New York Black Yankees, Philadelphia Stars, Pittsburgh Crawfords (USL), Newark Eagles
GORDON, CLYDE—1903—ss, Genuine Cuban Giants
GORDON, DAVID E. (JUMBO)—1883-87—of, St. Louis Black Stockings
GORDON, D.D.—1910—owner, Chicago Unions
GORDON, EDWARD L.—1891—of, Cuban Giants
GORDON, HERALD (BEE BOP)—1950-51, 1954—p, Chicago American Giants, Detroit Stars
GORDON, HERMAN CLAY—1923-24—p, of, 2b, Toledo Tigers, Birmingham Black Barons, St. Louis Stars, Cleveland Browns, Pittsburgh Keystones
GORDON, HERMAN EVAN—1917—p, Bacharach (AC) Giants
GORDON, JACKSON (JACK)—1884-87—secretary, Chicago Gordons
GORDON (LEFTY)—1928—p, Kansas City (KS) Giants
GORDON, SAMUEL SIMON (SAM, S.S.)—1901-15—c, 1b, manager, Indianapolis ABCs, West Baden (IN) Sprudels, Chicago Union Giants, French Lick (IN) Plutos, Illinois Giants, Winnipeg Giants, Calgary Black Sox
GORDON, TED—1929—p, Santop Broncos
GORDON, WALLACE CLIFFORD—1902-15—of, 2b, 3b, Cuban Giants, New York Black Sox, Lincoln (NY) Giants, Brooklyn All-Stars, Indianapolis ABCs, Chicago Black Sox, Cleveland Giants, Cleveland Starlight Champions
GORDY, TILLMAN (TED)—1946—of, Fresno/San Diego Tigers
GOREE, FRED—1925—manager, Chicago Independents
GORHAM, ____—1911-12—of, Philadelphia Giants
GORMAN, ____—1918—2b, Bacharach (AC) Giants
GORHAM, ALEXANDER—1886-89—owner, New York Gorhams
GORLEY, ____—1928—c, Buck Ewing's All-Stars
GOSHAY, SAMUEL—1949—of, Kansas City Monarchs
GOSHEN, ____—1931—of, Cuban Stars (East)
GOTTLIEB, EDWARD ISADORE (EDDIE)—1936-50—officer, promoter and booking agent, NNL; owner, Philadelphia Stars
GOULD, ____—1867—of, Camden Resolutes
GOULD, SR., HAROLD LORENZO (HAL, JOHN, BIG RED)—1947-48—p, Philadelphia Stars; author
GOULD, JR., LAYFAYETTE—1917—of, Bacharach (AC) Giants
GOVANTES, JOSÉ—1908-10—2b, of, New York Cuban Stars, Stars of Cuba
GOVEINS, ____—1907—of, Keystone (PA) Giants
GOVENS, ____—1909—of, Philadelphia Quaker City Giants
GOVERN, STANISLAUS KOSTKA (S.K., SIKI)—1886-88, 1891, 1896—manager, Philadelphia Pythians, New York Gorhams, Cuban Giants
GRACE, ____—1931—of, Chicago American Giants
GRACE, CHARLES ARTHUR—1888-89—p, 1b, of, Champaign (Ill.-Ind. League), Bloomington (IL) Reds
GRACE, DEWEY—1936-37—of, Chicago Giants
GRACE, ELLSWORTH—1950—2b, New York Black Yankees
GRACE, JAMES—1960—Birmingham Black Barons
GRACE, WILLIE (FIREMAN)—1942-50—of, Cincinnati-Cleveland Buckeyes, Cleveland Buckeyes, Louisville Buckeyes, Houston Eagles
GRACEY, ____—1927—umpire, NNL
GRADY, L.—1924—p, Washington Potomacs
GRAHAM, ____—1869—1b, Rockford (IL) Rockfords
GRAHAM, ____—1907-08—p, Chicago Union Giants, Minneapolis Keystones
GRAHAM, ____—1926—ss, Atlanta Black Crackers
GRAHAM, JOHN—1867-71—of, 3b—Philadelphia Pythians
GRAHAM, DENNIS WILSON (PEACHES)—1918-31—of, Washington Red Caps, Bacharach (AC) Giants St. Louis Stars, Homestead Grays, Pittsburgh Crawfords
GRAHAM, FOSTER—1958-59—ss, Memphis Red Sox
GRAHAM, MILTON—1956—c, Birmingham Black Barons
GRAHAM, VASCO—1895-99—c, of, Lansing (MI) Colored Capital All-Americans, Adrian (MI) Page Fence Giants,

Negro Leagues Book #2: The Players

Adrian Reformers (Michigan St. League), Dubuque (IA), Cuban Giants

GRANGER, (RABBIT)—1908-09—ss, of, Indianapolis ABCs, Louisville Giants

GRANSBERRY, BILL—1929—of, 1b, Chicago American Giants, Chicago Giants

GRANT, ____—1926—p, Washington Black Sox

GRANT, ART—1920-22, 1925—c, Baltimore Black Sox, Richmond Giants (NAA), Harrisburg Giants

GRANT, ARTHUR—1944—infield, Cleveland Buckeyes, Great Lakes Bluejackets

GRANT, BURTON—1916—of, West Baden (IN) Sprudels

GRANT, CALVIN LEWIS—1959-60—p, Detroit Stars, Kansas City Monarchs

GRANT, JR., CHARLES (CHARLIE, CHIEF TOKOHAMA)—1896-1916—2b, Adrian (MI) Page Fence Giants, Columbia Giants, Cuban X-Giants, Philadelphia Giants, New York Black Sox, Lincoln (NY) Giants, Philadelphia Quaker City Giants, Cincinnati Stars, Cuban Giants

GRANT, CLARENCE—1890—c, 3b, of, Cuban Giants

GRANT, DON—1919—of, Cleveland Giants

GRANT, FRANK—1890—c, Cuban Giants

GRANT, FRANKLIN—1946—c, San Francisco Sea Lions

GRANT, HARRY—1890-92—c, of, Cuban Giants

GRANT, JAMES—1875—of, p, St. Louis Blue Stockings

GRANT, LEROY—1908-25—1b, Pop Watkins Stars, Chicago American Giants, Lincoln (NY) Giants, Indianapolis ABCs, Cleveland Browns, Schenectady Mohawk Giants, Royal Poinciana (FL), Breakers Hotel (FL)

GRANT, PHIL—1923, 1927—p, All Nations, Kansas City Monarchs

GRANT, ULYSSES FRANKLIN (FRANK)—1886-1905—2b, ss, 3b, Meriden (Eastern League); Buffalo (International League); Cuban Giants, Harrisburg (Eastern Interstate League); Lansing (MI), Colored Capital All-Americans, New York Gorhams (Middle States League), Ansonia Cuban Giants (Connecticut St. League), Trenton (NJ) Cuban Giants (Middle States League), Philadelphia Giants, Genuine Cuban Giants, Cuban X-Giants, Cleveland Giants

GRANT, WARREN—1946—2b, Oakland Larks

GRATTIS, ____—1948—p, Birmingham Clowns

GRAVES, ____—1932—1b, John Donaldson All-Stars

GRAVES, ____—1942—of, 2b, Jacksonville Red Caps

GRAVES, BOB—1932-39—p, of, Indianapolis ABCs, Indianapolis Athletics, Baltimore Elite Giants

GRAVES, JOE—1914-16—p, of, All Nations

GRAVES, LAWRENCE (CANNON BALL)—1920-23—p, 2b, Harrisburg Giants, Nashville Elite Giants, New Orleans Crescent Stars

GRAVES, LONNIE [see GOODWIN, ALFRED ALONZO]

GRAVES, WESLEY—1946—owner, Little Rock Black Travelers

GRAVES, JR., WHIT ALLEN—1950-51—p, Indianapolis Clowns

GRAY, ____—1867, 1871—of, Mutuals of Washington, Chicago Uniques

GRAY, ABE—1931-32—c, 1b, Indianapolis ABCs, John Donaldson All-Stars

GRAY [GRAVES], CHESLEY (CHESTER)—1940-46—c, St. Louis Stars, New York Black Yankees, Harrisburg-St. Louis Stars, Kansas City Monarchs, Toledo Cubs/Rays, Boston Blues, New Orleans-St. Louis Stars

GRAY, EMERSON HENRY—1917, 1922—c, Bacharach (AC) Giants

GRAY [GREY], G. E. (WILLIE, DOLLY, LEFTY)—1920-34, 1936—of, 1b, Cleveland Tate Stars, Homestead Grays, Lincoln (NY) Giants, Penn Red Caps of NY, Dayton Marcos, Pittsburgh Keystones, Newark Stars, Columbus Buckeyes, Newark Browns, Brooklyn Royal Giants, Birmingham Black Barons, Chattanooga White Sox

GRAY, HOWARD—1951—infield, New Orleans Eagles

GRAY, JIM—1929-33—2b, 3b, Nashville Elite Giants, Montgomery Grey Sox

GRAY, JOHN ELLIOTT (JOHNNY)—1958—c, Indianapolis Clowns

GRAY, JOSÉ—1950—p, New York Cubans

GRAY, (PANCHO)—1951—p, Chicago American Giants

GRAY, REYNOLD—1939—officer, Norfolk Black Tars

GRAY, RICHARD—1945—2b, Chicago Brown Bombers (USL)

GRAY, ROOSEVELT (CHAPPY)—1920-23, 1932—1b, c, p, Cleveland Tate Stars, Toledo Tigers, Dayton Marcos, Kansas City Monarchs, Birmingham Black Barons, John Donaldson All-Stars, Kansas City (MO) Royals

GRAY, JR., ROOSEVELT (CHAPPY)—1946—ss, Fresno/San Diego Tigers

GRAY, WILLIAM—1884-87—of, c, Baltimore Atlantics, Baltimore Lord Baltimores (NCBBL)

GRAY, WILLIAM—1944, 1946—c, Pittsburgh Crawfords (USL), Homestead Grays

GRAY, WILLIE—1954—p, Detroit Stars

GRAYER [GREYER], GEORGE A.–1916-22–1b, Baltimore Black Sox

GREASON, [REV.] WILLIAM HENRY (WILLIE, BILL, BOOSTER)–1947-51, 1960–p, Birmingham Black Barons, Nashville Black Vols, Nashville Cubs, Raleigh (NC) Tigers, Asheville Blues

GREEN, ____ –1867–1b, Washington Alerts

GREEN, ____ –1872–p, Keystone Club of New Jersey

GREEN, ____ –1902–p, Cuban X-Giants

GREEN, ____ –1923–c, Nashville Elite Giants

GREEN, ____ –1927–c, Wilmington Potomacs

GREEN, ALPHONSE–1942–of New York Cubans

GREEN, ALVIN PARKER–1950, 1956–infield, Baltimore Elite Giants, Memphis Red Sox

GREEN, BILL–1946–p, Fresno/San Diego Tigers

GREEN, CARL–1934–of, Cincinnati Tigers

GREEN, CHARLES ALBERT (JOE, GREENIE)–1902-31–manager, of, owner, Leland Giants, Chicago Giants, Chicago American Giants, Chicago Union Giants, Columbia Giants, Philadelphia Giants, Genuine Cuban Giants

GREEN, CHARLIE–1940–2b, Philadelphia Stars

GREEN, CURTIS (CORNELIUS)–1923-29–1b, p, Birmingham Black Barons, Brooklyn Cuban Giants, Philadelphia Tigers, Schenectady Mohawk Giants, Bacharach (AC) Giants

GREEN, DAVE–1950–of, Baltimore Elite Giants

GREEN, DONALD–1952–of, Kansas City Monarchs

GREEN, SR., GEORGE–1959-60–of, ss, Indianapolis Clowns

GREEN, GEORGE WASHINGTON–1890s–manager, Cuban Giants

GREEN, HENRYENE (RENE) PROCTOR [Mrs. Vernon]–1949-50–owner, Baltimore Elite Giants

GREEN, HERMAN–1952-56, 1959–of, 1b, manager, Detroit Stars, Kansas City Monarchs, Satchel Paige All-Stars

GREEN, (HONEY)–1938-44–p, of, Newark Eagles, Cleveland Bears, Memphis Red Sox, Boston Royal Giants

GREEN [GREENE], JAMES–1950, 1955–3b, New York Black Yankees

GREEN, JOHN JULIUS (JUNIOR)–1927-30–of, 1b, Philadelphia Royal Giants, Cleveland Royal Giants, Memphis Red Sox, Detroit Stars

GREEN, LESLIE (CHIN)–1939-46–of, St. Louis Stars, New Orleans-St. Louis Stars, Cincinnati-Cleveland Buckeyes, New York Black Yankees, Memphis Red Sox, Chicago American Giants

GREEN, LOUIS–1946–c, San Francisco Sea Lions

GREEN, LUTHER–1931–of, Homestead Grays, Knoxville Giants

GREEN, NATHAN–1920–p, Detroit Stars

GREEN, PETER (ED)–1908-20–of, p, Pittsburgh Giants, Lincoln (NY) Stars, Brooklyn Royal Giants, Brooklyn Colored Giants, Philadelphia Giants, Lincoln (NY) Giants, Cuban Giants

GREEN, JR., SHEDRICK (BB)–1955–of, Indianapolis Clowns, New York Black Yankees

GREEN, THOMAS–1946–p, 2b, Fresno/San Diego Tigers

GREEN, VERNON (RUFUS, FAT, BABY)–1921, 1931, 1942-49–c, officer, owner, Nashville Giants, Cleveland Giants, Baltimore Elite Giants

GREEN, WILLIE (WIL)–1915-24–3b, Chicago Giants, Chicago American Giants, Chicago Union Giants, Detroit Stars, Kansas City Monarchs

GREEN, WILLIAM (WILLIE, THE EAT)–1906-12–c, St. Paul Colored Gophers, Minneapolis Keystones, St. Louis Giants, Chicago Giants, Chicago Union Giants, Leland Giants

GREENE, ____ –1950–umpire, East/West game

GREENE [GREEN], JAMES ELBERT (JOE, PEA, PIG)–1932-48–c, Kansas City Monarchs, Cleveland Buckeyes, Atlanta Black Crackers, Homestead Grays, Indianapolis ABCs

GREENE, JOHN (BIG RED)–1951–infield, Chicago American Giants

GREENE, TERRY–1929–p, Louisville Black Caps

GREENE, ULYSSES GRANT (DOUBLE DUTY)–1958-61–p, Indianapolis Clowns

GREENE, WALTER–1928–of, 1b, Brooklyn Cuban Giants, Bacharach (AC) Giants

GREENE, WILL–1910, 1912, 1915–p, Pittsburgh Giants, Philadelphia Giants, Lincoln (NY) Giants

GREENEY, ____ –1930–umpire, NSL

GREENIDGE, VICTOR (SLICKER)–1941-45–p, New York Cubans

GREENFIELD, FRANK (EGGIE)–1919–c, Baltimore Black Sox

GREENLEE, WILLIAM AUGUSTUS (GUS, BIG RED)–1931-46–officer, owner, Pittsburgh Crawfords; 1933-38–founder and president, second NNL; 1945–founder, vice-president, United States Baseball League

GREER, ____ –1938–of, Memphis Red Sox

GREER, J. B.–1939-42–officer, Cleveland Bears, Knoxville Red Caps, Jacksonville Red Caps

GREFFENREED, LEROY–1946–2b, Cleveland Clippers

GREGG, ____ –1932–1b, Austin Black Senators

GREGORY, ____—1870-71—p, Boston Resolutes
GREGORY, ____—1918—2b, Bacharach (AC) Giants
GREGORY, JOHN (SPEEDBALL)—1940—p, Birmingham Black Barons
GREY, EMERSON—1917—p, Bacharach (AC) Giants, Brooklyn Royal Giants
GREY, ____—1899—2b, Cuban Giants
GREY, M.—1888—utility, New York Gorhams
GREY, MILTON H.—1935—officer, NSL
GREY, WILLIAM [see GRAY, G. E. (WILLIE, DOLLY)]
GREYER, GEORGE A.—1920—1b, Baltimore Black Sox
GRIDIRON, DAVID—1953—p, Kansas City (KS) Giants
GRIER, ____—1906—1b, Chicago Union Giants
GRIER, CLAUDE BONDS (RED)—1924-28—p, Wilmington Potomacs, Bacharach (AC) Giants, Washington Potomacs, Pittsburgh Giants
GRIESMAN, ____—1929—2b, Schenectady Mohawk Giants
GRIFFIN, ____—1921, 1923, 1929—2b, of, ss, Nashville Elite Giants, Memphis Red Sox, Louisville Black Caps, Evansville Giants
GRIFFIN, ____—1943—p, Birmingham Black Barons
GRIFFIN, ____—1945—of, Detroit Motor City Giants
GRIFFIN, ____—1958—p, Birmingham Black Barons
GRIFFIN, CHARLES H. (CHARLEY)—1884-89—p, of, Pittsburgh Keystones (NCBBL), Cleveland Unions, Cleveland Blue Stockings
GRIFFIN, CLARENCE BERNARD (C.B.)—1932-35—of, Columbus Blue Birds, Cleveland Red Sox, Brooklyn Eagles, Columbus Elite Giants, Columbus Turfs, Columbus Stars
GRIFFIN, E.—1902-10—p, of, Philadelphia Giants, New York Black Sox
GRIFFIN, FRED—1945—p, Chicago Brown Bombers (USL)
GRIFFIN, JAMES (HORSE)-1911-21—2b, York (PA) Cuban Giants, Pittsburgh Giants, Philadelphia Giants, Cuban X-Giants
GRIFFIN, LEONARD—1902-13—p, of, Indianapolis ABCs, Louisville Giants
GRIFFIN, ROBERT—1931, 1937—p, Chicago American Giants, St. Louis Stars
GRIFFIN, ROLAND JAMES—1913—p, of, Indianapolis ABCs
GRIFFIN, SILAS—1947—3b, Birmingham Black Barons
GRIFFITH, ____—1888—p, Bloomington (IL) Reds
GRIFFITH, ____—1919-20—umpire, ECL
GRIFFITH, ROBERT LEE (BIG BILL, SCHOOLBOY)—1934-52—p, Nashville Elite Giants, Columbus Elite Giants, Washington Elite Giants, Baltimore Elite Giants, New York Black Yankees, Philadelphia Stars, Indianapolis Clowns, Denver Post Negro All-Stars, Trujillo All-Stars (Ciudad Trujillo Dragons)
GRIFFITH, TED—1943-45—p, of, Newark Eagles
GRIGGS, ACIE (SKEET)—1948, 1951—of, New York Cubans, Birmingham Black Barons
GRIGGS, BENJAMIN L. (BENNIE)—1947—p, Chattanooga Choo Choos
GRIGGS III, WILEY LEE (WILLIE, WALLY, DIAMOND JIM)—1948-59—2b, Birmingham Black Barons, Houston Eagles, Cleveland Buckeyes, New Orleans Eagles, Louisville Clippers, Detroit Stars
GRIGSBY, AUBREY—1955, 1958-59—p, New York Black Yankees, Kansas City Monarchs, Birmingham Black Barons
GRIGSBY, J. B.—1929—officer, Houston Black Buffaloes
GRIMES, ADOLPHUS—1944-45—1b, Atlanta Black Crackers, Nashville Black Vols
GRIMES, EUGENE—1947—c, of, Cleveland Buckeyes
GRIMES, LIONEL E.—1943, 47—of, p, Cleveland Buckeyes, Harrisburg-St. Louis Stars
GRIMES, WADDY—1920-21—c, Knoxville Giants, Birmingham Black Barons, Atlanta Black Crackers
GRIMM, ____—1921—of, Bacharach (AC) Giants
GRINNAGE, ALFRED—1887—2b, Wilmington Base Ball Club
GROSS, ____—1924—ss, Wilmington (DE) Black Sox, Newark Dusky Boys
GROSS, ____—1927—2b, Brooklyn Cuban Giants
GROSS, JR., BEN—1887—of, p, Pittsburgh Keystones (NCBBL)
GROSS, JAMES—1958-59—p, Birmingham Black Barons
GROSS, R.—1889—of, Cleveland Blue Stockings
GROSS, ROY—1946—3b, c, Fresno/San Diego Tigers
GROVE, ____—1931—ph, Cleveland Cubs
GROVES, ____—1922—umpire, ECL
GROVES, CHARLIE—1934—p, Padron's Cuban Giants
GUARINO, JOSÉ—1957—c, Detroit Stars
GRUEKENDLE, ____—1870—of, Boston Resolutes
GRUHLER, HENRY WHITEY—1918—3b, Bacharach (AC) Giants; writer *Atlantic City Daily Press*
GUEREDE, MANUEL—[see QUEVEDO, MANUAL SANTOS]
GUERRA, MARCELINO (JUAN)—1910-24—of, 1b, New York Cuban Stars, Almendares Cubans, Stars of Cuba, Cuban Stars (East & West), Cincinnati Cuban Stars

GUICE, LACEY KIRK (LARRY)—1951-52—of, New Orleans Eagles, Chicago American Giants

GUILBE, FELIX (FELO)—1946-47—of, Baltimore Elite Giants

GUILBE [GILBERT], JUAN (TELO)—1940, 1946-47—p, of, New York Cubans, New York Black Yankees, Indianapolis Clowns

GUILLEU, ____—1921—p, Cincinnati Cuban Stars

GUINN, ____—1867—2b, Ithaca (NY) Actives

GUIWN, JEFFERSON—1943-45—c, Cleveland Buckeyes

GULLEY, NAPOLEON (NAP, LEFTY, SCHOOL BOY)—1943-48—p, of, Cleveland Buckeyes, Newark Eagles, Cincinnati Crescents, Harlem Globetrotters, Seattle Steelheads, Detroit Senators, Cincinnati Crescents

GULLEY, R. —1946—of, Oakland Larks

GULLOESTL, ____—1930—of, Havana Red Sox

GUMBS, ____—1926—c, Newark Stars

GUNN, ____—1871—1b, Chelsea Auroras

GUNN, J. H.—1916—c, Bacharach (AC) Giants

GURLEY, ____—1925—of, Bacharach (AC) Giants

GURLEY, EARL C. (JAMES, GEORGE)—1922-32—of, p, Louis Stars, Memphis Red Sox, Chicago American Giants, Montgomery Grey Sox, Nashville Elite Giants, Birmingham Black Barons, Indianapolis ABCs, Cleveland Hornets, Harrisburg Giants, Chattanooga Black Lookouts, Chattanooga White Sox, Evansville Giants

GUTHRIE, WALLACE—1952-53—p, Memphis Red Sox, Birmingham Black Barons

GUTIÉRREZ, EUSTAQUIO—1913—of, Long Branch (NJ) Cubans

GUTIÉRREZ, LUIS (JOE)—1923-26—3b, of, All Cubans, Cuban Stars (West)

GUTZEIT [GUTILOS, GUETSCHAW, GUETZEHAVY], O.—1922-31—umpire, NNL

GUY, WESLEY—1927-29—p, Chicago Giants

GUYTON, MILLER—1951—3b, Kansas City Monarchs, Philadelphia Stars

H

HAASE, LEW—1913—of, All Nations
HACKETT, ____—1892—of, Cuban Giants
HACKETT, (SPEEDBALL)—1927-28, 1931-32—p, Washington Pilots, Philadelphia Tigers, Bacharach (Philly) Giants, ECL Stars, Schenectady Mohawk Giants, Harrisburg Giants, Brooklyn Royal Giants
HACKLEY, ALBERT W.—1884-96—of, ss, Chicago Unions, Chicago Unknowns
HACKNEY, ____—1945—of, Asheville Blues
HADDAD, JOSÉ—1931—p, of, Cuban House of David
HADLEY, HENRY (HARRY, RED)—1937-38—of, Atlanta Black Crackers
HAGGINS [HIGGINS] JR., RAYMOND (BILLY RAY)—1953-55, 1958—of, Memphis Red Sox
HAIN, ____—1924—p, Memphis Red Sox
HAINES, ____—1908—p, Chicago Union Giants
HAINES, ____—1920—p, Indianapolis ABCs
HAINES, ____—1926—p, Lincoln (NY) Giants
HAINES, ____—1934—c, Bacharach (Philly) Giants
HAINES, JESSE—1932—p, Little Rock Grays
HAINES, JESSE E.—1946—p, Homestead Grays
HAINEY, ____—1915—p, West Baden (IN) Sprudels
HAIR, JR., [REV.] HAROLD OSCAR—1953, 1957-58—3b, ss, Birmingham Black Barons, Kansas City Monarchs
HAIRSTON, HAROLD (HAL)—1946-47—p, Homestead Grays
HAIRSTON, NAPOLEON R. (RAP, NAP)—1934-35, 1938-40—of, manager, Pittsburgh Crawfords, Indianapolis Crawfords, Toledo Crawfords, Newark Dodgers, Schenectady Mohawk Giants
HAIRSTON, RICHARD (DICK)—1953-54—p, of, Indianapolis Clowns
HAIRSTON, SAMUEL HARDING (SAM)—1944-50—c, 3b, Birmingham Black Barons, Cincinnati-Indianapolis Clowns, Indianapolis Clowns; scout, Chicago White Sox, Chet Brewer's Kansas City Royals
HAIRSTONE, JAMES BURTON (J. B., HARRY)—1916-22—manager, of, Baltimore Black Sox, Bacharach (AC) Giants
HALE, ____—1909—p, Louisville Cubs
HALE, E. (RED)—1937-39—ss, Detroit Stars, Detroit Cubs, Chicago American Giants
HALEY, ____—1923—p, Detroit Stars
HALEY, GRANVILLE (RED)—1928-33—2b, 3b, Chicago American Giants, Birmingham Black Barons, Gilkerson's Union Giants, Cuban Stars (East), Chattanooga White Sox, Chattanooga Black Lookouts
HALL, ____—1880—ss, Washington Uniques
HALL, ____—1889—1b, New Orleans Pinchbacks
HALL, ____—1907—2b, Keystone (PA) Giants
HALL, ____—1918—1b, Pennsylvania Giants
HALL, ____—1920—ph, Knoxville Giants
HALL, ____—1922—c, Cuban X-Giants
HALL, ____—1923—umpire, NSL
HALL, ____—1942—ph, Jacksonville Red Caps
HALL, AUGUSTUS (GUS)—1882-83—president, Chicago Adelaides
HALL, CHARLEY—1945, 1948—of, Kansas City Monarchs
HALL, DELORES M.—1945—officer, Brooklyn Brown Dodgers
HALL, ELBERT RUFUS—1906—1b, Cuban X-Giants
HALL, EMORY—1887—2b, 1b, Philadelphia Pythians (NCBBL), Lancaster (PA) Giants
HALL, H.—1915—c, St. Louis Cubs
HALL, HARRY P.—1871-74—officer, Chicago Unions
HALL, HERMAN (BAD NEWS)—1940, 1944—3b, 1b, Indianapolis Crawfords, Cincinnati-Indianapolis Clowns, Atlanta Black Crackers
HALL, HORACE GREELEY—1933-42—officer, Chicago American Giants; vice president, NAL
HALL, JAMES—1956—c, Birmingham Black Barons
HALL, JAMES BLAINE (BLAINEY)—1913-25—of, 3b, Schenectady Mohawk Giants, Lincoln (NY) Giants, Philadelphia Giants, Baltimore Black Sox, Bacharach (AC) Giants, Royal, Breakers Hotel (FL)
HALL, JOSEPH W.—1945—co-owner, Philadelphia Hilldales (USL), Brooklyn Brown Dodgers (USL)
HALL, LANE [see HALL, JAMES BLAINE]
HALL, LESTER—1948—infield, Baltimore Elite Giants
HALL, O.—1889—utility, Cleveland Blue Stockings
HALL, PERRY—1921-47—p, 3b, of, St. Louis Giants, Milwaukee Bears, Memphis Red Sox, Cleveland Tigers, Gilkerson's Union Giants, Chicago Giants, Indianapolis Athletics, Chicago Columbia Giants, Birmingham Black Barons, Detroit Stars, Dayton Marcos, Bacharach (AC) Giants, Nashville Elite Giants, St. Louis Stars, Minneapolis-St. Paul Gophers
HALL, PRIM (BABE)—1942—1b, of, Twin Cities Gophers
HALL, SELLERS McKEE (SELL, SHADOW BALL)—1912-13, 1916-20, 1923—p, manager, Clays (PA) Giants, Pittsburgh Colored Giants, Homestead Grays, Chicago American Giants, Cuban X-Giants

HALL, THOMAS—1934—ss, Washington Pilots

HALL, W.—1936—1b, 2b, John Donaldson All Stars

HALL, WILLIE—1909—of, St. Louis Giants

HALL, WILSON (WILLIE)—1945—of, Detroit Motor City Giants (USL)

HALLIDAY, JOSH (SPIKE)—1928-31—umpire, ECL

HALLOWAY, KEN—1931—p, Newark Browns

HALTON, LUTHER—1935—c, Miami Giants

HAMBLETON, THOMAS—1871—2b, Chicago Uniques, Chicago Blue Stockings

HAMILTON, ____—1872—of, Amicable Club of New York

HAMILTON, ____—1932—player, John Donaldson's All-Stars

HAMILTON, JR., ARTHUR LEE (ART, PINKY)—1953-54, 1956-60—c, Indianapolis Clowns, Detroit Clowns, Detroit Stars, Detroit-New Orleans Stars, New York Black Yankees

HAMILTON, E.H.—1886—2b, New York Gorhams

HAMILTON, FRANK L.—1913—officer, Colored National Base Ball League of the United States

HAMILTON, GEORGE [see HAMPTON, EPPIE GEORGE (PEP)]

HAMILTON, J. C. (JOHN, ED, GATOR)—1939-42—p, of, Homestead Grays

HAMILTON, JOHN H. (J. H.)—1924-27—3b, 2b, ss, Washington Potomacs, Birmingham Black Barons, Indianapolis ABCs, Cleveland Elites, Wilmington Potomacs

HAMILTON, JIM—1946—ss, of, Kansas City Monarchs, San Francisco Sea Lions

HAMILTON, L.—1923-25—3b, of, Memphis Red Sox, Birmingham Black Barons

HAMILTON, MATTHEW—1888-89—manager, secretary, Bloomington (IL) Reds

HAMILTON, (PEE WEE)—1920—ss, Knoxville Giants

HAMILTON, STEWART—1888-89—3b, Bloomington (IL) Reds

HAMILTON, T.—1946—c, San Francisco Sea Lions, Los Angeles White Sox

HAMILTON, TED—1921-28—p, of, Kansas City Monarchs, Cleveland Browns, Cleveland Tate Stars, St. Louis Stars, Memphis Red Sox, Detroit Stars, Chicago Giants

HAMILTON, THERON BERTRAM—1934—vice president, Homestead Grays

HAMILTON, THOMAS—1871—ss, 2b, Chicago Uniques

HAMMAN, ED P.—1952-70—owner, Indianapolis Clowns

HAMMAN, JOYCE E.—1959-60—secretary, Negro American League

HAMMOND, DON—1923-26—3b, ss, of, Cleveland Tate Stars, Cleveland Browns, Toledo Tigers, Newark Stars

HAMMONS, JOHN M.—1930—officer, Louisville White Sox

HAMPTON, ____—1909-10—p, Harrisburg Giants, Brooklyn Royal Giants

HAMPTON [HAMILTON], EPPIE GEORGE (PEP)—1922-38—c, Memphis Red Sox, Washington Pilots, New Orleans Crescent Stars, Birmingham Black Barons, Cleveland Tigers, Atlanta Black Crackers, Houston Black Buffaloes

HAMPTON, FRED—1953—utility, Kansas City (KS) Giants

HAMPTON, LEWIS—1920-28—p, of, Atlanta Black Crackers, Columbus Buckeyes, Indianapolis ABCs, Bacharach (AC) Giants, Washington Potomacs, Lincoln (NY) Giants, Wilmington Potomacs

HAMPTON, THOMAS HENRY—1869-79, 2b, 3b, ss, of, Chicago Uniques, Chicago Blue Stockings

HAMPTON, WADE—1918-24—p, Pennsylvania Giants, Hilldale Club

HANADY, ____—1910—3b, New Orleans Eagles

HANCOCK, ARTHUR DELWORTH (CORN TRIMMER, SLIM)—1926-29—1b, of, ss, Colored House of David, Cleveland Elites, Cleveland Hornets, Gilkerson's Union Giants

HANCOCK, CHARLES WINSTON (CHARLEY)—1921, 1928-29, 1931-32—c, 1b, St. Louis Giants, Chicago American Giants, Colored House of David, John Donaldson All-Stars

HANCOCK, EDDIE L.—1952-55—p, Memphis Red Sox

HANCOCK, GENE—1954—of, Memphis Red Sox

HANCOCK, JOHN—1951—p, New Orleans Eagles

HANCOCK, LEROY J.—1951-54—p, of, New Orleans Eagles, Memphis Red Sox, Chicago American Giants, Kansas City Monarchs

HANCOCK, W.—1885—p, Brooklyn Remsens

HANDY, GEORGE WILLIAM—1946-49—infield, Memphis Red Sox, Houston Eagles

HANDY, WILLIAM OSCAR (BILL, BUCK, SCREAM, DUCKBREAST)—1910-27—2b, New York Black Sox, Brooklyn Royal Giants, St. Louis Giants, Lincoln (NY) Giants, Bacharach (AC) Giants, Philadelphia Royal Giants, Grand Central Terminal Red Caps, Breakers Hotel (FL)

HANES, ____—1946— p, Atlanta Black Crackers

HANEY, ____—1915—p, West Baden (IN) Sprudels

HANKE, ____—1858-60—1b, Henson Base Ball Club of Jamaica (NY)

HANKS, ____—1908—c, Brooklyn Colored Giants

HANLEY, SPENCER—1867-71—of, c, Philadelphia Pythians

HANNAH, ____—1921—c, St. Louis Giants
HANNIBAL, CARL—1934—p, Padron's Cuban Giants
HANNIBAL, JACK [nee FLOYD, PORTER LEE]—1913-17—of, Bowser's ABCs, Indianapolis ABCs, Louisville White Sox, Jewell's ABCs
HANNIBAL, LEO JACK (HIPPO)—1932, 1937-38—p, Indianapolis ABCs, Indianapolis Athletics, Homestead Grays, Memphis Red Sox
HANNON, JR., HENRY H.—1908-13, 1920-21, 1932—of, 3b, owner, officer, manager, Royal Poinciana (FL) Hotel, Pop Watkins Stars, Philadelphia Giants, St. Louis Giants, Montgomery Grey Sox, Chicago Giants, Louisville White Sox, French Lick (IN) Plutos
HANSENT, ____—1924—umpire, ECL
HANSON, ____—1915—ss, Chicago American Giants
HANSON, HARRY—1926—vice president, NSL
HARDAWAY, CURTIS O'NEAL—1952-53—3b, Indianapolis Clowns
HARDEN, ____—1867—of, Utica (NY) Fearless
HARDEN, ____—1944—ss, New York Black Yankees
HARDEN, BILLIE—1938-48—officer, Atlanta Black Crackers
HARDEN, JAMES—1947—p, Homestead Grays
HARDEN, [REV] JOHN H.—1938-48—officer, owner, Atlanta Black Crackers, Indianapolis ABCs, New York Black Yankees; treasurer, NSL
HARDEN, LOVELL (BIG PITCH)—1943-45—p, Cleveland Buckeyes
HARDEN, THOMAS T.—1886—manager, Southern League of Colored Base Ballists
HARDGROVE, F.—1912-13—3b, Kansas City (KS) Giants
HARDIMAN, ____—1911—of, 2b, St. Paul Colored Gophers
HARDIMAN, WESLEY—1937—p, St. Louis Stars, New Orleans Black Pelicans
HARDIN, ED—1884—3b, Chicago Unknowns
HARDIN, EUGENE (MULUTE)—1945-50—c, Cincinnati Crescents, Baltimore Elite Giants, Harlem Globetrotters, Asheville Blues, Portland (OR) Rosebuds, Seattle Steelheads
HARDING, ____—1917, 1921—p, All Nations, Calgary Black Sox
HARDING, WILLIAM CLAIRE (HALLIE, HALLEY)—1926-31, 1937—ss, 2b, 3b, Indianapolis ABCs, Detroit Stars, Kansas City Monarchs, Chicago Columbia Giants, Bacharach (AC) Giants, Baltimore Black Sox, Philadelphia Stars; Writer: *Los Angeles Sentinel*, *New Crusader* (Chicago), *Los Angeles Tribune*
HARDING, ROY—1938—p, Atlanta Black Crackers
HARDING, TOM—1940, 1945—of, Indianapolis Crawfords, New Orleans Black Pelicans
HARDING, WALTER—1946—ss, Boston Blues
HARDISON, ____—1906—of, Topeka (KS) Giants
HARDLEY, ____—1904—3b, Chicago Unions
HARDON, E.—1884—3b, Chicago Unknowns
HARDWICK, WILLIE—1959-64—of, Detroit Stars, Kansas City Monarchs, Satchel Paige All-Stars
HARDWICK, LEON HERBERT—writer, author, *Afro-American* newspapers
HARDY, ARTHUR WESLEY (ART)—1911—p, Kansas City (KS) Giants
HARDY, C.—1937—of, Chicago American Giants
HARDY, JOHN (DOC)—1950—infield, Cleveland Buckeyes
HARDY, PAUL JAMES (PICCOLO)—1931-52—c, manager, Montgomery Grey Sox, Detroit Stars, Birmingham Black Barons, Baltimore Elite Giants, Columbus Elite Giants, Chicago American Giants, Kansas City Monarchs, Memphis Red Sox, Nashville Elite Giants, Harlem Globetrotters, Cincinnati Crescents, Seattle Steelheads
HARDY, W.—1909-11—of, Leland Giants
HARDY, WALTER LEE—1944-47, 1949-50—ss, 2b, New York Black Yankees, New York Cubans, Kansas City Monarchs
HARDY, WHEELER—1926—p, Montgomery Grey Sox
HAREWAY, KEN—1931—p, Newark Browns
HARGETT, L.—1918—p, Hilldale Club
HARGETT, YOOK—1887—3b, Philadelphia Pythians (NCBBL)
HARGRAVE, ____—1914—of, Lincoln (NY) Stars, Philadelphia Giants
HARGROVE, ____—1928—p, Baltimore Black Sox
HARK'S, ____—1932—2b, Colored House of David
HARKINS, ____—1924—umpire, NSL
HARKINS, BILL—1907—2b, St. Paul Colored Gophers
HARLAND, BILL [see HOLLAND, ELVIS WILLIAM (BILL)]
HARMON, CHARLES (CHUCK) BYRON [a.k.a. CHARLIE FINE]—1944, 1947—of, Great Lakes Bluejackets, Indianapolis Clowns,
HARMON, LINCOLN—1944—p, Chicago American Giants
HARMON, TAYLOR—1934—of, New Orleans Crescent Stars
HARNESS, ROBERT MARSEILLES ("O")—1927-28—p, Chicago Giants
HARNEY, ____—1929—ss, Nashville Elite Giants

HARNEY, GEORGE—1923-31—p, Chicago Giants, Chicago Columbia Giants, Chicago American Giants

HAROLD, ____—1933—ss, John Donaldson All-Stars

HARPER, ____—1910, 1912, 1916, 1917, 1922—p, of, Leland Giants, Kansas City (KS) Giants, Chicago Union Giants, All Nations, Dayton Marcos

HARPER, ____—1916—1b, Lincoln (NY) Stars

HARPER, ____—1920—p, Peoria (IL) Black Devils

HARPER, CHARLES (CHICK, CHALKY)—1920-25—ss, of, p, Hilldale Club, Norfolk Stars, Kansas City Monarchs, Detroit Stars

HARPER, DAVID T. (DAVE, ROUGHOUSE)—1942-46—of, Kansas City Monarchs, Philadelphia Stars, Birmingham Black Barons, Atlanta Black Crackers

HARPER, HERSCHEL (BUBBA)—1942—of, Atlanta Black Crackers

HARPER, JOHN—1920-26—p, Hilldale Club, Bacharach (AC) Giants, Lincoln (NY) Giants, Richmond Giants

HARPER, LUCIUS CLINTON—1916—writer, *Chicago Defender*

HARPER, WALTER—1923, 1929-32, 1936—c, Chicago American Giants, Birmingham Black Barons, Chicago Columbia Giants

HARPSON, FRED—1923, 1928—3b, Lincoln (NY) Giants, Brooklyn Cuban Giants, Brooklyn Royal Giants

HARRELL, WILLIAM (BILLY)—1951—ss, Birmingham Black Barons

HARRELSON, ____—1919—of, Indianapolis ABCs [see HARRISON, ED]

HARRIDAY, ALEX—1959-61—p, Indianapolis Clowns

HARRIS, ____—1867—1b, Mutuals of Washington

HARRIS, ____—1883—2b, Louisville Falls City

HARRIS, ____—1907—1b, Cuban Giants

HARRIS, ____—1912—p, Baltimore Giants

HARRIS, ____—1916—3b, Penn Red Caps of NY

HARRIS, ____—1918—of, Bacharach (AC) Giants

HARRIS, ____—1919—of, Cleveland Giants

HARRIS, ____—1919-20—of, p, Chicago Union Giants

HARRIS, ____—1920—p, Jacksonville Stars

HARRIS, ____—1920-22—of, New Orleans Crescent Stars

HARRIS, ____—1920—of, Pensacola Giants

HARRIS, ____—1922—p, Bacharach (AC) Giants

HARRIS, ____—1926—p, Memphis Red Sox

HARRIS, ____—1932—3b, Monroe (LA) Monarchs

HARRIS, ____—1932—2b, John Donaldson All-Stars

HARRIS, ____—1934—1b, 2b, Philadelphia Stars

HARRIS, ____—1934—of, Pittsburgh Giants

HARRIS, ____—1947—3b, New York Black Yankees

HARRIS, ANANIAS ANDREW (ANDY, SIX BITS, JIMMY DYKES)—1917-27—p, 3b, 1b, manager, Brooklyn Royal Giants, Hilldale Club, Pennsylvania Giants, Harrisburg Giants, Baltimore Black Sox, Pennsylvania Giants, Penn Red Caps of NY, Newark Stars, Lincoln (NY) Giants, Breakers Hotel (FL), Pittsburgh Stars of Buffalo, Cleveland Elites

HARRIS, ARTHUR—editor, Atlantic City Press

HARRIS, BEN—1920-21, 1927—p, Atlanta Black Crackers, Chicago American Giants, Columbus Buckeyes, Indianapolis ABCs

HARRIS, BILFIELD (LEFTY)—1941—p, New York Cubans

HARRIS, BILL—1929-32—c, Memphis Red Sox, Indianapolis ABCs, Monroe (LA) Monarchs, St. Louis Stars

HARRIS, C.—1932—p, Indianapolis ABCs, San Antonio Black Indians

HARRIS, CHARLES (TEENIE)—1930-60— photographer, *Pittsburgh Courier*

HARRIS, CHARLIE—1938, 1941-44—2b, Philadelphia Stars, Chicago American Giants, Cincinnati Ethiopian Clowns (NML), Chicago Brown Bombers (NML), Jacksonville Red Caps, Cincinnati-Cleveland Buckeyes

HARRIS, (CHICK)—1910—p, Indianapolis ABCs

HARRIS, CLYDE—1958—p, Detroit Clowns

HARRIS, CORNELIUS (NEAL, NATE)—1928-31—of, 3b, Pittsburgh Crawfords

HARRIS, CURTIS—1926—p, Birmingham Black Barons, Memphis Red Sox

HARRIS, CURTIS (CHIVA, POPEYE, POPSICLE, MOOCHA)—1931-40—2b, ss, 3b, 1b, c, New Orleans Crescent Stars, Cleveland Stars, Pittsburgh Crawfords, Kansas City Monarchs, Philadelphia Stars

HARRIS, DONNIE EDWARD—1957-58—of, Birmingham Black Barons

HARRIS, DIXON—1932—utility, Homestead Grays

HARRIS, (DUMMY)—1929—p, Tulsa Black Oilers

HARRIS, E.—1884—player, Philadelphia Mutual B.B.C.

HARRIS, ED—1935-41—writer, *Philadelphia Tribune*

HARRIS, EDDIE—1946—owner, Oakland Larks (WCBA)

HARRIS, EDDIE—1955—infield, New York Black Yankees

HARRIS, ELANDER VICTOR (VIC)—1923-50—of, manager, coach, Cleveland Tate Stars, Cleveland Browns, Chicago American Giants, Homestead Grays, Pittsburgh Crawfords, Baltimore Elite Giants, Birmingham Black Barons, Toledo Tigers, Detroit Wolves

HARRIS, EARNEST (ONK)—1958-59—of, Birmingham Black Barons
HARRIS, FRANK—1884-85—p, Brooklyn Alpines, Argyle Hotel
HARRIS, GEORGE—1932-38—2b, Louisville Black Caps, Louisville Red Caps, Louisville Black Colonels
HARRIS, GEORGE BEN—1945-47—c, Pittsburgh Crawfords (USL), Detroit Motor City Giants, Chicago American Giants
HARRIS, H.—1882—ss, Philadelphia Orions
HARRIS, H. B.—1919—business manager, Brooklyn Royal Giants
HARRIS, H. C.—1916—manager, Baltimore Black Sox
HARRIS, HENRY (STUMP DADDY)—1928-34—ss, Memphis Red Sox, Louisville Black Caps, Baltimore Black Sox, Louisville White Caps
HARRIS, JR., HERBERT S.—1933-48—officer, New York Black Yankees
HARRIS, HORACE—1932—of, Birmingham Black Barons, Montgomery Grey Sox
HARRIS, ISIAH (IKE, LEFTY)—1949-56, 1959—p, 1b, Memphis Red Sox
HARRIS, J.—1936—of, Cincinnati Tigers
HARRIS, JAMES L. (JIMMY)—1942—of, Birmingham Black Barons
HARRIS, JAMES R.—1884-87—of, manager, Baltimore Atlantics, Baltimore Lord Baltimores (NCBBL)
HARRIS, JOE—1933—p, Bacharach (Philly) Giants
HARRIS, JOHN F.—1912—Manager, Kansas City (KS) Giants
HARRIS, JOHN I. (JOHNNY, STEEL ARM)—1919-21—p, of, Lincoln (NY) Giants, Fort Worth Black Panthers, Indianapolis ABCs, Brooklyn Royal Giants, Grand Central Terminal Red Caps
HARRIS, JOSEPH—1867—of, Camden Resolutes
HARRIS, JOSEPH—1883-87—manager, c, St. Louis Black Stockings, Chicago Gordons, Boston Resolutes (NCBBL), Long Island Alpine Club
HARRIS, L.J.—1910—p, Indianapolis ABCs
HARRIS, JR., LEON L. (THE STOPPER)—1954—p, Kansas City Monarchs
HARRIS, LONNIE (SHOWBOAT, DONNIE)—1954-59—of, p, Louisville Clippers, Memphis Red Sox, Detroit Stars
HARRIS, NATHAN (NATE)—1901-13—2b, Philadelphia Giants, Leland Giants, Chicago Giants, Cuban Giants, Columbia Giants, Genuine Cuban Giants, Paterson (NJ) Smart Set
HARRIS, PERRY H.—1919-21—owner, St. Louis Giants
HARRIS, R.—1929—c, Tulsa Black Oilers

HARRIS, RAYMOND M. (MO)—1916-45—2b, Homestead Grays, Pittsburgh Crawfords; umpire, EWL, NNL
HARRIS, RICHARD—1934—3b, ss, Philadelphia Stars, Baltimore Black Sox
HARRIS, ROBERT [see HARRIS, CURTIS (POPEYE)]
HARRIS, ROGER—1942—of, Birmingham Black Barons
HARRIS, SAMUEL (SAM)—1932, 1940-42, 1946—of, Monroe (LA) Monarchs, Chicago American Giants, Birmingham Black Barons, Cincinnati-Cleveland Buckeyes, Twin City Colored Giants (USL)
HARRIS, TOMMY—1946-49—c, Cleveland Buckeyes, Louisville Buckeyes
HARRIS, VIRGIL (SCHOOLBOY, SONNY)—1934-37—of, 2b, ss, Cincinnati Tigers, Cincinnati-Cleveland Buckeyes
HARRIS, WEBB—1901—c, Columbia Giants
HARRIS, WILLIAM (BILLY, BEAVER)—1955—infield, p, New York Black Yankees
HARRIS, WILLIAM A. (WOOGIE, BILL)—1928-31—of, Pittsburgh Crawfords, Homestead Grays
HARRIS, WILLIE—1920-21—p, Indianapolis ABCs, Kansas City Monarchs, Columbus Buckeyes, Chicago American Giants, Fort Worth Black Panthers, Atlanta Black Crackers, Dayton Marcos
HARRIS, WILLIE JAMES (RED)—1951-60—p, of, Philadelphia Stars, Detroit Stars, Detroit Clowns, Birmingham Black Barons, Memphis Red Sox, Louisville Clippers
HARRIS, WILMER JOSEPH (SCHOOLBOY, WILL)—1945-52—p, Philadelphia Stars
HARRIS, WIN—1922-28—1b, ss, Homestead Grays
HARRISON, ____—1918—3b, Bacharach (AC) Giants
HARRISON, ____—1927—ph, Gilkerson's Union Giants
HARRISON, ____—1933-34—3b, Baltimore Stars
HARRISON, ____—1939—p, Newark Eagles
HARRISON, ABRAHAM (ABE)—1885-97—ss, Philadelphia Orions, Argyle Hotel, Cuban Giants, Trenton (NJ) Cuban Giants (Middle States League), York (PA) Cuban Giants (Eastern Interstate League), York (PA) Colored Monarchs (Eastern Interstate League), Cuban X-Giants
HARRISON, BENNY (SMOKEY)—1946—p, Homestead Grays
HARRISON, ED—1910-16, 1919—1b, West Baden (IN) Sprudels, Bowser's ABCs, St. Louis Giants, Jewell's ABCs
HARRISON, HENRY—1924—ss, St. Louis Giants
HARRISON, JAMES ROBERT (JIM)—1954—of, Kansas City Monarchs

HARRISON, JOHNNY—1942—p, Philadelphia Daisies (NML)
HARRISON, TOMLINI—1927-30—p, St. Louis Stars, Kansas City Monarchs, Homestead Grays
HARRISON, VERNON—1946—3b, Newark Eagles
HARRISON, W.— 1910—secretary, Oklahoma City Giants
HARRISTON, CLYDE—[see HAIRSTON, SAM]
HARRY, ____–1924—p, All Nations
HARRY, [REV] EARL—1955—infield, Indianapolis Clowns, New York Black Yankees
HARSH, FENTON—1884—officer, Chicago Unknowns
HART, ____–1930—c, Santop Broncos
HART, ____–1941—c, Newark Eagles
HART, ____–1936—bus driver, Denver Post Negro League All-Stars
HART, ELZY—1887—c, Pittsburgh Keystones (NCBBL)
HART, FRANK H.—1883-84—ss, St. Louis Black Stockings
HART, WILLIAM (WILD BILL)—1946—p, Brooklyn Brown Dodgers
HARTS, ____–1918—p, Pennsylvania Giants
HARTMAN, GARRELL VERNELL—1944—3b, of, Philadelphia Stars
HARTMAN, J. C.—1955—ss, Kansas City Monarchs
HARTWELL, ____–1947—pr, Philadelphia Stars
HARVEY, ____–1917—utility, Royal Poinciana (FL)
HARVEY, ____–1929—of, Philadelphia Colored Giants of New York
HARVEY, AL (JIM, ANDY)—1935-38—ss, Philadelphia Stars, Pittsburgh Crawfords
HARVEY, B. T.—1950—secretary, NSL; 1946—umpire, NSL
HARVEY, CHARLES—1919—officer, Lincoln (NY) Giants
HARVEY, CHARLES—1950—ss, Cleveland Buckeyes
HARVEY, DAVID V.W.—1862—ss, Unknown Base Ball Club (of Weeksville, NY)
HARVEY, DAVID WILLIAM (BILL)—1931-46—p, of, Memphis Red Sox, Pittsburgh Crawfords, Baltimore Elite Giants, Cleveland Red Sox, Toledo Crawfords, Indianapolis Crawfords, Cleveland Giants, Monroe (LA) Monarchs, Brooklyn Brown Dodgers, New York Black Yankees
HARVEY, JAMES—1911—c, of, Chicago Union Giants
HARVEY, RICHARD (LEFTY, HOWLING HARVEY, LITTLE PITCH, FRANK)—1910-21—p, of, Illinois Giants, Chicago Union Giants, Chicago Giants, St. Louis Giants, Twin City Gophers, Brooklyn Royal Giants, Lincoln (NY) Stars, Lincoln (NY) Giants, Bacharach Giant, Grand Central Terminal Red Caps, Royal Poinciana (FL)

HARVEY, ROBERT A. (BOB)—1943-51—of, Newark Eagles, Houston Eagles, New Orleans Eagles
HARWOOD, ____–1935—p, Memphis Red Sox
HASKINS, ____–1931—of, Little Rock Black Travelers
HASKINS, EDWARD LEE—1957—p, Kansas City Monarchs
HASKINS, WILLIAM [see BASKINS, WILLIAM]
HASSLER, ____–1920—of, Knoxville Giants
HASTINGS, ____–1928—p, St. Louis Stars
HATCHETT, GENE—1948—of, New York Black Yankees
HATCHETT, RUFUS MAURICE—1913-20—2b, ss, Brooklyn Royal Giants, Philadelphia Giants, Cuban Giants
HATFIELD, ____–1869—ss, Mutuals of Washington
HATFIELD, ROSS—1887—pr, Pittsburgh Keystones
HATTEN, [HATTON] RUFUS (RUFE)—1942-47, 1952, 1959—c, manager, Minneapolis-St. Paul Colored Gophers, Raleigh (NC) Tigers, Asheville Blues, Chicago American Giants, Detroit Black Sox, Baltimore Elite Giants, Memphis Red Sox, Harlem Globetrotters
HATTERES, HENRY—1949—utility, Harlem Globetrotters
HATTON, WILLIAM H.—1880, 1883—p, Washington Manhattans
HAVENS, ____–1884—c, Brooklyn Alpines
HAVIS, CHESTER—1947—p, Memphis Red Sox
HAWK, ____–1915—3b, Chicago Union Giants
HAWK, WILLIE—1905—c, Brooklyn Royal Giants
HAWKINS, ____–1938—of, Indianapolis ABCs
HAWKINS, BUREL—1889—of, Chicago Unions
HAWKINS, C.W. (CHARLIE)—1926—2b, Atlanta Black Crackers
HAWKINS, DAVID (DAVE)— writer, *Cleveland Call & Post*
HAWKINS, J.—1913-14—3b, Philadelphia Giants, Cuban Giants
HAWKINS, JOHN—1940—ss, New York Black Yankees
HAWKINS, LEMUEL (LEM, HAWK, HAWKSHAW, alias LEONARD)—1919-29—1b, of, manager, Los Angeles White Sox, Kansas City Monarchs, Chicago Giants, Chicago American Giants, Shreveport Black Sports, Dallas Giants, Booker T's.
HAWKINS, ROBERT (BOB, PIGGIE)—1932, 1946—ss, 3b, 2b, John Donaldson's All-Stars, Sea Francisco Sea Lions
HAWKINS, ROOSEVELT—1947—of, Cleveland Buckeyes
HAWKINS, SAM—1915—p, Chicago Palmer House
HAWLEY, ____–1932—c, Memphis Red Sox
HAYDEN, JOE (SMOKEY JOE, GOOSE)—1945-46—p, New Orleans Black Pelicans, Fresno/San Diego Tigers, Portland (OR) Rosebuds

HAYDEN, WILLIAM BETHEL (BILL)—1945-47—p, Baltimore Elite Giants, New Orleans Black Pelicans
HAYES, ____—1925—3b, Gilkerson's Union Giants
HAYES, ____—1928—p, Birmingham Black Barons
HAYES, ____—1929—c, Chattanooga Black Lookouts
HAYES, ____—1931, 1937—3b, Chicago Giants
HAYES, ____—1938—ss, Indianapolis ABCs
HAYES, ____—1938—p, Jacksonville Red Caps
HAYES, ARTHUR (NAPPY)—1904—p, Philadelphia Giants
HAYES, BOB (BILL)—1926—umpire, ECL
HAYES, BURNALLE JAMES (BUN)—1928-35—p, manager, Baltimore Black Sox, Washington Pilots, Chicago American Giants, Newark Dodgers, Brooklyn Eagles, Jacksonville Red Caps, Pittsburgh Crawfords
HAYES, GERALD W.—1925—umpire, World Series
HAYES, JIMMY—1949—c, Kansas City Monarchs
HAYES, JOHN—1930—1b, Colored House of David
HAYES, JOHN W. (CHARLEY)—1938, 1940—ss, 2b, Philadelphia Stars, St. Louis-New Orleans Stars, Indianapolis ABCs
HAYES, JOHN (JOHNNY) WILLIAM—1934-51—c, Newark Dodgers, Newark Eagles, New York Black Yankees, Boston Blues, Baltimore Elite Giants, Pittsburgh Crawfords, Philadelphia Stars
HAYES, LORENZO B. (BENNY)—bus driver, Kansas City Monarchs
HAYES [HAYNES], MALVIN B. (BUDDY, ESCO)—1916-24—c, St. Louis Giants, Chicago American Giants, Jewell's ABCs Pittsburgh Keystones, Cleveland Browns, Milwaukee Bears, Toledo Tigers
HAYES, SAM (BUDDY)—1910-17—c, of, ss, Pittsburgh Giants, Philadelphia Giants, Havana Red Sox, Dayton Giants
HAYES, JR., THOMAS HENRY—1939-50—officer, owner, Birmingham Black Barons; vice president, NAL
HAYES, TOMMY—1958-59—c, Memphis Red Sox
HAYES, ULYSSES—1946—p, Pittsburgh Stars
HAYES, WILBUR FILLMORE—1942-50—officer, general manager, Cincinnati Buckeyes, Cleveland Buckeyes; sergeant-at-arms, NAL
HAYMAN, CHARLES (BUGS, SY)—1908-10—p, Philadelphia Giants
HAYNES, ____—1905—of, Brooklyn Royal Giants
HAYNES, ____—1906—of, Illinois Giants
HAYNES, ____—1920—2b, Jacksonville Stars
HAYNES, ____—1936—ph, Philadelphia Stars
HAYNES, JAMES—1946—p, Homestead Grays
HAYNES, JOHN H.—1917-21—owner, St. Louis Giants
HAYNES, LEROY—1939—of, Indianapolis ABCs
HAYNES, SAMMIE—1943-46—c, Kansas City Monarchs, Atlanta Black Crackers
HAYNES, WILLIAM (BILL, WILLIE)—1920-24—p, Dallas Giants, Hilldale Club, Harrisburg Giants, Baltimore Black Sox, Bacharach (AC) Giants, St. Louis Giants
HAYNES, WILLIS (BILL)—1932—p, 1b, Hilldale Club, Little Rock Grays
HAYS, ____—1880—of, Washington Manhattans
HAYS, ____—1880—1b, Washington Douglass Club
HAYSLETT [HASLETT, HAZLEY], CLAUDE—1936-38, 1941—p, Memphis Red Sox, Indianapolis Athletics, Birmingham Black Barons, New York Black Yankees
HAYWOOD, ____—1869—2b, Brooklyn Unique
HAYWOOD, ____—1887—p, of, c, Baltimore Lord Baltimores (NCBBL), South Baltimore Mutuals
HAYWOOD, ALBERT ELLIOTT (BUSTER)—1935-54—c, manager, Birmingham Black Barons, New York Cubans, Cincinnati-Indianapolis Clowns, Indianapolis Clowns, Cincinnati Ethiopian Clowns (NML), Memphis Red Sox, Brooklyn Eagles, Chet Brewer's Kansas City Royals
HAYWOOD, NATHANIEL—1958—of, Indianapolis Clowns
HAYWOOD, ROBERT (BOB, ROCKEYE)—1957-58, 1960—3b, Kansas City Monarchs, Raleigh (NC) Tigers, Detroit-New Orleans Stars
HAZZARD, AUGUSTUS—1868—player, Philadelphia Pythians
HEAD, ____—1931—c, Chicago American Giants
HEAD, COLEY—1928—owner, Atlanta Grey Sox
HEAD, JOHN W. (HOMEY)—1951—of, Kansas City Monarchs
HEADY, ISAAC—1867—of, Brooklyn Monitors
HEALY, ____—1888—p, Hoosier Black Stockings
HEARD, ____—1932—of, Atlanta Black Crackers
HEARD, JEHOSIE (JAY)—1946-51, 1953—p, Birmingham Black Barons, Memphis Red Sox, Houston Eagles, New Orleans Eagles
HEARN, ____—1923—ss, Richmond Giants
HEAT, ____—1941—p, New York Cubans
HEATH, ____—1914-15, 1919—of, 2b, French Lick (IN) Plutos, Louisville White Sox, Jewell's ABCs
HEATH, ____—1922-23—p, Cleveland Tate Stars, Baltimore Black Sox
HEBERT, ____—1932—ph, New York Black Yankees

HECHAVARRIA, GIL GUIDO (SIXTO)—1957—of, Mobile Havana Cuban Giants
HECKLE, WAYNE—1918—2b, Bacharach (AC) Giants
HEFNER, JR., JAMES CHESTER ARTHUR (ART)—1945-50—of, Nashville Black Vols, New York Black Yankees, Philadelphia Stars, Asheville Blues
HEISKELL, ____—1902—p, Algona (IA) Brownies
HELLER, MAC HELLAR—1931-32—1b, Monroe Monarchs
HELLUM, S.—1888—of, Providence Grays
HEMPHILL, ____—1914—p, Schenectady Mohawk Giants
HENDERSON, ____—1869—of, Philadelphia Excelsior
HENDERSON, ____—1887—1b, New York Gorhams
HENDERSON, ____—1929—umpire, ECL
HENDERSON, ____—1936—2b, Chicago Giants
HENDERSON, A.—1926—2b, Chattanooga White Sox
HENDERSON, ARMOUR—1914-15—p, Schenectady Mohawk Giants, Baltimore Giants
HENDERSON, ARTHUR CHAUNCEY (RATS)—1922-31, 1935—p, Richmond Giants (NAA), Bacharach (AC) Giants, Detroit Stars, Schenectady Mohawk Giants, Royal Poinciana (FL)
HENDERSON, BEN (RABBIT)—1928, 1931, 1936-37—p, St. Louis Giants, St. Louis Stars, Birmingham Black Barons, Memphis Red Sox
HENDERSON, (BUNK)—1924-26—c, Birmingham Black Barons, Houston Black Buffaloes
HENDERSON, C.—1925-29—p, 2b, ss, of, Atlanta Black Crackers, Chattanooga White Sox
HENDERSON, CURTIS LEE (DAN)—1936-42, 1946-47—ss, 3b, of, Penn Red Caps of NY, Philadelphia Stars, New York Black Yankees, Washington Black Senators, Toledo Crawfords, Indianapolis Crawfords, Homestead Grays, Brooklyn Royal Giants, Los Angeles White Sox, Indianapolis Clowns
HENDERSON, GEORGE E. (RUBE, RUDY, R.T.)—1920-24, 1929—of, p, officer, Cleveland Tate Stars, Toledo Tigers, Chicago Giants, Bacharach (AC) Giants
HENDERSON, H. (LONG)—1926, 1928-29, 1932—1b, Chattanooga Black Lookouts, Nashville Elite Giants, Chattanooga White Sox
HENDERSON, JACK—1926—of, Atlanta Black Crackers
HENDERSON, JACK—1942, 1946—2b, 3b, New Orleans Black Pelicans, Cleveland Clippers
HENDERSON, JAMES—1921—p, Detroit Stars
HENDERSON, JAMES (DUKE)—1949-53—of, Kansas City Monarchs (not to be confused with Neale Henderson of the Monarchs in 1949)
HENDERSON, LENON—1926, 1928-33—3b, ss, Chattanooga Black Lookouts, Nashville Elite Giants, Birmingham Black Barons, Montgomery Grey Sox, Louisville Black Caps, Indianapolis ABCs, Chattanooga White Sox
HENDERSON, LES (SOCCO)—1944-46—p, Memphis Red Sox, Fresno/San Diego Tigers
HENDERSON, LOUIS—1925-27—p, of, Bacharach (AC) Giants, Lincoln (NY) Giants, Atlanta Black Crackers
HENDERSON, III, NEALE (BOBO)—1949—of, ss, Kansas City Monarchs (not to be confused with James Henderson of the Monarchs in 1949)
HENDERSON, POWHATTEN—1883—of, Cleveland Blue Stockings
HENDERSON, ROBERT (ROPE, WIMPY)—1939, 1941—infield, Chicago Palmer House Stars, Chicago American Giants
HENDERSON, WILLIAMS H.—1886—ss, Chicago Unknowns
HENDRIX, SCOTT—1914, 1918, 1921-22—p, Chicago Giants, Baltimore Black Sox, Lincoln (NY) Giants, Calgary Black Sox
HENDRIX, SR., STOKES EDWARD—1934—p, Nashville Elite Giants
HENING, ____—1925—umpire, NSL
HENLEY, ____—1927—3b, Brooklyn Royal Giants
HENRIQUEZ, RICARDO (RICHARD, DICK)—1913-16—1b, manager, Long Branch (NJ) Cubans, Jersey City Cubans
HENRY, ____—1907, 1911—p, of, Philadelphia Giants, Pittsburgh Giants
HENRY, ALFRED—1950-51—of, Baltimore Elite Giants, Philadelphia Stars
HENRY, CHARLES (CHARLIE, KING SHABAMBI)—1922-42—p, manager, Hilldale Club, Harrisburg Giants, Detroit Giants, Bacharach (Philly) Giants, Detroit Black Sox, Louisville Black Colonels, Detroit Stars
HENRY, CORNELIUS—1867—of, Brooklyn Monitors
HENRY, H.—1888—infield, Providence Grays
HENRY, JAMES—1946—officer, Nashville Cubs
HENRY, JAY—1915—ss, All Nations
HENRY, SR., JOSEPH (PRINCE JOE)—1950-52, 1955, 1958-59—2b, 3b, Memphis Red Sox, Indianapolis Clowns, Detroit Stars, Detroit Clowns

HENRY, LEO (PREACHER)—1936-51—p, Jacksonville Red Caps, Cleveland Bears, Cincinnati Ethiopian Clowns (NML), Indianapolis Clowns, Harlem Globetrotters
HENRY, OTIS (RED)—1931-37—2b, 3b, Memphis Red Sox, Monroe (LA) Monarchs, Indianapolis Athletics
HENRY, ROY M.—1932—1b, Newark Browns
HENSEL, ____—1926—umpire, ECL
HENSLEY, LOGAN FRANK (EGGIE, SLAP)—1922-39—p, St. Louis Giants, St. Louis Stars, Toledo Tigers, Indianapolis ABCs, Detroit Stars, Cleveland Giants, Chicago American Giants, Cleveland Tate Stars, Cleveland Browns, Claybrook (AR) Tigers
HENSON, ____—1867—of, Washington Alerts
HENSON, ____—1887—1b, New York Gorhams
HENSON, ____—1935—p, Baltimore Black Sox
HENSON, ROBERT—1858-60—founder, p, Henson Base Ball Club of Jamaica (NY)
HEIDY, ____—1930—umpire, ECL
HEPBURN, VINCENT—1958-59—p, Indianapolis Clowns
HERBEL, ____—1923—2b, All Nations
HERBERT, JOSH—1896—1b, Danville (PA) Penn State Association
HEREDIA, RAMÓN (NAPOLEON)—1939-45—3b, ss, New York Cubans
HERIDAN, T.—1884—of, Chicago Gordons
HERMAN, [see ANDREWS, HERMAN (JABO)]
HERMAN, ALEXANDER LEE (ALEX)—1926, 1932—manager, 2b, of, Chattanooga White Sox, Memphis Red Sox
HERNÁNDEZ, ____—1930—p, Boston Black Sox
HERNÁNDEZ, ALBERTO (SAGUITA, LABACA LECHERA)—1941—of, New York Cubans
HERNÁNDEZ, BENNY—1946—3b, Fresno/San Diego Tigers
HERNÁNDEZ, JOSÉ (CHICO)—1920-22—p, of, Cuban Stars (West)
HERNÁNDEZ, RAMÓN—1920-30—3b, Cuban Stars (West), Havana Red Sox, Cincinnati Cuban Stars
HERNÁNDEZ, RICARDO (CHICO)—1908-16—2b, 3b, New York Cuban Stars, All Cubans, All Nations
HERNÁNDEZ y RAMOS, SALVADOR JOSÉ (CHICO, SAL)—1945—c, Cincinnati-Indianapolis Clowns
HERNDON, BEN—1931—p, Newark Browns
HERNDON, S.—1884—2b, Chicago Gordons
HERR, ____—1921, 1929—c, Kansas City Monarchs, Chattanooga Black Lookouts

HERRERA y VILLAVICENCIO, JUAN FRANCISCO (PANCHO, FRANK)—1952-54—c, 1b, Kansas City Monarchs
HERRERA y VALDÉS, RAMÓN (PAÍTO, MIKE)—1915-28—2b, 3b, Havana Reds, Jersey City Cubans, Cuban Stars (East & West), Cincinnati Cuban Stars
HERRERA, ROBERTO GUTIÉRREZ (MUSULUNGO)—1955-56—c, Indianapolis Clowns, Memphis Red Sox
HERRING, BOB—1959—p, Raleigh (NC) Tigers
HERRING, JIM—1960—p, Raleigh (NC) Tigers
HERRING, MOSES L.—1920—3b, St. Louis Giants
HERROLD, ____—1903—p, Chicago Union Giants
HERRON, ELMER FREEMAN (BABE)—1902-13—of, Indianapolis ABCs
HERRON, ROBERT LEE (BIG DADDY, BOBBY)—1950-51, 1959—of, Houston Eagles, New Orleans Eagles, Detroit Stars
HERRON, WALTER—1917—p, Hilldale Club
HERVE, C.—1954—utility, Indianapolis Clowns
HESLIP, JESSE—1945—President; Toledo Cubs/Rays
HEWITT, GEORGE—1946—c, Homestead Grays
HEWITT, JOSEPH WILLIAM (JOE)—1909-34—ss, of, 2b, manager, St. Louis Giants, Brooklyn Royal Giants, Lincoln (NY) Giants, Philadelphia Giants, Detroit Stars, Chicago American Giants, St. Louis Stars, Cleveland Cubs, Dayton Marcos, Milwaukee Bears, Birmingham Black Barons, Nashville Elite Giants, Lincoln (NY) Stars, Cleveland Browns, Chicago Giants, Louisville Red Caps, Grand Central Terminal Red Caps, Royal Poinciana (FL), Breakers Hotel (FL)
HEWLETT, JACOB—1858-60—of, Henson Base Ball Club of Jamaica (NY)
HEYWOOD, CHARLIE (DOBIE)—1925-26—p, Lincoln (NY) Giants
HIBBS, ____—1926—umpire, ECL
HICKLES [HICKLE], JAMES T.—1955—p, Detroit Stars
HICKOK, ____—1932—p, Gilkerson's Union Giants
HICKS, ____—1917—of, Brown's Tennessee Rats
HICKS, ____—1923—1b, Nashville Elite Giants
HICKS, ____—1931-of-, Detroit Giants
HICKS, ____—1946—1b, San Francisco Sea Lions
HICKS, (BUDDY)—1951—of, Indianapolis Clowns
HICKS, FRED—1920—3b, Kansas City Monarchs
HICKS, F.W.—1867—1b, Brooklyn Monitors
HICKS, JAMES EUGENE (JIMMY, DOBBY)—1939-41—p, Bacharach (Philly) Giants, Homestead Grays, New York Cuban Stars, Brooklyn Royal Giants
HICKS, L.C.—1931—officer, Norfolk Giants

HICKS, LOUIS—1941—p, Detroit Black Sox
HICKS, (PEE WEE)—1945—2b, New Orleans Black Pelicans
HICKS, WESLEY—1927-31—of, Chicago American Giants, Memphis Red Sox, Kansas City Monarchs, Houston Black Buffaloes
HICKS, WILBUR—1946-47—of, Fresno/San Diego Tigers, Homestead Grays
HICKS, WILLIAM EDWARD (BILL)—1950—p, Philadelphia Stars
HICKSON, ____—1931—2b, Newark Browns
HIDALGO, HELIODORO (JABUCO [SATCHEL])—1905-13—of, Stars of Cuba, New York Cuban Stars, All Cubans
HIGBEE, WILBUR—1908, 1911-13—p, of, Indianapolis ABCs, Cuban Giants
HIGDON, BARNEY (BONNIE)—1942-44—p, Cincinnati Ethiopian Clowns (NML), Detroit Black Sox, Minneapolis-St. Paul Colored Gophers, Chicago American Giants
HIGGINS, ____—1946—p, Montgomery Dodgers
HIGGINS, MARVIN—1957-58—of, Memphis Red Sox, Detroit Clowns
HIGGINS, N.—1887—c, Columbus (Ohio St. League), Lancaster (PA) Giants
HIGGINS, ROBERT (BOB)—1887-88, 1896—p, Syracuse Stars (International League), Cuban Giants
HIGGS, H. [a.k.a. WHIGGS or WIGGS]—1867—ss, Mutuals of Washington
HIGH, ____—1946—p, Chattanooga Choo Choos
HIGHTOWER, ____—1927—1b, Chappie Johnson All-Stars
HIGHTOWER, GUY HARRISON—1940—1b, New York Black Yankees
HIGHTOWER, JAMES—1890—1b, Lincoln (NE) Giants
HILL, ____—1915—ss, St. Louis Giants
HILL, ____—1922—p, Nashville Cubs, New Orleans Crescent Stars
HILL, BEN—1938-39, 1943-46—p, Bacharach (Philly) Giants, Philadelphia Stars, Pittsburgh Crawfords (USL), Philadelphia Hilldales (USL), New York Black Yankees
HILL, BILLY (STUMP)—1910—3b, of, St. Louis Giants, St. Paul Colored Gophers
HILL, CHARLEY (LEFTY)—1910-27—of, p, Chicago Union Giants, Dayton Marcos, Detroit Stars, St. Louis Giants, Chicago American Giants, West Baden (IN) Sprudels, Lincoln (NY) Giants, Dayton Giants, Chicago Giants, Philadelphia Royal Giants
HILL, CLINTON L.—1888-89—2b, captain, Bloomington (IL) Reds

HILL, FRED—1924—of, Kansas City Monarchs
HILL, GILBERT R.—1928-29—p, Pittsburgh Crawfords
HILL, GUS—1920—pr, Indianapolis ABCs
HILL, HERBERT EUGENE (HERB)—1949—of, p, Philadelphia Stars
HILL, JAMES (JIMMY, LEFTY, SQUAB)—1938-45—p, Newark Eagles, North All-Stars, Satchel Paige All-Stars
HILL, JESSE—1949—p, Homestead Grays
HILL, JOHN (JOHNNY)—1897-1910—3b, ss, Philadelphia Quaker City Giants, Baltimore Giants, Genuine Cuban Giants, Philadelphia Giants, Cuban X-Giants, Brooklyn Royal Giants, New York Black Sox, New York Colored Giants
HILL, JOHN PRESTON (PETE)—1904-25—of, manager, business manager, Philadelphia Giants, Philadelphia Royal Stars, Leland Giants, Chicago American Giants, Detroit Stars, Milwaukee Bears, Baltimore Black Sox, Oklahoma City Giants, Royal Poinciana (FL), Brooklyn Royal Giants, West Baden Sprudels
HILL, JOHNSON FREDERICK (J.H.)—1920-29—3b, of, St. Louis Giants, Detroit Stars, Milwaukee Bears, Brooklyn Royal Giants, Lincoln (NY) Giants, Fort Worth Black Cats, Philadelphia Colored Giants of New York
HILL, JONATHAN—1937—of, p, Atlanta Black Crackers, St. Louis Stars
HILL, LEE—1915, 1919-20—2b, 1b, West Baden (IN) Sprudels, Dayton Marcos, Jewell's ABCs, St. Louis Giants
HILL, LYNDON—1899, 1906—of, 1b, Chicago Columbia Giants, Wilmington Giants
HILL, MARK—1939—3b, Toledo Crawfords, Bacharach (Philly) Giants
HILL, SAMUEL LESLEY (SAM)—1946-49, 1952, 1956-58—of, Detroit Stars, Chicago American Giants, Memphis Red Sox, Birmingham Black Barons
HILL, VINCENT—1960—of, Raleigh (NC) Tigers
HILL, W. R.—1885—ss, Brooklyn Remsens
HILL, [REV.] WILLIAM ELLEBEE (BILL)—1955-56, 1958—p, Kansas City Monarchs, Birmingham Black Barons
HILSON, (ROCKY)—1944-45—umpire, NNL
HILTON, CHARLES (CHARLIE)—1929, 1931-32—2b, Colored House of David, John Donaldson All-Stars
HILTON, GEORGE—1887—officer, Philadelphia Pythians (NCBBL)
HINES, ____—1903—of, Philadelphia Giants
HINES, SR., C. W.—1887—manager, Louisville Falls City (NCBBL)

HINES, H.—1888—ss, 1b, of, Hoosier Black Stockings, Rockford (IL) Reds
HINES, JOHN (JACKHOUSE, MEXICAN)—1924-34—c, of, Chicago American Giants, Cole's Chicago American Giants, Chicago Giants
HINES, P.—1888—of, Rockford (IL) Reds
HINES, WILLIAM—1921—of, Houston Black Buffaloes
HINESMAN, ROBERT L.—1951-54—p, Chicago American Giants, Detroit Stars
HINKEY, ____—1926, 1929, 1932—p, Dayton Marcos, Cleveland Elites, Colored House of David, John Donaldson's All-Stars
HINSON, ____—1932—p, Newark Browns
HINSON, JOE—1941-42—of, Otto Brigg's All-Stars, Philadelphia Daisies (NML)
HINSON, FRANK—1896—p, Cuban X-Giants, Cuban Giants
HINTON, JOE—1930—p, Columbus Keystones
HINTON, ROLAND LEE (ARCHIE, CHARLIE)—1944-46—p, infield, Nashville Black Vols, Cleveland Buckeyes, Baltimore Elite Giants
HIRSCHFIELD, JOHN J.—1907-10—manager, president, St. Paul Colored Gophers
HOAGLAND, F. B.—1885—secretary, Brooklyn Remsens
HOARD, ____—1921—p, Kansas City Monarchs
HOARSLEY, PETE—1945—p, Pittsburgh Crawfords (USL)
HOBBLE, ____—1914—of, Philadelphia Giants
HOBERT, ____—1889—of, Chicago Unions
HOBGOOD [HOPGOOD], FREDERICK DOUGLASS (FREDDIE, LEFTY, JOHN)—1941-46—p, utility, Newark Eagles, New York Black Yankees, Philadelphia Stars
HOBSON, (BABE)—1937-42—infield, Schenectady Mohawk Giants
HOBSON [HOPSON], CHARLES (JOHNNY)—1922-25—p, ss, Lincoln (NY) Giants, Bacharach (AC) Giants, Richmond Giants (NAA), Schenectady Mohawk Giants
HOCKER, BRUCE WILLIAM—1913-20—1b, Bowser's ABCs, Lincoln (NY) Stars, Dayton Marcos, Louisville White Sox, Chicago American Giants, Hilldale Club, West Baden (IN) Sprudels, Penn Red Caps of NY, Chicago Black Sox
HOCKER. F. (LITTLE)—1915—p, Louisville White Sox
HOCKETT, ____—1918—2b, Brooklyn Royal Giants [see HEWITT, JOSEPH]
HOCKETT, (SPEEDBALL)—1932—p, Bacharach (Philly) Giants
HODGES, RAYMOND JASPER (JIM)—1917-25—p, Lincoln (NY) Giants, Baltimore Black Sox

HODSON, ____—1888-89—p, Philadelphia Giants
HOFFMAN, ____—1872—p, Amicable Club of New York
HOGAN, ____—1916—p, Louisville White Sox
HOGAN, ____—1918—of, Bacharach (AC) Giants
HOGAN, ____—1929—of, Chattanooga Black Lookouts
HOGAN, ____—1947—ph, Newark Eagles
HOGAN, JACK—1908—c, of, Indianapolis ABCs
HOGAN, JULIUS—1932—c, of, Bacharach (Philly) Giants
HOISTON [HOLSTON], FLOYD—1937—p, Birmingham Black Barons
HOKE, ____—1870—ss, Johnstown (NY) Wide Awakes
HOKE, (BUD)—1945—2b, Toledo Cubs/Rays
HOLCOMB, ____—1887—of, New York Gorhams
HOLCOMB, GEORGE EDWARD—1923—p, Detroit Stars
HOLDEN, ____—1910-11—of, St. Louis Giants, Philadelphia Giants
HOLDEN, SR., CARL (HOGHEAD, YOGI, DEEP FREEZER)—1960—c, of, Birmingham Black Barons
HOLDER, ____—1944-45—ss, Newark Eagles, Philadelphia Hilldales (USL)
HOLDER, CLYDE—1951—p, New Orleans Eagles
HOLDER, JR., WILLIAM (BILL) E.—1953-54—ss, Indianapolis Clowns, Kansas City Monarchs
HOLLAND, ____—1922—of, Bacharach (NY) Giants
HOLLAND, ELVIS WILLIAM (BILL, SPEED, DEVIL)—1919-41—p, manager, Wilmington Giants, Jewell's ABCs, Detroit Stars, Chicago American Giants, Lincoln (NY) Giants, Brooklyn Royal Giants, New York Harlem Stars, New York Black Yankees, Philadelphia Stars, Hilldale Club
HOLLAND, H.—1922—umpire, NNL
HOLLAND, LEW—1923—p, Toledo Tigers
HOLLAND, PERCY—1946—c, Cincinnati Crescents
HOLLAND, ROBERT—1887—utility, Washington Capital Citys
HOLLAND, WILLIAM (BILLY)—1894-1908, 1923—of, Adrian (MI) Page Fence Giants, Chicago Unions, Brooklyn Royal Giants, Leland Giants, Pop Watkins Stars, Algona (IA) Brownies, Chicago Columbia Giants; umpire, NNL
HOLLIDAY, ____—1891—ss, New York Colored Giants
HOLLIDAY, ____—1930—umpire [see HALLIDAY, JOSH]
HOLLIDAY, CHARLES DUROUCHER (FLIT)—1935, 1938—of, Atlanta Black Crackers
HOLLIDAY, JAMES—1921—c, Illinois Giants
HOLLIMON, ULYSSES (SLIM)—1950-54—p, Baltimore Elite Giants, Birmingham Black Barons
HOLLINGSWORTH, ____—1909—p, Louisville White Sox

HOLLINGSWORTH, CURTIS L.–1946-50–p, Birmingham Black Barons
HOLLINS, JAMES–1953–p, Birmingham Black Barons
HOLLINS, TOM (POPEYE)–1936–p, Birmingham Black Barons
HOLLMAN, SOOY–1946–utility, Pittsburgh Stars
HOLLOWAY, ____–1928–ph, Kansas City (KS) Giants
HOLLOWAY, CHRISTOPHER COLUMBUS (CRUSH)–1919-39–of, San Antonio Black Aces, Indianapolis ABCs, Baltimore Black Sox, Hilldale Club, Detroit Stars, Bacharach (AC) Giants, Brooklyn Eagles, New York Black Yankees, Brooklyn Royal Giants, Baltimore Elite Giants, Newark Browns
HOLLOWAY, KEN–1931–p, Newark Bears
HOLLUMS, ____–1923–umpire, NSL
HOLLY, J. STAMP–1945-46, 1950–of, Harlem Globetrotters, Seattle Steelheads, New Orleans Black Pelicans, Chicago American Giants
HOLMES, ____–1936–p, New York Cubans
HOLMES, ARTHUR L.–1956–Indianapolis Clowns
HOLMES, BENJAMIN F. (BEN)–1883-91–3b, Washington Manhattans, Argyle Hotel, Cuban Giants, Trenton (NJ) Cuban Giants (Middle States League), Ansonia Cuban Giants (Connecticut St. League)
HOLMES, EDDIE–1932–p, Baltimore Black Sox
HOLMES, EDDIE–1949–p, Durham (NC) Eagles
HOLMES, FRANK (SONNY, DUCKY, LEFTY)–1929-40–p, Bacharach (Philly) Giants, Philadelphia Stars, Lincoln (NY) Giants, Washington Elite Giants, Washington Black Senators, Brooklyn Royal Giants, New York Cubans
HOLMES, HERBERT ALPHONSE (CHINK)–1939, 1945–2b, Boston Royal Giants, New York Black Yankees
HOLMES, JOHNNY–1942–of, Newark Eagles, Baltimore Grays
HOLMES, LEROY THOMAS (PHILLIE)–1934-48–ss, Jacksonville Red Caps, Cleveland Bears, Atlanta Black Crackers, Kansas City Monarchs, Cincinnati-Indianapolis Clowns, Brooklyn Eagles
HOLMES, LES–1931–of, p, Cuban Stars (West)
HOLMES, RAYMOND WENDELL (RAY)–1957–p, Indianapolis Clowns
HOLMES, W.–1884-86–p, 1b, Chicago Gordons, Chicago Unknowns
HOLMES, WILLIE EUGENE (GENE)–1959-61–p, manager, Raleigh (NC) Tigers

HOLSCROFF, WILLIAM–1954–infield, Birmingham Black Barons
HOLSEY, ROBERT J. (FROG)–1928-32–p, Chicago American Giants, Chicago Columbia Giants, Chicago Giants, Cleveland Cubs, Nashville Elite Giants, Foster Memorial Giants
HOLT, DANA (DANNY)–1920-31–of, Pittsburgh Keystones, Toledo Tigers, Birmingham Black Barons, Pittsburgh Crawfords, Nashville White Sox
HOLT, GEORGE W.–1913–officer, Colored National Base Ball League of the United States
HOLT, JOHNNY–1920-24–of, Birmingham Black Barons, Pittsburgh Keystones, Toledo Tigers, Pittsburgh Crawfords, Nashville White Sox
HOLT, JOSEPH–1928–of, Brooklyn Cuban Giants
HOLTON, LUCIUS O.–1946–p, Cleveland Clippers, Brooklyn Brown Dodgers
HOLTZ [HOLT], EDWARD (EDDIE)–1918-24–2b, ss, St. Louis Giants, Chicago American Giants, St. Louis Stars, Lincoln (NY) Giants
HONG, LONG–1916–p, All Nations
HONICUTT, JR., [REV.] WILLIE JAMES-1954-61–infielder, Detroit Stars, Kansas City Monarchs
HOOD, DOZIER CHARLES–1945–c, Kansas City Monarchs
HOOD, GUY–1946-50–umpire, NNL
HOODS, WILLIAM [see WOODS, WILLIAM (BILLY)]
HOOGLAND, F. R.–1885–officer, Brooklyn Remsens
HOOKER, ____ [see HOCKER, BRUCE]
HOOKER, AL–1959-61–p, Indianapolis Clowns
HOOKER, LENIEL CHARLIE (LEN, ELBOW)–1940-49–p, Newark Eagles, Houston Eagles, Philadelphia Stars, North All-Stars
HOOPER, EARL–1943–1b, Cincinnati Ethiopian Clowns (NML)
HOOPER, GEORGE ROVEN–1924-28–owner, Cleveland Browns, Cleveland Elites, Cleveland Elite Giants
HOOVER, ____–1887–1b, Philadelphia Pythians (NCBBL)
HOPKINS, ____–1927–p, Chappie Johnson All-Stars
HOPKINS, CHARLES L. (C.L., HOP)–1924-25–secretary, Washington Potomacs, Wilmington Potomacs
HOPKINS, EMMETT (JOE)–1945–p, Newark Eagles
HOPKINS, GEORGE WILLIAM–1888-1909–p, 2b, of, Adrian (MI) Page Fence Giants, Algona (IA) Brownies, Chicago Unions, Chicago Union Giants, New Orleans Pinchbacks, Minneapolis Keystones, St. Paul Colored Gophers

HOPKINS, GORDON DERRICK (HOPPY)—1952-54—2b, 1b, Indianapolis Clowns
HOPKINS, JOHN—1888—umpire, Independent Colored teams
HOPSON, BOB—1913—2b, Homestead Grays
HOPWOOD, REGINALD LANIER (HOPPY)—1928—of, Kansas City Monarchs
HORDY [HARDY], J. H.—1887—ss, Baltimore Lord Baltimores (NCBBL)
HORN, EDWIN F.—1883-1890—publisher, *Indianapolis Colored World*
HORN, JR., HERMAN (DOC)—1950-54—of, Kansas City Monarchs
HORN, WILLIAM (WILL)—1896-1910—p, Chicago Unions, Philadelphia Giants, Leland Giants, Algona (IA) Brownies, Philadelphia Quaker City Giants, Cuban Giants, Columbia Giants, St. Paul Colored Gophers
HORNE, ____—1936—batboy, Denver Post Negro League All-Stars
HORNE, BILLY J. (LITTLE GRUMBLER)—1938-46—ss, 2b, Monroe (LA) Monarchs, Chicago American Giants, Cincinnati Buckeyes, Cincinnati-Cleveland Buckeyes, Cleveland Buckeyes, Harrisburg-St. Louis Stars
HORNE, CLYDE—1925—2b, Birmingham Black Barons
HORNE, ROY C.—1913—of, Homestead Grays
HORNER, ____—1920—p, New Orleans Crescent Stars
HORNER, ____—1913, 1918, 1923—3b, ss, Pennsylvania Giants, Milwaukee Bears
HORNS, JAMES J.—1887—3b, Boston Resolutes (NCBBL)
HORSLEY, ____—1945—3b, Detroit Motor City Giants
HORTIS, ____—1931—p, Cuban Stars (East)
HORTON, ____—1946—p, Knoxville Giants
HORTON, CLARENCE (SLIM)—1930—p, Pittsburgh Crawfords
HORVATH, ____—1937—umpire, NNL
HOSKINS, CLARENCE—1945—of, Detroit Motor City Giants
HOSKINS, DAVID TAYLOR (DAVE)—1942-49—of, p, Cincinnati Ethiopian Clowns (NML), Chicago American Giants, Homestead Grays, Louisville Buckeyes
HOSKINS, WILLIAM CHARLES (BILL)—1937-46—of, Detroit Stars, Memphis Red Sox, Baltimore Elite Giants, New York Black Yankees, St. Louis Stars, Kansas City Monarchs, Chicago American Giants, Washington Black Senators, Chet Brewer's Kansas City Royals
HOSTETTER, PAUL—1946—umpire, NAL
HOSTON, SAMUEL R. (SAM)—1908-27—manager, Philadelphia Giants; second vice-president, Inter City Base Ball Association (1909)
HOUCK [HOUKE], JAMES—1878, 1884, 1886—3b, 1b, ss, Chicago Unions, Chicago Gordons
HOULEMARD, SR., MICHAEL ANGELO—1943-54—p, New Orleans Black Pelicans, Birmingham Black Barons
HOUSE, CHARLES BARNER (RED)—1937, 1941, 1944-47—3b, Detroit Stars, Detroit Wolves, Detroit Black Sox, Detroit Motor City Giants, Homestead Grays
HOUSTON, TICK—1919-20—p, 2b, Jewell's ABCs, Kansas City Monarchs, Indianapolis ABCs
HOUSTON, BILL—1941-42—p, Homestead Grays
HOUSTON, E.—1934—of, Cincinnati Tigers
HOUSTON, NATHANIAL (JESS, JEFF, NAP)—1929-39—p, 2b, ss, of, Birmingham Black Barons, Memphis Red Sox, Cincinnati Tigers, Chicago American Giants, Schenectady Mohawk Giants
HOUSTON, WILLIAM—1910, 1914—c, ss, West Baden (IN) Sprudels, Louisville White Sox
HOVLEY, ____—1932—p, Nashville Elite Giants
HOWARD, ____—1922—1b, All Nations
HOWARD, CARRENZA [CARRANZA] M. (SCHOOLBOY)—1940-50—p, New York Cubans, Indianapolis Clowns, North Classic Team, New York Black Yankees
HOWARD, CARL—1935-36—of, Pittsburgh Crawfords, Birmingham Black Barons
HOWARD, CHARLES HENRY (DOC, THE OHIO WHIRLWIND)—1896-99—of, p, Cuban Giants, Cuban X-Giants
HOWARD, CLARENCE—1927, 1935—ss, Brooklyn Cuban Giants, Brooklyn Eagles
HOWARD, ED (SAILOR)—1946—p, Chicago American Giants
HOWARD, ELSTON GENE (ELLIE)—1948-53—of, c, Kansas City Monarchs
HOWARD, HERB—1948—p, of, Kansas City Monarchs
HOWARD, HERMAN (RED)—1932-48—p, Memphis Red Sox, Washington Elite Giants, Indianapolis Athletics, Jacksonville Red Caps, Indianapolis ABCs, Chicago American Giants, Birmingham Black Barons, Little Rock Black Travelers, Cleveland Bears, Chattanooga Choo Choos
HOWARD, J.D.—sports editor, *Indianapolis Ledger*
HOWARD, McKINLEY—1919-23, 1927—p, 3b, Detroit Stars, Indianapolis ABCs, Memphis Red Sox, Cleveland

Hornets, Cleveland Tate Stars, Chicago American Giants, Bacharach (AC) Giants

HOWARD, MITCHELL—1934—p, Memphis Red Sox

HOWARD, NAT—1920-29—p, 3b, Norfolk Giants, Harrisburg Giants, Baltimore Black Sox, Detroit Stars, Lincoln (NY) Giants, Norfolk Stars, Schenectady Mohawk Giants

HOWARD, PERCY—1942, 1946-47, 1949, 1954-55—c, of, Chicago American Giants, Cincinnati Crescents, Detroit Stars, Indianapolis Clowns, Memphis Red Sox

HOWARD, REGINALD ROBERT (REGGIE)—1956-57—2b, Indianapolis Clowns; 1944-50—batboy, Memphis Red Sox, '47 East-West All-Star game

HOWARD, T.—1932—utility, Little Rock Grays

HOWARD, TELOSH (or TWELOOSH)—1937-39—p, Atlanta Black Crackers, Indianapolis Athletics, Indianapolis ABCs

HOWARD, WILLIAM (BILL)—1931-33—1b, 3b, 2b, p, Birmingham Black Barons, Little Rock Grays

HOWARD, WILLIAM M.—1937-38—p, Memphis Red Sox, Jacksonville Red Caps

HOWARD, WILLIE—1948—of, Birmingham Black Barons [see MAYS, JR., WILLIE HOWARD]

HOWE, ____—1926—ph, Memphis Red Sox

HOWE, ____—1946—p, Chattanooga Choo Choos

HOWE, JOHN M.—writer, editor, *Philadelphia Tribune*

HOWELL, ____—1908—of, Brooklyn Royal Giants

HOWELL, HENRY REESE—1918-21—p, Pennsylvania Giants, Bacharach (AC) Giants, Penn Red Caps of NY, Brooklyn Royal Giants

HOWELL, HENRY FREDO (HEN)—1954-56—1b, Detroit Stars, Birmingham Black Barons

HOWELL, HORNSBY—1946—trainer, East-West All-Star game

HOYT, DANA—1932—1b, Bacharach (Philly) Giants

HUBBARD, DeHART—1934-37, 1942—officer, secretary, Cincinnati Tigers, Cincinnati-Cleveland Buckeyes

HUBBARD, JAMES (JIM)—1909-10—of, Oklahoma City Monarchs, Oklahoma City Giants, San Antonio Broncos

HUBBARD, JAMES D. (J.D.)—1938—3b, Birmingham Black Barons

HUBBARD, JESSE JAMES (MOUNTAIN MAN)—1919-35—p, of, Bacharach (AC) Giants, Brooklyn Royal Giants, Baltimore Black Sox, Hilldale Club, Homestead Grays, New York Black Yankees, Providence Giants, Lincoln (NY) Giants, Philadelphia Quaker City Giants

HUBBARD, LARRY—1946—of, Kansas City Monarchs

HUBBARD, PALMER W.—1957-60—of, Detroit Stars, Kansas City Monarchs

HUBBARD, RICHARD C. (DICK)—1885, 1889-90—1b, manager, Chicago Gordons, Chicago Resolutes

HUBBIE, (BUTCH)—1951—p, Birmingham Black Barons

HUBER [HUBERT], JOHN MARSHALL (BUBBA)—1939-50—p, c, Chicago American Giants, Birmingham Black Barons, Cincinnati Ethiopian Clowns (NML), Memphis Red Sox, Philadelphia Stars

HUBERT, C.—1926, 1930-31—c, of, 3b, Memphis Red Sox, Nashville Elite Giants, Birmingham Black Barons

HUBERT, WILBUR (WILLIE, HANK, BUBBER, BUTCH, BUFFER)—1935-48—p, Newark Eagles, Baltimore Elite Giants, Cincinnati Buckeyes, Baltimore Grays, Homestead Grays, Philadelphia Stars, Cincinnati-Cleveland Buckeyes, New York Black Yankees, Newark Dodgers, Pittsburgh Crawfords (USL), Brooklyn Brown Dodgers, Chattanooga Choo Choos, Louisville Black Caps

HUCKLEY, ____—1892—ss, Chicago Unions

HUDSON, ____—1908—of, Brooklyn Colored Giants

HUDSON, ____—1911—p, St. Paul Colored Gophers

HUDSON, A. G.—1922—umpire, Western League of Colored Baseball Clubs

HUDSON JR., ANDREW A.—1931-32—utility, Memphis Red Sox

HUDSON, CHARLES (KEEN LEGS)—1920, 1923, 1928-30—p, Atlanta Black Crackers, Milwaukee Bears, Louisville White Sox, Fort Worth Black Cats, Chattanooga White Sox

HUDSON, DICK—1931—p, Chicago American Giants

HUDSON, EDWARD LEE (ED)—1958, 1964—c, Detroit Clowns, Kansas City Monarchs, Satchel Paige All-Stars

HUDSON, EUGENE—1944-45—umpire, NAL

HUDSON, WILLIAM HENRY (LEFTY)—1937-42—p, of, Cincinnati Tigers, Chicago American Giants

HUDSPETH, ROBERT (HIGHPOCKETS)—1919-33—1b, San Antonio Black Aces, Indianapolis ABCs, Columbus Buckeyes, Bacharach (NY) Giants, Bacharach (AC) Giants, Lincoln (NY) Giants, Brooklyn Royal Giants, Hilldale Club, New York Black Yankees, Providence Giants

HUESTON, [JUDGE] WILLIAM CLARENCE—1926-31—president, NNL

HUFF, JR., EDWARD C. (EDDIE)—1922-32—c, of, manager, Indianapolis ABCs, Bacharach (AC) Giants, Dayton Marcos

HUFF, OSCAR [see HUTT, OSCAR]

HUGHBANKS, GEORGE—1890—2b, Lincoln (NE) Giants

Negro Leagues Book #2: The Players

HUGHBANKS [HUBANKS], HUGH—1890—2b, Lincoln (NE) Giants

HUGHES, ____—1921, 1923—p, c, Bacharach (AC) Giants

HUGHES, ____—1940—of, Memphis Red Sox

HUGHES, ARTHUR—1927—of, Kansas City Monarchs

HUGHES, CHARLES S. (CHARLIE)—1928-38, 1946—2b, ss, Cleveland Red Sox, Columbus Blue Birds, Washington Black Senators, Pittsburgh Crawfords, Baltimore Black Sox, Pittsburgh Stars

HUGHES, LEE TRACY—1950—p, Kansas City Monarchs

HUGHES, LUTHER (YOATEE)—1947—p, Detroit Wolves

HUGHES, PERCY—1942—p, Chicago Brown Bombers (NML)

HUGHES, ROBERT—1931-34, 1937—p, Louisville White Sox, Indianapolis Athletics, Little Rock Grays, Monroe (LA) Monarchs

HUGHES, SAMUEL THOMAS (SAMMY T.)—1929-46—2b, Louisville White Caps, Louisville Black Caps, Louisville White Sox, Washington Pilots, Nashville Elite Giants, Columbus Elite Giants, Washington Elite Giants, Baltimore Elite Giants, Homestead Grays

HULBERT, GEORGE—1890—utility, Chicago Unions

HULL, ____—1928—umpire, NNL

HUM'N, ____—1906—ss, Wilmington Giants

HUMBER, ____—1889—p, Philadelphia Giants

HUMBER, THOMAS WILLIAM (TOM, CHARLIE)—1942-45, 1950—2b, Newark Eagles, Baltimore Elite Giants, Baltimore Grays

HUMBLE, JOHN—1944-45—p, Chicago Brown Bombers (USL)

HUMES, JOHN (JOHNNY)—1937—p, Newark Eagles

HUMPHREY, ____—1870-71—1b, Boston Resolute

HUMPHREYS, CAREY—1952—of, Kansas City Monarchs

HUMPHREYS, FLOYD—1956—Indianapolis Clowns

HUMPHRIES, S.M.—1928, 1930, 1938—officer, of, Atlanta Grey Sox, Atlanta Black Crackers

HUNDLEY, GEORGE—1946—c, Cincinnati Crescents

HUNDLEY, JOHNNY LEE—1943, 1946—c, of, Cleveland Buckeyes, Chicago American Giants

HUNGO, FIDELIO— [see FIDEL UNGO]

HUNT, ____—1920—2b, Nashville White Sox

HUNT, ____—1920—1b, Nashville White Sox

HUNT, ____—1927—p, Wilmington Potomacs, Santop Broncos

HUNT, C. L.—1889-91—manager, Chicago Unions

HUNT, FRED—1946—utility, Pittsburgh Stars

HUNT, GROVER—1946—c, Chicago American Giants, Cincinnati Crescents

HUNT, JAMES—1946—utility, Pittsburgh Stars

HUNT, LEONARD DONALD (LEN)—1949-53—of, Kansas City Monarchs

HUNTER, ____—1931—of, Cincinnati Tigers

HUNTER, CLAUDE—1942, 1944—p, Philadelphia Stars, Birmingham Black Barons

HUNTER, BERTHUM (BERT, NATE, BUFFALO, BILL, WILLIE, BERTRUM)—1931-37—p, St. Louis Stars, Detroit Wolves, Pittsburgh Crawfords, Akron Grays, Kansas City Monarchs, Philadelphia Stars, Homestead Grays

HUNTER, D. F.—1867—officer, Brooklyn Monitors

HUNTER, EUGENE—1924—p, Memphis Red Sox, Cleveland Browns

HUNTLEY, ____—1936, 1939, 1942—c, St. Louis Stars, St. Louis Giants, New Orleans-St. Louis Stars

HURDEE, ____—1937—ph, Pittsburgh Crawfords

HURRA, ____—1929—p, Cuban Stars (East)

HURST, CHARLEY—1927—p, Boston Pilgrims

HUSBAND, VINCENT—1951-54—p, New Orleans Eagles, Chicago American Giants, Indianapolis Clowns

HUTCHINSON, ____—1867—of, Philadelphia Excelsior

HUTCHINSON, FRED (HUTCH, PUGGEY)—1907-25—ss, 3b, 2b, Leland Giants, Chicago American Giants, Indianapolis ABCs, Bacharach (AC) Giants, Bacharach (NY) Giants, Bowser's ABCs, Chicago Union Giants, Jewell's ABCs

HUTCHINSON, GEORGE I. - 1923-24—owner, Detroit Stars

HUTCHINSON, LOGAN—1902-07—p, Indianapolis ABCs

HUTCHINSON, LOUIS—1946-48—p, Portland (OR) Rosebuds, Harlem Globetrotters, Seattle Steelheads

HUTCHINSON, WILLIAM (BERT)—1886-87, 1890—of, Chicago Unknowns, Chicago Unions, Philadelphia Excelsior

HUTCHINSON, WILLIE D. (ACE)—1939-50—p, Kansas City Monarchs, Memphis Red Sox

HUTT, OSCAR—1919-24—1b, of, Dayton Marcos, Toledo Tigers, St. Louis Giants

HUXLEY, ____—1904—p, Chicago Unions

HYATTE, CURTIS L.—1940s—owner, Knoxville Smokies

HYDE, COWAN FONTELLA (BUBBA, BUBBER)—1926-30, 1937-51—of, 2b, Cincinnati Tigers, Memphis Red Sox, Chicago American Giants, Indianapolis Athletics, Houston Eagles, St. Louis Giants, Birmingham Black Barons, Atlantic Black Crackers, Chet Brewer's Kansas City Royals

HYDE, HARRY—1896-1909—3b, Chicago Unions, Chicago Union Giants, St. Paul Colored Gophers
HYLAND, ____—1915—p, Chicago Union Giants
HYMAN, ____—1908-09—p, Philadelphia Quaker City Giants
HYNE, ____—1935—c, Chicago American Giants
HYNES, ____—1897—p, Cuban Giants

I

IDLETT, ARTHUR LEROY (KID)—1925, 1928, 1932—utility, Atlanta Grey Sox, Atlanta Black Crackers,
INCERA, VICTOR—1955—of, Kansas City Monarchs
INGERSOLL, ____—1905—2b, Brooklyn Royal Giants
INGRAM, ALFRED (ALEX)—1942-44—p, Jacksonville Red Caps, Cincinnati Ethiopian Clowns (NML)
INGRAM, PRESTON—1943-47—utility, Atlanta Black Crackers, New York Black Yankees
INGRAM, WALTER B.—1918—p, Philadelphia Quaker City Giants
IRONS, ____—1867—of, Philadelphia Excelsior
IRONS, ____—1919—2b, Wilmington Giants
IRONS, CLIFF—1934—p, Philadelphia Stars
IRVIN, BILL—1919—manager, Cleveland Tate Stars
IRVIN, CALVIN COOLIDGE (CAL, BETTLE, MULLET)—1946—ss, Newark Eagles
IRVIN, MONFORD MERRILL (MONTE) [a.k.a. JIMMY NELSON]—1937-48—of, ss, 3b, Newark Eagles; scout New York Mets; author
IRVIN, WALTER—1923—trainer, New York Giants (MLB)
IRWIN, ALEXANDER CHARLES (ALEX, HAPPY, BUD)—1904-11—ss, infield, Chicago Unions, Chicago Union Giants, Leland Giants, Illinois Giants, Twin Cities Gophers, Minneapolis Keystones
IRWIN [IRVIN], EDDIE—1931—2b, Chicago Giants
IRWIN, G.—1886—ss, Unions of New Orleans
ISREAL, CLARENCE CHARLES (PINT)—1940-47—3b, 2b, Newark Eagles, Homestead Grays
ISREAL, ELBERT WILLIS (IZZY)—1946, 1948-50—infield, Homestead Grays, Philadelphia Stars
IVES, ____—1924—c, New Orleans-St. Louis Stars
IVORY, JAMES EDWARD (SAP)—1956-60—ss, Detroit Stars, Birmingham Black Barons
IVORY, KAYBEE—1936-37—p, 1b, Chicago American Giants, St. Louis Stars
IVORY, WILLIE LEE (BUDDY)—1954-59—ss, p, Louisville Clippers, Detroit Stars, Birmingham Black Barons
IZQUIERDO, ALBERTO—1927—c, Cuban Stars (East)

A rare 1954 Coca Cola 15" standup advertisement of Monte Irvin of the New York Giants. Courtesy of the author.

J

JACKMAN, WILLIAM (BILL, CANNONBALL)—1921-22, 1925-46—p, Houston Black Buffaloes, St. Louis Tigers, Lincoln (NY) Giants, Philadelphia Giants, Philadelphia Quaker City Giants, Brooklyn Eagles, Boston Royal Giants, Newark Eagles, Royal Poinciana (FL)

JACKSON, ____—1870—p, Johnstown (NY) Wide Awakes

JACKSON, ____—1890—c, Lincoln (NE) Giants

JACKSON, ____—1907—of, Brooklyn Royal Giants

JACKSON, ____—1910—of, New York Black Sox

JACKSON, ____—1910—ss, French Lick (IN) Plutos

JACKSON, ____—1913, 1922—of, Homestead Grays, Philadelphia Giants

JACKSON, ____—1920—player, Birmingham Black Barons

JACKSON, ____—1920—ss, New Orleans Crescent Stars

JACKSON, ____—1922—p, Chicago Giants

JACKSON, ____—1922—ss, Cuban X-Giants

JACKSON, ____—1926—p, Montgomery Grey Sox

JACKSON, ____—1931—p, Detroit Stars

JACKSON, ____—1936, 1942—p, Chicago American Giants

JACKSON, ____—1941—p, Havana Cuban Giants

JACKSON, ____—1942—p, Cincinnati Clowns

JACKSON, A.—1867—c, Utica (NY) Fearless

JACKSON, A. J.—1956-58—p, Kansas City Monarchs

JACKSON, A. MATTHEW—1931-36—3b, ss, Montgomery Grey Sox, Birmingham Black Barons, Cincinnati Tigers, Detroit Stars, Chicago American Giants

JACKSON, AL—1956-58—c, Kansas City Monarchs

JACKSON, ANDREW (AJAX, RANDOLPH)—1887-99—3b, Cuban Giants, Lansing (MI) Colored Capital All-Americans, Cuban X-Giants, York (PA) Cuban Giants (Eastern Interstate League), New York Gorhams (Middle States League) and (NCBBL), Otsego (International League)

JACKSON, BILLY—1934—1b, Cleveland Red Sox

JACKSON, BROWN (BENNIE, BUDNEY)—1958-60—of, 3b, Birmingham Black Barons

JACKSON, C.—1926, 1929—ss, 3b, Atlanta Black Crackers, Homestead Grays, Chicago American Giants

JACKSON, CARL—1935—1b, Philadelphia Stars

JACKSON, CARLTON—1928—officer, Harrisburg Giants

JACKSON, CHARLES (SLICK, BABY)—1908–11—p, Twin Cities Gophers, Minneapolis Keystones, St. Paul Colored Gophers

JACKSON, CHARLEY—1880—of, Washington Uniques

JACKSON, (DAD)—1945—utility, Philadelphia Hilldales (USL)

JACKSON, JR., DALLAS—1950—2b, of, Cleveland Buckeyes

JACKSON, DANIEL M. (DAN, HATCHET, THUMPER)—1949, 1951—of, Homestead Grays, Kansas City Monarchs

JACKSON, DENNIS—1920—officer, Bacharach (AC) Giants

JACKSON, DORIS ARLENE—1953—2b, Indianapolis Clowns

JACKSON, EARL—1927—1b, Chappie Johnson All Stars

JACKSON, EARL—1935—1b, Philadelphia Stars

JACKSON, EDGAR S.—1931-32, 1937—c, Little Rock Grays, Memphis Red Sox

JACKSON, EDWARD G.—1879-89—c, Chicago Uniques, Chicago Unions, Chicago Resolutes, Chicago Picketts

JACKSON, F.—1887—officer, Brooklyn Remsens

JACKSON, F.—1934—1b, Cincinnati Tigers, Cleveland Red Sox

JACKSON, FRED—1867—2b, Brooklyn Monitors

JACKSON, FRED HOWARD—1953-56—of, p, Birmingham Black Barons

JACKSON, FREDDIE—1944—p, New York Black Yankees

JACKSON, GENERAL (GEN)—1946-47—of, p, Portland (OR) Rosebuds, Baltimore Elite Giants

JACKSON, GEORGE (BAD EYE)—1910—p, Kansas City (KS) Giants

JACKSON, GEORGE—1950—infield, New York Black Yankees

JACKSON, GEORGE P.—1886-90—p, of, Philadelphia Pythians (NCBBL), Trenton (NJ) Cuban Giants (Middle States League), Cuban Giants, Lancaster (PA) Giants

JACKSON, (GUMBO)—1920, 1922—2b, 3b, ss, Birmingham Black Barons, New Orleans Crescent Stars

JACKSON, GUY—1910-15—ss, 3b, Chicago Giants, Chicago Union Giants, Lincoln (NY) Stars

JACKSON, H.—1897—p, Chicago Unions

JACKSON, HARRY—1932—3b, Atlanta Black Crackers

JACKSON, HARRY—1942—p, Richmond Hilldales

JACKSON, HAYWARD—1945-46—officer, United States Baseball League (USBL)

JACKSON, HENDERSON—1936-39—c, Birmingham Black Barons, Bacharach (Philly) Giants

JACKSON, HENRY—1936—p, Bacharach (Philly) Giants

JACKSON, HUBERT (LEFTY)—1909—p, Washington Giants

JACKSON, ISAIH (IKE, STONEWALL)—1951-53—c, of, Kansas City Monarchs
JACKSON, J.—1867—1b, Brooklyn Monitors
JACKSON, J. W. (BOOTY)—1924-26—p, Atlanta Black Crackers, Albany (GA) Giants
JACKSON, JACK—1927-28—of, Bacharach (AC) Giants, Baltimore Black Sox
JACKSON, JACKIE—1950—of, Homestead Grays
JACKSON, JAMES—1883—2b, Washington Manhattans
JACKSON, JAMES—1889—p, Cleveland
JACKSON, JAMES L.—1940, 1942—ss, Indianapolis Crawfords, Philadelphia Stars
JACKSON, JERRY BERT (BOZO, BABE)—1938-46—ss, Philadelphia Stars, Homestead Grays, Atlanta Black Crackers
JACKSON, JESS (CANNONBALL, JOE)—1911, 1914—p, of, Brown's Tennessee Rats, All Nations
JACKSON, JOE—1931—p, Philadelphia Quaker City Giants
JACKSON, JOHN—1889—of, Cleveland
JACKSON, JR., JOHN W. (BIG TRAIN)—1938-40—p, Kansas City Monarchs, Memphis Red Sox
JACKSON, JR., JOHN WESLEY (STONY)—1950-53—p, Houston Eagles, Kansas City Monarchs
JACKSON, J.T.—1926—officer, Birmingham Black Barons
JACKSON, (LEFTY)—1926-27—3b, p, Chappie Johnson All Stars, Philadelphia Giants
JACKSON, LESLIE—1921, 1926—p, c, of, Indianapolis ABCs, Newark Stars
JACKSON, LESTER E.—1933-41—p, of, Winston-Salem, Schenectady Mohawk Giants, Boston Colored Giants, Newark Eagles, New York Black Yankees
JACKSON, LINCOLN—1933-36, 1941—1b, Cuban Stars (East), Washington Pilots, Bacharach (Philly) Giants, Baltimore Black Sox, Otto Brigg's All-Stars
JACKSON, MAJOR ROBERT R.—1889-91—of, manager, Chicago Unions, Chicago Resolutes; 1910—officer, Leland Giants; 1938-42—commissioner, NAL; 1942—founder, Negro Major Baseball League of America (NML)
JACKSON, SR., MARTÍNEZ (SKIP)—1929-33—bus driver, Newark Eagles
JACKSON, MILFORD [MILLFORD]—1926—3b, Atlanta Black Crackers
JACKSON, N.—1935—1b, ss, Bacharach (Philly) Giants
JACKSON, NORMAN (JELLY)—1934-45—ss, Cleveland Red Sox, Homestead Grays, Washington Elite Giants, Pittsburgh Crawfords
JACKSON, OLLIE—1911—treasurer, St. Louis Giants

JACKSON, OSCAR (OSS, OJAX)—1887-03—of, 1b, New York Gorhams (NCBBL), Cuban Giants, Cuban X-Giants, York (PA) Cuban Giants (Eastern Interstate League), Philadelphia Giants
JACKSON, [DR.] R. B.—1931-50—president, vice president, NSL; officer, owner, Nashville Black Vols, Nashville Cubs, Nashville Black Sox
JACKSON, SR., RESTINE T. (R.T.)—1928-31—officer, owner Birmingham Black Barons; president, NSL
JACKSON, JR., RICHARD ALVIN (DICK, WORKIE)—1921-31—2b, ss, 3b, Bacharach (AC) Giants, Bacharach (NY) Giants, Harrisburg Giants, Baltimore Black Sox, Hilldale Club
JACKSON, RICHARD (DICK)—1947—p, Havana Las Palomas
JACKSON, ROBERT (BOB)—1886-99—c, of, New York Gorhams (NCBBL), Cuban X-Giants, Ansonia Cuban Giants (Connecticut St. League), York (PA) Colored Monarchs (Eastern Interstate League)
JACKSON, R.R.—1889—manager, Chicago Unions
JACKSON, RUFUS (SONNYMAN)—1934-49—president, treasurer, Homestead Grays
JACKSON, S.—1867—2b, Utica (NY) Fearless, Brooklyn Monitors
JACKSON, SAM—1887—c, Pittsburgh Keystones (NCBBL)
JACKSON, SAM—1926—c, Cleveland Elites
JACKSON, SAMUEL—1867—of, Brooklyn Monitors
JACKSON, SAMUEL—1942-47—p, 1b, Chicago American Giants
JACKSON, SAMUEL EARL (ICKY)—1951-52—1b, Philadelphia Stars
JACKSON, SANFORD OLANDER (JAMBO)—1923-31—of, ss, 3b, Memphis Red Sox, Chicago American Giants, Chicago Columbia Giants, Birmingham Black Barons
JACKSON, SONNY (LEFTY)—1931—p, Brooklyn Royal Giants
JACKSON, THOMAS—1916-28—officer, manager, Bacharach (AC) Giants
JACKSON, THOMAS H. (TOM)—1928, 1932—of, c, Indianapolis ABCs
JACKSON, THOMAS WALTON (TOM, JACK)—1924-29—p, Atlanta Black Crackers, St. Louis Stars, Cleveland Tigers, Nashville Elite Giants, Memphis Red Sox, Montgomery Grey Sox, New Orleans Black Pelicans, Louisville White Sox

JACKSON, TOBY—1916-26. 1931—c, of, Penn Red Caps of NY, Lincoln (NY) Giants, Lincoln (NY) Stars, Philadelphia Giants, Newark Stars, New York Black Yankees
JACKSON, TOMMY—1946, 1953-54—p, Cleveland Clippers, Louisville Clippers
JACKSON, VERNELL (STEEL ARM)—1950-51—p, Memphis Red Sox
JACKSON, WADE (LEFTY)—1926-43—p, ss, Philadelphia Giants, Brooklyn Royal Giants, Schenectady Mohawk Giants, Buck Ewing's All-Star
JACKSON, WALTER—1931—p, Knoxville Giants
JACKSON, WARDELL—1960—owner, general manager, Birmingham Black Barons
JACKSON, WILBUR—1914—3b, ss, Philadelphia Giants, Schenectady Mohawk Giants
JACKSON, WILLIAM—1906—p, of Philadelphia Quaker City Giants, Cuban X-Giants, Cuban Giants, Wilmington Giants
JACKSON, WILLIAM [WILBUR] (ASHES)—1909-17—3b, Kansas City (KS) Giants, Kansas City (MO) Royal Giants, Kansas City Colored Giants
JACKSON, WILLIAM (BILL)—1890-1905—c, of, 2b, Cuban Giants, Cuban X-Giants, Genuine Cuban Giants, York (PA) Cuban Giants (Eastern Interstate League), Ansonia Cuban Giants (Connecticut St. League), Famous Cuban Giants
JACKSON, WILLIE—1930-31—1b, 3b, Memphis Red Sox
JACOBIUS, WALTER—1886-89—officer, New York Gorhams
JACOBS, ____—1869—ss, Mutuals of Washington
JACOBS, ____—1919—p, of, Penn Red Caps of NY
JACOBS, EDDIE (RED)—1944—p, Newark Eagles
JACONT, ____—1891—2b, New York Colored Giants
JACOX, CALVIN MOSES (CAL)—writer, *Norfolk Journal and Guide*
JAGERS, CLARENCE—1926—ss, Baltimore Black Sox
JAMERSON, LONDELL (TINCY)—1950-51—p, Kansas City Monarchs
JAMES, ____—1896—p, Cuban X-Giants
JAMES, ____—1900—ss, Genuine Cuban Giants
JAMES, ____—1925—p, Cuban Stars (East)
JAMES, AUGUSTUS (GUS)—1905-12—2b, c, of, Paterson (NJ) Smart Set, Lincoln (NY) Giants, Brooklyn Royal Giants, Pop Watkins Stars, Pittsburgh Stars of Buffalo, Royal Poinciana Hotel
JAMES, HUBBARD—1938—3b, Birmingham Black Barons

JAMES, S.—1931-32—1b, Little Rock Black Travelers, Cleveland Cubs
JAMES, TICE LIVINGSTON (WINKY, TARZAN)—1936-42, 1946—ss, c, Cincinnati Buckeyes, Chicago American Giants, Cleveland Buckeyes, Memphis Red Sox, Chicago Brown Bombers (NML), Cincinnati Ethiopian Clowns (NML), Indianapolis Clowns
JAMES, WADE (BABE)—1942, 1946—p, Philadelphia Daisies (NML), Portland (OR) Rosebuds, Oakland Larks
JAMES, WILLIAM (NUX, KNUX)—1906-19—2b, manager, Cuban X-Giants, Royal Poinciana Hotel, Louisville White Sox, Lincoln (NY) Giants, Portsmouth (VA) Giants, Breakers Hotel, Philadelphia Giants, Philadelphia Quaker City Giants, Paterson (NJ) Smart Set, Schenectady Mohawk Giants
JAMES, WILLIAM WALTER—1882, 1887—1b, of, Philadelphia Orions, Philadelphia Pythians (NCBBL)
JAMIESON [JAMERSON], JOHN—1919—utility, Lincoln (NY) Giants
JAMISON, CAESAR—1923-32—umpire, NNL, EWL
JAMISON, EDDIE—1950—c, Cleveland Buckeyes
JANUARY, ALVIN—1929—c, Birmingham Black Barons
JARMON, DON—1933—p, Columbus Blue Birds
JARNIGAN, LOUIS—1934—of, Pittsburgh Giants
JARNIGAN, HORACE—1934—of, Homestead Grays, Pittsburgh Giants
JARRETT, FRANK—1946—p, Pittsburgh Crawfords (USL)
JARVIS, ____—1884-c, Brooklyn Alpines
JARVIS, JR., GIDEON—1958-61—of, Memphis Red Sox, Kansas City Monarchs
JASPER, ____—1926, 1932-33—p, Chattanooga White Sox, Nashville Elite Giants, Birmingham Black Barons, Memphis Red Sox
JAURON, ____—1928—p, Cleveland Tigers
JEFFCOAT, ALBERT—1953-56—p, New York Black Yankees, Indianapolis Clowns
JEFFERS, BOB—1940-41—1b, Chicago American Giants
JEFFERSON, CHUCK—1947—p, Detroit Wolves, Philadelphia Stars
JEFFERSON, DONALD C.—1920-21—c, Dayton Marcos, Pittsburgh Keystones
JEFFERSON, EDWARD L. (EDDIE)—1942-47—p, Philadelphia Stars, Detroit Motor City Giants, Detroit Wolves, Toledo Cubs/Rays
JEFFERSON, GEORGE LEO (JEFF)—1942-50—p, Jacksonville Red Caps, Cleveland Buckeyes, Louisville Buckeyes

JEFFERSON, GEORGE WASHINGTON—1926-34—p, Albany (GA) Giants, Birmingham Black Barons

JEFFERSON, R.—1939, 1945—3b, p, Indianapolis ABCs, Toledo Cubs/Rays

JEFFERSON, RALPH TENNYSON—1917-32—of, Indianapolis ABCs, Bacharach (AC) Giants, Philadelphia Royal Stars, Washington Potomacs, Philadelphia Giants, Philadelphia Royal Giants, Chicago Union Giants, Cuban Stars (East), Philadelphia Quaker City Giants, Foster's Hartford Giants

JEFFERSON, T. H.—1950-53—umpire, NNL

JEFFERSON, WAVERLY—1931—p, Bacharach (Philly) Giants

JEFFERSON, WILLIE (BILL)—1937-50—p, Cincinnati Tigers, Memphis Red Sox, Cincinnati-Cleveland Buckeyes, Cleveland Buckeyes, Philadelphia Stars

JEFFREYS, FRANK—1917-20—of, Chicago Giants

JEFFRIES, ____—1919—p, Bacharach (AC) Giants

JEFFRIES, ALEX—1932-33—3b, Newark Browns, Hilldale Club, Bacharach (Philly) Giants, New York Black Yankees, Newark Dodgers

JEFFRIES, CLAUDIS—1958—p, Detroit Clowns

JEFFRIES, E.—1921-22—c, Chicago Giants

JEFFRIES, HARRY—1928—of, Harrisburg Giants, Jacksonville Eagles

JEFFRIES, HARRY (LITTLE JEFF)—1920-49—3b, c, ss, 2b, p, of, 1b, manager, Chicago Giants, Chicago American Giants, Chicago Columbia Giants, Detroit Stars, Cleveland Tigers, Cleveland Tate Stars, Cleveland Browns, Bacharach (AC) Giants, Knoxville Giants, Toledo Tigers, Baltimore Panthers, Baltimore Black Sox, Newark Dodgers, Newark Browns, Brooklyn Royal Giants, Washington Potomacs, Cincinnati-Indianapolis Clowns, Schenectady Mohawk Giants, Hilldale Club, New York Black Yankees, Columbus Keystones, Richmond Hilldales

JEFFRIES, JAMES COURTNEY (JIM)—1913-31—p, of, Indianapolis ABCs, Jewell's ABCs, Baltimore Black Sox, Harrisburg Giants, Chicago American Giants, Chicago Black Sox, Royal Poinciana (FL)

JEFFRIES, JEFF—1940—p, Brooklyn Royal Giants, Homestead Grays

JEFFRIES, M.—1924-26—3b, of, Cleveland Browns, Baltimore Black Sox, Cleveland Elites

JEFFRIES, NATHANIEL (SONNY)—1940, 1942-43, 1948—c, p, of, Chicago Brown Bombers (NML), Richmond Hilldales (NML), New York Black Yankees

JELLY, ____—1928—c, Kansas City (KS) Giants

JEMISON [JAMESON], CHARLES HEARD—1934-35—p, Homestead Grays, Newark Dodgers

JENKINS, ____—1919—p, Philadelphia Quaker City Giants

JENKINS, BENNIE (CHICK)—1932, 1937—of, Pittsburgh Crawfords, Detroit Stars

JENKINS, CLARENCE (BARNEY)—1929—c, Detroit Stars

JENKINS, CLARENCE REGINALD (FATS)—1920-40, 1942, 1945-46—of, manager, co-owner, Lincoln (NY) Giants, Harrisburg Giants, Bacharach (AC) Giants, Bacharach (NY) Giants, Baltimore Black Sox, New York Harlem Stars, New York Black Yankees, Philadelphia Stars, Brooklyn Eagles, Brooklyn Royal Giants, Pittsburgh Crawfords, Toledo Crawfords, Penn Red Caps of NY; 1945-46, Philadelphia Hilldales or Daisies (USL)

JENKINS, D.—1935—2b, Detroit Cubs

JENKINS, DALE—1946—2b, Detroit Stars

JENKINS, (DOC)—1939—manager, Durham (NC) Lucky Strikes

JENKINS, GEORGE—1955—p, Detroit Stars

JENKINS, HORACE PALMER—1911-27—of, p, Chicago American Giants, Chicago Giants, Chicago Union Giants

JENKINS, JAMES (JIMMY)—1868—player, Philadelphia Pythians

JENKINS, JAMES (JIMMY)—1954—of, Detroit Stars

JENKINS, JAMES EDWARD (PREACHER, PEE WEE)—1944-54—p, Cincinnati-Indianapolis Clowns, New York Cubans, Birmingham Black Barons, Indianapolis Clowns

JENKINS, M.—1924—p, ss, Washington Potomacs, Cleveland Browns, Dayton Marcos

JENKINS, RAYMOND WENDELL (WENDY, PUSS)—1942-43, 1946—ss, Philadelphia Daisies (NML), Philadelphia Stars, Oakland Larks, Brooklyn Brown Dodgers

JENKINS, THOMAS (TOM)—1913-17, 1927-28—c, of, secretary, Hilldale Club

JENKINS, VAN—1940—2b, Cleveland Bears

JENNINGS, BOYCE—1950—officer, Delta Giants (Greenville, MS)

JENNINGS, CHARLES FRANK—1956—c, Memphis Red Sox

JENNINGS, J. (GEECH)—1924-26—p, Atlanta Black Crackers

JENNINGS, THURMAN (JACK)—1914-27—2b, ss, of, Chicago Giants

JERNTO, ____—1928—ph, Harrisburg Giants

JESSIE, W.—1887—3b, of, Louisville Falls City (NCBBL)

JESSON, ____—1917—1b, All Nations

JESSUP, CHARLES—1907-12—p, Chicago Union Giants, Minneapolis Keystones

JESSUP, JOSEPH GENTRY (JEEP)—1940-49—p, Chicago American Giants, Birmingham Black Barons

JETHROE, SAMUEL (SAM, THE JET)—1938, 1942-48—of, c, Cincinnati Buckeyes, Cleveland Buckeyes, Indianapolis ABCs

JETTER, ____—1931—of, Philadelphia Quaker City Giants

JEWELL, ____—1867—of, Brooklyn Unique

JEWELL, WARNER (WERNER)—1917-26—owner, officer, Jewell's ABCs, Indianapolis ABCs

JIMÉNEZ, BIENVENIDO (HOOKS, GAMBETA, PATA JOROBÁ)—1915-29—2b, Cuban Stars (East & West), Birmingham Black Barons, Havana Cubans, Cincinnati Cuban Stars

JIMÉNEZ y PEÑALVER, EUSEBIO—1920-22—of, Cuban Stars (East & West), Cincinnati Cuban Stars

JIMÉNEZ, PEDRO (NATILLAS)—1937-38—p, of, Havana Cubans, New York Cubans

JIMÉNEZ, RICARDO—1914—c, Long Branch (NJ) Cubans

JIMERSON, ____—1922—p, Buffalo Stars

JOHNNY BOY, ____—1920—p, Chicago Black Sox

JOHNS, LINCOLN—1944—c, Chicago American Giants

JOHNSON, ____—1867—of, Washington Alerts

JOHNSON, ____—1880, 1887—of, Washington Manhattans, Washington Mutuals

JOHNSON, ____—1894—player, Cuban Giants

JOHNSON, ____—1903—p, Chicago Union Giants

JOHNSON, ____—1909—p, Philadelphia Quaker City Giants

JOHNSON, ____—1910—of, New York Black Sox

JOHNSON, ____—1914—of, All Nations

JOHNSON, ____—1915—p, St. Louis Giants

JOHNSON, ____—1917—1b, Brown's Tennessee Rats

JOHNSON, ____—1919—1b, Grand Central Terminal Red Caps

JOHNSON, ____—1919—of, Wilmington Giants

JOHNSON, ____—1920—p, Atlanta Black Crackers

JOHNSON, ____—1922—of, Cuban X-Giants

JOHNSON, ____—1924, 1926—of, p, Bacharach (AC) Giants

JOHNSON, ____—1925—of, Chappie Johnson All-Stars

JOHNSON, ____—1926, 1929, 1934—1b, Pennsylvania Red Caps

JOHNSON, ____—1929-30—of, Gilkerson's Union Giants

JOHNSON, ____—1931—of, Monroe (LA) Monarchs

JOHNSON, ____—1932—of, Kansas City (KS) Giants

JOHNSON, ____—1932—c, Bacharach (Philly) Giants

JOHNSON, ____—1932—of, Harrisburg Giants

JOHNSON, ____—1934—p, Memphis Red Sox

JOHNSON, A.—1884—ss, Brooklyn Alpines

JOHNSON, A.—1914-17—2b, 3b, of, Lincoln (NY) Stars, Cuban Giants, Lincoln (NY) Giants

JOHNSON, A. (SAMPSON)—1911-24—c, Bacharach (AC) Giants, Pittsburgh Giants, Pennsylvania Giants, Homestead Grays, Philadelphia Giants, Washington Potomacs, Baltimore Giants

JOHNSON, ABDULLAH (SHOWBOAT, ROBERT)—1956-57—1b, ss, Kansas City Monarchs, Detroit Stars

JOHNSON, ADDIE—1930-31—c, of, Louisville White Sox

JOHNSON, A.J.—1928-30, 1932—of, 2b, c, Birmingham Black Barons, Houston Black Buffaloes, Austin Black Senators

JOHNSON, AJAY DEFOREST—1927—p, Philadelphia Royal Giants

JOHNSON, AL—1936-40—p, Washington Elite Giants, Baltimore Elite Giants, Washington Black Senators

JOHNSON, ALLEN—1936-46—officer, owner, Mound City Blues, St. Louis Stars, New York Black Yankees, Harrisburg-St. Louis Stars, Boston Blues, Indianapolis ABCs

JOHNSON, ARTHUR JOHN (JACK)—1903-04—1b, umpire, Philadelphia Giants, Johnson's Pets

JOHNSON, B.—1904—of, Philadelphia Giants

JOHNSON, BEN [see DANIEL SPENCIL JOHNSON]

JOHNSON, BERTRAM (BERT)—1932-38—of, Newark Dodgers, Baltimore Black Sox, Birmingham Black Barons, Washington Pilots

JOHNSON, BILL—1931-34—3b, ss, Little Rock Black Travelers, Akron Tyrites, Cleveland Red Sox

JOHNSON, BILL—1956—of, Kansas City Monarchs

JOHNSON, BLAZER [see TEASLEY, RONALD]

JOHNSON, BOB—1944-46—1b, Kansas City Monarchs, Brooklyn Brown Dodgers, Cleveland Clippers, Detroit Motor City Giants

JOHNSON, BUCKY—1939—2b, Newark Eagles

JOHNSON, BURTON [see BERTRAM JOHNSON]

JOHNSON, (BUSTER)—1943—of, New York Black Yankees

JOHNSON, BYRON WALDO EMERSON (MEX, JEW BABY)—1937-40—ss, Kansas City Monarchs

JOHNSON, C. [see JOHNSON, G. CLAUDE (HOOKS)]

JOHNSON, HERB—1942—3b, ss, New Orleans Black Pelicans

JOHNSON, C. HOWARD—1887—secretary, Philadelphia Pythians (NCBBL)

Negro Leagues Book #2: The Players

JOHNSON, CARLTON—1933—of, New York Black Yankees

JOHNSON, CECIL LEON (SESS)—1915-31—1b, of, Philadelphia Giants, Hilldale Club, Philadelphia Tigers, Philadelphia Royal Stars, Philadelphia Royal Giants, Baltimore Black Sox, Newark Stars, Norfolk Stars, Newark Browns, Cuban X-Giants, Bacharach (AC) Giants, Schenectady Mohawk Giants

JOHNSON, CHARLES—1859, 1862—of, Unknown Base Ball Club (of Weeksville, NY)

JOHNSON, CHARLES—1949-50—3b, Cleveland Buckeyes, Memphis Red Sox

JOHNSON, CHARLES—1953—c, Birmingham Black Barons

JOHNSON, CHARLES A.—1889—manager, 3b, Brooklyn Alpine

JOHNSON, CHARLES B.—1925-27—officer, Bacharach (AC) Giants

JOHNSON, CHARLIE—1952—p, Indianapolis Clowns

JOHNSON, CLARENCE—1946—infield, Pittsburgh Stars

JOHNSON, CLAUDE (TICK)—1928-31—infield, Pittsburgh Crawfords

JOHNSON, CLAUDE CECIL (HOOKS)—1916-32—3b, 2b, Lincoln (NY) Stars, Baltimore Black Sox, Harrisburg Giants, Detroit Stars, Memphis Red Sox, Birmingham Black Barons, Cleveland Tate Stars, Hilldale Club, Brooklyn Royal Giants, Nashville Elite Giants

JOHNSON, JR., CLIFFORD (CLIFF, CONNIE)—1940-50—p, Indianapolis Crawfords, Kansas City Monarchs

JOHNSON, CURTIS T. (COLT)—1950—p, 3b, of, Kansas City Monarchs

JOHNSON, D.—1912—of, Kansas City (KS) Giants

JOHNSON, DANIEL SPENCIL (DAN, SHANG, GATLING GUN)—1916-26—p, of, Bacharach (AC) Giants, Brooklyn Royal Giants, Lincoln (NY) Giants, Hilldale Club, Indianapolis ABCs, Harrisburg Giants

JOHNSON, DAVE (DUD)—1914-20—of, ss, 2b, p, Philadelphia Giants, Brooklyn Royal Giants

JOHNSON, DON (GROUNDHOG)—1952—2b, 3b, Chicago American Giants

JOHNSON, DONALD DALE—1952-53—p, Birmingham Black Barons

JOHNSON, E.—1920-22—1b, Nashville Elite Giants, Nashville White Sox

JOHNSON, E. (STONEWALL)—1919—p, of, Baltimore Black Sox

JOHNSON, EARL—1915—p, Baltimore Giants

JOHNSON, ED—1944—p, Homestead Grays

JOHNSON, EDDIE—1945-46, 1948—of, 2b, Chicago American Giants, Cleveland Clippers, Cleveland Buckeyes

JOHNSON, ELMER—1934—ss, 3b, Baltimore Black Sox

JOHNSON, ERNEST D. (SCHOOLEY, SCHOOLBOY)—1949-53—p, of, Kansas City Monarchs

JOHNSON, ERNIE—1934—3b, Bacharach (Philly) Giants

JOHNSON, EUGENE—1934—p, Memphis Red Sox

JOHNSON, EUGENE CLARK (GENE)—1956-57—1b, of, Detroit Stars

JOHNSON, FRANK—1889—1b, Cleveland

JOHNSON, FRANK—1929, 1932-37—of, manager, Shreveport Black Sports, Monroe (LA) Monarchs, Memphis Red Sox

JOHNSON, FRANKIE—1924—p, c, Harrisburg Giants, Homestead Grays

JOHNSON, FRED (RABBIT)—1945-48—p, ss, Pittsburgh Crawfords (USL), Boston Blues, Chicago American Giants, Cleveland Buckeyes

JOHNSON, FURMAN—1954—p, Indianapolis Clowns

JOHNSON, G.—1888—infield, Providence Grays

JOHNSON, JR., GEORGE (CHAPPIE, RAT)—1896-1939—c, 1b, manager, Columbia Giants, Chicago Union Giants, Brooklyn Royal Giants, Leland Giants, Chicago Giants, St. Louis Giants, Dayton Chappies, Custer's Baseball Club of Columbus, Philadelphia Royal Stars, Norfolk Stars, Algona (IA) Brownies, Adrian (MI) Page Fence Giants, Mohawk (NY) Giants, Philadelphia Giants, Penn Red Caps of NY, Chappie Johnson's Stars, Louisville White Sox, Philadelphia Quaker City Giants, Cuban X-Giants, Dayton Giants, St. Paul Colored Gophers, Bacharach (AC) Giants, Twin City Gophers, West Baden (IN) Sprudels, Columbus Giants

JOHNSON, GEORGE A.—1889—of, Brooklyn Alpines

JOHNSON, JR., GEORGE WASHINGTON (DIBO, JUNIOR)—1909-31—of, Fort Worth Wonders, Kansas City, (KS) Giants, Brooklyn Royal Giants, Hilldale Club, Lincoln (NY) Giants, Philadelphia Tigers, Philadelphia Giants, Bacharach (AC) Giants, Breakers Hotel (FL)

JOHNSON, GRAHAM—1942-44—2b, Newark Eagles

JOHNSON, GRANT U. (HOME RUN)—1894-1922—ss, 2b, manager, Adrian (MI) Page Fence Giants, Columbia Giants, Brooklyn Royal Giants, Cuban X-Giants, Philadelphia Giants, Lincoln (NY) Giants, Washington Giants, Lincoln (NY) Stars, Pittsburgh Colored Stars, Pittsburgh Stars of Buffalo, Chicago Unions, Schenectady Mohawk Giants, Brooklyn Colored Giants, Chicago Giants, Buffalo Stars, Leland Giants, Chicago American Giants

JOHNSON, H. (HAMP)—1933-34, 1946-47—of, Birmingham Black Barons, Detroit Senators

JOHNSON, HARRY—1914-15—p, 2b, Philadelphia Giants

JOHNSON, HARRY A.—1884-89—2b, of, c, St. Louis Black Stockings, Cuban Giants, Trenton (NJ) Cuban Giants (Middle States League)

JOHNSON, HANK—1938—of, Bacharach (Philly) Giants

JOHNSON, HERB L. (H.L.)—1942, 1946—ss, 3b, New Orleans Black Pelicans, Nashville Cubs, Montgomery Dodgers

JOHNSON, HOWARD (MONK)—1914-26—of, Penn Red Caps of NY, Lincoln (NY) Giants, Brooklyn All-Stars, New York Stars, Wilmington Potomacs, Grand Central Terminal Red Caps, Royal Poinciana (FL)

JOHNSON, HUBERT (LEFTY, CANNONBALL)—1911—of, Brown's Tennessee Rats

JOHNSON, J.—1903-07—c, 1b, Cuban X-Giants, Chicago Union Giants, Chicago Unions

JOHNSON, JACK (ROY)—1938-40, 1942-43—3b, Homestead Grays, Toledo Crawfords, Cincinnati Buckeyes, Philadelphia Daisies (NML)

JOHNSON, JAMES—1898—of, c, Adrian (MI) Page Fence Giants

JOHNSON, JAMES—1916, 1921-23, 1933—ss, of, Baltimore Black Sox, Bacharach (AC) Giants, Columbus Buckeyes

JOHNSON, JAMES (J. D.)—1950-53—p, Philadelphia Stars, Kansas City Monarchs, Birmingham Black Barons

JOHNSON, JAMES A.—1870-75—manager, St. Louis Blue Stockings

JOHNSON, JIM (BIG JIM)—1942—p, Twin Cities Gophers

JOHNSON, JIM (JIMMIE)—1932-35—ss, 3b, Hilldale Club, Bacharach (Philly) Giants, Newark Dodgers, Pittsburgh Crawfords

JOHNSON, JIM W. (J.W., LEFTY)—1929-34—of, p, Memphis Red Sox

JOHNSON, JIMMY (JEEP)—1943-47—ss, Philadelphia Stars, Pittsburgh Crawfords, Homestead Grays

JOHNSON, JIMMY (SLIM)—1939-43—p, Toledo Crawfords, Indianapolis Crawfords, Philadelphia Stars, Philadelphia Daisies (NML)

JOHNSON, J.J.—1932—2b, ss, 3b, Little Rock Black Travelers, Washington Pilots

JOHNSON, JOE—1884-85—p, c, Baltimore Atlantics

JOHNSON, JOE—1935-36—p, Mohawk Colored Giants

JOHNSON, JOHN—1950—p, New York Cubans

JOHNSON, JOHN (JOHNNY)—1938-47—p, Birmingham Black Barons, Homestead Grays, New York Black Yankees, Baltimore Elite Giants, New York Cubans, Newark Eagles

JOHNSON, JOHN BRADY—1925-28, 1939—president, manager, Brooklyn Cuban Giants; president, New York Black Yankees; president ECL

JOHNSON, JOHN H. (CANNONBALL, GOLD TOOTH)—1920-22—1b, Penn Red Caps, Lincoln (NY) Giants

JOHNSON, JOHN H.—1946—2b, Pittsburgh Crawfords (USL)

JOHNSON, [REV.] JOHN HOWARD—1947-48—president, Negro National League

JOHNSON, JOHN J.—1950s—writer, *Kansas City Call*

JOHNSON, JOHN ARTHUR (JACK)—1905—manager, 1b, Johnson's Pets

JOHNSON, JOHN THOMAS (TOPEKA JACK)—1901-22—1b, ss, of, manager, Chicago Unions, Chicago Union Giants, Algona Brownies, Topeka (KS) Giants, Minneapolis Keystones, Kansas City (MO) Royal Giants, Kansas City (KS) Giants, Jack Johnson's Giants

JOHNSON, JOHN WESLEY (SMOKE, LEFTY)—1922-32—p, 1b, Cleveland Tate Stars, Cleveland Elites, Cleveland Browns, Lincoln (NY) Giants, Cleveland Tigers, Chicago American Giants, Memphis Red Sox

JOHNSON, JOHNNY (JIMMIE)—1943—of, Cleveland Buckeyes

JOHNSON, JOHNNY (PEE WEE)—1939—2b, Newark Eagles

JOHNSON, JOSEPH B.—1937—officer, Indianapolis Athletics, 1939—president, Eastern Colored League

JOHNSON, JOSHUA (JOSH, BRUTE)—1934-42—c, of, Cincinnati Tigers, Homestead Grays, New York Black Yankees, Brooklyn Royal Giants, Philadelphia Stars

JOHNSON, JUDY [see JOHNSON, WILLIAM JULIUS]

JOHNSON, LEAMAN—1935, 1940-49—ss, 2b, Bacharach (AC) Giants, Memphis Red Sox, Newark Eagles, Birmingham Black Barons, New York Black Yankees, Minneapolis-St. Paul Colored Gophers, Harlem Globetrotters, Los Angeles White Sox, Cincinnati Crescents, Detroit Senators, Cincinnati Buckeyes, Chicago American Giants

JOHNSON, LEE—1941—p, c, Birmingham Black Barons

JOHNSON, LEE A.—1933—business manager, Cole's American Giants

JOHNSON, LENNIE—1928—c, of, Brooklyn Royal Giants

Negro Leagues Book #2: The Players

JOHNSON, LEONARD—1947-48—p, Chicago American Giants, Kansas City Monarchs

JOHNSON, LEROY D.—1950-51—p, Birmingham Black Barons

JOHNSON, LESTER—1929, 1932—of, 2b, Chattanooga Black Lookouts

JOHNSON, LOUIS (CHICK)—1927—p, Birmingham Black Barons

JOHNSON, LOUIS DECATUR (DICTA, SPITBALL)—1908-25—p, manager, coach, Twin City Gophers, Chicago American Giants, Indianapolis ABCs, Detroit Stars, Toledo Tigers, Pittsburgh Keystones, Milwaukee Bears, Bowser's ABCs, Louisville White Sox, Leland Giants, Chicago Giants, St. Paul Colored Gophers, Royal Poinciana (FL)

JOHNSON, LOUIS BROWN (SWEET LOU, SLICK)—1955—of, Kansas City Monarchs

JOHNSON, LUDWIG—1945-46—batboy, Indianapolis Clowns

JOHNSON, LUTHER—1946—2b, 3b, Portland (OR) Rosebuds

JOHNSON, M. [see JOHNSON, HOWARD (MONK)]

JOHNSON, MAMIE LEE (PEANUT)—1954—p, Indianapolis Clowns

JOHNSON, (MONK) [see JOHNSON, HOWARD (MONK)]

JOHNSON, N.—1906—ss, Philadelphia Quaker City Giants

JOHNSON, NATE (SPEEDBOY)—1922-24—p, Bacharach (AC) Giants, Cleveland Browns, Brooklyn Royal Giants, Harrisburg Giants

JOHNSON, OLLIE—1910-12, 15—of, c, p, 1b, 2b, Brooklyn Royal Giants, Cuban Giants, Pittsburgh Giants

JOHNSON, OSCAR (HEAVY)—1920-33—of, c, 1b, St. Louis Giants, Kansas City Monarchs, Baltimore Black Sox, Harrisburg Giants, Cleveland Tigers, Memphis Red Sox, Dayton Marcos

JOHNSON, OTHELLO—1915-22—1b, Bacharach (AC) Giants, Brooklyn Royal Giants, Philadelphia Giants, Lincoln (NY) Giants, Penn Red Caps of NY

JOHNSON, OZIAH—1946—of, Boston Blues

JOHNSON, P.—1886—c, Unions of New Orleans

JOHNSON, P.—1903-04—1b, Chicago Unions

JOHNSON, P.—1916—c, 3b, Cuban X-Giants

JOHNSON, P.—1933—p, Memphis Red Sox

JOHNSON, PEARLEY (TUBBY, PETER)—1920-31, 1941-44—of, Baltimore Black Sox, Boston Royal Giants, Providence Giants, Harrisburg Giants, Otto Brigg's All-Stars

JOHNSON, (PEE WEE)—1939—2b, Newark Eagles

JOHNSON, PHIL—1929—p, Santop Broncos

JOHNSON, PHIL—1960—manager, Raleigh (NC) Tigers

JOHNSON, R.—1906—3b, Philadelphia Quaker City Giants

JOHNSON, RALPH BURNETT (R. B., ROB, BIG CAT)—1950-54—ss, Indianapolis Clowns, Kansas City Monarchs

JOHNSON, RALPH O. (BOTTS)—1941—of, Philadelphia Stars

JOHNSON, RAY—1920-21—c, 1b, of, St. Louis Giants

JOHNSON, RAYMOND—1946—of, Seattle Steelheads, Cleveland Buckeyes

JOHNSON, RAYMOND K.—1942—p, Kansas City Monarchs

JOHNSON, (RAT) [see JOHNSON, GEORGE (CHAPPIE)]

JOHNSON, REUBEN—1926—3b, Albany (GA) Giants

JOHNSON, RICHARD (DICK) [a.k.a. DICK MALE, DICK NOYLE]—1886-90—c, of, Syracuse Stars, Zanesville (OH) (Ohio State League, Tri-State League; Lima (OH), Tri-State League; Peoria (IL), Springfield Senators (IL) (Central Interstate League)

JOHNSON, RICK—1938—of, Bacharach (NJ) Giants

JOHNSON, ROBERT—1869-76—2b, 3b, ss, Chicago Uniques, Chicago Blue Stockings

JOHNSON, ROBERT B.—1939-40—of, New York Black Yankees, Brooklyn Royal Giants, Bacharach (NJ) Giants

JOHNSON, ROBERT (BOB)—1928-37—3b, of, Brooklyn Cuban Giants, Philadelphia Tigers, Brooklyn Royal Giants, Washington Pilots

JOHNSON, ROBERT (SHOWBOAT)—[see JOHNSON, ABDULLAH]

JOHNSON, RODDIE (RUDDY)—1954—utility, Indianapolis Clowns

JOHNSON, ROY—1956—Detroit Stars

JOHNSON, ROY (BUBBLES)—1920—2b, Kansas City Monarchs

JOHNSON, RUDOLPH VALENTINO (RUDY)—1950—of, Cleveland Buckeyes

JOHNSON, S.—1886-87—of, New York Gorhams

JOHNSON, SESS [see JOHNSON, CECIL]

JOHNSON, SETH—1923—2b, Havana Red Sox

JOHNSON, SIMON—1871-76—of, Chicago Uniques

JOHNSON, (SPEED)—1928—p, Havana Red Sox

JOHNSON, TED—1933—of, Baltimore Black Sox

JOHNSON, THOMAS JEFFERSON (COLLEGE BOY)—1911-25—p, Chicago Union Giants, Lincoln (NY) Giants,

Indianapolis ABCs, Chicago American Giants, Pittsburgh Keystones, Schenectady Mohawk Giants, Chicago Giants, Royal Poinciana (FL), Detroit Stars; umpire, NNL

JOHNSON, [DR.] THOMAS FAIRFAX (LITTLE PROFESSOR, TOMMY)—1940—p, Philadelphia Stars, 1950—p, Indianapolis Clowns, 1963—scout, Pittsburgh Pirates

JOHNSON, TOBIE—1932—p, Indianapolis ABCs

JOHNSON, TOM (TOMMY)—1937-42—p, St. Louis Stars, Chicago American Giants

JOHNSON, TOPEKA JACK [see JOHNSON, JOHN THOMAS]

JOHNSON, TRACEY (BUCK)—1938—2b, Washington Black Senators

JOHNSON, UPTON—1905-06—3b, Brooklyn Royal Giants, Philadelphia Quaker Giants

JOHNSON, V.—1920—c, of, Nashville Elite Giants, Atlanta Black Crackers, Pensacola Giants, Nashville White Sox

JOHNSON, VERNADINE—1959—secretary, Newark Indians

JOHNSON, W.—1880—of, Washington Eagles

JOHNSON, W.—1931—1b, Newark Browns

JOHNSON, W.—1928 [see JOHNSTON, WILLIAM WADE]

JOHNSON, WALTER—1936—c, Birmingham Black Barons

JOHNSON, WALTER—1944-45, 1949-50—p, Homestead Grays, Memphis Red Sox

JOHNSON, WILL—1920—p, Jacksonville Stars, Atlanta Black Crackers

JOHNSON, WILLIAM—1858-62—c, Henson Base Ball Club of Jamaica (NY), Unknown Base Ball Club (of Weeksville, NY)

JOHNSON, WILLIAM—1871-74—p, Chicago Uniques, Philadelphia Pythians

JOHNSON, WILLIAM—1897—of, Cuban X-Giants

JOHNSON, WILLIAM—1919-23—of, Brooklyn Royal Giants, Bacharach (AC) Giants, Lincoln (NY) Giants

JOHNSON, WILLIAM (BILL)—1936-38—p, St. Louis Stars, Chicago American Giants

JOHNSON, WILLIAM (BUCK, BILL, WILLIE)—1938-40, 1945—ss, 2b, c, of, Washington Black Senators, Schenectady Mohawk Giants, Brooklyn Royal Giants, New York Black Yankees, Chicago American Giants, Philadelphia Stars

JOHNSON, WILLIAM H. (WISE, BILL, BIG C.)—1920-34—c, of, manager, Homestead Grays, Hilldale Club, Philadelphia Tigers, Penn Red Caps of NY, Wilmington Potomacs, Harrisburg Giants, Washington Potomacs, Dayton Marcos

JOHNSON, WILLIAM JULIUS (JUDY, PAPA, JING)—1918-38—3b, ss, manager, Hilldale Club, Homestead Grays, Darby Daisies, Breakers Hotel (FL), Pittsburgh Crawfords; 1951-54—scout, coach, Philadelphia Athletics

JOHNSON, WILLIE JAMES—1952—p, Chicago American Giants

JOHNSON, WILLIS—1953—p, Kansas City (KS) Giants

JOHNSON, WILLIS (SLIM)—1936—p, Washington Elite Giants

JOHNSON, W. J.—1926—c, of, Atlanta Black Crackers

JOHNSON, WOOD—1915—p, Chicago Palmer House Stars

JOHNSTON, ____—1889—1b, Trenton (NJ) Cuban Giants (Middle States League)

JOHNSTON [JOHNSTONE], ____—1911-13—c, Pittsburgh Giants, Philadelphia Giants

JOHNSTON, C.—1916—2b, Lincoln (NY) Stars

JOHNSTON [JOHNSON], JACK—1920, 1922, 1927—p, of, Detroit Stars, St. Louis Stars, St. Louis Black Sox

JOHNSTON, JIMMY—1946—p, Homestead Grays

JOHNSTON [JOHNSON], WILLIAM WADE (KID)—1921-34—of, p, Cleveland Tate Stars, Kansas City Monarchs, Baltimore Black Sox, Detroit Stars, Penn Red Caps of NY, Padron's Cuban Giants, St. Louis Stars, Indianapolis ABCs

JONES, ____—1907—of, Keystone (PA) Giants

JONES, ____—1909—p, Pittsburgh Giants

JONES, ____—1909—player, Harrisburg Giants

JONES, ____—1909—c, Indianapolis ABCs

JONES, ____—1911—ss, Chicago American Giants

JONES, ____—1915—p, of, All Nations

JONES, ____—1918—of, Bacharach (AC) Giants

JONES, ____—1920—1b, New Orleans Crescent Stars

JONES, ____—1920—2b, Chicago Union Giants

JONES, ____—1920—of, Philadelphia Giants

JONES, ____—1921—p, Memphis Red Sox

JONES, ____—1921—of, Chicago Union Giants

JONES, ____—1921—c, Cleveland Tate Stars

JONES, ____—1922—of, Cuban X-Giants

JONES, ____—1922-24—umpire, NNL

JONES, ____—1923—p, Nashville Elite Giants

JONES, ____—1929—of, Fort Worth Panthers

JONES, ____—1929—of, Dallas Black Giants

JONES, ____—1935—p, Memphis Red Sox

JONES, ____—1937—c, New York Black Yankees

JONES, ____—1939—of, St. Louis Stars

JONES, ____—1943—3b, St. Louis Stars

JONES, ____—1943—ss, Pittsburgh Crawfords

Negro Leagues Book #2: The Players

JONES, ____—1946—of, Birmingham Black Barons
JONES, ____—1948—ph, New York Black Yankees
JONES, A.—1926—p, Dayton Marcos
JONES, JR., AARON—1954-55—p, Detroit Stars
JONES, ABE— [see JONES, WILLIAM ALBERT]
JONES, ALEX—1926—2b, of, St. Louis Stars
JONES, ALBERT ALONZO (AL)—1944-46—p, Chicago American Giants, Memphis Red Sox, Cincinnati Crescents, Harlem Globetrotters, Portland Rosebuds, Seattle Steelheads, San Francisco Sea Lions
JONES, ALVIN—1928—officer, Harrisburg Giants
JONES, ANDREW—1903—p, Cuban Giants, Genuine Cuban Giants
JONES, ANDREW J.—1867-68—p, 2b, Philadelphia Excelsior, Philadelphia Pythians
JONES, ARCHIE—1940-42—2b, 3b, Philadelphia Stars, Baltimore Grays
JONES, ARTHUR BROWN (MUTT, DUMP)—1925-26, 1934—p, ss, Birmingham Black Barons
JONES, B. (SUG)—1932, 1934—1b, of, c, Little Rock Black Travelers, Cleveland Red Sox, Memphis Red Sox, Little Rock Grays
JONES, BAILEY—1951—c, New Orleans Eagles
JONES, BENJAMIN (BEN)—1950—ss, New York Black Yankees
JONES, BENNY [see JONES, ROSCOE (BENNY, HOGHEAD)]
JONES, BERT [see JONES, GEORGE ELBERTUS]
JONES, BOB (BUD)—1932, 1941—2b, ss, of, Hilldale Club, Philadelphia Stars, Detroit Stars
JONES, BOK—1932, 1934—3b, of, Memphis Red Sox
JONES, C.— 1886—utility, St. Louis Black Stockings
JONES, C.—1931—2b, Little Rock Black Travelers
JONES, C. (CHARLIE)—1927—2b, Royal Poinciana Hotel (FL)
JONES, CASEY—1934—of, 2b, Baltimore Black Sox
JONES, CHARLES—1883—officer, Washington Manhattans
JONES, CHARLES (FOX)—1946—of, 3b, Brooklyn Brown Dodgers, Seattle Steelheads
JONES, CHARLES D.—1950—3b, Cleveland Buckeyes
JONES, CHARLES W.—1934—ph, Philadelphia Stars
JONES, CHICO—1964—p, of, Satchel Paige All-Stars
JONES, CLARA—1935—officer, Boston ABCs
JONES, CLARENCE—1943—of, Baltimore Elite Giants
JONES, CLARENCE WOODROW (BUTSEY)—1960—ss, Detroit-New Orleans Stars, Raleigh (NC) Tigers

JONES, JR., CLEVELAND (FOUR-WAY)—1958—2b, Birmingham Black Barons
JONES, JR., CLINTON (CASEY)—1940-55—c, Memphis Red Sox
JONES, JR., COLLINS CHESTERFIELD (COLLIS)—1942-47—2b, ss, of, Harrisburg-St. Louis Stars, Cincinnati Ethiopian Clowns (NML), Birmingham Black Barons, Twin City Gophers, Detroit Black Sox, Philadelphia Stars, Harlem Globetrotters, Portland (OR) Rosebuds
JONES, COUNTRY [see JONES, SPENCER]
JONES, C.P.—1945—officer, Nashville Black Vols
JONES, CURTIS (BUD)—1941, 1946—p, Detroit Black Sox, Cleveland Buckeyes
JONES, D.—1882-84—of, Philadelphia Orions, Philadelphia Mutual B.B.C.
JONES, DICK—1932, 1935—of, manager, Memphis Red Sox
JONES, DICK—1938—officer, Indianapolis ABCs
JONES, EARL—1937—3b, Detroit Stars
JONES, EDDIE—1942—ss, Baltimore Grays
JONES, EDWARD (ED)—1915-19—c, of, Chicago American Giants, Chicago Giants, Bacharach (AC) Giants, Bowser's ABCs, Chicago Union Giants, Harrisburg Giants, Louisville White Sox, Indianapolis ABCs
JONES, E. R.—1888—manager, Providence Grays
JONES, ERNEST (MINT)—1934-42—1b, Jacksonville Red Caps, Cleveland Bears, Philadelphia Stars, Boston Royal Giants
JONES, EUGENE (LEFTY)—1943—of, p, Homestead Grays, Philadelphia Stars, Atlanta Black Crackers
JONES, JR., FAYTE [FATE]—1950—of, Birmingham Black Barons
JONES, FELIX—1946—p, San Francisco Sea Lions
JONES, FRANCIS (FRANK, J.R.)—1867-68—of, p, Philadelphia Pythians, Philadelphia Excelsior
JONES, FRANKLIN H.—1869—utility, Philadelphia Pythians, Philadelphia Excelsior
JONES, G.—1920—of, Hilldale Club
JONES, GEORGE—1932—p, John Donaldson All Stars
JONES, GEORGE ELBERTUS (BERT, YELLOW KID)—1896-1903, 1911, 1914—p, Chicago Unions, Atchison (Kansas St. League), Algona (IA) Brownies, Chicago Union Giants, Twin Cities Gophers, French Lick (IN) Plutos, West Baden (IN) Sprudels, Kansas City (KS) Giants
JONES, GERALD—1947—of, Nashville Cubs
JONES, H.—1914—p, c, Baltimore Giants

JONES, HANK—1927, 1939-40, 1946—p, of, Chicago Giants, Chicago American Giants, Fresno/San Diego Tigers, Chicago Palmer House Stars

JONES, HANZEL—1926—p, of, Chattanooga Black Lookouts, Nashville Elite Giants

JONES, HAROLD MARION (HANK, HAL)—1955-56—of, Kansas City Monarchs

JONES, HENRY N. (TEENAN)—1884-87—vice-president, Chicago Gordons; 1890—treasurer, Chicago Unions

JONES, HERMAN—1960—p, Detroit-New Orleans Stars

JONES, HURLEY—1931—p, Birmingham Black Barons

JONES, JR., JAMES EDWARD (JIMMY, LEFTY)—1943, 1946-47, 1949-52—of, Baltimore Elite Giants, Nashville Cubs, Philadelphia Stars

JONES, JIMMIE—1921—p, Cuban Stars (East)

JONES, JOHN L. (NIPPY, JOHNNY)—1922-34—of, 3b, ss, Detroit Stars, Baltimore Black Sox, Indianapolis ABCs, Bacharach (Philly) Giants, Washington Pilots, Memphis Red Sox, Detroit Giants

JONES, JOHN EDWARD (JOHNNY)—1951—p, New Orleans Eagles

JONES, JOHN PAUL—1920—p, Indianapolis ABCs

JONES, JOHN W.—1886—president, Southern League of Colored Base Ballists

JONES, J. T.—1931-32—of, c, Bacharach (Philly) Giants, Washington Pilots, Little Rock Travelers-Grays

JONES, JULIUS (JULES)—1938-40—of, Memphis Red Sox, Birmingham Black Barons

JONES, L.—1910, 1912—c, Chicago Union Giants

JONES, LAWRENCE—1927, 1931, 1936—3b, Cleveland Hornets, Nashville Elite Giants, Chicago Giants

JONES, LEE—1908-22—of, Brooklyn Colored Giants, Brooklyn Royal Giants, Dallas Giants

JONES, L.H.—1886—treasurer, Southern League of Colored Base Ballists

JONES, LINCOLN—1944—c, Chicago American Giants

JONES, LUCIOUS (SQUAB)—1920, 1932, 1937—of, 2b, manager, Jacksonville Stars, Atlanta Black Crackers

JONES, MARVIN T. (LEFTY, ROLLER)—1954-55—p, Kansas City Monarchs

JONES, NICK—1929-32—of, Colored House of David, John Donaldson All-Stars

JONES, ODA—1898—p, of, Celoron (NY) Acme Colored Giants (Iron & Oil League)

JONES, OLLIE—1918-19—3b, St. Louis Giants

JONES, PAUL C.—1952-55—officer, Birmingham Black Barons

JONES, PAUL HENRY—1946-50, 1958—p, Fresno Tigers, Cleveland Buckeyes, Homestead Grays, Louisville Buckeyes, Memphis Red Sox

JONES, R.—1898—of, Chicago Unions

JONES, RAY—1941—ph, New York Black Yankees

JONES, REUBEN [RUBEN]—1918-49—of, manager, Dallas Giants, Birmingham Black Barons, Indianapolis ABCs, Chicago American Giants, Little Rock Black Travelers, Memphis Red Sox, Houston Eagles, Cleveland Red Sox, Little Rock Grays, Fort Worth Black Panthers

JONES, REX—1964—1b, Satchel Paige All-Stars

JONES, RICHARD—1887—manager, Providence Grays

JONES, SR., ROBERT LEO (FOX)—1946—of, infield, Brooklyn Brown Dodgers

JONES, ROSCOE (BENNY, HOGHEAD)—1931-35—of, Newark Dodgers, Cleveland Red Sox, Hilldale Club, Brooklyn Eagles, Pittsburgh Crawfords, Homestead Grays

JONES, (ROUGHHOUSE)—1932—of, Austin Black Senators

JONES, RUTHERFORD HAYES—1901-09—owner, secretary, business manager, Washington Giants

JONES, S.—1884, 1887—utility, St. Louis Black Stockings

JONES, S.—1909-10—c, Illinois Giants

JONES, SAM—1941—p, Detroit Black Sox

JONES, SAM—1950—p, Homestead Grays

JONES, SAMUEL (RED, TOOTHPICK SAM, SAD SAM)—1947-48—p, Cleveland Buckeyes

JONES, SPENCER (COUNTRY)—1930-33—2b, c, Brooklyn Royal Giants, Providence Giants

JONES, STANLEY LEE—1956-58—p, Birmingham Black Barons

JONES, STUART [STEWART] (SLIM, COUNTRY)—1932-38—p, 1b, Baltimore Black Sox, Philadelphia Stars

JONES, TENAN [see JONES, HENRY (TEENAN)]

JONES, TOM (PETE)—1942, 1944, 1946—c, ss, Philadelphia Stars, Chicago Brown Bombers (NML & USL), Harlem Globetrotters

JONES, VOLLINS—1945, 1947—of, Detroit Motor City Giants, Detroit Senators

JONES, W.—1886—ss, St. Louis Black Stockings

JONES, W.—1909-16—p, of, Cuban Giants, West Baden (IN) Sprudels, St. Louis Giants, Cuban X-Giants

JONES, W.—1946—of, Cincinnati Crescents

JONES, WALT—1920-21—ss, p, Indianapolis ABCs, Fort Worth Black Panthers

JONES, WALTER—1947—p, Cleveland Buckeyes

JONES, WALTER—1948—of, Chattanooga Choo Choos

JONES, WALTER—1955—ss, Indianapolis Clowns

JONES, WILLIAM (BRER)—1932, 1934—of, Atlanta Black Crackers, Chattanooga Black Lookouts, Birmingham Black Barons, Memphis Red Sox

JONES, WILLIAM WALTER (FOX, BILL, WEE WILLIE)—1922-30—c, 3b, Chicago American Giants, Chicago Giants, Bacharach (AC) Giants, Hilldale Club, Chicago Union Giants, Royal Poinciana (FL)

JONES, WILLIAM ALBERT (ABE, AL, W.A.)—1884-94—c, manager, officer, Chicago Unions, Chicago Gordons, Chicago Unknowns

JONES, WILLIAM EUGENE—1942-43—of, Baltimore Grays, Baltimore Elite Giants

JONES, WILLIAM J.—1868—player, Philadelphia Pythians

JONES, WILLIAM NATHANIEL (BILL)—1956-58—p, of, 1b, Kansas City Monarchs

JONES, WILLIE (WEE WILLIE)—1946—p, Oakland Larks

JONES, WILLIS (WILL, LITTLE)—1895-1912—of, Leland Giants, Chicago Union Giants, Algona (IA) Brownies, St. Paul Colored Gophers

JORDAN, ____—1870-71—ss, 2b, Mutuals of Washington

JORDAN, CECIL—1946-48—ss, Memphis Red Sox

JORDAN, HENRY (HEN)—1921-25—c, Harrisburg Giants, Pittsburgh Stars of Buffalo, Baltimore Black Sox

JORDAN, LARNIE L. (BOO)—1936-42, 1945—ss, Philadelphia Stars, New York Black Yankees, Brooklyn Royal Giants, Bacharach (Philly) Giants, Philadelphia Hilldales (USL)

JORDAN, MAYNARD—1949-50—of, Houston Eagles

JORDAN, R.—1921—ss, Pittsburgh Stars of Buffalo

JORDAN, ROBERT—1896-1907—c, 1b, of, Cuban Giants, Cuban X-Giants, Philadelphia Giants, Brooklyn Royal Giants

JORDAN, VERDON—1945—infield, Cincinnati-Indianapolis Clowns

JORDAN, WILLIAM T.—1899-1912—president, business manager, Baltimore Giants

JORDAN, WILLIE—1933, 1938—p, Chicago American Giants, Louisville Black Colonels

JORDON, BERNARD—1948—p, Baltimore Elite Giants

JOSEPH, ____—1910—of, New York Black Sox

JOSEPH, W.L.—1934—officer, Atlanta Black Crackers

JOSEPH, WALTER LEE (NEWT, PEP, NIMROD, BLOOD & GUTS)—1920, 1922-39—p, 3b, manager, Montgomery Grey Sox, Kansas City Monarchs, Paige's All-Stars

JOSEPH, WILSON EMERSON—1929-30—3b, Kary All-Stars, Sioux City All-Stars, Colored House of David

JOSEPHS, W.H.—1939—officer, Washington Royal Giants

JOSEPHS, WILLIAM—1924-25—ss, 3b, Birmingham Black Barons, Cleveland Browns, Indianapolis ABCs

JOSH, ____—1917—p, Lincoln (NY) Giants

JOSHUA, ____—1871—of, Boston Resolutes

JOURNY, ____—1921—p, Knoxville Giants

JOYNES, JOSH—1930—p, Santop Broncos

JOYNER, JOHN—1946—utility, Pittsburgh Stars

JOYNER, WILLIAM—1893-1906—ss, Chicago Unions, Chicago Union Giants

JUANELO, ____ [see MIRABAL [MIRABEL], JUANELO]

JUDAH, ISAAC—1887—officer, Philadelphia Pythians (NCBBL)

JUDSON, ____—1916—p, St. Louis Giants

JUDSON, ____—1931—p, Indianapolis ABCs

JUDSON, CHARLES—1942, 1945—p, Detroit Motor City Giants, Detroit Black Sox

JUDSON, CLYDE W.—1942, 1945, 1948—c, Detroit Motor City Giants, Detroit Black Sox

JUNCO y CASANOVA, JOSÉ IRENE—1911-22—p, Cuban Giants, Cuban Stars (East & West), All Cubans

JUPITER, ____—1884—c, Brooklyn Remsens

JUPITER, ALFRED B.—1887-89, 1897-98—p, Boston Resolutes (NCBBL), Cuban Giants, Celoron (NY) Acme Colored Giants (Iron & Oil League), Cuban X-Giants, Trenton (NJ) Cuban Giants (Middle States League)

JURAN, ELI [EAGLE DURANT]—1921-43—p, 1b, of, Birmingham Black Barons, Newark Stars, Cleveland Browns, Washington Pilots, Hilldale Club, Baltimore Black Sox

JURAN, JOHN HENRY (B., JOHNNY)—1921-23—p, Birmingham Black Barons

JUSTICE, CHARLES PELL (CHARLEY)—1933-37—p, Akron Tyrites, Detroit Stars

K

KAISER, ____–1929–p, Evansville Giants

KAISER, CECIL (MINUTE MAN, ASPIRIN TABLET)–1939, 1945-49–p, Pittsburgh Crawfords (USL), Homestead Grays, Detroit Motor City Giants, Brooklyn Brown Dodgers, Detroit Stars

KALLIS, LENNIE–1940–ss, Cincinnati Buckeyes

KANE, ____–1944–ph, Cleveland Buckeyes

KATINA, ____–1916–p, All Nations

KAUTINES, ____–1913, 1916–of, All Nations

KEANE, WILLIAM (W.L.)–1929-31–2b, c, officer, Louisville White Sox

KEARNEY, ____–1932–p, Newark Browns

KEARNES, ____–1946–ph, Philadelphia Stars

KEARNS, JOHN–1930–of, Columbus Keystones

KEATING, ____ [see KEETON, EUGENE]

KECK, D. J.–1948–treasurer, Negro American Association

KEELER, [KEEFER] ____–1931–of, Bacharach (Philly) Giants

KEELEY, ____–1952–of, Memphis Red Sox

KEENAN, JAMES J. (JIM)–1914-30–business manager, owner, Lincoln (NY) Giants; secretary-treasurer, ECL

KEENE [KEEN], JOHNNY–1952–of, Chicago American Giants

KEENE, EDWARD–1915-16–3b, 1b, West Baden (IN) Sprudels, Bowser's ABCs

KEETON [KEATING], EUGENE ADERSON–1917, 1920-26–p, Dayton Marcos, Pittsburgh Stars of Buffalo, Cleveland Tate Stars, Indianapolis ABCs, Dayton Giants

KEIGER, [see KINKEIDE, JOHN]

KEITH, CLARENCE–1931, 1934–of, Knoxville Giants, Atlanta Black Crackers

KELCH, ____–1867–1b, Camden Resolutes

KELL, A.–1912–p, All Nations

KELL, W.–1912–ss, All Nations

KELLAR, MARION–1930–secretary, New Orleans Black Pelicans

KELLEY, COLAN–1954–p, Birmingham Black Barons

KELLEY [KELLY], HENRY–1932–p, Bacharach (Philly) Giants

KELLEY, HOLLAND F.–1945-46–general secretary, USL, business manager, Pittsburgh Crawfords (USL)

KELLEY, KLUG (KING)–1900-08–ss, of, 3b, 1b, Genuine Cuban Giants, Famous Cuban Giants, New York Colored Giants, Cuban Giants

KELLEY, PALMER–1916-18–p, Chicago Giants, Chicago Union Giants, Dayton Giants

KELLEY, RICHARD A. (CHARLES)–1889-91–1b, 2b, ss, Danville (Illinois-Indiana League); Jamestown (Pennsylvania-New York League)

KELLMAN, EDRIC LEON–1946-53–3b, Cleveland Buckeyes, Louisville Buckeyes, Memphis Red Sox, Indianapolis Clowns

KELLY, ____–1908–3b, New York Colored Giants

KELLY, ____–1913–c, Paterson (NJ) Smart Set

KELLY, ____–1918–1b, Pennsylvania Giants

KELLY, ____–1931–3b, Memphis Red Sox

KELLY, L. E.–1914–3b, Hilldale Club, Lincoln (NY) Stars

KELLY, (LEFTY) [see SEARCY, KELTON]

KELLY, RICHARD A.–1889–1b, 2b, ss, Danville (ILL-IND League)

KELLY, ROSCOE (SLIM)–1946–3b, Brooklyn Brown Dodgers

KELLY, W.H.–1937, 1941-42–p, Memphis Red Sox, Jacksonville Red Caps

KELLY, JR., WALTER COWAN–1950-53–p, Cleveland Buckeyes, Memphis Red Sox, Birmingham Black Barons

KELLY, WILLIAM–1944-47–c, New York Black Yankees, Homestead Grays

KELLY, WILLIAM H.–1898, 1902-03–3b, Celoron (NY) Acme Colored Giants (Iron & Oil League), Cuban Giants

KELSEY, ____–1912–of, All Nations

KEMP, ____–1946–umpire, NNL

KEMP, ED (DUCKY)–1914-31–of, manager, Philadelphia Royal Giants, Norfolk Stars, Norfolk Giants, Baltimore Black Sox, Lincoln (NY) Giants, Brooklyn Royal Giants, Schenectady Mohawk Giants

KEMP, GEORGE–1910, 1916-18–of, Hilldale Club

KEMP, GEORGE WALTER–1942-43–c, New York Black Yankees, North All-Stars

KEMP, JAMES ALBERT (GABBY)–1935-39–2b, Atlanta Black Crackers, Jacksonville Red Caps, Indianapolis ABCs

KEMP, JOHN–1920-28–of, Memphis Red Sox, Birmingham Black Barons

KENAN, ____–1929–p, Evansville Giants

KENDALL, ____–1918-20, 1925–2b, Lincoln (NY) Giants

KENDRICK, LEO–1943–c, Atlanta Black Crackers

KENDRICKS, L. H. (WILLIE)–1943–p, Atlanta Black Crackers

KENNARD [KENNA], DANIEL C. (DAN)–1913-27–c, Indianapolis ABCs, Chicago American Giants, St. Louis Giants,

Lincoln (NY) Giants, St. Louis Stars, Detroit Stars, Bowser's ABCs, West Baden (IN) Sprudels, Chicago Black Sox, Royal Poinciana (FL)
KENNEDY, ____–1905–of, Chicago Unions
KENNEDY, ____–1910–ss, St. Paul Colored Gophers
KENNEDY, [see CANNADY, WALTER I.]–1926-27–ss, 3b, Lincoln (NY) Giants, Harrisburg Giants
KENNEDY, DAVE–1915-17–of, All Nations, Havana Red Sox
KENNEDY, ERNEST D.–1950–infield, Memphis Red Sox
KENNEDY, JIM–1951–1b, Birmingham Black Barons
KENNEDY, JOHN IRWIN [IRVIN]–1949, 1954-56–3b, ss, Durham (NC) Eagles, Birmingham Black Barons, Kansas City Monarchs
KENNEDY, NED–1954–p, Kansas City Monarchs
KENNEDY, ROBERT–1945-46–p, Boston Blues
KENNEDY, WALTER–1945–officer, Knoxville Smokies
KENNEDY, SR., WALTER FOXSWORTH (FOX)–1950–of, Chicago American Giants
KENNER, BURRELL–1921–ss, 2b, Hilldale Club, Washington DC Braves
KENNARD, ____–1867–of, Brooklyn Unique
KENT, ____–1919–of, Philadelphia Giants, Brooklyn Royal Giants
KENT, [DR.] RICHARD WILLIAM–1922-31–officer, St. Louis Stars
KENWOOD, ____–1927–p, Hilldale Club
KENYON, [REV.] HARRY C.–1919-29–p, 2b, of, manager, Brooklyn Royal Giants, Hilldale Club, Indianapolis ABCs, Chicago American Giants, Lincoln (NY) Giants, Detroit Stars, Kansas City Monarchs, Memphis Red Sox
KERNER, JOHN F.–1931-34–of, Columbus Blue Birds, Detroit Stars, Indianapolis ABCs, Columbus Turfs, Columbus Stars
KERRIGAN, ____–1922–umpire, NNL
KERRY, ____–1929–ph, Bacharach (AC) Giants
KESSELL, ____–1930–3b, Havana Red Sox
KESSLER, JERRY–employee, Newark Eagles
KETCHUM, WILLIE–1954–of, Kansas City Monarchs
KEYES, GARVIN–1943–infield, Philadelphia Stars
KEYES, ROBERT–1941-46–p, Memphis Red Sox,
KEYES, STEVE EZEKIEL (YOUNGIE, ZEKE, KHORA)–1940-48–p, Memphis Red Sox, Philadelphia Stars, Indianapolis Crawfords, Cincinnati Ethiopian Clowns (NML), Cleveland Buckeyes

KEYS [KEYES], ALBERT (LEFTY, RED)–1915, 1918–p, St. Louis Giants, Chicago American Giants
KEYS, SR., [DR.] GEORGE B.–1922-32–officer, St. Louis Stars; officer, NNL
KEYS, LUDIE [LUDY]–1934-35–president, owner, Birmingham Black Barons
KEYS, NORMAN–1950–p, Houston Eagles
KILGORE, CHARLES–1929–of, Shreveport Black Sports
KILLIAN, ____–1922–umpire, NNL
KIMBALL, ROY–1956–New York Black Yankees
KIMBLE, HOLLIS–1946–p, Boston Blues
KIMBRO, HENRY ALLEN (KIMMIE, JUMBO)–1936-53–of, manager, Washington Elite Giants, Baltimore Elite Giants, New York Black Yankees, Birmingham Black Barons, Philadelphia Stars, South All-Stars
KIMBRO, HOWARD (HOWDY)–1928-32, 1945-46–p, Pittsburgh Crawfords (USL), Pittsburgh Stars
KIMBRO, TED [a.k.a. ARTHUR, JESS]–1914-18–3b, 2b, Bowser's ABCs, St. Louis Giants, Lincoln (NY) Giants, Louisville White Sox, West Baden (IN) Sprudels, Hilldale Club, Grand Central Terminal Red Caps
KIMBROUGH, (BOOTS)–1947–bus driver, Cleveland Buckeyes
KIMBROUGH, LARRY NATHANIEL (SCHOOLBOY)–1942-48–p, Philadelphia Stars, Homestead Grays, Richmond Giants
KIN, ____–1931–c, Cuban Stars (East)
KINARD, ROOSEVELT–1931-33–3b, Washington Pilots, Schenectady Mohawk Giants
KINCAIDE, C. J.–1945-47–officer, NSL; officer, Knoxville Smokies
KINCANNON, SR., [TINCANER], HARRY (TIN CAN)–1929-39–p, Pittsburgh Crawfords, Philadelphia Stars, New York Black Yankees, Washington Black Senators, Toledo Crawfords
KINDLE, WILLIAM HORACE (BILL)–1911-20, 1925–ss, 2b, of, Brooklyn Royal Giants, Indianapolis ABCs, Chicago American Giants, Lincoln (NY) Stars, Lincoln (NY) Giants, Brooklyn All-Stars, New York Stars, West Baden (IN) Sprudels, Cuban Giants
KINE, ____–1947–c, Cincinnati-Indianapolis Clowns
KING, ____–1938–p, Philadelphia Stars
KING, ____–1920–3b, Philadelphia Giants
KING, ALTON–1941-49–ss, Detroit Motor City Giants, Detroit Wolves, Detroit Stars

KING, B. LEE (BABY)—1923—officer, Birmingham Black Barons; 1920-38—umpire, NAL

KING, BOKLY—1944—p, Atlanta Black Crackers

KING, BRENNAN [BRENDAN] L.—1943-47—p, Cincinnati Ethiopian Clowns (NML), Nashville Cubs, Nashville Black Vols, Atlanta Black Crackers

KING, CHARLES—1937—p, Pittsburgh Crawfords

KING, CHARLES B.—1928—officer, Memphis Red Sox

KING, SR., CLARENCE EARL (CHARLEY, PIJO)—1947-54, 1958—of, Birmingham Black Barons, Detroit Clowns

KING, DANIEL—1926—of, Dayton Marcos

KING, DOUGLAS—1946—of, Pittsburgh Stars

KING, EZELLE (ZEKE)—1952, 1955—1b, Harlem Globetrotters, Detroit Stars

KING, G.—1929—2b, ss, Boston Black Sox

KING, HAL—1946—co-owner, 1946 San Francisco Sea Lions

KING TUT [see KING, RICHARD ELMER and FARRINGTON, FREDDIE]

KING, J.—1929—ss, 2b, Boston Black Sox

KING, LEON—1947—p, Detroit Wolves, Kansas City Monarchs

KING, LEONARD D.—1921—of, Kansas City Monarchs

KING, LEROY—1927-28—p, Chicago Giants

KING, PARIS BERNARD—1955—c, Memphis Red Sox

KING, RICHARD ELMER (KING TUT)—1931-32, 1937-60—clown, 1b, Bacharach (Philly) Giants, Cincinnati Ethiopian Clowns (NML), Schenectady Mohawk Giants, Indianapolis Clowns, Baltimore Grays

KING, SHERMAN G.—1921—owner, Memphis Union Giants

KING, WILBERT [WILBUR]—1944-47—of, 2b, Memphis Red Sox, Cleveland Buckeyes, Chicago American Giants, New York Black Yankees, Detroit Motor City Giants, Detroit Wolves

KING, WILLIAM (DOLLY)—1941, 1944, 1947—c, of, New York Black Yankees, Homestead Grays

KING, WILLIAM F.—1890-92—ss, Chicago Unions

KINGMAN, ____—1869—p, Rockford (IL) Rockfords

KINGSLEY, ____—1871—c, Chelsea Auroras

KINKEIDE, JOHN—1883, 1887—p, of, Louisville Falls City (NCBBL), Chicago Unions

KINNARD, DAN [see KENNARD, DAN C.]

KINNER, SR., H.B.—1946—owner, Milwaukee Tigers (USL)

KINNEY, BEN—1907-09—manager, Cuban Stars

KINNON, EDDIE—1946—3b, of, San Francisco Sea Lions

KINSON, ____—1937—p, New York Black Yankees

KIRBY, ____—1928—p, Cleveland Tigers

KIRKSEY [KIRKSLEY], ____—1926, 1928—c, Dayton Marcos

KIRKWOOD, HERSAL—1930—p, Houston Black Buffaloes

KITAMURA, RICHARD SHOJI (DICK)—1948-49—ss, Harlem Globetrotters

KITCHEN, M. (SONNY)—1951—of, Philadelphia Stars

KLEP [KLEPP], EDWARD JOSEPH (EDDIE, LEFTY)—1946—p, Cleveland Buckeyes

KLINE, ____—1914—1b, All Nations

KLISE, ____—1914—p, Chicago Giants

KLONDYKE, (DIXIE)—1914—c, Chicago American Giants

KNAPP, ____—1938—p, Indianapolis ABCs

KNIGHT, DAVID—1868—player, Philadelphia Pythians

KNIGHT, DAVE (MULE)—1921-23, 1930-31—p, Detroit Stars, Baltimore Black Sox, Chicago American Giants, Chicago Giants

KNIGHT, GEORGE—1942—p, Philadelphia Stars

KNIGHT, NATHAN—1908-10—p, c, 3b, St. Paul Colored Gophers, Indianapolis ABCs, St. Louis Giants, New York Black Sox

KNOWLES, SONNY—1942—3b, Baltimore Grays

KNOX, ____—1889—3b, Philadelphia Giants

KNOX, ____—1930—umpire, NSL

KNOX, ELMER—1943-1949—of, Atlanta Black Crackers, Jacksonville Red Caps, Knoxville Grays

KNOX, ELWOOD C.—1920—co-drafter of NNL constitution, sports editor, *Indianapolis Freeman*

KNOX, GEORGE L.—1892-1927, publisher, editor, *Indianapolis Freeman*

KOBEK, GEORGE—1927—of, Chicago American Giants

KOGER, JR., EUGENE ALLEN (GENE)—1950, 1954—utility, Philadelphia Stars, Indianapolis Clowns, Greensboro (NC) Red Wings, Winston-Salem Pond Giants, Satchel Paige All-Stars

KOLOZAR (KOLEZAR), ____—1937-38—umpire, NAL

KOOP, ____—1922—utility, Bacharach (AC) Giants

KOUNTZE, MABRAY (DOC)—writer, *Boston Chronicle, Boston Guardian, Boston Greater News, Medford Transcripts*

KRAMER, ____—1916—3b, All Nations

KRANSON [KRANSTON], ARTHUR LEE—1934-41—p, Monroe (LA) Monarchs, Kansas City Monarchs, Memphis Red Sox, Chicago American Giants

KREITER [KRIDER], J. MONROE—1890—manager, Cuban Giants, York (PA) Colored Monarchs (Eastern Interstate League)

Negro Leagues Book #2: The Players

KUEBLER, CONRAD—1907-16—owner, officer, St. Louis Giants, St. Louis Black Bronchos (female team)
KUNTZ, J.—1915—of, St. Louis Cubs
KYLE, ____—1917—ss, Los Angeles White Sox
KYLE, ANDY—1922—p, Baltimore Black Sox, Bacharach (AC) Giants

King Tut (aka Richard Elmer King) with Bebop (aka Ralph Bell) and Prince Joe Henry of the Indianapolis Clowns pray for clear skies.

L

LABAUX, TED—1946—ss, Los Angeles White Sox

LABBOT [LABOT, LABOR], BUMPTY—1934—c, New Orleans Crescent Stars

LACEY, ____—1907—3b, Indianapolis ABCs

LACEY, ____—1929—c, Cleveland Tigers

LACEY, ____—1939—c, Satchel Paige All-Stars

LACEY, PERCY (BOB)—1935, 1937—p, Newark Dodgers, Philadelphia Stars

LACEY, RAY—1940—ph, Cleveland Bears

LACKEY, OBIE EZEKIEL—1927-43—ss, 2b, 3b, Philadelphia Giants, Hilldale Club, Bacharach (Philly) Giants, Pittsburgh Crawfords, Homestead Grays, Baltimore Black Sox, Philadelphia Stars, Brooklyn Royal Giants, New York Black Yankees, Santop's Broncos, Newark Dodgers, Detroit Black Sox

LACY, RAYMON TAYLOR (SKIPPER)—1947-50—of, Homestead Grays, Newark Eagles, Houston Eagles

LACY, SAMUEL HAROLD (SAM)—1918-2001—writer, *Washington Tribune* (1918-39), *Baltimore Afro-American* (1939-40, 1943-2003), *Chicago Defender* (1940-43); sports commentator—1968-76—Baltimore's WBAL-TV; player—1917-44—LeDroit (DC) Tigers, Hilldale Athletic Club, Bacharach (AC) Giants; Director of Publicity—1938— Washington Black Sox

LADUNA, PHILOMENO TIMITHIO (PHIL, P.T.)—1954-55—p, Indianapolis Clowns

LaFLORA [LAFORE], LOUIS—1925—of, Kansas City Monarchs

LaFORCE, EDWARD (ED)—1901-1927—trainer, Pittsburgh Pirates (MLB)

LaGRANDE, LARRY [see LeGRANDE, LARRY EDWIN]

LAIR, ____—1925—of, Penn Red Caps of NY

LALLY, ____—1910—p, Illinois Giants

LAMAR, CLARENCE (LEMON)—1935-45, 1949—ss, manager, St. Louis Stars, Cleveland Bears, Jacksonville Red Caps, Birmingham Black Barons, Cincinnati Ethiopian Clowns (NML), Durham (NC) Eagles, Asheville Blues, Monroe (LA) Monarchs

LAMAR, JR., EDWARD B. (E.B.)—1895-1927—manager, club officer, agent, Cuban X-Giants, Cuban Stars (East), Bacharach (AC) Giants, Harrisburg Giants, Brooklyn Cuban Giants

LAMAR, HORATIO VINCENT—1939—2b, Indianapolis ABCs, Atlanta Black Crackers

LaMARQUE, JAMES HARDING (JIM, LEFTY, LIBERTAD)—1942-51—p, Kansas City Monarchs

LAMBERT, (CHICK)—1932—ss, Bacharach (Philly) Giants

LAMBERT, CHARLES—1887, 1b, Wilmington Base Ball Club

LAMBERTIS, NESTOR (PAPA)—1929-34—of, Cuban Stars (East), Schenectady Mohawk Giants

LAMBESTES, ____—1930—of, Havana Red Sox

LAMPKINS, WILLIAM—1943—utility, Kansas City Monarchs

LANCASTER, ____—1880—ss, Washington Eagles

LANCASTER, ELI ED—1908-11—manager, Louisville Giants, Louisville Cubs

LAND [LANG], WILLIAM MATHEW (BILL)—1908-22—of, 1b, New York Colored Giants, Cuban Giants, Paterson (NJ) Smart Set, Schenectady Mohawk Giants, Brooklyn Royal Giants, Buffalo Cuban Giants, Buffalo Stars

LANDERS, JOHN WILLLIAM BARKLEY—1917—p, Indianapolis ABCs

LANDERS, ROBERT HENRY (HENNY, LEFTY)—1949-52—p, Kansas City Monarchs

LANDRY, ____—1880—of, Washington Keystones

LANE, ____—1926—ss, Chattanooga White Sox

LANE, ALTO (BIG TRAIN)—1929-34—p, Memphis Red Sox, Indianapolis ABCs, Cincinnati Tigers, Louisville White Sox, Kansas City Monarchs, Louisville Black Caps

LANE, D.—1867—1b, Monrovia Club of Harrisburg

LANE, ISAAC SAPPE (I.S)—1917-24—of, 3b, Dayton Giants, Dayton Marcos, Columbus Buckeyes, Detroit Stars

LANE, JAMES (BIG JIM)—1947—of, Detroit Wolves

LANE, W.—1867—2b, Monrovia Club of Harrisburg

LANE, ROBERT F.—1931-38—secretary, Bedford Lane Company— Greenlee Field

LANE, WILLIAM HENRY (BILL)—1910-11—3b, ss, Leland Giants, Chicago Giants, Chicago American Giants

LANEY, W.H.—1934—officer, Little Rock Black Travelers

LANG, JOHN F.—1883-86—manager, Washington Manhattans, Argyle Hotel, Cuban Giants

LANGRAM [LANDRUM], ____—1939—2b, 3b, Kansas City Monarchs, Chicago American Giants

LANGRUM, [DR.] E. L.—1934—owner, Cleveland Red Sox

LANGRUM, LEE—1948-49—c, San Francisco Sea Lions

LANIER, A. S.—1921—officer, Cuban Stars (West)

LANKFORD [LANGFORD] LOUIS ADWARD (AD, SPITBALL)—1912-20—c, of, p, St. Louis Giants, Lincoln (NY) Stars, Brooklyn Royal Giants, Penn Red Caps of NY,

Lincoln (NY) Giants, Schenectady Mohawk Giants, Breakers Hotel (FL)

LANSING, WILBUR—1948-49—p, Newark Eagles, Houston Eagles

LANTIGUA, ENRIQUE (CARLOS)—1935, 1937—c, New York Cubans, Trujillo All-Stars (Ciudad Trujillo Dragons)

LANTZ, ____—1932—pr, Indianapolis ABCs

LANUZA, PEDRO (JUSTINE)—1928-32—c, 1b, Havana Red Sox, Cuban Stars (West), Cuban House of David

LARRINAGO, PÉREZ PRUDENCIO—1946—2b, ss, Cleveland Buckeyes, Atlanta Black Crackers

LaRUE, JAMES—1919, 1921—c, Jewell's ABCs, Detroit Stars

LARD, ____—1929—1b, Wichita Falls Black Spudders

LARZA, ____—1920—1b, Cuban Stars (East)

LASUE, ____—1910—of, New York Black Sox

LATTIMER, LLOYD—1921—p, Indianapolis ABCs

LATTIMORE, ALBERT (ALPHONSO, DUKE)—1929-36—c, Baltimore Black Sox, Brooklyn Royal Giants, Columbus Blue Birds, Columbus Stars, Columbus Turfs, Schenectady Mohawk Giants, Columbus Keystones

LAU, ____—1927—p, Cuban Stars (East)

LAURENT, MILFRED STEPHEN (MILT, RICK—1922-35—3b, 1b, of, 2b, c, Memphis Red Sox, Cleveland Cubs, Birmingham Black Barons, Nashville Elite Giants, New Orleans Crescent Stars, New Orleans Caulfield Ads, New Orleans Black Pelicans

LAVELLA, ____—1919—p, Atlanta Black Crackers

LAVERA, ____—1919—c, Cuban Stars [see RODRÍGUEZ y VALERA, VICENTE]

LAVOY, R. [see SAVOY, R.]

LAW, ____—1918—of, Pennsylvania Giants

LAWRENCE, H.—1884—utility, St. Louis Black Stockings

LAWRENCE, NATHANIEL (NATE)—1945—of, Detroit Motor City Giants

LAWSON, ____—1909—p, Leland Giants

LAWSON, ____—1932—of, John Donaldson All-Stars

LAWSON, GEORGE (BABE)—1946-47—1b, Chattanooga Choo Choos

LAWSON, L.B. (FLASH, CHICK)—1934, 1940, 1949—p, Washington Pilots, Philadelphia Stars, Memphis Red Sox

LAWYER, FLOYD (FRED)—1913-14—of, Schenectady Mohawk Giants

LAYTON, [REV] CLIFFORD AVON—1953-55—p, Indianapolis Clowns, New York Black Yankees

LAYTON, OBEDIAH (OBIE)—1931-32, 1934, 1939-41—p, Hilldale Club, Schenectady Mohawk Giants, Detroit Black Sox, Bacharach (Philly) Giants

LÁZAGA, AGAPITO (RAÚL)—1916-22—of, p, 1b, Cuban Stars (East & West)

LEACH, ____—1926—2b, Santop All-Stars

LEACH, R.E.—1914—c, Indianapolis ABCs

LEAK, CURTIS A.—1940-48, 1950—officer, New York Black Yankees; secretary, NNL; owner, New York Black Travelers

LEARY, ____—1922, 1925—p, ss, Philadelphia Giants, Penn Red Caps of New York

LEATHERBERRY, ____—1931—p, Philadelphia Giants

LEAVELL [LAVELLE], HARRY GOWAN (HA HA)—1907-12—c, 1b, New York Colored Giants, Genuine Cuban Giants, Cuban Giants, Cuban Stars

LeBEAUX, WILBERT—1936-37—ss, 2b, Chicago American Giants

LeBLANC, ____—1915—ss, 2b, of, Lincoln (NY) Giants, Philadelphia Giants

LeBLANC, HUGH—1951—p, New Orleans Eagles

LeBLANC, JOSÉ V. (JULIO, COUNT)—1918-21—p, of, Cuban Stars (West), Cincinnati Cuban Stars

LEE, ____—1898, 1902, 1906—ss, 3b, 2b, Cuban Giants, Cuban X-Giants

LEE, ____—1906—p, Illinois Giants

LEE, ____—1908—1b, Cuban Giants

LEE, ____—1918—1b, Philadelphia Giants

LEE, A.—1930—p, Santop Broncos

LEE, AMERICUS—1920—3b, Atlanta Black Crackers

LEE, ARCHIE—1911—2b, of, Brown's Tennessee Rats

LEE, BILL—1956—c, Memphis Red Sox

LEE, ED (KID)—1911, 1916—ss, 1b, Chicago Giants, Chicago Union Giants

LEE, FRED—1908, 1915—of, umpire, Kansas City (KS) Giants

LEE, GEORGE L.—1933-1948, 1970-1986— sports cartoonist, *Bang, Chicago American, Chicago Defender, Sport Eye*

LEE, SR., HOLSEY SCRANTON (SCRIP, SCRIPTUS, SPARKY)—1920-43—p, of, Norfolk Stars, Philadelphia Stars, Philadelphia Royal Giants, Hilldale Club, Norfolk Giants, Richmond Giants (NAA), Baltimore Black Sox, Bacharach (AC) Giants, Cleveland Red Sox, Philadelphia Giants; umpire, NNL

LEE, JIMMY—1942—umpire, USL

LEE, LOWN—1909—p, Kansas City (MO) Royal Giants

LEE, RICHARD S. (DICK)—1917-18—of, Chicago Union Giants

LEE, JR., ROY—1946—p, Durham (NC) Eagles

LEE, S.—1930—3b, Santop Broncos

LEE, VINCENT PERCY (SHORTY)—1931, 1933, 1939, 1942—c, Baltimore Black Sox, Baltimore Stars, Baltimore Elite Giants, Newark Eagles, Richmond Hilldales

LEE, WILLIAM—1888-89—ss, Chicago Unions

LEE, WILLIAM A. (WILLIE)—1943, 1946—infield, Atlanta Black Crackers, Homestead Grays

LEE, WILLIE JAMES—1956-59—of, Memphis Red Sox, Kansas City Monarchs, Birmingham Black Barons

LeFAVRE, ____—1884—of, Brooklyn Remsens

LEFGOWICH, SAM—1914—p, All Nations

LEFTWICH, JOHN (HYMIE)—1942, 1945—p, Homestead Grays, Biz Mackey All-Stars

LeGARE (LaGEAR), ____—1921—of, Chicago Union Giants

LeGRANDE, SR., LARRY EDWIN—1956-63—of, c, Memphis Red Sox, Detroit Clowns, Detroit Stars, Kansas City Monarchs, Satchel Paige All-Stars

LeGROIT, ____—1884—1b, Newark Dusky Boys

LEGROVE, ____—1937—of, Indianapolis Athletics

LELAND, FRANK C.—1887-1912—of, ss, manager, Washington Capital Citys, Chicago Union Giants, Leland Giants, Chicago Giants, Chicago Unions, Chicago Resolutes

LEMON, ____ [see LAMAR, CLARENCE]

LENNON, GEORGE E.—1911—officer, Twin City Gophers

LENOX, ____—1943—1b, New York Black Yankees

LEON, ____—1891—of, New York Gorhams

LEÓN, ____—1915, 1917-18—of, p, c, Almendares Cubans, Cuban Stars (East)

LEÓN y BECERRA, ISIDORO LESTER (IZZY)—1948—of, New York Cubans

LEONARD, ____—1943—of, New York Black Yankees

LEONARD, JAMES (BOBO, BULL)—1919-36—of, Cleveland Tate Stars, Cleveland Browns, Cleveland Tigers, Cleveland Hornets, Toledo Tigers, Chicago American Giants, Bacharach (AC) Giants, Lincoln (NY) Giants, Baltimore Black Sox, Penn Red Caps of NY, Brooklyn Royal Giants, Indianapolis ABCs, Cleveland Elites

LEONARD, L. K.—1929—officer, San Antonio Indians

LEONARD, WALTER FENNER (BUCK)—1932-50—1b, Baltimore Stars, Brooklyn Royal Giants, Homestead Grays, South All-Stars; author

LESTER, ____—1932—p, Nashville Elite Giants

LETT, ROGER—1943—p, Cincinnati Ethiopian Clowns (NML)

LETTLERS, GEORGE—1887—player, Washington Capital Citys

LEUSCHNER, WILLIAM A. (W. A., BILL)—1940-43—booking agent; owner, officer, New York Black Yankees

LEVELL, ____—1929—of, Evansville Giants

LEVIS [LEVY], OSCAR JOSEPH [OSCAL] (CHICK)—1921-34—p, manager, Cuban Stars (East), Hilldale Club, Darby Daisies, Baltimore Black Sox, All Cubans, New York Cuban Stars

LEVITT, ____—1939—1b, Homestead Grays

LEVY, OSCAR [see LEVIS, OSCAR J.]

LEWIS, ____—1867—ss, Brooklyn Monitors

LEWIS, ____—1890—of, Nebraska Lincoln Giants

LEWIS, ____—1920—ss, Baltimore Black Sox

LEWIS, ____—1923—p, All Nations

LEWIS, A. D.—1937-38, 1941—1b, Birmingham Black Barons, Louisville Black Colonels, Detroit Black Sox

LEWIS, AUSTIN—1950—p, Chicago American Giants

LEWIS, BERT—1933—1b, p, John Donaldson All-Stars, Louisville Red Caps

LEWIS, BILLY—1915—writer, *Indianapolis Freeman*

LEWIS, BURTON—1921—of, Houston Black Buffaloes

LEWIS, CARY B.—1920—co-drafter, constitution of NNL; secretary, NNL; writer, *Indianapolis Freeman*; editor, *Chicago Defender*

LEWIS, CHARLES (BABE)—1925-26—ss, Lincoln (NY) Giants, Philadelphia Giants

LEWIS, CLARENCE (FOOTS)—1931-37—ss, Memphis Red Sox, Cleveland Red Sox, Nashville Elite Giants, Pittsburgh Crawfords, Akron Tyrites, Cleveland Giants

LEWIS, COFIELD—1935—ss, Brooklyn Eagles

LEWIS, COLEMAN A.—1921—officer, Cleveland Tate Stars

LEWIS, EARL—1923—p, Indianapolis ABCs

LEWIS, ELMORE—1958—p, Kansas City Monarchs

LEWIS, ERNEST (ERNIE)—1957—p, Memphis Red Sox, Detroit Stars

LEWIS, FRANK—1932—of, Montgomery Grey Sox

LEWIS, GEORGE F. (PEACHES)—1917-22—p, Lincoln (NY) Giants, Bacharach (AC) Giants

LEWIS, GROVER—1928—3b, Homestead Grays

LEWIS, HENRY N.—1943-45—of, p, manager, officer, owner, Atlanta Black Crackers, Knoxville Smokies

LEWIS, IRA F. (TUCK)—1913-17—2b, 3b, Chicago Union Giants, Chicago Giants;—1922—secretary, Pittsburgh Keystones; 1914-48—writer, editor, *Pittsburgh Courier*

LEWIS, J.—1890—c, Lincoln (NE) Giants

LEWIS, JAMES D.—1885-87—3b, p, 1b, Chicago Gordons, Chicago Uniques, Chicago Unknowns

LEWIS, JAMES LOYD (JIM, JOE, SPEED KING, LANKY)—1936-38, 1943, 1945, 1947, 1953—2b, p, Pittsburgh Crawfords, Indianapolis Clowns, New York Black Yankees, Memphis Red Sox, Chicago Brown Bombers (USL), Baltimore Grays, Brooklyn Royal Giants, Philadelphia Stars

LEWIS, JEROME AMBROSE—1910-13—1b, West Baden (IN) Sprudels

LEWIS, JOEL (CHIEF)—1920—c, of, New Orleans Crescent Stars

LEWIS, JOHN—1945—p, Homestead Grays

LEWIS, JOHN LEONARD—1953—of, Birmingham Black Barons

LEWIS, JOSEPH HERMAN (SLEEPY, JOE)—1919-37, 1939, 1942, 1946-48—c, 3b, manager, Baltimore Black Sox, Baltimore Grays, Washington Potomacs, Homestead Grays, Hilldale Club, Lincoln (NY) Giants, Philadelphia Quaker City Giants, Darby Daisies, Bacharach (AC) Giants, Norfolk-Newport News Royals, Brooklyn Royal Giants, Belleville (VA) Grays

LEWIS, JR., JOSEPH WILLIAM (JOE)—1958—p, Kansas City Monarchs

LEWIS, LEON—1887—of, Boston Resolutes (NCBBL)

LEWIS, MILTON—1920-30—2b, 1b, Norfolk Giants, Wilmington Potomacs, Bacharach (AC) Giants, Richmond Giants (NAA), Harrisburg Giants, Philadelphia Giants, Philadelphia Quaker City Giants, Wilmington Quaker Giants

LEWIS, REUBEN—1958—utility, Kansas City Monarchs

LEWIS, ROBERT STEVENSON (BUBBLES, BUBBER)—1922-28—officer, owner, Memphis Red Sox; vice president, NNL

LEWIS, RUFUS (LOU, MISSISSIPPI)—1946-50—p, Newark Eagles, Houston Eagles

LEWIS, SIMON—1950-53—umpire, East/West game

LEWIS, WILL OLLIE (FRISCO)—1929—utility, Colored House of David

LICKERT, ____—1922—umpire

LIGGINS, ____—1879—2b, Johnstown (NY) Wide Awakes

LIGGINS, HENRY—1954—road secretary, Memphis Red Sox

LIGGONS, JAMES—1932-34—p, Monroe (LA) Monarchs, Memphis Red Sox, Little Rock Grays

LIGHTNER, CHARLES (CHARLEY)—1920—p, Kansas City Monarchs

LIGON, RUFUS C.—1932, 1934, 1944-46, 1958-59—p, manager, Austin Black Senators, Memphis Red Sox

LILLARD, JOSEPH L. (MIDNIGHT EXPRESS)—1932-34, 1937, 1946—p, of, manager, Cole's Chicago American Giants, Chicago American Giants, Cincinnati Tigers, Brooklyn Royal Giants, Brooklyn Brown Dodgers

LILLY, ____—1922—p, Illinois Giants

LILLY, JOHN—1925-26—of, Birmingham Black Barons

LILLY, ROOSEVELT—1949-51—p, Birmingham Black Barons

LIMA, JUAN—1906—of, All Cubans

LINARES, ABEL—1899, 1911-21—owner, president, All Cubans, Cuban Stars (West), Cincinnati Cuban Stars

LINARES, ROGELIO (ICE CREAM, MANTECADO)—1940-46—1b, of, Cuban Stars (East), North Classic Team, New York Cubans

LINEVILLE, OREN—1940—bus driver, Kansas City Monarchs

LINCOLN, [DR.] CHARLES ERIC—1948—road secretary, Birmingham Black Barons

LINCOLN, JAMES—1890-95—ss, 3b, Lincoln (NE) Giants, Adrian (MI) Page Fence Giants,

LINDER, WILLIAM—1922-23—p, Kansas City Monarchs

LINDSAY, CLARENCE HOLMES (C. H.)—1920-35—ss, Richmond Giants (NAA), Bacharach (AC) Giants, Bacharach (Philly) Giants, Baltimore Black Sox, Wilmington Potomacs, Penn Red Caps of NY, Lincoln (NY) Giants, Philadelphia Giants, Royal Poinciana (FL)

LINDSAY, LEONARD (YAHOODI, SLOPPY)—1934-35, 1942-47—1b, p, Newark Dodgers, Cincinnati Ethiopian Clowns (NML), Birmingham Black Barons, Indianapolis Clowns, San Francisco Sea Lions, Havana Las Palomas

LINDSAY, MERF—1910—of, Kansas City (KS) Giants

LINDSAY, P.—1910—1b, of, Kansas City (KS) Giants

LINDSAY, ROBERT ALEXANDER (FROG)—1908-17—ss, Kansas City (KS) Giants, Kansas City Colored Giants, Kansas City Cyclones

LINDSAY, WILLIAM (BILL, THE KANSAS CYCLONE)—1908-14—of, p, Kansas City (KS) Giants, Leland Giants, Chicago American Giants, Kansas City Cyclones

LINDSAY, WILLIAM HUDSON (RED, BILL)–1929-34–3b, ss, Bacharach (Philly) Giants, Washington Pilots, Hilldale Club, Lincoln (NY) Giants, Harrisburg Giants
LINDSEY, ____–1912-14–of, Lincoln (NY) Giants, West Baden (IN) Sprudels
LINDSEY, BEN–1928-29–ss, Bacharach (AC) Giants, Hilldale Club, Baltimore Black Sox
LINDSEY, JAMES–1887–of, Pittsburgh Keystones (NCBBL)
LINDSEY, JAMES–1943–1b, Birmingham Black Barons
LINDSEY, ROBERT–1929, 1931–p, of, 1b, Shreveport Black Sports, Indianapolis ABCs
LINDSEY, WILLIAM ALBERT (BILL)–1926–ss, Dayton Marcos
LINEVILLE, OREN–1940–bus driver, Kansas City Monarchs
LINTHICUM, ROSS–1959-60–p, Indianapolis Clowns
LINTON, BENJAMIN E.–1942-45–officer, owner, Detroit Motor City Giants, Detroit Black Sox
LIPKINS, ALPHONSE (AL)–1944–p, Cincinnati-Indianapolis Clowns
LIPSCOMB, GEORGE–1946–1b, 2b, Los Angeles White Sox
LIPSEY, HENRY–1942–p, Memphis Red Sox
LIPTON, J.–1870–2b, Utica (NY) Fairless
LIPTON, P.–1870–3b, Utica (NY) Fairless
LISBY, MAURICE CHARLES [MO]–1934–p, Newark Dodgers, Bacharach (Philly) Giants
LISTACH [LISTASH], NORA (FLYING FRENCHMAN)–1940-41–of, Birmingham Black Barons, Cincinnati Buckeyes
LISY, ____–1912–ss, All Nations
LITHET, ____–1942–of, New York Cubans
LITTLE, EARL–1938–p, Birmingham Black Barons
LITTLE, IRVIN–1959–p, Kansas City Monarchs
LITTLE, JESS–1956–of, Birmingham Black Barons
LITTLE, NORMAN–1911–1b, 3b, Brown's Tennessee Rats
LITTLE, WILLIAM–1937-50–officer, Chicago American Giants
LITTLE, WILLIAM (BILL) O.–1952-57–c, infield, Kansas City Monarchs, Memphis Red Sox
LITTLES, BEN HENRY–1947-51, 1956–of, Homestead Grays, New York Black Yankees, Philadelphia Stars, Memphis Red Sox
LITZSEY [LITSZEY, LETZSIE], JOHN (RED) W.–1946–p, Fresno/San Diego Tigers
LIVINGSTON, ____–1950–umpire, East/West game
LIVINGSTON, CURTIS–1950–of, Cleveland Buckeyes
LIVINGSTON, L. D. (LEE, GOO GOO)-1928-33–of, Kansas City Monarchs, New York Harlem Stars, Pittsburgh Crawfords, Penn Red Caps of NY
LLOYD, ANTHONY C. (TONY)–1958-59–2b, Birmingham Black Barons
LLOYD, JOHN HENRY (POP, BEMBA CUCHARA, SAM)–1905-32–ss, 1b, 2b, manager, Palatka Giants, Macon Acmes, Cuban X-Giants, Philadelphia Giants, Leland Giants, Lincoln (NY) Giants, Chicago American Giants, Brooklyn Royal Giants, Columbus Buckeyes, Bacharach (AC) Giants, Bacharach (NY) Giants, Hilldale Club, New York Harlem Stars, Lincoln (NY) Stars, Kansas City Monarchs, Royal Poinciana (FL), Breakers Hotel (FL)
LLOYD, T. CURTIS (BINGO)–1938-39–of, Chicago Palmer House Stars
LOATMAN, ____–1932–2b, Bacharach (Philly) Giants
LOCKE, CLARENCE VIRGIL (DAD)–1945-48–p, 1b, Chicago American Giants
LOCKE, EDDIE–1943-51–p, Cincinnati Ethiopian Clowns (NML), Kansas City Monarchs, New York Black Yankees, Chicago American Giants
LOCKE, JAMES–1921-26–umpire, ECL
LOCKE, PLINY–1867, 1871–of, 1b, Philadelphia Excelsior, Philadelphia Pythians, Utica (NY) Fearless
LOCKETT, LESTER (BUCK)–1937-50–3b, of, Chicago American Giants, Birmingham Black Barons, Cincinnati-Indianapolis Clowns, Baltimore Elite Giants, Memphis Red Sox, St. Louis Stars, Cincinnati Buckeyes
LOCKETT, LOU–1941, 1947–ss, Philadelphia Stars
LOCKETT, MONROE–1938–p, Indianapolis ABCs
LOCKETT, SAM–1946–p, Pittsburgh Stars
LOCKETT, WILLIE–1938–of, Indianapolis ABCs
LOCKHART, ____–1942–utility, Jacksonville Red Caps
LOCKHART, ADOLPHUS JOSEPH (A. J., DUKE, ARTHUR)–1924-26, 1928–p, 3b, Wilmington Potomacs, Philadelphia Quaker City Giants, Philadelphia Giants
LOCKHART, GEORGE HUBERT (JOE, PROF)–1920-29–p, Atlanta Black Crackers, Bacharach (AC) Giants, Chicago American Giants, Wilmington Potomacs
LOCKMAN, ____–1867–ss, Philadelphia Pythians
LOCKMAN, JAMES (TUT)–1943, 1946–ss, 1b, Memphis Red Sox
LOFTIN, LOUIS SANTOP [see SANTOP, LOUIS]
LOGAN, ____–1919–p, Chicago Union Giants

LOGAN, COLEY (CARL, NAT)—1934, 1937, 1940-42—infield, Bacharach (Philly) Giants, Schenectady Mohawk Giants, Philadelphia Stars, Brooklyn Royal Giants
LOGAN, FREDERICK CURTIS (FRED, SONNY)—1950—of, New York Black Yankees
LOGAN, NICHOLAS (NICK, STEEL ARM)—1920-25—p, Baltimore Black Sox, Atlanta Black Crackers
LOGAN, ROGERS—1947—p, Detroit Wolves
LOGSTON, ____—1929—umpire, NNL
LOLLA [LOLIA], JOHN HENRY (BIG BOY, SALLY LONG, KEGGIE)—1902-11—utility, of, Louisville Giants, Indianapolis ABCs
LOMAX, GRIFFIN [GRIFFITH, GRIFFORD] (GRIFF)—1942, 1946—of, p, San Francisco Sea Lions, Newark Eagles
LONDON, JULIUS L.—1909-11—2b, p, Houston Black Buffaloes, St. Paul Colored Gophers, Dallas Black Giants, Chicago American Giants
LONDON, LAFAYETTE—1883—p, of, Louisville Falls City
LONG, ____—1920—3b, Knoxville Giants
LONG, CARL RUSSELL—1952-53—of, Birmingham Black Barons, Philadelphia Stars
LONG, EARNEST SYLVESTOR (THE KID)—1948-50—p, Cleveland Buckeyes, Louisville Buckeyes
LONG, EMORY (BANG)—1932-40, 1945—3b, Atlanta Black Crackers, Chicago American Giants, Indianapolis Athletics, Philadelphia Stars, Kansas City Monarchs, Washington Black Senators, Memphis Red Sox
LONG, FRED THOMAS (BIG, POPS, BANG, BING)—1920-21, 1925-26, 1929—of, Detroit Stars, Indianapolis ABCs, Chattanooga Black Lookouts
LONG, LENNIE—1964—2b, Satchel Paige All-Stars
LONG, MATTHEW (BUCK)—1950—c, Memphis Red Sox
LONG, THOMAS (TOM)—1926—c, Kansas City Monarchs
LONGEST, BERNELL (CHICK, BARNEY)—1942-48—2b, Chicago Brown Bombers (NML), Chicago American Giants
LONGEST, CHARLES—1954—of, Detroit Stars
LONGEST, JIMMY—1942-43—1b, Chicago Brown Bombers (NML)
LONGLEY, WAYMAN (RED, RAY)—1932-53—2b, of, ss, c, 1b, 3b, Memphis Red Sox, Chicago American Giants, Little Rock Grays, New Orleans Eagles, Washington Elite Giants, Little Rock Black Travelers
LONGMEUR, ____—1926—umpire, NNL
LONGWARE, JR., ALONZO—1920, 1929—3b, manager, Detroit Stars, Shreveport Black Sports, Indianapolis ABCs

LOONEY, CHARLIE—1933, 1938—2b, Akron Tyrites, Louisville Black Colonels, Memphis Red Sox
LÓPEZ, ARMANDO—1923-24—p, Cuban Stars (East)
LÓPEZ, JOSÉ DIONISIO (LOPITO)—1920—2b, 3b, of, Cuban Stars (West)
LÓPEZ, JULIO (EL CARTERO)—1903—of, All Cubans
LÓPEZ y FREGUEDA, JUSTO CÁNDIDO (CANDO, POLICE CAR)—1926-39—of, Cuban Stars (East & West), New York Cubans, New York Cuban Stars
LÓPEZ, PEDRO—1938-39—of, New York Cubans
LÓPEZ, RAÚL—1948-50—p, New York Cubans
LÓPEZ, VENTURA—1929—p, Cuban Stars (West)
LORD, ____—1907—of, Philadelphia Giants
LORENZO, JÉSUS—1928-30—p, Cuban Stars (West)
LORITTY, CRAWFORD M.—1940, utility, Memphis Red Sox
LOTIS, ____—1943—p, Cincinnati Ethiopian Clowns (NML)
LOTT, HUGH BENJAMIN (BENNY, HONEY)—1949-51—2b, 3b, Indianapolis Clowns, New York Black Yankees
LOTT, RAYMOND D. (RAY)—1946-50—of, Los Angeles White Sox, Philadelphia Stars, New York Black Yankees, Chicago American Giants
LOTT, WALTER—1948—3b, New York Black Yankees
LOUDEN, LOUIS OLIVER (TOMMY, LOU)—1942-50—c, New York Cubans, North Classic Team, Birmingham Black Barons
LOUGARY, ____—1943—utility, New York Cubans
LOUIE, ____—1932—ph, Nashville Elite Giants
LOUIS, JOE [see AGNEW, JOE]
LOUIS, R.—1958—utility, Detroit Clowns
LOVE, ANDREW J. (ANDY)—1930-32, 1945—c, of, Detroit Stars, Washington Pilots, Toledo Cubs/Rays
LOVE, RICHARD—1902—of, Chicago Columbia Giants
LOVE, WILLIAM—1926-27—c, of, Chattanooga Black Lookouts, Memphis Red Sox, Chattanooga White Sox
LOVELACE, LARRY—1947—p, Chicago American Giants
LOVELL, ____—1927, 1930—p, Chappie Johnson's All-Stars
LOVILL, ____—1891—2b, Cuban Giants
LOVING, JOSEPH G.—1887—p, Washington Capital Citys
LOW, NAT—writer, *New York Daily Worker*
LOWE, ____—1921—3b, Chicago Union Giants
LOWE, GREGORY (GRADY)—1959-60—of, Detroit-New Orleans Stars
LOWE, WILLIAM McKINLEY (KID)—1919, 1921-33—3b, of, manager, Pennsylvania Giants, Indianapolis ABCs, Detroit

Stars, Memphis Red Sox, Chattanooga Black Lookouts, Nashville Elite Giants
LOWERS, ____—1928-29—umpire, NNL
LOWELL, ____—1915—1b, Cuban Giants
LOWELL, ____—1924—p, Bacharach (AC) Giants
LUAC'IMBE, ____—1921—c, All Nations
LUBERAS, GUSTAVO—1936—p, Cuban Stars (East)
LUCAS, ____—1887—of, South Baltimore Mutuals
LUCAS [LUGO], LORENZO—1926—p, Memphis Red Sox
LUCAS, MILES (PEPE)—1919-27—p, of, Cuban Stars (East & West), New Orleans Crescent Stars, Harrisburg Giants
LUCAS, SMITTY (SCOTTY)—1928—officer, Philadelphia Tigers
LUCENS, ____—1928—ss, Bacharach (AC) Giants, Brooklyn Royal Giants
LUGO, LEVINGELO XIQUES (LEO)—1943-46—of, Cincinnati-Indianapolis Clowns, Indianapolis Clowns
LUGO y LUGO, ORLANDO—1954-55—infield, Indianapolis Clowns, New York Black Yankees
LUKE, SLYVESTER—1943-50—batboy, Cleveland Buckeyes
LUMPKIN, SR., NORMAN FRANK (GERONIMO)—1938—p, of, Atlanta Black Crackers
LUMPKINS, WILLIAM (LEFTY)—1930-32—p, Newark Browns
LUNDY, RICHARD BENJAMIN (DICK, KING RICHARD, GERONIMO)—1916-48—ss, manager, Bacharach (AC) Giants, Bacharach (NY) Giants, Lincoln (NY) Giants, Hilldale Club, Baltimore Black Sox, Philadelphia Stars, Newark Dodgers, New York Cubans, Newark Eagles, Jacksonville Eagles, Brooklyn Royal Giants, Havana Red Sox, Atlanta Black Crackers, Royal Poinciana (FL), Breakers Hotel (FL)
LUNDY [LANDY], WALTER—1957-58—of, Detroit Stars, Detroit Clowns, Indianapolis Clowns
LUNGALOW, ____—1929—c, Chattanooga Black Lookouts
LUQUE, ADOLFO DOMINGO DeGUZMAN (DOLF, PAPA MONTERO, HARARA PERFECTO)—1912-13—p, of, Long Branch (NJ) Cubans
LUTHER, (LEFTY) [see FARRELL, LUTHER]
LUTZ, BILL—1948—umpire, NNL
LYDA, ____—1932—p, Coles' Chicago American Giants
LYLES, ____—1916—p, All Nations
LYLES, JOHN A. (THE BRUTE, THE CARBONDALE FLASH)—1932-43—of, ss, 2b, 3b, c, Homestead Grays, Indianapolis ABCs, Cleveland Bears, St. Louis Stars, Chicago American Giants, Cincinnati Buckeyes, Cleveland Buckeyes, Indianapolis Clowns, New Orleans-St. Louis Stars, Claybrook (AR) Tigers
LYMAN, ____—1926—p, Washington Black Sox
LYNCH, EARL—1931—c, Knoxville Giants
LYNCH, JAMES [THOMAS]—1914-19—of, 3b, 2b, Indianapolis ABCs, Dayton Marcos, West Baden (IN) Sprudels, Jewell's ABCs
LYNN, ____—1917—p, Jewell's ABCs
LYNN, ____—1943—p, Homestead Grays
LYONS, ____—1895—of, Adrian (MI) Page Fence Giants
LYONS, ____—1922-24—umpire, ECL
LYONS, ____—1929—of, San Antonio Black Indians
LYONS, ____—1947—ph, Chicago American Giants
LYONS, BENJAMIN JESTER (BENNIE)—1911-17—1b, of, ss, French Lick (IN) Plutos, West Baden (IN) Sprudels, Bowser's ABCs, Jewell's ABCs, Chicago Giants, All Nations, Louisville White Sox
LYONS, CHASE—1899-1910—p, Genuine Cuban Giants, Cuban Giants, West Baden (IN) Sprudels, Leland Giants, Columbia Giants, Chicago Union Giants
LYONS, JR., GRANVILLE (LEFTY)—1929-42—1b, Chattanooga Black Lookouts, Evansville Giants, Nashville Elite Giants, Louisville Black Caps, Detroit Stars, Louisville Red Caps, Philadelphia Stars, Memphis Red Sox, Baltimore Elite Giants
LYONS, JAMES HENRY (JIMMIE)—1909-32—c, p, of, manager, Kansas City (KS) Giants, Dayton Marcos, Indianapolis ABCs, Lincoln (NY) Giants, St. Louis Giants, Brooklyn Royal Giants, Chicago American Giants, Detroit Stars, Cleveland Browns, Washington Potomacs, Louisville Black Caps, Royal Poinciana (FL), Breakers Hotel (FL), Minneapolis Keystones
LYONS, LOUIS—1950—p, Cleveland Buckeyes
LYTLE, CLARENCE LESTER (DUDE)—1901-12—p, of, Chicago Union Giants, Leland Giants, St. Paul Colored Giants, Columbia Giants, St. Paul Colored Gophers, Minneapolis Keystones, St. Louis Giants, Twin Cities Gophers
LYTLE, JOHN ALLEN—1954-55—p, Detroit Stars, Indianapolis Clowns
LYZAN, ____—1928—p, Havana Red Sox

M

MABEN, BENNIE—1952—infield, Memphis Red Sox
MABON, LEROY (LEE, LUCKY)—1958-60—ss, Indianapolis Clowns
MacDONALD, ____—1929—umpire, ECL
MACK, ____—1926—umpire, ECL, Colored All-Stars
MACK, ____—1942—2b, Twin Cities Gophers
MACK, JOHN H.—1945—p, Kansas City Monarchs
MACK, PAUL—1916-17—of, 3b, Bacharach (AC) Giants, Jersey City Colored Giants
MACK, ROBERT GEORGE—1945-46—p, New York Black Yankees
MACK, ROY—1945—of, Detroit Motor City Giants
MACKALL, EDWARD (ED, LITTLE NAPOLEON)—1899-1922—trainer, Baltimore Orioles (MLB), New York Giants (MLB)
MACKEY [McKEY], JAMES RALEIGH (BIZ, RILEY)—1918-48—c, ss, 3b, of, 2b, 1b, p, manager, Dallas Black Giants, Waco Black Navigators, San Antonio Black Aces, Indianapolis ABCs, Hilldale Club, Darby Daisies, Philadelphia Stars, Washington Elite Giants, Baltimore Elite Giants, Newark Eagles, Newark Dodgers, Nashville Elite Giants, Homestead Grays, San Francisco Sea Lions, Philadelphia Royal Giants
MACKEY, GARLAND—writer, *Washington Tribune*
MACKLIN, ____—1924-29—3b, Chicago Giants
MADDIX, RAYDELL (RAY, BO, BLACK BEAU)—1949-50, 1953—p, Indianapolis Clowns
MADDOX, ARTHUR—1935-37—p, Cincinnati Tigers
MADDOX, FRANK (FLASH)—1946—1b, p, Oakland Larks
MADDOX, FORREST A. (ONE WING)—1920-26—p, of, Birmingham Black Barons, Montgomery Grey Sox, Knoxville Giants, Washington Braves, Atlanta Black Crackers
MADDOX, VERNON (FLASH)—1956—p, Kansas City Monarchs
MADERT, ____—1917—2b, Chicago Giants
MADISON, ____—1906—p, Chicago Union Giants
MADISON, ROBERT LEE (BOB)—1935-42, 1945—p, of, Kansas City Monarchs, Memphis Red Sox, Indianapolis Athletics, Birmingham Black Barons, Asheville Black Tourists
MAGEE, SHERRY—1927—umpire, World Series
MAGRIÑAT, JOSÉ MARÍA (HÉCTOR, KIKO)—1906-16—of, umpire, Cuban X-Giants, Havana Stars, All Cubans, Cuban Stars (West)
MAHNER, ____—1932—of, Monroe (LA) Monarchs
MAHICKTINO, ____—1914—c, All Nations
MAHOLEY, ____—1920—3b, Philadelphia Giants
MAHONEY, ____—1931—ss, Detroit Giants
MAHONEY, ANTHONY BARNES (TONY)—1920-23—p, Norfolk Giants, Indianapolis ABCs, Baltimore Black Sox, Brooklyn Royal Giants, Norfolk Stars
MAHONEY, ULYSSES (ULE)—1944—p, 1b, Philadelphia Stars
MAIDEN, ____—1932—c, Bacharach (Philly) Giants
MAINOR III, JOHN J. (HANK)—1950-51—p, Baltimore Elite Giants, Philadelphia Stars
MAJOR, ____—1918—of, Havana Red Sox
MAJORS, JAMES G.—1915-16—p, Chicago Union Giants
MAKELL (MACKELL), WILLIAM FRANK—1942-49—c, of, Baltimore Grays, Newark Eagles, Baltimore Elite Giants, Philadelphia Stars
MAKOMIS, ____—1917—of, Los Angeles White Sox
MALARCHER, DAVID JULIUS (CAP, GENTLEMAN DAVE)—1915-34—3b, of, 2b, manager, Indianapolis ABCs, Detroit Stars, Chicago American Giants, Cole's Chicago American Giants, Chicago Columbia Giants, Royal Poinciana (FL)
MALCOLM, ____—1939—ss, St. Louis Stars
MALCOLM, CLAUDE—1938—officer, Atlanta Black Crackers
MALCOLM, RUFUS—1938—officer, Atlanta Black Crackers
MALE, DICK [see JOHNSON, DICK]
MALLETTE [MELLETTE], WILLIAM BARNUM (WILLY)—1913-16—2b, ss, Schenectady Mohawk Giants, Lincoln (NY) Stars
MALLOY, CHARLES—1918, 1922—p, of, Bacharach (AC) Giants, All Cubans, Penn Red Caps of NY, Nashville Elite Giants
MALLOY, GERALD WARREN (JERRY)— 1946—1b, Chicago Brown Bombers (USL)
MALONE, ____—1930—p, Dallas Black Giants
MALONE, BILL (LUCKY)—1944, 1946—p, Kansas City Monarchs, Fresno/San Diego Tigers
MALONE, WILLIAM H.—1886-98—p, 1b, 3b, of, Cuban Giants, Pittsburgh Keystones (NCBBL), New York Gorhams (Middle States League), York (PA) Cuban Giants (Eastern Interstate League), Trenton (NJ) Cuban Giants (Middle States League), Philadelphia Pythians (NCBBL), York (PA) Colored Monarchs (Eastern Interstate League), Cuban X-Giants, Adrian (MI) Page Fence Giants, Shenandoah (Middle States League)
MALSON, ____— [see MALONE, WILLIAM H.]

MANELA [MANOLO, MANNO], CLAUDIO (MIKE)–1921, 1925–p, Cuban Stars (East), Cincinnati Cuban Stars

MANESE, ED–1923-26, 1936–2b, Detroit Stars, Kansas City Monarchs, Indianapolis ABCs; officer, Nashville Elite Giants

MANGRUM, (RIP)–1948–of, New York Cubans

MANGUN, ROSCOE–1956–2b, Birmingham Black Barons

MANHATTEN, W.H.–1883–officer, Washington Manhattans

MANINS, ____–1928–2b, Kansas City (KS) Giants

MANLEY, ABRAHAM LINCOLN (ABE)–1935-48–NNL vice-president, president, treasurer, owner, Brooklyn Eagles, Newark Eagles

MANLEY, EFFA BISHOP (a.k.a. EFFA BROOKS, EFFA COLE)–1935-48–NNL officer, owner, Brooklyn Eagles, Newark Eagles; author

MANN, FRANKLIN L.–1918–1b, Chicago Union Giants

MANNING, ALEXANDER–1890-1932–publisher, *Indianapolis World*

MANNING, CHASER–1931–32-1b, 2b, Montgomery Grey Sox

MANNING, FELIX (BIG)–1932, 1944–p, New York Black Yankees, Atlanta Black Crackers

MANNING, JOHN–1902-05–of, p, Philadelphia Giants, Genuine Cuban Giants

MANNING, JOHN–1945-46–p, Philadelphia Hilldales (USL), Brooklyn Brown Dodgers

MANNING, SR., MAXWELL CORNELIUS (MAX, MILEO)–1938-49–p, Newark Eagles, Houston Eagles

MANNING, THADDEUS–1868–player, Philadelphia Pythians

MANSFIELD, NOAH–1912, 1917–2b, Kansas City (KS) Giants, Kansas City Colored Giants

MANUAL, ____–1883–of, Louisville Falls City

MANUEL, (CLOWN)–1938-40–of, Louisville Black Colonels, Cleveland Bears

MANZANO, HILARIO–1918–c, 1b, Cuban Stars (East)

MAPP, CHARLIE–1955–p, Indianapolis Clowns

MAPP, RICHARD (DICKIE)–1935, 1942-44–ss, 3b, Boston Royal Giants

MARA, CANDIDO–1948–3b, Memphis Red Sox

MARAVALE, ____–1923–p, Cuban Stars (East)

MARBLEAN, ____–1867–c, Brooklyn Unique

MARBURY, JOSEPH (BULL)–1957-58–of, Indianapolis Clowns

MARBURY, JR., RENDON ALFONSO (JUG)–1956, 1958–2b, ss, Birmingham Black Barons, Indianapolis Clowns

MARCANO, ____–1912–of, All Nations

MARCELL, EVERETT (SAM, ZIGGY, JOE)–1939-49–c, 1b, Chicago American Giants, Newark Eagles, Baltimore Elite Giants, New York Black Yankees, Kansas City Monarchs, Homestead Grays, Philadelphia Hilldales (USL), Pittsburgh Crawfords (NNL & USL), Cincinnati Crescents, Harlem Globetrotters, Seattle Steelheads, Philadelphia Stars

MARCELL [MARCEL, MARCELLE], OLIVER HAZZARD (GHOST)–1918-32–3b, Brooklyn Royal Giants, Bacharach (AC) Giants, Bacharach (NY) Giants, Lincoln (NY) Giants, Detroit Stars, Baltimore Black Sox, Providence Giants

MARCELLO, ____–1921–p, All Cubans [see BARCELÓ, JOAQUÍN]

MARGOLIS, WILLIAM–1947–officer, Cincinnati Crescents

MARINE, W.C.–1923–officer, secretary, New Orleans Crescent Stars, NSL

MARINO, ALPHONSE–1949–p, New York Cubans

MARIST, ____–1932–2b, of, Chicago American Giants, Nashville Elite Giants

MARKHAM [MARCUM], JOHN MATTHEW (JOHNNY)–1929-47–p, Shreveport Black Sports, Kansas City Monarchs, Monroe (LA) Monarchs, Birmingham Black Barons, Cincinnati Crescents, Chicago American Giants, New Orleans Crescent Stars, Detroit Senators

MARKHAM, MELVIN (DUKE) [see NESBIT, MELVIN]

MARKS, ____–1928–p, Cleveland Tigers

MARKS, ERNIE–1948–p, Baltimore Elite Giants

MARLIN, ____–1923–p, Bacharach (AC) Giants

MARLOTA, J. F. (MARLOTICA)–1911–of, All Cubans, Cuban Stars

MARLOWE, ____ [see PARTLOW, ROY]–1938–of, Homestead Grays

MAROTO y MENA, ENRIQUE (RICKY)–1954-56–of, p, Kansas City Monarchs

MÁRQUEZ y SÁNCHEZ, LUIS ANGEL CANENA–1945-48–2b, of, New York Black Yankees, Homestead Grays, Baltimore Elite Giants

MARRERO, FELIPE–1915–p, Almendares Cubans

MARSANS y MENDIONDO, ARMANDO–1905-06–of, All Cubans, Cuban Stars

MARSELLAS, JR., DAVID–1941–c, New York Black Yankees

MARSH, ____–1932–of, Nashville Elite Giants

MARSH, CHARLIE–1936–p, Newark Eagles

MARSH, JR., FRANK (LEFTY)—1955-59—of, 1b, Birmingham Black Barons, Kansas City Monarchs, Detroit Stars
MARSH, LORENZO—1950—c, Cleveland Buckeyes
MARHSALL, ____—1867—ss, Camden Resolutes
MARSHALL, ____—1926—of, Washington Black Sox
MARSHALL, ____—1929—c, Birmingham Black Barons
MARSHALL, ____—1934—c, Bacharach (Philly) Giants
MARSHALL, GARRETT—1920—officer, Nashville Elite Giants
MARSHALL, HIRAM J.—1945-46—p, 3b, Boston Blues
MARSHALL, JACK (BOSS)—1920-29—p, Chicago American Giants, Detroit Stars, Kansas City Monarchs, Birmingham Black Barons, Royal Poinciana (FL)
MARSHALL, ROBERT WALLS (BOBBY, RUBE)—1907-11—1b, manager, St. Paul Colored Gophers, Leland Giants, Twin City Gophers, Chicago Giants, Minneapolis Keystones
MARSHALL, WILLIAM—1862—3b, Brooklyn Monitors
MARSHALL, WILLIAM JAMES (JACK, BOISY)-1926-45—2b, 3b, 1b, Dayton Marcos, Gilkerson's Union Giants, Chicago Columbia Giants, Cole's American Giants, Chicago American Giants, Philadelphia Stars, Cincinnati-Indianapolis Clowns, Kansas City Monarchs, Chicago Brown Bombers (USL)
MARSLEY, ____—1934—of, New Orleans Crescent Stars
MARTIN, ____—1869—p, Mutuals of Washington
MARTIN, ____—1911—p, utility, Cuban Giants
MARTIN, ____—1911—of, ss, Cleveland Cubs
MARTIN, ____—1912—of, Indianapolis ABCs
MARTIN, ____—1912—of, All Nations
MARTIN, ALEXANDER—1932—officer, Cleveland Cubs
MARTIN, [DR.] ARTHUR T. (A.T.)—1923-50—officer, Memphis Red Sox
MARTIN, [DR.] BEBEE (B.B.)—1933-51—officer, Memphis Red Sox; officer, New Orleans Eagles, officer, Negro Southern League (NSL)
MARTIN, BOB—1944—p, Atlanta Black Crackers
MARTIN, CHARLES (CHARLIE)—1934-35, 1937-43—p, 1b, of, Schenectady Mohawk Giants
MARTIN, CLEM—1939—ss, New York Black Yankees
MARTIN, EDWARD A. (ED, MARTY)—1951-52—p, Philadelphia Stars
MARTIN, FELIX—1925-28—p, of, Dayton Marcos, Chicago Giants
MARTIN, HAROLD DOUGLAS—1921—p, 3b, Pittsburgh Keystones

MARTIN, HARVEY L.—1902, 1908-09, 1912-13—c, of, p, 1b, 2b, Philadelphia Giants, Indianapolis ABCs, Chicago Giants, Leland Giants, Louisville Cubs, Louisville White Sox
MARTIN, HENRY—1944—c, Chicago American Giants
MARTIN, JACK (FAT)—1923—3b, Toledo Tigers
MARTIN, JACK (DICK)—1922, 1932—c, p, Indianapolis ABCs, Monroe (LA) Monarchs
MARTIN, JAMES—1919—umpire, ECL
MARTIN, SR., JAMES EDWARD—1944—ss, Philadelphia Stars
MARTIN, JIM (PEPPER, BEANY)—1935—infield, Brooklyn Eagles
MARTIN, JOHN—1964—3b, Satchel Paige All-Stars 1929-51—officer, owner, Memphis Red Sox, Chicago American Giants;—1940-60—president, NAL; president, Negro Dixie League, NSL
MARTIN, LAWRENCE (TEE, DAD)—1939—p, Indianapolis ABCs
MARTIN, R.—1885—p, Argyle Hotel
MARTIN, WILLIAM (STACK)—1925-34—1b, of, c, 3b, p, Indianapolis ABCs, Detroit Stars, Dayton Marcos, Philadelphia Royal Giants
MARTIN, JR., WILLIAM—1946—c, Fresno/San Diego Tigers
MARTIN, [DR.] WILLIAM SYLVESTER (W.S.)—1927-50—owner, officer, Memphis Red Sox; president, NSL, officer, NAL
MARTÍNEZ, CARLOS—1928—c, Cuban Stars (West)
MARTÍNEZ, FRANCISCO—1938-39—p, Cuban Stars (East), New York Cubans
MARTÍNEZ y ESTRELLA, HORACIO ANTONIO (RABBIT)—1935-47—ss, New York Cubans, North All-Stars
MARTÍNEZ, L.—1902—of, All Cubans
MARTÍNEZ, LINO—1906—of, Havana Stars, Cuban X-Giants, Cuban Stars
MARTÍNEZ, MAGDALENO (MALENO)—1921—3b, Bacharach (AC) Giants, All Cubans
MARTÍNEZ, MANUEL (MULATON)—1902—c, of, All Cubans, Havana Stars
MARTÍNEZ, MILLITO—1936—2b, p, Cuban Stars (East)
MARTÍNEZ, PABLO—1928—p, Cuban Stars (West)
MARTÍNEZ, PASQUAL—1924—p, Cuban Stars (West)
MARTÍNEZ y GÓMEZ, CARLOS PRUDENCIO—1918, 1920-22—p, Cuban Stars (East & West), All-Cubans
MARTÍNEZ, RAMÓN—1928—3b, Cuban Stars (West)
MARTINI, JOSÉ—1928—p, Cuban Stars (West)

MARVAREZ, FERNANDO—1945—ss, Pittsburgh Crawfords (USL)

MARVIN, ALFRED—1938—p, Kansas City Monarchs, Philadelphia Stars

MARVRAY, I, CHARLES JEFFERSON (HAWK)—1949-50—of, 1b, Louisville Buckeyes, Cleveland Buckeyes

MARVRAY, JOHN—1951-52—p, Indianapolis Clowns

MASHAW, FORREST WEDWARD—1920, 1923—of, Indianapolis ABCs, Homestead Grays

MASON, ____—1918—ss, Bacharach (AC) Giants

MASON, BENJAMIN (BERNIE)—1933—officer, Cleveland Giants

MASON, (BIG)—1921—p, Montgomery Grey Sox

MASON, CHARLES (CORPORAL, SUITCASE)—1922-29, 1932, 1934—of, Richmond Giants (NAA), Bacharach (AC) Giants, Bacharach (NY) Giants, Lincoln (NY) Giants, Newark Stars, Homestead Grays, Washington Pilots, Monroe (LA) Monarchs, Royal Poinciana (FL), Washington (Yakima) Browns

MASON, CHARLEY—1889—manager, Philadelphia Giants

MASON, EDWARD—1929—officer, Wichita Falls

MASON, GEORGE E.—writer, *Indianapolis Freeman*

MASON, [REV.] HENRY (HANK, PISTOL)—1951-54—p, Kansas City Monarchs

MASON, HUGH LEONARD—1908-09, 1912-13, 1924—p, of, Leland Giants, Illinois Giants, Indianapolis ABCs, Chicago Giants, Rockville (MD)

MASON, JAMES—1887—p, Pittsburgh Keystones (NCBBL)

MASON, JAMES CLIFFORD—1955, 1958—p, New York Black Yankees, Detroit Clowns, Indianapolis Clowns

MASON, JIM—1931-34—1b, of, Cuban Stars (West), Memphis Red Sox, Washington Pilots, Cuban House of David

MASON, JUAN (CHICO)—1957—of, Indianapolis Clowns

MASON, LEONARD H.—1924, 1927—3b, Baltimore Black Sox

MASON, MARCELIUS—1939-40—owner, Cleveland Bears

MASON, WILLIAM—1946—utility, Cleveland Clippers

MASSENGILL, LLOYD—1959—p, Raleigh (NC) Tigers

MASSEY, ____—1929-30—p, of, Evansville Giants, Louisville White Sox

MASSEY, C.S.—1887—officer, NCBBL

MASSINGALE, GARCÍA—1945—of, Kansas City Monarchs

MASSINGALE, MACK—1909-11—owner, Kansas City (KS) Giants

MASSIP, SALVADOR—1925, 1930-36—1b, of, Cuban Stars (East & West), Washington Pilots, Memphis Red Sox, New York Cubans, Havana Red Sox

MATCHETT, CLAUDE (JACK)—1940-45—p, Kansas City Monarchs, Cincinnati Ethiopian Clowns

MATHEWS, ____—1946—of, Memphis Red Sox

MATHEWS, ADELBERT RICHARD (DELL)—1904-07—of, Chicago Union Giants, Leland Giants, St. Paul Colored Gophers

MATHIS, SR., VERDELL (LEFTY)—1940-50—p, of, Memphis Red Sox, Philadelphia Stars, Chet Brewer's Kansas City Royals

MATLOCK, LEROY—1929-42—p, St. Louis Stars, Detroit Wolves, Washington Pilots, Homestead Grays, Pittsburgh Crawfords, New York Cubans, Trujillo All-Stars (Ciudad Trujillo Dragons)

MATSON, ____—1891—of, Cuban Giants

MATTHEWS, ADELBERT—1902-05—p, Chicago Unions

MATTHEWS, CLIFFORD—1945—officer, owner, New Orleans Black Pelicans

MATTHEWS, FRANCIS OLIVER (FRAN, MATTY, LEFTY)—1938-46—1b, Brooklyn Eagles, Philadelphia Giants, Newark Eagles, Boston Royal Giants, Baltimore Elite Giants, New York Cubans, Kansas City Monarchs, Los Angeles White Sox

MATTHEWS, GEORGE—1887—player, Cincinnati Browns (NCBBL)

MATTHEWS, JACK (DICK)—1932-34—p, Monroe (LA) Monarchs, New Orleans Crescent Stars

MATTHEWS, JACK (FAT)—1922-23—3b, c, Indianapolis ABCs, Toledo Tigers

MATTHEWS, JESSE—1942—1b, Birmingham Black Barons, Memphis Red Sox

MATTHEWS, JOE —1887—of, South Baltimore Mutuals

MATTHEWS, JOHN T. (BIG, BUNNY)—1919-33—owner, officer, Dayton Marcos

MATTHEWS, JOHNNY (JIMMIE)—1914-16—2b, ss, Baltimore Black Sox, Cuban Giants, Brooklyn All-Stars

MATTHEWS, JUNE—1916—2b, 3b, Baltimore Black Sox

MATTHEWS, JUNIUS—1942—p, Minneapolis-St. Paul Colored Gophers

MATTHEWS, LAWRENCE (GOATEE)—1947—p, Detroit Wolves

MATTHEWS, WILLIAM—1887—of, c, South Baltimore Mutuals

MATTHEWS, WILLIAM CLARENCE (BILLY)—1905-10—ss, 2b, Burlington (Vermont League); New York Black Sox

MATTHEWS, WILLIAM QUENCY (BIG BILL)—1958-63—p, Kansas City Monarchs, Detroit Stars, Detroit-New Orleans Stars, Detroit Clowns

MAUPINS, FRANK—1890-92—c, 3b, Lincoln (NE) Giants, Plattsmouth (Nebraska St. League)

MAVEY, ____—1929—of, Tulsa Black Oilers

MAXEY, RICE—1918—p, Foster's Hartford Giants

MAXWELL, ____—1914—of, Chicago American Giants

MAXWELL, SHERMAN (JOCKO)—1926-67—sports director, sportscaster, WNJR, WHOM, WWRL

MAXWELL, WILLIAM—1887—of, Wilmington Base Ball Club

MAXWELL, ZEARLEE (JIGGS, POPS)—1931-38—3b, Monroe (LA) Monarchs, Memphis Red Sox

MAY, BEVERLY D.—1868—player, Philadelphia Pythians

MAYA, ____—1907—of, Cuban Stars

MAYARÍ, ____ [see MONTALVO, ESTEBAN]

MAYBIE, ____—1898—p, Celoron (NY) Acme Colored Giants (Iron & Oil League)

MAYERS, GEORGE [see MEYERS, GEORGE (DEACON)]

MAYFIELD, II, FRED—1883, 1887—of, Louisville Falls City (NCBBL)

MAYO, ____—1906-07—p, Cuban X-Giants, Cuban Giants

MAYO, GEORGE (HOT STUFF)—1911-18, 1927-28—1b, of, officer, Pittsburgh Giants, Pittsburgh Colored Stars, Hilldale Club, Pittsburgh Stars of Buffalo

MAYS, DAUGHTON (DAVE)—1926, 1932, 1936-38—of, p, 2b, Kansas City Monarchs, St. Louis Stars, Memphis Red Sox, New Orleans Black Pelicans, Houston Black Buffaloes

MAYS, HORACE—1917—ss, p, Bacharach (AC) Giants

MAYS, JR., WILLIE HOWARD (BUCK)—1948-50—of, Chattanooga Choo Choos, Birmingham Black Barons

MAYWEATHER, ELDRIDGE EVERETT (CHILLI, ED, HEAD, SNAKE)—1934-46—1b, Monroe (LA) Monarchs, Kansas City Monarchs, St. Louis Stars, New Orleans-St. Louis Stars, New York Black Yankees, Boston Blues, Brooklyn Eagles

MAYWEATHER, ELLIOTT—1926-29—p, Memphis Red Sox

MAYWOOD, ____—1917—p, Lincoln (NY) Giants

MAZZER [MAZAER, MAZAAR], ROBERT J. (WHITEY)—1945—co-owner, president, Philadelphia Hilldales (USL)

McADOO, TULLIE—1906-27—1b, Salt Lake City Occidentals, Topeka (KS) Giants, Kansas City (KS) Giants, St. Louis Giants, St. Louis Stars, Cleveland Browns, Chicago American Giants, Chicago Giants, Chicago Union Giants, Oklahoma City Monarchs

McATEE [McAFEE], ULYSSES—1928-31—2b, Louisville White Sox

McALLEN, ____—1909—p, Louisville White Sox

McALLISTER, ____—1943—of, Pittsburgh Crawfords

McALLISTER, ALLYN M.—1910—officer, Stars of Cuba

McALLISTER, FRANK (CHIP, RED)—1938-46—p, Indianapolis ABCs, St. Louis Stars, New Orleans-St. Louis Stars, New York Black Yankees, Harrisburg-St. Louis Stars, Brooklyn Brown Dodgers, Cleveland Clippers, Boston Blues, Harlem Globetrotters

McALLISTER, GEORGE—1921-34—1b, Bessemer Braves, Birmingham Black Barons, Chicago American Giants, Indianapolis ABCs, Memphis Red Sox, Homestead Grays, Cleveland Red Sox, Detroit Stars, Cuban Stars (West)

McALLISTER, MIKE—1921—of, Kansas City Monarchs

McANTIE, ____—1930—p, Colored House of David

McBRIDE, ____—1913—of, All-Nations

McBRIDE, CHARLES H.—1941, 1943—p, of, Newark Eagles

McBRIDE, FRED—1931-40—1b, Indianapolis ABCs, Chicago American Giants, Birmingham Black Barons

McBRIDE, J. F.—1924—umpire, World Series

McCABB, ____—1923—p, St. Louis Stars

McCALL, HENRY (BUTCH)—1936-38, 1944-45—of, 1b, Chicago American Giants, Birmingham Black Barons, Indianapolis Athletics, Chicago Brown Bombers (USL), Harlem Globetrotters

McCALL, WILLIAM L. (BILL)—1922-31, 1934—p, Pittsburgh Keystones, Birmingham Black Barons, Kansas City Monarchs, Chicago American Giants, Indianapolis ABCs, Detroit Stars, Toledo Tigers, Cleveland Tigers, Cleveland Tate Stars, Padron's Cuban Giants

McCAMPBELL, ERNEST J.—1908—player, Kansas City (KS) Giants

McCAMPBELL, [DR.] THOMAS (TOM)—1908—player, Kansas City (KS) Giants

McCANTIE, ____—1930—p, Colored House of David

McCAREY, WILLIE—1943-45—p, Cleveland Buckeyes

McCARTHY, C. H.—1921—president, Southeastern Negro League

McCARTY, ____—1915-17—umpire, Independent Colored teams

McCARVER, FRED—1920-23—2b, Nashville White Sox, Montgomery Grey Sox, Memphis Red Sox

McCARY (McCRAY), JAMES—1925—umpire, NNL

McCAULEY, B. (ROSEY)—1930—p, Nashville Elite Giants

McCAULEY, BEN—1953—of, Kansas City Monarchs

M'CL'Y, ____—1906—of, Wilmington Giants

McCLAIN [McLAIN], EDWARD (BOOTS)—1920-36—ss, 3b, 2b, umpire, Dayton Marcos, Cleveland Tate Stars, Toledo Tigers, Cleveland Browns, Detroit Stars, Indianapolis ABCs, Columbus Buckeyes, Columbus Blue Birds, Columbus Stars

McCLAIN, EUGENE WALTER (JEEP)—1942, 1945-46—3b, Philadelphia Daisies (NML), Philadelphia Stars, New York Black Yankees

McCLAMMY, JOE (SMOKEY)—1918—p, Grand Central Terminal Red Caps

McCLAREN, ____—1945—p, Philadelphia Stars

McCLELLAN, JR., DANIEL J. (DAN)—1899-31—p, of, manager, Cuban X-Giants, Philadelphia Giants, Paterson (NJ) Smart Set, Lincoln (NY) Giants, Philadelphia Quaker City Giants, Washington Potomacs, Wilmington Potomacs, Brooklyn Royal Giants

McCLELLAN, L.E.—1913—player, All Nations

McCLELLAND, [DR.] J. W. (GEORGE)—1922—officer, St. Louis Stars

McCLENNON, HENRY—1959—p, Memphis Red Sox

McCLINIC [McCLINNIC], NATHANIEL (NAT)—1946-48—of, Cleveland Buckeyes

McCLURE, ROBERT E. (BOB, BIG BOY)—1920-30—p, Indianapolis ABCs, Cleveland Tate Stars, Baltimore Black Sox, Bacharach (AC) Giants, Brooklyn Royal Giants, Toledo Tigers

McCLURE, WILL—1947—officer, Chattanooga Choo Choos

McCOLLUM, DWIGHT (CALDONIA)—1946—c, Fresno/San Diego Tigers

McCOLLUM, FRANK—1954-58—p, Louisville Clippers, Birmingham Black Barons, Kansas City Monarchs, Memphis Red Sox

McCORD, JR., CLINTON HILL (BUTCH)—1946-50—of, 1b, Baltimore Elite Giants, Nashville Cubs, Chicago American Giants,

McCORMICK, BOB—1916, 1920-21, 1931—3b, Birmingham Black Barons, Montgomery Grey Sox

McCOURT, MARK—1941—of, Detroit Black Sox

McCOY, ____—1929—p, Cuban Stars (East)

McCOY, ____—1948—of, Chattanooga Choo Choos

McCOY, ALFRED BERNARD DEL RIO (AL)—1946-47—of, Indianapolis Clowns, New York Black Yankees

McCOY, CHARLES (CHARLIE)—1955—of, New York Black Yankees

McCOY, FRANK (CHINK)—1930-43, 1955—c, Newark Stars, Newark Dodgers, Harrisburg-St. Louis Stars, Bacharach (Philly) Giants, Newark Browns, Brooklyn Eagles, New York Black Yankees

McCOY, ROY A.—1932—officer, Washington Pilots

McCOY, WALTER LOREO—1945-48—p, Chet Brewer's Kansas City Royals, Chicago American Giants

McCRACKEN, ____—1931—p, Newark Browns

McCRARY [McCREARY], FRED D.—1921—of, Cleveland Tate Stars; 1935—officer, Nashville Elite Giants; —1938-49—umpire, NNL

McCRARY, GEORGE—1943-44—p, New York Black Yankees, Cleveland Buckeyes, Cincinnati-Indianapolis Clowns

McCRARY, WILLIAM LEROY. (YOUNGBLOOD, BILL)—1946-48—p, Kansas City Monarchs

McCRAY, ALBERT (BLACKGOLD)—1931-32, 1938—c, Colored House of David

McCRAY, TED—1954—p, Louisville Clippers

McCRAY, WILLIAM L.—1954—ss, Louisville Clippers

McCREARY, JAMES—1946—umpire, NNL

McCREE, EARL—1952—p, Kansas City Monarchs

McCULLEN, ____—1944—of, Charleston's Cuban Yanks

McCULLOUGH, AMOS M.—1928—officer, Memphis Red Sox

McCUNE, MILROY—1909-13—3b, St. Paul Colored Gophers, Minneapolis Keystones, Chicago Giants

McCURINE [McCURRINE], JR., JAMES (BIG JIM, BIG STICK)—1946-49—of, Chicago American Giants

McDANIEL, ROGER—1956—New York Black Yankees

McDANIEL, WILMER—1956—New York Black Yankees

McDANIEL[S], BOOKER TALIAFERRO (CANNONBALL)—1940-53—p, of, Kansas City Monarchs, Memphis Red Sox, Kansas City (KS) Giants, Chet Brewer's Kansas City Royals

McDANIEL, FRED YOUNGBLOOD—1940-51—of, 3b, Memphis Red Sox, Kansas City Monarchs, New Orleans Eagles, Houston Eagles, Cincinnati-Cleveland Buckeyes

McDANIEL, WILBUR (DOUGHBELLY)—1957-58—c, 1b, manager, Indianapolis Clowns, Los Angeles Hawks

McDANIEL, WILBUR (MAC)—1957-58—p, of, Indianapolis Clowns
McDAY, ____—1932, 1934—ss, 3b, New Orleans Caulfield Ads, New Orleans Black Pelicans
McDEVITT, BOB—1924-26—umpire, NNL
McDEVITT, DANIEL J. (DAN)—1924—27—umpire, World Series
McDEVITT, JOHN J.—1922—officer, Baltimore Black Sox
McDONALD, ____—1882—c, Philadelphia Orions
McDONALD, ____—1942—ph, Jacksonville Red Caps
McDONALD, EARL—1938—officer, Washington Black Senators
McDONALD, GIFFORD VAN HORN—1910-23—p, of, Philadelphia Giants, Philadelphia Royal Giants, Bacharach (AC) Giants, Lincoln (NY) Giants, Havana Red Sox, Baltimore Black Sox, Washington Potomacs, Chicago American Giants
McDONALD, HENRY—1914, 1921—of, Pittsburgh Stars of Buffalo
McDONALD, LUTHER (VET, OLD SOUL)—1926-37—p, St. Louis Stars, Chicago American Giants, Chicago Columbia Giants, Cole's American Giants, Detroit Stars, Memphis Red Sox, Albany (GA) Giants
McDONALD, RAY—1946—c, San Francisco Sea Lions
McDONALD, WEBSTER (MAC)—1918-46—p, manager, co-owner, officer-USL, Philadelphia Giants, Richmond Giants (NAA), Chicago American Giants, Hilldale Club, Darby Daisies, Washington Pilots, Philadelphia Stars, Wilmington Potomacs, Detroit Stars, Homestead Grays, Lincoln (NY) Giants, Norfolk Stars, Baltimore Black Sox, Philadelphia Daisies (NML), Otto Brigg's All-Stars, New York Harlem Stars, John Donaldson All-Stars
McDONALD, WILL—1946—officer, USL
McDONNELL, (IRONMAN)—1921—p, Bacharach (AC) Giants
McDOUGAL, JR., JAMES (JOHN)—1951-52—of, Chicago American Giants
McDOUGAL, LEMUEL GIRARD (LEM)—1917-20—p, Chicago American Giants, Indianapolis ABCs, Chicago Giants
McDOUGALL, ARTHUR (ARTIE, RABBIT)—1906, 1909-11, 1916—ss, St. Paul Colored Gophers, Twin Cities Gophers, St. Louis Giants
McDUFFIE, TERRIS CHESTER (THE GREAT, TC)—1930-45—p, of Birmingham Black Barons, Baltimore Black Sox, New York Black Yankees, Newark Eagles, Homestead Grays, Philadelphia Stars, Newark Dodgers, Brooklyn Eagles, Penn Red Caps of NY, Jacksonville Red Caps, North Classic Team, Bacharach (Philly) Giants, Hilldale Club, Cuban Stars (West)
McFALL, BOB—1940—of, Cincinnati Buckeyes
McFARLIN, JOHN—1926-29, 1932—1b, 2b, Atlanta Grey Sox, Atlanta Black Crackers
McFARLAND, JOHN—1944-47—p, 1b, New York Black Yankees, Atlanta Black Crackers
McGAR, HIRAM—1916, 1920—president, Colored Texas League; president Fort Worth Black Panthers, Texas Negro League
McGAVOCK [McGARVOCK], HERBERT T. (HUB)—1919-21—of, Jewell's ABCs, Montgomery Grey Sox, Nashville White Sox
McGEACHY, ____—1888—of, Hoosier Black Stockings
McGEE, HORACE—1887—manager, Cincinnati Browns
McGILL, ____—1912—of, Kansas City (KS) Giants
McCORMICK, ____—1889—1b, Philadelphia Giants
McGOWAN, CURTIS—1950—p, Memphis Red Sox
McGOWAN, MALCOLM E.—1923-41—owner, officer, Bacharach (AC) Giants
McGREW (McGRAW), H. H. (TED)—1924—umpire, World Series
McGUINN, JOHNNY—1946—of, Oakland Larks
McHALLON, ____—1922—p, New Orleans Crescent Stars
McHASKELL, J. C.—1926-29—1b, Memphis Red Sox, Atlanta Black Crackers
McHENRY, GEORGE—1930—officer, Louisville White Caps
McHENRY, HENRY LLOYD (CREAM)—1928-50—p, Houston Black Buffaloes, Kansas City Monarchs, New York Harlem Stars, New York Black Yankees, Philadelphia Stars, Indianapolis Clowns, Penn Red Caps of NY, Newark Browns, Bacharach (Philly) Giants
McHOMER, ____—1931—ss, Detroit Giants
McINTOSH, JIMMY—1937—c, Detroit Stars
McINTYRE, ____—1907—of, New York Colored Giants
McINTYRE, ____—1922—p, Bacharach (NY) Giants
McINTYRE, B.—1924-26—3b, of, Memphis Red Sox, Atlanta Black Crackers, Birmingham Black Barons
McKAMEY, ____—1946—ss, Kansas City Monarchs
McKANE, ____—1926—umpire, ECL
McKAY, ____—1939—ph, Chicago American Giants
McKEEVER, JOHN—1946—infield, Pittsburgh Stars
McKEG, ____—1897—ss, Cuban Giants
McKELVIN [McKELLAM], FRED—1942—p, Cincinnati-Cleveland Buckeyes

McKENNA [McKINLEY], ____–1929–p, Louisville Black Colonels
McKENZIE, HERBERT–1950–c, New York Black Yankees
McKINES, ____–1870–of, Johnstown (NY) Wide Awakes
McKINLEY, ____–1940–p, Chicago American Giants
McKINNEY, ____–1926–umpire, ECL
McKINNEY, JOE–1929–p, Dallas Black Giants
McKINNIS, GREADY (LEFTY)–1941-49–p, Birmingham Black Barons, Chicago American Giants, Pittsburgh Crawfords (USL), Minneapolis-St. Paul Colored Gophers
McKINNIS, HANK–1942-43–p, Kansas City Monarchs
McKNIGHT, ____–1910–treasurer, Oklahoma City Giants
McKNIGHT, ____–1915–of, All Nations
McKNIGHT, GEORGE–1949–c, Homestead Grays
McKNIGHT, JR., IRA D. (JOE)–1951-52, 1956-60–of, c, Memphis Red Sox, Kansas City Monarchs, Satchel Paige All-Stars, Birmingham Black Barons
McLAIN [McCLAIN], BILL–1933-34–p, Columbus Blue Birds, Columbus Stars
McLAIN, [see McCLAIN, EDWARD (BOOTS)]
McLANE, ____–1915–p, Pittsburgh Giants
McLAUGHLIN, DAN–1926–umpire, ECL
McLAUGHLIN, HENRY MACK–1914-19–p, 1b, of, Jewell's ABCs, Lincoln (NY) Giants, Louisville White Sox, West Baden (IN) Sprudels
McLAURIN, FELIX VERNON–1942-52–of, Jacksonville Red Caps, Birmingham Black Barons, New York Black Yankees, Chicago American Giants
McLAURIN, JOHNNIE (JACK)–1944, 1948–c, Newark Eagles, Jacksonville Red Caps
McLAWN, ____–1948–c, Newark Eagles
McLEAN, ____–1887–c, Baltimore Lord Baltimores (NCBBL)
McLEAN, TOM–1939–owner, Norfolk Black Tars
McLEMORE, ____–1938–p, Birmingham Black Barons, Kansas City Monarchs
McLEMORE, ____–1952–p, Birmingham Black Barons
McLLOYD, ____–1920–of, Peoria (IL) Black Devils
McLLOYD, ____–1922-23–p, Bacharach (AC) Giants
McMAHON, ____–1869–of, Mutuals of Washington
McMAHON, ____–1926-29–umpire, NNL
McMAHON, EDWARD (ED)–1906, 1911-13–owner, Lincoln (NY) Giants, Lincoln (NY) Stars, Philadelphia Quaker Giants
McMAHON, RODERICK JAMES (JESS)–1906, 1911-13–officer, owner, Lincoln (NY) Giants, Lincoln (NY) Stars, Philadelphia Quaker Giants
McMEANS, WILLIE–1945–p, Chicago American Giants
McMILLAN, EARL THOMAS–1923–of, Toledo Tigers
McMULLIN [McMULLEN], CLARENCE–1945-49–of, Kansas City Monarchs, Houston Eagles, Portland (OR) Rosebuds, Chicago Brown Bombers (USL)
McMURRAY, WILLIAM JOSEPH (WILLIE, WILL)–1906-15–c, 3b, St. Paul Colored Gophers, St. Louis Giants, Chicago Union Giants, West Baden (IN) Sprudels, Twin City Gophers
McNAIR, ALLEN HURLEY (MAC, BUGGER, WE WE, ERIC)–1910-46–of, Minneapolis Keystones, St. Paul Colored Gophers, Long Island Lake Giants, Chicago Giants, Gilkerson's Union Giants, Chicago American Giants, Detroit Stars, Chicago Union Giants, Kansas City Monarchs, Cincinnati Tigers, All Nations, Kansas City (KS) Giants, Brooklyn Royal Giants, John Donaldson All-Stars; umpire, NAL
McNAMEE, TOM C.–1913–officer, Colored National Base Ball League of the United States
McNEAL, ALBERT–1918-21–1b, c, Dayton Marcos, Columbus Buckeyes, Cleveland Tate Stars
McNEAL, CLYDE CLIFTON (JUNIOR)–1945-50–ss, 2b, Chicago American Giants
McNEAL, RUFUS LEE (ZIPPY)–1953-55–p, of, Indianapolis Clowns
McNEAL [McNEIL], WILLIAM (RED)–1926-33–of, p, Louisville Black Colonels, Louisville White Sox, Louisville Black Caps, Nashville Elite Giants, Louisville Red Caps, Evansville (IN) Giants
McNEELY, WILLIAM HENRY (LEFTY)–1946-47–of, Birmingham Black Barons, Miami Clowns
McNEIL, ____–1916–ss, Lincoln (NY) Giants
McNEIL, ____–1930–of, Baltimore Black Sox
McNEIL [McNEAL], JAMES EARL–1959-60–of, c, Raleigh (NC) Tigers
McNEIL, ROY–1939–of, Atlanta Black Crackers
McPHERSON, GEORGE–1958–utility, Memphis Red Sox
McQUADE, ____–1888–of, Rockford (IL) Rockfords
McQUEEN, ____–1931–p, Newark Browns
McQUEEN, JOHN HENRY (PETE)–1932-45–of, Memphis Red Sox, New York Black Yankees, Little Rock Grays, Pittsburgh Crawfords, Brooklyn Royal Giants
McQUEEN, PRESTEL–1949–p, Durham (NC) Eagles
McQUEEN, VERDENE–1958–p, Memphis Red Sox

McQUERY, FRED [see McCRARY, FRED]
McREE, JOE—1955—p, Detroit Stars
McREYNOLDS, ELZIE—1916—of, p, Bowser's ABCs, Indianapolis ABCs
McWOOR, ____—1930—p, Louisville Black Colonels
MEADE, ____—1884—ss, Newark Dusky Boys
MEADE, FREDERICK C. (FRED, CHICK) [a.k.a. Chick Fleming, Leslie A. Marshall]—1914-22—3b, Pittsburgh Colored Stars, Hilldale Club, Pittsburgh Stars of Buffalo, Baltimore Black Sox, Harrisburg Giants, Indianapolis ABCs, Brooklyn All-Stars, New York Stars, Cuban Giants, Philadelphia Giants
MEADOWS, ____—1928—p, Kansas City (KS) Giants
MEADOWS, HELBURN L.—1934-35, 1952—of, Cincinnati Tigers, Philadelphia Stars
MEAGHER, ____—1932—of, Washington Pilots
MEANS, CHARLES—1947—2b, ss, Detroit Wolves
MEANS, GEORGE S.—1871—vice-president, Chicago Uniques
MEANS, LEMUEL LEWIS (LOU)—1920-28, 1932—2b, c, Bacharach (AC) Giants, Birmingham Black Barons, Atlanta Black Crackers, Atlanta Grey Sox
MEANS, THOMAS (TOMMY)—1900-04, 1907-09, 1912—p, of, Chicago Unions, Chicago Union Giants, Kansas City (KS) Giants, Indianapolis ABCs, St. Paul Colored Giants, Columbia Giants, Leland Giants, All Nations
MEANS, WINSLOW—1947-48—p, Havana Las Palomas, Harlem Globetrotters
MECKLING, S.—1909—c, Kansas City (MO) Royal Giants
MEDEROS, JÉSUS (FRANK, LICO)—1910-20—p, of, All Cubans, Bacharach (AC) Giants, Cuban Stars
MEDERT, ____—1917—ss, Chicago Giants
MEDICE, JOSEPH—1945—infield, New Orleans Black Pelicans
MEDINA, LÁZARO [a.k.a. CHAPMAN] LEONARDO—1944-46—p, 1b, Cincinnati-Indianapolis Clowns, Indianapolis Clowns, Baltimore Elite Giants
MEDINA, PEDRO—1905-07—c, p, All Cubans, Cuban Stars, Havana Stars
MEDLEY, CALVIN R. (BABE)—1946-47—p, New York Black Yankees
MEDRO, ____—1910—1b, Minneapolis Keystones
MEEKS, GIBBIE (CY)—1946—ss, Brooklyn Brown Dodgers, Pittsburgh Crawfords (USL)
MEITIA, ____—1936—of, Cuban Stars
MELELL, ____—1947—p, Philadelphia Stars

MELLITO or MILLITO [see NAVARRO, EMILIO]
MELLIX, RALPH BOLEY (FELIX, LEFTY)—1922-35, 1943-46—p, manager, Homestead Grays, Newark Browns, Brooklyn Brown Dodgers, Pittsburgh Crawfords, Newark Dodgers, Pittsburgh Giants, Pittsburgh Stars, Chicago Brown Bombers (USL)
MELLO, HARRY [see MILLON, HERALD]
MELLOY, CHARLEY—1922—p, Bacharach Giants, All Cubans
MELTON, ____—1916—p, St. Louis Giants
MELTON, ELBERT (BABE)—1928-32, 1936—of, 2b, Brooklyn Cuban Giants, Lincoln (NY) Giants, Baltimore Black Sox, Brooklyn Royal Giants, Providence Giants, Washington Pilots, Newark Browns
MELVIN, ____—1867—ss, Ithaca (NY) Actives
MENARD, JOHN WILLIS—1886—founder, Southern League of Colored Baseballists
MENEESE, ED—1936—officer, Nashville Elite Giants
MÉNDEZ, ____—1922—p, All Cubans
MÉNDEZ, ____—1937—c, New York Cubans
MÉNDEZ, JOSÉ De La CARIDAD (JOE, EL DIAMANTE NEGRO, BLACK MATTY, MENDY, EL MONO AMARILLO)—1908-26—p, ss, 3b, 2b, manager, Cuban Stars (West), Stars of Cuba, All Nations, Los Angeles White Sox, Chicago American Giants, Detroit Stars, Kansas City Monarchs
MENDIETA, INOCENTE—1912-15—2b, Cuban Stars (East), Long Branch (NJ) Cubans, Havana Reds
MENTOR, JOHN—1928—p, Kansas City (KS) Giants
MERCER, ____—1907—3b, Keystone (PA) Giants
MERCHANT, HENRY LEWIS (FRANK, SPEED)—1940-54—of, 1b, Chicago American Giants, Cincinnati-Indianapolis Clowns, Indianapolis Clowns, Chicago Brown Bombers
MERIDA, JOHN H. (SNOWBALL, BIG BOY)—1907-11—c, 2b, Indianapolis ABCs, Minneapolis Keystones, Kansas City (MO) Royal Giants
MEREDITH, ____—1914—3b, West Baden (IN) Sprudels
MEREDITH, BUFORD (GEETCHIE)—1920-31—ss, 2b, Birmingham Black Barons, Nashville Elite Giants, Memphis Red Sox, Knoxville Giants
MERRICK, ZEKE—1953-54—of, Memphis Red Sox
MERRIL, ____—1921—of, Bacharach (AC) Giants
MERRITT, SCHUTE—1934-35—2b, of, Newark Dodgers
MERRITT, WILLIAM (BILL, TRIP)—1905-17—p, of, Brooklyn Royal Giants, Lincoln (NY) Giants

MERSHEIMER, FRED J. —1896-1904—officer, Cuban X-Giants

MESA, ANDRES R.—1947-48—of, Havana Las Palomas, Indianapolis Clowns

MESA, PABLO (CHAMPION)—1921-27—of, Cuban Stars (East), All Cubans, New York Cuban Stars

MESHAD, SR., FLOYD G.—1955—owner, Birmingham Black Barons

METZ, ____—1939—ph, Kansas City Monarchs

MEXIO, ____—1925—of, Cuban Stars (West)

MEYERS, ____—1946—ph, Cincinnati Crescents

MEYERS, C.—1908—of, Brooklyn Colored Giants

MEYERS, GEORGE ALLEN (DEACON)—1920-28—p, Nashville White Sox, St. Louis Stars, Dayton Marcos, St. Louis Giants, Toledo Tigers, Montgomery Grey Sox

MEYERS, WILLIAM [see MYERS, WILLIAM VANDEVEER]

MIARKA [MIERKO], STANLEY V.—1950—2b, p, Chicago American Giants

MICHAELS, ____—1954—p, Birmingham Black Barons

MICKEY, JAMES (HORACE)—1940—ss, Chicago American Giants, Birmingham Black Barons

MICKEY, JOHN BAPTIST—1898, 1907—p, Celoron (NY) Acme Colored Giants (Iron & Oil League), Philadelphia Giants

MICKLE, ____—1930—umpire, NNL

MIDDLETON, CHARLES—1929—2b, Birmingham Black Barons

MIKADO, JAP (Mikado translates to "Emperor" in Japanese) [see MIKAMI, GORO below]

MIKAMI, GORO [a.k.a. JAP JACOBS]—1916-18—2b, All Nations

MILES, ____—1913—of, Louisville White Sox

MILES, JACK (SONNY BOY)—1934-40—of, Chicago American Giants

MILES, JIMMY—1934—1b, Philadelphia Stars

MILES, JR., JOHN (MULE, SONNY BOY)—1946-49—of, Chicago American Giants

MILES, JONAS—1940—p, Cincinnati Buckeyes

MILES, TOM (CHERRY)—1946—1b, of, Chicago American Giants, Cleveland Clippers

MILES, WILLIE—1921-27—of, 1b, 3b, Pittsburgh Keystones, Toledo Tigers, Memphis Red Sox, Cleveland Tate Stars, Cleveland Browns, Cleveland Elites, Cleveland Hornets, Homestead Grays, St. Louis Giants, Albany (GA) Giants

MILES, ZELL—1946-51—of, Seattle Steelheads, Harlem Globetrotters, Chicago American Giants

MILHOUSE, ____—1932—of, Pittsburgh Crawfords

MILLER, ____—1906—of, 2b, Brooklyn Royal Giants [see MILLINER, EUGENE JAMES]

MILLER, ____—1910-20—c, of, Pittsburgh Giants, Dayton Marcos

MILLER, ____—1922—p, New Orleans Crescent Stars

MILLER, ____—1929—p, Bacharach Giants

MILLER, A.—1927-33—of, Memphis Red Sox, Birmingham Black Barons, Louisville Red Caps

MILLER, BUSTER—writer, *New York Age*

MILLER, C. B. (RUBY BOB)—1923-29—2b, 3b, Memphis Red Sox, Birmingham Black Barons, Atlanta Black Crackers, Atlanta Grey Sox

MILLER, CHARLES—1958—1b, Detroit Clowns

MILLER, CHARLIE—1929, 1932-38—2b, 3b, Evansville Giants, Nashville Elite Giants, New Orleans Crescent Stars, Louisville Black Caps, Cincinnati Tigers, St. Louis Stars, Louisville Red Caps

MILLER, CYRUS B.—1868—player, Philadelphia Pythians

MILLER, DALE—1955, 1957—p, of, New York Black Yankees, Detroit Stars

MILLER, DEMPSEY (DIMP)—[see MILLER, PERCY]

MILLER, (DUSTY)—1945—of, Toledo Ray/Cubs

MILLER, EDDIE (BUCK)—1924-31—p, ss, 3b, Chicago American Giants, Indianapolis ABCs, Homestead Grays, Chicago Columbia Giants

MILLER, ELIJAH DANIEL (LUCKY)—1926-45—batboy, Homestead Grays

MILLER, JR., FERNÁNDEZ RAYMOND (RAY)—1954—1b, Detroit Stars

MILLER, FRANK WILLIAM (CYCLONE)—1887-97—p, of, Pittsburgh Keystones (NCBBL), Cuban Giants (Trenton, NJ), Cuban X-Giants, New York Gorhams (Middle States League), Philadelphia Giants, Cuban Giants, Genuine Cuban Giants, York (PA) Colored Monarchs (Eastern Interstate League)

MILLER, FRANKLIN—1922—umpire, NNL

MILLER, HENRY JOSEPH (HANK, HENNIE)—1938-49—p, Philadelphia Daisies (NML), Philadelphia Stars, Otto Brigg's All-Stars, Newark Eagles, Chicago American Giants, Nashville Cubs, Brooklyn Brown Dodgers

MILLER, HERMAN—1924—2b, Chicago American Giants

MILLER, J.—1911-12, 1917—ss, 3b, All Nations, Pittsburgh Giants

MILLER, JAMES (BO)—1938-39—3b, Homestead Grays, Atlanta Black Crackers

MILLER, JAMSIE—1894—of, Cuban Giants

MILLER, JASPER (JOE)—1937-40—p, New Orleans Crescent Stars, St. Louis Stars, Cincinnati Tigers, Newark Eagles

MILLER, JOHN W.—1922—officer, Memphis Red Sox

MILLER, JOSEPH (JOE, KID)—1890-06—p, of, Lincoln (NE) Giants, Adrian (MI) Page Fence Giants, Columbia Giants, Adrian Reformers (Michigan St. League), Chicago Union Giants

MILLER, LOUIS LEE (RED, SHORTY)—1909-23—3b, Paterson (NJ) Smart Set, Lincoln (NY) Giants, Lincoln (NY) Stars, Brooklyn Royal Giants, Bacharach (AC) Giants, Baltimore Black Sox, Philadelphia Giants

MILLER, LEROY (FLASH)—1934-45—ss, 2b, Newark Dodgers, New York Black Yankees, Brooklyn Royal Giants, Schenectady Mohawk Giants

MILLER, JR., LEROY (PIRATE)—1959-60—p, Birmingham Black Barons, Philadelphia Stars

MILLER, MELVIN RAY—1960—of, Kansas City Monarchs

MILLER, NED (BUSTER)—1937, 1939—1b, 2b, Indianapolis Athletics, Detroit Stars, Toledo Crawfords, Indianapolis Crawfords

MILLER, OTHO (BUDDY)—1951—ss, Indianapolis Clowns

MILLER, PERCY M. (DIMP, DEMPSEY, DIMPLES, NOTHING BALL)—1921-45—p, of, 2b, St. Louis Stars, St. Louis Giants, Cleveland Hornets, Cleveland Tigers, Cleveland Cubs, Cleveland Elites, Detroit Stars, Nashville Elite Giants, Chicago Giants, Kansas City Monarchs, Birmingham Black Barons, Memphis Red Sox, Newark Browns, Toledo Crawfords; manager, Detroit Motor City Giants

MILLER, PLEAS C. (HUB, SPITBALL)—1911-17—p, of, West Baden (IN) Sprudels, St. Louis Giants, Pittsburgh Stars of Buffalo

MILLER, R.—1933—1b, Louisville Red Caps

MILLER, RAY [see MILLER, JR., FERNÁNDEZ RAYMOND]

MILLER, THEODORE THOMAS—1888-89—of, Bloomington (IL) Reds

MILLER, W.—1937, 1940-42—p, of, Chicago American Giants

MILLER, WILLIAM—1921—officer, Nashville Elite Giants

MILLIGAN, WALTER L.—1883—of, Cleveland Blue Stockings

MILLINER, EUGENE JAMES (GABBIE, GENE)—1902-12—of, 2b, Chicago Union Giants, St. Paul Colored Gophers, Kansas City (MO) Royal Giants, Brooklyn Royal Giants, Twin City Gophers, Kansas City (KS) Giants

MILLON [MILNER], RALPH HARRY—1946-47—pr, ph, Chicago American Giants

MILLS, C.—1869—of, Mutuals of Washington

MILLS, CHARLES ALEXANDER (CHUBBY)—1907-24—officer, manager, St. Louis Giants, St. Louis Black Stockings

MILLS, E.—1869—1b, Mutuals of Washington

MILTON, ____—1920—of, Chicago American Giants, Pensacola Giants

MILTON, ____—1946—3b, Brooklyn Brown Dodgers

MILTON, ART (SHOWBOAT)—1937-42—1b, Schenectady Mohawk Giants, Baltimore Grays

MILTON, BILL—1929—p, Santop Broncos

MILTON, C.—1933-34—p, Cleveland Red Sox, Columbus Blue Birds

MILTON, EDWARD—1926-28—of, 2b, Cleveland Elites, Cleveland Tigers

MILTON, HENRY WILLIAM E. (STREAK)—1932-43—of, Chicago Giants, Indianapolis ABCs, Chicago American Giants, Brooklyn Royal Giants, Kansas City Monarchs, New York Black Yankees, Brooklyn Eagles, Baltimore Grays, New Orleans Black Pelicans

MIMMS, ____—1932—p, 2b, Columbus Turfs

MIMS, ____—1910—of, St. Louis Giants

MIMS [MIMES], JOE (FIREBALL) NATHAN—1955-56—p, Detroit Stars

MIMS, RICHARD (LEFTY)—1945—p, Detroit Motor City Giants

MINCY, PURNELL CECIL (LEFTY, BOOSTER)—1939-40—p, Philadelphia Stars, Newark Eagles, New York Black Yankees

MINOR, GEORGE—1944-49—of, Chicago American Giants, Cleveland Buckeyes, Louisville Buckeyes

MINOR, ROBERT—1919-20—of, Baltimore Black Sox

MIÑOSO y ARRIETA, SATURNINO ORESTES ARMAS (MINNIE)—1946-48—3b, New York Cubans; author

MINTON, THEOPH J.—1868—player, Philadelphia Pythians

MINTON, WILLIAM H.—1868—player, Philadelphia Pythians

MIRABAL [MIRABLE, MIRABEL], ANTONIO—1937-40—1b, 2b, of, New York Cuban Stars

MIRABAL [MIRABEL], JUANELO—1920-34, 1949-50—p, president, Birmingham Black Barons, Cuban Stars (East), New York Cubans, All Cubans

MIRAKA, STANLEY [see MIERKO, STANLEY V.]

MIRALL, ____–1930–3b, Brooklyn Royal Giants

MIRANDA, FERNANDO (PITA)–1916–of, New York Cuban Stars

MIRO, PEDRO–1945-48–2b, New York Cubans, New Orleans Black Pelicans, Atlanta Black Crackers

MISSOURI, JAMES ALBERT (JIM)–1937-41–p, Philadelphia Stars

MITCHELL, ____–1872–3b, Amicable Club of New York

MITCHELL, ____–1913–1b, of, Louisville White Sox, St. Louis Giants

MITCHELL, ____–1914-16–p, Pittsburgh Giants, Baltimore Giants, Jersey City Colored Giants

MITCHELL, ____–1922–of, Richmond Giants

MITCHELL, ____–1922-25–umpire, ECL

MITCHELL, ____–1934–p, Pittsburgh Crawfords

MITCHELL, ____–1935–p, Chicago Giants

MITCHELL, A.–1884–player, Philadelphia Mutual B.B.C.

MITCHELL, ALONZO (FLUKE, MONTY)–1926-44–manager, p, 1b, officer, Cleveland Bears, Atlanta Black Crackers, Harrisburg Giants, Baltimore Black Sox, Birmingham Black Barons, Akron Tyrites, Indianapolis ABCs, Montgomery Grey Sox, Homestead Grays, Bacharach (AC) Giants, Jacksonville Red Caps, Breakers Hotel (FL), Newark Stars

MITCHELL, ARTHUR HAROLD–1939-43–infield, manager, New York Black Yankees, Schenectady Mohawk Giants

MITCHELL, BENJAMIN–1921–p, Dayton Marcos

MITCHELL, BENJAMIN ARNETT [ERNEST] (HOOKS)–1919-25–p, Jacksonville Stars, Jacksonville Red Caps, Grand Central Terminal Red Caps, Baltimore Black Sox, Bacharach (AC) Giants, Harrisburg Giants,

MITCHELL, CHARLIE–1942–c, Boston Royal Giants

MITCHELL, CHARLIE A.–1888-89–of, p, Bloomington (IL) Reds

MITCHELL, CLARENCE (STRINGBEAN)–1938–1b, p, Indianapolis ABCs

MITCHELL, EDWARD (KIDD)–1908-10–owner, Minneapolis Keystones

MITCHELL, FRANK–1932–2b, Montgomery Grey Sox

MITCHELL, GEORGE–1932-35–1b, of, Montgomery Grey Sox, Columbus Elite Giants, Akron Tyrites

MITCHELL, (BIG) GEORGE FREDRICK (MOUNTAIN DROP, TOAD)–1924-49–p, of, manager, business manager, USL officer, Chicago American Giants, Indianapolis ABCs, Cleveland Cubs, Mounds City (IL) Blues (became Indianapolis ABCs), St. Louis Stars, New Orleans-St. Louis Stars, Harrisburg-St. Louis Stars, New York Black Yankees, Cleveland Stars, Detroit Stars, Kansas City Monarchs, Jacksonville Red Caps, Detroit Black Sox, Harlem Globetrotters, Houston Eagles

MITCHELL, J.–1909–of, Louisville Cubs

MITCHELL, J. LEONARD OTTO–1926-40–2b, business manager, Birmingham Black Barons, Louisville White Sox, Louisville Black Colonels, Baltimore Black Sox, Indianapolis ABCs, Evansville Giants

MITCHELL, SR., JESSIE JAMES–1954-60–of, Birmingham Black Barons, Louisville Clippers, Kansas City Monarchs

MITCHELL, SR., JOHN–1957-60–of, Birmingham Black Barons

MITCHELL, JOHNNY–1932–of, c, Montgomery Grey Sox

MITCHELL, JOHNNY (BO)–1938–p, Birmingham Black Barons, Atlanta Black Crackers

MITCHELL, JR., JOSEPH (JOE)–1951–p, Chicago American Giants

MITCHELL, SR., JOSEPH (JOE, GOOSE)–1926–of, Birmingham Black Barons

MITCHELL, LEE–1900-01–c, Chicago Union Giants

MITCHELL, LLOYD–1930–of, Memphis Red Sox

MITCHELL, M.–1904–of, Chicago Unions

MITCHELL, SR., ROBERT LEE (BOB, PEACHHEAD, MOONBEAM)–1950-57–p, Cleveland Buckeyes, Kansas City Monarchs

MITCHELL, ROBERT SHEDRICK (PUDD)–1923-24–c, of, St. Louis Stars, Birmingham Black Barons

MITCHELL, S.–1932–p, Montgomery Grey Sox

MITCHELL, W.–1926–of, Nashville Elite Giants

MITCHELL, WILLIAM–1875–player, St. Louis Blue Stockings

MITCHELL, WILLIAM (BUD)–1926-36–of, p, c, Hilldale Club, Darby Daisies, Bacharach (AC) Giants, Washington Pilots, Newark Stars, Baltimore Black Sox, Philadelphia Stars, Harrisburg Giants, Washington Elite Giants

MIXON, ____–1928–of, Kansas City (KS) Giants

MOBLEY, AL (JOHNNY, JOE)–1953-55–1b, of, Birmingham Black Barons

MOBLEY, IRA T. (DICK)–1954–ss, 2b, of, Kansas City Monarchs

MOBLY, D.–1867–ss, Brooklyn Unique

MOBLY, H.–1867–c, Brooklyn Unique

MOISE, C.–1886–of, Unions of New Orleans

MOFFETT, (MUFF)–1920, 1926, 1928–p, New Orleans Crescent Stars, New Orleans Black Pelicans, Chattanooga Black Lookouts, Chattanooga White Sox

MOFFIT, (LEFTY)—1945—p, New Orleans Black Pelicans
MOLES, (LEFTY)—1935—p, Philadelphia Stars
MOLINA, ____—1903—of, All Cubans
MOLINA, G.—1929-30—p, Cuban Stars (West)
MOLINA y BECERRA, AGUSTÍN (TINTI)—1906-31—1b, of, c, manager, officer, Cuban Stars (West), Cuban X-Giants, Philadelphia Quaker Giants, Havana Stars, Cincinnati Cuban Stars, All Cubans
MOLINEAUX, ____—1870-71—3b, Boston Resolutes
MOLLETT, E. [see MALLETTE, WILLIAM]
MOLLOY, ____—1922—p, Bacharach (AC) Giants
MONCEVILLE____ [see CONCEPCION, RAMÓN]
MONDELL, ____—1945—p, Baltimore Elite Giants
MONEHILE, ____—1930—of, Boston Black Sox
MONGIN [MUNGIN], SAMUEL (SAM, POLLY)—1907-22—3b, Brooklyn Royal Giants, Lincoln (NY) Stars, Lincoln (NY) Giants, Bacharach (AC) Giants, St. Louis Giants, Philadelphia Giants, Chicago Giants, Breakers Hotel (FL)
MONROE, ____—1926—p, Philadelphia Giants
MONROE, ____—1936, 1939—3b, St. Louis Stars, St. Louis Giants
MONROE, AL—1937—secretary, NAL; writer, *Abbott's Monthly*; sports editor, *Chicago Whip*
MONROE, BILL—1920, 1927-28—3b, ss, Pittsburgh Stars of Buffalo, Baltimore Black Sox
MONROE, WILLIAM S. (BILL, DIAMOND BILL, MONIE)—1896-1914—2b, Chicago Unions, Philadelphia Giants, Brooklyn Royal Giants, Chicago American Giants, Cuban X-Giants, Chicago Giants, Philadelphia Quaker Giants
MONTALVO, ESTEBAN (MAYARÍ)—1920-28—of, p, Birmingham Black Barons, Lincoln (NY) Giants, Cuban Stars (East & West)
MONTGOMERY, ____—1923-30—umpire, NNL
MONTGOMERY, A. G.—1926—secretary, NSL
MONTGOMERY, GRADY (MONTY)—1948-52—infield, Chicago American Giants, Baltimore Elite Giants, Indianapolis Clowns
MONTGOMERY, JOE—1954-56—of, Detroit Stars, Kansas City Monarchs
MONTGOMERY, JOHN S.—1926—officer, Albany (GA) Giants
MONTGOMERY, LOUIS M. (HULA LOU, SLIM)—1942, 1945-46—p, of, Cincinnati Ethiopian Clowns (NML), Detroit Motor City Giants, Pittsburgh Stars
MONTICELLO, ____—1930—of, Newark Browns
MOODY, ____—1931—ss, Memphis Red Sox
MOODY, CHESTER—1956—c, New York Black Yankees
MOODY, FRANK R.—1940—p, Birmingham Black Barons
MOODY, LEICESTER (LEE)—1944-47—1b, Kansas City Monarchs, Birmingham Black Barons, Chet Brewer's Kansas City Royals
MOODY, WILLIS—1921-29—of, Pittsburgh Keystones, Homestead Grays, Pittsburgh Giants
MOONEY, FRANK—1913, 1917, 1919—3b, p, Chicago American Giants, Jewell's ABCs, Los Angeles White Sox
MOONEY, TOM (RABBIT FOOT, CIRCUS, IRON MAN)—1908-09—p, San Antonio Broncos
MOORE, ____—1867—of, Ithaca (NY) Actives
MOORE, ____—1913-15—c, All Nations
MOORE, ____—1918—1b, Bacharach (AC) Giants
MOORE, ____—1920—p, Pittsburgh Stars of Buffalo
MOORE, ____—1921—of, Norfolk Giants
MOORE, ____—1930—p, Santop Broncos
MOORE, A.—1912—2b, Chicago Giants
MOORE, ALLEN J.—1932—p, John Donaldson All-Stars
MOORE, [REV.] ARNOLD DWIGHT (GATEMOUTH)—1955—owner, Birmingham Black Barons
MOORE, BILLY JOE—1956—1b, ss, Birmingham Black Barons
MOORE, CHARLES—1943-44—umpire, NNL
MOORE, (CHINK)—1939—p, Bacharach (Philly) Giants
MOORE, C. L.—1924—umpire, NNL
MOORE, CLARENCE—1928—1b, Bacharach (AC) Giants
MOORE, CLARENCE LEE (C. L., COOL BREEZE, DAGO)—1944-48—p, manager, officer, owner, Asheville Blues; president, Negro American Association, Chicago American Giants
MOORE, EUGENE LUCILLE (DEER FOOT)—1910-20—of, St. Louis Giants, Bowser's ABCs, West Baden (IN) Sprudels, Louisville White Sox, Indianapolis ABCs, Chicago Black Sox, Detroit Stars
MOORE, EXCELL—1950-52—p, Cleveland Buckeyes, New Orleans Eagles, Indianapolis Clowns
MOORE, G.—1907—of, Harrisburg Giants
MOORE, H.—1920—2b, Knoxville Giants
MOORE, HENRY W. (HARRY, MIKE)—1894-1914—of, 1b, 3b, Chicago Unions, Algona (IA) Brownies, Cuban X-Giants, Philadelphia Giants, Leland Giants, Chicago Giants, Lincoln (NY) Giants, Chicago Union Giants
MOORE, HERBERT CATO—1942—p, Detroit Black Sox
MOORE, HENRY LOWERY—1932-38—officer, Memphis Red Sox, St. Louis Stars, Birmingham Black Barons

MOORE, J. (BUN)—1920, 1923—p, Knoxville Giants, Indianapolis ABCs
MOORE, JACK—1935, 1939, 1946—of, Monroe (LA) Monarchs, Cleveland Bears, Los Angeles White Sox
MOORE, JR., JAMES M. (BULLET JIM)—1942-48—p, Detroit Motor City Giants, Detroit Brown Bombers, New York Black Yankees, Philadelphia Daisies (NML)
MOORE, III, JAMES ROBERT (RED)—1935-42—1b, Chattanooga Choo Choos, Mohawk Giants, Atlanta Black Crackers, Baltimore Elite Giants, Newark Eagles, Indianapolis ABCs
MOORE, JIM—1914—of, Schenectady Mohawk Giants
MOORE, JIMMY—1932, 1934—1b, of, Atlanta Black Crackers, Gilkerson's Union Giants
MOORE, JOHN—1929—ss, Shreveport Black Sports, Birmingham Black Barons
MOORE, JOHNNY—1928-30—1b, Pittsburgh Crawfords
MOORE, JOHNNY—1946—3b, San Francisco Sea Lions
MOORE, JOHNSON—1950—of, Chicago American Giants
MOORE, KENZIE—1938, 1940—1b, Newark Eagles
MOORE, LAURENCE (LON)—1954—c, Kansas City Monarchs
MOORE, LEGOLIAN (BOOTS)—1948-49—p, of, Harlem Globetrotters
MOORE, L.W.—1919—owner, San Antonio Black Aces; 1930—owner, Shreveport Black Sports
MOORE, N. (STEEL ARM)—1926—of, Memphis Red Sox
MOORE, P.D.—1932-34—c, Monroe (LA) Monarchs, Louisville Red Caps
MOORE, PETE—1941—ss, 3b, Detroit Stars
MOORE, RALPH THOMAS (SQUIRE)—1920-28—p, Memphis Red Sox, Kansas City Monarchs, Cleveland Hornets, Cleveland Tigers, Cleveland Tate Stars, Birmingham Black Barons, Chicago American Giants, Cleveland Elites
MOORE, RICHARD—1932, 1935—ss, 2b, Bacharach (Philly) Giants, Philadelphia Stars
MOORE, ROBERT—1946—p, Philadelphia Stars
MOORE, ROY—1923—1b, of, Cleveland Tate Stars
MOORE, S.—1914—1b, Schenectady Mohawk Giants
MOORE, S.J.—1919-20—owner, San Antonio Black Broncos
MOORE, SHERLEY CARL (SNOW, LEFTY)—1907, 1914-16—p, Bowser's ABCs, Louisville White Sox, Indianapolis ABCs
MOORE, T. CLAY—1920—officer, Nashville Elite Giants
MOORE, W.—1907—3b, Harrisburg Giants
MOORE, WALTER (DOBIE, BLACK CAT, SCOOPS, FRECKLE)—1920-26—ss, Kansas City Monarchs
MORALES, ISMAEL (MULO)—1932, 1937—of, Cuban Stars (East), New York Cubans
MORÁN y BENAVIDES, CARLOS (CHICO)—1910-14—3b, Cuban Stars
MORÁN y BENAVIDES, FRANCISCO (FRANK, PANCHO)—1911—of, Cuban Stars
MOREFIELD, FRED (MUSCLES)—1945-46—of, Pittsburgh Crawfords (USL)
MOREHEAD [MOORHEAD], ALBERT—1923, 1925, 1932, 1943-45—c, manager, Chicago Giants, Cleveland Cubs, Birmingham Black Barons, Chicago Brown Bombers (USL), Foster Memorial Giants
MORELAND, NATHANIEL EDMUND (NATE)—1940-46—p, Baltimore Elite Giants, Kansas City Monarchs, Los Angeles White Sox
MORERA, LUIS—1928—p, Havana Red Sox
MORESELL, (MOUSE)—1928—of, Baltimore Black Sox
MORGAN, ____—1907—3b, Brooklyn Royal Giants
MORGAN, ____—1916—p, Louisville White Sox
MORGAN, ____—1917—p, Cuban Giants
MORGAN, ____—1928—of, Birmingham Black Barons
MORGAN, ____—1931—1b, Memphis Red Sox
MORGAN, ____—1932—of, Birmingham Black Barons
MORGAN, (BLACKIE)—1936—of, Philadelphia Stars
MORGAN, CONSTANCE ENOLA (CONNIE)—1954—2b, Indianapolis Clowns
MORGAN, JOHN L. (PEPPER, BLACKIE)—1937-38—of, Memphis Red Sox, Indianapolis Athletics
MORGAN, T.—1897-99—of, Chicago Unions
MORGAN, WILLIAM LEE (WILD BILL, SACK)—1943-49—p, Atlanta Black Crackers, Memphis Red Sox, Baltimore Elite Giants, Birmingham Black Barons
MORÍN, EUGENIO—1910-23—2b, 3b, c, Cuban Stars (East & West), Cincinnati Cuban Stars
MORLAND, ____—1889—of, Philadelphia Giants
MORMAN, ____—1921—2b, Calgary Black Sox
MORNEY, LEROY—1929-47—ss, 3b, 2b, Shreveport Black Sports, Monroe (LA) Monarchs, Columbus Blue Birds, Cleveland Giants, Pittsburgh Crawfords, Columbus Elite Giants, Washington Elite Giants, Baltimore Elite Giants, New York Black Yankees, Philadelphia Stars, Chicago American Giants, Birmingham Black Barons, Cincinnati Ethiopian Clowns (NML), Toledo Crawfords, Homestead Grays,

Nashville Elite Giants, Chicago Brown Bombers (USL), Detroit Senators

MORRIS, ____—1867—of, Philadelphia Pythians

MORRIS, ____—1907—c, All Havanas

MORRIS, ____—1921—of, Birmingham Black Barons

MORRIS, AL—1921, 1925, 1927-30—of, c, Birmingham Black Barons, Nashville Elite Giants, Louisville White Sox

MORRIS, AMBROSE HARRY (BROSE)—1909-14—2b, p, Indianapolis ABCs, Schenectady Mohawk Giants

MORRIS, BARNEY (BIG AD)—1932-48—p, Monroe (LA) Monarchs, Pittsburgh Crawfords, New York Cubans, Toledo Crawfords, New Orleans Crescent Stars

MORRIS, BRISTOL F. (BRIS)—1939—owner, Greensboro (NC) Red Sox, 1948—secretary, Negro American Association

MORRIS, CHARLIE—1936—p, Newark Eagles

MORRIS, HAROLD GOODWIN (HAL, YELLOWHORSE)—1924-36, 1946—p, Kansas City Monarchs, Detroit Stars, Chicago American Giants, Cleveland Royal Giants, Monroe (LA) Monarchs, Gilkerson's Union Giants, San Francisco Sea Lions (co-owner); 1949-?, scout, Chicago Cubs

MORRIS, HERBIE (SANTE FE, ED)—1946—p, Los Angeles White Sox

MORRIS, IKE—1928—1b, St. Louis Giants

MORRIS, JAMES H.—1883—of, Cleveland Blue Stockings

MORRIS, THOMAS (TOMMY)—1955-56—2b, New York Black Yankees

MORRIS, WILLIAM B.—1883—utility, Cleveland Blue Stockings

MORRISON, ____—1915—p, Cuban Giants

MORRISON, ____—1919—3b, Cleveland Giants

MORRISON, FELTON CRAIG—1943, 1946—of, Philadelphia Stars, Oakland Oaks (PCL), Oakland Larks

MORRISON, JIMMY—1930—of, Memphis Red Sox

MORRISON, ROY—1934—p, Bacharach (Philly) Giants

MORRISON, W.—1924—1b, Cleveland Browns

MORSE, ____—1867—of, Brooklyn Unique

MORSE, ROY T.—1917—1b, Brooklyn Royal Giants

MORTIN, R.—1885—p, Argyle Giants

MORTON, ____—1911—p, Brown's Tennessee Rats

MORTON, ____—1916—p, Chicago Union Giants

MORTON, ____—1917—2b, Havana Red Sox

MORTON, ____—1927—of, Chappie Johnson All Stars

MORTON, BERRY [see BERRY, MORTON]

MORTON, FERDINAND QUENTIN—1935-38—commissioner, NNL

MORTON, JOHN—1935-37—of, p, Brooklyn Eagles, Pittsburgh Crawfords, Philadelphia Stars

MORTON, SIDNEY DOUGLAS (SY)—1940-47—ss, 2b, Philadelphia Stars, Otto Brigg's All-Stars, Pittsburgh Crawfords (USL), Chicago American Giants, Newark Eagles, Brooklyn Brown Dodgers

MOSELEY, BEAUREGARD FITZHUGH—1910-11—attorney, officer, Leland Giants

MOSES, C. (LEFTY)—1938-40—p, Kansas City Monarchs

MOSES, JOE—1955—c, Birmingham Black Barons

MOSLEY, ____—1908—of, Cleveland Giants

MOSLEY, C. D. (GATEWOOD)—1932-38—p, of, New Orleans Crescent Stars, Homestead Grays, Kansas City Monarchs, Colored House of David

MOSLEY, LOU—1932—p, Bacharach (Philly) Giants, Cuban Stars (West)

MOSLEY, RUSSELL (HOWIE)—1955-57, 1961—utility, Memphis Red Sox, Raleigh (NC) Tigers

MOSLEY [MOSELEY], WILLIAM—1928-33—officer, Detroit Stars

MOSS, ____—1958—utility, Detroit Clowns

MOSS, ARNOLD L.—1930—owner, New Orleans Black Pelicans

MOSS, JAMES HUGH (JIMMY)—1917-21—p, Brooklyn Royal Giants, Chicago American Giants, Montgomery Grey Sox, Bessemer Braves

MOSS, PORTER (ANKLE BALL)—1932, 1934-44—p, Indianapolis ABCs, Cincinnati Tigers, Memphis Red Sox, Chicago American Giants, Kansas City Monarchs

MOTEN, ____—1926—of, Washington Black Sox

MOTEN, VATS—1937—c, Cincinnati Tigers

MOTHELL, CARROLL RAY (DINK, DEKE)—1918-34—of, 2b, 1b, ss, c, p, All Nations, Kansas City Monarchs, Cleveland Stars, Chicago American Giants, Topeka (KS) Giants

MOTLEY, ____—1910—ss, Illinois Giants, Chicago Union Giants

MOTLEY, ROBERT CARTER (BOB)—1947-58—umpire, NAL, East/West game; author

MOTT, ____—1918—ss, Bacharach (AC) Giants

MOTT, ____—1931—3b, p, Birmingham Black Barons

MOULTEN, ____—1897—of, Cuban Giants

MOUTON, ANTHONY—1946—p, Fresno/San Diego Tigers

MOUTON, STANLEY (MOOSE)—1946—1b, p, Fresno/San Diego Tigers

MOXIE, ____—1930—p, Dallas Black Giants

MOXLEY, ____—1920—of, Dayton Marcos

MUIR, WALTER—1920—p, Kansas City Monarchs
MULCAHY, ____—1891—of, Cuban Giants
MULCAY, ____—1913—utility, Long Branch (NJ) Cubans
MULLEN, A.—1925-28—of, umpire, Kansas City Monarchs, Birmingham Black Barons
MULLEN, GEORGE—1887—utility, Boston Resolutes (NCBBL)
MULLER, ____—1925—umpire, ECL
MULLINS, LEROY—1948—p, Memphis Red Sox
MULVEY, BEN—1934—manager, Penn Red Caps of NY
MUMPFORD, PEASTER (PETE)—1956-59—p, Birmingham Black Barons, Detroit Stars
MUNDY, GEORGE A.—1921—officer, Cleveland Tate Stars
MUNGIN, SAMUEL [see MONGIN, SAMUEL]
MUNGIN, JR., JOHN T. (BILL)—1925-27—p, Baltimore Black Sox, Harrisburg Giants, Hilldale Club
MUÑOZ, FRANCISCO (PACO)—1916—Jersey City Cubans, Long Branch (NJ) Cubans
MUÑOZ, JOSÉ (JOSEÍTO)—1904-16—p, of, 1b, Cuban Stars, Stars of Cuba, All Cubans, Cuban X-Giants
MUNROE, ELMER ALBERT (LEFTY)—1939, 42—p, Boston Royal Giants
MUNROE, WILLIAM [see MONROE, WILLIAM]
MUNSTON, ____—1920—of, Chicago Giants [see WINSTON, CLARENCE (BOBBY)]
MURDEN, SHUGARTY—1920-26—p, 2b, 3b, Atlanta Black Crackers
MURDOCK, ____—1924—p, Indianapolis ABCs
MURPHY, [see MILLER, PERCY M.]—1922—p, Kansas City Monarchs
MURPHY, ____—1889—p, Cuban Giants
MURPHY, ____—1907—2b, Cuban Giants
MURPHY, ____—1915—of, Chicago American Giants
MURPHY, ____—1930—ph, Birmingham Black Barons
MURPHY, AL—1937—p, Indianapolis Athletics
MURPHY, CARL TURLEY—1922-67—editor, *Afro-American* newspapers
MURPHY, JIMMY (AL)—1936-37, 1942, 1945—p, Indianapolis Athletics, Birmingham Black Barons, Cincinnati Tigers, Cincinnati-Cleveland Buckeyes, Philadelphia Daisies (NML), New Orleans Black Pelicans
MURPHY, SR., JOHN HENRY—1892-1922—editor, *Afro-American* newspapers
MURPHY, RONALD—1946—batboy, Newark Eagles
MURPHY, SYLVESTER—1950s—bus driver, secretary, Kansas City Monarchs

MURPHY, W. CHARLES (SPEEDBALL)—1900-17—p, of, Lincoln (NY) Stars, Lincoln (NY) Giants, Philadelphia Giants, Buffalo Giants, Brooklyn Colored Giants, Brooklyn Royal Giants, New York Black Sox, Chicago American Giants, Kansas City Monarchs, Bacharach (AC) Giants
MURRAY, ____—1872—ss, Amicable Club of New York
MURRAY, ____—1889—3b, New Orleans Pinchbacks
MURRAY, ____—1890—of, York Cuban Giants
MURRAY, ____—1907—of, Havana Cuban Stars
MURRAY, ____—1922—p, Kansas City Monarchs
MURRAY, ____—1938—p, Birmingham Black Barons [see MITCHELL, JOHNNY (BO)]
MURRAY, ____—1952—c, Kansas City Monarchs
MURRAY, CHARLES—[see MARVRAY, CHARLES]
MURRAY, CLAY—1934—p, Bacharach (Philly) Giants
MURRAY, JOHN JOSEPH (RED)—1932—p, Monroe (LA) Monarchs, Memphis Red Sox
MURRAY, MAL—1956-58—p, Indianapolis Clowns, Detroit Clowns
MURRAY, MITCHELL—1919-34—c, Indianapolis ABCs, Dayton Marcos, Cleveland Tate Stars, Toledo Tigers, St. Louis Stars, Chicago American Giants, Columbus Buckeyes, Indianapolis Monarchs
MURRAY [MURRY], RICHARD NATHANIEL (DICK, COWBOY)—1943-44, 1946, 1955—p, Baltimore Elite Giants, Cincinnati Ethiopian Clowns (NML), Cincinnati-Indianapolis Clowns, Nashville Cubs, New York Black Yankees
MURRYALL, JOHNNY—1952—p, Indianapolis Clowns
MUSE, E. E.—1922, 1933-34—p, 2b, New Orleans Crescent Stars, Hilldale Club, Monroe (LA) Monarchs
MUTRIE, J.—1871—ss, Chelsea Auroras
MUTRIE, R.—1871—of, Chelsea Auroras
MYALS, ____—1920—2b, Birmingham Black Barons
MYERS, ____—1888—of, Hoosier Black Stockings
MYERS, E.K.—1891—officer, Cuban Giants
MYERS, GEORGE A.—1883—manager, Cleveland Blue Stockings
MYERS, LEANDER—1908—2b, Brooklyn Colored Giants
MYERS, WILLIAM VANDEVEER (LEFTY)—1908-10, 1921—1b, of, Pop Watkins Stars, Brooklyn Royal Giants, Philadelphia Giants, Pennsylvania Red Caps, Calgary Black Sox, Cleveland Tate Stars

N

NAD, ____–1923–p, Milwaukee Bears
NAILS, C.W.–1934–officer, Monroe (LA) Monarchs
NAITO [NAIKA], JAP–1913–of, All Nations
NANCE, ____–1945–p, Harlem Globetrotters
NANCE, ____–1958–p, Detroit Clowns
NANCE, ARTHUR–1927-29–ss, 2b, Chicago Giants, Chicago American Giants
NANCE, J.A.–1934-35–officer, Knoxville Giants
NAPIER, EUTHUMN (EUDIE, NAP)–1935-50–c, Homestead Grays, Pittsburgh Crawfords (USL), Bacharach (Philly) Giants, Cincinnati Crescents
NAPOLEON, EDWARD–1947–p, Detroit Senators
NAPOLEON, LAWRENCE (LARRY, LEFTY)–1946-47–p, Cincinnati Crescents, Kansas City Monarchs
NARANJO y DÍAZ, PEDRO–1950, 1954–p, Indianapolis Clowns, Detroit Stars
NASH, ____–1908–c, Indianapolis ABCs
NASH, ____–1932–1b, Newark Browns
NASH, ____–1942–p, Jacksonville Red Caps
NASH, ____–1958–p, Kansas City Monarchs
NASH, LEONARD–1929–of, Memphis Red Sox
NASH, WILLIAM GREG–1928-34–p, Birmingham Black Barons, Memphis Red Sox, Nashville Elite Giants
NATCHEZ, ____–1941–ph, Satchel Paige's All-Stars
NATION, CARRIE (a.k.a. May Arbaugh)–1912–1b, All Nations
NATURE BOY [see WILLIAMS, JOHNNY]
NAVARRETTE, RAMUNDO–1950–p, New York Cubans
NAVARRO, EMILIO (MILLITO)–1928-29–2b, ss, Cuban Stars (East), Stars of Cuba
NAVARRO, RAÚL (RAYMOND)–1945-46–of, ss, c, Cincinnati-Indianapolis Clowns, Indianapolis Clowns
NAYLOR, ____–1919–3b, Wilmington Giants
NEAL, ____–1871–of, Philadelphia Pythians
NEAL, ____–1940–p, Homestead Grays
NEAL, CHARLES LENARD (CHARLIE)–1948, 1955–2b, ss, Raleigh (NC) Tigers, Atlanta Black Crackers
NEAL, GEORGE LAWRENCE–1909-11–3b, 2b, Buxton (IA) Wonders, Chicago Giants, Leland Giants, Kansas City (KS) Giants
NEAL, WILLIE FRANK–1952–infield, p, Memphis Red Sox
NEALY, BOOKER F. (PROF)–1944-46–p, of, Asheville Blues, Jacksonville Red Caps
NEALY, R.J.–1916-17–of, Kansas City Tigers
NEARS, HENRY (RED)–1940–c, of, Memphis Red Sox
NEASE [NIESE, NIESCE], ____–1908, 1911–c, of, Columbus Giants, Chicago Union Giants
NEBON, ____ [see NELSON, JOHN]–1902–ss, Philadelphia Giants
NED'A, ____–1906–2b, All Cubans
NEELEY, LOUIS–1944-45–c, Chicago Brown Bombers (USL), Harlem Globetrotters
NEELY, A.C. (BOOKER)–1932-33, 1946–p, Louisville Black Caps, Cuban Stars (East & West), Asheville Blues
NEHF, ____–1926–of, Cleveland Elites
NEIL, RAYMOND (AUSSA, TACKOLU, RAY)–1941-54, 1956–2b, clown, Cincinnati Ethiopian Clowns (NML), Indianapolis Clowns, St. Joseph (MI) Auscos, Chet Brewer's Kansas City Royals
NEILS, ____–1926–p, Cuban Stars (West)
NELSON, ____–1869–3b, Mutuals of Washington
NELSON, ____–1880–c, Washington Keystones
NELSON, ____–1934-35–p, Chicago American Giants
NELSON, ____–1938–ss, 3b, Newark Eagles
NELSON, ARTHUR (NAPPY, LEFTY)–1937–p, of, Atlanta Black Crackers
NELSON, CLYDE–1939, 1942-49–3b, 2b, 1b, of, Chicago Brown Bombers (NML), Chicago American Giants, Cleveland Buckeyes, Indianapolis Clowns, Indianapolis ABCs, Detroit Black Sox, Chet Brewer's Kansas City Royals
NELSON, ED–1943–of, Cincinnati Ethiopian Clowns (NML)
NELSON, EVERETT (ACE)–1922, 1928, 1931-33–p, Montgomery Grey Sox, Chattanooga Black Lookouts, Detroit Stars
NELSON, J.–1869–p, Washington Alerts
NELSON, JIMMY [see IRVIN, MONFORD]
NELSON, JOHN C. (NELLIE)–1884-1903, 1908–p, of, 2b, Chicago Gordons, Long Island Alpine Club, New York Gorhams (NCBBL), Cuban Giants, Cuban X-Giants, Philadelphia Giants, Philadelphia Gorhams (Middle States League) Ansonia Cuban Giants (Connecticut St. League), Trenton (NJ) Cuban Giants (Middle States League), Adrian (MI) Page Fence Giants, York (PA) Cuban Giants (Eastern Interstate League)
NELSON, P.–1869–c, Washington Alerts
NELSON, P.–1924–umpire, NNL
NELSON, P.–1924–2b, St. Louis Giants
NELSON, PAUL (FATS)–1929–c, Shreveport Black Sports

NELSON, RAYMOND (IKE)—1918—of, Bacharach (AC) Giants
NELSON, S.—1884—of, Brooklyn Alpines
NELSON, T. (FRENCHIE)—1908-of, Cleveland Giants
NELSON, W.—1889—c, Cleveland Blue Stockings
NESBIT, MELVIN (a.k.a. DUKE MARKHAM)—1935-37—of, Brooklyn Eagles, Newark Eagles, Newark Dodgers, Schenectady Mohawk Giants
NESBITT, ____—1921—of, Nashville Elite Giants
NESBITT, ____—1934—p, Bacharach (Philly) Giants
NESBITT, [DR.] EDWARD E.—1928-31—officer, Memphis Red Sox
NESTOR, S. (JACE) [see CRUZ, NESTOR]
NEUMAN(N), ____—1927-29—umpire, NNL
NEVELLE, GUS—1930—p, Pittsburgh Crawfords
NEWBERN [NEWBERRY], ____—1908—of, Chicago Union Giants, Cuban Giants
NEWBERRY, HENRY—1946-47—p, Montgomery Dodgers, Chicago American Giants
NEWBERRY, JAMES LEE (JIMMIE)—1943-50—p, Birmingham Black Barons, Chet Brewer's Kansas City Royals
NEWBERRY, RICHARD A.—1947—ss, Chicago American Giants
NEWCOMBE, DONALD (DON, BIG NEWK)—1944-45—p, Newark Eagles
NEWKIRK, ALEXANDER (ALEX, SLATS)—1946-49—p, New York Black Yankees, New York Cubans, Boston Blues
NEWMAN, ____—1888-90—c, Bloomington (IL) Reds, Lincoln (NE) Giants
NEWMAN, ____—1909—p, Leland Giants
NEWMAN, TAFT—1928, 1930—of, St. Louis Giants, Nashville Elite Giants
NEWMAN, WILLIAM—1937, 1940—p, Memphis Red Sox
NEWSKI, ____—1916—1b, All Nations
NEWSOME, OMER CURTIS—1920-29—p, Atlanta Black Crackers, Indianapolis ABCs, Washington Potomacs, Detroit Stars, Dayton Marcos, Memphis Red Sox, Wilmington Potomacs, Montgomery Grey Sox, Philadelphia Colored Giants of New York
NEWTON, ____—1867—1b, p, Ithaca (NY) Actives
NEWSON, ____—1940—of, Newark Eagles
NEWTON, ____—1909—1b, Illinois Giants
NEWTON, ____—1916—p, French Lick (IN) Plutos
NEWTON, ____—1924—umpire, NNL
NEWTON, J. A.—1921—officer, Nashville Elite Giants; 1922—manager, Chattanooga Tigers
NEWTON, JAMES—1946—p, Pittsburgh Stars
NICHOLAS, WILLIAM SPENCER (BILL, WILLIE)—1935-36—p, Newark Eagles, Brooklyn Eagles
NICHOLS, ____—1929—of, Louisville Black Caps
NICHOLS, (LEFTY)—1926—p, Chattanooga White Sox, Nashville Elite Giants
NICHOLS, CHARLES—1885—of, Argyle Hotel
NICHOLS, CHARLIE—1958—of, Memphis Red Sox
NICHOLSON, RUFORD (KUCO)—1955-56—p, Indianapolis Clowns
NICKENS, ____—1928-29—2b, p, Kansas City (KS) Giants, Washington Black Sox
NICOLAI, ____—1897—of, Adrian (MI) Page Fence Giants
NIMIN, [MIMIN] [see ESCALANTE, FRANCISCO]
NIMMONS, ERNEST J. (ERNIE, COKEY)—1952—of, Indianapolis Clowns, Kansas City Monarchs, Philadelphia Stars
NIRSA, ____—1923—of, Cuban Stars (West)
NIX, NATHANIEL (TANK, TOM)—1938-39—p, Brooklyn Royal Giants, Bacharach (Philly) Giants, Philadelphia Meteors
NIXON, ____—1904—of, Chicago Unions
NIXON, ____—1926—umpire, NNL
NIXON, ____—1937—of, Philadelphia Stars
NIXON, BILL (WILLIE)—1940-41—of, Birmingham Black Barons, Jacksonville Red Sox
NOBLE, CARLOS—1950—p, New York Cubans
NOBLE, JUAN (JOHN, GYP, GIP)—1944-47, 1949-50—p, of, New York Cubans, Havana Las Palomas, Chicago Brown Bombers (USL)
NOBLE y MAGEE, RAFAEL MIGUEL (RAY, SAM)—1945-50—c, New York Cubans
NOEL, EDDIE—1920-26, 1929—p, of, Nashville Elite Giants, Nashville White Sox
NOLAN, ____—1916-20—1b, c, St. Louis Giants, Kansas City Colored Giants, Kansas City Monarchs
NOLAND, ERNEST (BUDDY)—1932—officer, Little Rock Black Travelers
NOLAN [NOLON], JAMES—1957-58—p, Detroit Stars, Detroit Clowns
NOLES, ____—1921—p, Montgomery Grey Sox
NOLL, ____—1888—p, Rockford (IL) Rockfords
NORMAN, ____—1933—of, Kansas City Monarchs
NORMAN, B.—1909—p, Kansas City (KS) Giants
NORMAN, (BUD, ACE)—1940—p, Indianapolis Crawfords
NORMAN, ELBERT (ALTON, ED)—1919-26, 1929—ss, Chicago American Giants, Lincoln (NY) Giants, Cleveland Elites, Cleveland Tate Stars, Memphis Red Sox

NORMAN, GARNETT WESLEY (BUGHOUSE)—1923-24—of, Memphis Red Sox

NORMAN, GEORGE A. —1859—treasurer, 2b, Unknown Base Ball Club (of Weeksville, NY)

NORMAN, JAMES—1957-58—p, Detroit Stars, Detroit Clowns

NORMAN, JAMES (JIM)—1906-14—3b, manager, Kansas City (KS) Giants, Kansas City (MO) Royal Giants, Oklahoma City Monarchs, Louisville White Sox, Chicago American Giants, Topeka (KS) Giants, French Lick (IN) Plutos

NORMAN, WILLIAM (SHIN, CHIN, BILLY)—1906-11—p, of—Topeka (KS) Giants, Leland Giants, Chicago Union Giants, Kansas City (KS) Giants, Chicago Giants

NORRIS, EDWARD (SLIM, EDDIE)—1929-30—3b, Louisville White Sox, Louisville Black Caps

NORTH, L.—1922, 1926—of, p, Richmond Giants (NAA), Baltimore Black Sox

NORTHRUP [NORTHUP, NORTHROP], JOHN HENRY (HARRY, ZIP)—1902-05—p, 1b, 2b, Genuine Cuban Giants, Watsons (Weedsport, NY), Savannahs, Norwood, All-Auburn

NORTON, ____—1942—pr, New York Cubans

NORWOOD, C. H.—1887—of, Philadelphia Pythians (NCBBL)

NORWOOD, WALTER—1933—officer, Detroit Stars

NOVAL, TOMÁS DE LA (PIPO)—1935—of, Cuban Stars (East)

NOYLE, DICK [see JOHNSON, DICK]

NUÑEZ, DAGOBERTO (BERTO)—1953-54—p, of, Kansas City Monarchs

NUNLEY, BEAUFORD [BUFORD]—1931-34—1b, Little Rock Grays, Memphis Red Sox

NUNN, ____—1939—of, St. Louis Giants

NUNN, SR., WILLIAM GOLDWYN—1937—secretary, NNL; 1919-63—managing editor and writer, *Pittsburgh Courier*

NUTTALL, H. (BILL)—1924-26—p, Lincoln (NY) Giants, Bacharach (AC) Giants

NUTTER, ISAAC NELSON—1927-28—attorney, officer, Bacharach (AC) Giants; president, Eastern Colored League

NYASSES [see DAVIS, EDWARD]

O

OAKLEY, CHARLES—1940—p, New Orleans-St. Louis Stars
OBAUVAN, ____—1883—3b, St. Louis Black Stockings
OBIE, WILLIAM (BILL)—1931—p, [see LAYTON, OBEDIAH (OBIE)]
O'BRIAN, ____—1888—3b, Rockford (IL) Rockfords
O'BRIEN, ____—1922—umpire, NNL
O'BRYANT [O'BRIEN], WILLIAM (WILLIE)—1930-32—ss, of, Houston Black Buffaloes, Washington Pilots
O'DELL, ____—1891—p, 3b, New York Colored Giants
O'DELL, ____—1923—of, Richmond Giants
O'DELL, JOHN WESLEY—1949-50—p, Houston Eagles
ODEN, JOHNNY WEBB—1926-32, 1945—3b, Birmingham Black Barons, Knoxville Giants, Louisville Black Caps, Memphis Red Sox, Chicago Brown Bombers (USL)
ODOM, SAM—1946—p, Indianapolis Clowns
O'DONNELL, CHARLES K.—1887—manager, officer, Pittsburgh Keystones
O'FARRILL y GARCÍA, ORLANDO ESTEBAN (CHICO)—1949-51—ss, Indianapolis Clowns, Philadelphia Stars, Baltimore Elite Giants
OFFERT [OFFUTT], MOSE—1925-26—p, Indianapolis ABCs
OGARZON, ANDRÉS—1915—3b, Havana Reds
OGDEN, CHARLES—1886—of, Unions of New Orleans
OGLESBY, ____—1905—2b, Chicago Unions
OLAVE, PEDRO—1906—p, Cuban X-Giants, Havana Stars, Philadelphia Quaker Giants
OLDHAM, JAMES (JIMMY)—1920-23—p, St. Louis Giants, St. Louis Stars
O'LEE, ____—1934—c, Washington Pilots
OLIVER, ____—1917—3b, All Nations
OLIVER, JR., HUDSON J. (HUDDY)—1911, 1918—2b, p, Brooklyn Royal Giants, Philadelphia Quaker City Giants
OLIVER, JAMES FRANKLIN (PEE WEE, SELASSIE)—1941-46—ss, of, Cincinnati Ethiopian Clowns (NML), Birmingham Black Barons, Indianapolis Clowns
OLIVER, JOHN—1885-87—3b, of, Brooklyn Remsens, Trenton (NJ) Cuban Giants (Middle States League)
OLIVER, JOHN HENRY—1945-46—ss, of, Memphis Red Sox, Cleveland Buckeyes, Atlanta Black Crackers
OLIVER, LEONARD E.—1911-13—ss, Philadelphia Giants, Pittsburgh Giants, Paterson (NJ) Smart Set
OLIVER, LOU—1896, 1898, 1902—c, of, Cuban Giants, Cuban X-Giants
OLIVER, MARTIN—1930-34—c, infield, Birmingham Black Barons, Louisville Black Caps, Memphis Red Sox
OLSON, C.M. (CY)—1912, 1917, 1923—c, 3b, All Nations, Brooklyn Royal Giants
O'MARA, ____—1937—c, New York Cubans
O'MEADA, ____—1932—ph, Cuban Stars (West)
OMS y COSMES, ALEJANDRO (WALLA WALLA, EL CABALLERO [The Gentleman])—1917-35—of, Cuban Stars (East & West), New York Cubans, All Cubans
O'NEAL, LANDON—1927—president, Cleveland Hornets
O'NEIL, ____—1929—of, Chattanooga Black Lookouts
O'NEIL, JR., JOHN JORDAN (BUCK, NANCY)—1937-42, 1946-55—1b, manager, Memphis Red Sox, Kansas City Monarchs; 1955—coach, Chicago Cubs; author
O'NEIL, WARREN G. (DADD)—1944-45, 1947—c, Jacksonville Red Caps, Nashville Black Vols, Detroit Wolves
O'NEILL, ____—1929—umpire, ECL
O'NEILL [O'NEAL], CHARLES—1918-23—c, Atlanta Black Crackers, Jacksonville Stars, Columbus Buckeyes, Bacharach (AC) Giants, Bacharach (NY) Giants, Toledo Tigers, Chicago American Giants
O'NEILL, STEVE (BUCK)—1910-14—p, c, West Baden (IN) Sprudels, Louisville White Sox, Indianapolis ABCs
O'ROURKE, ____—1888—ss, Rockford (IL) Rockfords
O'ROURKE, JOHN A.—1889—3b, Philadelphia Giants, 1906—manager, Philadelphia Professionals
ORA, CLARENCE—1932—of, Cleveland Cubs, Chicago Giants, Foster Memorial Giants
ORANGE, ____—1928—of, Cleveland Tigers
ORANGE, ____—1939—1b, New York Cubans
ORANGE, [DR.] GRADY DIPLOMA (DIP, GERBER)—1925-31—ss, 2b, 3b, Birmingham Black Barons, Kansas City Monarchs, Detroit Stars
ORATER, ____—1862—2b, Brooklyn Monitors
OREN, ____—1903-5—p, Genuine Cuban Giants
ORENDORF, JAMES THOMAS (JIM)—1906—3b, Topeka (KS) Giants
ORME, ____—1932—ss, Kansas City (KS) Giants
ORMES, A. W.—1911—utility, Leland Giants
ORNES, ____—1920—2b, Kansas City Monarchs
ORR, ____—1882—3b, Philadelphia Orions
ORTÍZ y CORREA, FELIX—1957—ss, New Orleans Bears, Kansas City Monarchs
ORTÍZ, JULIO ARANGO (ORTIE, BILL)—1944-45—of, ss, Cincinnati-Indianapolis Clowns, Kansas City Monarchs, Harlem Globetrotters

ORTÍZ, RAFAELITO—1948—p, Chicago American Giants
OSBORN, A.C.—1921-22—ss, All Nations
OSBORNE, ____—1905—p, Philadelphia Giants
OSCAL, [see LEVIS, OSCAR J.]
OSLEY, JULIUS (SNOOKS)—1934, 1937-38, 1945—p, New Orleans Crescent Stars, Birmingham Black Barons, Detroit Motor City Giants, Nashville Black Vols
OSORIO y CEDEÑO, FERNANDO ALBERTO (MAMAVILA)—1949—p, Louisville Buckeyes
OSTOSKY, ____—1916—c, All Nations
OTIS, ____—1930—p, Brooklyn Royal Giants
OTIS, AMOS—1920-21—of, Nashville Giants
O'TOOLE, ____—1928—umpire, ECL
OUSLEY, GUY C.—1927, 1931-32—ss, Chicago Giants, Chicago American Giants, Cleveland Cubs, Memphis Red Sox, Louisville Black Caps, Harrisburg Giants, Foster Memorial Giants
OVERALLS, ____—1926—of, Memphis Red Sox
OVERLAND, GEORGE—1875-76, 1879—of, Chicago Uniques
OVERSTREET, ____—1912—of, Louisville Cubs
OVERTON, ALPHONSE ALBERT (AL, TEXAS)—1932, 1937, 1944, 1946—p, Little Rock Grays, Philadelphia Stars, Cincinnati-Indianapolis Clowns, Portland (OR) Rosebuds
OVERTON, JOHN L. 1920—officer, Nashville Elite Giants; 1925—officer, Indianapolis ABCs
OVERTON, RUBE—1924-26—owner, Indianapolis ABCs
OWENS, ____—1928—ph, Kansas City (KS) Giants
OWENS, ____—1943—3b, Atlanta Black Crackers
OWENS, A.—1927-28—ss, Cleveland Tigers, Birmingham Black Barons
OWENS, ALBERT—1930-31—p, Nashville Elite Giants
OWENS, ALFONSO (BUDDY)—1951-52—3b, Chicago American Giants
OWENS, ARTHUR C.—1954—p, Detroit Stars
OWENS, AUBRY PERCY—1920-26—p, Indianapolis ABCs, Chicago American Giants, New Orleans Caulfield Ads, Chicago Giants
OWENS, DeWITT—1926-38—ss, 3b, 2b, Birmingham Black Barons, Indianapolis Crawfords, Detroit Stars, Brooklyn Royal Giants, Austin Black Senators
OWENS, J.—1931—of, Cleveland Cubs
OWENS, JACKSON McCLELLAND (JACK)—1950-54—p, Chicago American Giants, Detroit Stars
OWENS, JAMES CLEVELAND (JESSE, JC)—1939, 1946-48—vice-president, Toledo Crawfords; officer, Detroit Senators; vice-president, co-owner, Portland (OR) Rosebuds (WCNBL), co-owner Kansas City Stars (Monarchs)
OWENS, JOHNNY—1920—p, 1b, 2b, Atlanta Black Crackers, Pensacola Giants
OWENS, JUDGE—1943—2b, Baltimore Elite Giants
OWENS, LANE AUGUSTUS—1952—infield, Indianapolis Clowns
OWENS, NATHAN (NATE)—1945-47—p,, Nashville Black Vols, Nashville Cubs, Mobile Black Bears
OWENS, RAYMOND (SMOKEY, KANKOL)—1938-42—p, of, Cleveland Bears, Cleveland Buckeyes, New Orleans-St. Louis Stars, Cincinnati Ethiopian Clowns (NML), Cincinnati Buckeyes, Jacksonville Red Caps
OWENS, ROOSEVELT (ROSIE)—1927, 1934, 1937—p, Lincoln (NY) Giants, Newark Dodgers, Newark Eagles, Washington Black Sox, Philadelphia Stars
OWENS, SYLVESTER (JOE, GOOD BLACK)—1939-42—of, Indianapolis ABCs, Atlanta Black Crackers, Philadelphia Stars, Jacksonville Red Caps
OWENS, TOM—1937—p, Newark Eagles
OWENS, W. E.—1887—player, Cincinnati Browns (NCBBL)
OWENS, WALT (COACH O)—1953-55—p, of, Detroit Stars
OWENS, WILLIAM JOHN (BILL)—1923-33—ss, 2b, p, Washington Potomacs, Chicago American Giants, Indianapolis ABCs, Dayton Marcos, Memphis Red Sox, Detroit Stars, Cleveland Elites, Harrisburg Giants, Brooklyn Royal Giants, Wilmington Potomacs, Cincinnati Giants
OWENS, WILLIAM OSCAR—1913-34—p, of, Homestead Grays, Indianapolis ABCs, Pittsburgh Keystones, Baltimore Black Sox, Pensacola Giants
OYSTER, JAMES F.— 1924—commissioner, Eastern Colored League

P

PACE, ____—1910—2b, French Lick (IN) Plutos

PACE, BENJAMIN HARRISON (BROTHER)—1913, 1917-20, 1921-25, 1930—c, Philadelphia Quaker City Giants, Pennsylvania Red Caps, Pittsburgh Keystones, Homestead Grays

PACE, GRAHAM (EDDIE)—1930-43—of, Nashville Elite Giants, Schenectady Mohawk Giants, Brooklyn Royal Giants

PADRÓN y ACOSTA, JUAN—1915-34—p, of, manager, Cuban Stars (East & West), Brooklyn Royal Giants, Almendares Cubans, Royal Poinciana (FL), Breakers Hotel (FL), Chicago American Giants, Birmingham Black Barons, Indianapolis ABCs, Detroit Giants, Padron's Cuban Giants, Cincinnati Cuban Stars, Havana Cubans, Lincoln (NY) Stars

PADRÓN y OTOREÑA, LUIS (EL MULO)—1909-16—p, 2b, of, Cuban Stars, Paterson (NJ) Smart Set, Long Branch (NJ) Cubans, Jersey City Cubans

PAGE, ____—1912—c, Chicago Union Giants, Cuban Giants

PAGE, ____—1930—ss, Wilmington Quaker Giants

PAGE, ____—1932—1b, Gilkerson's Union Giants

PAGE, ____—1945—of, Homestead Grays

PAGE, ALLEN—1945-51—vice president, treasurer, Negro Southern League; officer, New Orleans Creoles; promoter, New Orleans Eagles

PAGE, CHARLIE—1949—3b, Durham (NC) Eagles

PAGE, GAITHA—1905-1906—owner, Topeka (KS) Giants

PAGE, JAKE (PINKY)—1946—of, San Francisco Sea Lions

PAGE, R.—1925—officer, Indianapolis ABCs

PAGE, THEODORE ROOSEVELT (TERRIBLE TED)—1926-37—of, Newark Stars, Homestead Grays, Pittsburgh Crawfords, New York Black Yankees, Newark Eagles, Philadelphia Stars, Brooklyn Royal Giants, Baltimore Black Sox, Philadelphia Quaker City Giants, Brooklyn Eagles, Chappie Johnson's All-Stars

PAGÉS y RUIZ, PEDRO ARMANDO (GAMO)—1939, 1947—of, New York Cubans

PAIGE, ____—1927—1b, Brooklyn Cuban Giants

PAIGE, ALLEN — [see PAGE, ALLEN]

PAIGE, LEROY ROBERT (SATCHEL)—1926-47, 1950, 1954-61—p, Chattanooga Black Lookouts, Birmingham Black Barons, Cleveland Cubs, Pittsburgh Crawfords, Kansas City Monarchs, New York Black Yankees, Satchel Paige All-Stars, Philadelphia Stars, Baltimore Black Sox, Chicago American Giants, St. Louis Stars, Memphis Red Sox, Trujillo All-Stars (Ciudad Trujillo Dragons); author

PAIGE, JR., SATCHEL—1963-64 [a.k.a. DOSTER, LEROY or COTTINGHAM, SHERMAN]

PAIGE, WILLIAM—1891—of, Cuban Giants

PAINE, HENRY—1884—of, Brooklyn Remsens

PAINE, JOHN—1887—of, Philadelphia Pythians (NCBBL)

PALL, ____—1913—p, Royal Poinciana (FL)

PALM, CLARENCE (SPOONY, MIDNIGHT)—1927-46—c, manager, Birmingham Black Barons, St. Louis Giants, St. Louis Stars, Detroit Stars, Cleveland Giants, Homestead Grays, Brooklyn Eagles, New York Black Yankees, Philadelphia Stars, Cole's American Giants, Akron Tyrites, Pittsburgh Crawfords, Chicago American Giants, Brooklyn Brown Dodgers, Schenectady Mohawk Giants, Newark Eagles, Denver Post Negro All-Stars

PALM, ROBERT—1936—c, St. Louis Stars

PALMA, ALCIBIADES—1930—p, Cuban Stars (West)

PALMER, ____—1913—p, St. Louis Giants

PALMER, CURTIS—1945, 1948-50—of, Birmingham Black Barons, Harlem Globetrotters, New York Black Yankees

PALMER, EARL—1918-19—ss, of, Foster's Hartford Giants, Chicago Union Giants, Lincoln (NY) Giants

PALMER, GEORGE—1959—player, Indianapolis Clowns

PALMER, JOSEPH—1887—of, New York Gorhams (NCBBL)

PALMER, LEON—1926-30—of, Dayton Marcos, Louisville White Sox

PALMER, SR., RALPH LEON—1951-55—p, Chicago American Giants, Detroit Stars, Kansas City Stars

PALMER, RUDY—1936—2b, Chicago Giants

PALMORE, EARL—1959-61—p, Indianapolis Clowns

PALMORE, MORRIS (POP, NYASSIS)—1936-42—of, p, manager, Ethiopian Clowns

PALOMINO, EMILIO ANTONIO (PAK)—1904-06, 1908, 1911—of, p, All Cubans, Cuban X-Giants, All Havanas, New York Cuban Stars

PANIER, ____—1914, 1917-20—p, of, Cuban Giants, Philadelphia Giants, Baltimore Giants

PANGBORN, THOMAS CLARINGTON (LEFTY)—1909-12—p, St. Paul Colored Gophers, Twin Cities Gophers, French Lick (IN) Plutos

PANNELL, (HANDSOME)—1914—c, Cuban Giants, New York Stars, Brooklyn All-Stars

PANYAN, ____—1918—ph, Philadelphia Giants

PAPE, ED—1946—of, Homestead Grays

PARDEE, JOHN L.—1925—c, Birmingham Black Barons

PARDO, ____—1920—p, New Orleans Crescent Stars, Pensacola Giants, Atlanta Black Crackers
PAREDA [PARERA] y MORALES, PASTOR HÉCTOR (MONK)—1909-21—p, Stars of Cuba, Cuban Stars (West), All Cubans
PAREGO [PARAGO], GEORGE A.—1885-88—p, of, 1b, Argyle Hotel, Cuban Giants, Trenton (NJ) Cuban Giants (Middle States League), Cuban Stars
PARK, JAMES—1935—utility, Newark Dodgers
PARKE [PARK, PARKER], ____—1867-71—1b, 2b, of, Mutuals of Washington
PARKER, ____—1891—of, Chicago Unions
PARKER, ____—1908—of, New York Colored Giants
PARKER, ____—1927—umpire, NNL
PARKER, ARTHUR—1920—3b, Chicago Giants
PARKER, BILLY—1937—p, Indianapolis Athletics
PARKER, CHARLES (SONNY) [see PARKER, EMORY]
PARKER, E. —1920—p, Pittsburgh Stars of Buffalo
PARKER, EMMETT—1923—trainer, New York Giants (MBL)
PARKER, EMORY Z. (FOOTS, SONNY)—1942-43—p, Chicago Brown Bombers (NML), Harrisburg-St. Louis Stars
PARKER, (FEETS)—1958—1b, Kansas City Monarchs
PARKER, GEORGE—1943—c, Newark Eagles
PARKER, HARRISON—1919—p, Lincoln (NY) Giants
PARKER, JACK—1938, 1940, 1946—ss, Pittsburgh Crawfords, New York Black Yankees, Newark Eagles, Pittsburgh Stars
PARKER, ROY—1946—p, manager, owner, Fresno/San Diego Tigers
PARKER, THOMAS (TOM, BIG TRAIN)—1929-48—p, of, manager, Memphis Red Sox, Indianapolis ABCs, Monroe (LA) Monarchs, Homestead Grays, New Orleans-St. Louis Stars, New Orleans Crescent Stars, New York Black Yankees, North Classic Team, Harrisburg-St. Louis Stars, New York Cubans, Boston Blues, Indianapolis Athletics, Nashville Elite Giants, Columbus Elite Giants, Toledo Crawfords, Birmingham Black Barons, Detroit Senators, Alexandria (LA) Lincoln (NY) Giants
PARKER, WESLEY—1890-1908—of, 1b, Genuine Cuban Giants, Chicago Unions, New York Colored Giants, Cuban X-Giants, Cleveland Giants
PARKER, WILLIE (LEFTY)—1917-23, 1926, 1928-29—p, 1b, of, Lincoln (NY) Giants, Baltimore Black Sox, Pittsburgh Stars of Buffalo, Memphis Red Sox, Montgomery Grey Sox
PARKER, WILLIE JOHN—1952—1b, Philadelphia Stars

PARKINSON, (PARKY)—1950—p, Houston Eagles
PARKS, ____—1870—1b, Mutuals of Washington
PARKS, ____—1916—p, Lincoln (NY) Stars
PARKS, ____—1928—ph, Harrisburg Giants
PARKS, ARTHUR—1937—of, Chicago Giants
PARKS, CHARLES EDISON or EDERSON (CHARLIE, HUNKY)—1940-49—c, manager, Baltimore Elite Giants, Newark Eagles, Greensboro (NC) Goshen Red Wings, Asheville Blues
PARKS, JOHN—1939-47—c, of, p, New York Black Yankees, Newark Eagles
PARKS, JOSEPH B. (JOE, BILL)—1909-19—of, c, ss, Cuban Giants, Philadelphia Giants, Brooklyn Royal Giants, Penn Red Caps of NY, Bacharach (AC) Giants
PARKS, RALPH—1936-38—p, New York Black Yankees, Knoxville Giants
PARKS, SAM—1945-46—officer, owner, Memphis Grey Sox, Little Rock Black Travelers
PARKS, WILLIAM W. (BUBBER)—1910-20—ss, 2b, of, Chicago Giants, Lincoln (NY) Giants, Chicago American Giants, Lincoln (NY) Stars, Penn Red Caps of NY, Philadelphia Giants, Chicago Union Giants, Leland Giants, Twin City Gophers
PARNELL, ____—1934, 1939—p, Bacharach (Philly) Giants, Detroit Stars
PARNELL, BRYON—1958—of, Indianapolis Clowns
PARNELL, ROY ALEXANDER (RED)—1926-50—of, manager, Birmingham Black Barons, Monroe (LA) Monarchs, New Orleans Crescent Stars, Columbus Elite Giants, Philadelphia Stars, Pittsburgh Crawfords (USL), Houston Eagles, Nashville Elite Giants, Houston Black Buffaloes, Philadelphia Hilldales (USL), Detroit Senators, Denver Post Negro All-Stars, New Orleans Black Pelicans
PARPETTI, AGUSTÍN (PULPITA)—1908-23—1b, Cuban Stars (East & West), Kansas City Monarchs, Bacharach (AC) Giants, Richmond Giants (NAA), Havana Cubans, New York Cuban Stars
PARRA, JOSÉ—1911—p, All Cubans
PARRADO, TEODORO MANUEL (MANOLO)—1921-22, 1927—1b, Cincinnati Cuban Stars, Cuban Stars (East & West)
PARRETT, ____—1880—c, Washington Manhattans
PARRETT, ____—1880—of, Washington Eagles
PARRIS, JONATHAN CLYDE (THE DUDE)—1946-49—1b, 3b, of, New York Black Yankees, Louisville Buckeyes, Philadelphia Stars, Baltimore Elite Giants
PARRISH, ____—1938—2b, Indianapolis ABCs

PARSON, ____–1908–p, Genuine Cuban Giants
PARSONS, AGUSTUS [A. S.] (GUS)–1895-97–manager, Adrian (MI) Page Fence Giants
PARSONS, ELWOOD–1950–scout, Brooklyn Dodgers
PARTLOW, ROY (SILENT ROY) E.–1934-50–p, of, Cincinnati Tigers, Memphis Red Sox, Homestead Grays, Philadelphia Stars
PASCHAL, ____–1917–2b, Los Angeles White Sox
PASSON, HARRY–1933-35–officer, Bacharach (AC) Giants, Bacharach (Philly) Giants
PASTOR, PEDRO [a.k.a. JUAN MANUEL PASTORIZA]–1924–p, Cuban Stars (West), Detroit Stars
PATE, ARCHIE–1908-17–of, c, p, St. Paul Colored Gophers, Chicago Giants, Chicago American Giants, New York Stars, Bowser's ABCs, St. Louis Giants, Brooklyn All-Stars, Minneapolis Keystones, Chicago Union Giants, Leland Giants
PATMAN, ____–1914–of, Chicago American Giants
PATTERSON, ____–1867–1b, Brooklyn Unique
PATTERSON, ____–1886–of, New York Gorhams
PATTERSON, ____–1869–of, Mutuals of Washington
PATTERSON, ____–1919–of, Lincoln (NY) Giants
PATTERSON, ____–1920–ss, p, Atlanta Black Crackers, Jacksonville Stars, Pensacola Giants
PATTERSON, ____–1922–p, Bacharach (AC) Giants
PATTERSON, ____–1922–c, Richmond Giants
PATTERSON, ____–1926–ss, Memphis Red Sox
PATTERSON, ANDREW LAWRENCE (PAT)–1934-49–2b, 3b, of, coach, Penn Red Caps of NY, Cleveland Red Sox, Pittsburgh Crawfords, Kansas City Monarchs, Philadelphia Stars, Newark Eagles, Houston Eagles, Homestead Grays, Denver Post Negro All-Stars
PATTERSON, BEN (SAMPSON)–1927, 1929, 1931–p, Shreveport Black Sports, Montgomery Grey Sox
PATTERSON, GABLE (GABRIEL)–1941-50–of, Pittsburgh Crawfords (USL), Homestead Grays, New York Black Yankees, Philadelphia Stars
PATTERSON, JOE MICHAEL–1955–of, Kansas City Monarchs
PATTERSON, JOHN W. (PAT)–1890-1907–of, 3b, manager, Lincoln (NE) Giants, Adrian (MI) Page Fence Giants, Columbia Giants of Chicago, Philadelphia Giants, Cuban X-Giants, Cuban Giants, Philadelphia Quaker City Giants, Brooklyn Royal Giants, Chicago Union Giants, Plattsmouth (Nebraska St. League)

PATTERSON, WILLIAM BENJAMIN–1914-25–manager, Houston Black Buffaloes, Austin Black Senators, Birmingham Black Barons
PATTERSON, JR., WILLIE LEE (ROY, PAT)–1945-55, 1960–c, 1b, 3b, New York Cubans, Birmingham Black Barons, Philadelphia Stars, Memphis Red Sox, Chicago American Giants, Louisville Clippers, Kansas City Monarchs, Pittsburgh Crawfords (USL), Detroit Stars, Detroit-New Orleans Stars
PATTON, ____–1913–p, French Lick (IN) Plutos
PATTON, E.–1926–p, St. Louis Stars
PATTON, JAMES–1906-14–of, p, Cuban X-Giants, Philadelphia Giants, New York Stars, Brooklyn All-Stars
PATTON, JIM–1916-21–of, p, Montgomery Grey Sox
PAUL, ____–1891–of, Cuban Giants
PAUL, ____–1908–ss, Brooklyn Colored Giants
PAUL, ____–1911, 1914–2b, c, Chicago Union Giants, Philadelphia Giants, Cuban Giants
PAUL, ____–1946–ss, of, Brooklyn Brown Dodgers
PAUL, ROBERTO L.–1957, 1960–ss, Detroit Stars, Detroit-New Orleans Stars
PAYMOND, HERBERT–1960-61–p, Birmingham Black Barons
PAYNE, ____–1906–2b, Wilmington Giants
PAYNE, ____–1928–of, p, Birmingham Black Barons
PAYNE, ____–1948–p, Birmingham Clowns
PAYNE, ANDREW PATRICK (JAP)–1902-22–of, p, Philadelphia Giants, Cuban X-Giants, Leland Giants, Chicago American Giants, Chicago Union Giants, New York Central Red Caps, Brooklyn Royal Giants, Penn Red Caps of NY, Lincoln (NY) Stars, Chicago Giants, Lincoln (NY) Giants, Grand Central Terminal Red Caps, Schenectady Mohawk Giants
PAYNE [PAINE], ERNEST (RUSTY)–1937, 1940–of, Cincinnati Tigers, Indianapolis Crawfords
PAYNE, FELIX HALL–1909-10–utility, officer, Kansas City (KS) Giants
PAYNE, HOWARD–1926-31–2b, p, Brooklyn Royal Giants, Newark Stars, Philadelphia Giants, Baltimore Black Sox, Philadelphia Colored Giants of New York
PAYNE, JAMES–1887-88–of, Baltimore Lord Baltimores (NCBBL), Trenton (NJ) Cuban Giants (Middle States League), Cuban Giants, Philadelphia Pythians (NCBBL)
PAYNE, TOM–1933–of, Homestead Grays, Baltimore Black Sox, Pittsburgh Crawfords

PAYNE, WILLIAM (DOC)—1898—of, Celoron (NY) Acme Colored Giants (Iron & Oil League)
PAYTON, ____—1931—of, Cincinnati Tigers
PEACE, WILLIAM WARREN (FATHER DIVINE, BILL)—1945-48—p, Newark Eagles
PEACOCK, PETE—1933—3b, Homestead Grays
PEAK, RUFUS—1931—officer, Detroit Stars
PEAKS, ____—1931—p, Montgomery Grey Sox
PEARCE, JOHNNY (YOGI)—1957-58—of, Kansas City Monarchs
PEARSON, ____—1929—of, Wichita Falls Spudders
PEARSON, [see PATTERSON, JOHN W.]—1903-04—of, p, Philadelphia Giants, Cuban Giants
PEARSON, F.W.—1921—president, Blue Ridge Colored League
PEARSON, FRANK (IVY, WAHOO)—1945-54—p, Memphis Red Sox, Chicago American Giants, Louisville Clippers
PEARSON, JIMMY—1948-49—p, New York Cubans, New York Black Yankees
PEARSON, LEONARD CURTIS (LENNIE, HOSS)—1936-50—of, 3b, ss, 1b, manager, Newark Eagles, Baltimore Elite Giants, Philadelphia Stars, North All-Stars, North Classic Team, Biz Mackey All-Stars
PEARSON, RUTLEDGE HENRY—1951—1b, Chicago American Giants
PEATROS, PETE—1913—2b, Homestead Grays
PEATROS, MAURICE (BABY FACE, LEFTY)—1944-47—1b, Homestead Grays, Pittsburgh Crawfords (USL), Brooklyn Brown Dodgers (USL)
PEDA, ____—1915—of, Cuban Stars
PEDEMONTE, MARIO—1926—p, Cuban Stars (West)
PEDRERA, PAUL—1927, 1931—c, Cuban Stars (East), Newark Browns
PEDROS, ____—1913-14—3b, All Nations
PEDROSO, EUSTAQUIO (BOMBIA, BOMBIN)—1910-30—p, 1b, c, All Cubans, Cuban Stars (East & West)
PEDROSO, FERNANDO DÍAZ (EL BICHO) [see DÍAZ y PEDROSO, FERNANDO]
PEDROSO, RAFAEL (SUNGO)—1926-31, 1937, 1b, p, Newark Browns, Stars of Cuba, Cuban Stars (East)
PEEBLES, ARTHUR J.—1933—officer, Columbus Blue Birds
PEEKS, A. J.—1932—officer, Atlanta Black Crackers
PEEPLES, NATHANIEL (NAT)—1948-51—c, of, Kansas City Monarchs, Indianapolis Clowns, Memphis Red Sox
PEERMAN, W. DONALD—1946—p, Indianapolis Clowns

PEETE, CHARLES (MULE)—1950—of, Indianapolis Clowns
PELHAM, CHARLES—1939-41—2b, 3b, of, Schenectady Mohawk Giants
PELHAM, WILLIAM (DON)—1933-38—of, Bacharach (Philly) Giants, Atlanta Black Crackers
PELL, ____—1867—3b, Utica (NY) Fearless
PELL, THEODORE (TEED)—1894-95—of, Cuban Giants
PELL, WALTER J.—1886-89—officer, New York Gorhams
PELLAS, ____—1923—p, Cuban Stars (West)
PEÑA, L.—1929—c, 1b, Cuban Stars (West)
PEÑALVER, CUNALGIO (JULIO)—1947-48—umpire, NNL
PENDER, ____—1869—3b, Rockford (IL) Rockfords
PENDERGRAPH, HAYES—1929—officer, San Antonio Black Bears
PENDLETON, JAMES EDWARD (JIM)—1947-48—ss, Asheville Blues, Chicago American Giants
PENHAM, ____—1872—of, Keystone Club of New Jersey
PENN, ____—1922—1b, Bacharach (AC) Giants
PENNINGTON, ____—1929—p, Nashville Elite Giants
PENNINGTON, ARTHUR DAVID (ART, SUPERMAN)—1940-51—of, 1b, 2b, Chicago American Giants, Pittsburgh Crawfords, Birmingham Black Barons
PENNINGTON, JIM—1950—of, New York Black Yankees
PENNO [PANNA], DANIEL—1887-1898—p, of, 2b, ss, Boston Resolutes (NCBBL), Cuban Giants, Cuban X-Giants, Providence Grays
PENOY, ____—1932—c, Penn Red Caps of NY
PENTO, ____—1929—p, Boston Black Sox
PEOPLES, EDDIE—1933—p, Memphis Red Sox
PEPPERS, CHARLES—1955—of, Memphis Red Sox
PERDUE, FRANK M.—1920-34—president, NSL; president, manager, Birmingham Black Barons
PEREIRA, JOSÉ (PEPIN)—1947—p, Baltimore Elite Giants
PÉREZ, ____—1920—ss, Birmingham Black Barons
PÉREZ, INOCENCIO—1905-07—p, All Cubans, Cuban X-Giants, Havana Stars, Cuban Stars
PÉREZ, JAVIER (BLUE)—1933-45, 1948—2b, 3b, New York Cubans, Brooklyn Eagles, Homestead Grays, Bacharach (Philly) Giants, Indianapolis Clowns
PÉREZ, JOSÉ (PEPIN)—1911-37—1b, c, Cuban Stars (East & West), Harrisburg Giants, Hilldale Club, Madison Stars
PÉREZ, JULIÁN (FALLANCA)—1910-11—p, Stars of Cuba, Cuban Stars
PÉREZ, LUIS [see CABALLERO, LUIS]
PÉREZ, PROPENCIO—1949—p, Memphis Red Sox

PÉREZ, TEODORO—1915—of, Havana Reds

PERISEE, GEORGE—1942, 1945—of, Minneapolis-St. Paul Colored Gophers, Chicago Brown Bombers (USL), Detroit Motor City Giants

PERKINS, CECIL—1944—1b, Kansas City Monarchs

PERKINS, CHESTER—1946—3b, Detroit Stars

PERKINS, JOHN (JOHNNY)—1964—ss, Satchel Paige All-Stars

PERKINS, VERNE—1929—3b, Birmingham Black Barons

PERKINS, WILLIAM GAMIEL (BILL, CY)—1926-48—c, manager, Birmingham Black Barons, Cleveland Cubs, Pittsburgh Crawfords, Cleveland Stars, Philadelphia Stars, Baltimore Elite Giants, New York Black Yankees, Denver Post Negro All-Stars, Homestead Grays, Atlanta Black Crackers, Brooklyn Royal Giants, Montgomery Grey Sox, Trujillo All-Stars (Ciudad Trujillo Dragons)

PERNELL, ____—1916—p, Penn Red Caps of NY

PERRIGAN [PURGEN], JOHN ROBERT—1916-21—2b, Penn Red Caps of NY, Madison Stars, Hilldale Club

PERRY, ____—1916—of, All Nations

PERRY, SR., ALONZO THOMAS (TAPYA, SPEEDY, EL GIGANTA AZUL)—1946-50—p, 1b, of, Chattanooga Choo Choos, Homestead Grays, Birmingham Black Barons, San Francisco Sea Lions, Atlanta Black Crackers

PERRY, CARLISLE [CARYLE] (CARL, CASH, NATIVE SON)—1917-27, 1946—2b, 3b, ss, owner, manager, Detroit Stars, Bacharach (AC) Giants, Washington Potomacs, Lincoln (NY) Giants, Cleveland Browns, Baltimore Black Sox, Indianapolis ABCs, Hilldale Club, Cleveland Tate Stars, Richmond Giants (NAA), Norfolk Stars, Los Angeles White Sox, Breakers Hotel (FL)

PERRY, C. J.—1887—treasurer, Philadelphia Pythians (NCBBL)

PERRY, DON—1920-27—1b, Madison Stars, Washington Braves, Harrisburg Giants, Schenectady Mohawk Giants, Philadelphia Royal Giants

PERRY, ED—1887—3b, Washington Capital Citys, South Baltimore Mutuals

PERRY, EDDIE—1943-44—p, Baltimore Elite Giants, Philadelphia Stars

PERRY, HANK—1926—p, Hilldale Club

PERRY, LAWSON—1921—3b, Houston Black Buffaloes

PERRY, LEON (LYNN)—1934, 1937-40—p, Newark Dodgers, Schenectady Mohawk Giants

PERRY, WALTER—1936, 1941—1b, 2b, Homestead Grays, Schenectady Mohawk Giants

PERTELL [PURTELL], WILLIAM—1911—2b, Brown's Tennessee Rats

PERVIN, ____—1929—p, Fort Worth Panthers

PERVIS [PURVIS], ____—1931-32, 1937—of, Memphis Red Sox, Monroe (LA) Monarchs, Birmingham Black Barons

PERVIS, ____—1947—p, New Orleans Creoles

PETERS, ____—1869—p, Philadelphia Excelsior

PETERS, ____—1915—p, Pittsburgh Giants

PETERS, ____—1916—c, Lincoln (NY) Stars

PETERS, LEE B. (FRANK)—1914-23—ss, Chicago Union Giants, Chicago Giants

PETERS, RALPH—1939—of, Bacharach (Philly) Giants

PETERS, SAM—1920—of, Nashville White Sox

PETERS, WILLIAM STITT (W.S., HANDSOME WILLIE)—1887-1923—1b, owner, manager, Chicago Unions, Chicago Union Giants, Chicago Resolutes

PETERSON, ____—1867-68—1b, 2b, ss, Brooklyn Unique, Actives of Philadelphia, Utica (NY) Fearless

PETERSON, ____—1914—p, Chicago American Giants, Baltimore Giants

PETERSON, ____—1919—2b, Grand Central Terminal Red Caps

PETERSON, ALEX—1946—utility, Pittsburgh Stars

PETERSON, HARVEY (PETE)—1931-37, 1946—of, p, 1b, 2b, ss, Montgomery Grey Sox, Knoxville Giants, Birmingham Black Barons, Memphis Red Sox, Cincinnati Tigers, Cleveland Clippers, Brooklyn Brown Dodgers, Cleveland Cubs, Detroit Motor City Giants

PETERSON, L.—1885-86, 1888-91—1b, p, Brooklyn Remsens, Chicago Unions, New York Gorhams

PETERSON, NORMAN—1938—umpire, NAL

PETERSON, ROBERT W. (BOB)—1925—p, Cooperstown Giants

PETIT, RAFAEL—1906—3b, Havana Stars

PETREE, DENNIS—1927, 1930—of, Baltimore Black Sox, Columbus Keystones

PETRICOLA, ____—1924—p, Cuban Stars (West)

PETTIFORD, ____—1918—of, Dayton Marcos

PETTIS, W. H.—1920—officer, Nashville Elite Giants

PETTUS, WILLIAM THOMAS (ZACK, BILL)—1909-23—c, 1b, manager, Kansas City (KS) Giants, Philadelphia Giants, Leland Giants, Chicago Giants, Lincoln (NY) Stars, Lincoln (NY) Giants, St. Louis Giants, Hilldale Club, Bacharach (AC) Giants, Richmond Giants (NAA), Harrisburg Giants, Brooklyn Royal Giants, Chicago American Giants, Grand Central Terminal Red Caps, Breakers Hotel (FL)

PETWAY, BRUCE FRANKLIN (BUDDY)—1906-25—c, 1b, manager, Leland Giants, Brooklyn Royal Giants, Philadelphia Giants, Chicago American Giants, Detroit Stars, Cuban X-Giants, Royal Poinciana (FL)
PETWAY, HOWARD—1906, 1908—p, Leland Giants, St. Paul Colored Gophers
PETWAY, SHERLEY (CHARLIE)—1931-32, 1937-44—ss, 2b, c, of, manager, Nashville Elite Giants, Birmingham Black Barons, Louisville Black Caps, Detroit Stars, Chicago Brown Bombers (NML), Cleveland Buckeyes
PHELAN, ____—1918-19—umpire, Independent Colored teams
PHELPS, ____—1938—p, Baltimore Elite Giants
PHELPS, ROY—1945—of, Birmingham Black Barons
PHIFFER, ____—1937—3b, ss, St. Louis Stars
PHIFFER, JOHN—1921—p, Indianapolis ABCs [see FIFER, JOHN]
PHIFFER, LESTER J.—1951-53—ss, 3b, Kansas City Monarchs, Kansas City (KS) Giants
PHILLIPS, ____—1906—of, Philadelphia Quaker City Giants
PHILLIPS, ____—1910—c, Cuban Stars
PHILLIPS, ____—1920-27—ss, 2b, 3b, of, Nashville Elite Giants, Detroit Stars, Milwaukee Bears, Nashville White Sox, New Orleans-St. Louis Stars
PHILLIPS, CARD—1911—2b, ss, Minneapolis Keystones
PHILLIPS, ERNIE—1927—p, Birmingham Black Barons
PHILLIPS, HARRY—1916-17—2b, Hilldale Club
PHILLIPS, JOHN (FIFER)—1939-40—p, Baltimore Elite Giants, Memphis Red Sox
PHILLIPS, MOSES (MULE)—1946—1b, Homestead Grays
PHILLIPS, NORRIS (PLAYBOY)—1942-46—p, Kansas City Monarchs, Memphis Red Sox, Harlem Globetrotters, Portland Rosebuds
PHILLIPS, JR., RICHARD ALBASO (DICK)—1952-55—p, Kansas City Monarchs
PHILLIPS, VERNON—1946—p, Asheville Blues
PHILLIPS, WALTER—1920—officer, Nashville Elite Giants
PICCARD, ____—1941—c, New Orleans-St. Louis Stars
PICKENS, ____—1920-21—p, Birmingham Black Barons
PICKERING, F.D.—1940—officer, Cleveland Bears
PIERCE, ____—1921—p, Norfolk Giants
PIERCE, ALBERT—1876—ss, St. Louis Blue Stockings
PIERCE, HERBERT [see PIERCE, WILLIAM]
PIERCE, JOHNNIE—1937—owner, Ethiopian Clowns
PIERCE, LEONARD—1923-27—p, of, Wilmington Potomacs, Philadelphia Giants, Schenectady Mohawk Giants, Philadelphia Royal Giants
PIERCE, STEVE—1925-28—officer, owner, Detroit Stars
PIERCE, JR., WILLIAM HERBERT (BIG BILL, BONEHEAD)—1910-32—1b, c, umpire, Philadelphia Giants, Chicago American Giants, Lincoln (NY) Stars, Lincoln (NY) Giants, Penn Red Caps of NY, Bacharach (AC) Giants, Norfolk Giants, Detroit Stars, Homestead Grays, Baltimore Black Sox, Norfolk Stars, Schenectady Mohawk Giants, Pittsburgh Crawfords, Wilmington Potomacs, Royal Poinciana (FL)
PIERRE, JR., JOSEPH—1950-51—3b, Kansas City Monarchs
PIERRE [PERRY], ROGERS (SHARPE, ASKARI)—1934-48, 1954—p, Chicago American Giants, Colored House of David, Cincinnati-Indianapolis Clowns, Cincinnati Ethiopian Clowns (NML), Cincinnati Tigers, New Orleans Black Pelicans, Harlem Globetrotters, Seattle Steelheads, Memphis Red Sox
PIERSON, ____—1927, 1931, 1933, 1937, 1942, 1943—2b, of, 3b, St. Louis Giants, Homestead Grays, Birmingham Black Barons, St. Louis Stars, Chicago Brown Bombers (NML)
PIGG, LEONARD DANIEL (FATTY, LEN)—1947-51—c, Havana Las Palomas, Indianapolis Clowns, Cleveland Buckeyes
PIGGOTT, ____—1871—2b, Chelsea Auroras
PILLAR, ____—1931, 1938—ss, Nashville Elite Giants
PILLAR, JOSÉ—1917—p, Havana Cubans
PILLOT y MASSÓ, LUIS GUILLERMO (GUILLO)—1941, 1943-44—p, New York Black Yankees, Cincinnati Ethiopian Clowns (NML), Great Lakes Bluejackets
PILOTO, JOSÉ (POTOTO, HIDDEN BALL)—1948-50—p, Memphis Red Sox
PILUZO, ____—1935—of, p, New York Cubans [see DIHIGO y LLANOS, MARTÍN]
PINDER, ____—1887—2b, South Baltimore Mutuals
PINDER, ____—1934—3b, Homestead Grays
PINDER, EARNEST SYLVESTER (MONK)—1910, 1916—of, Hilldale Club
PINDER, EDDIE (POTATO)—1914-16—of, Hilldale Club
PINDER, FREDRICK (FRED)—1910-17—ss, Hilldale Club
PINE, FELIX—1954—p, Detroit Stars
PING, ____—1914—1b, Philadelphia Giants
PINGHAM, ____—1872—3b, Keystone Club of New Jersey
PINKNEY, ____—1880—c, Washington Douglass Club

PINKSTON, ALFRED CHARLES (AL)—1936, 1949-50—1b, St. Louis Stars, New Orleans Creoles
PINSON, F.E.—1909-10, 1914—p, Birmingham Giants, Philadelphia Giants
PINTO, ____—1914-15—p, of, New York Stars, Brooklyn All-Stars, Cuban Giants
PIPKINS, ROBERT M. (LEFTY, DIAMOND, BLACK DIAMOND)—1928-34, 1940-42, 1946-47—p, Birmingham Black Barons, Cleveland Cubs, New Orleans Crescent Stars, Cincinnati Crescents, Detroit Senators, Houston Black Buffaloes, New Orleans Black Pelicans
PIRTLE, JAMES W. (JW)—1949-51—p, Houston Eagles, New Orleans Eagles
PITMAN, ____—1916—p, West Baden (IN) Sprudels
PITTS, ____—1930—2b, of, Houston Black Buffaloes
PITTS, ____—1944-45—ss, 3b, New York Black Yankees, Newark Eagles
PITTS, CURTIS EUGENE—1950-51—c, ss, Chicago American Giants, Cleveland Buckeyes
PITTS, ED—1940—c, Philadelphia Stars
PITTS, JAMES—1921—officer, Cleveland Tate Stars
PITTS, WILLIAM A.—1875—of, St. Louis Blue Stockings
PLA, T.—1933—p, Cuban Stars (West)
PLAVE, ____—1906—p, Cuban X-Giants [see OLAVE, PEDRO]
PLOCK, ____—1889—of, Philadelphia Giants
PLUMMER, ____—1912—3b, Pittsburgh Giants
PLUMMER, ____—1933—of, Baltimore Stars
PLUMMER, ALEXANDER—1884—3b, Chicago Unknowns, Chicago Gordons
PLUMMER, ARTIS—1949—2b, Durham (NC) Eagles
PLUMMER, [BISHOP] HOWARD Z.—1938-39—owner, Belleville (VA) Grays, officer, ECL
PLUNO, [see PENNO, DAN]
POINDEXTER, ____—1891—p, New York Gorhams
POINDEXTER, CHET—1958—p, Detroit Clowns
POINDEXTER, H.—1888—of, Providence Grays
POINDEXTER, MALCOLM—1960-64—officer, Indianapolis Clowns
POINDEXTER, ROBERT ALBERT (ROY)—1924-29—p, Birmingham Black Barons, Chicago American Giants, Memphis Red Sox
POINSETTE, ROBERT—1939—of, p, New York Black Yankees, Toledo Crawfords
POINTER, ____—1887—p, 3b, Binghamton, NY (Int. League)

POINTER, ROBERT LEE—1960-62—p, Kansas City Monarchs
POLAMBO, FRANK—1910—owner, New Orleans Baseball Club
POLANCO y CRUZ, RAFAEL (RALPH)—1941-42—p, Newark Eagles, Philadelphia Stars
POLE (POOLE), JOHN—1859-62, p, Unknown Base Ball Club (of Weeksville, NY)
POLES, ____—1913—1b, Chicago Union Giants
POLES, EDWARD (POSSUM, GOOGLES)—1922-31—ss, 3b, Baltimore Black Sox, Harrisburg Giants, Schenectady Mohawk Giants
POLES, SPOTTSWOOD (SPOT)—1909-23, 1935—of, umpire, Philadelphia Giants, Lincoln (NY) Giants, Brooklyn Royal Giants, Lincoln (NY) Stars, Hilldale Club, Bacharach (AC) Giants, Harrisburg Giants, Richmond Giants, Breakers Hotel (FL)
POLLARD, ____—1905—2b, Chicago Unions, Illinois Giants
POLLARD, ____—1936—of, St. Louis Stars
POLLARD, SR., FREDERICK DOUGLASS (FRITZ)—1942—vice-president, Negro Major Baseball League of America
POLLARD, SR., [REV] NATHANIEL HAWTHORNE (NAT)—1946-50—p, Birmingham Black Barons, author
POLLOCK, SYDNEY SAMUEL (SYD)—1926-60—officer, owner, Havana Red Sox, Cuban House of David, Cuban Stars (West), Ethiopian Clowns, Cincinnati Ethiopian Clowns (NML), Indianapolis Clowns
POMPEZ, GONZALO ALEJANDRO (ALEX) [a.k.a ANTONIO MORENO]—1917-50—officer, Cuban Stars (East), New York Cubans; vice-president, NNL
PONCE, ____—1919—of, Cuban Stars
PONTELLO, ____—1927—p, Cuban Stars (East)
POOLE, ____—1921—2b, Chicago Union Giants
POOLE, CLAUDE—1945-46—p, of, New York Black Yankees
POOLE, DAN—1944—p, Jacksonville Red Caps
POOLE, EDGAR—1932—1b, Chicago American Giants
POOLE, MILT—1946—p, San Francisco Sea Lions
POPE, ____—1932—1b, Penn Red Caps
POPE, CHARLES—1920—3b, Pensacola Giants
POPE, DAVID (DAVE)—1946-48—2b, 3b, of, Homestead Grays, Detroit Senators, Pittsburgh Crawfords (USL)
POPE, EDGAR—1938—of, Atlanta Black Crackers
POPE, EDWARD (LITTLE)—1947—of, Detroit Senators

POPE, JAMES—1931-33—p, Louisville White Sox, Montgomery Grey Sox, Columbus Blue Birds
POPE, JOHN—1884—utility, St. Louis Black Stockings
POPE, WILLIAM ROBERT (WEE WILLIE, BILL)—1945-48—p, Pittsburgh Crawfords (USL), Pittsburgh Stars, Homestead Grays
POPLE, ____—1867—ss, Monrovia Club of Harrisburg
POREE [PORSEE], SALVADOR—1921—p, St. Louis Giants
PORTER, ____—1909—player, Harrisburg Giants
PORTER, ____—1925—p, Gilkerson's Union Giants
PORTER, ANDREW—1885—of, Chicago Gordons
PORTER, ANDREW V. (ANDY, PULLMAN)—1932-50—p, Little Rock Grays, Cleveland Cubs, Nashville Elite Giants, Washington Elite Giants, Baltimore Elite Giants, Indianapolis Clowns, Columbus Elite Giants, Louisville Black Caps, Newark Eagles, Foster Memorial Giants
PORTER, BERNARD (BERNIE) DON—1958—Detroit Clowns
PORTER, CHARLIE—1921—of, Cincinnati Cuban Stars
PORTER, CLARENCE [see FLOYD, PORTER LEE]—1913—of, Indianapolis ABCs
PORTER, JAMES H.—1889—2b, of, Brooklyn Alpine
PORTER, MERLE McKINLEY (BUGS BUNNY)—1949-50—1b, Kansas City Monarchs
PORTER, R. —1944—c, Chicago Monarchs
PORTER, THOMAS—1932—p, Chicago Giants, Colored House of David
PORTER, WALLACE—1954—p, Detroit Stars
PORTER, WILL H.—1894-1899—co-founder, *Indianapolis Recorder*
PORTIER, JR., JAMES AUDLEY (ROCKY)—1954-57—c, Indianapolis Clowns, New York Black Yankees
PORTLOCK, ____—1913—c, Dayton Marcos
PORTLOCK, ____—1933—c, Chicago American Giants
PORTUONDO [PORTUANDO], BARTOLOME (BARTOLO)—1915-27—3b, 1b, Almendares Cubans, Kansas City Monarchs, Cuban Stars (East)
POSEY, CUMBERLAND WILLIS (CUM, a.k.a. CUMBERLAND CUMBERT)—1911-46—of, officer, Homestead Grays, Detroit Wolves; founder, EWL; secretary, treasurer, NNL
POSEY, ETHEL SHAW TRUMAN—1947—officer, Homestead Grays
POSEY, JEFF RAY—1936—p, Birmingham Black Barons
POSEY, SEWARD HAYES (SEE, SEA)—1911-48—officer, business manager, Homestead Grays

POST, ____—1916—of, Lincoln (NY) Stars
POSTELL, ____—1934—2b, Cincinnati Tigers
POTTER, ____—1884—1b, Brooklyn Alpines
POTTER, ____—1921—c, Kansas City Monarchs
POTTER, LAMAR—1932-34—of, p, Atlanta Black Crackers, Monroe (LA) Monarchs, Louisville Red Caps, Louisville Black Caps
POTTER, WILLIAM H.—1894-1924—co-founder, publisher, *Indianapolis Recorder*
POTTS, ____—1926—umpire, ECL
POTTS, ____—1929—1b, Colored House of David
POVIE, SR., BENJAMIN C. —1858-59—president, c, Unknown Base Ball Club (of Weeksville, NY)
POVIE, F. —1859—of, Unknown Base Ball Club (of Weeksville, NY)
POWE, LIND—1926—p, of, New Orleans Black Pelicans
POWELL, ____—1914-15—p, Lincoln (NY) Giants
POWELL, ____—1928—p, Baltimore Black Sox
POWELL, ____—1928—ph, Cleveland Tigers
POWELL, BEN—1917-24—owner, Kansas City Royals
POWELL, EDWARD D. (EDDIE, BIG RED, BOCHE)—1936-38—c, New York Black Yankees, Washington Black Senators, New York Cubans, St. Louis Stars, Schenectady Mohawk Giants, Philadelphia Stars
POWELL, ELVIN (SHOELESS)—1931—2b, Memphis Red Sox
POWELL, JAMES—1874-79—p, c, 3b, Chicago Uniques
POWELL, JESSE—1931—officer, Little Rock Black Travelers
POWELL, JOHNNY—1946—c, Boston Blues
POWELL, LEROY—1933—p, Akron Tyrites
POWELL, MALVIN [MELVIN] (PUTT)—1929-45—p, of, Cole's American Giants, Chicago American Giants, Chicago Columbia Giants, Birmingham Black Barons, Chicago Brown Bombers (USL), Chicago Giants
POWELL, RICHARD DENNIS (DICK)—1938-52—officer, business manager, Baltimore Elite Giants, Nashville Elite Giants
POWELL, ROY (RED)—1938-39, 1941—p, of, Philadelphia Stars, Washington Black Senators, Newark Eagles
POWELL, RUSSELL HAROLD—1914-21—c, Indianapolis ABCs, Royal Poinciana (FL)
POWELL, WILLIAM—1874-76—ss, Chicago Uniques
POWELL, WILLIAM HENRY (BILL)—1946-52—p, Birmingham Black Barons

POWELL, WILLIE ERNEST (WEE WILLIE, PIGGY)–1925-36–p, Chicago American Giants, Detroit Stars, Cole's American Giants, Cleveland Red Sox, Chicago Giants

POWER, JR., JOHN–1858–treasurer, Unknown Base Ball Club (of Weeksville, NY)

POWERS, ____–1926–p, Nashville Elite Giants

PRACTOR [PRATER], AL–1887, 1890–player, Louisville Falls City (NCBBL)

PRADER, ____–1929–p, Houston Black Buffaloes

PRAGUE, ____–1939–of, New York Cuban [see PAGES, PEDRO]

PRATS [PRATZ, PRATO], ESTEBAN [ESTABAN]–1899, 1907–1b, All Cubans, Cuban Stars

PRATS, MIGUEL–1899, 1902, 1906-07–of, All Cubans, Cuban Stars

PRATT, ____–1872–of, Amicable Club of New York

PRATT, ____–1927–2b, Wilmington Potomacs

PRATT, P.L.–writer, *Pittsburgh Courier*

PRATT, RYLAND D.–1922-23–owner, Indianapolis ABCs

PRATT, WALTER–1929–p, Houston Black Buffaloes

PRESLEY, LAWSON–1958–Kansas City Monarchs, Detroit Clowns

PRESSWOOD, SR., HENRY (HANK, BABY)–1948-52–ss, Cleveland Buckeyes, Kansas City Monarchs

PRESTON, ____–1920–c, Montgomery Grey Sox

PRESTON, ____–1920–1b, Jacksonville Stars

PRESTON, ALBERT WEBBER (AL)–1943-52–p, New York Black Yankees, Chicago American Giants, Baltimore Elite Giants, Pittsburgh Crawfords (USL), Boston Blues, Brooklyn Brown Dodgers

PRESTON, LEROY–1932–batboy, Chicago American Giants

PRESTON, ROBERT–1950–p, Baltimore Elite Giants

PRICE, ____–1908–p, Cuban Giants

PRICE, ____–1916, 1923–of, Bacharach (AC) Giants

PRICE, ____–1920, 1922–c, 3b, Pensacola Giants, Pittsburgh Keystones

PRICE, ACIE–1884–p, St. Louis Eclipse

PRICE, DAVE–1884, 1887–c, St. Louis Eclipse, St. Louis Black Stockings

PRICE, EWELL–1951–c, New Orleans Eagles

PRICE, HENRY–1867-71–2b, 3b, ss, Philadelphia Excelsior, Philadelphia Pythians (NCBBL), Actives of Philadelphia

PRICE, JAMES–1942–p, Richmond Hilldales

PRICE, MARVIN DANIEL (BIG MERV, THUMPER)–1950-52, 1956–1b, Cleveland Buckeyes, Chicago American Giants, New Orleans Eagles, Memphis Red Sox

PRICE, WILLIE–1951–p, Birmingham Black Barons

PRIDE, CHARLEY FRANK (MINNIE)–1953-56, 1958-59–p, of, Memphis Red Sox, Birmingham Black Barons

PRIDE, JR., [REV.] MACK A.–1956–p, Kansas City Monarchs

PRIETO, GEORGE (BOBO)–1959–utility, Indianapolis Clowns

PRIMM [PRIM], WILLIAM (SHEENEY)–1902-11–c, Leland Giants, St. Louis Giants, Indianapolis ABCs, Chicago Union Giants, Cuban Giants

PRIMM, CHARLES RANDOLPH–1925-26–p, Kansas City Monarchs

PRIMROSE, WILLIAM–1892–manager, New York Gorhams

PRINCE, ____–1884–of, Newark Dusky Boys

PRINCE, JOHN (BUSTER)–1936, 1944–3b, p, Chicago American Giants

PRINGLE, GASTON–1957–Indianapolis Clowns

PRINGLE, RANSOM–1898–p, 3b, Celoron (NY) Acme Colored Giants (Iron & Oil League)

PRIOR, ROBERT A.–1916-17–p, St. Louis Giants, Bowser's ABCs; officer, St. Paul Colored Gophers

PRITCHETT, DEWITT–1943–p, Atlanta Black Crackers

PRITCHETT [PRITCHARD], WILBERT (WILBUR, LEFTY)–1921-33–p, Harrisburg Giants, Baltimore Black Sox, Brooklyn Royal Giants, Hilldale Club, Bacharach (AC) Giants, Brooklyn Cuban Giants, Philadelphia Tigers

PROCTOR, ____–1868–of, Actives of Philadelphia

PROCTOR, ____–1880–of, Washington Uniques

PROCTOR, CLARENCE–1913–p, St. Louis Giants

PROCTOR, GEORGE–1938, 1940–p, Philadelphia Stars, New York Black Yankees

PROCTOR, JAMES (CUB)–1884-87–p, c, ss, Baltimore Atlantics, Baltimore Lord Baltimores (NCBBL)

PROCTOR, JAMES ARTHUR (JIM)–1955–p, Indianapolis Clowns, New York Black Yankees

PROPHET, MALLIE (WILLIE)–1934–of, Bacharach (Philly) Giants

PROVENS, ____–1945–of, Cleveland Buckeyes

PRUE, ____–1951–1b, New Orleans Eagles

PRYOR, ____–1905–p, Chicago Columbia Giants

PRYOR, ALBERT–1946–infield, Homestead Grays

PRYOR, ANDERSON—1922-27, 1931-33, 1937—2b, ss, New Orleans Crescent Stars, Milwaukee Bears, Detroit Stars; umpire, 1935-36, 1945, NAL
PRYOR, BILL—1927-31—p, Memphis Red Sox, Detroit Stars, Detroit Giants
PRYOR, EDWARD—1925-34—2b, Lincoln (NY) Giants, Penn Red Caps of NY, Royal Poinciana (FL)
PRYOR, WESLEY (WHIP)—1905-17—3b, p, Chicago Columbia Giants, Cuban X Giants, Illinois Giants, Chicago Union Giants, Leland Giants, Chicago American Giants, St. Louis Giants, Chicago Giants, Schenectady Mohawk Giants, Brooklyn Royal Giants, Louisville White Sox, Lincoln (NY) Stars, Indianapolis ABCs, Jewell's ABCs, Bowser's ABCs, Cuban Stars, St. Paul Colored Gophers
PUCKETT, ____—1920—ss, Chicago Black Sox
PUGH, JOHN (JOHNNY)—1908, 1912-22, 1928—of, manager, Schenectady Mohawk Giants, Brooklyn Royal Giants, Philadelphia Giants, Bacharach (AC) Giants, Harrisburg Giants, Lincoln (NY) Giants, Lincoln (NY) Stars, Cuban Stars, Atlanta Grey Sox
PULLAM [PULLIAM], ARTHUR EUGENE (CHICK)—1908-15—c, Kansas City (KS) Giants, Kansas City (MO) Royal Giants
PULLEN, O'NEAL (NEAL)—1920-29, 1931, 1933-34—c, Brooklyn Royal Giants, Kansas City Monarchs, Baltimore Black Sox, Lincoln (NY) Giants, Philadelphia Royal Giants, Cleveland Royal Giants, Pullen's Royal Giants
PULLER, ____—1907—c, Harrisburg Giants
PUNCH, ____—1922-23—p, Baltimore Black Sox, Washington Potomacs
PURCELL, HERMAN D. [HARMON] (FLASH)—1944-47—3b, p, Cleveland Buckeyes, Memphis Red Sox, Kansas City Monarchs
PURNELL, ____—1919—p, Wilmington Giants
PURNELL, BYRON W.—1958-60—of, Indianapolis Clowns
PURNELL, JAMES W.—1867-69—officer, Philadelphia Pythians (NCBBL)
PURNSLEY, W. S.—1887—player, Louisville Falls City (NCBBL)
PURGEN, JOHN—1920-21—2b, Madison Stars, Hilldale Club [see PERRIGAN, JOHN ROBERT]
PURSON, ____—1883—c, Louisville Falls City
PUTNAM, ____—1884—of, Brooklyn Alpines

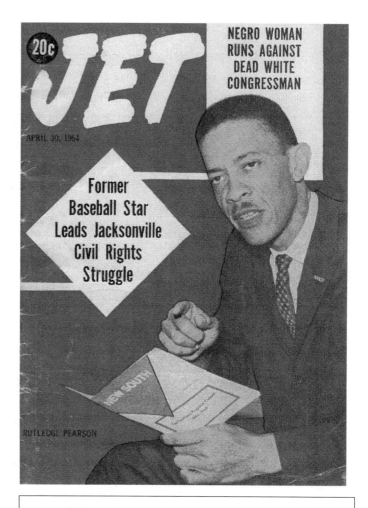

Rutledge Pearson, 1b, 1951 Chicago American Giant

Q

QUALDERS, ____—1926—umpire, NNL

QUARLES, ____—1917—umpire, Independent Colored teams

QUARTERMAN, JR., ISIAH [ISRAEL, IKE] CLIFFORD—1949, 1955—c, Durham (NC) Eagles, Indianapolis Clowns, Albany (NY) Black Sox, Jacksonville Braves, New York Black Yankees

QUATO [PLATO], ____—1928—1b, Havana Red Sox

QUEEN, ____—1898—of, Chicago Unions

QUEVEDO [GUEREDE], MANUAL SANTOS—1956—p, Detroit Stars

QUICKSLEY, ____—1937—of, Birmingham Black Barons

QUIDGLEY y RODRÍGUEZ, SANTIAGO—1954—p, Louisville Clippers

QUINCY, ____—1922—2b, ss, Bacharach (AC) Giants

QUINCY, C.—1915—of, St. Louis Cubs

QUINN (QUEST), BILL—1922-23—p, All Nations

QUINN, GEORGE—1939—manager, Quinn Stars

QUIÑONES, TOMÁS [THOMAS] PLANCHARON—1946-47—p, Indianapolis Clowns

QUINTANA, PEDRO SIERRA (PETE) [see SIERRA, PEDRO]

QUINTANA, RAFAEL (BUSTA)—1928-34—2b, Newark Dodgers, Cuban Stars (East & West)

QUINTERO (QUINTANO) y CAVADA, MOISES—1904—1b, c, All Cubans

R

RABBAR, ____—1939—ss, New York Cubans
RABBIT, ____—1917—2b, Lost Island (IA) Giants
RACKLIN, ABE—1913—of, Long Branch (NJ) Cubans
RADCLIFF [RADCLIFFE], ALEXANDER (ALEC)—1927-46—ss, 3b, Chicago Giants, Cole's American Giants, Chicago American Giants, New York Cubans, Kansas City Monarchs, Cincinnati-Indianapolis Clowns, Memphis Red Sox, Birmingham Black Barons, Detroit Senators
RADCLIFF, HENRY [see RICHARDSON, HENRY]
RADCLIFFE, EVERETT (RED, RIP)—1925-29, 1934-37—ss, Dayton Marcos, Chicago American Giants, Chicago Giants
RADCLIFFE, THEODORE ROOSEVELT (DOUBLE DUTY, TED)—1927-50—c, p, manager, Detroit Stars, St. Louis Stars, Pittsburgh Crawfords, Homestead Grays, Columbus Blue Birds, New York Black Yankees, Brooklyn Eagles, Cincinnati Tigers, Memphis Red Sox, Birmingham Black Barons, Chicago American Giants, Louisville Buckeyes, Kansas City Monarchs, Harlem Globetrotters, Nashville Elite Giants, Minneapolis-St. Paul Colored Gophers, Cincinnati Crescents, Baltimore Giants, Gilkerson's Union Giants, Brooklyn Royal Giants, Bismarck (ND)
RAFE, ____—1928—p, Cuban Stars (East)
RAGSDALE, ____—1916—p, Louisville White Sox
RAGSTER, CARL (LEFTY)—1946—p, Fresno/San Diego Tigers
RAGGS, HARRY [see ROBERTS, HARRY]
RAGLAND, HERLEN [HARLEN, HURLAND, HERBERT] (EARL)—1916-21—p, Kansas City (MO) Tigers, Kansas City (MO) Royals, Indianapolis ABCs, Kansas City Monarchs, Columbus Buckeyes, Dayton Marcos
RAINE, J.—1884-85—of, Baltimore Atlantics
RAINES, LAWRENCE GLENN HOPE (LARRY)—1951-52—ss, Chicago American Giants
RAMÍREZ, RAMIRO (ROME)—1916-48—of, manager, All Cubans, Bacharach (AC) Giants, Bacharach (NY) Giants, Baltimore Black Sox, Havana Red Sox, Cuban House of David, Indianapolis Clowns, Brooklyn Royal Giants, New York Cuban Stars, Richmond Giants (NAA), Cuban Stars (East & West), Havana La Palomas, New York Black Yankees
RAMOS, EZEQUIEL—1907-13—p, 2b, Cuban Stars (East), Long Branch (NJ) Cubans
RAMOS, JOSÉ (CHEO)—1921, 1929—of, All Cubans, Cuban Stars (East)
RAMSAY, WILLIAM—1889—of, Chicago Unions

RAMSEY, LAYMON (BIG LAD)—1946-51—p, Memphis Red Sox, Jacksonville Eagles, Chicago American Giants, Harlem Globetrotters, Chattanooga Choo Choos
RAMSEY, MACK—1906-16—of, 2b, Twin City Gophers, Chicago Union Giants
RAMSON, ____—1919—ph, Pittsburgh Stars of Buffalo
RAND, ____—1921—1b, Chicago Union Giants
RANDALL, ____—1945—c, Nashville Black Vols
RANDALL, WILLIAM TALTON (SONNY, BILL)—1942-44—of, Homestead Grays, Richmond Hilldales, Great Lakes Bluejackets
RANDELL [RANDALL], CHARLES (CHUCK)
RANDOLPH, ANDREW G.—1882-88—1b, of, Argyle Hotel, Trenton (NJ) Cuban Giants (Middle States League), Boston Resolutes (NCBBL), Actives of Philadelphia, Cuban Giants, Lancaster (PA) Giants
RANDOLPH, EUGENE—1938—p, Atlanta Black Crackers
RANDOLPH, PERCY—1939—p, Chicago American Giants
RANIER, ____—1921—p, Chicago Union Giants
RANKIN, BILL (BULLETS, SHORTY)—1923-27—p, c, Washington Potomacs, Richmond Giants (NAA), Philadelphia Giants
RANKIN, GEORGE—1887—player, Cincinnati Browns (NCBBL)
RANOTES, ____—1947—p, Indianapolis Clowns
RANSOM, ART—1909—c, Cuban Giants
RANSOM, JOE—1926—c, Cleveland Elites, Harrisburg Giants
RANSOM, JOE—1930—3b, 2b, Newark Browns
RANSOM, SAMUEL L. (SAMMIE)—1907-09—2b, 1b, St. Paul Colored Gophers, Cuban Giants
RARRAT, ____—1921—c, Cuban Stars (East)
RARZEN, ____—1906—1b, Cuban Stars
RASBERRY, CHARLES—1952—utility, Kansas City Monarchs
RASBERRY, TED ROOSEVELT—1954-64—owner, manager, Detroit Stars, Detroit Clowns, Kansas City Monarchs, Satchel Paige All-Stars
RASMUSSEN, ____—1915—p, All Nations
RATHEREE, HENRY—1948—p, Harlem Globetrotters
RAUPPIUS, ADAM—1941—umpire, NNL
RAUZE, ____—1937—c, Philadelphia Stars
RAWLINGS, ____—1880—of, Washington Uniques
RAWLINS, ____—1903-05—3b, of, Genuine Cuban Giants, Cuban Giants
RAY, ARTHUR—1918—ss, Bacharach (AC) Giants

RAY, FRANK—1932—of, Atlanta Black Crackers

RAY, JOHN (JOHNNY)—1931-45, 1951-of, Montgomery Grey Sox, Birmingham Black Barons, Cleveland Bears, Jacksonville Red Caps, Cincinnati-Indianapolis Clowns, Kansas City Monarchs, Pittsburgh Crawfords, Monroe (LA) Monarchs; Mgr., Louisville Dodgers, Cincinnati Ethiopian Clowns (NML), Harlem Globetrotters

RAY, OTTO C. (JAYBIRD)—1920-24—p, c, of, Kansas City Monarchs, Chicago Giants, St. Louis Stars, Cleveland Tate Stars, Cleveland Browns

RAY, SR., RICHARD—1943-45—2b, of, Chicago Brown Bombers (USL)

RAY, THOMAS—1887—ss, New York Gorhams (NCBBL)

RAYMOND, ____—1887—1b, Baltimore Lord Baltimores (NCBBL)

RAYMOND, ____—1920—ss, Jacksonville Stars

RAYMOND, LON—1941-50—officer, Memphis Red Sox

RAYMOND, W.—1921-22—p, Pittsburgh Keystones, Harrisburg Giants

REACH, ALBERT T.—1887—treasurer, Philadelphia Pythians (NCBBL)

READING, ____—1922—umpire, NNL

REAVIS, AL W.—1920-32—p, Lincoln (NY) Giants, Penn Red Caps of NY, Baltimore Black Sox

REBUSE, ____—1922-23—1b, ss, All Nations

RECASNER, J.—1886—2b, Unions of New Orleans

RECCIUS, J.W.—1910—owner, Louisville Cubs

RECTOR, CORNELIUS (CONNIE, BROADWAY, EDDIE)—1920-44—p, of, manager, Hilldale Club, Brooklyn Royal Giants, Lincoln (NY) Giants, New York Harlem Stars, New York Black Yankees, New York Cubans, Fort Worth Black Panthers

REDD, EUGENE (GENE)—1922-23—3b, Pittsburgh Keystones, Milwaukee Bears, New Orleans Crescent Stars, Kansas City Monarchs, Cleveland Tate Stars

REDD, ULYSSES ADOLPH (HICKEY, CHERRY, GUMBO)—1940-52—ss, Birmingham Black Barons, Chicago American Giants, Cincinnati Crescents, Harlem Globetrotters

REDDEN, WARD—1934—c, Cincinnati Tigers

REDDICK, (BUSTER)—1942-44—of, c, Boston Royal Giants

REDDING, JR., RICHARD (DICK, GRENADE, CANNONBALL)—1911-38—p, of, manager, Philadelphia Giants, Lincoln (NY) Giants, Lincoln (NY) Stars, Indianapolis ABCs, Chicago American Giants, Royal Poinciana (FL), Breakers Hotel (FL), Brooklyn Royal Giants, Bacharach (AC) Giants, Bacharach (NY) Giants

REDDING, SAM—1926, 1929—of, Albany (GA) Giants, Brooklyn Royal Giants

REDDON, BOB—1919-20, 1924—p, Cleveland Tate Stars, St. Louis Stars

REDHOUSE, CHARLES [see HOUSE, CHARLES]

REDMON, TOM—1911—p, Leland Giants

REDMOND, ____—1919—of, Cleveland Giants

REDUS, JR., WILSON ROBERT (FROG)—1924-40—of, manager, coach, St. Louis Stars, Cleveland Stars, Columbus Blue Birds, Cleveland Giants, Kansas City Monarchs, Cleveland Red Sox, Chicago American Giants, Cleveland Browns, Indianapolis ABCs

REDWINE, BERT—1926—p, Cleveland Elites

REDWOOD, J.P. (BABY JACK)—1910—owner, Bluff City (Memphis) Tigers

REED, ____—1929—c, Shreveport Black Sports

REED, ANDREW—1917-21—of, Chicago Union Giants, Detroit Stars, Chicago Giants, St. Louis Giants

REED, CHARLIE—1929—p, Dallas Black Giants

REED, COLONEL J.E.—1922-23—treasurer, Cleveland Tate Stars

REED, CURTIS—1937—of, St. Louis Stars

REED, DAVID—1945—p, Brooklyn Brown Dodgers

REED, DWIGHT—1942—umpire, USL

REED, EDWARD LEE (EDDIE)—1953-56—of, Memphis Red Sox

REED, JERRY—1932—2b, p, Atlanta Black Crackers, New Orleans Black Pelicans

REED, JOHN D.—1934-43—p, Cole's American Giants, Indianapolis ABCs, Chicago American Giants, Chicago Brown Bombers (NML), Atlanta Black Crackers, Indianapolis Athletics, St. Louis Stars, New Orleans Crescent Stars

REED, LeROY (LEE)—1946—utility, Cleveland Clippers, Cincinnati Crescents

REED, P.—1908—p, Columbus Giants

REED, PORTER A.—1930-40s, umpire, Negro National and American League

REED, PORTER LAVARE (GUT)—1947, 1949—of, Detroit Wolves, Houston Eagles

REED, WALTER—1942—p, Birmingham Black Barons

REED, WILL—1920—of, 3b, Atlanta Black Crackers

REEDY, JR., FLEMING (BUDDY)—1950-51—3b, Baltimore Elite Giants

REEL [REELE], JAMES (JIMMY)—1923—of, Toledo Tigers

REESE, ____—1905—ss, Chicago Columbia Giants

REESE, ____—1943—c, Atlanta Black Crackers

REESE, CHARLES—1910-14—p, of, Cuban Giants, Chicago Union Giants, New York Stars, Brooklyn All-Stars, Buffalo Cuban Giants

REESE, JAMES (BIG JIM, SLIM, SLEEKY, LEFTY)—1934-40—p, Cleveland Red Sox, Brooklyn Eagles, Atlanta Black Crackers, Baltimore Elite Giants, Brooklyn Royal Giants

REESE, JOHN EDWARD (SPEEDYBOY)—1918-31—of, Bacharach (AC) Giants, Hilldale Club, Chicago American Giants, Detroit Stars, Toledo Tigers, St. Louis Stars

REEVES, ____—1925—c, Gilkerson's Union Giants

REEVES, ____—1929—c, Hilldale Club [see LEWIS, JOSEPH HERMAN]

REEVES, BEN F. (CYCLONE)—1912-13—c, All Nations

REEVES, DONALD RAY (SOUP)—1935-41—of, Atlanta Black Crackers, Indianapolis ABCs, Chicago American Giants

REEVES, JOHN—1890-92—3b, of, p, Lincoln (NE) Giants, Plattsmouth (Nebraska St. League)

REEVES, TIM—1906-08, 1913—of, Brooklyn Colored Giants, Indianapolis ABCs, Chicago Union Giants

REGGIE, ____—1921—p, Indianapolis ABCs

REICHART, MASON—1927—officer, Evansville Giants

REID [REED], ALLEN (AL)—1938, 1940-41—p, Louisville Black Caps, Newark Eagles, Philadelphia Stars

REID [REED], AMBROSE LEEVOLIA—1920-32—of, 2b, 1b, 3b, Bacharach (AC) Giants, Hilldale Club, Pittsburgh Crawfords, Atlanta Black Crackers, Homestead Grays, Royal Poinciana (FL)

REID, MEL—1946—of, Oakland Larks

REID, PHILIP E. (DADDY)—1907-10—manager, president, St. Paul Colored Gophers

REID, PORTER [see REED, PORTER LAVAER]

REILLY, ____—1930—ss, Colored House of David

REIMER, ____—1931—umpire, NNL

REINAGLE, ____—1888—ss, Bloomington (IL) Reds

REMEY, ____—1934—p, New Orleans Crescent Stars

REMICK, ____—1871—3b, Chelsea Auroras

REMUR, ____—1921—p, Breakers Hotel (FL)

RENA, [see PEÑA, L.]

RENFRO, WILLIAM J.—1887-90—p, Binghamton, NY (International League), Chicago Resolutes, Chicago Unions

RENFROE, ____—1905—of, Chicago Columbia Giants

RENFROE, SR., OTHELLO NELSON (CHICO, CHAPPY)—1945-53—of, c, ss, Kansas City Monarchs, Cleveland Buckeyes, Indianapolis Clowns; scout, Montreal Expos; official scorer, Atlanta Braves; writer, *Atlanta Daily World*

RENSTROM, ____—1929—p, Chicago Giants

RESAUD, ____—1926—umpire, NNL

REYNOLDS, ____—1869—3b, Philadelphia Excelsior

REYNOLDS, JIMMY—1940, 1946, 1948-49—3b, 1b, of, Indianapolis Crawfords, Cleveland Buckeyes, Louisville Buckeyes, Birmingham Black Barons

REYNOLDS, JOE—1935—p, Philadelphia Stars

REYNOLDS, LOUIS THOMAS (LOU)—1897-99—of, Chicago Columbia Giants, Chicago Unions

REYNOLDS, R.—1878—of, Chicago Uniques

REYNOLDS, WILLIAM ERNEST (BILL, GUMP)—1948-50—2b, Cleveland Buckeyes, Louisville Buckeyes

REVADA, VELMA—1946—of, Los Ángeles White Sox

REVENN, ____—1930—p, Evansville Giants

REX, ____—1912—p, Brown's Tennessee Rats

RHOADES, CORNELIUS (NEAL)—1910-18—c, of, Bowser's ABCs, Hilldale Club

RHODES, CLAUDE (DUSTY, SCHOOLBOY)—1931-33—p, Louisville Black Caps, Columbus Blue Birds, Chattanooga Black Lookouts

RHODES, HARRY (ARMY, LEFTY)—1940-50—p, 1b, Chicago American Giants, Chicago Brown Bombers, Havana Las Palomas

RHODES, REUBEN—1916—of, Bowser's ABCs

RHONE, ____—1940—p, Indianapolis Crawfords

RHONE, WALTER (HACKEY)—1919—3b, Philadelphia Giants

RIAS, ____—1872—of, Keystone Club of New Jersey

RICARDO, ____—1930—p, Havana Red Sox

RICE, JIMMY—1926—p, Lincoln (NY) Giants

RICE, MILLER—1934-37—of, Cincinnati Tigers

RICH, ____—1867—3b, Camden Resolutes

RICH, ____—1918—p, Chicago Union Giants

RICHARDS, ____—1924—2b, New Orleans Crescent Stars

RICHARDS, ____—1926—p, Chattanooga White Sox

RICHARDS, ____—1935—3b, Bacharach (Philly) Giants

RICHARDS, JESSE—1950—officer, Atlanta Brown Crackers

RICHARDSON, ____—1869—of, Washington Alerts

RICHARDSON, ____—1908—of, Brooklyn Colored Giants

RICHARDSON, ____—1918—of, Pennsylvania Giants

RICHARDSON, ____—1947—p, Chattanooga Choo Choos

RICHARDSON, DESERIA "BOO BOO"—1953—2b, Indianapolis Clowns

RICHARDSON, DEWEY—1922—c, Hilldale Club

RICHARDSON, DON—1949—player, Homestead Grays

RICHARDSON, EARL—1943—ss, Newark Eagles

RICHARDSON, GEORGE—1900-03—2b, Chicago Union Giants, Algona (IA) Brownies, Chicago Unions
RICHARDSON, GEORGE—1925—officer, Detroit Stars
RICHARDSON, GLEMBY (GLENN, GENE)—1946-49—2b, New York Black Yankees
RICHARDSON, HENRY [a.k.a. RADCLIFF, HENRY]—1943—c, Chicago American Giants
RICHARDSON, HENRY LAYTON (LONG TOM)—1921-38—p, of, Baltimore Black Sox, Washington Pilots, Bacharach (AC) Giants, Washington Black Senators, Pittsburgh Crawfords, Cuban Stars (West), Richmond Giants (NAA), Cuban House of David, Philadelphia Stars
RICHARDSON, JIM—1933-34, 1939, 1946—p, Philadelphia Stars, New York Black Yankees, Pittsburgh Stars
RICHARDSON, JOHN—1929—c, Dallas Black Giants
RICHARDSON, JOHN J. (JOHNNY, BLACK SON)—1922-27—p, Birmingham Black Barons, Shreveport Black Sports, Hilldale Club
RICHARDSON, JOHNNY (BOB, DUDE)—1948-50—ss, Atlanta Black Crackers, Homestead Grays, Schenectady Mohawk Giants
RICHARDSON, NORVAL EUGENE (GENE, BRITCHES, SOUTHO)—1947-53—p, Kansas City Monarchs, Baltimore Elite Giants, Birmingham Black Barons
RICHARDSON, RAYFORD ARTHUR (RAY, YOUNG JOSH)—1954-56—c, Birmingham Black Barons, Detroit Stars
RICHARDSON, TALMADGE—1921-23—p, 2b, Bacharach (AC) Giants, Baltimore Black Sox
RICHARDSON, THEODORE (TED, LEFTY)—1953-54—p, Indianapolis Clowns, Louisville Clippers, Jackie Robinson All-Stars
RICHARDSON, THOMAS W. (T.W.)—1951-55- p, Baltimore Elite Giants, Memphis Red Sox, Birmingham Black Barons
RICHARDSON, VICIAL—1946—ss, Cleveland Buckeyes
RICHARDSON, WILLIAM—1875—3b, p, St. Louis Blue Stockings
RICHARDSON, WILLIAM EDGAR (BABA)—1953-55, 1957—p, Birmingham Black Barons, Detroit Stars
RICHBOURG, (LEFTY)—1939—Indianapolis ABCs
RICHMOND, ____—1880—of, Washington Keystones
RICHMOND, MORTON—1935—p, Brooklyn Eagles
RICHENBACH, ____—1909—p, Louisville White Sox
RICKHOFF, R. C.—1870—umpire, Independent Colored teams

RICKS, ____—1859—1b, Unknown Base Ball Club (of Weeksville, NY)
RICKS, ____—1870—c, Johnstown (NY) Wide Awakes
RICKS, CURTIS JEROME—1920-26—1b, Dayton Marcos, Cleveland Tate Stars, Indianapolis ABCs, Chicago American Giants, Cleveland Browns
RICKS, NAPOLEON—1887—ss, Louisville Falls City (NCBBL)
RICKS, PENDER—1924-28-1b, Philadelphia Giants, Harrisburg Giants
RICKS, WILLIAM (BILL, SCHOOLBOY)—1944-50—p, Philadelphia Stars, New York Black Yankees
RICO, OSCAR—1952-54—scout, Kansas City Monarchs; manager, Havana Cuban Giants
RIDDICK, VERNON WALTER (BIG SIX)—1938-41—ss, 3b, Newark Eagles, Schenectady Mohawk Giants
RIDDLE, SR., JOHN THOMAS—1927—infield, Philadelphia Royal Giants
RIDDLE, MARSHALL LEWIS (JIT)—1936-43, 1946—2b, Indianapolis ABCs, St. Louis Stars, New Orleans-St. Louis Stars, Cincinnati-Cleveland Buckeyes, Cleveland Buckeyes, Jacksonville Red Caps, Cincinnati Crescents
RIDER, ____—1932—3b, Indianapolis ABCs
RIDGELY, ____—1880—of, Washington Keystones
RIDGELY [RISLEY, RIDGLEY], RANDOLPH H. (BUCK)—1916-30—2b, Lincoln (NY) Giants, Baltimore Black Sox, Harrisburg Giants, Washington Potomacs, Schenectady Mohawk Giants, Brooklyn Royal Giants
RIDLEY, CHARLES—1947—bus driver, Cleveland Buckeyes
RIDLEY, JACK—1925-34—of, 1b, Nashville Elite Giants, Cleveland Cubs, Louisville Red Caps
RIGAL, MANUEL J.—1922-27—ss, 3b, Cuban Stars (West)
RIGBY, CHARLES—1950—of, New York Black Yankees
RIGGINS, ARVELL [ORVILLE] (BO, MULE, BILL)—1920-36—ss, 3b, manager, Detroit Stars, Cleveland Hornets, Homestead Grays, Lincoln (NY) Giants, New York Harlem Stars, New York Black Yankees, Brooklyn Royal Giants, Chicago American Giants
RIGNEY, H. G. (HANK)—1939-45—president/officer, Toledo Crawfords, Indianapolis Crawfords, Toledo Cubs/Rays
RIGSBY, ____—1917—ph, All Nations
RILE, EDWARD (ED, HUCK)—1919-36—p, 1b, Jewell's ABCs, Chicago American Giants, Lincoln (NY) Giants, Columbus Buckeyes, Detroit Stars, Cole's American Giants, Brooklyn Royal Giants, Kansas City Monarchs, Dayton Marcos, Homestead Grays, Pittsburgh Giants

RILEY, ____–1920–p, Penn Red Caps
RILEY, ____–1924–1b, New Orleans Crescent Stars
RILEY (REILLY), ____–1925-30–umpire, ECL
RILEY, JIM (JACK)–1945–2b, Birmingham Black Barons
RIMS, ____–1920–p, Bacharach (AC) Giants
RINGGOLD, ____–1872–c, Amicable Club of New York
RINGHOLM, ____–1869–of, Brooklyn Unique
RÍOS, MATÍAS [HERMAN]–1915-24–3b, ss, Cuban Stars (West), Cincinnati Cuban Stars
RITCHEY, JOHN FRANKLIN (HOSS)–1947–c, Chicago American Giants
RITCHIE, ____–1921–p, Chicago Union Giants, Indianapolis ABCs
RIVAS, FRANCISCO E. (CANILLO, PANCHO)–1917-18–2b, Almendares Cubans, Cuban Stars (East) Havana Cubans
RIVELL, ____–1934–umpire, NNL
RIVERA, ANICETO (NENENE)–1933–ss, Cuban Stars (East)
RIVERA, CARLOS LAVEZZARI (CHARLIE, SNOOKER)–1939-44–ss, 3b, New York Black Yankees, Baltimore Elite Giants, New York Cubans, Brooklyn Royal Giants, Ethiopian Clowns
RIVERA, SOL–1919–officer, Atlanta Cubs
RIVERO, ____–1929–3b, Boston Black Sox
RIVERO, MANUEL–1933–of, Cuban Stars (East)
RIVERS, ____–1925–p, Gilkerson's Union Giants
RIVERS (RIVERA), BILL–1944, 1948–of, Kansas City Monarchs, Chattanooga Choo Choos
RIVERS, DEWEY (DEEP)–1926-34–of, Hilldale Club, Schenectady Mohawk Giants, Baltimore Black Sox, Homestead Grays, Brooklyn Cuban Giants
RIVERS, LEO I.–1946–utility, Portland (OR) Rosebuds
RIVERS, SOL–1926–officer, Atlanta Black Crackers
ROACH, ____–1930–of, Colored House of David
ROANE, ALWIN (AL) URIEL–1959-60–p, Raleigh (NC) Tigers
ROANE, FREDDY–1919–of, Wilmington Giants
ROANE, I.–1919–of, Wilmington Giants
ROBAS, ____–1930–of, Boston Black Sox
ROBB, ENGLISH–1945–c, New Orleans Black Pelicans
ROBBINS, (SLIM)–1926, 1935, 1938–p, 2b, Harrisburg Giants, Bacharach (Philly) Giants
ROBELSON, BING–1934–p, Bacharach (Philly) Giants
ROBERSON, T. (CHARLEY)–1934–3b, Nashville Elite Giants

ROBERTS, ____–1884–of, Brooklyn Alpines
ROBERTS, ____–1914–1b, Philadelphia Giants
ROBERTS, ____–1926-27–umpire, NNL
ROBERTS, ____–1929–c, Fort Worth Panthers
ROBERTS, CHARLEY (SPECS)–1932, 1938, 1942, 1945–p, Atlanta Black Crackers, Washington Black Senators, Philadelphia Daisies (NML), Brooklyn Brown Dodgers
ROBERTS, SR., CURTIS BENJAMIN–1947-50–2b, Kansas City Monarchs
ROBERTS, ELIHU[E] D.–1916-20–of, Bacharach (AC) Giants, Hilldale Club
ROBERTS, EUGENE A.–1957–2b, of, Memphis Red Sox
ROBERTS, FRED DOUGLAS (POPS)–1902-16–2b, Chicago Union Giants, Chicago Unions, Leland Giants, St. Paul Colored Gophers, Minneapolis Keystones, Illinois Giants
ROBERTS, HARRY HAMLET (RAGGS)–1920-32–of, c, Norfolk Giants, Baltimore Black Sox, Schenectady Mohawk Giants, Harrisburg Giants, Homestead Grays, Chicago Columbia Giants, Pittsburgh Crawfords, Norfolk Stars, Breakers Hotel (FL)
ROBERTS, J. D.–1918-24–ss, Pennsylvania Giants, Hilldale Club, Bacharach (AC) Giants, Richmond Giants (NAA), Chicago Giants
ROBERTS, JESSE–1950–p, Chicago American Giants
ROBERTS, JR., LEO–1925–1b, Indianapolis ABCs
ROBERTS, LEROY (ROY, EVERREADY)–1916-35–p, Bacharach (AC) Giants, Bacharach (NY) Giants, Columbus Buckeyes, Brooklyn Royal Giants, Lincoln (NY) Giants, Hilldale Club, Cleveland Giants, Cleveland Red Sox, Madison Stars, Detroit Stars, Royal Poinciana (FL)
ROBERTS, RIC–writer, *Atlanta Daily World*
ROBERTS, ROBERT (ROB)–1928–3b, ss, Brooklyn Royal Giants
ROBERTS, SARAH MUTT–1936-39–p, Philadelphia Stars, Nashville Elite Giants, Baltimore Elite Giants, Bacharach (Philly) Giants
ROBERTS, TOM (SPECS)–1937-46–p, Homestead Grays, New York Black Yankees, Newark Eagles, Philadelphia Stars, Oakland Larks
ROBERTSON, ____–1903–ss, Cuban X-Giants
ROBERTSON, ____–1911–p, Twin City Gophers
ROBERTSON, ____–1919–c, Grand Central Terminal Red Caps
ROBERTSON, ____–1930–ss, Newark Browns
ROBERTSON, ____–1936–p, Birmingham Black Barons
ROBERTSON, BOBBY [see ROBINSON, WILLIAM]

ROBERTSON, CHARLES [see ROBINSON, CHARLES E.]

ROBERTSON, NORMAN—1901—1b, Columbia Giants

ROBERTSON, PETER (CREOLE PETE)—1920, 1933-34—of, p, manager, New Orleans Black Pelicans, New Orleans Crescent Stars

ROBINSON, ____—1880—of, Washington Douglass Club

ROBINSON, ____—1880—ss, Washington Manhattans

ROBINSON, ____—1909—of, Louisville Cubs

ROBINSON, ____—1911—p, Wilmington Giants

ROBINSON, ____—1917—p, Dayton Marcos

ROBINSON, ____—1918—1b, Philadelphia Giants

ROBINSON, ____—1926—1b, Memphis Red Sox

ROBINSON, ____—1926—c, New Orleans Black Pelicans

ROBINSON, ____—1926—of, Bacharach (AC) Giants

ROBINSON, ____—1929—p, Wichita Falls Spudders

ROBINSON, ____—1939—p, St. Louis Giants

ROBINSON, ____—1944—of, Charleston's Cuban Yanks

ROBINSON, ____—1946—3b, Cincinnati Crescents

ROBINSON, ____—1946—3b, San Francisco Sea Lions

ROBINSON, ALBERT EDWARD—1884, 1888, 1905-12, 1919—of, 3b, 1b, p, Chicago Gordons, Chicago Unions, Brooklyn Royal Giants, Philadelphia Giants, Cuban Giants, New York Black Sox

ROBINSON, ARZELL (ACE)—1953-59—p, Memphis Red Sox, Kansas City Monarchs

ROBINSON, BOB—1901-17—c, 1b, ss, Chicago Columbia Giants, Algona (IA) Brownies, Leland Giants, Chicago Union Giants, Illinois Giants, Cuban Giants, Chicago American Giants

ROBINSON, BOOKER TALIAFERRO (LITTLE BOOK, ROBBIE) [a.k.a. Edward Robinson]—1943-45—3b, c, New York Black Yankees, Atlanta Black Crackers, Seattle Steelheads, Homestead Grays

ROBINSON, CHARLES E. (CHARLIE, PAPA, LEFTY)—1920-26, 1932—p, New Orleans Crescent Stars, Birmingham Black Barons, St. Louis Stars, Atlanta Black Crackers, New Orleans Caulfield Ads

ROBINSON, CLARENCE—1943—c, Baltimore Elite Giants

ROBINSON, CLIFFORD—1946-48—batboy, Indianapolis Clowns

ROBINSON, CORNELIUS RANDALL (NEIL, NEAL, SHADOW)—1934-52—of, ss, Homestead Grays, Cincinnati Tigers, Memphis Red Sox, Baltimore Elite Giants, Padron's Cuban Giants, Kansas City Royals

ROBINSON, DESERIA (BOO BOO)—1953—2b, Indianapolis Clowns

ROBINSON (DIRT MAN)—1946—p, Fresno/San Diego Tigers

ROBINSON, EDWARD [see ROBINSON, BOOKER TALIAFERRO]

ROBINSON, EDWARD J. (SCOBY)—1931, 1934—of, Louisville White Sox, Homestead Grays

ROBINSON, FRANK—1957—Memphis Red Sox

ROBINSON, GEORGE—1910—stockholder—St. Louis Giants

ROBINSON, GEORGE WASHINGTON (SIS, THE SOUTHERN BEARCAT)—1910, 1918, 1923—p, New York Black Sox, Bacharach (AC) Giants; 1925—officer, Wilmington Potomacs

ROBINSON, H.—1886—utility, St. Louis Black Stockings

ROBINSON, HAROLD (HAL)—1940, 1945-46—ss, Philadelphia Stars, Philadelphia Hilldales (USL), Boston Blues, Brooklyn Brown Dodgers

ROBINSON, HARRY—1960—of, Raleigh (NC) Tigers

ROBINSON, HENRY FRAZIER (SLOW, HANK)—1939, 1942-50—c, Satchel Paige All-Stars, Baltimore Grays, Kansas City Monarchs, Baltimore Elite Giants, Nashville Cubs; author

ROBINSON, J. ROBERT (GINNEY)—1905-12—of, Brooklyn Royal Giants, Kansas City (KS) Giants, New York Black Sox, Oklahoma City Monarchs

ROBINSON, JACK ROOSEVELT (JACKIE)—1945—ss, Kansas City Monarchs

ROBINSON, JACOB (RED)—1946-47—3b, Chicago American Giants

ROBINSON, JAKE—1954—of, p, Detroit Stars

ROBINSON, JAMES DORSEY (BLACK RUSIE)—1893-1907—p, Lansing (MI) Colored Capital All-Americans, Cuban Giants, Cuban X-Giants, Brooklyn Royal Giants, Pawtucket (New England League), Philadelphia Giants

ROBINSON, JAMES EDWARD (JIM)—1950-53, 56-58—ss, 3b, 2b, Goshen Red Wings, Philadelphia Stars, Indianapolis Clowns, Kansas City Monarchs, Memphis Red Sox

ROBINSON, JOE—1946—c, New Orleans Algiers

ROBINSON, JOHN—1887—utility, St. Louis Black Stockings

ROBINSON, JOHNNY—1926, 1930-32, 1936, 1938-42—3b, of, Cleveland Elites, Memphis Red Sox, St. Louis Stars, Indianapolis ABCs, Little Rock Grays

ROBINSON, JOSHUA—1939—of, New York Black Yankees

ROBINSON, KENNETH (KEN)—1931-47—2b, 3b, of, Newark Browns, Brooklyn Royal Giants, New York Black Yankees, Newark Eagles, Jacksonville Eagles, Cleveland Bears, Bacharach (Philly) Giants, Jacksonville Red Caps, Atlanta Black Crackers

ROBINSON, L.—1946—ph, Baltimore Elite Giants

ROBINSON, LEROY—1945—of, Nashville Black Vols

ROBINSON, LEROY—1957—owner, New Orleans Bears, Kansas City Monarchs

ROBINSON, LUTHER (BILL, BOJANGLES)—1931—officer, New York Stars (Black Yankees)

ROBINSON, MELVIN—1919—p, Baltimore Black Sox

ROBINSON, NEAL or NEIL [see ROBINSON, CORNELIUS RANDALL]

ROBINSON, NEWT [see ROBINSON, WALTER WILLIAM]

ROBINSON, NORMAN WAYNE (BOBBY, NORM)—1939-52—of, 3b, Satchel Paige All-Stars, Baltimore Elite Giants, Baltimore Grays, Birmingham Black Barons

ROBINSON, O.—1941—p, Detroit Black Sox

ROBINSON, RAYMOND K. (RAY, NOT SUGAR)—1938-47—p, Newark Eagles, Cincinnati-Cleveland Buckeyes, Philadelphia Stars

ROBINSON, RICHMOND (BLACK DIAMOND)—1883-87—of, St. Louis Black Stockings, Trenton (NJ) Cuban Giants (Middle States League),, New York Gorhams

ROBINSON, ROBERT (BOB)—1954-56—of, Detroit Stars, Indianapolis Clowns

ROBINSON, SAMMY—1954—p, Detroit Stars

ROBINSON, SARGER—1946—p, Pittsburgh Stars

ROBINSON, T.—1906—of, Topeka (KS) Giants

ROBINSON, WALTER (SKINDOWN)—1938-42—3b, 2b, Jacksonville Red Caps, Cleveland Bears

ROBINSON, WALTER WILLIAM (NEWT, BILL)—1925-32—ss, Hilldale Club, Lincoln (NY) Giants, Harrisburg Giants, New York Harlem Stars, Bacharach (AC) Giants

ROBINSON, WILLIAM L. (BOBBY)—1925-42—3b, ss, Indianapolis ABCs, Cleveland Elites, Memphis Red Sox, Detroit Stars, Cleveland Stars, Cleveland Red Sox, Birmingham Black Barons, New Orleans-St. Louis Stars, St. Louis Stars, Padron's Cuban Giants

ROBINSON, WILLIE (BABE, WINDSHIELD)—1933-42—p, Bacharach (Philly) Giants, Cleveland Red Sox, Boston Royal Giants

ROCHELLE, ____—1920—of, Birmingham Black Barons

ROCHELLE, CLARENCE—1944-45—p, Kansas City Monarchs, Chicago Brown Bombers (USL)

ROCK, ____—1930—3b, Havana Red Sox

ROCKY, ____—1917—of, Dayton Marcos

RODDY, BERT M. (B.M.)—1922-27—officer, Memphis Red Sox, 1926-27—president, Negro Southern League

RODÉS, JOAQUÍN—1915—of, Havana Reds

RODGERS, [see PIERRE, ROGERS]—1939—p, Chicago American Giants

RODGERS, EDWARD—1883-87—1b, St. Louis Black Stockings

RODGERS, SILVESTER CLIFFORD (SPEEDIE)—1949-50—p, Baltimore Elite Giants

RODNEY, LESTER—1936-58—writer, *New York Daily Worker*

RODOUD, ____—1921—c, Cuban Stars (East)

RODRÍGUEZ, ARTURO ANTONIO (EL POLLO)—1935-39—ss, 3b, 2b, New York Cubans, New York Cuban Stars

RODRÍGUEZ, B. CONRADO (RED)—1920-22, 1927-34—p, of, Cuban Stars (East & West), Birmingham Black Barons

RODRÍGUEZ y GARCÍA, BIENVENIDO (BENNY)—1948—of, c, Chicago American Giants

RODRÍGUEZ, CARLOS—1915—p, Cuban Stars

RODRÍGUEZ y LÓPEZ, CONRADO (GENERAL SAGUA)—1909—p, Cuban Stars

RODRÍGUEZ y ORDEÑANA, HECTOR ANTONIO—1944—3b, North Classic Team, New York Cubans

RODRÍGUEZ, JOSÉ (JOE, JOSEÍTO, EL HOMBRE GOMA)—1915, 1935—1b, Havana Reds, Havana Stars

RODRÍGUEZ, JOSÉ AGUSTÍN (FRIJOLITO)—1920-22—p, of, Bacharach (AC) Giants, Cuban Stars (West)

RODRÍGUEZ, (LEFTY)—1946—p, Los Ángeles White Sox

RODRÍGUEZ, MARIO—1934—p, Cuban Stars (East)

RODRÍGUEZ, OSCAR—1935—2b, ss, Havana Stars

RODRÍGUEZ y VALERA, VICENTE (EL LOCO)—1913-23—c, Cuban Stars (East & West), Detroit Stars, Kansas City Monarchs, All Cubans

ROESINK, JOHN—1925-30—officer, owner, Detroit Stars

ROGAN, CHARLES WILBER[N] (BULLET)—1917-46—p, of, 1b, 2b, 3b, ss, manager, Kansas City Colored Giants, All Nations, Los Angeles White Sox, Philadelphia Royal Giants, Kansas City Monarchs; umpire, NAL, East/West game

ROGAN, WILBUR SIDNEY—1930s—batboy, Kansas City Monarchs

ROGERS, ____—1883—utility, 1b, Washington Manhattans

ROGERS, ____—1900—p, Genuine Cuban Giants

ROGERS, ____–1918–ss, 3b, Bacharach (AC) Giants
ROGERS, ____–1916–of, West Baden (IN) Sprudels
ROGERS, ____–1921–of, Illinois Giants
ROGERS, ____–1935–p, Memphis Red Sox
ROGERS, BRICE E. (NAT)–1907, 1913-14–2b, ss, 3b,1b, manager, Louisville White Sox, Louisville Giants, Chicago Royal Giants, Philadelphia Giants
ROGERS, JOHN (HEAVY)–1928–of, Memphis Red Sox
ROGERS, SID–1887–player, Cincinnati Browns (NCBBL)
ROGERS, (SNEAKY)–1934–of, p, Cincinnati Tigers
ROGERS, WILLIAM EARL (STUMP) –1933-34–c, of, Philadelphia Royal Giants
ROGERS, WILLIAM NATHANIEL (NAT)–1923-46–of, manager, Harrisburg Giants, Brooklyn Royal Giants, Memphis Red Sox, Chicago Columbia Giants, Cole's American Giants, Chicago American Giants, Birmingham Black Barons, Kansas City Monarchs, Knoxville Giants, Brooklyn Eagles, Philadelphia Giants, Chicago Palmer House Stars
ROJO, DOMINGO JULIO (CLOWN)–1916-38–c, 3b, Cuban Stars (East), Bacharach (AC) Giants, Bacharach (NY) Giants, Baltimore Black Sox, Lincoln (NY) Giants, New York Cubans
ROLAND, ____–1933–3b, John Donaldson All-Star
ROLAND, CARL–1926–utility, Memphis Red Sox
ROLAND, J.–1944-45, umpire, NNL
ROLLING [ROLLINS], CARL E.–1920–of, St. Louis Giants
ROLLS, CHARLES–1911–c, Leland Giants
ROMAGOSA, JÉSUS–1920–of, Cuban Stars (East)
ROMAÑACH, TOMÁS (EL ITALIANO)–1914-16–ss, Long Branch (NJ) Cubans
ROMBY, ROBERT L. (BOB)–1946-50–p, of, Baltimore Elite Giants
ROME, DOUGLAS–1945–p, New Orleans Black Pelicans
ROMELEY, ____–1947–c, Memphis Red Sox
ROMERO, JOSÉ (PEPILLO)–1902–p, of, All Cubans
RONNIE, ____–1958–utility, Detroit Clowns
ROONEY, CLEMMONS–1941–p, New Orleans-St. Louis Stars
ROQUE, JACINTO (BATTLING SIKI)–1928-32, 1935, 1937–of, Cuban Stars (East & West), Cuban House of David
ROSADO, RAFAEL (RALPH, FACHY)–1955–c, Detroit Stars
ROSADO [ROSADES], SALVADOR (YOYO)–1899, 1903–p, All Cubans
ROSCOE, ____–1919–of, Philadelphia Giants
ROSCOE, JR., JOHNNY–1942, 1949-50–ph, New York Black Yankees, Birmingham Black Barons
ROSE, ____–1935–p, Homestead Grays
ROSE, CECIL–1924–p, St. Louis Stars
ROSE, HAYWOOD (KISSING BUG)–1901-11–c, 1b, Algona (IA) Brownies, Leland Giants, Chicago Union Giants, St. Paul Colored Gophers, Minneapolis Keystones, Chicago Unions, Leland Giants
ROSELL [ROSSELLE, ROSELLO, ROSELLA, ROSELLE], BASILIO (BRUJO)–1920, 1925-35–p, Birmingham Black Barons, Cuban Stars (East & West), New York Cubans
ROSS, ____–1889–of, New Orleans Pinchbacks
ROSS, ____–1918–p, Indianapolis ABCs
ROSS, ALEX–1887-89–3b, of, Greenville (Northern Michigan League), and (Michigan St. League)
ROSS, ARTHUR C.–1902-05–p, Chicago Union Giants, Leland Giants
ROSS, [DR.] ANDERSON–1956–owner, Birmingham Black Barons
ROSS, CHARLIE–1921–owner, Calgary Black Sox
ROSS, DICK–1925-27–of, St. Louis Stars, St. Louis Giants
ROSS, E.–1919, 1923–of, Hilldale Club, Cuban Stars (East)
ROSS, FRANK–1939–p, Memphis Red Sox
ROSS, GARY–1952–of, Indianapolis Clowns
ROSS, HOWARD TULLUS (HAROLD, LEFTY)–1922-27–p, Indianapolis ABCs, Chicago American Giants, Cleveland Browns, Cleveland Hornets
ROSS [ROSE], HENRY–1883, 1888-89–1b, St. Louis Black Stockings, Bloomington (IL) Reds
ROSS, JERRY–1926–p, Cleveland Elites
ROSS, SAM–1923–p, Hilldale Club, Harrisburg Giants, Washington Potomacs
ROSS, WILLIAM M. (ZERO BALL, NACOGDOCHES)–1924-31, 1932-34–p, St. Louis Giants, Chicago American Giants, Homestead Grays, Detroit Stars, Cleveland Tigers, St. Louis Stars, Philadelphia Royal Giants
ROSSITER, GEORGE SYLVESTER–1922-31–officer, owner, Baltimore Black Sox
ROSSMAN, ____–1922–umpire, NNL
ROSSMAN, ____–1929–of, Fort Worth Panthers
ROTH, HERMAN JOSEPH (BOBBY)–1920-26, 1932–c, Pittsburgh Keystones, New Orleans Crescent Stars, Chicago American Giants, Milwaukee Bears, Detroit Stars, Birmingham Black Barons, Cleveland Tate Stars, New Orleans Black Pelicans

ROTHELL (ROTHWELL), ____–1891, 1907–of, p, c, Philadelphia Orions, Trusty (PA) Giants

ROTORET, ____–1950–p, New York Cubans

ROUSE, JR., HOWARD–1951–of, Philadelphia Stars

ROUSSELL [RONSELL, RUSSELL], JIMPSEY [JIMSEY]– 1926-31–of, New Orleans Crescent Stars, New Orleans Black Pelicans, Birmingham Black Barons, Memphis Red Sox, Nashville Elite Giants

ROUTT, SAMMY–1926-27–p, of, Montgomery Grey Sox, Nashville Elite Giants

ROUZEN (ROUZAN), ____–1922–umpire, NNL

ROVIRA, JAIME (EL MONO, JAMIE)–1911–3b, All Cubans, Cuban Stars

ROWAN, WILLIAM (BILL)–1951-53–of, Kansas City Monarchs, Kansas City (KS) Giants

ROWE, ____–1932–p, Nashville Elite Giants, Atlanta Black Crackers

ROWE, WILLIAM (SCHOOLBOY)–1943-45–p, Chicago Brown Bombers (USL), Pittsburgh Crawfords (USL), Cleveland Buckeyes

ROWE, WILLIAM LEON (BILLY)–1934-1951–writer, photographer, publicist, *Pittsburgh Courier*

ROWELL, BRUCE–1946–owner, Seattle Steelheads; second-vice president of West Coast Negro Baseball League

ROWLETT, CURTIS–1947–officer, Detroit Senators

ROY, ____–1880–p, Washington Uniques

ROY, ____–1932–of, Homestead Grays

ROY, HARVEY–1887–of, Pittsburgh Keystones (NCBBL)

ROY, ORMBY–1930-32, 1946–ss, Pittsburgh Crawfords, Homestead Grays, Pittsburgh Stars

ROYAL, CHARLES–1859–manager, Unknown Base Ball Club (of Weeksville, NY)

ROYALL, JR., JOSEPH JOHN (JOE)–1936-45–c, Indianapolis Athletics, Jacksonville Red Caps, New York Black Yankees, Cleveland Bears, Asheville Blues

ROYCE, ____–1926–3b, Harrisburg Giants

ROYER, CARLOS (BEBÉ)–1906, 1908–p, 1b, Havana Stars, Cuban Stars

ROYLAND, ____–1916–of, Lincoln (NY) Stars

RUDD, ____–1891–3b, of, New York Colored Giants

RUDD, CHARLES–1948-49, 1953–bus driver, Birmingham Black Barons, Indianapolis Clowns

RUDOLPH, ____–1920–of, Pensacola Giants [see ASH, RUDOLPH]

RUE, JOSEPH WILLIAM–1920–umpire, NNL

RUFFIN, CHARLES LEON (LASSAS)–1935-50–c, manager, Newark Eagles, Pittsburgh Crawfords, Philadelphia Stars, Houston Eagles, Brooklyn Eagles, Toledo Crawfords, North All-Stars

RUGUS, ____–1936–c, Cuban Stars (East)

RUIZ, ANTONIO (PÉREZ, LOCO)–1944–p, Cincinnati-Indianapolis Clowns

RUIZ, SILVINO (POPPA)–1928-42–p, Cuban Stars (East), New York Cubans

RUNKEL (RUNKEY), ____–1930–umpire, NNL

RUNYON, ____–1922–p, Hilldale Club

RUSAN, HARRY–1931–ss, Brooklyn Royal Giants, Detroit Giants

RUSH, JOE (UNCLE)–1923-26–officer, owner, Birmingham Black Barons; secretary, NNL; president, NSL

RUSHING, VANITY (VAN)–1958-60–c, Indianapolis Clowns

RUSLEY, ____–1913–1b, Philadelphia Giants

RUSS, PYTHIAS–1925-29–c, ss, Chicago American Giants, Memphis Red Sox, Birmingham Black Barons

RUSSELL, ____–1871–of, Chelsea Auroras

RUSSELL, ____–1892–of, Cuban Giants

RUSSELL, ____–1908–3b, Columbus Giants

RUSSELL, ____–1915–of, All Nations

RUSSELL, ____–1928–of, Nashville Elite Giants

RUSSELL, ____–1940–ph, New Orleans-St. Louis Stars

RUSSELL, A.–1926–c, of, Cleveland Elites

RUSSELL, AARON A. (ERIC)–1913-20–3b, Homestead Grays

RUSSELL, BOBBY–1931, 33–p, ss, Brooklyn Royal Giants

RUSSELL, BRANCH LOWELL (LEE)–1922-33–3b, of, Kansas City Monarchs, St. Louis Stars, Cleveland Stars, Cleveland Cubs, Montgomery Grey Sox, Nashville Elite Giants

RUSSELL, ERIE–1913, 1924-26–3b, Harrisburg Giants, Dayton Marcos

RUSSELL, EWING–1936–3b, Cincinnati Tigers

RUSSELL, FRANK (JUNIOR)–1943-56–2b, 3b, Baltimore Elite Giants, Memphis Red Sox, Birmingham Black Barons, Nashville Cubs

RUSSELL, JOHN HENRY (PISTOL)–1920-35–2b, 3b, Birmingham Black Barons, Knoxville Giants, Montgomery Grey Sox Memphis Red Sox, St. Louis Stars, Indianapolis ABCs, Pittsburgh Crawfords, Detroit Wolves, Cleveland Red Sox, Homestead Grays

RUSSELL, MOSLEY–1955–2b, Detroit Stars

RUSSELL, THOMAS—1944, 1950—p, Chicago American Giants, Cleveland Buckeyes
RUSSELL, WILLIAM JAMES (BILL)—1944—p, New York Black Yankees
RUSSIE, ____—1888—p, Hoosier Black Stockings
RUTHERFORD, ____—1926—ss, Memphis Red Sox
RUTLEDGE, ____—1920-21—p, Dayton Marcos
RYAN, ____—1917—3b, All Nations
RYAN, DAVE—1939-40, 1942-43—1b, of, Schenectady Mohawk Giants
RYAN, MERVEN JOHN (RED, JABAO)—1915-34—p, Pittsburgh Stars of Buffalo, Brooklyn Royal Giants, Hilldale Club, Harrisburg Giants, Bacharach (AC) Giants, Baltimore Black Sox, Lincoln (NY) Stars, Newark Browns, Lincoln (NY) Giants, New York Harlem Stars, Penn Red Caps of NY, Homestead Grays
RYLE, WILLIAM ABRAHAM—1919—ss, Jewell's ABCs

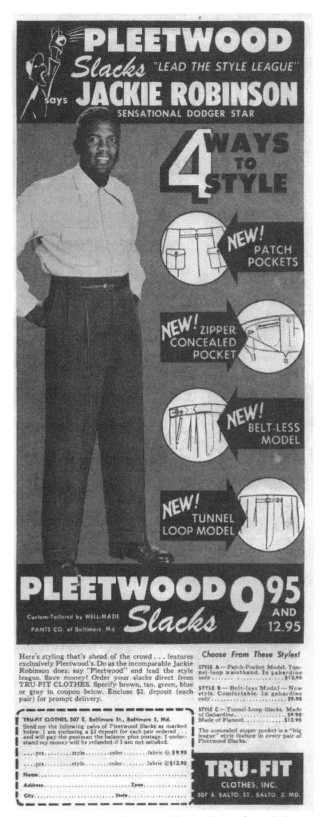

Author's collection, *Ebony*, December 1949

S

SAABIN, ____–1927–p, Cuban Stars (East)
SABALA, ____–1923–p, All Cubans
SABB, WILLIAM–1883–2b, Cleveland Blue Stockings
SADLER, ____–1909–p, St. Louis Giants
SADLER, WILLIAM A. (BILL, BUBBY)–1934-39–ss, Brooklyn Eagles, Washington Black Senators, Bacharach (Philly) Giants
SADLER, ULYSSES–1910–stockholder, St. Louis Giants
SAILS, ROSELL–1951–c, 1b, Philadelphia Stars
SALADER, ____–1929–of, Boston Black Sox
SALAS [SOLAS], WILFREDO–1948–p, New York Cubans, Chicago American Giants
SALAZAR, LÁZARO–1924-37–of, p, 1b, New York Cubans, Cuban Stars (East & West), Trujillo All-Stars (Ciudad Trujillo Dragons)
SALAZAR y CORREA, SANTIAGO (SANTOS)–1945-46–1b, New York Cubans, New Orleans Black Pelicans, Atlanta Black Crackers
SALDA, EMILLO–1929–p, Havana Red Sox
SALLEE, (SLIM)–1921–p, Montgomery Grey Sox
SALMON, HARRY LEE (BEANS, FISH)–1920-35–p, of, Birmingham Black Barons, Homestead Grays, Memphis Red Sox, Detroit Wolves, Pittsburgh Keystones
SALTERS, EDWARD–1937–of, Detroit Stars
SALTERW'E, ____–1929–2b, Fort Worth Panthers
SALVAT, MANUEL–1924-25–2b, Cuban Stars (East)
SALVERSON, HENRY [see SAVERSON, HENRY]
SAMA, PABLO–1950–3b, Indianapolis Clowns
SAMPSON, ____–1872–ss, Keystone Club of New Jersey
SAMPSON, ____–1913–of, All Nations
SAMPSON, ____–1922–of, Nashville Elite Giants
SAMPSON, CLARENCE (CLEM, CLAM HAND)–1896-1907–p, of, Genuine Cuban Giants, Cuban Giants, Famous Cuban Giants, Cuban X-Giants
SAMPSON, EMANUEL (EDDIE, LEO)–1938-46–of, Schenectady Mohawk Giants, Birmingham Black Barons
SAMPSON, JOHN–1942–of, New York Cubans
SAMPSON, ORMOND LEONARD (FLASH, GEORGE)–1932-38–ss, Atlanta Black Crackers, Brooklyn Royal Giants, Newark Dodgers, Bacharach (Philly) Giants, Cuban Stars (East)
SAMPSON, SAM–1940-43–2b, of, Cleveland Bears, Jacksonville Red Caps, Harrisburg-St. Louis Stars
SAMPSON, JR., THOMAS (TOMMY, TOOTS)–1938-49–2b, 1b, manager, Chicago American Giants, Birmingham Black Barons, New York Cubans, Chattanooga Choo Choos
SAMPSON, WELMON (STEEL ARM)–1931-32, 1938–p, Colored House of David
SAMUELO, ____–1930–1b, Boston Black Sox
SAMUELS, ____–1940–p, Philadelphia Stars
SAMUELS, JOHN–1926–president, Montgomery Grey Sox
SAN, PEDRO ALEJANDRO (ELI)–1926-28–p, Cuban Stars (East)
SÀNCHEZ, AMANDO–1948–p, Memphis Red Sox
SÀNCHEZ, GONZALO–1904-05, 1909–c, All Cubans, Cuban Stars
SÀNCHEZ, JOSÉ (JOE)–1913-14–of, 1b, Philadelphia Giants, Lincoln (NY) Stars
SANDERS, ____–1920–c, 2b, Knoxville Giants, Pensacola Giants
SANDERS, ____–1925–c, Penn Red Caps of New York
SANDERS, ____–1935–3b, Chicago Giants
SANDERS [SAUNDERS], BOBBY GENE–1957-59–of, ss, Birmingham Black Barons, Memphis Red Sox
SANDERS, D. D.–1953–2b, Kansas City (KS) Giants
SANDERS, EUGENE–1947–ss, New York Black Yankees
SANDERS, HUBERT–1913–1b, ss, Homestead Grays
SANDERS, JAMES E. (JAKE)–1955-59–of, Kansas City Monarchs, New Orleans Bears, Detroit Stars
SANDERS, JESS–1946, 1949–p, Asheville Blues, Durham (NC) Eagles
SANDERS, JOHN–1871–1b, Chicago Uniques
SANDERS, JOHN–1938–3b, Chicago Giants
SANDERS, WILLIE–1936–p, Memphis Red Sox
SANDERS, WILLIE–1958–ss, Birmingham Black Barons
SANDERSON, JOHNNY D.–1947–ss, Kansas City Monarchs
SANDS [SANDERS], SAMUEL–1932–p, Monroe (LA) Monarchs
SANDS, SAMUEL (PIGGY, SAM)–1950-54–ss, c, Indianapolis Clowns, Kansas City Monarchs
SANFORD, ____–1910–p, West Baden (IN) Sprudels
SANFORD, ____–1919–p, Dayton Giants
SANFORD, ____–1920–of, Pensacola Giants
SANFORD, ____–1925–c, Harrisburg Giants
SANTA CRUZ [SANTA], ESTEBAN–1908-10–of, Cuban Stars

SANTAELLA y CORREA, ANASTASIO (JUAN, TACHO)—1931, 1935-37—2b, 3b, ss, of, Philadelphia Royal Giants, New York Cubans
SANTIAGO, ____—1920—c, Birmingham Black Barons
SANTIAGO, ____—1954—of, p, Louisville Clippers
SANTIAGO, CARLOS MANUEL—1945-46—2b, New York Cubans
SANTIAGO y GUZMAN, JOSÉ GUILLERMO (PANTS)—1947-48—p, New York Cubans
SANTOP, LOUIS (TOP, BIG BERTHA, BLACK STAR RANGER)—(nee Louis Santop Loftin)—1909-31—c, manager, Fort Worth Wonders, Oklahoma City Monarchs, Oklahoma City Giants, Philadelphia Giants, Lincoln (NY) Giants, Chicago American Giants, Lincoln (NY) Stars, Brooklyn Royal Giants, Hilldale Club, Santop's Broncos, Breakers Hotel (FL)
SAPERSTEIN, ABRAHAM M. (ABE, A.M.)—1932-50—booking agent; officer, owner, Cleveland Cubs, Cincinnati Ethiopian Clowns (NML), Foster Memorial Giants, president WCBA; 1939—president, Negro Midwest League, 1946—president, West Coast Negro Baseball Association, Negro Major Baseball League of America; 1947—owner, Detroit Senators
SAPERSTEIN, MORRIE—1932—officer, Foster Memorial Giants
SARD, ____—1915—3b, Chicago Union Giants
SARDA, EMILIO ESTEBAN—1935—p, Cuban Stars
SARVIS, ____—1921-22—umpire, NNL
SARVIS, ANDREW (SMOKY, ANDY)—1939-44—p, Cleveland Bears, Jacksonville Red Caps
SATTERFIELD, ALFRED (TOAD, MIDGET)—1901-13—2b, ss, Famous Cuban Giants, Buffalo Cuban Giants, Cuban Giants, Genuine Cuban Giants, Brooklyn Royal Giants, Indianapolis ABCs
SAUCIER, (POPEYE)—1945—of, New Orleans Black Pelicans, Atlanta Black Crackers
SAULTER, ____—1916-18—p, St. Louis Giants
SAUNDERS, ____—1926-29—c, Penn Red Caps of NY
SAUNDERS, ALBERT—1925-28—c, 3b, Homestead Grays, Penn Red Caps of NY
SAUNDERS, AUGUSTUS L. (BOB)—1926-37—2b, Kansas City Monarchs, Detroit Stars, Bacharach (AC) Giants, Monroe (LA) Monarchs, Louisville Red Caps, Cleveland Hornets, Memphis Red Sox
SAUNDERS, G.—1871—of, Monrovia Club of Harrisburg
SAUNDERS, JACK—writer, *Philadelphia Tribune*
SAUNDERS, JOHN—1871—1b, Chicago Uniques
SAUNDERS, LEO—1940—p, ss, Chicago American Giants, Birmingham Black Barons
SAUNDERS, LESTER (YOUNGBLOOD)—1931-32, 1938—2b, Colored House of David
SAUNDERS, WILLIAM—1887—of, Pittsburgh Keystones (NCBBL)
SAUNDERS, WILLIAM (BILLY)—1950—c, Baltimore Elite Giants
SAUNDINE, ____—1929—p, Gilkerson's Union Giants
SAVAGE, ARTIE—1932—officer, Cleveland Stars
SAVAGE, AZEL (ACE)—1928—of, Cleveland Royal Giants
SAVAGE, BILL JUNIUS (JUNIOR)—1940—p, Memphis Red Sox
SAVAGE, JAMES—1925—p, Bacharach (AC) Giants, Wilmington Potomacs, Lincoln (NY) Giants
SAVAGE, JOHN—1944—p, New York Black Yankees
SAVERSON, HENRY L. (HANK)—1954-56—2b, Detroit Stars
SAVOY, ____—1880—2b, Washington Uniques
SAVOY, ____—1867—of, Washington Alerts
SAVOY, RUFUS—1884—ss, 2b, of, Chicago Gordons
SAWYER, ____—1921—2b, All Nations
SAWYER, CARL—1924—2b, Detroit Stars
SAXON, THOMAS (LEFTY)—1942—p, New York Cubans
SAYLOR, ALFRED (GREYHOUND, FOOTS)—1939-46—p, 1b, c, Atlanta Black Crackers, Birmingham Black Barons, Cincinnati Buckeyes, Cincinnati Ethiopian Clowns (NML), Seattle Steelheads, Claybrook (AR) Tigers
SAYTON, IRA P.—1867—officer, Brooklyn Unique
SCALES, ____—1897—utility, Chicago Unions
SCALES, BENNIE—1936—officer, Nashville Elite Giants
SCALES, GEORGE (JUNIOR)—1943—3b, Baltimore Elite Giants
SCALES, GEORGE LOUIS (TUBBY, EL MAGO)—1920-52—2b, 3b, of, ss, manager, Montgomery Grey Sox, St. Louis Giants, St. Louis Stars, Lincoln (NY) Giants, Newark Stars, Homestead Grays, New York Black Yankees, Philadelphia Stars, Baltimore Elite Giants, Pittsburgh Keystones, Birmingham Black Barons, Denver Post Negro All-Stars
SCALES, HARRY—1931—2b, Homestead Grays
SCALES, IRVIN ALFRED (RED)—1921—1b, Pittsburgh Keystones
SCANLON, ____—1915—umpire, NNL
SCANTLEBURY, PATRICIO ATHELSTAN (PAT)—1944-50—p, New York Cubans

SCHAEFER [SCHAEFFER], JESSE (BABE)—1904-11—c, of, Chicago Unions, Chicago Union Giants, Twin Cities Gophers, Minneapolis Keystones, St. Paul Colored Gophers, Chicago Union Giants, Leland Giants
SCHAINE, MICHAEL—1937-38—owner, Atlanta Black Crackers
SCHAUMBERG [SCHOMBURG] ____—1914—c, All Nations
SCHELL, ____—1923—p, Hilldale Club
SCHENCK, ____—1897—3b, Genuine Cuban Giants
SCHIFF, ____—1908—of, Genuine Cuban Giants
SCHLICHTER, HENRY WALTER—1902-10—officer, manager, Philadelphia Giants; president, National Association of Colored Base Ball Clubs of the United States and Cuba
SCHMIDT, EDWARD (JIMMY)—1933—p, Philadelphia Stars
SCHOENDORF, ____—1929—umpire, NNL
SCHOOLS, ____—1880—c, Washington Manhattans
SCHORLING, JOHN M.—1911-27—officer, Chicago American Giants
SCHOTEAU, ____—1914—of, All Nations
SCHREPPAL, ____—1922—umpire, NNL
SCHROEDER, ____—1918—p, All Nations
SCOFIELD, ____—1919—c, Wilmington Giants
SCOTLAND, JOE (OLD FORTY-FIVE)—1908-19—of, p, Pop Watkins Stars, Birmingham Giants, Chicago Union Giants, Indianapolis ABCs, Bowser's ABCs, Louisville White Sox, Jewell's ABCs Giants, Chicago American Giants
SCOTT, ____—1867—c, Philadelphia Excelsior
SCOTT, ____—1910—p, New Orleans Eagles
SCOTT, ____—1929—2b, Tulsa Black Oilers
SCOTT, A. F.—1934-35—officer, Louisville Red Caps
SCOTT, BOB—1942—c, Richmond Hilldales
SCOTT, C.—1937-38—p, of, Birmingham Black Barons
SCOTT, C. L.—1914-15—of, Schenectady Mohawk Giants
SCOTT, CHARLES—1918-20—of, St. Louis Giants
SCOTT, CHARLES W.—1885, 2b, p, of, Chicago Gordons
SCOTT, CLIFFORD—1920-21, 1924—c, Detroit Stars, Cleveland Browns
SCOTT, CORNELIUS ADOLPHUS—1934-97—editor, *Atlanta Daily World*
SCOTT, DANIEL W. (DAN)—1884-87—treasurer, Chicago Gordons
SCOTT, (DEATH VALLEY)—1914-16—p, Chicago
SCOTT, SR., EDWARD—1939-40—of, Miami Ethiopian Clowns; 1952-55—officer, Indianapolis Clowns
SCOTT, SR., ELISHA—1920—co-drafter, Negro National League constitution
SCOTT, ERNEST—1930—1b, Louisville White Sox
SCOTT, EUGENE—1920—c, Detroit Stars
SCOTT, FELIX—1947—p, Detroit Senators
SCOTT, FRANK L.—1887-94—2b, ss, of, vice-president, Chicago Unions
SCOTT, JIMMY—1950—p, Memphis Red Sox
SCOTT, JOHN—1944-50—of, Birmingham Black Barons, Kansas City Monarchs, Louisville Buckeyes, Chicago American Giants, Philadelphia Stars, Los Angeles White Sox, Pittsburgh Crawfords (USL), New York Black Yankees
SCOTT, JOHNNY—1940—of, Cincinnati Buckeyes
SCOTT, JOSEPH (JOE)—1947-50—1b, Birmingham Black Barons, Chicago American Giants, Detroit Senators
SCOTT, JOSEPH BURT (JOE)—1936-58—of, Chicago American Giants, Pittsburgh Crawfords, Memphis Red Sox, Philadelphia Stars, New York Black Yankees, Kansas City Monarchs, Satchel Paige All-Stars
SCOTT, LLOYD—1934-36—2b, 1b, Nashville Elite Giants, Chicago American Giants, Philadelphia Stars
SCOTT, OTTO—1931—3b, Montgomery Grey Sox
SCOTT, JR., PHILIP EDWIN (ED)—1962—scout, Boston Red Sox
SCOTT, REMY—1925—of, Philadelphia Giants
SCOTT, ROBERT (BOB)—1919-27—of, St. Louis Giants, Brooklyn Royal Giants, Lincoln (NY) Giants, Hilldale Club, Harrisburg Giants
SCOTT, ROBERT EUGENE (BOB)—1945-50—p, of, 1b, Boston Blues, New York Black Yankees, Pittsburgh Crawfords (USL)
SCOTT, THEODORE—1932—c, Washington Pilots
SCOTT, WILLIAM—1930—officer, Louisville White Sox
SCOTT, WILLIAM—1946—ss, Nashville Cubs
SCOTT, JR., WILLIAM (WILL)—1950-53—of, Philadelphia Stars, Birmingham Black Barons
SCOTT, WILLIAM C.—1890—secretary Chicago Unions
SCOTT, WILLIE LEE (JOE)—1927-41—1b, Evansville Giants, Memphis Red Sox, Louisville White Sox, Indianapolis ABCs, Columbus Blue Birds, Homestead Grays, Chicago American Giants, Jacksonville Red Caps, Louisville Black Caps

SCOTT, WINFIELD [see WELCH, WINFIELD [WINGFIELD] SCOTT]
SCOTTY, ____–1915–of, Chicago Giants
SCOTTY, ____–1921–of, Calgary Black Sox
SCRAGG, JESSE–1915–p, Philadelphia Giants
SCROGGINS, JOHN–1947–p, Kansas City Monarchs
SCRUGGS, DON JUAN–1954–utility, Kansas City Monarchs
SCRUGGS, EUGENE (DICK)–1956-58, 1960–p, Detroit Stars, Kansas City Monarchs, Birmingham Black Barons
SCRUGGS, H. C.–1924–1b, Birmingham Black Barons
SCRUGGS, ROBERT JAMES–1949-50–p, Cleveland Buckeyes
SCRUGGS, WILLIE C.–1949-54–p, Louisville Buckeyes, Cleveland Buckeyes, Houston Eagles, Birmingham Black Barons, Louisville Clippers, New Orleans Eagles
SCUDDER, E.–1887–c, 1b, of, Philadelphia Pythians (NCBBL), Lancaster (PA) Giants
SCURLY, ____–1929–of, Penn Red Caps of NY
SEARAY, ____–1942–ph, Cincinnati-Cleveland Buckeyes
SEARCY, ____–1929–c, Wichita Falls Black Spudders
SEARCY, KELTON (KELLY, LEFTY)–1950-55–p, Baltimore Elite Giants, Birmingham Black Barons
SEARS, HARRY–1950-51–umpire, NAL
SEATON, ____–1917–of, Dayton Marcos
SEAVERS, ____–1942–p, Jacksonville Red Caps
SEAY, RICHARD WILLIAM (DICKIE, ERKIE)–1925-47–2b, Penn Red Caps of NY, Newark Stars, Baltimore Black Sox, Brooklyn Royal Giants, Philadelphia Stars, Pittsburgh Crawfords, Newark Eagles, New York Black Yankees, Newark Browns, Philadelphia Giants, Schenectady Mohawk Giants, Bacharach (AC) Giants, Newark Stars
SEE, ____–1934–of, p, Cleveland Red Sox
SEERY, ____–1888–of, Hoosier Black Stockings
SEGRAVES [SEAGRAVES], JOHN CLAUDE (J. C.)–1937, 1942-43–of, 2b, ss, Indianapolis Athletics, Memphis Red Sox, Cincinnati Ethiopian Clowns (NML)
SEGRAVES [SEAGRAVES], SAMUEL D. (SAM)–1942, 1946–c, of, Twin Cities Gophers, Chicago American Giants, Cincinnati Crescents
SEGRIST, ____–1931–p, Cuban House of David
SEGULA, PERCY [see WILSON, PERCY LAWRANCE]
SELDEN, A. A.–1887–manager, Boston Resolutes (NCBBL)
SELDEN, WILLIAM A. (WILLIE, FATTY)–1886-99–p, of, Boston Resolutes (NCBBL), Cuban Giants, New York Gorhams (Middle States League), Lansing (MI) Colored Capital All-Americans, Cuban X-Giants, Trenton (NJ) Cuban Giants (Middle States League), York (PA); Cuban Giants (Eastern Interstate League), York (PA); Colored Monarchs (Eastern Interstate League)
SELDEN [SELDON], WILLIAM HENRY (BEE)–1908-14–ss, 2b, Chicago Giants, Chicago American Giants, Columbia Giants, Indianapolis ABCs, Schenectady Mohawk Giants, Leland Giants, Illinois Giants, French Link (IN) Plutos, Twin City Gophers
SELDON, CLARENCE E.–1955-56–of, New York Black Yankees, Indianapolis Clowns
SELF, JOHN–1958–1b, Kansas City Monarchs
SELLER, [see SUTTLES, GEORGE (MULE)]
SELLERS, ____–1891–of, Philadelphia Orions
SEMLER, JAMES ALOYSIUS (SOLDIER BOY, BILL, SARGE)–1933-48–officer, owner, New York Black Yankees
SEMLER, MAUDE–1947-48–officer, New York Black Yankees
SENGSTACKE, JOHN HERMAN HENRY–1940-97–editor, president, general manager, *Chicago Defender, Tri-State Defender*
SERBADE, ____–1941–of, Cincinnati Ethiopian Clowns (NML)
SERRELL [HOSKINS], BONNIE CLINTON (BARNEY, EL GRILLO [the CRICKET])–1941-51–2b, 3b, Kansas City Monarchs, Chicago American Giants
SERUBY, ____–1888–of, Cuban X-Giants
SETO, ____–1929–of, Cuban Stars (East)
SETTLE [GETTLE], ____–1869-71–of, Mutuals of Washington
SETTLE, JR., J.T.–1922-23–officer, Memphis Red Sox
SETTLES, ____–1927–3b, Evansville Giants
SEWELL, ____–1945–p, Asheville Blues
SEWELL, JIM–1956–ss, Birmingham Black Barons
SEXTON, ____–1893–2b, Chicago Unions
SEYMOUR, HELLEN–1913-14–of, ss, All Nations
SEYMOUR, SOLOMON (COOTIE)–1935–1b, 3b, Philadelphia Stars
SHACKELFORD [SHACKLEFORD], JOHN GERALD (GABLE, SHACK, ARK)–1924-30–3b, 2b, manager, Cleveland Browns, Chicago American Giants, Birmingham Black Barons, Harrisburg Giants, Cleveland Clippers, Cleveland Tigers;–1945-46–president, USL
SHADE, HAROLD–1956-57–ss, Detroit Stars

SHADNEY [SHODNEY], WILLIAM—1886-87—of, c, Trenton (NJ) Cuban Giants (Middle States League), Cuban Giants
SHADRICK, ____—1918—c, Bacharach (AC) Giants
SHAFER, ____—1915—3b, St. Louis Cubs
SHAMBERGER, CECIL—1938-40—3b, Atlanta Black Crackers, Indianapolis Crawfords, Kansas City Monarchs
SHANKS, ____—1945—ss, Chicago American Giants
SHANKS, HANK—1927—1b, Birmingham Black Barons
SHANNON, ____—1932—of, Pittsburgh Crawfords
SHARKEY, ____—1923-30—umpire, NNL
SHARKEY, LITTLE—1946—2b, Oakland Larks
SHARP, R.—1927-28—of, Gilkerson's Union Giants
SHARP, WILL (KID WONDER)—1920-21, owner, Birmingham Black Barons
SHARPE, R.—1923—ss, St. Louis Stars
SHARPE, ROBERT E. (PEPPER)—1940-49—p, of, Memphis Red Sox, Chicago American Giants, Chicago Brown Bombers
SHARTZ [SHORTS], ____—1908-14—c, 3b, Philadelphia Quaker City Giants, Philadelphia Giants
SHAW, ____—1909—p, St. Louis Giants
SHAW, ALBERT CHARLES—1942—ph, Birmingham Black Barons
SHAW, BOB—1944—of, c, Chicago Brown Bombers (USL)
SHAW, JOHN—1920—of, St. Louis Giants
SHAW, JOHN E.—1871-76—of, 1b, Chicago Uniques
SHAW, ROBERT (BOB)—1897-99—p, Adrian (MI), Page Fence Giants, Chicago Unions
SHAW, THEODORE (TED, LEFTY)—1927-31—p, Chicago American Giants, Chicago Giants, Detroit Stars, Memphis Red Sox, Pullen's Royal Giants, Philadelphia Royal Giants
SHAW, W. RUSSELL—1910—secretary, St. Louis Giants
SHAW, WILLIAM J.—1920—treasurer NSL, Atlanta Black Crackers officer
SHAWLER, JAMES—1902-13—of, Minneapolis Keystones, Leland Giants, Indianapolis ABCs, Chicago Union Giants
SHEELOR [SEELOR], WILLIE JAMES (PEE WEE)—1951-56—2b, ss, Chicago American Giants, Memphis Red Sox
SHEFFEY, DOUGLAS B. (DOUG)—1910, 1915-16—p, Hilldale Club
SHEFFER, JESSE—1907—C, St. Paul Colored Gophers
SHELBY, HIAWATHA LAVERN (BILL)—1941-46—of, Philadelphia Stars, Indianapolis Clowns
SHELLAFOO [SHULAFOO], ____—1913—of, All Nations
SHELTON, ____—1920—c, Dayton Marcos
SHELTON, JEFF L.—1943, 1946—of, p, Harrisburg-St. Louis Stars, Cleveland Buckeyes

SHEPARD, ____—1870—of, Boston Resolutes
SHEPARD, ____—1880—2b, Washington Manhattans
SHEPARD, BECK—1948—owner, Chattanooga Choo Choos
SHEPARD, SR., FREDDIE D.—1943-48—of, Knoxville, Grays, Atlanta Black Crackers, Birmingham Black Barons, Chattanooga Choo Choos
SHEPHARD, PRICE—1920, 1926, 1928—c, Atlanta Black Crackers, Chattanooga Black Lookouts
SHEPHERD, FREDERICK LEE (TUBHEAD, SNOOKS)—1944, 1947-48— p, Atlanta Black Crackers, Chicago American Giants
SHEPHERD, HARRY—1938—of, Indianapolis ABCs
SHEPHERD, WILLIE—1944—of, Atlanta Black Crackers
SHEPPARD, ____—1929—p, Dallas Black Giants
SHEPPARD, RAY—1924-32—ss, Birmingham Black Barons, Detroit Wolves, Homestead Grays, Detroit Stars, Kansas City Monarchs, Monroe (LA) Monarchs, Indianapolis ABCs
SHEPPARD, [DR.] SAMUEL (SAM)—1887-1926—ss, New York Gorhams (NCBBL); officer, business manager, St. Louis Stars, owner, Cleveland Elites
SHEPPARD, WILLIAM—1922-25—p, Kansas City Monarchs, Memphis Red Sox, Cleveland Browns
SHERBER, JACK—1951—infield, New Orleans Eagles
SHERKLIFF, ROY GEORGE (ED)—1931-34—p, Hilldale Club, Washington Pilots, Philadelphia Stars
SHERMAN, ART—1951—of, New Orleans Eagles
SHERRILL, ERNIE—1959-60—of, Memphis Red Sox
SHEWELL, ____—1925—umpire, ECL
SHIELDS, CHARLIE (LEFTY)—1941-45—p, Chicago American Giants, Homestead Grays, New York Cubans
SHIELDS, JAMES D. (JAYDEE)—1925-29—p, Schenectady Mohawk Giants, Bacharach (AC) Giants
SHIELDS, LONNIE—1916—p, Lincoln (NY) Giants
SHIELDS, R.—1890, 3b, Chicago Unions
SHINER, ____—1870—of, Chicago Blue Stockings
SHINN, WILLIAM A.—1941—2b, New York Black Yankees
SHIPP, JR., JESSE ALRIGHT—1907-12—p, Brooklyn Royal Giants, New York Colored Giants, 1920-21—umpire, NNL
SHIRLEY, ____—1914—of, Brooklyn Royal Giants
SHIVELY, GEORGE ANNER (RABBIT)—1911-25—of, Indianapolis ABCs, Bacharach (AC) Giants, Bacharach (NY) Giants, Washington Potomacs, Bowser's ABCs, Brooklyn Royal Giants, West Baden (IN) Sprudels
SHORT, ____—1907—c, Philadelphia Giants
SHORT, ____—1921—umpire, NNL
SHORTZ, ____—1891—of, Cuban Giants

SHORTER, HILDA MAE BOLDEN [see BOLDEN [SHORTER], HILDA]
SHORTER, JACK—1951—3b, New Orleans Eagles
SHREWSBERRY, ____—1918—of, Pennsylvania Giants
SHROPSHIRE, RALPH—1937—c, St. Louis Stars
SHUGARTY, MURDEN [see MURDEN, SHUGARTY]
SHULL, GLOVER—1911—owner, Twin City Gophers
SHUTT, ROBERT—1941-50—officer, Memphis Red Sox
SHYBAKER, ____—1942—p, New York Black Yankees
SIAS, GEORGE (CHARLEY, DIRTY SHIRT)—1929-34—3b, Shreveport Black Sports, Houston Black Buffaloes, Washington Pilots, Monroe (LA) Monarchs, New Orleans Crescent Stars
SIBLEY, ____—1910-13—p, c, Indianapolis ABCs
SIDDLE, JOSEPH JAMES (JUMPING JOE, LEFTY)—1944-45, 1947—infield, p, Kansas City Monarchs, Detroit Wolves
SIEBERT, ____—1937—of, St. Louis Stars, Pittsburgh Crawfords
SIERRA, FELIPE—1921-32—ss, 2b, 3b, of, All Cubans, Cuban Stars (East & West)
SIERRA y QUINTANA, PEDRO PASTOR (a.k.a. PETE QUINTANA)—1954-58—p, Indianapolis Clowns, Detroit Stars
SIGENERO, [see FIGUEROA, JOSÉ ANTONIO]
SIJO, [see GÓMEZ, RAFAEL EMILIO]
SILVA, PEDRO—1921-22—p, of, All Cubans, Cuban Stars (West)
SILVERS, LINDSAY—1933—2b, Philadelphia Stars
SILVERS, (PIE)—1946-47—p, Chattanooga Choo Choos
SILVERTO, ____—1930—p, Boston Black Sox
SILVIO [SILVIA], ORLANDO—1957—3b, Mobile Havana Cuban Giants
SIMERSON, ____—1936—p, St. Louis Stars
SIMMONDS, BOBBY—1955—batboy, Indianapolis Clowns
SIMMONS, ____—1923—ph, Toledo Tigers
SIMMONS, ____—1945—ph, Philadelphia Stars
SIMMONS, JR., ARTHUR LEE (BIG HUT)—1958—p, Kansas City Monarchs, Detroit Clowns
SIMMONS, HUBERT (BERT) VAN WYKE—1950—p, Baltimore Elite Giants
SIMMONS, JOSEPH R. (J. R.)—1887—of, 2b, Baltimore Lord Baltimores (NCBBL)
SIMMONS, PAUL—1914—of, Indianapolis ABCs
SIMMONS, ROSCOE CONKLIN (R. S.)—1942-49—officer, Chicago American Giants; secretary, statistician, public relations director, NAL
SIMMONS, SILAS JOSEPH (SI)—1915-18, 1926, 1929—p, of, Blue Ribbons of Germantown (PA), Lincoln (NY) Giants, Cuban Stars (East)
SIMMS, JOHN (JIM)—1871—of, Chicago Uniques
SIMMS, WILLIE (BILL, SIMMY, JEEP)—1934-44—of, Monroe (LA) Monarchs, Cincinnati Tigers, Kansas City Monarchs, Chicago American Giants, Atlanta Black Crackers
SIMPKINS, BOOKER—1920—p, Nashville White Sox
SIMPSON, ____—1930—c, Memphis Red Sox
SIMPSON, ____—1942—2b, Twin Cities Gophers
SIMPSON, DAVID—1933—1b, of, Cleveland Giants, Baltimore Black Sox, Akron Tyrites
SIMPSON, HARRY—1886—1b, Trenton (NJ) Cuban Giants
SIMPSON, HARRY—1956—of, Kansas City Monarchs
SIMPSON, HARRY LEON (GOODY, SUITCASE, PETACAS [Cases])—1946-48—of, Philadelphia Stars
SIMPSON, HERBERT HAROLD (HERB, BRIEFCASE)—1942-51—of, p, 1b, Birmingham Black Barons, Chicago American Giants, Homestead Grays, Harlem Globetrotters, Cincinnati Crescents, Seattle Steelheads
SIMPSON, JAMES—1886-87—of, Trenton (NJ) Cuban Giants, Philadelphia Pythians (NCBBL)
SIMPSON, LAWRENCE—1910-20—p, of, Chicago Union Giants, Chicago Giants, Bowser's ABCs, Schenectady Mohawk Giants, Indianapolis ABCs, West Baden (IN) Sprudels
SIMPSON, WILLIAM E.—1886-87—manager, Lancaster (PA) Giants, Cuban Giants
SIMS, ____—1920—c, Knoxville Giants
SIMS, FREDDIE—1926—p, Gilkerson's Union Giants
SIMS, HARRY FATE (PETE)—1951-54—c, 1b, of, 3b, Philadelphia Stars, Kansas City Monarchs, Memphis Red Sox
SIMS, (HAMBONE)—1944—p, Atlanta Black Crackers, Knoxville Giants
SIMS, LEO—1934, 1938—ss, New Orleans Crescent Stars, Atlanta Black Crackers
SINCLAIR, ____—1932-33—2b, 1b, Bacharach (AC) Giants, Newark Dodgers
SINCLAIR, HARRY—1930-31—secretary, NNL
SINGER, ORVILLE WILLICE (RED)—1921-32—of, 2b, Lincoln (NY) Giants, Cleveland Browns, Cleveland Tigers, Cleveland Cubs, Cleveland Stars, Pennsylvania Red Caps, Kansas City Monarchs
SINGLETON, ____—1896—c, Cuban X-Giants

SINGLETON, ALEX—1946—p, Cleveland Buckeyes
SINGLETON, JERRY—1959—p, Indianapolis Clowns
SINGLONG [SINGLAND], ____—1929-31—2b, of, Nashville Elite Giants, Montgomery Grey Sox
SISCO, MOSES (POP)—1913-18—of, Philadelphia Giants, Jersey City Colored Giants
SIVENS, G.—1884—of, Chicago Unknowns, Chicago Gordons
SKAGGS, ____—1913—of, All Nations
SKIDMOORE, ____—1869—of, Brooklyn Unique
SKINNER, [see BELFIELD, SKINNER]
SKINNER, ANDREW JOHN—1909-11—c, Leland Giants, Oklahoma City Monarchs, Kansas City (KS) Giants
SKINNER, FLOYD—1909, 1912, 1917—p, Kansas City Colored Giants
SKINNER, LOU—1959—of, Kansas City Monarchs
SLAUGHTER, ____—1913—c, Louisville Cubs
SLAUGHTER, ____—1928-29—1b, 2b, Louisville White Sox
SLAUGHTER, C.—1884-85—1b, ss, Baltimore Atlantics
SLAWSON, ____—1916—3b, 2b, Lincoln (NY) Stars
SLOAN, BOB—1927, 1929—of, Shreveport Black Sports, Wichita Falls Black Spudders
SLOAN, ROBERT LEE—1919-21—of, Brooklyn Royal Giants
SLOAN, WILLIAM GEORGE (W.G.)—1909—2b, Kansas City (KS) Giants, Illinois Giants, Leland Giants; owner, Dayton Marcos
SLOANE, ____—1908—p, Cleveland Giants
SMALL, ____—1910—p, Kansas City Cyclones
SMALL, JAMES—1919-22—umpire, NNL
SMALLEY, EVANS—1944, 1946—p, Pittsburgh Crawfords, Pittsburgh Stars
SMALLWOOD, DeWITT MARK (WOODY)—1951-55—of, New York Black Yankees, Philadelphia Stars, Indianapolis Clowns, Birmingham Black Barons
SMALLWOOD, LOWELL (LOUIS)—1923-24—2b, Milwaukee Bears, Chicago Giants
SMART [MART], (LEFTY)—1932—p, of, Indianapolis ABCs
SMATHERS, CHARLEY—1960—p, Detroit-New Orleans Stars
SMAULDING, BAZZ OWEN—1927-28—p, Kansas City Monarchs, Cleveland Tigers, Chicago American Giants, Birmingham Black Barons
SMELDING, CLARENCE—1946—player, Kansas City Monarchs

SMILEY, DOUG—1926-29—p, Montgomery Grey Sox, Nashville Elite Giants, Evansville Giants
SMITH, ____—1880—1b, Washington Keystones
SMITH, ____—1886—ss, Brooklyn Alpines
SMITH, ____—1887—p, Louisville Falls City (NCBBL)
SMITH, ____—1891—of, New York Gorhams
SMITH, ____—1898—of, Adrian (MI) Page Fence Giants
SMITH, ____—1908—of, New York Colored Giants
SMITH, ____—1909—3b, Kansas City (MO) Royal Giants
SMITH, ____—1913—1b, Paterson (NJ) Smart Set
SMITH, ____—1918—1b, Indianapolis ABCs
SMITH, ____—1918—of, Columbus Giants
SMITH, ____—1918—3b, Bacharach (AC) Giants
SMITH, ____—1919—of, Lincoln (NY) Giants, Grand Central Terminal Red Caps
SMITH, ____—1920—2b, ss, Jacksonville Stars
SMITH, ____—1920—of, Chicago Union Giants
SMITH, ____—1920—of, Chicago Black Sox
SMITH, ____—1920-21—p, Detroit Stars, Cleveland Tate Stars
SMITH, ____—1920—of, Chattanooga Black Lookouts
SMITH, ____—1920—of, Pittsburgh Stars of Buffalo
SMITH, ____—1921—of, Chicago American Giants
SMITH, ____—1921—p, St. Louis Giants
SMITH, ____—1921—1b, Illinois Giants
SMITH, ____—1921—p, Cleveland Tate Stars
SMITH, ____—1922—p, Nashville Cubs
SMITH, ____—1922—p, ss, Bacharach (NY) Giants
SMITH, ____—1924—c, St. Louis Stars
SMITH, ____—1924, 1927—of, Memphis Red Sox
SMITH, ____—1926—p, ss, Dayton Marcos
SMITH, ____—1926—3b, Atlanta Black Crackers
SMITH, ____—1928—3b, Harrisburg Giants
SMITH, ____—1929—p, Fort Worth Panthers, Houston Black Buffaloes
SMITH, ____—1931—p, Louisville White Sox
SMITH, ____—1932—p, Austin Black Senators
SMITH, ____—1932—ss, 3b, John Donaldson All-Stars
SMITH, ____—1932—p, Bacharach (Philly) Giants
SMITH, ____—1935—c, Chicago Giants
SMITH, ____—1939—p, Homestead Grays
SMITH, ____—1942—of, Baltimore Grays
SMITH, ____—1942—1b, Philadelphia Daisies
SMITH, ____—1942—p, Detroit Black Sox
SMITH, ____—1947—3b, Chattanooga Black Lookouts
SMITH, ____—1948—of, Kansas City Royals

SMITH, A.—1867-71—p, 3b, Mutuals of Washington, Ithaca (NY) Actives, Actives of Philadelphia

SMITH, A.—1931—c, Chicago Giants

SMITH, ALEX—1913—2b, Chicago American Giants

SMITH, ALLEN (NICODEMUS)—1936-40—1b, p, Miami Giants, Ethiopian Clowns, Royal Poinciana Hotel

SMITH, ALPHONSE EUGENE (AL, FUZZY)—1946-48—of, ss, Cleveland Buckeyes

SMITH, ART (WHEEZER)—1914-15—p, All Nations

SMITH, B.—1921—p, Baltimore Black Sox

SMITH, B.—1921—c, ss, Norfolk Giants, Richmond Giants

SMITH, B. (BUSTER)—1931-33—p, c, 1b, Birmingham Black Barons

SMITH, B. B. H. (BABE)—1887-89—p, New York Gorhams (NCBBL) and (Middle States League)

SMITH, BENJAMIN F. (BEN)—1939, 1947—p, St. Louis Giants, Detroit Senators

SMITH, BILL—1948—of, New York Black Yankees

SMITH, C.—1897, 1904—of, 3b, Cuban Giants, Cuban X-Giants

SMITH, C.—1915—p, St. Louis Cubs

SMITH, C.—1921—p, Baltimore Black Sox

SMITH, C.—1924, 1929, 1931—1b, 2b, Chicago Columbia Giants, Chicago American Giants

SMITH, C. CHARLES (RED)—1920, 1924-25—c, p, St. Louis Stars, Indianapolis ABCs

SMITH, CARL A. (CLYDE, BOOTNOSE, BOOTS)—1933-38, 1945—c, 3b, ss, Birmingham Black Barons, Homestead Grays, Pittsburgh Crawfords (USL), Monroe (LA) Monarchs

SMITH, CHARLES (CHARLIE)—1938—3b, Washington Black Senators, Newark Eagles

SMITH, CHARLES E. (CHINO, POSTITIO, CHARLIE)—1924-31—of, 2b, Philadelphia Giants, Brooklyn Royal Giants, Lincoln (NY) Giants, Brooklyn Cuban Giants

SMITH, CHARLIE—1888-89—ss, Bloomington (IL) Reds

SMITH, CLARENCE (SCALLY)—1919-33—of, manager, Columbus Buckeyes, Detroit Stars, Birmingham Black Barons, Baltimore Black Sox, Cleveland Cubs, Bacharach (AC) Giants, Chicago Columbia Giants

SMITH, CLEVELAND (CLEO)—1922-29—2b, 3b, ss, Baltimore Black Sox, Lincoln (NY) Giants, Homestead Grays, Philadelphia Tigers, Harrisburg Giants, Newark Stars, Schenectady Mohawk Giants, Philadelphia Royal Giants, Richmond Hilldales

SMITH, DeMORRIS (MICKEY)—1947-49— batboy, Kansas City Monarchs

SMITH, DODE M.—1942—p, Cincinnati-Cleveland Buckeyes

SMITH, DONALD—1953—p, Birmingham Black Barons

SMITH, DOUGLAS O.—1932-34, 1942-43—officer, Washington Pilots, Washington Black Senators, Baltimore Elite Giants

SMITH, E.—1919—2b, Brooklyn Royal Giants

SMITH, E.—1921—of, Norfolk Giants

SMITH, E.—1929—p, Schenectady Mohawk Giants

SMITH, EARNEST (ERNEST)—1934-40, 1944—c, of, Monroe (LA) Monarchs, Chicago American Giants, Detroit Senators, Chicago Giants

SMITH, EDWARD (ED)—1887, 1891—c, Boston Resolutes (NCBBL), Philadelphia Orions

SMITH, EUGENE F. (GENIE, SMITTY, GENE)—1939-51—p, St. Louis Stars, New Orleans-St. Louis Stars, New York Black Yankees, Homestead Grays, Havana Las Palomas, Cincinnati-Cleveland Buckeyes, Cleveland Buckeyes, Louisville Buckeyes, Chicago American Giants, Kansas City Monarchs

SMITH, EUGENE L. (GENE, CHEEVER, GOAT)—1936-46—3b, ss, 2b, 1b, of, Miami Giants, Ethiopian Clowns, Jacksonville Red Caps, Cincinnati Buckeyes, Cincinnati-Cleveland Buckeyes, Cleveland Buckeyes, Indianapolis Clowns

SMITH, F. L.—1890—ss, Chicago Unions

SMITH, FORD [see SMITH, JOHN FORD]

SMITH, FRANK (LEFTY)—1922-23—p, of, Richmond Giants (NAA)

SMITH, FRED—1936, 1946—c, St. Louis Stars, Kansas City Monarchs

SMITH, FRED (SOAPY)—1934—p, Cleveland Red Sox

SMITH, G. (LEFTY)—1927—p, Washington Black Sox

SMITH, GEORGE—1931, 1933, 1938—of, 2b, Chicago American Giants, Nashville Elite Giants

SMITH, GEORGE E. (SONNY)—1948-52—of, Chicago American Giants, Harlem Globetrotters

SMITH, GEORGE CORNELIUS—1956-57—2b, Indianapolis Clowns

SMITH, GUY—1920-21—of, Chicago American Giants, St. Louis Giants, Chicago Union Giants

SMITH, H.—1859, 1862, 1867-71—p, 3b, of, c, Unknown Base Ball Club (of Weeksville, NY), Chicago Blue Stockings, Mutuals of Washington, Brooklyn Monitors

SMITH, H.—1928, 1930—p, Buck Ewing's All-Stars, Birmingham Black Barons

SMITH, HANEY—1947—of, Havana Las Palomas

SMITH, HAROLD C.—1883-85—p, Cleveland Blue Stockings
SMITH, HARRY—1902-10—1b, of, Philadelphia Giants, Brooklyn Royal Giants, Genuine Cuban Giants, Philadelphia Quaker City Giants, New York Colored Giants
SMITH, HARRY—1921—officer, Montgomery Grey Sox
SMITH, HARRY A.—1902-06—officer, Philadelphia Giants, Wilmington Giants; writer, *Philadelphia Tribune*
SMITH, HARVEY—1937-38—p, Pittsburgh Crawfords, Washington Elite Giants
SMITH, HENRY—1942-47—2b, Jacksonville Red Caps, Chicago American Giants, Indianapolis Clowns, Cincinnati Ethiopian Clowns (NML), Cincinnati-Indianapolis Clowns, New York Black Yankees, Harlem Globetrotters, Memphis Red Sox
SMITH, HERBERT (SHINE, HERB)—1921-36—p, Washington Potomacs, Baltimore Black Sox, Bacharach (AC) Giants, Homestead Grays, Lincoln (NY) Giants, Harrisburg Giants, Schenectady Mohawk Giants, Hilldale Club, Philadelphia Stars, New York Harlem Stars
SMITH, HERBERT (LEFTY)—1920-21—p, Kansas City Monarchs, Chicago Giants, Chicago American Giants, St. Louis Giants, Cleveland Tate Stars
SMITH, [ALVIS, ELVIS] HILTON LEE (SMITTY)—1931-50, 1953—p, manager, Austin (TX) Black Senators, Monroe (LA) Monarchs, Kansas City Monarchs, Kansas City (KS) Giants, Kansas City Royals (winter), Fulda (MN), Bismarck (ND); 1980—associate scout, Chicago Cubs
SMITH, HY—1885—of, Brooklyn Remsens
SMITH, I.J.—1932—3b, John Donaldson All Stars
SMITH, J.—1859—ss, Unknown Base Ball Club (of Weeksville, NY)
SMITH, JACOB—1915—p, Philadelphia Giants
SMITH, JAKE—1921-31—2b, ss, 3b, Norfolk Giants, Brooklyn Royal Giants, Harrisburg Giants, Bacharach (AC) Giants
SMITH, JAMES (JIM)—1925, 1930—ss, 2b, Detroit Stars
SMITH, JAMES (JIMMY)—1942, 1950—p, New York Black Yankees, Asheville Blues
SMITH, JAMES H. (JIMMY)—1901-11—3b, ss, p, Cuban X-Giants, Leland Giants, Chicago Unions, Chicago Union Giants, St. Paul Colored Gophers, Illinois Giants
SMITH, JIM—1943, 1945—of, Newark Eagles, Brooklyn Brown Dodgers
SMITH, JOE—1913-16—p, St. Louis Giants
SMITH, JOE—1937—p, Indianapolis Athletics

SMITH, JOHN (LEFTY)—1942-48—of, Birmingham Black Barons, Chicago American Giants, New York Black Yankees, Cincinnati Crescents, Boston Blues
SMITH, JOHN FORD (GERONIMO, EL TENIENTE)—1938-48—of, p, Pittsburgh Crawfords, Indianapolis Crawfords, Kansas City Monarchs,
SMITH, JOHN WENDELL—1937-72—writer, *Pittsburgh Courier* (1937-47), *Chicago American* (1947-73), *Chicago Sun-Times* (1964-72), sports editor, WBBM-TV (1963), WGN-TV (1964-72).
SMITH, L.—1922-23, 1926—of, Baltimore Black Sox
SMITH, L.—1940-42—c, of, Cleveland Bears, Jacksonville Red Caps, Chicago American Giants, Kansas City Monarchs
SMITH, LEANDER—1916-17—of, Kansas City Tigers
SMITH, LEO—1945—1b, Brooklyn Brown Dodgers, Brooklyn Royal Giants
SMITH, MARSHALL (DARKNIGHT)—1919-27—p, of, ss, 3b, Philadelphia Quaker City Giants, Baltimore Black Sox, Homestead Grays, Richmond Giants (NAA), Madison Stars, Schenectady Mohawk Giants, Hilldale Club, Lincoln (NY) Giants
SMITH, MICHAEL—1955—3b, New York Black Yankees
SMITH, MILTON (MILT)—1949-51—3b, 2b, Philadelphia Stars
SMITH, MILTON (YOUNGBLOOD)—1925—c, St. Louis Stars, Indianapolis ABCs
SMITH, MONROE MANCE—1944—of, Kansas City Monarchs
SMITH, MORRIS—1933-34—p, Monroe (LA) Monarchs, New Orleans Crescent Stars
SMITH, NASHVILLE—1933—1b, Newark Dodgers
SMITH, O.—1926-27—of, 2b, 3b, Bacharach (AC) Giants, Montgomery Grey Sox, Brooklyn Royal Giants
SMITH, O. H.—1885—p, Brooklyn Remsens
SMITH, OLIVER (OLLIE)—1945—p, Cincinnati-Indianapolis Clowns
SMITH, OTIS—1942—of, Baltimore Grays
SMITH, PERCY—1952-54—p, Indianapolis Clowns
SMITH, PETE—1937-38—2b, ss, Pittsburgh Crawfords
SMITH, PHIL—1875—c, St. Louis Blue Stockings
SMITH, QUINCY O. (Q)—1943-46—of, Cleveland Buckeyes, Birmingham Black Barons, Cincinnati Crescents, Havana Las Palomas
SMITH, R.—1921—3b, Norfolk Giants
SMITH, R.—1943—of, Kansas City Monarchs
SMITH, R.—1945—p, Chicago American Giants

SMITH, R. (RED)—1914-25—p, of, Lincoln (NY) Giants, Lincoln (NY) Stars, Brooklyn Royal Giants, Hilldale Club, Philadelphia Giants, York (PA) Cuban Giants, Bacharach (AC) Giants, Pennsylvania Giants, Washington Potomacs
SMITH, RAYMOND D.—1945-46—p, Philadelphia Stars
SMITH, RED EAGLE—1920-21—c, p, Bacharach (AC) Giants, Cleveland Tate Stars
SMITH, RICHARD TOBIAS (TOBE)—1907-14—owner, Kansas City (KS) Giants
SMITH, ROBERT (JAKE, COOL)—1930-44—c, 3b, Birmingham Black Barons, Memphis Red Sox, Cincinnati Tigers, St. Louis Stars, New Orleans-St. Louis Stars, Pittsburgh Crawfords, Cleveland Cubs, Chicago Brown Bombers
SMITH, ROBERT LEE (BOB)—1954, 1964—c, of, Detroit Stars, Satchel Paige All-Stars
SMITH, RUSSELL—1939, 1942—1b, 3b, Bacharach (Philly) Giants, Philadelphia Daisies (NML), Richmond (VA) Daisies
SMITH, S. (SPOOK)—1942—c, Baltimore Grays
SMITH, SAM—1911—of, Pittsburgh Giants
SMITH, SAMUEL—1883—player, Cleveland Blue Stockings
SMITH, SCOTT—1920-21—of, p, Knoxville Giants, Atlanta Black Crackers
SMITH, STANLEY—1949—of, Durham (NC) Eagles
SMITH, TAYLOR—1948-53, 1956-58, 1960—p, Chicago American Giants, Birmingham Black Barons, Indianapolis Clowns, Kansas City Monarchs
SMITH, THEODORE—1921—1b, Illinois Giants
SMITH, THEODORE W.—1885—officer, Brooklyn Remsens
SMITH, THEOLIC (FIREBALL)—1936-51—p, Pittsburgh Crawfords, St. Louis Stars, New Orleans-St. Louis Stars, Cincinnati-Cleveland Buckeyes, Cleveland Buckeyes, Kansas City Monarchs, Toledo Crawfords, Chicago American Giants, Claybrook (AR) Tigers
SMITH, TOM—1870—3b, Johnstown (NY) Wide Awakes
SMITH, (TURKEY)—1934-36—1b, p, c, Cleveland Red Sox, Cincinnati Tigers, Chattanooga Black Lookouts
SMITH, VOLDIE—1920—2b, 1b, Pensacola Giants
SMITH, W.—1921—ss, Hilldale Club
SMITH, W.—1921—c, Washington DC Braves
SMITH, W.—1927—1b, Washington Black Sox
SMITH, W.—1931—3b, ss, Cincinnati Tigers
SMITH, W.A.—1922-23—c, Richmond Giants
SMITH, WALTER WALKER—1944—c, Cleveland Buckeyes
SMITH, WARDELL—1946—p, Chicago American Giants

SMITH, WAYMAN—1930—of, Columbus Keystones
SMITH, WENDELL— [see SMITH, JOHN WENDELL]
SMITH, WILL— 1920—p, Jacksonville Stars
SMITH, WILLIAM—1887—officer, Washington Capital Citys
SMITH, WILLIAM—1938—2b, ss, Newark Eagles
SMITH, WILLIAM C.—1888-90—p, 3b, of, officer, Chicago Unions
SMITH, WILLIAM T. (BIG BILL)—1883-1916—c, 1b, of, 3b, manager, Genuine Cuban Giants, Cuban X-Giants, Philadelphia Giants, Brooklyn Royal Giants, Schenectady Mohawk Giants, Chicago Unions, Memphis Giants, Cuban Giants, New York Stars, Brooklyn All-Stars, St. Louis Black Stockings, New York Black Sox
SMITH, WILLIE D. (WONDERFUL)—1957-60—p, of, Detroit Stars, Birmingham Black Barons
SMITH, WILLIE D.—1946-48—p, 3b, Homestead Grays, Cincinnati Crescents
SMITH, WORTHY—1909-10—officer, Kansas City (KS) Giants
SMITH, W.T.—1917-22—umpire, NNL
SMITH, WYMAN C. (LEFTY, SUBWAY)—1920-25—of, Baltimore Black Sox
SMOOT, ____—1886-87—ss, 1b, New York Gorhams
SNAER (SHAER, SNAIR, SWAIN), LUCIAN—1923—umpire, NNL
SNEAD [SNEED], SYLVESTER ALONZO (BO, GATOR)—1938-46, 57-58—of, 2b, ss, manager, Kansas City Monarchs, Cincinnati Ethiopian Clowns (NML), New York Black Yankees, Indianapolis Clowns, Schenectady Mohawk Giants, Detroit Black Sox
SNEED, EARL—1929—p, Dallas Black Giants
SNEED, EDDIE (LEFTY)—1940-42—p, Birmingham Black Barons
SNEEDON, JAMES—1891—player, Elmira (PONY League)
SNIPPERS, PHILIP—1888—manager, New York Gorhams
SNOW, FELTON (SKIPPER)—1929-47, 1950—3b, 2b, manager, Louisville White Sox, Louisville Black Caps, Nashville Elite Giants, Columbus Elite Giants, Washington Elite Giants, Baltimore Elite Giants, Nashville Cubs, New Orleans Crescent Stars, Philadelphia Stars, Cleveland Red Sox, South All-Stars, New Orleans Creoles
SNOWDEN, ____—1869—ss, Washington Alerts
SNOWDEN, ____—1921—of, Norfolk Giants
SNOWDEN, DAVE—1933—p, Detroit Stars
SNOWDEN, HELEN L.—1945-46—officer, Brooklyn Brown Dodgers

SNOWDEN, MOSES—1945—3b, Philadelphia Stars
SNYDER, ____—1888—c, Rockford (IL) Rockfords
SNYDER, ____—1915—c, All Nations
SNYDER, SMITH—1943—of, New York Cubans
SOCKARD, [see STOCKARD, THEODORE]
SOLBLUM, ____—1931—of, Birmingham Black Barons
SOLDERO, DIXON—1932—p, Cuban Stars (East & West)
SOLDIER, ____—1923—c, Richmond Giants
SOLER, JUAN REINOSO—1955-56—3b, Detroit Stars
SOLÍS, MIGUEL L.—1928-36, 1940—2b, 3b, Cuban Stars (East & West), New York Cubans, Stars of Cuba
SOMMERS, BILL—1946—Los Angeles White Sox [see SUMMERS, LONNIE]
SORRELL [DR.]—1936-37—owner, Birmingham Black Barons
SOSA, VICTORIANO (VICTOR, RAMON)—1948—c, Homestead Grays
SOSTRE y MORALES, FRANCISCO C. (CISCO KID)—1947—p, New York Cubans
SOTO, A. M. (TONEY)—1917—manager, Havana Cubans
SOTO, JOSEPH JÉSUS—1951—c, New Orleans Eagles
SOUELL [SOWELL], HERBERT (BALDY) [a.k.a. HERB CYRUS]—1940-51—3b, Kansas City Monarchs
SOURIE, FRED LEE—1947, 1949—p, Detroit Wolves, Houston Eagles
SOUTHALL, JOHN—1898—c, Celoron (NY) Acme Colored Giants (Iron & Oil League)
SOUTHWORTH, ____—1931—of, Little Rock Black Travelers
SOUTHY, ____—1921—ss, Lincoln (NY) Giants
SOWELL, CLYDE E.—1948—p, Baltimore Elite Giants
SOWEN, ____—1933—ss, Cuban Stars (East)
SOWLES, ____—1915—2b, All Nations
SPANN, ____—1932—2b, Indianapolis ABCs
SPARKEY, ____—1929—p, Oklahoma City Black Indians
SPARKS, JOE—1937-40—2b, ss, St. Louis Stars, Chicago American Giants
SPARROW, JAMES—1867-69, 1871—ss, of, Philadelphia Pythians
SPARROW, ROY W.—1938—officer, Washington Black Senators
SPEAR, ____—1905—of, Chicago Columbia Giants
SPEAR, CHARLES W.—1885, ss, Chicago Gordons
SPEARMAN, SR., ALVIN (AL) LOUIS—1944, 1949-51—p, Chicago Monarchs, Chicago American Giants, Kansas City Monarchs
SPEARMAN, [REV.] CHARLES KENSTON—1919-31—c, Brooklyn Royal Giants, Homestead Grays, Lincoln (NY) Giants, Penn Red Caps of NY, Fort Worth Black Panthers, Breakers Hotel (FL)
SPEARMAN, CLYDE (BIG SPLO)-1932-46—of, Pittsburgh Crawfords, New York Black Yankees, New York Cubans, Philadelphia Stars, Chicago American Giants, Birmingham Black Barons, Denver Post Negro All-Stars, Brooklyn Brown Dodgers, Brooklyn Royal Giants
SPEARMAN, CODIE—1924-26—3b, of, Cleveland Elites
SPEARMAN, FREDERICK D. (BABE)—1936—3b, ss, Memphis Red Sox
SPEARMAN, HENRY ALLEN (JAKE, LITTLE SPLO)—1932-46—3b, Homestead Grays, Pittsburgh Crawfords, Washington Black Senators, New York Black Yankees, Baltimore Elite Giants, Philadelphia Stars, Newark Eagles, Pittsburgh Crawfords (USL), South All-Stars, Brooklyn Brown Dodgers
SPEARMAN, WILLIAM (WILLIE)—1923-29—p, of, Cleveland Elites, Cleveland Hornets, Nashville Elite Giants, St. Louis Stars
SPEARS, FRANK—1878—ss, Chicago Uniques
SPEARS, L.—1890—ss, Chicago Unions
SPEARS, WALTER—1934, 1937—1b, Cincinnati Tigers, Detroit Stars
SPEASE, JAMES—1960—of, Raleigh (NC) Tigers
SPECKENBACH, ELEANOR M.—1945-46—officer, Brooklyn Brown Dodgers
SPEDDEN, CHARLES PRICE—1918-31—officer, owner, Baltimore Black Sox
SPEEDY, SR., WALTER—1914—infield, Chicago American Giants
SPENCER, ____—1899—of, Cuban X-Giants
SPENCER, ____—1926—p, Cleveland Elites
SPENCER, ____—1946—2b, Seattle Steelheads
SPENCER, A.—1887—utility, St. Louis Black Stockings
SPENCER, HENRY (SPIKE)—1923-26—umpire, NNL
SPENCER, JOHN WILLIAM (JOHNNY, MOUNTAIN GOAT)—1920-22—of, Baltimore Black Sox, Pittsburgh Keystones
SPENCER JR., JOSEPH B. (J.B., JOE)—1942-50—2b, Birmingham Black Barons, Homestead Grays, Pittsburgh Crawfords (USL), New York Cubans, Baltimore Elite Giants, New York Black Yankees, North Classic Team, Cincinnati Crescents, Harlem Globetrotters, Newark Eagles, New Orleans Creoles

SPENCER, WILLIAM (PEE WEE, WILLIE)—1933-40, 1945—c, 3b, manager, Chicago American Giants, Toledo Crawfords, Indianapolis Crawfords, Toledo Cubs/Rays

SPENCER, WILLIE—1941—of, Birmingham Black Barons

SPENCER, ZACK—1931-33—p, Chicago Columbia Giants, Columbus Blue Birds, Detroit Stars, Cleveland Cubs

SPERAN, ____—1932—c, Cuban Stars (East)

SPICER, J.—1887—of, Wilmington Base Ball Club

SPIKE, ____—1923—p, of, Washington Potomacs

SPINK, ____—1898—3b, Cuban Giants

SPOTTSVILLE, RAY [ROY] (BILL)—1950-51—p, Houston Eagles, New Orleans Eagles

SPRATT, ____—1922, 1927—ss, c, Nashville Elite Giants, Evansville Giants

SPRIGGS, ____—1868—1b, Actives of Philadelphia

SPRIGGS, GEORGE HERMAN—1959-60—of, Kansas City Monarchs, Detroit-New Orleans Stars

SPRIGGS, M.A.—1887—officer, Louisville Falls City (NCBBL)

SPRINGFIELD, WILLIAM—1950—2b, New York Black Yankees

SPRUILL [SPROUL], JOE (TONY)—1927-28, 1933, 1941—p, Schenectady Mohawk Giants, Lincoln (NY) Giants

ST. THOMAS, LARRY—1943, 1947—c, Newark Eagles, New York Black Yankees

STACK, ____—1917—2b, Chicago Union Giants

STACK, ____—1933—umpire, East/West game

STACK, ____—1934—c, Washington Pilots

STAFFORD, HUBERT—1929—p, Birmingham Black Barons

STALLARD, WALTER R.—1910-14—p, of, Louisville Cubs, Indianapolis ABCs, St. Paul Colored Gophers, Twin Cities Gophers

STALLWORTH, STERLING—1926, 1932—1b, Atlanta Black Crackers, Little Rock Grays

STAMMORE, ____—1926—p, Lincoln (NY) Giants

STAMPS, HULAN (LEFTY)—1924-33—p, Memphis Red Sox, Indianapolis ABCs, Detroit Stars

STAMPS, (JELLY)—1945—3b, New Orleans Black Pelicans

STANHOUSE, ____—1914—of, Schenectady Mohawk Giants

STANKIE, EDDIE—1951—of, Birmingham Black Barons

STANLEY, ____—1940—of, Chicago American Giants

STANLEY, CHARLES—1883—c, Cleveland Blue Stockings

STANLEY, JOHN WESLEY (NECK)—1928-49—p, Bacharach (AC) Giants, Lincoln (NY) Giants, Philadelphia Quaker City Giants, Brooklyn Royal Giants, Baltimore Black Sox, New York Black Yankees, New York Cubans, North Classic Team, Philadelphia Stars, Hilldale Club

STANNARD [STARMAND], WILLIAM—1887—of, Pittsburgh Keystones (NCBBL)

STANTON, ____—1891-92—c, Cuban Giants, New York Gorhams

STAPLES, JOHN—1920-21—manager, president, Montgomery Grey Sox

STAPLETON, ____—1888—1b, Bloomington (IL) Reds

STARK, CLIFFORD O.—1933—booking agent

STARK, LEE—1887—c, Cincinnati Browns (NCBBL)

STARKEY, ____—1907—1b, Trusty (PA) Giants

STARKS, JAMES (BRUISER)—1934-46—1b, of, Newark Dodgers, New York Black Yankees, Harrisburg-St. Louis Stars, Pittsburgh Crawfords, Brooklyn Royal Giants, Birmingham Black Barons, Homestead Grays, Brooklyn Eagles

STARKS, LESLIE (DOLLY)—1924, 1927, 1932-35—manager, of, 1b, Memphis Red Sox, Kansas City Monarchs, Newark Dodgers, John Donaldson All-Stars

STARKS, OTIS (LEFTY)—1919-39—p, Hilldale Club, Chicago American Giants, Brooklyn Royal Giants, Lincoln (NY) Giants, Bacharach (AC) Giants, Newark Stars, St. Louis Giants, Cuban Stars (East), Providence Giants, Brooklyn Eagles

STEARNES, GERALD—1951—c, New Orleans Eagles

STEARNES [STEARNS, STARNS, STORENO], NORMAN THOMAS (TURKEY)—1920-42, 45—of, Knoxville Giants, Nashville Elite Giants, Nashville White Sox, Montgomery Grey Sox, Detroit Stars, Lincoln (NY) Giants, Cole's American Giants, Chicago American Giants, Philadelphia Stars, Kansas City Monarchs, Detroit Black Sox, Toledo Cubs/Rays

STEDGRASS, ____—1937—p, Memphis Red Sox

STEEL, ____—1926—p, Memphis Red Sox

STEEL, HARRY—1938—p, Indianapolis ABCs

STEELE, EDWARD D. (ED, STAINLESS)—1941-58—of, manager, Cincinnati Crescents, Birmingham Black Barons, Detroit Stars, Detroit Clowns, Chet Brewer's Kansas City Royals

STEELE, WILLIE—1953—of, Kansas City Monarchs

STENO, ____—1914-16—cf, ss, All Nations

STEPHENS, ____—1926—p, Indianapolis ABCs [see STEVENS, FRANK]

STEPHENS, ALBERT—1948—p, New York Black Yankees

STEPHENS, BEAUREGARD G. (B.G.)—1955, 1959—p, of, Kansas City Monarchs

STEPHENS, FRANK [see STEVENS, FRANK]

Negro Leagues Book #2: The Players

STEPHENS, JAMES—1923—officer, Philadelphia Giants
STEPHENS, JOE (JUNIOR)—1949-50—p, New York Black Yankees
STEPHENS, JOHN SAMUEL—1921—p, Indianapolis ABCs
STEPHENS [STEVENS], PAUL EUGENE (COUNTRY JAKE, WIZARD OF YORK)—1921-37—ss, Hilldale Club, Philadelphia Giants, Homestead Grays, Pittsburgh Crawfords, Philadelphia Stars, New York Black Yankees
STEPHENS, ROBERT—1947-48—p, Cleveland Buckeyes, New York Black Yankees
STEPHENSON, ____—1945—2b, Philadelphia Hilldales (USL)
STERLING, ____—1889—p, Philadelphia Giants
STERMAN [STIRMAN], TOM—1908-12, 1915—of, Kansas City (MO) Royal Giants, Kansas City (KS) Giants
STEVENS, ____—1910—p, St. Louis Giants
STEVENS, ____—1925-29—c, Detroit Stars, Chicago Giants
STEVENS, ____—1950—p, Houston Eagles
STEVENS, CHARLES—1910—owner, New Orleans Eagles; 1922—manager, New Orleans Crescent Stars
STEVENS, DYKE—1944—umpire, NAL
STEVENS, FRANK L. (LEFTY) [a.k.a. Lefty Stevenson, Frank Stephens]—1923-31—p, of, 1b, Chicago American Giants, Cleveland Hornets, Toledo Tigers, St. Louis Stars, Cleveland Tigers, Cuban Stars (West), Bacharach (AC) Giants, Birmingham Black Barons, Detroit Stars
STEVENS, GEORGE—1924—ss, Philadelphia Giants
STEVENS, (JAKE), [see STEPHENS, PAUL EUGENE]
STEVENS [STEPHENS], JIM—1933—2b, Philadelphia Stars
STEVENS, LINCOLN—1929—p, Bacharach (AC) Giants, Schenectady Mohawk Giants
STEVENS, ROBERT [see STEPHENS, ROBERT]
STEVENSON, ____—1910—of, New Orleans Eagles
STEVENSON, (LEFTY) [see STEVENS, FRANK]
STEVENSON, WILLARD (WILLIE)—1940, 1943—p, Homestead Grays
STEWARD, ____—1940—of, Cleveland Bears
STEWARD, CLARENCE—1914, 1919—1b, c, Philadelphia Giants
STEWART, ____—1887—p, Baltimore Lord Baltimores
STEWART, ____—1907—1b, Trusty (PA) Giants
STEWART, ____—1910—p, Oklahoma City Giants
STEWART, ____—1919—of, Wilmington Giants
STEWART, ARCHIE (TANK)—1920-24—p, ss, St. Louis Giants, St. Louis Stars, Chicago American Giants, Austin Black Senators
STEWART, ARTIS—1950—p, Cleveland Buckeyes
STEWART, CHARLES W. (CHARLEY)—1951—of, Chicago American Giants
STEWART, FRANK—1866-67, 1870—of, Rochester Unexpected, Washington Alerts
STEWART, FRANK—1934-40—p, Homestead Grays, Washington Elite Giants, Indianapolis ABCs, Memphis Red Sox
STEWART, GEORGE—1926—officer, Atlanta Black Crackers
STEWART, GEORGE PHELDON—1894-1924—cofounder, publisher, *Indianapolis Recorder*
STEWART, LEON—1940-42—p, of, Newark Eagles, Birmingham Black Barons
STEWART, LESLIE—1916, 1922—c, Jersey City Colored Giants, Philadelphia Giants
STEWART, MANUEL—1946-47—3b, Baltimore Elite Giants
STEWART, OZZIE (OSSIE)—1943—p, Baltimore Elite Giants
STEWART, RICHARD—1946—of, Asheville Blues
STEWART, SR., RILEY ANDERSON—1946-50—p, Chicago American Giants, New York Cubans, Memphis Red Sox
STEWART, S.—1886—p, St. Louis Black Stockings
STEWART, SR., WILLIAM (BILL)—1946, 1949-51—p, Portland Rosebuds, Gretna (LA) Graystones
STIGGENS, ____—1921—p, Pittsburgh Stars of Buffalo
STIGGETTS, ____—1912—of, Philadelphia Giants
STILES, ____—1937—of, Detroit Stars
STILES, NORRIS—1950—p, Cleveland Buckeyes
STILL, JOE—1887—player, Philadelphia Pythians (NCBBL)
STILL, ROBERT G. (BOBBY)—1887— officer, National League of Colored Base Ball Clubs; 1b, manager, Philadelphia Pythians (NCBBL)
STILLS, JIMMY—1928-31—of, Pittsburgh Crawfords
STINSON, ____—1932—of, Atlanta Black Crackers
STINSON, CHARLES P.—1887—player, Philadelphia Pythians (NCBBL)
STIRMAN, TOM [see STERMAN, TOM]
STITTLER, ____—1922—p, Bacharach (AC) Giants
STIVERS, BILLIE WAYNE—1939—of, Chicago American Giants
STOCK, ____—1925—p, Penn Red Caps of New York
STOCKARD, THEODORE BERNARD (TED, LICKS)—1927-28, 1937-38—ss, 3b, Cleveland Hornets, Cleveland Tigers, Kansas City Monarchs, Colored House of David
STOCKLEY, LAWRENCE—1950—of, New York Black Yankees

STOKES, ____—1913—of, Paterson (NJ) Smart Set
STOKES, JIM—1933—p, c, Detroit Stars, Atlanta Black Crackers
STONE, ____—1929—c, Evansville Giants
STONE, ____—1943—p, Nashville Elite Giants
STONE, EDWARD DANIEL (ED, ACE, BLACK CAT)—1931-50—of, (bus driver), Bacharach (AC) Giants, Wilmington Hornets, Brooklyn Eagles, Newark Eagles, Philadelphia Stars, Pittsburgh Crawfords, New York Black Yankees, Baltimore Black Sox
STONE, MARCENIA LYLE ALBERGA (TONI)—1949-50, 1953-54—2b, New Orleans Creoles, Indianapolis Clowns, Kansas City Monarchs
STONE, NAT—1956—ss, Memphis Red Sox
STONER, ____—1922—umpire, NNL
STOPUGHERS, ____—1909—ss, Kansas City (MO) Royal Giants
STORY, ____—1930—p, Kansas City (KS) Giants
STOUCH, HARRY—1946—umpire, NNL
STOUT, ____—1888—of, New York Gorhams
STOVALL, ____—1924—p, Cleveland Browns
STOVALL, J.C. (FRED)—1930-35—owner, Monroe (LA) Monarchs
STOVES, WALTER WAITE—1958-60—c, Birmingham Black Barons
STOVEY, GEORGE WASHINGTON—1886-96—p, of, Jersey City (Eastern League); Newark (International League); Cuban Giants, New York Gorhams (Middle States League), Cuban X-Giants, Worchester (Northeastern League), Ansonia Cuban Giants (Connecticut St. League), Troy (NY St. League), York (PA) Cuban Giants (Eastern Interstate League), Trenton (NJ) Cuban Giants (Middle States League), York (PA) Colored Monarchs (Eastern Interstate League)
STRATHEM, CLIFF—1946—utility, Raleigh Tigers
STRATTON, ____—1930—c, Hilldale Club
STRATTON, FELTON (LEROY)—1920-33—ss, 3b, 2b, manager, Nashville White Sox, Milwaukee Bears, Birmingham Black Barons, Chicago American Giants, Nashville Elite Giants, Nashville Cubs, Cuban Stars (West)
STRAUCH, PETER—1946-51—umpire, NNL
STRAWBRIDGE, H.—1929-30—owner, officer, Birmingham Black Barons
STREET, ____—1916—2b, Montgomery Grey Sox
STREETER, SAMUEL (SAM, LEFTY)—1920-36—p, Montgomery Grey Sox, Atlanta Black Crackers, Chicago American Giants, Bacharach (AC) Giants, Lincoln (NY) Giants, Birmingham Black Barons, Homestead Grays, Cleveland Cubs, Pittsburgh Crawfords, Baltimore Black Sox, Breakers Hotel (FL)
STREET[S], ALBERT (GABBY)—1925, 1929-31—3b, p, Chicago American Giants, Colored House of David
STRICKER, ____—1920—p, Baltimore Black Sox
STRICKLAND, COLONEL T.—1929—officer, Dallas Giants
STRICKLAND, W.—1924-25—p, Indianapolis ABCs
STRINGBEAN, ____—1926—of, Memphis Red Sox
STRINGER, JAMES—1909—president, manager, Louisville Cubs
STRONG, GEORGE—1938—manager, Indianapolis ABCs; 1942—1b, Chicago Brown Bombers (NML)
STRONG, HENRY—1936—ss, Chicago American Giants
STRONG, J.C.—1921—of, Dayton Marcos
STRONG, JOSEPH TALTON [FULTON] (JOE, BABY FACE, J.T.)—1922-37—p, of, Cleveland Tate Stars, Chicago American Giants, New Orleans Crescent Stars, Milwaukee Bears, Hilldale Club, St. Louis Stars, Homestead Grays, Baltimore Black Sox, Pittsburgh Crawfords
STRONG, LINCOLN—1895-96—c, Cuban Giants
STRONG, NATHANIEL CALVIN (NAT)—1908-34—booking agent; officer, Brooklyn Royal Giants, New York Black Yankees, Cuban Stars
STRONG, OTHELLO LEAR—1947-52—p, Chicago American Giants, Harlem Globetrotters
STRONG, SR., THEODORE RELIGHN (TED)—1913—p, Chicago American Giants; 1937—manager, Indianapolis Athletics
STRONG, JR., THEODORE RELIGHN (T. R., TED)—1936-51—of, ss, 1b, 3b, 2b, Chicago American Giants, Indianapolis Athletics, Indianapolis ABCs, Kansas City Monarchs, Indianapolis Clowns, Harlem Globetrotters
STROTHERS, COLONEL WILLIAM—1924-27—officer, owner, Harrisburg Giants
STROTHERS, CHUCK—1948—p, Newark Eagles
STROTHERS, TIMOTHY SAMUEL (SAM, TIM)—1906-18—c, 1b, of, Topeka (KS) Giants, Leland Giants, Chicago American Giants, Chicago Giants, Chicago Union Giants, West Baden (IN) Sprudels
STROUD, NICK—1924—umpire, NNL
STROUD, PERCY—1948—umpire, NNL
STROZIER, JR., ALBERT ALTON (COOL PAPA)—1956-59—ss, Memphis Red Sox
STUART, ____—1900—ss, Cuban X-Giants
STUART, C.—1884—p, Baltimore Atlantics

STUART, H.D.—1954-55—officer, Birmingham Black Barons

STUART [STEWART], JOE—1884-87—p, c, Baltimore Atlantics, Baltimore Lord Baltimores (NCBBL)

STUBBLEFIELD, WILKER HARRISON THELBERT (MICKEY)—1947-49—p, Omaha Rockets, Kansas City Monarchs

STUDEVAN [STURDEVEN], MARK—1910, 1916, 1927-28—3b, 2b, of, treasurer, Hilldale Club

STUMM, ____—1937—utility, Philadelphia Stars

STURM, ____—1926—of, Indianapolis ABCs

STYLES, ____—1897—of, Genuine Cuban Giants

SUÁREZ, JOSÉ (CHECHE)—1916-21—p, Cuban Stars (East & West), New York Cuban Stars, Cincinnati Cuban Stars

SUBLETTE, WILLIAM HOWARD—1908, 1910—p, Leland Giants

SULLIVAN, ____—1888—of, Hoosier Black Stockings

SULLIVAN, ____—1914, 1918-20—2b, of, c, Chicago Union Giants, Foster's Hartford Giants

SULLIVAN, ____—1924—p, Indianapolis ABCs

SULLIVAN, ____—1937—p, Birmingham Black Barons

SUMMERALL, WILLIAM H. (BIG, RED)—1936-40—p, St. Louis Stars, Memphis Red Sox, Claybrook (AR) Tigers

SUMMEROW, STEPHEN—1944—infield, Cleveland Buckeyes, Great Lakes Bluejackets

SUMMERS, ANDY—1951—umpire, NNL, East/West game

SUMMERS, LONNIE (CARL)—1938-51—of, 3b, Baltimore Elite Giants, Chicago American Giants, Los Angeles White Sox

SUMMERS, SMITH (TACK, DRAG)—1923-29—of, Toledo Tigers, Cleveland Browns, Cleveland Elites, Cleveland Hornets, Cleveland Tigers, Chicago American Giants, Cleveland Elites

SUNKETT, JR., GOLDEN LEROY (PETE)—1942-45—p, of, Philadelphia Daisies (NML), Philadelphia Stars, Chicago American Giants

SUQUA, ____—1909—p, Cuban Stars

SURNER, ____—1883—1b, Louisville Falls City

SURRATT, SR., ALFRED G. (SLICK)—1949-51—of, Kansas City Monarchs, Detroit Stars

SUSINI, ANTONIO—1921, 1936—2b, ss, All Cubans, Cuban Stars

SUSSO, ____—1930—p, Colored House of David

SUTLIFFE, WILLIAM C. (W.C.)—1878, 1884-86—p, manager, Chicago Uniques, Chicago Gordons

SUTTLES, EARL—1950—1b, Cleveland Buckeyes

SUTTLES, GEORGE (MULE, MULO)—1918-48—1b, of, manager, Birmingham Black Barons, St. Louis Stars, Detroit Wolves, Washington Pilots, Chicago American Giants, Cole's American Giants, Newark Eagles, New York Black Yankees, Bacharach (AC) Giants, Baltimore Black Sox, Newark Buffaloes; umpire, East/West game

SUTTLES, J.T.—1923—officer, Memphis Red Sox, President, Negro Southern League

SUTTON, ____—1911—3b, St. Paul Colored Gophers

SUTTON, ____—1913—ph, Louisville Cubs

SUTTON, ____—1929—of, Nashville Elite Giants

SUTTON, E.—1883-87—c, St. Louis Black Stockings

SUTTON, LEROY—1940-46—p, New Orleans-St. Louis Stars, Chicago American Giants, Cincinnati-Indianapolis Clowns, Boston Blues

SUTTON, WILBUR—1949—owner, Richmond Giants (NAA)

SUYDAM, ____—1859—of, Unknown Base Ball Club (of Weeksville, NY)

SWACINA, ____—1923-25—umpire, NNL

SWAN, ____—1933—ss, Akron Tyrites

SWANDEL, ____—1869—2b, Mutuals of Washington

SWANCY, NOLAN—1924—p, Indianapolis ABCs

SWEATT, GEORGE ALEXANDER (NEVER, SHARKEY, THE TEACHER, BIG SWEAT)—1921-28, 1931—3b, 2b, of, Chicago Giants, Kansas City Monarchs, Chicago American Giants

SWEENEY, AL—writer, *Washington Tribune, Afro-American*

SWEENEY, W. ALLISON—1890-1932—editor, *Indianapolis World*

SWEETLAND, ____—1922—p, Lincoln (NY) Giants

SWEGETT, ____—1927—c, Santop Broncos

SWICKET, ____—1908-11, 1917—p, of, Philadelphia Quaker City Giants, Philadelphia Giants, Philadelphia All-Stars

SWIGGETT, MURRAY SIMPSON—1911, 1916—of, 1b, Philadelphia Giants, Penn Red Caps of NY

SYDNOR [SYDNEY], DOUGLAS (DOUG)—1943-44—of, New York Black Yankees

SYDNOR [SYNDOR], JOHNNY—1938—c, Louisville Black Caps

SYKES, ____—1913—ss, Louisville Cubs

SYKES, FRANKLIN JEHOY (DOC)—1913-26—p, of, Lincoln (NY) Stars, Hilldale Club, Baltimore Black Sox, Brooklyn Royal Giants, Philadelphia Giants, Penn Red Caps of NY, Lincoln (NY) Giants

SYKES, JOE (SIKI)—1942—of, Cincinnati Ethiopian Clowns (NML)

SYKES, MELVIN ELIJAH—1924-26—of, Hilldale Club, Lincoln (NY) Giants, Pittsburgh Crawfords, Atlanta Black Crackers

SYMORE, ____—1916—of, Dayton Marcos

T

TABOR, MONROE—1909-10, 1915—2b, Birmingham Giants, St. Louis Giants, All Nations

TABOR, R.H.—1920—vice-president NSL, officer Atlanta Black Crackers; officer, Nashville Elite Giants

TABORN, EARL (MICKEY, PIEL ROJA [red skin])—1946-51—c, Kansas City Monarchs

TALBERT, ____—1940—c, Birmingham Black Barons

TALBERT, DANGERFIELD F. (DANGER, TAI)—1900-11—3b, Leland Giants, Chicago Union Giants, Chicago Giants, Cuban X-Giants, Chicago Unions, Algona (IA) Brownies, Indianapolis ABCs, Philadelphia Giants

TALBOT, ____—1880—2b, Washington Douglass Club

TALBOT, JAMES—1883—ss, Washington Manhattans

TALBOTT, FRANK—1902-10—p, Chicago Union Giants, Indianapolis ABCs

TALIAFERRO, ____—1867—c, Washington Alerts

TALLEY, ____—1920—p, Pensacola Giants

TALLEY, RICHARD (KID)—1932-34—p, Bacharach (Philly) Giants, New York Black Yankees

TALLEY, STERLING—1946-48—ss, Chattanooga Choo Choos

TANNER, ____—1923—of, Richmond Giants

TAPLEY, JOHN THEODORE—1933—3b, Akron Tyrites

TAPLEY, TOWNSEND—1933—ss, Akron Tyrites

TARRANT, JAMUEL—1945—p, Baltimore Elite Giants

TATE, GEORGE JENNINGS—1918-23—officer, owner, Cleveland Tate Stars; vice president, NNL

TATE, ROOSEVELT (SPEED, BILL)—1931-37—of, Birmingham Black Barons, Nashville Elite Giants, Memphis Red Sox, Cincinnati Tigers, Knoxville Giants, Louisville Black Caps, Chicago American Giants, Claybrook (AR) Tigers

TATE, THOMAS—1958—p, Detroit Clowns

TATE, WILLIAM—1914-17—p, Brooklyn Royal Giants, Lincoln (NY) Giants, Philadelphia Giants, Pennsylvania Red Caps

TATE, WILLIAM (W. M.)—1944-1b, Chicago American Giants

TATUM, JR., REECE (GOOSE)—1939-49, 1958—1b, Louisville Black Colonels, Brooklyn Royal Giants, Birmingham Black Barons, Minneapolis-St. Paul Colored Gophers, Cincinnati Ethiopian Clowns (NML), Cincinnati-Indianapolis Clowns, Indianapolis Clowns, Chicago American Giants, Detroit Clowns

TAYLOR, ____—1871—of, Chicago Uniques

TAYLOR, ____—1902—of, Indianapolis ABCs

TAYLOR, ____—1907—of, Trusty (PA) Giants

TAYLOR, ____—1915—p, St. Louis Cubs

TAYLOR, ____—1919—2b, Dayton Marcos

TAYLOR, ____—1920—c, Peoria (IL) Black Devils

TAYLOR, ____—1929—ss, Louisville White Sox

TAYLOR, ____—1934—of, Kansas City Monarchs

TAYLOR, ALFRED—1932-33, 1936—p, 1b, Indianapolis ABCs, Akron Tyrites, Cincinnati Tigers

TAYLOR, BENJAMIN—1947—p, New York Black Yankees, Jacksonville Eagles

TAYLOR, BENJAMIN HARRISON (BEN)—1910-40—1b, manager, Birmingham Giants, Chicago American Giants, Indianapolis ABCs, St. Louis Giants, Bacharach (AC) Giants, Washington Potomacs, Washington Pilots, Washington Royal Giants, Harrisburg Giants, Baltimore Black Sox, Baltimore Stars, Brooklyn Eagles, Washington Black Senators, West Baden (IN) Sprudels, Hilldale Club, Lincoln (NY) Giants, Royal Poinciana (FL); umpire NNL, EWL, East/West game

TAYLOR, (BIG) [see TAYLOR, JOHN]

TAYLOR, CHARLES ISHAM (C. I.)—1904-22—2b, of, manager, owner, Birmingham Giants, West Baden (IN) Sprudels, Indianapolis ABCs, Royal Poinciana (FL); vice president, NNL

TAYLOR, CORBIN—1868—player, Philadelphia Pythians

TAYLOR, CULLEN E.—1931—owner, San Antonio Black Indians

TAYLOR, CYRUS G.—1922-25—of, Lincoln (NY) Giants, Harrisburg Giants, Baltimore Black Sox

TAYLOR, DAN—1946—ph, Brooklyn Brown Dodgers

TAYLOR, EARL—1931—manager, Little Rock Black Travelers

TAYLOR, G.—1920, 1923—of, p, Birmingham Black Barons, Cleveland Tate Stars

TAYLOR, GEORGE—1875—2b, St. Louis Blue Stockings

TAYLOR, GEORGE H.—1889-09—1b, c, infield, of, Aspen (Colorado St. League), Denver (Colorado St. League), Adrian (MI) Page Fence Giants, Chicago Union Giants, Leland Giants, Beatrice (Nebraska St. League), Lincoln (NE) Giants, St. Paul Colored Gophers, Chicago Columbia Giants, St. Louis Giants, Illinois Giants

TAYLOR, HARRY—1920—ph, Birmingham Black Barons

TAYLOR, HARRY C.—1887—p, of, secretary, Boston Resolutes (NCBBL)

TAYLOR, HERMAN (NORM)—1946-49, 1952, 1954—3b, manager, Asheville Blues, Greensboro (NC) Goshen Red Wings
TAYLOR, J.—1870—rf, Boston Resolutes
TAYLOR, J.H.—1920—vice president, Negro Southern League
TAYLOR, JAMES ALLEN (CANDY JIM)—1904-48—3b, 2b, manager, Birmingham Giants, St. Paul Colored Gophers, Leland Giants, Indianapolis ABCs, St. Louis Giants, Chicago American Giants, Chicago Black Sox, Dayton Marcos, Cleveland Tate Stars, St. Louis Stars, Cleveland Elites, Memphis Red Sox, Detroit Stars, Nashville Elite Giants, Columbus Elite Giants, Homestead Grays, Baltimore Elite Giants, Bowser's ABCs, Toledo Tigers, Louisville White Sox, Chicago Giants, West Baden (IN) Sprudels, Birmingham Black Barons, Washington Elite Giants, Royal Poinciana (FL); vice chairman, NNL
TAYLOR, JIM—1896—of, Cuban Giants
TAYLOR, JOE CEPHUS (CASH)—1949-51—c, of, Chicago American Giants
TAYLOR, JOHN—1943-45—of, Birmingham Black Barons
TAYLOR, JOHN—1947—ss, Detroit Senators
TAYLOR, JOHN (BIG RED)—1920-30—p, Chicago Giants, Lincoln (NY) Giants, Kansas City Monarchs, Penn Red Caps of NY, Chicago American Giants
TAYLOR, JR., JOHN ARTHUR (JOHNNY, SCHOOLBOY)—1935-45—p, Pittsburgh Crawfords, Toledo Crawfords, Homestead Grays, Bacharach (Philly) Giants, New York Cubans, Newark Eagles
TAYLOR, JONATHAN BOYCE (STEEL ARM JOHNNY)—1903-21—p, St. Paul Colored Gophers, Leland Giants, Chicago Giants, Chicago Black Sox, St. Louis Giants, Lincoln (NY) Giants, Indianapolis ABCs, Bowser's ABCs, West Baden (IN) Sprudels, Birmingham Giants, Louisville White Sox, Bacharach (AC) Giants, Hilldale Club, Peoria American Black Devils, Chicago American Giants
TAYLOR, JOSEPH (RED)—1921—p, Chicago Giants
TAYLOR, JUDSON—1870—Pittsburgh Rapids
TAYLOR, JULIUS F.—1913—officer, Colored National Base Ball League of the United States
TAYLOR, LEROY R. (BEN)—1925-36—of, Chicago American Giants, Indianapolis ABCs, Kansas City Monarchs, Detroit Wolves, Homestead Grays, Cleveland Red Sox, Detroit Stars, Birmingham Black Barons
TAYLOR, LOUIS R.—1942—president, owner, Detroit Black Sox
TAYLOR, M.—1922, 1924—of, St. Louis Stars
TAYLOR, MATTHEWS—1920—1b, Birmingham Black Barons
TAYLOR, O.—1935—p, Columbus Elite Giants
TAYLOR, OLAN (JELLY, SATAN)—1934-46, 1956-57—1b, manager, Cincinnati Tigers, Memphis Red Sox, Birmingham Black Barons, Pittsburgh Crawfords, Kansas City Monarchs
TAYLOR, OLIVIA HARRIS [MRS. C. I.]—1922-24—officer, owner, Indianapolis ABCs
TAYLOR, RAYMOND (BROADWAY)—1931-46—c, Memphis Red Sox, Cincinnati-Cleveland Buckeyes, Cleveland Buckeyes, Columbus Buckeyes, Kansas City Monarchs, Cleveland Clippers, Louisville Black Caps, New York Black Yankees, Little Rock Grays
TAYLOR, (RIP, ZEKE)—1931—of, Hilldale Club
TAYLOR, ROBERT (LIGHTNING, FLASH)—1938-42—c, Indianapolis ABCs, St. Louis Stars, New York Black Yankees, New Orleans-St. Louis Stars, Chicago American Giants
TAYLOR, ROBERT M.—1948—officer, New York Black Yankees
TAYLOR, ROSS (SHINE)—1939—of, Toledo Crawfords
TAYLOR, SAM—1926—1b, 3b, Dayton Marcos, Detroit Stars
TAYLOR, JR., SAMMIE T. (BAY)—1953-54—c, Kansas City Monarchs, Indianapolis Clowns
TAYLOR, SAMUEL—1912-32—p, manager, St. Louis Giants, Little Rock Black Travelers, Little Rock Grays
TAYLOR, T.—1909—ss, p, Kansas City (KS) Giants
TAYLOR, TIM—1934—officer, Nashville Elite Giants
TAYLOR, JR., THOMAS (TOMMY, TAILSPIN, MR. T.) LEE—1959-60—p, Kansas City Monarchs
TAYLOR, TRAVIS—1946-47—3b, Cleveland Clippers, Detroit Wolves
TAYLOR, W.—1870-71—c, Boston Resolutes
TAYLOR, WALTER—1905-06, 1909—p, Chicago Union Giants, Kansas City (KS) Giants
TAYLOR, ZACHARY—1937—p, Memphis Red Sox
TEAGUE, ____—1913—p, West Baden (IN) Sprudels
TEAMER, ____—1871—of, Philadelphia Pythians
TEAMOH, ROBERT—writer, *Boston Globe*
TEASLEY, RONALD (RON, SCHOOLBOY) [a.k.a. BLAZER JOHNSON]—1945, 1948—of, 1b, Toledo Cubs/Rays, Detroit Wolves, New York Cubans, Carman Cardinals (ManDak)
TEEL, JOSEPH L. (JOE)—1952—of, Philadelphia Stars
TENNY, WILLIAM ANDREW (BIG RED)—1909-12—c, Kansas City (KS) Giants

TERÁN, JULIÁN (RECURVON, JULIO)—1916-24—2b, 3b, Cuban Stars (East & West), Almendares Cubans, New York Cuban Stars, Bacharach (AC) Giants, Lincoln (NY) Giants
TERINO, ____—1914—p, All Nations
TERRELL, ____—1916—of, Cuban X-Giants
TERRELL, ____—1943—3b, Atlanta Black Crackers
TERRELL, J.B.—1931—1b, Memphis Red Sox
TERRELL, LAWRENCE—1924-25—p, Detroit Stars
TERRELL, SAM M. (S.M.)—1928—general manager, Cleveland Stars
TERRELL [TYRELL], WINDSOR WINSLOW (WW, GEORGE)—1887-96—ss, Boston Resolutes, Cuban X-Giants, York (PA) Cuban Giants (Eastern Interstate League), Ansonia Cuban Giants (Connecticut St. League), New York Gorhams
TERRY, (BABE)—1927-29—p, Nashville Elite Giants, Evansville Giants
TERRY, ERNEST—1931—manager, Pittsburgh Crawfords
TERRY, JOHN (TARCAT)—1931-39—2b, Indianapolis ABCs, Homestead Grays, Cincinnati Tigers, Newark Dodgers, Baltimore Elite Giants, Toledo Crawfords
TEVERA, [see TERAN, JULIAN RECURVON (JULIO)]
THEFIS, ____—1917—of, Dayton Marcos
THOMAS, ____—1869—c, Rockford (IL) Rockfords
THOMAS, ____—1871—of, Mutuals of Washington
THOMAS, ____—1880—of, Washington Keystones
THOMAS, ____—1880—of, Washington Manhattans
THOMAS, ____—1887—2b, 3b, Baltimore Lord Baltimores (NCBBL)
THOMAS, ____—1915—p, St. Louis Giants
THOMAS, ____—1916—ss, Cuban X-Giants
THOMAS, ____—1918—3b, Dayton Marcos
THOMAS, ____—1918—of, Philadelphia Giants
THOMAS, ____—1919-20—1b, Penn Red Caps of NY, Pittsburgh Stars of Buffalo
THOMAS, ____—1921—p, Brooklyn Royal Giants
THOMAS, ____—1920—of, Bacharach (AC) Giants
THOMAS, ____—1923—ss, Havana Red Sox
THOMAS, ____—1927, 1934—of, Gilkerson's Union Giants
THOMAS, ____—1931—2b, Chicago American Giants
THOMAS, ____—1934—ss, Homestead Grays
THOMAS, ____—1942—1b, 2b, Twin Cities Gophers
THOMAS, ALFRED (BUCK)—1944-49—p, Chicago American Giants
THOMAS, ART—1951—p, Kansas City Monarchs
THOMAS, ARTHUR—1883-91—c, 1b, of, Washington Manhattans, Washington Mutuals, Cuban Giants, New York Gorhams, Trenton (NJ) Cuban Giants (Middle States League), York (PA) Cuban Giants (Eastern Interstate League), York (PA) Colored Monarchs (Eastern Interstate League)
THOMAS, BEN—1917—of, Havana Red Sox
THOMAS, BOOKER—1924, 1926—p, New Orleans-St. Louis Stars, New Orleans Black Pelicans
THOMAS, C.—1936—c, New York Cubans
THOMAS, C.—1955—of, New York Black Yankees
THOMAS, CHARLES—1868—1b, Philadelphia Pythians
THOMAS, CHARLES (CHARLIE, TOOTIE)—1942—of, p, Chicago Brown Bombers (NML), Boston Colored Giants
THOMAS, [DR.] CHARLES LEE—1905—1b, c, of, Philadelphia Giants
THOMAS, CHARLES W. (C.W.)—1910-12—1b, p, Philadelphia Giants
THOMAS, CHARLEY—1916-22—c, Baltimore Black Sox
THOMAS, CLINTON CYRUS (CLINT, HAWK, BUCKEYE)—1920-38—of, 2b, Brooklyn Royal Giants, Columbus Buckeyes, Detroit Stars, Hilldale Club, Bacharach (AC) Giants, Lincoln (NY) Giants, Darby Daisies, New York Harlem Stars, New York Black Yankees, Newark Eagles, Philadelphia Stars, New York Cubans, Chicago American Giants, Royal Poinciana (FL)
THOMAS, D.—1932—2b, Kansas City (KS) Giants
THOMAS, DAN—1934-40—of, p, Jacksonville Red Caps, Chicago American Giants, Birmingham Black Barons, Cincinnati Tigers
THOMAS, DAN (BANCH)—1921-32—2b, 3b, Indianapolis ABCs, St. Louis Stars, Kansas City Monarchs, Cleveland Hornets, Memphis Red Sox
THOMAS, DAVE—1936—2b, Chicago Giants
THOMAS, DAVID (SHOWBOAT, DAVE)—1923-46—1b, manager, Montgomery Grey Sox, Birmingham Black Barons, Baltimore Black Sox, Baltimore Elite Giants, Nashville Elite Giants, New York Black Yankees, New York Cubans, North Classic Team, North All-Stars, Washington Black Senators, Brooklyn Royal Giants, Lincoln (NY) Giants, Denver Post Negro All-Stars, 1950—road secretary, New York Cubans
THOMAS, DAVY (KID)—1928—p, Lincoln (NY) Giants
THOMAS, DEAN—1944—p, Chicago American Giants
THOMAS, DON—1945—p, Detroit Motor City Giants
THOMAS, E.—1941—p, Satchel Paige's All-Stars
THOMAS, ERNEST—1945—of, Homestead Grays
THOMAS, EWELL—1922-27—2b, p, Kansas City Monarchs, New Orleans Stars, Nashville Elite Giants, New Orleans Black Pelicans, Evansville Giants

THOMAS, F.—1926—p, Chattanooga White Sox
THOMAS, FRANK—1945—p, Birmingham Black Barons
THOMAS, FRED—1946—p, of, Cincinnati Crescents
THOMAS, GEORGE—1959-60—p, Raleigh (NC) Tigers
THOMAS, HAL (LEFTY)—1931—1b, Baltimore Black Sox [see THOMAS, DAVID (SHOWBOAT, DAVE)]
THOMAS, HENRY—1931—of, New York Black Yankees [see THOMAS, CLINTON CYRUS]
THOMAS, HERB (BOY, LEFTY)—1928-32—p, Lincoln (NY) Giants, Hilldale Club, Havana Red Sox, Schenectady Mohawk Giants
THOMAS, J.—1932—3b, Kansas City (KS) Giants
THOMAS, JAMES—1921—p, Illinois Giants
THOMAS, JASON—1887—1b, Louisville Falls City (NCBBL)
THOMAS, JEROME—1887—c, Washington Capital Citys
THOMAS, JESSE—1945—manager, Birmingham Black Barons, Mobile Black Bears
THOMAS, JOE (IKE)—1932, 1937—2b, Indianapolis ABCs, Detroit Stars
THOMAS, JOHN—1946-47—of, Birmingham Black Barons
THOMAS, JOHN—1950-53—p, Cleveland Buckeyes, Birmingham Black Barons
THOMAS, JOHN W.—1910—vice-president, St. Louis Giants
THOMAS, [DR.] JOSEPH F.—1931-38, president, Bedford Land Company - Greenlee Field
THOMAS, [DR.] JOSEPH H.—1939—officer ECL, owner, Baltimore Black Sox;—1942—owner, Baltimore Black Orioles (NML)
THOMAS, JULIAN R. (JACK, JULES, HOME RUN)—1908-31—of, Brooklyn Royal Giants, Lincoln (NY) Giants, Penn Red Caps of NY, St. Louis Giants, Bacharach (AC) Giants, Hilldale Club, Lincoln (NY) Stars, Breakers Hotel (FL)
THOMAS, L. (FRISCO)—1928-30—1b, c, Birmingham Black Barons, Nashville Elite Giants
THOMAS, LACEY—1934-44—p, of, Jacksonville Red Caps, Cleveland Bears, Chicago American Giants
THOMAS, LARRY—[see ST. THOMAS, LARRY]
THOMAS, LEROY—1934—p, Jacksonville Red Caps
THOMAS, LOU (SCHOOLBOY)—1946—p, Los Angeles White Sox
THOMAS, M.—1918-19—p, Lincoln (NY) Giants, Washington Red Caps
THOMAS, NELSON—1947—p, Newark Eagles
THOMAS, ORANGE—1944—p, Kansas City Monarchs, Kansas City (KS) Giants

THOMAS, ORILLE E. (OREL, LITTLE DEAN)—1937—p, Detroit Stars
THOMAS, SAMUEL—1932—2b, Little Rock Grays
THOMAS, (SPEEDY)—1944—of, Jacksonville Red Caps
THOMAS, VERN—1958—of, Detroit Clowns, Memphis Red Sox
THOMAS, W.—1944—ss, Chicago Monarchs
THOMAS, WALTER LEWIS (BANCY, BANZI, HAZEL)—1935-47—p, of, Kansas City Monarchs, Memphis Red Sox, Birmingham Black Barons, Chicago American Giants, Detroit Motor City Giants, Detroit Wolves
THOMAS, WILLIAM (WILLIE)—1943, 1946—of, Chicago Brown Bombers (NML), Portland (OR) Rosebuds
THOMASON, CHARLES JOHN (CHARLIE)—1941-44—of, Newark Eagles
THOMPKINS [THOMPSON], ____—1920—p, 2b, Pensacola Giants, St. Louis Giants
THOMPKINS [THOMPSON], ____—1920-21—of, c, Dayton Marcos, Columbus Buckeyes, Nashville White Sox
THOMPKINS, ALLIE LEVY (MERK)—1928-29—of, Pittsburgh Crawfords
THOMPSON, ____—1869—3b, Washington Alerts
THOMPSON, ____—1906—p, Famous Cuban Giants
THOMPSON, ____—1920—p, Pensacola Giants [see 1906 THOMPKINS, ____ above]
THOMPSON, ____—1920—1b, Peoria (IL) Black Devils
THOMPSON, ____—1923-24—of, p, Bacharach (AC) Giants
THOMPSON, ____—1939—of, Homestead Grays
THOMPSON, A.—1914—ss, Baltimore Giants
THOMPSON, ALBERT—1859, 1862—p, 3b, Unknown Base Ball Club (of Weeksville, NY)
THOMPSON, AUSTIN DEVERE—1910-16—manager, ss, Hilldale Club
THOMPSON, BENNIE—1914, 1917—2b, ss, 1b, Cuban Giants, Baltimore Giants, Dayton Marcos
THOMPSON, BOBBY—1958—p, Detroit Clowns
THOMPSON, (BUDDY)—1942-43—c, p, Chicago Brown Bombers (NML)
THOMPSON, CARL W.—1954—officer, Louisville Clippers
THOMPSON, COPPERKNEE (WAHOO)—1941-42—of, infield, Cincinnati Ethiopian Clowns (NML), Minneapolis-St. Paul Colored Gophers
THOMPSON, EDWARD LEE (EDDIE, LEFTY)—1942—p, Chicago Brown Bombers (NML)
THOMPSON, JR., FRANK ANDREW (HOSS)—1951-54—p, Baltimore Elite Giants, Birmingham Black Barons

THOMPSON, FRANK PAYNE—1869, 1882—ss, 1b, Philadelphia Excelsior, Philadelphia Orions; 1885, 1887—organizer, Keystone Athletics of Philadelphia, Argyle Hotel of Babylon NY, Cuban Giants

THOMPSON, FRANK R. (GROUNDHOG)—1945-57—p, Birmingham Black Barons, Homestead Grays, Memphis Red Sox, Cincinnati Crescents

THOMPSON, GENE (WILL)—1947-50—p, Asheville Blues, Philadelphia Stars

THOMPSON, HAROLD LLOYD—1949—p, Kansas City Monarchs

THOMPSON, HAROLD R.—1931—p, Detroit Stars

THOMPSON, HENRY CURTIS (HAWK, HANK, AMETRALLADORA, YOUNGBLOOD)—1943-48—of, 2b, ss, Kansas City Monarchs

THOMPSON, H.R.—1929—of, Birmingham Black Barons

THOMPSON, J.W. (FRED, GUNBOAT)—1914-20—p, Lincoln (NY) Stars, Pittsburgh Stars of Buffalo, Detroit Stars, Lincoln (NY) Giants, Penn Red Caps of NY, Bacharach (AC) Giants, Cuban Giants, Pensacola Giants, Chicago American Giants, Chicago Union Giants

THOMPSON, JAMES (SANDY)—1923-33—of, Milwaukee Bears, Birmingham Black Barons, Chicago American Giants, Chicago Columbia Giants, Cole's American Giants, Cuban Stars (East)

THOMPSON, JIMMY—1945—umpire, NAL

THOMPSON, JOE—1956—2b, Kansas City Monarchs

THOMPSON, JOSEPH—1859, 1862—p, 3b, Unknown Base Ball Club (of Weeksville, NY)

THOMPSON, KENNON—1946—umpire, NSL

THOMPSON, LEONARD JAMES (LEN)—1940, of, Kansas City Monarchs, Baltimore Elite Giants

THOMPSON, LLOYD PAYNE—1910-16, 1922-32—of, ss, officer, Hilldale Club, Darby (PA) Daisies

THOMPSON, LUTHER—1945—p, New Orleans Black Pelicans

THOMPSON, MARSHALL—1887—manager, Boston Resolutes (NCBBL)

THOMPSON, NELSON—1947—p, New York Black Yankees

THOMPSON, (PEPPER)—1930—3b, Homestead Grays

THOMPSON, RANDOLPH—1949—p, Homestead Grays

THOMPSON, RICHARD VICTOR (VIC, DICK)—1954—ss, of, Kansas City Monarchs

THOMPSON, RUSSELL—stockholder—1920-31, The Negro National League of Professional Baseball Clubs (NNL);

THOMPSON, S.—1932-35—p, Cuban Stars (East), Brooklyn Eagles, Cleveland Cubs

THOMPSON, SAMPSON—1906—p, Cuban Giants

THOMPSON, JR., SAMUEL (SAM)—1957, 1959—of, p, New Orleans Bears, Raleigh (NC) Tigers, Kansas City Monarchs

THOMPSON, SAMUEL (SAMMY, RUNT)—1929-38—ss, 2b, Birmingham Black Barons, Memphis Red Sox, Little Rock Black Travelers, Cleveland Bears, Atlanta Black Crackers, Little Rock Grays, Kansas City Monarchs

THOMPSON, SAMUEL KING (HOME RUN, SAM)—1903-05, 1908-11—of, c, Philadelphia Giants, Louisville Giants, Indianapolis ABCs

THOMPSON, SAMUEL TOMMY (SAD SAM, LONG TOM)—1931-48—p, Kansas City Monarchs, Indianapolis ABCs, Detroit Stars, Columbus Elite Giants, Philadelphia Stars, Chicago American Giants, Monroe (LA) Monarchs, Nashville Elite Giants, Baltimore Elite Giants, Cleveland Buckeyes

THOMPSON, T.R.—1921—2b, Chicago Giants

THOMPSON, V.—1859, 1862—p, Unknown Base Ball Club (of Weeksville, NY)

THOMPSON, VIC—1954—ss, Kansas City Monarchs

THOMPSON, WADE—1922-26—p, of, Harrisburg Giants, Richmond Giants (NAA), Baltimore Black Sox

THOMPSON, WALDO—1947—p, Asheville Blues

THOMPSON, WILLIAM—1887—of, manager, Louisville Falls City (NCBBL)

THOMPSON, WILLIAM—1926—ss, Brooklyn Royal Giants

THOMPSON, WILLIAM PENN (BILL)—1900, 1911—of, Genuine Cuban Giants, Bellows Falls Sulphites (VT) (Twin State League)

THORNE, GERALD (a.k.a TOM THORN)—1946—of, Philadelphia Stars

THORNHILL, ____—1927—p, St. Louis Black Sox

THORNTON, ____—1939—p, Chicago American Giants

THORNTON, CHARLES—1887—p, Pittsburgh Keystones (NCBBL)

THORNTON, HAYWOOD—1931—of, Memphis Red Sox

THORNTON, JACK JOEL—1932-37—1b, Atlanta Black Crackers

THORNTON, JESSE LUTHER—1937—officer, Indianapolis Athletics

THORNTON, MILTON—1946—of, 2b, 3b, Fresno/San Diego Tigers

THORPE, ____—1938—1b, Bacharach (Philly) Giants

THORPE, CLARENCE JIM—1928, 1934—p, Hilldale Club, Bacharach (Philly) Giants
THORPE, WILLIAM—1929—p, Oklahoma City Black Indians
THURMAN, JIM—1932-33, 1937-38—of, 1b, Louisville Black Caps, Columbus Blue Birds, St. Louis Stars, Indianapolis ABCs
THURMAN, JOSEPH—1947—1b, Detroit Wolves
THURMAN, ROBERT BURNS (El MUCARO, BOB)—1946-49—p, of, Homestead Grays, Kansas City Monarchs
THURSTON, ____—1938—p, Birmingham Black Barons
THURSTON, BOBBY—1911—of, Chicago Giants
TIANT, SR., LUIS ELEUTERIO (LEFTY, SIR SKINNY)—1929-47—p, Cuban Stars (West), New York Cubans, Cuban House of David, Havana Red Sox
TIDDLE, MILTON—1955—c, Kansas City Monarchs
TIDMORE, OZZIE—1958-61—2b, of, Kansas City Monarchs
TIERNEY, ____—1915—3b, All Nations
TILLER, ARTHUR—1909—of, Indianapolis ABCs
TILLEY, CLIFFORD—1953—3b, Kansas City (KS) Giants
TILLEY, JASON—1879, 1887—of, Chicago Uniques, Louisville Falls City (NCBBL)
TILLMAN, SR., JAMES PINCKNEY (JIM P)—1941-43—c, Homestead Grays
TIMMONS, HUGH—1913—of, All Nations
TIMMONS, TIM—1913—player, All Nations
TINDLE, LEVY—1933—officer, Detroit Stars
TINKER, SR., [REV.] HAROLD C. (HOOKS)—1928-31—of, Pittsburgh Crawfords
TIPTON, ____—1942—ph, Birmingham Black Barons
TIPP, ____—1920—1b, Jacksonville Stars
TISCHMAN, ____—1924—utility, Hilldale Club
TISDALE, JULIUS (ALEC)—1943—of, New York Black Yankees
TITO, JOE—1931-38, treasurer, Bedford Land Company - Greenlee Field
TITO, RALPH—1931-38, concessionaire, Bedford Land Company— Greenlee Field
TITUS, JAMES—1937—owner, Detroit Stars, Titus Giants
TOBIE, ____—1922—of, Cuban Stars (East)
TODD, ELZIE ALPHONSO (JUNIOR, JOE)—1951-52—p, Indianapolis Clowns
TOBOLDT, C.W.—1898—owner, manager, Celoron (NY) Acme Colored Giants (Iron & Oil League)
TOESANG, ____—1870—c, Utica (NY) Fairless
TOLBERT, ____—1908—p, Chicago Union Giants
TOLBERT, ANDREW—1954—2b, Detroit Stars
TOLBERT, JAMES (JAKE)—1946-48, 1954—c, of, Chicago American Giants, New York Black Yankees, Detroit Stars
TOLBERT, S.—1944—3b, Pittsburgh Crawfords
TOLEDO, JULIO—1951-53—1b, Indianapolis Clowns
TOLES, JR., THEODORE (TED, LEFTY)—1946-47, 1949—p, of, Pittsburgh Crawfords (USL), Newark Eagles, Cleveland Buckeyes, Jacksonville Eagles
TOLIN, ____—1909—player, Harrisburg Giants
TOLIVER, ____—1921—p, Pittsburgh Keystones
TOLOSA, ABRAHAM—1919—p, Cuban Stars
TOL'R, ____—1907—of, Harrisburg Giants
TOMAR, VALDEZ—1932—2b, Atlanta Black Crackers
TOMCO, ____—1922—p, Chicago American Giants
TOME, ____—1908—p, Pop Watkins All Stars
TOMLIN, ____—1926-27—utility, Albany (GA) Giants, St. Louis Stars
TOMM, [TOWN]—1917-18—of, Brooklyn Royal Giants, Philadelphia Giants, Bacharach (AC) Giants
TOMPKINS, ____—1871—of, Boston Resolutes
TONEY, ____—1926—Memphis Red Sox
TONEY, ALBERT—1901-17—ss, 3b, of, Chicago Union Giants, Leland Giants, Chicago American Giants, Chicago Giants, Algona (IA) Brownies, Philadelphia Giants, Philadelphia Quaker City Giants, St. Paul Colored Gophers
TOOMER, ____—1958—of, Memphis Red Sox
TOOMEY, ____—1921—p, Illinois Giants
TOOSON, ROLAND LORENZO—1955—ss, of, p, Memphis Red Sox, Birmingham Black Barons
TOPLIN, ____—1926, 1928-29—c, Nashville Elite Giants, Evansville (IN) Giants, Louisville Black Caps, Nashville Giants
TORIAN [TORRIN, TORAN], LONNIE—1920—p, St. Louis Giants
TORRES, ____—1942—ph, New York Cubans
TORRES, ARMANDO (INDIAN)—1939—p, Cuban Stars (East), New York Cubans
TORRES, JOSÉ (GACHO)—1926—1b, of, Newark Stars
TORRES y MARTÍNEZ, RICARDO J.—1914-16—c, Long Branch (NJ) Cubans
TORRIENTE [TORRIENTI], CRISTÓBAL [CHRISTOBAL, CRISTOBEL] CARLOS—1913-33—of, p, manager, Cuban Stars (West), Chicago American Giants, Chicago Giants, Kansas City Monarchs, Detroit Stars, Gilkerson's Union Giants, Cleveland Cubs, All Nations, Havana Cubans, Foster Memorial Giants, Chicago's Falon Giants

TORRENTO, TY—1932—Atlanta Black Crackers [see ARENAS, SR., HIPOLITO KANTERRA]
TOUSSAINT, ____—1867—p, c, Ithaca (NY) Actives
TOWN, [see TOMM]
TOWNSEND, ____—1938—ph, Brooklyn Royal Giants
TOWNSEND, JESSIE B.—1958-59—p, Kansas City Monarchs
TRABUE, ____—1924—p, Indianapolis ABCs
TRAMMEL, NATHANIEL ELMER (NAT, STEEL ARM)—1926, 1930-32—1b, of, Memphis Red Sox, Birmingham Black Barons, Brooklyn Royal Giants
TRAMMELL, ____—1941—of, New York Black Yankees
TRAMMELL, ELMER—1928—p, Atlanta Grey Sox
TRAPP, JAMES—1935—of, Detroit Cubs
TRAVIS, ARTHUR—1940-41—2b, ss, Detroit Stars
TRAVIS, WILLIAM—1946—p, Homestead Grays, Brooklyn Brown Dodgers
TRAWICK, JOE—1950—2b, Cleveland Buckeyes
TREADWAY, ____—1888—of, Bloomington (IL) Reds
TREADWAY, ELBERT (TED)—1939-40—p, Kansas City Monarchs, Toledo Crawfords
TREADWELL, ____—1888—of, Bloomington (IL) Reds
TREADWELL, HAROLD E.—1919-28—p, Brooklyn Royal Giants, Bacharach (AC) Giants, Bacharach (NY) Giants, Harrisburg Giants, Chicago American Giants, Indianapolis ABCs, Dayton Marcos, Detroit Stars, Cleveland Browns, Lincoln (NY) Giants
TREALKILL [TRILKILL], CLARENCE, HARVEY—1929-31—ss, of, Nashville Elite Giants
TREHEARN, WALTER (BUNDY, LEFTY)—1944-45—1b, Harlem Globetrotters, Birmingham Black Barons, Chicago American Giants, New York Black Yankees
TRENT, THEODORE (TED, BIG FLORIDA, HIGHPOCKETS)—1927-39—p, St. Louis Stars, Detroit Wolves, Homestead Grays, Cole's American Giants, Chicago American Giants, Washington Pilots, New York Black Yankees, Kansas City Monarchs, Evansville Giants
TRESIVANT, WILLIAM [see WILLIAMS, TRESIVANT]
TRICE JR., ROBERT LEE (BOB)—1949-50—p, of, Homestead Grays
TRIGG, ALEX—1955—utility, Detroit Stars
TRIMBLE, FRANK—1931-32—2b, Montgomery Grey Sox
TRIMBLE, WILLIAM E.—1927-32—officer, owner, Chicago American Giants
TRIMONT, PERCY ODELL—1947—utility, New Orleans Black Creoles, New York Cubans

TRIPLETT, MAHLON—1917-18—p, Hilldale Club
TRIPLETT, NORMAN—1917-18—of, Hilldale Club
TRIPP, C.A.—1883—3b, 2b, Cleveland Blue Stockings
TROTTER, WILLIAM MONROE—1901-34—writer, *Boston Guardian*
TROUPE, ____—1930—p, Newark Browns
TROUPPE [TROUPE], QUINCY THOMAS (BIG TRAIN)—1929-49—c, of, p, 1b, 2b, ss, 3b, manager, St. Louis Stars, Detroit Wolves, Homestead Grays, Kansas City Monarchs, Chicago American Giants, Indianapolis ABCs, Cincinnati-Cleveland Buckeyes, Cleveland Buckeyes, New York Cubans; author
TROUT, ____—1927—p, Gilkerson's Union Giants
TROY, DONALD LEE—1944-46—p, Baltimore Elite Giants, Los Angeles White Sox
TRUESDALE, ____—1931—p, Colored House of David
TRUJILLO y MOLINA, (GENERALISSIMO) RAFAEL LEONIDAS—1937—owner, Trujillo All-Stars (Ciudad Trujillo Dragons)
TRUSTY, ____—1927—3b, Santop Broncos
TRUSTY, ED—1907—p, Trusty (PA) Giants
TRUSTY, JOB—1889-1907—3b, of, Ansonia Cuban Giants (Connecticut St. League), Trenton (NJ) Cuban Giants (Middle States League), Philadelphia Giants, Trusty (PA) Giants, Genuine Cuban Giants, York Cuban Giants
TRUSTY, SHEPPARD B. (SHEP)—1885-89—p, of, Philadelphia Orions, Argyle Hotel of Babylon NY, Cuban Giants
TUBBS, ____—1920, 1923—of, Birmingham Black Barons
TUCKER, ____—1891—ss, of, Philadelphia Orions
TUCKER, ____—1916—ss, Penn Red Caps of NY
TUCKER, EUGENE—1927—p, Philadelphia Royal Giants
TUCKER, HENRY—1916-24—officer, Bacharach (AC) Giants
TUCKER, JAMES HENRY—1940, 1944—1b, of, Indianapolis Crawfords, Newark Eagles
TUCKER, MICHAEL—1919-24—of, Bacharach (AC) Giants
TUCKER, ORVAL—1930-31, 1934, 1942—2b, Baltimore Black Sox, Hilldale Club, Bacharach (Philly) Giants, Boston Royal Giants
TUDELL, ____—1919—ss, Grand Central Terminal Red Caps
TUGERSON, JAMES CLARENCE (BIG JIM, SCHOOLBOY)—1951-53—p, Kansas City Monarchs, Indianapolis Clowns
TUGERSON, SR., LEANDER (TUG)—1950-52—p, Indianapolis Clowns

TURNER, ____—1908—2b, New York Colored Giants

TURNER, ____—1928—of, Havana Red Sox

TURNER, A. (JOE)—1947—p, Jacksonville Eagles

TURNER, B. (AGGIE)—1908-17—1b, 2b, of, New York Colored Giants, Indianapolis ABCs, Kansas City (KS) Giants, Cleveland Giants

TURNER, BOB—1946-50—c, Kansas City Monarchs, Houston Eagles, Newark Eagles

TURNER, CARL—1945—3b, Chicago Brown Bombers (USL)

TURNER, CLARENCE—1951-53, 1957—p, Indianapolis Clowns

TURNER, CLEM—1926, 1928-30—1b, 3b, c, Cleveland Tigers, Chicago Giants, Kansas City Monarchs

TURNER, CLIVE—1937-38—p, Chicago Giants

TURNER, ELBERT CARTER (E. C., POP, BERT) [a.k.a. BERT (BILLY, J.H.) Wagner for the Brooklyn Royal Giants]—1921-37—3b, 2b, ss, Bacharach (AC) Giants, Hilldale Club, Brooklyn Royal Giants, Homestead Grays, Birmingham Black Barons, Cleveland Cubs, Cole's American Giants, New York Harlem Stars; umpire, NNL, EWL

TURNER, ETWOOD—1923—of, Toledo Tigers

TURNER, G.—1875—utility, St. Louis Blue Stockings

TURNER, HENRY (FLASH, DAD)—1936-44—c, 2b, of, Jacksonville Red Caps, Cleveland Bears, Newark Eagles, Cleveland Buckeyes

TURNER, JAMES (TUCK)—1919-20, 1923, 1928—p, Dayton Marcos, Chicago American Giants, St. Louis Stars

TURNER, JAMES HENRY (LITTLE LEFTY)—1940-45—1b, Indianapolis Crawfords, Baltimore Elite Giants, Harrisburg-St. Louis Stars, Pittsburgh Crawfords (USL), Brooklyn Royal Dodgers

TURNER, JESS—1916-17—utility, All Nations, Chicago Union Giants, Chicago Giants

TURNER, JOE A.—1947—p, Jacksonville Eagles

TURNER, JOE O.—1887—c, of, Philadelphia Pythians (NCBBL), Lancaster (PA) Giants

TURNER, LORENZO DOW—1911—p, Philadelphia Giants

TURNER, OLIVER—1943—p, Chicago Brown Bombers (NML)

TURNER, RICHARD—1909—secretary, Louisville Cubs

TURNER, ROBERT (BOB)—1946—c, Kansas City Monarchs

TURNER, SONNY—1946—p, Pittsburgh Stars

TURNER, THOMAS (TEETUM)—1947—1b, Chicago American Giants

TURNER, WILSON—1914-16—1b, c, Chicago Union Giants

TURNER, WILLIAM J. (W.J.)—1884-88—3b, Chicago Gordons, Unions of New Orleans, New Orleans Pinchbacks

TURNER, WYATT JAMES (WHITEY)—1930-31, 1939, 1944—c, Pittsburgh Crawfords, Homestead Grays, Great Lakes Bluejackets

TURNSTALL, WILLIE—1950—p, Cleveland Buckeyes

TURPIN, BEN—1937—p, Memphis Red Sox

TUT, KING [nee RICHARD ELMER KING]—1931-32, 1937-60—clown, 1b, Cincinnati Ethiopian Clowns (NML), Schenectady Mohawk Giants, Indianapolis Clowns, Bacharach (Philly) Giants, Baltimore Grays

TWYMAN, OSCAR—1916—of, Lincoln (NY) Stars

TYE, DANIEL RICHARD (DAN)—1927, 1930-37—3b, Memphis Red Sox, Cincinnati Tigers, New York Black Yankees

TYE, DONALD (TIPPY)—1936—p, Cincinnati Tigers

TYES, JAMES—1954—umpire, NAL

TYLER, ____—1869-71—2b, c, Mutuals of Washington, Washington Keystones

TYLER, BILL—1942—c, Chicago Brown Bombers (NML)

TYLER, CHARLES H.—1934-35—officer, Newark Dodgers

TYLER, E.—1915—2b, St. Louis Cubs

TYLER, EDWARD (EDDIE)—1925-28—of, p, Brooklyn Cuban Giants, Hilldale Club, St. Louis Stars

TYLER, EUGENE—1939, 1942-43—c, ss, of, Cleveland Bears, Chicago Brown Bombers (NML), Kansas City Monarchs, Cincinnati-Cleveland Buckeyes

TYLER, J.—1871, 1876—of, c, Chicago Uniques

TYLER, J.—1911—of, Cuban Giants

TYLER, ROY—1925-26, 1931—of, Chicago American Giants, Cleveland Elites, Chicago Giants

TYLER, WILLIAM (STEEL ARM, BILL)—1925-33—p, Memphis Red Sox, Detroit Stars, Kansas City Monarchs, Cole's American Giants, Chicago American Giants, Columbus Blue Birds

TYMS, ____—1922—of, Chicago American Giants

TYNDALE, ____—1868—ss, Actives of Philadelphia

TYNOR, ____—1943—of, New York Cubans

TYREES [TYRESS], RUBY PEARL—1916-24—p, Brown's Tennessee Rats, All Nations, Chicago American Giants, Chicago Union Giants, St. Louis Giants, Cleveland Browns, Royal Poinciana (FL)

TYSON, SR., ARMAND CUPREE (CAP)—1936-42, 1945-46—c, Birmingham Black Barons, Detroit Black Sox,

Philadelphia Hilldales (USL), New York Black Yankees, Fresno/San Diego Tigers

TYSON, JOE—1953—p, Kansas City (KS) Giants

TYSON, OSCAR (BISH)—1942—of, Twin Cities Gophers

TYUS, JR., JULIUS—1947—p, Philadelphia Stars

U

UHLER, ____–1900–of, Chicago Unions
ULACIA, PEDRO–1947–trainer, New York Cubans
UMSTEAD, ROBERT–1913–of, All Nations
UNDERHILL, ____–1919–1b, Wilmington Giants
UNDERHILL, BOB–1924–p, Hilldale Club
UNDERWOOD, ____–1929–c, San Antonio Black Indians
UNDERWOOD, ELI [ELY] M.–1931-32, 1934–of, 2b, Pittsburgh Crawfords, Chattanooga Black Lookouts, Padron's Cuban Giants
UNDERWOOD, JIM–1954–3b, Detroit Stars, Louisville Clippers
UNDERWOOD, RAY–1937–of, p, Detroit Stars
UNDERWOOD, ROBERT LEE–1955–ss, Birmingham Black Barons
UNGO [HUNGO], FIDEL (FIDELIO) A.–1914-16–1b, 2b, of, Long Branch (NJ) Cubans
UN'TER, ____–1897–2b, Genuine Cuban Giants
URBAN, ____–1945–3b, Newark Eagles

V

VACTOR, JOHN—1886-88—p, ss, of, Philadelphia Pythians (NCBBL), New York Gorhams, Trenton (NJ) Cuban Giants, Cuban Giants (Middle States League), Lancaster (PA) Giants

VALA'O, ____—1931—p, Cuban Stars (East)

VALAS, ____—1917—3b, Cuban Giants

VALDÉS y CALZADILLA, FAUSTINO—1920—p, 1b, of, Cuban Stars (West)

VALDÉS y PEÑA, FERMÍN (STRIKE, STRICO, SWAT)—1931-44—2b, ss, Cuban Stars (West), Atlanta Black Crackers, New York Cubans, Cuban Havana Stars, Cuban House of David, Cincinnati-Indianapolis Clowns

VALDÉS, LUCIO A.—1920—p, Cuban Stars (East)

VALDÉS, PEDRO L.—1915—c, Almendares Cubans

VALDÉS, ROGELIO—1905-06, 1910-11—ss, of, Cuban X-Giants, Cuban Stars, All Cubans, Stars of Cuba

VALDÉS, SEVERINO—1920-21—of, Bacharach (AC) Giants

VALDÉS, SIMÓN—1905-06, 1911—2b, All Cubans, Havana Stars, Philadelphia Quaker Giants, Cuban X-Giants, Cuban Stars

VALDÉS y PÉREZ, EDUARDO (PEPE BALA)—1915, 1918-19—p, of, Cuban Stars (East), Havana Reds

VALDEZ, FELIX (MANUEL)—1951-52—p, Memphis Red Sox

VALDEZ, PABLO (TONY)—1910-20—of, p, Stars of Cuba, Cuban Stars (West), Havana Cubans

VALDEZ, P. J.—1917—president, Havana Cubans

VALENTINE, ____—1871—ss, Philadelphia Pythians

VALENTINE, JAMES E. (JIMMY)—1952-57—3b, 2b, Louisville Clippers, Detroit Stars, Memphis Red Sox, Kansas City Monarchs

VALENTINE, JAY—1914-18—of, p, Almendares Cubans, Hilldale Club, Philadelphia Giants

VALEZ, [see VARGAS, JUAN (TETELO)]—1941—of, New York Cubans

VALEZ, QIAQUIME—1927—p, Cuban Stars (East)

VALLEE, ____—1929—umpire, ECL

VALLION, RICHARD—1956—utility, New York Black Yankees

VALOS, ____—1917—3b, Cuban Giants

VAN, JOHN—1930—p, Colored House of David

VAN BUREN, MARK—1940s-50s—umpire, NAL, East/West game

VAN BUREN, WILLIAM (BILL)—1931—of, Memphis Red Sox

VAN BUREN, WILLIAM E. (BILL, COOL BREEZE)—1953—of, Kansas City Monarchs

VAN DYKE, FRED—1895-97—p, of, Adrian (MI) Page Fence Giants

VANCE, COLUMBUS S. (LUKE, DAZZY)—1927-34—p, Birmingham Black Barons, Homestead Grays, Detroit Wolves, Detroit Stars, Indianapolis ABCs, Atlanta Grey Sox

VANDERPOOL, ____—1872—of, Amicable Club of New York

VANEVER, BOBBY—1944—of, Kansas City Monarchs

VANLEW, ____—1884—3b, Newark Dusky Boys

VAN SICKLE, GEORGE—1887-89—Secretary, Trenton (NJ) Cuban Giants (Middle States League)

VANN, EARL—1953—umpire, NAL

VANN, ROBERT LEE—1910-40—editor, *Pittsburgh Courier, The* (Pittsburgh) *Competitor*

VANWYCK, JOHN—1858-60—2b, Henson Base Ball Club of Jamaica (NY)

VARGAS, GUILLERMO—1949—of, New York Cubans

VARGAS, JOSÉ (HUESITO)—1935, 1938-39—of, Cuban Stars (East), New York Cubans

VARGAS y MARCANO, JUAN ESTEBAN (TETELO, THE DOMINICAN DEER)—1927-44—of, ss, Cuban Stars (East & West), New York Cubans, Cuban House of David, Trujillo All-Stars (Ciudad Trujillo Dragons), scout, Pittsburgh Pirates

VARGAS y VÉLEZ, ROBERTO ENRIQUE—1948—p, Chicago American Giants, Memphis Red Sox

VARONA, ____—1948—p, Chicago American Giants

VARONA y SÁNCHEZ, CLEMENTE P.—1947—ss, Cleveland Buckeyes

VARONA y FLEITAS, GILBERTO (GIL)—1950-56—1b, Memphis Red Sox

VARONA y FLEITAS, ORLANDO CLEMENTE—1948-1952, 1955—ss, 3b, Memphis Red Sox

VASQUEZ, ARMANDO [see VÁZQUEZ, ARMANDO BERNANDO]

VASSER, ____—1922—of, All Nations

VASSETTI, ____—1934—c, New Orleans Crescent Stars

VAUGHAN, OSCAR—1951—of, New Orleans Eagles

VAUGHN, ____—1922—of, All Nations

VAUGHN, ____—1929—of, Louisville White Sox

VAUGHN, DONALD ORIN (DON, D.D.)—1955—p, Kansas City Monarchs

VAUGHN, EVERETT—1938—ph, Chicago American Giants

VAUGHN, HAROLD—1926-27—of, Kansas City Monarchs, Breakers Hotel (FL)
VAUGHN, JOE—1931—secretary, NSL
VAUGHN, RAY (SLIM)—1931-34—p, Newark Dodgers, Newark Browns
VAUGHN, SYLVESTER—1940s-50s—umpire NAL, East/West game
VAUGHN, JR., WILLIAM HENRY (BILLY)—1961-65—ss, 3b, Indianapolis Clowns
VÁZQUEZ, ANDRÉS—1935—of, Cuban Stars
VÁZQUEZ, ARMANDO BERNANDO—1944-52—1b, Cincinnati-Indianapolis Clowns, Indianapolis Clowns, New York Cubans, Havana Las Palomas
VEADEZ, HENRY—1952—infield, Kansas City Monarchs
VEALE, SR., ROBERT—1931—p, of, Birmingham Black Barons, Montgomery Grey Sox
VEALE JR., ROBERT (BOB)—1948—batboy, Birmingham Black Barons
VELÁSQUEZ y LARU, JOSÉ LUIS (JOE)—1948-50—p, Indianapolis Clowns
VENEY, ____—1874—of, Chicago Uniques
VENEY, JEROME (JERRY)—1908-17—of, manager, Homestead Grays
VENEY, JOHN W.—1913—c, Homestead Grays
VENNING, RICHARD E. D.—1868—player, Philadelphia Pythians
VENTURA, ____—1929—p, Cuban Stars (West)
VERNAL, (SLEEPY)—1941—p, New York Cubans
VERONA, ORLANDO [see VARONA, ORLANDO CLEMENTE]
VESSELS, G—1888—c, Providence Grays
VICTORY, GEORGE MILLER—1917-20—officer, Pennsylvania Giants, Peerless American Giants
VIDAL, ETIENNE C.—1868—of, Philadelphia Pythians
VIERIRA, SR., JUSTIN CHRISTOPHER (J.C., CHRIS)—1949—of, New York Black Yankees
VILLA y CAMPOS, MANUEL (MANOLO, ROBERTO, BOBBY)—1909-22—of, 2b, Stars of Cuba, All Cubans, Cuban Stars (West), Cuban Havana Stars, Cuban Stars
VILLAFANE, VICENTE—1947—utility, Indianapolis Clowns
VILLARÍN, M.—1921—2b, ss, Bacharach (AC) Giants
VILLAZÓN, ANGEL [MANUEL]—1913—p, of, Long Branch (NJ) Cubans
VILLODAS, LUIS (KING KONG)—1946-47—c, Baltimore Elite Giants
VINCENT, ____—1941—1b, St. Louis Giants
VINCENT, IRVING B. (LEFTY)—1934-35—p, Pittsburgh Crawfords
VINES, EDDIE BENJAMIN—1940—p, 3b, Chicago American Giants, Birmingham Black Barons
VIOLÁ [VIOLAT], JUAN—1902—1b, All Cubans; 1913-16—1b, of, Long Branch (NJ) Cubans
VIVENS, JOHNNIE—1929—p, St. Louis Stars
VIVIAN, ____—1911—p, Brown's Tennessee Rats
VOELKER, ____—1913—p, Louisville White Sox
VONEIS [VONELS], ____—1937—1b, Philadelphia Stars
VOORHEES (VORHEES), ____—1921-24—umpire, ECL
VUNANS, ____—1917—p, Brown's Tennessee Rats

W

WABUM, ____—1912—1b, of, All Nations

WADDY, EWING (IRVING, LEFTY)—1932-33—p, Indianapolis ABCs, Detroit Stars

WADE, BUDDY (SPEEDBALL)—1946—p, San Francisco Sea Lions, Oakland Larks

WADE, LEE—1908-20—p, of, 1b, Cuban Giants, Portsmouth (VA) Giants, Philadelphia Giants, St. Louis Giants, Lincoln (NY) Giants, Chicago American Giants, Lincoln (NY) Stars, Brooklyn Royal Giants, Penn Red Caps of NY, Columbus Black Tourist, Pittsburgh Giants, Grand Central Terminal Red Caps, Breakers Hotel (FL)

WAGNER, ____—1924-25—umpire, NNL

WAGNER, BERT (BILLY, J.H.) [see TURNER, ELBERT CARTER]

WAITES, ARNOLD—1936-37—p, Homestead Grays, Washington Elite Giants

WAITE, R.—1888—of, Providence Grays

WAKEFIELD, BURGESS (BERT)—1895-1908, 1915—1b, 2b, Chicago Unions, Kansas City (KS) Giants, Troy, Atchison, Salina and Emporia (Kansas State League), Algona (IA) Brownies, Chicago Union Giants

WALBROOK, ____—1946—of, San Francisco Sea Lions

WALDEN, GEORGE—1948—of, New York Cubans

WALDON, (ALLIE or OLLIE)—1944-45, 1948—of, Chicago American Giants, Kansas City Monarchs, New York Cubans

WALDRON, ____—1923—umpire, NNL

WALES, ____—1872—of, Keystone Club of New Jersey

WALKER, ____—1896—of, Adrian (MI) Page Fence Giants

WALKER, ____—1904—of, Cuban Giants

WALKER, ____—1905—c, Brooklyn Royal Giants

WALKER, ____—1913—of, Chicago Union Giants

WALKER, ____—1928—c, Kansas City (KS) Giants

WALKER, ____—1929—3b, Wichita Falls Spudders

WALKER, ____—1930—c, Houston Black Buffaloes

WALKER, ____—1932—1b, John Donaldson All-Stars

WALKER, ____—1942—of, Newark Eagles

WALKER, ____—1947—p, Newark Eagles

WALKER, ALBERT (FREDDO) M.—1936-37—manager, Birmingham Black Barons

WALKER, ADMIRAL D. (DEACON)—1923, 1927-28, 1933—p, of, Milwaukee Bears, Kansas City Monarchs, Newark Dodgers, Cleveland Tigers

WALKER, BILL (WILD BILL)—1955—p, 1b, manager, New York Black Yankees

WALKER, BOB—1946—p, Los Angeles White Sox

WALKER, CASEY—1935-37—c, Newark Dodgers, Indianapolis Athletics

WALKER, CHARLIE—1887—c, Pittsburgh Keystones

WALKER, JR., CHARLIE—1930-34—officer, owner, Homestead Grays

WALKER, CHARLIE—1945—pr, Baltimore Elite Giants

WALKER, CLARENCE—1940—p, Philadelphia Stars

WALKER, SR., EDSALL ELLIOTT (BIG, CATSKILL WILD MAN)—1936-45—p, Homestead Grays, Philadelphia Stars, Baltimore Elite Giants, South All-Stars

WALKER, ELON—1958—p, Memphis Red Sox

WALKER, FRANK—1919—officer, New Orleans Black Pelicans

WALKER, FREDDO—1934—owner, Birmingham Black Barons

WALKER, FREDERICK (FRED)—1868-69—of, Philadelphia Pythians

WALKER, GEORGE T. (SCHOOLBOY)—1937-52—p, Homestead Grays, Kansas City Monarchs

WALKER, H.—1926, 1932—c, of, Memphis Red Sox, Monroe (LA) Monarchs

WALKER, HARRY—1943—umpire, NNL

WALKER, HARRY J.—1940, 1945—utility, officer, Cleveland Bears

WALKER, [REV] HERBERT (PIANO RED)—1951, 1957-58—p, Jackie Robinson All-Stars, New York Black Yankees, Indianapolis Clowns

WALKER, HERBERT FRANKLIN (LAUDIE, LOTTIE, PETE)—1921-26—p, of, 2b, 3b, Pittsburgh Keystones, Homestead Grays

WALKER, HUGH—1938—ss, Memphis Red Sox

WALKER, ISAAC (IKE)—1960—c, Raleigh (NC) Tigers

WALKER, J.—1886—of, Unions of New Orleans

WALKER, JACK (JIM)—1940-43—p, Newark Eagles, Harrisburg-St. Louis Stars, New York Black Yankees, Schenectady Mohawk Giants

WALKER, JESSE T. (SELASSIE, HOSS, DEUCE, AUSSA)—1927-55—ss, 3b, manager, officer, Philadelphia Royal Giants, Bacharach (AC) Giants, Cleveland Cubs, Nashville Elite Giants, Washington Elite Giants, Baltimore Elite Giants, New York Black Yankees, Birmingham Black Barons, Cincinnati Ethiopian Clowns (NML), Cincinnati-Indianapolis Clowns, Nashville Cubs, Indianapolis Clowns, Columbus Elite Giants, Detroit Stars, Louisville Stars, Cleveland Royal Giants, Pullen's Royal Giants

WALKER, JOE—1943—p, Pittsburgh Crawfords
WALKER, JOHN OSCAR—1959-60—p, 2b, Raleigh (NC) Tigers, Satchel Paige All-Stars
WALKER, JOHNNY H.—1958-59—2b, Detroit Stars, Kansas City Monarchs
WALKER, LARRY [see DOBY, LAWRENCE (LARRY) EUGENE]
WALKER, LEON—1948—of, 1b, Harlem Globetrotters
WALKER, MOSES FLEETWOOD (FLEET)—1882-89—c, of, 1b, Newcastle, PA, Toledo Blue Stockings (Northwestern League and American Association); Cleveland Whites (Western League); Waterbury (Southern New England and Eastern Leagues); Newark Stars and Syracuse Stars (International League)
WALKER, MOSES [MOSE] L.—1928-31—officer, owner, Detroit Stars
WALKER, OSCAR [see WALKER, JOHN OSCAR]
WALKER, R. 1867-68—3b, Philadelphia Pythians
WALKER, RICHARD E.—1887—3b, Boston Resolutes (NCBBL)
WALKER, ROBERT TAYLOR (R. T.)—1943-49—p, Harrisburg-St. Louis Stars, Homestead Grays, Boston Blues, Harlem Globetrotters
WALKER, SAM—1958, 1960—p, Memphis Red Sox, Raleigh (NC) Tigers
WALKER, T.—1884, 1886—of, Chicago Gordons, Unions of New Orleans
WALKER, TOM (TONY, PRETTY BOY)—1942-45—p, Baltimore Elite Giants, New York Black Yankees, Philadelphia Stars, Homestead Grays
WALKER, W. C.—1931-33—of, Monroe (LA) Monarchs, Newark Dodgers
WALKER, WELDAY WILBERFORCE (WELDY)—1884-87—of, c, 2b, Toledo Blue Stockings (American Association); Akron (Ohio State League); Pittsburgh Keystones (NCBBL), Cleveland Whites (Western League)
WALKER, WILLIAM S.—1937—of, St. Louis Stars, Chicago American Giants
WALLA, GEORGE—1913-15—3b, ss, 1b, All Nations
WALLACE, ____—1904—c, Cuban Giants
WALLACE, ____—1918—c, Chicago Union Giants
WALLACE, ____—1919—3b, Pittsburgh Stars of Buffalo
WALLACE, DEMAS—1907, 1913-14—of, Louisville Giants, Louisville White Sox
WALLACE, FELIX— [see WALLACE, RICHARD]
WALLACE, HORACE—1940—2b, Cincinnati Buckeyes
WALLACE, HOWARD—1933—ss, Baltimore Stars
WALLACE, JAMES ALFRED (BO, JIM)—1948-49—c, Newark Eagles, Houston Eagles
WALLACE, McKINLEY (JACK)—1926-31—of, 2b, Bacharach (AC) Giants, Cleveland Cubs, Philadelphia Giants, Penn Red Caps of NY, Philadelphia Colored Giants of New York
WALLACE [WALLS], MICKEY—1951—p, Indianapolis Clowns
WALLACE, RICHARD FELIX (DICK, NOISY)—1906-25—ss, 2b, 3b, manager, St. Paul Colored Gophers, Leland Giants, St. Louis Giants, Bacharach (AC) Giants, Lincoln (NY) Giants, Famous Cuban Giants, Hilldale Club, Cuban Giants, Genuine Cuban Giants Minneapolis Keystones, Twin City Gophers, Philadelphia Giants, Chicago Giants, Breakers Hotel (FL)
WALLER, GEORGE—1936, 1943-45—of, 1b, Chicago Giants, Chicago Brown Bombers (NML & USL), Atlanta Black Crackers, Newark Eagles
WALLET, ____—1941—umpire, East/West game
WALLICK, WILLIAM—1924—owner, St. Louis Giants
WALLS, ____—1933—of, John Donaldson All-Stars
WALLS, ____—1944—c, New York Black Yankees
WALLS, GREENEY (GREENIE)—1923—manager, of, Memphis Red Sox, 1941-42—umpire, NNL
WALLS, JAMES D. (JIMMY)—1954—of, Kansas City Monarchs
WALLS, MAHLON E.—1947—Philadelphia Stars [see DUCKETT, MAHLON]
WALRATH, ____—1870—1b, Johnstown (NY) Wide Awakes
WALSH, ____—1913-14—2b, Long Branch (NJ) Cubans
WALSH, ____—1925—of, Bacharach (AC) Giants
WALSH, ____—1936—p, Newark Eagles
WALTERS, ____—1917—p, French Lick (IN) Plutos
WALTERS, ____—1921—1b, Calgary Black Sox
WALTERS, ____—1926—umpire, NNL
WALTERS, ____—1927—cf, Chappie Johnson's All-Stars
WALTERS, THEODORE F.—1923-24—p, Milwaukee Bears, Cleveland Browns
WALTON, RONIE—1909—of, Cuban Giants
WALTON, CLIFF (CHIEF)—1916, 1921—ss, Chicago Giants, Pittsburgh Keystones
WALTON, FRANK (FUZZY)—1930, 1938, 1946—of, Baltimore Black Sox, Pittsburgh Crawfords, Boston Blues, Brooklyn Brown Dodgers, Pittsburgh Stars
WALTON, JR., GEORGE—1946-48—of, San Francisco Sea Lions, Fresno/San Diego Tigers, Indianapolis Clowns

WALTON, JACK (JUNIOR)—1946—p, of, San Francisco Sea Lions
WALTON, JOHNNY—1942—p, Chicago Brown Bombers (NML)
WALTON, LESTER ALGAR—1908-14, 1917-19, 1932—writer, *New York Age*
WANNAMAKER, GEORGE—1954-55—3b, Indianapolis Clowns
WANZER, ____—1872—1b, Keystone Club of New Jersey
WARD, ____—1869—p, Brooklyn Unique
WARD, ____—1896—2b, Cuban Giants [see WHITE, KING SOLOMON]
WARD, ____—1913, 1915—1b, Louisville Cubs, West Baden (IN) Sprudels
WARD, ADDIS (ADDIE)—1932, 1935—of, Bacharach (Philly) Giants, Brooklyn Eagles, Philadelphia Stars
WARD, ALONZO—1887—p, Wilmington Base Ball Club
WARD, BRITT—1944-45—c, Kansas City Monarchs, New Orleans Black Pelicans
WARD, (CHERRY)—1927, 1930—p, Evansville Giants, Houston Black Buffaloes
WARD, ELIJAH (ELI)—1946—p, Pittsburgh Crawfords (USL)
WARD, HARRY (WOLFANG)—1934—of, Cincinnati Tigers; 1945—umpire, East/West game
WARD, IRA ELMO—1917-28, 1931—ss, 1b, Chicago Giants, Chicago Union Giants, Foster's Hartford Giants
WARD, NORRIS—1944—umpire, NAL
WARD, RALPH (STODY)—1942—p, Boston Royal Giants
WARD, THOMAS C. (PINKY, WILLY)—1923-35—of, Memphis Red Sox, Chicago Columbia Giants, Louisville Black Caps, Cincinnati Tigers, Birmingham Black Barons, Brooklyn Eagles, Indianapolis ABCs, Bacharach (AC) Giants, Washington Potomacs, Chicago American Giants
WARE, ARCHIE VIRGIL—1940-51—1b, Chicago American Giants, Kansas City Monarchs, Cleveland Buckeyes, Louisville Buckeyes, Indianapolis Clowns, Cincinnati Buckeyes
WARE, JOE (SHOWBOAT)—1920-23, 1932-36—of, Nashville Elite Giants, Cleveland Stars, Cleveland Giants, Memphis Red Sox, Akron Tyrites, Pittsburgh Crawfords, Newark Dodgers
WARE, JOHN—1941—p, Birmingham Black Barons
WARE, WILLIE LEE (SPIDER, LONG GEORGE)—1924-27—1b, Chicago American Giants, Nashville Elite Giants
WARFIELD, FRANCIS XAVIER (FRANK, WEASEL)—1914-32—2b, manager, St. Louis Giants, Indianapolis ABCs, Kansas City Monarchs, Detroit Stars, Hilldale Club, Baltimore Black Sox, Washington Pilots, Bowser's ABCs, Dayton Marcos, Royal Poinciana (FL), Chicago American Giants
WARMACK, HERMAN PETER (H.P.)—1910-11—1b, St. Louis Giants, Indianapolis ABCs
WARMACK, JAMES—1932—of, Washington Pilots
WARMACK, SAM—1921-38, 1941—of, c, ss, Richmond Giants (NAA), Hilldale Club, Bacharach (AC) Giants, Louisville Black Colonels, Washington Pilots, Columbus Blue Birds, Schenectady Mohawk Giants, St. Louis Stars, Cleveland Tate Stars, Detroit Black Sox
WARNER, ____—1922—umpire, NNL
WARREN, ____—1880—3b, Washington Eagles
WARREN, ____—1918—2b, Bacharach (AC) Giants, Pennsylvania Giants
WARREN, ____—1921—p, Kansas City Monarchs
WARREN, ____—1937—c, New York Black Yankees
WARREN, CISCERO THOMAS (LEFTY)—1946-48—p, Homestead Grays, Memphis Red Sox, Raleigh Tigers
WARREN, EDWARD A.—1910—owner, business manager, New York Black Sox
WARREN, JESSE—1940-47—3b, of, Memphis Red Sox, New Orleans-St. Louis Stars, Birmingham Black Barons, Cincinnati-Cleveland Buckeyes, Chicago American Giants, Boston Blues, Boston Royal Giants, Detroit Senators, Kansas City Monarchs, Brooklyn Royal Giants
WARREN, RON (BUNNY, BOB)—1952, 1956, 1959—2b, Detroit Stars
WARRICK [WARWICK], WILLIAM (OLD WAR HORSE)—1903-06—p, of, Philadelphia Giants, Brooklyn Royal Giants, Chicago Union Giants, Cuban X-Giants
WARRINGTON, NOAH—1910-11—president, St. Louis Giants
WARSHAM, ____—1949—p, Chicago American Giants
WASAW (WAUBAN, WALUM, WABUM), ____—1912—of, All Nations
WASHINGTON, ____—1869—c, Washington Alert
WASHINGTON, ____—1880—3b, Washington Keystones
WASHINGTON, ____—1880—1b, Washington Manhattans
WASHINGTON, ____—1926—p, Chattanooga White Sox
WASHINGTON, ____—1926—2b, Montgomery Grey Sox
WASHINGTON, ____—1926—p, Cuban Stars (West)
WASHINGTON, ____—1929—c, Nashville Elite Giants
WASHINGTON, ____—1931—of, Bacharach (Philly) Giants
WASHINGTON, ____—1932—2b, Chicago American Giants
WASHINGTON, ____—1945—c, Brooklyn Brown Dodgers

WASHINGTON, ALONZO [see GOODWIN, ALFRED ALONZO]

WASHINGTON, (BULL)—1909—1b, Cuban X-Giants, Cuban Giants

WASHINGTON, CHESTER L. (CHES)—1925-83—writer, *Chicago Defender, Pittsburgh Courier, Los Angeles Times, Los Angeles Wave*

WASHINGTON, EDDIE—1938—3b, Newark Eagles

WASHINGTON, EDGAR HUGHES (ED, BLUE)—1915, 1920—p, 1b, Chicago American Giants, Kansas City Monarchs

WASHINGTON, GEORGE (GEORGIA RABBIT)—1908—p, Philadelphia Giants

WASHINGTON, HAROLD REUBEN (RUBE, HARRY)—1906-12—p, Cuban X-Giants, Philadelphia Giants, Cuban Stars, Kansas City (KS) Giants, Indianapolis ABCs, Kansas City Royals, Oklahoma City Monarchs, St. Louis Giants, French Link (IN) Plutos

WASHINGTON, ISAAC (IKE)—1928-30—officer, Bacharach (AC) Giants

WASHINGTON, JR., JASPER (JAP)—1922-37—3b, 1b, Pittsburgh Keystones, Homestead Grays, Pittsburgh Crawfords, Newark Browns, Breakers Hotel (FL); umpire, NNL

WASHINGTON, JOE—1923—p, of, Washington Potomacs

WASHINGTON, JOHN—1947—1b, Jacksonville Eagles

WASHINGTON, JOHN G. (JOHNNY)—1933-51—1b, Montgomery Grey Sox, Birmingham Black Barons, Pittsburgh Crawfords, New York Black Yankees, Baltimore Elite Giants, Houston Eagles, New Orleans Eagles, Chicago American Giants

WASHINGTON, L.—1884-85—ss, Baltimore Atlantics

WASHINGTON, LAFAYETTE (FAY)—1940-46—p, Chicago American Giants, Birmingham Black Barons, Cincinnati-Indianapolis Clowns, Kansas City Monarchs, St. Louis Stars, New Orleans-St. Louis Stars, Seattle Steelheads

WASHINGTON, LAWRENCE—1945—1b, New York Black Yankees

WASHINGTON, NAMON ARTHUR (CY)—1920-31—of, ss, c, 2b, San Antonio Black Aces, Indianapolis ABCs, Hilldale Club, Brooklyn Cuban Giants, Philadelphia Tigers, Lincoln (NY) Giants, Brooklyn Royal Giants

WASHINGTON, PETER (PETE)—1923-39—of, Washington Potomacs, Wilmington Potomacs, Lincoln (NY) Giants, Albany (GA) Giants, Baltimore Black Sox, Philadelphia Stars, Bacharach (AC) Giants

WASHINGTON, TOM (TOMMY)—1904-15—c, Philadelphia Giants, Pittsburgh Giants, New York Black Sox

WASHINGTON, WILLIAM—1908-11—1b, c, Chicago Union Giants, Chicago Giants, Cuban Giants

WASHINGTON, WILLIAM (BILL, WILLIE, WILKES)—1950-60—ss, 3b, manager, New York Black Yankees, Philadelphia Stars, Memphis Red Sox, Detroit Stars, Kansas City Monarchs

WASNER, BILL—1928—umpire, ECL

WATERS, ____—1869—3b, Philadelphia Pythians

WATERS, ____—1919—c, Wilmington Giants

WATERS, DICK—1916—manager, St. Louis Giants

WATERS, GEORGE—1885-87—player, Philadelphia Manhatten Club, Boston Resolutes (NCBBL)

WATERS, JAMES—1938-39—of, Bacharach (Philly) Giants

WATERS, JACK—1939—secretary, New York Black Yankees

WATERS, JOCK—1926—manager, Brooklyn Royal Giants

WATERS, MARSHALL—1927-28—batboy, Harrisburg Giants

WATERS, THEODORE FRANCIS MULLEN (TED)—1916-28—p, of, Chicago Giants, Hilldale Club, Philadelphia Tigers, Bacharach (AC) Giants

WATKINS, ____—1891—of, Cuban Giants

WATKINS, ____—1926—umpire, ECL

WATKINS, ____—1928-29—c, Louisville White Sox

WATKINS, ____—1934—c, Padron's Cuban Giants

WATKINS, DAN WILLIAM (WILD BILL)—1910-17—p, Chicago American Giants, Indianapolis ABCs, West Baden (IN) Sprudels, All Nations

WATKINS, EDGAR (BUDDY, ED)—1946—of, Fresno/San Diego Tigers

WATKINS, ELMER—1946—pr, Philadelphia Stars

WATKINS, G. C.—1937—officer, Indianapolis Athletics

WATKINS, GEORGE—1946—ss, Philadelphia Stars

WATKINS, JOHN McCREARY (POP)—1899-1922—1b, c, manager, Genuine Cuban Giants, Cuban Giants, Havana Red Sox, Pop Watkins Stars, Famous Cuban Giants

WATKINS, JOHNNY—1931—of, Detroit Giants

WATKINS, MURRAY CLIFTON (SKEETER, MAURICE)—1942-50—3b, Newark Eagles, Philadelphia Stars, Baltimore Grays, North All-Stars

WATKINS, RICHARD—1948-50—1b, of, Memphis Red Sox

WATKINS, THOMAS—1874—1b, Chicago Uniques

WATROUS, SHERMAN—1952—of, Memphis Red Sox

WATSON, ____—1913—p, Washington Giants

WATSON, ____—1917—p, Chicago Union Giants

WATSON, ____—1951—1b, Philadelphia Stars

WATSON, AMOS (COUNTRY, BIG TRAIN)—1944-45-50—p, Cincinnati-Indianapolis Clowns, Baltimore Elite Giants, Indianapolis Clowns, Kansas City Monarchs, Durham (NC) Eagles, Boston Royal Giants, Cleveland Buckeyes
WATSON, CLAUDE—1946—p, Kansas City Monarchs
WATSON, DAVID—1923—p, Birmingham Black Barons
WATSON, EVERETT—1931—officer, Detroit Stars
WATSON, G.—1931—p, Santop Broncos
WATSON, GEORGE—1907, 1914-15—1b, c, Louisville Giants, Louisville White Sox, Brooklyn All Stars
WATSON, JIMMY [ROBERT]—1950—p, New York Cubans
WATSON, JOHNIE WALSTINE (GEORGE)—1922-26, 1931—of, Detroit Stars, Detroit Giants
WATSON, SR., JOSEPH LEE (JOE)—1953—of, Kansas City (KS) Giants
WATSON, WILLIAM—1888-89—c, of, Bloomington (IL) Reds
WATSON, WILLIAM (BILL)—1924-26, 1931, 1934—of, Brooklyn Royal Giants, Bacharach (AC) Giants, Penn Red Caps of NY
WATTERS, [WATERS] ____—1916—infield, Chicago Giants
WATTS, ____—1900—of, Chicago Unions
WATTS, ____—1920—3b, Pensacola Giants
WATTS, ANDREW (SONNY, BIG SIX)—1946-52—infield, Cleveland Buckeyes, Birmingham Black Barons, Indianapolis Clowns
WATTS, EDDIE—1924-27—2b, 1b, St. Louis Stars, Cleveland Hornets, Cleveland Elites
WATTS, HERMAN (LEFTY)—1941-42—p, Jacksonville Red Caps, Cincinnati-Cleveland Buckeyes, New York Black Yankees
WATTS, JACK—1911-21—c, 1b, Louisville Cubs, Chicago American Giants, Indianapolis ABCs, Dayton Marcos, Bowser's ABCs, West Baden (IN) Sprudels, Louisville White Sox, Pittsburgh Keystones, Madison Stars, Chicago Black Sox
WATTS, RICHARD (DICK)—1949-50—p, Birmingham Black Barons
WEATHERSPOON [WITHERSPOON], ____—1917—p, Bacharach (AC) Giants
WEATHERSPOON, LESTER—1948-49—of, Indianapolis Clowns, Homestead Grays
WEAVER, ____—1906-09—1b, of, Cuban X-Giants, Philadelphia Giants, Cuban Giants
WEAVER, DICK—1944—ph, Newark Eagles

WEAVER, MARY JO (JOSETTE)— 1940—queen, Kansas City Monarchs
WEBB, ____—1937—of, Chicago Giants
WEBB, B. (BABY, BLACK CAT)—1907-10—p, Oklahoma City Monarchs, Oklahoma City Giants, San Antonio Broncos
WEBB, DAVE (DAVIE)—1917-19—p, 1b, Lincoln (NY) Giants
WEBB, FLOYD—1916-17—player, Kansas City Tigers
WEBB, JAMES D.—1907-10—2b, Oklahoma City Monarchs, Leland Giants, San Antonio Broncos
WEBB, NORMAL (TWEED)—1926, 1931—historian, 2b, Fort Wayne Pirates, St. Louis Pullmans
WEBB, WILLIAM—1875—of, St. Louis Blue Stockings
WEBB, WILLIAM (SONNY)—1923—c, Bacharach (AC) Giants
WEBB, JR., WILLIAM LEE (SONNY)—1958—of, Detroit Clowns
WEBSTER, ____—1867—3b, Washington Alerts
WEBSTER, CHARLES—1950—of, Birmingham Black Barons
WEBSTER, DANIEL JIM (DOUBLE DUTY)—1933-38, 1945—c, p, Detroit Stars, Kansas City Monarchs, Louisville Black Colonels, Toledo Cubs/Rays
WEBSTER, ERNEST—1954—p, Kansas City Monarchs
WEBSTER, PEARL FRANKLYN (SPECKS)—1912-18—c, of, Brooklyn Royal Giants, Hilldale Club, Grand Central Terminal Red Caps, Breakers Hotel (FL)
WEBSTER, ROBERT—1936—p, Kansas City Monarchs
WEBSTER, RUFUS—1925-31—c, Detroit Stars
WEBSTER, S.—1915—of, St. Louis Giants
WEBSTER, WILLIAM (WEST, SPECKS)—1911-28—c, St. Louis Giants, Chicago Giants, Chicago American Giants, Schenectady Mohawk Giants, Lincoln (NY) Giants, Detroit Stars, Dayton Marcos, Brooklyn Cuban Giants, Jewell's ABCs, Bacharach (AC) Giants, Leland Giants, Indianapolis ABCs, Lincoln (NY) Stars
WEEKS, DUNCAN—1927—officer, Bacharach (AC) Giants
WEEKS [WICKS], E.—1918-24—2b, 3b, Pennsylvania Giants, Harrisburg Giants, Pittsburgh Stars of Buffalo, Brooklyn Royal Giants, Hilldale Club
WEEKS, REGINALD—1927—officer, Bacharach (AC) Giants
WEEKS, WILLIAM—1922-27—officer, Bacharach (AC) Giants
WEEMS, ____—1936—of, Memphis Red Sox
WEEMS, ____—1946—c, San Francisco Sea Lions

WEIDEL, ____–1916–p, All Nations
WELCH, ____–1938–of, Indianapolis ABCs
WELCH, ISAAC (IKE)–1952, 1954–1b, of, Indianapolis Clowns, Atlanta Black Crackers, New Orleans Black Pelicans
WELCH, PHIL (JEFF)–1958-61–p, Birmingham Black Barons
WELCH, WINFIELD [WINGFIELD] SCOTT (W. S., MOE, GUS)–1918-51–manager, of, New Orleans Black Pelicans, New Orleans Crescent Stars, Monroe (LA) Monarchs, Shreveport Giants, Cincinnati Buckeyes, Birmingham Black Barons, Cincinnati Crescents, New York Cubans, Chicago American Giants, Shreveport Black Sports, Alexandria (LA) Lincoln (NY) Giants, Detroit Senators, Atlanta Black Crackers
WELDON, LEON–1920–of, Bacharach (AC) Giants
WELLER, ____–1918–of, Pennsylvania Giants
WELLS, ____–1910–p, Indianapolis ABCs
WELLS, ____–1923–of, Havana Red Sox
WELLS, ____–1927–ss, Evansville Giants
WELLS, ____–1939–p, Detroit Stars
WELLS, A.E.–1922–secretary, treasurer, Montgomery Grey Sox
WELLS, A.S.–1920, 1929–president, Dallas & Texas Negro League
WELLS, C.–1918–2b, c, Lincoln (NY) Giants, Pennsylvania Giants
WELLS, CHARLES G.–1950-52–c, Philadelphia Stars
WELLS, IRA–1948–p, Memphis Red Sox
WELLS, T.–1935–p, Detroit Cubs
WELLS, WILLIAM–1956–3b, New York Black Yankees
WELLS, WILLIE BROOKS (JUNIOR)–1944-51–ss, Memphis Red Sox, New Orleans Eagles, Chicago American Giants
WELLS, WILLIE JAMES (THE DEVIL, CHICO)–1924-54–ss, manager, St. Louis Stars, Detroit Wolves, Kansas City Monarchs, Chicago American Giants, Cole's American Giants, Newark Eagles, Memphis Red Sox, New York Black Yankees, Baltimore Elite Giants, Indianapolis Clowns, Homestead Grays, St. Louis Giants, Birmingham Black Barons
WELMAKER, ROY HORACE (SNOOK, LEFTY)–1932-45–p, Atlanta Black Crackers, Homestead Grays, Philadelphia Stars
WERDEN (WERNER), PERRY–1922–umpire, NNL
WESLEY, ____–1945–3b, Detroit Motor City Giants
WESLEY, CHARLES (CONNIE, TWO SIDES)–1920-30–of, 2b, manager, Columbus Buckeyes, Pittsburgh Keystones, Indianapolis ABCs, Memphis Red Sox, Birmingham Black Barons, St. Louis Stars, Louisville White Caps, Louisville Red Caps, Atlanta Black Crackers, Montgomery Grey Sox
WESLEY, EDGAR (ED)–1918-31–1b, Detroit Stars, Cleveland Hornets, Bacharach (AC) Giants, Chicago American Giants, Harrisburg Giants, Indianapolis ABCs
WESLEY, EUGENE–1920, 1926–c, Birmingham Black Barons, Montgomery Grey Sox
WESLEY, GUY–1920, 1925-26, 1936–p, Chicago Union Giants, Chicago Giants
WESLEY, PETE–1910–of, 3b, St. Paul Colored Gophers
WESSON, LES–1948-49–p, New York Black Yankees
WEST, ART–1942–p, Chicago American Giants
WEST, BILL–1930–p, Nashville Elite Giants
WEST, C. [see WEST, JAMES (JIM, HINKEY, SHIFTY)]
WEST, CHARLIE–1942–of, Birmingham Black Barons
WEST, JAMES (JIM, HINKEY, SHIFTY)–1930-47–1b, manager, Birmingham Black Barons, Cleveland Cubs, Memphis Red Sox, Nashville Elite Giants, Columbus Elite Giants, Washington Elite Giants, Baltimore Elite Giants, Philadelphia Stars, New York Black Yankees, Oakland Larks
WEST, JOE–1942-44–3b, 2b, Boston Royal Giants
WEST, OLLIE EARNEST–1942-46–p, Chicago American Giants, Chicago Brown Bombers, Birmingham Black Barons, Homestead Grays, Pittsburgh Crawfords (USL)
WEST, JR., PRICE C.–1955, 1958-61–of, manager, New York Black Yankees, Detroit Clowns, Raleigh (NC) Tigers, Kansas City Monarchs, Indianapolis Clowns
WEST, RUSSELL–1925–1b, Wilmington Potomacs
WEST, WALKER–1948–umpire, East/West game
WEST, WILLIAM (WILD BILL, BIG BILL)–1907-14–of, p, Louisville White Sox, Chicago Union Giants, Louisville Cubs, Indianapolis ABCs, Leland Giants
WESTBROOK, GUS–1960–infield, Birmingham Black Barons
WESTBROOK, LEO–1959–p, Memphis Red Sox
WESTBROOK, LUTHER LEON (SUGAR)–1946–of, p, San Francisco Sea Lions, Los Angeles White Sox
WESTFIELD, ERNEST L. (ERNIE)–1960–p, Birmingham Black Barons
WESTFIELD, WALTER–1946–utility, Pittsburgh Stars
WESTMORELAND, ____–1926–c, Nashville Elite Giants
WESTON, ISAAC (DEACON)–1949–p, Louisville Buckeyes
WESTON, MOE–1930, 1937–p, Hilldale Club, Philadelphia Stars [see OVERTON, ALPHONSE ALBERT]

WEYMAN, J. B.—1887—1b, Baltimore Lord Baltimores (NCBBL)

WHARTON, ____—1904—p, Philadelphia Giants

WHARTON, ____—1921-23—of, Kansas City Monarchs

WHARTON, ____—1932—p, Bacharach (Philly) Giants

WHATLEY, DAVID SAMUEL (SPEED, DAVE, HAMMER MAN)—1936-48—of, Birmingham Black Barons, Homestead Grays, Cleveland Bears, Jacksonville Red Caps, Memphis Red Sox, New York Black Yankees, Philadelphia Hilldales (USL), Pittsburgh Crawfords (USL), San Francisco Sea Lions

WHEAT, ____—1916—of, All Nations

WHEAT, CHARLES—1945—p, Chicago Brown Bombers (USL)

WHEAT, JIMMIE—1947—2b, Cleveland Buckeyes

WHEATHERSPOON, ____—1917—p, Bacharach (AC) Giants

WHEELER, ____—1867—player, Philadelphia Excelsior

WHEELER, CHICK—1922-24—umpire, NNL

WHEELER, JOE (JODIE)—1921-30—p, Bacharach (AC) Giants, Baltimore Black Sox, Brooklyn Cuban Giants, Wilmington Potomacs, Homestead Grays, Schenectady Mohawk Giants

WHEELER, LEON—1948, 1951—p, Chicago American Giants, Harlem Globetrotters

WHEELER, LLOYD—1887—p, Chicago Gordons

WHEELER, MALLARD—1950—officer, Savannah Tigers

WHEELER, SAMUEL WALLACE (SAM, BOOM BOOM)—1946-50—of, Portland (OR) Rosebuds, Harlem Globetrotters, New York Cubans

WHIGGS, (WIGGS) [a.k.a. W. HIGGS]—1867—ss, Mutuals of Washington

WHITAKER, ENOS—owner, Dallas Black Giants

WHITE, ____—1880—1b, Washington Douglass Club

WHITE, ____—1880—2b, Washington Eagles

WHITE, ____—1880—of, Washington Keystones

WHITE, ____—1880—of, Washington Manhattans

WHITE, ____—1942—1b, Homestead Grays

WHITE, ADOLPHUS (DOLPH)—1910, 1914—p, New York Black Sox, New York Colored Giants

WHITE, ARNOLD—1936-37—p, Homestead Grays, Washington Elite Giants

WHITE, ARTEMIS ARSTANDO (ART, ANDY)—1948—p, Indianapolis Clowns, Memphis Red Sox

WHITE, ARTHUR—1934—p, Newark Dodgers

WHITE, B.—1902—p, Philadelphia Giants

WHITE, BURLIN—1912-44—c, manager, West Baden (IN) Sprudels, Bacharach (AC) Giants, Lincoln (NY) Giants, Philadelphia Royal Stars, Harrisburg Giants, Philadelphia Royal Giants, Philadelphia Giants, Philadelphia Quaker City Giants, Boston Royal Giants, Bowser's ABCs, Hilldale Club, Madison Stars, Cuban Stars (East), Chicago American Giants, Kansas City (KS) Giants, Birmingham Black Barons, Chicago Union Giants, Royal Poinciana (FL). Breakers Hotel (FL)

WHITE, BUTLER LEON—1920-24—1b, Chicago Giants

WHITE, C.—1915—p, St. Louis Cubs

WHITE, CARVER DEWITT—1954—c, Detroit Stars

WHITE, CHANEY LEONARD (REINDEER)—1920-36—of, Hilldale Club, Bacharach (AC) Giants, Wilmington Potomacs, Philadelphia Quaker City Giants, Homestead Grays, Darby Daisies, Philadelphia Stars, Baltimore Black Sox, New York Cubans, Brooklyn Royal Giants, Washington Potomacs, Breakers Hotel (FL)

WHITE, JR., CHARLES (CHARLIE, HOSS)—1950—3b, New York Black Yankees, Philadelphia Stars

WHITE, CLARENCE (RED)—1926-34—p, Nashville Giants, Nashville Elite Giants, Memphis Red Sox, Louisville White Sox, Louisville White Caps, Monroe (LA) Monarchs, Montgomery Grey Sox, Louisville Red Caps

WHITE, CLIFFORD—1916—p, West Baden (IN) Sprudels, Chicago Union Giants

WHITE, CURTIS—1959—p, Kansas City Monarchs, Detroit Stars

WHITE, EDDIE—1920—ph, Lincoln (NY) Giants

WHITE, EDDIE—1944—of, Homestead Grays

WHITE, EUGENE (STANK)—1950-51, 1956-57—2b, 1b, Chicago American Giants, Kansas City Monarchs

WHITE, EUGENE WILLIAM (BILL)—1935-36—3b, Brooklyn Eagles, Newark Eagles

WHITE, F. (LEFTY)—1912-16—p, Schenectady Mohawk Giants, Chicago Union Giants, Paterson (NJ) Smart Set

WHITE, GEORGE—1908-09—of, Columbus Giants, Chicago Union Giants

WHITE, GEORGE—1938, 1946—p, manager, Chicago American Giants, Twin City Colored Giants

WHITE, HENRY (LEFTY)—1940—p, Cleveland Bears

WHITE, J.—1936—p, Bacharach (Philly) Giants

WHITE, JR., JACOB C.—1867-68—player, Philadelphia Pythians

WHITE, JAMES (BABE)—1922-25—2b, Pittsburgh Keystones, Toledo Tigers, St. Louis Stars, Indianapolis ABCs

WHITE, JOHNNY—1936—p, Bacharach (Philly) Giants

WHITE, JOSEPH S.—1868—player, Philadelphia Pythians
WHITE, J. W.—1910, 1921—owner, Nashville Standard Giants; officer, Nashville Elite Giants
WHITE, KING SOLOMON (SOL)—1883-1912, 1920-26—2b, ss, 1b, manager, coach, executive, author, Bellaire (OH) Globes, Wheeling (WV) Green Stockings (Ohio State League); Pittsburgh Keystones (NCBBL), Washington Capital Citys, New York Gorhams (Middle States League), York (PA) Colored Monarchs & the York (PA) Cuban Giants (Eastern Interstate League), Genuine Cuban Giants, Fort Wayne (IN) (Western Interstate League); Adrian (MI) Page Fence Giants, Cuban X-Giants, Columbia Giants, Philadelphia Giants, Lincoln (NY) Giants, Philadelphia Quaker City Giants, Cleveland Browns, Newark Stars, Philadelphia Gorhams, Ansonia Cuban Giants (Connecticut St. League), Cuban Giants, Boston (NY) Giants, Brooklyn Royal Giants, Cuban X-Giants; writer, *Cleveland Advocate, New York Age, New York Amsterdam News*
WHITE, LAWRENCE EDWARD (EDDIE, LADD)—1944, 1946-49—p, Homestead Grays, Memphis Red Sox, Indianapolis Clowns
WHITE, M.—1886-87—p, c, of, New York Gorhams (NCBBL)
WHITE, MARTIN M.—1868—player, Philadelphia Pythians
WHITE, PERCY (RUNT)—1933—3b, Columbus Blue Birds
WHITE, R.—1923—2b, Toledo Tigers
WHITE, R. W.—1887—player, Washington Capital Citys, Cuban Giants
WHITE, RANDOLPH—1936-38—p, Homestead Grays
WHITE, (RED) [see WHITE, CLARENCE]
WHITE, ROBERT—1922, 1926—2b, 3b, St. Louis Stars, Pittsburgh Keystones, Philadelphia Giants
WHITE, SAM—1914, 1922—of, c, All Nations
WHITE, STEPHEN (STEVE)—1925—of, Indianapolis ABCs
WHITE, WILLIAM EDWARD (BILLY)—1879—1b, Providence Grays (National League)
WHITE, SR., WILLIAM EPHRIAM (BILL, WILLIE)—1952, 1957-59—of, Kansas City Monarchs, Memphis Red Sox
WHITE, WILLIE—1931—of, Memphis Red Sox
WHITE, ZARLIE—1934—of, Monroe (LA) Monarchs
WHITEHEAD (WHITEHILL), ____—1923-25—umpire, NSL
WHITEHEAD, JOHN—1960-62—p, manager, New York Stars, New York Royals
WHITEHEAD, O.—1915—p, Chicago Palmer House Stars

WHITFIELD, (LEFTY)—1950—p, Baltimore Elite Giants, Asheville Blues
WHITLEY, DAVE [see WHITNEY, DAVEY L.]
WHITLOCK, ____—1926—1b, Dayton Marcos
WHITLOCK, ROBERT—1947—p, Chicago American Giants
WHITLOR, M.C.—1919-21—owner, St. Louis Giants
WHITMAN, ____—1923—of, Brooklyn Royal Giants
WHITMORE, JAMES—1951—p, Baltimore Elite Giants
WHITNEY, CARL EUGENE—1939, 1942, 1946—of, St. Louis Giants, New York Black Yankees, Brooklyn Brown Dodgers
WHITNEY, DAVEY LEE (DAVE, WIZ)—1952-55—of, ss, Kansas City Monarchs
WHITTINGTON, DONALD LEE (DON)—1952-54—2b, 3b, Philadelphia Stars, Memphis Red Sox
WHITWORTH, RICHARD HENDERSON (BIG, DICK)—1912-24—p, Chicago American Giants, Chicago Giants, Hilldale Club, Bacharach (AC) Giants, Chicago Union Giants, Kansas City (KS) Giants, Detroit Stars, Royal Poinciana (FL)
WHYTE, WILLIAM T. (BILLY)-1883-1894—p, of, Cuban Giants, York (PA) Cuban Giants (Eastern Interstate League), Trenton (NJ) Cuban Giants (Middle States League), St. Louis Black Stockings, Boston Resolutes (NCBBL)
WICKES, W.—1888—infield, Providence Grays
WICKHAM [WICKMAN], ____—1914—of, Cuban Giants
WICKS [WEEKS], E.—1921—infield, Hilldale Club
WICKWARE, FRANK ELLIS (SMILEY, RED ANT, BIG RED, SMOKEY)—1910-25—p, Muskogee (OK), Dallas Black Giants, Leland Giants, St. Louis Giants, Philadelphia Giants, Schenectady Mohawk Giants, Lincoln (NY) Stars, Chicago American Giants, Chicago Giants, Brooklyn Royal Giants, Detroit Stars, Norfolk Stars, Lincoln (NY) Giants, Jewell's ABCs, Indianapolis ABCs, Louisville White Sox, Bacharach (AC) Giants, Chicago Union Giants, Royal Poinciana (FL), Wickware Colored Giants (Bridgeport, CN)
WIGGINS, ____—1920—ss, Chicago American Giants
WIGGINS, D.—1923—1b, Washington Potomacs
WIGGINS, JOE [a.k.a. JOE CHEVALIER—1927-34—3b, Nashville Elite Giants, Bacharach (AC) Giants, Baltimore Black Sox, New York Black Yankees, Hilldale Club, Pittsburgh Crawfords, Cleveland Cubs, Schenectady Mohawk Giants, Atlanta Grey Sox
WIGGINS, MAURICE CALDWELL—1932, 1939—ss, Gilkerson's Union Giants, Chicago Palmer House Stars

WIGGINS, ROBERT—1935—of, Detroit Cubs
WIGGINS, ROBERT (BOB)—1942-43—ss, Chicago Brown Bombers (NML)
WIGGINS, ROBERT L. (BOB)—1959-60—of, Raleigh (NC) Tigers
WIGGINS, (RUBE)—1938—p, New York Black Yankees
WIGGS, LEONARD DAVID (FATS)—1934, 2b, of, Cleveland Red Sox
WIGWARE, ____—1930—ss, 3b, Nashville Elite Giants
WILBERT, ANDREW (ART, MOFIKE)—1941-42—of, Cincinnati Ethiopian Clowns (NML), Minneapolis-St. Paul Colored Gophers
WILCOX, ____—1909—player, Harrisburg Giants
WILCOX, ____—1922—p, New Orleans Crescent Stars
WILDER, ____—1938, 1941—c, Bacharach (Philly) Giants, Otto Brigg's All-Stars
WILDER, WILLIAM E. (BEAR, BILL)—1946, 1949-50—utility, Raleigh Tigers, Harlem Globetrotters
WILDS, HORACE WILLIAM (BILLY)—1888, 1890, 1892, 1896—c, Stockton (California League), Oakland (California League), SF Pacifics, SF Imperials, SF Californias
WILES, ____—1927—umpire, NNL
WILEY, ____—1910—p, New Orleans Eagles
WILEY, ____—1929—of, Colored House of David
WILEY [WYLIE], FRED LEWIS (ATLANTA SURPRISE)—1920-28—2b, p, of, Lincoln (NY) Giants, Penn Red Caps of NY, Philadelphia Tigers
WILEY, JR., JOSEPH (JOE)—1945-50—3b, Baltimore Elite Giants, Memphis Red Sox, Cincinnati Crescents, New Orleans Black Pelicans, Chicago American Giants
WILEY, SAMUEL (SAM)—1910, 1919—1b, 3b, West Baden (IN) Sprudels, Detroit Stars
WILEY, [DR.] WABISHAW SPENCER (DOC)—1910-23—c, Brooklyn Royal Giants, Lincoln (NY) Giants, Philadelphia Giants, West Baden (IN) Sprudels, Schenectady Mohawk Giants, Bacharach (AC) Giants, Pittsburgh Stars of Buffalo, Breakers Hotel (FL)
WILEY, W.C.—1921-22—manager, St. Louis Tigers, Galveston (TX) Sand Crabbers
WILKERSON, ____—1931—2b, Bacharach (Philly) Giants
WILKES, (LEFTY)—1914—of, All Nations
WILKES, JAMES EUGENE (JIMMY, SEABISCUIT, CHIP)—1945-52—of, Newark Eagles, Houston Eagles, Indianapolis Clowns, Brooklyn Brown Dodgers

WILKINS [WILKES], BARRON DeWARE—1910, 1919-24—officer, co-owner, New York Black Sox, Bacharach (AC) Giants
WILKINS, BYRD J.—1910—treasurer—St. Louis Giants
WILKINS, JIM—1952—p, Philadelphia Stars
WILKINS, SAM (S. B.)—1931-32—secretary, Baltimore Black Sox, Washington Pilots
WILKINS, WALTER—1954, 1958—p, Detroit Stars, Louisville Clippers, Detroit Clowns
WILKINS, WESLEY C. (WEST, RABBIT)—1908-16—of, Kansas City (KS) Giants, All Nations
WILKINS, WILLIAM—1938—p, Schenectady Mohawk Giants
WILKINSON, ____—1906—of, Wilmington Giants
WILKINSON, ____—1929—2b, Santop Broncos
WILKINSON, JAMES LESLIE (J. L.)—1909-48—owner, officer, p (1912-15), All Nations, Kansas City Monarchs;—1920-31—stockholder, secretary, The Negro National League of Professional Baseball Clubs (NNL); treasurer, Negro American League (NAL)
WILKINSON, J.—1939—p, New York Black Yankees
WILLAS [WILLIS], ____—1923-24—p, of, Washington Potomacs
WILLAS, S.—1887—of, New York Gorhams (NCBBL)
WILLBURN, ____—1926—p, Baltimore Black Sox
WILLETT, PETE—1923-28—ss, 3b, Lincoln (NY) Giants, Cleveland Browns, Cleveland Tigers, Homestead Grays
WILLFORD, CLARENCE [see WILLIFORD [WILLFORD], CLARENCE]
WILLIAMS, ____—1867—of, Monrovia Club of Harrisburg
WILLIAMS, ____—1869—of, Rockford (IL) Rockfords
WILLIAMS, ____—1882—p, Philadelphia Orions
WILLIAMS, ____—1889—2b, New Orleans Pinchbacks
WILLIAMS, ____—1906—of, Topeka (KS) Giants
WILLIAMS, ____—1906—of, Brooklyn Royal Giants
WILLIAMS, ____—1908—c, Pop Watkins Stars
WILLIAMS, ____—1910—of, Oklahoma City Monarchs
WILLIAMS, ____—1911—p, Indianapolis ABCs
WILLIAMS, ____—1917-18—ss, c, 1b, Dayton Marcos
WILLIAMS, ____—1919—p, Pittsburgh Stars of Buffalo
WILLIAMS, ____—1919—c, Detroit Stars
WILLIAMS, ____—1920—of, Chattanooga Black Lookouts
WILLIAMS, ____—1920—of, Chicago Black Sox
WILLIAMS, ____—1920—ss, Chicago Union Giants
WILLIAMS, ____—1920—c, Montgomery Grey Sox
WILLIAMS, ____—1922—p, Buffalo Stars

WILLIAMS, ____–1926–p, Chattanooga White Sox
WILLIAMS, ____–1926–p, Albany Giants
WILLIAMS, ____–1928–p, St. Louis Giants
WILLIAMS, ____–1929–p, Evansville Giants
WILLIAMS, ____–1929–p, Pittsburgh Crawfords
WILLIAMS, ____–1931–1b, Philadelphia Quaker City Giants
WILLIAMS, ____–1932–p, Monroe (LA) Monarchs
WILLIAMS, ____–1932–of, Colored House of David
WILLIAMS, ____–1942–of, Baltimore Grays
WILLIAMS, ____–1945–2b, Atlanta Black Crackers
WILLIAMS, ____–1945–of, Philadelphia Daisies
WILLIAMS, A.–1929–of, Chicago Giants
WILLIAMS, A. D.–1925-26–officer, Indianapolis ABCs, officer, NNL; writer, *Indianapolis Ledger*
WILLIAMS, ALBERT SIDNEY (AL, SID)–1943-45, 1948–p, Newark Eagles, New York Black Yankees
WILLIAMS, ALEXANDER McDONALD (DON)–1921-22–owner, officer, Pittsburgh Keystones
WILLIAMS, ANDREW (ANDY)–1913-16–of, 2b, Brooklyn Royal Giants, Cuban Giants
WILLIAMS, ANDREW (RED)–1924, 1928–2b, Indianapolis ABCs, Cleveland Tigers
WILLIAMS, ANDREW (STRINGBEAN, ANDY)–1913-28–p, manager, Indianapolis ABCs, West Baden (IN) Sprudels, Louisville White Sox, St. Louis Giants, Lincoln (NY) Giants, Dayton Marcos, Chicago American Giants, Bacharach (AC) Giants, Bacharach (NY) Giants, Washington Potomacs, Penn Red Caps of NY, Brooklyn Royal Giants, Buck Ewing's All-Stars, Breakers Hotel (FL), 1940s–officer, Indianapolis Clowns
WILLIAMS, ARTHUR–1883–p, Washington Capital Citys
WILLIAMS, ARTHUR J. (SHORTNECK)–1954, 1956-59–owner, officer, Louisville Clippers, Birmingham Black Barons
WILLIAMS, B.–1931-39–of, Montgomery Grey Sox, St. Louis Stars, Indianapolis ABCs, Birmingham Black Barons, New York Black Yankees
WILLIAMS, (BACCO)–1914–ss, Philadelphia Giants
WILLIAMS, BERT–1891–of, New York Colored Giants
WILLIAMS, BILBO (BIGGIE)–1942-43–of, Chicago Brown Bombers (NML), Baltimore Elite Giants, Baltimore Grays
WILLIAMS, BILL–1894-1905–p, of, Genuine Cuban Giants, Cuban X-Giants
WILLIAMS, BILL–1946–of, Chicago American Giants
WILLIAMS, BILLY (WIL)–1902–1b, St. Cloud, MN

WILLIAMS, BOB–1933–p, Baltimore Black Sox
WILLIAMS, (BUCK)–1921-22–p, Bacharach (AC) Giants
WILLIAMS, (BUCK)–1923, 1925–p, Havana Red Sox, Houston Black Buffaloes
WILLIAMS, (BUCKY) [see WILLIAMS, WALLACE IGNATUS]
WILLIAMS, C.–1885–manager, 2b, Brooklyn Remsens
WILLIAMS, C.–1927–c, Brooklyn Cuban Giants
WILLIAMS, C.–1930-32–ss, Indianapolis ABCs, Chicago American Giants
WILLIAMS, CHARLES–1887–umpire, NCBBL; –2b, Boston Resolutes (NCBBL)
WILLIAMS, CHARLES (CHARLIE)–1917–manager, York (PA) Cuban Giants
WILLIAMS, CHARLES (CHARLIE)–1956–ss, Birmingham Black Barons
WILLIAMS, JR., CHARLES ARTHUR (CHARLIE, CHET)–1924-31–ss, 2b, Memphis Red Sox, Chicago American Giants, Chicago Columbia Giants
WILLIAMS, CHARLES H.–1919–officer, Grand Central Station Red Caps
WILLIAMS, CHARLES HENRY (LEFTY)–1915-35–p, Homestead Grays, Detroit Wolves
WILLIAMS, CHARLES MADISON–1885–of, Chicago Gordons
WILLIAMS, CHARLES R.–1887–2b, Boston Resolutes (NCBBL)
WILLIAMS, CHARLEY–1945–p, Toledo Cubs/Rays
WILLIAMS, CHESTER ARTHUR (CHES, CHET, CHOLLY)–1929-43–ss, 2b, Shreveport Black Sports, Memphis Red Sox, Indianapolis ABCs, St. Louis Stars, Pittsburgh Crawfords, Homestead Grays, Philadelphia Stars, Toledo Crawfords
WILLIAMS, CLARENCE–1952–infield, Chicago American Giants
WILLIAMS, CLARENCE (GEECHIE)–1936-45–p, of, Washington Elite Giants, Baltimore Elite Giants, Washington Black Senators, Richmond Hilldales (NML), Brooklyn Royal Giants
WILLIAMS, CLARENCE E. (WAXEY, BOW WOW)–1886-1913–c, manager, Cuban Giants, New York Gorhams, Cuban X-Giants, Philadelphia Giants, Lansing (MI) Colored Capital All-Americans, Paterson (NJ) Smart Set, Ansonia Cuban Giants (Connecticut St. League), Trenton (NJ) Cuban Giants (Middle States League), Harrisburg (Eastern Interstate League), Famous Cuban Giants, Brooklyn Royal Giants,

Buffalo Cuban Giants, York (PA), Colored Monarchs (Eastern Interstate League)

WILLIAMS, CLAUDE—1944—p, St. Louis Stars

WILLIAMS, CLYDE—1929—p, Homestead Grays

WILLIAMS, SR., CLYDE HENRY (LEFTY)—1947-50—p, Cleveland Buckeyes

WILLIAMS, (COTTON) [see WILLIAMS, ROBERT A.]

WILLIAMS, CRAIG (STRINGBEAN)—1927-28—p, Brooklyn Cuban Giants

WILLIAMS, (CURLY) [see WILLIAMS, WILLIE C.]

WILLIAMS, DEWEY—1926—p, Atlanta Black Crackers

WILLIAMS, D.L. (CURTIS, LEFTY)—1958-59—p, Memphis Red Sox, Birmingham Black Barons, Detroit Stars

WILLIAMS, DEE—1906, 1909-11—utility, Topeka (KS) Giants, Kansas City (KS) Giants

WILLIAMS, DELMAR (DEL)—1921—1b, 2b, of, officer, Cleveland Tate Stars

WILLIAMS, DICK—1927—p, Chappie Johnson All-Stars

WILLIAMS, DOUG—1958-59—p, Indianapolis Clowns, Kansas City Monarchs

WILLIAMS, E.—1902, 1904—1b, of, Cuban X-Giants, Cuban Giants

WILLIAMS, E.B.—1926—p, Albany (GA) Giants

WILLIAMS, EDWARD (FROGGIE, ED)—1928-29, 1932, 1938—p, Chicago Giants, Colored House of David, Foster Memorial Giants

WILLIAMS, E.J.—1887—c, Washington Capital Citys

WILLIAMS, ELBERT—1929-35—p, Louisville White Sox, Monroe (LA) Monarchs, Brooklyn Eagles, Detroit Stars, Philadelphia Stars, Havana Red Sox, Cuban House of David, Columbus Elite Giants

WILLIAMS, ELIJAH (EDDIE, BUDDY)—1943-46—of, Harrisburg-St. Louis Stars, Kansas City Monarchs, Newark Eagles, Cleveland Clippers, Pittsburgh Stars

WILLIAMS, ENNIS (STEW)—1947-48, 1951—utility, Baltimore Elite Giants, Chattanooga Choo Choos

WILLIAMS, EUGENE (GENE, FIREBALL)—1956-61—p, 1b, Memphis Red Sox, Birmingham Black Barons

WILLIAMS, FELIX [see WILLIAMS, NORLDON [NOLAN] LEROY]

WILLIAMS, FINDALE (DOCK)—1926-27—of, p, Memphis Red Sox, Birmingham Black Barons, Kansas City Monarchs

WILLIAMS, FRANK (SHORTY)—1942-46—of, Cincinnati-Cleveland Buckeyes, Homestead Grays, Chicago American Giants

WILLIAMS, FRANKLIN DELANO (HANK)—1958-60—of, Memphis Red Sox, Kansas City Monarchs

WILLIAMS, FRED—1920-25—c, Columbus Buckeyes, Indianapolis ABCs, Washington Potomacs, Harrisburg Giants, Brooklyn Royal Giants, Indianapolis ABCs

WILLIAMS, G.—1921—of, Cleveland Tate Stars

WILLIAMS, GEORGE—1885—2b, Chicago Gordons

WILLIAMS, GEORGE—1928—ss, 3b, Cleveland Tigers

WILLIAMS, GEORGE—1941—p, New York Black Yankees

WILLIAMS, GEORGE—1948—2b, Newark Eagles

WILLIAMS, GEORGE (BABE)—1952—c, Chicago American Giants

WILLIAMS, GEORGE L.—1883-1906—2b, 1b, 3b, c, manager, Washington Manhattans, Philadelphia Orions, Argyle Hotel, Cuban Giants, New York Gorhams, Cuban X-Giants, York (PA) Cuban Giants (Eastern Interstate League), Trenton (NJ) Cuban Giants (Middle States League), Philadelphia Giants, York (PA) Colored Monarchs (Eastern Interstate League), Wilmington (DE) Giants

WILLIAMS, GERARD—1921-28—ss, Indianapolis ABCs, Homestead Grays, Lincoln (NY) Giants, Pittsburgh Keystones

WILLIAMS, GRAHAM H.—1929-34—p, Homestead Grays, Monroe (LA) Monarchs, New Orleans Crescent Stars, Nashville Elite Giants

WILLIAMS, GUY—1934—3b, Cleveland Red Sox

WILLIAMS, H.—1930, 1932—of, Houston Black Buffaloes, Austin Black Senators

WILLIAMS, HAM—1901—p, Cuban X-Giants

WILLIAMS, HANK—1928—ss, Lincoln (NY) Giants

WILLIAMS, HARRY LOVETT—1930-50—3b, 2b, ss, manager, Pittsburgh Crawfords, Toledo Crawfords, Baltimore Black Sox, Homestead Grays, Brooklyn Eagles, Newark Eagles, New York Black Yankees, Harrisburg-St. Louis Stars, Baltimore Elite Giants, New York Cubans, New Orleans Creoles, Denver Post Negro All-Stars, Trujillo All-Stars (Ciudad Trujillo Dragons)

WILLIAMS, HENRY—1937—p, Chicago American Giants

WILLIAMS, HENRY (HANK, HARRY)—1911-14, 1917-22—3b, 2b, 1b, Schenectady Mohawk Giants, Brooklyn Royal Giants, Cuban Giants, New York Stars, Brooklyn All-Stars, Baltimore Black Sox

WILLIAMS, HENRY (FLICK)—1922-32, 1937—c, coach, Kansas City Monarchs, St. Louis Stars, Indianapolis ABCs, Pittsburgh Crawfords

WILLIAMS, HERMAN—1958—of, Detroit Clowns

WILLIAMS, I. C.—1932—of, Indianapolis ABCs, New York Cubans

WILLIAMS, IRA—1927, 1929—ss, Shreveport Black Sports, San Antonio Black Indians

WILLIAMS, IRVING—1907-10—traveling secretary, St. Paul Colored Gophers

WILLIAMS, ISAAC (IKE)—1949-52—p, Philadelphia Stars

WILLIAMS, J.—1909—ss, Kansas City (KS) Giants

WILLIAMS, J.—1951—of, Baltimore Elite Giants

WILLIAMS, JAMES—1862, 1867—ss, p, Brooklyn Monitors

WILLIAMS, JAMES—1885, 1891—c, Brooklyn Remsens, New York Gorhams

WILLIAMS, JAMES —1910—stockholder—St. Louis Giants

WILLIAMS, JAMES (BIG JIM)—1929, 1932-48, 1957—of, 1b, manager, Indianapolis ABCs, Detroit Stars, Brooklyn Eagles, Memphis Red Sox, Homestead Grays, Toledo Crawfords, Cleveland Bears, New York Black Yankees, New York Cubans, Birmingham Black Barons, Durham (NC) Eagles, Atlanta Black Crackers, Jacksonville Eagles, Jacksonville Red Caps, Florida Stars, Newark Dodgers, Chet Brewer's Kansas City Royals, Philadelphia Stars, Otto Briggs's All-Stars

WILLIAMS, JAMES H.—1918—manager, Grand Central Terminal Red Caps

WILLIAMS, JAMES R. (JOHNNY, NATURE BOY)—1948-61, 1965—ss, Cincinnati-Indianapolis Clowns, Indianapolis Clowns

WILLIAMS, JEFF—1954—p, Kansas City Monarchs

WILLIAMS, JESSE HORACE (BILL)—1939-51—ss, Kansas City Monarchs, Indianapolis Clowns, Harlem Globetrotters, Chet Brewer's Kansas City Royals

WILLIAMS, JESSE SHARON—1942-48—c, Cincinnati-Cleveland Buckeyes, Cleveland Buckeyes, Cleveland Clippers, Chicago American Giants

WILLIAMS, JIM—1901-04—officer, Chicago Unions

WILLIAMS, JIM (BULLET)—1929-33—p, of, Nashville Elite Giants, Cleveland Cubs, Detroit Wolves, Homestead Grays

WILLIAMS, JIMMY—1952—p, Chicago American Giants

WILLIAMS, JOE—1939-41—ss, Homestead Grays, Chicago American Giants

WILLIAMS, JOHN—1948-59—1b, Chicago American Giants, Birmingham Black Barons, Detroit Stars

WILLIAMS, JOHN (BIG BOY, BIG PITCH)—1926-38—of, p, St. Louis Stars, Homestead Grays, Dayton Marcos, Columbus Elite Giants, Jacksonville Red Caps, Detroit Wolves, Houston Black Buffaloes

WILLIAMS, JOHN HENRY (STINKY)—1951-54—3b, of, Birmingham Black Barons, Louisville Clippers

WILLIAMS, JOHN R.—1913-17—secretary-treasurer, Baltimore Black Sox

WILLIAMS, JOHN WILLIAM (JOHNNY)—1942-55—p, Chicago Brown Bombers (NML), Chicago American Giants, Harlem Globetrotters, Birmingham Black Barons, Kansas City Monarchs, Indianapolis Clowns, Cincinnati-Indianapolis Clowns

WILLIAMS, JOHNNY—1921—of, Cleveland Tate Stars

WILLIAMS, JOSEPH (CYCLONE, SMOKY, SMOKEY JOE, CÍCLON)—1905-34—p, manager, San Antonio Black Broncos, Birmingham Giants, Washington Giants, Royal Poinciana (FL), Breakers Hotel (FL), Leland Giants, Chicago Giants, Lincoln (NY) Giants, Chicago American Giants, Brooklyn Royal Giants, Homestead Grays, Detroit Wolves, Hilldale Club, Schenectady Mohawk Giants

WILLIAMS, JOSEPH (JOE)—1946—of, New York Black Yankees

WILLIAMS, KONEY—1948—3b, Indianapolis Clowns

WILLIAMS, L.—1906—of, Famous Cuban Giants

WILLIAMS, L. C. [see WILLIAMS, LINCOLN]

WILLIAMS, JR., LAWRENCE (LARRY)—1954-55—of, Kansas City Monarchs, Birmingham Black Barons

WILLIAMS, (LEFTY)—1915—p, Baltimore Black Sox

WILLIAMS, (LEFTY)—1924—p, Kansas City Monarchs

WILLIAMS, LEMUEL—1937-39—p, St. Louis Stars, Chicago American Giants

WILLIAMS, LEMUEL RUSSELL (L.R.)—1904-14, 1921, 1923, 1931-32—of, umpire, officer, Cuban Giants, Brooklyn All-Stars, Famous Cuban Giants, owner, Cleveland Stars, Cleveland Tate Stars, Philadelphia Giants

WILLIAMS, LENNIE—1920, 1929—p, Knoxville Giants, Nashville Elite Giants

WILLIAMS, LEO—1925, 1928, 1930, 1932—c, Kansas City Monarchs, Memphis Red Sox, Homestead Grays

WILLIAMS, LEONARD D. (LEN, PREACHER)—1950-51—1b, of, Indianapolis Clowns

WILLIAMS, LEROY [see WILLIAMS, NORLDON [NOLAN] LEROY]

WILLIAMS, LILLY—1941—infield, Philadelphia Stars

WILLIAMS, LINCOLN (L.C., MOFIKE)—1939-42—of, New York Cubans; 1950s—officer, Indianapolis Clowns

WILLIAMS, LONNIE—1932, 1937—1b, Chicago American Giants

WILLIAMS, LOUIS—1929, 1931—c, Colored House of David, John Donaldson All-Stars
WILLIAMS, M.—1938-44—3b, ss, of, Birmingham Black Barons, New York Black Yankees, Newark Eagles
WILLIAMS, M. (JESS)—1931-32—ss, 2b, Pittsburgh Crawfords, Nashville Elite Giants
WILLIAMS, MACK—1946—of, Chicago American Giants
WILLIAMS, MAE—1935—officer, Brooklyn Eagles
WILLIAMS, MARSHALL J.—1928-29, 1944-45—c, Detroit Stars, Pittsburgh Crawfords, Homestead Grays, Detroit Motor City Giants
WILLIAMS, MARVIN (TEX, COQUETA)—1943-50—2b, Philadelphia Stars, Cleveland Buckeyes, North Classic Team, North All-Stars
WILLIAMS, MATHIS (MATT)—1921-24—ss, 3b, Cleveland Tate Stars, Pittsburgh Crawfords
WILLIAMS, MORRIS (STRINGBEAN, MAURICE)—1920-23—p, Indianapolis ABCs, Washington Potomacs
WILLIAMS, N.—1912-13—3b, Paterson (NJ) Smart Set
WILLIAMS, N.—1937—of, Birmingham Black Barons
WILLIAMS, NELSON M.—1887— officer, National League of Colored Base Ball Clubs; manager, Washington Capital Citys
WILLIAMS, NISH [see WILLIAMS, VICINIUS]
WILLIAMS, SR., NORLDON [NOLAN] LEROY (JEFF, FLOYD)—1947-54—2b, 3b, Newark Eagles, Houston Eagles, Kansas City Monarchs
WILLIAMS, NORM—1930—of, c, Nashville Elite Giants
WILLIAMS, OSCAR—1946—p, San Francisco Sea Lions
WILLIAMS, PERCY—1936—officer, Atlanta Black Crackers
WILLIAMS, PETE—1926—officer, Houston Black Buffaloes
WILLIAMS, PHIL (PETE)—1931-39—3b, Baltimore Black Sox, Toledo Crawfords, Jacksonville Red Caps, Indianapolis ABCs
WILLIAMS, SR., POINDEXTER—1920-33—c, manager, umpire, Chicago American Giants, Detroit Stars, Kansas City Monarchs, Birmingham Black Barons, Louisville White Sox, Nashville Elite Giants, Homestead Grays, Montgomery Grey Sox
WILLIAMS, JR., POINDEXTER—1950—infield, Chicago American Giants
WILLIAMS, R.—1884—ss, Chicago Unknowns
WILLIAMS, R.—1901, 1905—1b, Cuban X-Giants
WILLIAMS, RAY—1932—2b, of, Indianapolis ABCs, Pittsburgh Crawfords
WILLIAMS, RAYMOND (RAY)—1933-43, 1950—p, New York Black Yankees
WILLIAMS, REUBEN E. (RUBE)—1952-53—ss, Chicago American Giants, Indianapolis Clowns
WILLIAMS, RHINY (RED)—1938—manager, Indianapolis ABCs
WILLIAMS, ROBERT (BOB)—1954—officer, Louisville Clippers
WILLIAMS, ROBERT A. (COTTON)—1943-51—p, ss, 2b, 3b, Newark Eagles, Houston Eagles, New Orleans Eagles, Philadelphia Stars
WILLIAMS, ROBERT LAWNS (BOBBY)—1918-45—ss, 2b, 3b, manager, Chicago American Giants, Indianapolis ABCs, Homestead Grays, Pittsburgh Crawfords, Cleveland Red Sox, Cleveland Tigers, Columbus Blue Birds, Akron Tyrites, Cleveland Giants, Bacharach (AC) Giants, Royal Poinciana (FL), Breakers Hotel (FL)
WILLIAMS, SR., ROBERT ROSEL—1954—ss, Birmingham Black Barons
WILLIAMS, RODNEY—1905, 1910—c, 2b, of, Chicago Columbia Giants, St. Louis Giants, Chicago Union Giants
WILLIAMS, ROGER—1939—3b, Kansas City Monarchs
WILLIAMS, ROY (BOB)—1952-55—of, 3b, Birmingham Black Barons, Chicago American Giants, Indianapolis Clowns
WILLIAMS, ROY KENNETH—1933-44—p, Columbus Blue Birds, Brooklyn Royal Giants, Philadelphia Stars, New York Black Yankees, Baltimore Elite Giants, Homestead Grays, Columbus Turfs, Columbus Keystones, Schenectady Mohawk Giants
WILLIAMS, ROY S.—1927-35—p, Homestead Grays, Pittsburgh Crawfords, Baltimore Black Sox, Brooklyn Eagles
WILLIAMS, S.—1936—3b, Pittsburgh Crawfords
WILLIAMS, SAMUEL CLARENCE (SAMMY C.)—1947-52—p, Birmingham Black Barons
WILLIAMS, SIDNEY (AL) [see WILLIAMS, ALBERT SIDNEY]
WILLIAMS, (SLIM)—1928—p, Brooklyn Royal Giants
WILLIAMS, SLOAN—1920, 1926—1b, New Orleans Crescent Stars, Atlanta Black Crackers
WILLIAMS, SOLOMON (SOL)—1884-85—of, Baltimore Atlantics
WILLIAMS, STANLEY (STANKEY)—1955, 1959—of, Birmingham Black Barons
WILLIAMS, STUART—1950—2b, Cleveland Buckeyes
WILLIAMS, T.—1896-05—c, of, Cuban X-Giants, Philadelphia Giants

WILLIAMS, T.—1932-34—3b, c, of, Pittsburgh Crawfords, Homestead Grays
WILLIAMS, THOMAS (TOM, WRIST)—1916-26—p, Bacharach (AC) Giants, Chicago American Giants, Brooklyn Royal Giants, Hilldale Club, Chicago Giants, Detroit Stars, Pete Hill All-Stars, Lincoln (NY) Giants
WILLIAMS, TOM—1956-58—2b, Indianapolis Clowns, New York Black Yankees
WILLIAMS, TRESIVANT—1929—commissioner, Texas-Oklahoma-Louisiana League (TOL)
WILLIAMS, VERN—1953—p, Indianapolis Clowns
WILLIAMS, VICINIUS J. (NISH, ZEKE)—1926-39, 1943—c, of, 3b, 1b, Atlanta Black Crackers, Nashville Elite Giants, Cleveland Cubs, Columbus Elite Giants, Washington Elite Giants, Indianapolis ABCs
WILLIAMS, VICTOR—1932-33—p, Baltimore Black Sox
WILLIAMS, W.—1918-19—p, St. Louis Giants
WILLIAMS, W.L.—1930—1b, Baltimore Black Sox
WILLIAMS, WALLACE—1951-52—umpire, East/West game
WILLIAMS, WALLACE IGNATUS (BUCKY)—1930-31, 36—infield, p, Pittsburgh Crawfords, Pittsburgh Monarchs, Homestead Grays
WILLIAMS, WALTER—1898—p, Celoron (NY) Acme Colored Giants (Iron & Oil League)
WILLIAMS, WALTER—1913-17—business manager, Baltimore Black Sox
WILLIAMS, JR., WALTER TURNER (BUDDY)—1937-40—p, 3b, Newark Eagles, Philadelphia Stars, Washington Black Senators, Atlanta Black Crackers
WILLIAMS, (WHIRLWIND)—1911-14—p, West Baden (IN) Sprudels, Indianapolis ABCs
WILLIAMS, WILLIAM—1937—president, NNL
WILLIAMS, WILLIAM (BILL)—1954—3b, Louisville Clippers
WILLIAMS, (WILLIE)—1929-38—ss, 2b, Bacharach (AC) Giants, Brooklyn Royal Giants, Schenectady Mohawk Giants
WILLIAMS, WILLIE—1937-43—p, Washington Elite Giants, Baltimore Elite Giants, Birmingham Black Barons, Newark Eagles
WILLIAMS, WILLIE C. (CURLEY, CURLY)—1945-54—of, Newark Eagles, Houston Eagles, New Orleans Eagles, Birmingham Black Barons
WILLIAMS, WILMORE—1943—of, Newark Eagles
WILLIAMS, WOODROW WILSON (WOODY)—1933, 1940—p, Akron Tyrites, Baltimore Elite Giants
WILLIAMS, ZACK—1939—p, New York Black Yankees
WILLIAMS, (ZEKE) [see WILLIAMS, NISH]
WILLIAMSON, ____—1924—p, Washington Potomacs
WILLIAMSON, R.—1945—p, Detroit Motor City Giants
WILLIFORD, ____—1926—ss, Atlanta Black Crackers, Memphis Red Sox, Birmingham Black Barons
WILLIFORD [WILLFORD], JR., CLARENCE—1952—of, Philadelphia Stars
WILLIS, ____—1931—of, Chattanooga Black Lookouts
WILLIS, CHARLES LEE (COOT)—1950—of, Birmingham Black Barons
WILLIS, JAMES—1910-11—c, of, Minneapolis Keystones
WILLIS [WILLETTS], JIM (CANNONBALL, SMOKEY)—1925-39—p, New Orleans Crescent Stars, Birmingham Black Barons, Nashville Elite Giants, Cleveland Cubs, Philadelphia Stars, Columbus Elite Giants, Washington Elite Giants, Baltimore Elite Giants, New Orleans Black Pelicans
WILLIS, (REB)—1926—p, Memphis Red Sox
WILLIS, S.—1887—of, New York Gorhams
WILLIS-GEDDES, GERTRUDE—1930—treasurer, New Orleans Black Pelicans
WILLISTON, [DR.] E.D.—1905—president, Metropolitan Colored Baseball League
WILLITT, ____—1919—ss, Cleveland Giants
WILLOUGHBY, ____—1936—p, Homestead Grays
WILLS, JAMES A. (BUCK)—1910-11—3b, c, Brooklyn Royal Giants, Minneapolis Keystones
WILMORE, ALFRED GARDNER (APPLES)—1943, 1946-50—p, Newark Eagles, Philadelphia Stars, Baltimore Elite Giants
WILMORE, ELIAS—1858-60—of, Henson Base Ball Club of Jamaica (NY)
WILSON, ____—1867—of, Philadelphia Pythians
WILSON, ____—1887—p, South Baltimore Mutuals
WILSON, ____—1910—2b, New Orleans Eagles
WILSON, ____—1917—c, Brown's Tennessee Giants
WILSON, ____—1918—2b, Philadelphia Giants
WILSON, ____—1919—of, St. Louis Giants
WILSON, ____—1927—c, Harrisburg Giants
WILSON, ____—1936—3b, ss, Birmingham Black Barons
WILSON, ____—1938—of, Brooklyn Royal Giants
WILSON, ____—1942—ss, Philadelphia Daisies
WILSON, ____—1945—of, Asheville Blues
WILSON, ____—1947—of, New York Black Yankees
WILSON, ____—1948—pr, Indianapolis Clowns

WILSON, ALEC—1939-40—of, c, ss, New York Black Yankees
WILSON, ALFRED—1940—of, New York Cubans
WILSON, ANDREW—1919, 1922-31—of, p, San Antonio Black Aces, New Orleans Crescent Stars, Milwaukee Bears, Chicago Giants
WILSON, ARTHUR LEE (ARTIE, SNOOP)—1944-48—ss, Birmingham Black Barons, New York Black Yankees
WILSON, BENJAMIN (BENNY)—1923-28—of, Lincoln (NY) Giants, Penn Red Caps of NY, Bacharach (AC) Giants, Newark Stars
WILSON, BILL—1945-46—c, Philadelphia Stars, Philadelphia Hilldales (USL)
WILSON, BOB—1957—c, of, Kansas City Monarchs
WILSON, CARTER (COLTIE)—1920-23, 1926—of, p, Gilkerson's Union Giants, Chicago Union Giants, Chicago Giants
WILSON, JR., CHARLES (CHARLEY)—1917-22—p, Dayton Giants, Dayton Marcos, Columbus Buckeyes, Detroit Stars, Indianapolis ABCs, Chicago Giants
WILSON, CHARLES (CHUCK)—1948-49—of, 3b, Indianapolis Clowns
WILSON, CLAUDE—1930—p, Columbus Keystones
WILSON, DANIEL RICHMAN (DAN)—1937-47—of, 3b, 2b, ss, Pittsburgh Crawfords, St. Louis Stars, New Orleans-St. Louis Stars, New York Black Yankees, Harrisburg-St. Louis Stars, Homestead Grays, Philadelphia Stars, Claybrook (AR) Tigers
WILSON, DON—1955—p, New York Black Yankees
WILSON, DOUG—1953—of, Kansas City (KS) Giants
WILSON, SR., EARL—1938—p, Birmingham Black Barons
WILSON, EDWARD—1883—3b, 2b, of, Cleveland Blue Stockings
WILSON, EDWARD MATHEW (ED)—1896-1907—p, 1b, of, Cuban X-Giants, Lansing (MI) Colored Capital All-Americans, Adrian (MI) Page Fence Giants, Celoron (NY) Acme Colored Giants (Iron & Oil League), Cuban Giants, Philadelphia Giants
WILSON, ELMER ELLSWORTH—1921-26—2b, Dayton Marcos, Detroit Stars, St. Louis Stars
WILSON, SR., EMMETT DABNEY—1936-46—of, Pittsburgh Crawfords, Cincinnati-Cleveland Buckeyes, Cleveland Buckeyes, Cincinnati Ethiopian Clowns (NML), Boston Blues, Claybrook (AR) Tigers, Kansas City Monarchs, Memphis Red Sox
WILSON, SR., ERNEST JUDSON (JUD, BOOJUM, JOROCÓN)—1922-45—3b, 1b, manager, Baltimore Black Sox, Homestead Grays, Philadelphia Stars, Pittsburgh Crawfords
WILSON, FELTON—1932-33, 1937—c, Akron Tyrites, Cleveland Stars, Detroit Stars
WILSON, FRANK (CHINK)—1910-17—ss, of, p, Bacharach (AC) Giants, Hilldale Club
WILSON, FRED (SARDO)—1938-47—of, p, manager, New York Black Yankees, Newark Eagles, Cincinnati Ethiopian Clowns (NML), Cincinnati-Indianapolis Clowns, Detroit Senators
WILSON, GEORGE—1922—of, New Orleans Crescent Stars
WILSON, GEORGE H.—1946-47, 3b, of, Boston Blues, Chicago American Giants, Philadelphia Stars
WILSON, GEORGE H. (CANNONBALL, BLACK RUSIE)—1895-1905—p, of, Adrian (MI) Page Fence Giants, Columbia Giants, Chicago Union Giants, Adrian Reformers (Michigan St. League)
WILSON, HARRY—1950—p, Cleveland Buckeyes
WILSON, HARVEY—1939—infield, Toledo Crawfords
WILSON, HENRY (SKILLET)—1938-39—utility, Philadelphia Stars
WILSON, HUBERT (HERB, TACK, PUG)—1928-29—p, Kansas City Monarchs
WILSON, J.—1919—1b, St. Louis Cubs
WILSON, J. FINLEY—1928-1930—co-owner, Detroit Stars
WILSON, JACK—1943, 1945—of, Memphis Red Sox, Nashville Black Vols
WILSON, JAMES—1943, 1947—p, Atlanta Black Crackers, Memphis Red Sox
WILSON, JAMES (CHUBBY)—1926, 1929-33—of, Lincoln (NY) Giants, Bacharach (AC) Giants, Newark Dodgers
WILSON, JAMES (NIP)—1936-41—of, Chicago American Giants, Indianapolis Crawfords, Birmingham Black Barons
WILSON, [REV.] JAMES WILLIAM (J. H.)—1887—of, Baltimore Lord Baltimores (NCBBL)
WILSON, JAY—1945-48—ss, Birmingham Black Barons
WILSON, SR., JOHN EDWARD (JUMPIN' JOHNNY)—1948-49—of, Chicago American Giants; author
WILSON, JOHNNY—1921, 1926-27—of, p, Cleveland Tate Stars, Nashville Elite Giants, Detroit Stars
WILSON, JOSEPH—1887—player, Washington Capital Citys
WILSON, LIONEL J. (LEFTY)—1946—p, Oakland Larks
WILSON, M.H. (CHAUFF)—1950's—bus driver, Indianapolis Clowns
WILSON, MOSE—1958, 1960—of, Memphis Red Sox, Raleigh (NC) Tigers

WILSON, NOBLE—1911-12, 1918-19—c, of, Brown's Tennessee Rats, St. Louis Giants
WILSON, PERCY LAWRANCE (PETE) (a.k.a. PERCY SEGULA)—1920-26, 1932-33—1b, p, New Orleans Crescent Stars, New Orleans Caulfield Ads, Kansas City Monarchs, New Orleans Black Pelicans, Milwaukee Bears, Baltimore Black Sox
WILSON, R.—1918—of, Foster's Hartford Giants, Dayton Marcos
WILSON, RAYMOND V. (RAY)—1902-10—1b, p, Cuban X-Giants, Cuban Giants, Philadelphia Giants
WILSON, ROBERT (BOB)—1947-50—3b, Newark Eagles, Houston Eagles, Memphis Red Sox
WILSON, T.—1929—of, Baltimore Black Sox
WILSON, THOMAS—1952—c, Philadelphia Stars
WILSON, THOMAS T. (SMILING TOM)—1918-47—officer, owner, Cincinnati Crescents, Nashville Standard Giants, Nashville Elite Giants, Cleveland Cubs, Cincinnati Tigers, Baltimore Elite Giants; 1933-46—vice-chairman,—1936-38—treasurer,—1939-46+—president, NNL; secretary, president, NSL
WILSON, TOMMY—1944, 1948—ss, New York Black Yankees, Philadelphia Stars
WILSON, [DR.] WESLEY ROLLO [a.k.a. Franklin Penn]—1929-34—secretary, ANL;—1934—Commissioner, NNL; writer—1914-56—*Pittsburgh Courier, Philadelphia American, Philadelphia Tribune*
WILSON, WILLIAM H.—1883, 1887—ss, Cleveland Blue Stockings, Pittsburgh Keystones (NCBBL)
WILSON, WOODROW WILLIAM (LEFTY)—1931, 1936-40—p, Kansas City Monarchs, Memphis Red Sox, Cuban Stars (West)
WILSON, W.T.—1900—p, of, Genuine Cuban Giants
WINDOM, MOSE—1909—ss, St. Louis Giants
WINESBERRY, ____—1924—3b, New Orleans Crescent Stars
WINFIELD, ____—1931—2b, Montgomery Grey Sox
WINFREY, ROY—1947-51—p, Atlanta Black Crackers
WING, CHARLES—1869-71—p, 3b, Mutuals of Washington, Chicago Blue Stockings
WINGATE, JOHN WALKER (J. W., WINDY)—1951—3b, Kansas City Monarchs
WINGFIELD, DAVID—1920-23, 1931—2b, of, ss, p, Dayton Marcos, Detroit Stars, Toledo Tigers, Cleveland Tate Stars, Memphis Red Sox
WINGFIELD, DAVID (MINGO)—1920—of, Atlanta Black Crackers

WINFIELD, WILLIE—1930—p, Colored House of David
WINGO, JOHN (DOC)—1944—c, Kansas City Monarchs
WINKLE, ____—1946—3b, Indianapolis Clowns
WINN, ____—1869—2b, Rockford (IL) Rockfords
WINN, ____—1932—ss, Chattanooga Black Lookouts
WINNIE, ____—1870—of, Johnstown (NY) Wide Awakes
WINSTON, CLARENCE HENRY (BOBBY)—1905-23—of, Philadelphia Giants, Leland Giants, Chicago Giants, Cuban X-Giants
WINSTON, JAMES (HACK, LEFTY)—1929-32—p, of, Chicago Giants, Chicago Columbia Giants, Atlanta Black Crackers, Detroit Stars, Foster Memorial Giants
WINSTON, JOSEPH JOHN (JOHNNY, BOOBY)—1955-60—p, infield, of, Detroit Stars, Kansas City Monarchs, Detroit Clowns, Satchel Paige All-Stars
WINTERS, ____—1891—of, New York Gorhams
WINTERS, JAMES HENRY (JESS, JESSE, BIG JIM, NIP)—1919-33—p, Washington Braves, Norfolk Stars, Bacharach (AC) Giants, Bacharach (NY) Giants, Norfolk Giants, Hilldale Club, Philadelphia Stars, Harrisburg Giants, Lincoln (NY) Giants, Darby Daisies, Newark Browns, Washington Pilots, Baltimore Black Sox, Philadelphia Royal Giants, Schenectady Mohawk Giants, Homestead Grays
WINTHROP, ____—1939—of, Homestead Grays
WISE, ____—1920—of, Jacksonville Stars
WISE, (LEFTY)—1921, 1925-29, 1932—p, Schenectady Mohawk Giants, Chicago American Giants
WISE, RUSSELL—1940—1b, Indianapolis Crawfords
WISE, WALTER—1913-17—manager, Baltimore Black Sox
WISE, WILLIAM—1888-89—of, c, Bloomington (IL) Reds
WISHER, ____—1923—of, Harrisburg Giants
WISWELL, ____—1888—of, Bloomington (IL) Reds
WITHERSPOON, ____—1921—ph, Washington Braves
WITHERSPOON, LESTER (LES)—1948-50—p, of, Indianapolis Clowns, Homestead Grays
WITTLESEY, ____—1871—of, Chelsea Auroras
WIZARD, ____—1912—of, All Nations
WOMACK, JAMES—1923-36—1b, Cleveland Tigers, Indianapolis ABCs, Cuban Stars (West), Columbus Turfs, Columbus Blue Birds, Baltimore Black Sox, Richmond Giants (NAA), Bacharach (AC) Giants, Columbus Stars, Columbia Keystones, St. Louis Stars
WOMBECK, ____—1927—c, St. Louis Giants
WOOD, BRITT—1945—c, New Orleans Black Pelicans
WOODARD, ____—1928—infield, Cleveland Tigers
WOODRUFF, JOE—1956—p, Birmingham Black Barons

WOODS, BERT—1908-11, 1916—p, Louisville Cubs, Minneapolis Keystones, Chicago American Giants, Indianapolis ABCs, French Lick (IN) Plutos, West Baden (IN) Sprudels
WOODS, BUD—1887—c, of, Louisville Falls City (NCBBL)
WOODS, C.—1933—2b, John Donaldson All Stars
WOODS, ED (DOGGIE)—1891-1904—p, 1b, of Ansonia Cuban Giants (Connecticut St. League), Chicago Unions, Adrian (MI) Page Fence Giants, Algona (IA) Brownies, Grey Eagle (MN)
WOODS, EDWARD (EDDIE)—1959—of, Memphis Red Sox
WOODS, JAMES LEON—1955, 1958—of, Birmingham Black Barons, Kansas City Monarchs
WOODS, JOHN—1920—p, New Orleans Crescent Stars, New Orleans Black Pelicans
WOODS, JULIUS—1947—3b, Detroit Wolves
WOODS, K.—1933—of, John Donaldson All Stars
WOODS, MILTON—1952—of, Kansas City Monarchs
WOODS, PARNELL L.—1933-51—3b, manager, Birmingham Black Barons, Cleveland Bears, Jacksonville Red Caps, Cincinnati-Cleveland Buckeyes, Cleveland Buckeyes, Louisville Buckeyes, Memphis Red Sox, Chicago American Giants, Harlem Globetrotters
WOODS, ROBERT (DOGGY)—1902, 1904—p, Algona (IA) Brownies, Gray Eagle (MN)
WOODS, SAMUEL NELSON (BUDDY, SAM)—1945-54—p, Detroit Motor City Giants, Brooklyn Brown Dodgers, Cleveland Buckeyes, Memphis Red Sox, Kansas City Monarchs, Detroit Wolves
WOODS, TOM—1945—3b, 2b, Philadelphia Stars
WOODS, VIRGIL RAY—1955—p, Detroit Stars
WOODS, WILLIAM J. (BILLY)—1887, 1890-91—ss, p, Philadelphia Pythians (NCBBL), Washington Capital Citys, Ansonia Cuban Giants (Connecticut St. League), York Cuban Giants, New York Gorhams
WOODS, WILLIAM J. (WILLIE)—1919-27—of, Brooklyn Royal Giants, Indianapolis ABCs, Columbus Buckeyes, St. Louis Stars, Washington Potomacs, Bacharach (AC) Giants, Chicago American Giants, St. Louis Giants, Chappie Johnson's All Stars
WOODSON, HARRY (BLACK DIAMOND)—1885—of, St. Louis Black Stockings
WOODSON, WILLIAM—1904—of, Philadelphia Giants
WOODWORTH, ____—1917—p, Chicago Union Giants
WOOLFOLK, LEWIS E.—1923-24—p, Chicago American Giants

WOOTEN, NATHANIEL (NATE)—1949, 1954—p, Memphis Red Sox, Louisville Clippers
WORK, ____—1937—ph, Chicago American Giants
WORLEY, ERNEST (BILLY)—1929, 1932—ss. Colored House of David, John Donaldson All Stars
WORMLEY, ____—1867—of, Washington Alerts
WORTENBERRY, ALEX—1887—c, Wilmington Base Ball Club
WORTHINGTON, ROBERT LEE (BOB)—1959-61—c, Raleigh (NC) Tigers
WORTHY, FRED—1946, 1950-53—ss, Asheville Blues, Raleigh (NC) Tigers
WOULDRIDGE [WOOLRIDGE, WOOLDRIDGE], CHARLES JAMES (CHARLEY)—1926-28—ss, 1b, of, Cleveland Elites, Cleveland Tigers
WRIGHT, ____—1869—ss, Rockford (IL) Rockfords
WRIGHT, ____—1917—p, Kansas City (KS) Giants
WRIGHT, ____—1929—2b, of, Wichita Falls Black Spudders, Colored House of David
WRIGHT, AMOS (BIG TRAIN)—1929-37—p, Schenectady Mohawk Giants, Chappie Johnson's All-Stars
WRIGHT, BILL—1948—of, Kansas City Monarchs
WRIGHT, BRUCE—1943-46—3b, Cincinnati Ethiopian Clowns (NML), Harlem Globetrotters, New York Cubans, Portland (OR) Rosebuds, Seattle Steelheads, Chicago Brown Bombers (USL), Brooklyn Brown Dodgers
WRIGHT, BURNIS (WILD BILL)—1932-45—of, Nashville Elite Giants, Columbus Elite Giants, Washington Elite Giants, Baltimore Elite Giants, Philadelphia Stars
WRIGHT, CHARLEY—1931—p, Birmingham Black Barons
WRIGHT, CLARENCE (BUGGY)—1898—1b, Celoron (NY) Acme Colored Giants (Iron & Oil League)
WRIGHT, DANNY—1951-59—p, Chicago American Giants, Birmingham Black Barons, Detroit Stars, Memphis Red Sox
WRIGHT, DON—1933-34—of, Louisville Red Caps
WRIGHT, ERNEST (ERNIE)—1941-49—officer, owner, Cleveland White Sox, Cincinnati Buckeyes, Cleveland Buckeyes; vice-president, NAL
WRIGHT, GEORGE—1898—1b, Celoron (NY) Acme Colored Giants (Iron & Oil League)
WRIGHT, GEORGE MARTIN (ED, JESS)—1905-13—ss, Philadelphia Quaker City Giants, Brooklyn Royal Giants, Leland Giants, Chicago Giants, Lincoln (NY) Giants, Chicago Union Giants
WRIGHT, GLEN—1953—c, Kansas City (KS) Giants

WRIGHT, HENRY—1928-35—p, Nashville Elite Giants, Cleveland Cubs, Columbus Elite Giants, Birmingham Black Barons

WRIGHT, JR., HENRY L. (RED)—1948, 1954—c, Baltimore Elite Giants, Birmingham Black Barons

WRIGHT, HOWARD—1931-33—p, Bacharach (Philly) Giants, Nashville Elite Giants

WRIGHT, SR., JOHN RICHARD (NEEDLE NOSE, JOHNNY)—1937-54—p, Newark Eagles, Indianapolis Crawfords, Pittsburgh Crawfords, Homestead Grays, Toledo Crawfords, Indianapolis Clowns, New York Cubans, Brooklyn Brown Dodgers, Great Lakes Bluejackets

WRIGHT, J.—1905, 1908—1b, Chicago Unions, Brooklyn Colored Giants

WRIGHT, JOSEPH—1923—of, Bacharach (AC) Giants

WRIGHT, L.—1934—of, ss, Nashville Elite Giants, New Orleans Crescent Stars

WRIGHT, MORGAN—1921, 1926—p, Chicago Giants, Dayton Marcos

WRIGHT, O.C. NORMAN—1924—of, Atlanta Black Crackers

WRIGHT, RICHARD (RED)—1954—c, Birmingham Black Barons

WRIGHT, ROBERT—1915—c, Chicago American Giants

WRIGHT, SILAS—1858-59—vice-president, president, Unknown Base Ball Club (of Weeksville, NY); 1859, 1862—2b, of, Unknown Base Ball Club (of Weeksville, NY)

WRIGHT, THOMAS—1960—p, Raleigh (NC) Tigers

WRIGHT, WALTER J. (BRICKTOP)—1940, 1943—of, 1b, New York Black Yankees

WRIGHT, WALTER C.—1920—p, New Orleans Black Pelicans

WRIGHT, ZOLLIE COFFER—1931-43—of, Memphis Red Sox, Monroe (LA) Monarchs, New Orleans Crescent Stars, Columbus Elite Giants, Washington Elite Giants, Washington Black Senators, New York Black Yankees, Philadelphia Stars, Nashville Elite Giants, Baltimore Elite Giants

WROTHER, ____—1934—1b, New Orleans Crescent Stars

WYATT, ____—1910—of, Pittsburgh Giants

WYATT, ____—1941—p, New York Black Yankees

WYATT, ____—1942—of, New Orleans Crescent Stars

WYATT, DAVID (DAVE, CHARLIE)—1896-1920—of, 2b, ss, Celoron (NY) Acme Colored Giants (Iron & Oil League), Chicago Unions, Cuban X-Giants, Chicago Union Giants, Leland Giants, St. Paul Colored Gophers; co-drafter, constitution of NNL; 1907-1922—writer, *Indianapolis Freeman, Chicago Whip*

WYATT, JOHN THOMAS—1953-55—p, Indianapolis Clowns

WYATT, LEON—1947-48—p, Atlanta Black Crackers

WYATT, RALPH ARTHUR (PEPPER)—1941-46—ss, Chicago American Giants, Homestead Grays, Cleveland Buckeyes

WYATT, WILLIAM (BILL) EDWARD—1956-58—2b, ss—Birmingham Black Barons

WYATT, WILLIE C.—1929—c, Detroit Stars

WYCKOFF, ____—1913—ss, Paterson (NJ) Smart Set

WYLIE, FRED [see WILEY [WYLIE], FRED LEWIS]

WYLIE, STEVE ENLOE—1944-47—p, Kansas City Monarchs, Memphis Red Sox

WYNDER, A.—1920—p, Pensacola Giants

WYNDER, CLARENCE—1950—c, Cleveland Buckeyes

WYNDER, P.—1920—ss, Pensacola Giants

WYNN, CALVIN—1949—of, Louisville Buckeyes

WYNN, EMERSON—1946—owner, Milwaukee Tigers (USL)

WYNN, SIDNEY—1952—utility, Kansas City Monarchs

WYNN, WILLIAM W. (FOURTEEN, WILLIE)—1939, 1942, 1944-50—c, Bacharach (Philly) Giants, Newark Eagles, New York Cubans, Philadelphia Stars

WYNNE, ARTHUR—1932—president, Cleveland Stars

X

XIQUES, LEOVIGILDO [see LUGO, LEVINGELO XIQUES]

Y

YANCEY, ____–1907–3b, Keystone (PA) Giants

YANCEY, WILLIAM JAMES (BILL, YANK)–1923-36, 1946–ss, manager, Philadelphia Giants, Hilldale Club, Philadelphia Tigers, Lincoln (NY) Giants, Darby Daisies, New York Black Yankees, Brooklyn Eagles, Philadelphia Stars, New York Cubans, Bacharach (AC) Giants, Atlanta Black Crackers, Philadelphia Quaker City Giants; scout, New York Yankees

YANCY, ____–1911-12–of, Philadelphia Giants

YANK, [see DEAS, JAMES ALVIN]

YARBOROUGH, (GEECH)–1932, 1940–c, Atlanta Black Crackers, Newark Eagles

YARNALL, ____–1919–umpire, ECL

YARYAN, ____–1926–c, Birmingham Black Barons

YELLOT, CHARLES H.–1859–secretary, p, Unknown Base Ball Club (of Weeksville, NY)

YENDES, ROBERT–1917–of, All Nations

YOAKUM, ____–1946–ss, Fresno/San Diego Tigers

YOKELY [YOKELEY], LAYMON SAMUEL (CORNER POCKET, NORMAN)–1926-46–p, Baltimore Black Sox, Bacharach (AC) Giants, Philadelphia Stars, Washington Black Senators, Brooklyn Eagles, Baltimore Elite Giants, Boston Blues, Havana Red Sox, Brooklyn Brown Dodgers

YOKUM, LEWIS FRANK–1922–p, Kansas City Monarchs

YORK, JAMES HENRY (JIM)–1919-22–c, of, Norfolk Giants, Hilldale Club, Bacharach (NY) Giants

YOUNG, ____–1926–p, Gilkerson's Union Giants

YOUNG, ____–1945–of, Detroit Motor City Giants

YOUNG, A.–1926–of, Colored All Stars

YOUNG, A.D.–1925–p, Indianapolis ABCs

YOUNG, A.W.–1924-26–of, Atlanta Black Crackers

YOUNG, ADAM–1951–p, Philadelphia Stars

YOUNG, ALLEN–1947–p, Detroit Senators

YOUNG, ANDREW SPURGEON NASH (A.S., DOC)–1943-66–author, writer, Los Angeles Sentinel, Cleveland Call and Post, Chicago Defender, New York Amsterdam News

YOUNG, SR., ARCHIE HUE (DROPO)–1954-57–c, 1b, Louisville Clippers, Birmingham Black Barons

YOUNG, BENJAMIN H.–1938-39–officer, manager, Belleville (VA) Grays

YOUNG, BERDELL [BUDELL, BURDELL]–1922-28, 1935–of, Bacharach (AC) Giants, Lincoln (NY) Giants, Philadelphia Quaker City Giants

YOUNG, BILL (BUDDY)–1946–3b, ss, Los Angeles White Sox

YOUNG, BOB–1950–infield, Cleveland Buckeyes

YOUNG, C.H.–1910–Oklahoma Monarchs Baseball Club

YOUNG, D.–1929–p, Colored House of David

YOUNG, EDWARD GEORGE (PEP)–1936-47–c, 1b, 3b, Chicago American Giants, Kansas City Monarchs, Homestead Grays

YOUNG, EUGENE–1926, 1932–c, Little Rock Black Travelers, Chattanooga White Sox

YOUNG, FRANK (SI)–1907-10–of, p, Indianapolis ABCs, Chicago Union Giants, Minneapolis Keystones

YOUNG, FRANK ALBERT (FAY, alias MISTER FAN, born JOHN LAKE CAUTION, JR.)–1939-48–secretary, NAL; writer, 1907-57–*Chicago Defender, Kansas City Call, Abbott's Monthly*

YOUNG, [DR.] HOWARD E.–1913-17–president, Baltimore Black Sox

YOUNG, JAMES–1936–p, Washington Elite Giants, New York Cubans

YOUNG, JOHN–1920-24–p, Montgomery Grey Sox, St. Louis Stars, Memphis Red Sox, New Orleans Crescent Stars

YOUNG, LEANDY (LEE)–1940-46–of, Birmingham Black Barons, Kansas City Monarchs, Memphis Red Sox, Satchel Paige All-Stars, Oakland Larks

YOUNG, SR., LEROY A.–1946–ss, Homestead Grays

YOUNG, MONROE D.–1920–secretary, Knoxville Giants

YOUNG, MORRISE DOOLITTLE (MAURICE)–1927, 1929, 1931–of, 1b, p, Kansas City Monarchs, Colored House of David

YOUNG, MONROE D.–1920-21–officer, Knoxville Giants

YOUNG, NORMAN HARVEY–1941-44, 1946–ss, Baltimore Elite Giants, Cleveland Buckeyes, New York Black Yankees, Atlanta Black Crackers, Kansas City Monarchs, Nashville Cubs

YOUNG, ROY–1938, 1942-48–umpire, NAL

YOUNG, ROY–1930–ss, Lincoln (NY) Giants

YOUNG, THOMAS JEFFERSON (T.J., TOM, SHACK PAPPY)–1925-41–c, Kansas City Monarchs, St. Louis Stars, Detroit Wolves, Homestead Grays, Newark Eagles, Philadelphia Stars, Philadelphia Royal Giants

YOUNG, [REV.] ULYSSES SAMUEL–1960-61–p, 1b, Indianapolis Clowns

YOUNG, WILBUR—1945—p, Birmingham Black Barons
YOUNG, WILLIAM—1927—p, Kansas City Monarchs
YOUNG, [DR.] WILLIAM H.—1949-50—officer, owner, Houston Eagles
YOUNG, WILLIAM PENNINGTON (PEP, BLIMP)—1918-36—c, Homestead Grays, Pittsburgh Giants, Grand Central Terminal Red Caps; owner, president, Cleveland Stars; umpire, EWL; editor, *Pittsburgh American*
YOUNG, JR., WILLIE C.—1945-46, 1948—p, Birmingham Black Barons, Pittsburgh Stars, Memphis Red Sox
YVANES, ARMANDO—1949-50—ss, New York Cubans

Z

ZAPP, STEPHEN JAMES (ZIPPER)—1945-46, 1948-51, 1954—of, 3b, Nashville Cubs, Birmingham Black Barons, Homestead Grays, Baltimore Elite Giants
ZEIGLER, ____—1914—of, West Baden (IN) Sprudels
ZEIGLER, FRED—1944—p, Newark Eagles
ZEIGLER, GORDON JAMES—1920, 1928-29—p, Birmingham Black Barons, Detroit Stars
ZEIGLER, SR., VERTIS R.—1928-29—batboy, Detroit Stars
ZEIGLER, WILLIAM (DOC)—1925, 1927-29, 1931, 1935-37—p, of, Chicago Giants
ZIMMERMAN, ____—1906—of, Philadelphia Giants
ZIMMERMAN, GEORGE—1887—c, Pittsburgh Keystones (NCBBL)
ZINSER, ____—1916—p, Baltimore Giants
ZIPP, ____—1920—of, Jacksonville Stars
ZOMPHIER, CHARLES (ZOMP)—1926-31—p, 2b, 3b, ss, of, Cleveland Elites, Cleveland Hornets, Cleveland Tigers, Memphis Red Sox, Cleveland Cubs, Birmingham Black Barons, St. Louis Giants, St. Louis Stars, Cuban Stars (West); umpire, NAL
ZOSS, BARNEY—1951—umpire, NNL
ZUBER, ____—1909—p, Birmingham Giants

All-Time Register

LEGEND:

ANL - American Negro League, 1929

ECL - Eastern Colored League, 1923-1928

EWG – East-West Game, 1933-1960

EWL – East-West League, 1933

NAL – Negro American League, 1937-1960

NACBBC - National Association of Colored Base Ball Clubs of the United States and Cuba, 1907-1909, a.k.a. International League of Independent Professional Base Ball Clubs - ILBCAC

NCBBL - National Colored Base Ball League or the League of Colored Base Ball Players, 1887

NML – Negro Major Baseball League of America, 1942

NNL – Negro National League, 1920-1931; 1933-1948

NSL – Negro Southern League, 1926, 1932, 1945

SLCB - Southern League of Colored Baseballists, 1886

USL –United States League, 1945-1946

WCBA – West Coast Baseball Association, 1946

Pitcher - p

Catcher - c

First baseman - 1b

Second baseman - 2b

Third baseman - 3b

Shortstop - ss

Outfielder – of

Pinch runner – pr

Pinch hitter – ph

NOTES:

Names in [brackets] are other names used in box scores, or post-career titles, i.e. "Dr." or "Rev."

Names in (parentheses) are nicknames

Very Special Appreciation to Gary Ashwill, Bob Bailey, James Brunson, Tony Kissel, Kevin Johnson, Lawrence McCray, Patrick Rock and John Russell for their tremendous contributions to this Register update.

APPENDIX A: WOMEN IN BLACK BASEBALL

There have been roughly a dozen female owners in Major League Baseball; Joan Kroc, the wife of McDonald's restaurant founder and San Diego Padres owner Ray Kroc, Joan Payson, the original owner of the expansion New York Mets, Marge Schott, the controversial majority owner of the Cincinnati Reds from 1984 to 1999 and Jean Yawkey of the Boston Red Sox upon the death of her husband Tom Yawkey in 1976 were perhaps the most recognizable. Other executives include Helen Hathaway Britton, president of the St. Louis Cardinals in 1916, and Lorinda "Linda" de Roulet, Payson's daughter, served as president of the New York Mets.

With the exception of Newark Eagles owner Effa Manley, the only female in the National Baseball Hall of Fame, other female Negro League team owners and officers, listed below, are seldom acknowledged for their contributions to the national game.

Owners:

OLIVIA HARRIS TAYLOR (1885 - 1935). Indianapolis ABCs, 1922-24

When Negro League pioneer Charles Ishum (C.I.) Taylor, 46, died in February of 1922, his widow Olivia assumed ownership of the Indianapolis ABCs. Her brother-in-law and future Hall of Famer, Ben Taylor was named manager. That season, led by future Hall of Famers Oscar Charleston and Biz Mackey, the ABCs finished in second place with a 50-34 won/lost record. After two seasons of battling over player salaries and the reluctant acceptance by the male-dominant ownerships, Olivia sold the team.

However during her tenure as team owner she earned the respect of the Circle City's African American business community. Two years later, with letters of support from the Better Indianapolis League and the Indianapolis Negro Business League, Ms. Taylor was elected president of the Indianapolis NAACP chapter. In view of the resurgence by the Ku Klux Klan in central Indiana during the mid-1920s, under Governor Edward L. Jackson (1925-1929) and Indianapolis Mayor John L. Duvall (1926-27), Taylor held a challenging position of authority for any man or woman. Jackson and Duvall, endorsed by the David Curtiss Stephenson state Grand Dragon of the KKK (in 1923), were both later accused of taking bribes from the White supremacist hate group. In 1926, Olivia Taylor and the NAACP raised $2500 to protest enacted segregation sanctions initiated by said administration. In June of 1927, she became the first woman to host the historic NAACP's national convention albeit in Klan country.

In 1935, the 50-year-old Birmingham native and fearless civil rights activist died in her home at 434 No. California Street in Indianapolis. Ms. Taylor's role in Black Baseball history has been relatively unknown and underappreciated. As the first female owner of a Negro League team she deserves a greater historical truth and recognition for her role in Black Baseball history. More than 75 years after her death, through efforts led by Dr. Jeremy Krock, of the Negro Leagues Baseball Grave Marker Project, funds were raised to place a headstone on her unmarked grave in 2013. Olivia is buried in Indianapolis' Crown Hill Cemetery alongside her husband Charles Ishum.

EFFA BROOKS COLE MANLEY (1897 - 1981) Brooklyn Eagles, Newark Eagles, 1935-48

Effa Manley was co-owner, along with her husband Abraham, of the 1935 Brooklyn Eagles and the Newark Eagles, from 1936 to 1948. Ms. Manley handled the day-to-day business operations of the team, arranged playing schedules, traveling accommodations, negotiated contracts and managed the payroll, along with promotions and advertisements. Year in and year out the Newark Eagles finished in the first division of the Negro National League, except for 1944. Their tenure of managers included National Baseball Hall of Fame inductees, Biz Mackey, Willie Wells and Mule Suttles. In 1946, her Eagles won the Negro World Series championship, with a trio of future Hall of Famers on the club; Leon Day, Monte Irvin and Larry Doby. For her success in negotiating Major League contracts for her players, she was crowned "Queen of the Negro Leagues" by author Jim Overmyer.

Before there was a recognized Civil Rights Movement, Manley supported various boycotts and protests for equality. As part of her work for the Citizens' League for Fair Play, Manley organized a 1934 boycott of stores that refused to hire Black salesclerks. In 1935, she walked a picket line in nearby New York in a successful bid for local businesses to hire African American employees with a "Don't Buy Where You Can't Work" campaign. After six weeks, the owners of Blumstein's Department Store gave in, and by the end of 1935 some 300 stores on 125th Street employed Black clerks.

Manley was treasurer of the Newark chapter of the National Association for the Advancement of Colored People (NAACP) and often used Eagles games to promote civic causes. In 1939, as federal anti-lynching legislation went before Congress, Ms. Manley had ticket takers at Ruppert Stadium wear satin beauty pageant sashes with the phrase "Stop Lynching" across their chest and sold "Stop Lynching" lapel buttons to promote passage of the Federal law. The Manley's later admitted soldiers free to their home games during World War II. They also hosted a benefit game for world class sprinter John Borican in 1941.

Effa also got behind other campaigns initiated by President Harry Truman like the anti-poll tax and desegregation of the military. She supported A. Philip Randolph, chair of the Committee Against Jim Crow in Military Service and Training African Americans in his efforts to convince Truman to end segregation in the armed forces. In July of 1948, President Truman issued Executive Order 9981, declaring equality of treatment and opportunity for all persons in the military regardless of race, color, religion or national origin.

By 1949, her highest flying Eagles had left the nest for the White Major Leagues. The team was sold to Houstonians Dr. W. H. Young and Hugh Cherry, ending the Queen's reign in baseball circles. In 2006, Effa Manley became the first woman to be elected into the National Baseball Hall of Fame and Museum in Cooperstown, New York.

Effa Manley is buried in Holy Cross Cemetery & Mausoleum in Calvert City, California.

HENRYENE "RENE" PROCTOR GREEN (1920 - 2001) Baltimore Elite Giants, 1949-50

After the fatal heart attack of her husband Vernon Green, at age 49, on May 29, 1949, ownership of the Baltimore Elite Giants passed to Henryene. Realizing her lack of experience as a club owner, she gave Richard Powell, the Elite's business manager, power of attorney and the titles of General Manager and Vice-President.

In her two seasons of ownership, 1949 and 1950, the Elite Giants finished in first place with a 59-30 won/lost record and then fell to fifth place the next season with a 24-20 won/lost record, its final season in the Negro American League. In 1951, she married Richard Powell, but their marriage ended in divorce. Ms. Green, a Nashville native, died in her hometown of Tennessee. She is buried in Metropolitan Bordeaux Cemetery in Nashville, TN.

DR. HILDA MAE BOLDEN SHORTER (1904 - 1986). Philadelphia Stars, 1951-52

In 1951, Dr. Bolden inherited the Philadelphia Stars from the estate of her father, Edward Bolden, who had died a year earlier. At the time she was Director of the Parkside Clinic for children. The pediatrician-specialist owner of the Stars had recently been named as one of the *AFRO's* 10 best-dressed women by the *Washington Afro-American* newspaper. The auburn-haired lady also inherited a great manager in Oscar Charleston.

Back in 1946, Bolden earned the distinction of receiving a commission as a captain in the U.S. Army. At the time she was associated with Infant Welfare clinics and was a social hygiene worker with the Chicago Health Department. Bolden also worked with Dr. Ralph Spaeth, famed pediatrician from the University of Illinois.

During her scholastic career, Hilda Bolden was valedictorian of her Darby High School class and member of the debating team. Listed as "Tillie" and "Sheba" in her high school yearbook, Hilda's maxim was "Forever working, but willing to help others." This aspiration led her to the University of Pennsylvania and Meharry Medical College, where she earned various honors and awards. She was the recipient of a two-year Rosenwald Fellowship for advanced study in pediatrics at the University of Chicago and the historic Provident Hospital in Chicago (the first African American owned and operated, non-segregated hospital in America in 1891).

In addition to her medical profession, Bolden was an accomplished pianist, vocalist and composer. She was also an active member of the NAACP, the Urban League, the National Council of Negro Women and the Delta Sigma Theta sorority.

During Dr. Shorter's two-year tenure (1951-52) with co-owner Eddie Gottlieb, the Stars finished in fourth place with a 28-28 won/lost record and in last place the next season with a 22-38 won/lost record. After Gottlieb purchased the NBA Philadelphia Warriors in 1952, he was more concerned with the struggling franchise than putting money into a slowly dying Negro League organization.

After the sale of the team, Dr. Hilda Shorter continued her contributions to the medical community. One such example was during the 69th Annual Convention of the National Medical Association, August 2-6, 1964, in Washington DC, where she presented a white paper entitled *Infant Mortality*. It was an informative paper about the chief causes of death among babies; asphyxia and atelectasis, premature birth, congenital malformations and birth injuries, et al.

Dr. Hilda Bolden Shorter died in March of 1986 in Cambridge, Dorchester County, Maryland. She is buried East New Market Cemetery in East New Market, MD.

MINNIE L. WATKINS FORBES - Detroit Stars, 1956

Minnie Forbes was born in 1932 in Cedar Bluff near West Point, Mississippi. She became owner of the 1956 Detroit Stars, when the league informed her uncle Ted Rasberry, it was a conflict of interest for him to own two teams in the same league, the Stars and the Kansas City Monarchs. In 1956, incomplete records show a won/lost record of 13 wins against 11 losses under manager Ed Steele.

MINNIE FORBES (right) with Uncle Ted Rasberry and his wife Edith.

When Forbes moved to Grand Rapids at the age of 12, she provided child labor to Uncle Ted behind the scenes with the Grand Rapids Black Sox, a semi-pro team. At the age of 18, Forbes was officially hired as the Detroit Stars' secretary, booking agent and contract negotiator for Rasberry Enterprises. Her tasks also included managing her uncle's pre-paid legal plans, Amway sales, Aloe Vera juice distribution, and life insurance policies. Meanwhile, Forbes was also an owner and third basewoman/manager of several Grand Rapids area softball teams.

In 1959, with the apparent demise of the Negro Leagues forthcoming, she became an office manager at Jacobson's, a regional department store based in Jackson, Michigan, and retired in 1998. In 2012, Forbes made a rare public appearance at the 15th annual Jerry Malloy Negro League Conference in Cleveland, Ohio. Later in August 2013, she was among a selected dozen Negro League players and executives invited to the White House for a meet and greet in the Blue Room with President Barack Obama.

Officers:

- LEONA DIXON, officer, Louisville Black Caps, 1929
- GERTRUDE WILLIS-GEDDES, treasurer, New Orleans Black Pelicans, 1930
- MAE WILLIAMS, officer, Brooklyn Eagles, 1935
- CLARA JONES, officer, Boston ABCs, 1935
- BILLIE HARDEN, officer, Atlanta Black Crackers, 1938-48
- DELORES M. HALL, officer, Brooklyn Brown Dodgers, 1945
- HELEN L. SNOWDEN, officer, Brooklyn Brown Dodgers, 1945-46
- ELEANOR M. SPECKENBACH, officer, Brooklyn Brown Dodgers, 1945-46
- ETHEL SHAW TRUMAN POSEY, officer, Homestead Grays, 1947
- MAUDE SEMLER, officer, New York Black Yankees, 1947-48
- EVA CARTMAN, secretary, treasurer, Memphis Red Sox, 1954
- VERNADINE JOHNSON, secretary, Newark Indians, 1959
- JOYCE E. HAMMAN, secretary, Indianapolis Clowns, 1959-60

Negro Leagues Book #2: The Players

Players:

The ladies listed below have been discovered to have salaried contracts with their respective teams.
- CARRIE NATION (a.k.a. May Arbaugh), 1912, All Nations
- PEARL BARNETT, 1917, Havana Stars
- ISABELLE BAXTER, 1932, Cleveland Colored Giants
- DORIS ARLENE JACKSON, 1953, Indianapolis Clowns
- TONI STONE, 1953-54, Indianapolis Clowns, Kansas City Monarchs (pictured below looking at camera).

DESERIA "BOO BOO" ROBINSON, pictured with right hand in back pocket, 1953, Indianapolis Clowns.

CONSTANCE ENOLA MORGAN - Prior to coming to the Indianapolis Clowns in 1954, she was an outstanding softball player for the North Philadelphia Honey Dippers. Morgan played one season with the Clowns as a second base person.

Women in Black Baseball

MAMIE JOHNSON - Shown with son Butch, Mamie "Peanut" Johnson pitched one season in the Negro Leagues, 1954, with the Indianapolis Clowns. She was drafted by the Washington Nationals in 2008 in a mock draft of Negro League veterans. Hall of Fame baseball outfielder Dave Winfield hatched the idea to have a draft for the Negro Leagues players, and Commissioner Bud Selig and Jimmie Solomon, baseball's executive vice president, helped spearhead the event.

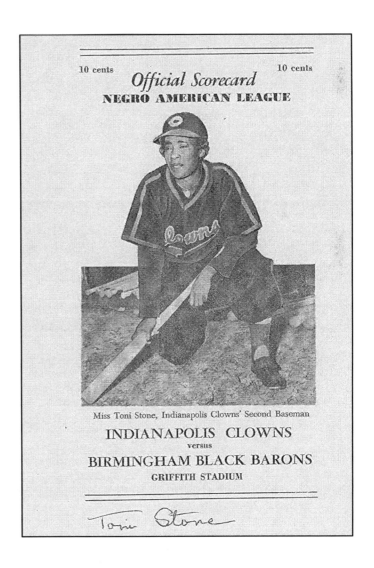

Negro Leagues Book #2: The Players

APPENDIX B:

MAJOR LEAGUE AND NEGRO LEAGUE CONNECTIONS

98 former players from Negro teams with at least one cup of coffee in Major League Baseball:

Hank Aaron
Rafael Almeida *
Sandy Amoros
Gene Baker
Ernie Banks
Joe Black
Bob Boyd
Ike Brown
Billy Bruton, (a.k.a. James or Bill Johnson)
Bill (Chief Chouneau) Cadreau *
Jacinto Calvo *
Frank (José) Campos
Vibert Clarke
Clarence (Choo Choo) Coleman
George Crowe
Charlie Dees
Larry Doby, (a.k.a. Larry Walker)
Sammy Drake
Luke Easter
Junior Gilliam
Miguel "Mike" González *
Sam Hairston
Billy Harrell
Jay Heard
Pancho Herrera
Dave Hoskins
Monte Irvin, (a.k.a. Jimmy Nelson)
Connie Johnson
Clarence W. Jones
John Kennedy
Luis Márquez
Armando Marsans *
Willie Mays
Charlie Neal
Ray Noble
Charles Peete
Jim Pendleton
Jim Proctor
Curt Roberts

José Acosta *
George Altman
Angel Aragón *
Dan Bankhead
Frank Barnes
Walt Bond
Marshall Bridges
Willard Brown
Alfredo Cabrera *
Joe Caffie
Roy Campanella
Paul Casanova
Buster Clarkson
Wes Covington
Tomás Cruz *
Pedro Dibut *
Lino Donoso
Winn (Pop) Durham
Oscar Estrada *
Eusebio González *
Bill Greason
Chuck Harmon
J.C. Hartman
Sal (Chico) Hernández *
Ramón "Mike" Herrera *
Elston Howard
Sam Jethroe
Sweet Lou Johnson
Toothpick Sam Jones
Dolf Luque *

Hank Mason
Minnie Miñoso
Don Newcombe
Satchel Paige

Dave Pope
Larry Raines
Jackie Robinson

Héctor Rodríguez
Patricio Scantlebury
Al Smith
Milt Smith
George Spriggs
Hank Thompson
Ricardo Torres *
Quincy Trouppe
Moses Fleetwood Walker *
Charles White
Bob Wilson

José Santiago
Harry "Suitcase" Simpson
George C. Smith
Willie Smith
Joe Taylor
Bob Thurman
Bob Trice
Roberto Vargas
Welday Walker *
Artie Wilson
John Wyatt

Names with asterisks in bold denote the 18 men who played in Major League Baseball prior to Jackie Robinson's debut in 1947 with the Brooklyn Dodgers.

Negro Leagues Book #2: The Players

Debut Dates of Black Players onto Major League Teams

In present-day commentary about the national pastime, the term "organized" is often used when describing Jackie Robinson's and Larry Doby's entries into the National and American Leagues. The term is contentious and demeaning in that it implies that African Americans who played in the Negro Leagues were "unorganized" before their immigration into Major League baseball.

Let us also note the term "organized" is problematic as it has become a dog whistle to imply that Negro League baseball was unorganized. The term is contentious and demeaning in that it implies that African Americans who played in the Negro Leagues were "unorganized" before their migration into Major League baseball. This coded language taps into and reinforces stereotypes.

The implication that the Black leagues were unorganized is unfounded. Religiously, the Black leagues used the same official rules of play set forth by the National Association of Professional Baseball Leagues of 1901, and purchased their Wilson baseballs, their Louisville sluggers and Spalding uniforms and other equipment from the same suppliers. Adding, their league games were played on regulation size fields in Major League ball parks and stadiums. The players had contracts, statistics were kept, and schedules were printed in the newspapers. The infrastructure of the Black leagues and the White leagues during apartheid was identical!

The term "organized" erroneously implies that the all-Black leagues did not have player contracts, nor any formal team charters or state incorporation papers. Simply untrue! This term assumes that baseball historians possess subjectivity of what qualities define "organized". Consequently, it is considered a judgmental term whose meaning is dependent on the user's perspective, and thus best avoided. Let us be mindful of what Hall of Fame first baseman Walter "Buck" Leonard (1932-50) once proclaimed, "We were not unorganized, we were just unrecognized!".

Below is a chronological list of players with African American heritage who played in *both* the Negro Leagues and the Major Leagues. At 18 years old, **William Edward White**, a first baseman, is the first known Black player to integrate a major league team, the **Providence Grays** of the National League, on June 21, 1879. He played in one game. However, White is not included in this list because he never played for a Negro League, or for an all-Black team.

Brothers, Moses (from the Newark Little Giants) and Welday Walker (from the Pittsburgh Keystones), are the first known Black players to integrate the Major Leagues. Others who followed the Walkers, but before Jackie Robinson, are mostly of Cuban heritage, and were considered "white" by the big league teams.

HANK THOMPSON & WILLARD "HOME RUN" BROWN were the third and fourth Negro Leaguers to break the Majors' color barrier when they joined the St. Louis Browns in 1947. Thompson was the hard-hitting thumper for the K.C. Monarchs, playing both infield and outfield. He possessed a powerful throwing arm and covered the outfield pasture with gazelle-like grace.

A national treasure in Puerto Rico, Willard Brown, in the 1948/49 winter season, smashed a record 27 home runs in 60 games. He erased Josh Gibson's old record of 13. His seasonal record still stands today, with his closest challenge coming from Reggie Jackson's 20 home runs in 1971. Both men were members of the Satchel Paige All-Stars that toured the Midwest against the Bob Feller All-Stars in a series of games in 1946.

Major League & Negro League Connections

PLAYERS	Major League team	DEBUT DATE
Moses Fleetwood Walker	Toledo Blue Stockings	May 1, 1884
Welday Walker	Toledo Blue Stockings	July 1, 1884
Wm. "Chief Chouneau" Cadreau	Chicago White Sox	October 9, 1910
Rafael Almeida	Cincinnati Reds	July 4, 1911
Armando Marsans	Cincinnati Reds, St. Louis Terriers, St. Louis Browns, New York Yankees, Cincinnati Reds	July 4, 1911
Mike González	Boston Braves	September 28, 1912
Jack Calvo	Washington Senators	May 9, 1913
Alfredo Cabrera	St. Louis Cardinals	May 16, 1913
Adolf Luque	Boston Braves	May 20, 1914
Ángel Aragón	New York Yankees	August 20, 1914
Eusebio González	Boston Red Sox	July 26, 1918
Richardo Torres	Washington Senators	May 18, 1920
José Acosta	Washington Senators	July 28, 1920
Pedro Dibut	Cincinnati Reds	May 1, 1924
Ramon Herrera	Boston Red Sox	September 22, 1925
Oscar Estrada	St. Louis Browns	April 21, 1929

Negro Leagues Book #2: The Players

Salvador "Chico" Hernández	Chicago Cubs	April 16, 1942
Tomás de la Cruz	Cincinnati Reds	April 20, 1944
Jackie Robinson - ROY, MVP '49	Brooklyn Dodgers	April 15, 1947
Larry Doby	Cleveland Indians, Chicago White Sox, Detroit Tigers	July 5, 1947
Hank Thompson	St. Louis Browns, New York Giants	July 17, 1947
Willard Brown	St. Louis Browns	July 19, 1947
Dan Bankhead	Brooklyn Dodgers	August 6, 1947
Roy Campanella - MVP '51, '53, '53	Brooklyn Dodgers	April 20, 1948
Satchel Paige	Cleveland Indians, St. Louis Browns, Kansas City A's	July 9, 1948
Minnie Miñoso	Chicago White Sox, Cleveland Indians, St. Louis Cardinals, Washington Senators	April 19, 1949
Don Newcombe - ROY, MVP '56	Brooklyn Dodgers, Los Angeles, Cincinnati Reds, Cleveland Indians	May 20, 1949
Monte Irvin	New York Giants, Chicago Cubs	July 8, 1949
Luke Easter	Cleveland Indians	August 11, 1949
Sam Jethroe - ROY	Boston Braves, Pittsburgh Pirates	April 18, 1950
Luis Márquez	Boston Braves, Chicago Cubs, Pittsburgh Pirates	April 18, 1951
Ray Noble	New York Giants	April 18, 1951
Artie Wilson	New York Giants	April 18, 1951

Major League & Negro League Connections

Harry "Suitcase" Simpson	Cleveland Indians, Kansas City A's, New York Yankees, Chicago White Sox, Pittsburgh Pirates	April 21, 1951
Willie Mays – ROY, MVP '54, '65	New York Giants, San Francisco Giants, New York Mets	May 25, 1951
Sam Hairston	Chicago White Sox	July 21, 1951
Bob Boyd	Chicago White Sox, Baltimore Orioles, Kansas City A's, Milwaukee Braves	September 8, 1951
José Campos	Washington Senators	September 11, 1951
Toothpick Sam Jones	Cleveland Indians, Chicago Cubs, St. Louis Cardinals, San Francisco Giants, Detroit Tigers, Baltimore Orioles	September 22, 1951
Héctor Rodríguez	Chicago White Sox	April 15, 1952
George Crowe	Boston Braves, Milwaukee Braves, Cincinnati Reds, St. Louis Cardinals	April 16, 1952
Buster Clarkson	Boston Braves	April 30, 1952
Quincy Trouppe	Cleveland Indians	April 30, 1952
Joe Black – ROY	Brooklyn Dodgers, Cincinnati Reds, Washington Senators	May 1, 1952
Dave Pope	Cleveland Indians, Baltimore Orioles	July 1, 1952
Sandy Amoros	Brooklyn Dodgers, Los Angeles Dodgers, Detroit Tigers	August 22, 1952
Billy Bruton	Milwaukee Braves, Detroit Tigers	April 13, 1953
Junior Gilliam – ROY	Brooklyn Dodgers, Los Angeles Dodgers	April 14, 1953
Connie Johnson	Chicago White Sox, Baltimore Orioles	April 17, 1953
Jim Pendleton	Milwaukee Braves, Pittsburgh Pirates, Cincinnati Reds, Houston Colt .45's	April 17, 1953

Negro Leagues Book #2: The Players

Dave Hoskins	Cleveland Indians	April 18, 1953
Al Smith	Cleveland Indians, Chicago White Sox, Baltimore Orioles, Boston Red Sox	July 10, 1953
Bob Trice	Philadelphia A's, Kansas City A's	September 13, 1953
Ernie Banks – MVP '58, '59	Chicago Cubs	September 17, 1953
Gene Baker	Chicago Cubs, Pittsburgh Pirates	September 20, 1953
Hank Aaron – MVP '57	Milwaukee Braves, Atlanta Braves	April 13, 1954
Curt Roberts	Pittsburgh Pirates	April 13, 1954
Chuck Harmon	Cincinnati Reds, St. Louis Cardinals, Philadelphia Phillies	April 17, 1954
José Santiago	Cleveland Indians, Kansas City A's	April 17, 1954
Charles White	Milwaukee Braves	April 18, 1954
Jay Heard	Baltimore Orioles	April 24, 1954
Bill Greason	St. Louis Cardinals	May 31, 1954
Joe Taylor	Philadelphia A's, Cincinnati Reds, St. Louis Cardinals, Baltimore Orioles	August 26, 1954
Winn Durham	Baltimore Orioles, St. Louis Cardinals	September 10, 1954
Elston Howard	New York Yankees, Boston Red Sox	April 14, 1955
Bob Thurman	Cincinnati Reds	April 14, 1955
Roberto Vargas	Milwaukee Braves	April 17, 1955

Major League & Negro League Connections

Lino Donoso	Pittsburgh Pirates	June 18, 1955
Milt Smith	Cincinnati Reds	July 21, 1955
Billy Harrell	Cleveland Indians, Boston Red Sox	September 2, 1955
Vibert Clarke	Washington Senators	September 4, 1955
Charlie Neal	Brooklyn Dodgers, Los Angeles Dodgers, New York Mets, Cincinnati Reds	April 17, 1956
Wes Covington	Milwaukee Braves, Chicago White Sox, Kansas City A's, Philadelphia Phillies, Chicago Cubs, L.A. Dodgers	April 19, 1956
Patricio Scantlebury	Cincinnati Reds	April 19, 1956
Charles Peete	St. Louis Cardinals	July 17, 1956
Joe Caffie	Cleveland Indians	September 13, 1956
Larry Raines	Cleveland Indians	April 16, 1957
John Kennedy	Philadelphia Phillies	April 22, 1957
Frank Barnes	St. Louis Cardinals	September 22, 1957
Pancho Herrera	Philadelphia Phillies	April 15, 1958
Bob Wilson	Los Angeles Dodgers	May 17, 1958
Henry Mason	Philadelphia Phillies	September 12, 1958
George Altman	Chicago Cubs, St. Louis Cardinals, New York Mets	April 11, 1959
Marshall Bridges	St. Louis Cardinals, Cincinnati, New York Yankees, Washington Senators	June 17, 1959

Negro Leagues Book #2: The Players

Jim Proctor	Detroit Tigers	September 14, 1959
Sammy Drake	Chicago Cubs	April 17, 1960
Sweet Lou Johnson	Chicago Cubs, Los Angeles Dodgers, Milwaukee Braves, Cleveland Indians, California Angels	April 17, 1960
Walt Bond	Cleveland Indians, Houston Colts .45's, Minnesota Twins	April 19, 1960
Choo Choo Coleman	Philadelphia Phillies, New York Mets	April 19, 1961
John Wyatt	Kansas City A's, Boston Red Sox, New York Yankees, Detroit Tigers, Oakland A's	September 8, 1961
J.C. Hartman	Houston Colts .45's	July 21, 1962
Charlie Dees	Los Angeles Angels	May 26, 1963
Willie Smith	Detroit Tigers, Los Angeles Dodgers, California Angels, Cleveland Indians, Chicago Cubs, Cincinnati Reds	June 18, 1963
George C. Smith	Detroit Tigers, Boston Red Sox	August 4, 1963
George Spriggs	Pittsburgh Pirates, Kansas City Royals	September 15, 1965
Paul Casanova	Washington Senators, Atlanta Braves	September 18, 1965
Clarence W. Jones	Chicago Cubs	April 20, 1967
Ike Brown	Detroit Tigers	June 17, 1969

Negro League Players Who Went Directly into the Major Leagues

Larry Doby, 1947
Hank Thompson, 1947
Willard Brown, 1947
Dan Bankhead, 1947
Satchel Paige, 1948
Ernie Banks, 1953

MINNIE MIÑOSO - If one were to combine all hits from the Major Leagues, Negro Leagues, Cuban Leagues and the Mexican Leagues, Minnie Miñoso would have close to 4,000 hall-of-fame hits. Miñoso played in Major League All-Star games in 1951-54, 1957, 1959-60. An excellent hitter, he led the American League in total bases in 1954 with 304. Miñoso was also a standout in left field, winning Gold Gloves in 1957, 1959, and 1960.

Negro Leagues Book #2: The Players

BARRIER BREAKERS in Major League Baseball

The First Latinos or African Americans to play for the original 16 Major League teams.

As the sport's caste system is broken.

Team	Black	Date	Latino	Country	Date
Brooklyn Dodgers	Jackie Robinson	4/15/47	Sandy Amoros	Cuba	8/22/52
Cleveland Indians	Larry Doby	7/5/47	Minnie Minoso	Cuba	4/19/49
St. Louis Browns	Hank Thompson (j)	7/17/47	NONE (f)		
New York Giants	Hank Thompson (a)	7/8/49	Ray Noble	Cuba	4/18/51
Boston Braves	Sam Jethroe	4/18/50	Luis Marquez	Puerto Rico	4/18/51
Chicago White Sox	Sam Hairston	7/21/51	Minnie Minoso	Cuba	5/1/51
Philadelphia A's	Bob Trice	9/13/53	Vic Power	Puerto Rico	4/13/54
Chicago Cubs	Ernie Banks (k)	9/17/53	Luis Marquez	Puerto Rico	5/11/54
Pittsburgh Pirates	Curt Roberts	4/13/54	Carlos Bernier	Puerto Rico	4/22/53
St. Louis Cardinals (b)	Tom Alston (l)	4/13/54	Memo Luna	Mexico	4/20/54
Cincinnati Reds	Chuck Harmon	4/17/54	Nino Escalera	Puerto Rico	4/17/54
Washington Senators (e)	Joe Black	8/6/57	Carlos Paula	Cuba	9/6/54
New York Yankees	Elston Howard	4/14/55	Hector Lopez	Panama	5/26/59
Philadelphia Phillies	John Kennedy	4/22/57	Chico Fernandez	Cuba	4/16/57
Detroit Tigers	Larry Doby	4/10/59	Ozzie Virgil	Dom. Rep.	6/6/58
Boston Red Sox (c)	Pumpsie Green (h)	7/21/59	Felix Mantilla	Puerto Rico	12/11/62

FIRST NON-WHITE PLAYER AT EACH POSITION

PLAYER	AL	NL	PLAYER
P Satchel Paige - 1948	**Cleveland Indians**	**Brooklyn Dodgers**	Dan Bankhead - 1947
C Sam Hairston - 1951	**Chicago White Sox**	**Brooklyn Dodgers**	Roy Campanella - 1948
1B Larry Doby - 1947	**Cleveland Indians**	**Brooklyn Dodgers**	Jackie Robinson - 1947
2B Hank Thompson - 1947	**St. Louis Browns**	**Brooklyn Dodgers**	Jackie Robinson - 1948
3B Minnie Minoso - 1951	**Chicago White Sox**	**New York Giants**	Hank Thompson - 1949
SS Larry Doby - 1947	**Cleveland Indians**	**New York Giants**	Artie Wilson - 1951
OF Willard Brown - 1947	**St. Louis Browns**	**New York Giants**	Monte Irvin - 1949
OF Larry Doby - 1948	**Cleveland Indians**	**New York Giants**	Hank Thompson - 1950
OF Minnie Minoso - 1949	**Cleveland Indians**	**Boston Braves**	Sam Jethroe - 1950

FIRST NON-WHITE REGULAR AT EACH POSITION
(100 games or 154 innings)

PLAYER	AL	NL	PLAYER
P - Connie Johnson - 1956 (g)	Baltimore Orioles	Brooklyn Dodgers	Don Newcombe - 1949
C - Earl Battery - 1960 (d)	Washington Senators	Brooklyn Dodgers	Roy Campanella - 1949
1B - Luke Easter - 1950	Cleveland Indians	Brooklyn Dodgers	Jackie Robinson - 1947
2B - Jake Wood - 1961	Detroit Tigers	Brooklyn Dodgers	Jackie Robinson - 1948
3B - Hector Lopez - 1956	Kansas City A's	New York Giants	Hank Thompson - 1950

Major League & Negro League Connections

SS - Chico Fernandez - 1960	Detroit Tigers	Chicago Cubs	Ernie Banks - 1954
OF - Larry Doby - 1948	Cleveland Indians	Boston Braves	Sam Jethroe - 1950
OF - Minnie Minoso - 1952	Chicago White Sox	New York Giants	Monte Irvin - 1951
OF - Harry Simpson - 1952	Cleveland Indians	New York Giants	Willie Mays - 1951

(a) Monte Irvin, former Newark Eagle, also debuted July 8, 1949 for the New York Giants.

(b) Rev. Bill Greason was the first former Negro League player, with the St. Louis Cardinals, on May 31, 1954.

(c) John Wyatt (on June 13, 1966) and Elston Howard (on August 3, 1967) were the first pitcher and non-pitcher, from the Negro Leagues, to play for the Boston Red Sox in 1967.

(d) New York Yankees' Elston Howard caught 91 games in 1960 and 111 games in 1961.

(e) Panamanian Vibert Clarke was the first ex-Negro Leaguer to play for the Washington Senators on September 4, 1955.

(f) Valmy Thomas, from the Virgin Islands, (although born in Puerto Rico) was the first black player for the Baltimore Orioles in 1960.

(g) Satchel Paige appeared in 138 innings in 46 games for the St. Louis Browns in 1952.

(h) Pitcher Earl "No Hit" Wilson debuted with the Boston Red Sox on July 28, 1959, seven days after Pumpsie Green.

(i) Pitcher Brooks Lawrence debuted with the St. Louis Cardinals two months after Tom Alston

(j) Willard "Home Run" Brown debuted with the St. Louis Browns two days after Hank Thompson.

(k) Gene Baker from the Kansas City Monarchs was the first African American with the Chicago Cubs, but Ernie Banks appeared on the field first.

Special note: Luis Marquez was the first Latin American to play for the Boston Braves, Chicago Cubs, and the Pittsburgh Pirates.

Negro Leagues Book #2: The Players

BROWN BARRIER BREAKERS

Light enough for the Major Leagues and dark enough for the Negro Leagues.
Before Jackie Robinson and Larry Doby

15 Tan players who played in both the Major & Negro Leagues before 1947

1905, 1923—of, All Cubans, Cuban Stars (East)	**ARMANDO MARSANS** * B/T: R/R 5' 10" 157 lbs. B: October 3, 1887 Matanzas, Cuba D: September 3, 1960 Havana, Cuba	July 4, 1911-18—of, inf Cincinnati Reds, St. Louis Browns, New York Yankees
1904-07—3b All Cubans, Havana Cuban Stars	**RAFAEL D. (MIKE) ALMEIDA** * B/T: R/R 5' 9" 164 lbs. B: July 30, 1887 Havana, Cuba D: March 19, 1968 Havana, Cuba	July 4, 1911-13—3b, ss, of, 2b Cincinnati Reds
1911-14—c, 1b Cuban Stars, Long Branch (NJ) Cubans	**MIGUEL ANGEL (MIKE, BAGUETTE, PANDE FLAUTA) GONZÁLEZ y CORDERO*** B/T: R/R 6' 1" 200 lbs. B: September 24, 1890 Havana, Cuba D: February 19, 1977 Havana, Cuba	September 28, 1912, 1914-21, 1924-29, 1931-32—c, 1b, of, 2b Boston Braves, Cincinnati Reds, New York Giants, Chicago Cubs
May 9, 1913, 1920—of Washington Senators	**JACINTO (JACK) CALVO** * B/T: L/L 5' 10" 156 lbs. B: June 11, 1894 Havana, Cuba D: June 15, 1965 Miami, Florida	1913-16—of Long Branch (NJ) Cubans
1905—1b All Cubans	**ALFREDO A. (PAJARO) CABRERA** * B/T: R/R 5' 10" W:? B: May 11, 1881 Canary Islands, Spain D: 1964 Batabano, Cuba	May 16, 1913 – ss St. Louis Cardinals
1911, 1917 – p Chicago Union Giants	**WILLIAM (CHIEF CHOUNEAU) CADREAU** B/T: R/R 5' 9" 150 lbs. B: September 2, 1888 Cloquet, MN D: September 17, 1946 Cloquet, MN	1910 – p Chicago White Sox
1912-13—p, of Cuban Stars, Long Branch (NJ) Cubans	**ADOLFO DOMINGO (DOLF, PAPA MONTERO, HARARA PERFECTO) LUQUE** * B/T: R/R 5' 7" 160 lbs. B: August 4, 1890 Havana, Cuba D: July 3, 1957 Havana, Cuba	May 20, 1914-15, 1918-35—p Boston Braves, Cincinnati Reds, Brooklyn Dodgers, New York Giants
1913—3b Long Branch (NJ) Cubans	**ÁNGEL (PETE) ARAGÓN y VALDES SR.** B/T: R/R 5' 5" 150 lbs. B: August 2, 1890 Havana, Cuba D: January 24, 1952 New York, NY	August 20, 1914, 1916-17—3b, of, ss New York Yankees
1914-15—p Long Branch (NJ) Cubans	**JOSÉ ACOSTA** * B/T: R/R 5' 7" 140 lbs. B: March 4, 1891 San Antonio Rio Blanco, Cuba D: November 16, 1977 Havana, Cuba	July 28, 1920-22—p Washington Senators, Chicago White Sox

Major League & Negro League Connections

1914-16—c Long Branch (NJ) Cubans	RICARDO TORRES B/T: R/R 5' 11" 160 lbs. B: April 16, 1891, Regal, Cuba D: April 17, 1960, Regal, Cuba	May 18, 1920-22—1b, c Washington Senators
1923—p Cuban Stars (West)	**PEDRO DIBUT y VILLAFANA*** B/T: R/R 5' 8" 190 lbs. B: November 18, 1892 Cienfuegos, Cuba D: December 4, 1979 Hialeah, Florida	May 1, 1924-25—p Cincinnati Reds
1915-28—2b, 3b Jersey City Cubans, Cuban Stars (West), Cuban Stars (East), Cincinnati Cubans	**RAMON (PAITO, MIKE) HERRERA** * B/T: R/R 5' 6" 147 lbs. B: December 19, 1897 Havana, Cuba D: February 3, 1978 Havana, Cuba	September 22, 1925-26—2b, 3b, ss Boston Red Sox
1924-25, 1931—p, of Cuban Stars (East), Cuban Stars (West)	OSCAR ESTRADA B/T: L/L 5' 8" 160 lbs. B: February 15, 1904 Havana, Cuba D: January 2, 1978 Havana, Cuba	April 21, 1929 – p St. Louis Browns
1934—p Havana Cuban Stars	TOMÁS (TOMMY) de la CRUZ y RIVERO B/T: R/R 6' 1" 168 lbs. B: September 18, 1910 Marianao, Cuba D: September 6, 1958 Havana, Cuba	April 20, 1944 – p Cincinnati Reds
April 16, 1942-43 – c Chicago Cubs	SALVADOR JOSÉ (CHICO) HERNÁNDEZ y RAMOS B/T: R/R, 6'1" 195 lbs. B: January 3, 1916, Havana, Cuba D: January 3, 1986, Havana, Cuba	1945—c Indianapolis Clowns
	* CUBAN BASEBALL HALL OF FAME	

Negro Leagues Book #2: The Players

Special Negro Leagues Draft by MLB

On June 5, 2008, at Disney's Wide World of Sports Complex, in Lake Buena Vista, Florida, Major League Baseball held a ceremonial draft of Negro League players. Below is a list of living players drafted.

American League Teams:

Baltimore Orioles - HUBERT (BERT) SIMMONS—1950—p, Baltimore Elite Giants

Boston Red Sox - JIM COLZIE—1937-49—p, Atlanta Black Crackers, Cincinnati-Indianapolis Clowns, Indianapolis Clowns

Chicago White Sox - HANK PRESSWOOD—1948-52—ss, Cleveland Buckeyes, Kansas City Monarchs

Cleveland Indians - OTHA BAILEY—1950-59—c, Cleveland Buckeyes, Houston Eagles, New Orleans Eagles, Birmingham Black Barons

Detroit Tigers - CECIL KAISER—1939, 1945-49—p, Pittsburgh Crawfords (USL), Homestead Grays, Detroit Motor City Giants, Brooklyn Brown Dodgers, Detroit Stars

Kansas City Royals - ULYSSES HOLLIMON—1950-54—p, Baltimore Elite Giants, Birmingham Black Barons

L.A. Angels of Anaheim - NEALE (BOBO) HENDERSON—1949—of, Kansas City Monarchs (not to be confused with James Henderson of the Monarchs in 1949)

Minnesota Twins - BILL BELL—1949-54—p, Kansas City Monarchs, Birmingham Black Barons

New York Yankees - EMILIO NAVARRO—1928-29—2b, ss, Cuban Stars (East), Stars of Cuba. He was the *oldest* player to attend at 102 years old. Navarro is a member of the 1992 Puerto Rican Baseball Hall of Fame and 2004 Puerto Rican Sports Hall of Fame.

Oakland Athletics - IRVIN CASTILLE—1951-53—ss, 3b, Birmingham Black Barons

Seattle Mariners - JOHN (MULE) MILES, JR.—1946-49—of, Chicago American Giants

Tampa Bay Rays - WALTER LEE (DIRK) GIBBONS—1948-49—p, Indianapolis Clowns

Texas Rangers - CHARLEY PRIDE—1953-56, 1958-59—p, of, Memphis Red Sox, Birmingham Black Barons

Toronto Blue Jays - HAROLD (BIG RED) GOULD, SR.—1947-48—p, Philadelphia Stars

Major League & Negro League Connections

National League Teams:

Arizona Diamondbacks - BOB (PEACHHEAD) MITCHELL, SR.—1950-57—p, Cleveland Buckeyes, Kansas City Monarchs

Atlanta Braves - JAMES (RED) MOORE, III—1935-48—1b, Atlanta Black Crackers, Baltimore Elite Giants, Philadelphia Daisies (NML), Newark Eagles

Chicago Cubs - WALT (COACH O) OWENS—1953-55—p, of, Detroit Stars

Cincinnati Reds - CHARLES DAVIS—1953-55—p, Memphis Red Sox

Colorado Rockies - MACK PRIDE, JR.—1956—p, Kansas City Monarchs

Florida Marlins - RICKY MAROTO—1954-56—of, p, Kansas City Monarchs

Houston Astros - BILL BLAIR, JR.—1947-48—p, Detroit Senators, Indianapolis Clowns, Portland (OR) Rosebuds

Los Angeles Dodgers - ANDY PORTER—1932-50—p, Little Rock Greys, Cleveland Cubs, Nashville Elite Giants, Washington Elite Giants, Baltimore Elite Giants, Indianapolis Clowns, Columbus Elite Giants, Louisville Black Caps, Newark Eagles

Milwaukee Brewers - JOE B. SCOTT—1944-49—of, Memphis Red Sox

New York Mets - BOB SCOTT—1945-50—p, of, 1b, Boston Blues, New York Black Yankees, Pittsburgh Crawfords (USL)

Philadelphia Phillies - MAHLON DUCKETT—1940-50—3b, 2b, ss, Philadelphia Stars, Homestead Grays

Pittsburgh Pirates - JAMES TILLMAN-1941-42—c, Homestead Grays

St. Louis Cardinals - PRINCE JOE HENRY—1950-52, 1955, 1958-59—2b, 3b, Memphis Red Sox, Indianapolis Clowns, Detroit Stars, Detroit Clowns

San Diego Padres - WALTER McCOY—1945-48—p, Chicago American Giants

San Francisco Giants - CARLOS SANTIAGO—1945-46—2b, New York Cubans

Washington Nationals - MAMIE JOHNSON—1954—p, Indianapolis Clowns

APPENDIX C:

All-Star Register for the annual East-West Classic, 1933-1960

HOF - designates the player is a National Baseball Hall of Fame and Museum inductee.

Players with a (2) following a year indicates that there were two East-West games that year, and that they played in both games.

Robert "James" Abernathy: Kansas City Monarchs, 1947

Ray Aguillard: Detroit Stars, 1957

Newt "Colt" Allen: Kansas City Monarchs, 1936, 1937, 1938, 1941

Eddie Alston: Detroit Clowns, 1958

Dave Amaro: Indianapolis Clowns, 1953

Juan Armenteros: Kansas City Monarchs, 1953, 54, 1955

Buddy Armour: St. Louis Stars, 1941; Cleveland Buckeyes, 1944; Chicago American Giants, 1947 (2)

Paul Arnold: Newark Dodgers, 1935

Frank "Pee Wee" Austin: Philadelphia Stars, 1945, 1946, 1947 (2), 1948 (2)

Otha Bailey: Birmingham Black Barons, 1952, 1953, 1954, 1955, 1956 (2), 1957, 1958

Robert Baldwin: Detroit Stars, 1957

Dan Bankhead: Birmingham Black Barons, 1941; Memphis Red Sox, 1946 (2), 1947

Fred Bankhead: Memphis Red Sox, 1942 (2)

Sam Bankhead: Nashville Elite Giants, 1933, 1934; Pittsburgh Crawfords, 1936, 1938; Homestead Grays, 1942 (2), 1943, 1944, 1946

Ernie Banks - HOF: Kansas City Monarchs, 1953

James Banks: Memphis Red Sox, 1956, 1957, 1958

Marvin Barker: New York Black Yankees, 1940, 1945, 1948

Isaac Barnes: Memphis Red Sox, 1957, 1958

Dave "Impo" Barnhill: New York Cubans, 1941, 1942 (2), 1943, 1948

Jesse Bass: Birmingham Black Barons, 1958; Detroit Stars, 1959, 1960

Lloyd "Pepper" Bassett: Pittsburgh Crawfords, 1937; Chicago American Giants, 1939 (2), 1941; Birmingham Black Barons, 1947, 1948, 1950; Memphis Red Sox, 1953

Hank Baylis: Kansas City Monarchs, 1952, 1953, 1955

Herman Bell: Birmingham Black Barons, 1949

James "Cool Papa" Bell - HOF: Pittsburgh Crawfords, 1933, 1934, 1935, 1936; Chicago American Giants, 1942 (2); Homestead Grays, 1943, 1944

Jerry Benjamin: Homestead Grays, 1937, 1943, 1945

Gene Benson: Philadelphia Stars, 1940, 1945, 1946 (2)

Bill "Fireball" Beverly: Chicago American Giants, 1952

Rainey Bibbs: Cincinnati Tigers, 1937

Joe Black: Baltimore Elite Giants, 1947, 1948, 1950

Heberto "Harry" Blanco: New York Cubans, 1942 (2)

Don Bonner: Detroit Stars, 1959, 1960

Lyman Bostock: Birmingham Black Barons, 1941

Bob Boyd: Memphis Red Sox, 1947, 1948 (2), 1949

Gene "Flash" Bremer: Memphis Red Sox, 1940; Cincinnati Buckeyes, 1942 (2); Cleveland Buckeyes, 1944, 1945

Chet Brewer: Kansas City Monarchs, 1934; Cleveland Buckeyes, 1947

Sherwood Brewer: Indianapolis Clowns, 1949, 1950; Kansas City Monarchs, 1951, 1953; Detroit Clowns, 1958

George "Chippy" Britton: Homestead Grays, 1933

Eddie Brooks: Birmingham Black Barons, 1952, 1953, 1954, 1955

Barney "Brinquitos" Brown: New York Black Yankees, 1937, 1938; Philadelphia Stars, 1942, 1946 (2)

Ike Brown: Kansas City Monarchs, 1960

John W. Brown: Cleveland Buckeyes, 1946

Larry "Iron Man" Brown: Chicago American Giants, 1933, 1934; Memphis Red Sox, 1938, 1939 (2), 1940, 1941

Ray Brown - HOF: Homestead Grays, 1935, 1940

T.J. Brown: Memphis Red Sox, 1942

Willard "Home Run" Brown - HOF: Kansas City Monarchs, 1936, 1937, 1942 (2), 1943, 1948 (2), 1949

Willie Brown: Indianapolis Clowns, 1953

José Antonio Burgos: Birmingham Black Barons, 1949

Thomas "Pee Wee" Butts: Baltimore Elite Giants, 1944, 1946, 1947 (2), 1948, 1949, 1950; Birmingham Black Barons, 1953

Richard "Subby" Byas: Chicago American Giants, 1936, 1937

Bill Byrd: Washington Elite Giants, 1936; Baltimore Elite Giants, 1939 (2), 1941, 1944, 1945, 1946 (2)

Marion "Sugar" Cain: Kansas City Monarchs, 1958

Walter "Lefty" Calhoun: New Orleans-St. Louis Stars, 1940

Roy Campanella: Baltimore Elite Giants, 1941, 1944, 1945

Walter "Rev" Cannady: New York Black Yankees, 1938

Caldonia Canatienzo: Detroit Stars, 1957

Andrew Carpenter: Detroit Stars, 1954

Ernest "Spoon" Carter: Memphis Red Sox, 1947, 1948

Marlin Carter: Memphis Red Sox, 1942 (2)

Manny Cartledge: Birmingham Black Barons, 1953, 1955

Al Cartmill: Kansas City Monarchs, 1955

Bill "Ready" Cash: Philadelphia Stars, 1948 (2), 49

Irvin Castille: Birmingham Black Barons, 1953

Joe Castille: Detroit Stars, 1957

Oscar Charleston - HOF: Pittsburgh Crawfords, 1933, 1934, 1935

Marvin Chalmers: Detroit Stars, 1959

Robert "Eggie" Clarke: New York Black Yankees, 1940

Vibert Clarke: Cleveland Buckeyes, 1946, 1947, 1948; Memphis Red Sox, 1950, 1951

James "Bus" Clarkson: Newark Eagles, 1940; Philadelphia Stars, 1949

Howard "Duke" Cleveland: Jacksonville Red Caps, 1941

Nat "Sweetwater" Clifton: Detroit Clowns, 1958

James "Fireball" Cohen: Indianapolis Clowns, 1948

Francisco "Pancho" Coimbre: New York Cubans, 1941, 1944

José Luis Colas: Memphis Red Sox, 1947 (2), 1948, 1951

Elliott Coleman: Birmingham Black Barons, 1955

Andy Cooper - HOF: Kansas City Monarchs, 1936

Tom Cooper: Kansas City Monarchs, 1950, 1951, 1953

William "Sug" Cornelius: Chicago American Giants, 1935, 1936, 1938

Alex Crespo: New York Cubans, 1940

George Crowe: New York Black Yankees, 1948

Negro Leagues Book #2: The Players

Jimmie Crutchfield: Pittsburgh Crawfords, 1934, 1935, 1936; Chicago American Giants, 1941

Nate Dancey: Kansas City Monarchs, 1959, 1960

Ray Dandridge - HOF: Newark Dodgers, 1935; Newark Eagles, 1937, 1944

Isaac Barnes: Memphis Red Sox, 1959

Lloyd "Ducky" Davenport: Cincinnati Tigers, 1937; Memphis Red Sox, 1939; Birmingham Black Barons, 1942; Chicago American Giants, 1943, 1944; Cleveland Buckeyes, 1945

Charlie Davis: Memphis Red Sox, 1954, 1955

John "Cherokee" Davis: Newark Eagles, 1944, 1945; Houston Eagles, 1949

Lorenzo "Piper" Davis: Birmingham Black Barons, 1946 (2), 1947 (2), 1948 (2), 1949

Robert "Butch" Davis: Baltimore Elite Giants, 1949

Walter "Steel Arm" Davis: Chicago American Giants, 1933

Leon Day - HOF: Brooklyn Eagles, 1935; Newark Eagles, 1937, 1939 (2), 1942 (2), 1943, 1946 (2)

Wesley "Doc" Dennis: Birmingham Black Barons, 1951, 1952, 1953, 1954

Lou Dials: Chicago American Giants, 1936

Pedro "Manny" Díaz: New York Cubans, 1946, 1949, 1950

Martín Dihigo - HOF: New York Cubans, 1935, 1945

Herbert "Rap" Dixon: Philadelphia Stars, 1933; Pittsburgh Crawfords, 1934

Larry Doby - HOF: Newark Eagles, 1946 (2)

Jesse Douglas: Chicago American Giants, 1950

Verdes Drake: Indianapolis Clowns, 1953, 1954

Claro Duany: New York Cubans, 1947 (2)

Frank Duncan, Jr.: Chicago American Giants, 1938

Herman Dunlap: Chicago American Giants, 1936

Jake Dunn: Philadelphia Stars, 1937, 1938

Winn Durham: Chicago American Giants, 1952

Eddie Dwight: Kansas City Monarchs, 1936

Luke Easter: Homestead Grays, 1948 (2)

Howard Easterling: Cincinnati Tigers, 1937; Homestead Grays, 1940, 1943, 1946 (2); New York Cubans, 1949

Eugene Elliott: Kansas City Monarchs, 1956

Harry "Speed" Else: Kansas City Monarchs, 1936

Frank Ensley: Indianapolis Clowns, 1954

Felix "Chin" Evans: Memphis Red Sox, 1946

Frank Evans: Detroit Stars, 1956

John Evans: Kansas City Monarchs, 1957

Wilmer "Red" Fields: Homestead Grays, 1948

Jimmy Ford: St. Louis Stars, 1941

Pedro Formental: Memphis Red Sox, 1949

Ralph Fortson: Raleigh Tigers, 1960

Willie Foster - HOF: Chicago American Giants, 1933, 1934

Kenny Free: Raleigh Tigers, 1959

Jonas "Lefty" Gaines: Baltimore Elite Giants, 1942 (2), 1946 (2); Philadelphia Stars, 1950

Willy "Willie" Gaines: Indianapolis Clowns, 1953

Raúl Galata: New York Cubans, 1950

Silvio García: New York Cubans, 1946 (2), 1947 (2)

Henry Garrett: Raleigh Tigers, 1960

Josh Gibson - HOF: Pittsburgh Crawfords, 1933, 1934, 1935, 1936; Homestead Grays, 1939 (2), 1942 (2), 1943, 1944, 1946 (2)

JOSH GIBSON is reported to have hit a baseball out of Yankee Stadium, or was it Grand Canyon? Regardless of whether this feat is factual or mythical, Gibson stands the tallest amongst the trees in baseball's slugger forest. When fans saw Gibson squat in the on-deck circle, palms got sweaty, feet got happy and cheeks got yeasted in anticipation of expectations. Gibson's power was legendary. His stroke blended the power of a piston with the smoothness of a cue ball. Without any doubt, one of Black baseball's most prolific hitters.

Paul Gilbert: Kansas City Monarchs, 1959
George Giles: Brooklyn Eagles, 1935
Junior Gilliam: Baltimore Elite Giants, 1948 (2), 1949, 1950
Alvin "Bubber" Gipson: Birmingham Black Barons, 1942
Rufus Gipson: Louisville Black Clippers, 1954; Birmingham Black Barons, 1955; Memphis Red Sox, 1956, 1957, 1958, 1959; Raleigh Tigers, 1960
Tom "Lefty" Glover: Baltimore Elite Giants, 1945
Hiram "Rene" González: New York Cubans, 1950
Harold Gordon: Detroit Stars, 1954
Willie "Fireman" Grace: Cleveland Buckeyes, 1946 (2), 1948
Calvin Grant: Kansas City Monarchs, 1960
Bill Greason: Birmingham Black Barons, 1949
Herman Green: Detroit Stars, 1955, 1956, 1959
Leslie "Chin" Green: New Orleans-St. Louis Stars, 1940
Joe Greene: Kansas City Monarchs, 1940, 1942 (2)
Robert "Schoolboy" Griffith: Columbus Elite Giants, 1935; New York Black Yankees, 1948; Philadelphia Stars, 1949
Wiley Griggs: New Orleans Eagles, 1951; Birmingham Black Barons, 1956, 1957
Aubrey Grisby: Kansas City Monarchs, 1958
Manuel Santos Guerede: Detroit Stars, 1956
Larry Guice: New Orleans Eagles, 1951
Billy Ray Haggins: Memphis Red Sox, 1953, 1954, 1955
Sam Hairston: Indianapolis Clowns, 1948
Art Hamilton: Detroit Clowns, 1958; Detroit Stars, 1959, 1960
Curtis Hardaway; Birmingham Black Barons, 1953
Donnie Harris: Birmingham Black Barons, 1957
J.C. Hartman: Kansas City Monarchs, 1955
Chick "Popsickle" Harris: Kansas City Monarchs, 1936

Negro Leagues Book #2: The Players

Earnest Harris: Birmingham Black Barons, 1959
Isiah Harris: Memphis Red Sox, 1953, 1954, 1955
Lonnie Harris: Louisville Black Clippers, 1954; Memphis Red Sox, 1957, 1958
Vic Harris: Homestead Grays, 1933, 1934, 1938, 1939, 1942, 1943, 1947
Willie Harris: Louisville Black Clippers, 1954; Memphis Red Sox, 1955; Detroit Stars, 1956, 1959; Detroit Clowns, 1958; Birmingham Black Barons, 1960
Wilmer Harris: Philadelphia Stars, 1951, 1952
David "Bill" Harvey: Baltimore Elite Giants, 1943
Bob Harvey: Newark Eagles, 1948; Houston Eagles, 1950
Johnny Hayes: New York Black Yankees, 1947 (2); Baltimore Elite Giants, 1951
Buster Haywood: Indianapolis Clowns, 1946, 1951, 1953
Jehosie "Jay" Heard: New Orleans Eagles, 1951
Curtis "Dan" Henderson: Toledo-Indianapolis Crawfords, 1940
James "Duke" Henderson: Kansas City Monarchs, 1952
Leo "Preacher" Henry: Jacksonville Red Caps, 1941
Prince Joe Henry: Detroit Clowns, 1958
Francisco "Pancho" Herrera: Kansas City Monarchs, 1953, 1954
Jimmy Hill: Newark Eagles, 1941
Sam Hill: Chicago American Giants, 1948 (2); Memphis Red Sox, 1958
Bill Holland: New York Black Yankees, 1939
Eugene Holmes: Raleigh Tigers, 1959
Billy Horne: Chicago American Giants, 1939 (2), 1941
Dave Hoskins: Cleveland Buckeyes, 1949
William "Big Bill" Hoskins: Baltimore Elite Giants, 1941
Carrenza "Schoolboy" Howard: New York Cubans, 1944
Palmer Hubbard: Birmingham Black Barons, 1957; Kansas City Monarch, 1958, 1960
William Henry "Lefty" Hudson: Chicago American Giants, 1941
Sammy T. Hughes: Nashville Elite Giants, 1934; Columbus Elite Giants, 1935; Washington Elite Giants, 1936; Baltimore Elite Giants, 1938, 1939 (2)
Bertrum Hunter: Pittsburgh Crawfords, 1933
Willie "Ace" Hutchinson: Memphis Red Sox, 1949
Cowan "Bubba" Hyde: Memphis Red Sox, 1943, 1946 (2)
Monte Irvin - HOF: Newark Eagles, 1941, 1946 (2), 1947 (2), 1948
James "Sap" Ivory: Detroit Stars, 1955, 1956, 1957, 1960; Birmingham Black Barons, 1958
Willie Lee "Bud" Ivory: Detroit Stars, 1954
A.J. Jackson: Kansas City Monarchs, 1956
Brown Jackson: Birmingham Black Barons, 1958, 1960
Isiah "Ike" Jackson: Kansas City Monarchs, 1952
John "Stony" Jackson, Jr.: Kansas City Monarchs, 1952, 1953
Gideon Jarvis: Kansas City Monarchs, 1958
Clarence "Fats" Jenkins: New York Black Yankees, 1933; Brooklyn Eagles, 1935
Charlie Jennings: Memphis Red Sox, 1956
Gentry "Jeep" Jessup: Chicago American Giants, 1944, 1945, 1946, 1947, 1948
Sam "The Jet" Jethroe: Cincinnati Buckeyes, 1942 (2); Cleveland Buckeyes, 1944, 1946 (2), 1947 (2)
Abdulla "Showboat" Johnson: Detroit Stars, 1957
Byron "Mex" Johnson: Kansas City Monarchs, 1938

Connie Johnson: Toledo-Indianapolis Crawfords, 1940; Kansas City Monarchs, 1950

Ernest "Schooley" Johnson: Kansas City Monarchs, 1953

Gene Johnson: Detroit Stars, 1956, 1957

Jimmy "Slim" Johnson: Toledo-Indianapolis Crawfords, 1939

Judy Johnson - HOF: Pittsburgh Crawfords, 1933, 1936

Sweet Lou Johnson: Kansas City Monarchs, 1955

Aaron Jones: Detroit Stars, 1955

Bill Jones: Kansas City Monarchs, 1956

Jimmie Jones: Philadelphia Stars, 1952

Stuart "Slim" Jones: Philadelphia Stars, 1934; Philadelphia Stars, 1935

Casey Jones, Jr.: Memphis Red Sox, 1950, 1951

Leon Kellman: Cleveland Buckeyes, 1947, 1948, 1949; Memphis Red Sox, 1950

John Kennedy: Birmingham Black Barons, 1954

Henry "Jimbo" Kimbro: New York Black Yankees, 1941; Baltimore Elite Giants, 1943, 1944, 1946 (2), 1947 (2); Birmingham Black Barons, 1951, 1952, 1953

Harry "Tin Can" Kincannon: Pittsburgh Crawfords, 1934

Clarence "Pijo" King: Detroit Clowns, 1958

Ezell King: Detroit Stars, 1955

Arthur Lee Kranson: Kansas City Monarchs, 1936

James "Lefty" LaMarque: Kansas City Monarchs, 1948 (2), 1949

Larry LeGrande: Detroit Stars, 1959

Walter "Buck" Leonard - HOF: Homestead Grays, 1935, 1937, 1938, 1939 (2), 1940, 1941, 1943, 1944, 1945, 1946 (2), 1948

Rufus Lewis: Newark Eagles, 1947, 1948

Rogelio "Ice Cream" Linares: New York Cubans, 1945

Ben Littles: Philadelphia Stars, 1950, 1951; Memphis Red Sox, 1956

Lester "Buck" Lockett: Birmingham Black Barons, 1943, 1945; Baltimore Elite Giants, 1948 (2)

Carl Long: Birmingham Black Barons, 1953

Cando "Police Car" López: New York Cubans, 1939

Louis Louden: New York Cubans, 1946, 1947 (2), 1948 (2), 1950

Dick Lundy: Philadelphia Stars, 1933; Newark Dodgers, 1934

John Lyles: Cleveland Bears, 1939

Raleigh "Biz" Mackey - HOF: Philadelphia Stars, 1933, 1935; Washington Elite Giants, 1936; Baltimore Elite Giants, 1938; Newark Eagles, 1947

Max Manning: Newark Eagles, 1947, 1948

Ricky Maroto: Kansas City Monarchs, 1955, 1956

Frank Marsh: Birmingham Black Barons, 1956

Luis Ángel Márquez: Homestead Grays, 1947 (2), 1948 (2)

Henry "Pistol" Mason: Kansas City Monarchs, 1954

Horacio "Rabbit" Martínez: New York Cubans, 1940, 1941, 1943, 1944, 1945

Verdell "Lefty" Mathis: Memphis Red Sox, 1941, 1942, 1944, 1945

Leroy Matlock: Pittsburgh Crawfords, 1935, 1936

Big Bill Matthews: Detroit Stars, 1960

Eldridge "Chili" Mayweather: Kansas City Monarchs, 1937; New Orleans-St. Louis Stars, 1940

Booker "Cannonball" McDaniel: Kansas City Monarchs, 1945

Terris "The Great" McDuffie: New York Black Yankees, 1939; Homestead Grays, 1941; Newark Eagles, 1944

Negro Leagues Book #2: The Players

Henry "Cream" McHenry: Philadelphia Stars, 1940, 1941
Gread "Lefty" McKinnis: Birmingham Black Barons, 1943; Chicago American Giants, 1944, 1949
Ira McKnight: Kansas City Monarchs, 1956, 1957, 1958, 1960
Felix McLaurin: Chicago American Giants, 1952
Clyde McNeal: Chicago American Giants, 1950
James McNeil: Raleigh Tigers, 1959
Henry "Speed" Merchant: Indianapolis Clowns, 1950, 1952
Hank Miller: Philadelphia Stars, 1947 (2)
Ray Miller: Detroit Stars, 1954
Henry Milton: Kansas City Monarchs, 1936, 1937, 1938, 1939, 1949
Minnie Miñoso: New York Cubans, 1947 (2), 1948 (2)
George "Big" Mitchell: St. Louis Stars, 1941
Jessie Mitchell: Detroit Stars, 1956; Birmingham Black Barons, 1957; Kansas City Monarchs, 1959
John Mitchell: Birmingham Black Barons, 1958, 1960
Al "Johnny" Mobler: Birmingham Black Barons, 1955
Joe Montgomery: Detroit Stars, 1954, 1955
Bill Moore: Birmingham Black Barons, 1956
Leroy Morney: Cleveland Giants, 1933; Toledo-Indianapolis Crawfords, 1939; Chicago American Giants, 1940
Barney "Big Ad" Morris: Pittsburgh Crawfords, 1937; New York Cubans, 1944
Porter "Ankleball" Moss: Cincinnati Tigers, 1937; Memphis Red Sox, 1942, 1943
Ray Neil: Indianapolis Clowns, 1947, 1951, 1953
Clyde Nelson: Chicago American Giants, 1946
Dagoberto Nuñez: Kansas City Monarchs, 1954
John "Buck" O'Neil: Kansas City Monarchs, 1942 (2), 1943, 1949
Alejandro "Walla Walla" Oms: New York Cubans, 1935
Felix Ortiz: New Orleans Bears, 1957
Raymond "Smoky" Owens: Cleveland Bears, 1939
Leroy Robert "Satchel" Paige - HOF: Pittsburgh Crawfords, 1934, 1936; Kansas City Monarchs, 1941, 1942, 1943, 1955
Roy "Red" Parnell: Nashville Elite Giants, 1934; Philadelphia Stars, 1939
Roy Partlow: Homestead Grays, 1939
Andy "Pat" Patterson: Cleveland Red Sox, 1934; Kansas City Monarchs, 1936; Philadelphia Stars, 1939 (2), 1942 (2)
Willie "Pat" Patterson: Chicago American Giants, 1952; Memphis Red Sox, 1953; Detroit Stars, 1960
Lennie Pearson: Newark Eagles, 1941, 1942 (2), 1943, 1945, 1946; Baltimore Elite Giants, 1949
Art "Superman" Pennington: Chicago American Giants, 1942 (2), 1950
Cy Perkins: Pittsburgh Crawfords, 1934; Baltimore Elite Giants, 1940
Alonzo Perry: Birmingham Black Barons, 1950
Richard "Dick" Phillips: Kansas City Monarchs, 1952
Andy "Pullman" Porter: Indianapolis Clowns, 1949
Bernard Porter: Detroit Clowns, 1958
Jim Portier: Indianapolis Clowns, 1954
Malvin "Putt" Powell: Chicago American Giants, 1934
Bill Powell: Birmingham Black Barons, 1948, 1950
Charley Pride: Memphis Red Sox, 1956, 1958

ALEC RADCLIFF a record holder of many batting records in the East-West All-Star classic. In a John Holway interview, Radcliff told one of his secrets to batting success, "I wasn't a great home run hitter. I'd hit the ball for average. I had a 40-ounce bat, I didn't swing as hard as the average fellow. I'd just meet the ball most of the time. We used to have our bats made by Spalding. Each player was allowed six bats; I had two 40-ounces and four 36's. I'd get a pitcher and he had a good number-one - fastball - I'd get a 36-ounce bat. If a fellow like to throw a lot of curve balls, I'd use the 40-ounce."

Alec Radcliff: Chicago American Giants, 1933, 1934, 1935, 1936, 1937, 1938, 1939 (2), 1943; Cincinnati Clowns, 1944; Cincinnati Indianapolis Clowns, 1945; Memphis Red Sox, 1946 (2)

Ted "Double Duty" Radcliffe: Cincinnati Tigers, 1937; Memphis Red Sox, 1938, 1939, 1941; Chicago American Giants, 1943; Birmingham Black Barons, 1944

Larry Raines: Chicago American Giants, 1952
Wilson "Frog" Redus: Chicago American Giants, 1936, 1937
Eddie Lee Reed: Memphis Red Sox, 1953, 1955
Donald "Soup" Reeves: Chicago American Giants, 1940
Othello "Chico" Renfroe: Kansas City Monarchs, 1946
Gene "Britches" Richardson: Kansas City Monarchs, 1949
Ray Richardson: Detroit Stars, 1956
Ted "Lefty" Richardson: Indianapolis Clowns, 1952
Bill Ricks: Philadelphia Stars, 1945
Marshall "Jit" Riddle: St. Louis Stars, 1939; New Orleans-St. Louis Stars, 1940
Arzell "Ace" Robinson: Memphis Red Sox, 1956
Neal Robinson: Memphis Red Sox, 1938, 1939 (2), 1940, 1941, 1943, 1944, 1945, 1948
Jackie Robinson: Kansas City Monarchs, 1945
James Robinson: Kansas City Monarchs, 1957, 1958
Norman "Bobby" Robinson: Birmingham Black Barons, 1951
Wilber "Bullet" Rogan - HOF: Kansas City Monarchs, 1936

Negro Leagues Book #2: The Players

The Rogan Family. Seated is Wilber "Bullet" Rogan with wife, Kathryn. The little fellow is son Wilbur, who played a part in his father missing the 1925 Negro World Series. Engaging in a little horseplay, "Little Bullet" accidentally struck his father in the knee with a sewing needle, just before the start of the series. Rogan missed the series and the Monarchs missed Rogan, as they lost the best of a nine-game series in six games to the Hilldale Club. Rogan was inducted into the National Baseball Hall of Fame in 1998.

Robert "Bob" Romby: Baltimore Elite Giants, 1947 (2)
Ralph Rosado: Detroit Stars, 1955
Leon Ruffin: Newark Eagles, 1946
Silvino "Poppa" Ruiz: New York Cubans, 1940
John "Pistol" Russell: Pittsburgh Crawfords, 1933
Tommy "Toots" Sampson: Birmingham Black Barons, 1940, 1941, 1942 (2), 1943
Bobby Gene Sanders: Memphis Red Sox, 1957; Birmingham Black Barons, 1958, 1959
Jake Sanders: Detroit Stars, 1959
Samuel "Piggy" Sands: Indianapolis Clowns, 1953
George "Tubby" Scales: Baltimore Elite Giants, 1943
Patricio "Pat" Scantlebury: New York Cubans, 1946 (2), 1949, 1950
John Scott: Kansas City Monarchs, 1946
Kelly "Lefty" Searcy: Baltimore Elite Giants, 1951
Dickie Seay: Philadelphia Stars, 1935; New York Black Yankees, 1940, 1941
John Self: Kansas City Monarchs, 1958
Bonnie Serrell: Kansas City Monarchs, 1944
Harold Shade: Detroit Stars, 1956, 1957
Pedro Sierra: Detroit Stars, 1956
Harry Sims: Memphis Red Sox, 1953
Gene Smith: New York Black Yankees, 1942
Hilton Smith - HOF: Kansas City Monarchs, 1937, 1938, 1939 (2), 1940, 1941, 1942
John Ford Smith: Kansas City Monarchs, 1947
Milt Smith: Philadelphia Stars, 1951
Theolic "Fireball" Smith: St. Louis Stars, 1939; Cleveland Buckeyes, 1943; Kansas City Monarchs, 1951
Willie Smith: Birmingham Black Barons, 1958, 1959
Felton "Skipper" Snow: Columbus Elite Giants, 1935; Washington Elite Giants, 1936
Juan Soler: Detroit Stars, 1955, 1956
Herb Souell: Kansas City Monarchs, 1947 (2), 1948 (2), 1950
Norman "Turkey" Stearnes - HOF: Chicago American Giants, 1933, 1934, 1935; Detroit Stars, 1937; Kansas City Monarchs, 1939
Ed Steele: Birmingham Black Barons, 1950, 1951

Paul "Jake" Stephens: Philadelphia Stars, 1935
Ed Stone: Brooklyn Eagles, 1935; Newark Eagles, 1939, 1940
Alton "Cool Papa" Strozier: Memphis Red Sox, 1956, 1957, 1958
Sam Streeter: Pittsburgh Crawfords, 1933
Ted Strong: Indianapolis Athletics, 1937; Indianapolis ABCs, 1938; Kansas City Monarchs, 1939 (2), 1941, 1942 (2)
Lonnie Summers: Chicago American Giants, 1949; Chicago American Giants, 1951
George "Mule" Suttles - HOF: Chicago American Giants, 1933, 1934, 1935; Newark Eagles, 1937; Baltimore Elite Giants, 1939
Reece "Goose" Tatum: Indianapolis Clowns, 1947
Johnny "School Boy" Taylor: Pittsburgh Crawfords, 1938
LeRoy "Ben" Taylor: Kansas City Monarchs, 1936
Olan "Jelly" Taylor: Memphis Red Sox, 1939, 1940, 1941
Tommy Taylor: Kansas City Monarchs, 1959, 1960
Frank "Groundhog" Thompson: Birmingham Black Barons, 1952, 1954; Memphis Red Sox, 1957
Luis Tiant, Sr.: New York Cubans, 1935, 1947 (2)
Ozzie Tidmore: Kansas City Monarchs, 1958
Ted "Highpockets" Trent: Chicago American Giants, 1934, 1935, 1936, 1937
Quincy Trouppe: Indianapolis ABCs, 1938; Cleveland Buckeyes, 1945, 1946 (2), 1947 (2); Chicago American Giants, 1948 (2)
Leander Tugerson: Indianapolis Clowns, 1951
Manuel Valdez: Memphis Red Sox, 1952
Jimmy Valentine: Memphis Red Sox, 1957
Juan "Tetelo" Vargas: New York Cubans, 1942 (2), 1943
Roberto Vargas: Chicago American Giants, 1948
Gilberto Varona: Memphis Red Sox, 1951, 1952, 1955
Orlando Varona: Memphis Red Sox, 1949
Edsall Walker: Homestead Grays, 1938
George Wanamaker: Indianapolis Clowns, 1954
Archie Ware: Cleveland Buckeyes, 1944, 1945, 1946 (2)
Bill Washington: Memphis Red Sox, 1955
Johnny Washington: Pittsburgh Crawfords, 1936; Baltimore Elite Giants, 1947 (2); Houston Eagles, 1950
Peter Washington: Philadelphia Stars, 1952
Willie Washington: Kansas City Monarchs, 1958, 1959
Murray "Skeeter" Watkins: Newark Eagles, 1945; Philadelphia Stars, 1946 (2)
Sherman Watrous: Memphis Red Sox, 1952
Willie "the Devil" Wells - HOF: Chicago American Giants, 1933, 1934, 1935; Newark Eagles, 1937, 1938, 1939 (2), 1942 (2), 1945
Roy "Snook" Welmaker: Homestead Grays, 1945
Jim West: Washington Elite Giants, 1936; Philadelphia Stars, 1942 (2)
Ernie Westfield: Birmingham Black Barons, 1960
Charlie "Hoss" White: Philadelphia Stars, 1950
Eugene "Stank" White: Kansas City Monarchs, 1957, 1958
Davey Whitney: Kansas City Monarchs, 1955
Don Whittington: Philadelphia Stars, 1952; Memphis Red Sox, 1954
James "Seabiscuit" Wilkes: Newark Eagles, 1948; Indianapolis Clowns, 1952

Negro Leagues Book #2: The Players

Charlie Williams: Birmingham Black Barons, 1956
Chester Williams: Pittsburgh Crawfords, 1934, 1935, 1936, 1937
Eugene Williams: Memphis Red Sox, 1956, 1957
Frank Williams: Memphis Red Sox, 1959; Kansas City Monarchs, 1960
"Big Jim" Williams: Toledo-Indianapolis Crawfords, 1939 (2)
Jesse Williams: Kansas City Monarchs, 1943, 1945, 1951
John Williams: Louisville Black Clippers, 1954; Birmingham Black Barons, 1955, 1956, 1957
Johnny "Nature Boy" Williams: Indianapolis Clowns, 1946 (2), 1947
Marvin "Tex" Williams: Philadelphia Stars, 1944
Willie "Curley" Williams: Houston Eagles, 1950; New Orleans Eagles, 1951
Artie "Snoop" Wilson: Birmingham Black Barons, 1944, 1946 (2), 1947 (2), 1948 (2)
Bob Wilson: Houston Eagles, 1949
Dan Wilson: St. Louis Stars, 1939 (2), 1941; New York Black Yankees, 1942 (2)
Jud "Boojum" Wilson - HOF: Philadelphia Stars, 1933, 1934, 1935
Fred "Sardo" Wilson: Cincinnati Clowns, 1943
Robert Wilson: Kansas City Monarchs, 1957
John "Bobby" Winston: Kansas City Monarchs, 1957; Detroit Clowns, 1958
Parnell Woods: Birmingham Black Barons, 1938; Cleveland Bears, 1939; Birmingham Black Barons, 1940; Jacksonville Red Caps, 1941; Cincinnati Buckeyes, 1942 (2); Chicago American Giants, 1951
Sam "Buddy" Woods: Memphis Red Sox, 1953
Robert Worthington: Raleigh Tigers, 1960
Burnis "Wild Bill" Wright: Columbus Elite Giants, 1935; Washington Elite Giants, 1936, 1937; Baltimore Elite Giants, 1938, 1939 (2), 1942 (2), 1945
Danny Wright: Birmingham Black Barons, 1957
Johnny Wright: Homestead Grays, 1943, 1947
Zollie Wright: Washington Elite Giants, 1936
Ralph "Pepper" Wyatt: Chicago American Giants, 1942
William Wyatt: Birmingham Black Barons, 1956, 1957

East-West All-Stars by Team, 1933 to 1960

Listed below are teams with their representatives for each year. Teams placing players on the All-Star teams for more than 10 consecutive years were the Chicago American Giants (20 years), Kansas City Monarchs (18 years), and the Memphis Red Sox (22 years). In fact, the American Giants are the only team having players participate every year until their franchise folded in 1952. From 1933 to 1960, the teams with the most representatives were the Kansas City Monarchs with 132, the Memphis Red Sox with 110, and the Birmingham Black Barons with 104 players.

Teams with only one representative were the Cincinnati-Indianapolis Clowns, Cleveland Giants, Cleveland Red Sox, Indianapolis Athletics and the New Orleans Bears. In 1936, the Kansas City Monarchs, not a member of any league, had a record 11 players in the East-West Classic. Players with (2) beside their names indicate they played in both games that year.

BALTIMORE ELITE GIANTS - 46 players
1938: Sammy T. Hughes, 2b; Raleigh "Biz" Mackey, c; Burnis "Wild Bill" Wright, rf
1939: Bill Byrd, p (2); Sammy T. Hughes, 2b (2); George "Mule" Suttles, rf; Burnis "Wild Bill" Wright, cf (2)
1940: Cy Perkins, c
1941: Bill Byrd, p; Roy Campanella, c; Bill Hoskins, lf
1942: Jonas Gaines, p (2); Burnis "Wild Bill" Wright, rf (2)
1943: David "Bill" Harvey, p; Henry Kimbro, cf; George "Tubby" Scales, ph
1944: Robert "Pee Wee" Butts, ss; Bill Byrd, p; Roy Campanella, 3b; Henry Kimbro, rf
1945: Bill Byrd, ph; Roy Campanella, c; Tom Glover, p; Burnis "Wild Bill" Wright, rf
1946: Robert "Pee Wee" Butts, ss; Bill Byrd, p (2); Jonas Gaines, p (2); Henry Kimbro, cf (2)
1947: Joe Black, p; Robert "Pee Wee" Butts, ss (2); Henry Kimbro, cf (2); Bob Romby, ph (2); Johnny Washington, 1b (2)
1948: Joe Black, p; Robert "Pee Wee" Butts, ss; Junior Gilliam, 2b (2); Lester Lockett, rf, lf (2)
1949: Robert "Pee Wee" Butts, ss; Robert "Butch" Davis, lf; Junior Gilliam, 2b; Lennie Pearson, 1b
1950: Joe Black, p; Robert "Pee Wee" Butts, ss; Junior Gilliam, 2b
1951: Johnny Hayes, c; Kelly Searcy, p

BIRMINGHAM BLACK BARONS - 104 players
1938: Parnell Woods, ph
1940: Tommy Sampson, Jr., 2b; Parnell Woods, 3b
1941: Dan Bankhead, p; Lyman Bostock, Sr., 1b; Tommy Sampson, Jr., 2b
1942: Lloyd "Ducky" Davenport, ph; Alvin "Bubber" Gipson, p; Tommy Sampson, Jr., 2b (2)
1943: Lester Lockett, lf; Gread McKinnis, p; Tommy Sampson, Jr., 2b
1944: Ted "Double Duty" Radcliffe, c; Artie Wilson, ss
1945: Lester Lockett, lf
1946: Lorenzo "Piper" Davis, 2b (2); Artie Wilson, ss (2)
1947: Lloyd "Pepper" Bassett, c; Lorenzo "Piper" Davis, 2b (2); Artie Wilson, ss (2)
1948: Lloyd "Pepper" Bassett, c; Lorenzo "Piper" Davis, 2b (2); Bill Powell, p; Artie Wilson, ss (2)
1949: Herman Bell, ph; José Antonio Burgos, ss; Lorenzo "Piper" Davis, 2b; Bill Greason, p
1950: Lloyd "Pepper" Bassett, c; Alonzo Perry, 1b; Bill Powell, p; Ed Steele, lf
1951: Wesley "Doc" Dennis, 1b; Henry Kimbro, cf; Norman "Bobby" Robinson, lf; Ed Steele, rf
1952: Otha Bailey, c; Eddie Brooks, 2b; Wesley "Doc" Dennis, 1b; Henry Kimbro, cf; Frank "Groundhog" Thompson, p

Negro Leagues Book #2: The Players

1953: Otha Bailey, c; Eddie Brooks, 2b; Robert "Pee Wee" Butts, ss; Menske "Manny" Cartledge, p; Irwin Castille, 3b; Wesley "Doc" Dennis, 1b; Curtis Hardaway, 3b; Henry Kimbro, rf; Carl Long, lf

1954: Otha Bailey, c; Eddie Brooks, 2b; Wesley Dennis, 1b; John Kennedy, ss; Frank "Groundhog" Thompson, p

1955: Eddie Brooks, 2b; Otha Bailey, c; Elliott Coleman, p; Menske "Manny" Cartledge, p; Rufus Gipson, 3b; Al "Johnny" Mobley, 1b; John Williams, rf

1956: Claude Barnes, p; Otha Bailey, c (2); Wiley Griggs, 3b, 2b (2); Jim Hall, c; Willie Lee "Bud" Ivory, 2b; Frank Marsh, cf, rf (2); Gene Johnson, 1b; Roscoe Mangun, 2b; Bill Moore, 1b (2); Charlie Williams, p (2); John Williams, 2b (2); William Wyatt, 2b, ss (2)

1957: Otha Bailey, c; Joe Elliott, p; Donnie Harris, cf; Jessie Mitchell, lf; John Williams, lf; Danny Wright, p; William Wyatt, 2b

1958: Otha Bailey, c; Jesse Bass, pr, 3b; Wiley Griggs, 3b; James "Sap" Ivory, 1b, 3b; Brown Jackson, lf; Jessie Mitchell, rf; Bobby Gene Sanders, ph, ss; Willie Smith, p

1959: Ernest "Onk" Harris, cf; James "Sap" Ivory, infield; Pete Mumpford, p; Bobby Gene Sanders, ss; Willie Smith, p

1960: Jesse Bass, ss; Willie Harris, lf; James "Sap" Ivory, 3b; Brown Jackson, rf; John Mitchell, cf; Herbert Paymond, p; Walter Stoves, c; Philip Welch, p; Gus Westbrook, infield; Ernie Westfield, p

BROOKLYN EAGLES - 4 players
1935: Leon Day, p; George Giles, 1b; Clarence "Fats" Jenkins, lf; Ed Stone, ph

CHICAGO AMERICAN GIANTS - 73 players
1933: Larry "Iron Man" Brown, c; Walter "Steel Arm" Davis, lf; Willie Foster, p; Alec Radcliff, 3b; Norman "Turkey" Stearnes, cf; George "Mule" Suttles, 1b; Willie "the Devil" Wells, ss

1934: Larry "Iron Man" Brown, c; Willie Foster, p; Alec Radcliff, 3b; Norman "Turkey" Stearnes, cf; George "Mule" Suttles, 1b; Ted "Highpockets" Trent, p; Willie "the Devil" Wells, ss

1935: William "Sug" Cornelius, p; Alec Radcliff, 3b; Norman "Turkey" Stearnes, rf; George "Mule" Suttles, lf; Ted "Highpockets" Trent, p; Willie "the Devil" Wells, ss

1936: Richard "Subby" Byas, c; William "Sug" Cornelius, p; Lou Dials, rf; Herman Dunlap, lf; Alec Radcliff, 3b; Wilson "Frog" Redus, rf; Ted "Highpockets" Trent, p

1937: Richard "Subby" Byas, ph; Alec Radcliff, 3b; Wilson "Frog" Redus, rf; Ted "Highpockets" Trent, p

1938: William "Sug" Cornelius, p; Frank Duncan, Jr., c; Alec Radcliff, 3b

1939: Lloyd "Pepper" Bassett, c (2); Billy Horne, 2b (2); Alec Radcliff, 3b, ss (2)

1940: Leroy Morney, ss; Donald "Soup" Reeves, lf

1941: Lloyd "Pepper" Bassett, c; Jimmie Crutchfield, lf; Billy Horne, ss; William Henry Hudson, ph

1942: James "Cool Papa" Bell, cf, rf (2); Art "Superman" Pennington, ph, cf (2); Ralph "Pepper" Wyatt, ss

1943: Lloyd "Ducky" Davenport, rf; Alec Radcliff, 3b; Ted "Double Duty" Radcliffe, c

1944: Lloyd "Ducky" Davenport, rf; Gentry Jessup, p; Gread McKinnis, p

1945: Gentry Jessup, p

1946: Gentry Jessup, p; Clyde Nelson, 3b

1947: Buddy Armour, p, rf (2); Gentry Jessup, p

1948: Sam Hill, rf (2); Gentry Jessup, p; Quincy Trouppe, c (2); Roberto Enrique, p

1949: Gready McKinnis, p; Lonnie Summers, c

1950: Jesse Warren, 3b; Clyde McNeal, ss; Art "Superman" Pennington, cf

1951: Andy Anderson, lf; Parnell Woods, 3b

1952: William "Fireball" Beverly, p; Winn Durham, lf; Felix McLaurin, lf; Willie "Pat" Patterson, 1b; Larry Raines, ss

CINCINNATI BUCKEYES - 3 players
1942: Gene Bremer, p (2); Sam "the Jet" Jethroe, ph, cf (2); Parnell Woods, 3b (2)

CINCINNATI CLOWNS - 2 players
1943: Fred Wilson, ph
1944: Alec Radcliff, 3b

CINCINNATI TIGERS - 5 players
1937: Rainey Bibbs, 2b; Lloyd "Ducky" Davenport, rf; Howard Easterling, ss; Porter Moss, p; Ted "Double Duty" Radcliffe, c

CINCINNATI -INDIANAPOLIS CLOWNS - 1 player
1945: Alec Radcliff, 3b

CLEVELAND BEARS - 3 players
1939: John Lyles, ss; Raymond "Smoky" Owens, p; Parnell Woods, 3b

CLEVELAND BUCKEYES - 25 players
1943: Theolic "Fireball" Smith, p
1944: Buddy Armour, lf; Gene Bremer, p; Sam "the Jet" Jethroe, cf; Archie Ware, 1b
1945: Gene Bremer, p; Lloyd "Ducky" Davenport, rf; Quincy Trouppe, c; Archie Ware, 1b
1946: John W. Brown, ph; Vibert Clarke, p; Willie Grace, rf (2); Sam "the Jet" Jethroe, cf (2); Quincy Trouppe, c (2); Archie Ware, 1b (2)
1947: Chet Brewer, p; Vibert Clarke, p; Sam "the Jet" Jethroe, rf, cf (2); Leon Kellman, 2b; Quincy Trouppe, c (2)
1948: Vibert Clarke, p; Willie Grace, lf; Leon Kellman, 3b
1949: Dave Hoskins, ph; Leon Kellman, ph

CLEVELAND GIANTS - 1 player
1933: Leroy Morney, 2b

CLEVELAND RED SOX - 1 player
1934: Andy "Pat" Patterson, 2b

COLUMBUS ELITE GIANTS - 4 players
1935: Robert "Schoolboy" Griffith, p; Sammy T. Hughes, 2b; Felton Snow, ph; Burnis "Wild Bill" Wright, ph

DETROIT CLOWNS - 9 players
1958: Eddie Alston, ss; Sherwood Brewer, 2b; Nat "Sweetwater" Clifton, 1b; Arthur Lee Hamilton, c; Willie "Red" Harris, p; Prince Joe Henry, ph, rf; Clarence "Pijo" King, cf; Bernard Porter, 1b; John "Booby" Winston, p

DETROIT STARS - 48 players
1937: Norman "Turkey" Stearnes, cf

Negro Leagues Book #2: The Players

1954: Andrew Carpenter, p; Herald "Beebop" Gordon, p; Willie Lee "Bud" Ivory, ss; Ray Miller, lf; Joe Montgomery, ph

1955: Herman Green, lf; James "Sap" Ivory, ss; Aaron Jones, p; Ezelle King, 1b; Joe Montgomery, cf; Ralph Rosado, c; Juan Soler, 3b

1956: Frank Evans, lf (2); Herman Green, lf (2); Manuel Santos Guerede, p; Willie Harris, p; James "Sap" Ivory, 2b; Gene Johnson, 1b; Joe Mims, p; Jessie Mitchell, cf (2); Ray Richardson, c (2); Harold Shade, 3b (2); Pedro Sierra, p; Juan Soler, ss (2)

1957: Ray Aguillard, c; Robert Baldwin, 1b; Joe Castillo, c; Palmer Hubbard, rf; Abdullah Johnson, 1b; Gene Johnson, cf; Harold Shade, ss

1959: Ben Adams, p; Jesse Bass, 2b; Don Bonner, lf; Ronald Busch, infield; Marion "Sugar" Cain, p; Marvin Chalmers, ss; Earl Cunningham, infield; Earl Floyd, infield; Calvin Gant, p; Herman Green, 1b; Arthur Lee Hamilton, c; Willie Harris, p; Larry LeGrande, cf; Bill Matthews, p; Jake Sanders, of; Ron Warren, infield

DETROIT - NEW ORLEANS STARS - 9 players

1960: Don Bonner, lf; Hezikia Evans, infield; Arthur Lee Hamilton, c; Bob Haywood, infield; Herman Jones, p; Gregory Lowe, infield; Bill Matthews, p; Willie "Pat" Patterson, 1b; George Spriggs, of

HOMESTEAD GRAYS - 47 players

1933: George "Chippy" Britton, p; Vic Harris, lf
1935: Ray Brown, p; Walter "Buck" Leonard, 1b
1937: Jerry Benjamin, rf; Walter "Buck" Leonard, 1b
1938: Vic Harris, lf; Walter "Buck" Leonard, 1b; Edsall Walker, p
1939: Josh Gibson, c (2); Vic Harris, lf; Walter "Buck" Leonard, 1b (2); Roy Partlow, p
1940: Ray Brown, p; Howard Easterling, 3b; Walter "Buck" Leonard, 1b
1941: Walter "Buck" Leonard, 1b; Terris "The Great" McDuffie, p
1942: Sam Bankhead, 2b, cf (2); Josh Gibson, c (2); Vic Harris, ph
1943: Sam Bankhead, 2b; James "Cool Papa" Bell, lf; Jerry Benjamin, ph; Howard Easterling, 3b; Josh Gibson, c; Vic Harris, ph; Walter "Buck" Leonard, 1b; Johnny Wright, p
1944: Sam Bankhead, 2b, ss; James "Cool Papa" Bell, lf; Josh Gibson, c; Walter "Buck" Leonard, 1b
1945: Jerry Benjamin, cf; Walter "Buck" Leonard, 1b; Roy Welmaker, p
1946: Sam Bankhead, ss; Howard Easterling, 3b (2); Josh Gibson, c (2); Walter "Buck" Leonard, 1b (2)
1947: Vic Harris, pr; Luis Márquez, rf (2); Johnny Wright, p
1948: Luke Easter, rf, lf (2); Wilmer Fields, p; Walter "Buck" Leonard, 1b; Luis Márquez, cf, rf (2)

HOUSTON EAGLES - 5 players
1949: Johnny "Cherokee" Davis, cf; Bob Wilson, 3b, ss
1950: Bob Harvey, rf; Johnny Washington, 1b; Willie "Curley" Williams, ss

INDIANAPOLIS ABCS - 2 players
1938: Ted Strong, 1b; Quincy Trouppe, lf

INDIANAPOLIS ATHLETICS - 1 player
1937: Ted Strong, 1b

INDIANAPOLIS CLOWNS - 29 players
1946: Buster Haywood, c; Johnny "Nature Boy" Williams, p (2)
1947: Ray Neil, 2b; Goose Tatum, 1b; Johnny "Nature Boy" Williams, p

1948: Jim "Fireball" Cohen, p; Sam Hairston, ph

1949: Sherwood Brewer, rf; Andy Porter, p

1950: Sherwood Brewer, 3b, rf; Henry "Speed" Merchant, lf

1951: Buster Haywood, c; Ray Neil, 2b; Leander Tugerson, p

1952: Henry "Speed" Merchant, rf; T.W. Richardson, p; Armando Vázquez, 2b; Jimmy "Seabiscuit" Wilkes, 1b

1953: Dave Amaro, p; Willie Brown, ss; Reynaldo Drake, cf; Willy Gaines, p; Buster Haywood, ph; Ray Neil, 2b; Sam "Piggy" Sands, c

1954: Reynaldo Drake, cf; Frank Ensley, lf; Jim Portier, c; George Wanamaker, 3b

JACKSONVILLE RED CAPS - 3 players

1941: Howard "Duke" Cleveland, ph; Leo "Preacher" Henry, p; Parnell Woods, 3b

KANSAS CITY MONARCHS - 132 players

1934: Chet Brewer, p

1936 - record 11 players: Newt Allen, 2b, ss; Willard "Home Run" Brown, ss; Andy Cooper, p; Eddie Dwight, cf; Harry "Speed" Else, c; Curtis "Popsickle" Harris, 1b; Art Kranson, p; Henry Milton, cf; Andy "Pat" Patterson, 2b; Wilber "Bullet" Rogan, lf; Leroy Taylor, rf

1937: Newt Allen, 2b ss; Willard "Home Run" Brown, lf; Eldridge "Chili" Mayweather, ph; Henry Milton, ph; Hilton Smith, p

1938: Newt Allen, 2b; Byron "Mex" Johnson, ss; Henry Milton, rf; Hilton Smith, p

1939: Henry Milton, rf; Hilton Smith, p (2); Norman "Turkey" Stearnes, rf; Ted Strong, 1b, ss (2)

1940: Joe Greene, c; Henry Milton, rf; Hilton Smith, p

1941: Newt Allen, ss; Satchel Paige, p; Hilton Smith, p; Ted Strong, rf

1942: Willard "Home Run" Brown, lf (2); Joe Greene, c (2); John "Buck" O'Neil, 1b (2); Satchel Paige, p; Hilton Smith, p; Ted Strong, rf (2)

1943: Willard "Home Run" Brown, cf; John "Buck" O'Neil, 1b; Satchel Paige, p; Jesse Williams, ss

1944: Bonnie Serrell, 2b

1945: Booker McDaniel, p; Jackie Robinson, ss; Jesse Williams, 2b

1946: Chico Renfroe, ss; John Scott, lf

1947: Robert "James" Abernathy, lf; John Ford Smith, p; Herb Souell, 3b (2)

1948: Willard "Home Run" Brown, cf (2); Jim "Lefty" LaMarque, p (2); Herb Souell, 3b (2)

1949: Willard "Home Run" Brown, 3b, lf; Jim "Lefty" LaMarque, p; John "Buck" O'Neil, ph; Gene Richardson, p

1950: Tom Cooper, c, rf; Connie Johnson, p; Herb Souell, 3b

1951: Sherwood Brewer, 3b; Tom Cooper, c 1b; Theolic "Fireball" Smith, p; Jesse Williams, 2b

1952: Hank Baylis, 3b; James "Duke" Henderson, cf; Ike "Stonewall" Jackson, c; John "Stony" Jackson, p; Dick Phillips, p

1953: Juan Armenteros, c; Ernie Banks, ss; Hank Baylis, 3b; Sherwood Brewer, 2b; Tom Cooper, lf; Pancho Herrera, 1b; John "Stony" Jackson, p; Ernie "Schooley" Johnson, rf

1954: Juan Armenteros, c; Pancho Herrera, 1b; Hank "Pistol" Mason, p; Dagoberto Nuñez, lf

1955: Juan Armenteros, c; Hank Baylis, 3b; Al Cartmill, 2b; J.C. Hartman, ss; Sweet Lou Johnson, rf; Ricky Maroto, p; Satchel Paige, p; Davey Whitney, lf

1956: Walt Bond, lf; Andy Carpenter, p; Eugene Elliott, 3b; A.J. Jackson, p (2); Bill Jones, lf; John Kennedy, ss; Ricky Maroto, cf (2); Ira McKnight, rf, 3b, c (2); Joe Montgomery, rf; Jim Robinson, 3b

1957: John Evans, 3b; Ira McKnight, c; Jim Robinson, 2b; Willie White, 1b; Bob Wilson, cf; John "Booby" Winston, p

1958: Marion "Sugar" Cain, p; Aubrey Grigsby, p; Palmer Hubbard, pr; Gideon Jarvis, lf, 3b; Ira McKnight, c; Jim Robinson, ss; John Self, 1b; Ozzie Tidmore, 2b; Willie Washington, 3b; Willie White, rf

1959: Nate Dancey, infield; Paul Gilbert, 1b; Palmer Hubbard, of; Jessie Mitchell, lf; Tommy Taylor, p; Willie Washington, 3b; John "Booby" Winston, p

1960: Ike Brown, ss; Nate Dancey, 2b; Leon Franklin, p; Calvin Grant, p; Palmer Hubbard, cf; Ira McKnight, 3b; Mel Miller, of; Tommy Taylor, p; Frank Williams, rf

ERNIE "SCHOOLEY" JOHNSON, despite his slender build, was a home run hitter extraordinaire. Give him a table leg or a broom handle, this slugger could hit. In 1953, the talented outfielder led the Negro American League in home runs with 11, out slugging teammate Ernie Banks.

LOUISVILLE BUCKEYES - 2 players
1949: Dave Hoskins, ph; Leon Kellman, ph

LOUISVILLE CLIPPERS - 4 players
1954: Lonnie Harris, cf; Rufus Gipson, 2b; John Williams, ss; Willie "Red" Harris, ph

MEMPHIS RED SOX - 110 players
1938: Larry "Iron Man" Brown, c; Ted "Double Duty" Radcliffe, p; Neil Robinson, cf
1939: Larry "Iron Man" Brown, c (2); Lloyd "Ducky" Davenport, ph; Ted "Double Duty" Radcliffe, p; Neil Robinson, cf (2); Olan "Jelly" Taylor, 1b
1940: Gene Bremer, p; Larry "Iron Man" Brown, c; Neil Robinson, cf; Olan "Jelly" Taylor, ph
1941: Larry "Iron Man" Brown, c; Verdell Mathis, p; Ted "Double Duty" Radcliffe, p; Neil Robinson, cf; Olan "Jelly" Taylor, 1b
1942: Fred Bankhead, 2b (2); T.J. Brown, ss; Marlin Carter, 3b (2); Verdell Mathis, p; Porter Moss, p
1943: Cowan "Bubba" Hyde, pr; Porter Moss, p; Neil Robinson, cf
1944: Verdell Mathis, p; Neil Robinson, cf
1945: Verdell Mathis, p; Neil Robinson, cf
1946: Dan Bankhead, p (2); Felix "Chin" Evans, p; Cowan "Bubba" Hyde, lf (2); Alec Radcliff, 3b (2)
1947: Dan Bankhead, p; Bob Boyd, 1b; Ernest "Spoon" Carter, p; José Colas, lf, cf (2)
1948: Bob Boyd, 1b (2); Ernest "Spoon" Carter, pr; José Colas, ph; Neil Robinson, lf
1949: Bob Boyd, 1b; Pedro Formental, cf; Willie "Ace" Hutchinson, p; Orlando Varona, ss
1950: Vibert Clarke, p; Casey Jones, c; Leon Kellman, 3b
1951: Vibert Clarke, p; José Colas, cf; Casey Jones, c; Gilberto Varona, 1b
1952: Gilberto Varona, 1b; Sherman Watrous, rf
1953: Lloyd "Pepper" Bassett, c; Billy Ray Haggins, rf; Isiah Harris, p; Willie "Pat" Patterson, 1b; Eddie Reed, cf; Fate Sims, lf; Sam "Buddy" Woods, p

1954: Billy Ray Haggins, lf; Don Whittington, 3b; Isiah Harris, p; Charlie Davis, p

1955: Willie "Red" Harris, lf; Bill Washington, ss, c; Billy Ray Haggins, rf; Gilbert Varona, 1b; Eddie Reed, cf; Charlie Davis, p; Isiah Harris, p; Ricky Maroto, p

1956: James Banks, 1b, rf (2); Rufus Gipson, 2b (2); Alvin Green, p; Lonnie Harris, cf; Willie Harris, lf; Charlie Jennings, c (2); Bill Lee, c; Willie Lee, cf; Ben Littles, pr; Frank McCollum, p; Charley Pride, rf (2); Arzell "Ace" Robinson, p (2); Alton "Cool Papa" Strozier, ss (2); Gilbert Varona, 1b; Bill Washington, 3b; Eugene Williams, ph

1957: James Banks, 1b; Isaac Barnes, c; Rufus Gipson, 2b; Lonnie Harris, pr; Bobby Gene Sanders, lf; Jimmy Valentine, 3b; Eugene Williams, p

1958: James Banks, 1b; Isaac Barnes, c; Rufus Gipson, 2b; Lonnie Harris, cf; Sam Hill, lf; Charley Pride, p; Alton "Cool Papa" Strozier, ph

1959: Isaac Barnes, c; Elbert Fowler, infield; Rufus Gipson, 2b; Arzell "Ace" Robinson, p; Bill White, of; Eugene Williams, p; Frank Williams, rf

NASHVILLE ELITE GIANTS - 4 players
1933: Sam Bankhead, rf
1934: Sam Bankhead, rf; Sammy T. Hughes, 2b; Roy "Red" Parnell, lf

NEW ORLEANS BEARS - 1 player
1957: Felix Ortiz, ss

NEW ORLEANS EAGLES - 3 players
1951: Larry Guice, rf; Jehosie "Jay" Heard, p; Willie "Curley" Williams, ss

NEW ORLEANS-ST. LOUIS STARS - 4 players
1940: Walter "Lefty" Calhoun, p; Leslie "Chin" Green, cf; Eldridge "Chili" Mayweather, 1b; Marshall "Jit" Riddle, 2b

NEW YORK BLACK YANKEES - 19 players
1933: Clarence "Fats" Jenkins, lf
1937: Barney "Brinquitos" Brown, p
1938: Barney "Brinquitos" Brown, p; Walter "Rev" Cannady, 3b
1939: Elvis "Bill" Holland, p; Terris "The Great" McDuffie, p
1940: Marvin Barker, cf, rf; Robert "Eggie" Clarke, c; Richard "Dickie" Seay, 2b
1941: Henry Kimbro, cf; Richard "Dickie" Seay, 2b
1942: Eugene L. "Gene" Smith, p; Dan Wilson, lf (2)
1945: Marvin Barker, 3b
1947: Johnny Hayes, c (2)
1948: Marvin Barker, ph; George Crowe, 1b; Robert "Schoolboy" Griffith, p

NEW YORK CUBANS - 43 players
1935: Martín Dihigo, p, cf; Alejandro Oms, rf; Luis Tiant, Sr., p
1939: Candido "Police Car" López, lf
1940: Alejandro "Alex" Crespo, lf; Horacio "Rabbit" Martínez, ss; Silvino "Poppa" Ruiz, p
1941: Dave "Impo" Barnhill, p; Francisco "Pancho" Coimbre, rf; Horacio "Rabbit" Martínez, ss
1942: Dave "Impo" Barnhill, p (2); Harry Blanco, 2b, p (2); Juan "Tetelo" Vargas, cf (2)
1943: Dave "Impo" Barnhill, p; Horacio "Rabbit" Martínez, 2b; Juan "Tetelo" Vargas, cf

1944: Francisco "Pancho" Coimbre, rf; Carranza "Schoolboy" Howard, p; Horacio "Rabbit" Martínez, ss; Barney "Big Ad" Morris, p

1945: Martín Dihigo, p; Rogelio Linares, rf; Horacio "Rabbit" Martínez, ss

1946: Pedro "Manny" Díaz, ph; Silvio García, ss; Louis Louden, c; Patricio Scantlebury, p, ph (2)

1947: Claro Duany, rf, ph (2); Silvio García, 2b (2); Louis Louden, c (2); Minnie Miñoso, 3b (2); Luis Tiant, Sr., p (2)

1948: Dave "Impo" Barnhill, p; Louis Louden, c (2); Minnie Miñoso, 3b (2)

1949: Pedro "Manny" Díaz, cf; Howard Easterling, 3b; Patricio Scantlebury, p

1950: Pedro "Manny" Díaz, c; Raul Galata, p; Hiram "Rene" González, 1b; Louis Louden, c; Patricio Scantlebury, p

NEWARK DODGERS - 3 players
1934: Dick Lundy, ss
1935: Paul Arnold, cf; Ray Dandridge, 2b

LEON DAY - Despite his low-key demeanor, the hard-throwing right hander, without a wind-up, mesmerized batters with his arsenal of assorted pitches. Known to short-arm his pitches, which made the ball appear quicker to the plate, Day had a blazing fastball and snapping curve. A calm technician with a bulldog attitude toward winning ball games, Day was equally feared as a hitter. Consistent competitiveness was a day-to-day affair with Mr. Day.

NEWARK EAGLES - 39 players
1937: Ray Dandridge, 3b; Leon Day, p; George "Mule" Suttles, lf; Willie "the Devil" Wells, ss
1938: Willie "the Devil" Wells, ss
1939: Leon Day, p (2); Ed Stone, rf; Willie "the Devil" Wells, ss (2)
1940: Buster Clarkson, ss; Ed Stone, rf
1941: Jimmy Hill, p; Monte Irvin, 3b; Lennie Pearson, cf
1942: Leon Day, p (2); Lennie Pearson, ph, cf (2); Willie "the Devil" Wells, ss (2)
1943: Leon Day, p; Lennie Pearson, rf
1944: Ray Dandridge, 2b, 3b; Johnny "Cherokee" Davis, cf; Terris "The Great" McDuffie, p
1945: Johnny "Cherokee" Davis, lf; Lennie Pearson, ph; Murray "Skeeter" Watkins, 3b; Willie "the Devil" Wells, 2b
1946: Leon Day, p (2); Larry Doby, 2b (2); Monte Irvin, lf (2); Lennie Pearson, rf; Charles Ruffin, c
1947: Monte Irvin, lf (2); Rufus Lewis, p; Raleigh "Biz" Mackey, ph; Max Manning, p
1948: Bob Harvey, rf; Monte Irvin, rf; Rufus Lewis, p; Max Manning, p; Jimmy "Seabiscuit" Wilkes, cf

PHILADELPHIA STARS - 46 players
1933: Rap Dixon, rf; Dick Lundy, ss; Raleigh "Biz" Mackey, c; Jud Wilson, 3b
1934: Stuart "Slim" Jones, p; Jud Wilson, 3b
1935: Stuart "Slim" Jones, p; Raleigh "Biz" Mackey, c; Richard "Dickie" Seay, 2b; Paul "Jake" Stephens, ss; Jud Wilson, 3b
1937: Joseph "Jake" Dunn, 2b
1938: Joseph "Jake" Dunn, ph

1939: Roy "Red" Parnell, lf (2); Andy "Pat" Patterson, 3b (2)

1940: Gene Benson, cf; Henry "Cream" McHenry, p

1941: Henry "Cream" McHenry, p

1942: Barney "Brinquitos" Brown, p; Andy "Pat" Patterson, 3b (2); Jim West, 1b (2)

1944: Marvin "Tex" Williams, ph

1945: Frank "Pee Wee" Austin, ss; Gene Benson, lf; Bill Ricks, p

1946: Frank "Pee Wee" Austin, pr; Gene Benson, rf (2); Barney "Brinquitos" Brown, p (2); Murray "Skeeter" Watkins, ph, pr (2)

1947: Frank "Pee Wee" Austin, ss (2); Henry Miller, p (2)

1948: Frank "Pee Wee" Austin, ss (2); Bill "Ready" Cash, c (2)

1949: Bill "Ready" Cash, c; Buster Clarkson, rf; Robert "Schoolboy" Griffith, p

1950: Jonas Gaines, p; Ben Littles, rf; Charlie White, Jr., 3b

1951: Wilmer Harris, p; Ben Littles, ph; Milt Smith, 3b

1952: Wilmer Harris, p; Jimmie Jones, rf; Ted Washington, ss; Don Whittington, 3b

LEROY ROBERT "SATCHEL" PAIGE, pitched a few games in Yankee pinstripes. In an article published by the New York Daily Worker on September 13, 1937, Joe DiMaggio told sportswriter Lester Rodney that "Satchel Paige is the greatest pitcher I ever batted against." The Yankee Clipper was recalling those dark days in the batter's box when he faced Paige in the West Coast league during the off-season.

PITTSBURGH CRAWFORDS - 36 players

1933: James "Cool Papa" Bell, cf; Oscar Charleston, 1b; Josh Gibson, c; Bertrum Hunter, p; Judy Johnson, 3b; John Henry Russell, 2b; Sam Streeter, p

1934: James "Cool Papa" Bell, cf; Oscar Charleston, 1b; Jimmie Crutchfield, rf; Josh Gibson, c, lf; Vic Harris, lf; Harry Kincannon, p; Satchel Paige, p; Cy Perkins, c; Ches Williams, 2b

1935: James "Cool Papa" Bell, cf; Oscar Charleston, 1b; Jimmie Crutchfield, rf; Josh Gibson, c; Leroy Matlock, p; Ches Williams, ss

1936: Sam Bankhead, lf; James "Cool Papa" Bell, cf; Jimmie Crutchfield, rf; Josh Gibson, c; Judy Johnson, 3b; Leroy Matlock, p; Satchel Paige, p; Johnny Washington, 1b; Ches Williams, ss

1937: Lloyd "Pepper" Bassett, c; Barney "Big Ad" Morris, p; Ches Williams, 2b

1938: Sam Bankhead, cf; Johnny "School Boy" Taylor, p

RALEIGH TIGERS- 16 players

1959: Ronald Busch, infield; Bobby Carter, of; Kenny Free, 3b; Eugene Holmes, p; Bill Matthews, p; James McNeil, rf; Alvin Roane, p

1960: Jimmy Durante, infield; Ralph Fortson, 1b; Henry Garrett, p; Rufus Gipson, 2b; Harry Robinson, of; Price West, of; Mose Wilson, of; Robert Worthington, c; Thomas Wright, of

ST. LOUIS STARS - 7 players

1939: Marshall "Jit" Riddle, 2b; Theolic "Fireball" Smith, p; Dan Wilson, lf, rf (2)

1941: Buddy Armour, cf; Jimmy Ford, 2b; "Big George" Mitchell, ph; Dan Wilson, lf

TOLEDO CRAWFORDS - 3 players

1939: Jimmy "Slim" Johnson, p; Leroy Morney, 2b, ss; "Big Jim" Williams, rf, ph (2)

Negro Leagues Book #2: The Players

TOLEDO-INDIANAPOLIS CRAWFORDS - 2 players
1940: Curtis Henderson, ss; Connie Johnson, p

WASHINGTON ELITE GIANTS - 8 players
1936: Bill Byrd, p; Sammy T. Hughes, 2b; Raleigh "Biz" Mackey, c; Felton Snow, 3b; Jim West, 1b; Burnis "Wild Bill" Wright, cf; Zollie Wright, rf
1937: Burnis "Wild Bill" Wright, cf

MLB players who played in the East-West All-Star Classic

Dan Bankhead: Birmingham Black Barons, 1941; Memphis Red Sox, 1946, 1947
Ernie Banks: Kansas City Monarchs, 1953
Joe Black: Baltimore Elite Giants, 1947, 1948, 1950
Ike Brown: Kansas City Monarchs, 1960
Willard "Home Run" Brown: Kansas City Monarchs, 1936, 1937, 1942, 1943, 1948, 1949
Walt Bond: Kansas City Monarchs, 1956
Roy Campanella: Baltimore Elite Giants, 1941, 1944, 1945
Vibert Clarke: Cleveland Buckeyes, 1946, 1947, 1948; Memphis Red Sox, 1950, 1951
Buster Clarkson: Newark Eagles, 1940; Philadelphia Stars, 1949
George Crowe: New York Black Yankees, 1948
Larry Doby: Newark Eagles, 1946
Winn Durham: Chicago American Giants, 1952
Luke Easter: Homestead Grays, 1948
Junior Gilliam: Baltimore Elite Giants, 1948, 1949, 1950
Bill Greason: Birmingham Black Barons, 1949
Sam Hairston: Indianapolis Clowns, 1948
J.C. Hartman: Kansas City Monarchs, 1955
Jehosie "Jay" Heard: New Orleans Eagles, 1951
Pancho Herrera: Kansas City Monarchs, 1953, 1954
Dave Hoskins: Louisville Buckeyes, 1949
Monte Irvin: Newark Eagles, 1941, 1946, 1947, 1948
Sam Jethroe: Cincinnati-Cleveland Buckeyes, 1942; Cleveland Buckeyes, 1944, 1946, 1947
Connie Johnson: Toledo-Indianapolis Crawfords, 1940; Kansas City Monarchs, 1950
Sweet Lou Johnson: Kansas City Monarchs, 1955
John Kennedy: Birmingham Black Barons, 1954; Kansas City Monarchs, 1956
Luis Márquez: Homestead Grays, 1947, 1948
Hank "Pistol" Mason: Kansas City Monarchs, 1954
Minnie Miñoso: New York Cubans, 1947, 1948
Satchel Paige: Pittsburgh Crawfords, 1934, 1936; Kansas City Monarchs, 1941, 1942, 1943, 1955
Larry Raines: Chicago American Giants, 1952
Jackie Robinson: Kansas City Monarchs, 1945
Patricio Scantlebury: New York Cubans, 1946, 1949, 1950
Milt Smith: Philadelphia Stars, 1951
Willie Smith: Birmingham Black Barons, 1958, 1959
George Spriggs: Detroit-New Orleans Bears, 1960

Quincy Trouppe: Indianapolis ABCs, 1938; Cleveland Buckeyes, 1945, 1946, 1947; Chicago American Giants, 1948

Charles White, Jr.: Philadelphia Stars, 1950

Artie Wilson: Birmingham Black Barons, 1944, 1946, 1947, 1948

Bob Wilson: Houston Eagles, 1949; Kansas City Monarchs, 1957

Negro Leagues Book #2: The Players

Future NBBHOF Inductees who played in the East-West All-Star Classic

Sunday, September 10, 1933 in Chicago at Comiskey Park
- James "Cool Papa" Bell: Pittsburgh Crawfords
- Oscar Charleston: Pittsburgh Crawfords
- Willie Foster: Chicago American Giants
- Josh Gibson: Pittsburgh Crawfords
- Judy Johnson: Pittsburgh Crawfords
- Raleigh "Biz" Mackey: Philadelphia Stars
- Norman "Turkey" Stearnes: Chicago American Giants
- George "Mule" Suttles: Chicago American Giants
- Willie "the Devil" Wells: Chicago American Giants
- Jud Wilson: Philadelphia Stars

Sunday, August 26, 1934 in Chicago at Comiskey Park
- James "Cool Papa" Bell: Pittsburgh Crawfords
- Oscar Charleston: Pittsburgh Crawfords
- Willie Foster: Chicago American Giants
- Josh Gibson: Pittsburgh Crawfords
- Leroy "Satchel" Paige: Pittsburgh Crawfords
- Norman "Turkey" Stearnes: Chicago American Giants
- George "Mule" Suttles: Chicago American Giants
- Willie "the Devil" Wells: Chicago American Giants
- Jud Wilson: Philadelphia Stars

Sunday, August 11, 1935 in Chicago at Comiskey Park
- James "Cool Papa" Bell: Pittsburgh Crawfords
- Ray Brown: Homestead Grays
- Oscar Charleston: Pittsburgh Crawfords
- Ray Dandridge: Newark Dodgers
- Leon Day: Brooklyn Eagles
- Martín Dihigo: New York Cubans
- Josh Gibson: Pittsburgh Crawfords
- Walter "Buck" Leonard: Homestead Grays
- Raleigh "Biz" Mackey: Philadelphia Stars
- Norman "Turkey" Stearnes: Chicago American Giants
- George "Mule" Suttles: Chicago American Giants
- Willie "the Devil" Wells: Chicago American Giants
- Jud Wilson: Philadelphia Stars

Sunday, August 23, 1936 in Chicago at Comiskey Park
- James "Cool Papa" Bell: Pittsburgh Crawfords
- Willard "Home Run" Brown: Kansas City Monarchs
- Andy Cooper: Kansas City Monarchs
- Josh Gibson: Pittsburgh Crawfords
- Judy Johnson: Pittsburgh Crawfords
- Raleigh "Biz" Mackey: Washington Elite Giants
- Leroy "Satchel" Paige: Pittsburgh Crawfords
- Wilber "Bullet" Rogan: Kansas City Monarchs

Sunday, August 8, 1937 in Chicago at Comiskey Park
- Willard "Home Run" Brown: Kansas City Monarchs
- Ray Dandridge: Newark Eagles
- Leon Day: Newark Eagles
- Walter "Buck" Leonard: Homestead Grays
- Hilton Smith: Kansas City Monarchs
- Norman "Turkey" Stearnes: Detroit Stars
- George "Mule" Suttles: Newark Eagles
- Willie "the Devil" Wells: Newark Eagles

Sunday, August 21, 1938 in Chicago at Comiskey Park
- Walter "Buck" Leonard: Homestead Grays
- Raleigh "Biz" Mackey": Baltimore Elite Giants
- Hilton Smith: Kansas City Monarchs
- Willie "the Devil" Wells: Newark Eagles

Sunday, August 18, 1940 in Chicago at Comiskey Park
- Ray Brown: Homestead Grays
- Walter "Buck" Leonard: Homestead Grays
- Hilton Smith: Kansas City Monarchs

Sunday, July 27, 1941 in Chicago at Comiskey Park
- Roy Campanella: Baltimore Elite Giants
- Monte Irvin: Newark Eagles
- Walter "Buck" Leonard: Homestead Grays
- Leroy "Satchel" Paige: Kansas City Monarchs
- Hilton Smith: Kansas City Monarchs

Sunday, August 16, 1942 in Chicago at Comiskey Park
- James "Cool Papa" Bell: Chicago American Giants
- Willard "Home Run" Brown: Kansas City Monarchs
- Leon Day: Newark Eagles
- Josh Gibson: Homestead Grays
- Leroy "Satchel" Paige: Kansas City Monarchs
- Hilton Smith: Kansas City Monarchs
- Willie "the Devil" Wells: Newark Eagles

Tuesday, August 18, 1942 in Cleveland at Municipal Stadium
    James "Cool Papa" Bell: Chicago American Giants
    Willard "Home Run" Brown: Kansas City Monarchs
    Leon Day: Newark Eagles
    Josh Gibson: Homestead Grays
    Willie "the Devil" Wells: Newark Eagles

Sunday, August 1, 1943 in Chicago at Comiskey Park
    James "Cool Papa" Bell: Homestead Grays
    Willard "Home Run" Brown: Kansas City Monarchs
    Leon Day: Newark Eagles
    Josh Gibson: Homestead Grays
    Walter "Buck" Leonard: Homestead Grays
    Leroy "Satchel" Paige: Kansas City Monarchs

Sunday, August 13, 1944 in Chicago at Comiskey Park
    James "Cool Papa" Bell: Homestead Grays
    Roy Campanella: Baltimore Elite Giants
    Ray Dandridge: Newark Eagles
    Josh Gibson: Homestead Grays
    Walter "Buck" Leonard: Homestead Grays

Sunday, July 29, 1945 in Chicago at Comiskey Park
    Roy Campanella: Baltimore Elite Giants
    Martín Dihigo: New York Cubans
    Walter "Buck" Leonard: Homestead Grays
    Jackie Robinson: Kansas City Monarchs
    Willie "the Devil" Wells: Newark Eagles

Thursday, August 15, 1946 in Washington, DC, at Griffith Stadium
    Leon Day: Newark Eagles
    Larry Doby: Newark Eagles
    Josh Gibson: Homestead Grays
    Monte Irvin: Newark Eagles
    Walter "Buck" Leonard: Homestead Grays

Sunday, August 18, 1946 in Chicago at Comiskey Park
    Leon Day: Newark Eagles
    Larry Doby: Newark Eagles
    Josh Gibson: Homestead Grays
    Monte Irvin: Newark Eagles
    Walter "Buck" Leonard: Homestead Grays

Sunday, July 27, 1947 in Chicago at Comiskey Park
    Monte Irvin: Newark Eagles

Raleigh "Biz" Mackey: Newark Eagles

Tuesday, July 29, 1947 in New York at Polo Grounds
Monte Irvin: Newark Eagles

Sunday, August 22, 1948 in Chicago at Comiskey Park
Willard "Home Run" Brown: Kansas City Monarchs
Monte Irvin: Newark Eagles
Walter "Buck" Leonard: Homestead Grays

Tuesday, August 24, 1948 in New York at Yankee Stadium
Willard "Home Run" Brown: Kansas City Monarchs

Sunday, August 14, 1949 in Chicago at Comiskey Park
Willard "Home Run" Brown: Kansas City Monarchs

Sunday, August 16, 1953 in Chicago at Comiskey Park
Ernie Banks: Kansas City Monarchs

Sunday, July 31, 1955 in Chicago at Comiskey Park
Leroy "Satchel" Paige: Kansas City Monarchs

Sunday, August 20, 1961 in New York at Yankee Stadium
Leroy "Satchel" Paige: Kansas City Monarchs

Latin American players in the East-West All-Star Classic

CUBA
Dave Amaro: Indianapolis Clowns, 1953
Juan Armenteros: Kansas City Monarchs, 1953, 1954, 1955
Heberto "Harry" Blanco: New York Cubans, 1942 (2)
Alex Crespo: New York Cubans, 1940
Pedro "Manny" Díaz: New York Cubans, 1946, 1949, 1950
Martín Dihigo: New York Cubans, 1935, 1945
Verdes Drake: Indianapolis Clowns, 1953, 1954
Claro Duany: New York Cubans, 1947 (2)
Pedro Formental: Memphis Red Sox, 1949
Raúl Galata: New York Cubans, 1950
Silvio García: New York Cubans, 1946 (2), 1947 (2)
Hiram "Rene" González: New York Cubans, 1950
Francisco "Pancho" Herrera: Kansas City Monarchs, 1953, 1954
Rogelio "Ice Cream" Linares: New York Cubans, 1945
Cando "Police Car" López: New York Cubans, 1939
Minnie Miñoso: New York Cubans, 1947 (2), 1948 (2)
Alejandro "Walla Walla" Oms: New York Cubans, 1935
Silvino "Poppa" Ruiz: New York Cubans, 1940
Luis Tiant, Sr.: New York Cubans, 1935, 1947 (2)
Gilberto Varona: Memphis Red Sox, 1951, 1952, 1955
Orlando Varona: Memphis Red Sox, 1949

PUERTO RICO
José Antonio Burgos: Birmingham Black Barons, 1949
Francisco "Pancho" Coimbre: New York Cubans, 1941, 1944
Luis Ángel Márquez: Homestead Grays, 1947 (2), 1948 (2)

PANAMA
Vibert Clarke: Cleveland Buckeyes, 1946, 1947, 1948; Memphis Red Sox, 1950, 1951
Leon Kellman: Cleveland Buckeyes, 1947, 1948, 1949; Memphis Red Sox, 1950
Patricio "Pat" Scantlebury: New York Cubans, 1946 (2), 1949, 1950

DOMINICAN REPUBLIC
Horacio "Rabbit" Martínez: New York Cubans, 1940, 1941, 1943, 1944, 1945

1949 to 1999, 50 Years of Major League All-Star History

In 1949, former stars from the Negro Baseball Leagues Jackie Robinson, Larry Doby, Roy Campanella and Don Newcombe became the first African Americans to play in a Major League Baseball All-Star game. In the next 50 years, 175 Blacks have been honored to play in baseball's most elite showcase. Listed below are the All-Stars; with former Negro League players in **BOLD**. The number in parenthesis represents the number of All-Star appearances.

Hank Aaron (25)	Tommy Agee
Dick Allen	**George Altman (3)**
Harold Baines	Dusty Baker
Ernie Banks (14)	Jesse Barfield
Kevin Bass	Earl Battey
Don Baylor	Albert Belle
Jim Bibby	Paul Blair
Vida Blue	Bobby Bonds
Barry Bonds	Bobby Bonilla
Phil Bradley	Hubie Brooks
Chris Brown	Don Buford
Al Bumbry	Ellis Burks
Joe Carter	Dave Cash
Cito Gaston	Chris Chambliss
Royce Clayton	Nate Colbert
Vince Coleman	Cecil Cooper
Joey Cora	**George Crowe (one year, 1958)**
Tommy Davis	Willie Davis
Chili Davis	Eric Davis
Andre Dawson	Al Downing
Shawon Dunston	Leon Durham
Ray Durham	Mike Easler
Damion Easley	Dock Ellis
Cecil Fielder	Curt Flood
George Foster	Ron Gant
Ralph Garr	Clarence Gaston
Bob Gibson	**Jim Gilliam (2)**
Dwight Gooden	Tom Gordon
Jim Grant	Ken Griffey, Jr.
Ken Griffey, Sr.	Alfredo Griffith
Marquis Grissom	Tony Gwynn
Tommy Harper	Jim Ray Hart
Rickey Henderson	Dave Henderson
George Hendrick	Ken Hill
Larry Hisle	Al Holland
Willie Horton	**Elston Howard (12)**

Negro Leagues Book #2: The Players

Reggie Jackson	Grant Jackson
Bo Jackson	Ferguson Jenkins
Derek Jeter	Alex Johnson
Charles Johnson	Lance Johnson
Sam Jones (2)	Cleon Jones
Ruppert Jones	David Justice
Pat Kelly	Ken Landreaux
Ray Lankford	Barry Larkin
Ron LeFlore	Chet Lemon
Jeffrey Leonard	Kenny Lofton
Davey Lopes	Bill Madlock
Gary Matthews	Carlos May
Lee May	Dave May
John Mayberry	**Willie Mays (24)**
Bake McBride	Willie McCovey
Willie McGee	Lynn McGlothen
Hal McRae	Kevin Mitchell
Donnie Moore	Joe Morgan
Lloyd Moseby	Jerry Mumphrey
Eddie Murray	**Charlie Neal (3)**
Dave Nelson	Mike Norris
Blue Moon Odom	Ben Oglivie
Al Oliver	Amos Otis
Satchel Paige (2)	Dave Parker
Terry Pendleton	Gerald Perry
Vida Pinson	Kirby Puckett
Tim Raines	Willie Randolph
Johnny Ray	Harold Reynolds
Jim Rice	J.R. Richards
Mickey Rivers	Bip Roberts
Frank Robinson	John Roseboro
Reggie Sanders	George Scott
Mike Sharperson	Gary Sheffield
Harry Simpson (one year, 1956)	Wayne Simpson
Ken Singleton	Heathcliff Slocumb
Al Smith (3)	Reggie Smith
Ozzie Smith	Lonnie Smith
Lee Smith	Willie Stargell
Dave Stewart	Darryl Strawberry
Garry Templeton	Frank Thomas
Andre Thornton	Ellis Valentine
Mo Vaughn	Gregg Vaughn
Bob Veale	Leon Wagner
Gary Ward	Claudell Washington

Bob Watson	Lou Whitaker
Bill White	Roy White
Devon White	Billy Williams
Maury Wills	Don Wilson
Willie Wilson	Dave Winfield
Tony Womack	**John Wyatt (one year, 1964)**
Jimmy Wynn	Eric Young

APPENDIX D:

All-Time World Series Rosters by players

Ted (Red) Alexander: 1946, 1948 K.C. Monarchs, Homestead Grays
Newt (Colt) Allen: 1924-25, 1942 Kansas City Monarchs
Tom Allen, Sr.: 1924 Hilldale Club
Mario (Homero) Ariosa: 1947 New York Cubans
Alfred (Buddy) Armour: 1945 Cleveland Buckeyes
Joe Atkins 1947: Cleveland Buckeyes
Sam Bankhead: 1942-45, 1948 Homestead Grays
Dave (Impo) Barnhill: 1947 New York Cubans
Lloyd (Pepper) Bassett: 1948 Birmingham Black Barons
Ray Battles 1945: Homestead Grays
Cliff (Cherry) Bell: 1924-25 Kansas City Monarchs
Herman Bell 1948: Birmingham Black Barons
James (Cool Papa) Bell: 1943-45 Homestead Grays
William (W) Bell, Sr.: 1924-25 Kansas City Monarchs
Jerry Benjamin: 1942-45 Homestead Grays
Alonzo (Buster) Boone: 1944 Birmingham Black Barons
Herb (Doc) Bracken: 1947 Cleveland Buckeyes
James Bray: 1927 Chicago American Giants
Gene Bremer, Sr.: 1945, 1947 Cleveland Buckeyes
Chet Brewer: 1947 Cleveland Buckeyes
Otto Briggs: 1924-25 Hilldale Club
Johnny Britton: 1944, 1948 Birmingham Black Barons
Jim Brown: 1926-27 Chicago American Giants
Larry (Iron Man) Brown :1927 Chicago American Giants
Ray Brown: 1942-45 Homestead Grays
Willard (Home Run) Brown: 1942, 1946 Kansas City Monarchs
Clarence Bruce: 1948 Homestead Grays
Elias (Country Brown) Bryant: 1926 Bacharach (AC) Giants
Earl Bumpus: 1944 Birmingham Black Barons
Lorenzo (Chiquitin) Cabrera: 1947 New York Cubans
Bill (Zip) Campbell: 1924 Hilldale Club
Avelino Canizares: 1945 Cleveland Buckeyes
Jesse (Hoss) Cannady: 1944 Homestead Grays
Matt Carlisle: 1942-43 Homestead Grays
George (Tank) Carr: 1924-25 Hilldale Club
Frank Carswell: 1945 Cleveland Buckeyes
Alfred Carter: 1942 Homestead Grays
Ernest (Spoon) Carter: 1943-44 Homestead Grays
Cleveland Clark: 1947 New York Cubans
Vibert (Webbo) Clarke: 1947 Cleveland Buckeyes
James (Buster) Clarkson:1942 Homestead Grays

Phil Cockrell: 1924-25 Hilldale Club
Johnnie Cowan: 1945, 1947 Cleveland Buckeyes
Sam Crawford: 1926 Chicago American Giants
Martín Crue: 1947 New York Cubans
Nap (Chance) Cummings: 1926 Bacharach (AC) Giants
Rube Currie: 1924-25, 1926-27 Hilldale Club; Chicago American Giants
Maurice (Eggie) Dallard: 1927 Bacharach (AC) Giants
Austin Davis: 1945 Homestead Grays
John (Cherokee) Davis:1946 Newark Eagles
Lorenzo (Piper) Davis:1943-44, 1948 Birmingham Black Barons
Ross (Satchel) Davis: 1947 Cleveland Buckeyes
Walter (Steel Arm) Davis:1927 Chicago American Giants
Leon Day: 1942, 1946 Homestead Grays, Newark Eagles
Nelson Dean: 1925 Kansas City Monarchs
Fernando (El Bicho) Díaz: 1947 New York Cubans
Larry Doby, Sr. : 1946 Newark Eagles
Lino Donoso: 1947 New York Cubans
Bill (Plunk) Drake: 1924-25 Kansas City Monarchs
Claro Duany: 1947 New York Cubans
Frank Duncan, Jr.: 1924-25 Kansas City Monarchs
Al (Blue) Dunn: 1943 Birmingham Black Barons
Luke Easter: 1948 Homestead Grays
Howard Easterling: 1942-43 Homestead Grays
Luther (Red) Farrell: 1926-27 Bacharach (AC) Giants
Benny Felder: 1946 Newark Eagles
Wilmer (Red) Fields: 1948 Homestead Grays
Willis (Pud) Flournoy: 1944 Birmingham Black Barons
Sylvester (Hooks) Foreman: 1925 Kansas City Monarchs
Willie Foster: 1926-27 Chicago American Giants
Ramondo (Chano) García: 1926 Bacharach (AC) Giants
Silvio García: 1947 New York Cubans
Floyd (Jelly) Gardner: 1926 Chicago American Giants
Rab Roy Gaston: 1942-43 Homestead Grays
Josh Gibson: 1942-45 Homestead Grays
Alvin (Bubber) Gipson: 1943 Birmingham Black Barons
Willie Grace: 1945, 1947 Cleveland Buckeyes
Joe Greene: 1942, 1946 Kansas City Monarchs
Claude (Red) Grier: 1926 Bacharach (AC) Giants
Jim Hamilton: 1946 Kansas City Monarchs
George Harney: 1926-27 Chicago American Giants
Vic Harris: 1942-43, 1945 Homestead Grays
Bob Harvey: 1946 Newark Eagles
Lem Hawkins: 1924-25 Kansas City Monarchs
Rats Henderson: 1926 Bacharach (AC) Giants
John (Jackhouse) Hines: 1926 Chicago American Giants
Len Hooker: 1946 Newark Eagles

Negro Leagues Book #2: The Players

Dave Hoskins: 1944-45 Homestead Grays
Jesse (Mountain Man) Hubbard: 1927 Bacharach (AC) Giants
John (Bubber) Huber: 1943-44 Birmingham Black Barons
Monte Irvin: 1946 Newark Eagles
Clarence (Pint) Isreal: 1946 Newark Eagles
Jerry (Bozo) Jackson: 1945 Homestead Grays
Norm (Jelly) Jackson: 1944-45 Homestead Grays
Stanford (Jambo) Jackson: 1926-27 Chicago American Giants
George Jefferson: 1945 Cleveland Buckeyes
Willie Jefferson: 1945 Cleveland Buckeyes
Gentry Jessup: 1943 Birmingham Black Barons
Sam (the Jet) Jethroe: 1945, 1947 Cleveland Buckeyes
George (Dibo) Johnson: 1924-25 Hilldale Club
Oscar (Heavy) Johnson: 1924 Kansas City Monarchs
Judy Johnson: 1924-25 Hilldale Club
Wade Johnston: 1925 Kansas City Monarchs
Collis Jones: 1944 Birmingham Black Barons
Sam (Toothpick) Jones: 1947 Cleveland Buckeyes
Willie (Fox) Jones: 1926-27 Bacharach (AC) Giants
Newt Joseph: 1924-25 Kansas City Monarchs
Leon Kellman: 1947 Cleveland Buckeyes
Jim (Lefty) LaMarque: 1946 Kansas City Monarchs
Scrip Lee: 1924-25 Hilldale Club
Walter (Buck) Leonard: 1942-45, 1948 Homestead Grays
Joe (Sleepy) Lewis: 1924, 1926 Hilldale Club, Bacharach (AC) Giants
Milton Lewis: 1927 Bacharach (AC) Giants
Rufus Lewis: 1946 Newark Eagles
Leonard (Yahoodi) Lindsay: 1943 Birmingham Black Barons
James Lindsey: 1943 Birmingham Black Barons
Lester Lockett: 1943-44 Birmingham Black Barons
George (Prof) Lockhart: 1926-27 Bacharach (AC) Giants
Lou Louden: 1947 New York Cubans
Richard Lundy 1926-27 Bacharach (AC) Giants
Raleigh (Biz) Mackey: 1924-25; 1946 Hilldale Club, Newark Eagles
Gentleman Dave Malarcher: 1926-27 Chicago American Giants
Max Manning, Sr. : 1946 Newark Eagles
Oliver (Ghost) Marcell: 1926-27 Bacharach (AC) Giants
Johnny Markham: 1943-44 Birmingham Black Barons
Luis Márquez: 1948 Homestead Grays
Horacio (Rabbit) Martínez: 1947 New York Cubans
Jack Matchett: 1942 Kansas City Monarchs
Willie Mays: 1948 Birmingham Black Barons
Bill McCall: 1924 Kansas City Monarchs
Webster McDonald: 1926-27 Chicago American Giants
Gready (Lefty) McKinnis: 1943 Birmingham Black Barons
Felix McLaurin: 1943-44 Birmingham Black Barons

Hurley McNair: 1924-25 Kansas City Monarchs
José Méndez: 1924-25 Kansas City Monarchs
Eddie (Buck) Miller: 1927 Chicago American Giants
Minnie Miñoso :1947 New York Cubans
Alonzo Mitchell: 1926 Bacharach (AC) Giants
Walter (Dobie) Moore: 1924-24 Kansas City Monarchs
Leroy Morney: 1944 Birmingham Black Barons
Barney (Big Ad) Morris: 1947 New York Cubans

CARROLL MOTHELL - The quiet and soft-spoken Deke Mothell was a black knight in white satin. A cerebral player, Mothell was the master of versatility. Mothell was an excellent fielder and could play every position. The dedicated disciple of the game was known for his line drive hits. As a streak hitter, he had an unbelievable knack for getting the clutch hit. His playing style would be described as "crumbling elegance" – finding ugly ways to beat you.

Carroll (Deke) Mothell: 1924 Kansas City Monarchs
Eudie Napier: 1948 Homestead Grays
Clyde Nelson: 1947 Cleveland Buckeyes
Jimmy Newberry: 1948 Birmingham Black Barons
Ray Noble: 1947 New York Cubans

John (Buck) O'Neil, Jr.: 1942, 1946 Kansas City Monarchs
Leroy (Satchel) Paige: 1942, 1946 Kansas City Monarchs
Charlie Parks: 1946 Newark Eagles
Roy Partlow: 1942-43 Homestead Grays
Pat Patterson: 1946 Newark Eagles
Lennie Pearson: 1942, 1946 Homestead Grays, Newark Eagles
Alonzo Perry: 1948 Birmingham Black Barons
Dave Pope: 1948 Homestead Grays
Bill Powell: 1948 Birmingham Black Barons
Willie Powell: 1926-27 Chicago American Giants
Ted (Double Duty) Radcliffe: 1943-44 Birmingham Black Barons
Ambrose Reid: 1926-27 Bacharach (AC) Giants
Othello (Chico) Renfroe, Sr.: 1946 Kansas City Monarchs
Roy Roberts: 1926-27 Bacharach (AC) Giants
Bill Robinson: 1925 Hilldale Club
Wilber (Bullet) Rogan: 1924 Kansas City Monarchs
Nat Rogers: 1927 Chicago American Giants
Leon Ruffin: 1946 Newark Eagles
Pythias Russ: 1927 Chicago American Giants
Merven (Red) Ryan :1924-25 Hilldale Club
Tommy Sampson: 1943 Birmingham Black Barons

Negro Leagues Book #2: The Players

Louis Santop: 1924-25 Hilldale Club
Alfred (Greyhound) Saylor: 1943-44 Birmingham Black Barons
Pat Scantlebury: 1947 New York Cubans
Joe Scott: 1948 Birmingham Black Barons
John Scott: 1946 Kansas City Monarchs
Bonnie Serrell: 1942 Kansas City Monarchs
Willie Simms: 1942 Kansas City Monarchs
Al Smith: 1947 Cleveland Buckeyes
Clarence (Scally) Smith: 1927 Bacharach (AC) Giants
Eugene (Gene) Smith: 1947 Cleveland Buckeyes

HILTON SMITH was a rich manager's promise, or a poor manager's dream. Satchel got the headlines, while Hilton got the win. Hilton was a poor man's version of Satchel Paige. However, there was nothing cheap or shy about Smithy's game. Catcher Quincy Trouppe claimed Hilton had a better fastball than Sal "The Barber" Maglie. With a sinking fastball, curve, slider and a change thrown both sidearm and overhand, Trouppe bragged, "Hilton, in my estimation, had the most ability of any pitcher of my time." Smith was inducted into the National Baseball Hall of Fame in 2001.

Hilton Smith: 1942, 1946 Kansas City Monarchs
John Ford (Geronimo) Smith: 1946 Kansas City Monarchs
Herb Souell: 1942, 1946 Kansas City Monarchs
Clyde (Big Splo) Spearman: 1943 Birmingham Black Barons
Ed Steele: 1943-44, 1948 Birmingham Black Barons
Paul (Jake) Stephens: 1924-25 Hilldale Club
Ed Stone: 1942 Homestead Grays
Ted (T.R.) Strong, Jr.: 1942, 1946 Kansas City Monarchs
George Sweatt: 1924-25; 1926-27 K.C. Monarchs, Chicago American Giants
Earl Taborn: 1946 Kansas City Monarchs
Clint Thomas: 1924-25 Hilldale Club
Hank Thompson: 1946 Kansas City Monarchs
James (Sandy) Thompson: 1926 Chicago American Giants
Bob Thurman: 1948 Homestead Grays
Luis Tiant, Sr.: 1947 New York Cubans
Quincy Trouppe: 1945, 1947 Cleveland Buckeyes
Bert [Pop Turner] Wagner: 1927 Bacharach (AC) Giants
Jesse (Hoss) Walker :1943 Birmingham Black Barons
Edsall Walker, Sr.: 1943-44 Homestead Grays
Archie Ware: 1945, 1947 Cleveland Buckeyes
Frank Warfield: 1924-25 Hilldale Club
Namon Washington: 1925 Hilldale Club
Roy Welmaker: 1942, 1944-45 Homestead Grays
Dave (Speed) Whatley: 1942 Homestead Grays
Chaney White: 1926-27 Bacharach (AC) Giants
Jimmy Wilkes: 1946 Newark Eagles

Chester (Ches) Williams: 1942 Homestead Grays
Jesse Horace Williams: 1942 Kansas City Monarchs
Jesse Sharon Williams: 1947 Cleveland Buckeyes
Charlie Williams, Jr.: 1926-27 Chicago American Giants
Robert (Cotton) Williams: 1946 Newark Eagles
Clyde (Lefty) Williams, Sr.: 1947 Cleveland Buckeyes
Artie Wilson: 1944, 1948 Birmingham Black Barons
Jud Wilson: 1942-45 Homestead Grays
Nip Winters: 1924-25 Hilldale Club
Parnell Woods: 1945 Cleveland Buckeyes
Johnny Wright: 1942-43, 1945 Homestead Grays
Ralph (Pepper) Wyatt: 1943 Homestead Grays
Steve Wylie: 1946 Kansas City Monarchs
Jim Zapp: 1948 Birmingham Black Barons

Negro Leagues Book #2: The Players

MLB players who played in the Negro League World Series

Willard "Home Run" Brown: Kansas City Monarchs, 1942, 1946

Vibert "Webbo" Clarke: Cleveland Buckeyes, 1947

James "Buster" Clarkson: Homestead Grays, 1942

Larry Doby: Newark Eagles, 1946

Lino Donoso: New York Cubans, 1947

Luke Easter: Homestead Grays, 1948

Dave Hoskins: Homestead Grays, 1944, 1945

Monte Irvin: Newark Eagles, 1946

Sam "the Jet" Jethroe: Cleveland Buckeyes, 1945, 1947

Sam "Toothpick" Jones: Cleveland Buckeyes, 1947

Luis Márquez: Homestead Grays, 1948

Willie Mays: Birmingham Black Barons, 1948

Minnie Miñoso: New York Cubans, 1947

Ray Noble: New York Cubans, 1947

Satchel Paige: Kansas City Monarchs, 1942, 1946

Pat Scantlebury: New York Cubans, 1947

Hank Thompson: Kansas City Monarchs, 1946

Quincy Trouppe: Cleveland Buckeyes, 1945, 1947

Artie Wilson: Birmingham Black Barons, 1944, 1948

All-Time Negro League World Series Rosters - by Teams

Bacharach (AC) Giants
Elias (Country Brown) Bryant 1926
Napoleon (Chance) Cummings 1926
Maurice (Eggie) Dallard 1927
Luther Farrell 1926-27
Ramondo (Chano) García 1926
Claude (Red) Grier 1926
Arthur (Rats) Henderson 1926
Jesse (Mountain Man) Hubbard 1927
William (Fox) Jones 1926-27
Joe (Sleepy) Lewis 1926
Milton Lewis 1927
George (Prof) Lockhart 1926-27
Richard (Dick) Lundy 1926-27
Oliver (Ghost) Marcell 1926-27
Alonzo Mitchell 1926
Ambrose Reid 1926-27
Roy Roberts 1926-27
Clarence (Scally) Smith 1927
Bert (Billy) Wagner [Pop Turner] 1927
Chaney (Reindeer) White 1926-27

Birmingham Black Barons
Lloyd (Rocking Chair) Bassett 1948
Herman Bell 1948
Alonzo (Buster) Boone 1944
Johnny Britton 1944, 1948
Earl Bumpus 1944
Lorenzo (Piper) Davis 1943-44, 1948
Alphonse (Blue) Dunn 1943
Willis (Pud) Flournoy 1944
Alvin (Bubber) Gipson 1943
John (Bubba) Huber 1943-44
Joseph (Jeep) Jessup 1943
Collis Jones 1944
Leonard (Yahoodi) Lindsay 1943
James Lindsey 1943
Lester (Buck) Lockett 1943-44
John Markham 1943-44
Willie (Buck) Mays 1948
Gready (Lefty) McKinnis 1943
Felix McLaurin 1943-44
Leroy Morney 1944

Jimmy Newberry 1948
Alonzo (Tapya) Perry 1948
William (Bill) Powell 1948
Ted (Double Duty) Radcliffe 1943-44
Tommy (Toots) Sampson 1943
Al (Greyhound) Saylor 1943-44
Joe Scott 1948
Clyde (Big Splo) Spearman 1943
Ed (Stainless) Steele 1943-44, 1948
Jesse (Hoss) Walker 1943
Artie Wilson 1944, 1948
Jim Zapp 1948

Chicago American Giants
James Bray 1927
James (Jim) Brown 1926-27
Larry (Iron Man) Brown 1927
Sam Crawford 1926
Rube Currie 1926-27
Walter (Steel Arm) Davis 1927
Willie (Bill) Foster 1926-27
Floyd (Jelly) Gardner 1926
George Harney 1926-27
John (Jackhouse) Hines 1926
Stanford (Jambo) Jackson 1926-27
Gentleman Dave Malarcher 1926-27
Webster McDonald 1926-27
Eddie (Buck) Miller 1927
Willie (Pee Wee) Powell 1926-27
Nat Rogers 1927
Pythias Russ 1927
George (Never) Sweatt 1926-27
James (Sandy) Thompson 1926
Ches Williams 1926-27

Cleveland Buckeyes
Alfred (Buddy) Armour 1945
Joe Atkins 1947
Herb (Doc a.k.a. Alfred Bragana) Bracken 1947
Gene Bremer 1945, 1947
Chet Brewer 1947
Avelino Canizares 1945
Frank Carswell 1945
Vibert (Webbo) Clarke 1947

Johnnie Cowan 1945, 1947
Ross (Satchel) Davis 1947
Willie (Fireman) Grace 1945, 1947
George (Jeff) Jefferson 1945
Willie (Bill) Jefferson 1945
Sam (The Jet) Jethroe 1945, 1947
Toothpick Sam Jones 1947
Edric Leon Kellman 1947
Clyde Nelson 1947
Al (Fuzzy) Smith 1947
Eugene F. (Genie) Smith 1947
Quincy Trouppe 1945, 1947
Archie Ware 1945, 1947
Jesse Sharon Williams 1947
Clyde (Lefty) Williams 1947
Parnell Woods 1945

Hilldale Club
Tom Allen 1924
Otto Briggs 1924-25
Bill (Bullet) Campbell 1924
George (Tank) Carr 1924-25
Phil (Fish) Cockrell [Williams] 1924-25
Currie Rube 1924-25
George (Dibo) Johnson Jr. 1924-25
William (Judy) Johnson 1924-25
Holsey (Scrip) Lee 1924-25
Joe (Sleepy) Lewis 1924
Raleigh (Biz) Mackey 1924-25
Newt Robinson 1925
Merv (Red) Ryan 1924-25
Louis (Top) Santop [Loftin] 1924-25
Paul (Jake) Stephens 1924-25
Clint (Hawk) Thomas 1924-25
Frank (Weasel) Warfield 1924-25
Namon (Cy) Washington 1925
Jesse (Nip) Winters 1924-25

Homestead Grays
Ted (Red) Alexander 1948
Sam Bankhead 1942-45, 1948
Ray Battles 1945
James (Cool Papa) Bell 1943-45
Jerry Benjamin 1942-45
Ray Brown 1942-45
Clarence Bruce 1948

Jesse (Hoss) Cannady 1944
Matt (Lick) Carlisle 1942-43
Alfred Carter 1942
Ernest (Spoon) Carter 1943-44
Buster Clarkson 1942
Austin Davis 1945
Leon Day 1942
Luke Easter 1948
Howard Easterling 1942-43
Wilmer Fields 1948
Roy Gaston 1942-43
Josh Gibson 1942-45
Vic Harris 1942-43, 1945
Dave Hoskins 1944-45
Jerry (Bozo) Jackson 1945
Norman (Jelly) Jackson 1944-45
Walter (Buck) Leonard 1942-45, 1948
Luis (Canena) Márquez 1948
Euthumn (Eudie) Napier 1948
Roy (Silent Roy) Partlow 1942-43
Lennie (Hoss) Pearson 1942
David Pope 1948
Ed Stone 1942
Robert (Bob) Thurman 1948
Edsall Walker 1943-44
Roy (Snook) Welmaker 1942, 1944-45
Dave (Speed) Whatley 1942
Ches Williams 1942
Ernest (Jud) Wilson 1942-45
Johnny Wright 1942-43, 1945
Ralph (Pepper) Wyatt 1943

Kansas City Monarchs
Ted (Red) Alexander 1946
Newt (Colt) Allen 1924-25, 1942
Cliff (Cherry) Bell 1924-25
William (W) Bell 1924-25
Willard (Home Run) Brown 1942, 1946
Nelson Dean 1925
Bill (Plunk) Drake 1924-25
Frank Duncan Jr. 1924-25
Sylvester (Hooks) Foreman 1925
Joe Greene 1942, 1946
Jim Hamilton 1946
Lem (Hawk) Hawkins 1924-25
Oscar (Heavy) Johnson 1924

Wade (Kid) Johnston 1925
Newt Joseph 1924-25
Jim (Lefty) LaMarque 1946
Claude (Jack) Matchett 1942
Bill McCall 1924
Hurley McNair 1924-25
José Méndez 1924-25
Dobie Moore 1924-25
Carroll (Dink Deke) Mothell 1924
John (Buck) O'Neil Jr. 1942, 1946
Leroy (Satchel) Paige 1942, 1946
Othello (Chico) Renfroe 1946
Wilber (Bullet) Rogan 1924
John Scott 1946
Bonnie (Barney) Serrell 1942
Bill (Jeep) Simms 1942
Hilton Smith 1942, 1946
John Ford Smith 1946
Herb Souell [Cyrus] 1942, 1946
Ted Strong, Jr. 1942, 1946
George (Never) Sweatt 1924-25
Earl (Mickey) Taborn 1946
Hank Thompson 1946
Jesse (Bill) Williams 1942
Steve Enloe Wylie 1946

New York Cubans
Mario (Homero) Ariosa 1947
Dave (Impo) Barnhill 1947
Lorenzo (Chiquitin) Cabrera 1947
Cleveland Clark 1947
Martín Crue 1947
Fernando (El Bicho) Díaz 1947
Lino Donoso 1947
Claro Duany 1947
Silvio García 1947
Lou Louden 1947
Horacio (Rabbit) Martínez 1947
Minnie Miñoso 1947
Barney (Big Ad) Morris 1947
Ray Noble 1947
Patricio Scantlebury 1947
Luis (Lefty) Tiant 1947

Newark Eagles
Johnny (Cherokee) Davis 1946
Leon Day 1946
Larry Doby 1946
Benny Felder 1946
Bob Harvey 1946
Len Hooker 1946
Monte Irvin 1946
Clarence (Pint) Isreal 1946
Rufus Lewis 1946
Raleigh (Biz) Mackey 1946
Max Manning 1946
Charles Parks 1946
Andrew (Pat) Patterson 1946
Len Pearson 1946
Charles (Lassas) Ruffin 1946
James (Seabiscuit) Wilkes 1946
Robert A. (Cotton) Williams 1946

APPENDIX E:

Hall of Fame Inductees

TED WILLIAMS - 1966
NATIONAL HALL OF FAME INDUCTION SPEECH:

I guess every player thinks about going into the Hall of Fame. Now that the moment has come for me I find it difficult to say what is really in my heart. But I know it is the greatest thrill of my life. I received two hundred and eighty-odd votes from the writers. I know I didn't have two hundred and eighty-odd friends among the writers. I know they voted for me because they felt in their minds and in their hearts that I rated it, and I want to say to them: Thank you, from the bottom of my heart.

Today I am thinking about a lot of things. I am thinking about my playground director in San Diego, Rodney Luscomb, my high school coach, Wos Caldwell, and my managers, who had so much patience with me—fellows like Frank Shellenback, Donie Bush, Joe Cronin, and Joe McCarthy. I am thinking of Eddie Collins, who had so much faith in me—and to be in the Hall with him particularly, as well as those other great players, is a great honor. I'm sorry Eddie isn't here today.

I'm thinking of Tom Yawkey. I have always said it: Tom Yawkey is the greatest owner in baseball. I was lucky to have played on the club he owned, and I'm grateful to him for being here today.

But I'd not be leveling if I left it at that. Ballplayers are not born great. They're not born great hitters or pitchers or managers, and luck isn't a big factor. No one has come up with a substitute for hard work. I've never met a great player who didn't have to work harder at learning to play ball than anything else he ever did. To me it was the greatest fun I ever had, which probably explains why today I feel both humility and pride, because God let me play the game and learn to be good at it.

The other day Willie Mays hit his five hundred and twenty-second homerun. He has gone past me, and he's pushing, and I say to him, 'go get 'em Willie.'

Baseball gives every American boy a chance to excel. Not just to be as good as anybody else, but to be better. This is the nature of man and the name of the game. **I hope someday Satchel Paige and Josh Gibson will be voted into the Hall of Fame as symbols of the great Negro players who are not here only because they weren't given the chance.**

As time goes on I'll be thinking baseball, teaching baseball, and arguing for baseball to keep it right on top of American sports, just as it is in Japan, Mexico, Venezuela, and other Latin American and South American countries. I know Casey feels the same way.... I also know I'll lose a dear friend if I don't stop talking. I'm eating into his time, and that is unforgivable. So in closing, I am grateful and know how lucky I was to have been born an American and had the chance to play the game I love, the greatest game.

Ted Williams
July 25, 1966
Cooperstown, New York

International Baseball Hall of Fames

American, Cuban, Mexican, and Puerto Rican Baseball Hall of Fame Inductees

Inductee	Hall(s) of Fame
Hank Aaron	US:1982
José (Acostica) Acosta	Cuba:1958 (a)
Rafael Almeida	Cuba:1939 (a)
Santos Amaro	Cuba:1967 (b), Mexico:1977
Edmundo (Sandy) Amoros	Cuba:1978 (b)
Luis Pedro Arango	Cuba:1986 (b)
Homero Mario Ariosa	Mexico:1982
Ernie Banks	US:1977
Dave (Impo) Barnhill	Cuba:2007 (b)
Bernardo Baro	Cuba:1945 (a)
Agustín Bejerano	Cuba:1997 (b), Mexico:1973
James (Cool Papa) Bell	US:1974 (a), Cuba:2007 (b)
Joe Black	Cuba:2007 (b)
Carlos Blanco	Cuba:1997 (b)
Heberto Blanco	Cuba:1997 (b)
Ramón (El Profesor) Bragaña	Cuba:1960 (a), Mexico:1964
Ray (Jabao) Brown	US:2006 (c), Cuba:1998 (b), Puerto Rico:1996
Willard (Ese Hombre) Brown	US:2006 (c), Puerto Rico:1991 & 2014
Luis (Anguilla) Bustamante	Cuba:1939 (a)
Armando Cabañas	Cuba:1959 (a)
Alfredo (Pájaro) Cabrera	Cuba:1942 (a)
Lorenzo (Chiquitín) Cabrera	Cuba:1985 (b)
Jacinto Calvo	Cuba:1948 (a)
Roy Campanella	US:1969, Mexico:1971
Avelino Canizares	Cuba:1997 (b)
Julian Castillo	Cuba:1943 (a)
Pelayo Chacón	Cuba:1949 (a)
Oscar Charleston	US:1976 (a), Cuba:1997 (b)
Bus Clarkson	Puerto Rico:1996
Francisco (Pancho) Coimbre	Puerto Rico:1991
Andy Cooper	US:2006 (c)
Francisco (Cuco) Correa	Cuba:1986 (b)
Rogelio Crespo	Cuba:1962 (b)
Alejandro Crespo	Cuba:1973 (b)
Raymond (Mamerto) Dandridge	US:1987 (b), Cuba:2007 (b), Mexico:1989
Leon Day	US:1995 (b), Puerto Rico:1993
Heliodoro (Yoyo) Díaz	Cuba:1964 (b)
Pedro Dibut	Cuba:1963 (b)
Martín Dihigo	US:1977 (a), Cuba:1951 (c), Mexico:1964
Larry Doby	US:1998
Lino Donoso	Mexico:1988

Valentin Dreke	Cuba:1945 (a)
Claro Duany	Cuba:1997 (b)
Isidro Fabre	Cuba:1957 (a)
José María Fernández, Sr.	Cuba:1965 (b)
Rodolfo Fernández	Cuba:1966 (b)
Rafael Figarola	Cuba:1950 (a)
José Antonio (Tito) Figueroa	Puerto Rico:1992
Pedro Formental	Cuba:1972 (b)
Andrew (Rube) Foster	US:1981 (b)
Willie Foster	US:1996 (b)
Antonio María (El Ingles) García	Cuba:1939 (a)
Manuel (Cocaina) García	Cuba:1969 (b), Puerto Rico:1993
Regino (Mamelo) García	Cuba:1941 (a)
Silvio García	Cuba:1975 (b)
Josh Gibson	US:1972 (a), Cuba:2007 (b), Mexico:1971, Puerto Rico:1996
Gervasio (Strike) González	Cuba:1939 (a)
Valentín (Sirique) González	Cuba:1939 (a)
Hiram Rene González	Mexico:1993
Miguel Angel González	Cuba:1956 (a)
Frank Grant	US:2006 (c)
Marcelino Guerra	Cuba:1986 (b)
Juan Guilbe	Puerto Rico:1992
Eustaquio Gutiérrez	Cuba:1950 (a)
Ramón (Napoleon) Heredia	Cuba:1997 (b)
Francisco (Pancho) Herrera	Cuba:1997 (b)
Ramón (Paito) Herrera	Cuba:1963 (b)
Heliodoro (Jabuco) Hidalgo	Cuba:1943 (a)
Pete Hill	US:2006 (c)
Monte Irvin	US:1973 (a), Cuba:1997 (b), Mexico:1971
Bienvenido (Pata Joroba) Jiménez	Cuba:1951 (a)
Eugenio Jiménez	Cuba:1950 (a)
Judy Johnson	US:1975 (a)
Walter (Buck) Leonard	US:1972 (a)
Oscar Levis	Cuba:2007 (b)
Abel Linares	Cuba:1985 (b)
John Henry (Pop) Lloyd	US:1977 (a), Cuba:2007 (b)
Julio (El Cartero) López	Cuba:1949 (a)
Justo (Cando) López	Cuba:1984 (b)
Adolfo Luque	Cuba:1958 (a), Mexico:1985
Raleigh (Biz) Mackey	US:2006 (c)
Oliver (Ghost) Marcell	Cuba:2007 (b)
Luis Angel (Canena) Márquez	Puerto Rico:1991
Armando Marsans	Cuba:1939 (a)
Willie Mays	US:1979

Effa Manley	US:2006 (c)
Terris McDuffie	Cuba:2007 (b)
José de la Caridad **Méndez**	US:2006 (c), Cuba:1939 (a)
Pablo (Champion) Mesa	Cuba:1964 (b),
Minnie Miñoso	Cuba:1983 (b) & 2014 (a), Mexico:1996
Juanelo Mirabal	Cuba:2007 (b)
Agustín (Tinti) Molina	Cuba:1942 (a)
Esteban (Mayarí) Montalvo	Cuba:1964 (b)
Carlos (Chino) Morán	Cuba:1945 (a)
José (Joseíto) Muñoz	Cuba:1940 (a)
Emilio Navarro	Puerto Rico:1992
Rafael (Ray) Noble	Cuba:1985 (b)
Alejandro Oms	Cuba:1944 (a)
Rafaelito (Rafael) Ortiz	Puerto Rico:1992
Luis (Mulo) Padrón	Cuba:1943 (a)
Pedro Pagés	Cuba:1997 (b)
Satchel Paige	US:1971 (a), Puerto Rico:1993
Emilio Palomino	Cuba:1957 (a)
Agustín Parpetti	Cuba:1962 (b)
Juan Manuel Pastoriza	Cuba:1945 (a)
Eustaquio (Bombín) Pedroso	Cuba:1962 (b)
Alfred Pinkston	Mexico:1974
Alex Pompez	US:2006 (c), Cuba:1997 (b)
Bartolo Portuondo	Cuba:1985 (b)
Cumberland Posey	US:2006 (c)
Tomás (Planchardon) Quinonez	Puerto Rico:1993
Moises Quintero	Cuba:1953 (a)
José (Cheo) Ramos	Cuba:1986 (b)
Jackie Robinson	US:1962
Antonio (El Pollo) Rodríguez	Cuba:1997 (b)
Héctor Antonio Rodríguez	Cuba:1974 (b)
José (Joseíto) Rodríguez	Cuba:1951 (a)
Oscar Rodríguez	Cuba:1961 (a), Mexico:1993
Wilber (Bullet) Rogan	US:1998 (b)
Julio Rojo	Cuba:1984 (b)
Tomás (Italiano) Romañach	Cuba:1948 (a)
Basilio (Brujo) Rosell	Cuba:1985 (b), Mexico:1979
Carlos (Bebe) Royer	Cuba:1939 (a)
Lázaro Salazar	Cuba:1958 (a), Mexico:1964
Gonzalo Sánchez	Cuba:1949 (a)
Carlos Manuel Santiago	Puerto Rico:1993
José Guillermo Santiago	Puerto Rico:1993
Louis Santop	US:2006 (c)
George Scales	Puerto Rico:1993

Hilton Smith	US:2001 (b)
Miguel Solís	Mexico:1998
Norman (Turkey) Stearnes	US:2006 (c)
George (Mule) Suttles	US:2006 (c)
Ben Taylor	US:2006 (c)
Hank (Ametralladora) Thompson	Cuba:2007 (b)
Robert (El Mucaro) Thurman	Puerto Rico:1991 & 2014
Luis Tiant, Sr.	Cuba:1965 (b)
Cristóbal Torriente	US:2006 (c), Cuba:1939 (a)
Rogelio Valdés	Cuba:1946 (a)
Juan Esteban (Tetelo) Vargas	Cuba:1998 (b), Puerto Rico:1992
Manuel (Roberto) Villa	Cuba:1949 (a)
Luis (King Kong) Villodas	Puerto Rico:1993
Juan Violá	Cuba:1953 (a)
Willie (Devil) Wells	US:1997 (b), Cuba: 2007 (b)
Sol White	US:2006 (c)
Smokey Joe Williams	US:1999 (b), Cuba:2007 (b)
Artie Wilson	Cuba:2007 (b), Puerto Rico:1993
Jud Wilson	US:2006 (c), Cuba: 2007 (b)
J.L. Wilkinson	US:2006 (c)
Burnis (Wild Bill) Wright	Mexico:1982

(A) National Baseball Hall of Fame and Museum and Museum, Cooperstown, NY

   (a) Elected by the Veterans Committee

   (b) Elected by a special Negro Leagues Committee; the original committee members included Roy Campanella, Monte Irvin, Judy Johnson, Eppy Barnes, Bill Yancey, Frank Forbes, Eddie Gottlieb, Alex Pompez and writers Sam Lacy and Wendell Smith

   (c) Elected by the Negro Leagues Researchers and Authors Group (NLRAG); the original committee members included Todd Bolton, Greg Bond, Dick Clark, Ray Doswell, Leslie Heaphy, Larry Hogan, Larry Lester, Sammy Miller, Jim Overmyer, Rob Ruck and recently deceased Robert Peterson. Former Commissioner Fay Vincent served as non-voting Chairman.

(B) Cuban Baseball Hall of Fames

   (a) Salón de la Fama del Béisbol Cubano (1939 to 1961, 2014)

   (b) Federación de Peloteros Profesionales Cubanos en el Exilio (1962-1986, 1997-98, 2007)

(C) Mexican Professional Baseball Hall of Fame (1939, 1964, 1971, 1973-74, 1976-2011)

(D) Salón de la Fama del Béisbol Profesional de Puerto Rico (1991-93, 1996)

Negro Leaguers in the Naismith Memorial Basketball Hall of Fame

The Naismith Memorial Basketball Hall of Fame in Canton, Ohio, has inducted six men with connections to Negro League Baseball:
1971 - Abe Saperstein
1972 - Eddie Gottlieb
2011 - Reece "Goose" Tatum
2014 - Nat "Sweetwater" Clifton
2016 - Cumberland Posey
2017 - Zack Clayton

National Baseball Hall of Famers who played in both the Negro Leagues and the Major Leagues

A natural All-Star at each of the nine positions.
- Satchel Paige - p
- Roy Campanella - c
- Jackie Robinson - 1b
- Larry Doby - 2b
- Monte Irvin - 3b
- Ernie Banks - ss
- Willard Brown - of
- Hank Aaron - of
- Willie Mays – of

The Timeline of Negro League players Selected to the Hall of Fame.

On June 10, 1971, the National Baseball Hall of Fame and Museum, adopted by a resolution from its Board of Directors to establish a special selection committee for Negro League players. Below is the resolution verbatim.

Official Rules for Election by Hall of Fame Committee on Negro Leagues

The Committee shall serve until it shall dissolve itself of its own motion or until further notice from the Board of Directors of the National Baseball Hall of Fame and Museum, Inc.

Duties: The Committee shall consider all eligible candidates and shall annually conduct an election among its members for election to the Baseball Hall of Fame and Museum. It shall have such further duties as may be assigned to it from time to time by the Board of Directors of the National Baseball Hall of Fame and Museum, Inc.

Eligible Candidates – Candidates to be eligible must be selected from players:
a) who played at least 10 years in the Negro Baseball Leagues prior to 1946; or
b) whose service in the Negro Baseball Leagues prior to 1946 and in the Major Leagues thereafter aggregates at least 10 years; and
c) who are not otherwise eligible for election to the Hall of Fame.

Voting – The affirmative vote of at least 75 percent of the members, or such higher percentage as the Committee may determine, of the Committee shall be necessary for election of a candidate to membership in the National Baseball Hall of Fame. Elections may be by mail with signed copies of the ballots being filed with the Secretary of the Committee.

Negro Leagues Book #2: The Players

No automatic selection based on performances, such as batting average of .400 or more for one year, pitching a perfect game or similar outstanding achievements, shall be permitted.

The original nine members were former Major Leaguer Everett "Eppy" Duane Barnes, executives Eddie Gottlieb and Alex Pompez, former players Roy Campanella, Monte Irvin, Frank Forbes, William Julius "Judy" Johnson along with writers Sam Lacy and Wendell Smith. Leroy "Satchel" Paige was the first selection and formally inducted into the Hall of Fame on August 9, 1971.

Over the years, the committee would elect an all-star at each position before disbanding:
- 1971, Satchel Paige (p)
- 1972, Josh Gibson (c) and Walter "Buck" Leonard (1b)
- 1973, Monte Irvin (of)
- 1974, James "Cool Papa" Bell (of)
- 1975, Judy Johnson (3b)
- 1976, Oscar Charleston (of)
- 1977, Martín Dihigo (2b) and John Henry "Pop" Lloyd (ss)

In 1979, the special committee was absorbed by the Veterans' Committee with Campanella joining the Vets in 1978, John "Buck" O'Neil in 1981, and later Irvin in 1983. In effect, the Negro Leaguers were added to the melting pot of Major League veterans, managers, executives and umpires, of which only one selection made each year.

This Veterans' Committee selected the following Negro leaguers:
- 1981, Andrew "Rube" Foster
- 1987, Ray Dandridge

In 1995, the Veterans' Committee began a five-year plan to provide an extra slot to elect a Negro Leaguer, which was eventually extended two more years.
- 1995, Leon Day
- 1996, Willie Foster
- 1997, Willie Wells
- 1998, Wilber "Bullet" Rogan
- 1999, "Smokey" Joe Williams
- 2000, Norman "Turkey" Stearnes
- 2001, Hilton Smith

On July 26, 2005, per its press release, the National Baseball Hall of Fame approved to hold a special election of Negro Leagues and pre-Negro Leagues candidates. The announcement came on the near completion of a landmark study (2001-2005) about the history African Americans in baseball, from 1860 to 1960. Based on the study, the Board of Directors felt it was time to hold a special election. A five-member screening committee was named: Adrian Burgos, Dick Clark, Lawrence Hogan, Larry Lester and Jim Overmyer. The screening committee selected 39 candidates from a pool of 94 nominees.

On February 25-27, 2006, a 12-member voting committee gathered, under security, at the Grand Hyatt in Tampa, Florida. The committee consisting of scholars, authors and historians included: Todd Bolton, Greg Bond, Adrian Burgos, Dick Clark, Ray Doswell, Leslie Heaphy, Lawrence Hogan, Larry Lester, Sammy Miller, Jim Overmyer, Rob Ruck and Robert Peterson, who mailed in his ballot, due to illness. Former Major League Baseball Commissioner Fay Vincent served as the non-voting Chairman of the committee.

After three days of discussions, a record 17 players, managers and executives were selected to the National Baseball Hall of Fame. They were official inducted in Cooperstown, New York, on July 30, 2006.

Hall of Fame Inductees

2006, Ray Brown, Willard Brown, Andy Cooper, Frank Grant, Pete Hill, Biz Mackey, Effa Manley, José Méndez, Alex Pompez, Cum Posey, Louis Santop, Mule Suttles, Ben Taylor, Cristóbal Torriente, Sol White, J.L. Wilkinson and Jud Wilson.

Please note, other Negro League veterans such as Hank Aaron, Ernie Banks, Roy Campanella, Larry Doby, Willie Mays and Jackie Robinson were inducted into the National Baseball Hall of Fame as Major League players, not as Negro Leaguers.

Negro Leagues Book #2: The Players

List of National Baseball Hall of Famers by cities

Teams listed under Cuba had no home fields and were basically traveling teams.

CITY/STATE	TEAM	PLAYER
Adrian, MI	Page Fence Giants	White, Sol
Atlantic City, NJ	Bacharach Giants	Campanella, Roy
		Gómez, Rafael "Sijo"
		Lloyd, Pop
		Parpetti, Agustin
		Rojo, Julio "Clown"
		Suttles, Mule
		Taylor, Ben
		Williams, Smokey Joe
Baltimore, MD	Baltimore Black Sox	Day, Leon
		Dihigo, Martín
		Hill, Pete
		Paige, Satchel
		Rojo, Julio "Clown"
		Suttles, Mule
		Taylor, Ben
		Wilson, Jud
	Baltimore Elite Giants	Campanella, Roy
		Day, Leon
		Mackey, Biz
		Marquez, Luis
		Scales, George
		Villodas, Luis
		Wells, Willie
		Wright, Wild Bill
	Baltimore Stars	Taylor, Ben
Bellaire, OH	Bellaire Globes	White, Sol
Birmingham, AL	Birmingham Black Barons	Foster, Willie
		Jiménez, Bienvenido "Hooks"
		Mays, Willie
		Montalvo, Esteban
		Padrón, Luis
		Paige, Satchel
		Perry, Alonzo
		Rosell, Basilio
		Scales, George
		Suttles, Mule
		Wells, Willie
		Wilson, Artie
	Birmingham Giants	Taylor, Ben
Boston, MA	Boston Giants	White, Sol

Hall of Fame Inductees

Brooklyn, NY	Brooklyn Eagles	Taylor, Ben
	Brooklyn Brown Dodgers	Charleston, Oscar
	Brooklyn Eagles	Day, Leon
		Manley, Effa
		Taylor, Ben
	Brooklyn Royal Giants	Bustamente, Luis
		Figarola, José Rafael
		Leonard, Buck
		Lloyd, Pop
		Padrón, Luis
		Santop, Louis
		White, Sol
		Williams, Smokey Joe
Buffalo, NY	Buffalo (INT)	Grant, Frank
Chicago, IL	Chicago American Giants	Bell, Cool Papa
		Charleston, Oscar
		Cooper, Andy
		Fernández, José Maria "Cuso"
		Foster, Rube
		Foster, Willie
		Hill, Pete
		Lloyd, Pop
		Méndez, Jose
		Ortiz, Rafaelito
		Paige, Satchel
		Santop, Louis
		Stearnes, Turkey
		Suttles, Mule
		Taylor, Ben
		Torriente, Cristóbal
		Wells, Willie
		Williams, Smokey Joe
	Chicago Giants	Williams, Smokey Joe
	Chicago Union Giants	Foster, Rube
	Leland Giants	Foster, Rube
		Hill, Pete
		Lloyd, Pop
		Williams, Smokey Joe
Cincinnati, OH	Cincinnati Cubans	Baro, Bernardo
		Dreke, Valentin
		Herrera, Ramon "Mike"
		Jiménez, Bienvenido "Hooks"
		Jiménez, Eugenio
		Molina, Agustin "Tinti"
Cleveland, OH	Cleveland Browns	White, Sol
	Cleveland Buckeyes	Canizares, Avelino

Negro Leagues Book #2: The Players

	Cleveland Cubs	Paige, Satchel
		Torriente, Cristóbal
Columbus, OH	Columbus Buckeyes	Lloyd, Pop
	Columbus Elite Giants	Wright, Wild Bill
Cuba	All Cubans	Almeida, Rafael
		Bustamente, Luis
		Cabrera, Alfredo (Pajaro)
		Castillo, Julian
		Chacon, Pelayo
		Fabre, Isidro "Papi"
		Fernández, José Maria "Cuso"
		Figarola, José Rafael
		García, Antonio Maria
		García, Regino (Mamelo)
		Hidalgo, Heliodoro "Jabuco"
		Marsans, Armando
		Mesa, Pablo "Champion"
		Molina, Agustin "Tinti"
		Muñoz, Jose
		Oms, Alejandro "Walla Walla"
		Padrón, Luis
		Palomino, Emilio
		Pedroso, Eustaquio (Bombin)
		Ramos, Jose
		Sánchez, Gonzalo
		Valdes, Rogelio
		Viola, Juan
	Ansonia Cuban Giants	Grant, Frank
		White, Sol
	Columbia Giants	White, Sol
	Cuban Giants	Grant, Frank
		Molina, Agustin "Tinti"
		White, Sol
	Cuban Stars West	Arango, Pedro
		Baro, Bernardo
		Chacon, Pelayo
		Correa, Marcelino
		Díaz, Yoyo
		Dibut, Pedro
		Dreke, Valentin
		Fabre, Isidro "Papi"
		Fernández, José Maria "Cuso"
		Fernández, Rodolfo "Rudy"
		García, Manuel (Cocaina)
		González, Gervasio "Strike"
		Herrera, Ramon "Mike"

Hall of Fame Inductees

	Jiménez, Bienvenido "Hooks"
	Jiménez, Eugenio
	López, Cando
	López, Vidal
	Méndez, Jose
	Molina, Agustin "Tinti"
	Montalvo, Esteban
	Oms, Alejandro "Walla Walla"
	Pedroso, Eustaquio (Bombin)
	Rosell, Basilio
	Salazar, Lazaro
	Tiant, Sr., Luis
	Torriente, Cristóbal
	Vargas, Tetelo
Cuban Stars East	Arango, Pedro
	Baro, Bernardo
	Bejerano, Agustín (Pijini)
	Bragana, Ramon
	Chacon, Pelayo
	Correa, Marcelino
	Crespo, Alejandro "Filete"
	Díaz, Yoyo
	Dihigo, Martín
	Fabre, Isidro "Papi"
	Fernández, José Maria "Cuso"
	Fernández, Rodolfo "Rudy"
	García, Manuel (Cocaina)
	Gómez, Rafael "Sijo"
	Herrera, Ramon "Mike"
	Jiménez, Bienvenido "Hooks"
	Jiménez, Eugenio
	López, Cando
	López, Vidal
	Marsans, Armando
	Mesa, Pablo "Champion"
	Montalvo, Esteban
	Navarro, Emilio
	Oms, Alejandro "Walla Walla"
	Padrón, Luis
	Pedroso, Eustaquio (Bombin)
	Pompez, Alex
	Portuondo, Bartolome
	Ramos, Jose
	Rojo, Julio "Clown"
	Romanach, Tomás
	Rosell, Basilio

	Salazar, Lazaro
	San, Pedro "Eli"
	Torriente, Cristóbal
	Vargas, Tetelo
Cuban Stars of Havana	Almeida, Rafael
	Chacon, Pelayo
	Crespo, Alejandro "Filete"
	Dreke, Valentin
	Fernández, José Maria "Cuso"
	Figarola, José Rafael
	González, Valentin
	González, Gervasio "Strike"
	Jiménez, Bienvenido "Hooks"
	Muñoz, Jose
	Padrón, Luis
	Parpetti, Agustin
	Pedroso, Eustaquio (Bombin)
	Rojo, Julio "Clown"
	Torriente, Cristóbal
Cuban X-Giants	Foster, Rube
	García, Antonio Maria
	Grant, Frank
	Hill, Pete
	Lloyd, Pop
	Muñoz, Jose
	Palomino, Emilio
	Valdes, Rogelio
	White, Sol
Genuine Cuban Giants	García, Antonio Maria
	Grant, Frank
	White, Sol
Havana Cuban Stars	Bustamente, Luis
	Chacon, Pelayo
Havana Red Sox	Rodriguez, Oscar "Joe"
	Tiant, Sr., Luis
Long Branch (NJ) Cubans	Acostca, Jose
	Calvo, Jacinto
	González, Valentin
	González, Gervasio "Strike"
	González, Miguel "Mike"
	Luque, Dolf
	Muñoz, Jose
	Padrón, Luis
	Romanach, Tomás
	Viola, Juan
Stars of Cuba	Arango, Pedro

Hall of Fame Inductees

		Bragana, Ramon
		Cabanas, Armando
		Chacon, Pelayo
		Figarola, José Rafael
		García, Manuel (Cocaina)
		Hidalgo, Heliodoro "Jabuco"
		Méndez, Jose
		Muñoz, Jose
		Navarro, Emilio
Dayton, OH	Dayton Marcos	Brown, Ray
Detroit, MI	Detroit Black Sox	Stearnes, Turkey
	Detroit Senators	Bell, Cool Papa
	Detroit Stars	Cooper, Andy
		Dandridge, Ray
		Hill, Pete
		Méndez, Jose
		Stearnes, Turkey
		Torriente, Cristóbal
	Detroit Wolves	Bell, Cool Papa
		Brown, Ray
		Suttles, Mule
		Wells, Willie
		Williams, Smokey Joe
		Posey, Cum
Fort Wayne, IN	Fort Wayne (IN)	White, Sol
French Lick Township, IN	West Baden Sprudels	Taylor, Ben
Harrisburg, PA	Harrisburg Ponies	Grant, Frank
	Harrisburg Giants	Charleston, Oscar
		Taylor, Ben
	Harrisburg Gorhams	Grant, Frank
		White, Sol
Indianapolis, IN	Indianapolis ABCs	Brown, Ray
		Charleston, Oscar
		Mackey, Biz
		Padrón, Luis
		Taylor, Ben
	Indianapolis Clowns	Aaron, Hank
		Casanova, Paul
		Charleston, Oscar
		Guilbe, Juan
		Quinones, Tomás
		Wells, Willie
	Indianapolis Crawfords	Charleston, Oscar
Kansas City, MO	Kansas City Monarchs	Banks, Ernie
		Baro, Bernardo
		Bell, Cool Papa

		Brown, Willard
		Cooper, Andy
		Foster, Willie
		Herrera, Pancho
		Lloyd, Pop
		Méndez, Jose
		Paige, Satchel
		Parpetti, Agustin
		Portuondo, Bartolome
		Robinson, Jackie
		Rogan, Bullet
		Smith, Hilton
		Stearnes, Turkey
		Thurman, Bob
		Torriente, Cristóbal
		Wells, Willie
		Wilkinson, J.L.
Louisville, KY	Louisville White Sox	Foster, Rube
Memphis, TN	Memphis Red Sox	Bell, Cool Papa
		Formental, Pedro
		Foster, Willie
		Paige, Satchel
		Wells, Willie
Milwaukee, WI	Milwaukee Bears	Hill, Pete
Nashville, TN	Nashville Elite Giants	Dandridge, Ray
		Mackey, Biz
		Stearnes, Turkey
		Wright, Wild Bill
New York, NY	Lincoln Giants	Bejerano, Agustín (Pijini)
		Charleston, Oscar
		Lloyd, Pop
		Montalvo, Esteban
		Rojo, Julio "Clown"
		Santop, Louis
		Scales, George
		Stearnes, Turkey
		Suttles, Mule
		Taylor, Ben
		White, Sol
		Williams, Smokey Joe
	Lincoln Stars	Charleston, Oscar
		Lloyd, Pop
		Padrón, Luis
		Santop, Louis
	New York Black Yankees	Fernández, Rodolfo "Rudy"
		Lloyd, Pop

Hall of Fame Inductees

	Marquez, Luis
	Paige, Satchel
	Suttles, Mule
	Wells, Willie
	Wilson, Artie
New York Cuban Stars	Baro, Bernardo
	Bustamente, Luis
	Castillo, Julian
	Chacon, Pelayo
	Fabre, Isidro "Papi"
	Fernández, José Maria "Cuso"
	Figarola, José Rafael
	García, Antonio Maria
	González, Miguel "Mike"
	Guerra, Marcelino
	Hidalgo, Heliodoro "Jabuco"
	López, Cando
	Luque, Dolf
	Méndez, Jose
	Mesa, Pablo "Champion"
	Moran, Carlos
	Muñoz, Jose
	Palomino, Emilio
	Parpetti, Agustin
	Portuondo, Bartolome
	Rodriguez, Antonio "El Pollo"
	Rojo, Julio "Clown"
	Torriente, Cristóbal
New York Cubans	Amaro, Santos
	Amoros, Sandy
	Arango, Pedro
	Ariosa, Homero
	Baez, Andres Julio
	Blanco, Carlos
	Blanco, Heberto
	Bragana, Ramon
	Cabrera, Lorenzo (Chiquitin)
	Coimbre, Pancho
	Correa, Marcelino
	Crespo, Alejandro "Home Run"
	Dandridge, Ray
	Díaz, Yoyo
	Dihigo, Martín
	Donoso, Lino
	Duany, Claro
	Fabre, Isidro "Papi"

		Fernández, José Maria "Cuso"
		Fernández, Rodolfo "Rudy"
		García, Manuel (Cocaina)
		García, Silvio
		González, Hiram Rene
		Guilbe, Juan
		Heredia, Ramon "Napoleon"
		Lantiqua, Enrique "Carlos"
		López, Cando
		Miñoso, Minnie
		Noble, Ray
		Oms, Alejandro "Walla Walla"
		Pages, Pedro
		Pompez, Alex
		Rodriguez, Antonio "El Pollo"
		Rodriguez, Héctor
		Rojo, Julio "Clown"
		Rosell, Basilio
		Salazar, Lazaro
		Santiago, Carlos
		Santiago, Jose
		Taylor, Ben
		Tiant, Sr., Luis
		Torriente, Cristóbal
		Vargas, Tetelo
	New York Gorhams	Grant, Frank
		White, Sol
Newark, NJ	Newark Dodgers	Dandridge, Ray
		Mackey, Biz
	Newark Eagles	Dandridge, Ray
		Day, Leon
		Doby, Larry
		Irvin, Monte
		Mackey, Biz
		Manley, Effa
		Suttles, Mule
		Wells, Willie
	Newark Stars	Scales, George
		White, Sol
Philadelphia, PA	Hilldale Club	Charleston, Oscar
		Dihigo, Martín
		Johnson, William "Judy"
		Lloyd, Pop
		Santop, Louis
		Taylor, Ben
		Williams, Smokey Joe

Hall of Fame Inductees

	Hilldales (USL)	Charleston, Oscar
	Philadelphia Giants	Foster, Rube
		Grant, Frank
		Hill, Pete
		Jiménez, Eugenio
		Lloyd, Pop
		Santop, Louis
		White, Sol
	Philadelphia Gorhams	White, Sol
	Philadelphia Quaker Giants	White, Sol
	Philadelphia Royal Giants	Hill, Pete
	Philadelphia Stars	Bragana, Ramon
		Campanella, Roy
		Charleston, Oscar
		Mackey, Biz
		Paige, Satchel
		Scales, George
		Stearnes, Turkey
		Wilson, Jud
		Wright, Wild Bill
Pittsburgh, PA	Homestead Grays	Bell, Cool Papa
		Brown, Ray
		Charleston, Oscar
		Dihigo, Martín
		Foster, Willie
		Gibson, Josh
		Johnson, William "Judy"
		Leonard, Buck
		Mackey, Biz
		Marquez, Luis
		Perry, Alonzo
		Scales, George
		Thurman, Bob
		Wells, Willie
		Williams, Smokey Joe
		Wilson, Jud
		Posey, Cum
	Pittsburgh Crawfords	Bell, Cool Papa
		Charleston, Oscar
		Foster, Willie
		Gibson, Josh
		Johnson, William "Judy"
		Paige, Satchel
		Wilson, Jud
	Pittsburgh Keystones	Scales, George
		White, Sol

Negro Leagues Book #2: The Players

San Antonio, TX	San Antonio Broncos	Williams, Smokey Joe
St. Louis, MO	St. Louis Giants	Charleston, Oscar
		Scales, George
		Taylor, Ben
		Wells, Willie
	St. Louis Stars	Bell, Cool Papa
		Cooper, Andy
		Paige, Satchel
		Pinkston, Al
		Scales, George
		Suttles, Mule
		Wells, Willie
Toledo, OH	Toledo Crawfords	Charleston, Oscar
	Toledo Rays	Stearnes, Turkey
Trenton, NJ	Trenton Cuban Giants	Grant, Frank
Washington DC	Washington Black Senators	Taylor, Ben
	Washington Capital Citys	White, Sol
	Washington Elite Giants	Campanella, Roy
		Mackey, Biz
		Wright, Wild Bill
	Washington Pilots	Suttles, Mule
		Taylor, Ben
	Washington Potomacs	Taylor, Ben
	Washington Royal Giants	Taylor, Ben
Wheeling, WV	Wheeling Green Stockings	White, Sol
York, PA	Colored Monarchs	White, Sol

List of Cooperstown Hall of Famers by Teams

All Cubans
1908 José Méndez

All Havanas
1908 José Méndez

All Nations
1912-14, 1916-17, 1922 José Méndez
1917, 1922 Wilber "Bullet: Rogan
1916-17 Cristóbal Torriente
1916 J.L. Wilkinson

Almendares Blues
1913 José Méndez
1913 Cristóbal Torriente

Ansonia Cuban Giants
1891 Frank Grant
1891 Sol White

Bacharach (AC) Giants
1920, 1927 Oscar Charleston
1919, 1924-25 John Henry "Pop" Lloyd
1920 Louis Santop
1921 George "Mule" Suttles
1919, 1929 Ben Taylor
1921 Cristóbal Torriente
1919 Smokey Joe Williams

Bacharach (NY) Giants
1922 John Henry "Pop" Lloyd

Bacharach (Phila) Giants
1932 John Henry "Pop" Lloyd

Baltimore Black Sox
1927-28, 1931 Oscar Charleston
1934 Leon Day
1931 Martín Dihigo
1924-25 Pete Hill
1928, 1930 Raleigh "Biz" Mackey
1930 Robert "Satchel" Paige
1930, 1932 George "Mule" Suttles
1926-28 Ben Taylor
1922-31 Jud "Boojum" Wilson

Baltimore Elite Giants
1938-42, 1944-45 Roy Campanella
1938-39 Raleigh "Biz" Mackey
1946 Willie "The Devil" Wells

Baltimore Stars
1933 Walter "Buck" Leonard
1933 Ben Taylor

Birmingham Black Barons
1925 Willie Foster
1948 Willie Mays
1927-1930 Leroy "Satchel" Paige
1923-25 George "Mule" Suttles
1941 Willie "The Devil" Wells

Bowser's ABCs
1916 Oscar Charleston

Breakers Hotel – FL
1923 Judy Johnson
1921 John Henry "Pop" Lloyd
1916-18 Louis Santop
1913 Ben Taylor
1916-18 Smokey Joe Williams

Bright's Cuban Giants
1892-98, 1900, 1904 Frank Grant
1893-94, 1896, 1898 Sol White

Brooklyn Eagles
1935 Leon Day

Brooklyn Royal Giants
1918-20 John Henry "Pop" Lloyd
1915-19 Louis Santop
1924 Smokey Joe Williams

Chattanooga Black Lookouts
1926 Leroy "Satchel" Paige

Chattanooga Choo Choos
1948 Willie Mays

Chicago American Giants
1929, 1942 James "Cool Papa" Bell
1918-19, 1923, 1930 Oscar Charleston
1923-30, 1932-1935, 1937 Willie Foster
1911-17 Andrew "Rube" Foster
1911-18 Pete Hill
1911, 1914-17 John Henry "Pop" Lloyd

1918 José Méndez
1930, 1944 Leroy "Satchel" Paige
1915 Louis Santop
1932-34, 1935, 1937-38 Norman "Turkey" Stearnes
1929, 1933-35 George "Mule" Suttles
1913-14 Ben Taylor
1918-25 Cristóbal Torriente
1929, 1933-35 Willie "The Devil" Wells
1915-16 Smokey Joe Williams

Chicago Columbia Giants
1900 Frank Grant
1900 Sol White

Chicago Giants
1910-11 Smokey Joe Williams

Chicago Leland Giants
1907-10 Andrew "Rube" Foster
1908-10 Pete Hill
1910 John Henry "Pop" Lloyd

Chicago Union Giants
1902 Andrew "Rube" Foster

Cincinnati-Indianapolis Clowns
1947 Willie "The Devil" Wells

Cleveland Cubs
1931 Leroy "Satchel" Paige

Colored All Stars
1928 Judy Johnson

Columbus Buckeyes
1921 John Henry "Pop" Lloyd

Cuban Stars
1906, 1909, 1911-12 José Méndez
1913-16 Cristóbal Torriente

Cuban Stars East
1923-27, 1930 Martín Dihigo

Cuban Stars of Havana
1916 Cristóbal Torriente

Cuban Stars West
1918 Cristóbal Torriente

Detroit Stars
1919 Oscar Charleston
1920—28, 1930 Cooper, Andy
1933 Dandridge, Ray
1919-21 Pete Hill
1919 José Méndez
1923-31, 1937 Norman "Turkey" Stearnes
1920, 1927-28 Cristóbal Torriente

Detroit Wolves
1932 James "Cool Papa" Bell
1932 Ray Brown
1932 George "Mule" Suttles
1932 Willie "The Devil" Wells
1932 Smokey Joe Williams

Foster's Cleveland Cubs
1932 Cristóbal Torriente

Gilkerson's Union Giants
1929-31 Cristóbal Torriente

Harrisburg Giants
1924-27 Oscar Charleston
1925 Ben Taylor

Havana Red Sox
1923 John Henry "Pop" Lloyd

Hilldale Club
1926, 1928-29 Oscar Charleston
1929, 1930 Martín Dihigo
1918, 1921-29, 1932 Judy Johnson
1923 John Henry "Pop" Lloyd
1923-30 Raleigh "Biz" Mackey
1917-26 Louis Santop
1919 Ben Taylor
1917 Smokey Joe Williams

Homestead Grays
1932, 1943-46 James "Cool Papa" Bell
1932-45 Ray Brown
1929-1932 Oscar Charleston
1937 Ray Dandridge
1937, 1942 Leon Day,
1927-28 Martín Dihigo
1931 Willie Foster
1930-32, 1934, 1937-40, 1942-46 Josh Gibson
1929, 1930, 1932 Judy Johnson
1934-1948 Walter "Buck" Leonard
1927 Raleigh "Biz" Mackey

1942 Leroy "Satchel" Paige
1913 Cum Posey
1932, 1937 Willie "The Devil" Wells
1925-32, 1934 Smokey Joe Williams
1931-32, 1940-45 Jud "Boojum" Wilson

Indianapolis ABCs
1931 Ray Brown
1915-18, 1920, 1922-23 Oscar Charleston
1914 John Henry "Pop" Lloyd
1920-22 Raleigh "Biz" Mackey
1914-18, 1920-22 Ben Taylor

Indianapolis Crawfords
1940 Oscar Charleston,

Kansas City Monarchs
1953 Ernie Banks
1932 James "Cool Papa" Bell
1935-44, 1946-49 Willard Brown
1928-29, 1931, 1933-39 Andy Cooper
1931 Willie Foster
1921 John Henry "Pop" Lloyd
1920-26 José Méndez
1935, 1939-47 Leroy "Satchel" Paige
1945 Jackie Robinson
1920-1938 Wilber "Bullet" Rogan
1937-1948 Hilton Smith
1930-31, 1934, 1938-40 Norman "Turkey" Stearnes
1926 Cristóbal Torriente
1932 Willie "The Devil" Wells

Kansas City Royals
1948 James "Cool Papa" Bell
1948 Leroy "Satchel" Paige
1948 Hilton Smith

Knoxville Giants
1920 Norman "Turkey" Stearnes

Lamar's Cuban X Giants
1903, 1905 Rube Foster
1898-99 Frank Grant
1905 Pete Hill
1906 John Henry "Pop" Lloyd
1896-99, 1901, 1903 Sol White

Los Angeles White Sox
1917, 1921 Wilber "Bullet" Rogan

Louisville White Sox
1914 Rube Foster

Memphis Red Sox
1923-24 Willie Foster
1943 Leroy "Satchel" Paige
1945, 1948 Willie "The Devil" Wells

Milwaukee Bears
1923 Pete Hill

Monroe Monarchs
1934 Willard Brown
1932, 1934 Hilton Smith

Montgomery Grey Sox
1921 Norman "Turkey" Stearnes

Nashville Elite Giants
1933 Ray Dandridge

Nashville White Sox
1920 Norman "Turkey" Stearnes

New York Black Yankees
1941 Leroy "Satchel" Paige
1941 George "Mule" Suttles
1945-46 Willie "The Devil" Wells

New York Colored Giants
1921 Wilber "Bullet" Rogan

New York Cubans
1935-36, 1945 Martín Dihigo
1936 Jud "Boojum" Wilson

New York Gorhams
1891 Frank Grant
1889, 1891-92 Sol White

New York Harlem Stars
1931 John Henry "Pop" Lloyd

New York Lincoln Giants
1911-14, 1918-19, 1926-30 John Henry "Pop" Lloyd
1911-14, 1916-17 Louis Santop
1930 Norman "Turkey" Stearnes
1912 Ben Taylor
1912-23, 1925 Smokey Joe Williams
1927 Jud "Boojum" Wilson

New York Lincoln Stars
- 1916 Oscar Charleston
- 1915 John Henry "Pop" Lloyd
- 1915-16 Louis Santop

Newark Dodgers
- 1934-35 Ray Dandridge

Newark Eagles
- 1936-38, 1942, 1944 Ray Dandridge
- 1936-39, 1941-43, 1946 Leon Day
- 1942-44, 1946-47 Larry Doby
- 1938-42, 1945-48 Monte Irvin
- 1939-41, 1945-47 Raleigh "Biz" Mackey
- 1936-40, 1942-44 George "Mule" Suttles
- 1936-39, 1942, 1945 Willie "The Devil" Wells

Otsego Michigan
- 1902 Rube Foster

Page Fence (Adrian, MI) Giants
- 1895 Sol White

Philadelphia Giants
- 1904-06 Rube Foster
- 1902-03 Frank Grant
- 1904-07 Pete Hill
- 1907-09, 1918 John Henry "Pop" Lloyd
- 1911 Louis Santop
- 1902-07 Sol White

Philadelphia Hilldale Daisies
- 1931 Martín Dihigo
- 1931 Judy Johnson
- 1931 Raleigh "Biz" Mackey

Philadelphia Quaker City Giants
- 1906 Rube Foster

Philadelphia Stars
- 1944 Roy Campanella
- 1941 Oscar Charleston
- 1943 Leon Day
- 1933-35, 1937 Raleigh "Biz" Mackey
- 1936 Norman "Turkey" Stearnes
- 1933-39 Jud "Boojum" Wilson

Pittsburgh Crawfords
- 1932-37 James "Cool Papa" Bell
- 1932-38 Oscar Charleston
- 1936 Willie Foster
- 1930, 1932-36 Josh Gibson
- 1932-36 Judy Johnson
- 1931-34, 1936 Leroy "Satchel" Paige
- 1932 Jud "Boojum" Wilson

Pittsburg[h] Keystones
- 1887 Sol White

Pittsburg[h] Stars of Buffalo
- 1919 Smokey Joe Williams

Royal Poinciana - FL
- 1917 Oscar Charleston
- 1917-18 Pete Hill
- 1917 John Henry "Pop" Lloyd
- 1916 Ben Taylor
- 1927 Smokey Joe Williams

San Antonio Black Broncos
- 1909 Smokey Joe Williams

St. Louis Giants
- 1920-21 Oscar Charleston
- 1920 Raleigh "Biz" Mackey
- 1911 Ben Taylor
- 1924 Willie "The Devil" Wells
- 1922-31 James "Cool Papa" Bell
- 1922 Oscar Charleston
- 1926-31 George "Mule" Suttles
- 1924-31 Willie "The Devil" Wells

St. Paul Colored Gophers
- 1907-08 Rube Foster

Stars of Cuba
- 1910 José Méndez

Toledo Crawfords
- 1939 Oscar Charleston

Trenton (NJ) Cuban Giants
- 1889 Frank Grant

Waco (TX) Yellow Jackets
- 1899 Rube Foster

Washington Black Senators
- 1938 Willie Foster

Washington Elite Giants
- 1937 Roy Campanella
- 1936-37 Raleigh "Biz" Mackey

Washington Pilots
1932 George "Mule" Suttles

Washington Potomacs
1923-24 Ben Taylor

West Baden (IN) Sprudels
1913 Pete Hill

1910, 1912-13 Ben Taylor

York Colored Monarchs
1886 Sol White

York Cuban Giants
1890 Frank Grant
1890 Sol White

Teams with the Most Negro League Hall of Famers in the National Baseball Hall of Fame in Cooperstown, New York.

1934 Kansas City Monarchs
1. James "Cool Papa" Bell – of
2. Andy Cooper – p
3. Willie Foster – p
4. Wilber "Bullet" Rogan – p
5. Norman "Turkey" Stearnes – of
6. Willie "the Devil" Wells – ss
7. J.L. Wilkinson – owner

1942 Newark Eagles
1. Ray Dandridge – 3b
2. Leon Day – p
3. Larry Doby – 2b
4. Monte Irvin – cf
5. George "Mule" Suttles – 1b
6. Willie "the Devil" Wells – ss
7. Effa Manley – co-owner

Runner-up teams include the **1931 Homestead Grays** with Oscar Charleston (1b), Josh Gibson (c), Jud Wilson (3b) and pitchers Willie Foster and Smokey Joe Williams; and the **1935 Pittsburgh Crawfords** with Cool Papa Bell (cf), Oscar Charleston (1b), Josh Gibson (c), Judy Johnson (3b) and Satchel Paige on the mound.

Shrine of the Eternals with Negro League Connections

The **Baseball Reliquary** is a nonprofit, educational organization dedicated to fostering an appreciation of American art and culture through the context of baseball history and to exploring the national pastime's unparalleled creative possibilities.

The highest honor afforded an individual by the Baseball Reliquary is election to the Shrine of the Eternals. Similar in concept to the National Baseball Hall of Fame, the Shrine of the Eternals differs philosophically in that statistical accomplishment is not the principal criterion for election. It is believed that the election of individuals on merits other than statistics and playing ability will offer the opportunity for a deeper understanding and appreciation of baseball than has heretofore been provided by "Halls of Fame" in the more traditional and conservative institutions.

Following is a list of individuals with Negro League connections, who have been inducted into the Shrine of the Eternals between 1999 and 2020. Year of induction appears to the right of each name.

Rube Foster (2020), executive
Minnie Miñoso (2002), player
Don Newcombe (2016), player
Buck O'Neil (2008), manager
Satchel Paige (2001), player
Jackie Robinson (2005), player
Rachel Robinson (2014), activist
Lester Rodney (2005), writer

APPENDIX F: Family Connections & Crossover Skills

Two-Timers (Before Vincent "Bo" Jackson and Deion "Prime Time" Sanders):

Negro Leaguers and executives who participated in other professional sports.

TOM BAIRD
 Baseball—1938-1954—officer, owner, Kansas City Monarchs; booking agent for Negro American League exhibition games
 Basketball—1954/1958—owner, Harlem Stars

JOE BANKHEAD
 Baseball—1948—p, Birmingham Black Barons
 Basketball—1947/1948—g, Harlem Globetrotters

ERNIE BANKS
 Baseball—1950, 1953—ss, Kansas City Monarchs
 Basketball—1951/1952—f, Harlem Globetrotters

BILL BATTLES
 Baseball—1938-39, 1947-1949—p, ss, Mohawk Giants, Chicago American Giants
 Tennis—1958-1988—United States Tennis Association pro

HARRY BAUCHMAN
 Baseball—1911-1923—2b, 3b, Minneapolis Keystones, All Nations, Chicago American Giants, Chicago Union Giants, Chicago Giants
 Boxing— 1912, Heavyweight, record unknown

VIRGIL BLUEITT
 Baseball—1915-1920, 1937-1949—2b, of, Chicago Union Giants; umpire, NAL
 Basketball—1940s—official, referee for Chicago semi-pro and pro teams.
 Football—1940s, official for Chicago college and semi-pro teams

ELMORE "SCRAPPY, BILL DICK" BROWN
 Baseball—1918-1932—ss, Washington Red Caps, Lincoln Giants, Baltimore Black Sox, Brooklyn Royal Giants, Hilldale Club, Homestead Grays
 Basketball—1926/1927—Baltimore Athenians

WILLIAM "CAP" BROWN
 Baseball—1952-1955—infield, Birmingham Black Barons, Indianapolis Clowns
 Basketball—Coach, Parker High School, Birmingham, AL, 1958-96, 891-259 Won/Lost record

EARNEST BURKE
 Baseball—1946-1948—p, of, 3b, Baltimore Elite Giants
 Tennis—[Years not known]—Professional coach

SOL BUTLER
Baseball—1925—p, Kansas City Monarchs
Football—1923-1926—qb, Hammond Pros, Rock Island Independents, Akron Pros, Canton Bulldogs
Olympian—1920—long jump [broad jump]

ZACHARY M. "SMILEY" CLAYTON - In 1939, he led the New York Rens and the 1943 Washington Bears to a World Basketball Championships. In 1949, Clayton became the first Black man to receive a referee's boxing license from the state of Pennsylvania. Later in 1952, he became the first African American to referee a heavyweight title fight; Ezzard Charles versus Jersey Joe Walcott in their fourth meeting. However, he is best remembered for officiating the "Rumble in the Jungle" bout in Zaire, Africa, between George Foreman and Muhammad Ali. The multi-talented man began his humble baseball career in 1931 with the semi-pro [Louis] Santop's Broncos at the age of 14.

ZACK CLAYTON
Baseball—1932-1944—1b, c, Bacharach Giants, Cole's American Giants, Chicago American Giants, New York Black Yankees, Brooklyn Eagles, Brooklyn Royal Giants.
Basketball—1935/1937, 1939/1946—g, f, Chicago Crusaders, New York Rens, Philadelphia Lumberjacks, 1932/1944 Harlem Globetrotters
Boxing—Referee of several Heavyweight Championship fights, including the 1974 "Rumble in the Jungle," Muhammad Ali vs. George Foreman, and the Jersey Joe Walcott vs. Ezzard Charles championship fight in 1952.
1993 Pennsylvania Sports Hall of Fame
1996 New York City Basketball Hall of Fame
2017 Naismith Memorial National Basketball Hall of Fame

NAT "SWEETWATER" CLIFTON
Baseball—1949, 1958—1b, Chicago American Giants, Detroit Clowns
Basketball—c, 1946/1947 New York Rens, 1947/1950 Harlem Globetrotters, 1950/1957 New York Knicks, 1957/1958 Detroit Pistons, 1961/1962 Chicago Majors (ABL)

GEORGE CROWE
Baseball—1947-1949—1b, New York Cubans, New York Black Yankees
Basketball—c, f, 1946/1949, Los Angeles Red Devils, 1947/1948 New York Rens, 1948/1949 Dayton Rens, 1950/1951 Harlem Globetrotters

PIPER DAVIS
Baseball—1942-1950, 1958-1959—1b, 2b, ss, manager, Birmingham Black Barons
Basketball—g, f, 1942/1943, Bob's Savoy Café, 1943/1946 Harlem Globetrotters

LOU DIALS
Baseball—1925-1936—1b, of, Detroit Stars, Chicago American Giants, Memphis Red Sox, Hilldale Club, Cleveland Giants, Homestead Grays, Akron Tyrites, Birmingham Black Barons, New York Black Yankees
Football—1936-1937—end, New York Brown Bombers

JOSH DEVOE
Baseball—1915-1922—c, Chicago Giants, Pittsburgh Keystones
Baseball umpire—1923-1924, 1934-1941
Golf—1935-79—pro golfer and trainer

TED DIXON
Baseball—1955—of, Detroit Stars
Basketball—1953/1954—g, Harlem Globetrotters

LARRY DOBY
Baseball—1942-1947—2b, Newark Eagles
Basketball—1943/1944, 1947/1948—g, f, Paterson Panthers (ABL), Paterson Crescents, Manhattan Nationals (ABL)

BILL "SHOWBOAT" DUMPSON
Baseball—1950-1952—p, Indianapolis Clowns, Philadelphia Stars, New York Black Yankees
Basketball—1953/1959—f, Harlem Globetrotters, Dumpson's Court Jesters (Long Island, NY)

GEORGE FIALL
Baseball—1918-1929—ss, 3b, Lincoln Giants, Harrisburg Giants, Baltimore Black Sox, Birmingham Black Barons, Penn Red Caps of NY
Basketball—1924/1929—f, New York Rens

CHARLES "BLACK CYCLONE FROM WOOSTER" FOLLIS
Baseball—1908-1909—of, c, Cleveland Giants, Cuban Giants
Football—1902—hb, Shelby Athletic Association

FRANK FORBES
Baseball—1913-1928—ss, Lincoln Stars, Harrisburg Giants, Royal Poinciana, Brooklyn Royal Giants, Penn Red Caps, Bacharach Giants, Chappie Johnson's Stars; 1929-1943—umpire; owner, business manager, New York Cubans; NNL & ANL promoter
Basketball—1917/1918—g, New York Incorporators, 1919/1920—New York Spartan Braves, 1922/23, Forbes' Commonwealth Big Five, 1923/25—New York Rens (a.k.a. Renaissance Big 5)
Boxing—promoter, judge at 1947 Jersey Joe Walcott - Joe Louis fight at Madison Square Garden.
Writer—1938-1948, *Chicago Defender*
Referee/Official— [1938 - ?] —Basketball, Football, Boxing

GREENE FARMER, JR.,
Baseball—1942-1947—of, p, Cincinnati Clowns, New York Cubans, New York Black Yankees, Jacksonville Red Caps, Cincinnati Crescents
Basketball, 1946/1947—g, Kansas City Stars, Harlem Globetrotters

Negro Leagues Book #2: The Players

BILL "HIPPO" GALLOWAY
Baseball—1899-1906, of, 3b, 2b, Cuban X Giants, Cuban Giants
Hockey—1899, Woodstock (Central Ontario Hockey Association)

JOE GANS (born Joseph Gant)
Baseball—1905—captain, 1b, Middle Section Giants of Baltimore
Boxing—1893-1909—World lightweight champion 145-10-16 Won-Lost-Draw

ROBERT GARRETT
Baseball—1951-1952—umpire, Negro National League
Basketball, [Years not known]—Harlem Globetrotters

SAMMY GEE
Baseball—1948, 1955—ss, New York Cubans, Detroit Stars
Basketball—1947/1951, Harlem Globetrotters

OSCAR "GIBBY" GIVENS
Baseball— 1939, 1944-1948—ss, Newark Eagles
Football—1947, qb, Los Angeles Dons pre-season (AAFC)

EDDIE GOTTLIEB
Baseball—1933-1952—co-owner, Philadelphia Stars
Basketball—1947/1949—coach, general manager, Philadelphia Warriors (BAA); 1951/1979—owner, Philadelphia Warriors (NBA)

GUS GREENLEE
Baseball—1931-46—officer, owner, Pittsburgh Crawfords; founder and president, second NNL; founder, United States Baseball League
Football—1938, owner, New York Black Yankees (Independent)

JACK HANNIBAL (born Porter Lee Floyd)
Baseball—1913-1917—of, Bowser's ABCs, Indianapolis ABCs, Louisville White Sox, Jewell's ABCs
Boxing—1911-30, Middleweight champion, 9-5-0 Won/Lost/Draw

HALLEY HARDING
Baseball—1926-1931—ss, 2b, 3b, Indianapolis ABCs, Detroit Stars, Kansas City Monarchs, Chicago Columbia Giants, Bacharach Giants, Baltimore Black Sox
Basketball—1927/1930, Thomas Brookins' Globetrotters; 1931/1932, Savoy Big Five; 1933/1934 Los Angeles Hottentots
Football—1937—rb, New York Brown Bombers, Chicago Black Hawks, tryout with Chicago Cardinals
Writer: 1940s, *New Crusader* (Chicago), *Los Angeles Sentinel, Los Angeles Tribune*

CHUCK HARMON
Baseball—1947—of, Indianapolis Clowns
Basketball—1951/1952, Saratoga Harlem Yankees (ABL)

BILLY HARRELL
Baseball—1951—ss, Birmingham Black Barons
Basketball—1951/1952, Saratoga Harlem Yankees (ABL)

Family Connections & Crossover Skills

DeHART HUBBARD
Baseball—1934-1937, 1942—NNL official, secretary, Cincinnati Tigers, Cleveland-Cincinnati Buckeyes
Track & Field—1924—Olympic Long Jump Gold Medalist, 24' 5".

MONTE IRVIN
Baseball—1937-48—of, ss, 3b, Newark Eagles
Basketball—1938/39—f, Orange (NJ) Triangles

CLARENCE "FAT or FATS" JENKINS
Baseball—1920-1940—of, manager, Lincoln Giants, Harrisburg Giants, Bacharach Giants, Baltimore Black Sox, New York Black Yankees, Philadelphia Stars, Brooklyn Eagles, Brooklyn Royal Giants, Pittsburgh Crawfords, Toledo Crawfords, Penn Red Caps of NY; 1945-1946, Philadelphia Hilldales (USL)
Basketball—1923/1939—g, New York Rens, Washington Bears
Boxing—1920—middleweight, U.S. Olympic trials

WADE "KID" JOHNSTON
Baseball—1919-1934—2b, of, p, Indianapolis ABCs, Cleveland Tate Stars, Kansas City Monarchs, Baltimore Black Sox, Detroit Stars, Penn Red Caps of NY, Padron's Cuban Giants
Boxing—1915-1922—Welterweight, 1-3-0 Won/Lost/Draw

GEORGE "CHAPPIE" JOHNSON, JR.
Baseball— 1896-1939—c, 1b, manager, Columbia Giants, Chicago Union Giants, Brooklyn Royal Giants, Leland Giants, Chicago Giants, St. Louis Giants, Dayton Chappies, Custer's Baseball Club of Columbus, Philadelphia Royal Stars, Norfolk Stars, Algona (IA) Brownies, Adrian (MI) Page Fence Giants, Mohawk (NY) Giants, Philadelphia Giants, Penn Red Caps of NY, Chappie Johnson's Stars, Louisville White Sox, Philadelphia Quaker City Giants, Cuban X-Giants, Dayton Giants, St. Paul Colored Gophers, Bacharach Giants, Twin City Gophers, West Baden (IN) Sprudels, Columbus Giants
Boxing—1908, Heavyweight

JACK JOHNSON born John Arthur Johnson
Baseball—1905—manager, 1b, Johnson's Pets
Boxing—1897-1931, Heavyweight champion, 74-13-10 Won/Lost/Draw

JOHN "TOPEKA JACK" JOHNSON, born John Thomas Johnson
Baseball—1901-1912, 1917—1b, ss, of, manager, Chicago Unions, Chicago Union Giants, Algona Brownies, Topeka (KS) Giants, Minneapolis Keystones, Kansas City (MO) Royal Giants, Kansas City (KS) Giants
Boxing—1905-1925, Heavyweight

COLLINS JONES
Baseball—1942-1947—2b, ss, of, Harrisburg-St. Louis Stars, Cincinnati Ethiopian Clowns (NML), Birmingham Black Barons, Twin City Gophers, Detroit Black Sox, Philadelphia Stars, Harlem Globetrotters, Portland (OR) Rosebuds
Basketball—1946/1947—g, Kansas City Stars

JAMES J. KEENAN
Baseball—1914-1930—owner, business manager, Lincoln Giants; secretary and treasurer of Eastern Colored League
Basketball, promoter, business manager of New York Rens

WILBERT "WILBUR" KING

Baseball—1944-1947—of, 2b, Memphis Red Sox, Cleveland Buckeyes, Chicago American Giants, New York Black Yankees, Detroit Motor City Giants, Detroit Wolves, Monterrey Reds

Basketball—??—Harlem Globetrotters, 1946/1947, Detroit Gems

WILLIAM "DOLLY" KING

Baseball—1941, 1944, 1947—c, rf, New York Black Yankees, Homestead Grays

Basketball—1942/1943, 1945/1946, 1947/1948 New York Rens; 1946/1947, Rochester Royals (NPL); 1948/1949 Dayton Rens

Football—1941— [All years not known]—Long Island (APFA)

WILLIAM LAMPKINS

Baseball—1943—utility, Kansas City Monarchs

Basketball—1940/1941, Washington Bruins (Bears)

SAM LACY

Baseball—1917-1944—Le Droit (DC) Tigers, Hilldale Athletic Club, Bacharach Giants, Washington Black Sox

Basketball—1940/1941—general manager, Washington Bruins (Bears)

JOE "MIDNIGHT EXPRESS" LILLARD

Baseball—1932-1934, 1937, 1946—p, of, c, manager, Cole's American Giants, Chicago American Giants, Cincinnati Tigers, Brooklyn Brown Dodgers

Football—1932-1933—rb, Chicago Cardinals (NFL), 1934 Westwood (PCFL), 1938 Clifton (AA), 1939 Union City Rams (AA), Brooklyn Eagles (AA), 1941 New York (AA), 1936-1938 New York Brown Bombers (Independent)

Basketball—1927/1928—f, Savoy Big Five, 1934/1935—f, Chicago Hottentots

L. D. "GOO GOO" LIVINGSTON

Baseball—1928-1933—of, Kansas City Monarchs, New York Black Yankees, Pittsburgh Crawfords, Penn Red Caps of NY

Football—1936-1937—tackle, New York Brown Bombers

EVERETT "ZIGGY" MARCELL

Baseball—1939-1948—c, Chicago American Giants, Newark Eagles, Baltimore Elite Giants, New York Black Yankees, Kansas City Monarchs, Homestead Grays, Pittsburgh Crawfords (NNL & USL)

Basketball—1946/1947, 1950s—g, Harlem Clowns, Harlem Globetrotters, Bellingham Fircrest (Pacific Coast Professional Basketball League), Los Angeles Red Devils

Football—1944, 1946—Los Angeles Bulldogs (Pacific Coast Football League)

BOBBY MARSHALL

Baseball—1909-1911—1b, manager, St. Paul Colored Gophers, Leland Giants, Twin City Gophers, Chicago Giants

Football—1920-1925—g, Rock Island Independents, Duluth (MN) Kelleys, Minneapolis Marines

ED MARTIN

Baseball—1951-1952—p, Philadelphia Stars

Basketball—1955/1989—coach, South Carolina State, Tennessee State University (National Coach of the Year, 1972), Vanderbilt University

HENRY McDONALD

Baseball— 1914—of, Pittsburgh Stars of Buffalo

Football—1911-1917—hb, Rochester Jefferson

JESS McMAHON
Baseball—1911-1913—officer, owner, Lincoln Giants
Basketball—1922/1924— owner, Commonwealth Five
Boxing—1932—promoter, Kid Chocolate vs. Fidel LaBarba (world featherweight title)

MARION MOTLEY
Baseball—1942—1b, Reno (NV) Colored Giants
Football—1946-1953, 1955—fb, Cleveland Browns, Pittsburgh Steelers

LOU MONTGOMERY
Baseball—1942, 1945—p, of, Cincinnati Clowns. Detroit Motor City Giants
Football—1937-1941—hb, Boston College Eagles

JOHN "BUCK" O'NEIL
Baseball—1948-1955—manager, Kansas City Monarchs
Basketball—1955/1957—assistant business manager, Harlem Stars

GUY OUSLEY
Baseball—1931-1932—ss, 3b, Chicago American Giants, Cleveland Cubs, Memphis Red Sox, Louisville Black Caps
Basketball—[years not known]—Harlem Globetrotters

JESSE OWENS
Baseball—1939, 1946-1947—vice president, Toledo Crawfords; officer, Detroit Senators; vice president, co-owner, Portland Rosebuds
Track & Field—1936 Olympic Gold medalist
Basketball—1946/1947—owner, Kansas City Stars

LENNIE PEARSON
Baseball—1936-1950—of, 3b, ss, 1b, manager, Newark Eagles, Baltimore Elite Giants, St. Louis Stars
Basketball—1944/1946—f, New York Rens

BILL "ZACK" PETTUS
Baseball—1909-1923—c, 1b, 2b, ss, manager, Kansas City (KS) Giants, Philadelphia Giants, Leland Giants, Chicago Giants, Lincoln Stars, Lincoln Giants, St. Louis Giants, Hilldale Club, Bacharach Giants, Richmond Giants, Harrisburg Giants, Brooklyn Royal Giants, Chicago American Giants
Boxing—1909—Heavyweight challenger (minimum 170 lbs.)

FRITZ POLLARD, SR.
Baseball—1942—vice-president, Negro Major Baseball League of America
Football—1920/1926—qb, 1920/1921 Akron Pros, 1922 Milwaukee Badgers; 1923, 1925 Hammond Pros; 1925 Providence Steam Roller; 1925/1926 Akron Pros; coach, 1921 Akron Pros; 1925 Hammond Pros; 1936-1938 New York Brown Bombers

CUM POSEY
Baseball—1911-1946—of, officer, Homestead Grays, Detroit Wolves; co-founder of East-West League; secretary and treasurer, NNL
Basketball—1909/1920—Monticello Delaney Rifles, Loendi Big Five

Negro Leagues Book #2: The Players

DICK POWELL
Baseball—1938-1952—officer, owner, Baltimore Elite Giants, Nashville Elite Giants
Boxing—[years not known]—judge

TED RASBERRY
Baseball—1954-1960— owner, Kansas City Monarchs, Detroit Stars, Detroit Clowns
Basketball—1956/1958—owner, Harlem Satellites, Harlem Magicians, Harlem Travelers

In May of 1966, JACKIE ROBINSON is named General Manager of the Brooklyn Dodgers of the Continental Football League. The *Associated Press* claims he is the first Negro to hold such a post in professional sports. Robinson carried the pigskin as a halfback for the Honolulu Bears and the Los Angeles Bulldogs in the 1940s.

JACKIE ROBINSON
Baseball—1945— ss, Kansas City Monarchs
Football—1941, 1944—hb, Honolulu Bears, Los Angeles Bulldogs (Pacific Coast Football League); 1966—General Manager, Brooklyn Dodgers (Continental Football League)
Basketball—1946/1947—f, Los Angeles Red Devils

ABE SAPERSTEIN
Baseball—1932-1950—booking agent, officer, Cleveland Cubs, Cincinnati Clowns, Foster Memorial Giants; president, Negro Midwestern League, West Coast Negro Baseball Association; owner, Detroit Senators
Basketball—1927/1956, 1961/1962—owner, Harlem Globetrotters, Chicago Majors (ABL)

GEORGE "SONNY" SMITH
Baseball—1951-1952—of, Chicago American Giants, Harlem Globetrotters
Basketball— [Years not known]—Harlem Globetrotters

HENRY SMITH
Baseball—1942-1947—2b, Jacksonville Red Caps, Chicago American Giants, Indianapolis Clowns, Cincinnati Clowns, Cincinnati-Indianapolis Clowns, New York Black Yankees
Basketball— [Years not known]—Harlem Globetrotters

JOHN FORD SMITH
Baseball—1939-1948—of, p, Indianapolis Crawfords, Kansas City Monarchs
Basketball— [Years not known]—Harlem Globetrotters

Family Connections & Crossover Skills

OTHELLO STRONG
Baseball—1949-1952—p, Chicago American Giants, Harlem Globetrotters baseball team
Basketball—1949/195?—Harlem Globetrotters

TED STRONG, JR.
Baseball—1937-1951—of, 1b, manager, Indianapolis Athletics, Indianapolis ABCs, Kansas City Monarchs, Indianapolis Clowns, Chicago American Giants
Basketball—1937/1948—g, Harlem Globetrotters, Chicago Studebakers

REECE "GOOSE" TATUM
Baseball—1939-1949, 1958—of, 1b, Louisville Black Colonels, Brooklyn Royal Giants, Birmingham Black Barons, Minneapolis-St. Paul Colored Gophers, Cincinnati Clowns, Cincinnati-Indianapolis Clowns, Indianapolis Clowns, Chicago American Giants, Detroit Clowns
Basketball—1942/1957—c, Harlem Globetrotters, Harlem Stars

CLARENCE TURNER
Baseball—1951-1954—p, Indianapolis Clowns, Jackie Robinson All-Stars
Basketball—coach, Camden High School, New Jersey

BILL WATSON
Baseball—1924-1926, 1931—of, Brooklyn Royal Giants, Bacharach Giants, Penn Red Caps of NY
Basketball—1927/1930—Harlem Globetrotters

JACK WATTS
Baseball—1911-1921—c, Louisville Cubs, Chicago American Giants, Indianapolis ABCs, Dayton Marcos, Bowser's ABCs, West Baden (IN) Sprudels, Louisville White Sox, Pittsburgh Keystones
Boxing—1910-1915—Middleweight, 5-3-0 Won/Lost/Draw

WINFIELD WELCH
Baseball—1918-1951—manager, of, New Orleans Black Pelicans, Monroe (LA) Monarchs, Shreveport Giants, Cincinnati Buckeyes, Birmingham Black Barons, Cincinnati Crescents, New York Cubans, Chicago American Giants, Shreveport Black Sports, Alexandria (LA) Lincoln Giants
Basketball—coach, asst. manager, Harlem Globetrotters (11 years)

SAM "BOOM BOOM" WHEELER
Baseball—1946, 1948—of, Seattle Steelheads, New York Cubans
Basketball—1946/1959—g, f, Harlem Globetrotters, Harlem Magicians

DAVEY "WIZ" WHITNEY
Baseball—1952-1955—of, Kansas City Monarchs
Basketball—Head coach—1964/1969, Texas Southern University; 1969/1989—Alcorn A&M/State University; 562-364 Won/Lost record

JOHN "JUMPING JOHNNY" WILSON
Baseball—1948-1949—of, Chicago American Giants
Basketball—1942/1954—Orange (NJ) Triangles, Washington Bears, Harlem Globetrotters, New York Rens

HARRY "BLACK DIAMOND" WOODSON
Baseball—1885—of, St. Louis Black Stockings
Boxing—1882-1885—heavyweight, 11-6-3 Won/Lost/Draw

WALTER J. "BRICKTOP" WRIGHT
Baseball—1940, 1943—of, 1b, New York Black Yankees
Basketball—1939/1943—Chicago Crusaders, Washington Bears, New York Rens, Hammarlund (New York) All-Stars

WILLIAM W. "FOURTEEN, WILLIE" WYNN
Baseball—1944-1950—c, Newark Eagles, New York Cubans
Basketball—1943/1945—New York Rens

BILL YANCEY
Baseball—1923-1936, 1946—ss, manager, Philadelphia Giants, Hilldale Club, Philadelphia Tigers, Lincoln Giants, Darby Daisies, New York Black Yankees, Brooklyn Eagles, Philadelphia Stars, New York Cubans, Bacharach Giants, Atlanta Black Crackers, Philadelphia Quaker City Giants
Basketball—1929/1937, 1945/1946—g, New York Rens, San Francisco All-Nations

WILLIAM "PEP" YOUNG
Baseball—1919-1936—c, Homestead Grays, Pittsburgh Giants; owner, president, Cleveland Stars; umpire, East-West League
Basketball—1919/1923—g, Loendi (Pittsburgh)

NOTES:

In 1963, the **New York Rens** were selected as a team to the Naismith Memorial Basketball Hall of Fame in Springfield, Massachusetts.

In 2002, the **Harlem Globetrotters** were selected as a team to the Naismith Memorial Basketball Hall of Fame in Springfield, Massachusetts.

List of Relatives in the Black Leagues

[HOF] - National Baseball Hall of Famer

DAN BANKHEAD - In 1947, he became the first African American pitcher in the Major Leagues, as a teammate of Jackie Robinson with the Brooklyn Dodgers (1947-51). A top-notch pitcher in the Negro Leagues, joined a selected circle when he hit a home run in his first major league at bat on August 26, 1947, in Ebbets Field off the Pirates' Fritz Ostermueller. Bankhead was also bombed for 10 hits in 3-1/3 innings pitching in relief that day. During World War II, he served in the Marine Corps.

SAM BANKHEAD is best known as Josh Gibson's closest friend and the character portrayed in dramatist August Wilson's award winning play *Fences*. In 1951, he became the first African American manager in Minor League Baseball when he was a player-manager for the Farnham Pirates of the Provincial League. An outstanding player in many ways, Bankhead played in nine East-West All-Star games from 1933 to 1946.

Negro Leagues Book #2: The Players

BROTHERS:
Daniel and Robert Adjer
Tom and Eddie Alston
George and James Anthony
Pete and George Armstrong
Dan, Fred, Garnett, Jr., Joe, and Sam Bankhead (5)
S. and G. Banks
Richard and Norman Banks
Ben and Ernie Banks [HOF]
Bud and Lamb Barbee
Frank, Isaac and Joe Barnes (3)
Sherman and Eugene Barton
Ray and Bill Battle
J. and W. Bear
Stanley and John Beckwith
John and Sam Billingsley
Garnett and Lonnie Blair
Carlos and Heberto Blanco
Bob (Rope) and James (Jimmy) Boyd
John and Marshall Bridges
Harry and Thomas "Pee Wee" Butts
Luis and Rafael Cabrera
Benjamin and Marion Cain
Jacinto and Tomás del Calvo
Floyd and Paul Nick Carter
John and Joseph Chapman
Bennie and Oscar Charleston [HOF]
Benny, Charlie and William Clark
José and Carlos Colas
Benny and Carl Coleman
William and Walter I. Cook, team officers
Anthony and Darltie Cooper
Johnny, Marion and Herman (Rounder) Cunningham (3)
David Deal and Bob Mitchell
Rap and Paul Dixon
Frank and R.J. Ensley
Don and Marvin Fearbry
José, Sr., and Rodolfo Fernández
George and Tom Fiall, Jr.
José Antonio and Luis Enrique Figueroa
John and Gerald Fitzgerald
Frank and Joe Forbes
Rube [HOF] and Willie Foster [HOF]
Oran and Severn Frazier
W.W. and Jimmy Fuller

Family Connections & Crossover Skills

Herbert and W. Gay
Richard and Tom Gee
Jerry and Josh Gibson [HOF]
Clarence and Frank Grant [HOF]
Eugene and Lionel Grimes
Felix and Juan Guilbe
John and Leroy Hancock
Arthur and Charles Hancock
Vic, Bill, and Neal Harris (3) (a)
Sonny and Virgil Harris
William "Woogie" and Charles "Teenie" Harris (b)
Bob and Jim Herring
Frank and Leroy Holmes
F. (Little) and Bruce William Hocker
Cal and Monte Irvin [HOF]
Clarence (Pint) and Elbert Isreal
Willie (Bud) and James (Sap) Ivory
Ajax, Ojax and William Jackson (3)
Willie and George Jefferson
Newt and Wilson Joseph
Johnny and Eli Juran
Clyde and Charles Judson
Alton and Wilbur King
Robert, Merf and Bill Lindsay (3)
J. and P. Lipton
Ben and Ray Lott
Rendon, Joseph and Morris Marbury (3)
A.T. and B.B. and J.B. and W.S. Martin (4)
John and Charles Marvray
Ernest and Tom McCampbell
Jess and Ed McMahon
Winslow and Charles Means
Alonzo and Ben Mitchell
Bob Mitchell and David Deal
Jessie and John Mitchell
Joe and Johnny Mitchell
Robert and George Mitchell (twins)
Bullet Jim and Herbert Cato Moore
Walter "Dobie" and Pete Moore
Ralph and Roy Moore
Sherley Carl and Lucile Moore
J. and R. Mutrie
Leander and William Myers
Juan and Ray Noble
Howard and Bruce Petway
Ernest, Eddie and Fred Pinder (3)

Negro Leagues Book #2: The Players

Dave and Willie Pope
Merle and Andy Porter
Cumberland and Seward Posey (owners)
Benjamin and F. Povie

CHARLEY PRIDE, is one of the few African Americans to have enjoyed considerable success in the country music industry. Between 1969 and 1971, Pride had eight singles that reached number one on the US Country Hit Parade. Elvis Presley may be the only artist who sold more records than Pride for the RCA label. He was inducted into the Country Music Hall of Fame in 2000. Pride pitched and played outfield in the Negro Leagues, often entertaining his teammates with a little guitar solo on the bus ride between towns.

Charley and Mack, Jr., Pride
Ted Radcliffe and Alec Radcliff
Ted and Charles Rasberry
Frazier, Neal and Norman Robinson (3)
José (Joscíto) and Oscar Rodríguez
Branch and John Henry Russell
Abe and Morrie Saperstein
Clyde, Willie, Charles, Codie, and Henry Spearman (5)
Allen (Nicodemus) and Eugene L. "Cheever" Smith
Quincy and Eugene F. Smith
John and Paul (Jake) Stephens
Ted and Othello Strong
Melvin and Franklin "Doc" Sykes
Townsend and John Tapley
Charles Isham (C.I.), Jonathan (Steel Arm), Ben [HOF] and (Candy) Jim Taylor (4)
Orel and Walter Thomas
A. and J. Thompson
Mahlon and Norman Triplett
James and Leander Tugerson
Eli and Ray Underwood
Orlando and Gilberto Varona
John W. and Jerome Veney
Ike and Oscar Walker
Weldy and Fleetwood Walker
Duncan, Reginald and William Weeks (team officers)
Harry and Roy S. Williams
Clarence and George Williams

Family Connections & Crossover Skills

Dan and Emmett Wilson
T.J. and Maurice Young
(a) Bill Harris was an umpire and a non-player.
(b) Teenie Harris was a photographer and non-player

FATHER and SONS:
    Harry "Mooch" and Harry, Jr., Barnes
    Green and Bill (Fireball) Beverly
    Robert and Alonzo Boone
    Lyman Sr., and Lyman, Jr., Bostock
    Floyd and Chester Buchanan
    Pelayo (father) and Elio (son) and Pelayo, Jr. (son), Chacón
    Lorenzo "Piper" Sr., and Lorenzo, Jr., Davis
    Valentín and Reynardo Dreke
    Frank Jr., and Frank III Duncan
    José Sr., and José, Jr., Fernández
    Josh [HOF] and Josh, Jr. **Gibson**
    George and Brian Giles (grandson)
    George L. and Elwood C. Knox
    Oliver and Everett "Ziggy" Marcell
    Joseph (Goose) and Joseph, Jr., Mitchell
    William S. and Frank Peters
    Charles Kenston Spearman and Frederick Spearman
    Ted, Sr., and sons Ted Strong, Jr.; Othello Strong
    Willie [HOF] and Willie Brooks **Wells, Jr.**
    Poindexter, Sr., and Poindexter, Jr., Williams
    Andrew and Percy Wilson
    Henry and Henry L. "Red" Wright
    Gordon and Vertis Ziegler

UNCLES and NEPHEWS:
    Ernie Banks and Bobby Earl Jackson (Texas Rangers, 1981-83)
    Herb Barnhill and Carl J. Dent
    Rufus E. Battle, and Anthony and Darltie Cooper
    Charles Beverly and Bill (Fireball) Beverly
    Tom Cooper and Bill (Fireball) Beverly
    Willis Crump and Dick Lundy
    Rap and Paul Dixon and grandnephew Tom Goodwin (Major league teams, 1991-2004)
    Andy Porter and Don Porter
    Ted Rasberry and Johnny H. Walker (John's mother Irene was Ted's sister)
    Earl and **George "Mule" Suttles [HOF]**
    Uncles Willie, Codie, Henry and Clyde Spearman and nephew Frederick Spearman
    Charles Kenston Spearman and Sam "Boom Boom" Wheeler
    Jim West and Henry Elmore (grand-nephew)
    Marshall and Frank Williams (Frank's brother is former Chicago Cub **Billy Williams [HOF]**)

Negro Leagues Book #2: The Players

UNCLES and NIECES:

Ted Rasberry, owner of the Monarchs and Detroit Stars, and Minnie Forbes (owner of 1956 Detroit Stars)

IN-LAWS:

Ted Radcliffe & Alec Radcliff (uncles-in-law) and HOFer **Norman "Turkey" Stearnes** (nephew-in-law). [Radcliffe's niece Nettie married Norman Stearnes.]

Al Spearman married Cecelia Nelson, who was the niece of Ted Radcliffe.

Henry Richardson was nephew of Ted Radcliffe and Alec Radcliff, and not a brother as often reported in the press.

Dewitt "Woody" Smallwood and John Wyatt (brothers-in-law). [Wyatt married Smallwood's sister, Patricia.]

John Francis "Hap" Allen's niece Mae Louise Allen married **Willie Mays** [HOF].

Ray Brown [HOF] was Cum Posey's son-in-law. [Ray married Posey's daughter Ethel Shaw Truman.]

Harold Hairston married Erma Dee Hayes, the daughter of Wilbur Filmore Hayes, owner of the Cleveland Buckeyes.

Ernest and Thomas McCampbell, brother-in-laws of Gaitha Page. Page married the brothers' sister Olivia.

COUSINS:

John Bissant and Bob Bissant
Henry Elmore and Birmingham Sam Brison
Minnie Forbes and Hank Saverson and Johnny H. Walker
Edward Poles and Spottswood Poles
Sylvester and Zack Foreman (not brothers as often printed in newspapers)
Acie (Skeet) Griggs and Wiley Lee Griggs
Robert Hudspeth and **Raleigh "Biz" Mackey [HOF]**
Arthur Simmons and Willie Lee (their mothers were sisters)
Frederick Spearman and Sam "Boom Boom" Wheeler
J.B. Spencer and Bill Stewart

MAJOR LEAGUE CONNECTIONS (Major Leaguers listed in bold):

Hank [HOF] and **Tommy Aaron** (brothers)
José Acosta and **Merito Acosta** (brothers)
Eddie and **Tom Alston** (brothers)
Ángel "Pete" Aragón and **Ángel "Jack" Aragón** (father & son)
Lyman Bostock, Sr. and **Lyman Bostock, Jr.** (father & son)
James (Jimmy) and **Bob (Rope) Boyd** (brothers)
Willie James and **Dennis "Oil Can" Boyd** (father & son)
Joe Caffie and cousins Ed Stroud and **Oscar Gamble**
Perucho (Latin American leagues) and **Orlando Cepeda [HOF]** (father & son)
Pelayo and **Elio Chacon** (father & son)
Leroy and **Warren Cromartie** (father & son)
Ray Dandridge and **Brad Dandridge** (uncle and nephew)
Artis and **Larry Demery** (father & son)
Sammy and **Solly Drake** (brothers)
Gil Gonzalo L. Garrido, Sr., and **Gil Gonzalo Garrido, Jr.** (father & son)
George and **Brian Giles** (father & grandson)

Roberto Gutiérrez Herrera and **Ricardo Gutiérrez** (father & son)

Sam and sons **Jerry**, **John** Hairston (father & sons) [*All three played in the Majors*]

Sam and son **Jerry** and grandsons **Jerry, Jr.**, **Scott** Hairston (grandfather, father and two sons) [*All four played in the Majors*]

Martínez "Skip" Jackson, Sr., bus driver and **Reginald Martínez Jackson [HOF]** (father & son)

James and **Nat Oliver** (father & son)

Amos Otis and **Amos Joseph "A.O." Otis** (father & son)

Willie and **Dave Pope** (brothers)

Walter "Bancy" Thomas and **Richie Martin** (grandfather and son)

Luis, Sr. and **Luis, Jr.**, **Tiant** (father & son)

Frank and **Billy Williams [HOF]** (brothers)

Marshall and **Billy Williams [HOF]** (uncle and nephew)

Nish Williams and **Donn Clendenon** (father & son)

Earl Wilson, Sr. and **Earl Wilson, Jr.** (father & son)

Robert Veale, Sr. and **Bob Veale, Jr.** (father & son)

There are 10 National Baseball Hall of Famers with relatives who played in the Negro Leagues:

Ernie Banks

James Bell

Oscar Charleston

Willie and Rube Foster

Josh Gibson

Frank Grant

Monte Irvin

Ben Taylor

Willie Wells

Negro Leagues Book #2: The Players

Negro Leaguers with relatives in the Major Leagues, NBA, and NFL, along with entertainment and political connections

NBA connections:
Hipolito "Torrento" Arenas and Washington Wizards point guard **Gilbert Arenas** (grandson).
Ernie Banks and Atlanta Hawks point guard **Acie Law IV,** the son of niece Dolores Law (grandnephew).
James "Cool Papa" Bell and **Chad Bell** (Atlanta Hawks summer league) (grandnephew).
Gene Bremer and Boston Celtics point guard **J.R. Bremer** (grandnephew).
Austin Carr, Sr., and Cleveland Cavaliers point guard **Austin Jr.** (son).
Creole Pete Robertson and Harlem Globetrotters Pablo Robertson and Cleveland Cavaliers 1970 draft pick **Walter Robertson** (father and sons).

COLLEGIATE basketball:
James "Cool Papa" Bell and **Chad Bell** (University of Nevada [Reno] Wolfpack) (grandnephew).
J.C. Hartman and **Jasmine Hartman** (University of Oklahoma Sooners) (granddaughter).
Josh Gibson and **Naje Gibson** (University of Pittsburgh Panthers) (great-granddaughter).
Josh Gibson and **Petie Gibson** (University of New Mexico Lobos), 1999 inductee to the New Mexico Sports Hall of Fame (grandson).

NFL and USFL football connections:
Ernie Banks's mother Essie and **O.J. Simpson's** mother Eunice were first cousins. Banks and Simpson are second cousins.
Jim Colzie and Oakland Raiders, Tampa Bay Bucs defensive back **Neil Colzie** (father and son).
Jim Colzie and New York Jets, middle linebacker **Marvin Jones** (grandnephew).
Raleigh "Biz" Mackey and **Riley Odom**, tight-end, Denver Broncos (grandson).
Walt Owens and Los Angeles Rams guard **Mel Tyrae Owens** (father and son).
Ozzie Tidmore and 1962-63 Cleveland Browns linebacker **Sam Tidmore** (brothers)
Norman Triplett and **Wally Triplett**, Detroit Lions and Chicago Cardinals halfback (uncle and nephew).
Mahlon Triplett and **Wally Triplett**, Detroit Lions and Chicago Cardinals halfback (father and son).
Edgar "Blue" Washington and Los Angeles Rams running back **Kenny Washington** (father and son).
William "Bill" White, p, 1952, 1958-59, Kansas City Monarchs and **Billy White**, running back, 1983-84, Birmingham Stallions and the Memphis Showboats (father and son).

BOXING connections:
Roy Charleston, heavyweight boxer, from 1911-12, is brother of Oscar and Bennie Charleston.
Ted Toles, Jr., is brother of **Roscoe Toles**, heavyweight boxer (fought Joe Louis).
Heavyweight champion **Joe Louis** managed the 1935 Joe Louis Brown Bombers in Detroit at Mack Park.

ENTERTAINMENT connections:
Louie Armstrong sponsored the semi-pro 1931 Armstrong Secret 9, based on New Orleans, Louisiana.
Pusey Dell Arnett, 19th century Chicago Union infielder was married to **Florence Beatrice Price**, America's first known African American female classical composer.
Roosevelt "Booga" Barnes, blues guitarist and harmonica player, was brother to players Isaac, Joe and Frank Barnes.
Cab Calloway played shortstop and sponsored an amateur team called the "Hi-De-Ho" in 1935. They played around the Midwest until 1942.

Family Connections & Crossover Skills

Tap dancer **Savion Glover's** great-grandfather was Richard "Dick" Lundy.

Warren "Birdland" Suttles, co-founder of The Ravens, a R&B vocal group, is the nephew of George "Mule" Suttles

Actress, activist and Duchess of Sussex, **Meghan Markle** is the great-great niece of William Demont "Happy" Evans, II, outfielder and middle infielder for several teams, 1924-36.

Singer **Julia Lee**, known as the "Princess of the Boogie Woogie" was married to Frank Duncan, Kansas City Monarch catcher and manager.

Vincent McMahon, founder of the World Wide Wrestling Federation (WWWF), is son of Jess McMahon, and nephew of Ed McMahon, co-owners of the Lincoln Giants.

Rev. Dwight "Gatemouth" Moore, blues singer, and Birmingham Black Barons owner.

Bartolo Portuondo and daughter **Omara Portuondo Peláez**, singer and Grammy winner with the Buena Vista Social Club.

Charley Pride, 2000 Country Music Hall of Fame singer, pitched for the Memphis Red Sox and the Birmingham Black Barons.

Bill "Bojangles" Robinson, dancer, actor and co-owner of the New York Black Yankees.

Actor **Blair Underwood** is the grandnephew of Pittsburgh Crawfords infielder Eli Underwood.

Vaudeville entertainer and black-faced comedians **Bert A. Williams** and **George Walker** organized the Williams and Walker Base Ball Club of New York City, NY, in 1900. Sometimes known as the New York Colored Giants.

POLITICAL Connections:

Edward W. Brooke, the first African American senator (R-Massachusetts) elected since Reconstruction, was the nephew of **Alex Pompez**. Uncle Alex was married to Ruth Seldon whose sister Helene was Brooke's mother.

Charles Remond Douglass (pictured), third baseman and pitcher for the Washington Alerts and Mutuals of Washington was the third and youngest son of abolitionist Frederick Douglass. Charles Remond served with the 54th Massachusetts Regiment during the Civil War.

MEDIA Connections:

William G. Nunn, Sr., *Pittsburgh Courier* writer, and Negro National League secretary, William G. Nunn, Jr., Pittsburgh Steelers' Assistant Personal Director, and **Bill Nunn III**, actor best known for his appearance as "Radio Raheem" in Spike Lee's movie *Do The Right Thing*.

ART, AERONAUTICS, ENGINEERING Connections:

Eddie Dwight, Jr., renown sculptor and former test pilot who was the first African American to be trained as an astronaut under President John F. Kennedy's administration, is the son of Indianapolis ABCs and Kansas City Monarchs outfielder Eddie Dwight Sr.

APPENDIX G: Uniform Numbers

Major League Baseball players began wearing numbers on the back of their uniforms permanently in 1929. The Cleveland Indians sported the look first, on April 16 (for home games only), and the New York Yankees following suit two days later. New York was the first club to wear numbers on both their home and road uniforms. By 1934, all major league clubs displayed the digits, the New York Giants being the last holdout.

The Chicago American Giants were the first Negro League team to display uniform numbers in 1928, a year before the Indians and the Yankees. The earliest photographic evidence of uniform numbers appeared in the 1909 *Chicago Daily News*, which pictured Cuban pitcher and future Hall of Famer José Méndez. In the photo, Méndez appears in a Cuban Stars uniform with the number "12" on his left sleeve.

Listed below are the Minor and Major League uniform numbers of former Negro Leaguers who are now in the National Baseball Hall of Fame and Museum in Cooperstown, New York.

Name	Induction Year	Uniform Numbers	Primary position
Hank Aaron	1982	6 (1952) - Eau Claire 5 (1953) - Jacksonville 5 (1954) - Milwaukee Braves 44 (1955-74) - Milwaukee/Atlanta Braves 44 (1975-76) - Milwaukee Brewers	Outfielder
Ernie Banks	1977	14 (1953-71) - Cubs	Shortstop
Willard Brown	2006	15 (1947) - Browns	Outfielder
Roy Campanella	1969	2 and 7 (1946) - Nashua Dodgers 7, (1947) - Montreal Royals ?, (1948) - St. Paul Saints 33 (1948) - Dodgers 56 (1948) - Dodgers 39 (1948-57) - Dodgers	Catcher
Larry Doby	1998	14 (1947-55) - Cleveland Indians 37 (1949) - Cleveland Indians 14 (1950) - Cleveland Indians 6 (1953) - Cleveland Indians 14 (1956-57) - Chicago White Sox 14 (1958) - Cleveland Indians 3 or 25 (1959) - San Diego Padres 25 (1959) - Detroit Tigers 32 (1959) - Chicago White Sox	Outfielder
Monte Irvin	1973	?? (1949-50) - Jersey City Giants 7 (1949) - New York Giants 20 (1950-55) - New York Giants	Outfielder

		24 (1955) - Minneapolis Millers 39 (1956) - Chicago Cubs ?? (1957) - Los Angeles Angels (PCL)	
Willie Mays	1979	12 (1950) - Trenton Giants 28 (1951) - Minneapolis Millers 14 (1951) - New York Giants 24 (1951-1972) - New York & San Francisco Giants 24 (1972-73) - New York Mets	Outfielder
Satchel Paige	1971	31 (1951) - Cleveland Indians 29 (1948-49) - Cleveland Indians 22, 29 & 47 (1951) - St. Louis Browns 29 (1952-53) - St. Louis Browns 29 (1956-58) Miami Marlins (retired) 29 (1965) - Kansas City Athletics	Pitcher
Jackie Robinson	1962	9 and 30 (1946) - Montreal Royals 42 (1947-56) - Dodgers	Second Baseman

Retired Major League Uniform Numbers of former Negro League players.

Name	Number	Team	Year
Hank Aaron	44	Atlanta Braves	1977
	44	Milwaukee Brewers	1976
Ernie Banks	14	Chicago Cubs	1982
Roy Campanella	39	Los Angeles Dodgers	1972
Larry Doby	14	Cleveland Indians	1994
Jim Gilliam	19	Los Angeles Dodgers	1978
Elston Howard	32	New York Yankees	1984
Monte Irvin	20	San Francisco Giants	2010
Willie Mays	24	San Francisco Giants	1972
Minnie Miñoso	9	Chicago White Sox	1983
Jackie Robinson	42	Los Angeles Dodgers	1972

Hank Aaron is the only former Negro Leaguer to have more than one Major League team retire his number.

Jim "Junior" Gilliam's number is the only one retired by the Dodgers of a player not in the National Baseball Hall of Fame and Museum.

Jackie Robinson is the first and currently the only player to have his number permanently retired by all Major League Baseball teams, on April 15, 1997, the 50th anniversary of his debut with the Brooklyn Dodgers.

Uniform numbers of players compiled from photographs and printed rosters, home and road numbers

Player	Year	Club	Home	Road
Abernathy, Robert	1946	Boston Blues	28	
	1947	Indianapolis Clowns	20	
Adams, Ben	1959	Detroit Stars	30	
Adams, Emery	1939	Baltimore Elite Giants	18	
	1940	Baltimore Elite Giants	15	
	1941	Baltimore Elite Giants	15	
	1942	Baltimore Elite Giants	15	
	1946	New York Black Yankees	15	
	1948	Baltimore Elite Giants	26	
Alexander, Spencer	1940	Newark Eagles	12	
	1941	Newark Eagles	9	
Alexander, Ted	1946	Kansas City Monarchs	18	35
	1947	Kansas City Monarchs	35	
Allen, Newt	1936	Kansas City Monarchs	2	
	1942	Kansas City Monarchs	19	
	1943	Kansas City Monarchs	19	
	1944	Kansas City Monarchs	19	
	1947	Indianapolis Clowns	4	
Amaro, Dave	1953	Indianapolis Clowns	31	
	1954	Indianapolis Clowns	34	
	1955	Indianapolis Clowns	23	
Amoros, Sandy	1950	New York Cubans	1	
Anderson, Bill	1941	New York Cubans	8	
	1943	New York Cubans	14	
	1944	New York Cubans	20	
	1946	New York Cubans	14	
	1947	New York Cubans	14	
Aguillard, Ray	1958	Detroit Clowns	10	
Arencibia, Edward	1948	New York Cubans	17	
Ariosa, Homero	1947	New York Cubans		23
Armenteros, Juan	1954	Kansas City Monarchs	12	
Armour, Alfred	1941	New Orleans-St. Louis Stars	5	
	1945	Cleveland Buckeyes	26	
	1946	Cleveland Buckeyes	26	
	1947	Chicago American Giants	14	
Armstead, Jimmie	1940	Baltimore Elite Giants	10	
	1949	Philadelphia Stars	7	
Ascanio, Carlos	1946	New York Black Yankees	3	
Ashby, Earl	1947	Homestead Grays	22	
	1948	Newark Eagles	36	
Austin, Frank	1944	Philadelphia Stars	10	29
	1945	Biz Mackey's M.L. All Stars	28	

	1945	Philadelphia Stars	2	29
	1946	Philadelphia Stars	2	
	1947	Philadelphia Stars	3	
	1948	Philadelphia Stars	3	
Awkard, Russell	1940	New York Cubans	18	
Bailey, Otha	1958	Birmingham Black Barons	4	
Baker, Edgar	1946	Cleveland Clippers	15	
Baker, Gene	1948	Kansas City Monarchs	26	
	1949	Kansas City Monarchs	30	
Baker, Rufus	1946	New York Black Yankees	2	4
	1947	New York Black Yankees	2	
Ballestro, Miguel	1948	New York Cubans	9	
Bankhead, Fred	1942	West All-Stars	9	
	1943	Memphis Red Sox	20	
Bankhead, Garnett	1948	Homestead Grays	32	
Bankhead, Sam	1936	Pittsburgh Crawfords	7	
	1939	Homestead Grays	7	7
	1942	Homestead Grays	5	
	1942	East All-Stars	8	
	1943	Homestead Grays	5	
	1944	Homestead Grays	5	
	1945	Homestead Grays	21	
	1946	Homestead Grays	28	
	1947	Homestead Grays	28	
	1948	Homestead Grays	28	
	1949	Homestead Grays	28	
Banks, Earl	1945	Newark Eagles	35	
Banks, Ernie	1950	Kansas City Monarchs	28	
	1953	Kansas City Monarchs	28	
Banks, James	1957	Memphis Red Sox	2	
	1958	Memphis Red Sox	5	
Barbee, Lamb	1940	New York Black Yankees	23	
	1942	Philadelphia Stars	28	
	1945	Cincy-Indy Clowns	23	
	1946	New York Black Yankees		41 & 8
	1947	New York Black Yankees	19	
Barbee, Quincy	1943	Baltimore Elite Giants	3	
Barber, Samuel	1946	Cleveland Clippers	19	
Barker, Marvin	1939	New York Black Yankees	6	
	1940	New York Black Yankees	5	
	1941	New York Black Yankees	6	
	1942	Philadelphia Stars	21	
	1945	New York Black Yankees	3	
	1946	New York Black Yankees	5	
	1947	New York Black Yankees	1	
Barnes, Frank	1949	Kansas City Monarchs	19	

	1950	Kansas City Monarchs	19	
Barnes, Isaac	1957	Memphis Red Sox	3	
	1959	Memphis Red Sox	3	
Barnes, William	1939	Baltimore Elite Giants	31	
	1940	Baltimore Elite Giants	7	
	1942	Baltimore Elite Giants	7	
	1946	Baltimore Elite Giants	30	
Barnhill, Dave	1941	New York Cubans	3	
	1942	East All-Stars	17	
	1943	New York Cubans	1	
	1944	New York Cubans	1	
	1946	New York Cubans	1	
	1947	New York Cubans	1	
	1948	New York Cubans	1	
Barrow, Wesley	1947	Baltimore Elite Giants	31	
Bass, Jesse	1959	Detroit Stars	14	
	1960	Detroit-New Orleans Stars	35	
Bass, Leroy	1940	Homestead Grays	9	
Bassett, Lloyd	1943	Cincinnati Clowns	16	
	1944	Birmingham Black Barons		47
	1944	Indy-Cincy Clowns	17	
	1946	Birmingham Black Barons	9	
	1947	Birmingham Black Barons	1	
	1948	Birmingham Black Barons	1	
	1949	Birmingham Black Barons	1	
	1950	Birmingham Black Barons	8	
	1953	Memphis Red Sox	22	
Battle, Ray	1944	Homestead Grays	19	
	1945	Homestead Grays	19	
Baylis, Henry	1949	Baltimore Elite Giants	17	23
	1950	Birmingham Black Barons	2	
	1954	Kansas City Monarchs	14	
Beach, Roy	1958	Memphis Red Sox	2	
Beal, Giovanni	1947	Newark Eagles	7	
Beckwith, John	1934	New York Black Yankees	8	
Belfield, Skinner	1948	Newark Eagles	9	
Bell, Charles	1948	Homestead Grays	33	
Bell, Herman	1946	Birmingham Black Barons	14	
	1947	Birmingham Black Barons	8	
	1948	Birmingham Black Barons	3	
	1949	Birmingham Black Barons	3	
	1950	Birmingham Black Barons	3	
Bell, James	1928	St. Louis Stars	17	
	1934	Pittsburgh Crawfords	8	
	1936	Pittsburgh Crawfords	8	
	1943	Homestead Grays	1	

	1944	Homestead Grays	1	
	1945	Homestead Grays	18	
	1946	Homestead Grays	24	
Bell, William	1948	Newark Eagles	40	
	1954	Kansas City Monarchs	16	
Benjamin, Jerry	1939	Homestead Grays		1
	1940	Homestead Grays	2	
	1941	Homestead Grays	2	
	1942	Homestead Grays	2	
	1943	Homestead Grays	2	
	1944	Homestead Grays	2	
	1945	Homestead Grays	15	
	1946	Homestead Grays	15	
	1947	Homestead Grays	15	
	1948	New York Cubans	18	
Bennett, Bransford	1941	New Orleans-St. Louis Stars	3	
	1942	New York Black Yankees	19	20
	1946	Boston Blues	27	
Bennett, Jim	1947	Indianapolis Clowns		9
Benson, Gene	1939	Philadelphia Stars	24	
	1940	Philadelphia Stars	24	
	1941	Philadelphia Stars	24	
	1942	Philadelphia Stars	24	
	1943	Philadelphia Stars	24	
	1944	Philadelphia Stars	24	
	1945	Philadelphia Stars	16	24
	1946	Philadelphia Stars	9	
	1947	Philadelphia Stars	9	
	1948	Philadelphia Stars	9	
Bernal, Plácido	1941	New York Cubans	5	
Bernard, Pablo	1949	Louisville Buckeyes	26	
Berry, Mike	1947	Kansas City Monarchs	26	
Betts, Russel Boyd	1950	Kansas City Monarchs	18	
Bibbs, Rainey	1941	Kansas City Monarchs	3	
Binder, Jim	1946	Cleveland Clippers	2	
Biot, Charles	1940	New York Black Yankees	6	
	1941	Baltimore Elite Giants	5	
Bissant, John	1947	Chicago American Giants	3	
Bizzle, James	1947	Birmingham Black Barons	16	
Black, Joe	1946	Baltimore Elite Giants	22	
	1947	Baltimore Elite Giants	22	
	1948	Baltimore Elite Giants	22	
	1949	Baltimore Elite Giants	21	
Blackmon, Clifford	1941	Homestead Grays	17	
	1941	New Orleans-St. Louis Stars	12	
Blair, Garnet	1945	Homestead Grays	26	

	1946	Homestead Grays	29	
Blake, Frank	1934	New York Black Yankees	16	
	1935	New York Cubans	32	
Blanco, Carlos	1941	New York Cubans	2	
Blanco, Heberto	1941	New York Cubans	10	
	1942	East All-Stars	19	
Bond, Walter	1956	Kansas City Monarchs	20	
Bonner, Don	1959	Detroit Stars	15	
	1960	Detroit-New Orleans Stars	25	
Boone, Alonzo	1944	Birmingham Black Barons		10
	1948	Cleveland Buckeyes	21	
	1949	Louisville Buckeyes	21	
Boone, Charles	1941	New Orleans-St. Louis Stars	11	
	1942	New York Black Yankees	12	28
	1944	Philadelphia Stars		16
Boone, Oscar	1939	Baltimore Elite Giants	13	
Bostock Lyman	1946	Birmingham Black Barons	27	
	1947	Chicago American Giants	5	
Bowers, Julius	1947	New York Black Yankees	23	
Boyd, Bob	1949	Memphis Red Sox	16	
Boyd, James	1946	Newark Eagles	15	
Boyd, Lincoln	1951	Indianapolis Clowns	32	
Bracken, Doc	1944	Great Lakes Bluejackets	14	
Bradley, Frank	1941	Kansas City Monarchs	11	
	1942	Kansas City Monarchs	11	
Braithwaite, Alonzo	1947	Philadelphia Stars	10	
	1948	Philadelphia Stars	10	
Branham, Luther	1949	Birmingham Black Barons	13	
	1950	Chicago American Giants		18
Breda, Bill	1950	Kansas City Monarchs	20	
Bremer, Eugene	1942	West All-Stars	19	
	1946	Cleveland Buckeyes	31	
Brewer, Chet	1941	Philadelphia Stars	30	
	1948	Cleveland Buckeyes	19	
Brewer, Sherwood	1949	Indianapolis Clowns	23	
	1951	Indianapolis Clowns	23	
	1953	Kansas City Monarchs	17	
	1954	Kansas City Monarchs	17	
	1960	Kansas City Monarchs	30	
Britton, John	1943	Cincinnati Clowns	6	
	1944	Birmingham Black Barons	12	12
	1946	Birmingham Black Barons	3	
	1947	Birmingham Black Barons	11	
	1948	Birmingham Black Barons	11	
	1949	Birmingham Black Barons	11	
	1950	Indianapolis Clowns	26	

Uniform Numbers

Brooks, Alex	1939	New York Black Yankees	2	
Brooks, Ameal	1943	New York Cubans	8	
	1944	New York Cubans	10	
Brooks, Wallace	1948	Baltimore Elite Giants	20	
Broome, J.B.	1947	New York Black Yankees	22	
Brown, Barney	1942	Philadelphia Stars	14	
	1943	Philadelphia Stars	14	
	1944	Philadelphia Stars	25	
	1945	Philadelphia Stars	1	
	1946	Philadelphia Stars	1	
	1947	Philadelphia Stars	1	
	1948	Philadelphia Stars	1	
	1949	Philadelphia Stars	2	
Brown, Curtis	1947	New York Black Yankees	6	
Brown, D.	1955	New York Black Yankees	37	
Brown, Ike	1960	Kansas City Monarchs	51	
Brown, James	1941	Newark Eagles	15	
	1944	Great Lakes Bluejackets	27	
	1947	Indianapolis Clowns	8	
Brown, Jesse	1940	New York Black Yankees	2	
	1941	Baltimore Elite Giants	11	
	1942	Baltimore Elite Giants	18	
Brown, John	1946	Cleveland Buckeyes	26	
Brown, Larry	1934	Chicago American Giants	8	
	1936	Philadelphia Stars	16	
	1943	Memphis Red Sox	10	
	1945	Memphis Red Sox	24	
Brown, Ray	1939	Homestead Grays		11
	1940	Homestead Grays	11	
	1941	Homestead Grays	11	
	1942	Homestead Grays	11	
	1944	Homestead Grays	11	
	1945	Homestead Grays	31	
Brown, T.J.	1942	West All Stars	14	
	1947	Indianapolis Clowns	16	
	1949	Louisville Buckeyes	19	
Brown, Willard	1941	Kansas City Monarchs	10	
	1942	Kansas City Monarchs	30	
	1942	West All Stars	3	
	1943	Kansas City Monarchs	30	
	1946	Kansas City Monarchs	5	36
	1947	Kansas City Monarchs	30	
	1948	Kansas City Monarchs	23	
	1949	Kansas City Monarchs	12	
	1958	Kansas City Monarchs	42	
Brown, Willie	1953	Indianapolis Clowns	26	

Bruce, Clarence	1948	Homestead Grays	31	
Bruton, Charles	1939	New York Black Yankees	20	
	1941	New Orleans-St. Louis Stars	8	
Bryant, Allen	1941	Kansas City Monarchs	8	
Buchanan, Chester	1941	Philadelphia Stars	11	
	1942	Philadelphia Stars	29	
	1943	Philadelphia Stars	29	
Buckner, Joseph	1946	Boston Blues	22	
Bumpus, Earl	1944	Kansas City Monarchs	29	
	1947	Chicago American Giants	19	
	1948	Chicago American Giants	19	
Burch, Walter	1946	Cleveland Buckeyes	24	
Burgin, Ralph	1939	New York Black Yankees	1	
Burgos, José	1949	Birmingham Black Barons	5	
	1950	Birmingham Black Barons	5	
Burke, Ernest	1947	Baltimore Elite Giants	23	28
	1948	Baltimore Elite Giants		28
Burnett, Fred	1941	New York Black Yankees	9	
	1942	New York Black Yankees	4	16
Burns, Willie	1943	Baltimore Elite Giants	17	
	1944	Indy-Cincy Clowns	15	8
Busch, Ronald	1959	Raleigh Tigers	4	
Butts, Harry	1949	Indianapolis Clowns	21	
	1950	Indianapolis Clowns	21	
	1951	Indianapolis Clowns	21	
Butts, Thomas	1939	Baltimore Elite Giants	6	
	1940	Baltimore Elite Giants	9	
	1941	Baltimore Elite Giants	9	
	1942	Baltimore Elite Giants	9	
	1942	East All Stars	18	
	1945	Baltimore Elite Giants	10	
	1946	Baltimore Elite Giants	10	
	1947	Baltimore Elite Giants	10	
	1948	Baltimore Elite Giants	10	
	1949	Baltimore Elite Giants	10	
	1953	Birmingham Black Barons	27	
Byas, Subby	1936	Chicago American Giants	7	
Byrd, Bill	1936	Washington Elite Giants	10	
	1939	Baltimore Elite Giants	22	
	1941	Baltimore Elite Giants	20	
	1942	Baltimore Elite Giants	10	
	1943	Baltimore Elite Giants	11	
	1943	Philadelphia Stars	27	
	1945	Baltimore Elite Giants	25	34
	1945	Biz Mackey's M.L. All Stars	34	
	1946	Baltimore Elite Giants	25	

Uniform Numbers

	1947	Baltimore Elite Giants	32	
	1948	Baltimore Elite Giants	32	20
	1949	Baltimore Elite Giants	20	20
Cabrera, Lorenzo	1947	New York Cubans	21	
	1948	New York Cubans	21	
Cabrera, Luis	1948	Indianapolis Clowns	8	
Cabrera, Rafael	1944	Indy-Cincy Clowns	24	11
Cain, Marion	1939	New York Black Yankees	19	
	1959	Detroit Stars	11	
Calhoun, Walter	1941	New Orleans-St. Louis Stars	7	
	1942	New York Black Yankees	10	32
	1946	Cleveland Buckeyes	35	
Caballero, Luis	1950	New York Cubans	5	
Campanella, Roy	1939	Baltimore Elite Giants	19	
	1940	Baltimore Elite Giants	14	
	1941	Baltimore Elite Giants	22	
	1942	Baltimore Elite Giants	11	
	1945	Baltimore Elite Giants	28	27 & 23
	1945	Biz Mackey's M.L. All Stars	27	
Campbell, Dave	1939	New York Black Yankees	5	
	1941	Philadelphia Stars	26	
Campini, Joe	1948	Baltimore Elite Giants	25	
Canada, Ernie	1951	Philadelphia Stars	17	
Canada, James	1943	Memphis Red Sox	11	
Canizares, Avelino	1945	Cleveland Buckeyes	23	
Cannady, Jesse	1944	Homestead Grays	7	
	1944	Indy-Cincy Clowns	6	
Cannady, Walter	1934	New York Black Yankees	3	
	1939	New York Black Yankees	3	
Cárdenas, Oscar	1956	Kansas City Monarchs	16	
Carlisle, Matthew	1940	Homestead Grays	7	
	1941	Homestead Grays	8	
	1942	Homestead Grays	7	
	1946	Homestead Grays		17
Carreras, Clemente	1940	New York Cubans	3	
	1941	New York Cubans	6	
Carswell, Frank	1946	Cleveland Buckeyes	30	
	1953	Indianapolis Clowns	36	12
Carter, Alfred	1935	Pittsburgh Crawfords	19	
	1940	New York Cubans	16	
Carter, Bobby	1959	Raleigh Tigers	2	
Carter, Ernest	1940	Newark Eagles	11	
	1943	Homestead Grays	17	
	1944	Homestead Grays	7	
	1945	Homestead Grays	20	
Carter, James	1948	Newark Eagles	14	

Carter, Marlin	1942	West All Stars	5	
	1943	Memphis Red Sox	1	
	1948	Chicago American Giants	2	
Carter, Mathew	1954	Kansas City Monarchs	19	
Carter, Paul	1934	Philadelphia Stars	15	
Casey, William	1934	Philadelphia Stars	11	
	1940	New York Cubans	17	
Cash, Bill	1943	Philadelphia Stars	33	
	1944	Philadelphia Stars	33	
	1945	Philadelphia Stars	10	33
	1946	Philadelphia Stars	8	
	1947	Philadelphia Stars	8	
	1948	Philadelphia Stars	8	
	1949	Philadelphia Stars	10	8
	1950	Philadelphia Stars	30	
Cathey, Willis	1948	Indianapolis Clowns	3	
	1949	Indianapolis Clowns	34	24
Chalmers, Marvin	1959	Detroit Stars	34	
Charleston, Oscar	1934	Pittsburgh Crawfords	3	
	1944	Philadelphia Stars	19	
	1948	Philadelphia Stars		22
	1951	Philadelphia Stars	53	
	1954	Indianapolis Clowns	40	
Chism, Elijah	1946	Cleveland Buckeyes	4	
	1947	Birmingham Black Barons	18	
Chism, Joe	1957	Detroit Stars	12	
	1958	Detroit Clowns	12	
Christopher, Thad	1941	Newark Eagles	4	
Clark, Chifian	1945	New York Cubans	2	
	1946	New York Cubans	20	
	1947	New York Cubans	20	
	1948	New York Cubans	20	
Clark, Cleveland	1950	New York Cubans	20	
Clark, Elmer	1957	Kansas City Monarchs	24	
Clark, M.	1958	Memphis Red Sox	6	
Clarke, Robert	1934	New York Black Yankees	9	
	1939	New York Black Yankees	9	
	1940	New York Black Yankees	9	
	1941	Baltimore Elite Giants	10	
	1942	Baltimore Elite Giants	8	
	1943	Baltimore Elite Giants	10	
	1943	Philadelphia Stars	17	
	1945	Baltimore Elite Giants	16	
	1946	Baltimore Elite Giants	16	
Clarke, Vibert	1948	Cleveland Buckeyes	4	
	1949	Louisville Buckeyes	27	

Name	Year	Team	Number	Also
Clarkson, James	1940	Newark Eagles	17	
	1942	Philadelphia Stars	19	
	1946	Philadelphia Stars	18	
	1949	Philadelphia Stars	16	21 & 20
	1950	Philadelphia Stars	34	
Clayton, Zack	1944	Great Lakes Bluejackets	31	
Cleveland, Howard	1946	Indianapolis Clowns	19	
Clifford, Luther	1948	Homestead Grays	40	
Coates, Leroy	1944	Great Lakes Bluejackets	21	
Coffey, Howard	1954	Indianapolis Clowns	23	
Cohen, Jim	1949	Indianapolis Clowns	30	
	1951	Indianapolis Clowns	30	
Coimbre, Francisco	1940	New York Cubans	8	
	1941	New York Cubans	17	
	1943	New York Cubans	4	
	1944	New York Cubans	14	
Colas, Carlos	1941	New York Cubans	18	
Cole, Cecil	1946	Newark Eagles	14	
Coleman, Clarence	1956	Indianapolis Clowns	34	
Collins, Gene	1947	Kansas City Monarchs		15 & 21
	1948	Kansas City Monarchs	21	
	1949	Kansas City Monarchs	21	
	1950	Kansas City Monarchs	21	
Collins, Willie	1950	Birmingham Black Barons	16	
Colthirst, Alejandro	1948	Indianapolis Clowns		18
Colzie, Jim	1946	Indianapolis Clowns	4	
	1947	Indianapolis Clowns	10	
Connors, Doc	1954	Kansas City Monarchs	25	
Cooper, Andy	1936	Kansas City Monarchs	14	
Cooper, Anthony	1941	New York Black Yankees	12	
Cooper, George	1946	Boston Blues	36	
Cooper, Tom	1947	Kansas City Monarchs	38	24
	1948	Kansas City Monarchs	24	
	1949	Kansas City Monarchs	23	
	1950	Kansas City Monarchs	23	
	1953	Kansas City Monarchs	21	
Cooper, W.T.	1939	Philadelphia Stars	15	
	1941	Philadelphia Stars	15	
	1942	Philadelphia Stars	15	
	1946	New York Black Yankees	16	
Cornelius, Willie	1934	Chicago American Giants	11	
	1936	Chicago American Giants	13	
Correa, Francisco	1935	New York Cubans	20	
Cos, Caldonia	1957	Detroit Stars	22	
	1958	Detroit Clowns	22	
Costello, Joe	1957	Detroit Stars	45	

Cox, Roosevelt	1943	New York Cubans	10	
	1944	New York Cubans	13	
Cozart, Haywood	1939	Newark Eagles	19	
Craig, Joe	1946	Philadelphia Stars	10	
Creacy, Dewey	1934	Philadelphia Stars	5	
Crespo, Alejandro	1940	New York Cubans	4	
	1946	New York Cubans	18	
Cromartie, Leroy	1945	Cincy-Indy Clowns	6	
Crowe, George	1947	New York Black Yankees	21	
Crue, Martín	1943	New York Cubans	19	
	1946	New York Cubans	6	
	1947	New York Cubans	6	
	1948	New York Cubans	6	
Crutchfield, Jimmie	1934	Pittsburgh Crawfords	9	
	1936	Pittsburgh Crawfords	9	
Cunningham, Earl	1954	Kansas City Monarchs	29	
	1959	Detroit Stars	5	
Curry, Homer	1936	Washington Elite Giants	12	
	1939	New York Black Yankees	11	
	1940	New York Black Yankees	1	
	1941	Baltimore Elite Giants	4	
	1942	Philadelphia Stars	20	
	1943	Philadelphia Stars	22	
	1944	Philadelphia Stars	34	22
	1945	Philadelphia Stars	4	22
	1946	Philadelphia Stars	4	17 & 21
	1947	Philadelphia Stars	17	
Dailey, James	1948	Baltimore Elite Giants	11	
Dancy, Nat	1959	Kansas City Monarchs	33	
	1960	Kansas City Monarchs	55	
Daniels, Eddie	1946	New York Cubans	8	
	1947	New York Cubans	7	
Daniels, James	1943	Birmingham Black Barons	3	
Davenport, Lloyd	1945	Cleveland Buckeyes	34	
Davidson, Charles	1946	New York Black Yankees		15
	1947	New York Black Yankees	14	
	1949	Baltimore Elite Giants	19	
Davis, Bill	1945	Philadelphia Stars	5	
Davis, Eddie	1946	Indianapolis Clowns	14	
	1949	Indianapolis Clowns	26	28
Davis, Fritz	1947	Detroit Wolves	33	
Davis, George	1960	Kansas City Monarchs	57	
Davis, Johnny	1945	Biz Mackey's M.L. All Stars	31	
	1945	Newark Eagles	31	
	1946	Newark Eagles	17	
	1947	Newark Eagles	17	

Uniform Numbers

Name	Year	Team	#	#
	1948	Newark Eagles	17	
	1949	Houston Eagles	20	17
Davis, Lorenzo	1943	Birmingham Black Barons	26	
	1944	Birmingham Black Barons	4	4
	1946	Birmingham Black Barons	5	
	1947	Birmingham Black Barons	20	
	1948	Birmingham Black Barons	15	
	1949	Birmingham Black Barons	15	
	1950	Birmingham Black Barons	13	
Davis, Nat	1949	Philadelphia Stars		19 & 10
	1950	Philadelphia Stars	8	
Davis, Otis	1946	Cleveland Clippers	7	
Davis, Robert	1947	Baltimore Elite Giants	30	
	1949	Baltimore Elite Giants	27	
Davis, Roosevelt	1934	Pittsburgh Crawfords	15	
	1935	Pittsburgh Crawfords	10	
	1940	Baltimore Elite Giants	6	
	1943	Cincinnati Clowns	11	
	1944	Indy-Cincy Clowns	23	23
Davis, Ross	1946	Boston Blues	33	
Day, Leon	1939	Newark Eagles	10	
	1941	Newark Eagles	10	
	1942	East All Stars	16	
	1946	Newark Eagles	7	
	1949	Baltimore Elite Giants	12	
Dean, Charlie	1947	New York Black Yankees	10	
Dean, Jimmy	1949	Philadelphia Stars	9	
Debran, Roy	1940	New York Black Yankees	20	
Dedeaux, Russ	1941	Newark Eagles	12	
	1946	New York Black Yankees		41
Dennis, Wesley	1945	Baltimore Elite Giants	23	
	1946	Philadelphia Stars	6	
	1947	Philadelphia Stars	6	
	1948	Philadelphia Stars	6	
	1953	Birmingham Black Barons	19	
Dent, Carl	1951	Philadelphia Stars	32	
Dials, Lou	1936	Chicago American Giants	1	
Díaz, El Bicho	1950	New York Cubans	9	
Díaz, Heliodoro	1935	New York Cubans	0	
Díaz, Pablo	1935	New York Cubans	22	
	1945	New York Cubans	9	
Diggs, Leon	1951	Raleigh Tigers	6	
	1953	Indianapolis Clowns		6
	1955	New York Black Yankees	35	
Dihigo, Martín	1935	New York Cubans	15	
	1945	New York Cubans	17	

343

Name	Year	Team		
Dismukes, William	1942	Kansas City Monarchs	13	
	1947	Detroit Wolves	22	
	1958	Kansas City Monarchs	1	
Dixon, Eddie Lee	1939	Baltimore Elite Giants	14	
Dixon, Rap	1935	New York Cubans	21	
Doby, Larry	1944	Great Lakes Bluejackets	7	
	1946	Newark Eagles	6	
	1947	Newark Eagles	6	
Donoso, Lino	1947	New York Cubans	2	
Douglas, Jesse	1945	Chicago American Giants	1	
	1950	Chicago American Giants		6
Drake, Reynaldo	1945	Cincy-Indy Clowns	11	
	1946	Indianapolis Clowns	11	
	1947	Indianapolis Clowns	11	
	1948	Indianapolis Clowns	11	
	1949	Indianapolis Clowns	20	
	1950	Indianapolis Clowns	20	
	1951	Indianapolis Clowns	20	
	1953	Indianapolis Clowns	20	
	1954	Indianapolis Clowns	21	
Drake, Verdes	1955	Indianapolis Clowns	20	
Duany, Claro	1944	New York Cubans	19	
	1947	New York Cubans	19	
Duckett, Mahlon	1941	Philadelphia Stars	20	
	1942	Philadelphia Stars	22	
	1944	Philadelphia Stars	27	12
	1945	Philadelphia Stars	3	21
	1946	Philadelphia Stars	3	
	1947	Philadelphia Stars	2	
	1948	Philadelphia Stars	2	
	1949	Homestead Grays	33	
Duncan, Frank	1935	New York Cubans	24	
	1941	Kansas City Monarchs	14	
	1942	Kansas City Monarchs	29	
	1943	Kansas City Monarchs	29	
	1944	Kansas City Monarchs	26	
	1945	Kansas City Monarchs	26	44 & 3
	1946	Kansas City Monarchs	38	
	1947	Kansas City Monarchs	1	37
Duncan, Mel	1949	Kansas City Monarchs	17	
	1950	Kansas City Monarchs	17	
Dunlap, Herman	1936	Chicago American Giants	4	
Dunn, Alphonse	1943	Birmingham Black Barons	30	
Dunn, Joseph	1934	Philadelphia Stars	10	
	1939	Philadelphia Stars	19	
	1940	Philadelphia Stars	30	

Uniform Numbers

	1941	Philadelphia Stars	19	
Easter, Luke	1947	Homestead Grays	30	
	1948	Homestead Grays	30	
Easterling, Howard	1940	Homestead Grays	6	
	1941	Homestead Grays	6	
	1942	Homestead Grays	6	
	1943	Homestead Grays	7	
	1946	Homestead Grays	21	18
	1949	New York Cubans	6	
Echols, Joe	1939	Newark Eagles	5	
Edwards, George	1946	Boston Blues	21	
Elliott, Eugene	1956	Kansas City Monarchs	24	
Elliott, Joe	1958	Birmingham Black Barons	10	
Ellis, Rocky	1934	Philadelphia Stars	9	
	1940	Homestead Grays	14	
Else, Henry	1936	Kansas City Monarchs	19	
Ensley, Frank	1953	Indianapolis Clowns	28	
	1954	Indianapolis Clowns	28	
	1955	Indianapolis Clowns	28	
Evans, Felix	1939	Newark Eagles		12
	1943	Memphis Red Sox	9	
Evans, Hezikia	1960	Detroit-New Orleans Stars	30	
Evans, Johnny	1954	Indianapolis Clowns	38	
Evans, Robert	1939	Newark Eagles	15	
	1940	New York Black Yankees	16	
	1941	New York Black Yankees	15	
	1942	New York Black Yankees	16	24
	1942	Philadelphia Stars	35	
	1943	Philadelphia Stars	16	
Evelyn, Lionel	1955	New York Black Yankees	25	
Fallings, John	1947	New York Black Yankees	20	
Farmer, Greene	1947	New York Black Yankees	3	
Favors, Thomas	1947	Kansas City Monarchs		20
Fearbry, Don.	1955	Indianapolis Clowns	26	
Felder, James	1948	Indianapolis Clowns		10
Felder, William	1946	Newark Eagles	3	
	1951	Philadelphia Stars	31	
Fernández, José María	1940	New York Cubans	14	
	1941	New York Cubans	14	
	1943	New York Cubans	13	
	1944	New York Cubans	15	
	1946	New York Cubans	2	
	1950	New York Cubans	15	
Fernández, Renaldo	1950	New York Cubans	2	
Fernández, Rodolfo	1943	New York Cubans	3	
	1944	New York Cubans	17	

	1946	New York Black Yankees		40
Ferrell, Leroy	1948	Baltimore Elite Giants		24
	1949	Baltimore Elite Giants	11	
Ferrell, Willie	1939	Homestead Grays		12
	1940	Homestead Grays	12	
Ferrer, Efigenio	1946	Indianapolis Clowns		8
	1947	Indianapolis Clowns		6
	1948	Indianapolis Clowns	9	
Fields, Tom	1946	Homestead Grays		21
Fields, Wilmer	1942	Homestead Grays	17	
	1946	Homestead Grays	33	
	1947	Homestead Grays	34	
	1948	Homestead Grays	41	
Figueroa, Enrique	1946	Baltimore Elite Giants	23	
Figueroa, José	1940	New York Cubans	10	
Fillmore, Joe	1941	Philadelphia Stars	33	
	1942	Philadelphia Stars	33	
	1946	Philadelphia Stars	19	
Finch, Rayford	1949	Louisville Buckeyes	30	
Finney, Ed	1948	Baltimore Elite Giants	19	
	1949	Baltimore Elite Giants		23
Flores, Conrad	1954	Kansas City Monarchs	24	
Flowers, Johnny	1942	New York Black Yankees	11	22
Floyd, Earl	1956	Kansas City Monarchs	22	
	1959	Detroit Stars	40	
Ford, Ervin	1954	Indianapolis Clowns	38	
	1955	Indianapolis Clowns	25	
Ford, Jimmy	1941	New Orleans-St. Louis Stars	6	
	1942	New York Black Yankees	5	4
Formental, Pedro	1949	Memphis Red Sox	29	
Forrest, Percy	1946	New York Black Yankees	6	
Fortson, Ralph	1959	Raleigh Tigers	14	
	1960	Raleigh Tigers	7	
Foster, Willie	1928	Chicago American Giants	2	
	1934	Chicago American Giants	5	
Fowler, Elbert	1959	Memphis Red Sox	4	
Franklin, Leon	1960	Kansas City Monarchs	59	
Free, Kenneth	1959	Raleigh Tigers	11	
Gaines, Jonas	1939	Baltimore Elite Giants	31	
	1940	Baltimore Elite Giants	17	
	1941	Baltimore Elite Giants	8	
	1942	Baltimore Elite Giants	3	
	1942	East All Stars	9	
	1946	Baltimore Elite Giants	11	15
	1947	Baltimore Elite Giants	16	
	1948	Baltimore Elite Giants		16

Uniform Numbers

	1949	Philadelphia Stars		7 & 3
	1950	Philadelphia Stars	1	
	1951	Philadelphia Stars	1	
Gaines, Willie	1953	Indianapolis Clowns	30	
	1954	Indianapolis Clowns	30	
	1955	Indianapolis Clowns	30	
Galata, Raúl	1949	Indianapolis Clowns		25
Gant, Calvin	1959	Detroit Stars	22	
Garay, José	1950	New York Cubans	18	
García, Atires	1945	Cincy-Indy Clowns	2	
	1946	Indianapolis Clowns		9
	1948	Indianapolis Clowns	1	
García, Manuel	1935	New York Cubans	18	
García, Silvio	1940	New York Cubans	1	
	1946	New York Cubans	17	
	1947	New York Cubans	17	
Garner, Horace	1949	Indianapolis Clowns	35	
Garrido, Gil	1944	New York Cubans	4	
	1945	New York Cubans	4	
Gary, Charles	1948	Homestead Grays	21	
	1949	Homestead Grays	31	
Gaston, Robert	1939	Homestead Grays		9
	1940	Homestead Grays	5	
	1941	Homestead Grays	2	
	1942	Homestead Grays	14	
	1944	Homestead Grays	14	
	1945	Homestead Grays	4	
	1947	Homestead Grays	29	
	1949	Homestead Grays	27	
Gay, William Howard	1944	Great Lakes Bluejackets	11	
Gerrard, Alphonso	1947	Indianapolis Clowns	19	
	1947	New York Black Yankees	7	
	1948	Chicago American Giants	5	
	1949	Indianapolis Clowns		35
Gibbons, Walter	1948	Indianapolis Clowns	4	
	1949	Indianapolis Clowns	28	
Gibson, Josh	1934	Pittsburgh Crawfords	11	
	1936	Pittsburgh Crawfords	11	
	1939	Homestead Grays		4
	1942	Homestead Grays	20	
	1942	East All Stars	3	
	1943	Homestead Grays	20	
	1944	Homestead Grays	20	
	1945	Homestead Grays	20	
	1946	Homestead Grays	30	
Gibson, Ralph	1956	Memphis Red Sox	11	

	1957	Memphis Red Sox	13	
Gilbert, Paul	1959	Kansas City Monarchs	45	
Gilliam, Jim	1946	Baltimore Elite Giants		12
	1947	Baltimore Elite Giants	18	
	1948	Baltimore Elite Giants	18	16
	1949	Baltimore Elite Giants	16	
Gilmore, James	1954	Kansas City Monarchs	20	
Gipson, Alvin	1943	Birmingham Black Barons	12	
	1944	Birmingham Black Barons	36	36
	1946	Birmingham Black Barons	17	
Gipson, Rufus	1957	Memphis Red Sox	1	
	1958	Memphis Red Sox	7	
	1959	Memphis Red Sox	7	
	1960	Raleigh Tigers	1	
Gist, Romie	1955	New York Black Yankees	30	
Givens, Oscar	1946	Newark Eagles	11	
	1948	Newark Eagles	15	
Gladstone, Granville	1950	Indianapolis Clowns	31	
Glenn, Hubert	1944	Philadelphia Stars	32	
	1945	Philadelphia Stars	20	11
Glenn, Stanley	1944	Philadelphia Stars	12	17
	1945	Philadelphia Stars	15	14
	1947	Philadelphia Stars	12	
	1948	Philadelphia Stars	12	
	1949	Philadelphia Stars	6	
Glover, Thomas	1939	Baltimore Elite Giants	16	
	1942	Baltimore Elite Giants	14	
	1943	Baltimore Elite Giants	15	
	1945	Baltimore Elite Giants	12	
Godinez, Manuel	1946	Indianapolis Clowns	16	
	1947	Indianapolis Clowns	16	
	1948	Indianapolis Clowns	16	
	1949	Indianapolis Clowns	25	
Golden, Clyde	1948	Newark Eagles	10	
González, Rene	1950	New York Cubans	17	
Gould, John	1947	Philadelphia Stars	19	
	1948	Philadelphia Stars	19	
Grace, Willie	1946	Cleveland Buckeyes	43	
	1948	Cleveland Buckeyes	43	
	1949	Louisville Buckeyes	43	
Grant, Arthur	1944	Great Lakes Bluejackets	24	
Graham, Foster	1958	Memphis Red Sox	16	
Grant, Calvin	1960	Kansas City Monarchs	53	
Graves, Whitt	1951	Indianapolis Clowns	39	
Gray, Chesley	1942	New York Black Yankees	9	6
	1945	Kansas City Monarchs		2

	1946	Boston Blues	26	
Greason, William	1948	Birmingham Black Barons	18	
	1949	Birmingham Black Barons	18	
	1950	Birmingham Black Barons	18	
Green, Herman	1959	Detroit Stars	20	
Green, Leslie	1942	New York Black Yankees	1	11
Green, Shedrick	1955	Indianapolis Clowns	29	
Greene, James	1942	Kansas City Monarchs	23	
	1942	West All Stars	2	
	1946	Kansas City Monarchs	19	22
	1947	Kansas City Monarchs	28	35
	1948	Cleveland Buckeyes	12	
Greenidge, Victor	1944	New York Cubans	15	
Griffith, Robert	1936	Washington Elite Giants	10	
	1941	Baltimore Elite Giants	7	
	1942	New York Black Yankees	23	25
	1946	New York Black Yankees	15	16
	1947	New York Black Yankees	15	
	1949	Philadelphia Stars	11	20 & 33
	1951	Philadelphia Stars		33
Griggs, Wiley	1958	Kansas City Monarchs	18	
Guilbe, Felix	1946	Baltimore Elite Giants		11
	1947	Baltimore Elite Giants	11	
Guilbe, Juan	1940	New York Cubans	12	
	1947	Indianapolis Clowns	18	
Haggins, Ray	1958	Memphis Red Sox	9	
Hair, Harold	1957	Kansas City Monarchs	19	
	1958	Kansas City Monarchs	29	
Hairston, Dick	1953	Indianapolis Clowns		8
	1954	Indianapolis Clowns	39	
Hairston, Harold	1946	Homestead Grays	14	8
Hairston, Sam	1945	Cincy-Indy Clowns	17	
	1946	Indianapolis Clowns	17	
	1947	Indianapolis Clowns	17	
	1948	Indianapolis Clowns	19	
	1949	Indianapolis Clowns	36	
	1950	Indianapolis Clowns	32	
Hamilton, Arthur Lee	1953	Indianapolis Clowns		2
	1954	Indianapolis Clowns	24	
	1959	Detroit Stars	12	
	1960	Detroit-New Orleans Stars	23	
Hamilton, J.C.	1940	Homestead Grays	15	
	1941	Homestead Grays	15	
	1942	Homestead Grays	15	
Hardaway, Curtis	1953	Indianapolis Clowns	32	
Hardy, Paul	1943	Birmingham Black Barons	24	

Hardy, Walter	1946	New York Black Yankees	9	18
	1947	New York Black Yankees	18	
	1950	New York Cubans	7	
Harmon, Chuck	1944	Great Lakes Bluejackets	8	
Harney, George	1928	Chicago American Giants	24	
Harris, Curtis Popsicle	1935	Pittsburgh Crawfords	17	
	1936	Kansas City Monarchs	8	
	1939	Philadelphia Stars	26	
	1940	Philadelphia Stars	26	
Harris, Donnie	1958	Birmingham Black Barons	12	
Harris, Eddie	1955	New York Black Yankees	38	
Harris, Ernest	1959	Birmingham Black Barons	21	
Harris, Lonnie	1958	Memphis Red Sox	1	
Harris, Tommy	1948	Cleveland Buckeyes	38	
	1949	Louisville Buckeyes	38	
Harris, Vic	1934	Pittsburgh Crawfords	14	
	1940	Homestead Grays	3	
	1941	Homestead Grays	3	
	1942	Homestead Grays	3	
	1942	East All Stars	24	
	1943	Homestead Grays	3	
	1944	Homestead Grays	3	
	1945	Homestead Grays	25	
	1946	Homestead Grays	25	
	1947	Homestead Grays	25	
	1948	Homestead Grays	25	
	1949	Baltimore Elite Giants	24	
Harris, Willie	1959	Detroit Stars	37	
	1960	Birmingham Black Barons	38	
Harris, Wilmer	1945	Philadelphia Stars	7	26
	1946	Philadelphia Stars	5	
	1947	Philadelphia Stars	5	
	1948	Philadelphia Stars	5	
	1949	Philadelphia Stars	3	
	1950	Philadelphia Stars	3	
	1951	Philadelphia Stars	23	
Harriston, Clyde	1944	Birmingham Black Barons	30	
	1944	Indy-Cincy Clowns		12
Hartman, Garrel	1944	Philadelphia Stars	14	
Harvey, Bob	1945	Biz Mackey's M.L. All Stars	21	
	1945	Newark Eagles	21	
	1946	Newark Eagles	18	
	1947	Newark Eagles	18	
	1948	Newark Eagles	18	
	1949	Houston Eagles	19	
Harvey, David	1942	Baltimore Elite Giants	4	

Uniform Numbers

	1943	Baltimore Elite Giants	20	
Haskin, Edward	1957	Kansas City Monarchs	10	
Hawkins, Lemuel	1928	Chicago American Giants	3	
Hayes, John	1939	Newark Eagles	8	
	1940	New York Black Yankees	11	
	1941	New York Black Yankees	8	
	1942	New York Black Yankees	8	9
	1942	East All Stars	7	
	1946	Boston Blues	20	
	1946	New York Black Yankees		16
	1947	New York Black Yankees	8	
	1949	Baltimore Elite Giants	25	26
Haynes, Sammy	1943	Kansas City Monarchs	32	
	1944	Kansas City Monarchs	17	
	1945	Kansas City Monarchs		10
Haywood, Albert	1943	Cincinnati Clowns	3	
	1944	Indy-Cincy Clowns	10	10
	1945	Cincy-Indy Clowns	24	
	1946	Indianapolis Clowns	10	
	1947	Indianapolis Clowns	6	
	1948	Indianapolis Clowns	5	
	1949	Indianapolis Clowns	27	28
	1951	Indianapolis Clowns	27	
	1953	Indianapolis Clowns	27	
Haywood, Bob	1960	Detroit-New Orleans Stars	19	
Heard, Jehosie	1946	Birmingham Black Barons	10	
	1947	Birmingham Black Barons	5	
Hechavarria, Gil	1957	Mobile Havana Cuban Giants	18	
Heffner, Arthur	1949	Philadelphia Stars	13	
Henderson, Jack	1946	Cleveland Clippers	5	
Henry, Alfred	1951	Philadelphia Stars	15	
Henry, Leo	1943	Cincinnati Clowns	5	
	1946	Indianapolis Clowns	6	
	1947	Indianapolis Clowns	1	
	1951	Indianapolis Clowns	24	
Henry, Prince Joe	1952	Memphis Red Sox	29	
	1955	Indianapolis Clowns	24	
Heredia, Ramón	1940	New York Cubans	9	
	1941	New York Cubans	9	
Hernández, Alberto	1941	New York Cubans	16	
Herrera, Pancho	1954	Kansas City Monarchs	10	
Herrera, Roberto	1955	Indianapolis Clowns	21	
Herve, C.	1954	Indianapolis Clowns	28	
Hicks, Eugene	1940	Homestead Grays	17	
	1941	New York Cubans	1	
Hill, Herb	1949	Philadelphia Stars	18	

Hill, Jimmy	1940	Newark Eagles	10	
	1941	Newark Eagles	1	
	1945	Newark Eagles	32	
Hill, Sam	1947	Chicago American Giants	7	
	1948	Chicago American Giants	7	
Hines, John	1928	Chicago American Giants	6	
Hinton, Roland	1945	Baltimore Elite Giants	20	
	1946	Baltimore Elite Giants	20	
Hobgood, Freddie	1941	Newark Eagles	14	
	1944	Philadelphia Stars	31	
	1946	New York Black Yankees	12	
Holder, Bill	1953	Indianapolis Clowns	3	
	1954	Indianapolis Clowns	29	
Holland, Bill	1934	New York Black Yankees	10	
	1939	New York Black Yankees	10	
	1940	New York Black Yankees	10	
	1941	New York Black Yankees	10	
Hollingsworth, Curtis	1946	Birmingham Black Barons	40	
	1947	Birmingham Black Barons	4	
Holmes, Eugene	1959	Raleigh Tigers	5	
Holmes, Frank	1934	Philadelphia Stars	16	
Holsey, Robert	1928	Chicago American Giants	23	
Holton, Lucious	1946	Cleveland Clippers	14	
Hooker, Leniel	1940	Newark Eagles	9	
	1941	Newark Eagles	11	
	1945	Biz Mackey's M.L. All Stars	33	
	1945	Newark Eagles	33	
	1946	Newark Eagles	5	
	1947	Newark Eagles	5	
	1948	Newark Eagles	5	
Hopkins, Gordon	1953	Indianapolis Clowns	1	1
	1954	Indianapolis Clowns	35	
Horn, Herman	1954	Kansas City Monarchs	23	
Horne, Billy J.	1942	West All Stars	12	
Hoskins, Bill	1939	Baltimore Elite Giants	8	
	1940	Baltimore Elite Giants	1	
	1941	Baltimore Elite Giants	1	
	1942	Baltimore Elite Giants	1	
	1943	Baltimore Elite Giants	1	
	1945	Baltimore Elite Giants	24	
	1946	Baltimore Elite Giants	24	
Hoskins, Clarence	1947	Detroit Wolves	28	
Hoskins, Dave	1944	Homestead Grays	6	
	1945	Homestead Grays	27	
	1946	Homestead Grays	27	
	1949	Louisville Buckeyes	48	

Name	Year	Team	#	
House, Charles	1947	Detroit Wolves	23	
Howard, Carrenza	1941	New York Cubans	7	
	1943	New York Cubans	5	
	1946	New York Cubans	19	
	1947	Indianapolis Clowns	9	
Howard, Elston	1948	Kansas City Monarchs	32	
	1949	Kansas City Monarchs	10	
	1950	Kansas City Monarchs	10	
Hubbard, Palmer	1958	Detroit Clowns	33	
	1958	Kansas City Monarchs	37	
	1959	Kansas City Monarchs	30	
	1960	Kansas City Monarchs	49	
Huber, John	1943	Birmingham Black Barons	44	
	1944	Birmingham Black Barons	8	50
Hubert, Willie	1939	Baltimore Elite Giants		1
	1940	Baltimore Elite Giants	8	
Hughes, Sammy T.	1936	Washington Elite Giants	2	
	1939	Baltimore Elite Giants	2	
	1940	Baltimore Elite Giants	2	
	1942	Baltimore Elite Giants	5	
	1946	Baltimore Elite Giants		28
Humber, Tom	1945	Newark Eagles	25	
Hunter, Bertrum	1934	Pittsburgh Crawfords	7	
Hutchinson, Willie	1943	Memphis Red Sox	2	
	1949	Memphis Red Sox	21	
Hyde, Cowan	1943	Memphis Red Sox	12	
Irvin, Monte	1939	Newark Eagles	18	
	1940	Newark Eagles	6	
	1941	Newark Eagles	18	
	1945	Biz Mackey's M.L. All Stars	35	
	1946	Newark Eagles	16	
	1947	Newark Eagles	16	
Isreal, Clarence	1940	Newark Eagles	2	
	1941	Newark Eagles	2	
	1946	Newark Eagles	8	
	1947	Homestead Grays	31	
Ivory James Sap	1959	Birmingham Black Barons	43	
	1960	Birmingham Black Barons	44	
Ivory, Willie	1958	Birmingham Black Barons	3	
Jackson, General	1947	Baltimore Elite Giants	21	
Jackson, A.J.	1956	Kansas City Monarchs	29	
	1958	Kansas City Monarchs	30	
Jackson, Al	1956	Kansas City Monarchs	30	
	1958	Kansas City Monarchs	35	
Jackson, Brown	1960	Birmingham Black Barons	42	
Jackson, Dan	1949	Homestead Grays	30	

Negro Leagues Book #2: The Players

Name	Year	Team	Col1	Col2
Jackson, John	1953	Kansas City Monarchs	24	
Jackson, Lester	1940	New York Black Yankees	8	
Jackson, Norman	1939	Homestead Grays		8
	1940	Homestead Grays	8	
	1944	Homestead Grays	18	
	1945	Homestead Grays	17	
Jackson, Stanford	1928	Chicago American Giants	9	
Jackson, Thomas	1946	Cleveland Clippers	16	
Jeffcoat, Albert	1955	New York Black Yankees	31	
Jefferson, Eddie	1946	Philadelphia Stars	12	
	1947	Detroit Wolves	20	
Jefferson, George	1946	Cleveland Buckeyes	20	22
	1949	Louisville Buckeyes	22	
Jefferson, Willie	1946	Cleveland Buckeyes	21	
Jeffries, Harry	1944	Indy-Cincy Clowns		17
Jenkins, Clarence	1934	New York Black Yankees	1	
	1940	Philadelphia Stars	19	
Jenkins, James (Pee Wee)	1946	New York Cubans	4	
	1947	New York Cubans	4	
	1948	New York Cubans	4	
	1950	New York Cubans	4	
Jessup, Gentry	1947	Chicago American Giants	17	
	1948	Chicago American Giants	17	
Jethroe, Sam	1946	Cleveland Buckeyes	27	
	1948	Cleveland Buckeyes	27	
Johnson, Abdulla (Showboat)	1956	Kansas City Monarchs	12	
	1957	Detroit Stars	11	
Johnson, Connie	1942	Kansas City Monarchs	4	
	1943	Kansas City Monarchs	31	
	1946	Kansas City Monarchs	17	21
	1947	Kansas City Monarchs	39	38
	1948	Kansas City Monarchs	38	
	1949	Kansas City Monarchs	15	
	1950	Kansas City Monarchs	15	
Johnson, Ernest	1953	Kansas City Monarchs	19	
Johnson, John	1950	New York Cubans	11	
Johnson, John (Johnny)	1939	Baltimore Elite Giants	23	
	1941	New York Cubans	18 & 5	
	1944	Homestead Grays	16	
	1946	New York Black Yankees	10	
Johnson, Judy	1934	Pittsburgh Crawfords	5	
	1936	Pittsburgh Crawfords	5	
Johnson, Leaman	1941	Newark Eagles	5	
	1942	New York Black Yankees	35	39
Johnson, Leonard	1947	Chicago American Giants	18	
Johnson, Mamie	1954	Indianapolis Clowns	25	

Johnson, Oziah	1946	Boston Blues	19	
Johnson, Roddie	1954	Indianapolis Clowns	25	
Johnson, Willie	1945	Philadelphia Stars	8	31
Johnston, Wade	1928	Detroit Stars	2	
Jones, Harold	1956	Kansas City Monarchs	14	
Jones, Herman	1960	Detroit-New Orleans Stars	28	
Jones, James	1943	Baltimore Elite Giants	9	
	1949	Philadelphia Stars	15	11
	1950	Philadelphia Stars	15	
Jones, Marvin	1954	Kansas City Monarchs	30	
Jones, Paul	1949	Louisville Buckeyes	20	
Jones, Paul Henry	1958	Memphis Red Sox	8	
Jones, Reuben	1928	Chicago American Giants	12	
Jones, Stuart	1934	Philadelphia Stars	17	
Jones, Tom	1946	Philadelphia Stars	20	
Jones, William	1957	Kansas City Monarchs	23	
Jordan, Larnie	1940	Philadelphia Stars	22	
	1941	Philadelphia Stars	22	
	1942	New York Black Yankees	7	35
Kaiser, Cecil	1947	Homestead Grays	17	
Kellman, Leon	1946	Cleveland Buckeyes	8	
	1948	Cleveland Buckeyes	8	
	1949	Louisville Buckeyes	10	
Kennedy, John	1956	Kansas City Monarchs	21	
Kennedy, Robert	1946	Boston Blues	15	
Keyes, Robert	1943	Memphis Red Sox	7	
Kimbro, Henry	1939	Baltimore Elite Giants	12	
	1940	Baltimore Elite Giants	12	
	1941	New York Black Yankees	1	
	1942	Baltimore Elite Giants	17	
	1943	Baltimore Elite Giants	12	
	1943	Philadelphia Stars	30	
	1945	Baltimore Elite Giants	14	
	1946	Baltimore Elite Giants	14	
	1947	Baltimore Elite Giants	14	
	1948	Baltimore Elite Giants	14	
	1949	Baltimore Elite Giants	14	
	1953	Birmingham Black Barons	14	
Kimbrough, Larry	1946	Philadelphia Stars	11	
Kincannon, Harry	1934	Pittsburgh Crawfords	10	
	1935	Pittsburgh Crawfords	15	
King, Alton	1947	Detroit Wolves	32	
King, Clarence	1950	Birmingham Black Barons	4	
King, Wilbur	1947	Detroit Wolves	34	
	1947	Homestead Grays	27	
Laduna, Phil	1954	Indianapolis Clowns	26	

Lamar, Clarence	1943	Cincinnati Clowns	17	
LaMarque, Jim	1942	Kansas City Monarchs	10	
	1944	Kansas City Monarchs	33	
	1945	Kansas City Monarchs	25	16
	1946	Kansas City Monarchs	16	32
	1947	Kansas City Monarchs	29	23
	1948	Kansas City Monarchs	34	
	1949	Kansas City Monarchs	26	
	1950	Kansas City Monarchs	26	
Lansing, Wilbur	1948	Newark Eagles		2
Lee, Willie	1958	Kansas City Monarchs	40	
LeGrande, Larry	1959	Detroit Stars	10	
Leon, Isidore	1948	New York Cubans	2	
Leonard, Walter	1939	Homestead Grays		3
	1940	Homestead Grays	4	
	1941	Homestead Grays	4	
	1943	Homestead Grays	4	
	1944	Homestead Grays	4	
	1945	Homestead Grays	32	
	1946	Homestead Grays	32	
	1947	Homestead Grays	32	
	1948	Homestead Grays	27	
	1949	Homestead Grays	32	
Lewis, Jim	1953	Indianapolis Clowns	4	4
Lewis, Rufus	1946	Newark Eagles	12	
	1947	Newark Eagles	12	
	1948	Newark Eagles	12	
	1949	Houston Eagles	13	12
Ligon, Rufus	1958	Memphis Red Sox	21	
Lillard, Joe	1944	Birmingham Black Barons	31	
Linares, Rogelio	1940	New York Cubans	7	
	1943	New York Cubans	7	
	1944	New York Cubans	7	
	1945	New York Cubans	7	
	1946	New York Cubans	7	
Lindsay, Leonard	1943	Cincinnati Clowns	19	
	1946	Indianapolis Clowns	12	
Littles, Ben	1949	Philadelphia Stars	5	3
	1950	Philadelphia Stars	19	
	1951	Philadelphia Stars	30	
Locke, Clarence	1947	Chicago American Giants	16	
	1948	Chicago American Giants	16	
Locke, Eddie	1945	Kansas City Monarchs	15	
Lockett, Lester	1943	Birmingham Black Barons	40	
	1944	Birmingham Black Barons	40	40
	1945	Birmingham Black Barons	18	

	1947	Baltimore Elite Giants	29	
	1948	Baltimore Elite Giants	20	29
	1949	Baltimore Elite Giants	29	
Logan, Carl	1940	Philadelphia Stars	20	
Long, Carl	1953	Birmingham Black Barons	11	
Long, Earnest	1949	Louisville Buckeyes	17	
Longest, Bernell	1947	Chicago American Giants	15	
Longley, Wayman	1943	Memphis Red Sox	14	
López, Raúl	1948	New York Cubans	5	
	1949	New York Cubans	5	
Lott, Benjamin	1951	Indianapolis Clowns	28	
Lott, Raymond	1950	Philadelphia Stars	7	
Louden, Louis	1944	New York Cubans	16	
	1946	New York Cubans	12	
	1947	New York Cubans	12	
	1948	New York Cubans	12	
	1950	New York Cubans	12	
Lowe, Gregory	1960	Detroit-New Orleans Stars	24	
Lugo, Levingelo	1944	Indianapolis-Cincinnati Clowns	20	20
	1946	Indianapolis-Cincinnati Clowns	7	
Lugo, Orlando	1954	Indianapolis Clowns	39	33
	1955	New York Black Yankees	20	
Lundy, Dick	1939	Newark Eagles	14	
	1940	Newark Eagles	18	
Lytle, John	1955	Indianapolis Clowns	32	
Mackell, Frank	1943	Baltimore Elite Giants	8	
Mackey, Raleigh	1934	Philadelphia Stars	2	
	1936	Washington Elite Giants	14	
	1939	Baltimore Elite Giants	20	
	1939	Newark Eagles	25	
	1940	Newark Eagles	25	
	1941	Newark Eagles	20	
	1945	Biz Mackey's M.L. All Stars	7	
	1945	Newark Eagles	7	
	1946	Newark Eagles	40	
	1947	Newark Eagles	40	
Maddix, Raydell	1949	Indianapolis Clowns	31	
	1950	Indianapolis Clowns	40	
Mahoney, Ulysses	1944	Philadelphia Stars	26	27
Mainor, Hank	1951	Philadelphia Stars	11	
Malarcher, Dave	1928	Chicago American Giants	1	
	1934	Chicago American Giants	10	
	1936	Chicago American Giants	25	
Manning, Maxwell	1939	Newark Eagles	16	
	1940	Newark Eagles	14	
	1941	Newark Eagles	16	

	1946	Newark Eagles	4	
	1947	Newark Eagles	4	
	1948	Newark Eagles	4	
Marcell, Everett	1940	Homestead Grays	18	
	1941	New York Black Yankees	20	
	1947	Baltimore Elite Giants	20	
Markham, John	1943	Birmingham Black Barons	39	
	1944	Birmingham Black Barons	11	11
Maroto, Enrique	1954	Kansas City Monarchs	19	
	1956	Kansas City Monarchs	19	
Márquez, Luis	1946	Homestead Grays	16	14
	1947	Homestead Grays	16	
	1948	Homestead Grays	16	
Marsh, Frank	1957	Kansas City Monarchs	28	
Marshall, Hiram	1946	Boston Blues	13	
Marshall, Jack	1928	Detroit Stars	9	
Marshall, William	1934	Chicago American Giants	4	
	1944	Indy-Cincy Clowns		15
Martin, William	1928	Detroit Stars	7	
Martínez, Horacio	1935	New York Cubans	22	
	1940	New York Cubans	18	
	1941	New York Cubans	12	
	1943	New York Cubans	18	
	1945	New York Cubans	18	
	1946	New York Cubans	15	
	1947	New York Cubans		2
Marvray, Charles	1949	Louisville Buckeyes	19	
Mason, Hank	1954	Kansas City Monarchs		29
Mason, Jim	1955	Indianapolis Clowns	33	
Matchett, Jack	1942	Kansas City Monarchs	27	
	1943	Kansas City Monarchs	27	
	1944	Kansas City Monarchs	9	
	1945	Kansas City Monarchs	40	4
Mathis, Verdell	1942	West All Stars	18	
	1943	Memphis Red Sox	18	
	1945	Memphis Red Sox	15	
Matlock, Leroy	1934	Pittsburgh Crawfords	12	
	1935	Pittsburgh Crawfords	16	
	1936	Pittsburgh Crawfords	16	
Matthews, Bill	1959	Detroit Stars	45	
	1960	Detroit-New Orleans Stars	22	
Matthews, Francis	1940	Newark Eagles	1	
	1941	Newark Eagles	6	
	1945	Newark Eagles	27	
Mays, Willie	1948	Birmingham Black Barons	21	
	1949	Birmingham Black Barons	21	

Uniform Numbers

	1950	Birmingham Black Barons	21	
Mayweather, Eldridge	1941	New Orleans-St. Louis Stars	9	
	1946	Boston Blues	6	
McAllister, Frank	1941	New Orleans-St. Louis Stars	17	
	1942	New York Black Yankees	17	34
McCollum, Frank	1957	Memphis Red Sox	11	
	1958	Kansas City Monarchs	44	
McCord, Clinton	1948	Baltimore Elite Giants		17
	1949	Baltimore Elite Giants		19
	1950	Chicago American Giants		24
McCoy, Chink	1955	New York Black Yankees	32	
McCoy, Walter	1947	Chicago American Giants	12	
	1948	Chicago American Giants	12	
McCurine, Jim	1947	Chicago American Giants	6	
	1948	Chicago American Giants	15	
McDaniel, Booker	1942	Kansas City Monarchs	21	
	1943	Kansas City Monarchs	21	
	1944	Kansas City Monarchs	20	
	1945	Kansas City Monarchs	29	14
	1949	Kansas City Monarchs	18	
McDaniel, Fred	1943	Memphis Red Sox	3	
McDonald, Webster	1934	Philadelphia Stars	1	
	1939	Philadelphia Stars	14	
	1940	Philadelphia Stars	14	
McDuffie, Terris	1939	New York Black Yankees	12	
	1941	Homestead Grays	12	
	1942	Philadelphia Stars	17	
McFarland, John	1947	New York Black Yankees		5
McHenry, Henry	1939	Philadelphia Stars	28	
	1940	Philadelphia Stars	28	
	1941	Philadelphia Stars	28	
	1946	Philadelphia Stars	14	
	1947	Philadelphia Stars	15	14
	1948	Philadelphia Stars	14	
McKinnis, Gready	1942	West All Stars	19	
	1943	Birmingham Black Barons	31	
	1949	Chicago American Giants	14	
McKnight, Ira	1956	Kansas City Monarchs	17	
	1957	Kansas City Monarchs	19	
	1958	Kansas City Monarchs	44	
	1960	Kansas City Monarchs	47	
McLaurin, Felix	1943	Birmingham Black Barons	2	
	1944	Birmingham Black Barons	2	2
	1946	New York Black Yankees	1	
McLawn, ?	1948	Newark Eagles		9
McNair, Hurley	1928	Detroit Stars	6	

Name	Year	Team		
McNeal, Clyde	1947	Chicago American Giants	10	
	1948	Chicago American Giants	10	
	1950	Chicago American Giants		10
McNeal, Rufus	1953	Indianapolis Clowns		11
	1954	Indianapolis Clowns	31	
	1955	Indianapolis Clowns	22	
McNeely, William	1946	Birmingham Black Barons	6	
McNeil, James	1959	Raleigh Tigers	6	
McQueen, Verdene	1958	Memphis Red Sox	15	
Medina, Lazarus	1944	Indy-Cincy Clowns		4
	1945	Cincy-Indy Clowns	18	
Medley, Calvin	1946	New York Black Yankees		40
Merchant, Henry	1944	Indy-Cincy Clowns	21	21
	1945	Cincy-Indy Clowns	21	
	1946	Indianapolis Clowns	21	
	1947	Indianapolis Clowns	21	
	1948	Indianapolis Clowns	21	
	1949	Indianapolis Clowns	34	27
	1951	Indianapolis Clowns	37	
	1953	Indianapolis Clowns	37	
	1954	Indianapolis Clowns	37	
Mesa, Andrés	1948	Indianapolis Clowns	6	
Miles, Cherry	1946	Cleveland Clippers	6	
Miles, Jack	1934	Chicago American Giants	1	
Miles, John	1947	Chicago American Giants	2	
Miller, Henry	1939	Philadelphia Stars	21	
	1940	Philadelphia Stars	21	
	1941	Philadelphia Stars	21	
	1944	Philadelphia Stars		31
	1945	Philadelphia Stars	5	17
	1946	Philadelphia Stars	16	
	1947	Philadelphia Stars	16	
	1948	Philadelphia Stars	16	
	1949	Philadelphia Stars	14	16
Miller, Leroy	1939	New York Black Yankees	7	
	1940	New York Black Yankees	7	
Miller, Melvin Ray	1960	Kansas City Monarchs	46	
Millon, Herald	1947	Chicago American Giants	4	
Milton, Henry	1936	Kansas City Monarchs	5	
Minor, George	1946	Cleveland Buckeyes	19	
	1948	Cleveland Buckeyes	3	
Miñoso, Minnie	1946	New York Cubans	10	
	1947	New York Cubans	10	
	1948	New York Cubans	10	
Mirabal, Antonio	1940	New York Cubans	2	
Miro, Pedro	1948	New York Cubans	19	

Name	Year	Team	#	#
Missouri, Jim	1939	Philadelphia Stars	29	
	1940	Philadelphia Stars	29	
Mitchell, Bob	1954	Kansas City Monarchs	11	
	1956	Kansas City Monarchs	25	
	1957	Kansas City Monarchs	25	
Mitchell, George	1941	New Orleans-St. Louis Stars	18	
Mitchell, Jesse	1957	Birmingham Black Barons	5	
	1958	Birmingham Black Barons	5	
	1959	Kansas City Monarchs	36	
Mitchell, John	1960	Birmingham Black Barons	32	
Mobley, Ira	1954	Kansas City Monarchs		24
Montgomery, Joe	1956	Kansas City Monarchs	18	
Moody, Lee	1944	Kansas City Monarchs	30	
	1945	Kansas City Monarchs	30	19
	1946	Kansas City Monarchs	31	30
	1947	Birmingham Black Barons	12	
Moore, James	1939	Baltimore Elite Giants		10
	1940	Baltimore Elite Giants	11	
Moore, Laurence	1954	Kansas City Monarchs	29	
Morgan, Connie	1954	Indianapolis Clowns	20	
Morgan, William	1945	Baltimore Elite Giants	19	
Morney, Leroy	1934	Pittsburgh Crawfords	6	
	1936	Pittsburgh Crawfords	9	
	1943	Cincinnati Clowns	14	
	1944	Birmingham Black Barons	60	
Morris, Barney	1943	New York Cubans	16	
	1944	New York Cubans	12	
	1946	New York Cubans	16	
	1947	New York Cubans	16	
Morton, Sidney	1943	Philadelphia Stars	10	
Moss, Porter	1936	Cincinnati Tigers	15	
	1942	West All Stars	27	
	1943	Memphis Red Sox	21	
Mumpford, Pete	1959	Birmingham Black Barons	33	
Murray, Mitch	1928	Chicago American Giants	7	
Murry, Dick	1955	New York Black Yankees	26	
Napier, Eudie	1946	Homestead Grays	36	9
	1947	Homestead Grays	26	
	1948	Homestead Grays	26	
Naranjo, Pedro	1951	Indianapolis Clowns	29	
Navarrette, Ramundo	1950	New York Cubans	10	
Navarro, Raymond	1945	Cincy-Indy Clowns	19	
Neil, Ray	1946	Indianapolis Clowns	2	
	1947	Indianapolis Clowns	2	
	1948	Indianapolis Clowns	2	
	1949	Indianapolis Clowns	22	

	1950	Indianapolis Clowns	22	
	1951	Indianapolis Clowns	22	
	1952	Indianapolis Clowns	22	
	1953	Indianapolis Clowns	22	
	1954	Indianapolis Clowns	27	
Nelson, Clyde	1948	Cleveland Buckeyes	26	
	1949	Indianapolis Clowns		34
Newberry, Jimmy	1943	Birmingham Black Barons	17	
	1944	Birmingham Black Barons	49	49
	1946	Birmingham Black Barons	7	
	1947	Birmingham Black Barons	15	
	1948	Birmingham Black Barons	17	
	1949	Birmingham Black Barons	17	
	1950	Birmingham Black Barons	17	
Newcombe, Don	1945	Biz Mackey's M.L. All Stars	23	
	1945	Newark Eagles	23	
Newkirk, Alexander	1946	New York Black Yankees	11	
	1947	New York Black Yankees	11	
Noble, Rafael	1946	New York Cubans	21	
	1947	New York Cubans	22	
	1948	New York Cubans	22	
Nolan, James	1958	Detroit Clowns	36	
Nuñez, Dagoberto	1954	Kansas City Monarchs	15	
O'Farrill, Orlando	1949	Philadelphia Stars		12
Oms, Alejandro	1935	New York Cubans	26	
O'Neil, Buck	1941	Kansas City Monarchs	1	
	1942	Kansas City Monarchs	20	
	1942	West All Stars	4	
	1943	Kansas City Monarchs	20	
	1946	Kansas City Monarchs	20	28
	1947	Kansas City Monarchs	22	
	1948	Kansas City Monarchs	33	
	1949	Kansas City Monarchs	22	
	1950	Kansas City Monarchs	22	
	1954	Kansas City Monarchs	22	
Orange, Grady	1928	Detroit Stars	4	
Ortiz, Felix	1957	Kansas City Monarchs	17	
Ortiz, Julio Arango	1945	Cincy-Indy Clowns	7	
Ortiz, Rafaelito	1948	Chicago American Giants	11	
Osorio, Alberto	1949	Louisville Buckeyes	28	
Overton, Albert	1944	Indy-Cincy Clowns	18	
Page, Ted	1934	Pittsburgh Crawfords	10	
Pagés, Pedro	1947	New York Cubans	18	
Paige, Leroy	1934	Pittsburgh Crawfords	1	
	1936	Pittsburgh Crawfords	1	
	1941	Kansas City Monarchs	15	

	1942	Kansas City Monarchs	25	
	1942	West All Stars	16	
	1943	Kansas City Monarchs	25	
	1944	Kansas City Monarchs	12	
	1945	Kansas City Monarchs	0	7
	1947	Kansas City Monarchs		21
Palm, Clarence	1939	New York Black Yankees	8	
	1941	Philadelphia Stars	27	
	1942	Philadelphia Stars	27	
	1944	Philadelphia Stars	18	
	1945	Philadelphia Stars	15	
	1946	New York Black Yankees	14	
Parker, Tom	1939	Homestead Grays		18
	1942	New York Black Yankees	21	10
	1946	Boston Blues	24	
	1948	Homestead Grays	43	
Parks, Charles	1940	Newark Eagles	8	
	1941	Newark Eagles	8	
	1946	Newark Eagles	36	
	1947	Newark Eagles	36	
Parnell, Roy	1939	Philadelphia Stars	25	
	1940	Philadelphia Stars	25	
	1941	Philadelphia Stars	25	
	1942	Philadelphia Stars	25	
	1943	Philadelphia Stars	25	
Parris, Clyde	1946	New York Black Yankees		7
	1947	New York Black Yankees	16	
Partlow, Roy	1939	Homestead Grays		16
	1941	Homestead Grays	16	
	1942	Homestead Grays	16	
	1943	Homestead Grays	12	
	1945	Biz Mackey's M.L. All Stars	30	
	1945	Philadelphia Stars	9	27
	1947	Philadelphia Stars	21	
	1948	Philadelphia Stars	21	
	1949	Homestead Grays	15	
Paschal, Alvin	1944	Great Lakes Bluejackets	14	
Patterson, Andrew	1936	Kansas City Monarchs	3	
	1939	Philadelphia Stars	22	
	1941	Philadelphia Stars	16	
	1942	Philadelphia Stars	30	
	1942	East All Stars	12	
	1946	Newark Eagles	10	
	1947	Newark Eagles	10	
	1949	Houston Eagles	3	
Patterson, Gabriel	1947	Homestead Grays	19	

	1947	New York Black Yankees		7
	1947	Philadelphia Stars		20
Patterson, Willie Lee	1950	New York Cubans	19	
	1953	Memphis Red Sox	8	
	1960	Detroit-New Orleans Stars	26	
Paul, Robert	1958	Detroit Clowns	4	
Peace, Warren	1945	Newark Eagles	28	
	1946	Newark Eagles	2	
	1947	Newark Eagles	2	
	1948	Newark Eagles	2	
Pearson, Leonard	1939	Newark Eagles	17	
	1940	Newark Eagles	7	
	1941	Newark Eagles	17	
	1942	East All Stars	1	
	1945	Biz Mackey's M.L. All Stars	24	
	1945	Newark Eagles	22	32
	1946	Newark Eagles	22	
	1947	Newark Eagles	22	
	1948	Newark Eagles	22	
	1949	Baltimore Elite Giants	30	
Pedroso, Fernando	1946	New York Cubans	9	
	1947	New York Cubans	9	
	1949	New York Cubans	9	
Peeples, Nat	1950	Kansas City Monarchs	29	
	1951	Indianapolis Clowns	36	
Peete, Charles	1950	Indianapolis Clowns	34	
Pendleton, Jim	1948	Chicago American Giants	18	
Pennington, Art	1942	Chicago American Giants	13	
	1945	Chicago American Giants	4	
	1950	Chicago American Giants		17
Pereira, José	1947	Baltimore Elite Giants	17	
Pérez, Javier	1943	New York Cubans	6	
	1944	New York Cubans	6	
Perkins, Bill	1940	Baltimore Elite Giants	3	
	1946	New York Black Yankees		8
	1946	Philadelphia Stars		12
	1948	Baltimore Elite Giants		21
Perry, Alonzo	1946	Homestead Grays	44	2
	1947	Birmingham Black Barons	7	
	1948	Birmingham Black Barons	7	
	1949	Birmingham Black Barons	7	
	1950	Birmingham Black Barons	7	
Peterson, Harvey	1946	Cleveland Clippers	18	
Phillips, Dick	1954	Kansas City Monarchs	18	
Phillips, John	1939	Baltimore Elite Giants	4	
Pigg, Leonard	1947	Indianapolis Clowns		7

	1948	Indianapolis Clowns	22	
	1949	Indianapolis Clowns	38	
	1951	Indianapolis Clowns	38	
Pillot, Luis	1941	New York Black Yankees	14	
	1943	Cincinnati Clowns	7	
	1944	Great Lakes Bluejackets	20	
Pitts, Curtis	1950	Chicago American Giants		44
Pitts, Ed	1940	Philadelphia Stars	15	
Pollard, Nat	1946	Birmingham Black Barons	12	
	1947	Birmingham Black Barons	10	
Poole, Claude	1946	New York Black Yankees	41	4
Pope, Willie	1947	Homestead Grays	36	
	1948	Homestead Grays	23	
Porter, Andrew	1942	Baltimore Elite Giants	6	
	1943	Baltimore Elite Giants	5	
	1945	Baltimore Elite Giants	18	
	1946	Baltimore Elite Giants	18	
	1947	Newark Eagles	14	
	1948	Indianapolis Clowns	17	
	1949	Indianapolis Clowns	37	
Portier, James	1954	Indianapolis Clowns	25	
Powell, Bill	1946	Birmingham Black Barons	11	
	1947	Birmingham Black Barons	19	
	1948	Birmingham Black Barons	19	
	1949	Birmingham Black Barons	4	19
	1950	Birmingham Black Barons	19	
Powell, Malvin	1934	Chicago American Giants	6	
Powell, Willie	1928	Chicago American Giants	13	
Presswood, Henry	1948	Cleveland Buckeyes	30	
Preston, Albert	1946	New York Black Yankees	40	
	1947	New York Black Yankees	5	
Pride, Charlie	1956	Memphis Red Sox	6	
	1958	Memphis Red Sox	12	
Pride, Mack	1956	Kansas City Monarchs	15	
Proctor, Jim	1955	New York Black Yankees	34	
Quarterman, Isiah	1955	Indianapolis Clowns	34	
Quiñones, Thomas	1947	Indianapolis Clowns	14	
Radcliff, Alex	1934	Chicago American Giants	3	
	1936	Chicago American Giants	6	
	1944	Indy-Cincy Clowns	14	14
	1945	Cincy-Indy Clowns	14	
Radcliffe, Everett	1934	Chicago American Giants	9	
Radcliffe, Ted	1928	Detroit Stars	8	
	1942	West All Stars	8	
	1944	Birmingham Black Barons	34	8
	1945	Kansas City Monarchs	27	

	1946	Homestead Grays	31	
Randall, Sonny	1944	Great Lakes Bluejackets	22	
Ray, John	1943	Cincinnati Clowns	15	
	1944	Indy-Cincy Clowns	25	5
Rector, Cornelius	1934	New York Black Yankees	11	
	1941	New York Black Yankees	11	
Redus, Wilson	1934	Chicago American Giants	17	
	1936	Chicago American Giants	18	
Reed, Eddie	1953	Memphis Red Sox	12	
Reed, Leroy	1946	Cleveland Clippers	4	
Renfroe, Othello	1945	Kansas City Monarchs	28	12
	1946	Kansas City Monarchs	11	25
	1947	Kansas City Monarchs	31	32
	1948	Cleveland Buckeyes	18	
Reynolds, William	1949	Louisville Buckeyes	15	
Rhodes, Harry	1947	Chicago American Giants	1	
	1948	Chicago American Giants	1	
	1950	Chicago American Giants		20
Richardson, Gene	1947	Kansas City Monarchs		27 & 3
	1948	Kansas City Monarchs	27	
	1949	Kansas City Monarchs	20	
Richardson, Glemby	1946	New York Black Yankees		3
	1947	New York Black Yankees	9	
Richardson, Johnny	1949	Homestead Grays	16	
Richardson, T.W.	1953	Indianapolis Clowns	23	
	1954	Indianapolis Clowns	23	
	1955	Indianapolis Clowns	27	
Ricks, Bill	1944	Philadelphia Stars	15	
	1945	Philadelphia Stars	17	15
	1946	Philadelphia Stars	15	
	1948	Philadelphia Stars	15	
	1949	Philadelphia Stars	12	15
Riddle, Marshall	1941	New Orleans-St. Louis Stars	1	
Rile, Ed	1928	Detroit Stars	5	
Ritchey, John	1947	Chicago American Giants	9	
Rivero, Carlos	1939	Baltimore Elite Giants	9	
	1943	New York Cubans	20	
Roane, Alvin	1959	Raleigh Tigers	12	
Roberts, Curt	1947	Kansas City Monarchs		33
	1948	Kansas City Monarchs	22	
	1949	Kansas City Monarchs	24	
	1950	Kansas City Monarchs	24	
Roberts, Eugene	1957	Memphis Red Sox	8	
Roberts, Tom	1939	Homestead Grays		17
Robinson, Arzell	1959	Memphis Red Sox	8	
Robinson, Booker	1945	Homestead Grays	29	

Uniform Numbers

Robinson, Cornelius	1943	Memphis Red Sox	4	
	1945	Memphis Red Sox	22	
Robinson, Frazier	1943	Baltimore Elite Giants	7	
Robinson, Henry	1946	Baltimore Elite Giants	26	
	1947	Baltimore Elite Giants	26	
	1948	Baltimore Elite Giants	26	
	1949	Baltimore Elite Giants	26	
Robinson, Jackie	1945	Kansas City Monarchs	23 & 5	39 & 8
Robinson, Jim	1956	Kansas City Monarchs	11	
	1957	Kansas City Monarchs	11	
	1958	Kansas City Monarchs	31	
Robinson, Neal	1936	Cincinnati Tigers	17	
Robinson, Norman	1945	Baltimore Elite Giants	21	
	1946	Baltimore Elite Giants	21	
	1947	Birmingham Black Barons	17	
	1950	Birmingham Black Barons	12	
Robinson, Ray	1947	Philadelphia Stars	20	
Rodríguez, Antonio	1944	New York Cubans	2	
Rodríguez, Benvienido	1948	Chicago American Giants	4	
Rogers, William	1943	Memphis Red Sox	17	
Romby, Robert	1946	Baltimore Elite Giants	19	
	1947	Baltimore Elite Giants	15	
	1948	Baltimore Elite Giants	15	18
	1949	Baltimore Elite Giants	18	
Ruffin, Leon	1939	Philadelphia Stars	27	
	1940	Philadelphia Stars	27	
	1946	Newark Eagles	9	
	1949	Houston Eagles	12	
Ruiz, Antonio	1944	Indy-Cincy Clowns	16	16
Ruiz, Silvino	1940	New York Cubans	11	
	1941	New York Cubans	12	
Russ, Pythias	1928	Chicago American Giants	5	
Russell, Frank	1943	Baltimore Elite Giants	4	
	1946	Baltimore Elite Giants	28	4
	1948	Baltimore Elite Giants	27	17
	1949	Baltimore Elite Giants	17	
Sails, Rosell	1951	Philadelphia Stars	18	
Salas, Wilfredo	1948	New York Cubans	11	
Salazar, Lázaro	1935	New York Cubans	17	
Sama, Pablo	1950	Indianapolis Clowns	24	
Sampson, Tommy	1943	Birmingham Black Barons	34	
	1944	Birmingham Black Barons	5	5
	1946	Birmingham Black Barons	35	
	1947	Birmingham Black Barons	13	
Sanders, Bobby	1959	Birmingham Black Barons	34	
Sanders, Jake	1959	Detroit Stars	21	

Name	Year	Team		
Sanderson, Johnny	1947	Kansas City Monarchs		16 & 39
Sands, Sam	1953	Indianapolis Clowns	39	
Santaella, Anastasio	1935	New York Cubans	23	
Santiago, José	1948	New York Cubans	7	
Saylor, Alfred	1943	Birmingham Black Barons	20	
	1944	Birmingham Black Barons	20	20
Scales, George	1934	New York Black Yankees	17	
	1939	New York Black Yankees	18	
	1940	Baltimore Elite Giants	16	
	1941	Baltimore Elite Giants	16	
	1942	Baltimore Elite Giants	16	
	1943	Baltimore Elite Giants	16	
	1946	Baltimore Elite Giants	29	
Scantlebury, Pat	1944	New York Cubans	3	
	1946	New York Cubans	3	
	1947	New York Cubans	3	
	1948	New York Cubans	3	
	1949	New York Cubans	3	
	1950	New York Cubans	3	
Scott, Bill	1951	Philadelphia Stars	6	
Scott, Joe	1948	Birmingham Black Barons	10	
	1949	Birmingham Black Barons	10	
	1950	Chicago American Giants		22
Scott, John	1944	Birmingham Black Barons		35
	1945	Kansas City Monarchs	16	18
	1946	Kansas City Monarchs	6	39
	1947	Kansas City Monarchs	24	25
	1948	Kansas City Monarchs	25	
	1949	Louisville Buckeyes	44	
Scott, Robert	1946	Boston Blues	29	
	1946	New York Black Yankees	3	
Scott, Willie Lee	1934	Chicago American Giants	18	
Scroggins, John	1947	Kansas City Monarchs		30 & 34
Scruggs, Don	1954	Kansas City Monarchs	30	
Scruggs, William	1949	Birmingham Black Barons	2	
	1949	Louisville Buckeyes	33	
Seay, Richard	1934	Philadelphia Stars	4	
	1939	Newark Eagles	2	
	1941	New York Black Yankees	7	
	1942	New York Black Yankees	2	2
	1946	New York Black Yankees	8	9
	1947	New York Black Yankees	4	
Self, John	1958	Kansas City Monarchs	36	
Serrell, Barney	1942	Kansas City Monarchs	26	
	1943	Kansas City Monarchs	26	
	1944	Kansas City Monarchs	11	

	1949	Kansas City Monarchs	16	
	1950	Kansas City Monarchs	16	
Shade, Harold	1958	Detroit Clowns	14	
Sharpe, Robert	1943	Memphis Red Sox	15	
Shaw, Ted	1928	Detroit Stars	13	
Shepard, Fred	1946	Birmingham Black Barons	8	
Sierra, Pedro	1954	Indianapolis Clowns	26	
Silvio, Orlando	1957	Mobile Havana Cuban Giants	5	
Simmons, Arthur Lee	1958	Kansas City Monarchs	45	
Simms, Bill	1942	Kansas City Monarchs	17	
	1943	Kansas City Monarchs	17	
Simpson, Harry	1946	Philadelphia Stars	7	
	1947	Philadelphia Stars	7	
	1948	Philadelphia Stars	7	
Smallwood, Dewitt	1951	Indianapolis Clowns	17	7
	1953	Indianapolis Clowns		7
	1955	New York Black Yankees	27	
Smith, Al	1948	Cleveland Buckeyes	29	
Smith, Eugene	1941	New Orleans-St. Louis Stars	16	
	1942	New York Black Yankees	20	26
	1942	East All Stars	14	
	1946	Homestead Grays	18	5
	1946	Indianapolis Clowns	18	18
	1947	Homestead Grays	18	
Smith, Henry	1943	Cincinnati Clowns	12	
	1944	Indy-Cincy Clowns	12	4
	1945	Cincy-Indy Clowns	12	
Smith, Hilton	1941	Kansas City Monarchs	12	
	1942	Kansas City Monarchs	24	
	1942	West All Stars	17	
	1943	Kansas City Monarchs	24	
	1944	Kansas City Monarchs	24	
	1945	Kansas City Monarchs	31	20
	1946	Kansas City Monarchs	3	23
	1947	Kansas City Monarchs		23 & 31
	1948	Kansas City Monarchs	31	
Smith, John Ford	1941	Kansas City Monarchs	13	
	1946	Kansas City Monarchs	10	37
	1947	Kansas City Monarchs		20 & 35
	1948	Kansas City Monarchs	35	
Smith, John Lefty	1946	New York Black Yankees		19
	1947	New York Black Yankees	12	
Smith, Milt	1949	Philadelphia Stars		7 & 4
	1950	Philadelphia Stars	32	
Smith, Monroe	1944	Kansas City Monarchs	4	
Smith, Percy	1953	Indianapolis Clowns	24	

Name	Year	Team		
Smith, Raymond	1945	Philadelphia Stars	7	
Smith, Robert	1941	New Orleans-St. Louis Stars	4	
	1943	Memphis Red Sox	8	
Smith, Willie	1948	Homestead Grays	34	
	1958	Birmingham Black Barons	7	
	1959	Birmingham Black Barons	36	
Snead, Sylvester	1943	Cincinnati Clowns	12	
	1946	New York Black Yankees		19 & 1
Snow, Felton	1936	Washington Elite Giants	5	
	1939	Baltimore Elite Giants	15	
	1940	Baltimore Elite Giants	5	
	1941	Baltimore Elite Giants	2	
	1942	Baltimore Elite Giants	2	
	1943	Baltimore Elite Giants	2	
	1943	Philadelphia Stars	26	
	1945	Baltimore Elite Giants	17	
	1946	Baltimore Elite Giants	17	
Snyder, Smith	1943	New York Cubans	9	
Souell, Herb	1942	Kansas City Monarchs	22	
	1943	Kansas City Monarchs	22	
	1944	Kansas City Monarchs	22	
	1945	Kansas City Monarchs	22	21
	1946	Kansas City Monarchs	15	24
	1947	Kansas City Monarchs	27	42
	1948	Kansas City Monarchs	42	
	1949	Kansas City Monarchs	25	
	1950	Kansas City Monarchs	25	
Sowell, Clyde	1948	Baltimore Elite Giants	17	
Spearman, Clyde	1934	New York Black Yankees	2	
	1935	New York Cubans	16	
	1943	Birmingham Black Barons	4	
	1944	Philadelphia Stars	11	11
	1945	Philadelphia Stars		11
	1946	New York Black Yankees	18	
Spearman, Henry	1939	Homestead Grays		6
	1940	New York Black Yankees	22	
	1941	Baltimore Elite Giants	3	
	1942	Philadelphia Stars	11	
	1943	Philadelphia Stars	11	
Spencer, Joe	1944	Homestead Grays	12	
	1947	Baltimore Elite Giants	33	
Spriggs, George	1960	Detroit-New Orleans Stars	21	
St. Thomas, Larry	1947	New York Black Yankees	24	
Stanley, John	1934	New York Black Yankees	15	
	1935	New York Cubans	27	
	1939	New York Black Yankees	17	

Name	Year	Team	#	#
	1940	New York Black Yankees	17	
	1941	New York Black Yankees	17	
	1942	New York Black Yankees	22	31
	1946	New York Black Yankees	17	
	1947	New York Black Yankees	17	
Starks, James	1941	New York Black Yankees	22	
Stearnes, Turkey	1928	Detroit Stars	3	
	1930	Detroit Stars	8	
	1934	Chicago American Giants	15	
Steele, Ed	1944	Birmingham Black Barons	28	26
	1945	Birmingham Black Barons	6	
	1946	Birmingham Black Barons	31	
	1947	Birmingham Black Barons	3	
	1948	Birmingham Black Barons	20	
	1949	Birmingham Black Barons	20	
	1950	Birmingham Black Barons	20	
Stephens, Paul	1934	Philadelphia Stars	6	
Stevenson, Willie	1940	Homestead Grays	16	
Stewart, Leon	1940	Newark Eagles	16	
Stewart, Riley	1947	Chicago American Giants	11	
	1948	Chicago American Giants	21	
	1950	New York Cubans	21	
Stone, Ed	1939	Newark Eagles	3	
	1940	Newark Eagles	3	
	1944	Philadelphia Stars	28	
	1945	Philadelphia Stars	12	28
Stone, Toni	1953	Indianapolis Clowns	29	
	1954	Kansas City Monarchs	30	4
Streeter, Sam	1934	Pittsburgh Crawfords	2	
Strong, Othello	1950	Chicago American Giants		39
Strong, T.R.	1941	Kansas City Monarchs	9	
	1942	Kansas City Monarchs	28	
	1942	West All Stars	7	
	1946	Kansas City Monarchs	8	40
	1947	Kansas City Monarchs	40	30
	1948	Indianapolis Clowns	14	
Strozier, Albert	1957	Memphis Red Sox	15	
	1958	Memphis Red Sox	11	
Summerow, Stephen	1944	Great Lakes Bluejackets	17	
Summers, Lonnie	1949	Chicago American Giants	9	
Sunkett, Pete	1943	Philadelphia Stars	20	
	1944	Philadelphia Stars	16	
	1945	Philadelphia Stars	1	25
Suttles, George	1934	Chicago American Giants	2	
	1939	Newark Eagles	4	
	1940	Newark Eagles	4	

		1941	New York Black Yankees	2	
Sutton, Leroy		1941	New Orleans-St. Louis Stars	11	
		1946	Boston Blues	23	
Taborn, Earl		1946	Kansas City Monarchs	9	31
		1947	Kansas City Monarchs	25	28
		1948	Kansas City Monarchs	28	
		1949	Kansas City Monarchs	29	
Talbert, James		1947	Chicago American Giants	8	
		1948	Chicago American Giants	8	
Talley, Richard (Kid)		1934	New York Black Yankees	12	
Tatum, Reece		1943	Cincinnati Clowns	4	
		1946	Indianapolis Clowns	15	
		1947	Indianapolis Clowns	12	
		1948	Indianapolis Clowns	20	
		1949	Indianapolis Clowns	33	
Taylor, Candy Jim		1943	Homestead Grays	9	
		1944	Homestead Grays	9	
		1946	Homestead Grays	10	
		1947	Chicago American Giants	21	
Taylor, Herman		1947	Asheville Blues	11	
Taylor, Joe		1954	Kansas City Monarchs		28
Taylor, Johnny		1935	New York Cubans	29	
		1940	New York Cubans	5	
Taylor, Leroy		1936	Kansas City Monarchs	1	
Taylor, Olan		1956	Kansas City Monarchs	50	
Taylor, Raymond		1946	Cleveland Clippers	8	
Taylor, Robert		1941	New Orleans-St. Louis Stars	2	
Taylor, Sam		1954	Indianapolis Clowns	22	
Taylor, Tommy		1959	Kansas City Monarchs	43	
		1960	Kansas City Monarchs	56	
Taylor, Travis		1946	Cleveland Clippers	11	
Thomas, C.		1955	New York Black Yankees	24	
Thomas, Clint		1934	New York Black Yankees	4	
Thomas, Dave		1934	New York Black Yankees	6	
		1935	New York Cubans	25	
		1944	New York Cubans	11	
		1945	Biz Mackey's M.L. All Stars	26	
		1946	New York Cubans	11	
Thomas, John		1947	Birmingham Black Barons	14	
Thomas, Nelson		1947	Newark Eagles	15	
Thomas, Vern		1958	Memphis Red Sox	34	
Thomas, Walter		1944	Kansas City Monarchs	15	
		1945	Kansas City Monarchs	10	5
		1947	Detroit Wolves	29	
Thomason, Charles		1941	Newark Eagles	3	
Thompson, Frank		1946	Homestead Grays	17	14

Uniform Numbers

Name	Year	Team	#	#
	1947	Homestead Grays	14	
	1948	Homestead Grays	17	
Thompson, Gene	1949	Philadelphia Stars	8	4
Thompson, Henry	1943	Kansas City Monarchs	33	
	1946	Kansas City Monarchs	33	
	1947	Kansas City Monarchs	33	
	1948	Kansas City Monarchs	37	
Thompson, James	1928	Chicago American Giants	8	
Thompson, Jr., Sam	1957	New Orleans Black Bears	5	
Thompson, Richard	1954	Kansas City Monarchs	28	
Thompson, Sad Sam	1939	Philadelphia Stars	31	
	1940	Philadelphia Stars	31	
	1948	Cleveland Buckeyes	15	
Thurman, Bob	1946	Homestead Grays	20	
	1947	Homestead Grays	20	
	1948	Homestead Grays	20	
	1949	Kansas City Monarchs	28	
Tiant Sr., Luis	1935	New York Cubans	30	
	1944	New York Cubans	5	
	1945	New York Cubans	5	
	1946	New York Cubans	5	
	1947	New York Cubans	5	5
Tidmore, Ozzie	1958	Memphis Red Sox	34	
Tolbert, Jake	1946	New York Black Yankees		12
Toledo, Julio	1953	Indianapolis Clowns	25	
Torriente, Cristóbal	1928	Detroit Stars	12	
Townsend, Jessie	1958	Kansas City Monarchs	32	
Trent, Ted	1934	Chicago American Giants	14	
	1936	Chicago American Giants	12	
Trouppe, Quincy	1945	Cleveland Buckeyes	11	
	1946	Cleveland Buckeyes	10	
	1948	Chicago American Giants	28	
Troy, Donald	1945	Baltimore Elite Giants	15	
Tugerson, James	1951	Indianapolis Clowns	26	
	1953	Indianapolis Clowns	14	14
Tugerson, Leander	1951	Indianapolis Clowns	33	
Turner, Clarence	1953	Indianapolis Clowns	35	10
Turner, Wyatt	1944	Great Lakes Bluejackets	2	
Valdés, Fermín	1944	Indy-Cincy Clowns	4	6
Vargas, Juan	1941	New York Cubans	15	
	1942	East All Stars	6	
	1943	New York Cubans	2	
	1944	New York Cubans	8	
Vargas, Roberto	1948	Chicago American Giants	9	
Varona, Orlando	1949	Memphis Red Sox	19	
Vázquez, Armando	1944	Indy-Cincy Clowns	9	19

	1945	Cincy-Indy Clowns	16	
	1948	New York Cubans	14	
Velásquez, José Laru	1948	Indianapolis Clowns	10	
Villafane, Vicente	1947	Indianapolis Clowns		8
Villodas, Luis	1946	Baltimore Elite Giants	27	
	1947	Baltimore Elite Giants	27	
Walker, Edsall	1939	Homestead Grays		10
	1940	Homestead Grays	10	
	1941	Philadelphia Stars	14	
	1943	Homestead Grays	11	
	1944	Homestead Grays	10	
	1945	Homestead Grays	28	
Walker, George	1941	Kansas City Monarchs	7	
	1950	Kansas City Monarchs	12	
Walker, Jesse	1939	Baltimore Elite Giants	6	
	1940	New York Black Yankees	3	
	1943	Birmingham Black Barons	5	
	1944	Indy-Cincy Clowns	3	3
	1945	Cincy-Indy Clowns	3	
	1946	Indianapolis Clowns	3	
	1947	Indianapolis Clowns	3	
	1948	Baltimore Elite Giants	31	28
	1949	Baltimore Elite Giants	28	
Walker, John	1959	Raleigh Tigers	15	
Walker, Robert	1945	Homestead Grays	24	
	1947	Homestead Grays	21	
	1948	Homestead Grays	21	
Walker, Tom	1945	Baltimore Elite Giants	11	
Wallace, Mickey	1951	Indianapolis Clowns	31	
Walls, James	1954	Kansas City Monarchs	25	
Walton, George	1948	Indianapolis Clowns	18	
Wannamaker, George	1954	Indianapolis Clowns	63	
Ware, Archie	1945	Cleveland Buckeyes	23	
	1946	Cleveland Buckeyes	25	
	1948	Cleveland Buckeyes	25	
	1949	Louisville Buckeyes	25	
	1950	Indianapolis Clowns	25	
Warren, Bob	1959	Detroit Stars	20	
Warren, Cicero	1946	Homestead Grays	38	19
	1947	Homestead Grays	29	
Warren, Jesse	1941	New Orleans-St. Louis Stars	15	
	1946	Boston Blues	7	
Washington, John	1936	Pittsburgh Crawfords	12	
	1939	New York Black Yankees	14	
	1941	Baltimore Elite Giants	17	
	1946	Baltimore Elite Giants	12	

Uniform Numbers

	1947	Baltimore Elite Giants	12	
	1948	Baltimore Elite Giants	12	
	1949	Houston Eagles	13	
Washington, Lafayette	1944	Birmingham Black Barons	17	
	1945	Cincy-Indy Clowns	20	
Washington, Peter	1934	Philadelphia Stars	8	
Washington, Willie	1958	Detroit Clowns	24	
	1958	Kansas City Monarchs	43	
	1959	Kansas City Monarchs	44	
Watkins, Murray	1945	Biz Mackey's M.L. All Stars	29	
	1945	Newark Eagles	28	29
	1946	Philadelphia Stars	21	4 & 13
	1947	Philadelphia Stars	4	
	1948	Philadelphia Stars	4	
	1949	Philadelphia Stars	1	
Watson, Amos	1945	Cincy-Indy Clowns	15	
	1946	Indianapolis Clowns	1	
	1947	Baltimore Elite Giants	26	25
Watson, Jimmy Robert	1950	New York Cubans	22	
Watts, Dick	1949	Birmingham Black Barons	4	
	1950	Birmingham Black Barons	6	
Watts, Herman	1941	New York Black Yankees	18	
Webster, Ernest	1954	Kansas City Monarchs	21	
Welch, Winfield	1942	West All Stars	26	
	1943	Birmingham Black Barons	45	
	1944	Birmingham Black Barons	45	45
	1945	Birmingham Black Barons	21	
Wells, Willie	1934	Chicago American Giants	16	
	1939	Newark Eagles	6	
	1942	East All Stars	4	
	1945	Biz Mackey's M.L. All Stars	20	
	1945	New York Black Yankees	2	
	1945	Newark Eagles	20	
	1946	Baltimore Elite Giants		27 & 26
	1946	New York Black Yankees	4	
Welmaker, Roy	1939	Philadelphia Stars	17	
	1940	Philadelphia Stars	17	
	1942	Homestead Grays	12	
	1945	Homestead Grays	15	
West, Jim	1936	Washington Elite Giants	11	
	1939	Baltimore Elite Giants	11	
	1939	Philadelphia Stars	34	
	1940	Philadelphia Stars	34	
	1941	Philadelphia Stars	34	
	1942	Philadelphia Stars	34	
	1942	East All Stars	5	

	1943	Philadelphia Stars	34	
	1944	Philadelphia Stars	35	34
	1945	Philadelphia Stars	19	34
West, Price	1955	New York Black Yankees	21	
Westfield, Ernie	1960	Birmingham Black Barons	41	
Weston, Isaac	1949	Louisville Buckeyes	31	
Whatley, David	1939	Homestead Grays		5
	1940	Homestead Grays	1	
	1941	Homestead Grays	1	
White, Artemis	1948	Indianapolis Clowns		1
White, Bill	1959	Memphis Red Sox	2	
White, Chaney	1934	Philadelphia Stars	7	
White, Charlie	1950	Philadelphia Stars	33	
White, Edward	1944	Homestead Grays	15	
White, Eugene	1956	Kansas City Monarchs	28	
Whittington, Don	1953	Memphis Red Sox	4	
Wiley, Joe	1947	Baltimore Elite Giants	19	
Wilkes, James	1946	Newark Eagles	1	
	1947	Newark Eagles	1	
	1948	Newark Eagles	1	
	1949	Houston Eagles	1	
Williams, Bilbo	1942	Baltimore Elite Giants	12	
Williams, Albert	1945	Newark Eagles	34	
Williams, Charles	1928	Chicago American Giants	4	
Williams, Chester	1934	Pittsburgh Crawfords	4	
	1936	Pittsburgh Crawfords	6	
	1939	Philadelphia Stars	23	
	1940	Philadelphia Stars	23	
	1941	Homestead Grays	7	
	1942	Homestead Grays	9	
Williams, Elijah Eddie	1945	Kansas City Monarchs		1
	1946	Cleveland Clippers	1	
Williams, Eugene	1959	Memphis Red Sox	12	
Williams, Frank Shorty	1946	Homestead Grays	19	29
Williams, Frank Delano	1959	Memphis Red Sox	6	
Williams, Harry	1942	New York Black Yankees	3	27
	1945	Baltimore Elite Giants	26	
Williams, James	1941	New York Black Yankees	4	
Williams, Jeff	1954	Kansas City Monarchs		21
Williams, Jesse	1942	Kansas City Monarchs	18	
	1943	Kansas City Monarchs	18	
	1944	Kansas City Monarchs	31	
	1945	Kansas City Monarchs	19	6
	1949	Indianapolis Clowns	29	
Williams, John	1948	Chicago American Giants	14	
	1955	Indianapolis Clowns	31	

Williams, Johnnie	1958	Birmingham Black Barons	11	
Williams, Johnny	1944	Indy-Cincy Clowns	11	18
	1945	Cincy-Indy Clowns	10	
	1946	Indianapolis Clowns	5	
	1947	Indianapolis Clowns	22	
	1948	Indianapolis Clowns	12	
Williams, Joseph	1946	New York Black Yankees	7	
Williams, Leroy	1947	Newark Eagles	3	
	1948	Newark Eagles	6	
Williams, Marvin	1943	Philadelphia Stars	19	
	1944	Philadelphia Stars	21	
	1945	Philadelphia Stars	18	
	1949	Philadelphia Stars	4	12
Williams, Robert	1947	Newark Eagles	11	
	1948	Newark Eagles	11	
	1949	Houston Eagles	11	
	1951	Philadelphia Stars	35	
Williams, Roy K.	1934	New York Black Yankees	14	
	1939	New York Black Yankees	16	
	1940	Baltimore Elite Giants	4	
	1941	Baltimore Elite Giants	12	
Williams, Sam	1947	Birmingham Black Barons	6	
	1948	Birmingham Black Barons	6	
	1949	Birmingham Black Barons	6	
	1950	Birmingham Black Barons	6	
Williams, Sidney	1945	Newark Eagles	24	
Williams, Walter	1939	Newark Eagles	11	
Williams, Willie	1939	Baltimore Elite Giants	1	
	1948	Newark Eagles	3	
	1949	Houston Eagles	9	
	1951	New Orleans Eagles	3	
Willis, Jim	1939	Baltimore Elite Giants	10	
Wilmore, Alfred	1947	Philadelphia Stars	18	
	1948	Baltimore Elite Giants	21	11
	1949	Baltimore Elite Giants	21	
Wilson, Arthur	1944	Birmingham Black Barons	24	24
	1945	Birmingham Black Barons	19	
	1946	Birmingham Black Barons	4	
	1947	Birmingham Black Barons	2	
Wilson, Bob	1957	Kansas City Monarchs	13	
Wilson, Chuck	1948	Indianapolis Clowns		12
	1949	Indianapolis Clowns	32	
Wilson, Dan	1941	New Orleans-St. Louis Stars	14	
	1942	New York Black Yankees	66	33
	1946	Homestead Grays	22	
	1947	Philadelphia Stars	11	

Wilson, Emmett	1946	Boston Blues	25	
Wilson, Fred	1939	Newark Eagles	7	
	1943	Cincinnati Clowns	9	
Wilson, Jud	1934	Philadelphia Stars	3	
	1939	Philadelphia Stars	20	
	1942	Homestead Grays	8	
	1943	Homestead Grays	8	
	1944	Homestead Grays	8	
	1945	Homestead Grays	22	
Wilson, Mose	1958	Memphis Red Sox	17	
Wilson, Robert	1947	Newark Eagles	8	
	1948	Newark Eagles	8	
	1949	Houston Eagles	17	16
	1957	Kansas City Monarchs	13	
Winston, John	1957	Kansas City Monarchs	20	
	1959	Kansas City Monarchs	38	
Witherspoon, Lester	1948	Indianapolis Clowns		14
	1949	Homestead Grays	42	
	1949	Indianapolis Clowns	39	
Woods, Sam	1946	Cleveland Buckeyes	12	
	1953	Memphis Red Sox	17	
Woods, Parnell	1942	West All Stars	1	
Woods, Tom	1945	Philadelphia Stars	6	16
Worthington, Robert	1960	Raleigh Tigers	5	
Wright Jr., Henry	1948	Baltimore Elite Giants	21	
Wright, Burnis	1936	Washington Elite Giants	8	
	1939	Baltimore Elite Giants	21	
	1942	Baltimore Elite Giants	20	
	1945	Baltimore Elite Giants	27	
Wright, John	1941	Homestead Grays	18	
	1942	East All Stars	2	
	1943	Homestead Grays	18	
	1944	Great Lakes Bluejackets	18	
	1947	Homestead Grays	24	
Wright, Zollie	1936	Washington Elite Giants	1	
	1939	New York Black Yankees	15	
	1940	New York Black Yankees	15	
	1941	Philadelphia Stars	18	
Wyatt, John	1953	Indianapolis Clowns		9
Wyatt, Ralph	1942	West All Stars	15	
	1946	Cleveland Buckeyes	17	
Wyatt, William	1957	Birmingham Black Barons	1	
	1958	Birmingham Black Barons	1	
Wylie, Enloe	1945	Kansas City Monarchs	8	17
	1946	Kansas City Monarchs	2	26
	1947	Kansas City Monarchs	32	

Wynn, Willie	1945	Newark Eagles	30	
	1947	Newark Eagles	9	
Yancey, Bill	1934	New York Black Yankees	7	
Young, Edward	1947	Homestead Grays	35	
Young, Leandy	1944	Birmingham Black Barons		41
Young, Norman	1941	New York Black Yankees	3	
Young, Tom	1941	Newark Eagles	19	
Yvanes, Armando	1950	New York Cubans	8	

APPENDIX H: Military Service of African American Players

The military history of African Americans spans from the arrival of the first enslaved Africans during the colonial history of the United States to the present day. This section only covers African American baseball players who served the Spanish-American War, both World Wars, and the Korean War.

Charles Remond Douglass, the third and youngest son of abolitionist Frederick Douglass, was a third baseman and pitcher for the Washington Alerts and Mutuals of Washington clubs. Charles Remond, along with his brother Lewis Henry served with the all-Colored 54th Massachusetts Regiment, led by a White officer, Colonel Robert Gould Shaw, during the Civil War. Despite the assertion that Black servicemen were inferior to Whites, the Regiment's charge of the Confederate station Fort Wagner, South Carolina, in 1863 proved to be a pivotal point in validating their battle worthiness and encouraged recruitment of African Americans by the Union.

Conversely, Charles Remond's father Frederick, wrote of Black Confederate soldiers in the August 1861 issue of his newspaper, *Douglass' Monthly*, that "among rebels were Black troops, no doubt pressed into service by their tyrant masters." Douglass added, "It is now pretty well established that there are at the present moment many Colored men in the Confederate army doing duty not only as cooks, servants and laborers, but as real soldiers, having muskets on their shoulders, and bullets in their pockets."

Some of the most notable segregated units during both World Wars were:
- 92nd Infantry Division
    - 351st Field Artillery
    - 366th Infantry Regiment
    - 370th Infantry Regiment
- 93rd Infantry Division
    - 369th Infantry Regiment, a.k.a. the Harlem Hellfighters or the Men of Bronze (formerly the 15th New York National Guard)
    - 370th Infantry Regiment (formerly the 8th Illinois) a.k.a. The Black Devils
    - 371st Infantry Regiment
    - 372nd Infantry Regiment
    - 25th Infantry Regiment (Buffalo Soldiers)
- 2nd Cavalry Division
    - 4th Cavalry Brigade
        - 10th Cavalry Regiment (the original Buffalo Soldiers)
        - 27th Cavalry Regiment
    - 5th Cavalry Brigade
        - 9th Cavalry Regiment
        - 28th Cavalry Regiment
- Air Corps Unit
    - 332d Fighter Group (Tuskegee Airmen)
- Marine Unit

The first African American U.S. Marines were trained at Camp Montford Point, in Jacksonville, North Carolina, from 1942 to 1949. They included pitcher Bill Greason and umpire Bob Motley.
- Navy Unit boot camp

Larry Doby, formerly of the Newark Eagles and the Cleveland Indians, is perhaps the most prominent African American trainee at Camp Robert Smalls at the Naval Station Great Lakes in Lake County, Illinois.

Civil War, 1861 to 1865

Douglass, Charles Remond - 3b, Washington Alerts, from the 54th Massachusetts Regiment, Camp Meigs, Readville, Massachusetts, 1863

Spanish American War, April to August 1898

Connor, John W. - owner, Brooklyn Royal Giants, Bacharach (AC) Giants (b) - Navy, 1898
Taylor, C.I. - owner, manager, Indianapolis ABCs (b) – Army, 1898

World War I, 1914 to 1918

PLAYER	POS.	TEAM	BRANCH	YEAR
Allen, Toussaint	1b	Hilldale Club	Army	1917-18
Arnett, Pusey Dell	ss	Chicago Unions	Army	1917-18
Bostick, Fred	of	Milwaukee Bears (b)	Army	1918
Briggs, Otto	of	Hilldale Club	Army	1917-19
Brooks, Irvin	of	Brooklyn Royal Giants (b)	Navy	1909-17
Brooks, Sidney	of	St. Louis Giants (b)	Army	1918-19
Burch, Edgar Daniel	p	Indianapolis ABCs	Army	1917-18
Charleston, Oscar	of	Indianapolis ABCs	Army	1912-15, 1918
Clark, Morten	ss	Indianapolis ABCs	Army	1918-19
Cobb, Lorenza	c, officer	St. Louis Giants	Army	1918-19
Cooper, Alfred "Army" (b)	p	Kansas City Monarchs	Army	1922
Crawford, Sam	p	Chicago Union Giants	Army	1917-18
Day, Wilson C.	1b	Indianapolis ABCs	Army	1917-18
Deas, James "Yank"	c	Lincoln Giants	Army	1918
Dismukes, Wm. "Dizzy"	p	Chicago American Giants	Army	1917-18
Donaldson, John	p	Indianapolis ABCs	Army	1917
Downs, McKinley "Bunny"	2b	Hilldale Club	Army	1918
Eggleston, Macajah "Mac"	c	Dayton Marcos	Army	1918-19
Forrest, James	c	Lincoln Giants	Army	1918-19
Francis, Otis W.	2b	Indianapolis ABCs	Army	1917-18
Fuller, James	c	Bacharach Giants	Army	1918-19
Gans, Robert "Jude"	lf	Lincoln Stars	Army	1918-19
Gillespie, Henry	p	Hilldale Club (b)	Army	1918-19
Gatewood, Ernest	c	Brooklyn Royal Giants	Army	1919
Gordon, Samuel	c	Chicago Union Giants	Army	1917-18
Grant, Leroy	1b	Chicago American Giants	Army	1918-19
Green, Peter "Ed"	of	Philadelphia Giants	Army	1918
Harris, Ananias Andrew	3b, p	Hilldale Club	Navy	1917-19
Hawkins, Lemuel	1b	Chicago Amer. Giants (b)	Army	1918-19
Herring, Moses	3b	St. Louis Giants	Army	1915-20
Hubbard, Jess	p	Brooklyn Royal Giants (b)	Army	1918
Johnson, Cecil	of	Philadelphia Tigers	Army	1918-19

Johnson, Oscar "Heavy"	of	Kansas City Monarchs (b)	Army	1913-22
Johnson, Tom "Schoolboy"	p	Chicago American Giants	Army	1918-19
Johnson, William H.	c	Harrisburg Giants	Army	1915-19
Kimbro, Ted (d)	3b	St. Louis Giants	Army	1918
Kindle, William "Bill"	2b	Lincoln Stars	Army	1918
Lewis, Jerome Ambrose *	1b	West Baden (IN) Sprudels	Army	1917-18
Lyons, James "Jimmie"	of	Chicago American Giants	Army	1918-19
Long, Fred T.	of	Detroit Stars	Army	1918-19
Longware, Alonzo	3b	Detroit Stars	Army	1918-19
Mahoney, Anthony "Tony"	p	Baltimore Black Sox (b)	Army	1918-19
Malarcher, David "Dave"	3b	Indianapolis ABCs	Army	1918-19
McGavock, Herbert	of	Jewell's ABCs	Army	1918-19
McLaughlin, Henry	p	Lincoln Giants	Army	1917-18
Moore, Walter "Dobie"	ss	Kansas City Monarchs (b)	Army	1916-20
Murray, Mitchell	c	St. Louis Stars	Army	1918-19
Myers, William	1b	Brooklyn Royal Giants(a)	Army	1918
Newsome, Omer	p	Indianapolis ABCs (b)	Army	1917-19
Norman, Elbert	ss	Lincoln Giants (b)	Army	1918
Oldham, Jimmy	p	St. Louis Giants	Army	1918-19
Oliver, Hudson	ss	Philadelphia Giants (a)	Army	1918
Orendorf, James T.	3b	Topeka (KS) Giants	Army	1917-18
Owens, Oscar	p, of	Homestead Grays (b)	Army	1918-19
Poles, Spottswood	of	Lincoln Giants	Army	1917-19
Pullen, Neil	c	Brooklyn Royal Giants (b)	Army	1918-19
Ragland, Herlen	P	Indianapolis ABCs	Army	1917-18
Ray, Otto	c	Kansas City Monarchs (b)	Army	1918-19
Redding, "Cannonball Dick"	p	Brooklyn Royal Giants	Army	1918-19
Riggins, Arvell	ss	Lincoln (NY) Giants	Army	1917-18
Rogan, Wilber "Bullet"	p, of	Kansas City Monarchs (b)	Army	1911-20
Rolling, Carl	of	St. Louis Giants (b)	Army	1918
Ross, William	p	Philadelphia Royal Giants	Army	1918-19
Russell, Branch	of	St. Louis Stars (b)	Army	1919-22
Santop, Louis Loftin	c	Hilldale Club	Navy	1918-19
Saunders, Hubert	1b	Homestead Grays (c)	Army	1918
Scott, Robert	of	Brooklyn Royal Giants	Army	1918
Simpson, Lawrence	p	Chicago Union Giants	Army	1917-18
Sloan, Robert Lee	of	Brooklyn Royal Giants	Army	1917-18
Smith, James H. "Jimmy"	ss	Leland Giants (a)	Army	1917-18
Starks, Otis	p	Brooklyn Royal Giants (b)	Army	1918
Stewart, Archie "Tank"	2b	St. Louis Giants	Army	1920
Stratton, Felton	3b	Birmingham Black Barons	Army	1918
Sweatt, George	of	Kansas City Monarchs (b)	Army	1918-19
Thomas, Clint	of	Hilldale Club (b)	Army	1918-19
Treadwell, Harold	p	Lincoln Club (b)	Army	1918
Triplett, Norman (d)	of	Hilldale Club	Army	1918
Tucker, Eugene	p	Philadelphia Royal Giants	Army	1918

Military Service

Tyrees, Ruby	p	Cleveland Browns	Army	1918
Webster, Pearl "Specks" (d)	c	Brooklyn Royal Giants	Army	1919
White, Butler	1b	Chicago Giants	Army	1918-19
Wickware, Frank	p	Detroit Stars	Army	1918-19
Wiley, Wabishaw "Doc"	c	Lincoln Giants	Army	1918-19
Williams, Bobby	ss	Chicago American Giants	Army	1918-19
Williams, John T.	Executive	Baltimore Black Sox	Army	1919
Wilson, Elmer	2b	St. Louis Stars	Army	1918
Wilson, Judson "Boojum"	3b	Baltimore Black Sox (b)	Army	1918

a) Served after baseball career ended.
b) Served before baseball career begun.
c) Hubert Saunders played for Homestead in 1913 but didn't play for a pro team again until 1925
d) Died of influenza during the war (Norman Triplett and Pearl Webster while serving in France, Ted Kimbro at Fort Dix, New Jersey)
(KIA)— Killed in Action

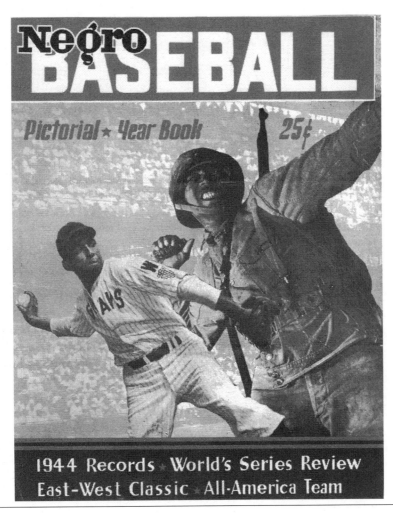

Ernest "Spoon" Carter on the cover of the 1945 *Negro Baseball Yearbook*

Defense Workers during World War II

PLAYER	POSITION	TEAMS	DEFENSE ROLE	YEARS
Harris, Vic	of, manager	Homestead Grays	Factory worker	1943-44
Charleston, Oscar	Manager	Philadelphia Stars	PQMD worker	1943-44

*** - Philadelphia Quarter Master Depot

World War II, 1939 to 1945

PLAYER	POS.	TEAM	BRANCH	YEARS
Awkard, Russell	of	Newark Eagles	Army	1941-45
Baker, Gene	2b	Kansas City Monarchs	Navy	1943
Baker, Hudson	of	Philadelphia Stars	Army	1944
Bankhead, Dan	p	Birmingham Black Barons	Marines	1943-45
Banks, Richard	c	Richmond Giants	Army	1941-45
Barbee, Walter "Lamb"	1b	Baltimore Elite Giants	Army	1943-46
Barber, Sam	p	Cleveland Buckeyes	Army	1942-45
Barnes, Bill	p	Baltimore Elite Giants	Army	1944-45
Barnes, Sr., Joe *	p	Memphis Red Sox**	Army	1944-46
Bass, Leroy "Red"	c	Homestead Grays	Air Force	1942-67
Bennett, Jeremiah	p	Philadelphia Stars	Army	1942-45
Biot, Charlie *	of	Baltimore Elite Giants*	Army	1942-46
Black, Joe	p	Baltimore Elite Giants	Army	1943-45
Blair, Garnett	p	Homestead Grays	Army	1943-45
Blair, William	p	Indianapolis Clowns	Army	1945
Bolden, Jim	p	Cleveland Buckeyes	Army	1942-46
Bostock, Sr., Lyman	1b	Birmingham Black Barons	Army	1942-45
Boyd, Bob	1b	Memphis Red Sox	Army	1944-46
Bracken, Herb	p	Cleveland Buckeyes	Navy	1944-45
Brewer, Sherwood	2b	Kansas City Monarchs	Army	1943
Brown, Barney	p	Philadelphia Stars	Army	1943
Brown, James	p	Newark Eagles	Army	1944-45
Brown Lawrence "Lefty"	p	Memphis Red Sox	USAAC	1942-45
Brown, Willard "Home Run"	of	Kansas City Monarchs	Army	1944-45
Bryant, Allen "Lefty"	p	Kansas City Monarchs	Army	1941-44
Buchanan, Chester	p	Philadelphia Stars	Navy	1944-45
Burke, Ernest	p	Baltimore Elite Giants	Marines	1943-46
Burton, William "Billy" **	of	Louisville Buckeyes	Army	1946
Carlisle, Matthew "Lick"	2b	Homestead Grays	Navy	1945
Cartmill, Jr., Alfred Franklin	2b	Kansas City Monarchs	Air Force	1950-54
Carter, Elmer	ss	Kansas City Monarchs	Army	1942-45
Carter, Marlin	3b	Memphis Red Sox	Coast Guard	1943-45
Clarkson, James "Bus"	ss	Philadelphia Stars	Army	1943-45
Clay, Alton **	of	NY Black Yankees	Army	1943-46
Cole, Cecil	p	Newark Eagles	Army	1941-46
Cohen, Jim	p	Indianapolis Clowns	Army	1942-46

Military Service

Name	Pos	Team	Branch	Years
Colzie, Jim	p	Indianapolis Clowns	Army Air Force	1943-45
Cooper, Bill	c	Philadelphia Stars	Army	1943-45
Crutchfield, Jimmie	of	Chicago American Giants	Army	1943-44
Cueria, Basilio	1b	Havana Red Sox	Army	1942-43
Davis, Ross "Satchel"	p	Cleveland Buckeyes	Army	1944-45
Davis, Spencer	of	New York Black Yankees	Army	1944-45
Day, Leon	p	Newark Eagles	Army	1944-45
Dean, Jimmy **	p	Philadelphia Stars	Army	1943-45
Doby, Larry	ss	Newark Eagles	Navy	1943-46
Douglas, Jesse	2b	Birmingham Black Barons	Army	1943
Duckett, Mahlon	3b	Philadelphia Stars	Army	1944-45
Duncan, Jr., Frank	c	Kansas City Monarchs	Army	1942-43
Duncan, III, Frank	p	Kansas City Monarchs	Army	1942-43
Dunn, Alphonse	1b	Birmingham Black Barons	Army Air Force	1943
Dunn, Joseph "Jake"	ss	Philadelphia Stars	Army	1942-45
Easterling, Howard	3b	Homestead Grays	Army	1943-45
Elam, Jim	p	Newark Eagles	Army	1944-45
Fields, Wilmer "Red"	p	Homestead Grays	Army	1944-45
Fillmore, Joe	p	Philadelphia Stars	Army	1943-46
Flowers, Jake	1b	New York Black Yankees	Army	1944
Gaines, Jonas	p	Baltimore Elite Giants	Army	1943-45
Gary, Charles	P	Homestead Grays	Navy	1944-46
Gibson, Jerry	of	Cincinnati Tigers	Army	1944-45
Gillis, Louis "Seaboy"	c	Birmingham Black Barons	USAAC	1943-46
Greason, William "Bill"	p	Birmingham Black Barons	Marines	1943-45
Greene, James "Pea"	c	Kansas City Monarchs	Army	1943-45
Griffith, Bob	p	New York Black Yankees	Army	1944-45
Griggs, Acie "Skeet"	of	New York Cubans	Navy	1942-44
Hairston, Harold	p, ss	Homestead Grays	USAAC	1944-45
Hardy, Paul	c	Birmingham Black Barons	Army	1944-45
Harmon, Charles **	of	Indianapolis Clowns	Navy	1943-45
Harvey, David "Bill"	p	Baltimore Elite Giants	Army	1944-45
Hayes, Johnny	c	New York Black Yankees	Army	1944-45
Hayslett, Claude	p	Atlanta Black Crackers	Army	1942-46
Henderson, Curtis	ss	New York Black Yankees	Army	1944-45
Hendrix, Stokes	p	Nashville Elite Giants	Army	1945-48
Henry, Leo "Preacher"	p	Indianapolis Clowns	Army	1944-45
Hopwood, Reginald	of	Kansas City Monarchs	Army	1942-45
Horne, Billy	2b	Cleveland Buckeyes	Army	1945
Hughes, Sammy T.	2b	Baltimore Elite Giants	Army	1943-46
Irvin, Monte	of	Newark Eagles	Army	1943-45
Israel, Clarence "Pint"	infield	Homestead Grays	Army	1943-45
Jefferson, Willie	p	Cleveland Buckeyes	Army	1942-43
Johnson, Bryon	ss	Kansas City Monarchs	Army	1941-45-
Johnson, Clifford "Connie"	p	Kansas City Monarchs	Army	1943-45
Johnson, Josh	c	New York Black Yankees	Army	1942-45

Name	Pos	Team	Service	Years
Johnson, Ralph (KIA)	p	Philadelphia Stars	Army	1942-44
Johnson, Walter *	of	Birmingham Black Barons	Army	1943-46
Kimbrough, Larry	p	Philadelphia Stars	Army	1944-45
King, Clarence "Pijo" **	of	Birmingham Black Barons	Army	1942
Lacy, Raymon **	of	Houston Eagles	Army	1944-45
Lewis, Rufus	p	Newark Eagles	Army Air Force	1943-45
Manning, Max	p	Newark Eagles	Army Air Force	1942-45
Martin, Harold (killed in plane crash)	3b, p	Pittsburgh Keystones*	Army Air Force	1942-45
McClinic, Nat	of	Cleveland Buckeyes	Army	1944-45
McCord, Clint "Butch"	1b	Baltimore Elite Giants	Navy	1944-45
McCoy, Walter	p	Chicago American Giants	Army	1943-44
McMillan, Earl *	of	Toledo Tigers	Army	1942
Miles, John "Mule"	of	Chicago American Giants	Army Air Force	1942-45
Moore, James "Red"	1b	Baltimore Elite Giants	Army	1941-45
Norman, Elbert	ss	Memphis Red Sox	Army	1942
O'Neil, John "Buck"	1b	Kansas City Monarchs	Navy	1943-45
Parker, Tom	p	New York Cubans	Army	1943-44
Parks, Charlie	c	Newark Eagles	Army	1943-45
Patterson, Andrew "Pat"	3b	Philadelphia Stars	Army	1942-45
Peatros, Maurice	1b	Pittsburgh Crawfords	Air Force	1946-47
Perkins, Bill	c	Philadelphia Stars	Army	1944-45
Pigg, Leonard "Len"	c	Indianapolis Clowns	Army	1940-45
Pollard, Nat	p	Birmingham Black Barons	Army	1944-45
Powell, Bill	P	Birmingham Black Barons	Army	1942-45
Presswood, Hank	3b	Cleveland Buckeyes	Army	1945-47
Randall, Wm. "Sonny"	of	Homestead Grays	Navy	1943-46
Redd, Ulysses	ss	Birmingham Black Barons	Army	1941-46
Reed, Porter L. **	of	Houston Eagles	Army	1942-46
Richardson, Earl	ss	Newark Eagles	Navy	1944-45
Ritchey, John	c	Chicago American Giants	Army	1943-45
Robinson, Henry Frazier	c	Baltimore Elite Giants	Army	1943-45
Robinson, Jackie **	ss	Kansas City Monarchs	Army	1942-44
Romby, Robert	p	Baltimore Elite Giants	Army	1943-45
Ruffin, Leon	c	Newark Eagles	Navy	1943-45
Russell, Frank	2b	Baltimore Elite Giants	Army	1945
Scott, Joe	1b	Birmingham Black Barons	Army	1941-45
Seay, Dick	2b	New York Black Yankees	Army	1944-45
Sharpe, Robert	p	Memphis Red Sox	Army	1945-46
Simmons, Bert	p	Baltimore Elite Giants	Army	1943-45
Simpson, Harry	of	Philadelphia Stars	Army	1942-45
Simpson, Herb	1b	Homestead Grays	Air Force	1943-45
Smith, Gene	p	New York Black Yankees	Army	1943-45
Smith, John Ford	p	Kansas City Monarchs	USAAC	1942-45
Smith, Raymond	p	Philadelphia Stars	Army	1943-45
Snead, Sylvester	of	Cincinnati Clowns	Army	1944-45

Military Service

Name	Pos	Team	Branch	Years
Spearman, Alvin **	p	Kansas City Monarchs	Army	1945-46
Spearman, Clyde	of	Philadelphia Stars	Army	1944-46
Strong, Jr., T.R. "Ted"	of	Kansas City Monarchs	Navy	1943-46
Summers, Lonnie	c	Chicago American Giants	Army	1942-45
Tatum, Reece "Goose"	1b	Indianapolis Clowns	Air Force	1943-45
Taylor, Johnny "Schoolboy"	p	New York Cubans	Army	1942-44
Taylor, Olan "Jelly"	1b	Memphis Red Sox	Air Force	1943-45
Thompson, Frank Hoss	p	Baltimore Elite Giants	Army	1942-44
Thompson, Henry "Hank"	2b	Kansas City Monarchs	Army	1944-45
Thurman, Robert "Bob" **	of	Homestead Grays	Army	1942-45
Trice, Bob	p	Homestead Grays	Navy	1947-48
Turner, Thomas **	1b	Chicago American Giants	Army	1940-45
Washington, Johnny	1b	Baltimore Elite Giants	Army	1942-45
Watts, Andy "Big Six"	3b	Cleveland Buckeyes	Navy	1944-45
Welmaker, Roy	p	Homestead Grays	Army	1942-45
Whatley, Dave "Speed"	of	Homestead Grays	Army	1944-45
Wilkes, James "Jimmy" **	of	Newark Eagles	Navy	1943
Williams, Frank	of	Homestead Grays	Army	1944-45
Williams, Jesse	ss	Kansas City Monarchs	Army	1943-45
Williams, Jr., Walter Turner	p	Newark Eagles	Army	1941-45
Williams, Wilmore	of	Newark Eagles	Navy	1944-45
Wilmore, Al "Apples"	p	Philadelphia Stars	Army	1943-46
Wilson, Emmett	of	New York Black Yankees	Army	1944-45
Wilson, Fred	of	Indianapolis Clowns	Army	1944
Wilson, Robert L.	of	Raleigh Tigers	Army	1953-54
Wright, Johnny	p	Homestead Grays	Navy	1944-45
Wright, Walter (Bricktop)	of	New York Black Yankees	Army	1943-46
Zapp, Jim	of	Baltimore Elite Giants	Navy	1942-45

*- Served after baseball career had ended.
**- Served before baseball career had begun.

Negro Leagues Book #2: The Players

LARRY DOBY - Doby joined the Navy towards the end of the 1943 season. He trained at the Great Lakes Naval Training Station in Illinois, where he played with the segregated Negro baseball team. Doby was also stationed at Camp Sam Roberts in California, before reaching Ulithi Atoll, which served as the central port and staging area for the Navy in the closing battles of the Pacific. Doby was inducted into the National Baseball Hall of Fame in 1998.

JOHN "BUCK" O'NEIL - From 1943 to 1945, O'Neil served his country as a member of the US Navy, working in a construction battalion. He was an outstanding manager of the Kansas City Monarchs. During his playing career, O'Neil was known primarily for his defense, above average speed, and contact hitting, while lacking the power expected from the first base position. He is best known for his elegant appearance in chapter five of the PBS documentary entitled *Baseball* by Ken Burns.

SPOTS POLES - In 1930, in the *Pittsburgh Courier*, William "Dizzy" Dismukes wrote, "Spottswood Poles, he of that nervous type, was the fastest man I ever saw in getting to first base. With all his speed, however, he was an ordinary base runner, seemingly awkward, but a good fly chaser and one of the game's greatest lead-off men. And truly, he was a great hitter." In 1917, at age 30, he became one of the Men of Bronze, enlisting with the 369th Infantry. While stationed in France, he (on far left) won five battle stars and the coveted Purple Heart.

Korean War, 1950 to 1953

PLAYER	POS.	TEAM	BRANCH	YEARS
Banks, Ernie	ss	Kansas City Monarchs	Army	1951-52
Brown, Cleophus	1b	Louisville Clippers	Army	1950-53
Bunch, Jr., Sidney	of	Baltimore Elite Giants	Army	1955-57
Fearbry, Jr., Marvin	2b	Indianapolis Clowns	Army	1953-54
Haggins, Ray	of	Memphis Red Sox	Army	1951-52
Henderson, Neale	of	Kansas City Monarchs	Army	1950
Jones, Marvin	p	Kansas City Monarchs	Army	1958
Jordan, Maynard	of	Houston Eagles	U.S. Air Force	1951-1971
Lloyd, Tony	2b	Birmingham Black Barons	Army	1951
Matthews, Fran*	1b	Newark Eagles	Army	1950-72
Newcombe, Don	p	Newark Eagles	Army	1952-53
Reed, Eddie	of	Memphis Red Sox	Army	1950
Robinson, James	3b	Kansas City Monarchs	Army	1953-55
Santiago, Carlos	2b	New York Cubans	Army	1951-53
Taylor, Sammie T.	c	Kansas City Monarchs	Army	1951-52
White, William E.	of	Kansas City Monarchs	Army	1953-54
Williams, Reuben	ss	Chicago American Giants	Army	1952
Williams, Robert Rosel	ss	Birmingham Black Barons	Army	1951
Young, Archie	c	Birmingham Black Barons	Army	1951-52

* - Career military; also served in Vietnam War.

APPENDIX I: Collegians

Sometimes portrayed as illiterate men by the press, these Black men listed below used their grey matter at many institutions of higher learning to earn several degrees.

NAME	COLLEGE OR UNIVERSITY
Adams, Bill "Packinghouse"	Wiley College (Marshall, TX)
Alexander, Harvey "Chuffy"	Samuel Huston College (Austin, TX)
Alexander, Spencer	Shaw University (Raleigh, NC)
Allen, Major	Howard University (Washington, DC)
Allen, Newt	Western Baptist College (Kansas City, MO)
Allen, Toussaint	Morris Brown College, (Atlanta, GA)
Alston, Tom	North Carolina A&T (Greensboro, NC)
Altman, George	Tennessee A&I (Nashville, TN)
Anderson, William	Alabama State University (Montgomery, AL)
Armstead, James	University of Louisville (KY)
Ash, Rudolph	University of Michigan (Ann Arbor, MI)
Bailey, Percy	Alcorn A&M (Alcorn, MS)
Banks, Ernie	Bishop College [now Paul Quinn] (Dallas, TX) Prairie View A&M College (Hempstead, TX)
Barnes, I.V.	Piney Woods Junior College (Piney Woods, MS)
Barnes, Sanford L.	Alcorn A&M (Alcorn, MS)
Bass, Leroy P. "Red"	Piney Woods Junior College (Piney Woods, MS) Tougaloo College (Tougaloo, MS) Lincoln University Law School (Jefferson City, MO) San José State College (San Jose, CA) Monterey Institute of International Studies (Monterey, CA)
Baynard, William (Frank)	Morris Brown College (Atlanta, GA)
Bell, Julian	Tennessee State College (Nashville, TN) University of Michigan (Ann Arbor, MI)
Bethea, Bill	Brooklyn Community College (Brooklyn, NY)
Beverly, Bill	Fisk University (Nashville, TN)
Bibbs, Rainey	Indiana State University (Terre Haute, IN) a.k.a. Indiana State Teachers College Bachelor of Science degree in Biology
Billingsley, Sam	Arkansas State College (Jonesboro, AR)
Bissant, John	Wiley College (Marshall, TX)
Black, Joe	Morgan State University (Baltimore, MD)
Blair, Garnett	Virginia Union University (Richmond, VA)
Bleach, Larry	University of Detroit (Detroit, MI)
Bond, Tim	Bluefield State College (Bluefield, WV)
Bond, Walter F.	Lane College (Jackson, TN)
Booker, Rich	Lincoln University, (Jefferson City, MO)
Bradley, "Red"	Morris Brown College (Atlanta, GA)

Collegians

Bragg, Eugene	Florida A&M (Tallahassee, FL)
Brandon, Mack	Alcorn A&M (Alcorn, MS)
Breda, Bill	Southern University (Baton Rouge, LA) Louisiana State University (Baton Rouge, LA) Bradley University (Peoria, IL)
Breedlove, Leroy	Texas Southern University (Houston, TX)
Brice, George Edward	Howard University (Washington, DC)
Brodie, Milledge	Biddle University (Charlotte, NC)
Brown, Country	Morris Brown College (Atlanta, GA)
Brown, Earl	Harvard University (Cambridge, MA)
Brown, Ray	Wilberforce University (Wilberforce, OH)
Brown, Willie	Tuskegee Institute (Tuskegee, AL)
Browning, James R. "Skink"	Western University (?) Shaw University (Raleigh, NC)
Busby, Jimmy	Wiley College (Marshall, TX)
Byas, Subby	Crane Junior College (Chicago, IL) Northwestern University (Evanston, IL) Roosevelt University (Chicago, IL)
Capers, George	Howard University (Washington, DC)
Casey, William "Mickey"	Johnson C. Smith University (Charlotte, NC)
Castone, William	Kansas State Agricultural College (Manhattan, KS)
Clark, Albert	Morehouse University (Atlanta, GA)
Clark, Maceo	Morehouse University (Atlanta, GA)
Clark, Morten	Knoxville College (Knoxville, TN)
Clarkson, James "Bus"	Wilberforce University (Wilberforce, OH)
Clay, Alton	Pittsburg (KS) State (Pittsburg, KS)
Clifton, Nat	Xavier University (New Orleans, LA)
Cockrell, Phil	Paine College (Atlanta, GA)
Collins, Atkins	Alabama State University (Montgomery, AL)
Collins, George	Coe College (Cedar Rapids, IA)
Cooley, Walter	Alabama A&M University (Normal, AL)
Cooper, Andy	Paul Quinn College (Dallas, TX)
Cooper, Tom	West Virginia State College (Charleston, WV)
Cooper, William (Bill)	Morris Brown College (Atlanta, GA)
Cornelius, Willie	Clark College (Atlanta, GA)
Cox, Comer	Fisk University (Nashville, TN)
Craddock, Walter (Tiny Tim)	Livingstone College (Salisbury, NC)
Cromartie, Leroy	Florida A&M (Tallahassee, FL)
Crossant, George	Boston University (Boston, MA)
Crowe, George	Indiana Central College (Indianapolis, IN)
Dandridge, Richard "Ping"	University of Pennsylvania (Philadelphia, PA)
Davis, Johnny "Cherokee"	City College of New York (New York, NY)
Davis, Lorenzo "Piper"	Alabama State University (Montgomery, AL)
Deal, David	Florida A&M (Tallahassee, FL)

Dean, Jimmy	Morris Brown College (Atlanta, GA)
DeWitt, Fred	Wilberforce University (Wilberforce, OH)
Dials, Oland "Lou"	University of California (Berkeley, CA) Santa Barbara College (Santa Barbara, CA)
Dickerson, John W.	Clark University (Atlanta, GA), Jackson State College, Mississippi Industrial College
Dismukes, William "Dizzy"	Talladega College (Talladega, AL)
Dixon, Eddie	Morris Brown College (Atlanta, GA)
Dixon, George	Brewer College (Greenwood, SC)
Doby, Larry	Long Island University (New York, NY) Virginia Union College (Richmond, VA)
Donald, George	Morris Brown College (Atlanta, GA)
Donaldson, John	George R. Smith College (Sedalia, MO)
Downer, Fred	Morehouse University (Atlanta, GA)
Downs, McKinley	Morris Brown College (Atlanta, GA)
Drake, Solly	Philander Smith College (Little Rock, AR)
Dudley, Charles	Meharry Medical College (Nashville, TN)
Dudley, Edward	Bishop College [now Paul Quinn] (Dallas, TX)
Dumpson, William	South Carolina State University (Orangeburg, NC)
Duncan, Warren	North Carolina A&T (Greensboro, NC) Alabama State University (Montgomery, AL)
Durham, Joseph V.	Shaw University (Raleigh, NC)
Dykes, A.	Paul Quinn (Dallas, TX)
Eaddy, Don	University of Michigan (Ann Arbor, MI)
Echols, Joe	Virginia State College (Petersburg, VA)
Edwards, Chancellor	Jarvis Christian College (Hawkins, TX)
England, Charlie	Shaw University (Raleigh, NC)
Ensley, Frank	Grambling University (Grambling, LA)
Evans, William Demont	Livingston College (Salisbury, NC)
Everett, J.W. "Jim"	Edward Waters College (Jacksonville, FL) Florida A&M (Tallahassee, FL)
Farmer, Jr., Greene	Knoxville College (Knoxville, TN) Sonoma State (Rohnert Park, CA) University of San Francisco (CA)
Favors, Thomas	Clark College (Atlanta, GA)
Fields, Wilmer	Virginia State College (Petersburg, VA)
Follis, Charles	College of Wooster (Wooster, OH)
Forbes, Frank	Howard University (Washington, DC)
Force, William	Knoxville College (Knoxville, TN)
Ford, Erwin L.	North Carolina A&T (Greensboro, NC)
Foreman, Zack	Langston University (Langston, OK)
Foster, Willie	Alcorn A&M (Alcorn, MS); Dean of Men
Farmer, Greene	Knoxville College (Knoxville, TN) Sonoma State University (Rohnert Park, CA)

Collegians

	University of San Francisco (San Francisco, CA)
Farmer, Walter Moran	Lincoln University Law School (Jefferson City, MO)
	Washington University (St. Louis, MO)
Frazier, Oran	Alabama A&M University (Normal, AL)
Frazier, Severn	Alabama A&M University (Normal, AL)
Gaines, Jonas	Southern University (Baton Rouge, LA)
Gans, Judy	Washington & Jefferson College (Washington, PA)
Gardner, Floyd "Jelly"	Arkansas Baptist College (Little Rock, AR)
Gettys, Spencer	Temple University (Philadelphia, PA)
	Delaware State (Dover, DE)
Gillard, Hamp	Talladega College (Talladega, AL)
Gilmore, Quincy	Wilberforce University (Wilberforce, OH)
Givens, Oscar	Morgan College [State] (Baltimore, MD)
Gomes, Joe	Providence College (Providence, RI)
Goodgame, John	Atlanta Baptist College (Atlanta, GA)
	Talladega College (Talladega, AL)
Gordon, Sam	Wabash College (Crawfordsville, IN)
Gould, Harold	Glassboro (now Rowan) State College (Glassboro, NJ)
Graham, Dennis	Shaw University (Raleigh, NC)
Gray, George	Clark College (Atlanta, GA)
Greason, Bill	Stanton College (Birmingham, AL), now Homewood & Baptist Bible College
Greene, John "Big Red"	Stowe Teachers College (St. Louis, MO)
Grier, Claude "Red"	North Carolina A&T (Greensboro, NC)
Griffith, Robert	Tennessee State University (Nashville, TN)
Grimes, Waddy	Morehouse University (Atlanta, GA)
Hadley, Henry "Red"	Morris Brown College (Atlanta, GA)
Hair, Harold	North Carolina A&T (Greensboro, NC)
Hairston, Napoleon	Winston-Salem State University (Winston-Salem, NC)
Hall, Elbert	Northern Illinois University (DeKalb, IL)
Harding, William Clair (Halley)	Wilberforce University (Wilberforce, OH)
	Knox College (Galesburg, IL)
	Wiley College (Marshall, TX)
	Fisk University (Atlanta, GA)
Hardy, Arthur	Washburn College (Topeka, KS)
Harmon, Chuck	University of Toledo (Toledo, OH)
Harrell, Billy	Siena College (Loudonville, NY)
Harris, Donald "Donnie"	Alabama A&M (Huntsville, AL)
Harvey, Bob	Bowie State University (Bowie, MD)
Hayes, Burnalle	Johnson C. Smith University (Charlotte, NC)
	North Carolina Central University (Durham, NC)
Hayes, Jr., Thomas Henry	Atlanta University (Atlanta, GA)
	Lincoln University (Jefferson City, MO)
Haynes, Leroy	Morehouse University (Atlanta, GA)

Hendricks, Jack	Northwestern University (Evanston, IL)
	Butler University (Indianapolis, IN)
	North Central College (Naperville, IL)
Henry, Otis	Jarvis Christian College (Hawkins, TX)
Hines, John	Wilberforce University (Wilberforce, OH)
	Wiley College (Marshall, TX)
Holden, Carl	Alabama A&M (Huntsville, AL)
Holmes, Leroy "Philly"	Bethune-Cookman College (Daytona Beach, FL)
Hopkins Gordon	Bowie State University (Bowie, MD)
Horn, Herman "Doc"	Howard University (Washington, DC)
Horton, Clarence	Bluefield College (Bluefield, WV)
Houlemard, Michael A.	Xavier University (New Orleans, LA)
Houston, William	Bowling Green State Univ. (Bowling Green, KY)
Howard, Carrenza	Shaw University (Raleigh, NC)
Hubbard, DeHart	University of Michigan (Ann Arbor, MI)
Huff, Eddie	Meharry Medical College (Nashville, TN)
	Wilberforce University (Wilberforce, OH)
Hunt, Leonard	Kentucky State University (Frankfort, KY)
Hyde, Cowan "Bubba"	Morris Brown College (Atlanta, GA)
	Rust College (Holly Springs, MS)
Irvin, Cal	Morgan State University (Baltimore, MD)
Irvin, Monte	Lincoln University (Oxford, PA)
Jackson, John W. Stony	Southern University (Baton Rouge, LA)
Jackson, Verdell	St. Augustine College (Raleigh, NC)
Jefferson, George	Langston University (Langston, OK)
Jefferson, Ralph	Morris Brown College (Atlanta, GA)
	Atlanta University (Atlanta, GA)
Jenkins, Clarence "Fats"	Columbia University (New York, NY)
Johnson, Bertram	Prairie View A&M College (Hempstead, TX)
Johnson, Byron	Wiley College (Marshall, TX)
Johnson, Daniel "Shang"	Morris Brown College (Atlanta, GA)
Johnson, "Topeka Jack"	Washburn University (Topeka, KS)
Johnson, John Wesley	Jarvis Christian College (Hawkins, TX)
Johnson, Josh	Cheyney University (Cheyney, PA),
	Penn State University (Pittsburgh, PA)
Johnson, Lou	Kentucky State College (Frankfort, KY)
Johnson, Dr. Thomas Fairfax	Springfield College (Springfield, MA)
	Howard University (Washington, DC)
Johnson, Thomas Jefferson	Morris Brown College (Atlanta, GA)
Johnson, William "Wise"	South Carolina State University (Orangeburg, NC)
Jordan, Maynard	LeMoyne College (Memphis, TN)
Keeton, Eugene	Kentucky State University (Frankfort, KY)
Kennedy, John	Edward Waters College (Jacksonville, FL)
Kennedy, Ned	Xavier University (New Orleans, LA)

Collegians

Kenyon, Harry	Arkansas Baptist College (Little Rock, AR)
Kimbrough, Larry	Wilberforce University (Wilberforce, OH)
Kindle, Bill	Fisk University (Nashville, TN)
	Springfield College (Springfield, MA)
King, Brennan	North Carolina A&T (Greensboro, NC)
King, Ezell	Grambling College (Grambling, LA)
Lacy, Raymon	Texas College (Tyler, TX)
	Stephen F. Austin State College (Nacogdoches, TX)
Lacy, Sam	Howard University (Washington, DC)
Lacy, Thurman	Prairie View A&M College (Hempstead, TX)
Lamar, Horatio	Morehouse University (Atlanta, GA)
Lane, Isaac S.	Wilberforce University (Wilberforce, OH)
Lee, Holsey S.	Virginia Union University (Richmond, VA)
Leland, Frank	Fisk University (Nashville, TN)
Levis, Oscar	City College of New York (New York, NY)
Lewis, Austin	Mississippi State College
Lewis, Clarence	Lemoyne College (Memphis, TN)
Lewis, Jerome	Talladega College (Talladega, AL)
Lillard, Joe	University of Oregon (Eugene, OR)
Lindsay, William Hudson	Johnson C. Smith University (Charlotte, NC)
Lisby, Maurice	Morgan State University (Baltimore, MD)
Livingston, L.D.	Wiley College (Marshall, TX)
Lloyd, Tony	Tuskegee Institute (Tuskegee, AL)
Lockhart, A.J.	Howard University (Washington, DC)
	Morris Brown College (Atlanta, GA)
Lockhart, George Hubert	Talladega College (Talladega, AL)
	Stillman Institute (Tuscaloosa, AL)
Long, Fred T.	Millikin University (Decatur, IL)
Lundy, Dick	Edward Waters College (Jacksonville, FL)
	Florida Normal State College (Tallahassee, FL)
Maddox, Forrest "One Wing"	Morehouse University (Atlanta, GA)
Malarcher, Dave	Dillard University (New Orleans, LA)
	Englewood Evening College (Chicago, IL)
Manning, Max	Lincoln University (Oxford, PA)
	Glassboro (now Rowan) State College (Glassboro, NJ)
Marcell, Everett	Southern University (Baton Rouge, LA)
Marsh, Frank	Grambling University (Grambling, LA)
Marshall, Bobby	University of Minnesota (Minneapolis, MN)
Marshall, Jack	Wilberforce University (Wilberforce, OH)
Martin, Edward A.	North Carolina AT&T (Greensboro, NC),
	Temple University (Philadelphia, PA)
Mathews, Dell	University of Wisconsin (Madison, WI)
Matthews, William Clarence	Harvard University (Cambridge, MA)
Matthews, Francis	Boston University (Boston, MA)

Negro Leagues Book #2: The Players

McCampbell, Dr. Thomas	University of Kansas School of Pharmacy
McCord, Clinton	Tennessee A&I (Nashville, TN)
McDonald, Gifford	Claflin College (Orangeburg, SC)
McNeal, Rufus	North Carolina A&T (Greensboro, NC)
Means, Lewis	Morris Brown College (Atlanta, GA)
Medley, Calvin R. "Babe"	Morgan State College (Baltimore, MD)
Merchant, Henry	Henderson Institute (Henderson, TX)
Merritt, William A.	Virginia Union University (Richmond, VA)
Miles, John	St. Phillips Junior College (San Antonio, TX)
Milton, Henry	Wiley College (Marshall, TX)
Mitchell, Alonzo	Morris Brown College (Atlanta, GA)
Monroe, Bill	Howard University (Washington, DC)
Moore, Clarence	Shaw University (Raleigh, NC) Arkansas Baptist College (Little Rock, AR) Virginia Union (Richmond, VA)
Moore, Henry L.	Mississippi Industrial College (Holly Spring, MS) Northwestern University (Evanston, IL)
Moore, Legolian (Boots)	Grambling College (Grambling, LA)
Moreland, Nate	Redlands Baptist College (Redlands, California)
Morton, Ferdinand Q.	Harvard University (Cambridge, MA) Law School of Boston University (Boston, MA)
Mosley, Lou	Lincoln University (Chester County, PA)
Murray, John Joseph "Red"	Lock Haven University (Lock Haven, PA) University of Notre Dame (South Bend, IN)
O'Neil, John "Buck"	Edward Waters College (Jacksonville, FL)
Oliver, Hudson	Howard University (Washington, DC)
Oliver, Martin	Howard University (Washington, DC)
Orange, Dr. Grady Diploma	Wiley College (Marshall, TX) Fisk University (Nashville, TN)
Owens, Aubry	Meharry Medical College (Nashville, TN) Alcorn A&M (Alcorn, MS)
Owens, Alphonso "Buddy"	College of DePaul (Chicago, IL)
Owens, Jackson	Millikin University (Decatur, IL)
Page, Gaitha	State Normal School (Emporia State University)
Paige, Leroy "Satchel"	Knoxville College (Knoxville, TN)
Palmer, Ralph	Philander Smith College (Little Rock, AR)
Pardee, John	Wiley College (Marshall, TX)
Patterson, Andrew Lawrence	Wiley College (Marshall, TX)
Patterson, Joe	Fort Valley State University (Ft. Valley, GA) Bellevue College (Omaha, NB) University of Nebraska (Lincoln, NB)
Peace, Warren	Kittrell AME College (Chapel Hill, NC)
Peeples, Nat	LeMoyne College (Memphis, TN)
Petway, Bruce	Meharry Medical College (Nashville, TN)

Pfiffer, Lester J.	Lincoln University (Jefferson City, MO)
Phillips, Richard	Morris Brown College (Atlanta, GA)
Posey, Cumberland	Duquesne (formerly Holy Ghost College) (Pittsburgh, PA)
	Penn State University (Pittsburgh, PA)
Powell, Bill	Miles College (Birmingham, AL)
Powell, Melvin	Alcorn A&M (Alcorn, MS)
Powell, Willie	Northwestern University (Evanston, IL)
Proctor, Jim	University of Maryland Eastern Shore (Princess Anne, MD)
Redd, Hickey	Leland College (Baker, LA)
Redding, Dick	Morris Brown College (Atlanta, GA)
Reese, Johnny	Morris Brown College (Atlanta, GA)
Reeves, Donald	Clark College (Atlanta, GA)
Renfroe, Chico	Clark College (Atlanta, GA)
Richardson William	Clark College (Atlanta, GA)
Riddle, Marshall	Hubbard Business College
Ritchey, John	San Diego State (San Diego, CA)
Rivero, Manuel	Columbia University (New York, NY)
Roberts, Elihu	Morris Brown College (Atlanta, GA)
Roberts, Jesse	Alcorn A&M (Alcorn, MS)
Robinson, Jackie	Pasadena Junior College (Los Angeles, CA)
	UCLA (Los Angeles, CA)
Robinson, James	North Carolina A&T (Greensboro, NC)
	City College of New York (New York, NY)
Rodgers, Silvester	Compton College (Los Angeles, CA)
	El Camino Junior College (Los Angeles, CA)
Rouse, Jr., Howard	North Carolina A&T (Greensboro, NC)
Roth, Herman	New Orleans University (New Orleans, LA)
	Southern University (Baton Rouge, LA)
Russ, Pythias	Samuel Huston College (Austin, TX)
	Walden University (Minneapolis, MN)
	Meharry Medical College (Nashville, TN)
Santiago, José	Modern Business College (New York, NY)
Scott, Joe	Virginia Normal (Petersburg, VA)
Scott, Lloyd	Alcorn A&M (Alcorn, MS)
Shackelford, John	Wiley College (Marshall, TX)
Sheffey, Doug	University of Pennsylvania (Philadelphia, PA)
Shepherd, Frederick Lee	Morris Brown College (Atlanta, GA)
Sheppard, Ray	Paul Quinn College (Dallas, TX)
Shields, Jimmy	Virginia Union University (Richmond, VA)
	Howard University (Washington, DC)
Simmons, Hubert "Bert"	North Carolina A & T (Greensboro, NC)
Simpson, Lawrence	Wilberforce University (Wilberforce, OH)
Smaulding, Owen	University of Washington (Seattle, WA)
Smith, Al	Indiana University (Bloomington, IN)

Smith, George (Sonny)	Western Kentucky or Kentucky State
Smith, Hilton	Prairie View A&M College (Hempstead, TX)
Smith, John Ford	University of Arizona (Tucson, AZ)
Smith, William T.	Fisk University (Nashville, TN)
Spearman, Alvin	Kentucky State University (Frankfurt, KY)
Spencer, Joe	Xavier University (New Orleans, LA)
Spruill, Joe	Morris Brown College (Atlanta, GA)
Stewart, Riley	Bishop College [now Paul Quinn] (Dallas, TX) Leland College (Baker, LA)
Streeter, Sam	Alabama A&M University (Normal, AL)
Street, Albert	Atlanta University (Atlanta, GA)
Strong, Joe	Wilberforce University (Wilberforce, OH)
Sublette, William	Fisk University (Nashville, TN)
Sweatt, George	Kansas State Normal School (Pittsburg KS)
Sykes, Franklin Jehoy	Morehouse University (Atlanta, GA) Howard University (Washington, DC)
Sykes, Melvin	Morehouse University (Atlanta, GA) Atlanta Baptist College (Atlanta, GA)
Taylor, C.I.	Clark College (Atlanta, GA) Benedict College (Columbia, SC)
Taylor, Jim	Greeley Institute (Greeley, CO)
Taylor, Steel Arm Johnny	Biddle University [now Johnson C. Smith] (Charlotte, NC)
Taylor, LeRoy R.	Wiley College (Marshall, TX)
Taylor, Sam	Clark College (Atlanta, GA)
Taylor, Jr., Tommie	Brevard Junior College (Brevard, NC) Lane College (Jackson, TN) B.S. Degree
Teasley, Ron	Wayne State University (Detroit, MI)
Terry, John	Wilberforce University (Wilberforce, OH)
Thomas, Charles	Boston University (Boston, MA)
Thomas, Fred	Assumption College (Windsor, Ontario, Canada)
Thompson, Samuel "Long Tom"	Wiley College (Marshall, Texas)
Trent, Ted "Highpockets"	Bethune-Cookman College (Daytona Beach, FL)
Trouppe, Quincy	Lincoln University (Jefferson City, MO)
Tucker, Orval	Johnson C. Smith University (Charlotte, NC)
Turner, Clarence	Johnson C. Smith University (Charlotte, NC)
Turner, E.C.	West Virginia State College (Charleston, WV)
Turner, Lorenzo Dow	Howard University (Washington, DC)
Turner, Thomas	Tuskegee Institute (Tuskegee, AL)
Varona, Clemente	North Carolina A & T (Greensboro, NC)
Walker, Moses Fleetwood	University of Michigan (Ann Arbor, MI) Oberlin College (Oberlin, OH)
Walker, Welday	University of Michigan (Ann Arbor, MI) Oberlin College (Oberlin, OH)
Ware, Joe	Howard University (Washington, DC)

Ware, William Lee	Wiley College (Marshall, TX)
Warmack, Herman Peter	Tuskegee Institute (Tuskegee, AL)
Watson, Amos	Florence Villa College (Winter Haven, FL)
Webb, Normal "Tweed"	Washington Technical School (St. Louis, MO)
Welch, Wingfield	New Orleans University (Dillard University) (New Orleans, LA)
Wells, Willie	Samuel Huston College (Austin, TX) Paul Quinn College (Dallas, TX)
Welmaker, Roy	Clark College (Atlanta, GA)
Westfield, Ernest	Eastern Illinois University (Charleston, IL), Roosevelt University (Chicago, IL)
Wheeler, Sam	Philander Smith College (Little Rock, AR)
White, Eugene	Edward Waters College (Jacksonville, FL) Stanton College Preparatory School (Jacksonville, FL)
White, Solomon	Wilberforce University (Wilberforce, OH)
Whitney, Davey	Kentucky State University (Frankfort, KY)
Wiggins, Joe	Virginia Normal (Petersburg, VA)
Wiley, Wabishaw Spencer	Arkansas Baptist College (Little Rock, AR) Howard University (Washington, DC)
Willet, Pete	Wilberforce University (Wilberforce, OH)
Williams, Bobby	Dillard University (New Orleans, LA)
Williams, Gerard	Morehouse University (Atlanta, GA)
Williams, Nish	Morehouse University (Atlanta, GA)
Williams, Phil	Morgan State University (Baltimore, MD)
Williams, Robert Rosel	So. Carolina State University (Orangeburg, SC) Benedict College (Columbia, SC) Bachelor of Arts
Williams, Tom	Morris Brown College (Atlanta, GA)
Willis, Charles L.	Miles College (Fairfield, AL) University of Montevallo (Montevallo, AL) Master, 1972 University of Montevallo (Montevallo, AL) AA (EDS) 1976
Wilson, Carter	Crane Junior College (Chicago, IL) Armour Institute (Chicago, IL)
Wilson, Herbert	Tyler Junior College (Tyler, TX)
Wilson, James William (J.H.)	Lincoln University (Oxford, PA), 1882 BA, 1888 MA
Wilson, Percy	Leland University (Baker, LA)
Wouldridge, Charley	Wilberforce University (Wilberforce, OH)
Wright, Walter	Xavier University (New Orleans, LA) Duquesne University (Pittsburgh, PA)
Wright, Zollie	Paul Quinn College (Dallas, TX)
Wyatt, Dave	Indiana State University (Terre Haute IN)
Wyatt, Ralph	Wilson Junior College (Chicago, IL)
Yokely, Layman	Livingstone College (Salisbury, NC)
Young, William P.	Lincoln University (Oxford, PA)
Ziegler, William	Fisk University (Nashville, TN)

APPENDIX J: Tributes to Negro Leaguers & Teams

Streets and Highways named after Black Ballplayers

Hank Aaron
- Hank Aaron Lane, Round Rock, TX
- Hank Aaron Drive Southwest, Atlanta, GA
- Hank Aaron Stadium Drive, Mobile, AL
- Hank Aaron State Trail, Milwaukee, WI
- 755 Hank Aaron Drive SE, Atlanta, GA

Ernie Banks
- Ernie Banks Drive, El Paso, TX
- Ernie Banks Street, Capitol Heights, MD

James "Cool Papa" Bell
- J. 'Cool-Papa' Bell Ave., St. Louis, MO
- James 'Cool Papa' Bell Ave., St. Louis, MO
- James (Cool Papa) Bell Drive, Jackson, MS

Ray Dandridge
- Dandridge Way, Newark, NJ

Leon Day
- Leon Day Way, Camden Yards, Baltimore, MD
- Day Way, Newark, NJ

Larry Doby
- Larry Doby Highway, near Camden, SC
- Doby Place, Newark, NJ
- Larry Doby Route 120 Meadowlands Sport Complex, NJ
- Larry Doby Way (Eagle Ave.) adjacent to Progressive Field, Cleveland, OH

Josh Gibson
- Josh Gibson Place, Pittsburgh, PA

Bud Fowler
- Bud Fowler Way at Doubleday Field, Cooperstown, NY

Junior Gilliam
- Jim Gilliam Way, Nashville, TN

Chuck Harmon
- Chuck Harmon Way, Cincinnati, OH

Roadways, Statues & Landmarks

Monte Irvin
- Irvin Way, Newark, NJ

"Sweet" Lou Johnson
- Sweet Lou Johnson Way, Los Angeles, CA
- Lou Johnson Way, Lexington, KY

Buck Leonard
- Buck Leonard Boulevard, Rocky Mount, NC

John Henry "Pop" Lloyd
- Pop Lloyd Boulevard, Atlantic City, NJ

Willie Mays
- Willie Mays Highway, Orlando, FL
- Willie Mays Plaza, San Francisco, CA
- Willie Mays Lane, Round Rock, TX
- Willie Mays Street, Shreveport, LA
- Willie Mays Drive, El Paso, TX
- Willie Mays Drive, Birmingham, AL

Terris McDuffie
- McDuffie Lane, Newark, NJ

Don Newcombe
- Newcombe Lane, Newark, NJ

John "Buck" O'Neil
- John "Buck" O'Neil Way, Kansas City, MO
- Buck O'Neil Way, Surprise, AZ

Satchel Paige
- Satchel Paige Drive, Mobile, AL
- Satchel Paige Way, Hollywood, MD

Lennie Pearson
- Pearson Lane, Newark, NJ

Spottswood Poles
- Spottswood Poles Drive in Jim Barnett Park, Winchester, PA

Jackie Robinson
- Jackie Robinson Parkway, Glendale, NY
- Jackie Robinson Parkway, Queens, NY
- Jackie Robinson Parkway, Brooklyn NY
- Jackie Robinson Plaza, Round Rock, TX
- Jackie Robinson Street, Austin, TX

Negro Leagues Book #2: The Players

- Jackie Robinson Street, DeRidder, LA
- Jackie Robinson Street, Bogalusa, LA
- Jackie Robinson Drive, Shreveport, LA
- Jackie Robinson Avenue, Dodgertown, Vero Beach, FL

Moses Fleetwood Walker
- Moses Fleetwood Walker Square, Toledo, OH

Willie "the Devil" Wells
- Willie Wells Avenue, Austin, TX

Ball Parks, Historic Markers, Statues and Other Landmarks named in honor of Negro League players and Teams

Hank Aaron
- Hank Aaron statue at Milwaukee Brewers' Miller Park (designer Brian Maughan)
- Milwaukee Brewers' Wall of Honor
- Hank Aaron statue at Atlanta Braves' site of former Turner Field (designer Eddie Dwight, Jr.)
- Hank Aaron statue at Atlanta Braves, SunTrust Park, Cobb County, GA
- Hank Aaron Stadium, Mobile, AL
- Hank Aaron Childhood Home Museum, Mobile, AL
- Hank Aaron 715 Home Run marker, Summerhill neighborhood, Atlanta, GA
- Hank Aaron Field, Newark, NJ
- W.C. Council Traditional School marker in Mobile, AL
- Hot Springs: The Birthplace of Spring Baseball marker near old Whittington Park, Hot Springs, AR
- Wisconsin Athletic Walk of Fame marker located on east side of the UW-Panther Arena, Milwaukee, WI
- Heinemann Park/Pelican Stadium historical marker in New Orleans, LA
- [Joe] Tinker Field historical Marker, Orlando, FL

James Abernathy
- 100th anniversary plaque honoring Nashvillians from the Negro Leagues, at E.S. Rose Park Baseball Pavilion, Nashville, TN

Tom Alston
- Original Home Place of the Greensboro Red Wings historical marker

Ernie Banks
- Ernie Banks statue at Chicago Cubs' Wrigley Field (designer Lou Cella)
- Ernie Banks statue at Booker T. Washington High School, Dallas, TX (designer Emmanuel Gillespie)

Wesley "Biggie" Barrows
- Wesley Barrows Stadium, Pontchartrain Park, New Orleans, LA

John Beckwith
- Harrisburg Giants marker, Harrisburg, PA

James "Cool Papa" Bell
- Cool Papa Bell statue at St. Louis Cardinals' Busch Stadium (designer Harry Weber)
- Cool Papa Bell statue at Pittsburgh Pirates' PNC Park (designer John Forsythe) (removed in 2015)
- Cool Papa Bell statue at Sports Museum of Los Angeles, CA (designer John Forsythe)
- James "Cool Papa" Bell birthplace marker, Starkville, MS
- Bell exhibit at Friends of Oktibbeha County Heritage Museum, in McKee Park, Starkville, MS
- Cool Papa Bell metal sign on the Homestead Grays Bridge, Pittsburgh, PA
- Bronze star marker on Delmar Boulevard in University City, MO
- Hot Springs: The Birthplace of Spring Baseball marker near old Whittington Park, Hot Springs, AR
- Hamtramck Stadium marker, Hamtramck, MI
- James "Cool Papa" Bell Baseball League at Fairground Park, St. Louis, MO

- James "Cool Papa" Bell Stadium at the Matthew Dickey and Girls Club, St. Louis, MO
- Cool Papa Bell mural at the KC Urban Youth Academy, Kansas City, MO
- Ring of Honor at Washington Nationals Park in Washington, DC

William Bell
- Willie Bell Park, El Campo, TX

Joe Black
- Joe Black Baseball Field at Hub Stine Sports Complex, Plainfield, NJ

Ed Bolden
- Hilldale Athletic Club (Darby Daisies) marker

Frank E. Bolden
- Marker on Centre Avenue in Pittsburgh, PA

Chet Brewer
- Chet Brewer Field, Los Angeles, CA

Bill Blair
- William Blair, Jr., Park in Dallas, TX

William "Soo" Bridgeforth
- 100th anniversary plaque honoring Nashvillians from the Negro Leagues, at E.S. Rose Park Baseball Pavilion, Nashville, TN

Ray Brown
- Ray Brown metal sign on the Homestead Grays Bridge, Pittsburgh, PA
- Ring of Honor at Washington Nationals Park in Washington, DC

Willard "Home Run" Brown
- Monroe Monarchs Field marker, Monroe, LA

Clarence Bruce
- Clarence Bruce metal sign on the Homestead Grays Bridge, Pittsburgh, PA

Sidney Bunch
- 100th anniversary plaque honoring Nashvillians from the Negro Leagues, at E.S. Rose Park Baseball Pavilion, Nashville, TN

Roy Campanella
- Roy Campanella Park, Los Angeles County, Compton, CA
- Roy Campanella Conference Room, Dodgertown, Vero Beach, FL
- Addisleigh Park Historical District (Landmarks Preservation Commission), Borough of Queens, NY

- Roy Campanella statue at the National Baseball Hall of Fame and Museum, Cooperstown, NY (designer Stanley Bleifeld)

Octavius V. Catto
- Octavius V. Catto statue at City Hall, Philadelphia, PA (designer Branly Cadet)

Oscar Charleston
- Oscar Charleston statue at Pittsburgh Pirates' PNC Park (designer John Forsythe) (removed in 2015)
- Oscar Charleston statue at the Negro Leagues Baseball Museum, Kansas City, MO (designer Kwan Wu)
- Oscar Charleston statue at the Sports Museum of Los Angeles, CA (designer John Forsythe)
- Oscar Charleston Park, Indianapolis, IN
- Oscar Charleston metal sign on the Homestead Grays Bridge, Pittsburgh, PA
- Hot Springs: The Birthplace of Spring Baseball marker near old Whittington Park, Hot Springs, AR
- Harrisburg Giants marker, Harrisburg, PA

Elliott Coleman
- 100th anniversary plaque honoring Nashvillians from the Negro Leagues, at E.S. Rose Park Baseball Pavilion, Nashville, TN

Crawford Grill
- Marker at the intersection of Wylie Avenue and Elmore Avenue in Pittsburgh, PA

Nelson Crews
- Nelson C. Crews Square, Kansas City, MO

George Crowe
- Resident Hall at the University of Indianapolis renamed "Ray and George Crowe Hall". Brother Ray coached future NBA star Oscar Robertson at Crispus Attucks High School.

Cuban Giants Marker
- Site of Argyle Hotel, Babylon (NY) Village Historic and Preservation Society

Ray Dandridge
- Ray E. Dandridge, Sr. Baseball Field, Newark, NJ
- Ring of Honor, Bears & Eagles Riverfront Stadium in Newark, NJ (removed in 2013)
- Ray Dandridge statue at the Negro Leagues Baseball Museum, Kansas City, MO (designer Kwan Wu)
- Mural on Perry Hilltop at Wilson Avenue and West Burgess Street, Pittsburgh, PA

Leon Day
- Leon Day Park, Baltimore, MD
- Ring of Honor, Bears & Eagles Riverfront Stadium in Newark, NJ (removed in 2013)
- Leon Day statue at the Negro Leagues Baseball Museum, Kansas City, MO (designer Kwan Wu)

Dayton Marcos
- Dayton Walk of Fame in the Wright-Dunbar Business District, Dayton, OH

Wesley "Doc" Dennis

Negro Leagues Book #2: The Players

- 100th anniversary plaque honoring Nashvillians from the Negro Leagues, at E.S. Rose Park Baseball Pavilion, Nashville, TN

Ed "Lefty" Derrick
- 100th anniversary plaque honoring Nashvillians from the Negro Leagues, at E.S. Rose Park Baseball Pavilion, Nashville, TN

Detroit Stars
- Hamtramck Stadium historical marker, Hamtramck, MI

Martín Dihigo
- Martín Dihigo statue at the Negro Leagues Baseball Museum, Kansas City, MO (designer Kwan Wu)

Rap Dixon
- First base dugout at Reich Little League Field, Steelton, PA
- Harrisburg Giants marker, Harrisburg, PA

Larry Doby
- Larry Doby statue at Cleveland Indians' Progressive Field (designer David Deming)
- Larry Doby statue at Larry Doby Field in Paterson, NJ (designer Phil Sgobba)
- Larry Doby Athletic Field, Camden, SC
- Larry Doby Highway, near Camden, SC
- Larry Doby Field, Eastside Park, Paterson, NJ
- Larry Doby Post Office, Paterson, NJ
- Larry Doby mural at Hinchliffe Stadium, Paterson, NJ
- Larry Doby Wing at the Yogi Berra Museum and Learning Center, campus of Montclair State University in Little Falls, NJ
- Larry Doby sign at Corbett Field (Cleveland Indians spring training site), Tucson, AZ
- Ring of Honor, Bears & Eagles Riverfront Stadium in Newark, NJ (removed in 2013)
- Hot Springs: The Birthplace of Spring Baseball marker near old Whittington Park, Hot Springs, AR
- Plaque at Padres' Hall of Fame at Petco Park, San Diego, CA
- Larry Doby statue at Cleveland Indians' Progressive Field (designer David Deming)

John Donaldson
- John Wesley Donaldson statue, Glasgow, MO (designer Kwan Wu)
- John Donaldson Field for Glasgow School District, Glasgow, MO

Clifford DuBose
- Clifford DuBose Field #4 at Stephens Park, Montevallo, AL

Luke Easter
- Luke Easter bust in Luke Easter Park
- Luke Easter Park, Cleveland, OH
- Luke Easter plaque, Cleveland Indians' Heritage Park
- Luke Easter's name on Offerman Stadium historic marker, Buffalo, NY

Roadways, Statues & Landmarks

Andrew "Rube" Foster
- Rube Foster statue at the Negro Leagues Baseball Museum, Kansas City, MO (designer Kwan Wu)
- Rube Foster Memorial Field, Fort Huachuca, AZ
- Andrew "Rube" Foster banner, Bronzeville, Chicago, IL
- Bronzeville Walk of Fame, "Andrew 'Rube' Foster," Chicago, IL
- Hot Springs: The Birthplace of Spring Baseball marker near old Whittington Park, Hot Springs, AR
- Andrew "Rube" Foster mural at Hamtramck Stadium, Hamtramck, MI
- Mural on Perry Hilltop at Wilson Avenue and West Burgess Street, Pittsburgh, PA

Willie Foster
- Hot Springs: The Birthplace of Spring Baseball marker near old Whittington Park, Hot Springs, AR

Josh Gibson
- Josh Gibson statue at the Sports Museum of Los Angeles, CA (designer John Forsythe)
- Josh Gibson statue at Pittsburgh Pirates' PNC Park (designer John Forsythe) (removed in 2015)
- Josh Gibson statue at Washington Nationals' Nationals Park, Washington, DC (designer Studio Amrany)
- Josh Gibson statue at the Negro Leagues Baseball Museum, Kansas City, MO (designer Kwan Wu)
- Josh Gibson Water Tower, Buena Vista, GA
- Josh Gibson Field, 2217 Bedford Avenue, Pittsburgh, PA
- Joshua (Josh) Gibson marker on Bedford Avenue, Pittsburgh, PA
- Josh Gibson Youth and Family Resource Center, Buena Vista, GA
- Josh Gibson metal sign on the Homestead Grays Bridge, Pittsburgh, PA
- Josh Gibson Heritage Park at Station Square, Pittsburgh, PA
- Mural on Lincoln Theatre at U Street across from Ben's Chili Bowl, Washington, DC
- Mural at Dorsey Park, Miami, FL by Kadir Nelson
- Mural on Perry Hilltop at Wilson Avenue and West Burgess Street, Pittsburgh, PA
- Mural on Lincoln Theatre at U Street across from Ben's Chili Bowl, Washington, DC
- Mirrored Marker at Navy Yard, Washington, DC.
- Griffith Stadium Marker in LeDroit Park, on Georgia Avenue NW near Howard University Hospital, Washington, DC
- Hot Springs: "The Birthplace of Spring Baseball" marker near old Whittington Park, Hot Springs, AR
- Hamtramck Stadium marker, Hamtramck, MI
- Ring of Honor at Washington Nationals Park in Washington, DC

Junior Gilliam
- Jim Gilliam #19 sign, Dodgertown, Vero Beach, FL
- Jim Gilliam Room, Dodgertown, Vero Beach, FL
- Jim Gilliam Park, Los Angeles, CA
- Jim Gilliam Senior Citizen Center, Los Angeles, CA
- Jim Gilliam Park & Recreation Center, Los Angeles, CA
- Jim Gilliam Child Care Center, Los Angeles, CA
- Junior Gilliam Way, Nashville, TN
- 100th anniversary plaque honoring Nashvillians from the Negro Leagues, at E.S. Rose Park Baseball Pavilion, Nashville, TN

Negro Leagues Book #2: The Players

Eddie Gottlieb
- Eddie Gottlieb Historical Marker - South Philadelphia High School, St Philadelphia PA

Greensboro Red Wings
- Original Home Place of the Greensboro Red Wings historical marker

Gus Greenlee
- Greenlee Field marker, Pittsburgh, PA (pictured)
- Crawford Grill marker, Pittsburgh, PA
- Gus Greenlee metal sign on the Homestead Grays Bridge, Pittsburgh, PA
- Mural on Perry Hilltop at Wilson Avenue and West Burgess Street, Pittsburgh, PA

Raymond Haggins
- Raymond "Ray" Haggins Field #3 at Stephens Park, Montevallo, AL

Sam Hairston
- Samuel Harding "Sam" Hairston Park in Lowndes County (Columbus) MS
- Sam Hairston Historic Marker, Columbus, MS

Sellers Hall
- Sellers Hall metal sign on the Homestead Grays Bridge, Pittsburgh, PA

Hamtramck Stadium
- Marker for the Detroit Stars at intersection of Joseph Campau Avenue and Goodson Street, Hamtramck, MI

Chuck Harmon
- Chuck Harmon statue at the Cincinnati Reds' urban youth baseball academy in Roselawn, OH (designer Tom Tsuchiya)

Bill "Woogie" Harris
- Bill Harris metal sign on the Homestead Grays Bridge, Pittsburgh, PA

Vic Harris
- Vic Harris metal sign on the Homestead Grays Bridge, Pittsburgh, PA

Harrisburg Giants
- Harrisburg Giants marker, Harrisburg, PA

Thomas Hayes
- T.H. Hayes and Sons Funeral Home marker at the intersection of Lauderdale and Mississippi Boulevard in Memphis, TN

Pete Hill
- Pete Hill birthplace marker, Buena, Culpeper County, VA
- Pete Hill highway marker, Richmond, VA
- Hot Springs: The Birthplace of Spring Baseball marker near old Whittington Park, Hot Springs, AR

(The) Hilldale Athletic Club (Darby Daisies) Marker
- Hilldale Athletic Club, Darby, PA

Homestead Grays
- Homestead Grays West Street, Pittsburgh, PA
- Homestead Grays Street, Pittsburgh, PA
- The Homestead Grays marker, Pittsburgh, PA

Homestead Grays Bridge
- Also known as the High Level Bridge, was built in 1936 and spans the Monongahela River between Homestead Borough and the southernmost tip of Pittsburgh's Squirrel Hill neighborhood. Historic metal signs honored the Grays, Pittsburgh Crawfords, Satchel Paige, Cool Papa Bell, Cum Posey, Sellers Hall, Vic Harris, Ray Brown, Buck Leonard, Clarence Bruce, Smokey Joe Williams, Gus Greenlee, Oscar Charleston, Ted Page, Bill Harris, Harold Tinker, Judy Johnson and Josh Gibson, Pittsburgh, PA.

Elston Howard
- Mural on storefronts in the 501 See Streets Projects, New York, NY, by Lexi Bella

Indianapolis ABCs
- Washington Park Baseball marker, Indianapolis, IN

Cal Irvin
- North Carolina A&T Aggies basketball court

Monte Irvin
- Monte Irvin statue at Monte Irvin Orange Park, East Orange, NJ (designer Jay Warren)
- Monte Irvin Field, East Orange, NJ
- Monte Irvin Orange Park, 47.5 acres, East Orange, NJ
- Ring of Honor, Bears & Eagles Riverfront Stadium in Newark, NJ (removed in 2013)
- Hot Springs: The Birthplace of Spring Baseball marker near old Whittington Park, Hot Springs, AR

Fats Jenkins
- Harrisburg Giants marker, Harrisburg, PA

Don "Groundhog" Johnson
- Don Johnson Field at the P&G Cincinnati Urban Youth Academy, Cincinnati, OH

Sweet Lou Johnson
- Lou Johnson Park, Lexington, KY
- Lou Johnson T-Ball League, Lexington, KY

Judy Johnson
- Judy Johnson statue at the Negro Leagues Baseball Museum, Kansas City, MO (designer Kwan Wu)
- Judy Johnson statue at Wilmington Blue Rocks, Daniel S. Frawley Stadium, Wilmington, DE (designer Phil Sumpter)
- Judy Johnson statue at Pittsburgh Pirates' PNC Park (designer John Forsythe) (removed in 2015)

Negro Leagues Book #2: The Players

- Judy Johnson Historic Home marker on Kiamensi Ave and Newport Road, Newport, DE
- Judy Johnson Memorial Park, Wilmington, DE
- Judy Johnson Field, at Daniel S. Frawley Stadium in Wilmington
- Judy Johnson metal sign on the Homestead Grays Bridge, Pittsburgh, PA
- Hot Springs: The Birthplace of Spring Baseball marker near old Whittington Park, Hot Springs, AR
- Judy Johnson Memorial Monument at Snow Hill Library by the Worchester County Public Library and Historical Society

Mamie "Peanut" Johnson
- Mamie "Peanut" Johnson Field at Rosedale Recreation Center, Washington, DC
- Mural on Lincoln Theatre at U Street across from Ben's Chili Bowl, Washington, DC

Kansas City Monarchs
- Buck O'Neil Education and Research Center, south side mural at 18th & The Paseo, Kansas City, MO
- Power & Light District mural, Downtown, Kansas City, MO

Henry Kimbro
- 100th anniversary plaque honoring Nashvillians from the Negro Leagues, at E.S. Rose Park Baseball Pavilion, Nashville, TN

Walter "Buck" Leonard
- Buck Leonard statue at Sports Museum of Los Angeles, CA (designer John Forsythe)
- Buck Leonard statue at Negro Leagues Baseball Museum, Kansas City, MO (designer Kwan Wu)
- Buck Leonard statue at Pittsburgh Pirates' PNC Park (designer John Forsythe) (removed in 2015)
- Buck Leonard Park, Rocky Mount, NC
- Buck Leonard metal sign on the Homestead Grays Bridge, Pittsburgh, PA
- Walter Fenner "Buck" Leonard historic marker in Rocky Mount, NC
- Ring of Honor at Washington Nationals Park in Washington, DC

John Henry "Pop" Lloyd
- Pop Lloyd statue at Negro Leagues Baseball Museum, Kansas City, MO (designer Kwan Wu)
- Pop Lloyd Baseball Stadium, Atlantic City, NJ
- Mural on Perry Hilltop at Wilson Avenue and West Burgess Street, Pittsburgh, PA

Raleigh "Biz" Mackey
- Ring of Honor, Bears & Eagles Riverfront Stadium in Newark, NJ (removed in 2013)
- Hot Springs: The Birthplace of Spring Baseball marker near old Whittington Park, Hot Springs, AR

Effa Manley
- Ring of Honor, Bears & Eagles Riverfront Stadium in Newark, NJ (removed in 2013)

Max Manning
- Max Manning Sports Complex, Pleasantville, NJ
- Mural at Dorsey Park, Miami, FL by Kadir Nelson

Roadways, Statues & Landmarks

Ed Martin
- 100th anniversary plaque honoring Nashvillians from the Negro Leagues, at E.S. Rose Park Baseball Pavilion, Nashville, TN

J.B. Martin and brothers
- Bronzeville Walk of Fame for "Dr. J.B. Martin," Chicago, IL
- Martin Hotel marker on M. L. King Boulevard (Tennessee Route 2), Chattanooga TN
- Martin Stadium marker, formerly known as Lewis Park, Memphis, TN

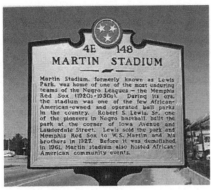

MARTIN STADIUM was built in the mid-'30s and was named after the Martin brothers who purchased the Memphis Red Sox in 1932. The Marker is located on Danny Thomas and Boss Crump Avenue. Martin Stadium had an original capacity of 3,000 with later renovations increasing capacity to approximately 7000. Stadium dimensions have been listed as Left Field: 360 feet; Left Center: 371; Center Field: 422; Right Center: 450; and Right Field: 301. Despite segregation sanctions of the period, Martin Stadium was without racial restrictions. Uniquely, the stadium had dormitories for their players that were located under the left field seats.

Willie Mays
- Willie Mays statue at Regions Field, Birmingham, AL (designer Caleb O'Connor)
- Willie Mays statue at San Francisco Giants' Pacific Bell Park (designer William Behrends)
- Willie Mays Park, Orlando, FL
- Willie Mays Park, Fairfield, AL
- Java House marker is on The Embarcadero near Townsend in San Francisco, CA
- Steamboat Point marker in sidewalk at AT&T Park's Willie Mays Plaza
- African American owned (Walter) Harmon Hotel marker in Hagerstown, MD

Clint "Butch" McCord
- 100th anniversary plaque honoring Nashvillians from the Negro Leagues, at E.S. Rose Park Baseball Pavilion, Nashville, TN

Milwaukee Bears
- Borchert Field/The Milwaukee Bears: Negro National League, 1923 historic marker, Milwaukee, WI

Minnie Miñoso
- Minnie Miñoso statue at Chicago White Sox's US Cellular Field (designer Maritza Hernández)
- Minnie Miñoso All-Star Stand, concessions stand at Comiskey Park
- Minnie Miñoso plaque, Cleveland Indians' Heritage Park

Monroe Monarchs Field marker
- Monroe Monarchs Historical Foundation, Monroe, LA

Negro Leagues Book #2: The Players

Bob Motley
- Bob Motley statue at Negro Leagues Baseball Museum, Kansas City, MO (designer Kwan Wu)
- "The Motley Family Field" at the KC Urban Youth Academy, connected to the Arrington "Bubble" Klice Community Center, Kansas City, MO

Nashville Players tribute
- 100th anniversary plaque honoring Nashvillians from the Negro Leagues, at E.S. Rose Park Baseball Pavilion, Nashville, TN

Negro Leagues tribute
- 6 ft x 8 ft bronze collage of Negro League legends at the entrance of Sand Castle Baseball Stadium, Atlantic City, NJ, by sculptor Jennifer Frudakis

The Negro National League of Professional Baseball Clubs founding
- The Paseo YMCA, 18th & The Paseo, Kansas City, MO (architect Charles A. Smith)
- Proposed Buck O'Neil Education and Research Center, formerly The Paseo YMCA

Buck O'Neil
- Buck O'Neil statue at Negro Leagues Baseball Museum, Kansas City, MO (designer Kwan Wu)
- John "Buck" O'Neil statue at National Baseball Hall Fame and Museum, Cooperstown, NY (designer William Behrends)
- Buck O'Neil statue at Kansas City Royals Hall of Fame Museum at Kauffman (designer Harry Weber)
- Buck O'Neil Baseball Complex at Twin Lakes Park, Sarasota, FL, home of the Baltimore Orioles
- Buck O'Neil bust at the Hall of Famous Missourians, Jefferson City, MO (sculptor E. Spencer Schubert)
- John Jordan "Buck " O'Neil marker and bust at the Missouri Sports Hall of Fame, Springfield, MO
- John Jordan Buck O'Neil (a.k.a. Broadway) Memorial Bridge, Kansas City, MO
- Buck O'Neil Education and Research Center, south side mural at 18th & The Paseo, Kansas City, MO
- Kansas City Royals Legacy Seat, Section 127, Seat 9, Row C, at Kauffman Stadium

Ted Page
- Ted Page metal sign on the Homestead Grays Bridge, Pittsburgh, PA

Satchel Paige
- Satchel Paige statue at Eagle Loan Company, Mentor-on-the-Lake, OH (designer John Forsythe)
- Satchel Paige statue at Negro Leagues Baseball Museum, Kansas City, MO (designer Kwan Wu)
- Leroy "Satchel" Paige statue at National Baseball Hall Fame and Museum, Cooperstown, NY (designer Stanley Bleifeld)
- Satchel Paige statue at Pittsburgh Pirates' PNC Park (designer John Forsythe) (removed in 2015)
- Satchel Paige Memorial Stadium, Kansas City, MO
- The Leroy "Satchel" Paige room at the Southmoreland Hotel, Kansas City, MO
- Satchel Paige Elementary School, Kansas City, MO
- Satchel Paige Field, Sprint Campus, Overland Park, KS
- Satchel Paige sign at Corbett Field (Cleveland Indians spring training site), Tucson, AZ
- Satchel Paige plaque, Cleveland Indians' Heritage Park
- Satchel Paige metal sign on the Homestead Grays Bridge, Pittsburgh, PA
- Artwork "Mound Magician" at the Nelson-Atkins Museum in Kansas City, MO by Radcliffe Bailey

Roadways, Statues & Landmarks

- Mural at Dorsey Park, Miami, FL by Kadir Nelson
- Mural on storefronts in the 501 See Streets Projects, New York, NY by Andre Trenier
- Mural at Downs-Mabson Fields in Austin, TX by Reginald Adams
- Mural on Perry Hilltop at Wilson Avenue and West Burgess Street, Pittsburgh, PA
- Economy Parking Lot A, Kiosk A4 marker, at Kansas City International Airport (MCI), Kansas City, MO
- W.C. Council Traditional School marker in Mobile, AL
- Hot Springs: The Birthplace of Spring Baseball marker near old Whittington Park, Hot Springs, AR
- Hamtramck Stadium marker, Hamtramck, MI
- Power & Light District mural, Downtown, Kansas City, MO
- Leroy and Lahoma Paige home at 2626 East 28th St., Kansas City, MO. Proposed National Register of Historic Places
- Satchel Paige mural at the KC Urban Youth Academy, Kansas City, MO

Charles Peete
- Charles Peete Little League Park, Portsmouth, VA

Art "Superman" Pennington
- Oak Hill Jackson Brickstones; Adam Todd and Art Pennington Apartments, Cedar Rapids, IA
- Superman Pennington mural at Convention Center Parking Ramp/Garage, Cedar Rapids, IA (artist Thomas Agran)

Bruce Petway
- 100th anniversary plaque honoring Nashvillians from the Negro Leagues, at E.S. Rose Park Baseball Pavilion, Nashville, TN

Philadelphia Giants, Hilldales, Stars Marker & Statue
- African American Baseball in Philadelphia historical marker, Philadelphia, PA
- Philadelphia Stars Negro League Memorial Park, Philadelphia, PA
- Philadelphia Phillies Citizens Bank Park exhibit
- Mural at Belmont and Leidy Streets in Philadelphia, PA

Philadelphia Pythians
- Jefferson Street Ballparks marker for the Jefferson Street Grounds and Athletic Park. Site of the first interracial baseball game, Pythians versus Olympic Club in 1869, North Philadelphia, PA
- A plaque of the team is stationed behind the Octavius Catto statue at City Hall in Philadelphia, PA.

Spottswood Poles
- Harrisburg Giants marker, Harrisburg, PA
- Spottswood Poles historic birthplace marker, Winchester, PA

Cum Posey
- Cum Posey metal sign on the Homestead Grays Bridge, Pittsburgh, PA
- Hot Springs: The Birthplace of Spring Baseball marker near old Whittington Park, Hot Springs, AR
- Mural on Perry Hilltop at Wilson Avenue and West Burgess Street, Pittsburgh, PA
- Ring of Honor at Washington Nationals Park in Washington, DC

Negro Leagues Book #2: The Players

Charley Pride
- Charley Pride Highway, North Sledge, MS

Ted Rasberry
- Ted Rasberry Field, Grand Rapids, MI

Rickwood Field Marker
- America's Oldest Baseball Park, Birmingham, AL
- Rickwood Field Opening Day marker, Birmingham, AL

John Ritchey
- John Ritchey bust and plaque in The Draft at Petco Park, San Diego, CA

Jackie Robinson
- Jackie Robinson statue at Jackie Robinson Ballpark in Daytona, FL (designer Jules LaSalle)
- Jackie Robinson statue at Parc Olympique, Montreal, Canadá (designer Jules LaSalle) Note, this is the same statue design as the one in the Jackie Robinson Ballpark in Daytona, FL.
- Jackie Robinson statue at Jackie Robinson Park of Fame, Stamford, CT (designer Maceo Jeffries)
- Jackie Robinson statue at Jackie Robinson Stadium, UCLA, in Los Angeles, CA (designer Richard Ellis)
- Jackie Robinson statue at Journal Square, Jersey City, NJ (designer Susan Wagner)
- Jackie and Mack Robinson Memorial Monuments, Centennial Square, Pasadena, CA (designers Ralph Helmick and John Outterbridge)
- Jackie Robinson statue at Brooklyn Cyclones, Cyclone Park, Brooklyn, NY (designer William Behrends) Note, alongside statue of Pee Wee Reese.
- Jackie Robinson statue at Los Angeles Dodgers' Dodger Stadium (designer Branly Cadet)
- Jackie Robinson Center, Pasadena, CA
- Jackie Robinson plaque at boyhood home site, Pasadena, CA
- Jackie Robinson football statue #55 at Rose Bowl Stadium, Pasadena, CA (designer Brian Hanlon)
- Jackie Robinson plaque at Montreal Royals home in Canada
- Jackie Robinson Community Center, New York, NY
- Jackie Robinson Elementary School, Chicago, IL
- Jackie Robinson Academy, Long Beach, CA
- Jackie Robinson Field (Cairo High School Syrupmakers) in Cairo, GA
- Jackie Robinson House in Brooklyn, NY, National Historic Landmark
- Jackie Robinson plaque at 5224 Tilden Avenue, Brooklyn, NY
- Jackie Robinson Housing, New York, NY
- Jackie Robinson Memorial at former site of Delorimier Stadium, Montreal, Canada
- Jackie Robinson Memorial Field, Pasadena, CA
- Jackie Robinson Park & Pool, New York, NY
- Jackie Robinson Radiology Associates Field, Daytona Tortugas (formerly Cubs), Daytona Beach, FL
- Jackie Robinson Athletic & Recreation Complex, at UCLA, Los Angeles, CA
- Jackie Robinson Park, Manhattan, NY
- Jackie Robinson PS 375 School, Brooklyn, NY
- Jackie Robinson Rotunda, New York Mets' Citi Field, New York, NY
- Jackie Robinson Museum, New York, NY

Roadways, Statues & Landmarks

- Jackie Robinson Senior Citizen Center, New York, NY
- Jackie Robinson Stadium (Susan Miller Dorsey High School), in Rancho La Cienega Park, Los Angeles, CA
- Jackie Robinson Stadium, Daytona Beach, FL
- Jackie Robinson YMCA, Milwaukee, WI
- Jackie Robinson YMCA, New Haven, CT
- Jackie Robinson YMCA, Robinson, MS
- Jackie Robinson YMCA, San Diego, CA
- Jackie Robinson Youth Center, Harlem, NY
- Addisleigh Park Historical District (Landmarks Preservation Commission), Borough of Queens, NY
- Hot Springs: The Birthplace of Spring Baseball marker near old Whittington Park, Hot Springs, AR
- Heinemann Park/Pelican Stadium marker in New Orleans, LA
- Tinker Field marker, Orlando, FL
- The Character and Courage statues, one of three, at the National Baseball Hall of Fame and Museum, Cooperstown, NY
- Mural on Perry Hilltop at Wilson Avenue and West Burgess Street, Pittsburgh, PA
- Jackie Robinson Room I and II, Dodgertown, Vero Beach, FL
- Historic Dodgertown renamed Jackie Robinson Training Complex, Vero Beach, FL, in 2019
- Jackie Robinson mural at the KC Urban Youth Academy, Kansas City, MO

WILBER "BULLET" ROGAN - This memorial bust was casted in bronze and is located on the west side of Chickasaw Bricktown (formerly RedHawks) Ballpark in the Bricktown area of Oklahoma City. This memorial honors this Oklahoma-born baseball hero. This memorial which was part of the Oklahoma 2007 statehood Centennial celebration consists of a head and shoulders statue of Rogan in his cap and uniform.

Wilber "Bullet" Rogan
- Wilber Joe Rogan bust at Redhawks Ballpark, Oklahoma City, OK
- Hot Springs: The Birthplace of Spring Baseball marker near old Whittington Park, Hot Springs, AR

Billy Rowe
- Plaque with Wendell Smith at Jackie Robinson Ballpark & Museum, Daytona Beach, FL

Al Smith
- Al Smith plaque, Cleveland Indians' Heritage Park

Chino Smith
- Marker at Fluor Field, Heritage Plaza, in Greenville, SC

Hilton Smith
- Hot Springs: The Birthplace of Spring Baseball marker near old Whittington Park, Hot Springs, AR
- Hilton Lee Smith Field in Simmang Northwest Park, Giddings, TX
- The Hilton Lee Smith Baseball Hall of Fame Display in Giddings, TX
- "Hometown of Hilton Smith" marker, Giddings, TX
- Mural at Downs-Mabson Fields in Austin, TX, by Reginald Adams

Negro Leagues Book #2: The Players

- Monroe Monarchs Field marker, Monroe, LA
- Hilton Smith mural at the KC Urban Youth Academy, Kansas City, MO

Taylor Smith
- 100th anniversary plaque honoring Nashvillians from the Negro Leagues, at E.S. Rose Park Baseball Pavilion, Nashville, TN

Wendell Smith
- Plaque with Billy Rowe at Jackie Robinson Ballpark & Museum, Daytona Beach, FL

St. Louis Stars Marker
- Stars Park, St. Louis, MO

Turkey Stearnes
- Hamtramck Stadium marker, Hamtramck, MI
- Norman "Turkey" Stearnes mural at Hamtramck Stadium, Hamtramck, MI
- Norman "Turkey" Stearnes Field at Hamtramck Stadium, Hamtramck, MI
- Norman "Turkey" Stearnes plaque outside of Comerica Park, Detroit, MI
- 100th anniversary plaque honoring Nashvillians from the Negro Leagues, at E.S. Rose Park Baseball Pavilion, Nashville, TN

Toni Stone
- Toni Stone Field, Dunning Baseball Complex, St. Paul, MN
- Mural at Dorsey Park, Miami, FL, by Kadir Nelson
- Mural at Downs-Mabson Fields in Austin, TX, by Reginald Adams

George "Mule" Suttles
- Ring of Honor, Bears & Eagles Riverfront Stadium in Newark, NJ (removed in 2013)
- Hot Springs: The Birthplace of Spring Baseball marker near old Whittington Park, Hot Springs, AR
- Mural on Perry Hilltop at Wilson Avenue and West Burgess Street, Pittsburgh, PA

Reece Goose Tatum
- Power & Light District mural, Downtown, Kansas City, MO

Ben Taylor
- Harrisburg Giants marker, Harrisburg, PA

Rev. Harold Tinker
- Harold Tinker metal sign on the Homestead Grays Bridge, Pittsburgh, PA

Cristóbal Torriente
- Hot Springs: The Birthplace of Spring Baseball marker near old Whittington Park, Hot Springs, AR

Jim Tugerson
- Tugerson Baseball Field at the Winter Haven Recreational and Cultural Center, Winter Haven, FL

Robert Lee Vann
- Marker on Centre Avenue in Pittsburgh, PA

Moses Fleetwood Walker
- Mural at Dorsey Park, Miami, FL by Kadir Nelson
- Historical Marker in Toledo, OH
- Moses Fleetwood Walker Birthplace sign, Mount Pleasant, OH
- Fleetwood's Tap Room, Toledo, OH
- Island Sanctuary for the Ghost of Moses Mural at Toledo Mudhens Stadium, OH
- Life-size mannequin in Toledo uniform at the Nutcracker Village and Advent Market in Steubenville, OH
- https://hensvilletoledo.com/fleetwoods-tap-room

Washington Park Marker
- Home of the Indianapolis ABCs and first NNL game in 1920. Near Indianapolis Zoo.

Willie "the Devil" Wells
- Ring of Honor, Bears & Eagles Riverfront Stadium in Newark, NJ (removed in 2013)
- Willie Wells mural on home in South Austin, TX. Painted by artist Tim Kerr.
- Mural at Downs-Mabson Fields in Austin, TX by Reginald Adams

Dave Whitney
- Davey L. Whitney Complex, multi-purpose center at Alcorn State University, Lorman, MS

J.L. Wilkinson
- Hot Springs: The Birthplace of Spring Baseball marker near old Whittington Park, Hot Springs, AR
- Buck O'Neil Education and Research Center, south side mural at 18th & The Paseo, Kansas City, MO

George L. Williams
- Original member of the 1885 Cuban Giants, was honored with a Police Hero Plaque at 16th and South Street in Philadelphia. Williams, Philadelphia's first African American detective, was killed in the line of duty on January 9, 1918. Plaque installed in June 2011.

Smokey Joe Williams
- Smokey Joe Williams statue at Pittsburgh Pirates' PNC Park (designer John Forsythe) (removed in 2015)
- Smokey Joe Williams Field, Seguin, TX
- Smokey Joe Williams metal sign on the Homestead Grays Bridge, Pittsburgh, PA
- Hot Springs: The Birthplace of Spring Baseball marker near old Whittington Park, Hot Springs, AR
- Hamtramck Stadium marker, Hamtramck, MI
- Mural at Downs-Mabson Fields in Austin, TX by Reginald Adams

John Wilson
- Jumpin' Johnny Wilson statue at Anderson High School in Anderson, IN (designer Kenneth G. Rydis) in honor of being named "Mr. Basketball".

Jud Wilson
- Hot Springs: The Birthplace of Spring Baseball marker near old Whittington Park, Hot Springs, AR
- Ring of Honor at Washington Nationals Park in Washington, DC

Negro Leagues Book #2: The Players

Tom Wilson
- Tom Wilson Park marker in Nashville, TN
- 100th anniversary plaque honoring Nashvillians from the Negro Leagues, at E.S. Rose Park Baseball Pavilion, Nashville, TN

Nip Winters
- James Henry "Nip" Winters marker, at Valley Road & Evanson Road, Hockessin, DE

Burnis "Wild Bill" Wright
- Wild Bill Wright bust at Parque Alberto Romo Chavez Stadium in Aguascalientes, Mexico
- Burnis "Wild Bill" Wright Sports Complex, Nashville TN

Frank "Fay" Young
- The Frank A. Young Poultry Plant at Tennessee State University, Nashville, TN

Jim Zapp
- 100th anniversary plaque honoring Nashvillians from the Negro Leagues, at E.S. Rose Park Baseball Pavilion, Nashville, TN

Honors, Awards and Postage Stamps of Negro Leaguers

Presidential Medal of Freedom Award
The Presidential Medal of Freedom is the nation's highest civilian honor, presented to individuals who have made especially meritorious contributions to the security or national interests of the United States, to world peace, or to cultural or other significant public or private endeavors. Former Negro League recipients include:
- 1984 - Jackie Robinson (posthumously) by President Ronald Reagan
- 2002 - Hank Aaron by President George W. Bush
- 2006 - Buck O'Neil by President George W. Bush
- 2013 - Ernie Banks by President Barack Obama
- 2015 - Willie Mays by President Barack Obama

Negro League players and executives honored at the White House
March 21, 1981 with President Ronald Reagan
- Walter "Buck" Leonard

February 19, 1992 with President George H. W. Bush
- Leon Day
- Jimmie Crutchfield
- Josh Gibson, Jr.
- Monte Irvin

February 8 and 22, 1994 with Vice-President Al Gore
- Russell Awkard
- Gene Benson
- Bill "Ready" Cash
- Jim "Fireball" Cohen
- Leon Day
- Mahlon Duckett
- Wilmer "Red" Fields
- Stanley "Doc" Glenn
- Max Manning

March 30, 2001 with President George W. Bush
- Hank Aaron
- Ernie Banks
- Buck O'Neil
- Monte Irvin

August 5, 2013 with President Barack Obama
- Ms. Leon Day
- Ms. Minnie Forbes
- Ms. Mamie "Peanut" Johnson
- Cliff Layton
- Larry LeGrande
- Carl Long

Negro Leagues Book #2: The Players

- James "Red" Moore
- Minnie Miñoso
- Jim Robinson
- Pedro Sierra
- Bob Scott
- Ron Teasley

Note: On June 23, 2009, the Brooklyn Cyclones, a minor league affiliate of the New York Mets changed their name to the "Baracklyn Cyclones" for a Barack Obama Bobblehead Day. Additionally, all proceeds from the auctioned off red-white-blue Cyclone jerseys went to the Jackie Robinson Foundation.

NAACP's Spingarn Medal

The Spingarn Medal, a gold medal awarded annually by the National Association for the Advancement of Colored People (NAACP) since 1915 to honor "the man or woman of African descent and American citizenship who shall have made the highest achievement during the preceding year or years in any honorable field" (as it was phrased when the award was founded). The award was intended both to draw the attention of the general public to African American achievement and to inspire young African Americans. The Spingarn Medal, which was established on June 29, 1914, is named for Joel Elias Spingarn, a writer, literary critic, educator, and civil rights activist who served as chairman of the Board of Directors (1913–19), treasurer (1919–30), and president (1930–39) of the NAACP.

- 1956 - Jackie Robinson
- 1976 - Hank Aaron

Congressional Gold Medal

A Congressional Gold Medal is an award bestowed by the United States Congress; the Congressional Gold Medal and the Presidential Medal of Freedom are the highest civilian awards in the United States. It is awarded to persons "who have performed an achievement that has an impact on American history and culture that is likely to be recognized as a major achievement in the recipient's field long after the achievement."

- 2003 - Jackie Robinson (posthumously) by President George W. Bush
- 2012 - Umpire Bob Motley as a Montford Point Marine by President Barack Obama
- 2012 - Rev. Bill Greason as a Montford Point Marine by President Barack Obama
- 2012 - Reuben Smartt (semi-pro Grand Rapids Black Sox) as a Montford Point Marine by President Barack Obama
- 2018 - Larry Doby (posthumously) by Representatives Jim Renacci, R-Ohio and Bill Pascrell, D-New Jersey

The Buck O'Neil Lifetime Achievement Award

This award is presented by the National Baseball Hall of Fame and Museum's Board of Directors not more than once every three years to honor an individual whose extraordinary efforts enhanced baseball's positive impact on society, broadened the game's appeal, and whose character, integrity and dignity are comparable to the qualities exhibited by O'Neil. The Award, named after Buck O'Neil, was first given in 2008, with O'Neil as the first recipient.

- 2011 - Roland Hemond
- 2014 - Joe Garagiola
- 2017 - Rachel Robinson
- 2019 – David Montgomery

Hank Aaron Award

The Hank Aaron Award is given annually to the Major League Baseball (MLB) players selected as the top hitter in each league, as voted on by baseball fans and members of the media. It was introduced in 1999 to commemorate the 25th anniversary of Hank Aaron's surpassing of Babe Ruth's career home run mark of 714 home runs. For the 1999 season, a winner was selected using an objective points system. Hits, home runs, and runs batted in (RBI) were given certain point values and the winner was the player who had the highest tabulated points total. The first winners of the award were **Manny Ramirez** from the Cleveland Indians and **Sammy Sosa** from the Chicago Cubs. In 2000, the system was changed to a ballot in which each MLB team's radio and television play-by-play broadcasters and color analysts voted for three players from each league.

The Rube Foster Award is presented by the Texas Black Sports Hall of Fame in Dallas, Texas, to a non-African American coach, player or supporter who has contributed greatly to the Texas black sports history. **R.C. Slocum**, the winningest football coach in Texas A&M history, and legendary Dallas Cowboys quarterback and Hall of Famer **Roger Staubach** were co-recipients of the inaugural award in 2016.

Jackie Robinson Rookie of the Year Award

The Rookie of the Year Award, or Jackie Robinson Award is given to the individual player from each League who has the best rookie season; pitching, hitting or fielding, that is during his first year of eligibility. The award was officially renamed the Jackie Robinson Award in July 1987, forty years after Jackie Robinson broke the baseball color line. This is the first MLB award named after a former Negro League player.

Willie Mays World Series Most Valuable Player Award

This is an annual award that celebrates the life and career of a World Series legend. The first World Series MVP was awarded in 1955, the year after Willie Mays made his famous over-the-head basket catch in deep center field, in Game 1 of the 1954 World Series at the Polo Grounds. Willie Mays played in four World Series during his 22-year Major League career, winning a championship with the Giants in the 1954 Fall Classic.

- 2017 - George Springer, Houston Astros
- 2018 - Steve Pearce, Boston Red Sox
- 2019 - Stephen Strasburg, Washington Nationals

Major League Baseball's All-Century Team

In 1999, the Major League Baseball All-Century Team was chosen by popular vote of fans. To select the team, a panel of experts first compiled a list of the 100 greatest Major League Baseball players from the past century. Over two million fans then voted on the players using paper and online ballots.

- Hank Aaron
- Ernie Banks
- Willie Mays
- Jackie Robinson

Keys to the City

- Moses Fleetwood Walker Day, from the Ohio State House of Representatives
- Chet Brewer Day from the City of Angels, CA

National Association of Black Journalists (NABJ)

The NABJ is an organization of African American journalists, students, and media professionals. Founded in 1975 in Washington, D.C., the NABJ's stated purpose is to provide quality programs and services to and advocate on behalf of Black journalists.

The NABJ offers The Sam Lacy Pioneer award which is named for the famed sports editor and columnist for the *Afro-American Newspapers*, a weekly produced paper based in Baltimore. It is given annually to individuals making great strides in their professional career, but more importantly, creating a positive change within their communities.

Listed below are writers, journalists and photojournalists who covered Negro League baseball that have been selected to NABJ Hall of Fame.

NABJ Hall of Famers
- 1990 Mal H. Goode
- 2005 Charles "Teenie" Harris
- 2013 Wendell Smith

NABJ Lifetime Achievement Awards
- 1978 Mal H. Goode
- 1991 Sam Lacy (pictured)

SAM LACY - A personal hero and mentor was a persuasive figure in the movement to racially integrate sports. In 1948, Lacy became the first African American member of the Baseball Writers' Association of America (BBWAA). In 1997, he received the National Baseball Hall of Fame's J. G. Taylor Spink Award for outstanding baseball writing from the BBWAA, joining the writers' and broadcasters' wing of the Hall of Fame. Few humans can claim interaction with **Jesse Owens'** gold-medal-winning performances at the 1936 Berlin Summer Olympics, covering world heavyweight title fights of boxer **Joe Louis** (including his victory over Max Schmeling) and traveling as a roommate with **Jackie Robinson**. In 1999, Lacy teamed with colleague Moses J. Newson, a former executive editor at the *Afro-American*, to write his autobiography, *Fighting for Fairness: The Life Story of Hall of Fame Sportswriter Sam Lacy*.

According to the **National Sports Media Association**, Lacy has received the following awards and honors.
- Became the first Black member of the Baseball Writers Association of America.
- Became the first Black journalist to be enshrined in the Maryland Media Hall of Fame.
- Was inducted into the Black Athletes Hall of Fame in Las Vegas.
- Received the Lifetime Achievement Award from the National Association of Black Journalists in 1991.
- Selected for the Society of Professional Journalists Hall of Fame by the Washington chapter in 1994.
- Honored with the A.J. Liebling Award by the Boxing Writers Association of America in 1995.
- Received an honorary doctorate from Loyola University Maryland (Baltimore) in 1997.
- Honored by the Smithsonian Institute with a lecture series in 1997.
- Received the J. G. Taylor Spink Award for outstanding baseball writing from the Baseball Writers Association of America in 1997.

- Was inducted into the writers and broadcasters wing of the Baseball Hall of Fame, and Lacy was formally enshrined on July 26, 1998.
- Lacy received the Frederick Douglass Award from the University System of Maryland in 1998.
- Had a scholarship program established in his name by the United Negro College Fund in 1998.
- Received the Red Smith Award from the *Associated Press* in 1998.
- Honored by the Sports Task Force wing of the National Association of Black Journalists which instituted the Sam Lacy Pioneer Award in 2003.
- Served on the President's Council on Physical Fitness.
- Served on the Baseball Hall of Fame's selection committee for the Negro Leagues.
- Honored by the University of Maryland's Philip Merrill College of Journalism which created "The Sam Lacy-Wendell Smith Award" to be presented annually to a sports journalist or broadcaster who has made significant contributions to racial and gender equality in sports.

J.G. Taylor Spink Award winners by the Baseball Writers' Association of America.

Listed are African American honorees for the award named in honor for the late publisher of *The Sporting News*, in recognition of meritorious contributions to baseball.
- Wendell Smith, 1993
- Sam Lacy, 1997
- Larry Whiteside, 2008
- Claire Smith, 2017

The **Red Smith Award** is awarded by the *Associated Press Sports Editors* (APSE) for outstanding contributions to sports journalism. It has been awarded annually at the APSE convention since 1981.

Below are awarded writers who wrote extensive editorials and game coverage during the heyday of the Negro Leagues.
- 1983 - Shirley Povich - *Washington Post*
- 1998 - Sam Lacy - *Baltimore Afro-American*
- 2014 - Wendell Smith - *Pittsburgh Courier, Chicago Herald-American, Chicago Sun-Times*

Sam Lacy-Wendell Smith Award is presented by the Shirley Povich Center for Sports Journalism. The award is given to a sports journalist who has made significant contributions to racial and gender equality in sports.
- Claire Smith, 2013

Society for American Baseball Research (SABR) committees and chapters related to the Negro Leagues
Committees:
- Asian Baseball Research Committee
- Latino Baseball Research Committee
- Negro Leagues Research Committee
- West Coast Negro Leagues Baseball Research Committee

Chapters:
- Luke Easter Chapter in Rochester, NY
- Sweet Lou Johnson Lexington Chapter in Lexington, KY
- Monarchs Chapter in Kansas City, MO
- North Florida Buck O'Neil Chapter in Tallahassee, FL
- Oscar Charleston Chapter in Indianapolis, IN
- Larry Doby Chapter in Aiken, SC
- Ernie Banks-Bobby Bragan DFW in Dallas, TX
- Cool Papa Bell Chapter, Starkville, MS

U.S. Postage stamps issued depicting Negro Leaguers

Jackie Robinson, stamps issued in 1982 (20 cents) Scott #2016; 1999 (33 cents) Scott #3186c; 2000 (33 cents), Scott #3408a

Josh Gibson, 2000 (33 cents), Scott #3408r

Satchel Paige, 2000 (33 cents), Scott #3408p

Roy Campanella, 2006 (39 cents), Scott #4080

Rube Foster, 2010 (44 cents se-tenant), Scott #4465-4466

Larry Doby, 2012 (forever), Scott #4695

Black Stars on the Silver Screen

DOCUMENTARIES:

A Century of Change: The Negro Leagues Centennial by KCPT, Kansas City, MO, Producer Kerry Rounds, 2020

After Jackie: Black Baseball in the 1950's by WILL TV12/Channel 12. Urbana, IL, University of Illinois, 1994.

Ain't Seen Nothin' Like It Since by KCPT-TV, Executive Producer Ted Dibble, Associate Producer Carla Searcy, Writer Scott O'Kelley, Narrated by Danny Cox, 1994.

American Giants: Legends of the Negro Leagues by WGN-TV. Narrated by Morgan Freeman, 1992.

Baseball, Black and White. ABC News with Ted Koppel, Ken Burns and Buck O'Neil, 1994.

Baseball, Bottom of the Second. Ken Burns. Alexandria, VA: PBS Films, 1994.

The Bases are Loaded: Divided by Politics, United by Baseball. Jeffrey Nagel and Anthony Lynch. 4th Street Films, 2005. Narrated by Kit Kreiger.

Before You Can Say Jackie Robinson: Black Baseball in America in the Era of the Color Line by Dr. Lawrence Hogan and Thomas Guy, 1993.

Behind the White Lines: The Negro Baseball Leagues by CNN Sports. Narrated by Tom Kirtland, 1991.

Biography: Jackie Robinson by CEL Communications and A&E Network. Narrated by Peter Graves. Executive Producer Charles Grinker, 1989.

Birmingham's Black Barons. Tim Stout. Birmingham: Time Warner Cable, 1996.

Black Diamonds - Blues City: Stories of the Memphis Red Sox by the University of Memphis. Narrated by Samuel L. Jackson, 1996.

The Boys in the Field. Karl Coleman, et al. Chapel Hill, NC: UNC Center for Public Television, 1980. (Included is an interview with Buck Leonard).

Brooklyn Dodgers: The Original America's Team series. *Twilight at Noon: The Jackie Robinson Story.* Produced by ESPN, 90 minutes, 1996.

Brooklyn Dodgers: The Original America's Team series. *At Nightfall: The Roy Campanella Story.* Produced by ESPN, 60 minutes, 1996.

Buck O'Neil and Black Baseball in Chicago. John Owens, Producer; Dr. David Fletcher, Executive Producer. Produced by the Chicago Baseball Museum, 30 minutes, 2008.

Bud Fowler and the Page Fence Giants. Directed by Michael Nash, 2017, 51 minutes.

A Celebration of Life: Buck O'Neil's Memorial Service. Negro Leagues Baseball Museum, 2006.

Closed Doors: The Integration of Baseball. Kimshi Productions and produced by Rick Morris, 1995.

Colored Champions on Parade. William Alexander, date unknown, 1920s.

Colored Champions of Sport. Newsreel produced by Edward W. Lewis and distributed by Alfred N. Sack Amusement Enterprise. Script written by St. Clair Bourne, narration by Jack Caldwell. 1939, 1940.

Negro Leagues Book #2: The Players

Colored Championship Baseball Game. Newsreel produced by Foster Photoplay Company. Negro League Championship game played in Chicago, Illinois, 1914.

A Conversation with Joe Scott: Memories of the Negro League with Reggie Williams. Produced by Mid-South Public Communications, WKNO – Memphis, 2008.

The Court-Martial of Jackie Robinson. TNT Producers, 21 October 1990.

Dramatic Moments in Black Sports History by Darryl Pitts, BlackBall Productions. Narrated by Fred Hickman, 1995.

An Evening With Buck O'Neil and His Memories of the Negro Baseball League. Colorado Springs, CO: Pikes Peak Library District and Community Video Center, 1999.

For the Love of the Game by Margaret Ford-Taylor and Karen Crocheron of Karamu Performing Arts Theatre, 1994.

Frank Bolden: The Man Behind the Words by Nancy Travis Bolden, Executive Director, David Love, filmmaker. The Pittsburgh Foundation and Howard Heinz Endowments. 27 minutes, 2001.

Greatest Sports Legends: Jackie Robinson by Sports Legend Video, Inc. Narrated by Ken Howard, 30 minutes. Date unknown.

Hard Road to Glory by Arthur Ashe. Narrated by James Earl Jones, 1989.

The Heart & Soul of Baseball: The Kansas City Monarchs by ABC-TV. Narrated by Mike Mahoney, 1991.

The History of Great Black Baseball Players by Melvin B. Bergman and William M. Speckin. Directed by Justin "Bud" Morgan and distributed by Fries Home Video. Narrated by Ernie Banks, 1990.

In Sports, Black and White. ESPN with Ted Koppel. February 28, 1997.

Is This Heaven: The Pete Hill Story. Directed by Keith Carmack, 2016, 75 minutes.

***Jackie Robinson* ABC News, Nightline Tributes.** Al Campanis interview with Ted Koppel. MPI Home Video, 1990.

Jackie Robinson. Mert Koplin and Charles Grinker. Time-Life Films, 1970.

Jackie Robinson, Baseball's First Black. Plymouth, MN: Simitar, 1997.

Jap Mikado: The First Japanese Professional Baseball Player by MBS (Mainichi Broadcasting System) Masayuki Nakanishi. Historian Kazuo Sayama. Japanese version only, 1995.

Josh Gibson: The Legend Behind the Plate by Duquesne University students, Pittsburgh, PA, 2009.

The Journey of the African-American Athlete by HBO Sports. Written by William C. Rhoden, 1996.

Kids First: How We Played the Game by KRON-TV (San Francisco, CA) with Craig Franklin and Karyne Holmes, 1994.

Kings on the Hill: Baseball's Forgotten Men by Rob Ruck and Molly Youngling. Music by Nathan Davis. Narrated by Ossie Davis, 1993.

A Life in the Negro Leagues. St. Louis, MO: Missouri Historical Society, 1995.

Life of a Young Ball Player, Willie Grace. Erie, PA: Erie Art Museum and Ducky Bearman Productions, 1994.

The Long Summers of Lou Dials by David E. Carter. Narrated by Dave Diles, 1986.

Documentaries

Magic Memories, Compilation. Brian S. McDaniel, et al. Birmingham: New World WVTM Communications of Alabama, 1996.

The Man Named Judy: The Judy Johnson Story by Dave Tiberi. Produced TNT Video Productions, 2000.

Major League Baseball Magazine: The Negro Leagues by Major League Baseball Properties, 1989.

Mister Kansas City, The Life of Buck O'Neil Merriam, KS: IBT Media, 2000.

Negro Leagues Baseball Museum: Discover Greatness by NLBM, 1990.

The Negro Leagues by First Generation Video and the Negro Leagues Baseball Museum. Producer Edward Scheele, Writer Martha Slater, Narrated by CNN's Bernard Shaw, 1994.

Nightline: Baseball in Black & White by ABC News, 2007.

No League of Their Own by KSHB-TV, NBC-41 (Kansas City, MO). Narrated by Linda Hamblin-Denton, 1995.

Not in Our League: The Negro Baseball Leagues by Group W Television, Inc., WJZ-TV in Baltimore, Maryland. Narrated by Al Sanders, 1993.

Only The Ball Was White by WTTW-Chicago. Narrated by Paul Winfield, 1980.

The Other Boys of Summer by Tumbleweed Pictures. Produced by Lauren Meyer. Color, 42 minutes. Narrated by Cicely Tyson, 2019.

Outside The Lines: A League Second to None by ESPN. Produced by Justin "Bud" Morgan, Narrated by Keith Olbermann, Robin Roberts and Chris Berman, 1994.

Pride Against Prejudice: The Larry Doby Story by Bud Greenspan and Cappy Productions, Inc. Executive Producer, Nancy Beffa. Narrated by Louis Gossett Jr. Showtime, 2007, 90 minutes.

The Playing Field by BlackBall, Inc. Executive producer Darryl Pitts, Narrated by Harry Porterfield, 1992.

Reaching the Finish Line: Black Athletes and Civil Rights.

Sports Profile: Artie Wilson. Evanston, IL: The Altschul Group, 1982.

There Was Always Sun Shining Someplace: Life in the Negro Baseball Leagues by Refocus Films Productions and Craig Davidson. Narrated by James Earl Jones, 1984.

They were All Stars: An Historic Narrative of Negro Leagues Baseball, Negro Leagues Baseball Museum, 16 minutes, 1990.

This Is Your Life: Leroy 'Satchel' Paige by Ralph Edwards Productions. Hosted by Ralph Edwards, 1972.

Records in the Sand: The 1945 Cleveland Buckeyes by Classic Teleproduction. Producer Debbie Bacon. Narrated by Jim Kisicki, 1995.

Safe at Home Plate by WPBA-Atlanta Public Television. Producers Conne Ward-Cameron and Toni Lee. Narrated by Charlie Pride, 1993.

Swingin' Timber: The Story of the Claybrook (AR) Tigers by David Duane Dawson, University of Arkansas' Fullbright College Advising Center, 2001.

Upstate Memories. Nancy Ogle and Annie V. Williams. Spartanburg, SC: WRET-TV, 1992.

ViewPoint: Celebrates the 75th Anniversary of Negro League Baseball by WOSU-TV (Columbus, OH). Producers Edwin Page and Willis Parker, 1995.

Negro Leagues Book #2: The Players

Wylie Avenue Days (Hill District of Pittsburgh) by WQED. QED Communications, Inc. Producers Doug Bolin and Christopher Moore, 1991

MOVIES:

As the World Rolls On (1921), with Jack Johnson and Blanche Thompson. Jack Johnson plays himself, as he assists Joe Walker, a physically weak young man, who learns physical fitness and the art of self-defense from the former heavyweight champion. Walker eventually wins the love of Molly Moran, played by Blanche Thompson. This film has footage of a game between the Kansas City Monarchs and the Detroit Stars. Produced by Andlauer Productions/Elk Photo Plays. It is a silent, black and white, 35 mm, 5600 foot or 1706.88 meter (7 reels) film.

The Ballad of Satchel Paige (1949), by Richard Durham. An NBC production. Also called *Destination Freedom*. From the recordings entitled *Ballads of Black America*.

The Court Martial of Jackie Robinson (1990), produced by Turner Pictures, Inc. This film stars Andre Braughter as Jackie Robinson and Stan Shaw as Joe Louis. It traces Robinson's college days, along with highlights and lowlights of his military career, plus his days with the Kansas City Monarchs. Ruby Dee, who had played Jackie's wife in *The Jackie Robinson Story*, in 1950, stars as his mother in this made for cable TV movie. Two hours in length.

Don't Look Back: The Story of Leroy "Satchel" Paige (1981), with Louis Gossett, Jr. (Satchel Paige), Beverly Todd (Lahoma Brown Paige), Ernie Barnes (Josh Gibson), Clifton Davis (Cool Papa Bell) and Jim Davis (J.L. Wilkinson). The slender Gossett does an admirable job in portraying Satchel Paige in this made-for-TV movie. The movie was adapted from the book *Maybe I'll Pitch Forever*. Satchel Paige served as a technical consultant. Produced by TBA/Satics/Triseme Productions in color, 98 minutes in length. Directed by Richard A. Colla.

It's Good to Be Alive: The Story of Roy Campanella (1974), with Paul Winfield, Ruby Dee and Louis Gossett, Jr. This made-for-TV movie tells the story of former Baltimore Elite Giant and Brooklyn Dodger Roy Campanella's life after his career-ending automobile accident in 1958. Winfield plays Campanella, with Dee as his wife, Ruthie, while Gossett plays the never-quit therapist (Sam Brockington). Produced by Larry Harmon Pictures/Metromedia in color, 100 minutes in length. Directed by Michael Landon.

The Jackie Robinson Story (1950), with Jackie Robinson and Ruby Dee This movie debuted soon after Robinson won the National League Most Valuable Player Award. An excellent biography of Mr. Robinson, who plays himself surprisingly well, while Ruby Dee stars as his supportive wife, Rachel. Produced by Jewel Productions/Eagle-Lion, this film is in black and white and 76 minutes in length.

The Kid from Cleveland (1950) with Satchel Paige and the Cleveland Indians. Bill Veeck gives a superb performance in this sentimental journey to rehabilitate Johnny Barrows as their new batboy. The film was produced by Republic Films in black and white. It is 89 minutes in length. Paige makes frequent appearances throughout the film.

The Wonderful Country (1959) with Robert Mitchum and Julie London. Satchel Paige portrays a U.S. Cavalry sergeant in this movie filmed on location in Durango, Mexico. Paige gave an outstanding performance but was never asked to act again.

ESPN's SportsCentury: Top 50 American Athletes of the 20th Century (Original series)

In 1999, ESPN counted down the Top 50 Athletes of the 20th Century, selected from North American athletes and voted on by a panel of sports journalists and observers, premiering a new biography highlighting each top athlete every week throughout the year. The 30- to 60-minute series ran from 1999 to 2007.

The original list of 100 athletes included:

#8, Willie Mays
#14, Hank Aaron
#15, Jackie Robinson
#63, Satchel Paige
#73, Josh Gibson

Negro Leagues Book #2: The Players

Screen credits for Negro League veterans
[not listed in eBook version]

Listed below are former Negro League players who had speaking roles, voiceovers and/or cameo appearances.

Hank Aaron
"MacGyer" Back from the Dead, 1987
"The Incredible Ida Earley" Drama, 1987
"Happy Days" The Hucksters, Comedy, 30 minutes, 1980
"Mr. Belvedere" The Field, 16 September 1989
"Summer Catch" Comedy/Drama, 108 minutes, 2001
"Touched by an Angel" The Perfect Game, 2001

Dero Austin
"The Bingo Long Traveling All-Stars & Motor Kings" Comedy, 110 minutes, 1976

Ernie Banks
"The Shooting of Dan McGrew" Animation, 7 minutes, 1965 (voiceover)
"Blackjack" Action, 104 minutes, 1978
"Diminished Capacity" Comedy, 92 minutes, 1978
"Pastime" Drama, 94 minutes, 1990
"Married … with Children" Dancing with Weezy, 21 November 1993, TV
"Promised Land" Drama, 99 minutes, 2004
"Reversal of Misfortune" Drama, 73 minutes, 2005
"Roman" Drama/Thriller, 92 minutes, 2006
"Yes Dear" Hustlin' Hughes, 17 February 2003, TV

Joe Black
"The Ed Nelson Show" 90 minutes, 1969
"The Dick Cavett Show" 30 minutes, 5 May 1972, TV, himself
"Cosby Show" There's Still No Joy in Mudville, 30 minutes, 1991, played Joe "Payday" Sims

Birmingham Sam Brison
"The Bingo Long Traveling All-Stars & Motor Kings" Comedy, 110 minutes, 1976

Roy Campanella
"This Is Your Life!" Ralph Edwards, 29 October 1952
"Roogie's Bump" Comedy, 71 minutes, 1954
"What's My Life", 6 September 1953
"Person to Person" by Edward R. Murrow, 2 October 1953 and 2 January 1959
"The Name's the Same" 27 July 1954
"Lassie" The Mascot, 27 September 1959, TV
"It's Good to Be Alive: The Story of Roy Campanella" Biography, 100 minutes, 1974, prologue only

Larry Doby

"The Kid From Cleveland" Action/Drama, 89 minutes, 1949
"It's My Turn" Comedy, 91 minutes, 1980

Monte Irvin
"It's My Turn" Comedy, 91 minutes, 1980

Willie Mays
"When Nature Calls" Comedy, 85 minutes, 1985
"The Donna Reed Show"
    1) Play Ball, 1 October 1964
    2) My Son the Catcher, 16 April 1964 and
    3) Calling Willie Mays, 29 January 1966, TV shows
"My Two Dads" You Love Me, Right? 7 May 1989, TV
"Mr. Belvedere" The Field, 16 September 1989, TV

Don Newcombe
"Pastime" Drama, 94 minutes, 1990.

Satchel Paige
"The Kid From Cleveland" Action/Drama, 89 minutes, 1949
"The Wonderful Country" Romance/Western, 98 minutes, 1959
"Don't Look Back: The Story of Leroy 'Satchel' Paige" Biography, 98 minutes, 1981, TV only
"This is Your Life" by Ralph Edwards, 1 October 1958 and 26 January 1972

Jackie Robinson
"The Jackie Robinson Story" Biography/Drama, 75 minutes, 1950 (black & white), and 1974 (color)
"The Court-Martial of Jackie Robinson" Biography/Drama, 100 minutes, 1990, TV only
"Jackie Robinson: An American Journey" Documentary, 15 minutes, 1988, TV only
"Jackie Robinson: Breaking Barrier" Documentary/Biography, 115 minutes, 1997, Video

Pedro Sierra
"Major League II" Comedy/Sport, 95 minutes, 1994

Edgar Blue Washington (courtesy of IMDbTV)
Actor (87 credits)
1961 *The Hustler,* Limping Attendant at Ames Billiards (uncredited)
1957 *The Wings of Eagles,* Bartender at Officer's Club (uncredited)
1953 *The Kid from Left Field,* Train Station Porter (uncredited)
1953 *Siren of Bagdad,* Palace Servant (uncredited)
1952 *Stars and Stripes Forever,* Crowd Spectator (uncredited)
1951 *Golden Girl,* Lola's Coachman (uncredited)
1951 *Angels in the Outfield.* Doorman (uncredited)
1951 *I Was a Communist for the F.B.I.,* Black Man at Union Meeting (uncredited)
1950 *Tarzan and the Slave Girl,* Randini Bearer Shot by Arrow (uncredited)
1949 *Pinky,* Minor Role (uncredited)
1949 *Bomba, the Jungle Boy,* Native Bearer (uncredited)

Negro Leagues Book #2: The Players

1949 *Tarzan's Magic Fountain,* Native Bearer (uncredited)
1948 *To the Ends of the Earth,* Binda Sha Henchman (uncredited)
1942 *Road to Morocco,* Nubian Slave (uncredited)
1942 *Tales of Manhattan,* Shantytown Man (Robeson sequence) (uncredited)
1942 *It Happened in Flatbush,* Courtroom Spectator (uncredited)
1942 *Drums of the Congo,* Native Bearer (uncredited)
1942 *Law of the Jungle,* Native (uncredited)
1942 *Lady for a Night,* Man Sitting Next to Chloe (uncredited)
1941 *Sundown,* Askari Veteran (uncredited)
1941 *A Girl, a Guy, and a Gob,* Opera House Doorman (uncredited)
1940 *The Long Voyage Home,* Black Cook on Glencairn (uncredited)
1939 *The Light That Failed,* Bit Part (uncredited)
1939 *Gone with the Wind,* Renegade's Companion (uncredited)
1939 *Stanley and Livingstone,* Mombay (scenes deleted)
1939 *Way Down South,* Slave (uncredited)
1939 *Charlie Chan in Reno,* Man in Line-Up (uncredited)
1939 *Rose of Washington Square,* Prisoner (uncredited)
1939 *Twelve Crowded Hours,* First Bartender (uncredited)
1938 *Charlie Chan in Honolulu,* Crewman (uncredited)
1938 *Kentucky,* Bill (uncredited)
1938 *The Cowboy and the Lady,* Dock Worker (uncredited)
1938 *Too Hot to Handle,* Native (uncredited)
1938 *Over the Wall,* Convict Playing Guitar (uncredited)
1938 *Tarzan's Revenge,* Bearer Bringing Olaf Poison Darts (uncredited)
1937 *Wells Fargo,* Sam - Coachman (uncredited)
1937 *Ali Baba Goes to Town,* Arab (uncredited)
1937 *Charlie Chan on Broadway,* Doorman at Hottentot Club (uncredited)
1937 *Souls at Sea,* Ship Slave (uncredited)
1937 *Nancy Steele Is Missing!,* Convict (uncredited)
1936 *White Hunter,* Wanderobi Native (uncredited)
1936 *The Plainsman,* Black Man Dropping Box (uncredited)
1936 *The Prisoner of Shark Island,* Black Soldier at Prison (uncredited)
1935 *Escape from Devil's Island,* Convict (uncredited)
1935 *Annie Oakley,* Cook (uncredited)
1935 *The Virginia Judge,* 1st Black Man (uncredited)
1935 *The Crusades,* One of Saladin's Guards (uncredited)
1935 *Love Me Forever,* Doorman (scenes deleted)
1935 *The Whole Town's Talking,* Bank Doorman (uncredited)
1934 *Menace,* Kenya Manservant (uncredited)
1934 *Belle of the Nineties,* Doorman at Sensation House (uncredited)
1933 *Roman Scandals,* Litter Bearer (uncredited)
1933 *Good-bye Love,* Jail Steward (uncredited)
1933 *One Year Later,* Train Porter (uncredited)
1933 *Her Bodyguard,* Chauffeur (uncredited)
1933 *King of the Arena,* Sambo (uncredited)
1933 *King Kong,* Warrior (uncredited)

1932 *Haunted Gold,* Clarence
1932 *The Saddle Buster,* Ranch Cook (uncredited)
1931 *Guilty Hands,* Johnny (uncredited)
1931 *Kiki* (uncredited)
1931 *Desert Vengeance,* Train Porter (uncredited)
1930 *The Cohens and the Kellys in Africa,* Native Golf Champion (uncredited)
1930 *Mountain Justice,* Mose (uncredited)
1930 *Lucky Larkin,* Hambone
1930 *Parade of the West,* Sambo
1929 *Welcome Danger,* Thorne's Black Henchman (uncredited)
1929 *Rio Rita,* Fremont Bank Robber (uncredited)
1929 *Hallelujah,* Church Member (uncredited)
1929 *Black Magic,* Unit
1929 *Weary River,* Prisoner in Bathtub (uncredited)
1928 *The Phantom City,* 'Blue'
1928 *Passion Song,* Ulambo
1928 *Do Your Duty,* Dude Jackson
1928 *Beggars of Life,* Black Mose (as Edgar Washington Blue)
1928 *Ransom,* Oliver
1928 *Wyoming,* Mose
1928 *The Smart Set,* Horse Groom (uncredited)
1928 *There It Is* (Short), The Butler (as Edgar Blue)
1927 *The Haunted Ship,* Mose
1927 *By Whose Hand?,* Eli
1927 *The Blood Ship,* Negro
1925 *Water Wagons* (Short), Chicken Thief (uncredited)
1922 *When Summer Comes* (Short), Hotel Porter (unconfirmed, uncredited)
1921 *A Virginia Courtship*
1920 *Haunted Spooks* (Short), Butler (uncredited)
1919 *Rowdy Ann* (Short), The Train Porter (as Edgar Blue)

Soundtrack (1 credit)
1938 *Over the Wall* ("Have You Met My Lulu?" (1938), uncredited)

Pictured **Blue Washington** in *Beggars of Life,* 1928

APPENDIX K: Cemeteries

"They say the dead don't rest without a marker of some kind." - **High Plains Drifter**

Each year funds are raised to buy headstones for unmarked graves of Negro League players and executives. Starting in September of 2004, led by the efforts of anesthesiologist **Dr. Jeremy Krock**, a dozen headstones were installed at Burr Oak Cemetery in Alsip, IL, over the next nine months. Dr. Krock had heard, from relatives, about the great outfielder **Jimmie Crutchfield** from his hometown of Ardmore, Missouri. Upon visiting Crutchfield's grave in Burr Oak Cemetery, Krock discovered the grave site was without a headstone. While at the cemetery, he also found two other Negro League greats, **John Donaldson** and **James "Candy Jim" Taylor** without proper recognition. Today, this trio of stars have headstones thanks to Krock's efforts. As Krock so eloquently put it, *"They played in anonymity, and now they're anonymous in death."*

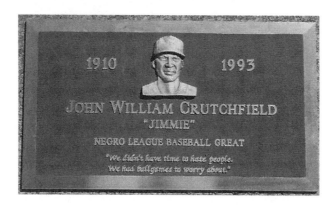

THE JIMMIE CRUTCHFIELD HEADSTONE - "A person dies three times," Dr. Jeremy Krock says. "First when their body stops functioning, second when they are buried, and finally, the last time someone says their name. My goal is to keep the names of Negro Leagues ballplayers and others connected to it alive." Krock, an anesthesiologist in Peoria, IL, grew up listening to relatives' stories of Jimmie Crutchfield, an outfielder who began his career with the Birmingham Black Barons, and fellow resident of Ardmore, MO. His family spoke proudly of Crutchfield, a Negro Leagues player who "escaped the hard, dangerous life of the coal mines to play baseball." Krock found that Crutchfield and his wife, Julia, had been buried in unmarked graves, at Burr Oak Cemetery in Alsip, IL, a disappointing ending to the story. It was then that the Negro Leagues Baseball Grave Marker Project was born.

Since 2004, with efforts led by Dr. Jeremy Krock, more than three dozen headstones have been installed in various parts of the country, by the Negro Leagues Research Committee of the Society for American Baseball Research (SABR). Coverage of marker dedications has been featured on the front page of the *New York Times* and featured in Phil Taylor's *Point After* commentary in *Sports Illustrated* and showcased on Brian Williams' *NBC Nightly News* segment entitled *Making a Difference*.

These articles and videos can be found at: https://www.larrylester42.com/grave-markers.html. Installation dates and locations about Jeremy Krock's Grave Marker Project can be found at Shakeia Taylor's website: https://tht.fangraphs.com/speak-their-names/

"There is no good in good-bye." — Larry Lester

Cemeteries

ALABAMA

Alabama National Cemetery, Montevallo, AL
Brown, Sr., Roger (Stud); 1940 - 2012

Bridgeforth Cemetery, Tanner, AL
Bridgeforth, William Sousa (Soo); 1907 - 2004

Crestview Memorial Gardens, Adamsville, AL
Meshad, Sr., Floyd G.; 1914 - 1997

El Shaddai [Spring Hill] Cemetery, Morgan County, AL
Vaughn, Jr., William Henry (Billy); 1944 - 2017

Elmwood Cemetery, Birmingham, AL
Barnes, Sr., Harry (Mooch, Tackhead); 1915 - 1993
Bostock, Sr., Lyman Wesley; 1918 - 2005
Brown, William Harris (Willie, Cap); 1923 - 1996
Davis, Lorenzo (Piper); 1917 - 1997
Eatmon, Elbert (Boe); 1914 - 1998
Griggs, III, Wiley Lee (Diamond Jim); 1925 - 1996
Hairston, Samuel Harding (Sam); 1920 - 1997
Ivory, James Edward (Sap); 1939 - 2008
Patterson, Jr., Willie Lee (Pat, Roy, Birmingham); 1919 - 2004
Shepard, Sr., Freddie D. (Tommy); 1916 - 1999

Elmwood Mausoleum, Birmingham, AL
Powell, William Henry (Bill); 1919 - 2004

Empire Cemetery, Empire, AL
Bankhead, Joseph Calvin (Joe); 1926 - 1986

Fairlawn Memory Gardens, Selma, AL
Frazier, Oran Franklin; 1908 - 1992

First Baptist Church of Williams Cemetery, Jacksonville, AL
Thomason, Charles John (Charlie); 1918 - 1993

George Washington Carver Memorial Gardens Cemetery, Birmingham, AL
Curry, William Jackson (Bo Jack, Willie); 1924 - 2007
Harris, William James (Red, Willie); 1932 - 2006

Lee, Willie James; 1935 - 2017
Mitchell, Sr., Jessie James; 1934 - 2010
Mitchell, Sr., John; 1937 - 2020
Pollard, Sr. Rev. Nathaniel Hawthorne (Nat); 1915 - 1996
Young, Sr., Archie Hue; 1928 - 2017

Gethsemane Cemetery, Mobile, AL
Harris, James L. (Jimmy); ???? - 2004

Grace Hill Cemetery, Birmingham, AL
Meredith, Buford (Geetchie); 1899 - 1932
Ivory, Willie Lee (Buddy); 1932 - 1975

Highland Memorial Gardens Park, Bessemer, AL
King, Sr., Clarence Earl (Pijo); 1923 - 1993

Maple Grove Cemetery, Anniston, AL
Smith, Willie D. (Wonderful); 1939 - 2006

Little Magnolia Cemetery, Mobile, AL
Williams, Jr., Charles Arthur (Charlie, Chet); 1903 - 1931

Montevallo City Cemetery, Montevallo, AL
DuBose, Clifford Joe; 1937 - 2013

Mount Silla Cemetery, Chesson, AL
Evans, Frank Bower; 1921 - 2012

New Grace Hill Cemetery, Birmingham, AL
Canada, James (Cat, Flash, Jim, Shortneck); 1914 - 1975
Griggs, Acie (Skeet); 1924 - 2007
Heard, Jehosie (Jay); 1920 - 1999

Shadow Lawn Memorial Gardens, Birmingham, AL
Bell, Herman; 1915 - 1970
Carter, Ernest C. (Spoon); 1902 - 1974
Hawkins, David (Dave); 1898 - 1942

Sykes Cemetery, Decatur, AL
Sykes, Melvin Elijah; 1901 - 1984

Valhalia Memory Gardens, Huntsville, AL
Holden, Sr., Carl (Hoghead); 1941 - 2015

Woodlawn Cemetery, Birmingham, AL
Jackson, Sr., Restine T. (R.T.); 1878 - 1936

Zion Memorial Gardens, Birmingham, AL
Brown, Sr., Cleophus (Buddy Buddy); 1933 - 2017
Gillis, Sr., Louis Charles (Sea Boy); 1924 - 2005
Perry, Sr., Alonzo Thomas (Tapya, Speedy); 1922 - 1982

ARIZONA
Greenwood Memorial Lawn Cemetery, Phoenix, AZ
Mesa, Andres R.; 1918 - 1994
Smith, John Ford (Geronimo, El Teniente); 1919 - 1983

ARKANSAS
Friendship Cemetery, Hot Springs, AR
Battle, Rufus E.; 1896 - 1954

Helms Cemetery, Arkadelphia, AR
Cooper, Darltie Ray (Dolly, Daltie); 1895 - 1944

Little Rock National Cemetery, Little Rock, AR
Clark, Loney; 1895 - 1937
Buster, Herbert; 1914 - 1976

New Hope Cemetery, Pollard, AR
Matchett, Clarence W.; 1916 - 1970

Odd Fellows Cemetery, Morrilton, AR
Kenyon, Rev. Harry C.; 1894 - 1973

Pleasant Hill Cemetery, Kenwood, AR
McDaniel, Booker Taliaferro (Cannonball); 1913 - 1974

Cemeteries

CALIFORNIA

Angeles Abbey Memorial Park Cemetery, Compton, CA
Davis, Martin Luther; 1917 - 2001

Angelus-Rosedale Cemetery, Los Angeles, CA
Fillmore, Joe Alexander (Fireball); 1914 - 1992
Sweatt, George Alexander (Sharkey, Never); 1893 - 1983

Arbor Vitae Cemetery, Madera, CA
Kinard, Roosevelt; 1901 - 1984

Camellia Memorial Lawn Cemetery, Sacramento, CA
Williams, Franklin Delano (Hank); 1936 - 2008

Cypress Lawn Memorial Park, Colma, CA
Morris, Harold Goodwin (Yellowhorse, Hal); 1900 - 1970

Eternal Valley Memorial Park, Newhall, CA
Harris, Elander Victor (Vic); 1905 - 1978

Evergreen Cemetery, Los Angeles, CA
Carr, George Henry (Tank); 1894 - 1948
Mackey, James Raleigh (Biz, Riley, McKey); 1897 - 1965
Washington, Edgar Hughes (Blue); 1898 - 1970

Evergreen Cemetery, Oakland, CA
Roberts, Sr., Curtis Benjamin (Curt); 1929 - 1969

Fairmont Memorial Park, Fairfield, CA
Ray, Sr., Richard; 1920 - 2002

Forest Lawn Long Beach Memorial Park, Long Beach, CA
Rodgers, Sylvester Clifford (Speedie); 1927 - 1992

Forest Lawn Memorial Park- Covina Hills, Covina, CA
Young, Andrew Spurgeon Nash (A.S., Doc); 1919 - 1996

Forest Lawn Memorial Park, Hollywood Hills, Los Angeles, CA
Campanella, Roy (Campy); 1921 – 1993
Marcell, Everett (Ziggy, Sam); 1916 - 1990

Fort Rosecrans National Cemetery, San Diego, CA
Farmer, Jr., Greene (Greenie); 1919 - 1982

Golden Gate National Cemetery, San Bruno, CA
Alberga, Marcenia Lyle (Toni Stone); 1921 - 1996
Butcher, Spencer (Butch); 1896 - 1967
Whatley, David Samuel (Speed); 1914 - 1961

Greenwood Memorial Park Mausoleum, San Diego, CA
Ritchey, John Franklin (Hoss); 1923 - 2003

Greenwood Memorial Park, San Diego, CA
Smith, Milton (Milt); 1929 - 1997

Holy Cross Cemetery & Mausoleum, Culver City, CA
Henderson, James (Duke); 1923 - 1984
Manley, Effa Brooks [Cole] (Effie); 1900 - 1981
Thompson, Samuel Tommy (Sad Sam, Long Tom); 1908 - 1978

Inglewood Park Cemetery, Inglewood, CA
Brewer, Chester Arthur (Chet); 1907 - 1990
Gilliam, James William (Junior); 1927 - 1978
Haynes, Sammie; 1920 - 1997
Haywood, Albert Elliott (Buster); 1910 – 2000
Scott, Joseph (Joe); 1918 - 1997
Souell [Cyrus], Herbert (Herb, Baldy); 1913 - 1978
Summers, Lonnie (Carl); 1915 - 1999
Ungo [Hungo], Fidel A. (Fidelio); 1893 - 1980
Ware, Archie Virgil; 1918 - 1990

Lincoln Memorial Park Cemetery, Carson, CA
Bell, Clifford W. (Cliff, Cherry, Cee Bell); 1896 - 1952
Donaldson, William Wilson (Billy, W.W.); 1891 - 1959
Dunn, Jr., Joseph P. (Jake); 1909 – 1984
Porter, Andrew V. (Andy, Pullman); 1910 - 2010
Porter, Merle McKinley (Bugs Bunny); 1921 - 2000
Scales, George Louis (Tubby, El Mago); 1900 - 1976
Taylor, LeRoy R. (Ben); 1902 - 1968

Los Angeles National Cemetery, Los Angeles, CA
Clark, Morten Avery (Specs, Morty); 1889 - 10129
Longware, Jr., Alonzo; 1891 - 1961
Moreland, Nathaniel Edmund (Nate); 1914 - 1973
Pullen, O'Neal (Neal); 1892 - 1944

Memory Gardens of the Valley, Santa Teresa, NM
Bass, Leroy Percy (Red, Roy); 1918 - 2003

Mount Hope Cemetery, San Diego, CA
Madison, Robert Lee (Bob); 1911 - 1973
Sharpe, Robert E. (Pepper); 1918 - 1997

Odd Fellows Cemetery, Fresno, CA
Thompson, Henry Curtis (Hank, Hawk); 1925 - 1969

Paradise Memorial Park, Santa Fe Springs, CA
Evans, II, William Demont (Bill, Happy, Gray Ghost); 1899 - 1986

Park Lawn Cemetery, City of Commerce, CA
Branham, Luther Humphrey; 1921 - 2000

Perris Valley Cemetery, Perris, CA
Simms, Willie (Bill, Jeep, Simmy); 1908 - 2002

Riverside National Cemetery, Riverside, CA
Hubbard, Jesse James (Mountain Man); 1895 - 1982
Matthews, Francis Oliver (Fran, Matty, Lefty); 1916 - 1999

Roosevelt Memorial Park, Gardena, CA
Bassett, Lloyd Pepper (Tarzan, Rocking Chair); 1910 - 1980

Rose Hills Cemetery, Whittier, CA
Douglas, Jesse Warren; 1922 - 1979

Shafter Memorial Park, Shafter, CA
Demery, Artis T.; 1914 - 1995

Suisun-Fairfield Cemetery, Fairfield, CA
Laduna, Philomeno Timithio (P.T.); 1935 - 1990

Sunset Lawn Memorial Park, Sacramento, CA
Carter, Elmer (Snake Eyes); 1911 - 2011

Union Cemetery, Bakersfield, CA
Boyd, Ollie; ???? - 1941

Westminster Memorial Park, Westminster, CA
Nutter, Isaac Nelson; 1894 - 1987

Woodlawn Cemetery, Compton, CA
Smith, Theolic (Fireball); 1913 - 1981
Stockard, Theodore Bernard (Ted, Licks); 1903 - 1962

Woodlawn Cemetery, Santa Monica, CA
Markham, John Matthew (Johnny); 1908 - 1975

COLORADO
Fairmount Cemetery, Denver, CO
Albright, Thomas (Pistol Pete); 1909 - 1986
Anderson, Theodore M. (Bubbles); 1904 - 1943

Fort Logan National Cemetery, Denver, CO
Hutchinson, Willie D. (Ace); 1921 - 1992
Johnson, Byron Waldo Emerson (Mex, Jew Baby); 1911 - 2005
Newkirk, Alexander (Alex, Slats); 1916 - 1996

Mountain View Cemetery, Pueblo, CO
Williams, Samuel Clarence (Sammy C.); 1922 - 2007

Riverside Cemetery, Denver, CO
Marcell, Oliver Hazzard (Ghost); 1895 - 1949

CONNECTICUT
Fairview Cemetery, New Britain, CT
Vierira, Sr., Justin Christopher (J.C.); 1925 - 2002

Oak Lawn Cemetery, Fairfield, CT
Baker, Rufus (Scoop); 1918 - 1992

Rose Hill Memorial Park, Rocky Hill, CT
Taylor, Jr., John Arthur (Schoolboy); 1916 - 1987

CUBA
Cementerio de Cristóbal Cólon, Havana, CU
Baró, Bernardo; 1896 - 1930
Cabrera, Alfredo A. (Pájaro); 1881 - 1964
Castillo, Julián; 1880 - 1948
Fernández, Sr., José María (Cuso); 1896 - 1972
García, Antonio María (El Ingles, A.M.); 1868 - 1923
González, Miguel Angel (Mike); 1890 - 1977
Hernández, Ricardo (Chico); 1885 - ????
Herrera, Ramón (Paíto, Mike); 1897 - 1978
Jiménez, Bienvenido (Hooks, Pata Joroba); 1890 - ????
Luque, Adolfo Domingo de Guzman (Dolf, Papa Montero); 1890 - 1957
Magriñat, José María (Héctor, Kiko); 1878 - 1950
Marsans, Armando; 1887 - 1960
Méndez, José De La Caridad (Black Diamond, Joe); 1887 - 1928
Molina, Agustín (Tinti); 1873 - 1961
Muñoz, José (Joseíto); 1881 - 1945
Parpetti, Agustín (Pulpita); 1887 - ????
Ramos, Ezequiel; 1885 - ????
Sama, Pablo; 1932 - 1951
Sánchez, Gonzalo; 1883 - ????

Cementerio Municipal Cruce, Cienfuegos, CU
Dihigo, Martín Magdaleno; 1906 - 1971

Cementerio Santa Clara, Santa Clara, CU
Oms, Alejandro (Walla Walla, Caballero); 1895 - 1946

National Cemetery, Havana, CU
Soler, Juan Reinoso; 1937 – 1959

DELAWARE
Delaware Veterans Memorial Cemetery, Bear, DE
Ferrell, Jr., Howard Leroy (Toots); 1929 - 2002

Emmanuel United Methodist Church Cemetery, Cheswold, DE
Carney, Clement (Ted); 1900 - 1966

Gracelawn Memorial Park, New Castle, DE
Bruton, William Haron (Billy); 1925 - 1995
Sadler, William A. (Bill, Bubby); 1909 - 1987

Silverbrook Cemetery, Wilmington, DE
Johnson, William Julius (Judy); 1899 - 1989

DISTRICT OF COLUMBIA
Mount Olivet Cemetery, Washington, DC
Lee, Holsey Scranton Scriptus (Script); 1899 - 1974
Piloto, José (Potato, Hidden Ball); 1926 - 2009

Rock Creek Cemetery, Washington, DC
Johnson, Thomas Fairfax (Tommy, L'il Professor); 1917 - 2007

Woodlawn Cemetery, Washington, DC
Morton, Ferdinand Quentin; 1881 - 1949

FLORIDA

Barrancas National Cemetery, Pensacola, FL
Marvray, I, Charles Jefferson (Hawk); 1928 - 1998

Bonifay Cemetery, Bonifay, FL
McDuffie, Terris Chester (The Great, TC); 1906 - 1968

Boynton Beach Memorial Park, Boynton Beach, FL
Campbell, William Henry (Zip, Bullet); 1896 - 1973

Dade Memorial Park, Miami, FL
Armenteros, Juan Francis; 1928 - 2003
Everett, James William (Jimmy, Blue Dean); 1908 - 1996
Herrera,, Juan Francisco (Pancho, Frank); 1934 - 2005

Dade North Memorial Park, Miami, FL
Wynn, Sidney; 1924 - 2008

Daytona Memorial Park, Daytona Beach, FL
Marshall, Hiram J.; 1922 - 1977

Edgewood Cemetery, Jacksonville, FL
Green, Jr., Shedrick (BB); 1932 - 2015
Henry, Leo (Preacher); 1911 - 1992
Jones, William Nathaniel (Bill); 1938 - 1996

Evergreen Cemetery, Jacksonville, FL
Hamilton, Jr., Arthur Lee (Art); 1934 - 2014
Kennedy, John Irvin; 1926 - 1998
White, Eugene (Stank); 1926 - 2002

Evergreen Memorial Cemetery, Miami, FL
Farrell, Luther Alaner (Buck, Red, Fats, Lefty); 1893 - 1956

Flagg-Serenity Memorial Chapel at Evergreen Cemetery, Palatka, FL
Turner, James Henry (Little Lefty); 1912 - 2000

Flagler Memorial Park, Miami, FL
Calvo, Jacinto del (Jack); 1894 - 1965
Campos, Francisco José (Frank); 1924 - 2006

Florida National Cemetery, Bushnell, FL
Brisker, William Lee; 1911 – 1996
Cooper, William Thomas (Bill, W.T.); 1918 - 2003
Williams, Sr., Norldon Leroy (Jeff, Floyd); 1927 - 1994

Fountainhead Memorial Park, Palm Bay, FL
Dandridge, Raymond Emmett (Ray); 1913 - 1994

Galilee Cemetery, Sarasota, FL
Hughes, Luther (Yoatee); 1918 - 1998

Gifford Cemetery, Vero Beach, FL
Barnwell, Ernest (Gator); 1910 - 1996

Glenwood Memorial Cemetery, West Palm Beach, FL
Bailey, Alonza; 1904 - 1984

Greenwood Cemetery, Jacksonville, FL
Lundy, Richard Benjamin (Dick, King Richard, Geronimo); 1898 - 1962

Hollywood Memorial Gardens Cemetery, Hollywood, FL
Pollock, Sydney Samuel (Syd); 1901 - 1968

Lakeside Memorial Park, Winter Haven, FL
Tugerson, James Clarence (Big Jim, Schoolboy); 1923 - 1983

Lincoln Cemetery, Gulfport, FL
Smith, George Cornelius; 1937 - 1987

Lincoln Cemetery, St. Petersburg, FL
Oliver, James Franklin (Pee Wee, Selassie); 1919 - 1971

Memorial Park Cemetery, Tampa, FL
Allen, Hosea Walter (Buster, Long Boy); 1918 - 1948
Gibbons, Walter Lee (Dirk); 1928 - 2015
Wiggs, Leonard David (Fats); 1913 - 2000

Miami Memorial Park, Miami, FL
Leon, Isidoro Lester (Izzy); 1911 - 2002

Morrison Cemetery (Florida Colored Cemetery), Ft. Meade, FL
Robinson, Booker Taliaferro (Little Book, Robbie); 1918 - 1998

Oak Grove Cemetery, Lake Alfred, FL
Watson, Amos (Country, Big Train); 1926 - 1997

Oak Ridge Cemetery, Ft. Myers, FL
Cannady, Walter I. (Rev, Sam); 1904 - 1981

Oak Ridge Cemetery, Inverness, FL
Hamman, Ed P.; 1907 - 1989

Old Jacksonville City Cemetery, Jacksonville, FL
Jamison, Caesar; 1877 - 1934

Orange Hill Cemetery, Tampa, FL
Sails, Rosell; 1921 - 2002

Rest Haven Memorial Park, Tampa, FL
Arenas, Sr., Hipolito Kanterra (Pops, Torrento); 1907 - 1995
Felder, Benjamin Franklin (Benny); 1926 - 2009

Restlawn Memorial Park, Jacksonville, FL
Barnhill, Herbert Edward (Herb, Barney); 1913 - 2004
Frazier, Albert Edwin (Cool Papa, Pops); 1915 - 1999

Rolling Hills Cemetery, Winter Haven, FL
Williams, Reuben E.; 1925 - 2005

Sunnyvale Cemetery, Quincy, FL
Snead, Sylvester Alonzo (Bo Gator); 1914 - 1995

Vista Memorial Gardens, Hialeah, FL
Dibut, Pedro; 1892 - 1979

Woodlawn Cemetery, Fort Myers, FL
Earle, Charles Babcock (Peles, Frank); 1884 - 1972

Woodland Cemetery, Tampa, FL
Rigney, H.G. (Hank); 1900 - 1958

Woodlawn Park Cemetery North, Miami, FL
Amoros, Edmundo (Sandy); 1930 - 1992

GEORGIA
Body shipped to Macon, GA
Hawkins, Lemuel (Hawk, Lem); 1895 - 1934

Cedar Grove Cemetery, Augusta, GA
Lamar, Horatio Vincent; 1911 - 1998

College Park Memorial Garden, Atlanta, GA
O'Kelley, Willie James (Stretch); 1920 - 1991

Crest Lawn Memorial Park, Atlanta, GA
Kemp, James Albert (Gabby); 1919 - 1993

East View Cemetery, Rome, GA
Long, Earnest Sylvestor (The Kid); 1927 - 2000
McClinic, Nathaniel (Nat); 1924 - 2004

Fairview Cemetery, Fort Valley, GA
Davis, Charles (Lefty); 1927 - 2016

Lincoln Cemetery, Atlanta, GA
Knox, Elmer; 1914 - 2007
Renfroe, Sr., Othello Nelson (Chico); 1923 - 1991
Scott, Cornelius Adolphus; 1908 - 2000
Welmaker, Roy Horace (Snook); 1913 - 1998

Lincoln Memorial Cemetery, Atlanta, GA
Gray, George; 1927 - 2001
Winfrey, Roy; 1932 - 2000

Monte Vista Biblical Gardens Cemetery, Atlanta, GA
Moore, III, James Robert (Red); 1916 - 2016

South-View Cemetery, Atlanta, GA
Butts, Thomas Lee (Pee Wee); 1919 - 1972
Favors, Thomas (Monk); 1920 - 2001
Glenn, Hubert (Country); 1916 - 2007
Ingram, Alfred (Alex); 1918 - 1995
Johnson, Ralph Burnett (R.B., Big Cat); 1924 - 2007
Phillips, Jr., Richard Albaso (Dick); 1930 - 2006
Reeves, Donald Ray (Soup); 1911 - 1973

Stone Mountain Cemetery, Stone Mountain, GA
Greene, James Elbert (Joe, Pea, Pig); 1911 - 1989

Unknown, Buford, GA
Lockhart, George Hubert (Prof); 1899 - 1968

West Hill Cemetery, Dalton, GA
Simpson, Harry Leon (Suitcase, Goody); 1924 - 1979

Zeta Cemetery, Tennille, GA
Johnson, Rudolph Valentino (Rudy); 1926 - 2000

ILLINOIS
Abraham Lincoln National Cemetery, Elwood, IL
Brewer, Sherwood (Woody); 1923 - 2003
Wiggins, Maurice Caldwell; 1910 - 2002

Burr Oak Cemetery, Alsip, IL
Brazelton, Clarkson (John); 1892 - 1940
Burley, Daniel Gardner (Dan); 1907 - 1962
Cornelius, William McKinley (Sug); 1906 - 1989
Crutchfield, John William (Jimmie, Colonel); 1910 - 1993
Davis, Roosevelt (Rosey, Duro, Macan); 1904 - 1968
DeMoss, Elwood (Bingo); 1889 - 1965
Donaldson, John Wesley; 1891 - 1970
Garrett, Robert Wayne (Fuzzy); 1907 - 1997
Green, Charles Albert (Joe); 1878 - 1962
Harding, William Claire (Hallie, Halley); 1904 - 1967
Hardy, Paul James; 1910 - 1979
Lewis, Jerome Ambrose; 1890 - 1962
Mann, Franklin L.; 1894 - 1965
Marshall, William James (Jack, Boisy); 1908 - 1990
McAdoo, Tullie; 1884 - 1961
McCurine, Jr., James (Big Jim, Big Stick); 1921 - 2002
Ousley, Guy C.; 1912 - 1964
Phillips, John (Fifer); 1915 - 2001
Radcliff, Alexander (Alec); 1905 - 1981
Smith, John Wendell; 1914 - 1972
Strong, Othello Lear; 1926 - 1986
Taylor, James Allen (Candy Jim); 1884 - 1948
Trent, Theodore (Ted, Highpockets, Big Florida); 1905 - 1944
Tyson, Sr., Armand Cupree (Cap); 1903 - 1973
Walker, Admiral D. (Deacon); 1898 - 1901
Williams, Woodrow Wilson (Woody); 1911 - 1992

Calvary Cemetery, Evanston, IL
Duany, Claro; 1917 - 1997

Camp Butler National Cemetery, Springfield, IL
Johnson, Joshua (Brute, Josh); 1913 - 1999

Cook County Cemetery for the Indigent, Oak Forest, IL
C. (Steel Arm); 1891 - 1941

East Linwood Cemetery, Galesburg, Knox County, IL
Thompson, Edward Lee (Eddie, Lefty); 1914 - 1979

Elmwood Cemetery, Centralia, IL
Burris, Jr., Samuel James (Speed); 1919 - 1982

Graceland Cemetery, Chicago, IL
Johnson, Arthur John (Jack); 1878 - 1946

Grandview Cemetery, Lakeview, IL
Banks, Ernest (Ernie); 1931 - 2015

Green Lawn Memorial Gardens, Cairo, IL
McAllister, Frank (Chip, Red); 1918 - 1987

Greenwood Cemetery, Chicago, IL
Schorling, John M.; 1865 - 1940

Greenwood Cemetery, Decatur, IL
Owens, Jackson McClelland (Jack); 1929 - 2007

Holy Sepulchre Cemetery, Alsip, IL
Hill, John Preston (Pete); 1882 - 1951
McMurray, William Joseph (Will); 1882 - 1945

Holy Sepulchre Cemetery, Worth, IL
Harness, Robert Marseilles (O); 1908 - 1991

Lincoln Cemetery, Blue Island, IL
Abbott, Robert Sengstacke; 1870 - 1940
Arnett, Pusey Dell; 1875 - 1957
Ball, Walter Thomas; 1878 - 1946
Bauchman, Harry (Pick); 1890 - 1931
Bennette, George Clifford (Jew Baby); 1901 - 1984
Dewberry, William James; 1874 - 1946
Dougherty, Charles (Pat, King); 1879 - 1939
Farmer, Walter Moran; 1867 - 1923
Foster, Andrew Bishop (Rube, Chief, Jock); 1879 - 1930
Francis, William Henry (Billy); 1878 - 1942

Goliah, Fred; 1888 - 1935
Johnson, Thomas Jefferson (College Boy); 1889 - 1926
Leland, Frank C.; 1869 -- 1914
McDonald, Luther (Vet, Old Soul); 1906 - 1976
Moseley, Beauregard Fitzhugh; 1868 - 1919
Petway, Bruce Franklin (Buddy); 1885 - 1941
Ross, Arthur C.; 1878 - 1916
Simpson, Lawrence; 1890 - 1921
Strong, Jr., Theodore Relighn (Ted, T.R.); 1917 - 1978
White, Carver DeWitt; 1931 - 2013

Miller Cemetery, Spring Valley, IL

Gilkerson, Robert Paul (Gilky); 1886 - 1944

Montrose Cemetery, Chicago, IL

Blueitt, Virgil Finley; 1896 - 1952

Mount Glenwood Memory Gardens South, Glenwood, IL

Barnes, Sr., Joseph (Joe); 1926 - 1995
Booker, James (Pete); 1886 - 1922
McMillan, Earl Thomas; 1908 - 1999
Moore, Henry W. (Harry, Mike); 1875 - 1917
Payne, Andrew Patrick (Jap); 1879 - 1942
Peters, William Stitt (W.S., Handsome Willie); 1867 - 1933
Strothers, Timothy Samuel (Sam, Tim); 1879 - 1942
Young, Frank Albert (Fay); 1884 - 1957

Mount Glenwood Memory Gardens West, Willow Springs, IL

Hall, Perry; 1898 - 1993

Mount Hope Cemetery, Chicago, IL

Rhodes, Harry; 1922 - 2001

Oak Woods Cemetery, Chicago, IL

Barnes, Isaac (Ike); 1932 - 1992
Binga, Jesse C.; 1865 - 1950
Britton, Jr., John A. (Jack); 1919 - 1990
Butler, Frank; 1872 - 1899
Jackson, Major Robert R.; 1870 - 1942
Lockett, Lester (Buck); 1912 - 2005
Newberry, James Lee (Jimmie); 1919 - 1983
Owens, James Cleveland (Jesse); 1913 - 1980
Radcliffe, Theodore Roosevelt (Double Duty, Ted); 1902 - 2005

Oakland Cemetery, Carbondale, IL

Armour, Alfred Allen (Buddy); 1915 - 1974

Pleasant View Cemetery, Kewanee, IL

Reynolds, Louis Thomas (Lou); 1872 - 1948

Restvale Cemetery, Alsip, IL

Clifton, Nat (Sweetwater, nee Clifton Nathaniel); 1922 -- 1990
Dial, Kermit Nathern; 1910 - 1982
Pate, Archie; 1886 - 1936
Robinson, William L. (Bobby); 1903 - 2002
Williams, Thomas (Wrist, Tom); 1896 - 1937

Resurrection Cemetery, Justice, IL

Dyll, Frank R.; 1929 - 1991

Rock Island National Cemetery, Rock Island Arsenal, IL

Baker, Eugene Walter (Gene); 1925 - 1999

Saint Mary's Cemetery, Evergreen Park, IL

Gardner, Floyd (Jelly); 1895 - 1977

Springdale Cemetery, Peoria, IL

Taylor, Jonathan Boyce (Steel Arm, Johnny); 1880 - 1956

Sunset Gardens of Memorial Cemetery, Millstadt, IL

Jones, Sr., Robert Leo (Fox); 1915 - 1992
Moody, Leicester (Lee); 1917 - 1998

Westlawn Cemetery, Chicago, IL

Saperstein, Abraham M. (Abe, A.M.); 1902 - 1966

Negro Leagues Book #2: The Players

INDIANA
Circle Grove Cemetery, Spiceland, IN
Merida, John H. (Snowball, Big Boy); 1879 - 1911

Crown Hill Cemetery, Indianapolis, IN
Allen, Herbert Todd; 1885 - 1971
Baldwin, Robert West (Tiny); 1904 - 1959
Bibbs, Junius Alexander Lloyd (Rainey); 1910 - 1980
Bowser, Thomas A.; 1869 - 1943
Brewer, McKinley; 1896 - 1955
Charleston, Benjamin Franklin (Bennie); 1907 - 1988
Francis, Otis Wilber (Cat); 1891 - 1940
Hannibal, Jack (nee Porter Lee Floyd); 1891 - 1949
Hutchinson, Fred (Hutch, Puggey); 1886 - 1954
Jewell, Warner (Werner); 1887 - 1960
Smith, George E. (Sonny); 1927 - 2011
Taylor, Charles Isham (C.I.); 1875 - 1922
Taylor, Olivia (Harris); 1885 - 1935
Warmack, Herman Peter (H.P.); 1882 - 1963

Floral Park Cemetery, Indianapolis, IN
Bennett, James Thomas (Jim, Fireball); 1919 - 1991
Charleston, Oscar McKinley (Charlie); 1896 - 1954

Hamline Chapel Cemetery, Monroe City, IN
Byrd, Prentice C. (Prime); 1903 - 1983

Highland Cemetery, South Bend, IN
Ash, Rudolph Theodeus; 1899 - 1977

Holy Cross and Saint Joseph Cemetery, Indianapolis, IN
Owens, William John (Bill); 1901 - 1999

New Crown Cemetery, Indianapolis, IN
Day, Wilson Connie; 1897 - 1961
Segraves, Samuel D.; 1920 - 1994
Shelby, Hiawatha Lavern (Bill); 1921 - 1996

Oak Hill Cemetery, Evansville, IN
Holtz, Edward (Eddie); 1899 - 1924
Wouldridge, Charles James (Charley); 1892 - 1969

Oaklawn Memorial Gardens, Fishers, IN
Barnes, Thomas B. (Tom); 1930 - 1997

Riverview Cemetery, South Bend, IN
Casey, Joseph Sylvester (Joe); 1900 - 1987
Robinson, Edward J. (Scoby); 1908 - 1990

Rosehill Cemetery, Bloomington, IN
Shively, George Anner (Rabbit); 1893 - 1962

IOWA
Cedar Memorial Park Cemetery, Cedar Rapids, IA
Garner, Horace T.; 1923 - 1995
Pennington, Arthur David (Art, Superman); 1923 - 2017

Glendale Cemetery, Des Moines, IA
Hall, Elbert Rufus; 1882 - 1935

Logan Park Cemetery, Sioux City, IA
Hancock, Charles Winston (Charlie); 1902 - 1974

Oak Hill Cemetery, Coon Rapids, IA
Thomas, Orille E. (Orel, Little Dean); 1909 - 1993

Oakland Cemetery, Fort Madison, IA
Cartmill, Jr., Alfred Franklin (Al); 1930 - 2016

KANSAS
Fairview Cemetery, Coffeyville, KS
Foreman, F. Sylvester (Hooks); 1895 - 1940

Fort Leavenworth National Cemetery, Fort Leavenworth, KS
Baylis, Henry Junior (Hank); 1924 - 1980
Bryant, Jr., Allen (Lefty); 1918 - 1992
Cooper, Alfred Mayart (Army); 1899 - 1966
Johnson, Jr., Clifford (Connie); 1922 - 2004
Mayweather, Eldridge Everett (Chili, Ed, Head, Snake); 1909 - 1966
Phiffer, Lester J.; 1934 - 1982
Ragland, Herlen (Hurland, Herbert, Earl); 1896 - 1960
Ray, Otto C. (Jaybird); 1894 - 1976
Rolling, Carl E.; 1893 - 1979
Surratt, Sr., Alfred G. (Slick); 1922 - 2010
Tyrees, Ruby Pearl; 1891 - 1965

Gypsum Hill Cemetery, Salina, KS
Primm, Charles Randolph; 1896 - 1986

Highland Park Cemetery, Kansas City, KS
McNair, Allen Hurley (Mac, Bugger); 1888 - 1948

Maple Grove Cemetery, Wichita, KS
Butler, Solomon W. (Sol, K.C.); 1895 - 1954
Guice, Lacy Kirk (Larry); 1931 - 1993

Mount Auburn Cemetery, Topeka, KS
Johnson, John Thomas (Topeka Jack); 1883 - 1940
Scott, Sr., Elisha; 1890 - 1963

Mount Hope Cemetery, Topeka, KS
Mothell, Carroll Ray (Dink, Deke); 1897 - 1980

Mount Olive Cemetery, Troy, KS
Wakefield, Burgess (Bert); 1870 - 1926

Old Mission Cemetery, Wichita, KS
Boyd, Robert Richard (Bob, Rope); 1925 - 2004
Thurman, Robert Burns (Bob); 1917 - 1998

Osage City Cemetery, Osage City, KS
Orendorf, James Thomas (Jim); 1876 - 1938

Sunrise Cemetery, SW of Manhattan, KS
Giles, Sr., George Franklin; 1909 - 1992

Topeka Cemetery, Topeka, KS
Williams, Dee; 1884 - 1911

Woodland Cemetery, Kansas City, KS
Smith, Richard Tobias (Tobe); 1862 - 1926

KENTUCKY
Bagdad Cemetery, Bagdad, KY
Gilbert, Paul Dean; 1938 - 1997

Cap Anderson Cemetery, Brandenburg, KY
Blackwell, Charles H. (Rucker); 1894 - 1935

Cave Hill Cemetery, Louisville, KY
Armstead, Jr., James (Jimmie); 1919 - 2006

Cherry Grove Cemetery, Cynthiana, KY
Russ, Pythias; 1904 - 1930

Davidson Memorial Gardens, Ivel, KY
Watts, Richard (Dick); 1927 - 2000

Eastern Cemetery, Louisville, KY
Mobley, Ira T.; 1928 - 1984
Snow, Felton (Skipper); 1905 - 1974

Evergreen Cemetery, Louisville, KY
Henry, Roy M.; 1912 - 1999

Greenwood Cemetery, Owensboro, KY
Wallace, Richard Felix (Dick, Noisy); 1882 - 1925

Louisville Cemetery, Louisville, KY
Hughes, Samuel Thomas (Sammy T.); 1910 - 1981

Monticello Cemetery, Monticello, KY
Bolden, Jr., Frank E.; 1912 - 2003

Ray Family Cemetery, Pike County, KY
Akers, Charley; 1897 - 1977

Saint Agnes Cemetery, Route 140, Uniontown, KY
Bumpus, Earl; 1914 - 1985

Saint Agnes Cemetery, Uniontown, KY
Walls, Mahlon E.; 1916 - 1976

LOUISIANA

Alexandria National Cemetery, Pineville, LA
Parker, Thomas (Tom, Big Train); 1912 - 1964

Calvary Missionary Baptist Church Cemetery, Benton, LA
Stewart, Sr., Riley Anderson; 1919 - 2000

Carrollton Cemetery (Green St.), New Orleans, LA
Bissant, John L.; 1914 - 2006
Wiley, Jr., Joseph (Joe); 1918 - 1993

Hi-Mount Cemetery, Lake Charles, Calcasieu Parish, LA
Fowlkes, Samuel (Buddy, Jimmy); 1926 - 1987
Williams, Chester Arthur (Ches, Cholly, Chet); 1906 - 1952

Jefferson Memorial Gardens, River Road, Saint Rose, LA
Johnson, Curtis T. (Colt); 1932 - 2004

Magnolia Cemetery, Monroe, LA
Saunders, Augustus L. (Bob); 1902 - 1999

McDonoghville Cemetery, Gretna, LA
Spencer, Jr., Joseph B. (Joe, J.B.); 1922 - 2003

Mount Olivet Cemetery, New Orleans, LA
Roth, Herman Joseph (Bobby); 1896 - 1988
Sias, George (Charley, Dirty Shirt); 1906 - 1985
Wright, Walter C.; 1912 - 2002

New Hope Baptist Church Cemetery, Gretna, LA
Barrow, Wesley (Biggie); 1900 - 1965

New Prosperity Baptist Church Cemetery, Clay, LA
Ensley, Frank James; 1927 - 2011

Port Hudson National Cemetery, Zachary, LA
Dunn, Alphonse (Blue, Allie, Al); 1911 - 2004
Gaines, Jonas George (Lefty); 1915 - 1998

Providence Memorial Park, Metairie, LA
Bissant, Robert Normand (Bob); 1913 - 1999

Restlawn Cemetery, Gretna, LA
Stewart, Sr., William (Bill); 1913 - 2017

Saint James United Methodist Church Cemetery, Convent, LA
Malarcher, David Julius (Gentleman Dave); 1894 - 1982

Southern Memorial Gardens, Baton Rouge, LA
Clarke, Sr., Albert D.; 1911 - 1988

Sunset Memorial Gardens, Baton Rouge, LA
Redd, Ulysses Adolph (Hickey, Cherry, Gumbo); 1914 - 2002

MARYLAND

Adams Chapel Cemetery, Baltimore, MD
Watkins, Murray Clifton (Skeeter, Maurice); 1915 - 1987

Arbutus Memorial Park, Arbutus, MD
Day, Leon; 1916 - 1995
Evans, Charles Alexander (Alec); 1897 - ????
Taylor, Benjamin Harrison (Ben); 1888 - 1953
Thomas, Dr. Joseph H. (Joe); 1884 - 1963

Baltimore National Cemetery, Baltimore, MD
Mungin, Jr., John T. (Bill); 1904 - 1976

East Market Cemetery, East Market, MD
Shorter, Hilda M.; 1904 - 1986

Fort Lincoln Cemetery, Brentwood, MD
Ellerbe, Lacy (Fox); 1919 - 2000
Tillman, Sr., James Pinckney (Jim P.); 1919 - 2009

Garrison Forest Veterans Cemetery, Owings Mills, MD
Burke, Ernest Alexander (Little Abner); 1924 - 2004
Carroll, Jr., Reginald Randolph (Sonny); 1928 - 2003
Powell, Richard Dennis (Dick); 1911 - 2004
Simmons, Hubert Van Wyke (Bert); 1924 - 2009

Gate of Heaven Cemetery, Silver Spring, MD
Awkard, Sr., Russell Alfred; 1917 - 2002
Carr, Austin George; 1923 - 1994
Isreal, Clarence Charles (Pint); 1918 - 1987
Isreal, Elbert Willis (Izzy); 1927 - 1996

George Washington Cemetery, Adelphi, MD
Williams, Jr., Walter Turner (Buddy); 1914 - 2014

Lincoln Memorial Cemetery, Suitland, MD
Lacy, Samuel Harold (Sam); 1903 - 2003
Medley, Calvin R. (Babe); 1923 - 1983
Williams, Joseph (Smokey Joe, Cyclone); 1886 - 1951

Marley Neck Road Cemetery, Glen Burnie, MD
Poles, Edward (Possum, Googles); 1904 - 1932

Maryland National Memorial Park, Laurel, MD
Harvey, David William (Bill); 1908 - 1989

Mount Auburn Cemetery, Baltimore, MD
Howe, John M.; 1898 - 1928
Warfield, Frank Xavier (Weasel); 1899 - 1932

Mount Calvary Cemetery, Baltimore, MD
Holloway, Christopher Columbus (Crush); 1896 – 1972
Jones, Stuart (Stewart) (Slim, Country); 1913 - 1938
McClure, Robert E. (Bob, Big Boy); 1895 - 1931

Mount Calvary United Methodist Church Cemetery, Fruitland, MD
Mainor, III, John J. (Hank); 1927 - 1998

Mount Olivet Cemetery, Baltimore, MD
Spedden, Charles Price; 1875 - 1960

National Harmony Memorial Park Cemetery, Hyattsville, MD
Dandridge, Richard Albert (Ping); 1891 – 1978
Jackson, Norman (Jelly); 1909 - 1980

Sharp Street Memorial United Methodist Church Cemetery, Baltimore, MD
Davis, Riley Marcilous (Peaches); 1894 - 1997

MASSACHUSETTS
Milton Cemetery, Milton, MA
Tiant, Sr., Luis Eleuterio (Sir Skinny, Lefty); 1906 - 1976

Mount Hope Cemetery, Mattapan, MA
Brown, Jesse J. (Lefty, Professor); 1914 - 1980
Johnson, Pearley (Tubby, Peter); 1902 - 1991

Pine Hill Cemetery, Westfield, MA
McGowan, Malcolm E; 1886 - 1942

Saint Joseph's Cemetery, Boston, MA
Jupiter, Alfred B.; 1871 - 1911

Unknown, Boston, MA
Matthews, William Clarence (Billy); 1877 - 1928

MEXICO
Panteon Jardin, Veracruz, MX
Donoso, Lino; 1922 - 1990

MICHIGAN
Bailey-Vergennes Cemetery, Lowell, MI
Miller, Jr., Fernández Raymond (Ray); 1927 - 2004

Chapel Hill Memorial Gardens, Grand Rapids, MI
Rasberry, Ted Roosevelt; 1913 - 2001

Crystal Springs Cemetery, Benton Harbor, MI
Neil, Raymond (Ray, Aussa, Tackolu); 1920 - 1998

Detroit Memorial Park Cemetery, Detroit, MI
King, Wilbert; 1914 - 2012

Detroit Memorial Park East, Warren, MI
Moore, Walter (Dobie); 1896 - 1947
Williams, Sr., Clyde Henry (Lefty); 1920 - 2005

Evergreen Cemetery, Detroit, MI
Williams, Jr., Lawrence (Larry); 1933 - 2003

Forest Lawn Cemetery, Saginaw, MI
Malone, William H.; 1868 - 1917

Fort Custer Military Cemetery, Battle Creek, MI
Adams, Benjamin Franklin (Ben); 1926 - 2005

Garfield Park Cemetery, Grand Rapids, MI
Ewell, Sr., Russell Lewis ; 1930 - 2007
Purcell, Herman D. (Flash); 1923 - 2005

Gethsemane Cemetery, Detroit, MI
Gordon, Herald (Bee Bop); 1925 - 2012
Lewis, Rufus (Lou, Mississippi); 1919 - 1999

Grand Lawn Cemetery, Detroit, MI
Arnold, Charles Edward (Chuck); 1930 - 2003
King, Alton; 1922 - 2012

Lincoln Memorial Park Cemetery, Clinton Township, MI
Stearnes, Norman Thomas (Turkey); 1901 - 1979

Mount Hope Cemetery, Lansing, MI
Raines, Lawrence Glenn Hope (Larry); 1930 - 1978

Mount Hope Memorial Gardens, Livonia, MI
Watts, Andrew (Andy, Big Six); 1922 - 1991

Oak Hill Cemetery, Battle Creek, MI
Patterson, John W. (Pat); 1872 - 1940

Oak Hill Cemetery, Pontiac, MI
Vines, Eddie Benjamin; 1918 - 1992

Oakwood Cemetery, Adrian, MI
Brooks, Gustavus B. (Gus); 1869 - 1895

GUS BROOKS, an Adrian (MI) Page Fence Giants center fielder, died of a heart attack while running to catch a fly ball during their inaugural season in 1895. Black baseball teams often performed skits during games to entertain fans. Because of this, many in attendance did not realize Brooks had died; they thought his collapse was part of the entertainment. Brooks' family was unable to claim his body, and in 1895 he was buried in an unmarked grave in Oakwood Cemetery in Michigan. This headstone was installed in the Oakwood Cemetery of Adrian, Michigan, in 2016.

Palmyra Village Cemetery, Palmyra, MI
Wilson, George H.; 1875 - 1915

Parkville Cemetery, Three Rivers, MI
Powell, Willie Ernest (Pee Wee, Pigmeat); 1903 - 1987

Perry Mount Park Cemetery, Pontiac, MI
Tapley, John Theodore; 1913 - 1956

River Rest Cemetery, Flint, MI
Hoskins, David Taylor (Dave); 1922 - 1970

Riverside Cemetery, Three Rivers, MI
Tyler, Roy; 1899 - 1984

United Memorial Gardens, Plymouth, MI
Gray, Chesley (Chester); 1914 - 1996
Webster, Daniel Jim (Double Duty); 1912 - 1988

Woodlawn Cemetery, Detroit, MI
House, Charles Barner (Red); 1913 - 2001
Martin, Dr. John B. (J.B.); 1885 - 1973

Moore, Herbert Cato; 1921 - 2003

Woodlawn Cemetery, Grand Rapids, MI
Padrón, Juan; 1892 - 1981

Woodlawn Cemetery, Highland Park, MI
Layton, Obediah (Obie); 1910 - 1997

Woodmere Cemetery, Detroit, MI
Duncan, III, Frank Lee; 1920 - 1999
Jones, Marvin T. (Lefty, T-Roller); 1932 - 2010

MINNESOTA

Crystal Lake Cemetery, Minneapolis, MN
Binga, William Henry; 1869 - 1950
Breedlove, Maceo; 1900 - 1993
Jones, George Elbertus (Bert); 1877 - 1943

Elmhurst Cemetery, St. Paul, MN
Castone, George William; 1867-1967
Matlock, Leroy; 1907 - 1968

Fort Snelling National Cemetery, South Minneapolis, MN
Hopwood, Reginald Lanier (Hoppy); 1906 - 1984
Johnson, Ralph O. (Botts); 1914 - 1944
Newberry, Richard A.; 1926 - 1982

Lakewood Cemetery, Minneapolis, MN
Marshall, Robert Walls (Bobby, Rube); 1880 - 1958

LaPrairie Cemetery, Cloquet, MN
Cadreau, William (Bill, Chief Chouneau); 1888 - 1946

MISSISSIPPI

Big Quarters Cemetery, Lumberton, MS
Dukes, Sr., Tommie (Dixie); 1906 - 1991

Biloxi National Cemetery, Biloxi, MS
Trimont, Percy Odell; 1928 - 2001

Carbondale Cemetery, Lorman, MS
Foster, Willie Hendrick (Bill); 1904 - 1978

Cedar Hill Cemetery, Vicksburg, MS
Gardner, Glover C. (Gus); 1898 - 1990

Garden Memorial Park, Jackson, MS
Bridges, Marshall; 1931 - 1990
Moore, Rev. Arnold Dwight (Gatemouth); 1913 - 2004

Green Lawn Memorial Park, Greenwood, MS
Bradley, Provine (Red); 1907 - 1986

Mount Pleasant C.M.E. Church Cemetery, Mount Olive, MS
Easterling, Howard Willis; 1911 - 1993

Public Cemetery, Bigbee Valley, MS
Tate, Roosevelt (Speed, Bill); 1909 - 1978

MISSOURI

Berry Cemetery, Ash Grove, MO
Yokum, Lewis Frank; 1893 - 1966

Blue Ridge Lawn Memorial Gardens, Kansas City, MO
Blackburn, Hugh R.; 1887 – 1950
Hayes, Lorenzo B. (Benny); 1915 – 1991
Rogan, Charles Wilber(n) (Bullet); 1893 - 1967

Calvary Cemetery, St. Louis, MO
Green, Leslie (Chin); 1914 - 1985
Trouppe, Quincy Thomas (Big Train); 1912 - 1993
Wheeler, Samuel Wallace (Boom Boom, Sam); 1923 - 1989
Whitney, Carl Eugene; 1913 - 1986

Forest Grove Cemetery, Lexington, MO
Lindsay, William (Bill, The Kansas Cyclone); 1891 - 1914

Forest Hill & Calvary Cemetery, Kansas City, MO
Hudson, Jr., Andrew A.; 1910 - 1995
LaMarque, James Harding (Jim, Lefty, Libertad); 1920 - 2000
O'Neil, Jr., John Jordan (Buck, Nancy); 1911 - 2006
Paige, Leroy Robert (Satchel); 1906 - 1982
Thompson, Orange; 1903 - 1989
Weaver, Mary Jo (Josette); 1921 - 2004
Young, Morrise Doolittle (Maurice); 1904 - 1984

Highland Cemetery, Kansas City, MO
Duncan, Jr., Frank Lee; 1901 - 1973
Gilmore, Quincy Jordan (Sect); 1882 - 1954
Joseph, Walter Lee (Newt); 1899 - 1953
Page, Gaitha; 1879 - 1970
Redd, Eugene (Gene); 1899 - 1955

Jefferson Barracks National Cemetery, Lemay, MO
Bostick, Fred; 1884 - 1965
Bracken, Herbert (Doc, a.k.a. Alfred Bragana); 1915 - 1994
Brooks, Sidney William; 1893 - 1949
Drake, William P. (Plunk, Bill); 1895 - 1977
Henry, Joseph (Prince Joe); 1930 - 2009

Herring, Moses L.; 1895 - 1931
Holliday, Charles Durocher (Flit); 1914 - 1992
Oldham, James (Jimmy); 1893 - 1930
Riddle, Marshall Lewis (Jit); 1918 - 1988
Russell, Branch Lowell (Lee); 1895 - 1959
White, Sr., William Ephraim; 1934 - 2006
Wilson, Sr., Emmett Dabney; 1913 - 1991
Zomphier, Charles (Zomp); 1906 - 1973

Lincoln Cemetery, Kansas City, MO
Foster, Leland Charles (Wow); 1909 - 1967
Hensley, Logan (Slap, Eggie); 1900 - 1971
Hicks, Fred; 1888 - 1950
Jamerson, Londell (Tincy); 1931 - 1975
Landers, Robert Henry (Henny, Lefty); 1930 - 1998

Longview Cemetery, Jefferson City, MO
Robinson, Charles E. (Papa, Lefty, Charlie); 1891 - 1974

Memorial Park Cemetery, Calvary Section, Columbia, MO
Gatewood, William Miller (Big Bill); 1881 - 1962

Missouri Veterans Cemetery, Springfield, MO
Horn, Jr., Herman (Doc); 1927 - 2006

Mount Moriah Cemetery, Kansas City, MO
Smallwood, Dewitt Mark (Woody); 1933 - 1995
Smith, Hilton [Alvis] Lee (Smitty); 1907 - 1983
Wilkinson, James Leslie (J.L.); 1878 - 1964
Williams, Jesse Horace (Bill); 1913 - 1990

Oakdale Cemetery, St. Louis, MO
Hewitt, Joseph William (Joe); 1885 - 1948

Ozark Memorial Park Cemetery, Joplin, MO
Clay, Alton Broyal (A.B.); 1923 - 1998

Parkway Cemetery, Joplin, MO
Thompson, Leonard James (Len); 1919 - 1973

Richmond Memory Gardens, Richmond, MO
King, Paris Bernard; 1931 - 1992

Southside Cemetery, Fulton, MO
Van Buren, William E. (Bill, Cool Breeze); 1935 - 2007

Saint James Catholic Church Cemetery, Catawissa, MO
Murphy, Jr., Sylvester J.; 1920 - 1988

Saint Jude Cemetery, Monroe City, MO
Robinson, Johnson K. (Buck); 1920 - 1998

Saint Peter's Cemetery, Normandy, MO
Askew, Jesse; 1914 - 2000
Bell, James Thomas (Cool Papa); 1903 - 1991
Bridgewater, Henry; 1845 - 1904
Cox, Comer Lane (Hannibal, Russ); 1905 – 1971
Ewing, Columbus Spurlock; 1902 - 1947
Head, John W. (Homey); 1929 - 2003
Hubbard, Palmer W.; 1936 - 1996
Hyde, Cowan Fontella (Bubba, Bubber); 1908 - 2003
Kennard, Daniel C. (Dan); 1883 - 1947
Mills, Charles Alexander (Chubby); 1878 - 1944
Palm, Clarence (Spoony, Midnight); 1907 - ????
Palm, Robert; 1914 - 1976
Vincent, Irving B. (Lefty); 1909 - 1977

Washington Park Cemetery, Berkeley, MO
Boswell, William Lee (Ducky); 1902 - 1982
Edwards, Frank Nutinous (Tenny); 1904 - 1977
Jones, Arthur Brown (Mutt, Dump); 1905 - 1984

MONTANA
Highland Cemetery, Great Falls, MT
Reed, Edward (Eddie) Lee; 1929 - 2009

NEW JERSEY

Atlantic City Cemetery, Pleasantville, NJ
Jackson, Thomas H. (Tom); 1868 - 1931
Lloyd, John Henry (Pop); 1884 - 1964
Manning, Sr., Maxwell Cornelius (Max, Mileo); 1918 - 2003
Trusty, Sheppard B. (Shep); 1863 - 1890
Williams, Clarence E. (Waxey, Bow Wow); 1866 - 1934

Beverly National Cemetery, Beverly, NJ
Allen, Sr., Toussaint L'Ouverture (Tom); 1894 - 1960
Banks, Sr., John T. (Johnny); 1922 - 2011
Flournoy, Willis Jefferson (Pud, Jesse); 1895 - 1964
Gans, Robert Edward (Jude); 1886 - 1949
Gillespie, Henry; 1896 - 1963
Wilson, [Dr.] Wesley Rollo; 1880 - 1956

East Ridgelawn Cemetery, Clifton, NJ
Grant, Ulysses Franklin (Frank); 1865 - 1937

Ewing Cemetery, Ewing, NJ
Harrison, Abraham (Abe); 1867 - 1932

Fair Lawn Cemetery, Fair Lawn, NJ
Barnes, Tobias (Ted); 1911 - 1979

Fairmount Cemetery, Newark, NJ
Belfield, Skinner; 1916 - 1995
Biot, Jr., Charles Augustus (Charlie); 1917 - 2000
Dabney, Sr., John Milton; 1867 - 1967
Louden, Louis Oliver (Tommy, Lou); 1919 - 1989
Manley, Abraham Lincoln (Abe); 1885 - 1952
Wiley, Wabishaw Spencer (Doc, Bill); 1892 - 1944

Forest Green Cemetery, Morganville, NJ
Williams, D.L. (Curtis, Lefty); 1938 - 2009

George Washington Memorial Park, Paramus, NJ
Fennar, Albertus Avant (Cleffie); 1911 - 2001
Howard, Elston Gene (Ellie); 1929 - 1980

Glendale Cemetery, Bloomfield, NJ
Christopher, Thadist B. (Ted); 1913 - 1967
Frazier, Joshua (Pop); 1886 - 1945
Hooker, Leniel Charlie (Len, Elbow); 1919 - 1977
Scantlebury, Patricio Athelstan (Pat); 1917 - 1991
Suttles, George (Mule, Mulo); 1900 - 1966

Gouldtown Memorial Park, Fairfield Township, NJ
Gould, Sr., Harold Lorenzo (Hal, John. Big Red); 1924 - 2012

Greenwood Cemetery, Pleasantville, NJ
Cummings, Napoleon (Nap, Chance); 1893 - 1974

Hillside Cemetery, Scotch Plains, NJ
Black, Joseph (Joe, Chico); 1924 - 2002

Holy Cross Cemetery, North Arlington, NJ
Dedeaux, Russell Lewis (Russ); 1913 - 1956

Lincoln Memorial Park, Mays Landing, NJ
Roberts, Elihu(e) D.; 1897 - 1975

Mercer Cemetery, Trenton, NJ
Cook, Walter I.; 1854 - 1888

Mount Holiness Memorial Park, Butler, NJ
Stone, Edward Daniel (Ed, Ace, Black Cat); 1909 - 1983

New Camden Cemetery, Camden, NJ
Wynn, William M. (Willie, Fourteen); 1917 - 1992

Perth Amboy, NJ
Figueroa, José Antonio (Tono); 1914 - 2004

Riverview Cemetery, Trenton, NJ
Whyte, William T. (Billy); 1860 - 1911

Rosedale Cemetery, Orange, NJ
Harvey, Robert A. (Bob); 1918 - 1992
Pearson, Leonard Curtis (Lennie, Hoss); 1918 - 1980

Rosehill Cemetery, Linden, NJ
Dent, Carl Jonvon; 1927 - 1995
Fernández, Rodolfo (Rudy, Ven Pordios); 1911 - 2000
Givens, Oscar C. (Gibby); 1922 - 1967
Wallace, James Alfred (Bo, Jim); 1930 - 2000

Sunset Memorial Park, Pennsauken, NJ
Yancey, William James (Bill, Yank); 1902 - 1971

Negro Leagues Book #2: The Players

NEW MEXICO
Memory Gardens of the Valley, Santa Teresa, NM
Bass, Leroy Percy (Red, Roy); 1918 - 2003

Unknown, Albuquerque, NM
Thomas, [Dr.] Charles Lee; 1881 - 1971

NEW YORK
Beverly Hills Cemetery, Lake Mohegan, NY
Fiall, George Goodwin; 1900 - 1936
Riggins, Arvell (Orville, Bill. Bo, Mule); 1900 - 1943

Calvary Cemetery, Queens, NY (in dispute)
Torriente, Cristóbal (Carlos); 1893 - 1938

Calverton National Cemetery, Calverton, NY
Brown, James Philip; 1919 - 1990
Johnson, William H. (Bill, Wise, Big C); 1895 - 1988
Spearman, Frederick D. (Babe); 1917 - 2010

Cypress Hills National Cemetery, Brooklyn, NY
Douglass, Edward (Eddie); 1887 - 1936
Hudspeth, Robert (Highpocket); 1894 - 1935
Mongin [Mungin], Samuel (Sam, Polly); 1884 - 1936
Noble, Rafael Miguel (Ray, Sam); 1919 - 1998
Robinson, Jack Roosevelt (Jackie); 1919 - 1972

Evergreen Cemetery, Brooklyn, NY
García, John (Juan); 1876 - 1904
King, William (Dolly); 1916 - 1969
Lindsay, Clarence Holmes (C.H.); 1898 - 1944
Robinson, Luther (Bill, Bojangles); 1878 - 1949

Ferncliff Cemetery, Hartsdale, NY
Stanley, John Wesley (Neck); 1905 - 1958

Flushing Cemetery, Queens, NY
Thomas, Julian (Jules, Jack. Home Run); 1886 - 1943

Forest Lawn Cemetery & Gardens, Buffalo, NY
Hardy, Arthur Wesley (Art); 1891 - 1980
Lockhart, Adolphus Joseph (A.J., Duke, Arthur); 1901 - 1993

Frederick Douglass Memorial Park Cemetery, Staten Island, NY
Bryant, Elias (Country Brown); 1895 - 1937
White, King Solomon (Sol); 1868 - 1955

Fresh Pond Crematory, Queens, NY
Gardner, James (Chappy); 1897 - 1943

Greenwood Cemetery, Brooklyn, NY
McHenry, Henry Lloyd (Cream); 1910 - 1981
Strong, Nathaniel Calvin (Nat); 1874 - 1935

Lakeside Cemetery, Hamburg, NY
Johnson, Grant U. (Home Run); 1872 - 1963

Long Island National Cemetery, East Farmingdale, NY
Brooks, Irvin Woodberry; 1891 - 1966
Buchanan, Chester Floyd (Buck); 1906 - 1964
Cueria, Basilio; 1898 - 1959
Deas, James Alvin (Yank); 1895 - 1972
Forrest, James Daniel; 1897 - 1977
Fuller, James (Jimmy); 1892 - 1987
Harris, Ananias Andrew (Andy, Six Bits); 1896 - 1957
Henderson, Curtis Lee (Dan); 1913 - 1960
Norman, Elbert (Alton, Ed); 1897 - 1962
Pace, Benjamin Harrison (Brother); 1894 - ????
Redding, Richard (Cannonball, Dick, Grenade); 1893 - 1948
Semler, James Aloysius (Soldier Boy, Bill, Sarge); 1891 – 1955
Semler, Maude; 1893 - 1973
Scott, Robert (Bob); 1892 - 1949
Spearman, Clyde (Big Splo); 1912 - 1955
Starks, Otis (Lefty); 1896 - 1965
Wright, Walter J. (Bricktop); 1908 - 1972

Memory Gardens, Colonie, NY
Mitchell, Arthur Harold; 1914 - 1994
Walker, Sr., Edsall Elliott (Big, Catskill, Wild Man); 1910 - 1997

Mount Hope Cemetery, Rochester, NY
King, Leonard D.; 1900 - 1984

Mount Olivet Cemetery, Maspeth, Queens, NY
Dunbar, Ashby Columbus; 1879 - 1925
Pettus, William Thomas (Zack, Bill); 1884 - 1924
Wilkins, Barron DeWare; 1865 - 1924

Mount Olivet Cemetery, Tonawanda, NY
Miro, Pedro; 1918 - 1996

Oakview Cemetery, Frankfort, NY
Fowler, John W. (Bud); 1858 - 1913

Oakwood Cemetery, Troy, NY
Harrell, William (Billy); 1928 - 2014

Park View Cemetery, Schenectady, NY
Ewing, William Monroe (Buck, Bill); 1903 - 1979

Pine Hill Cemetery, Throop, NY
Northrup, John Henry (Harry, Zip); 1882 - 1944

Pinelawn Memorial Park, Farmingdale, NY
Parris, Jonathan Clyde (The Dude); 1922 - 2016
Robertson, Peter (Creole Pete); 1905 - 1980

Saint Matthew's Cemetery, West Seneca, NY
McQueen, John Henry (Pete); 1909 - 1985

Saint Raymond Cemetery, Bronx, NY
McMahon, Roderick James (Jess); 1882 - 1954
Vázquez, Armando Bernando; 1922 - 2008

Spring Forest Cemetery, Binghamton, NY
Taylor, Robert (Lightning, Flash); 1916 - 1999

Vale Cemetery, Schenectady, NY
Wickware, Frank Ellis (Red Ant, Big Red); 1888 - 1967

Woodlawn Cemetery, Bronx, NY
Beckwith, Christopher John (Beck); 1900 - 1956
Connor, John Wilson.; 1876 - 1926
Johnson, Rev. John Howard; 1897 - 1995
Pompez, Gonzalo Alejandro (Alex); 1888 - 1974
Shipp, Jr., Jesse Alright; 1881 - 1922

Woodlawn Cemetery, Syracuse, NY
Anderson, Andrew W. (Andy); 1902 - 1989

NORTH CAROLINA
Ashelawn Gardens of Memory, Asheville, NC
Moore, Clarence Lee (C.L., Cool Breeze, Dago); 1908 - 1992

Beatties Ford Memorial Garden, Charlotte, NC
Parks, Charles Edison (Hunkie); 1917 - 1987

Beechwood Cemetery, Durham, NC
Turner, Elbert Carter (Pop, E.C., Bert); 1901 - 1970

Bridgeton Cemetery, Bridgeton, NC
Holton, Lucius O.; 1910 - 1989

Brownhill Cemetery, Greenville, NC
Barnhill, David (Impo, Dave); 1913 - 1983

Carolina Biblical Gardens of Guilford, Jamestown, NC
Chandler, Jr., John E. (Lefty, Dutch); 1926 - 2005

Carolina Biblical Gardens, Raleigh, NC
Warren, Ciscero Thomas (Lefty); 1919 - 2009
Wilder, William E. (Bear, Bill); 1928 - 2008

Cooper Cemetery, Brevard, Transylvania County, NC
Hefner, Jr., James Chester Arthur (Art); 1913 - 1988

Evergreen Cemetery, Winston-Salem, NC
Downs, McKinley (Bunny); 1894 - 1973
Yokely, Laymon Samuel (Norman, Corner Pocket); 1906 - 1975

First Baptist Church Cemetery, Kannapolis, NC
Sheelor, Willie James (Pee Wee); 1928 - 2014

Gardens of Gethsemane, Rocky Mount, NC
Leonard, Walter Fenner (Buck); 1907 - 1997

George Cemetery, Western Prong, NC
Ford, Sr., Ervin (Erwin) Lee; 1926 - 2002

Glennview Memorial Park, Durham NC
Barbee, John Quincy Adams (Bud); 1914 - 2000
Barbee, Walter Bratcher (Lamb); 1916 - 1986

Green Lawn Memorial Park Cemetery, Wilmington, NC
Fiall, Jr., Thomas Vivian (Tom); 1894 - 1978

Greenview Cemetery, Reidsville, NC

Negro Leagues Book #2: The Players

Koger, Jr., Eugene (Gene) Allen; 1930 - 2005

Lowndes Hill Baptist Church Cemetery, Greenville, NC
Drummond, James J.; 1940 - 2007

Mount Olin A.M.E. Zion Church Cemetery, Newton, NC
Grier, Claude Bonds (Red); 1904 - 1967

New Goshen United Methodist Church Cemetery, Greensboro, NC
Alston, Thomas Edison (Tom); 1926 - 1993

New Smith Grove Baptist Church Cemetery, Linwood, NC
Hartman, Garrell Vernell; 1913 - 1979

Northeastern Cemetery, Rocky Mount, NC
Battles, Raymond (Ray); 1918 - 1973

Oak Grove Cemetery, Elizabeth City, NC
Sampson, Jr., Thomas (Tommy, Toots); 1912 - 2002

Oak Hill Memorial Park, Kinston, NC
Long, Carl Russell; 1935 - 2015

Oak Ridge First Baptist Church Cemetery, Oak Ridge, NC
Siddle, Joseph James (Jumpin Joe, Lefty); 1921 - 2006

Pinelawn Memorial Park, Kinston, NC
McNeal, Rufus Lee (Zippy); 1915 - 2002

Pleasant Grove Baptist Church Cemetery, Wendell, NC
Hayes, Burnalle James (Bun); 1903 - 1969

Robinson Estates, King's Mountain, NC
Robinson, Henry Frazier (Slow, Pep, Hank); 1910 - 1997

Southview Cemetery, Kinston, NC
Hobgood, Frederick Douglass (Fred); 1921 - 1965

Sunset Memorial Park, Pennsauken, NC
Sunkett, Jr., Golden Leroy (Pete); 1918 - 1993

Viola Park Cemetery, Durham, NC

Watkins, John McCreary (Pop); 1856 - 1924

Violet Hill Cemetery, Asheville, NC
Gatewood, Ernest Willis; 1890 - 1949

OHIO

Alliance City Cemetery, Alliance, OH
Grimes, Lionel E.; 1918 - 1993

Body donated to Wright State Univ. Medical School, Dayton, OH
Parsons, Elwood; 1911 - 1995

Dayton National Cemetery, Dayton, OH
Boston, Robert Lee (Bob); 1918 - 2002
Murray, Mitchell (Mitch); 1896 - 1940

Dorset Cemetery, Dorset, OH
Singer, Orville Willice (Red); 1898 - 1985

Elmwood Cemetery, Lorain, OH
Ross, Howard Tullus (Harold, Lefty, Zero Ball); 1903 - 1963

Evergreen Cemetery, Columbus, OH
Johnson, John Wesley (Smoke, Lefty); ???? - 1943

Evergreen Memorial Park, Bedford Heights, OH
Bremer, Sr., Eugene Joseph (Gene, Flash); 1916 - 1971

Green Lawn Cemetery, Columbus, OH
Griffin, Clarence Bernard (C.B.); 1911 - 1991
Jackson, Jr., Dallas; 1925 - 2004

Greencastle Cemetery, Dayton, OH
Brown, Raymond L. (Ray); 1908 - 1965

Highland Park Cemetery, Highland Hills, OH
Boone, Alonzo Darn (Buster); 1908 - 1982
Calhoun, Walter Allen (Lefty); 1911 - 1976
Easter, Luscious (Luke); 1915 - 1979
Hayes, Wilbur Filmore; 1898 - 1957
Holcomb, George Edward; 1900 - 1983
Taylor, Olan (Jelly, Satan); 1910 - 1976

Hillside Memorial Park, Akron, OH
Cash, Wayman Treadwell L.; 1910 - 1998

Lake View Cemetery, Cleveland, OH
Hoiston, Floyd; 1913 - 1999
Pope, David (Dave); 1921 - 1999
Woods, Parnell L.; 1912 - 1977

Mount Hope Park Cemetery, Youngstown, OH
Dismukes, William (Dizzy); 1890 - 1961

Mount Peace Cemetery, Akron, OH
Finney, Edward Lewis (Mike); 1924 - 1998

Mount Pleasant Cemetery, Mount Pleasant, OH
Powell, Russell Harold; 1893 - 1961

Oakland Cemetery, Sandusky, OH
Haley, Granville (Red); 1901 - 1976

Ohio City Cemetery, Ohio City, OH
Smith, Dode M.; 1908 - 1996

Resthaven Memory Gardens, Avon, OH
Holder, Jr., William E. (Bill); 1931 - 1993

Spring Grove Cemetery, Cincinnati, OH
Grant, Jr., Charles (Tokohama, Charlie); 1874 - 1932
Reed, Percy A.; 1910 - 2000

Spring Grove Cemetery, East Liverpool, OH
Howard, Charles Allen (Doc); 1868 - 1904

Saint James United Methodist Church Cemetery, Cleveland, OH
Dimes, Edwin Charles; 1904 - 1999

Union Baptist Cemetery, Cincinnati, OH
Allen, Newton Henry (Colt); 1901 - 1988
Meadows, Helburn L.; 1907 - 1989

Union Cemetery, Steubenville, OH
Johnston, William Wade (Kid, Tick Houston); 1897 - 1978
Walker, Moses Fleetwood (Fleet); 1856 - 1924
Walker, Welday Wilberforce (Weldy); 1860 - 1937

Walnut Hills Cemetery, Cincinnati, OH
Robinson, Cornelius Randall (Neal, Shadow, Neil); 1907 - 1983

Negro Leagues Book #2: The Players

Wesleyan Cemetery, Cincinnati, OH
Merchant, Henry Lewis (Speed); 1918 - 1982

West Memory Gardens Cemetery, Dayton, OH
Blanchard, Chester Augustus; 1903 - 1996

Woodland Cemetery, Dayton, OH
Sloan, William George (W.G.); 1886 - 1931

Woodland Union Cemetery, Van Wert, OH
Selden, William Henry (Bee); 1885 - 1941

Woodlawn Cemetery, Cleveland, OH
Bright, Johnny; 1888 - 1908

Wooster Cemetery, Wooster, OH
Follis, Charles W. (Black Cyclone); 1879 - 1910

OKLAHOMA

Booker T. Washington Cemetery, Muskogee, OK
Taylor, Travis; 1929 - 1992

Booker T. Washington Cemetery, Tulsa, OK
Robinson, Norman Wayne (Bobby); 1913 - 1984

Center Point Cemetery, Redland, OK
Foreman, Jr., Zachariah L. (Zack); 1893 - 1921

Crown Hill Cemetery, Tulsa, OK
Redus, Jr., Wilson Robert (Frog); 1905 - 1979

Fort Gibson National Cemetery, Fort Gibson, OK
Dumas, Lafayette Napoleon (Jim); 1921 - 1943
Sourie, Fred Lee; 1928 - 2005

Parier Springs Cemetery, Boley, OK
Jefferson, George Leo (Jeff); 1922 - 1985

PENNSYLVANIA
Allegheny Cemetery, Pittsburgh, PA
Beale, Harry; 1906 - 1939
Clark, Charles W. (Sensation); 1902 - 1962
Dandy, George; 1890 - 1946
Garrison, Ross; 1867 - 1932
Gibson, Sr., Joshua (Josh); 1911 - 1947
Graham, Dennis Wilson (Peaches); 1896 - 1967
Greenlee, William Augustus (Gus, Big Red); 1895 - 1952

Hall, Sellers McKee (Sell); 1888 - 1951
Harris, Willie James (Red); 1909 - 1980
Hill, Gilbert R.; 1904 - 1930
Page, Theodore Roosevelt (Terrible Ted); 1903 - 1984
Sparrow, Roy; 1900 - 1943
Tinker, Sr., Rev. Harold C. (Hooks); 1905 - 2000
Turner, Wyatt James (Whitey); 1909 - 1986
Walton, Frank (Fuzzy); 1912 - 1995
Washington, Jr., Jasper (Jap); 1896 - 1960

Braddock Cemetery, Braddock, PA
Binder, James (Jimmy); 1902 - 1979

Brush Creek Cemetery, Irwin, PA
Clarkson, James Buster (Bus); 1915 - 1989

Calvary Cemetery, Pittsburgh, PA
Williams, Wallace Ignatus (Bucky); 1906 - 2009

Charles Evans Cemetery, Reading, PA
Day, Edward E. (Eddie); 1870 - 1906

Chelton Hills Cemetery, Philadelphia, PA
Morrison, Felton Craig; 1914 - 1981

Chitre Municipal Cemetery, Chitre, Herrera, PA
Osorio, Fernando Alberto (Mamavila); 1926 - 2010

Coraopolis Cemetery, Coraopolis, PA
Bowman, Emmett (Scotty); 1885 - 1912

East Cedar Hill Cemetery, Philadelphia, PA
Jenkins, Clarence Reginald (Fats); 1898 - 1968

Eden Cemetery, Collingdale (Delaware County) PA
Albritton, Alexander C. (Alex); 1892 - 1940
Berkley, John Randolph; 1899 - 1965
Bolden, Edward (Ed, Chief); 1882 - 1950
Catto, Octavius Valentine; 1839 - 1871
Dallard, Maurice Julius (Eggie, Morris); 1899 - 1933
Drew, John M. (Johnny); 1881 - 1976
Finley, John Thomas (Tom); 1903 - 1933
Forbes, Frank Lindsey (Strangler, Iron Man); 1891 - 1983
Fortune, Timothy Thomas; 1856 - 1928
Govern, Stanislaus Kostka (S.K., Siki); 1854 - 1924
Hill, John (Johnny); 1870 - 1922

King, Richard Elmer (King Tut); 1907 - 1966
McClellan, Jr., Daniel J. (Danny); 1878 - 1962
Parnell, Roy Alexander (Red); 1905 - 1954
Perry, Leon Lynn; 1916 - 1940

Erie Cemetery, Erie, PA
Jethroe, Samuel (Sam, The Jet); 1917 - 2001
Wright, Ernest (Ernie); 1901 - 1985

Erie County Memorial Gardens Cemetery, Erie, PA
Grace, Willie (Fireman); 1918 - 2006

Fairview Cemetery, Upper Dublin, PA
Bell, Elisha B. (Jake, Preacher); 1918 - 1997

Fairview Colored Cemetery, Willow Grove, PA
Glenn, Stanley Rudolf (Doc); 1926 – 2011
Hopkins, Gordon Derrick (Hoppy); 1934 - 2006
McDonald, Webster (Mac); 1900 - 1982
Pinder, Fredrick (Fred); 1891 - 1955
Schmidt, Edward (Jimmy); 1906 - 1985
Triplett, Norman; 1893 - 1918

Green Ridge Memorial Park, Pennsville, PA
Cole, Cecil Edward; 1919 - 2002

Green Lawn Cemetery, Chester, PA
Hayman, Charles (Bugs, Sy); 1885 - 1910

Green Lawn Cemetery, Feltonville, PA
Perrigan, John Robert; 1892 - 1966

Greenwood Cemetery, Pittsburgh, PA
Bankhead, Samuel Howard (Sam); 1910 - 1976
Gaston, Robert (Rab Roy, Jack); 1910 - 2000
Patterson, Gable (Gabriel); 1919 - 1991
Taylor, Joe Cephus (Cash); 1926 - 1993
Williams, Harry Lovett; 1905 - 1964

Greenwood Cemetery, Wilkinsburg, PA
Walker, Herbert Franklin (Laudie); 1898 - 1962

Har Nebo Cemetery, Philadelphia, PA
Gottlieb, Edward Isadore (Eddie); 1898 - 1979

Haven Memorial Cemetery, Chester, PA
Charleston, Porter R.; 1904 - 1986
Farrell, John R.; 1893 - 1961
Reid, Ambrose Leevolia; 1895 - 1966

Highwood Cemetery, Pittsburgh, PA
Fearbry, Jr., Marvin James (Butch); 1923 - 2008
Gibson, Jerry William; 1915 - 1952

Holy Sepulchre Cemetery, Cheltenham, PA
Clayton, Zachary M. (Zack); 1917 - 1997

Homestead Cemetery, Munhall, PA
Bruce, Clarence; 1924 - 1990
Jackson, Rufus (Sonnyman); 1900 - 1949
Mellix, Ralph Boley (Felix, Lefty); 1896 - 1985
Posey, Cumberland Willis (Cum); 1890 – 1946
Posey, Ethel Shaw Truman; 1893 - 1986

Homewood Cemetery, Pittsburgh, PA
Atkins, Joseph Oscar (Joe, Leroy); 1922 - 1970
Carlisle, Matthew (Lick, Matt); 1910 - 1973
Gibson, Jr., Joshua (Josh); 1930 - 2003
Harris, Charles (Teenie); 1908 - 1998
Mashaw, Forrest Wedward; 1898 - 1970
Streeter, Samuel (Lefty, Sam); 1900 - 1985
Vann, Robert Lee; 1879 - 1940
Young, William Pennington (Pep, Blimp); 1900 - 1968

Ivy Hill Cemetery, Philadelphia, PA
Byrd, William (Bill); 1907 - 1991
Duckett, Mahlon Newton (Mal); 1922 - 2015
Martin, Sr., James Edward; 1923 - 1996

Lakeside Cemetery, Erie, PA
Harden, Lovell (Big Pitch); 1917 - 1996

Lakewood Memorial Gardens, Dorseyville, PA
Calhoun, Roland C.; 1913 - 1985

Lincoln Cemetery, Harrisburg, PA
Mickey, John Baptist; 1876 - 1928
Strothers, Colonel William (C.W., Chief); 1868 – 1933
Wilson, Raymond V. (Ray); 1870 - 1912

Lincoln Memorial Park, Philadelphia, PA
Johnson, Jr., George Washington (Dibo; Junior); 1890 - 1940

Negro Leagues Book #2: The Players

National Cemetery of the Alleghenies, Cecil, PA
Pope, William Robert (Willie); 1918 - 2010

Merion Memorial Park, Bala Cynwyd, PA
Swiggett, Murray Simpson; 1888 - 1941
White, Jr., Jacob C.; 1837 - 1902
Williams, George L.; 1863 - 1918

Midland Cemetery, Steelton, PA
Dixon, Herbert Albert (Rap); 1902 - 1944

Monongahela Cemetery, North Braddock, PA
Gooden, Ernest E. (Pud); 1900 - 1934

Montefiore Cemetery, Jenkintown, PA
Passon, Harry; 1901 - 1954

Montour Presbyterian Cemetery, Oakdale, PA
Blair, Lonnie J. (Chico); 1929 - 1992

Mount Lawn Cemetery, Sharon Hill, PA
Cockrell [Williams], Philip (Fish, Georgia Rose); 1895 - 1951
Craig, Joseph P. (Joe); 1918 - 1991
Harris, Wilmer Joseph (Schoolboy, Wil); 1924 - 2004
McClain, Eugene Walter (Jeep); 1922 - 1997
Morgan, Constance Enola (Connie); 1934 - 1996
White, Chaney Leonard (Reindeer); 1894 - 1967
Woods, William J. (Willie); 1898 - 1927

Mount Peace Cemetery, Philadelphia, PA
Partlow, Roy E. (Silent Roy); 1911 - 1987

Mount Zion Cemetery, Collingdale, PA
Burbage, Knowlington Ottoway (Buddy); 1907 - 1989
Mayo, George (Hot Stuff); 1893 - 1987

Mount Zion Cemetery, Delta, PA
Stephens, John Samuel; 1897 - 1911
Stephens, Paul Eugene (Jake, Speed, Country); 1900 - 1981

National Cemetery of the Alleghenies, Cecil, PA
Pope, William Robert (Wee Willie, Bill); 1918 - 2010

New Evergreen Cemetery, Hayti, PA
Carter, Sr., Herman Leroy (Lee); 1920 - 2011

Philadelphia National Cemetery, Philadelphia, PA
Briggs, Otto (Mirror); 1891 - 1943
Johnson, Cecil Leon (Sess); 1893 - 1977
Santop [Loftin], D. Louis (Top, Big Bertha); 1889 - 1942

Restland Memorial Park, Monroeville, PA
Thompkins, Allie Levy (Merk); 1908 - 2001

Robinson's Run Cemetery, McDonald, PA
Campbell, Emmet Granville; 1887 - 1929

Rolling Green Memorial Park, West Chester, PA
Gettys, Spencer; 1916 - 2004
Waters, Theodore Francis Mullen (Ted); 1902 - 1966

Rose Valley Cemetery, Ambler, PA
Ford, John Dallas Cecil (Chink); 1894 - 1947

Round Hill Cemetery, Elizabeth, PA
Armstrong, George Isaac (Mule, Army); 1885 - 1954

Union Dale Cemetery, Pittsburgh, PA
Napier, Euthumn (Eudie, Nap); 1913 - 1983

Union Hill Cemetery, Kennett Square, PA
Winters, James Henry (Nip, Jesse); 1899 - 1971

West Laurel Hill Cemetery, Bala Cynwyd, PA
Schlichter, Henry Walter; 1865 - 1944

Westland Memorial Park, Wilmerding, PA
Pierce, Jr., William Herbert (Bonehead, Big Bill); 1890 - 1962

Westminister Cemetery, Bala Cynwyd, PA
Wilmore, Alfred Gardner (Apple); 1924 - 1996

Wildwood Cemetery, Williamsport, PA
Stovey, George Washington; 1863 - 1936

William Howard Day Cemetery, Steelton, PA
Dixon, Sr., Paul Perry (Dick); 1907 - 1994

Wintergreen Gorge Cemetery, Erie, PA
Crosby, Jr., Walter Charles (W.C.); 1921 - 2006

PUERTO RICO

Álvarez Memorial Cemetery, Ponce, PR
Coimbre, Francisco Atiles (Pancho); 1909 - 1989

Borinquen Memorial Park, Caguas, PR
Vargas, Roberto Enrique; 1929 - 2014

Cementerio Civil de Ponce, Ponce, PR
Guilbe, Juan (Telo); 1914 - 1994
Quiñones, Tomás Planchardon (Thomas); 1923 - 1967
Villodas, Luis (King Kong); 1918 - 1994

Guayama Cemetery, Guayama, PR
Vargas,, Juan Esteban (Tetelo, José, the Dominican Deer); 1906 - 1971

Municipal Cemetery, Aguadilla, PR
Márquez, Luis Angel (Canena); 1925 - 1988

Puerto Rico National Cemetery, Bayamon, PR
Delgado, Felix Rafael (Felle); 1909 - 2001

Vivaldi Cemetery, Mayaguez, PR
Santiago, Carlos Manuel; 1926 - 2008

SOUTH CAROLINA

Beaufort National Cemetery, Beaufort, SC
Holmes, Leroy Thomas (Philly); 1914 - 1964

Brooklyn C.M.E Church Cemetery, Chesnee, SC
Alexander, Theodore Roosevelt (Ted, Red); 1912 - 1999

Greenvile Memorial Gardens, Piedmont, SC
Tarrant, Jamuel; 1914 - 2012

Kings Chapel AME Methodist Church Cemetery, Pendleton, SC
Johnson, Jr., George (Chappie, Rat); 1877 - 1949

New Hopewell Baptist Church Cemetery (unmarked), Darlington County, SC
Smith, Charles E. (Chino, Postalita); 1901 - 1932

Old Mount Zion Baptist Church Cemetery, 96, SC
Williams, Robert Rosel; 1932 - 2018

Richland Cemetery, Greenville, SC
Jackson, Jr., Richard Alvin (Workie, Dick); 1897 - 1939

SOUTH DAKOTA

Black Hills National Cemetery, Sturgis, SD
Jackson, Daniel M. (Hatchet, Thumper, Dan); 1922 - 1992

TENNESSEE

Calvary Cemetery, Memphis, TN
Longley, Wayman (Red, Ray); 1909 - 1977
Pearson, Frank (Wahoo, Ivy); 1919 - 1997

Chattanooga National Cemetery, Chattanooga, TN
Richardson, Earl; 1924 - 1946

Crestview Cemetery, Knoxville, TN
Cleage, Ralph Pete; 1898 - 1977

Elmwood Cemetery, Memphis, TN
Carter, Marlin Theodore (Pee Wee, Mel); 1912 - 1993
Claybrook, Jr., John C.; 1872 - 1951
Hayes, Jr., Thomas Henry (Tom); 1902 - 1982
Lewis, Robert Stevenson (Bubbles, Bubber); 1883 - 1971
Martin, Dr. Arthur T. (A.T.); 1886 - 1975
Martin, Dr. Bebee (B.B.); 1889 - 1976
Martin, Dr. William Sylvester (W.S.); 1879 - 1958

Forest Hill Cemetery Midtown, Memphis, TN
Long, Matthew (Buck); 1927 - 1999

Forest Hills Cemetery, Chattanooga, TN
Monroe, William S. (Diamond Bill, Monie); 1876 - 1915
Norman, Garnett Wesley (Bughouse); 1900 - 1925

Greenwood Cemetery, Nashville, TN
Bunch, Jr., Sidney Thomas; 1931 - 2009
Kimbro, Henry Allen (Jimbo, Kimmie); 1912 - 1999
Lyons, Granville (Lefty); 1902 - 1950
Wilson, Thomas T. (Smiling Tom); 1889 - 1947

Greenwood Cemetery, Paris, TN
Guthrie, Wallace; 1922 - 1999

Hurricane Hill Cemetery, Dyer County, TN
Smith, William T. (Big Bill); 1869 - 1939

Memphis Memorial Gardens Cemetery, Memphis, TN

Davis, Sr., George Carter (Chin); 1938 - 2008
Mathis, Sr., Verdell (Lefty); 1914 - 2007

Memphis National Cemetery, Memphis, TN

Taylor, Jr., Sammie T. (Bay); 1929 - 1963

Metropolitan Bordeaux Cemetery, Nashville, TN

Proctor, Henryene; 1920 - 2001

Middle Tennessee Veterans Cemetery, Pegram, TN

Hendrix, Sr., Stokes Edward; 1914 - 2003
Martin, Edward A. (Ed, Marty); 1929 - 2002
Murry, Richard Nathaniel (Dick, Cowboy); 1921 - 1994
Thompson, Jr., Frank Andrew (Hoss); 1923 - 2002

Midtown Cemetery (Forest Hills Cemetery), Memphis, TN

Chatman, Charles Howard (Sleepy); 1933 - 2004

Mount Ararat Cemetery, Nashville, TN

Ray, John (Johnny); 1911 - 1957

Mount Carmel Cemetery, Memphis, TN

Curry, Homer (Blue Goose); 1905 - 1974

Nashville National Cemetery, Madison, TN

McGavock, Herbert T. (Hub); 1896 - 1954
Searcy, Kelton (Kelly, Lefty); 1931 - 1978
Stratton, Felton (Leroy); 1895 - 1974

New Park Cemetery, Memphis, TN

Bankhead, Fred; 1912 - 1972
Brown, Isaac (Ike); 1942 - 2001
Brown, Larry (Iron Man); 1901 - 1972

New Zion Cemetery, Etowah, TN

Dickey, Walter Claude (Steel Arm, John); 1894 - 1923

Oak Ridge Memorial Park, Oak Ridge, TN

Williams, Eugene (Gene, Fireball); 1932 - 2008

Salem Baptist Church Cemetery, Liberty, TN

Griffith, Robert Lee (Schoolboy, Big Bill); 1911 - 1977

Sherwood Memorial Gardens, Alcoa, TN

Bell, Julian (Jute); 1900 - 1991

Southwoods Memorial Park, Memphis, TN

Harris, Isiah (Ike, Lefty); 1925 – 2001
Jones, Jr., Clinton (Casey); 1918 - 1998

Unknown, Nashville, TN

Green, Vernon (Fat, Baby, Rufus); 1900 - 1949

West Tennessee State Veterans Cemetery, Memphis, TN

Peeples, Nathanial (Nat); 1926 - 2012
Scott, Joseph Burt (Joe); 1920 - 2013

Woodlawn Memorial Park, Nashville, TN

Abernathy, Robert William (James); 1918 - 1997
Dennis, Wesley Lewis (Doc); 1918 - 2001

TEXAS

Body shipped to Dallas, Texas for burial.
Blackmon, Henry (Galloping Ghost); 1891 - 1924

Brookshire Cemetery, Brookshire, TX
Beverly, Charles Green (Hooks, Wooger); 1900 - 1981

Corrigan Cemetery, Corrigan, TX
Ross, William M. (Zero Ball); 1893 - 1964

Cottonwood Community Cemetery, Honda, TX
Ligon, Rufus C.; 1903 - 1992

El Campo Community Cemetery, El Campo, TX
Bell, William (W); 1897 - 1969

Evergreen Cemetery, Victoria, TX
Dudley, Jr., Charles Arthur (C.A., Doc); 1894 - 1975

Fort Bliss National Cemetery, El Paso, TX
Tatum, Jr., Reece (Goose); 1921 - 1967

Fort Gibson National Cemetery, Fort Gibson, TX
Littles, Ben Henry; 1920 - 1952

Fort Sam Houston National Cemetery, San Antonio, TX
Cobb, Lorenza Samuel Nathaniel; 1888 – 1953
McNeal, Clyde Clifton (Junior); 1928 - 1996
Taborn, Earl (Mickey); 1922 - 1996
Walker, Jesse T. (Hoss, Selassie, Deuce, Aussa); 1912 - 1984

Glen Oak Cemetery, Dallas, TX
Sloan, Robert Lee; 1889 - 1951

Grace Hill Cemetery, Longview, TX
Neal, Charles Lenard (Charlie); 1931 - 1996

Greenwood Cemetery Annex, Waco, TX
Cooper, Andrew Lewis (Andy); 1896 - 1941
Walker, George T. (Schoolboy); 1915 - 1967

Grove Hill Memorial Park, Dallas, TX
Hill, Samuel Leslie (Sam); 1929 - 1992

Haven of Memories Cemetery, Canton, TX
Lewis, George F. (Peaches); 1890 - 1972

Hopewell Cemetery, Round Rock, TX
Johnson, Bertram; 1905 - 1976

Holy Cross Cemetery, Houston, TX
Bilao, Stephen Libore; 1885 - 1946

Houston Memorial Gardens, Houston, TX
Danage, Lunie D.; 1895 - 1982

Houston National Cemetery, Houston, TX
Bankhead, Daniel Robert; 1920 - 1976
Bond, Walter Franklin (Walt); 1937 - 1967
Brown, Jr., Thomas Jefferson (Tom, T.J.); 1922 - 1989
Brown, Willard Jessie (Home Run); 1915 - 1996
Davis, Otis (Fritz); 1919 - 1992
Pendleton, James Edward (Jim); 1924 - 1996
Watrous, Sherman; 1925 - 1997

Lakeview Cemetery, Wichita Falls, TX
Herron, Robert Lee (Big Daddy); 1924 - 1994

Lincoln Memorial Park, Dallas, TX
McMeans, Willie; 1910 - 1983
Wilson, Robert (Bob); 1925 - 1985

Meadowland Memorial Park, San Antonio, TX
Miles, Jr., John (Mule, Sonny Boy); 1922 - 2013

Mineral Wells, TX
Bobo, Willie Alphonso; 1902 - 1931

Oakwood Cemetery, Terrell, TX
Else, Harry Elmo (Speed); 1906 - 1986

Paradise Cemetery, South Houston, TX
Patterson, Andrew Lawrence (Pat); 1911 - 1984

Plummes Cemetery, Austin, TX
Wells, Willie Brooks (Junior); 1922 - 1994

Resthaven Memorial Park, Midland, Midland County, TX
Flournoy, Fred Emmet; 1905 - 1999

Restlawn Cemetery, Houston, TX
Jefferson, Willie; 1904 - 1979

Rosewood Cemetery, Conroe, TX
Williams, Marvin (Tex, Coqueta); 1923 - 2000

San Leon Cemetery, San Leon, TX
Munroe, Elmer Albert; 1916 - 1995

San Marcos - Blanco Cemetery, San Marcos, TX
Brown, James R. (Jim); 1892 - 1943

Shannon Rose Hill Memorial Park, Fort Worth, TX
Jackson, Sanford Olander (Jambo); 1900 - 1984

Texas State Cemetery, Austin, TX
Wells, Willie James (Devil, Chico); 1906 - 1989

Tyler Memorial Park and Cemetery, Tyler, TX
Smith, Eugene L. (Cheever, Goat, Gene); 1919 - 1996

Valley View Cemetery, Hubbard, Hill County, TX
Westbrook, Luther Leon (Sugar); 1912 - 1995

Van Alstyne Cemetery, Van Alstyne, TX
Wilson, Hubert (Tack, Pug, Herb); 1902 - 1981

VENEZUELA
Cementerio General del Sur, Caracas, VZ
Chacón, Pelayo; 1888 - 1971

VERMONT
South Newfane Cemetery, South Newfane, VT
Applegate, Gideon Spence (Red); 1927 - 2016

VIRGIN ISLAND
Christiansted Cemetery, St. Croix, VI
Gerard, Alphonso (Harlem Flash, Piggy, Chico); 1917 - 2002

VIRGINIA
Arlington National Cemetery, Arlington, VA
Mahoney, Anthony Barnes (Tony); 1893 - 1924
Martin, Harold Douglas; 1899 - 1945
Owens, William Oscar; 1893 - 1960
Poles, Spottswood (Spot); 1887 - 1962
Spearman, Rev. Charles Kenston; 1891 - 1963
Webster, Pearl Franklyn (Specks); 1889 - 1918
Wilson, Sr., Ernest Judson (Boojum, Jud, Jorocon); 1896 - 1963

Augusta Memorial Park, Waynesboro, VA
Daniels, Fred; 1893 -1993

Calvary Cemetery, Norfolk, VA
Cousins, Jr., Claude; 1938 - 2005
Jacox, Calvin Moses (Cal); 1923 - 1989
Riddick, Vernon Walter (Big Six); 1917 - 1979

Evergreen Cemetery, Richmond, VA
Evans, Robert J. (Bob); 1910 - 1947

Forest Hills Cemetery, Lynchburg, VA
Dyke, Jr., William Robert (Lefty); 1906 - 1984

Forest Lawn Cemetery, Richmond, VA
Blair, Sr., Garnett E. (Schoolboy); 1921 - 1996

Green Lawn Cemetery, Chesapeake, VA
Todd, Elzie Alphonso (Junior, Joe); 1935 - 2011

Hampton National Cemetery, Hampton, VA
Force, William (Buddie, Bill); 1895 - 1969

Lincoln Memorial Cemetery, Portsmouth, VA
Ruffin, Charles Leon (Lassas); 1912 - 1970

Magnolia Cemetery, Norfolk, VA
Lattimore, Albert (Alphonso, Duke); 1904 - 1986

Maury Cemetery, Richmond, VA
Banks, Norman Earl (Skeeter); 1918 - 1964
Graves, Jr., Whit Allen; 1927 - 1997

Meadowbrook Memorial Gardens, Suffolk, VA
Epps, Harvey; 1917 - 2002

Quantico National Cemetery, Triangle, VA
Cohen, James Clarence (Fireball); 1918 - 2002

Richmond National Cemetery, Richmond, VA
Elam, Jr., James Thomas (Jim); 1920 - 1961

Roosevelt Memorial Park, Chesapeake, VA

Cemeteries

Godfrey, Sr., James Edward Cleveland (Cleve); 1922 - 2011

Lundy, Walter; 1935 - 2005

Rosemont Cemetery, Suffolk, VA
Wilson, Rev. James William; 1861 - 1940

Shiloh Baptist Church Cemetery, Ashland, VA
Jackson, Lester E.; 1915 - 1991

Williams Memorial Park, Roanoke, VA
Eggleston, Jr., Macajah Marchand (Mack, Cager, Egg); 1896 - 1980

Woodlawn Cemetery, Beaverdam, VA
Brice, George Edward (Three Finger); 1888 - 1962

WASHINGTON
Acacia Memorial Park, Seattle, WA
Berry, Michael C. (Mike, Red); 1912 - 1995

Oakwood Hill Cemetery, Tacoma, WA
Claxton, James Edward (Jimmy); 1892 - 1970

Terrace Heights Memorial Park, Yakima, WA
Barnes, Sanford L.; 1913 - 2000

WEST VIRGINIA
Cunningham Memorial Park, St. Albans, WV
Thomas, Clinton Cyrus (Hawk, Clint); 1896 - 1990

Greenwood Memorial Cemetery, Beckley, WV
Kincannon, Harry (Tin Can); 1910 - 1965

Mount Moriah Cemetery, Albright, WV
Williams, James R. (Johnny, Nature Boy); 1929 - 1980

Saint Paul Catholic Church Cemetery, Wierton, WV
Trice, Jr., Robert Lee (Bob); 1926 - 1988

Spring Hill Cemetery, Charleston, WV
Roberts, Harry Hamlet (Raggs); 1895 - 1963

Spring Hill Cemetery, Huntington, WV
Gordon, Samuel Simon (Sam, S.S.); 1878 - 1962

Unknown, Paynesville, WV
Vance, Columbus S. (Luke, Dazzy); 1902 - 1982

Woodlawn Cemetery, Fairmont, WV
Jones, Samuel (Sad Sam, Toothpick Sam, Red); 1923 - 1971

WISCONSIN
Wood National Cemetery, Milwaukee, WI
Brown, Lawrence James (Lefty); 1910 - 1986

CREMATIONS
Benson, Eugene (Gene, Spider); 1913 - 1999
Benton, James Elbert; 1926 - 1999
Black, Joseph (Joe, Chico); 1924 - 2002
Campanella, Roy (Campy); 1921 - 1993
Canton, Denio (Toto); 1919 - 2005
Creacy, Albert Dewey (A.D.); 1900 - 1984
Dandridge, Troy Rasmussen (Dan); 1904 - 1993
Davis, John Howard (Cherokee); 1917 - 1982
Dials, Oland Cecil (Lou); 1904 -1994
Doby, Sr., Lawrence (Larry); 1923 - 2003
Fields, Sr., Wilmer Leon; 1922 - 2004
Gardner, James (Chappy); 1879 - 1943
Gaston, Hiram Allen; 1932 - 2005
Hardaway, Curtis O'Neal; 1928 - 2000
Hardwick, Leon Herbert; 1912 – 1981
Johnson, Oscar (Heavy); 1895 - 1960
Jones, Jr., James Edward; 1926 – 2002
Kimbrough, Larry Nathaniel (Schoolboy); 1923 - 2001
Kitamura, Richard Shoji (Dick); 1928 - 1981
Klep, Edward Joseph (Eddie); 1918 - 1981
McKnight, Jr., Ira D.; 1935 - 2018
Mitchell, Sr., Robert Lee (Peachhead); 1932 - 2019
Morrison, Felton; 1914 - 1981
Peace, William Warren (Father Devine); 1921 - 2002
Pereira, José (Pepin); 1927 - 2006
Santiago, José Guzman; 1928 - 2018
Scott, Joseph Bert; 1920 - 2013
Simmons, Silas Joseph (Si); 1895 - 2006
Streeter, Samuel; 1900 - 1985
Sykes, Franklin Jehoy (Doc); 1892 - 1986
Underwood, Eli M.; 1908 - 1985
Walton, Frank (Fuzzy); 1912 - 1995
Watkins, Richard; 1932 - 1991
Wyatt, John Thomas; 1935 – 1998

APPENDIX L: BOOKS, THESES, DISSERTATIONS, and NEWSPAPERS RESEARCHED

Books Authored by former Negro League Players:

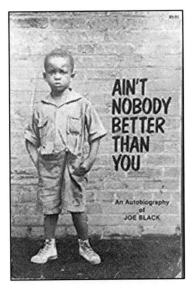

Altman, George with Lew Freedman. *My Baseball Journey from the Negro Leagues to the Majors and Beyond.* (Jefferson, North Carolina: McFarland & Company, 2013).

Black, Joe. *Ain't Nobody Better Than You.* (Scottsdale, Arizona: Ironwood Lithographers, 1983). (OP).

Cash, Bill "Ready" and Al Hunter, Jr. *Thou Shalt Not Steal: The Baseball Life and Times of a Rifle-Armed Negro League Catcher.* Philadelphia, Pennsylvania: Love Eagle Books, 2012).

Duncan, Melvin "Buck" with David E. Miller. *I Was Born a Grown Man* (Chicago, Illinois: Joshua Tree Publishing, 2018).

Fields, Wilmer. *My Life in the Negro Leagues.* (Westport, Connecticut: Meckler Books, 1992).

Fordham, Willie. *I Gave It My Best Shot.* (Harrisburg, PA: Wordshop Press, 1996).

Glenn, Stanley. *Don't Let Anyone Take Your Joy Away: An Inside Look at Negro League Baseball and Its Legacy.* (Lincoln, Nebraska: iUniverse, Inc, 2006).

Gould, Harold with Dr. Bob Allen. *He Came From Gouldtown . . . To Become a Philadelphia Star of the Negro Baseball Leagues.* (Millville, New Jersey: The Harold Gould Family, 2009).

Irvin, Monte with James A. Riley. *Nice Guys Finish First: The Autobiography of Monte Irvin.* (New York, New York: Carroll & Graf, 1996).

Irvin, Monte with Phil Pepe. *Few and Chosen: Defining Negro League Greatness.* (Chicago, Illinois: Triumph Books, 2007).

LeGrande, Larry with M.M. Angelo. *I Found Someone to Play with: Larry LeGrande, the Last Member of the Satchel Paige All-Stars.* (Mustang, Oklahoma: Tate Publishing & Enterprises, LLC, 2015).

Leonard, Buck with James A. Riley. *Buck Leonard: The Black Lou Gehrig, An Autobiography.* (New York, New York: Carroll & Graf, 1995).

Long, Carl with Diane Taylor. *A Game of Faith: The Story of Negro League Baseball Player Carl Long.* (Greenville, North Carolina: Taylor Made Publishing, 2013).

Manley, Effa & Leon Herbert Hardwick. *Blacks in Baseball.* (Los Angeles, California: The Pilot Historical Assn., 1980). (OP).

Minoso, Minnie with Herb Fagen. *Just Call Me Minnie: My Six Decades in Baseball.* (Champaign, Illinois: Sagamore Publishing, 1994).

Motley, Bob with Bryon Motley. ***Ruling Over Monarchs, Giants & Stars: Umpiring in the Negro Leagues & Beyond.*** (Champaign, Illinois: Sports Publishing, L.L.C, 2007).

Navarro, Millito with Daliana Muratti. ***Millito Navarro: A Century Old Legend.*** (Carolina, Puerto Rico: Terranova Editores, Cuartel de Ballaja, 2007) In Spanish only.

O'Neil, Buck with Steve Wulf & David Conrads. ***I Was Right On Time!*** (New York, New York: Simon & Schuster, 1996).

Paige, LeRoy "Satchel" (as told to David Lipman). ***Maybe I'll Pitch Forever.*** (Garden City, New York: Doubleday & Company, 1961). (OP). Reprint by University of Nebraska, 1993.

Pollard, Rev. Nathaniel Hawthorne (Nat). ***The Revelations of God: As Revealed to Reverend N.H. Pollard, Sr.*** (Detroit, MI, Venia Publications, 1995).

Robinson, Frazier "Slow" with Paul Bauer. ***Catching Dreams: My Life in the Negro Baseball Leagues.*** (Syracuse, New York: Syracuse University Press, 1999).

Robinson, Jackie with Wendell Smith. ***My Own Story.*** (New York, New York: Greenberg, 1948). (OP).

Robinson, Jackie with Carl T. Rowan. ***Wait Till Next Year.*** (New York, New York: Random House Inc., 1960). (OP).

Robinson, Jackie with Charles Dexter. ***Baseball Has Done It.*** (New York, New York: J.B. Lippincott Company, 1964). (OP).

Robinson, Jackie with Alfred Duckett. ***I Never Had It Made.*** (New York, New York: G.P. Putnam's Sons, 1972).

Toles, Jr., Ted with Michael T. Swank. ***Living on Borrowed time: The Life & Times of Negro League Player Ted Toles, Jr.*** (www.48HrBooks.com, 2014).

Trouppe, Quincy. ***Twenty Years Too Soon.*** (Los Angeles, California: Sands Enterprises, 1977). (OP). Reprint: St. Louis, Missouri: Missouri Historical Society, with introduction by Larry Lester, 1995.

White, Sol. ***Sol White's Official Baseball Guide: History of Colored Baseball.*** (Philadelphia, Pennsylvania: H. Walter Schlichter, 1907). (OP). Reprint, Columbia, South Carolina: Camden House, 1990.

White, Sol. ***Sol White's History of Colored Base Ball: With Other Documents of the Early Black Game, 1886-1936***, with introduction by Jerry Malloy. (Lincoln, Nebraska: University of Nebraska Press, 1995).

Wilson, Johnny with Dick Burdette. ***Jump, Johnny, Jump: The Story of Johnny Wilson.*** (Bloomington, Indiana: Author House, 2007).

Other authors with connections to Black Baseball:

Quincy Troupe (with one "P") author of ***Miles: the Autobiography*** and ***Earl the Pearl: My Story***, is the son of Quincy Trouppe, (who added a second "P" to the family name while playing in Mexico to accommodate the Spanish pronunciation of "Trou-pay"), who was a catcher for the Cleveland Buckeyes (Negro American League) and Cleveland Indians (Major American League).

Solomon Northrup, author of ***12 Years A Slave***, is the grandfather of Henry "Zip" Northrup, a pitcher for the Cuban Giants, 1902-1906.

Reference Sources

Selected Bibliography of Theses & Dissertations

Compiled by Dr. Leslie Heaphy, Kent State University

Bohlen, Carolyn Davidica. "**The Unsung Heroes: A Study of the Nonformal Educational Strategies Used by Negro League Baseball Players, 1920-1960.**" Doctoral Dissertation, Northern Illinois University, DeKalb, Illinois, 1999.

Bond, Gregory. "**Whipped Curs and Real Men: Race, Manliness and the Segregation of Organized Baseball in the Nineteenth Century.**" Master Thesis, University of Wisconsin – Madison, 1999.

Bond, Gregory. "**Jim Crow at Play: Race, Manliness, and the Color Line in American Sports, 1876-1916.**" Doctoral Dissertation, University of Wisconsin – Madison, 2008.

Bower, Scott Clayton. "**The History and Influence of Black Baseball in the United States and Indianapolis.**" Bachelor Thesis, Butler University, Indianapolis, Indiana, 1991.

Burgos, Jr., Adrian. "**Playing America's Game: Latinos and the Performance and Policing of Race in North American Professional Baseball, 1858-1959.**" Doctoral Dissertation, University of Michigan, Ann Arbor, Michigan, 2000.

Cable, Dale. "**Jackie Robinson and the Integration of Organized Baseball.**" Master Thesis, Allegheny College, Meadville, Pennsylvania, 1979.

Carroll, Brian. "**When to Stop the Cheering?: The Black Press, the Black Community, and the Integration of Professional Baseball.**" Doctoral Dissertation, University of North Carolina, Chapel Hill, NC, 2003.

Chenier, Robert P. "**Before Jackie Robinson: African-American Athletes in Northern Ohio.**" Master Thesis, Kent State University, Kent, Ohio, 1993.

Cornwell, Willard Jacob. "**Playing Between the Lines: An Examination of Negro League Baseball in Oklahoma, 1892-1965.**" Master Thesis. Oklahoma State University, Tulsa, OK, 2013.

Essington, Amy. "**Segregation, Race and Baseball: The Desegregation of the Pacific Coast League, 1948-1952.**" Doctoral Dissertation, The Claremont Graduate University, 2013.

Farmer, Jr., Greene. "**Social Implications of Black Professional Baseball in the United States.**" Doctoral Dissertation, United States International University, San Diego, California, 1975.

Fleet-Liscio, Stephanie M. "**Forgotten Champions: The Integration of the Cleveland Indians and the Demise of the Cleveland Buckeyes.**" Master Thesis, Shippensburg University, Shippensburg, Pennsylvania, 2007.

Fullerton, Christopher Dean. "**Striking Out Jim Crow: The Birmingham Black Barons.**" Master Thesis, University of Mississippi, Oxford, Mississippi, 1994.

Goldman, Marty. "**If Only You Was White: Sixty Years of Baseball Apartheid.**" Master Thesis, College Unknown, (BL-3376.82), 1981.

Goldstein, Cynthia Rose. **The Press Coverage of the Entrance of Jackie Robinson into Baseball as the First Black**. Master Thesis, Michigan State University, East Lansing, Michigan, 1973.

Harvey, John Albert. "**The Role of American Negroes in Organized Baseball.**" Doctoral Dissertation, Columbia University, New York, NY, 1961.

Heaphy, Leslie A. "**The Growth and Decline of the Negro Leagues.**" Master Thesis, University of Toledo, Toledo, Ohio, 1989.

Heaphy, Leslie A. **"Shadowed Diamonds: The Growth and Decline of the Negro Leagues."** Doctoral Dissertation, University of Toledo, Toledo, Ohio, 1995.

Hindman, Scott C. **"Blacks in Blue: The Saga of Black Baseball's Umpires, 1885-1951."** bachelor thesis, Princeton University, Princeton, NJ, 2003.

Hull, John. **"Baseball: The Negro Leagues and Racism in America."** Master Thesis. University of Michigan-Flint, 1999.

Johnson, Douglas. **"We are the Ship, All Else the Sea."** Baseball's Blackout." Master Thesis, Humboldt State University, Arcata, California, 2005.

Joyce, Allan E. **"The Atlanta Black Crackers."** Master Thesis, Emory University, Atlanta, Georgia, 1975.

Kaufman, Dina R. **"Breaking Down Barriers: The Negro Leagues' Fate and Baseball's Integration."** Bachelor Thesis, Amherst College, Amherst, Massachusetts, 2002.

Kaufmann, Kevin Colin. **"The Role of Pittsburgh Crawfords As A Means of Self-Help in Inner City Pittsburgh, 1931-1937."** Master Thesis, Michigan State University, East Lansing, Michigan, 1995.

Kinsey, Daniel C. **"The History of Physical Education in Oberlin College, 1833-1890."** Master Thesis, Oberlin College, Oberlin, Ohio, date unknown. [Moses Fleetwood Walker]

Klippel, Dave. **"Obscured Seasons: The Historical Impact of the Negro Baseball Leagues."** Bachelor Thesis, Eckerd College, St. Petersburg, Florida, 1994.

Lanctot, Neil. **"Helping the Race Morally and Financially: Black Professional Baseball and The Philadelphia Stars, 1933-1952."** Doctoral Dissertation, University of Delaware, Newark, Delaware, 2002.

Lea, George. **"Taylor Field: A Diamond in the Rough."** Master Thesis. University of Arkansas at Little Rock, 2008.

Leffler, Jr., Robert V. **"History of Black Baseball in Baltimore, from 1913 to 1951."** Master Thesis, Morgan State University, Baltimore, Maryland, 1974.

Lerner, Daniel J. **"Visions of A Sporting City: Shadowball and Black Chicago, 1887-1952."** Doctoral Dissertation, Michigan State University, East Lansing, Michigan, 2002.

Levy, Scott Jarman. **"Lily Dippers, Sockamayocks, and the Blue Goose: Black Baseball and the Color Line."** Master Thesis, Washington University, St. Louis, Missouri, 1989.

Lomax, Michael Eugene. **"Black Baseball, Black Community, Black Entrepreneurs: History of the Negro National and Eastern Colored Leagues, 1880-1930."** Doctoral Dissertation, Ohio State University, Columbus, Ohio, 1996.

Mack-Washington, Marta Notai. **"From Both Sides of the Plate: Negro League Baseball's Effa Manley Disrupts the American Mythology of Race and Ethnicity, 1897-1948."** Doctoral Dissertation. University of Iowa, 2015.

Mander, Maurice Robert. **"The Cuban Giants: Baseball Heroes and Second Class Citizens, 1865 – 1890."** Master Thesis, Morgan State University, Baltimore, Ohio, 1996.

Matheney, Timothy Michael. **"Heading for Home: Moses Fleetwood Walker's Encounter with Racism in America."** Senior Thesis, Princeton University, Princeton, New Jersey, 1989.

Reference Sources

McBee, Montgomery Kurt. **"They Also Played the Game: A Historical Examination of the Memphis Red Sox Baseball Organization, 1922-1959."** Doctoral Dissertation, University of Memphis, Memphis, Tennessee, 2001.

Newman, John Rolin. **"Negro League Baseball."** Master Thesis, University of Southern Florida, Tampa, Florida, 2000.

Ostenby, Peter Marshall. **"Other Games, Other Glory: The Memphis Red Sox and the Trauma of Integration, 1948-1955."** Master Thesis, University of North Carolina, Chapel Hill, North Carolina, 1989.

Pascoe, William Wesley. **Seasons in the Sun: The Negro Baseball Leagues.** Master Thesis, The University of Western Ontario, Canada, 1995.

Pfundstein, Thomas E. **"Black Baseball in Cleveland, 1920-1950."** Master Thesis, John Carroll University, University Heights, Ohio, 1996.

Rafferty-Osaki, Terumi A. **"What Price Color? African American History 1872-1960 Through the Eyes of Baseball."** Master Thesis, Boston College, Boston, Massachusetts, 2003.

Richardson, Andrew. **"A Retrospective Look at the Negro Leagues and Professional Negro Baseball Players."** Master Thesis, San José State University, San José, California, 1980.

Rogosin, William Donn. **"Black Baseball: The Life in the Negro League."** Doctoral Dissertation, University of Texas, Austin, Texas, 1981.

Ruck, Robert. **"Sandlot Seasons: Sport in Black Pittsburgh."** Doctoral Dissertation, University of Pittsburgh, Pittsburgh, Pennsylvania., 1987.

Rusinack, Kelly Elaine. **"Baseball on the Radical Agenda: The Daily and Sunday Worker on the Desegregation of Major League Baseball, 1933 to 1947."** Master Thesis, Clemson University, Clemson, South Carolina, December 1995.

Rutz, Miguel. **"The Ritual Significance of the National Pastime over the Long Duration: Democracy, Racial Progress and African Americans in Baseball."** Doctoral Dissertation, University of California, Davis, 2014.

Schell, Connor William. **"Kansas City Monarchs: An Examination of the Decline of Black Baseball's Preeminent Franchise."** B.A. Honors Thesis, Harvard University, Cambridge, Massachusetts, 2000.

Sedgewick, Austin Keefe. **"Shame and Pride, Degradation and Achievement: Exhibiting the Contested Memory of Black Baseball in America."** Honors Thesis, College of William and Mary, Williamsburg, Virginia, 2001.

Sheingold, Peter M. **"In Black and White: Sam Lacy's Campaign to Integrate Baseball."** Partial Fulfillment for Bachelor of Arts Degree in American History. Hampshire College, Amherst, Massachusetts, 1992.

Shoemaker, Martha McArdell. **"Propaganda or Persuasion: The Communist Party and Its Campaign to Integrate Baseball."** Master Thesis, University of Nevada at Las Vegas, 1999.

Shortelle, Dennis, P. **"They Also Played."** Master Thesis, Wesleyan University, Middletown, Connecticut, 1985.

Shults, Frederick David. **"The History and Philosophy of Athletics for Men at Oberlin College."** Doctoral Dissertation, Indiana University, South Bend, Indiana, 1967. [Moses Fleetwood Walker]

Smith, Courtney Michelle. **A Faded Memory: The Philadelphia Stars, 1933-1953**. Master Thesis, Lehigh University, Bethlehem, Pennsylvania, 2002.

Snyder, Brad Mitchell. **"They Took Back Griffith Stadium: The Homestead Grays in Washington, D.C. during the 1940s."** Senior Honor Thesis, Duke University, Durham, North Carolina, 1994.

Stillwell, Jr., Russell. **"Baseball: Its Historical Importance to the United States: Politically, Socially, and Economically."** Master Thesis, Southern Connecticut State University, New Haven, Connecticut, 2009.

Stoneberg, Eric Mark. **"The Denver Post Tournament and Pre-Organized Baseball Integration."** Master Thesis, Arizona State University, Phoenix, Arizona, 2009.

Trembanis, Sarah Lorraine. **"They Opened the Door Too Late."** Doctoral Dissertation, The College of William and Mary, Williamsburg, Virginia, 2006.

Williams, Whit M. **"Jackie Robinson."** Bachelor's Thesis, Dartmouth College, Hanover, New Hampshire, 1950.

Other Related Theses & Dissertations

Anderson, Daniel Roger. *"Renaissance Men: The Harlem Intelligentsia, the African-American Press and the Culture of Sport, 1918-1940."* Doctoral Dissertation. University of Minnesota, Minneapolis, Minnesota, 2005.

Anderson, Torben. *"Race Discrimination by Major League Baseball Fans."* Doctoral Dissertation, University of Washington, Seattle, Washington, 1988.

Brooks, Max. *"Content Analysis of Leading Negro Newspapers."* Doctoral Dissertation, Ohio State, Columbus, Ohio, 1953.

Bryant, Richard A. *"A Diamond in the Rough: the Integration of Major League Baseball and How Negro League Baseball was Arguably One of the Largest Contributors to the Desegregation of America."* Master Thesis, Delta State University, Cleveland, Mississippi, 2001.

Case, Alex K. *"Jackie Robinson: Baseball, America and Memory."* B.A. Honors Thesis, Lake Forest College, Lake Forest, Illinois, 1994.

Coates Jr., James Roland. *"Recreation and Sport in the African-American Community of Baltimore, 1890-1920."* Doctoral Dissertation, University of Maryland, College Park, Maryland, 1991.

Coursey, Leon M. *"The Life of Edwin Bancroft Henderson and His Professional Contributions to Physical Education."* Doctoral Dissertation, Ohio State University, Columbus, Ohio, 1971.

Deardorff, Donald. *"The Newspaper Press and Black Athletes."* Master Thesis, University of Maryland, College Park, Maryland, 1990.

Ellis, Brian. *"Racial Segregation in American Professional Sports: A Tipping Analysis."* Doctoral Dissertation. Howard University, 2014.

Ellman, Tracy D. *"The Influence of Race/Ethnicity in the Salary Arbitration Process in Major League Baseball."* Master Thesis, Illinois State University, Normal, Illinois, 1991.

Fink, Robert C. *"African-American Baseball in Texas, 1900-1950."* Master Thesis, Texas Tech University, Lubbock, Texas, 1999.

Fisher, Adam Gordon. *"Pride and Shame: Black Sportswriters' Coverage of Integration and the Negro Leagues, 1944-1952."* B. A. Honors Thesis, Harvard University, Cambridge, Massachusetts, 2001.

Foreman, Thomas Elton. *"Discrimination Against the Negro in American Athletics."* Master Thesis, Fresno State College, Fresno, California, 1957.

Gottlieb, Peter. *"Making Their Own Way: Southern Blacks Migration to Pittsburgh, 1916-1930."* Doctoral Dissertation, University of Pittsburgh, Pennsylvania, 1977.

Grossman, James R. *"A Dream Deferred: Black Migration to Chicago, 1916-1921."* Doctoral Dissertation, University of California at Berkeley, 1982.

Hardy, III, Charles. *"Race and Opportunity: Black Philadelphia During the Era of the Great Migration, 1916-30, Volume 1 and II."* Doctoral Dissertation, Temple University, Philadelphia, Pennsylvania, 1989.

Hutchinson, G. *"Black Athletes' Contribution Towards Social Change in the United States."* Doctoral Dissertation, United States International University, San Diego, California, 1977.

Irani, Daraius Sarosh. *"Three Essays on Sports Economics (Black Studies, Discrimination)."* Doctoral Dissertation, University of California, Santa Barbara, California, 1996.

Jansson, Kyle. *"Amateur and Semi-Professional Baseball in North Dakota Communities."* Master Thesis, Arizona State University, Phoenix, Arizona, 1994.

Kahn, Abraham. *"Baseball in the Black Public Sphere: Curt Flood and the Disappearance of Race."* Doctoral Dissertation. University of Minnesota, Minneapolis, Minnesota, 2010.

Klinetobe, Charles. *"Diamond Mine: Segregation, Alabama and the Making of the Players Who 'Saved Baseball.'"* Doctoral Dissertation. University of Nebraska-Lincoln, 2018.

Mallory, Patrick. *"The Game they all Played: Chicago Baseball, 1876-1906."* Doctoral Dissertation. Loyola University, Chicago, Illinois, 2013.

McCormick, Michael Dillon. *"Full Court Press: Rebellion, Resistance and the Black Athletes of the Civil Rights Movement."* Master Thesis. California State University, Fullerton, California, 2016.

McKenna, Christopher Michael. *Reluctance to Change: A Study in Social Exclusion, The Power of Jim Crow, and Baseball in America*. M.A. Thesis, California State University, Dominguez Hills, California, 2011.

Mendonca, Lenny. *"Social Racial Discrimination in Major League Baseball."* Senior Honors thesis, College Unknown, 1983.

Nabil, P.A. *"Emergence and Arrival of the Afro-American in the National Game: His Participation in Sport in General and Baseball in Particular as a Positive Mechanism for Socio-Economic Mobility in American Society."* Doctoral Dissertation, University of Illinois-Urbana-Champagne, Champagne, Illinois, 1979.

Naze, David. *"Kansas City, Congress and Cooperstown: Re-remembering the Cultural Legacy of Jackie Robinson."* Doctoral Dissertation. Indiana University, Bloomington, Indiana, 2012.

Neal, Richard Lee. *"America's Game in Middletown, USA: Baseball in Muncie, Indiana, 1876-1953."* Doctoral Dissertation, Ball State University, Muncie, Indiana, 1989.

Parsons, Nicholas Lawrence. *"From Jackie to Pumpsie and Beyond: An Institutional Analysis of the Integration of Black Players into Major League Baseball."* Master Thesis, Washington State University, Pullman, Washington, 2003.

Pascal, Anthony H. and Leonard A. Rapping. *"Racial Discrimination in Organized Baseball."* RAND Memorandum RM-6227-RC. Santa Monica, CA, Rand Corporation, 1970, 53 pages.

Price, Clement Alexander. *"The Afro-American Community of Newark, 1917-1947: A Social History."* Doctoral Dissertation, Rutgers University, Piscataway, NJ, 1975.

Pride, Armistead S. *"A Register and History of Negro Newspapers in the United States, 1827-1950."* Doctoral Dissertation, Northwestern University, Evanston, Illinois, 1950. 426 pages. Pride found more than 2700 newspapers in his search.

Rayl, Susan Jane. *"The New York Renaissance Professional Black Basketball Team, 1923-1950."* Doctoral Dissertation, Pennsylvania State University, McKeesport, Pennsylvania, 1996.

Roth, Hope. *"Wendell Smith and the Integration of Major League Baseball."* Master Thesis. Tufts University, Medford, Massachusetts, 2013.

Rutz, Jonathan Edward. "***Fields of Gray: An Examination of Jackie Robinson's First Season in Major League Baseball.***" Bachelor's Thesis, James Madison University, Harrisonburg, Virginia, 1998.

Saatsaz, Cyrus. "***Sports Journalists as the Gatekeepers of Social and Cultural Movements: A comparative Analysis of the Medias Coverage of Jackie Robinson, Jason Collins and Michael Sam.***" Master Thesis. San Diego State University, San Diego, California, 2015.

Slusser, James H. "***The Sports Page in American Life in the 1920s.***" Master Thesis, University of California at Berkeley, 1954.

Smith, Jeffrey E. "***Industrial League Baseball and Employee Welfare Work, 1910-1930.***" Doctoral Dissertation, University of Akron, Ohio, 1991.

Stainbrook, David. "***Mixing of Black and White in the World of Baseball.***" Bachelor's Thesis, California Polytechnic State University, San Luis Obispo, California, 1993.

Stillwell, Russell Jr. ***Baseball, Its Historical Importance to the United States: Politically, Socially and Economically***. M. S. Thesis, Southern Connecticut State University, New Haven, Connecticut, 2009.

Stoneberg, Eric. ***The Denver Post Tournament and Pre-Organized Baseball Integration***. M. A. Thesis, Arizona State University, Phoenix, Arizona, 2009.

Stroud, Daniel. "***From Dachau to the Dugout: Black America's Diamond-lined Response to Racism.***" Master Thesis. University of Missouri-Kansas City, 2011.

Sullivan, Dean Alan. "***The Growth of Sport in a Southern City: A Study of the Original Evolution of Baseball in Louisville, Kentucky, as an Urban Phenomenon, 1860-1900.***" Master Thesis, George Mason University, Fairfax, Virginia, 1989.

Swanson, Ryan. "***Jim Crow on Deck: Baseball During America's Reconstruction.***" Doctoral Dissertation. Georgetown University, Washington, DC, 2008.

Troiano, Laura T. "***Give Me A 'Ball Park Figure': Creating Civic Narratives Through Stadium Building in Newark, New Jersey***." Doctoral Dissertation, Newark-Rutgers, The State University of New Jersey, 2017.

Wiggins, David K. "***Sport & Popular Pastimes in the Plantation Community: The Slave Experience.***" Doctoral Dissertation, University of Maryland, College Park, Maryland, 1979.

Williams, Dorothy W. ***The Jackie Robinson Myth: Social Mobility and Race in Montreal, 1920-1960***. Master Thesis, Concordia University (Canada), 1999.

Major & Minor Newspapers Researched

Nearly 400 "Sacred Scrolls"

Akron Beacon–Journal (OH)
Alabama Journal (Montgomery)
Albany Evening Journal (NY)
Alliance Review (OH)
Altoona Mirror (PA)
Altoona Tribune (PA)
Amherst Record (MA)
Amsterdam Daily Democrat (NY)
Anderson Daily Bugle (IN)
Anderson Daily Bulletin (IN)
Anderson Herald (IN)
Appleton Post-Crescent (WI)
Arkansas Gazette (Little Rock)
Atchison Daily Globe (KS)
Atlanta Constitution (GA)
Atlanta Daily World (GA)
Atlanta Journal (GA)
Atlantic City Daily News (NJ)
Atlantic City Press (NJ)
Auburn Bulletin (IL)
Baltimore Afro American (MD)
Baltimore News-Post (MD)
Baltimore Sun (MD)
Bayard Advocate (IA)
Beaver Falls News Tribune (PA)
Beckley Post Herald (WV)
Belleville Daily Advocate (IL)
Berkshire Eagle (Pittsfield, MA)
Birmingham Age-Herald (AL)
Birmingham Eagles (AL)
Birmingham Mirror (AL)
Birmingham News (AL)
Birmingham Post (AL)
Birmingham Post-Herald (AL)
Birmingham Reporter (AL)
Birmingham Weekly Review (AL)
Birmingham World (AL)
Bismarck Tribune (ND)
Boston Globe (MA)
Boston Guardian (MA)

Brandon Daily Sun (Manitoba)
Bridgeport Post (CN)
Brockton Enterprise (MA)
Brooklyn Eagle (NY)
Buffalo Express (NY)
California Eagle (Los Angeles)
Camden Daily Courier (NJ)
Camden Democrat (NJ)
Camden Post-Telegram (NJ)
Canton Repository (OH)
Chambersburg Public Opinion (PA)
Charleroi Mail (PA)
Charleston Gazette (WV)
Charleston Mercury (Mt. Pleasant, SC)
Chattanooga Defender (TN)
Chester Times (PA)
Chicago American (IL)
Chicago Broad Ax (IL)
Chicago Daily Herald (IL)
Chicago Daily News (IL)
Chicago Daily Tribune (IL)
Chicago Defender (City & National) (IL)
Chicago Evening Post (IL)
Chicago Heights Star (IL)
Chicago Herald American (IL)
Chicago Herald Examiner (IL)
Chicago Negro Digest (IL)
Chicago Sun-Times (IL)
Chicago Tribune (IL)
Chicago Whip (IL)
Chicago's Abbott's Monthly (IL)
Chicago's Abbott's Weekly and Illustrated News (IL)
Cincinnati Enquirer (OH)
Clearfield (PA) Progress (OH)
Cleveland Advocate (OH)
Cleveland Call & Post (OH)
Cleveland Gazette (OH)
Cleveland Herald (OH)
Cleveland Plain Dealer (OH)
Cleveland Press (OH)

Reference Sources

Columbus Dispatch (OH)
Connellsville Daily Courier (PA)
Cortland Standard (NY)
Council Bluff Nonpareil (IA)
Crawfordsville Daily Journal (IN)
Cumberland Evening Times (MD)
Dallas Express (TX)
Dallas Morning News (TX)
Danville Bee (VA)
Davenport Democrat & Leader (IA)
Dayton Daily News (OH)
Dayton Forum (OH)
Dayton Herald (OH)
Dayton Journal (OH)
Delaware County Daily Times (PA)
Des Moines Register (IA)
Detroit Contender (MI)
Detroit Courier (MI)
Detroit Free Press (MI)
Detroit Times (MI)
Dixon Evening Telegraph (IL)
Dowagiac Daily News (MI)
Doylestown Democrat (PA)
Doylestown Intelligencer (PA)
Duluth News Tribune (MN)
Easton Daily Express (PA)
Erie Dispatch (PA)
Findlay Daily Republican (OH)
Findlay Morning Republican (OH)
Florida Times-Union (Jacksonville)
Fort Wayne Journal Gazette (TX)
Fort Wayne News and Sentinel (TX)
Fort Worth Press (TX)
Fort Worth Star Telegram (TX)
Fort Worth Star-Telegram (TX)
Frederick News-Post (MD)
Fresno Bee (CA)
Gettysburg Times (PA)
Grand Folks Daily Herald (MI)
Grand Rapids Press (MI)
Greensburg Daily Tribune (PA)
Hammond Times (IN)
Harrisburg Evening News (PA)
Harrisburg News (PA)
Harrisburg Patriot (PA)
Harrisburg Telegraph (PA)

Hartford Courant (CN)
Haverhill Evening Gazette (PA)
Helena Daily Independent (MT)
Herald-Press (St. Joseph, MI)
Hilldale Club, Darby (PA) - Lloyd Thompson Scorebooks
Holland Evening Sentinel (MI)
Homestead Daily News (PA)
Hopewell Herald (NJ)
Houston Informer (TX)
Huntsville Times (AL)
Illinois State Journal (Springfield)
Indiana Evening Gazette (PA)
Indiana Weekly Messenger (PA)
Indianapolis Freeman (IN)
Indianapolis Ledger (IN)
Indianapolis News (IN)
Indianapolis Record (IN)
Indianapolis Recorder (IN)
Indianapolis Star (IN)
Indianapolis Times (IN)
Indianapolis World (IN)
Iowa City Press-Citizen (IA)
Ironwood Daily Globe (MI)
Jackson Advocate (MS)
Jacksonville Journal (FL)
Jersey City Evening Journal (NJ)
Johnston Democrat (PA)
Johnstown Tribune (PA)
Joplin Globe (MO)
Kansas City American (MO)
Kansas City Call (MO)
Kansas City Journal-Post (MO)
Kansas City Kansas (KS)
Kansas City Plaindealer (KS)
Kansas City Star (MO)
Kansas City Sun (MO)
Kansas City Times (MO)
Kokomo Tribune (IN)
Lake Park News (Dickinson County, Iowa)
Leavenworth (KS) Times
Lebanon Daily Reporter (IN)
Lima News (OH)
Lincoln Journal (NE)
Lincoln Star (NE)
Long Branch Daily Record (NJ)

Negro Leagues Book #2: The Players

Los Angeles Times (CA)
Louisiana Weekly (NOLA)
Louisville Courier-Journal (KY)
Louisville Defender (KY)
Louisville Leader (KY)
Louisville Times (KY)
Lowell Sun (MA)
Lynn Daily Evening Item (MA)
Macon Daily Telegraph (GA)
Manchester Union (NH)
Mansfield News-Journal (OH)
Marysville Advocate-Democrat (KS)
Maryville Daily Forum (MO)
Massillon Evening Independent (OH)
Meadville Tribune-Republican (PA)
Memphis Commercial Appeal (TN)
Memphis News-Scimitar (TN)
Memphis World (TN)
Michigan Chronicle (Detroit)
Middletown Times-Herald (NY)
Milwaukee Journal (WI)
Milwaukee Sentinel (WI)
Monessen Daily Independent (PA)
Monroe Morning World (LA)
Monroe News-Star (LA)
Montgomery Advertiser (AL)
Montgomery Alabama Tribune
Morning Herald (Hagerstown, MD)
Morning Oregonian (Portland, Oregon)
Morristown County Chronicle (NJ)
Morristown Jerseyman (NJ)
Muncie Star (IN)
Nashville Banner (TN)
Nashville Clarion (TN)
Nashville Defender (TN)
Nashville Globe & Independent (TN)
Nashville Tennessean (TN)
Nashville World (TN)
Nassau Daily Review (NY) *
National (NOLA) Times
Nebraska State Journal (Lincoln)
New Jersey Afro American (Newark)
New Jersey Herald News (Newton)
New Orleans Courier (LA)
New Orleans Informer and Sentinel (LA)
New Orleans Item (LA)

New Orleans Times-Picayune (LA)
New York Age
New York American
New York Amsterdam Evening Recorder
New York Amsterdam News
New York Clipper
New York Courier
New York Daily Democrat & Recorder
New York Daily Eagle
New York Daily Mirror
New York Daily News
New York Daily Worker
New York Evening Telegram
New York Gazette
New York Herald
New York Herald-American
New York People's Voice
New York Press
New York Recorder
New York Times
New York World
Newark Afro American (NJ)
Newark Evening News (NJ)
Newark Herald (NJ)
Newark News (NJ)
Newark Star Eagle (NJ)
Newark Star-Ledger (NJ)
Newburg News (NY)
Newport News Daily Press (VA)
Newport News Times-Herald (VA)
News-Journal Sports (Longview, TX)
News-Palladium (Benton Harbor, MI)
Niagara Falls Gazette (NY)
Norfolk Journal & Guide (VA)
Norfolk Landmark (VA)
Norfolk Virginia-Pilot (VA)
Norristown Daily Journal (PA)
Norristown Herald (PA)
Norristown Times Herald (PA)
North Adams Evening Transcript (MA)
Norwich Bulletin (CN)
Oakland Tribune (CA)
Ohio State Journal (Columbus)
Oil City Blizzard (PA)
Oklahoma City Oklahoman (OK)
Olean Times-Herald (NY)

Reference Sources

Omaha Daily World (NE)
Opelika Daily News (AL)
Oswego Palladium (NY)
Otsego Union (MI)
Palatine Enterprise (IL)
Palladium-Item and Sun-Telegram (Richmond, IN)
Parkersburg News & Sentinel (WV)
Paterson Evening News (NJ)
Paterson Morning Call (NJ)
Paterson Morning News (NJ)
Penn's Grove Record (NJ)
Philadelphia Afro-American (PA)
Philadelphia Evening Item (PA)
Philadelphia Independent (PA)
Philadelphia Inquirer (PA)
Philadelphia Item (PA)
Philadelphia Record (PA)
Philadelphia Tribune (PA)
Piqua Daily Call (OH)
Pittsburgh American (PA)
Pittsburgh Competitor (PA)
Pittsburgh Courier (PA)
Pittsburgh Daily Press (PA)
Pittsburgh Post-Gazette (PA)
Pittsburgh Press (PA)
Pittsburgh Sun Telegraph (PA)
Plain Speaker (Hazleton, PA)
Plainfield Courier News (NJ)
Plattsburgh Press (NY)
Port Arthur News (TX)
Portland Oregonian (Oregon)
Portsmouth Daily Times (OH)
Portsmouth Stars (VA)
Post (Frederick, MD)
Pottstown Daily News (PA)
Poughkeepsie Free Press (NY)
Quincy Herald-Whig (IL)
Racine Journal Times (WI)
Reading Eagle (PA)
Red Bank Register (NJ)
Regina Leader-Post (Saskatchewan)
Reno Evening Gazette (NV)
Richfield Springs Mercury (NY)
Richmond Afro-American (VA)
Richmond Item (IN)
Richmond Palladium (IN)

Richmond Planet (VA)
Richmond Sun-Telegram (IN)
Richmond Times Dispatch (VA)
Rochester Chronicle (NY)
Salina Journal (KS)
San Antonio Express (TX)
San Antonio Light (TX)
Sandusky Star-Journal (OH)
Seattle Post-Intelligencer (WA)
Sedalia Democrat (MO)
Sheboygan Press (WI)
Shreveport Sun (LA)
South Bend Tribune (IN)
Springfield News Sun (OH)
Springfield Republican (MA)
St. Albans Daily Messenger (VT)
St. Augustine Evening News (FL)
St. Joseph Gazette (MO)
St. Joseph News-Press (MO)
St. Louis American (MO)
St. Louis Argus (MO)
St. Louis Gazette (MO)
St. Louis Globe-Democrat (MO)
St. Louis Post-Dispatch (MO)
St. Louis Times (MO)
St. Paul Recorder (MN)
Stamford Advocate (CN)
Statesville Record & Landmark (NC)
Sunbury Daily Item (PA)
Syracuse Herald Journal (NY)
Syracuse Post Standard (NY)
Tattler (St. Augustine, FL)
Titusville Herald (PA)
Toledo Blade (OH)
Toledo News Bee (OH)
Topeka Daily Capital (KS)
Trenton Daily True American (NJ)
Trenton Evening News (NJ)
Trenton Evening Times (NJ)
Trenton State Gazette (NJ)
Tribune Sports (Coshocton, OH)
Troy Daily Times (PA)
Tulsa Daily World (OK)
Tulsa Tribune (OK)
Uniontown Morning Herald (PA)
Uniontown Standard (PA)

Utica Herald-Dispatch (NY)
Vineland Independent (NJ)
Vineland News (NJ)
Walla Walla Union Bulletin (WA)
Warren Times-Mirror (PA)
Washington Afro American (DC)
Washington Bee (DC)
Washington Post (DC)
Washington Star (DC)
Washington Tribune (DC)
Weirton Daily Times (WV)
Wellsville Daily Reporter (NY)
West Chester Daily News (PA)
Wheeling Daily News (WV)
Wheeling Intelligencer (WV)
Wheeling Register (WV)

Williamsport Gazette and Bulletin (PA)
Wilmington Evening News (DE)
Wilmington Every Evening (DE)
Wilmington Journal (DE)
Wilmington Morning News (DE)
Wilmington Morning Star (DE)
Wilmington News-Journal (DE)
Winnipeg Free Press (Manitoba, Canada)
Wisconsin State Journal (Madison)
Xenia Evening Gazette (OH)
York Dispatch (PA)
York Gazette (PA)
Youngstown Vindicator (OH)
Zanesville Signal (OH)
Zanesville Times Recorder (OH)

*Note: The *Nassau (NY) Daily Review* is also known as the *Long Island Review* and the *Long Island Daily Press*.

Reference Sources

Contributing Libraries located in non-major Negro League cities:

Alabama Department of Archives and History, Montgomery, AL (Dr. Norwood A. Kerr)
Allen County Public Library, Fort Wayne, IN (Linda Chapman)
Altoona Public Library, Altoona, PA (Georgia Kuhn)
Anniston Public Library, Anniston, AL (Tom Mullins)
Appleton Public Library, Appleton, WI (Karen Probst)
Bismarck Public Library, Bismarck, ND (Kate Waldera)
Brighton Memorial Library, Rochester, NY (Lynne Fretz)
Cambria County Library, Johnstown, PA (Esther Vorhauer)
Daniel Boone Regional Library, Columbia, MO (Nina Sappington)
Davenport Public Library, Davenport, IA (Richardson-Sloan Special Collection)
Dayton Metro Library, Dayton, OH (Jack Carlson)
Decatur Public Library, Decatur, IL (Margaret G. Wollitz)
Dowagiac District Library, Dowagiac, MI (Kay)
Fort Wayne Public Library, Fort Wayne, IN (Linda Chapman)
Fort Worth Public Library, Fort Worth, TX (Shirley Apley)
Greensburg Hempfield Area Library, Greensburg, PA (Cindy Dull)
Huntsville Public Library, Huntsville, AL (Thomas Hutchens)
Irvington Public Library, Irvington-on-Hudson, NY (Elizabeth Sadewhite)
Jackson/Madison County Library, Jackson, TN (Jack D. Wood)
Jacksonville Public Library, Jacksonville, FL (Theresa Rooney)
Lake County Public Library, Merrillville, IN (Nancy Campbell)
Manhattan Public Library, Manhattan, KS
Martinsburg-Berkeley County Public Libraries (Keith Hammersla)
Marysville Public Library, Marysville, KS (Kathryn Hatfield)
Metropolitan Library System, Oklahoma City, OK (Katrina Price)
Middle George Archives, Macon, GA (Muriel M. Jackson)
Middletown Public Library, Middletown, OH (Deirdre Bray Root)
Morrison-Reeves Library, Richmond, IN (Marilyn Nobbe)
National Archives and Records Administration, Kansas City, MO (David Nowlin)
The National WWI Museum and Memorial, Kansas City, MO (Jonathan Casey)
Onondaga County Public Library, Syracuse, NY (Holly Sammons, Dennis McGraw)
Paterson Public Library, Paterson, NJ (Bruce R. Bardarik)
Port Arthur Public Library, Port Arthur, TX (Yolanda Clayton)
Public Library of Youngstown & Mahoning County (Barb Smith & Debra Bushmire)
Quincy Public Library, Quincy, IL (Nancy Dolan)
Research Center for Beaver County and Local History, Beaver Falls, PA (Alice Kern)
San Antonio Public Library, San Antonio, TX (Andy Crews)
St. Joseph Public Library, St. Joseph, MO (Vicki L. Thornton)
The Ferguson Library, Stamford, CN (William Miller)
Tulsa City-County Library, Tulsa, OK (Kathy Heng)
West Virginia Archives & History Library, Charleston, WV (Susan Scouras)
Wilmington Public Library, Wilmington, DE (Ben Prestianni)

Contributing Researchers:

Gary Ashwill (Durham, NC)
Pam Bakker (Savanna, GA)
Jeremy Beer (Chester, PA)
Melissa Booker (Cincinnati, OH)
Morgan Brenner (Havertown, PA)
Frederico Brillhart (Harrisburg, PA)
Rosilyn Stearnes Brown (Detroit, MI)
James Brunson III (DeKalb, IL)
Jack Carlson (Beavercreek, OH)
Brian Carroll (Rome, GA)
Paul Debono (Cincinnati, OH)
Jorge Colon Delgado (Toa Baja, PR)
Mark E. Eberle (Hays, KS)
Thomas Garrett (Portsmouth, VA)
Michael and Christian Garvey (Chicago, IL)
Timothy Gay (Northern VA)
Dan Gulden (York, PA)
Michael Haupert (La Crosse, WI)
Leslie Heaphy (Canton, OH)
John Holway (Alexandria, VA)
Dwayne Isgrig (St. Louis, MO)
Lisa Feder (Ingleside, IL)
Charlemagne Fouche (Dalton, GA)
Calobe Jackson (Harrisburg, PA)
Kevin Johnson (Broken Arrow, OK)
Jan Johnson (Topeka, KS)
Frank Keetz (Schenectady, NY)
Rick Kenney (St. Petersburg, FL)
Tony Kissel (Cortland, NY)
Ted Knorr (Harrisburg, PA)
Signe Knutson (Albany, NY)
David Krell (Jersey City, NJ)
Jeremy Krock (Peoria, IL)
Chris Lamb (Indianapolis, IN)
Neil Lanctot (King of Prussia, PA)
Michael E. Lomax (Iowa City, IA)
Mitch Lutzke (Williamston, MI)
Jerry Malloy (Mundelein, IL)
Peter Mancuso (New Hope, PA)
Louis Manley (Detroit, MI)
Ken Mars (Parkville, MD)
Bob May (Cincinnati, OH)
Lawrence McCray (Lexington, MA)
Pamela Paige O'Neal (Kansas City, MO)

Jim Overmyer (Tucson, AZ)
Robert Paige (St. Louis, MO)
Todd Peterson (Kansas City, MO)
Bill Plott (Montevallo, AL)
Richard Puerzer (Metuchen, NJ)
Tim Rives (Abilene, KS)
Patrick Rock (Kansas City, MO)
Philip Ross (Jamaica, NY)
Susan Rayl (Cortland, NY)
Kazuo Sayama (Japan)
Rick Swaine (Crawfordville, FL)
Layton Revel (Carrollton, TX)
Courtney Michelle Smith (Radnor Township, Pennsylvania)
DeMorris Smith (Kansas City, MO)
Lucky Smith (Auburn Hills, MI)
Donald Spivey (Palmetto Bay, FL)
George Skornickel (Pittsburgh, PA)
Bryan Steverson (Maryville, TN)
Joyce Stearnes Thompson (Auburn Hills, MI)
John A. Thorn (Catskill, NY)
Thomas Van Hyning (Florence, MS)
Preston Washington (Kansas City, MO)
Clarence Watkins (Birmingham, AL)
Ryan Whirty (New Orleans, LA)
Lyle Wilson (Seattle, Washington)

Authors:

Larry Lester has authored, co-authored and/or been editor of nine books on Black Baseball history. Lester has written forewords to several books and has served as an editor/fact checker to many doctoral dissertations and theses on sports history. He is listed as a contributing researcher to more than 200 publications on African American history, and has served as a consultant with ESPN, ESPN2, PBS, C-SPAN, History Channel and CNN.

Lester is the co-founder of the Negro Leagues Baseball Museum (NLBM) in Kansas City, Missouri, and served as their Research Director and Treasurer in their embryonic years. He was instrumental in the development of the NLBM's business plan, licensing program, static exhibits, and its Incorporation in 1990. He left the NLBM in 1995 to launch **NoirTech Research, Inc.,** combining his expertise in research and technology to strategically track the African American experience in sports, history and entertainment.

He is chairman of the **Society for American Baseball Research**'s (SABR) Negro Leagues Committee which annually host the **Jerry Malloy Negro League Conference**, the *only academic symposium dedicated exclusively to the examination and promotion of Black baseball history.*

In 2016, Lester received SABR's national **Henry Chadwick Award**, named after the "Father of Baseball." The following year, Lester was recipient of SABR's **Bob Davids Award**, the society's highest honor for his contributions to baseball that reflect the ingenuity, integrity and self-sacrifice of its founder. He lives in Raytown, Missouri. More information about Lester can be found at: https://www.larrylester42.com/authors-bio.html

Wayne Stivers is a native of rural Davis County in Southern Iowa. After attending the University of Colorado, he worked in corporate America until 1987. Upon leaving the business world, he started "Mister Sports Collectible," a sports memorabilia business with special emphases on women in sports and Negro League personalities. A member of the Society for American Baseball Research (SABR) since the early 1990s, Stivers has served as an editor of *The Courier*, a quarterly newsletter from the Negro Leagues Research Committee of SABR.

Stivers was one of the key researchers and contributing editors for the Negro League Researchers and Authors Group (NLRAG) during its five-year comprehensive study, funded by Major League Baseball Properties. He helped lead the efforts for the selection of a record seventeen (17) Negro League players and executives to the National Baseball Hall of Fame in Cooperstown, New York, in 2006. Over the past dozen years, he has continued to a major contributor to the online statistical databases, https://www.baseball-reference.com/ and http://www.seamheads.com/NegroLgs/ . Stivers currently lives in Plano, Illinois, approximately fifty-five (55) miles southwest of Chicago. Stivers is an avid follower of the Chicago Cubs and the Chicago Blackhawks.

Made in the USA
Columbia, SC
18 December 2020